To Steve & Shawna

Paul Steinberg

ACCOUNTING INFORMATION SYSTEMS

EIGHTH EDITION

Marshall B. Romney
Brigham Young University

Paul John Steinbart
Arizona State University

Prentice Hall, Upper Saddle River, New Jersey 07458

Library of Congress Cataloging-in-Publication Data

Romney, Marshall B.
Accounting information systems / Marshall B. Romney, Paul John Steinbart.—8th ed.
p. cm.
Includes bibliographical references and index.
ISBN 0–201–35721–6 (hardcover)
1. Accounting—Data processing. 2. Information storage and retrieval systems—Accounting. I. Steinbart, Paul John. II. Title.
HF5679.A34 1999
657'.0285—dc21 99–32593
CIP

Executive Editor: Annie Todd
Editor in Chief: P. J. Boardman
Acquisitions Editor: Deborah Hoffman Emry
Assistant Editor: Kathryn Sheehan
Editorial Assistant: Jane Avery
Marketing Manager: Beth Toland
Managing Editor: James Rigney
Print Buyer: Tim McDonald
Designer: Electronic Publishing Services Inc., NYC
Cover Design: Gina Hagen
Cover Photograph: Chigmaroff/Davison/Superstock
Composition: Electronic Publishing Services Inc., NYC

Simon & Schuster/A Viacom Company
Upper Saddle River, New Jersey 07458

Printed in the United States of America

10 9 8 7 6 5 4 3 2 1

ISBN 0-201-35721-6

Prentice-Hall International (UK) Limited, *London*
Prentice-Hall of Australia Pty. Limited, *Sydney*
Prentice-Hall Canada Inc., *Toronto*
Prentice-Hall Hispanoamericana, S.A., *Mexico*
Prentice-Hall of India Private Limited, *New Delhi*
Prentice-Hall of Japan, Inc., *Tokyo*
Pearson Education Asia Pte. Ltd., *Singapore*
Editora Prentice-Hall do Brasil Ltda., *Rio de Janeiro*

To

Our Wives and Families

for Their Support and Encouragement

CONTENTS

PREFACE

Today, professional accountants work in an exciting and complex environment that is constantly changing. Progress in information technology is occurring at an ever-increasing rate. Business organizations are changing their methods of operation and their management structures to meet the demands of an increasingly competitive environment. The economic and legal environment that accountants work in is also changing in unpredictable ways. All of these changes require that today's accounting students be better prepared than ever before to enter the challenging world of the accounting profession.

A central feature of accounting in today's business world is the interaction of accounting professionals with computer-based information systems. As primary users of information systems in organizations, accountants must participate in their design and understand their operation. Accounting managers must measure and evaluate the performance of information systems. Internal and external auditors must assess the quality of information processing and evaluate the accuracy of information input and output. The major share of the work of accounting consultants is in the design, implementation, and evaluation of information systems.

The eighth edition of *Accounting Information Systems* provides students with the knowledge and skills they need to pursue successful careers in accounting. The text reflects how information technology (IT) is altering the nature of accounting. Specifically, we discuss how such developments as the Internet, electronic commerce, EDI, data bases, and artificial intelligence are fundamentally transforming the way organizations conduct their business activities. We also explain how these IT developments are changing the way that businesses account for the results of those activities.

In addition to technology-driven changes, companies are responding to the increasingly competitive business environment by reexamining every internal activity in an effort to reap the most value at the least cost. As a result, accountants are being asked to do more than just report the results of past activities. They must take a more proactive role in both providing and interpreting financial and nonfinancial information about the organization's activities. Therefore, throughout this text we discuss how accountants can improve the design and functioning of the accounting information system (AIS) so that it truly adds value to the organization. For example, each cycle chapter uses data modeling to illustrate how accounting information systems can effectively integrate internally generated financial and nonfinancial data about organizational activities with other, externally generated data (e.g., customer credit ratings and satisfaction).

As with the first seven editions, this book is written to help students acquire the understanding and knowledge of accounting information systems that they must have to succeed in their chosen field. Today's accounting students will become tomorrow's users, auditors, and managers of computer-based information systems. To be successful in pursuing an accounting career, students must possess a basic knowledge of computer-based information systems and their role in performing the accounting function in contemporary business organizations. Graduating students must understand the following key concepts:

- The business activities performed in the five major business cycles as well as the flow of accounting data and information in those systems
- The collection and processing of data about those business activities
- The use of the latest information technology (IT) developments to improve the efficiency and effectiveness of business activities
- The development, implementation, and maintenance of accounting information systems (AIS)
- Internal control objectives and the effects of IT on these objectives
- Fundamental concepts of data base technology and its effect on AIS
- The design of an AIS to provide the information needed to make key decisions in each business cycle
- The tools of AIS work, such as data flow diagrams and flowcharting

This book is intended for use in a one-semester course in accounting information systems at the undergraduate or graduate level. Introductory financial and managerial accounting courses are suggested prerequisites, and an introductory course in data processing that covers a computer language or a software package is helpful. The book can also be used as the main text in graduate or advanced undergraduate courses in management information systems.

MAJOR CHANGES IN THE EIGHTH EDITION

The eighth edition of the book has been reorganized. The 21 chapters in the seventh edition were divided into five major sections or parts. The 19 chapters of the eighth edition are divided into four major parts. A number of reviewers have asked that the application (cycle) chapters be presented earlier in the text. Accordingly, we have moved the chapters on systems development to the end of the text and moved the other parts forward in the book. Therefore, Part One is Conceptual Foundations and consists of Chapters 1 through 7. Part Two is now Control and Audit and consists of Chapters 8 through 11. Part Three, AIS Applications, consists of Chapters 12 through 16. Finally, Part Four is Systems Development and consists of Chapters 17 through 19. The chapters on development can now be taught from the perspective of the students already having studied the applications that are to be developed.

The three-chapter Part Two of the Seventh Edition, "The Technology of Accounting Information Systems," no longer exists. The chapter on Personal Information Systems was deleted and the material was spread throughout the book as appropriate. The review of computer hardware and software is now an appendix to Chapter 4. The material in the chapter on data communication systems is now in the new chapter on electronic commerce, Chapter 7.

A significant effort was expended in this edition to make the book shorter and even easier for students to read and use. The whole text was reexamined with a view to tightening the exposition and presenting every concept in as clear and straightforward a manner as possible.

Another way we shortened the book's length was to move the five comprehensive cases to our new web site. Each case contains a list of requirements that correspond to specific chapters. This organization allows the instructor to tailor the case requirements to his or her choice of course objectives and topical coverage.

NEW FEATURES

Companion web site. A web site provides additional information and support to users of our text. Please feel free to visit the web site at http://www.prenhall.com/romney.

Increased coverage of business strategy. The concept of the value chain classifies information technology as a support activity. This means that investments in information technology are not an end in themselves, but must be linked to an organization's strategy and strategic position. Chapter 1 has been rewritten to discuss basic strategies and the strategic positions that firms can pursue. This material is placed in the first chapter so that students immediately begin to think about how information technology can be used to help organizations achieve their goals.

Improved coverage of data bases and data modeling. Accountants are increasingly becoming involved in data base design. The discussion of relational data bases in Chapter 5 has been improved by using ACCESS to illustrate the concepts and by moving the SQL material to the chapter appendix. Chapter 6 has been revised to more clearly explain the REA approach to data modeling. Many more examples are provided. Additional homework problems designed to help students progressively hone their data modeling skills are also included.

Enhanced coverage of e-commerce. Chapter 7 has been revised to focus on e-commerce. Topics covered include FEDI and control issues. The discussion of information technology concepts about networking and data communications has been rewritten to focus on how IT supports and enables e-commerce.

Continued focus on transaction cycles from a business process perspective. Chapters 12 through 15 cover the revenue, expenditure, production, and human resource business processes. In-depth coverage of how those processes are executed is combined with a thorough discussion of control issues. Improved REA diagrams illustrate how data about these processes can be stored in integrated data bases. Chapter 16 discusses both traditional general ledger systems and also enterprise resource planning (ERP) systems. Additional measurement topics that are part of the "New Finance," such as the balanced scorecard, are also covered.

Updated coverage of computer fraud and security. The chapter on computer fraud was updated to include the new techniques that perpetrators are using to defraud companies. Many of these involve the Internet and other electronic commerce applications. Many examples of recent frauds have been included to illustrate the fraud techniques.

Improved presentation of the systems development process. The three chapters on systems development have been reorganized to provide a more logical flow to the information. Chapter 17 provides an overview of the development process and discusses systems analysis concepts, concluding with a definition of user needs. Chapter 18 discusses the many options an organization has for acquiring or developing an AIS to meet those needs (e.g., purchasing software, writing software, end-user developed software, and outsourcing) or speeding up or improving the development process (business process reengineering, prototyping, and computer-assisted software engineering). Chapter 19 concludes with a discussion of how to design, implement, operate, and maintain a system to meet user needs.

CONTINUING FEATURES

Each chapter begins with an integrative case, based on one of four fictional companies, that introduces the chapter's key concepts and topics. This case is integrated throughout the chapter, and a description of how the issues are resolved is provided in the summary and case conclusion.

We continue to include one to four focus boxes in each chapter. The focus boxes are summaries of articles describing how specific companies are using the latest IT developments to improve their AIS. Numerous real-world examples, featuring both large and small companies in a variety of industries, have also been added to each chapter to highlight and reinforce key concepts.

Each chapter continues to have at least two end-of-chapter cases. One is a stand-alone case. The other is the AnyCompany case, which provides students with the opportunity to apply their knowledge to the specific problems and challenges faced by a business in their local area. The AnyCompany case also gives students the chance to practice their written and oral communication skills in a realistic setting. The requirements for each AnyCompany case are tailored to the topics offered in its chapter. These suggested requirements are too extensive to permit assignment of multiple AnyCompany cases in one semester. Instead, we encourage instructors to select the case(s) with requirements that most closely match their course objectives. Alternatively, instructors can choose selected requirements from several chapters to create a customized term project that reflects the topics they stress in their course.

The end-of-chapter material is designed to help students develop and test their knowledge. It includes both new and revised discussion questions, problems, and cases that integrate material from various parts of the chapter. Many problems were developed from reports in current periodicals. Other problems were selected from the various professional examinations, including the CPA, CMA, CIA, and SMAC exams. In addition, each chapter includes a short multiple-choice quiz, with answers provided at the end of the chapter. Students can use the quiz to test their understanding of the main topics in the chapter.

The text contains hundreds of figures, diagrams, flowcharts, and tables that illustrate the concepts taught in the chapters. At the end of the book is an extensive bibliography, organized by chapter. This list contains references to the real-world examples used in each chapter and provides students with a starting point for further research on topics of interest.

Finally, the comprehensive glossary at the back of the book has been extensively revised.

AN OVERVIEW OF THE EIGHTH EDITION

Part One: Conceptual Foundations of Accounting Information Systems

Part One consists of seven chapters that present the underlying concepts fundamental to an understanding of AIS. Chapter 1 introduces basic terminology and discusses how an AIS can add value to an organization. It also discusses basic strategies and the strategic positions that firms can pursue, so that students can understand how information technology can be used to help organizations achieve their goals.

Chapter 2 provides an overview of AIS topics, illustrated in the context of a simple manual system. This information helps students to understand what an accounting information system does; as they read the remainder of the book, they see how advances in information technology affect the manner in which those functions are performed. This coverage is especially useful if the curriculum has been changed so that the AIS course is now the first class accounting majors take after Principles.

Chapter 3 covers systems development and documentation techniques, focusing on data flow diagrams and flowcharts.

Chapter 4 discusses transaction processing in automated systems, presenting basic information processing and data storage concepts. An appendix to Chapter 4 reviews hardware and software concepts for any students that did not learn this material in another course.

Chapter 5 introduces students to data bases, with a particular emphasis on the relational data model and query languages.

Chapter 6 discusses data modeling and the design of a data base AIS. This chapter illustrates how the data base technology covered in Chapter 5 can be used to design an AIS that more fully meets the information needs of managers. Chapter 6 also demonstrates how traditional financial statements and managerial reports can be derived from a data base AIS.

Chapter 7 discusses the role of electronic commerce in today's business organizations. The chapter also discusses telecommunications concepts and applications as well as the Internet and the World Wide Web.

Part Two: Control and Audit of Accounting Information Systems

Part Two consists of four chapters. Chapter 8 provides a conceptual overview of controls and control theory. The material was written to reflect the terminology used in the COSO report.

Chapter 9 discusses the many specific computer controls used in business organizations.

Chapter 10 focuses on computer fraud and security, explaining how and why fraud occurs and the methods for preventing and detecting it.

Chapter 11 reviews principles and techniques for audit evaluation of internal control in computer-based AIS and introduces the topic of computer-assisted auditing.

Part Three: Accounting Information Systems Applications

Part Three consists of five chapters, each of which focuses on one of the business cycles. Chapter 12 covers the revenue cycle, including sales, billing, accounts receivable, and cash receipts.

Chapter 13 covers the expenditure cycle, including purchases, receiving, accounts payable, and cash disbursements.

Chapter 14 covers the production cycle, with a special focus on the implications of recent cost accounting developments, such as activity-based costing, for the design of the production cycle information system.

Chapter 15 discusses the human resources management (HRM)/payroll cycle and explores the ways in which these two systems can be integrated.

Chapter 16 focuses on the general ledger and reporting activities in an organization.

All five chapters have been written to reflect the three basic functions performed by the AIS: (1) efficient transaction processing, (2) provision of adequate internal controls to safeguard assets (including data), and (3) preparation of information useful for effective decision making. Both batch and on-line processing systems are presented. A data model for each cycle is described, as are the effects of data bases on the design and functioning of an AIS. The role of information technology in providing a competitive advantage is stressed and numerous real-world examples are incorporated throughout these five chapters.

Part Four: The Systems Development Process

As explained previously, the material in Part Four has been reorganized into three chapters. Chapter 17 introduces the systems development life cycle and discusses the introductory steps of this process (systems analysis, feasibility, and planning). Particular emphasis is placed on the behavioral ramifications of change.

Chapter 18 discusses the various development strategies used to obtain a new AIS.

Chapter 19 covers the remaining stages of the systems development life cycle (design, implementation, and operation) and emphasizes the interrelationships among the phases.

Many real-world examples are included in all three of these chapters to enable students to understand the accountant's role in the systems development process.

Instructional Supplements

Our objective in preparing this textbook has been to simplify the teaching of AIS by enabling instructors to concentrate on classroom presentation and discussion, rather than on locating, assembling, and distributing teaching materials. As further support, a number of supplementary materials, listed below, are also available free of charge to adopters of the text.

Solutions Manual prepared by authors

Instructors Manual/Test Item File (TIF) by Ashutosh Deshmukh, Pennsylvania State University at Erie

PH Custom Text Manager for Windows computerized test item file

PowerPoint Presentation by Olga Quintana, University of Miami

Companion Web Site/On-line Study Guide by Scott Summers, Brigham Young University

ACKNOWLEDGMENTS

We wish to express our appreciation to all supplements authors for preparing the various supplements that accompany this edition. We also thank Martha M. Eining of the University of Utah and Carol F. Venable of San Diego State University for preparing the comprehensive cases included on our web site. We are grateful to Iris Vessey for her contributions to the problem material.

We appreciate the help of Alexandria Wagley of Brigham Young University in typing and preparing the various drafts of the book and the *Solutions Manual.*

Perhaps most importantly, we are indebted to the numerous faculty members throughout the world who have adopted the earlier editions of this book and who have been generous with their suggestions for improvement. We are especially grateful to those who participated in reviewing the eighth edition throughout various stages of the revision process:

Benny R. Copeland, University of North Texas
F. Todd DeZoort, University of South Carolina
Cheryl L. Dunn, Florida State University
David R. Fordham, James Madison University
Leon J. Hanouille, Syracuse University
Dena W. Johnson, Texas Tech University
J. Edward Ketz, Pennsylvania State University
Bonnie W. Morris, West Virginia University

Paul J. Robertson, New Mexico State University
David H. Sinason, Northern Illinois University
Anthony M. Tinker, CUNY–Baruch College
Jon Woodroof, Middle Tennessee State University
Jeanne H. Yamamura, University of Nevada, Reno

We are grateful for permission received from four professional accounting organizations to use problems and unofficial solutions from their past professional examinations in this book. Thanks are extended to the American Institute of Certified Public Accountants for use of the CPA Examination materials, to the Institute of Certified Management Accountants for use of CMA Examination materials, to the Institute of Internal Auditors for use of CIA examination materials, and to the Society of Management Accountants of Canada for use of SMAC Examination materials.

Of course, any errors in this book remain our responsibility. We welcome your comments and suggestions for further improvement.

Finally, we want to thank our wives and families for their love, support, and encouragement. We also want to thank God for giving us the ability to start and complete this book.

Marshall B. Romney
Provo, Utah
Paul John Steinbart
Tempe, Arizona

PART ONE

CHAPTER 1

Accounting Information Systems: An Overview

LEARNING OBJECTIVES

After studying this chapter, you should be able to

- Explain what an accounting information system (AIS) is.
- Explain why studying AIS is important.
- Describe the two basic strategies and the three basic strategic positions a business can adopt.
- Discuss the role played by the AIS in a company's value chain and explain how the AIS can add value to a business.

Integrative Case: S&S, Inc.

After working for several years as a regional manager for a national retailing organization, Scott Parry decided to open his own business. Susan Gonzalez, one of his district managers, had also wanted to go into business for herself. Together they formed S&S, Inc. to sell home appliances to the public. S&S's product line includes both large kitchen and laundry appliances as well as smaller items like toasters and radios. Scott and Susan rented a large and attractive building in a busy part of the town. They each contributed enough money to see them through the first six months of business.

Scott and Susan arranged to carry many major brand names of appliances. Because of limited capital, however, they will only display a few models of each appliance in their showroom. The manufacturers will also supply parts, since S&S wants to provide full service for everything it sells. Scott and Susan estimate that they need to hire 10 to 15 employees—2 or 3 to work in the office, 2 or 3 in delivery, 2 to provide service and repairs, and 4 to 6 in sales. They plan to begin hiring these employees within the next two weeks.

Scott and Susan plan to hold the grand opening of S&S in five weeks. As they review what remains to be done to meet that deadline, Scott and Susan realize that they have not yet made a number of important decisions:

1. How to organize their accounting records so that the financial statements required by their banker can be easily produced.
2. How to design a set of procedures to ensure that they meet all of their government obligations, such as remitting sales, income, and payroll taxes.

3. How to price their products to be competitive yet earn a profit.
4. Whether to extend credit, on what terms, and how to accurately track what customers owe and have paid.
5. How to hire, train, and supervise their employees; what compensation and benefits packages to offer them; and how to process payroll.
6. How to keep track of cash inflows and outflows so that S&S is not caught in a cash squeeze.
7. The appropriate product mix and quantities to carry given S&S's limited showroom space.

Although Scott and Susan could make many of these decisions on the basis of an educated guess or gut feel, they will probably make better decisions if they obtain additional information. A well-designed accounting information system (AIS) can solve some of these issues. Moreover, if properly designed, the AIS can provide some of the information needed to make the remaining decisions.

INTRODUCTION

We begin this chapter by defining what an accounting information system (AIS) is. Next we discuss why AIS is an important topic to study. Then we describe how an AIS adds value to an organization.

WHAT IS AN AIS?

A **system** is a set of two or more interrelated components that interact to achieve a goal. Systems are almost always composed of smaller subsystems, each performing a specific function important to and supportive of the larger system of which it is a part. For example, the College of Business is a system composed of various departments, each of which is a subsystem. Yet, at the same time, the College itself is a subsystem of the university.

An **accounting information system (AIS)** consists of people, procedures, and information technology. The AIS performs three important functions in any organization:

1. It collects and stores data about activities and transactions so that the organization can review what has happened.
2. It processes data into information that is useful for making decisions that enable management to plan, execute, and control activities.
3. It provides adequate controls to safeguard the organization's assets, including its data. These controls ensure that the data is available when needed and that it is accurate and reliable.

Most organizations engage in many similar and repetitive transactions. These transaction types can be grouped into the five basic cycles, each of which constitutes a basic subsystem in the AIS:

1. The **expenditure cycle** consists of the activities involved in buying and paying for goods or services used by the organization.

2. The **production cycle** consists of the activities involved in converting raw materials and labor into finished products. (*Note:* Only manufacturing companies have a production cycle; retail organizations, like S&S, simply buy finished goods for resale to others.)
3. The **human resources/payroll cycle** consists of the activities involved in hiring and paying employees.
4. The **revenue cycle** consists of the activities involved in selling goods or services and collecting payment for those sales.
5. The **financing cycle** consists of those activities involved in obtaining the necessary funds to run the organization and in repaying creditors and distributing profits to investors.

As shown in Fig. 1.1, the basic activities in each of the five cycles can be described in terms of a give-to-get relationship.[1] For example, the expenditure cycle entails giving up cash in order to get goods and services. Similarly, the revenue cycle entails giving up goods and services in order to get cash. Figure 1.1 also shows how the five cycles (or subsystems) of the AIS are related to one another and how each feeds data to the **general ledger and reporting system** that provides information to both internal and external users. Each of the AIS subsystems (cycles) is described in more detail in Chapter 2 and in Part III of the text.

WHY STUDY AIS?

Many universities require accounting majors to take an AIS course. Many universities also require accounting students to take one or more other information systems courses. Some universities even require information systems majors to take the AIS course. This section explains why the AIS course is important and how it fits into both the accounting and information systems curriculum.

The Study of AIS Is Fundamental to Accounting

In *Statement of Financial Accounting Concepts No. 2,* the Financial Accounting Standards Board defined accounting as being an information system. It also stated that the primary objective of accounting is to provide information useful to decision makers. Therefore, it is not surprising that the Accounting Education Change Commission recommended that the accounting curriculum should emphasize that accounting is an information identification, development, measurement, and communication process. The commission suggested

[1]The idea of modeling an AIS as a set of give-to-get exchanges was developed in Cheryl L. Dunn and William E. McCarthy, "Conceptual Models of Economic Exchange Phenomena: History's Third Wave of Accounting Systems," *Collected Papers of the Sixth World Congress of Accounting Historians*, Volume 1 (Kyoto, Japan): 133–164; and in Guido Geerts and William E. McCarthy, "Modeling Business Enterprises as Value-Added Process Hierarchies with Resource-Event-Agent Object Templates," *Business Object Design and Implementation: OOPSLA 1995 Workshop Proceedings,* October 16, 1995 (Austin, Tex.: Springer).

FIGURE 1.1
An AIS and Its Subsystems
Adapted from classroom materials developed by Julie Smith David at Arizona State University, and based on ideas developed in the sources identified in footnote 1.

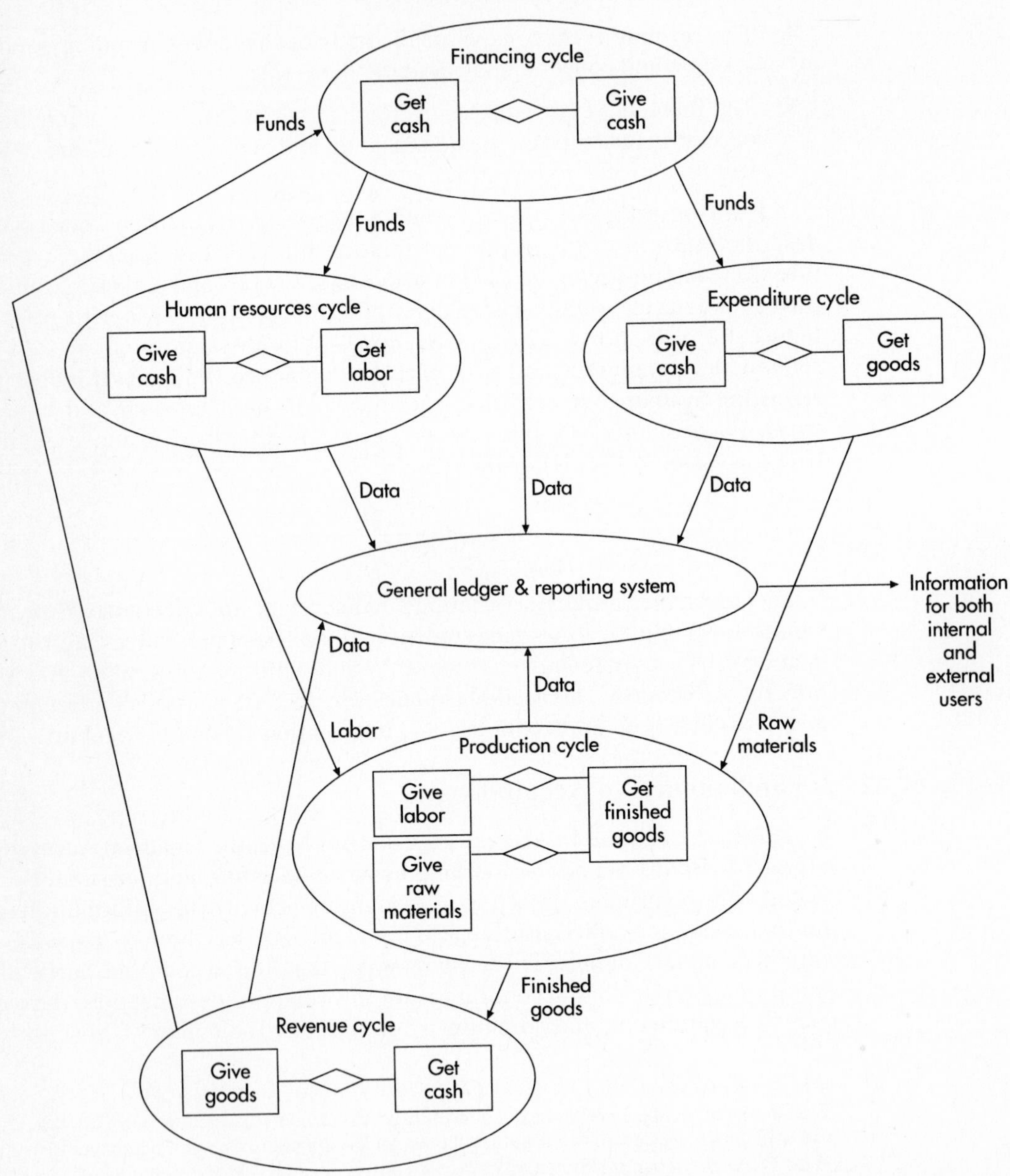

that the accounting curriculum should be designed to provide students with a solid understanding of three essential concepts:

1. The use of information in decision making
2. The nature, design, use, and implementation of an AIS
3. Financial information reporting

The other accounting courses that you take (financial accounting, managerial accounting, tax, and audit) focus on your role as a preparer or reporter of information. In contrast, the AIS course focuses on understanding how the accounting system works: how to collect data about an organization's activities and transactions; how to transform that data into information that management can use to run the organization; and how to ensure the availability, reliability, and accuracy of that information. Thus the AIS course complements the other accounting courses you will take.

Some of you intend to pursue careers in the public accounting profession. If so, you may become an auditor. Auditors need to understand the systems that are used to produce a company's financial statements. This course provides you with that knowledge; indeed, that is why many universities make the AIS course a prerequisite to the auditing course. Alternatively, you may want to specialize in tax. If so, you will need to understand enough about your clients' AIS to be confident that the information used for tax planning and compliance work is complete and accurate. A third career option for accounting majors is management consulting. Indeed, many CPA firms now derive less than half of their revenues from traditional auditing and tax services; the majority of their revenue now comes from providing various types of consulting services. One of the fastest growing types of consulting services entails the design, selection, and implementation of new AISs. Consequently, many CPA firms and other consulting organizations are interested in hiring students who have specialized in AIS. This course is an important component of such a specialization.

Not all accounting majors pursue careers in public accounting, however. Many of you will eventually find yourselves working in private industry or for not-for-profit organizations. Recently, the Institute of Management Accountants (IMA) conducted an intensive analysis of the job duties of corporate accountants. Table 1.1 presents the responses to a question asking respondents to indicate the five most critical work activities performed by accountants. Notice that respondents clearly indicated that work relating to accounting systems was the single most important activity performed by corporate accountants.

The AIS Course Complements Other Systems Courses

There are many other systems courses that cover the design and implementation of information systems, and that help you develop specialized skills in such areas as data bases, expert systems, and telecommunications. The AIS course differs from these other information systems courses in its focus on accountability and control. These issues are important, because in most large businesses the managers are not the owners. Instead, the owners have entrusted

TABLE 1.1 Ten Most Important Work Activities Performed by Accountants

1. Accounting systems and financial reporting
2. Long-term strategic planning
3. Managing the accounting and finance function
4. Internal consulting
5. Short-term budgeting
6. Financial and economic analyses
7. Process improvement
8. Computer systems and operations
9. Performance evaluation (of the organization)
10. Customer and product profitability analyses

Source: "The Practice Analysis of Management Accounting," An IMA Research Project, conducted by the Gary Siegel Organization (March 1996), p. 9.

management with assets and hold them accountable for their proper use. Therefore, Part II of the text addresses the design of controls to ensure the safeguarding of an organization's assets.

Data and information are among an organization's most valuable assets. To see why, consider what would happen if an organization lost all information about what its customers owed it, or if a list of its most profitable customers was obtained by a competitor. Clearly, the AIS must include controls to ensure safety and availability of the organization's data. Controls are also needed to ensure that the information produced from that data is both reliable and accurate. These topics usually receive little attention in other systems courses. Thus the AIS course complements other systems courses you may take.

Concerns about data reliability and security are relevant not only to accountants, but also to all information systems professionals. Moreover, since typically the AIS is one of the largest systems in most organizations, information systems professionals should have a basic understanding of how it works. Thus the AIS course is an important part of the education of information systems students.

INFORMATION TECHNOLOGY AND CORPORATE STRATEGY

Refer back to Table 1.1; notice that the second most important job activity of corporate accountants is long-term strategic planning. One important aspect of this topic is covered in this course: how to align information technology (IT) with an organization's strategy. As Fig. 1.2 shows, corporate strategy is one of the factors that should influence the design of an AIS.

Figure 1.2 also shows that new developments in IT affect the design of an AIS. Indeed, in the past decade, IT has profoundly changed the way that accounting and many other business activities are performed. Moreover, that

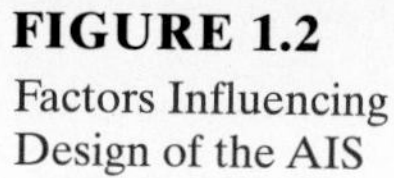

FIGURE 1.2
Factors Influencing Design of the AIS

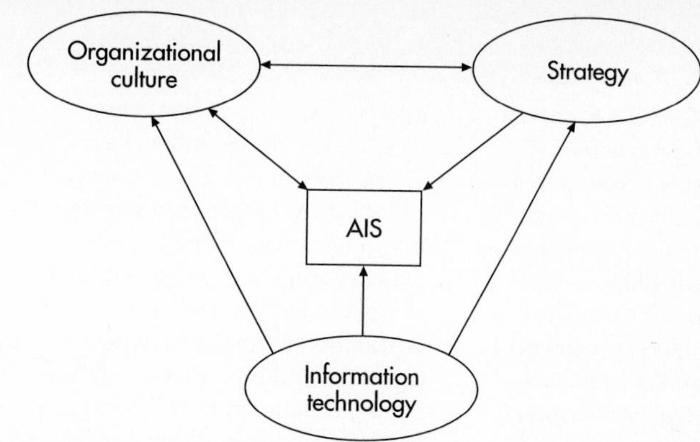

impact is likely to continue in the future. Therefore, this text focuses on understanding how IT can be used to accomplish the basic functions of the AIS.

The AIS course, however, is more than a computer course. To be sure, your professor will likely include out-of-class projects designed to help you to refine and improve your computer skills. Nevertheless, you also need to know how to evaluate the costs and benefits of new IT developments. This requires developing a basic understanding of corporate strategies and how IT developments can be used to implement existing organizational strategies or create an opportunity to modify those strategies (note the arrow from IT to strategy in Fig. 1.2).

Moreover, because an AIS functions within an organization, it should be designed to reflect the values of that organizational culture. Thus Fig. 1.2 also shows that the organizational culture influences the design of the AIS. Note, however, that unlike the case with strategy and IT, the arrow between organizational culture and the AIS is bidirectional. This reflects the fact that the AIS influences the organizational culture. One way it does so is through choices on how, and to whom, it disseminates information. For example, an AIS that makes information easily accessible and widely available is likely to increase pressures for more decentralization and autonomy. Throughout this text, therefore, we discuss the potential behavioral ramifications of making changes to a company's AIS. Focus 1.1 describes some of the difficulties in transferring an AIS designed for one organizational culture to another.

THE AIS AND CORPORATE STRATEGY

There are many opportunities to invest in IT so that the AIS can be improved to add value to an organization. Most organizations, however, do not have unlimited resources. Therefore, an important decision involves identifying which potential AIS improvements are likely to yield the greatest return. Making this decision wisely requires that accountants and information systems professionals understand their organization's strategy.

FOCUS 1.1 7-Eleven Discovers Difficulty in Transferring IS Across Cultures

ITO-YOKADO CO., the Japanese company that controls 7-Eleven stores, is learning that attempting to transplant successful changes in business processes to another culture is difficult. In Japan, average 7-Eleven store sales have doubled over the past two decades. At the same time, inventory turnover has dropped from 25 days to 7.

Toshifumi Suzuki, CEO of Ito-Yokado Co., credits much of that success to the use of an advanced point-of-sale (POS) system that helps each store to run a just-in-time inventory system. Store managers use the system to identify and respond to changes in sales trends. Food is delivered three times a day, to minimize waste.

Mr. Suzuki is encountering resistance to his plans to implement the same system in the United States, however. A major problem is that the POS system enables corporate headquarters to closely monitor the daily activities of each store manager. Indeed, headquarters tracks how much time each manager spends using the analytical tools provided by the system. Stores are ranked by time of use, and mangers who do not use the computer enough are warned to increase their usage.

Managers of U.S. stores bristle at such control. They also argue that the system is linked too tightly to current sales trends, and would not allow them the flexibility to stock shelves in response to special events like a local basketball tournament. Some also criticize the system for being too slow.

Mr. Suzuki shrugs off the complaints and says: "American 7-Elevens don't have a choice: It's either adopt our plans or die." Time will tell if he is right.

Source: Norihiko Shirouzu and Jon Bigness, "7-Eleven Operators Resist System to Monitor Managers," *Wall Street Journal* (June 16, 1997): B1, B3

Strategy and Strategic Positions[2]

Michael Porter, world-renowned professor of business at Harvard, notes that to be successful in the long run, a company "must deliver greater value to customers or create comparable value at a lower cost, or do both."[3] In other words, companies must choose to follow one of two strategies: (1) to be a lower-cost producer than their competitors, or (2) to differentiate their products and services from their competitors. Sometimes, a company can succeed in both producing a better product than its competitors and in doing so at costs below its industry average. Usually, however, companies must choose between these two basic strategies. If they concentrate on being the lowest-cost producer, they will have to forgo some value-added features that might differentiate their product. If they focus on product differentiation, they most likely will not have the lowest costs in their industry. Thus strategy involves making choices.

Porter argues that the fundamental choice companies must make involves selecting the strategic position they wish to adopt. He describes three basic strategic positions:

1. A *variety-based* strategic position involves producing or providing a subset of the industry's products or services. Jiffy Lube International is

[2]The material in this section is based on Michael E. Porter, "What Is Strategy?" *Harvard Business Review* (November–December 1996): 61–78.

[3] Michael E. Porter, "What Is Strategy?" *Harvard Business Review* (November–December 1996): 62.

an example of a company that has adopted a variety-based strategic position: it does not provide a wide range of automotive repair services, but focuses on oil changes and lubrication services.

2. A *needs-based* strategic position involves trying to serve most or all of the needs of a particular group of customers. For example, AARP focuses on retirees.
3. An *access-based* strategic position involves serving a subset of customers who differ from other customers in terms of factors, such as geographic location or size, which create different requirements for serving those customers. Edward Jones is an example of a company that has adopted an access-based strategic position: its stock brokerage offices are located primarily in smaller towns and cities not served by the larger brokerage houses.

Porter explains that these three basic strategic positions are not mutually exclusive and, indeed, often overlap. For example, although Jiffy Lube can be described as having a variety-based strategic position, it also has a needs-based focus by appealing to convenience-oriented customers who do not want to change their oil themselves and who can afford to pay a higher price for quicker service than would be provided at a company that offered a wider range of automobile repair services. Similarly, Southwest Airlines appears to have adopted elements of all three strategic positions. It does not offer first-class seating or meals (variety-based); it does offer low fares, attracting price-sensitive customers (needs-based); and it avoids large airports (access-based).

Porter argues that the specific strategic position selected is not important. Rather, the key is to design all of a company's activities so that they mutually reinforce one another in achieving the corporate strategy. When this occurs, a company reaps the benefits of synergy—the entire system of activities performed by the company is greater than the sum of each individual part. This makes it difficult for competitors to successfully imitate, because they must do more than just mimic specific procedures. Indeed, companies that have achieved a high degree of fit among their activities often do not worry about keeping their processes secret from competitors, because they know that they cannot be adopted piecemeal. This explains why Toyota, for example, regularly allows executives of other automobile manufacturers to tour its facilities.

The AIS plays an important role in helping an organization adopt and maintain a strategic position. Achieving a close fit among activities requires that data be collected about each activity. That data must then be transformed into information that can be used by management to coordinate those activities. To be of value, that information must be reliable and always available. Thus a well-designed AIS is essential to successfully adopting a sustainable strategic position.

Choosing a strategic position is important because it enables a company to focus its efforts. Otherwise, the company risks trying to be everything to everybody. Once a strategic position has been chosen, however, a company must seek to design its operations to maximize both efficiency and effectiveness. The value chain is a tool that can be used to help a company understand its essential activities and, thereby, identify those areas where additional investments in IT are likely to have the greatest effect.

THE VALUE CHAIN[4]

The ultimate goal of any business is to provide value to its customers. A business will be profitable if the value it creates is greater than the cost of producing its products or services. An organization's **value chain** consists of nine interrelated activities that collectively describe everything it does. As shown in Fig. 1.3, the nine activities in the value chain can be divided into two basic categories: primary activities and support activities.

The five **primary activities** in the value chain consist of the activities performed in order to create, market, and deliver products and services to customers and also to provide post-sales service and support:

1. *Inbound logistics* consists of receiving, storing, and distributing the materials that are inputs used by the organization to create the services and products that it sells. For example, the activities of receiving, handling,

[4] This section is based on Michael E. Porter and Victor E. Millar, "How Information Gives You Competitive Advantage," *Harvard Business Review* (July–August 1985): 149–160.

FIGURE 1.3
The Value Chain

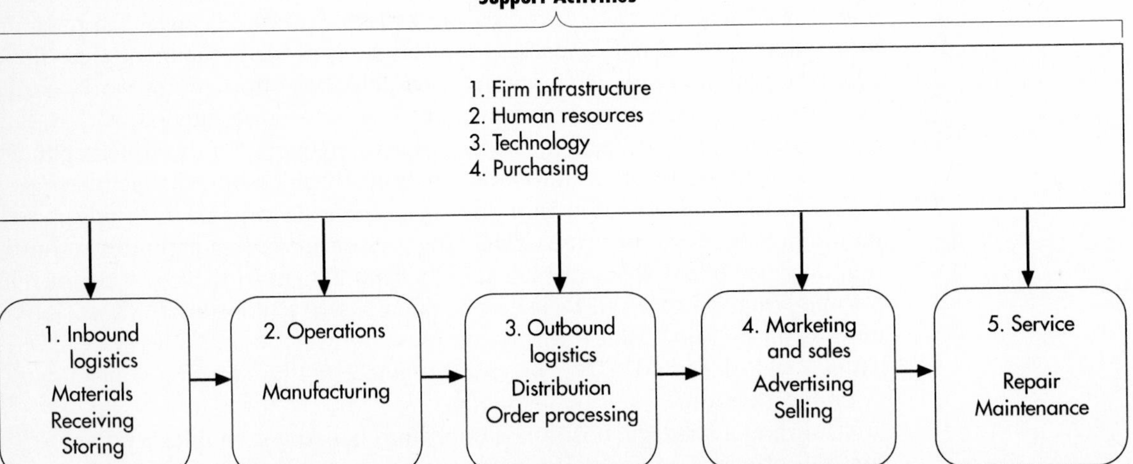

and storing the steel, glass, and rubber make up the inbound logistics activities for an automobile manufacturer.

2. *Operations* activities transform inputs into final products or services. For example, the assembly line activities in an automobile company convert raw materials into a finished car.
3. *Outbound logistics* are the activities involved in distributing finished products or services to customers. For example, shipping automobiles to car dealers is an outbound logistics activity.
4. *Marketing and sales* refers to the activities involved in helping customers to buy the organization's products or services. Advertising is an example of a marketing and sales activity.
5. *Service* activities provide post-sale (after the sale) repair and maintenance functions to customers.

The four **support activities** in the value chain make it possible for the primary activities to be performed efficiently and effectively:

1. *Firm infrastructure* refers to the accounting, finance, legal support, and general administration activities that are necessary for any organization to function. The AIS is part of the firm infrastructure. Thus the AIS plays a key role in the value chain by providing much of the information needed to perform the five primary activities.
2. *Human resources* activities include recruiting, hiring, training, and providing employee benefits and compensation.
3. *Technology* activities improve a product or service. Examples include research and development, information technology, and product design.
4. *Purchasing* includes all the activities involved in procuring raw materials, supplies, machinery, and the buildings used to carry out the primary activities.

The Value System

The value chain concept can be extended by recognizing that organizations must interact with suppliers, distributors, and customers. Thus as shown in Fig. 1.4, an organization's value chain and the value chains of its suppliers, distributors, and customers collectively form a **value system**. By paying attention to the interorganizational linkages in its value system, a company can add value to itself by helping the other organizations in its value system to improve their value chains. In our opening case, for example, S&S can reduce its purchasing and inbound logistics costs by implementing a just-in-time inventory management system and linking those systems directly to its suppliers' information systems. S&S benefits in two ways. First, costs are reduced because its own purchasing and inbound logistics activities are performed more efficiently, and with a reduction in the amount of capital tied up in inventory. Second, S&S's suppliers can more efficiently plan their production schedules to meet S&S's needs.

FIGURE 1.4
The Value System

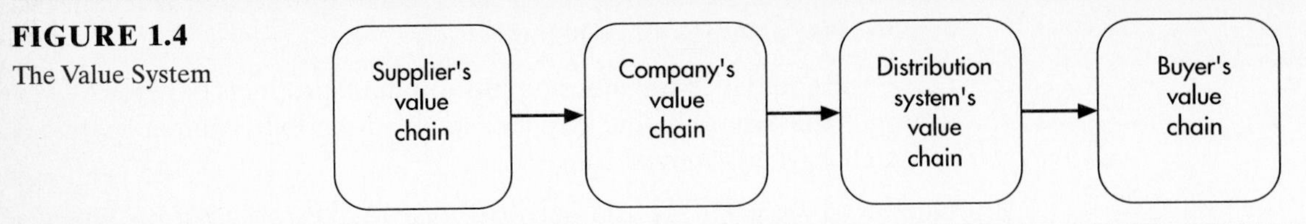

This reduces their costs, and part of that reduction is likely to be passed on to S&S in the form of lower product costs.

HOW AN AIS CAN ADD VALUE TO AN ORGANIZATION

Developments in information technology illustrate one way in which improvements in support activities can dramatically transform how an organization performs its primary activities. For example, the development of the Internet enables software companies to conduct their outbound logistics activities electronically. This change simultaneously reduces both the costs and time of delivering products to customers.

Recall that the AIS is part of the firm infrastructure that supports the performance of an organization's other value chain activities. To see this, note how the various subsystems of the AIS depicted in Fig. 1.1 can be linked to different parts of the value chain. For example, the expenditure cycle captures and processes information about the purchasing and inbound logistics activities. The human resources cycle and the production cycle support the human resources and operations portions of the value chain, respectively. The revenue cycle captures and processes information about the outbound logistics, sales and marketing, and service activities. The financing cycle supports the other firm infrastructure activities necessary to any organization.

One way the AIS adds value is by providing accurate and timely information to perform the various value chain activities. A well-designed AIS can further improve the efficiency and effectiveness of those activities by

1. *Improving the quality and reducing the costs of products or services.* For example, an AIS can monitor machinery so that operators are notified immediately when the process falls outside acceptable quality limits. This simultaneouly helps maintain product quality and reduce the amount of wasted materials and the costs of rework.

2. *Improving efficiency.* A well-designed AIS can help improve the efficiency of operations by providing more timely information. For example, a just-in-time manufacturing approach requires constant, accurate, and up-to-date information about raw materials inventories and their locations.

3. *Improved decision making.* An AIS can improve decision making by providing accurate information in a timely manner to appropriate

employees. For example, Frito-Lay collects data about customer inventories on a daily basis so that managers can better analyze sales trends. This enables Frito-Lay to quickly identify the causes of changes in sales and initiate corrective action. Thus, when sales of Tostitos tortilla chips declined in Texas, Frito-Lay launched an investigation and found that a small competitor had introduced a new white corn tortilla chip. Within three months, Frito-Lay introduced its own white corn chip and won back its lost market share.

4. *Sharing of knowledge.* A well-designed AIS can help to share knowledge and expertise, thereby improving operations and even providing a competitive advantage. For example, public accounting firms use a corporate intranet to share best practices and to support communication among people located at different offices. Employees can search the company-wide data base to identify the relevant experts to provide assistance for a particular client; thus, all of the firm's accumulated international expertise can be available to any local client.

A well-designed AIS can also help an organization profit by improving the efficiency and effectiveness of its value system. For example, allowing customers to directly access the company's inventory and sales order entry systems can reduce the costs of sales and marketing activities. Moreover, if such access reduces customers' costs and time of ordering, both sales and customer retention rates may increase. Of course, creating such interorganizational information systems raises new control concerns that must be addressed. It also requires increased reliability and accuracy of the data in the AIS.

Focus 1.2 describes how Wal-Mart linked improvements in its AIS to its strategy, so that its AIS contributed to its success by both improving its own value chain activities and by improving the operations of its value system.

INFORMATION AND DECISION MAKING

We have repeatedly emphasized how a well-designed AIS can add value by providing information useful for decision making. This section defines information and discusses the information needed to make various kinds of decisions.

What Is Information?

The term **data** refers to any and all of the facts that are collected, stored, and processed by an information system. **Information** is data that has been organized and processed so that it is meaningful. Table 1.2 lists six characteristics that make information useful and meaningful.

Decision Making

Researchers have developed many models of the decision-making and problem-solving process. All those models depict decision making as a complex,

FOCUS 1.2 How Wal-Mart Uses IT and Its AIS to Succeed

WAL-MART is the most successful and fastest growing retail chain in history. In part, this success is due to the way it uses its AIS and IT to improve the efficiency and effectiveness of its value chain activities. Wal-Mart has spent billions of dollars implementing one of the most sophisticated communications and distribution networks in the world. The system gives Wal-Mart a technological and competitive advantage over most other discounters. Consequently, Wal-Mart has increased productivity, lowered costs, and raised profitability.

Wal Mart uses a centralized distribution system for products that are not shipped directly to individual stores. When boxes of merchandise arrive at the distribution center, they are placed on conveyor belts. Laser scanners read the bar codes on each box to identify where each package should go. The boxes are then routed to the appropriate shipping location. Point-of-sale (POS) scanners reduce customer wait time at check out and provide accurate monitoring of inventory levels. Most purchases and payments are done electronically.

Wal-Mart's system also has improved the efficiency of its value system. The AIS allows some suppliers, such as Procter & Gamble (P&G), to directly manage the inventory of their products. Whenever a P&G product falls below the reorder level, the AIS automatically notifies the nearest P&G factory. P&G's system then checks inventory levels, notifies Wal-Mart when the products will be delivered, and ships them to the appropriate store. This arrangement reduces the amount of buffer inventory Wal-Mart needs to carry and also helps P&G better plan its own production. Thus both Wal-Mart and P&G reap the benefits of lower costs.

Source: Arthur A. Thompson, Jr., and A. J. Strickland III, *Strategic Management—Concepts and Cases,* 6th ed. (Boston: Irwin, 1992): 955–987.

multistep activity. First, the problem has to be identified. Then the decision maker must select a method for solving the problem. Next, the decision maker needs to collect the data needed to execute the decision model. Then he or she must interpret the outputs of the model and evaluate the merits of each alternative. Finally, the decision maker chooses and executes the preferred solution.

The AIS can provide assistance in all phases of the decision-making and problem-solving processes. Reports can help to identify potential problems. Different decision models and analytical tools can be provided to users. Query languages can facilitate the gathering of relevant data upon which to make the decision. Various tools, such as graphical interfaces, can help the decision maker interpret the results of a decision model and in evaluating alternative courses of action. Finally, the AIS can provide feedback on the results of actions.

Types of Decisions

One objective of the AIS is to provide information useful for decision making. To design an AIS to meet that objective, you must understand the different kinds of decisions that are made in organizations. Decisions can be categorized either in terms of the degree of structure that exists or by the scope of the decision.

TABLE 1.2 Characteristics of Useful Information

Relevant	Information is relevant if it reduces uncertainty, improves decision makers' ability to make predictions, or confirms or corrects their prior expectations.
Reliable	Information is reliable if it is free from error or bias and accurately represents the events or activities of the organization.
Complete	Information is complete if it does not omit important aspects of the underlying events or activities that it measures.
Timely	Information is timely if it is provided in time to enable decision makers to use it to make decisions.
Understandable	Information is understandable if it is presented in a useful and intelligible format.
Verifiable	Information is verifiable if two knowledgeable people acting independently each produce the same information.

Decision Structure. Decisions vary in terms of the degree to which they are structured. **Structured decisions** are repetitive, routine, and understood well enough that they can be delegated to lower-level employees in the organization. For example, the decision about extending credit to established customers requires only knowledge about the customer's credit limit and current balance. Indeed, structured decisions can often be automated.

Semistructured decisions are characterized by incomplete rules for making the decision and the need for subjective assessments and judgments to supplement formal data analysis. Setting a marketing budget for a new product is an example of a semistructured decision. Although semistructured decisions usually cannot be fully automated, they are often be supported by computer-based decision aids.

Unstructured decisions are nonrecurring and nonroutine. Examples include choosing the cover for a magazine, hiring senior management, and the choice of basic research projects to undertake. No framework or model exists to solve such problems. Instead, they require considerable judgment and intuition. Nevertheless, they can be supported by computer-based decision aids that facilitate gathering information from diverse sources.

Decision Scope. Decisions vary in terms of the scope of their effect. **Operational control** is concerned with the effective and efficient performance of specific tasks. Decisions relating to inventory management and extending credit are examples of operational control activities. **Management control** is concerned with the effective and efficient use of resources for accomplishing organizational objectives. Budgeting, developing human resource practices, and deciding on research projects and product improvements are examples of management control activities. **Strategic planning** is concerned with establishing organizational objectives and policies for accomplishing those objectives. Setting financial and accounting policies, developing new product lines, and acquiring new businesses are examples of strategic planning decisions.

A correspondence exists between a manager's level in an organization and his or her decision-making responsibilities. Top management faces unstructured and semistructured decisions involving strategic planning issues. Middle managers deal with semistructured decisions involving management control. Lower-level supervisors and employees face semistructured or structured decisions involving operational control.

Each type of decision occurs in all five of the basic accounting cycles described earlier:

- *Revenue cycle.* How much should be charged for each product? What discount and credit terms, if any, should be offered? What should warranty policies be? Which items are the most and least profitable? How much should be spent on advertising and market research?
- *Expenditure cycle.* How much inventory should be purchased? When? From which vendors? How should vendors be selected?
- *Production cycle.* How much of each product should be made? When? Which methods should be used? How should common costs be allocated? Should new investments in advanced technologies be made?
- *Human resource/payroll cycle.* How many hours did employees work, and how much should they be paid? What deductions should be made from each employee's paycheck? Are all employees continuing to adequately improve their skills? How effective and efficient are current training programs? What skills are in short supply? What are trends in turnover and absenteeism? Are we complying with all applicable government employment regulations? Are appropriate tax regulations being complied with?
- *Financing cycle.* What are current cash inflows and outflows? Is there a need for short- or long-term borrowing? What sources of funding should the organization use for scheduled capital expenditures? Do we have adequate insurance coverage? What should credit and collection policies be?

All these decisions require information that can come from a well-designed AIS. Accounting information plays two major roles in managerial decision making. First, it identifies situations requiring management action. For example, a cost report with a large variance might stimulate management to investigate and, if necessary, take corrective action. Second, by reducing uncertainty, accounting information provides a basis for choosing among alternative actions. For example, accounting information is often used to set prices and determine credit policies. It is important, however, to consider the potential value of information when designing an AIS to meet the many decision needs of management.

Value of Information

The **value of information** is the benefit produced by the information minus the cost of producing it. The benefits of information include a reduction in uncertainty, improved decisions, and a better ability to plan and schedule the organization's activities. The costs of producing information include the time and resources spent in collecting, processing, and storing data as well as the time and resources used to distribute the resulting information to decision makers.

Unfortunately, determining the value of information is not as easy as it sounds. It is hard to identify and quantify all of the costs, especially the indirect ones, associated with producing information. It is often even harder to quantify the benefits of providing additional information.

Information Overload

It is true that more information is better, but only to a point. There are limits to the amount of information that the human mind can effectively absorb and process. **Information overload** occurs when those limits are passed. Information overload is costly, because decision-making quality declines while the costs of providing that information increase. Thus information overload reduces the value of information.

Decision aids are designed to help people process information. Even with such tools, however, there are limits to the amount of information that can be effectively processed. Consequently, information systems designers need to consider how advances in information technology can help decision makers more effectively filter and condense information, thereby avoiding information overload. Case 1.2, at the end of this chapter, presents a classic discussion of information overload and how a well-designed information system can help solve this problem.

THE FUTURE OF AIS

Traditionally, the AIS has been referred to as a transaction processing system because it was concerned only with financial data and accounting transactions. For example, when a sale took place, the AIS would record a journal entry showing only the date of the sale, a debit to either cash or accounts receivable, and a credit to sales. Other potentially useful information about the sale, such as the time of day that it occurred, would traditionally be collected and processed outside of the AIS. Consequently, many organizations developed additional information systems to collect, process, store, and report information not contained in the AIS.

Unfortunately, the existence of multiple systems creates a number of problems and inefficiencies. Often, the same data must be captured and stored by more than one system. Not only does this result in redundancy across systems, it also can lead to discrepancies if the data is changed in one system but not in others. In addition, it is difficult to effectively integrate data from the various systems.

Enterprise resource planning systems are a recent development designed to overcome these problems. **Enterprise resource planning (ERP) systems** integrate all aspects of a company's operations with its traditional AIS. Thus, when the sales force enters an order, the effect of the transaction automatically flows to all affected parts of the company. Inventory is updated, production schedules are adjusted, and purchase orders are initiated to acquire any needed raw materials and supplies.

The important point underlying enterprise resource planning systems is the need for and value of cross-functional integration. Financial data must be linked to other nonfinancial operating data. This means that the traditionally separate functions of information systems and accounting need to become much more closely connected. Indeed, many organizations are beginning to combine these two functions. For example, several universities have recently merged their accounting and information systems departments. This text adopts a similar viewpoint. Therefore, we do not try to distinguish between an AIS and other organizational information systems. Instead, we assume that the AIS is *the* information system of the organization and that it will provide users with the information they need.

SUMMARY AND CASE CONCLUSION

Scott and Susan need a well-designed AIS to provide the information they need to effectively plan, manage, and control their business. S&S's AIS must be able to process data about sales and cash receipts, the purchase and payment for merchandise and services, payroll and tax-related transactions, and the acquisition of and payment for fixed assets, and it must be able to prepare financial statements.

Fortunately, there are many computer-based accounting packages available for the retail industry. Scott and Susan quickly learn, however, that considerable accounting knowledge is required to choose the specific package that will best fit their business. Thus, since they both have little background in accounting, their next task will be to hire an accountant to design an AIS for S&S, Inc.

KEY TERMS

- system
- accounting information system (AIS)
- expenditure cycle
- production cycle
- human resources/payroll cycle
- revenue cycle
- financing cycle
- general ledger and reporting system
- value chain
- primary activities
- support activities
- value system
- data
- information
- structured decisions
- semistructured decisions
- unstructured decisions
- operational control
- management control
- strategic planning
- value of information
- information overload
- enterprise resource planning (ERP) systems

CHAPTER QUIZ

1. Data differs from information in that
   a. data is output and information is input.
   b. information is output and data is input.
   c. data is meaningful information.
   d. there is no difference.

2. All of the following are characteristics of information *except*
   a. reliable.
   b. timely.
   c. inexpensive.
   d. relevant.

3. Which of the following is a primary activity in the value chain?
   a. Purchasing
   b. Accounting
   c. Service
   d. Human resource management

4. The subsystem of the AIS that includes inbound logistics activities is the
   a. revenue cycle.
   b. expenditure cycle.
   c. production cycle.
   d. human resource management cycle.

5. Information overload involves
   a. having too much information.
   b. not having enough information.
   c. structured decisions.
   d. unstructured decisions.

6. In the value chain concept, information technology is a
   a. primary activity.
   b. support activity.
   c. service activity.
   d. structured activity.

7. Lower-level management employees are most likely to make
   a. structured decisions involving strategic planning.
   b. unstructured decisions involving managerial control.
   c. structured decisions involving operational control.
   d. unstructured decisions involving strategic planning.

8. The value of information equals
   a. the costs of producing the information minus its benefits.
   b. the benefits of the information minus the costs to produce it.
   c. the price at which the information could be sold to some outside party.
   d. the cost of producing the information.

9. A firm, its suppliers, and its customers collectively form a(n)
   a. value system.
   b. value chain.
   c. ERP system.
   d. AIS.

10. A company that provides weekly maid service to upper-middle and upper-income dual-career families is most likely implementing which of the following strategic positions?
   a. Variety-based
   b. Needs-based
   c. Access-based
   d. Low-cost

DISCUSSION QUESTIONS

1.1 Apply the value chain concept to S&S, Inc. Explain how it performs the various primary and supporting activities.

1.2 The value of information was defined to equal the difference between the decision benefits and the costs of producing that information. Would you, or any organization, ever produce information if its expected costs exceeded its benefits? Provide some examples.

1.3 One of the functions of the AIS is to provide adequate controls to ensure the safety of organizational assets, including data. Many people, however, often view control procedures as "red tape." Discuss how well-designed controls, instead of being red tape, can improve overall efficiency and effectiveness.

1.4 How can recent developments in information technology affect the ways that organizations accomplish their primary value chain activities?

1.5 Focus 1.1 described 7-Eleven's difficulty in transferring its POS system from Japan to the United States. Do you think that an AIS can ever be successfully transferred across cultures? Why or why not? What could 7-Eleven headquarters have done differently to improve the chances of successful transfer of its POS system to the United States?

1.6 Give an example of each type of decision (operational control, management control, and strategic planning) that is made at S&S, Inc. Describe the degree of structure inherent in each of your examples. What kinds of information can S&S's AIS provide?

1.7 Focus 1.2 described how investments in IT contributed to Wal-Mart's success. How can a company determine whether it is spending too much, too little, or just enough on IT?

1.8 Table 1.2 lists several characteristics that make information useful. Can all those characteristics be simultaneously met? If not, what kinds of trade-offs might sometimes be required?

1.9 Information technology enables organizations to easily collect large amounts of information about employees. Discuss the following issues:

a. To what extent should management monitor employees' e-mail?
b. To what extent should management monitor which web sites are visited by employees?
c. To what extent should management monitor employee performance by, for example, using software to track keystrokes per hour or other unit of time? If such information is collected, how should it be used?
d. Should companies use software to electronically "shred" all traces of e-mail?
e. Under what circumstances and to whom is it appropriate for a company to distribute information it collects about the people who visit its web site?

PROBLEMS

1.1 Write a two-page report explaining the two basic strategies that S&S, Inc. can pursue and the three different strategic positions that it can adopt. Include in your report a discussion and examples of how information technology can be used to support the different strategies and strategic positions.

1.2 Information technology is continually changing the nature of accounting and the role of accountants. Write a two-page report describing what you think it will be like to be a controller or CFO in the year 2010.

1.3 The annual report is considered by some to be the single most important printed document that companies produce. In recent years annual reports have become large documents. They now include such sections as letters to the stockholders, descriptions of the business, operating highlights, financial review, management discussion and analysis, segment reporting, and inflation data as well as the basic financial statements. The expansion has been due in part to a general increase in the degree of sophistication and complexity in accounting standards and disclosure requirements for financial reporting.

The expansion also is reflective of the change in the composition and level of sophistication of users. Current users include not only stockholders, but financial and securities analysts, potential investors, lending institutions, stockbrokers, customers, employees, and, whether the reporting company likes it or not, competitors. Thus a report that was originally designed as a device for communicating basic financial information now attempts to meet the diverse needs of an ever-expanding audience.

Users hold conflicting views on the value of annual reports. Some argue that annual reports fail to provide enough information, whereas others believe that disclosures in annual reports have expanded to the point where they create information overload. The future of most companies depends on acceptance by the investing public and by its customers; therefore, companies should take this opportunity to communicate well-defined corporate strategies.

Required:

a. The goal of preparing an annual report is to communicate information from the corporation to its targeted users.
   1. Identify and discuss the basic factors of communication that must be considered in the presentation of this information.
   2. Discuss the communication problems a corporation faces in preparing the annual report that result from the diversity of the users being addressed.
b. Select two types of information found in an annual report, other than the financial statements and

accompanying footnotes, and describe how they are useful to the users of annual reports.

c. Discuss at least two advantages and two disadvantages of stating well-defined corporate strategies in the annual report.

d. Evaluate the effectiveness of annual reports in fulfilling the information needs of the following current and potential users:
   1. Shareholders
   2. Creditors
   3. Employees
   4. Customers
   5. Financial analysts

e. Annual reports are public and accessible to anyone, including competitors. Discuss how this affects decisions about what information should be provided in annual reports.
(CMA Examination, adapted)

1.4 Research how a company is using information technology to improve the efficiency and effectiveness of its value chain activities. Write a two-page report summarizing what you learn.

1.5 Write a two-page report about a company that is successfully using information technology to exploit and improve its value system.

CASES

The first case at the end of each chapter is an assignment that allows you to apply key concepts to a local company. This case, then, may become an ongoing case study that you work on throughout the term.

CASE 1.1 ANYCOMPANY, INC.—AN ONGOING COMPREHENSIVE CASE

Visit a small- to medium-sized business in your community and explain that you have been assigned to study a local company. Ask for permission to study the company and explain that you will need to meet with company employees several times during the term to get pertinent information. However, you will not need a great deal of their time or disrupt their business. Offer to share your findings and to make suggestions as a way of motivating the firm to allow you to study them.

Required:

Once you have lined up a company, answer the following questions.

1. What types of information systems does the company have? What subsystems does it have? Describe each information system and explain its purpose.
2. Who are the major external users of company information? The major internal users? What information is produced for each set of users?
3. For two system outputs, identify the decisions that are made with that information, the data collected to produce the information, how the data are stored and processed to produce the information, and how instructions and procedures are given to the system and its users. Use the characteristics of information (reliable, timely, etc.) to evaluate the usefulness of the information provided.
4. What information does the company lack that it would like to have?
5. How does the company's information system add value to the organization?

CASE 1.2 ACKOFF'S MANAGEMENT MISINFORMATION SYSTEMS

This case is adapted from a classic article entitled "Management Misinformation Systems." It was written by Russell L. Ackoff and appeared in *Management Science*. In the article, Ackoff identified five common assumptions about information systems and then explained why he disagreed with them.

REQUIRED:

Read the five assumptions, contentions, and Ackoff's explanation. For each of the five, decide whether you agree or disagree with Ackoff's contentions. Defend the stand you take by preparing a report that explains why you believe what you do. Be prepared to defend your beliefs in class.

ASSUMPTION 1: MANAGEMENT NEEDS MORE INFORMATION

Assumption 1. Most MISs [Management Information Systems] are designed based on the assumption that the critical deficiency under which most managers operate is the lack of relevant information.

Contention 1. I do not deny that most managers lack a good deal of information that they should have, but I do deny that this is the most important informational deficiency from which they suffer. It seems to me that they suffer more from an overabundance of irrelevant information.

This is not a play on words. The consequences of changing the emphasis of an MIS from supplying relevant information to eliminating irrelevant information is considerable. If one is preoccupied with supplying relevant information, attention is almost exclusively given to the generation, storage, and retrieval of information: Hence emphasis is placed on constructing data banks, coding, indexing, updating files, using access languages, and so on. The ideal that has emerged from this orientation is an infinite pool of data into which managers can reach to pull out any information they want. If, on the other hand, one sees the manager's information problem primarily, but not exclusively, as one that arises out of an overabundance of irrelevant information, most of which was not asked for, then the two most important functions of an information system become filtration (or evaluation) and condensation. The literature on the MIS seldom refers to these functions, let alone considers how to carry them out.

My experience indicates that most managers receive much more data (if not information) than they can possibly absorb even if they spend all of their time trying to do so. Hence they already suffer from an information overload. They must spend a great deal of time separating the relevant documents. For example, I have found that I receive an average of 43 hours of unsolicited reading material each week. The solicited material is usually half again this amount.

I have seen a daily stock status report that consists of approximately six hundred pages of computer printout. The report is circulated daily across managers' desks. I've also seen requests for major capital expenditures that come in book size, several of which are distributed to managers each week. It is not uncommon for many managers to receive an average of one journal a day or more. One could go on and on.

Unless the information overload to which managers are subjected is reduced, any additional information made available by an MIS cannot be expected to be used effectively.

Even relevant documents have too much redundancy. Most documents can be considerably condensed without loss of content. My point here is best made, perhaps, by describing briefly an experiment that a few of my colleagues and I conducted on the operations research (OR) literature several years ago. By using a panel of well-known experts, we identified four OR articles that all members of the panel considered to be "above average" and four articles that were considered to be "below average." The authors of the eight articles were asked to prepare "objective" examinations (duration 30 minutes) plus answers for graduate students who were to be assigned the articles for reading. (The authors were not informed about the experiment.) Then several experienced writers were asked to reduce each article to two-thirds and one-third of its original length only by eliminating words. They also prepared a brief abstract of each article. Those who did the condensing did not see the examinations to be given to the students.

A group of graduate students who had not previously read the articles were then selected. Each one was given four articles randomly selected, each of which was in one of its four versions: 100%, 67%, 33%, or abstract. Each version of each article was read by two students. All were given the same examinations. The average scores on the examinations were compared.

For the above-average articles there was no significant difference between average test scores for the 100%, 67%, and 33% versions, but there was a significant decrease in average test scores for those who had read only the abstract. For the below-average articles there was no difference in average test scores among those who had read the 100%, 67%, and 33% versions, but there was a significant increase in average test scores of those who had read only the abstract.

The sample used was obviously too small for general conclusions, but the results strongly indicate the extent to which even good writing can be condensed without loss of information. I refrain from drawing the obvious conclusions about bad writing.

It seems clear that condensation as well as filtration, performed mechanically or otherwise, should be an essential part of an MIS, and that such a system should be capable of handling much, if not all, of the unsolicited as well as solicited information that a manager receives.

ASSUMPTION 2: MANAGERS NEED THE INFORMATION THEY WANT

Assumption 2. Most MIS designers "determine" what information is needed by asking managers what information they would like to have. This is based on the assumption that managers know what information they need and want.

Contention 2. For a manager to know what information he needs, he must be aware of each type of decision he should (as well as does) make and he must have an adequate model of each. These conditions are seldom satisfied.

Most managers have some conception of at least some of the types of decisions they must make. Their conceptions, however, are likely to be deficient in a very critical way, a way that follows from an important principle of scientific economy: The less we understand a phenomenon, the more variables we require to explain it. Hence managers who do not understand the phenomena they control play it "safe" and, with respect to information, want "everything." The MIS designer, who has even less understanding of the relevant phenomena than the manager, tries to provide even more than everything. She thereby increases what is already an overload of irrelevant information.

For example, market researchers in a major oil company once asked their marketing managers what variables they thought were relevant in estimating the sales volume of future service stations. Almost 70 variables were identified. The market researchers then added about half again this many variables and performed a large multiple linear regression analysis of sales of existing stations against these variables and found about 35 to be statistically significant. A forecasting equation was based on this analysis. An OR team subsequently constructed a model based on only one of these variables, traffic flow, which predicted sales better than the 35-variable regression equation. The team went on to explain sales at service stations in terms of the customers' perception of the amount of time lost by stopping for service. The relevance of all but a few of the variables used by the market researchers could be explained by their effect on such a perception.

The moral is simple: One cannot specify what information is required for decision making until an explanatory model of the decision process and the system involved has been constructed and tested. Information systems are subsystems of control systems. They cannot be designed adequately without taking control into account. Furthermore, whatever else regression analyses can yield, they cannot yield understanding and explanation of phenomena. They describe and, at best, predict.

ASSUMPTION 3: GIVING MANAGERS THE INFORMATION THEY NEED IMPROVES THEIR DECISION MAKING

Assumption 3. It is frequently assumed that if managers are provided with the information they need, they will then have no problem in using it effectively.

Contention 3. Operations research (an academic subject area dealing with the application of mathematical models and techniques to business decisions) stands to the contrary.

Give most managers an initial tableau of a typical "real" mathematical programming, sequencing, or network problem and see how close they come to an optimal solution. If their experience and judgment have any value, they may not do badly, but they will seldom do very well. In most management problems there are too many possibilities to expect experience, judgment, or intuition to provide good guesses, even with perfect information.

Furthermore, when several probabilities are involved in a problem, the unguided mind of even a manager has difficulty in aggregating them in a valid way. We all know many simple problems in probability in which untutored intuition usually does very badly (e.g., What are the correct odds that 2 of 25 people selected at random will have their birthdays on the same day of the year?). For example, very few of the results obtained by queuing theory, when arrivals and service are probabilistic, are obvious to managers; nor are the results of risk analysis where the managers' own subjective estimates of probabilities are used.

The moral: It is necessary to determine how well managers can use needed information. When, because of the complexity of the decision process, they can't use it well, they should be provided with either decision rules or performance feedback so that they can identify and learn from their mistakes.

ASSUMPTION 4: MORE COMMUNICATION MEANS BETTER PERFORMANCE

Assumption 4. The characteristic of most MISs is that they provide managers with better current information about what other managers and their departments are doing. Underlying this provision is the belief that better interdepartmental communication enables managers to coordinate their decisions more effectively and hence improves the organization's overall performance.

Contention 4. Not only is this not necessarily so, but it seldom is so. One would hardly expect two competing companies to become more cooperative because the information each acquires about the other is improved.

For example, consider the following very much simplified version of a situation I once ran into. The simplification of the case does not affect any of its essential characteristics. A department store has two "line" operations: buying and selling. Each function is performed by a separate department. The Purchasing Department primarily controls one variable: how much of each item is bought. The Merchandising Department controls the price at which it is sold. Typically, the measure of performance applied to the Purchasing Department was the turnover rate of inventory. The measure applied to the Merchandising Department was gross sales; this department sought to maximize the number of items sold times their price.

Now by examining a single item, let us consider what happens in this system. The merchandising manager, using his knowledge of competition and consumption, set a price that he judged would maximize gross sales. In doing so, he utilized price-demand curves for each type of item. For each price the curves show the expected sales and values on an upper and lower confidence band as well. [See Fig. 1.5.] When instructing the Purchasing Department about how many items to make available, the merchandising manager quite naturally used the value on the upper confidence curve. This minimized the chances of his running short, which, if it occurred, would hurt his performance. It also maximized the chances of being overstocked, but this was not his concern, only the purchasing manager's. Say, therefore, that the merchandising manager initially selected price P_1 and requested that amount Q_1 be made available by the Purchasing Department.

In this company the purchasing manager also had access to the price-demand curves. She knew that the merchandising manager always ordered optimistically. Therefore, using the same curve, she read over from Q_1 to the upper limit and down to the expected value, from which she obtained Q_2, the quantity she actually intended to make available. She did not intend to pay for the merchandising manager's optimism. If merchandising ran out of stock, it was not her worry. Now the merchandising manager was informed about what the purchasing manager had done, so he adjusted his price to P_2. The purchasing manager in turn was told that the merchandising manager had made this readjustment, so she planned to make only Q_3 available. If this process (made possible only by perfect communication between departments) had been allowed to continue, nothing would have been bought and nothing would have been sold. This outcome was avoided by prohibiting communication between the two departments and forcing each to guess what the other was doing.

I have obviously caricatured the situation in order to make the point clear: When organizational units have inappropriate measures of performance that put them in conflict with each other, as is often the case, communication between them may hurt organizational performance, not help it. Organizational structure and performance measurement must be taken into account before opening the floodgates and permitting the free flow of information between parts of the organization.

ASSUMPTION 5: MANAGERS NEED ONLY TO UNDERSTAND HOW TO USE AN INFORMATION SYSTEM

Assumption 5. A manager does not have to understand how an information system works, only how to use it.

Contention 5. Managers must understand their MIS or they are handicapped and cannot properly operate and control their company.

Most MIS designers seek to make their systems as innocuous and unobtrusive as possible to managers, lest they become frightened. The designers try to provide managers with very easy access to the system and assure them that they need to know nothing more about it. The designers usually succeed in keeping managers ignorant in this regard. This leaves managers unable to evaluate the MIS as a whole. It often makes them afraid to even try to do so, lest they display their ignorance publicly. In failing to evaluate their MIS, managers delegate much of the control of the organization to the system's designers and operators—who may have many virtues, but managerial competence is seldom among them.

FIGURE 1.5

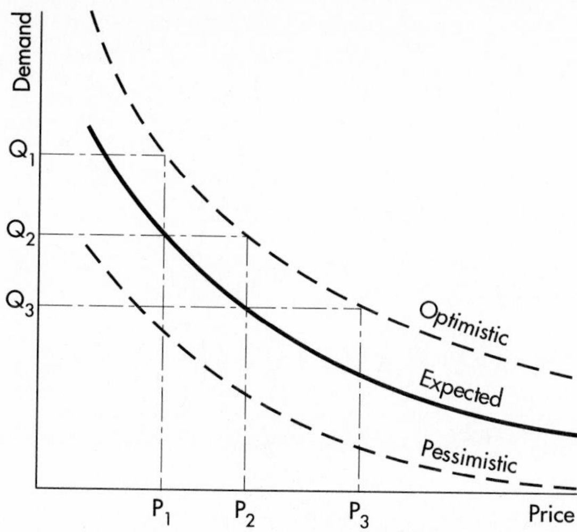

Let me cite a case in point. A chairman of the board of a medium-size company asked for help on the following problem. One of his larger (decentralized) divisions had installed a computerized production inventory control and manufacturing manager information system about a year earlier. It had acquired about $2 million worth of equipment to do so. The board chairman had just received a request from the division for permission to replace the original equipment with newly announced equipment that would cost several times the original amount. An extensive "justification" for so doing was provided with the request. The chairman wanted to know whether the request was justified. He admitted to complete incompetence in this connection.

A meeting was arranged at the division, at which I was subjected to an extended and detailed briefing. The system was large but relatively simple. At the heart of it was a reorder point for each item and a maximum allowable stock level. Reorder quantities took lead time as well as the allowable maximum into account. The computer kept track of stock, ordered items when required, and generated numerous reports on both the state of the system it controlled and its own "actions."

When the briefing was over, I was asked if I had any questions. I did. First I asked if, when the system had been installed, there had been many parts whose stock level exceeded the maximum amount possible under the new system. I was told there were many. I asked for a list of about 30 and for some graph paper. Both were provided. With the help of the system designer and volumes of old daily reports I began to plot the stock level of the first listed item over time. When this item reached the maximum "allowable" stock level, it had been reordered. The system designer was surprised and said that by sheer "luck" I had found one of the few errors made by the system. Continued plotting showed that because of repeated premature reordering the item had never gone much below the maximum stock level. Clearly, the program was confusing the maximum allowable stock level and the reorder point. This turned out to be the case in more than half of the items on the list.

Next I asked if they had many paired parts, ones that were only used with each other, for example, matched nuts and bolts. They had many. A list was produced and we began checking the previous day's withdrawals. For more than half of the pairs the differences in the numbers recorded as withdrawn were very large. No explanation was provided.

Before the day was out it was possible to show by some quick and dirty calculations that the new computerized system was costing the company almost $150,000 per month more than the hand system that it had replaced, most of this in excess inventories.

The recommendation was that the system be redesigned as quickly as possible and that the new equipment not be authorized for the time being.

The questions asked of the system had been obvious and simple ones. Managers should have been able to ask them, but—and this is the point—they felt themselves incompetent to do so. They would not have allowed a hand-operated system to get so far out of their control.

No MIS should ever be installed unless the managers for whom it is intended are trained to evaluate and hence control it rather than be controlled by it.

Source: Reprinted by permission of Russell Ackoff, "Management Misinformation Systems," *Management Sciences* Vol. 14, No. 4, December 1967, The Institute of Management Sciences, 290 Westminster Street, Providence, R.I. 02903.

ANSWERS TO CHAPTER QUIZ

1. b **3.** c **5.** a **7.** c **9.** a
2. c **4.** b **6.** b **8.** b **10.** b

CHAPTER 2

Elements and Procedures of General Ledger-Based Accounting Information Systems

LEARNING OBJECTIVES

After studying this chapter, you should be able to

- Explain the three basic functions performed by an accounting information system (AIS).
- Describe the documents and procedures used in an AIS to collect and process transaction data.
- Discuss the types of information that can be provided by an AIS.
- Describe the basic internal control objectives of an AIS and explain how they are accomplished.

Integrative Case: S&S, Inc.

The grand opening of S&S, Inc. is two weeks away. Scott Parry and Susan Gonzalez are working long hours to make the final arrangements for the store opening. They are hiring salespeople, both to work in the store and to call on outside businesses such as builders, apartment complex owners, and others who may need large volumes of appliances. The training for both sets of salespeople is scheduled to begin next week. Several people experienced in appliance repair are also being hired.

Susan has ordered what she thinks will be an adequate amount of inventory for the first month. The store is being remodeled and will have a bright, cheery decor. All seems to be in order. All, that is, except the accounting records.

Like many entrepreneurs, Scott and Susan have not given as much thought to their accounting records as they have to other parts of their business. They recognize that they need qualified accounting help and have hired a full-time accountant, Ashton Fleming. Scott and Susan think Ashton is perfect for the job because of his two years' experience with a national CPA firm. Ashton is looking forward to working for S&S because he has always wanted to be involved in building a company from the ground up.

On Ashton's first day on the job, Susan shows him where all the invoices for the inventory that she purchased are located. Scott explains that the sales staff are paid a fixed salary plus commissions and that all other employees are paid hourly rates. Employees are paid every two weeks, with their first paychecks due next week. Susan then pulls out several folders and hands them to Ashton. One contains the documentation on their bank loan, with the first payment due several days after the grand opening. The other folders contain information on rental payments, utilities, and other expenses. Susan tells Ashton that she and Scott do not know much about accounting and are relying on him to help them decide how to run the accounting end of S&S. She adds that the only thing they have done so far is to open a checking account for S&S and that they have kept the check register up to date so that they can monitor their cash flow.

Ashton asks Scott to show him where the computer is, because he wants to see what type of system he will have to assist him in his responsibilities. Scott replies that with all the challenges they have had in opening S&S, he and Susan have not had time to tackle that aspect yet. Scott adds that they will get a computer as soon as the store opens and business stabilizes. That could take several months, however, so for now Ashton will have to keep the books by hand. Scott wants Ashton to design the manual accounting system, however, so that it can be easily automated when S&S acquires a computer.

After Scott leaves, Ashton feels both excited and a little nervous about his responsibility for creating an accounting information system (AIS) for S&S. Although Ashton has audited many companies, he has never organized a company's books and is unsure how to go about it. Nor does he really understand how to plan for a computer-based AIS. A million questions run through his head. Here are just a few of them:

1. How am I going to organize things? Where do I start? What information do Scott and Susan need to run S&S effectively? How can that information be provided?
2. How am I going to collect and process data about all the types of transactions that S&S will engage in?
3. How do I organize all the data that will be collected?
4. How should I design the AIS so that the information provided is reliable and accurate?

INTRODUCTION

The introductory story indicates that Ashton needs to design an accounting information system for S&S. We have chosen to begin with a manual AIS so that you can clearly see all the components of the system and how they interact with one another. Moreover, many commercially available accounting packages work in basically the same way as a manual AIS. Thus, when we discuss automated systems in later chapters, you will already understand the basic functions and objectives of an AIS and can concentrate on learning how developments in information technology provide opportunities to improve system efficiency and effectiveness.

This chapter addresses the three basic functions performed by an AIS:

1. To collect and store data about the organization's business activities and transactions efficiently and effectively.
2. To process data into information that is useful for decision making and make it available to all those who need it. For example, management will need information to plan, execute, and control business activities.
3. To provide adequate controls to ensure that data about business activities are recorded and processed accurately and to safeguard those data and other organizational assets.

This chapter provides an overview of how an AIS fulfills these three functions. We begin by discussing the basic types of business activities in which an organization engages, the key decisions that must be considered when managing those activities, and the information needed to make those decisions. In doing so, we show that the nature and objectives of an organization affect the design of its AIS. The next section then describes the documents and procedures that are needed to capture and process data about the typical business activities engaged in by an organization. Then we discuss the types of information reports that can be produced by the AIS for use in decision making. We conclude the chapter with a brief discussion of internal controls in a manual AIS.

BUSINESS ACTIVITIES AND INFORMATION NEEDS

Ashton decides that before designing an AIS for S&S, he must first understand how the company functions. This insight will enable him to identify the kinds of information Scott and Susan will need to manage S&S effectively. Then Ashton can determine the types of data and procedures that will be needed to collect that information.

Ashton creates a three-column table to summarize the results of his analysis. In the left column, he lists some of the basic business activities that S&S will engage in. In the middle column, he writes down some of the key decisions that need to be made for each of these activities. Finally, in the right column, he lists some of the information that Scott and Susan will need to make these decisions. Table 2.1 shows the results of this effort.

Ashton realizes that his list is not exhaustive, but he is satisfied that it provides a good overview of S&S. He also recognizes that not all the information needs listed in the right-hand column will be produced internally by S&S's AIS. Information about payment terms for merchandise purchases, for example, will be provided by vendors. Thus the AIS must be designed for effective integration of such external data with internally generated data so that Scott and Susan can use both types of information to run S&S.

Next, Ashton reorganizes the business activities listed in Table 2.1 into groups of related transactions. For example, the sale of merchandise is related to the collection of payments from customers. Similarly, the acquisition of merchandise is related to the payment of vendors. These groups of related business activities form what are called **transaction cycles.** Each transaction cycle typi-

TABLE 2.1 Overview of S & S's Business Activities, Key Decisions, and Information Needs

Business Activities	Key Decisions	Information Needs
Acquire capital	How much? Invest or borrow? If borrow, best terms?	Cash flow projections Pro-forma financial statements Loan amortization schedule
Acquire building and equipment	Size of building? Amount of equipment? Rent or buy? Location? How to depreciate?	Capacity needs Prices Market study Tax tables and regulations
Hire and train employees	Experience requirements? How to assess integrity and competence of applicants? How to train?	Job description Applicant job history and skills
Acquire inventory	What models to carry? How much to purchase? Which vendors? How to manage inventory (store, control, etc.)	Market analyses Inventory status reports Vendor performance and payment terms
Engage in advertising and marketing	Which media? Content?	Cost analyses Market coverage
Sell merchandise	Markup percentage? Offer in-house credit? Which credit cards to accept?	Pro-forma income statement Credit card costs Customer credit status
Collect payments from customers	If offer credit, what terms? How to handle cash receipts?	Customer account status Accounts receivable aging report
Pay employees	Amount to pay? Deductions and withholdings? Process payroll in-house or use outside service?	Sales (for commissions) Time worked (for hourly employees) W4 forms Costs of external payroll service
Pay taxes	Payroll tax requirements Sales tax requirements	Government regulations Total wage expense Total sales
Pay vendors	Whom to pay? When to pay? How much to pay?	Vendor invoices Accounts payable

cally processes a large number of individual transactions. Most of these transactions, however, can be categorized into a relatively small number of distinct types. For example, the majority of the individual transactions processed in the revenue cycle relate either to the sale of goods or services to customers or to the collection of cash from customers in payment for those sales.

Ashton draws Fig. 2.1 to illustrate S&S. This figure groups business activities into transaction cycles and identifies common external relationships for each cycle. The figure also lists the basic types of transactions in each cycle.

The four transaction cycles shown in Fig. 2.1 (revenue, expenditure, financing, and human resources) are found in most organizations, not just in retail merchandising companies like S&S. Other types of organizations, however, may have additional transaction cycles. Manufacturing companies, for example, have a production cycle consisting of all transactions involved in the manufacture of products. Financial institutions have demand-deposit and installment-loan cycles that relate to the transactions involving customer accounts and loans, respectively. In addition, the nature of a given transaction cycle differs across types of organizations. For example, the expenditure cycle

FIGURE 2.1
Typical Transaction Cycles and External Relationships for a Retail Company

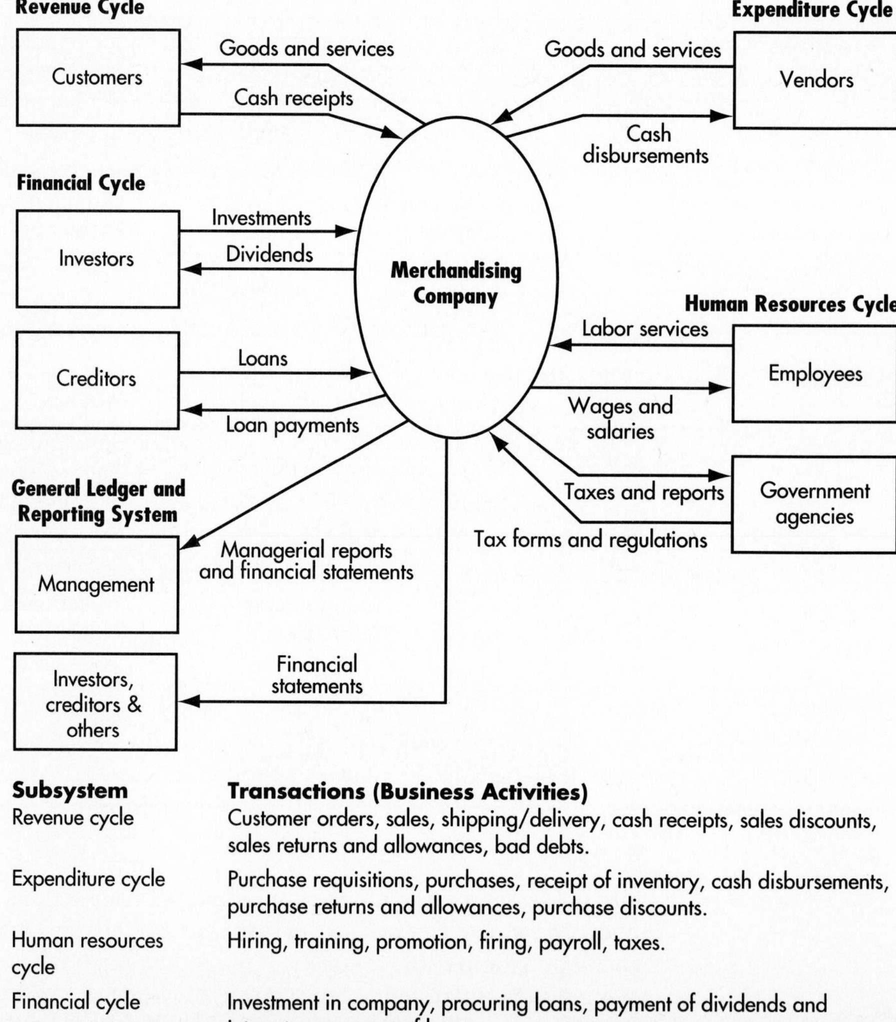

Subsystem	Transactions (Business Activities)
Revenue cycle	Customer orders, sales, shipping/delivery, cash receipts, sales discounts, sales returns and allowances, bad debts.
Expenditure cycle	Purchase requisitions, purchases, receipt of inventory, cash disbursements, purchase returns and allowances, purchase discounts.
Human resources cycle	Hiring, training, promotion, firing, payroll, taxes.
Financial cycle	Investment in company, procuring loans, payment of dividends and interest, repayment of loans.

of a service company, such as a public accounting or a law firm, does not involve processing transactions related to the purchase, receipt, and payment for merchandise that will be resold to customers.

As explained in Chapter 1, all five cycles feed information into a subsystem called the general ledger and reporting system. It is in this subsystem that all information is summarized and managerial reports and financial statements are prepared to meet the needs of internal and external users.

After preparing Table 2.1 and Fig. 2.1, Ashton believed that he understood S&S well enough to begin designing its AIS. In the next three sections, we examine the components of the manual system he developed. Although this discussion is set in the context of S&S, the components of the system represent the features typically found in any manual AIS.

TRANSACTION PROCESSING: DOCUMENTS AND PROCEDURES

One basic function of the AIS is the efficient and effective processing of data about a company's transactions. Transaction processing consists of three basic steps, performed in the following sequence:

1. Capture transaction data on source documents.
2. Record transaction data in journals, which present a chronological record of what occurred.
3. Post data from journals to ledgers, which sort data by account type.

We now examine the documents and procedures used to perform each step.

Capture Transaction Data on Source Documents

Although data about business activities could be recorded on blank pieces of paper, in notepads, or even on blackboards, better control and accuracy is provided by using special forms called **source documents.** An example of a source document used in the expenditure cycle is the purchase order (see Fig. 2.2), which is used to request merchandise from suppliers. Table 2.2 lists other common source documents used in each transaction cycle and describes their function.

Control over data collection is improved by prenumbering each source document (note the upper-right corner of the purchase order). Prenumbering simplifies verifying that all transactions have been recorded and that none of the documents have been misplaced. Accuracy is improved because source documents specify which information to collect, preprint standard information, such as addresses, and provide directions for completing the form.

Accuracy and efficiency in recording transaction data can be further improved if source documents are properly designed. Ashton recalled learning about forms design in his college AIS course. He scanned his old AIS textbook and found a checklist of principles for forms design that applied to both paper documents and computer input screens (see Table 2.3).

Now refer back to Fig. 2.2 to see how the principles listed in Table 2.3 are reflected in the sample purchase order Ashton developed. Notice that the top

FIGURE 2.2
Sample Purchase Order for S&S (bold items are preprinted)

PURCHASE ORDER **No. 101**

S&S, Inc.
Phone: (314) 555-2238
Fax: (314) 555-9863

Ship To:
S&S, Inc.
2533 Farthington Dr.
St. Louis, MO 63104-2345

Bill To:
S&S, Inc.
P.O. Box 457
St. Louis, Mo 63104-0457

Reference this number on all correspondence

To: Appliance Wholesalers
4533 Telegraph Rd.
St. Louis, MO 63129-2290

Date:	**Date Needed By:**	**Terms:**
11/23/99	12/05/2000	2/10, net 30

Item Number	**Description**	**Quantity**	**Unit Price**	**Extension**
1344	Maytag Dishwasher Model 907	10	399.95	3,999.50
2455	Maytag Freezer Model 211	5	799.95	3,999.75
			Total	$7,999.25

Shipping Instructions

____UPS
____Federal Express
____U.S. Postal Service
__x__Other: *Acme Freight*

Distribution of Copies:

white — vendor
yellow — accounts payable
blue — receiving
green — purchasing

Ashton Flemming	*Heather Finney*
Approved by	**Purchasing Agent**

of the form clearly indicates that this document is a purchase order from S&S. The heading also specifies where the merchandise should be shipped and where the invoice should be sent. Also note that the purchase order is prenumbered to facilitate tracking its status and that the vendor is instructed to reference this purchase order number in all correspondence.

Notice how the main body of the purchase order uses lines and boxes to group logically related information together. This design facilitates completing the form correctly, and it helps the recipient correctly read it. Thus adequate space is provided to record the date of the order, the date the merchandise is needed, and the terms desired. Below that, column headings indicate all the important data that needs to be entered. For example, each row in the purchase order has a space for the product number, description, quantity, and unit price

TABLE 2.2 Common Source Documents and Functions

Source Document	Function
Revenue Cycle	
Sales order	Record customer order.
Delivery ticket	Record delivery of merchandise to customer.
Credit memo	Support adjustments to customer accounts for sales returns and allowances, sales discounts, and write-off of uncollectible accounts.
Deposit slip	Record amounts of cash and checks deposited in company bank accounts.
Expenditure Cycle	
Purchase requisition	Request that purchasing department order specific goods.
Purchase order	Request merchandise from vendors.
Receiving report	Record receipt of merchandise from vendors.
Human Resources Cycle	
Time cards	Record time worked by employees.
W4 forms	Collect employee withholding data.
General Ledger & Reporting System	
Journal voucher	Record entry posted to general ledger.

of the ordered item, plus a column for an extension (quantity times price) of each line item. Toward the bottom of the purchase order, there is a box for the total amount of the order.

The bottom of the purchase order provides a space to check off the desired shipping option so that the purchasing agent need not write out the desired delivery method. Three carbon copies of the purchase order are prepared, and the distribution list for each copy is clearly indicated at the bottom of the form. Finally, there is a space at the bottom of the purchase order for the signature of the person placing the order. There is also a space for a person to indicate that the order has been reviewed and approved.

Record Transaction Data in Journals

After transaction data have been captured on source documents, the next step is to record the data in a journal. A journal entry is made for each transaction showing the accounts and amounts to be debited and credited. Ashton decided that S&S will follow the practice of most companies and use both a general journal and a set of specialized journals. The **general journal** records infrequent or nonroutine transactions, such as loan payments and end-of-period adjusting and closing entries. **Specialized journals** simplify the process of recording large numbers of repetitive transactions. S&S, like most organizations, will use specialized journals to record the four most common types of transactions: credit sales, cash receipts,

TABLE 2.3 Principles of Good Forms Design

General Considerations
- Are preprinted data used to the maximum extent possible?
- Are the weight and grade of the paper appropriate for the planned use?
- Are bold type, double-thick lines, and shading used appropriately to highlight different parts of the form?
- Is the form a standard size?
- Is the size of the form consistent with requirements for filing, binding, or mailing?
- If the form is intended to be mailed to external parties, is the address positioned so that the form can be used in a window envelope?
- Are copies of the form printed in different colors to facilitate proper distribution?
- Are there clear instructions on how to fill out the form?

Introductory Section of Form
- Does the name of the form appear at the top, in bold type?
- Is the form prenumbered consecutively?
- If the form is to be distributed to external parties, is the company's name and address preprinted on the form?

Main Body of Form
- Is logically related information (e.g., customer name, address) grouped together?
- Is there sufficient room to record each data item?
- Is the ordering of data items consistent with the sequence in which those items are most likely to be acquired?
- Are standardized explanations preprinted so that codes or checkoffs can be used instead of requiring written user entries?

Conclusion Section of Form
- Is space provided to record the final disposition of the form?
- Is space provided for a signature or signatures to indicate final approval of the transaction?
- Is space provided to record the date of final disposition or approval?
- Is space provided for a dollar or other numeric total?
- Is the distribution of each copy of the form clearly indicated?

purchases on account, and cash disbursements. To see how these specialized journals can save time, examine Table 2.4, which shows an example of a sales journal.

Notice that the sales journal has only one column to record the transaction amount. The reason is that the sales journal is used only for recording credit sales of inventory or services; consequently, every entry represents a debit to accounts receivable and a credit, for the same amount, to sales revenue. This also means that there is no need to write an explanation of each entry, as would be the case if credit sales were recorded in the general journal. Instead, all the information about the transaction is recorded in one line: the date, invoice number, name and account number of the customer, and the amount of the sale. When we consider the number of sales transactions likely to occur every day, the time saved by recording these transactions in a sales journal, rather than in the general journal, is considerable.

The remaining column in the sales journal, titled Post Ref., indicates completion of the next step in transaction processing: posting from the journals to the appropriate ledgers.

TABLE 2.4 Sample Sales Journal

Sales Journal					Page 5
Date	**Invoice Number**	**Account Debited**	**Account Number**	**Post Ref.**	**Amount**
Oct. 15	151	Brown Hospital Supply	120-035	✓	798.00
15	152	Greenshadows Hotel Suites	120-122	✓	1,267.00
15	153	Heathrow Apartments	120-057	✓	5,967.00
15	154	LMS Construction	120-173	✓	2,312.50
15	155	Gardenview Apartments	120-084	✓	3,290.00
15	156	KDR Builders	120-135	✓	1,876.50
		TOTAL			15,511.00
				120/502	

Post Transactions to Ledgers

Ledgers are used to summarize the financial status, including the current balance, of individual accounts. In a manual system, ledgers are actually books; hence, the phrase "keeping the books" refers to the process of maintaining the ledgers.

Ashton decided that S&S, like most companies, should have both a general ledger and a set of subsidiary ledgers. The **general ledger** contains summary-level data for every asset, liability, equity, revenue, and expense account of the organization. A **subsidiary ledger** records all the detailed data for any general ledger account that has many individual subaccounts. Subsidiary ledgers are commonly used for accounts receivable, inventory, fixed assets, and accounts payable.

The general ledger account corresponding to a subsidiary ledger, called a **control account,** contains the total amount for all individual accounts in the subsidiary ledger. Thus the accounts payable control account in the general ledger represents the total amount owed to all vendors. The balances in the subsidiary accounts payable ledger indicate the amount owed to each specific vendor.

The relationship between the general ledger control account and the individual account balances in the subsidiary ledger plays an important role in maintaining the accuracy of the data stored in the AIS. Specifically, the sum of all entries in the subsidiary ledger should equal the amount in the corresponding general ledger control account. For example, the inventory subsidiary ledger would contain dollar balances and quantities for each inventory item carried by S&S. The sum of all the dollar balances in the inventory subsidiary ledger should equal the total dollar balance in the inventory control account in the general ledger. Any discrepancy between the total of the subsidiary ledger and the balance in the corresponding general ledger control account indicates that an error in the recording and posting process has occurred.

The Posting Process. Ashton drew Fig. 2.3 to show Scott and Susan how the process of journalizing and posting sales transactions works. As shown in the top portion of the figure, each credit sale is first recorded in the sales journal. Each

FIGURE 2.3
Recording and Posting a Credit Sale

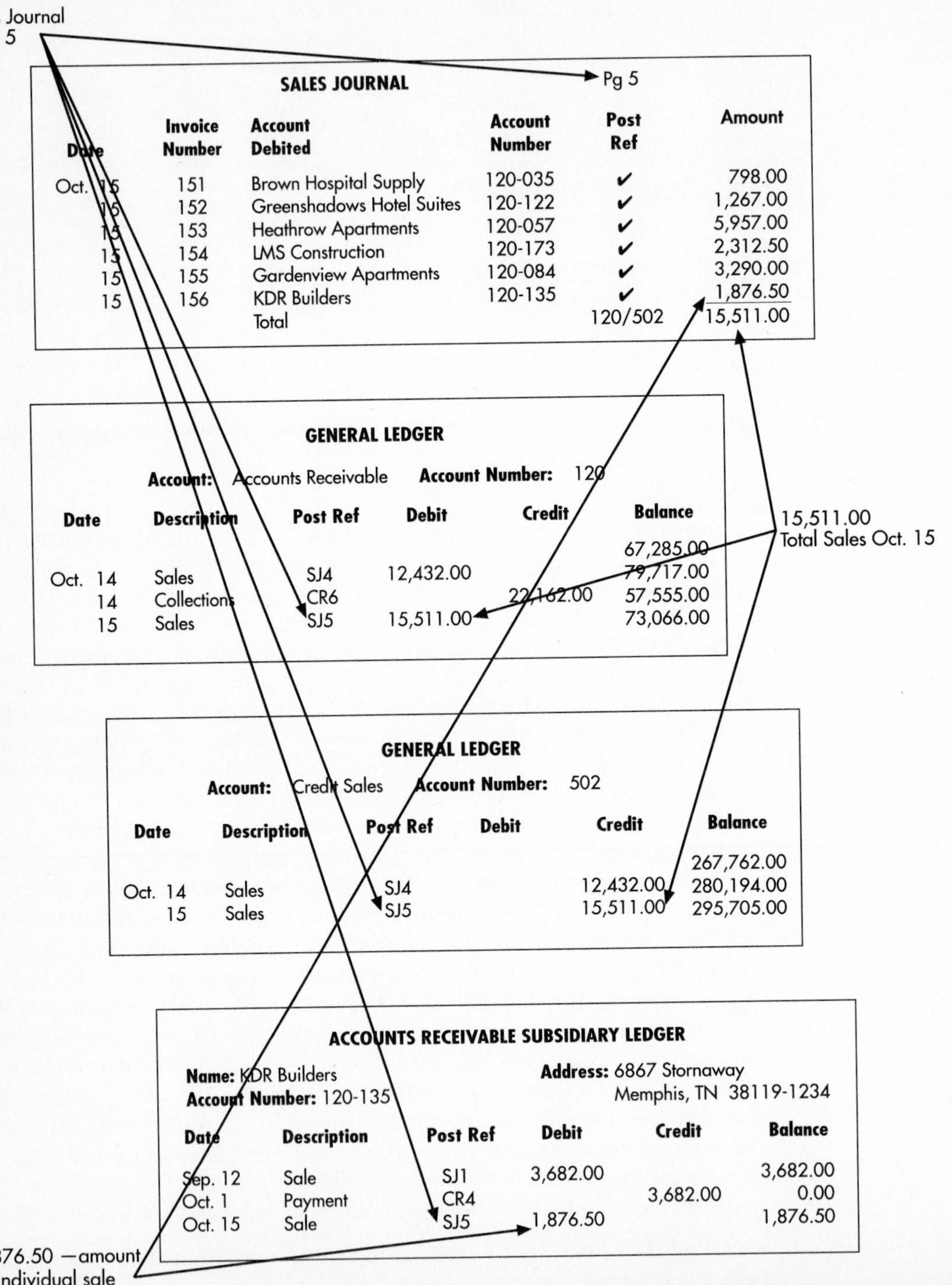

SALES JOURNAL Pg 5

Date	Invoice Number	Account Debited	Account Number	Post Ref	Amount
Oct. 15	151	Brown Hospital Supply	120-035	✔	798.00
15	152	Greenshadows Hotel Suites	120-122	✔	1,267.00
15	153	Heathrow Apartments	120-057	✔	5,957.00
15	154	LMS Construction	120-173	✔	2,312.50
15	155	Gardenview Apartments	120-084	✔	3,290.00
15	156	KDR Builders	120-135	✔	1,876.50
		Total		120/502	15,511.00

GENERAL LEDGER

Account: Accounts Receivable **Account Number:** 120

Date	Description	Post Ref	Debit	Credit	Balance
					67,285.00
Oct. 14	Sales	SJ4	12,432.00		79,717.00
14	Collections	CR6		22,162.00	57,555.00
15	Sales	SJ5	15,511.00		73,066.00

GENERAL LEDGER

Account: Credit Sales **Account Number:** 502

Date	Description	Post Ref	Debit	Credit	Balance
					267,762.00
Oct. 14	Sales	SJ4		12,432.00	280,194.00
15	Sales	SJ5		15,511.00	295,705.00

ACCOUNTS RECEIVABLE SUBSIDIARY LEDGER

Name: KDR Builders
Account Number: 120-135
Address: 6867 Stornaway
Memphis, TN 38119-1234

Date	Description	Post Ref	Debit	Credit	Balance
Sep. 12	Sale	SJ1	3,682.00		3,682.00
Oct. 1	Payment	CR4		3,682.00	0.00
Oct. 15	Sale	SJ5	1,876.50		1,876.50

individual entry in the sales journal is then posted to the appropriate customer's account in the accounts receivable subsidiary ledger (note the arrow at the top of Fig. 2.3 linking the $1,876.50 sale to KDR Builders in the sales journal to the debit for $1,876.50 in the accounts receivable subsidiary ledger at the bottom of the figure). The same process is followed for credit sales to all other customers. Periodically, the total of all entries recorded in the sales journal is then posted to the general ledger (note the debit of $15,511, representing total sales on October 15, linked by the arrow to the accounts receivable general ledger account in the middle of Fig. 2.3 and to the corresponding credit to the general ledger sales account for the same amount).

The Audit Trail. Figure 2.3 also shows how the posting references and document numbers provide what is known as an **audit trail.** An audit trail provides a means to check the accuracy and validity of ledger postings. To illustrate this process, observe that the posting reference for the $15,511 credit to the sales account in the general ledger, SJ5, refers back to page 5 of the sales journal. By checking page 5 of the sales journal, it is possible to verify that $15,511 represents the total credit sales recorded on October 15. Similarly, the posting reference for the $1,876.50 debit to the KDR Builders account in the subsidiary accounts receivable ledger also refers to page 5 of the sales journal as the source of that entry. Furthermore, note that the sales journal lists the invoice numbers for each individual entry. Invoice numbers provide the means for locating and examining the appropriate source documents in order to verify that the transaction did occur and was recorded accurately.

The Chart of Accounts. Figure 2.3 also shows that each general ledger account has its own number. The **chart of accounts** is a list of all general ledger accounts used by an organization. The structure of the chart of accounts is one of the most important aspects of an AIS, because it affects the preparation of financial statements and reports. Data stored in individual accounts can easily be summed for presentation in reports, but data stored in summary accounts cannot be easily broken down and reported in more detail. Consequently, it is important that the chart of accounts contain sufficient detail to meet the information needs of the organization.

To illustrate, consider the consequences if S&S were to use only one general ledger account for all sales transactions. It would be easy to produce reports showing the total amount of sales for a given time period, but it would be very difficult to prepare reports separating cash and credit sales. Indeed, the only way to produce these latter reports would be to trace the audit trail back to the journals and source documents to identify the nature of each sales transaction. Clearly, this approach would not be very practical. If, however, S&S used separate general ledger accounts for cash and credit sales, then reports showing both types of sales could be easily produced. Total sales could also be easily reported by summing each type of sale.

Table 2.5 shows the chart of accounts Ashton developed for S&S. Let us examine its structure. Each account number is three digits long, with each digit serving a specific purpose. The first digit represents the major account categories as they appear on S&S's financial statements: current assets, noncurrent assets, liabilities, equity accounts, revenues, expenses, and summary accounts. Notice that each major category is assigned a separate block of numbers, which corresponds to the sequence in

TABLE 2.5 Sample Chart of Accounts for S&S

Account Code	Account Name	Account Code	Account Name
100–199	Current Assets	400–499	Equity Accounts
101	Checking Account	400	Parry, Capital
102	Savings Account	410	Gonzalez, Capital
103	Petty Cash		
120	Accounts Receivable	500–599	Revenues
125	Allowance for Doubtful Accounts	501	Cash Sales
130	Notes Receivable	502	Credit Sales
150	Inventory	503	Service Revenues
160	Supplies	510	Sales Returns & Allowances
170	Prepaid Rent	511	Sales Discounts
180	Prepaid Insurance	520	Interest Revenue
		530	Miscellaneous Revenue
200–299	Noncurrent Assets		
200	Land	600–799	Expenses
210	Buildings	600	Cost of Goods Sold
215	Accumulated Depreciation —Buildings	611	Wages Expense
		612	Commissions Expense
230	Equipment	613	Payroll Tax Expense
235	Accumulated Depreciation —Equipment	620	Rent Expense
		630	Insurance Expense
240	Furniture and Fixtures	640	Supplies Expense
245	Accumulated Depreciation —Furniture & Fixtures	650	Bad Debt Expense
		701	Depreciation Expense—Buildings
250	Other Assets		
		702	Depreciation Expense—Equipment
300–399	Liabilities		
300	Accounts Payable	703	Depreciation Expense—Furniture & Fixtures
310	Wages Payable		
321	Employee Income Tax Payable	710	Income Tax Expense
322	FICA Tax Payable		
323	Federal Unemployment Tax Payable	900–999	Summary Accounts
324	State Unemployment Tax Payable	901	Drawing, Parry
330	Accrued Interest Payable	902	Drawing, Gonzalez
360	Other Liabilities	910	Income Summary

which it appears in the financial statements. Thus all current assets are numbered in the 100s, noncurrent assets are numbered in the 200s, and so on.

The second digit in each account code represents the primary financial subaccounts within each category. Again, the accounts are assigned numbers to match the order of their appearance in financial statements (in order of decreasing liquidity). Thus account 120 represents accounts receivable and account 150 represents inventory.

Finally, the third digit identifies the specific account to which the transaction data will be posted. For example, account 501 represents Cash Sales of appliances, account 502 represents Credit Sales of appliances, and account 503 represents Service Revenues (revenues from service calls). Similarly, accounts 101 through 103 represent the various cash accounts used by S&S.

It is important to realize that the chart of accounts will differ, depending on the nature and purpose of the organization it represents. For example, the sample chart of accounts for S&S reflects the fact that the company is a partnership. Corporations would not have separate capital and drawing accounts but, instead, accounts for common stock and retained earnings. Likewise, since S&S is a retail organization, it has only one type of general ledger inventory account. A manufacturing company, in contrast, would have separate general ledger accounts for raw materials, work in process, and finished goods inventories.

A chart of accounts should also provide room for growth. Notice that Ashton left a number of gaps in S&S's chart of accounts to allow for later insertion of additional accounts. For example, S&S does not currently have enough excess cash to invest in marketable securities. Later, when it can do so, a new general ledger account for marketable securities can be created and assigned the number 110. Ashton also knows that Scott and Susan hope to open additional stores in the future. When this occurs, he plans to add two more digits to the chart of accounts to represent each store in the chain, so that S&S can track sales, expenses, inventory, and other items in each individual store.

Finally, accounts in the subsidiary ledgers often have longer account codes than those used in the general ledger. For example, notice in Fig. 2.3 that each individual account receivable has a six-digit code. The first three digits are 120, the code for accounts receivable in the general ledger. The additional three digits provide a means for identifying up to 999 individual customers. The accounts payable and inventory subsidiary ledgers would be organized in a similar manner.

This concludes our description of the documents and procedures that Ashton developed for S&S's AIS. In a small company like S&S, it will be Ashton's responsibility not only to design and manage the AIS but also to perform most of the procedures we have just described. These tasks are only part of Ashton's responsibilities, however. As Focus 2.1 explains, controllers in small businesses must play a number of roles. Similarly, we pointed out earlier that transaction processing is only one of three key functions of the AIS.

PROVIDING INFORMATION FOR DECISION MAKING

A second function of the AIS is to provide management with information useful for decision making. In manual systems, this information is provided in the form of reports that fall into two main categories: financial statements and managerial reports.

Financial Statements

The preparation of financial statements consists of a sequence of activities. First, all the accounts in the general ledger and their balances are listed in a report called a **trial balance.** It is so named because one of its purposes is to allow the accountant to verify that the total debit balances in various accounts equal the total credit balances in other accounts. Once the trial balance has

FOCUS 2.1 What Does a Small Business Controller Do?

CONTROLLERS in small businesses play at least four distinct roles. The first role can be characterized as a technician. In this role, the controller is responsible for collecting and processing the data needed to prepare financial statements and, in addition, a wide variety of managerial reports. Moreover, just turning out those reports is not enough. The controller must understand the business issues behind the numbers well enough to be able to help management interpret those numbers correctly. He or she must also work with various managers to learn exactly what information they really need to do their jobs effectively, and then devise the means for providing that information.

A second role of the controller is to act as "company cop." This entails ensuring that the company is in compliance with all applicable regulations and that assets, including data, are adequately safeguarded. It also involves establishing procedures to ensure that business activities are performed correctly and efficiently and that data about them are recorded accurately.

A third role played by the controller in a small business is that of booster and trainer. This entails helping managers and staff to understand how their individual duties fit into the company's overall goals and objectives. It also involves overseeing sufficient cross-training of staff so that in the event of an employee's absence, due to vacations or illness, the business can continue to function smoothly. It may even include providing advice to young employees about career development, such as encouraging them to go back to school for further training. Moreover, in a small business, the controller may get involved in the kinds of employee counseling that in larger companies would be the province of a separate human resource management department.

A fourth role played by the small business controller is that of technology and accounting expert. The controller must keep abreast of technology and accounting developments and how they affect both business operations and employee responsibilities. Developing and maintaining a good personal network is essential to meeting this role, because no one individual can keep abreast of all the accounting and technological changes that occur each year. One way to develop such a network is to get involved in the local Institute of Management Accountants (IMA) chapter.

In summary, the small business controller is responsible for more than just keeping the books.

Source: Bonnie D. Labrack, "Small Business Controller," *Management Accounting* (November 1994): 38–41.

been prepared and checked, any necessary adjusting entries are made. Then another trial balance, called the **adjusted trial balance** because it reflects the effects of all adjusting entries, is prepared. The adjusted trial balance is examined to verify the equality of debits and credits and the accuracy of all adjusting entries. The income statement can then be produced from the adjusted trial balance. Next, closing entries are made to zero out all revenue and expense accounts and transfer the amount of net income (or loss) to the appropriate equity account. The balance sheet is then produced. Finally, the statement of cash flows is prepared, using information from the income statement and balance sheet.

Managerial Reports[1]

In addition to preparing financial statements, the AIS must be able to provide managers with detailed operational information about the organization's performance. For example, Scott and Susan need reports about inventory status, relative profitability of products, the relative performance of each salesperson, cash collections and pending obligations, and S&S's performance in meeting its delivery and service commitments.

Often, both traditional financial measures and operational data are required for proper and complete evaluation of performance. To illustrate, consider the evaluation of sales staff. Dividing sales revenue by the number of sales staff provides one measure of productivity. Dividing the number of sales by the same denominator provides another way to look at productivity. Dividing sales revenue by the number of hours worked by sales staff provides yet another measure of productivity. Additional perspective is gained by calculating the average sale amount and the cost of sales staff salaries as percentages of sales revenue. All these measures are valid, and all five together provide a better overall evaluation of performance than any one does alone.

Most source documents capture both financial and operational data about business transactions. The key is to design the AIS so that both kinds of data are stored in a manner that facilitates their integration in reports. Traditionally, most AIS systems have failed in this regard because they were designed primarily to support the preparation of financial statements, rather than the decision needs of internal management.

Corporate accountants must also know how to reorganize existing internally generated data and present it in a manner that sheds new light on operational results. For example, innovation is one vital requirement for continued long-term growth. One way that companies like Rockwater, a subsidiary of Brown & Root/Halliburton and a worldwide leader in underwater engineering and construction projects, measure innovation success is to track and report the percentage of sales revenues that are generated by new products.

Some important data must be collected from external sources, however. Data about customer satisfaction is one good example. It is not sufficient simply to measure and track how long it takes to fill and deliver customer orders. That merely provides information about how well a company is meeting its own goals for customer service. Information about whether the company is meeting its customers' requirements and expectations is also needed. The only way to find out the real story is to ask customers directly. Consequently, companies like Apple Computer regularly survey their customers. Other firms, such as U.S. automobile manufacturers, hire market research firms like J. D. Powers to collect that data. Once again, it is important to design the AIS so that such externally generated data are integrated with internally generated measures in a manner that facilitates the preparation of reports based on both kinds of data.

---

[1] The material in this section is drawn largely from two articles by Robert S. Kaplan and David P. Norton: "The Balanced Scorecard—Measures that Drive Performance," *Harvard Business Review* (January–February 1992): 71–79; and "Putting the Balanced Scorecard to Work," *Harvard Business Review* (September–October 1993): 134–147.

Budgets and Performance Reports. Two important types of managerial reports are budgets and performance reports. A **budget** is the formal expression of goals in financial terms. One of the most common and important types of budgets is the cash budget. A **cash budget** shows projected cash inflows and outflows (see Table 2.6). This information is especially important to a small business, because cash flow problems are one of the principal causes of small-business failures. A cash budget can provide advance warning of cash flow problems in time to permit corrective action to be taken.

Another commonly used budget is the operating budget. An **operating budget** projects an organization's revenues and expenses for a given time period, usually a month or a year. Typically, operating budgets are structured along the lines of financial statements.

Budgets are financial planning tools. Performance reports, in contrast, are used for financial control. A **performance report** lists the budgeted and actual amounts of revenues and expenses and also shows the variances, or differences, between these two amounts (see Table 2.7).

Budgeted amounts, however, are estimates; consequently, there are almost certain to be variances for each item in the performance report. Therefore, the principle of **management by exception** should be used to interpret those variances. If the performance report shows actual performance to be at or near budgeted figures, a manager can assume that the item is under control and that no action needs to be taken. On the other hand, significant deviations from budgeted amounts, in either direction, signal the need to investigate the cause of the discrepancy and take whatever action is appropriate to correct the problem.

Behavioral Implications of Managerial Reports. There is an old saying that measurement affects behavior. As applied to business, this means that employees tend to focus their efforts primarily on those tasks that are measured

TABLE 2.6 Sample Cash Budget

	January	February	March	April
Beginning Balance	10,000	11,000	8,000	8,000
Projected Cash Receipts:				
Cash Sales	7,000	8,500	8,000	9,000
Collections on Account	26,000	29,000	28,000	30,000
Total Cash Available (A)	43,000	48,500	44,000	47,000
Projected Cash Disbursements (B)	(32,000)	(41,000)	(39,000)	(36,000)
Projected Ending Cash Balance (C = A – B)	11,000	7,500	5,000	11,000
Desired Minimum Balance (D)	8,000	8,000	8,000	8,000
Amount Needed to Borrow (E =D – C)	0	500	3,000	0
Ending Balance (C + E)	11,000	8,000	8,000	11,000

TABLE 2.7 Sample Performance Report

L & P, Inc.: Monthly Performance Report						
	Current Month			**Year-to-Date**		
	Budget	**Actual**	**Variance**	**Budget**	**Actual**	**Variance**
Sales	$55,000	$56,500	1,500	$500,000	$512,000	12,000
Cost of Goods	39,000	39,400	400	350,000	354,000	4,000
Gross Margin	$16,000	$17,100	1,100	$150,000	$158,000	8,000
Selling Expenses	8,000	8,500	500	75,000	81,000	6,000
Other Operating Expenses	5,000	6,000	1,000	45,000	46,000	1,000
Income Before Taxes	$ 3,000	$ 2,600	(400)	$ 30,000	$ 31,000	1,000

and evaluated. This can be either good or bad, depending on the relationship between the behavior being measured and the organization's overall goals. To illustrate, consider the task of customer complaint resolution. The organization wants to satisfy its customers to the greatest extent possible at the lowest possible cost. If customer service representatives are evaluated solely in terms of the number of complaints resolved per unit of time, however, two types of problems may arise. The customer service representatives may be so focused on quickly resolving each complaint in the store's favor that they alienate some customers in the process. Or customer service representatives may "give away the store" just to appease and please every customer who has a complaint.

Budgets can often result in dysfunctional behavior. For example, the managers at a company who did not budget funds to purchase all the equipment needed to meet performance goals decided to rent the equipment. This allowed them to meet their performance targets and remain within budget, although a subsequent review by the company's internal auditors disclosed that renting the equipment cost the organization, over a period of years, $684,000 more than if the equipment had been purchased outright!

Indeed, the budgeting process itself can be dysfunctional. Management may expend a great deal of effort in number crunching, trying to get the budget numbers to turn out as desired, rather than focusing on how to accomplish the organization's mission and goals. Focus 2.2 discusses how to avoid this potential problem and turn the budgeting process into a value-added activity.

We have presented several examples of how reports produced by the AIS can unintentionally result in dysfunctional behavior. The key point to remember is that the AIS does not just neutrally report on employee performance. Rather, it directly affects behavior. In the next section, we look at how the AIS can be designed to encourage employees to behave in ways congruent with the organizational goals of providing accurate, reliable information and safeguarding assets.

FOCUS 2.2 Avoiding Dysfunctional Budgeting Behavior

TO FLY an airplane safely, you need to concentrate on where you are going, not on the instrument panel. Similarly, the key to running a business effectively is to focus on attaining the organization's goals, not on the budget process. This does not mean that budgeting has no value. Just as the instrument panel in a plane alerts the pilot about potential problems, budgets provide warning signs about organizational performance. The key to success in flying a plane or running a business, however, is not to spend too much time examining the instrument panel or budget. Accountants can use the following five-step process to help managers develop the proper perspective toward budgeting.

First, explain that the purpose of the budget is to identify and allocate the resources needed to accomplish the organization's goals. Moreover, stress that the objective is not only to accomplish those goals, but to do so as efficiently as possible.

Second, begin the budget process by identifying measurable goals. Each department manager needs to specify the unit's goals and how they relate to those of the entire organization.

Third, have each department manager develop several alternative strategies for accomplishing these goals. No cost data should be involved at this time, however. Instead, the focus should be solely on identifying alternative methods for accomplishing objectives.

Fourth, the accounting department, rather than the department managers, should assign costs to each alternative strategy. This keeps the department managers focused on how their unit's goals and strategies relate to those of the entire organization, not on playing games to get the budget numbers "right."

Fifth, the department manager reviews the budget figures prepared by the accounting department. Each manager should be encouraged to develop alternative strategies that may more efficiently achieve their unit's goals. Any such changes are then returned to the accounting department for assignment of costs. Steps four and five are repeated until the manager is satisfied with the final budget.

The key to this process is a division of responsibilities between the accounting department and unit managers. Managers focus on setting goals and developing strategies to meet those goals; accountants do the number crunching to translate those goals and strategies into a budget. The result is that managers focus on running the organization, not on budgeting. The accountant becomes a flight instructor, teaching managers to fly the plane instead of watching the instrument panel.

Source: Stephen M. Rehnberg, "Keep Your Head Out of the Cockpit," *Management Accounting* (July 1995): 34–37.

INTERNAL CONTROL CONSIDERATIONS

The third function of an AIS is to provide adequate internal controls to accomplish three basic objectives:

1. Ensure that the information produced by the system is reliable.
2. Ensure that business activities are performed efficiently and in accordance with management's objectives while also conforming to any applicable regulatory policies.
3. Safeguard organizational assets, including its data.

Two important methods for accomplishing these objectives are to provide for adequate documentation of all business activities and to design the AIS for effective segregation of duties. Additional aspects of internal control are covered in Chapters 8 and 9.

Adequate Documentation

Adequate documentation of all business transactions is the key to accountability. Documentation allows management to verify that assigned responsibilities were completed correctly. Ashton recalls an example he encountered while working as an auditor that gave him a firsthand glimpse of the types of problems that can arise from inadequate documentation. One of his audit clients sold and serviced computers, providing free repairs during the warranty period. Service personnel were instructed to treat repairs as being under warranty unless explicitly informed otherwise. The client had no procedures, however, for tracking warranty periods. Consequently, the company was completing a great deal of free repair work that should have been charged to customers. Indeed, the results of the audit estimated that the client had failed to bill almost $1 million worth of repair work! The client has since hired a new employee whose primary responsibility is to track warranty records for all computer sales.

Well-designed documents and records can also enhance the accuracy and efficiency of transaction processing. That is why Ashton took such care in designing S&S's source documents. Prenumbering source documents is especially important, because it facilitates accounting for them. Any gaps in the sequence of completed source documents should be promptly investigated. Missing documents may have been misplaced, in which case some transactions may have not been recorded. They may also, however, be a sign of a more serious problem. For example, a missing check may have been written for fraudulent purposes.

The use of posting references in journals and ledgers is also important, because it facilitates checking the accuracy of all entries posted to the ledgers. Finally, the use of specialized journals can improve the efficiency of recording business transactions.

Adequate documents and records can also ensure that an organization does not make commitments it cannot keep. For example, Ashton wants S&S to avoid promises to sell and deliver appliances that it does not currently have in stock. Consequently, he wants S&S to use a perpetual inventory system. To maintain the accuracy of those records, he will periodically reconcile recorded amounts with physical counts of inventory on hand.

Adequately written descriptions of company procedures are also important. Ashton recalls another audit problem he encountered that related to a weakness in this area. The clerk responsible for processing customer payments had not been instructed how to handle checks for which no match could be found in the accounts receivable records. Consequently, the clerk had decided that the proper thing to do was to return such checks to customers along with a note requesting additional information about why the check had been sent. This added more than a week to the time it took to turn accounts receivable into cash. After this situation was uncovered, the clerk was instructed to endorse restrictively and deposit all such checks and then to initiate correspondence with the customer for resolution of the matter. The company also put this policy in writing in the procedures manual, to avoid similar problems in the future.

Segregation of Duties

Segregation of duties refers to dividing responsibility for different portions of a transaction among several people. The objective is to prevent one person from having total control over all aspects of a business transaction. Specifically, the functions of authorizing transactions, recording transactions, and maintaining custody of assets should be performed by different people. Segregation of these three duties helps to safeguard assets and improve accuracy because each person can look at and thereby limit the others' actions. Effective segregation of duties should make it difficult for an individual employee to steal cash or other assets successfully.

Segregation of duties is especially important in business activities that involve the receipt or disbursement of cash, because it can be stolen so easily. For example, in processing cash receipts from customers, one person should be responsible for handling and depositing those receipts (the custody function) and another person should be responsible for updating the accounts receivable records (the recording function). Otherwise, a person who performed both functions could divert customer payments for personal use and conceal the theft by falsifying the accounts. Similarly, in the realm of cash disbursements, one person should be responsible for preparing and approving checks for payment (the authorization function), and another person should be responsible for signing and subsequently mailing those checks (the custody function). Indeed, Ashton recalls a fraud that occurred at one of his former audit clients because these cash disbursement functions were not adequately segregated. In that case, the treasurer signed all checks prepared by accounts payable, but instead of mailing them out himself, he returned them to accounts payable. After receiving the signed checks, however, the accounts payable manager would change the payee name by using the erase feature on the typewriter that had been used to prepare those checks! After the fraud was detected, the treasurer was instructed to mail all checks after signing them.

As this example shows, inadequate segregation of duties can create opportunities for the theft of organizational assets. Focus 2.3 provides an example of how bad this situation can get.

Small organizations like S&S, however, do not always have enough staff to segregate duties effectively. In such cases, effective control can still be achieved through close supervision and owner-performance of some key business activities. For example, Ashton intends to recommend that Scott and Susan be the only ones authorized to write checks on the company's account. In addition, only Scott and Susan should have the authority to approve the granting of credit to new customers or the extension of additional credit to existing ones.

SUMMARY AND CASE CONCLUSION

An AIS plays three key roles in any organization: (1) collecting and storing data about the organization, (2) processing the data to provide information useful for decision making, (3) including adequate internal control procedures to ensure the reliability of information produced and to safeguard the organization's assets. Ashton was confident that the AIS he had designed for S&S would fulfill those three

FOCUS 2.3 Stealing the Entire Company

THE CASE of Thomas Brimberry and Stix & Co. illustrates how severe the problem of employee fraud can become. Brimberry began working at Stix & Co. as a clerk earning $20,000 a year. He had greater ambitions, however, and with other family members he borrowed heavily to buy into a nightclub. It failed, saddling him with $3,000 monthly debt payments. To make ends meet, he started to steal from his employer.

He began by opening a margin account in his wife's maiden name. He increased the account's borrowing power by inflating stockholdings or erasing debt. The documents authorizing these transactions were added to batches of similar transactions, all of which were processed by an unsuspecting clerk who did not always carefully examine each transaction.

At first, Brimberry succeeded in his illegal stock trades and was able to cover his debt payments. A run of bad trades, however, eventually left him $1 million in debt to Stix & Co. To cover this shortage, he began to counterfeit stock certificates. He carefully selected firms that did not pay dividends, so that no one at Stix would notice the failure to receive a dividend check. Stix's policy requiring two people to be present whenever stock certificates were put into or removed from the bank vault was not a problem. Brimberry says he simply chose clerks to accompany him who were "too busy or too dumb" to ask any questions about what he was doing!

Eventually, the illusion of rapid growth created by Brimberry's fake accounts made Stix & Co. a takeover target. Brimberry then contacted James Massa, a lawyer, and introduced him to the Stix & Co. board of directors as a big investor. Massa eventually bought a controlling interest in the firm, using $1 million that he and Brimberry had embezzled from Stix & Co.! They then proceeded to steal at will, using their position as owners to fool the external auditors.

The scheme finally fell apart several years later when Brimberry and Massa began to argue about their relative share of the profits. Both were eventually convicted of embezzlement and sentenced to prison.

Source: John Curley, "How a Clerk Built Up a Brokerage Business by Hook or by Crook," *Wall Street Journal* (February 7, 1985): A1, A22.

functions. Table 2.8 lists the documents, journals, and ledgers that would comprise that system. Further details about these items will be provided in Chapters 12–16.

Ashton reflected on the steps he had followed to build the system. He began by obtaining an understanding of the basic business activities engaged in by S&S and of the key decisions that Scott and Susan would need to make to run the business effectively. Since S&S is a retail merchandising company, its operations could be described in terms of four basic transaction cycles:

1. The *revenue cycle* encompasses all transactions involving the sales of goods and services to customers and the collection of cash receipts in payment for those sales.

2. The *expenditure cycle* encompasses all transactions involving the purchase of and payment for the merchandise sold and other services consumed by S&S, such as rent and utilities.

3. The *human resources cycle* encompasses all the transactions involving the hiring, training, and payment of employees.

4. The *financing cycle* encompasses all transactions involving the investment of capital in the company, borrowing money, payment of dividends and interest, and loan repayments.

TABLE 2.8 Documents, Journals, and Ledgers for S&S

Title	Purpose
Documents	
Sales Invoice	Record cash and credit sales of appliances and parts
Service Invoice	Record sales of repair services
Delivery Ticket	Record delivery of appliances to customers
Monthly Statement	Inform customers of outstanding account balances
Credit Memo	Support adjustments to customer accounts for sales returns & allowances and sales discounts; also support write-off of uncollectible accounts
Purchase Order	Order merchandise from vendors
Receiving Report	Record receipt of merchandise from vendors, indicating both quantity and condition of items received
Time Card	Record time worked by employees
Specialized Journals	
Sales	Record all credit sales
Cash Receipts	Record cash sales, payments from customers, and other cash receipts
Purchases	Record all purchases from vendors
Cash Disbursements	Record all cash disbursements
General Journal	Record infrequent, nonroutine transactions; also record adjusting and closing entries.
Subsidiary Ledgers	
Accounts Receivable	Maintain details about each individual customer
Accounts Payable	Maintain details about each individual vendor
Inventory	Maintain details about each inventory item
Fixed Assets	Maintain details about each piece of equipment and other fixed assets
General Ledger	Maintain details about all major asset, liability, equity, revenue, and expense accounts

The *general ledger and reporting subsystem* includes all activities related to the preparation of financial statements and other managerial reports, as well as nonroutine transactions and various adjusting entries.

Ashton used this knowledge to identify the types of data that needed to be collected for each transaction. He then followed general principles of forms design to create source documents that would be easy to complete when capturing transaction data. He also designed a set of journals and ledgers in which to record and organize the data.

An important step had been designing the chart of accounts. Ashton had coded the general ledger accounts so that they would support not only the preparation of financial statements, but also a variety of other managerial reports for S&S. In addition, although the chart of accounts reflected the current structure of S&S, it could be easily expanded as the organization grew.

In the end, Ashton felt satisfied with the system's fundamental controls. Scott and Susan would perform certain key functions, such as approving credit and signing checks. The posting references in the various journals and ledgers, together with prenumbering all source documents, would provide an adequate audit trail. The use of specialized journals would facilitate the recording process. Finally, the periodic reconciliation of subsidiary ledger totals with their respective general ledger control accounts would provide a check on the accuracy of transaction processing.

Nevertheless, Ashton realized that the manual AIS he designed would not be adequate in the long run. As S&S grew and the volume of transactions increased, the system would have to be automated. Thus he began to gather information about how to make that transition. Although he is not yet sure exactly what computer equipment and programs S&S will need, Ashton is confident that with a little more study (see Chapters 3–7) he will be able to handle this transition.

KEY TERMS

transaction cycles
source documents
general journal
specialized journals
general ledger
subsidiary ledger
control account
audit trail
chart of accounts
trial balance
adjusted trial balance
budget
cash budget
operating budget
performance report
management by exception
segregation of duties

CHAPTER QUIZ

1. The set of transactions involving interactions between an organization and its suppliers is the
   a. revenue cycle.
   b. expenditure cycle.
   c. human resources cycle.
   d. financing cycle.

2. Transaction data are first captured and recorded on
   a. specialized journals.
   b. subsidiary ledgers.
   c. journal vouchers.
   d. source documents.

3. Adjusting entries are recorded first in
   a. specialized journals.
   b. the general journal.
   c. the general ledger.
   d. a subsidiary ledger.

4. Which of the following is most likely to be a general ledger control account?
   a. Accounts Receivable
   b. Petty Cash
   c. Prepaid Rent
   d. Retained Earnings

5. Which of the following is useful for projecting the need for short-term borrowing?
   a. Operating budget
   b. Performance report
   c. Cash budget
   d. Statement of cash flows

6. A report that expresses goals in financial terms is called a
   a. performance report.
   b. financial statement.
   c. budget.
   d. chart of accounts.

7. The chart of accounts lists general ledger accounts in
   a. alphabetical order.
   b. chronological order.
   c. order by size.
   d. the order in which they appear in financial statements.

8. Which of the following is the best way to compensate for inadequate segregation of duties?
   a. Maintaining a complete audit trail
   b. Preparing a trial balance

c. Directly involving ownership in key functions
d. Maintaining sound hiring practices

9. Which of the following is one of the three key functions of the AIS?
a. Processing transactions efficiently
b. Providing adequate segregation of duties
c. Ensuring that business activities are performed in a manner consistent with management's desires and regulatory rules
d. Developing a chart of accounts

10. Which of the following is the most important step in developing an AIS?
a. Developing well-designed source documents
b. Developing a sound chart of accounts
c. Developing subsidiary ledgers
d. Developing specialized journals

DISCUSSION QUESTIONS

2.1 Examine Table 2.1 and discuss how the various information items would be collected and reported by a company's AIS.

2.2 Many restaurants use customer checks with prenumbered sequence codes. Each food server is given a packet of these checks on which to write up customer orders. Food servers are told not to destroy any customer checks; if a mistake is made, they are to void that check and write a new one. All voided checks are to be turned in to the manager daily. How does this policy help the restaurant control cash receipts?

2.3 Look at the principles of forms design listed in Table 2.3. Which apply only to paper documents? Which apply to both paper documents and information presented on computer screens? What modifications, if any, do you think are needed to adapt those principles to the design of computer input screens?

2.4 How does an organization's line of business affect the design of its AIS? Give several examples of how differences among organizations are reflected in their AIS.

2.5 At most movie theaters, one employee is usually responsible for issuing tickets and collecting cash and another person collects those tickets when patrons enter the theater. What is the reason for this practice?

2.6 Some individuals argue that accountants should focus on producing financial statements and leave the design and production of managerial reports to information systems specialists. What are the advantages and disadvantages of following this advice? To what extent should accountants be involved in producing reports that include more than just financial measures of performance? Why?

PROBLEMS

2.1 The chart of accounts must be tailored to the specific needs of an organization. Discuss how the chart of accounts for each of the following organizations would differ from the one presented for S&S in Table 2.5:
a. A university
b. A bank
c. A government unit (city or state)
d. A manufacturing company
e. The expansion of S&S to a chain of 23 stores

2.2 Specialized journals should include columns for accounts commonly debited or credited. Refer to Table 2.4, which depicts an example of a sales journal, and use your knowledge of basic journal entries to design the following specialized journals:
a. Cash receipts journal (to include cash sales)
b. Purchases journal
c. Cash disbursements journal

2.3 Ollie Mace has recently been appointed controller of S. Dilley & Company, a family-owned manufacturing firm founded 28 years ago. The firm manufactures automotive parts. Its four major operating divisions are Heat Treating, Extruding, Small Parts Stamping, and Machining. Last year's sales from each division ranged from $150,000 to over $3 million. Each division is physically and managerially independent, except for the constant surveillance of S. Dilley, the firm's founder.

The accounting system for each division has evolved according to its needs and the abilities of its accounting staff. Mace is the first controller in the firm's history to have responsibility for overall financial management. Dilley expects to retire in a few years and wants Mace to improve the AIS before he retires so that it will be easier to monitor performance in each division.

Mace decides that the financial reporting system should be redesigned to include the following features:

- It should give managers uniform, timely, and accurate reports of business activity. Monthly reports should be uniform across divisions and be completed by the fifth of the following month, to provide enough time to take corrective actions to affect the next month's performance. Company-wide financial reports should be available at the same time.
- Reports should provide a basis for measuring the return on investment for each division. Thus, in addition to revenue and expense accounts, reports should show assets assigned to each division.
- The system should generate meaningful budget data for planning and decision making purposes. Budgets should reflect managerial responsibility and show costs for major product groups.

Mace believes that a new chart of accounts is required to accomplish these goals. He wants to divide asset accounts into six major categories, such as Current Assets and Plant and Equipment. He does not foresee a need for more than 10 control accounts within each of these categories. From his observations to date, 100 subsidiary accounts are more than adequate for each control account.

No division now has more than five major product groups. Mace foresees a maximum of six cost centers within any product group, including both the operating and nonoperating groups. He views general divisional costs as a non-revenue-producing product group. Altogether, Mace estimates that about 44 expense accounts plus about 12 specific variance accounts would be adequate.

Required:

Design a chart of accounts for S. Dilley & Company. Explain how you structured the chart of accounts to meet the company's needs and operating characteristics. Keep total account code length to a minimum, while still satisfying all of Mace's desires.

(CMA Examination, adapted)

2.4 Washington County Hospital is located in a well-known summer resort area. The county population doubles during the summer months, and hospital activity increases correspondingly. A new administrator has decided to implement a responsibility accounting system. This program was announced when the quarterly cost reports were presented to department heads. Previously, cost data were infrequently supplied to department heads. Excerpts from the announcement of the new program follow:

> *The hospital has adopted a responsibility accounting system. From now on you will receive quarterly reports comparing actual with budgeted costs for your department. The reports will highlight the variances so that you can zero in on departures from budget (this is called management by exception). Responsibility accounting means that you are accountable for keeping your department's costs within budget. Variations from budget will help you identify which costs are out of line, and the size of the variance will indicate the relative importance of the deviations. Your first report accompanies this announcement. [See Table 2.9.]*

The new administrator constructed the annual budget for 2000 and set quarterly budgets at one-fourth the annual budget. The administrator compiled the budget by analyzing costs for the past three years. The analysis showed that all costs increased each year, with a dramatic increase this past year. The administrator considered setting the budget at the average amount for the past three years, hoping that the new system would help to control cost increases. He finally decided, however, to set the budget at 3% below last year's actual costs. The activity level measured by patient days and pounds of laundry was set at last year's level too, because these numbers had remained basically constant over the past three years.

Required:

a. Comment on the method used to set the budget.
b. What do budget variances mean? Is the administrator interpreting this information correctly? Explain.
c. Does the report presented in Table 2.9 accurately represent the department's performance efficiency? Why or why not?

(CMA Examination, adapted)

2.5 Denny Daniels is production manager for the jazz division of QRS, Inc., which manufactures audio CDs. Daniels is dissatisfied with the reports provided by the accounting department, because they are virtually useless for helping him manage the production process. He also feels that the reports do not accurately reflect

TABLE 2.9 Washington County Hospital: Performance Report, Laundry Department, July–September 2000

	Budget	Actual	(Over) Under Budget	Percent (Over) Under Budget
Patient Days	9,500	11,900	(2,400)	(25)
Pounds Processed—laundry	125,000	156,000	(31,000)	(25)
Costs:				
Laundry labor	$9,000	$12,500	$(3,500)	(39)
Supplies	1,100	1,875	(775)	(70)
Water, heating, & softening	1,700	2,500	(800)	(47)
Maintenance	1,400	2,200	(800)	(57)
Supervisor's salary	3,150	3,750	(600)	(19)
Allocated administrative costs	4,000	5,000	(1,000)	(25)
Equipment depreciation	1,200	1,250	(50)	(4)
Totals	$21,550	$29,075	$(7,525)	(35)

Administrator's Comments: Costs are significantly above budget for the quarter. Particular attention needs to be paid to labor, supplies, and maintenance.

how hard or how effectively he works as a production manager. Daniels tried to discuss these perceptions and concerns with June Smith, the controller for the jazz division. He told her, "I think the cost report is misleading. I know I've had better production over a number of periods, but the cost report still says I have excessive costs. Look, I'm not an accountant, I'm a production manager. I know how to get a good-quality product out. Over a number of years, I've even cut the amount of raw materials used to do it. But the cost report doesn't show any of this. Basically, it's always negative, no matter what I do. There's no way you can win with accounting or the people at corporate who use these reports."

Smith gave Daniels little consolation. She stated that the accounting system and cost reports are designed by headquarters and cannot be changed. She added, "Although these accounting reports are pretty much the basis for evaluating the efficiency of your division and the means that corporate uses to determine whether you have done a good job, you shouldn't worry too much. You haven't been fired yet! Besides, these reports have been used for the last 25 years."

After talking with the production manager at the country division of QRS, Daniels concluded that most of what June Smith said was probably true. However, the country division was able to get corporate to agree to some minor cost reporting changes. Daniels also knew from the trade grapevine that turnover of production managers at QRS was considered high, even though relatively few were ever fired. Most seemed to end up quitting, usually in disgust, because they believed they were being evaluated unfairly. The following comment sums up the general feeling of production managers who had left QRS:

> *Corporate headquarters doesn't really listen to us. All they consider are those misleading cost reports. They don't want them changed, and they don't want any supplemental information. The accountants may be quick with numbers, but they don't know anything about production. As it was, I either had to ignore the cost reports entirely or pretend they were important, even though they didn't reflect how well I had done my job. No matter what they say about not firing people, negative reports mean negative evaluations. I'm better off working for another company.*

Table 2.10 is an example of the cost report that has Daniels in such an agitated state.

Required:

a. Comment on how Denny's perceptions of the following elements are likely to affect his behavior and performance: June Smith, the controller;

TABLE 2.10 Sample Cost Report for Problem 2.5

QRS, Inc. Jazz Division Cost Report April 2000 (000 omitted)			
	Master Budget	**Actual Cost**	**Excess Cost**
Materials	$ 400	$ 437	$37
Labor	560	540	(20)
Overhead	100	134	34
Total	$1060	$1111	$51

corporate headquarters; the cost report; himself; and the AIS.

b. Identify and explain three changes that should be made in the cost report to make the information more meaningful and useful to production managers like Daniels.

(CMA Examination, adapted)

2.6 You have recently hired a full-time employee to assist you in the opening of Katie's Flower Shop. Because you anticipate that the majority of sales will be made over the phone, collection of accounts is likely to be a challenge for your business. To help solve this problem, you have asked your newly hired assistant to design a form that can be used to record sales transactions. Your assistant has just completed the form shown in Fig. 2.4.

Required:

a. Which principles of form design are followed by this form?
b. Suggest at least three changes to the form that would make it more useful in collecting accounts.

2.7 An audit trail is a set of references that enables a person to trace a source document to its ultimate effect on the financial statements or vice versa. Describe in detail the audit trail for the following:

a. Purchases of inventory
b. Sale of inventory
c. Employee payroll

2.8 Search the Internet or recent newspapers or magazines for an article about employee fraud. Write a two-page report summarizing how the fraud occurred and what control procedures could have prevented it.

2.9 Search popular business magazines (*Business Week, Fortune, Forbes*) for an article that describes some dysfunctional behavior that resulted from a poorly designed managerial reporting and performance evaluation system. Write a two-page report summarizing the problem and explaining how the managerial report led to the unplanned (and undesired) behavior.

2.10 Shauna Washington started a business to sell art supplies and related curricula to home school families. The business grew quickly, with sales doubling three times during a five-year period. At that point, she sold the business because it had grown too large to manage from her home. Under the new owners, sales doubled again during the next two years. Profits, however, did not keep pace with sales. In addition, the firm borrowed heavily to open a warehouse. Inventory costs and operating expenses at the warehouse were higher than anticipated, and the monthly payments on the loan were proving to be burdensome. Recently, the number and amount of past due accounts had risen dramatically. Together, these problems created a severe cash flow problem. If the cash flow situation does not improve quickly, the firm may have to declare bankruptcy, even though sales are continuing to increase.

Required:

Describe some of the information that a good AIS could have provided for this firm and that, if provided in a timely manner, could have helped it avoid some of its problems.

FIGURE 2.4
Sample Form for Katie's Flower Shop

KATIE'S FLOWER SHOP **No. 1234**
123 Elm St. 456-7890

Sold To: **Order Date** ______

Terms:
____ **Paid**
____ **30 Day Account**
____ **C.O.D.**

Deliver To: **Delivery Date** ______

Delivered By ______

Quantity	Description	Amount
Goods Received By	**Tax**	
	Total	

CASE 2.1 ANYCOMPANY, INC.—AN ONGOING COMPREHENSIVE CASE

Identify a local company (you may use the same company that you identified to complete Case 1.1) and answer the following questions:

1. How many transaction cycles does the company have? Does it have any additional ones that were not discussed in this chapter? If so, identify and describe them.
2. Select any two transaction cycles and list the major transactions that occur in each. Trace how those transactions are processed by explaining what happens at each step in the cycle. Evaluate the adequacy of the audit trail related to those transactions.
3. What source documents does the company use to capture the relevant data for the transactions you identified in step 2? Comment on the adequacy of their design, using the criteria listed in Table 2.3.
4. What reports are produced in the two business cycles that you identified in step 2? What decisions are influenced by these reports? Comment on the adequacy of the reports for their intended purpose.
5. Examine the company's chart of accounts. How is it structured? How well does that structure meet the information needs of decision makers? How flexible is it in terms of providing for future growth?

CASE 2.2 S&S, INC.

You have been hired to assist Ashton Fleming in designing a manual accounting system for S&S. Ashton has developed a list of all the reports and documents that he thinks S&S needs (see Table 2.8). He asks you to complete the following tasks:

1. Prepare a preliminary design of the following documents, specifying which data elements should be captured on each:
   - **a.** Sales invoice
   - **b.** Repair services invoice
   - **c.** Receiving report
   - **d.** Employee time card
2. Design a report to manage appliance inventory.
3. Design a report to assist in managing credit sales and cash collections.
4. Design a report to track machines requiring service and warranty repairs.
5. Visit a local office supply store and identify what types of journals, ledgers, and blank forms are available. Describe how easily they could be adapted to meet S&S's needs.

ANSWERS TO CHAPTER QUIZ

1. b	**3.** b	**5.** c	**7.** d	**9.** a
2. d	**4.** a	**6.** c	**8.** c	**10.** b

CHAPTER 3

Systems Development and Documentation Techniques

LEARNING OBJECTIVES

After studying this chapter, you should be able to

- Prepare and utilize data flow diagrams to understand, evaluate, and design information systems.
- Prepare and utilize flowcharts to understand, evaluate, and design information systems.
- Prepare and utilize decision tables.

Integrative Case: S&S, Inc.

What a hectic few months it has been for Ashton Fleming! He was very busy beginning his new job and preparing for the week-long grand opening of S&S. Then he was swamped processing all the transactions from the highly successful opening. To top it all off, he became confused and discouraged after an impromptu visit to Computer Applications (CA), a local computer company.

Ashton spoke with Kimberly Serra, CA's manager. She explained that CA developed systems ranging from simple general ledger operations to highly integrated software. The company handles a wide variety of accounting applications, including accounts receivable and payable, inventory, payroll, cost accounting, fixed assets, and cash receipts and disbursements.

When Kimberly asked about S&S's system requirements and management's expectations, Ashton could not answer her specifically. He had not yet thought through these issues. When she asked how S&S's system worked, Ashton plunged into a discussion about how the various company documents were utilized. However, Kimberly seemed unable to follow his explanation. Ashton felt that part of his discussion was helpful, but that overall it was irrelevant to the issue at hand.

Ashton came away impressed by CA and Kimberly. She offered to begin studying how S&S worked so she could assist him in finalizing the company's system needs. Unfortunately, he does not have the official go-ahead from Susan to begin work on a new system. Besides, Ashton had the distinct impression that S&S was not quite ready to develop or acquire a system. Ashton's first priority is to understand S&S's information needs more clearly.

From his days as an auditor, Ashton knows the value of good system documentation in assisting unfamiliar users with both understanding and evaluating a system. Good system documentation would be a big help to him and Kimberly as well as Scott and Susan as they evaluate the current and proposed system.

After sharing his conclusions with Susan and Scott, Ashton's plan to document the current and proposed systems was well received. They support his taking a leadership role in moving toward a new system and were especially interested in diagrams or charts that would help them quickly grasp how the system worked. Ashton was given the following assignment:

1. What types of tools and techniques should S&S use to document its existing system so it is easy to understand and evaluate?
2. What development tools and techniques should S&S use to design its new computer-based information system?

INTRODUCTION

Documentation is the narratives, flowcharts, diagrams, and other written material that explain how a system works. This information covers the who, what, when, where, why, and how of data entry, processing, storage, information output, and system controls. Since a picture is worth a thousand words, one popular means of documenting a system is to develop diagrams, flowcharts, tables, and other graphical representations of information. They are then supplemented by a **narrative description** of the system, a written step-by-step explanation of system components and interactions. In this chapter we explain the most common systems documentation tools and techniques. They include data flow diagrams, flowcharts, and decision tables. These tools save both time and money, adding value to an organization.

Depending on your job function, you will need to understand documentation tools on one or more of the following levels:

1. At a minimum, you must be able to *read* documentation so that you can determine how the system works.

2. You may be required to *evaluate* internal control system documentation to identify control strengths and weaknesses and recommend improvements. Alternatively, you may have to evaluate the documentation for a proposed system to determine whether the system meets your needs.

3. The greatest amount of skill is needed to *prepare* documentation. If you are a member of a team that is developing a new system, you will have to prepare documentation to show how the existing as well as the proposed new system operates. You also may be required to document your understanding of a company's system of internal controls for others to review.

An understanding of documentation tools is required no matter what accounting career you choose. For example, Statement on Auditing Standards (SAS) 55, *Consideration of the Internal Control Structure in a Financial Statement Audit,* requires that independent auditors understand a client's system of internal controls before conducting an audit. SAS 55 recommends that auditors use flowcharts and decision tables to document large, complex systems. Auditors can spot internal control weaknesses and strengths more easily from such graphic portrayals.

This chapter discusses the following five documentation tools:

1. *Data flow diagrams,* a graphical description of the source and destination of data, how data flows within an organization, the processes performed on the data, and how data is stored.
2. *Document flowcharts,* a graphical description of the flow of documents and information between departments or areas of responsibility within an organization.
3. *Computer system flowcharts,* a graphical description of the relationship among the input, processing, and output in an information system.
4. *Program flowcharts,* a graphical description of the sequence of logical operations that a computer performs as it executes a program.
5. *Decision tables,* a tabular representation of the logic used in a computer program.

These tools are used extensively in the systems development process. According to Microsoft, systems development is an extremely complex process, one that is far more complicated than building a Boeing 747. These tools are used to bring order out of chaos and complexity. In addition, the people on the teams that develop information systems projects often change and these documentation tools help the new people on the team get up to speed quickly.

The documentation tools explained in this chapter are used throughout the book. Data flow diagrams and systems flowcharts, for example, are used extensively to show how systems work and how data and information flow. They are also tested on professional examinations—as you can see by noting the number of questions in the book that are adapted from these exams. Learning about these tools will better prepare you for these examinations.

DATA FLOW DIAGRAMS[1]

A **data flow diagram (DFD)** graphically describes the flow of data within an organization. It is used to document existing systems and to plan and design new ones. There is no ideal way to develop a DFD; different problems call for different methods. Some general guidelines for developing data flow diagrams are shown in Focus 3.1.

[1] Parts of this discussion are based on Tom DeMarco, *Structured Analysis and System Specification* (Englewood Cliffs, N.J.: Prentice-Hall, 1979). DeMarco has been at the forefront of structural analysis and design techniques and is a well-respected authority on the subject.

Elements in a Data Flow Diagram

A DFD is composed of four basic elements: data sources and destinations, data flows, transformation processes, and data stores. Each is represented on a DFD by one of the symbols shown in Fig. 3.1.

These four symbols are combined to show how data are processed. For example, the DFD in Fig. 3.2 shows that the input to process C is data flow B, which comes from data source A. The outputs of process C are data flows D and E. Data flow E is sent to data destination J. Process F uses data flows D and G as input and produces data flow I and G as output. Data flow G comes from and returns to data store H. Data flow I is sent to data destination K.

Figure 3.3 assigns specific titles to each of the processes depicted in Fig. 3.2. Figures 3.2 and 3.3 will be used to examine the four basic elements of a DFD in more detail.

Data Sources and Destinations. A source or destination symbol on the DFD represents an organization or individual that sends or receives data used or produced by the system. An entity can be both a source and a destination. **Data sources** and **data destinations** are represented by squares, as illustrated by items A (customer), J (bank), and K (credit manager) in Fig. 3.3.

Data Flows. A **data flow** represents the flow of data between processes, data stores, and data sources and destinations. Data that pass between data stores and either a data source or a destination must go through some form of data

FIGURE 3.1
Data Flow Diagram Symbols

Symbol	Name	Explanation
□ (square)	Data sources and destinations	The people and organizations that send data to and receive data from the system are represented by square boxes. Data destinations are also referred to as data sinks.
↗ (curved arrow)	Data flows	The flow of data into or out of a process is represented by curved or straight lines with arrows.
○ (circle)	Transformation processes	The processes that transform data from inputs to outputs are represented by circles. They are often referred to as bubbles.
═ (two lines)	Data stores	The storage of data is represented by two horizontal lines.

FOCUS 3.1 Guidelines for Drawing a DFD

1. *Understand the System.* An understanding of how the system works can be obtained by observing the flow of information through an organization and by interviewing the individuals who use and process the data.
2. *Ignore Certain Aspects of the System.* The purpose of a DFD is to diagram the origins, flow, transformation, storage, and destinations of data. Therefore, all control processes and control actions should be ignored. Only very important error paths should be included in the DFD; details of unimportant error paths should be ignored. Determining how the system starts and stops is usually deferred to a later stage in the development process.
3. *Determine System Boundaries.* Determine what is to be included and what is to be excluded from the system. Include all relevant data elements in the DFD, since anything excluded will not be considered during system development. When in doubt about whether to include data elements, do so until a definitive decision can be made to discard them.
4. *Develop a Context Diagram.* A context diagram is a good way of depicting system boundaries. It has the system of concern in a circle in the middle of the diagram. The outside entities the system interacts with directly are in boxes on either side, connected by data flows depicting the data passed between them. (See Fig. 3.5 and its attendant discussion.) DFDs are prepared, in successively more detail, to depict how data flows in the system.
5. *Identify Data Flows.* Identify all data flows entering or leaving the system's boundary, including where the data originates and its final destination. Any significant movement of information is usually a data flow. All data flows come from and go to either a transformation process, a data store (file), or a data source or destination. As each of these is identified, it should be connected to the appropriate data flow. Data flows can move in two directions; this is shown with a line with arrows on both ends (see G in Fig. 3.3).
6. *Group Data Flows.* A data flow can consist of one or more pieces of datum; data elements that always flow together should be grouped together and shown as one data flow until they are separated. If the data elements do not always flow together, they should be shown as two separate data flows.
7. *Identify Transformation Processes.* Place a circle wherever work is required to transform one data flow into another. All transformation processes should have one or more incoming and outgoing data flows.
8. *Group Transformation Processes.* Transformation

processing—that is, through a transformation process. Data flow arrows are labeled to indicate the type of data being passed. Thus the reader knows exactly what information is flowing; no inferences are required. Data flows are represented in Fig. 3.3 by items B (customer payment), D (remittance data), E (deposit), G (unlabeled; represents information entered into or retrieved from an accounts receivable data file), and I (receivables information).

A data flow can consist of one or more pieces of datum. For example, data flow B (customer payment) consists of two parts: a payment and remittance data. Process 1.0 (process payment) splits these two data elements and sends them in different directions. The remittance data (D) flows to another process, where it is used to update accounts receivable records, and the payment (E) is sent to the bank with a deposit slip.

Because data flows may be composed of more than one data element, it must be determined whether to show one or more lines. The determining factor is processes that are logically related or occur at the same time and place should be grouped together. Never combine unrelated items into a single transformation process; if data are not processed together, or are sometimes processed differently, separate them.

9. *Identify All Files or Data Stores.* Data is stored temporarily or permanently in most systems. Each data repository, and each data flow into and out of it, should be identified.
10. *Identify All Data Sources and Destinations.* All sources and destinations of data should be identified and included on the DFD.
11. *Name All DFD Elements.* All DFD elements (except data flows into or out of data stores; the data store name is sufficient for identification) should be given unique and descriptive names representing what is known about them. This makes a DFD easier to read and understand and provides the reader with key information. Naming data flows first forces the developer to concentrate on the all-important data flows, rather than on the processes or stores. Once data flows have been labeled, naming the processes and data stores is usually easy, since they typically take their names from the data inflows or outflows. Choose active and descriptive names, like "daily inventory update" and "validate transaction," rather than "input data" or "update process." Process names should include action verbs such as update, edit, prepare, reconcile, and record.
12. *Subdivide the DFD.* A cluttered DFD is hard to read and understand. If you have more than five to seven processes on a single page, then use higher- and lower-level DFDs. Decompose the context diagram into high-level processes, and then explode these high-level processes into successively lower-level processes. This is explained in greater detail in the chapter.
13. *Give Each Process a Sequential Number.* In a completed DFD, as shown in Figs. 3.6 and 3.7, each process is given a sequential number that helps readers move back and forth between the different DFD levels. Data flows should only go from lower-numbered to higher-numbered processes.
14. *Repeat the Process.* DFD developers must work through organization data flows several times. Each subsequent pass helps refine the diagram and identify the fine points. As you refine the DFD, organize it so that it flows from top to bottom and from left to right.
15. *Prepare a Final Copy.* Draw a final copy of the DFD. Do not allow data flow lines to cross over each other; if necessary, repeat a data store or destination to accomplish this. Place the name of the DFD, the date prepared, and the preparer's name on each page.

whether the data elements always flow together. For example, if customers sometimes send inquiries about the processing of their payments, the DFD could be revised as shown in Fig. 3.4. The figure shows two lines because customer inquiries, although interacting with the same elements of the DFD, do not always accompany a payment. The two data elements have different purposes, and customer inquiries occur less frequently. If represented by the same data flow, the separate elements would be obscured, and the DFD would be more difficult to interpret.

Processes. **Processes** represent the transformation of data. Figure 3.3 shows that process payment (C) takes the customer payment and splits it into the remittance data and the deposit (which includes the checks and deposit slip created within process payment). The updating process (F) takes the remittance data and the accounts receivables data, producing an updated receivables record and sending receivables information to the credit manager.

FIGURE 3.2
Basic Data Flow Diagram Elements

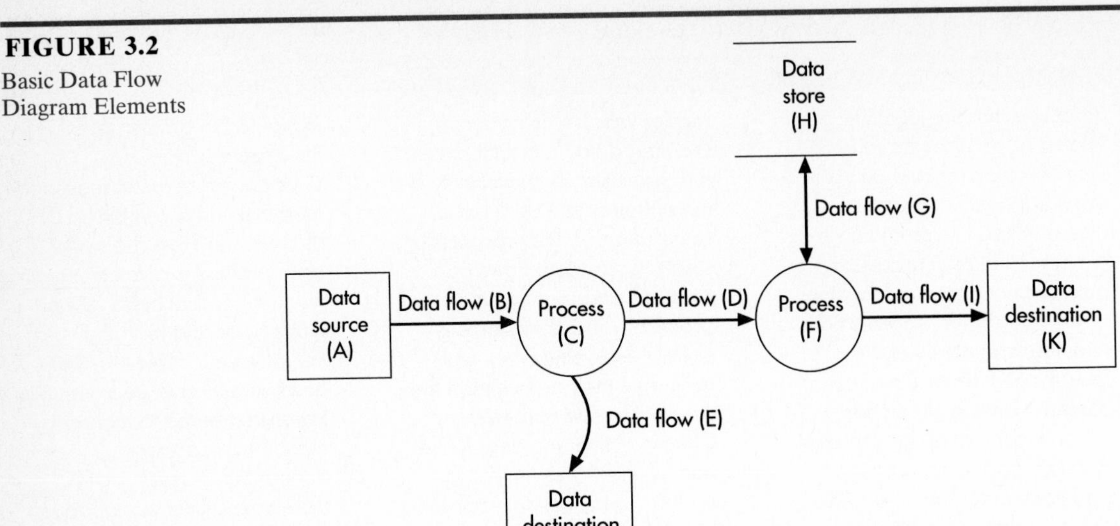

Data Stores. A **data store** is a temporary or permanent repository of data. DFDs do not show the physical storage medium (disks, paper, and the like) used to store the data. As with the other DFD elements, data store names should be descriptive. As shown in Fig. 3.3, item H, data stores are represented by horizontal lines, with the data store's name recorded inside.

FIGURE 3.3
Data Flow Diagram of Customer Payment Process

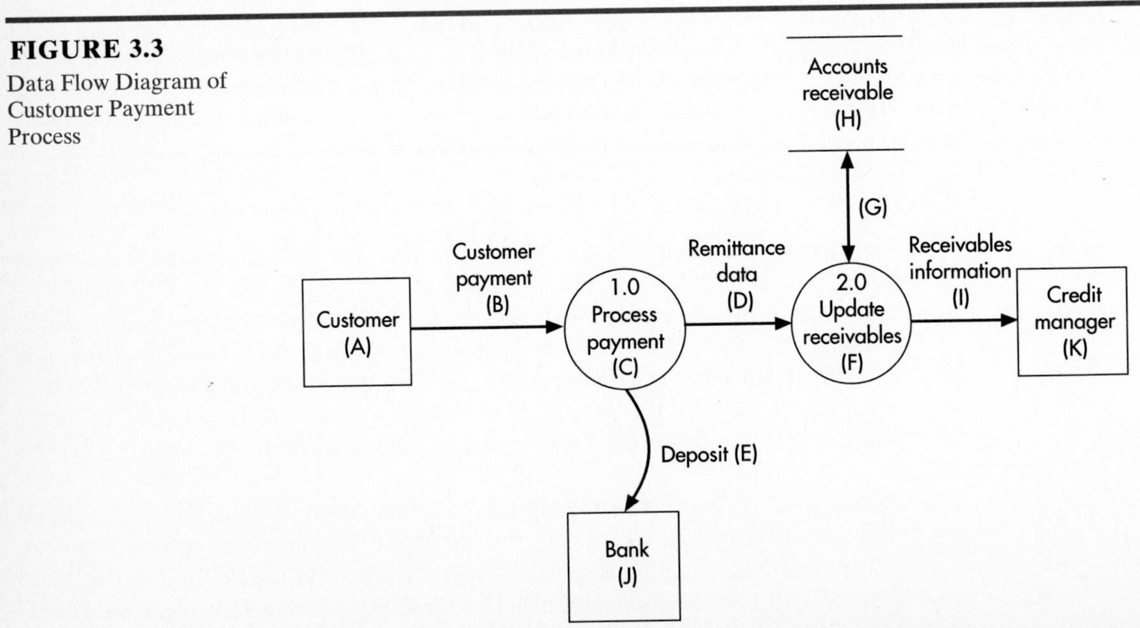

FIGURE 3.4
Splitting Customer Payments and Inquiries

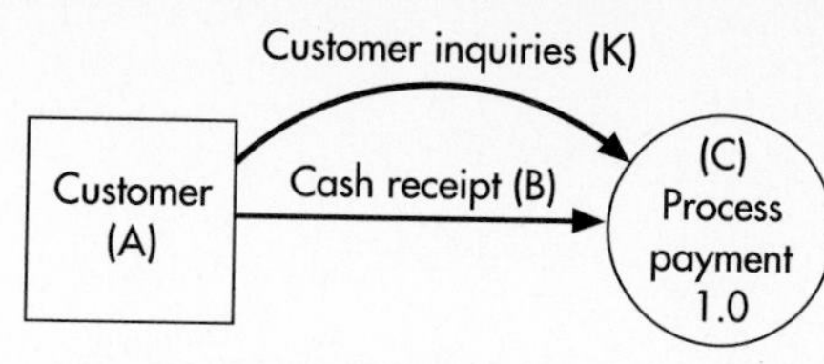

Data Dictionary. Data flows and stores are typically collections of data elements. For example, a data flow labeled "Employee information" might contain elements such as name, address, job title, and birth date. A **data dictionary** contains a description of all the data elements, stores, and flows in a system, including the storage and processing of data, the documents, and physical items such as inventory. Typically, a master copy of the data dictionary is maintained to ensure consistency and accuracy throughout the development process.

Subdividing the DFD

DFDs are subdivided into successively lower levels in order to provide ever-increasing amounts of detail, since few systems can be fully diagrammed on one sheet of paper. Since users have differing needs, a variety of levels can better satisfy these requirements.

The highest-level DFD is referred to as a **context diagram.** A context diagram provides the reader with a summary-level view of a system. It depicts a data processing system as well as the external entities that are the sources and destinations of the system's inputs and outputs.

Figure 3.5 is the context diagram that Ashton Fleming drew as he was analyzing the payroll processing procedures at S&S. It shows that the payroll processing system receives time cards from different departments and employee data from the human resources department. When these data are processed, the system produces (1) tax reports and payments for governmental agencies, (2) employee paychecks, (3) a check to deposit in the payroll account at the bank, and (4) management payroll reports.

Ashton also wants to diagram the details of the system. To do so, he decides to decompose the context diagram into successively lower levels, each with an increasing amount of detail. In preparation for this task, he wrote the narrative description of S&S's payroll processing procedures contained in Table 3.1. Take a few minutes to read this description and determine the following:

- The number of major data processing activities involved
- The data inputs and outputs of each activity (ignoring all references to people, departments, and document destinations)

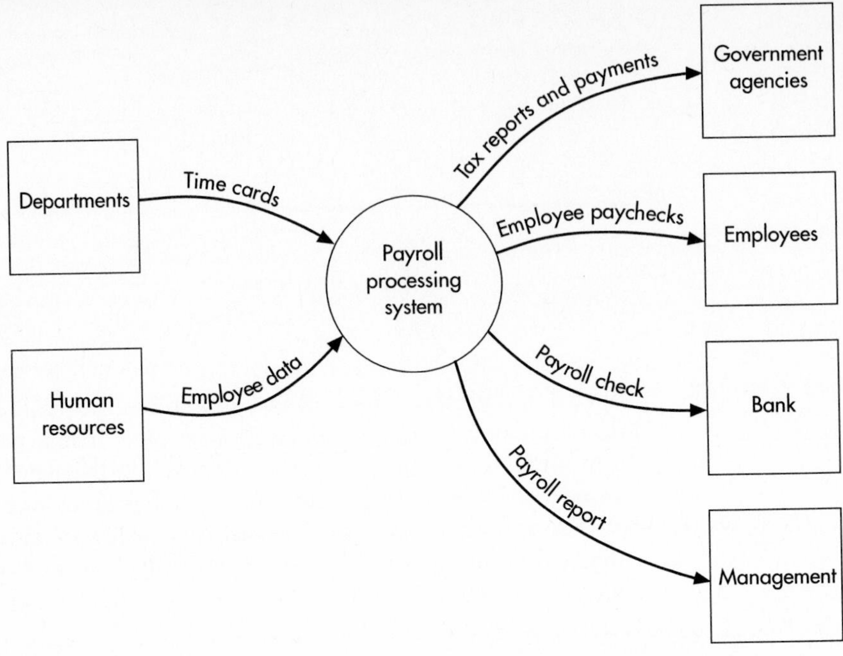

FIGURE 3.5
Context Diagram for S&S Payroll Processing

Based on Ashton's description, you should have identified approximately five data processing activities. You may have noted more or less, depending on how you identified the activities. The first is updating the employee/payroll master file (first paragraph of the narrative). The second is employee compensation (second, fifth, and sixth paragraphs). Later in the chapter, you will see that this activity is broken out into smaller parts in a lower-level DFD. A third is the generation of management reports (third paragraph). A fourth is the payment of taxes (fourth paragraph). A fifth is posting entries to the general ledger (last paragraph). All the data inflows and outflows, as well as the five activities, form the basis of the DFD and are summarized in Table 3.2.

Using this information, Ashton exploded his context diagram and created the DFD shown in Fig. 3.6. The data coming from the human resources department were grouped together and called "Employee data." Notice that some data inputs and outputs have been excluded from this DFD. For example, in process 2.0 the data inflows and outflows that are not related to an external entity or to another process are not depicted (tax tables and payroll register in this case). These data flows are internal to the "Pay employees" activity and are shown on the next DFD level.

Not fully satisfied with the level of detail he had captured, Ashton exploded process 2.0 (pay employees). Figure 3.7 provides more detail about the data processes involved in paying employees, and it includes the tax tables and the payroll register data flow left out of Fig. 3.6. In a similar fashion, each of the processes shown in Fig. 3.6 could be exploded to show a greater level of detail.

TABLE 3.1 Narrative Description of Payroll Processing at S&S

When employees are hired, they fill out a new employee form. When a change to an employee's payroll status occurs, such as a raise or a change in the number of exemptions, human resources fills out an employee change form. A copy of these forms is sent to payroll. These forms are used to create or update the records in the employee/payroll file and are then stored in the file. Employee records are stored alphabetically.

Some S&S employees are paid a salary, but most are hourly workers who record the times they work on time cards. At the end of each pay period department managers send the time cards to the payroll department. The payroll clerk uses the time card data, data from the employee file (such as pay rate and annual salary), and the appropriate tax tables to prepare a two-part check for each employee. The clerk also prepares a two-part payroll register showing gross pay, deductions, and net pay for each employee. The clerk updates the employee file to reflect each employee's current earnings. The original copy of the employee paychecks are forwarded to Susan. The payroll register is forwarded to the accounts payable clerk. The time cards and the duplicate copies of the payroll register and paychecks are stored by date in the payroll file.

Every pay period the payroll clerk uses the data in the employee/payroll file to prepare a payroll summary report for Susan so that she can control and monitor labor expenses. This report is forwarded to Susan along with the original copies of the employee paychecks.

Every month the payroll clerk uses the data in the employee/payroll file to prepare a two-part tax report. The original is forwarded to the accounts payable clerk, and the duplicate is added to the tax records in the payroll file. The accounts payable clerk uses the tax report to prepare a two-part check for taxes and a two-part cash disbursements voucher. The tax report and the original copy of each document are forwarded to Susan. The duplicates are stored by date in the accounts payable file.

The accounts payable clerk uses the payroll register to prepare a two-part check for the total amount of the employee payroll and a two-part disbursements voucher. The original copy of each document is forwarded to Susan, and the payroll register and the duplicates are stored by date in the accounts payable file.

Susan reviews each packet of information she receives and approves and signs the checks. She forwards the cash disbursements vouchers to Ashton, the tax reports and payments to the appropriate governmental agency, the payroll check to the bank, and the employee checks to the employees. She files the payroll report chronologically.

Ashton uses the payroll tax and the payroll check cash disbursement vouchers to update the general ledger. He then cancels the journal voucher by marking it "posted" and files it numerically.

FLOWCHARTS

A **flowchart** is an analytical technique used to describe some aspect of an information system in a clear, concise, and logical manner. Flowcharts use a standard set of symbols to describe pictorially the transaction processing procedures used by a company and the flow of data through a system. General guidelines for preparing flowcharts so that they are readable, clear, concise, consistent, and understandable are presented in Focus 3.2, on page 74.

TABLE 3.2 Activities and Data Flows in Payroll Processing at S&S

Activities	Data Inputs	Data Outputs
Update employee/payroll file	New employee form Employee change form Employee/payroll file	Updated employee/payroll file
Pay employees	Time cards Employee/payroll file Tax tables	Employee checks Payroll register Updated employee/payroll file Payroll check Payroll cash disbursements voucher
Prepare reports	Employee/payroll file	Payroll report
Pay taxes	Employee/payroll file	Tax report Tax payment Payroll tax cash disbursements voucher Updated employee/payroll file
Update general ledger	Payroll tax cash disbursements voucher Payroll cash disbursements voucher	Updated general ledger

Flowchart Symbols

The symbols used to create flowcharts are shown in Fig. 3.8. Each symbol has a special meaning that is easily conveyed by its shape. The shape indicates and describes the operations performed and the input, output, processing, and storage media employed. The symbols are drawn by a software program or with a **flowcharting template,** a piece of hard, flexible plastic on which the shapes of symbols have been cut out.

Flowcharting symbols can be divided into the following four categories, as shown in Fig. 3.8:

1. *Input/output symbols* represent devices or media that provide input to or record output from processing operations.
2. *Processing symbols* either show what type of device is used to process data or indicate when processing is completed manually.
3. *Storage symbols* represent the devices used to store data that the system is not currently using.
4. *Flow and miscellaneous symbols* indicate the flow of data and goods. They also represent such operations as where flowcharts begin or end, where decisions are made, and when to add explanatory notes to flowcharts.

FIGURE 3.6
DFD for S&S Payroll Processing

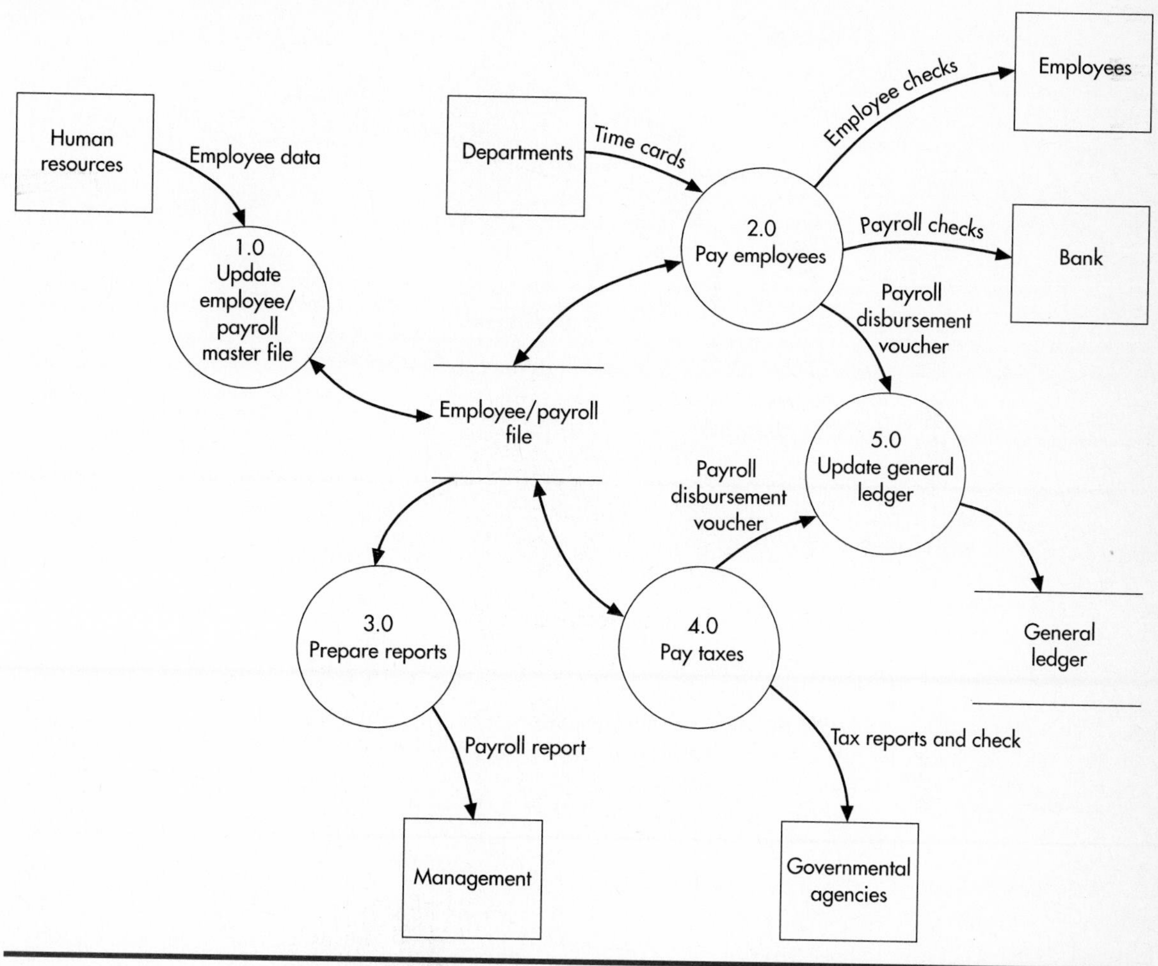

Document Flowcharts

A **document flowchart** illustrates the flow of documents and information between areas of responsibility within an organization. Document flowcharts trace a document from its cradle to its grave. They show where each document originates, its distribution, the purposes for which it is used, its ultimate disposition, and everything that happens as it flows through the system.

A document flowchart is particularly useful in analyzing the adequacy of control procedures in a system, such as internal checks and segregation of functions. Flowcharts that describe and evaluate internal controls are often

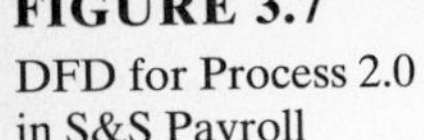

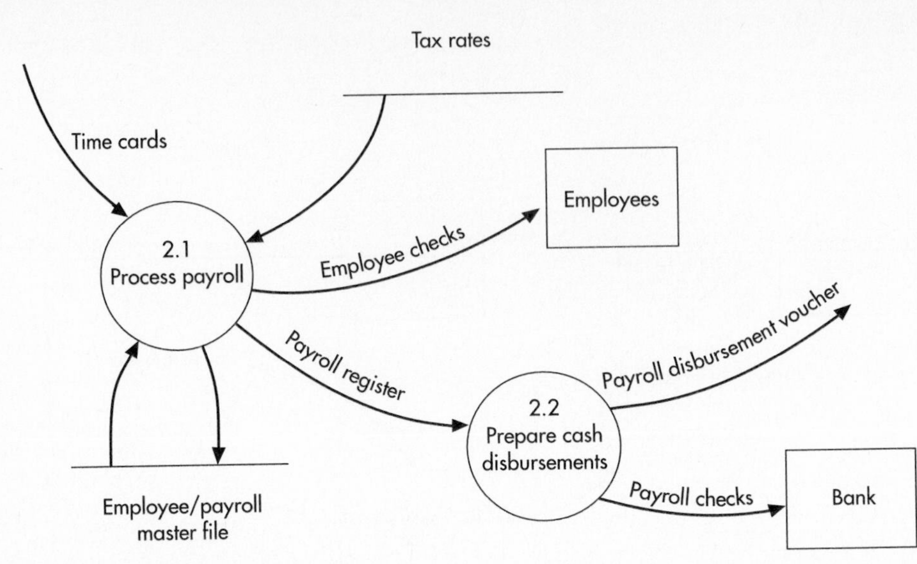

FIGURE 3.7
DFD for Process 2.0 in S&S Payroll Processing

referred to as **internal control flowcharts.** The document flowchart can reveal weaknesses or inefficiencies in a system, such as inadequate communication flows, unnecessary complexity in document flows, or procedures responsible for causing wasteful delays. Document flowcharts can also be prepared as part of the systems design process and should be included in the documentation of an information system.

The document flowchart that Ashton developed for the payroll process at S&S, as described in Table 3.2, is shown in Fig. 3.9.

Computer System Flowcharts

System flowcharts depict the relationship among the input, processing, and output of an AIS. A system flowchart begins by identifying both the inputs that enter the system and their origins. The input can be new data entering the system, data stored for future use, or both. The input is followed by the processing portion of the flowchart—that is, the steps performed on the data. The logic used by the computer to perform the processing task is shown on a program flowchart (explained in the following section). The resulting new information is the output component, which can be stored for later use, displayed on a screen, or printed on paper. In many instances, the output from one process is an input to another.

The sales processing system flowchart in Fig. 3.10 represents Ashton's proposal to capture sales data using state-of-the-art sales terminals. These

FIGURE 3.8
Common Flowcharting Symbols

Symbol	Name	Explanation
Input/Output Symbols		
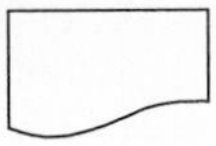	Document	A document or report; the document may be prepared by hand or printed by a computer
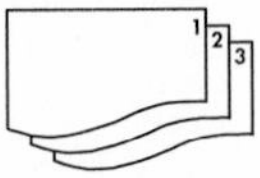	Multiple copies of one document	Illustrated by overlapping the document symbol and printing the document number on the face of the document in the upper-right corner
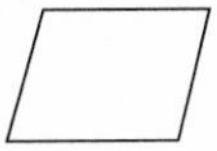	Input/output; Journal/ledger	Any function of input or output on a program flowchart Represents accounting journals and ledgers on document flowchart
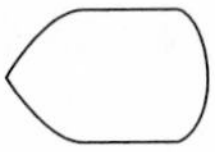	Display	Information displayed by an on-line output device such as a CRT terminal or personal computer monitor
	On-line keying	Data entry by on-line devices such as a CRT terminal or personal computer
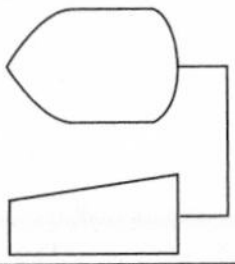	CRT terminal, personal computer	The display and on-line keying symbols are used together to represent CRT terminals and personal computers
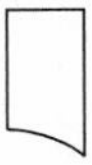	Transmittal tape	Manually prepared control totals; used for control purposes to compare to computer-generated totals
Processing Symbols		
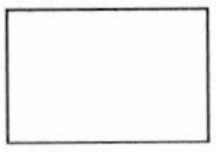	Computer processing	A computer-performed processing function; usually results in a change in data or information
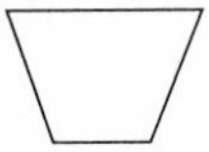	Manual operation	A processing operation performed manually
	Auxiliary operation	A processing function done by a device that is not a computer
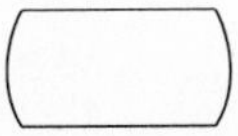	Off-line keying operation	An operation utilizing an off-line keying device (e.g., key to disk, cash register)

continues

FIGURE 3.8
Continued

Symbol	Name	Explanation
Storage Symbols		
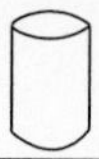	Magnetic disk	Data stored permanently on a magnetic disk; used for master files
	Magnetic tape	Data stored on a magnetic tape
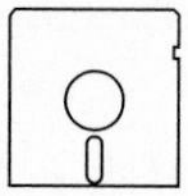	Magnetic diskette	Data stored on a diskette
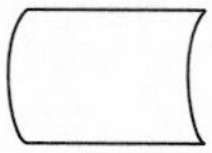	On-line storage	Data stored in a temporary on-line file in a direct-access medium such as a disk
 N	File	File of documents manually stored and retrieved; inscribed letter indicates file-ordering sequence: N = numerically A = alphabetically D = by date
Flow and Miscellaneous Symbols		
	Document or processing flow	Direction of processing or document flow; normal flow is down and to the right
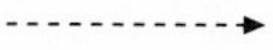	Data/information flow	Direction of data/information flow; often used to show data copied from one document to another
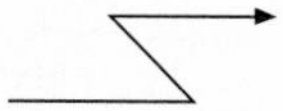	Communications link	Transmission of data from one location to another via communication lines
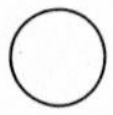	On-page connector	Connects the processing flow on the same page; its usage avoids connecting lines crisscrossing a page
	Off-page connector	An entry from, or an exit to, another page
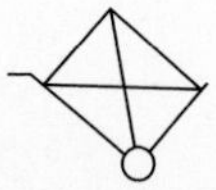	Flow of goods	Physical movement of goods; used primarily with document flowcharts

continues

FIGURE 3.8
Continued

Symbol	Name	Explanation
Flow and Miscellaneous Symbols (continued)		
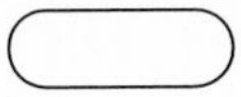	Terminal	A beginning, end, or point of interruption in a process or program; also used to indicate an external party
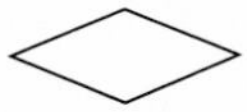	Decision	A decision-making step; used in a computer program flowchart to show branching to alternative paths
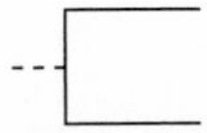	Annotation	Addition of descriptive comments or explanatory notes as clarification

terminals will edit the sales data (e.g., ensuring that all necessary sales data are collected) and print out a customer receipt. All sales data will be stored in a sales data file on a disk. At the end of each day, the data will be forwarded to S&S's computers, where it will be summarized and batch totals will be printed. A batch total is the sum of a numerical item contained in each transaction being processed; an example is total sales for all sales transactions. The summary data will then be processed, and batch totals will again be generated and printed. These amounts will be compared with the batch totals generated prior to processing, and all errors and exceptions will be reconciled. The accounts receivable, inventory, and sales marketing master files and the general ledger will be updated. Users can access the files at any time by using an inquiry processing system. This system will produce standard reports and allow the user to access the data needed for special analyses.

System flowcharts are an important tool of systems analysis, design, and evaluation. They are universally employed in systems work and provide an immediate form of communication among workers. The systems flowchart is an excellent vehicle for describing information flows and procedures within an AIS.

Program Flowcharts

A **program flowchart** illustrates the sequence of logical operations performed by a computer in executing a program. The relationship between systems and program flowcharts is shown in Fig. 3.11.

Program flowcharts employ a subset of the symbols shown in Fig. 3.8. As shown in Fig. 3.12, a flow line connects the symbols and indicates the sequence of operations. The processing symbol represents a data movement or arithmetic calculation. The input/output symbol represents either the reading of input or the writing of output. The decision symbol represents a comparison of one or

FIGURE 3.9

Document Flowchart of Payroll Processing at S&S *continues*

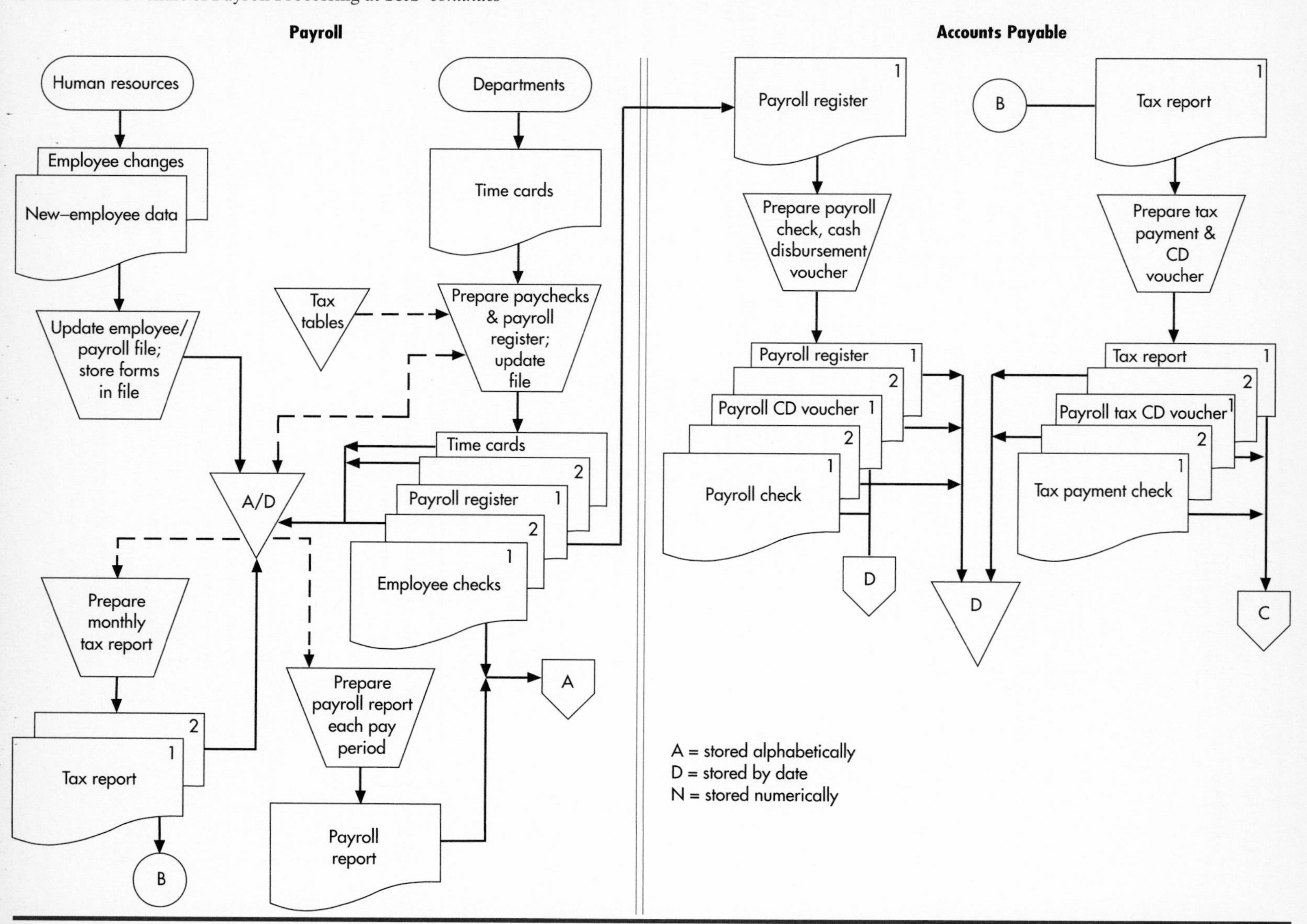

FIGURE 3.9
Continued

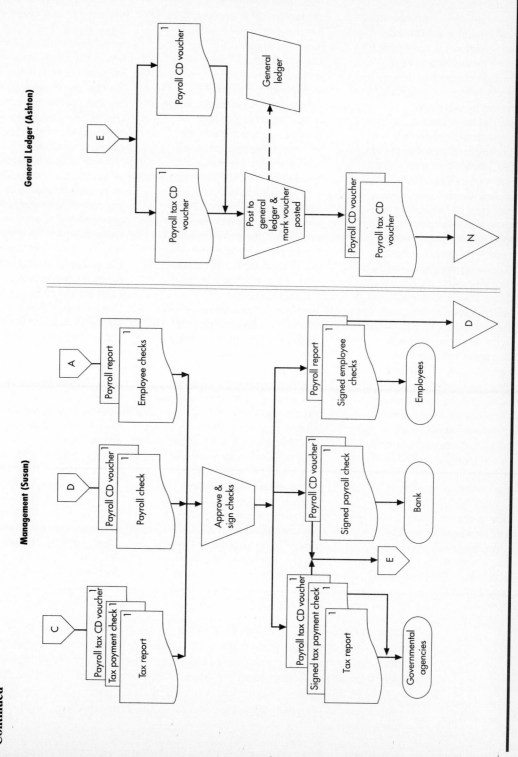

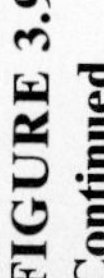

FOCUS 3.2 General Guidelines for Preparing Flowcharts

1. Understand a system before flowcharting it. Interview users, developers, auditors, and management, or have them fill out a questionnaire; read through a narrative description of the system; or walk through system transactions.
2. Identify the entities to be flowcharted, such as departments, job functions, or external parties. Identify documents and information flows in the system as well as the activities or processes performed on the data. (For example, when reading a description of the system, the preparer could draw a box around the entities, a circle around the documents, and a line under the activities.)
3. When several entities, such as departments or functions, need to be shown on a flowchart, divide the flowchart into columns with a label for each. Flowchart the activities of each entity in its respective column.
4. Flowchart only the normal flow of operations, making sure that all procedures and processes are in the right order. Identify exception procedures by using the annotation symbol.
5. Design the flowchart so that flow proceeds from top to bottom and from left to right.
6. Give the flowchart a clear beginning and ending. Designate where each document originated, and show the final disposition of all documents so there are no loose ends that leave the reader dangling.
7. Use the standard flowcharting symbols; draw them with a template or a computer.
8. Clearly label all symbols. Write a description of the input, process, or output inside the symbol. If the description will not fit, use the annotation symbol. Print neatly, rather than writing in freehand.
9. When using multiple copies of a document, place document numbers in the top right-hand corner of the symbol. The document number should accompany the symbol as it moves through the system.
10. Each manual processing symbol should have an input and an output. Do not directly connect two documents, except when moving from one column to another. When a document is moved to another column, show the document in both.
11. Use on-page connectors to avoid flow lines that go all over the page and make it look cluttered. Use off-page connectors to move from one flowchart page to another. Clearly label all connectors to avoid confusion.
12. Use arrowheads on all flow lines. Do not assume that the reader will know the direction of the flow.
13. If a flowchart cannot fit on a single page, clearly label the pages 1 of 3, 2 of 3, and so on.
14. Show documents or reports first in the column in which they are created. They can then be shown moving to another column for further processing. A manual process is not needed to show documents being forwarded.
15. Show all data entered into or retrieved from a computer file as passing through a processing operation (a computer program) first.
16. Use a line from the document to a file to indicate that it is being filed. A manual process is not needed to show a document entering a file.
17. Draw a rough sketch of the flowchart as a first effort. You should be more concerned with capturing content than a perfect drawing. Few systems can be flowcharted in a single draft.
18. Redesign the flowchart to avoid clutter and a large number of crossed lines.
19. Verify the flowchart's accuracy by reviewing it with those familiar with the system. Be sure all uses of flowcharting conventions are consistent.
20. Draw a final copy of the flowchart. Place the name of the flowchart, the date, and the preparer's name on each page.

more variables and the transfer of flow to alternative logic paths. All points where the flow begins or ends are represented by the terminal symbol. Connectors, labeled with a digit or a capital letter—represent the continuation of the logic flow at a different location. Several exit connectors may have the same label, but labels can have only one entry connector. Once designed and approved, the program flowchart serves as the blueprint for coding the computer program.

FIGURE 3.10
Systems Flowchart of Sales Processing System at S&S

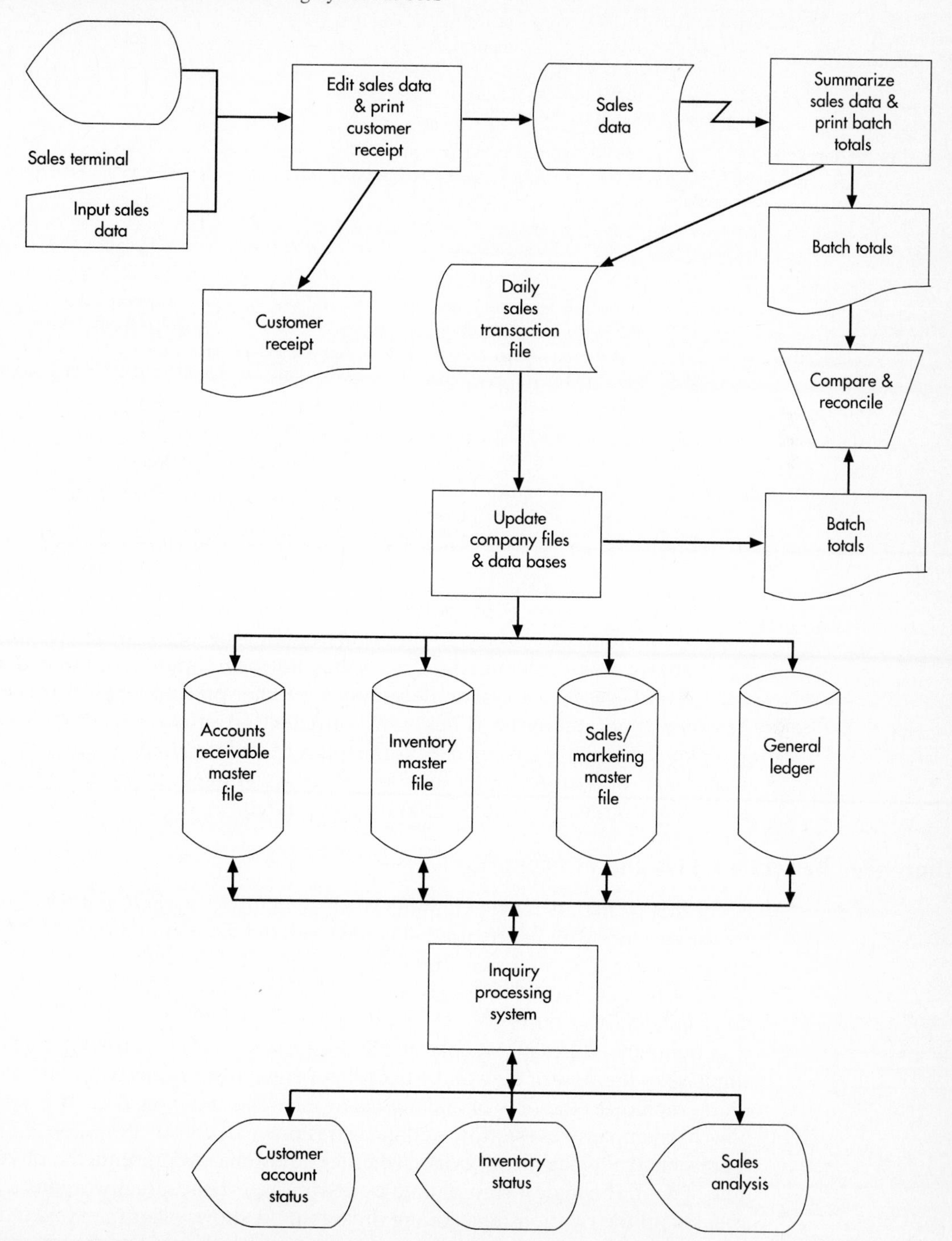

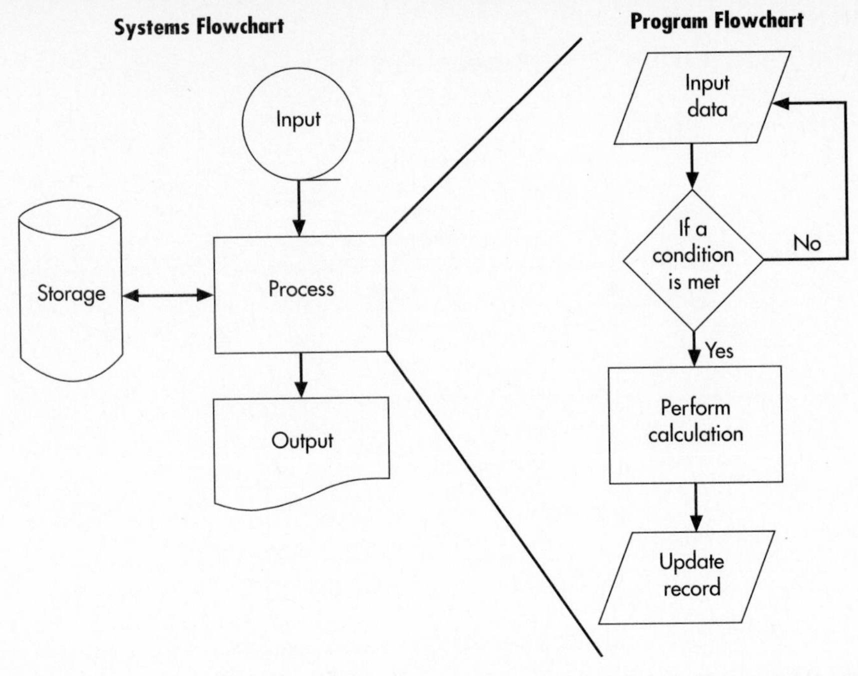

FIGURE 3.11
Relationship Between Systems and Program Flowcharts. A program flowchart describes the specific logic to perform a process shown on a systems flowchart.

The flowchart in Fig. 3.12 shows a simple example of the logic S&S's computer could use to process credit orders. After entering a sales order, customer credit approval is determined. If credit has not been approved, the order is rejected. Otherwise, the system determines whether present inventory can fill the order. If not, the order is held until sufficient inventory arrives. If there is enough inventory, the system checks the quantity ordered to determine if a discount is appropriate. An order for 500 units or less is filled; an order for greater than 500 units receives a 20% discount and is filled.

Differences Between DFDs and Flowcharts

According to a study by Kievit and Martin, data flow diagrams and flowcharts are the two most frequently used development and documentation tools. Their study shows that 62.5% of information professionals use DFDs and that 97.6% use flowcharts. Over 92% of users were satisfied with the use of both DFDs and flowcharts and use both.

A number of differences separate DFDs and systems flowcharts. First, a DFD emphasizes the flow of data and what is happening in a system, whereas a flowchart emphasizes the flow of documents or records containing data. A program flowchart emphasizes the flow of data as it is processed by a computer. A DFD represents the logical flow of data, whereas a flowchart represents the physical flow of data. The **logical view** of data is the way users conceptually organize and understand the relationships among data items. It shows what the system does with data—where data originate and are subsequently stored, the processes data undergo, and what ultimately happens to the processed data. The **physical view**

FIGURE 3.12
A Simple Program Flowchart for Processing Credit Orders

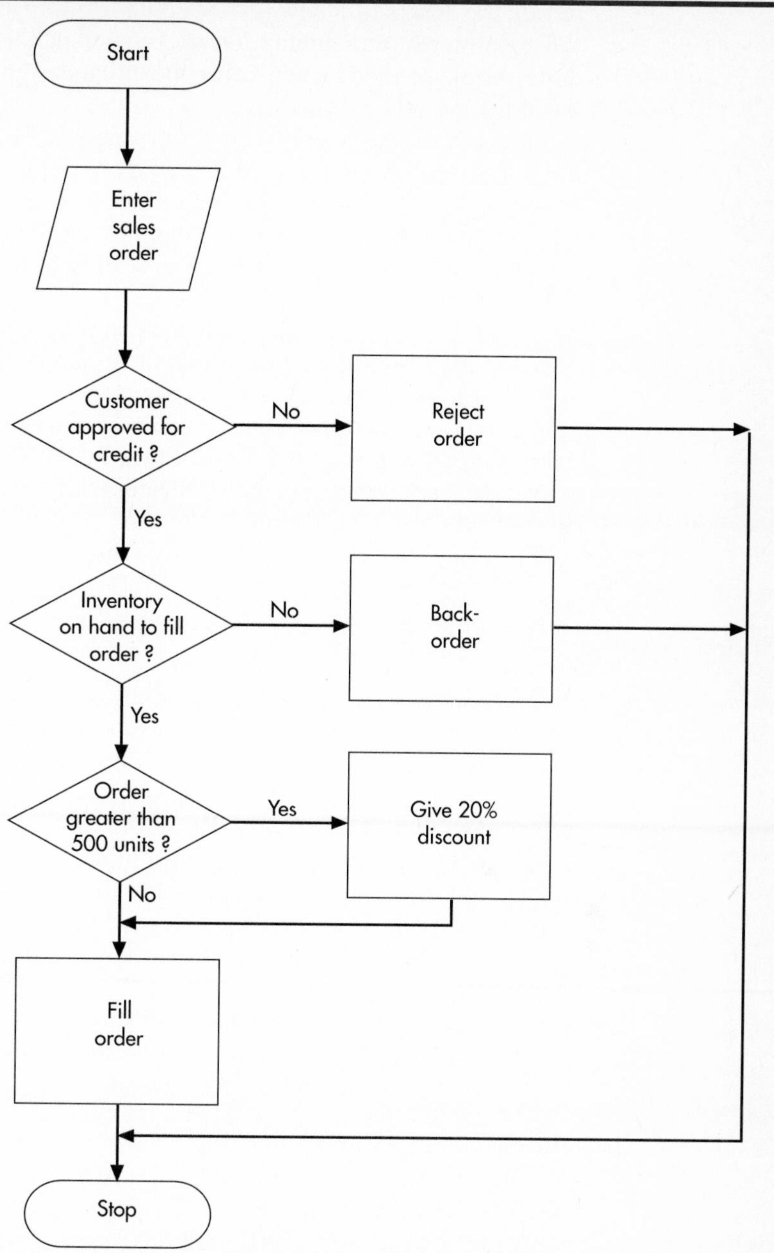

refers to how, where, and by whom data are physically arranged and stored. It is concerned with the physical aspects of the system, such as hardware, software, data structure, storage media (disks, tapes, etc.), and file organization.

Second, flowcharts are used primarily to document existing systems, since they emphasize how data are processed and stored. DFDs, in contrast, are primarily used in the design of new systems and do not concern themselves with the physical devices used to process, store, and transform data. Using a flowchart during the design of a new system could result in a premature physical design; that is, physical implementation decisions (such as *how* something should be done) would be made when only conceptual design issues (such as *what* should be done) should be discussed.

Third, DFDs make use of only four symbols. Flowcharts, on the other hand, use many symbols and thus can show more details pictorially than can DFDs. Consequently, it is imperative that DFD labels and accompanying descriptions effectively communicate what is happening. Finally, a flowchart shows the sequence of processes and data flows; DFDs do not. Nor do DFDs convey the timing of events, as a flowchart can.

Both DFDs and flowcharts are easy to prepare and revise when one of the recently developed DFD or flowcharting software packages is used. These packages are easier to use, in fact, than most word processors. Once a few basic commands are mastered, users can quickly and easily prepare, store, revise, and print presentation-quality DFDs or flowcharts. To create a flowchart, the user selects the appropriate symbol, indicates where it should be placed, enters the appropriate text, and moves to the next symbol. Editing a flowchart is easy; users merely click on the appropriate symbol and add, delete, or move it.

DECISION TABLES

A **decision table** is a tabular representation of decision logic. For any given situation, a decision table lists all the conditions (the ifs) that are possible in making a decision. It also lists the alternative actions (the thens) as well. Each unique relationship (if this condition exists, then take this action) is referred to as a **decision rule.** The general form of the decision table is illustrated in Table 3.3. The decision table in Table 3.4 outlines potential decisions and actions by S&S when filling credit orders. It corresponds with the program flowchart in Fig. 3.12.

A decision table has four parts: the condition and action stubs and the condition and action entries. The condition stub contains the various logic conditions for which the input data are tested. For example, there are three entries in the condition stub in Table 3.4. Note that they correspond to the three decision symbols in the program flowchart in Fig. 3.12.

The condition entry consists of a set of vertical columns, each representing a decision rule in which the entries must be either yes (Y), no (N), or a dash (—). The dash indicates an indifferent result of the condition test. For example, when credit is not approved, the quantity or inventory on hand is not relevant.

The action stub contains the actions the program should take. Table 3.4 indicates that four actions can be undertaken: reject the order, back-order, fill the order, or give a discount. The action entry columns indicate when an action is to occur. They display an X if the action is performed (if the input data meet the condition tests). A blank indicates the action is not performed.

Systems personnel use decision tables to illustrate the set of conditions present in most data processing programs and the corresponding courses of action for each condition. The advantage of decision tables is they indicate clearly all possible logical relationships among the input data. As a result, a program can be prepared to recognize and respond properly to each decision

TABLE 3.3 General Form of a Decision Table

Stub	Entry								
	Condition Rule								
Condition	**1**	**2**	**3**	**4**	**5**	**6**	**7**	**8**	**9**
(Specific conditions)									
	Action Rule								
Action	**1**	**2**	**3**	**4**	**5**	**6**	**7**	**8**	**9**
(Specific actions)									

rule. Decision tables, however, do not reflect the sequence of operations within a program and may become unmanageably large for complex programs. Program flowcharts and decision tables are often used together to help design and code computer programs.

Auditors can use decision tables to evaluate a client's application programs. If a decision table already exists, it can be reviewed for completeness and accuracy. If not, an auditor can create a decision table and then review it for weaknesses or errors in the computer program. Some studies have shown that up to 70% of application programs contain logic or syntax errors. For example, one savings and loan computer program failed to recognize that there were not 31 days in each month, resulting in over $100,000 in excess interest payments. Using a decision table, an auditor can create transaction data that can be processed by the system on a test basis. One or more transactions can be developed to test each separate decision rule, in this way assuring the auditor that the program actually meets its objectives. These concepts are discussed in more depth in Chapter 11.

TABLE 3.4 Simple Decision Table for Processing Credit Orders

	a	b	c	d
Credit approved	N	Y	Y	Y
Order ≤ inventory on hand	—	N	Y	Y
Order > 500 units	—	—	N	Y
Reject order	X			
Back-order		X		
Fill order			X	X
Give 20% discount				X

SUMMARY AND CASE CONCLUSION

Ashton prepared the DFDs and flowcharts of S&S's payroll processing system (Figs. 3.6, 3.7, 3.9, and 3.10) to document and explain the operation of the existing system. He was pleased to see that Scott and Susan were able to grasp the essence of the system from this documentation. The DFDs indicated the logical flow of data, and the flowcharts illustrated the physical dimensions of the system—the origin and final disposition as well as what happened to the documents in each department were clear.

Susan and Scott agreed to have Ashton document the remainder of the system. The documentation would help all three not only understand but improve the current system. In fact, the payroll documentation had already helped them identify a few minor changes they wanted to make in their system. Using the information from Fig. 3.9, Susan now understood why the payroll clerk sometimes had to borrow the only copy of the payroll report that was prepared. She thus recommended that a second copy be made and kept in the payroll department. Susan also questioned the practice of keeping all the payroll records in one employee/payroll file. To keep the file from becoming unwieldy, she recommended that it be broken up into three files: personal employee data, pay period documentation, and payroll tax data. A discussion with the payroll clerk verified that this approach would make payroll processing easier and more efficient.

Over the next few weeks, Ashton was able to document the rest of the accounting cycles. This process helped him identify inefficiencies and unneeded reports. He also found that some system documents were inadequately controlled. In addition, he got several ideas about how an automated system could help him reengineer the business processes at S&S. Outdated processes and procedures could be eliminated to make the system more effective by substituting technology for manpower.

When Ashton completed his analysis and documentation of the current system, Susan and Scott asked him to take the lead in moving the company from a manual to a computerized system. To do that, Ashton will need to gain a thorough understanding of the information needs of the various employees in the company. He will then need to design a new system using the tools, such as DFDs and flowcharts, that were examined in this chapter (systems development is discussed in Chapters 17–19, and data bases and data modeling are discussed in Chapters 5 and 6). He will also need to begin investigating the hardware and software options that are available to S&S (information technology is discussed in Chapter 4 and its appendix, and electronic commerce is discussed in Chapter 7).

KEY TERMS

- documentation
- narrative description
- data flow diagram (DFD)
- data sources
- data destinations
- data flow
- processes
- data store
- data dictionary
- context diagram
- flowchart
- flowcharting template
- document flowchart
- internal control flowchart
- system flowchart
- program flowchart
- logical view
- physical view
- decision table
- decision rule

CHAPTER QUIZ

1. A DFD is a representation of
   a. the physical view of data.
   b. the logical view of data.
   c. the decision rules in a computer program.
   d. a computer hardware configuration.

2. Documentation methods such as DFDs and flowcharts save both time and money, adding value to an organization.
   a. True
   b. False

3. Which of the following statements is false?
   a. DFDs make use of only four symbols; flowcharts make use of many symbols.
   b. A DFD emphasizes the flow of data and what is happening in a system, whereas a flowchart emphasizes the flow of documents or records containing data.
   c. DFDs can convey the timing of events; flowcharts cannot.
   d. A flowchart shows the sequence of processes and data flows; DFDs do not.

4. A DFD is composed of the following four basic elements: data sources and destinations, data flows, transformation processes, and data stores. Each is represented on a DFD by a different symbol.
   a. True
   b. False

5 Which of the following is not one of the guidelines that should be followed in naming DFD data elements?
   a. If a name cannot completely describe the data or process, then decompose the flow or process further.
   b. Make sure the names describe all the data or the entire process.
   c. Name only the most important DFD elements.
   d. Choose active and descriptive names.

6. The understanding of documentation skills that accountants need varies with their job function. However, they should at least be able to
   a. read documentation to determine how the system works.
   b. critique and correct documentation prepared by others.
   c. prepare documentation for a newly developed information system.
   d. teach others how to prepare documentation.

7. Which of the following statements is false?
   a. A flowchart is an analytical technique used to describe some aspect of an information system in a clear, concise, and logical manner.
   b. Flowcharts use a standard set of symbols to describe pictorially the flow of data through a system.
   c. Flowcharts are easy to prepare and revise when prepared with a flowcharting software package.
   d. A systems flowchart is a narrative representation of an information system.
   e. A program flowchart shows the logic used in computer programs.

8. Which of the following flowcharts illustrates the flow of information among areas of responsibility in an organization?
   a. Program flowchart
   b. Computer configuration chart
   c. Systems flowchart
   d. Document flowchart

9. Which of the following is not one of the recommended guidelines for making flowcharts more readable, clear, concise, consistent, and understandable?
   a. Divide the flowchart into columns with labels.
   b. Flowchart all information flows, especially exception procedures and error routines.
   c. Design the flowchart so that flow proceeds from top to bottom and from left to right.
   d. Show the final disposition of all documents so that there are no loose ends that leave the reader dangling.
   e. Each manual processing symbol should have an input and an output.

10. Which of the following is a false statement about decision tables?
   a. Auditors can use decision tables to evaluate a client's application programs.
   b. A decision table lists the conditions (the ifs) and the alternatives (the thens) that are possible in making a decision.
   c. Decision tables do not indicate logical relationships among the input data, but they do reflect the sequence in which the operations shown are to be performed.
   d. A decision table has four parts: the condition and action stubs, and the condition and action entries.
   e. Decision tables may become unmanageably large if a program is complex.

DISCUSSION QUESTIONS

3.1 Prepare arguments for and against the use of flowcharts and DFDs, and explain when it is most appropriate to use each documentation technique.

3.2 Identify the DFD elements in the following narrative: A customer purchases a few items from a local grocery store. Jill, a salesclerk, enters the transaction in the cash register and takes the customer's money. At closing, Jill gives both the cash and the register tape to her manager.

3.3 Do you agree with the following statement: "Any one of the systems documentation procedures, such as a DFD, can adequately document a given system"? Explain.

3.4 Compare the guidelines for preparing flowcharts and DFDs. What general design principles and limitations are common to both documentation techniques?

3.5 Your classmate asks you to explain flowcharting conventions using real-world examples. Draw each of the major flowchart symbols from memory, placing them into one of five categories: input, output, processing, storage, data flow, and miscellaneous. For each symbol, suggest several uses.

PROBLEMS

3.1 Prepare systems flowcharting segments for each of the following operations:

a. Processing transactions stored on magnetic tape to update a master file stored on magnetic tape
b. Processing transactions stored on magnetic tape to update a master file stored on a disk
c. Converting source documents off-line to magnetic tape using an optical character reader (OCR)
d. Processing OCR documents on-line to update a master file on magnetic disk
e. Reading data from a disk file into the computer to be listed on a printed report
f. Keying data from source documents to magnetic tape using an off-line, key-to-tape encoder
g. Manually sorting and filing invoices
h. Processing source data on-line using a terminal from a remote location that is connected to a central computer system for updating and recording source data on a magnetic disk master file

3.2 The Happy Valley Utility Company uses turnaround documents in its computerized customer accounting system. Meter readers are provided with preprinted computer forms, each containing the account number, name, address, and previous meter readings. Each form also contains a formatted area in which the customer's current meter reading can be marked in pencil. After making their rounds, meter readers turn in batches of these documents to the Computer Data Preparation Department, where they are processed by a mark-sense document reader that transfers their contents to magnetic tape.

This magnetic tape file is then sent to the computer center, where it is used as input for two computer runs. The first run sorts the transaction records on the tape into sequential order by customer account number. On the second run, the sorted transaction tape is processed against the customer master file, which is stored on a magnetic disk. Second-run outputs are (1) a printed report listing summary information and any erroneous transactions detected by the computer and (2) customer bills printed in a special OCR-readable font. Bills are mailed, and customers are requested to return the stub portion along with payment.

Customer payments are received in the mail room and checked for consistency against the returned stubs. Checks are then sent to the cashier's office. The mail room provides the Computer Data Preparation Department with three sets of records: (1) stubs with agreeing amounts, (2) stubs with differing amounts, and (3) a list of amounts received from customers without stubs. For the latter two types of records, data preparation personnel use a special typewriter to prepare corrected stubs. An OCR document reader then processes all the stubs and transfers their contents onto magnetic tape.

The magnetic tape containing the payment records is then sent to the computer center, where it is sorted on the computer into sequential order by customer account number and processed against the customer master file to post the payment amounts. Two printed outputs from this second process are (1) reports listing erroneous transactions and summary information and (2) past-due customer balances.

Required:

a. Draw a systems flowchart of the billing operations, commencing with the computer preparation of the meter reading forms and ending with the mailing of customer bills.

b. Draw a systems flowchart depicting customer payments processing, starting with the mail room operations and ending with the computer run that posts the payment amounts to the customer master file.

3.3 Prepare a program flowchart and a decision table for the following operation: Input to the program consists of an accounts receivable file containing (among other things) the amount due, date due, and customer credit limit. The program checks the due date of each customer record against the current date and prepares an aging schedule. Each customer's record is listed on a separate line of the aging schedule, with the amount due printed in one of three columns: (1) less than 60 days past due; (2) 61–180 days past due; or (3) more than 180 days past due.

The program compares the amount due with the customer's credit limit. Customer records that are more than 180 days past due and have an amount due in excess of the credit limit are printed on a Bad Debts Report for possible write-off by the credit manager. Other accounts that have an amount due in excess of the credit limit are printed on a Credit Review Report that goes to the treasurer. After the last record in the accounts receivable file is processed, the program is halted.

3.4 The Andy Dandy Company is a retailer that purchases goods from wholesalers and resells them to the public. The company wishes to purchase from the most reliable wholesaler. The following information was compiled and stored in the computer:

- A quality rating from 1 to 4 for each wholesaler (1 is considered the highest)
- Percentage of times each wholesaler has been late in delivering an Andy Dandy Company order
- Whether each wholesaler's prices have been stable or unstable
- Whether each wholesaler is in an economically rich or depressed area
- Whether each vendor has periodically suggested new products

The purchasing department has established the following criteria to be used in wholesaler selection:

- If the quality rating is 1, award the wholesaler 20% of the business.
- If the quality rating is 2 and the wholesaler is late less than 10% of the time, award that vendor 15% of the business.
- If the quality rating is 2 and the wholesaler is late more than 25% of the time, reject the vendor.
- If the quality rating is 2 and the wholesaler is late between 10% and 25% of the time, award that vendor 10% of the business, but only if prices have been stable.
- If the quality rating is 3 and the wholesaler is late less than 5% of the time, award that vendor 10% of the business, but only if the vendor is in a depressed area and has consistently suggested new products.
- If the quality rating is 4, reject the wholesaler.

Required:

Prepare a decision table to show the computer logic that is needed to write a program for vendor selection. (SMAC Examination, adapted)

3.5 The Dewey Construction Company processes its payroll transactions to update both its payroll master file and its work-in-process master file in the same computer run. Both the payroll master file and the work-in-process master file are maintained on disk and accessed randomly.

Data to be input to this system are keyed onto a tape using a key-to-tape encoder. The tape is then processed to update the files. This processing run also produces a payroll register on magnetic tape, employee paychecks and earnings statements, and a printed report listing error transactions and summary information.

Required:

Prepare a systems flowchart of the process described.

3.6 Prepare a document flowchart to reflect how ANGIC insurance company processes its casualty claims. The process begins when the Claims Department receives a notice of loss from a claimant. Claims prepares and sends the claimant four copies of a proof-of-loss form on which the claimant must detail the cause, amount, and other aspects of the loss. Claims also initiates a record of the claim, which is sent with the notice of loss to Data Processing, where it is filed by claim number.

The claimant must fill out the proof-of-loss forms with the assistance of an adjuster, who must concur with the claimant on the estimated amount of loss. The claimant and adjuster each keep one copy of the proof-of-loss form. The claimant sends the two remaining copies to the Claims Department. Separately, the adjuster submits a report to the Claims Department confirming the estimates on the claimant's proof-of-loss form.

The Claims Department authorizes a payment to the claimant, forwards a copy of the proof-of-loss form to Data Processing, and files the original proof-of-loss form and the adjuster's report alphabetically. The Data Processing Department prepares payment checks and mails them to the customers, files the proof-of-loss with the claim record, and prepares a list of disbursements, which it transmits to the Accounting Department.

3.7 Beccan Company is a discount tire dealer operating 25 retail stores in the metropolitan area. Beccan sells both private-brand and name-brand tires. The company operates a centralized purchasing and warehousing facility and employs a perpetual inventory system. All purchases of tires and related supplies are placed through the company's central Purchasing Department to take advantage of quantity discounts. The tires and supplies are received at the central warehouse and distributed to the retail stores as needed. The perpetual inventory system at the central facility maintains current inventory records, designated reorder points, and optimum order quantities for each type and size of tire and other related supplies. Beccan uses five documents in its inventory control system.

Retail stores requisition. The retail stores submit this document to the central warehouse whenever they need tires or supplies. The shipping clerks in the Warehouse Department fill the orders from inventory and authorize delivery to the stores.

Purchase requisition. The inventory control clerk in the Inventory Control Department prepares this document when the quantity on hand for an item falls below the designated reorder point. It is then forwarded to the Purchasing Department.

Purchase order. The Purchasing Department prepares this document when items need to be ordered. It is then submitted to an authorized vendor.

Receiving report. The Warehouse Department prepares this document when ordered items are received from vendors. The receiving clerk completes the document by indicating the vendor's name and the date and quantity of the shipment received.

Invoice. An invoice is received from vendors, specifying the amounts owed by Beccan.

The following departments are involved in Beccan's inventory control system:

Inventory Control Department. Responsible for the maintenance of all perpetual inventory records for all stock items. This inventory includes current quantity on hand, reorder point, optimum order quantity, and quantity on order for each item carried.

Warehouse Department. Maintains the physical inventory of all items carried in stock. All orders from vendors are received (receiving clerk) and all distributions to retail stores are filled (shipping clerks) in this department.

Purchasing Department. Places all orders for items needed by the company.

Accounts Payable Department. Maintains all open accounts with vendors and other creditors, in addition to processing payments.

Required:

Prepare a document flowchart that indicates the interaction and use of these documents among all departments at the central facility of Beccan Company. It should provide adequate internal control over the receipt, issuance, replenishment, and payment of tires and supplies. You may assume that there are a sufficient number of document copies to ensure that the perpetual inventory system has the necessary basic internal controls.
(CMA Examination, adapted)

3.8 As the internal auditor for No-Wear Products of Hibbing, Minnesota, you have been asked by your supervisor to document the company's current payroll processing system. Based on your documentation, No-Wear hopes to develop a plan for revising the current information system to eliminate unnecessary delays in the processing of paychecks. Your best explanation of the system came from an interview with the head payroll clerk:

> *The payroll processing system at No-Wear Products is fairly simple. Time data are recorded in each department using time cards and clocks. It is annoying, however, when people forget to punch out at night and we have to record their time information by hand. At the end of the period, our payroll clerks enter the time card data into a payroll file for processing. Our clerks are pretty good—though I've had to make my share of corrections when they mess up the data entry.*
>
> *Before the payroll file is processed for the current period, human resources sends us data on personnel changes, such as increases in pay rates and new employees. Our clerks enter this information into the payroll file so it is available for processing. Usually, when mistakes get back to us, it's because human resources is recording the wrong pay rate or an employee has left and they forget to remove the record.*
>
> *The data are then processed and individual employee paychecks are generated. Several important reports are also generated for management—though I don't know exactly what they do with*

them. In addition, the government requires regular federal and state withholding reports for tax purposes. Currently, the system generates these reports automatically, which is nice.

Required:

a. Prepare a context diagram for the current payroll processing system at No-Wear Products.
b. Develop a DFD to document the payroll processing system at No-Wear Products.

3.9 Ashton Fleming has decided to analyze the accounts payable process at S&S. His intent is to document how the present system works so the transition to a computerized system will be easier. He also hopes to improve on any weaknesses he discovers in the system. He has written the following narrative to explain what happens at S&S.

Before a vendor invoice is paid by S&S, it must be matched against the purchase order used to request the goods and the receiving report prepared by the Receiving Department. Since all three of these documents enter the Accounts Payable Department at different times, a separate alphabetical file is kept for each type of document. The purchase orders that are forwarded from purchasing are stored in a purchase order file. The receiving reports are stored in a receiving report file. When vendor invoices are received, the accounts payable clerk records the amount due in the accounts payable ledger and then files the invoices in the vendor invoice file.

The policy at S&S is to make sure all accounts are paid within 30 days to take advantage of the early-payment discounts that suppliers offer. When it comes time to pay a particular bill, the accounts payable clerk retrieves the vendor invoice and attaches the purchase order and the receiving report. These matched documents are forwarded to Ashton Fleming.

Ashton reviews the documents to ensure they are complete and prepares a two-part check. The checks as well as the other three documents are forwarded to Susan for her approval and signature. Ashton records the check amount in the cash disbursements journal.

Susan reviews the documents to ensure they are valid payables and then signs the checks. She forwards the check to the vendor and returns the documents as well as the second copy of the check to the accounts payable clerk. The clerk files the documents alphabetically in a paid invoice file.

At the end of every month, the accounts payable clerk uses information from the accounts payable ledger to prepare an accounts payable report. This report is forwarded to Susan for her review. After she is finished with the report, Susan files it chronologically.

Required:

a. Prepare a DFD to document accounts payable processing at S&S.
b. Prepare a document flowchart to document accounts payable processing at S&S.

3.10 Since opening its doors in Hawaii two years ago, Oriental Trading has enjoyed tremendous success. As a wholesaler, Oriental Trading purchases textiles from Asian markets and resells the textiles to local retail shops. To keep up with the strong demand for textiles in the Hawaiian Islands, Oriental Trading is expanding its local operations. At the heart of the expansion is the introduction of a new information system to handle the tremendous increase in purchases.

You have conducted several interviews with supervisors in the departments that interact with the acquisition/payment system. The following is a summary of your discussions.

A purchase requisition is sent from the inventory system and is received by Sky Ishibashi, a clerk in the Purchasing Department. Sky prepares a purchase order from information in the vendor and inventory files and mails it to the vendor. The vendor returns a vendor acknowledgment to Sky indicating receipt of the purchase order. Sky then sends a purchase order notification to Elei Mateaki, a clerk in the Accounts Payable Department.

When the Receiving Department accepts vendor goods, the inventory system notifies Elei by sending him a receiving report. Elei also receives the invoices that are mailed by the various vendors. Elei matches the invoices with the purchase order notification and the receiving report and updates the accounts payable master file.

Elei then sends a payment authorization to the Accounting Department. In the Accounting Department, Andeloo Nonu prepares and mails a check to the vendor. When the check is issued, the system automatically updates the accounts payable master file and the general ledger.

Required:

Develop a context diagram and a DFD of the acquisition/payment system at Oriental Trading.

3.11 Ashton Fleming has worked furiously for the past month trying to completely document the major business information flows at S&S. Upon completing his personal interviews with cash receipts clerks, Ashton asks you to develop a comprehensive DFD for the cash receipts system. Ashton's narrative of the system follows:

> *Customer payments include cash received at the time of purchase as well as account payments received in the mail. At the end of the day, all checks are endorsed by the treasurer and a deposit slip is prepared for the checks and the cash. The checks, cash, and deposit slip are then deposited daily at the local bank by a clerk.*
>
> *When checks are received as payment for accounts due, a remittance slip is included with the payment. The remittance slips are used to update the accounts receivable file at the end of the day. The remittance slips are stored in a file drawer by date.*
>
> *Every week, a cash receipts report and an aged trial balance are generated from the data in the accounts receivable ledger. The cash receipts report is sent to Scott and Susan. A copy of the aged trial balance by customer account is sent to the Credit and Collections Department.*

Required:

Develop a context diagram and a DFD for the cash receipts system at S&S.

3.12 A mail order skin and body care company advertises in magazines. Most orders are initiated by magazine subscribers who fill in and send coupons directly to the company. The firm also takes orders over the phone, answers inquiries about products, and handles payments and cancellations of orders. Products that have been ordered are sent either directly to the customer or to regional offices of the company that handle the required distribution. The mail order company has three basic data files that retain customer mailing information, product inventory information, and billing information based on invoice number. During the next few years, the company expects to become a multimillion-dollar operation. Recognizing the need to computerize much of the mail order business, the company has begun the process by calling you.

Required:

Draw a context diagram and at least two levels of logical DFDs for the preceding operations.

3.13 The local community college requires that each student complete a registration request form and mail or deliver it to the registrar's office. A clerk enters the request into the system. First, the accounts receivable subsystem is checked to ensure that no fees are owed from the previous quarter. Next, for each course, the student transcript is checked to ensure that the course prerequisites are completed. Then class position availability is checked and the student's Social Security number is added to the class list.

The report back to the student shows the result of registration processing: If fees are owed, the student is sent a bill and the registration is rejected. If prerequisites for a course are not fulfilled, the student is notified and that course is not registered. If the class is full, the student request is annotated with "course closed." If a student is accepted into a class, the day, time, and room are printed next to the course number. Student fees and total tuition are computed and printed on the form. Student fee information is interfaced to the accounts receivable subsystem. Course enrollment reports are prepared for the instructors.

Required:

Prepare a context diagram and at least two levels of logical DFDs for this operation.

3.14 Charting, Inc., a new audit client of yours, processes its sales and cash receipts documents in the following manner.

1. *Payment on account.* The mail is opened each morning by a mail clerk in the sales department. The mail clerk prepares a remittance advice (showing customer and amount paid) if one is not received. The checks and remittance advices are then forwarded to the sales department supervisor, who reviews each check and forwards the checks and remittance advices to the accounting department supervisor.

   The accounting department supervisor, who also functions as credit manager in approving new credit and all credit limits, reviews all checks for payments on past-due accounts and then forwards the checks and remittance advices to the accounts receivable clerk, who arranges the advices in alphabetical order. The remittance advices are posted directly to the accounts receivable ledger cards. The checks are endorsed by stamp and totaled. The total is posted to the cash receipts journal. The remittance advices are filed chronologically. After receiving the cash from the previous day's cash sales, the accounts receivable clerk prepares the daily deposit slip in triplicate. The third copy of the deposit slip is filed by date, and the second copy and the original accompany the bank deposit.

2. *Sales.* Sales clerks prepare sales invoices in triplicate. The original and second copy are presented to the cashier. The third copy is retained by the sales clerk in the sales book. When the sale is for cash, the customer pays the sales clerk, who presents the money to the cashier with the invoice copies.

   A credit sale is approved by the cashier from an approved credit list after the sales clerk prepares the three-part invoice. After receiving the cash or approving the invoice, the cashier validates the original copy of the sales invoice and gives it to the customer. At the end of each day, the cashier recaps the sales and cash received and forwards the cash and the second copy of the sales invoices to the accounts receivable clerk.

   The accounts receivable clerk balances the cash received with cash sales invoices and prepares a daily sales summary. The credit sales invoices are posted to the accounts receivable ledger, and then all invoices are sent to the inventory control clerk in the sales department for posting to the inventory control cards. After posting, the inventory control clerk files all invoices numerically. The accounts receivable clerk posts the daily sales summary to the cash receipts journal and sales journal and files the sales summaries by date.

   The cash from cash sales is combined with the cash received on account to make up the daily bank deposit.

3. *Bank deposits.* The bank validates the deposit slip and returns the second copy to the accounting department, where it is filed by date by the accounts receivable clerk.

   Monthly bank statements are reconciled promptly by the accounting department supervisor and filed by date.

Required:

You recognize that there are weaknesses in the existing system and believe a document flowchart would be beneficial in evaluating this client's internal control in preparing for your examination of the financial statements.

a. Complete the flowchart, given in Fig. 3.13, for sales and cash receipts of Charting, Inc. by labeling the appropriate symbols and indicating information flows. The chart is complete as to symbols and document flows.
   (CPA Examination, adapted)
b. Using the General Guidelines for Preparing Flowcharts discussed in Focus 3.2 and the flowcharting symbols shown in Fig. 3.8, critique the flowchart shown in Fig. 3.13. List all the ways the flowchart violates the guidelines or uses improper symbols.

3.15 A partially completed charge sales systems flowchart appears in Fig. 3.14. The flowchart depicts the charge sales activities of the Bottom Manufacturing Corporation.

A customer's purchase order is received, and a six-part sales order is prepared therefrom. The six copies are initially distributed as follows:

COPY NO. 1—BILLING COPY, TO BILLING DEPARTMENT

COPY NO. 2—SHIPPING COPY, TO SHIPPING DEPARTMENT

COPY NO. 3—CREDIT COPY, TO CREDIT DEPARTMENT

COPY NO. 4—STOCK REQUEST COPY, TO CREDIT DEPARTMENT

COPY NO. 5—CUSTOMER COPY, TO CUSTOMER

COPY NO. 6—SALES ORDER COPY, FILE IN SALES ORDER DEPARTMENT

When each copy of the sales order reaches the appropriate department or destination, it calls for specific internal control procedures and related documents. Some of the procedures and related documents are indicated on the flowchart. Other procedures and documents are labeled by the letters *a* to *r*.

Required:

List the procedures or the internal documents that are labeled letters *c* to *r* in the flowchart of Bottom Manufacturing Corporation's charge sales system. Organize your answer as follows. (Note that the explanations of the letters *a* and *b* in the flowchart are entered as examples.)
(CPA Examination, adapted)

Flowchart Symbol Letter	*Procedures or Internal Document*
a	Prepare six-part sales order.
b	File by order number.

FIGURE 3.13

Charting, Inc. Flowchart for Sales and Cash Receipts

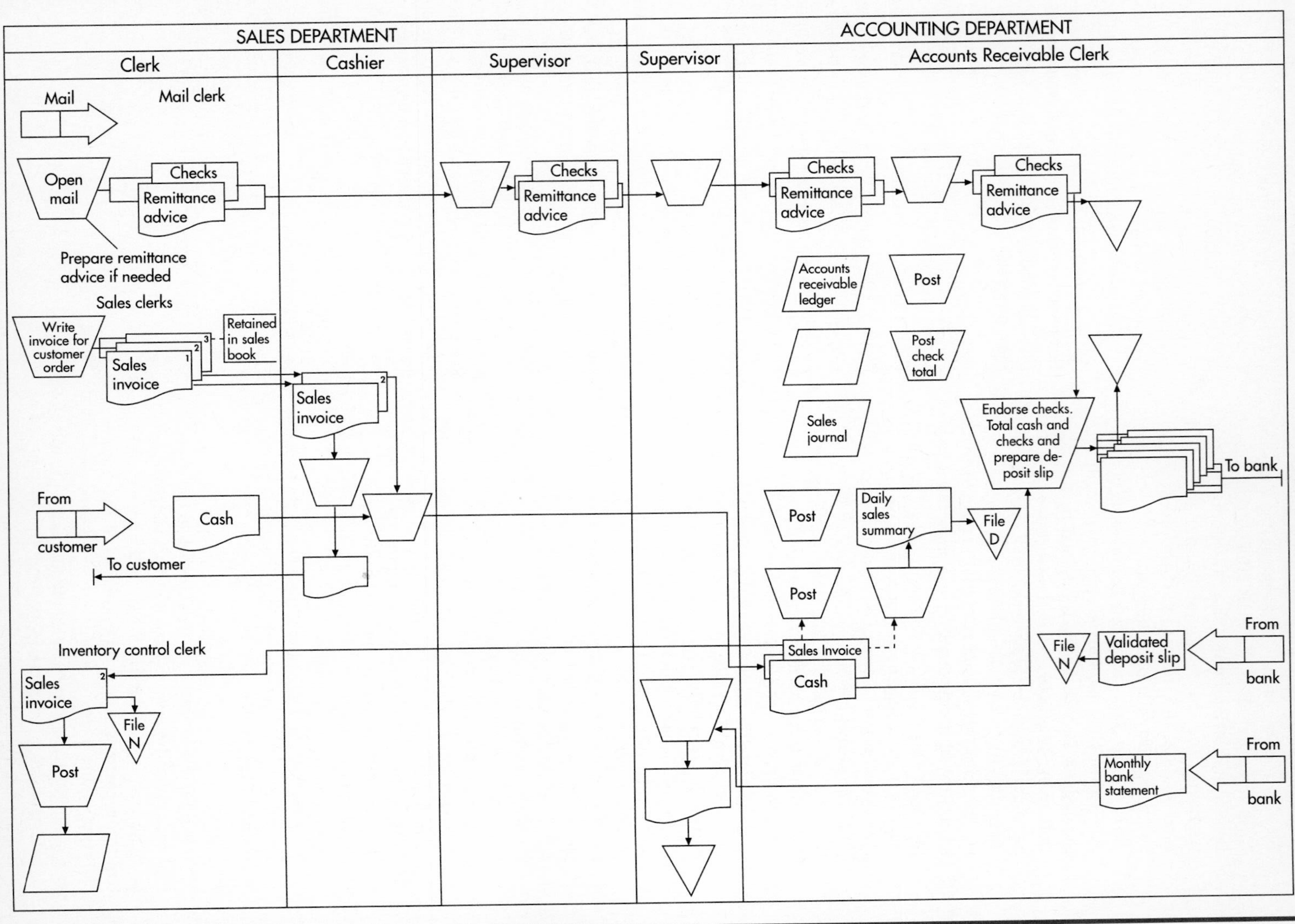

FIGURE 3.14
Bottom Manufacturing Corporation Flowchart of Credit Sales Activities

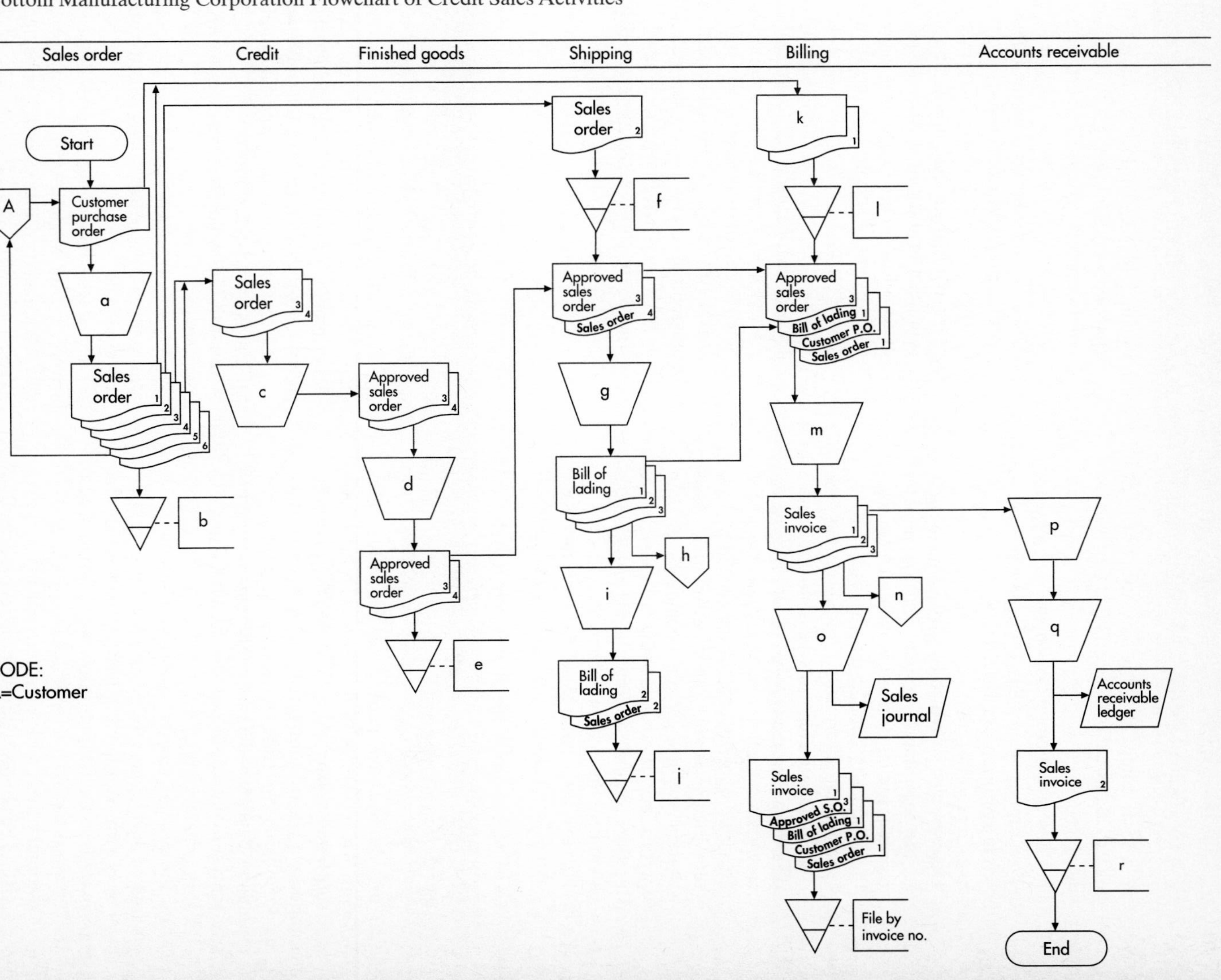

CASE 3.1 ANYCOMPANY, INC.—AN ONGOING COMPREHENSIVE CASE

Identify a local company (you may use the same company you identified in Case 1.1) and perform the following steps:

1. Select one of the company's business cycles for study. Examine all available documentation of the cycle's information system.
2. Prepare a report as follows:
   a. Describe who is involved in processing the data in the information system. Include in your report a partial organizational chart showing the relationships among employees.
   b. Describe the information flowing through the organization. Include in your report a context diagram and as many levels of DFDs as necessary to show the flow of information in the cycle.
   c. Describe what documents are used in the system. Include in your report a document flowchart showing the main documents used in processing transactions in the cycle, from origination to final destination. Also include a sample of the system documents.
   d. Identify the master files the company uses, and describe how and when they are updated. Include in your report a systems flowchart that shows the following: (1) all inputs to the computerized system, (2) all processing performed, and (3) all system output.
   e. Describe any other development tools used to create and document the system.
3. Select one of the software programs or applications the company uses. Do not choose anything too complex or difficult to understand. You may want to select only a portion of a program. As directed by your instructor, do one or more of the following steps:
   a. Draw a program flowchart showing the logic used in the program.
   b. Create a decision table that shows the conditions tested in the program and the actions to be taken when each unique condition is met.
4. In assignments 2 and 3, you used techniques and tools with a system that already existed. As an alternative to those assignments, analyze a system that is currently being developed.

CASE 3.2 DUB 5

You are the systems analyst for the Wee Willie Williams Widget Works (also known as Dub 5, which is a shortened version of 5 W's). Dub 5 produces computer keyboard components. It has been producing keyboards for IBM, its biggest customer, for more than 20 years and has recently signed an exclusive ten-year contract to provide the keyboards for all IBM personal computers.

As the systems analyst, you have been assigned the task of developing a DFD for Dub 5's order processing system. You have finished gathering all the information you need to develop the first-pass DFD and have just sat down to complete the diagram.

Customer orders, which are all credit sales, arrive via mail and by phone. When an order is processed, a number of other documents are prepared. You have diagrammed the overall process and the documents produced, as shown in Fig. 3.15.

The following documents are created.

- A packing slip is prepared by the Order Processing Department and then used by the Warehouse Department to fill the order. The packing slip accompanies the goods shipped from the warehouse.
- A customer invoice is prepared and mailed once the goods have been shipped.
- A monthly customer statement is mailed to the customer.
- When orders are not accepted, an order rejection is sent to the customer explaining why the order cannot be filled.
- A receivables notice, which is a copy of the customer invoice, is sent to the Accounting Department so that accounts receivable records can be updated.

After reviewing your notes, you write the following narrative summary:

When an order comes in, the order processing clerk checks the customer's credit file to confirm credit approval and ensure the amount falls within the credit limit. If either of these conditions is not met, the order is sent to the Credit Department. If an order meets both conditions, the order processing clerk enters it into the system on a standard order form. The information on the form is used to update the company's customer file (in which the name, address, and other information is stored), and the form is then placed in the company's order file.

When a rejected order is received by the Credit Department, the credit clerk first determines why the order has been rejected. If the credit limit has been exceeded, the customer is sent a personalized copy of a standard letter explaining that his or her credit limit has been exceeded and that the merchandise will be shipped as soon as Dub 5 receives payment. If the customer has not been approved for credit, a credit application is sent to the customer along with a letter stating that the order will be shipped as soon as credit approval is granted.

Before preparing a packing slip, the order processing employee checks the inventory records to determine whether the company has the products ordered on hand. If the items are in stock, a packing slip is prepared for every order form that is completed.

Once notification of shipped goods has been received, a customer invoice is prepared. One copy of the customer invoice is kept by the Order Processing Department, one is sent to the customer, and one is sent to the Accounting Department so that the receivables file can be updated. The receivables file contains all account information except name and address. A note is made in the customer file that the invoice has been sent. Every month, customer statements are sent by Dub 5.

From the information just discussed, complete a DFD for Dub 5.

FIGURE 3.15
Overall Process for Dub 5

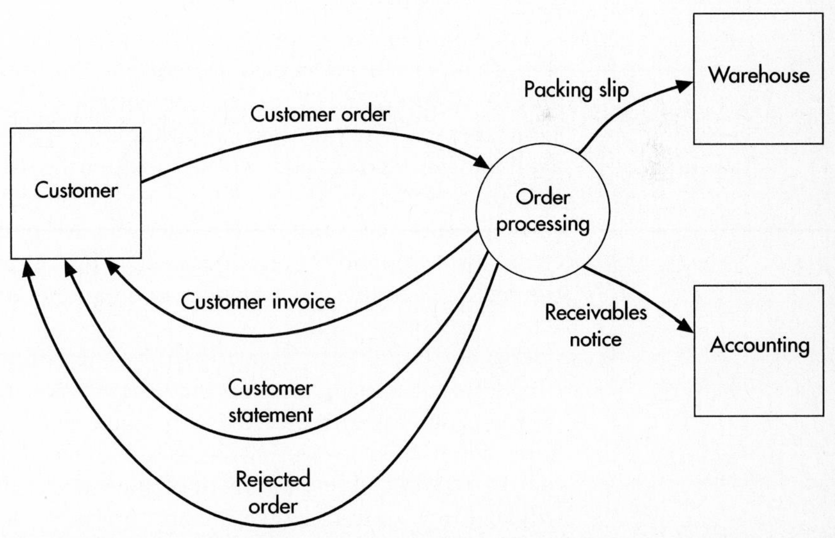

ANSWERS TO CHAPTER QUIZ

1. b **3.** c **5.** c **7.** d **9.** b
2. a **4.** a **6.** a **8.** d **10.** c

CHAPTER 4

Introduction to Data Processing

LEARNING OBJECTIVES

After completing this chapter, you should be able to

- Describe and give examples of the basic activities that take place in the data processing cycle.
- Explain how data is stored in files.
- Describe how data files are maintained.

Integrative Case: S&S, Inc.

Susan Gonzalez is frustrated. Over the past few months she has spent a great deal of time managing the store. She has just received the sales figures for October, and sales are down for the second month in a row. She is trying to figure out what is wrong and what she can do to reverse the trend.

For example, the special television promotion S&S ran in October was not as successful as past promotions. Susan believes that if she is able to compare the TV promotion with prior ones, she can find some answers. The problem is that the data she needs just are not available in a usable form. The store still processes its accounting data using a manual system. This does not provide much of the strategic information she needs, such as information about individual customer tastes and preferences, special discounts and promotions run by S&S's numerous suppliers, and national economic trends that affect purchasing patterns.

Susan's thoughts are interrupted by a telephone call. It is an old friend, Denise Ainge, who has made several recent purchases. She is having problems with one of the appliances and has a question about her account. Denise does not have the invoice number of the sale, but she does recall buying the appliance in October. Susan knows it will take time to track down the appropriate invoice. Since she has a meeting in just a few minutes with Scott and Ashton, she tells Denise she will have one of her staff call her back after they have found the information needed to answer her question.

During the meeting, Susan expresses her frustrations and wants to know how S&S can gather and store the necessary data. Susan explains her experience with trying to compare the monthly promotions and her call from Denise Ainge. She argues that this type of information should be available at her fingertips. For example, searching for information and then returning phone calls wastes valuable time. In addition, there will be other information needs in the future, and Susan wants quick access to the information to meet those needs.

Ashton thinks many of Susan's needs can be met with a computer system. Susan agrees that S&S may be ready for a computer-based AIS. Neither she nor Scott know much about computers, however. Therefore, Susan asks Ashton to research computer-based AIS and find answers to the following questions:

1. How are transactions processed using a computer?
2. What is the best way to enter data into a computer-based AIS?
3. How are reports generated from such a system, and what reports are needed?
4. How can S&S store the data it needs and make it readily available to those who need it?

INTRODUCTION

Figure 4.1 shows the four stages of the **data processing cycle:** data input, data storage, data processing, and information output.

Accountants play a significant role in the data processing cycle. They must interact with systems analysts to help answer questions such as the following: What data should be entered and stored by the organization? Who should have access to the data? Which data storage approach should be used: manual, file-based, or data base? How should the data be organized, updated, stored, accessed, and retrieved? How can both scheduled and unanticipated information needs be met? To answer these and related questions, accountants must understand the data processing cycle concepts explained in this chapter. Focus 4.1 shows why such knowledge is important: a well-designed AIS can save an organization a significant amount of money.

The next four sections discuss each of the stages of the data processing cycle in more detail. This discussion assumes that you already have a basic understanding

FIGURE 4.1
Four Stages of the Data Processing Cycle

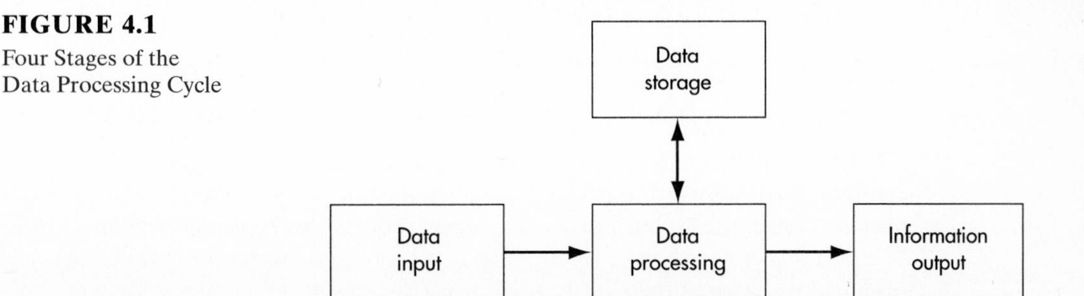

FOCUS 4.1 Information Systems Can Reduce Health Care Costs

MOST of the country's 6,000 hospitals have a hospital information system (HIS) that collects and processes information internally. However, the way hospitals move patient information from their HIS to the billing department and then to the insurance companies differs greatly. Many insurance company systems print billing data and drop it in the mail. The hospitals key the data into their HIS and process the claim. The printing, mailing, and rekeying process takes a great deal of time, slows the payment cycle, and introduces errors into the process. For example, at the Lake Charles Memorial Hospital, more than 12,000 claims errors occurred when claims were misplaced, mailed to the wrong office, or returned by Medicare or insurance companies due to inaccurate information on payment forms. Less than 5% of the estimated 3.5 billion health care claims are filed electronically each year.

Due to their current billing and collection systems, hospitals face a number of problems. Often they must use different methods of billing, depending on the payer's billing preference. The result is a great deal of confusion and a high error rate. Moreover, systems developers at hospitals have so much to do in terms of running the hospital and providing patients with adequate health care that the billing and collection areas of the hospital system take a backseat.

So what can be done? Hospitals and insurance companies are hammering out electronic billing and payment standards that can be applied consistently across the industry. Such efforts can yield sizable benefits. For example, after Lake Charles Memorial Hospital installed a new medical claims processing system, its error rate dropped 90%. Similarly, at Miami's Baptist Hospital, a more efficient system cut in half the 30 to 35 days it took to receive reimbursements for medical services from government agencies.

of computer hardware and software concepts. If you do not, or feel a need to refresh your knowledge, please refer to the appendix at the end of this chapter.

DATA INPUT

During the data input stage, transaction data are captured and converted to machine-processible form. To facilitate subsequent processing, data input may also require the following preparation:

- *Classification* by assigning identification codes (account number, department number, etc.) to data records based on a predetermined system, such as a chart of accounts.
- *Verification* to ensure data accuracy. It is less costly and more efficient to prevent data entry errors than to detect and correct them at the time of entry or once they are in the system.
- *Transmittal* from one location to another. For example, most bank ATMs capture and forward transaction data to their main office for processing.

Traditionally, transaction data has been captured on preprinted forms called **source documents.** Examples of internal source documents include sales orders, purchase requisitions, receiving reports, and employee time cards. External source documents include invoices from suppliers and checks and remittance advices from customers.

Data captured on source documents must be transformed into machine-readable format. Keying the data into an on-line terminal or microcomputer is one way this is done. Well-designed computer screens can improve the accuracy, completeness, and speed of data entry. The layout of these screens should resemble that of the source documents. The accuracy and speed of keying can be further improved by having the system prompt the user to input all necessary data. Often the nature of a succeeding question depends on the answer to a previous one. For example, consider a system built to help automobile insurance agents update their client's insurance policies. A "yes" response to the question "Is the insured adding a new driver?" leads to a series of questions about the new driver. Conversely, a "no" response precludes any additional questions about new drivers.

Data input accuracy and efficiency can be further improved by the use of scanning devices instead of keying. One way to do this is to use a **turnaround document,** a record of company data sent to an external party and then returned to the system as input. Turnaround documents are prepared in machine-readable form to facilitate their subsequent processing as input records. An example is a utility bill that is read by a special scanning device when it is returned with its payment.

Source data automation is yet another means to improve the accuracy and efficiency of data input. Source data automation devices capture transaction data in machine-readable form at the time and place of their origin. Examples include ATMs used by banks and scanners used in retail stores. Focus 4.2 describes how one insurance company has successfully implemented scanning technology. This example illustrates the need for accountants to keep abreast of how new developments in information technology can be used to improve the efficiency and effectiveness of their organization's AIS.

FOCUS 4.2 An Insurance Company Is Eliminating Paperwork

INSURANCE underwriters at Central Life Assurance Company (CLA) were drowning in paper. For 96 years CLA manually wrote insurance applications and associated documentation and forwarded them to data processing for entry into the system. Documents were frequently misplaced, misfiled, or mixed with outdated documents. The filing cabinets took up valuable floor space, and finding a document that was being processed was difficult.

CLA is solving its paper glut by moving to a paperless system that captures data as it is received in the office. When documents are received, they are scanned in the mail room and their images are stored on magnetic disks. Each document is indexed and checked for accuracy as it is scanned. After documents are scanned, they are routed to the proper department based on an assigned index number.

Scanned underwriting files contain all the information about a specific account: applications, financial reports, medical information, photographs, and so on. Because each scanned image (document) is indexed, the system organizes images by case. Agents can quickly access this information at any time using their PCs. After a case is closed, the images are archived on an optical disk instead of in a filing cabinet.

The new system has benefited CLA in several ways. Customer service has improved, because applications are processed faster and more accurately. In the past, when a customer would call an agent about a claim, the agent would have to look up the necessary information and call the person back. Now agents can access the information instantly while the customer is on the phone. The voluminous paperwork have been eliminated, and the new system is much more organized and easier to use. The result is better service and more efficient processing at significant cost savings.

DATA STORAGE

A company's data is one of its most important resources. However, the mere existence of relevant data does not guarantee its usefulness. An organization must have ready and easy access to its data in order to function properly. Therefore, accountants need to understand how data is organized and stored in an AIS and how that data can be accessed. In essence, accountants need to know how to manage data for maximum corporate use.

Fundamental Data Storage Concepts and Definitions

Imagine how difficult a textbook would be to read if it were not organized into chapters, sections, paragraphs, and sentences. Now imagine how hard it would be for S&S to find a particular invoice if all of its key documents were randomly dumped into file cabinets. Fortunately, most textbooks and company files are organized for easy retrieval. Likewise, information in an AIS can be organized for easy and efficient access. This section explains basic data storage concepts and definitions using accounts receivable information as an example.

An **entity** is something about which information is stored. Examples of entities include employees, inventory items, and customers. Each entity has **attributes,** or characteristics of interest, which need to be stored. An employee pay rate and a customer address are examples of attributes. Generally, each type of entity possesses the same set of attributes. For example, all employees possess an employee number, pay rate, and home address. The specific data values for those attributes, however, will differ among entities. For example, one employee's pay rate might be $8.00, whereas another's might be $8.25.

Computers store data by organizing smaller units of data into larger, more meaningful ones. This data storage hierarchy, beginning with fields (the smallest element) and ending with data bases (the largest), is shown in Fig. 4.2. Data values are stored in a physical space called a **field.** A number of fields are grouped together to form a **record,** a collection of data values that describe specific attributes of one entity. In Fig. 4.3, each row represents a different record and each column represents an attribute, or field. Thus each intersecting row and column in Fig. 4.3 is a field within a record and contains a **data value.**

Related records are grouped together to form a **file.** For example, all customer receivable records are stored in an accounts receivable file. Files containing related data are combined to form a **data base.** A set of interrelated, centrally coordinated data files facilitate both updating of the data and user access to the data. For example, the accounts receivable file might be combined with customer, sales analysis, and related files to form a customer data base.

Types of Files

Two basic types of files are used to store data. The first, a **master file,** is conceptually similar to a ledger in a manual system. A master file contains all the data that a company needs about an item of interest. For example, records in an accounts receivable master file include such information as customer name, address, current account balance, and credit limit. Decision makers frequently query master files to extract information for analysis. Most company reports

FIGURE 4.2
Hierarchy of Data Storage Elements

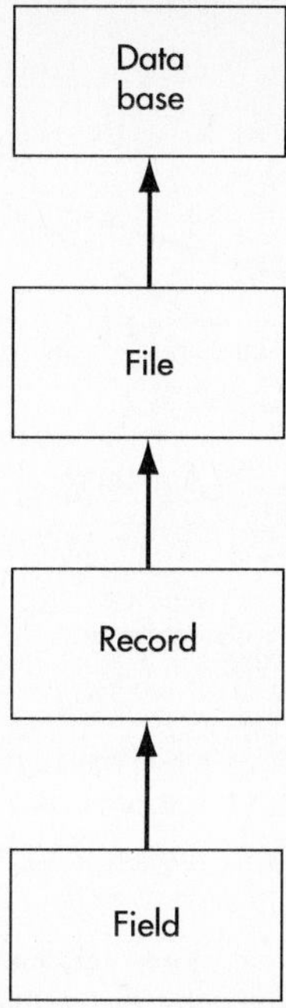

are prepared by printing out information contained in one or more master files. A master file is permanent in that it will exist indefinitely, although individual records within it may frequently be inserted, deleted, or changed. The most common type of change made to records in master files involves updating the data to reflect the effect of transactions. For example, a customer's account balance is updated to reflect new sales and payments received.

The second basic type of file is a **transaction file,** which is conceptually similar to a journal in a manual system. Transaction files are so named because they contain data about a specific type of transaction. For example, the sales transaction file contains data about all sales during a specific time period; similarly, the cash receipts transaction file contains data about all payments received by the company. Since they are used to update master files, transaction files must contain all the transaction data needed for that purpose. For example, a sales transaction file that updates the accounts receivable master file would contain the customer number and the amount and date of the sale.

File Access and Organization

All computer systems must have some formalized means of organizing data so that it can be accessed easily and efficiently. This section describes several ways of organizing and accessing files.

Accessing Individual Records: Primary and Secondary Keys. Records are typically updated, stored, and retrieved using an identifier called a **primary key,** which is the attribute that uniquely identifies each record. The appropriate

FIGURE 4.3
Accounts Receivable File

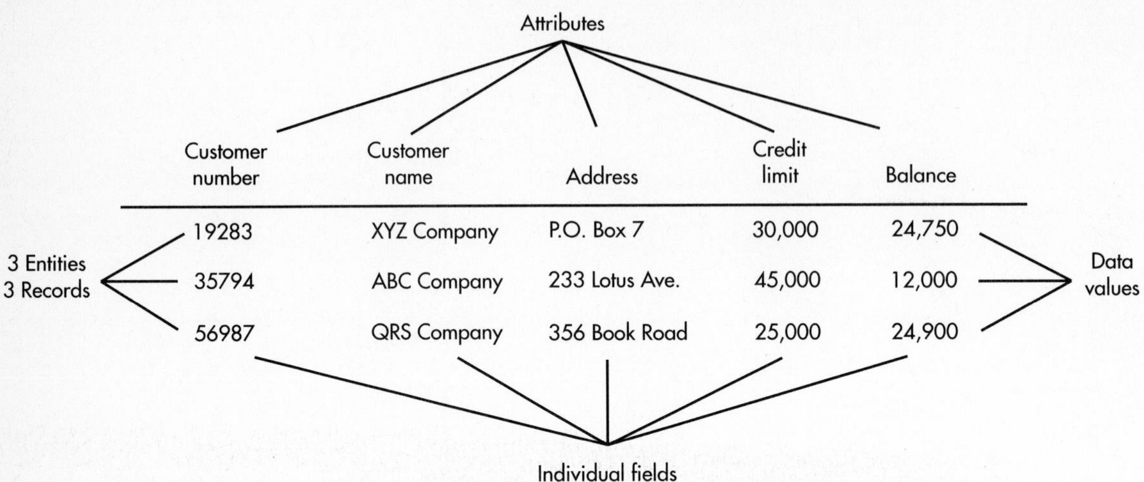

This accounts receivable file stores information about three separate entities: XYZ Company, ABC Company, and QRS Company. As a result, there are three records in the file. Five separate attributes are used to describe each customer: customer number, customer name, address, credit limit, and balance. There are therefore five separate fields in each record. Each field contains a data value that describes an attribute of a particular entity (customer). For example, the data value 19283 is the customer number for the XYZ Company.

primary key for each record is generally obvious. For example, customer number for the customer file and invoice number for the invoice file.

A **secondary key** is another field used to identify a record, although it is not unique. Secondary keys do not uniquely identify individual records, but identify a *group* of records. Secondary keys can be used to sort records. For example, zip code might be a secondary key in the accounts receivable file. This allows the file to be sorted by zip code to facilitate sales analyses.

The selection of secondary keys is important, because well-chosen secondary keys can significantly enhance data processing efficiency and facilitate information retrieval. The most appropriate secondary keys are those data elements that identify certain properties held in common by groups of records. Examples include invoice due date, employee department number, and inventory location code. Table 4.1 lists some common data records in a business organization and identifies a primary key and two or more secondary keys for each one.

File Organization. **File organization** refers to the way data are stored on the physical storage media. There are three basic ways that files are organized. **Sequential access files** store records in order according to their primary key (e.g., customer numbers from 00001 to 99999). **Indexed sequential access method (ISAM) files** store records in sequential order, but also have an index that links primary keys with their physical addresses. Figure 4.4 shows an example of an ISAM file and its accompanying index file. **Direct access files** store records in no particular order. Instead, a mathematical algorithm is applied to the primary key to determine the physical address at which to store that record.

File Access. **File access** refers to the way a computer locates stored records. The manner in which this is accomplished depends on the file organization. Records stored in sequential access files can only be accessed by starting at the beginning of the file and reading each record until the one desired is located. Because the search process is so inefficient, it is impractical for applications that require immediate access to records.

Both ISAM and direct access file organizations permit the direct access of individual records. In the case of ISAM files, a specific record is located by looking up its address in the index file. In the case of direct access files, the same algorithm used to originally store the record is used to calculate that record's address.

Multiattribute Search File Organization. The file organizations described thus far allow the file to be accessed by the primary key, but they do not facilitate accessing a set of data records based on one or more secondary keys. When access through secondary keys is desired, a multiattribute search file organization is used. Two methods are discussed here: linked lists and inverted lists (also called inverted files).

In a **linked list,** each data record has a **pointer field** containing the address of the next record in the list. Thus pointers link all related records. A group of records connected by pointers is referred to as a **chain.** Table 4.2 illustrates the use of embedded pointers to chain together records having the same secondary keys. The links in each chain are pointers contained in the fields labeled Next S and Next PL. Each of these fields points to the storage address of the next record having the same value for supplier and product line, respectively. For example, the chain for all parts supplied by ABC Co. contains the records at machine addresses 11, 16, 17, 21, and 30.

TABLE 4.1 Examples of Record Keys for Typical Business Records

4-1 : Table

Record Type	Primary Key	Secondary Keys
Payroll	employee number	"employee name, payroll date, department"
Customer	account number	"customer name, balance, credit limit"
Parts inventory	stock number	"location, description, vendor number"
Work in process	job number	"location, start date"
Finished goods	product number	"location, sales price"
General ledger	account code	"department number, current balance"
Fixed assets	asset number	"location, date of acquisition, vendor number"
Accounts payable	Vendor number	"payment due date, vendor number"

Record: 9 of 9

FIGURE 4.4
An Indexed Sequential File

Index

Key	Address
1482	4061
1487	4062
1492	4063
1497	4064
1502	4065

Data Storage Area

Address No. 4061	Customer No. 1478	Customer No. 1479	Customer No. 1480	Customer No. 1481	Customer No. 1482
Address No. 4062	Customer No. 1483	Customer No. 1484	Customer No. 1485	Customer No. 1486	Customer No. 1487
Address No. 4063	Customer No. 1488	Customer No. 1489	Customer No. 1490	Customer No. 1491	Customer No. 1492
Address No. 4064	Customer No. 1493	Customer No. 1494	Customer No. 1495	Customer No. 1496	Customer No. 1497
Address No. 4065	Customer No. 1498	Customer No. 1499	Customer No. 1500	Customer No. 1501	Customer No. 1502

Linked lists and pointers are commonly used in AIS to connect a set of detail records to a master record. For example, an accounts receivable record may have associated with it a number of transaction records, which could be connected to it by means of linked lists. Similarly, an invoice or purchase order record could have line-item records connected to it using pointers. Chains may also be used to link all records in a file that have the same secondary key, such as all employees who work in the same department.

Whereas linked lists use pointers embedded within the records, **inverted lists** use pointers stored in an index. An **inverted file** maintains inverted lists for some of the attributes. Table 4.3 shows inverted lists for the secondary keys supplier and product line, created from the sample data records in Table 4.2. There is one list for each value of each attribute, and each list contains the machine addresses of all records having that value. Using these inverted lists, any or all records containing a particular supplier or product line can be easily and quickly accessed.

DATA PROCESSING

The most common data processing activity is data maintenance, which is the periodic processing of transactions to update stored data. Four types of data maintenance are commonly used. *Additions* insert new records into a master file. *Deletions* remove records from a master file. *Updates* revise current balances in master files, generally by adding or subtracting an amount that is

TABLE 4.2 Use of Secondary Keys to Link Embedded Pointers

4-2 : Table

Address	Part #	Supplier	Next S	Product Line	Next PL
11	125	ABC Co.	16	Widget	17
12	164	XYZ Inc.	14	Doodad	16
13	189	GHI Corp.	18	Clavet	15
14	205	XYZ Inc.	24	Lodix	18
15	271	RST Mfg.	19	Clavet	22
16	293	ABC Co.	17	Doodad	20
17	316	ABC Co.	21	Widget	23
18	348	GHI Corp.	20	Lodix	19
19	377	RST Mfg.	22	Lodix	21
20	383	GHI Corp.	23	Doodad	24
21	451	ABC Co.	30	Lodix	25
22	465	RST Mfg.	25	Clavet	27
23	498	GHI Corp.	26	Widget	
24	521	XYZ Inc.	28	Doodad	26
25	572	RST Mfg.		Lodix	28
26	586	GHI Corp.	27	Doodad	29
27	603	GHI Corp.	29	Clavet	
28	647	XYZ Inc.		Lodix	30
29	653	GHI Corp.		Doodad	
30	719	ABC Co.		Lodix	

Record: 1 of 20

stored in a transaction record. *Changes* modify the data values of other fields in master files, such as changing customer credit ratings and addresses.

Figure 4.5 depicts the data maintenance steps required to update an accounts receivable master file record to reflect a sales transaction. The account number field is used to match each transaction file record with the appropriate record in the master file. In this example, account 0123 is being updated to reflect the effects of a sales transaction that occurred on February 19, 1999, as recorded on invoice number 9876. The sale amount ($360) is added

TABLE 4.3 Inverted Lists for the Secondary Keys of Table 4.2

4-3 : Table

Supplier	Address	Product Line	Address2
Supplier	Addresses	Product Line	Addresses
ABC Co.	"11, 16, 17, 21, 30"	Clavet	"13, 15, 22, 27"
GHI Corp.	"13, 18, 20, 23, 26, 27, 29"	Doodad	"12, 16, 20, 24, 26, 29"
RST Mfg.	"15, 19, 22, 25"	Lodix	"14, 18, 19, 21, 25, 28, 30"
XYZ Inc.	"12, 14, 24, 28"	Widget	"11, 17, 23"

Record: 6 of 6

FIGURE 4.5
File Update Example

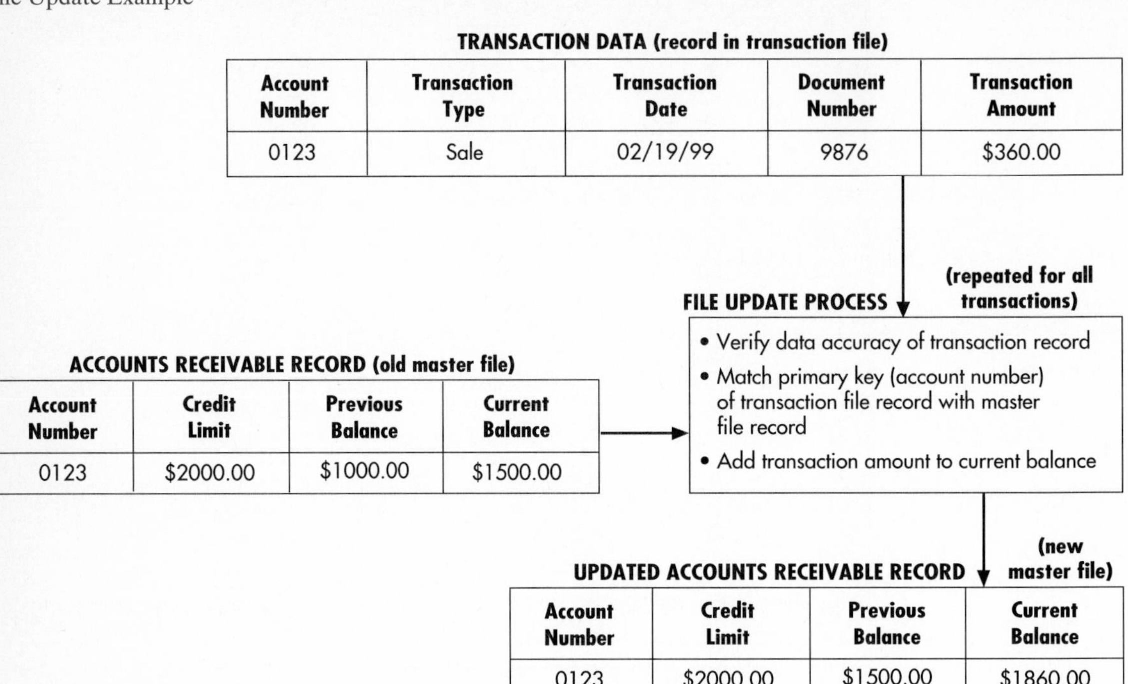

to the existing account balance ($1,500) to produce the updated current account balance ($1,860).

TRANSACTION DATA (record in transaction file)
Account Number
Transaction Type
Transaction Date
Document Number
Transaction Amount
0123
Sale
02/19/99
9876
$360.00
FILE UPDATE PROCESS
(repeated for all transactions)
• Verify data accuracy of transaction record
• Match primary key (account number) of transaction file record with master file record
• Add transaction amount to current balance
ACCOUNTS RECEIVABLE RECORD (old master file)
Account Number
Credit Limit
Previous Balance
Current Balance
0123
$2000.00
$1000.00
$1500.00
UPDATED ACCOUNTS RECEIVABLE RECORD
(new master file)
Account Number
Credit Limit
Previous Balance
Current Balance
0123
$2000.00
$1500.00
$1860.00

Figure 4.6 shows that master files can be updated in two ways: (1) periodically using all transactions that occurred during a given time period, or (2) as each individual transaction occurs. These two approaches are now explained.

Batch Processing

Updating master files periodically to reflect all transactions that occurred during a given time period is called **batch processing.** The master file is updated at set times (such as hourly or daily) or whenever a manageable number (50 to 100, for example) of transactions are gathered. As shown in Fig. 4.6, the transactions data can either be entered as a batch or as each transaction occurs. The latter approach is called on-line batch processing.

Batch processing requires that the master file be organized as either a sequential access or an ISAM file. In either case, the first step in batch processing is to sort the transaction file so that it is in sequential order by the primary key of the master file being updated. For example, before updating the accounts receivable master file, the transaction file containing records of all sales and payments transactions should be sorted so that it is in order by customer number. Doing so allows the simple program logic illustrated in Table 4.4 to be followed.

To simplify the illustration, Table 4.4 shows only the primary key (customer account number), account balance, and transaction amount fields. A positive transaction amount represents a sale; a negative amount represents a payment. Notice how steps 7, 9, and 11 can only be performed accurately if the transaction file is sorted to be in the same order as the master file. This enables the program to (1) determine when all transactions pertaining to a given master file record have been processed (step 7), (2) identify master file records for which no activity occurred (step 9), and (3) recognize transaction file records that do not correspond to any master file records (step 11).

FIGURE 4.6
Batch and On-line Processing

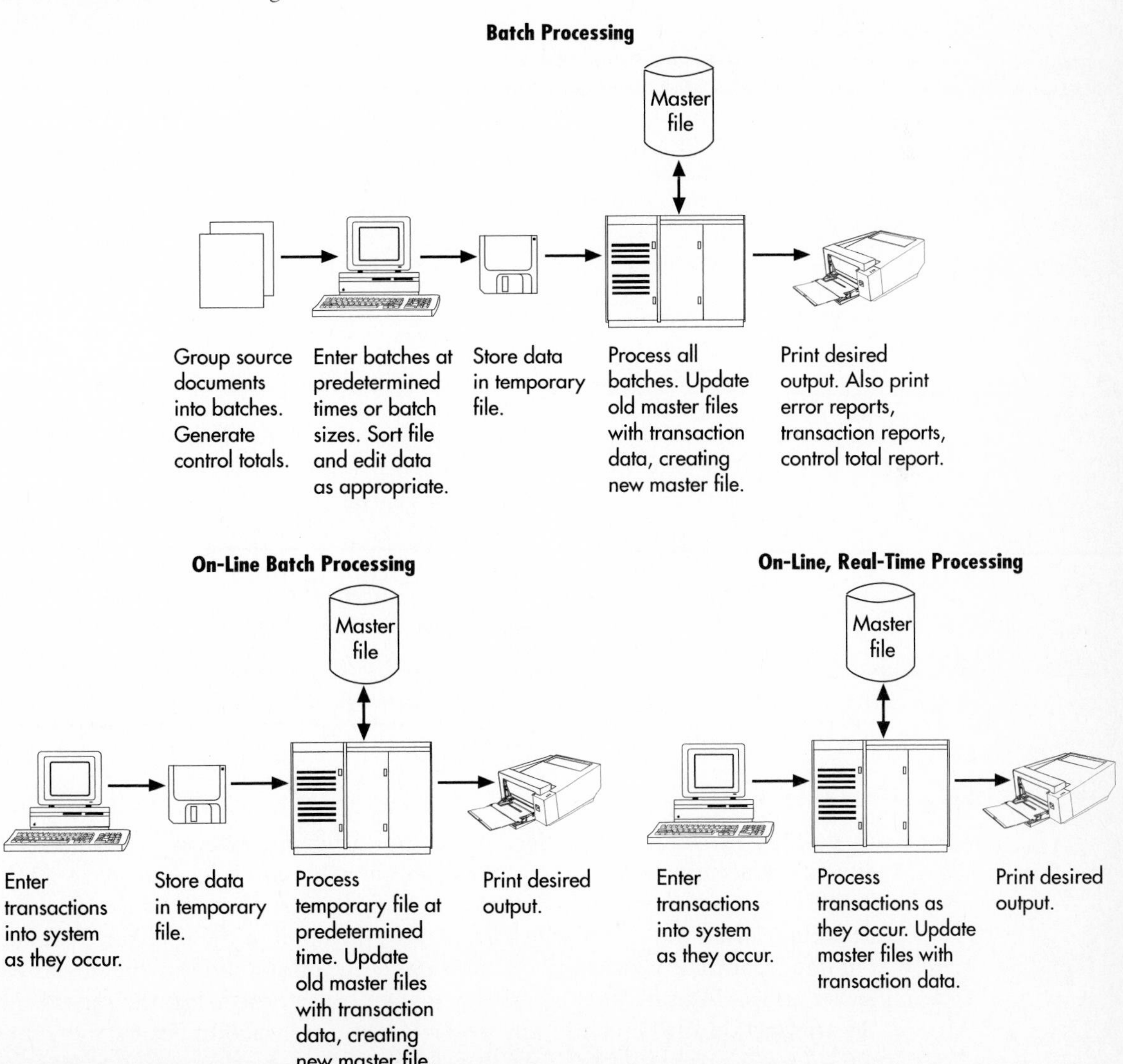
Batch Processing
Master file
Group source documents into batches. Generate control totals.
Enter batches at predetermined times or batch sizes. Sort file and edit data as appropriate.
Store data in temporary file.
Process all batches. Update old master files with transaction data, creating new master file.
Print desired output. Also print error reports, transaction reports, control total report.
On-Line Batch Processing
Master file
Enter transactions into system as they occur.
Store data in temporary file.
Process temporary file at predetermined time. Update old master files with transaction data, creating new master file.
Print desired output.
On-Line, Real-Time Processing
Master file
Enter transactions into system as they occur.
Process transactions as they occur. Update master files with transaction data.
Print desired output.

TABLE 4.4 Example of Sequential Batch Processing

Files Before Update

Master File		Transaction File	
Account #	**Balance**	**Account #**	**Amount**
101	1000	101	+700
102	600	101	−1000
104	1900	103	+500
		104	+1600

Update Process

		Master File		Transaction File	
Step	**Action**	**Acct #**	**Balance**	**Acct #**	**Amount**
1	Read master file record	101	1000		
2	Read transaction file record			101	700
3	Match and update	101	1700		
4	Read transaction file record			101	−1000
5	Match and update	101	700		
6	Read transaction file record			103	500
7	No match; write 101 to new master file	—	—		
8	Read master file record	102	600		
9	No match; write 102 to new master file	—			
10	Read master file record	104	1900		
11	No match; write 103 to error file	—			
12	Read transaction file record			104	1600
13	Match and update	104	3500		

Files After Update

Master File		Error File	
Account #	**Balance**	**Account #**	**Amount**
101	700	103	500
102	600		
104	3500		

On-line, Real-Time Processing

In **on-line, real-time processing,** the computer captures data electronically, edits it for accuracy and completeness, and immediately processes it. In addition, the computer processes information requests from users by locating the desired information in the data files and displaying it in the specified format. On-line, real-time processing requires that the master file be organized as either an ISAM or a direct access file. Unlike batch processing, the records in the transaction file can be in any order. When a transaction occurs, the computer uses the primary key of the transaction file (such as account number) to search the master file for the desired record. The appropriate record is then retrieved, updated, and written back to the master file. Figure 4.7 shows the steps involved in on-line, real-time processing.

It is important to distinguish between on-line, real-time processing and on-line batch processing. Both approaches enter transaction data at the time the event occurs. The difference lies in when the master files are updated. On-line, real-time processing updates the master file as each transaction occurs; in contrast, on-line batch processing only updates the master file periodically. Thus only on-line, real-time processing ensures that the master file always contains up-to-date information.

Advantages of Each Method

Batch processing is a legacy method that was primarily used for applications, like payroll, in which every or almost every record in the master file needed to

FIGURE 4.7
Generalized Direct Access File Processing Program Flowchart

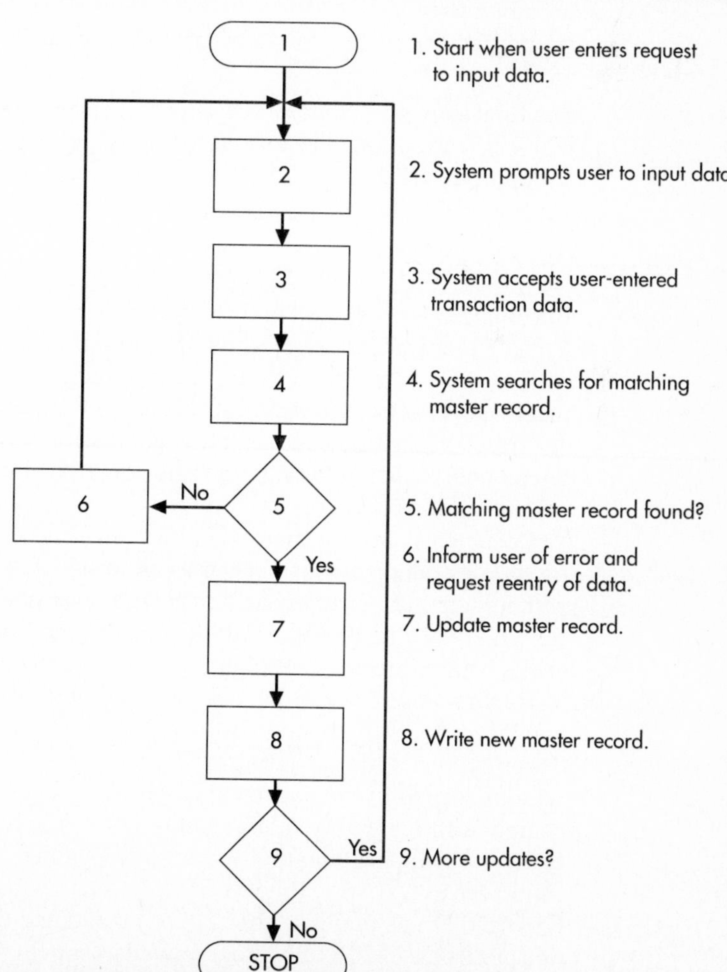

1
2
3
4
6
No
5
Yes
7
8
9
Yes
No
STOP
1. Start when user enters request to input data.
2. System prompts user to input data.
3. System accepts user-entered transaction data.
4. System searches for matching master record.
5. Matching master record found?
6. Inform user of error and request reentry of data.
7. Update master record.
8. Write new master record.
9. More updates?

be updated. Its main advantage was efficiency in processing. Its primary disadvantage is that the master files do not contain current information, except immediately after the periodic batch updating. Consequently, most companies are switching to on-line, real-time processing for most applications. On-line data entry is more accurate than periodic batch input because the system can refuse incomplete or erroneous entries and, since the data is being entered at the time the transaction occurs, the errors can be easily corrected. Real-time processing ensures that the information in master files is always current, thereby increasing its usefulness for making decisions.

Indeed, many companies are using on-line, real-time processing because of the competitive advantages it offers. For example, a few years ago Federal Express updated its mission statement to include the phrase "positive control of each package will be maintained by utilizing real-time electronic tracking and tracing systems." The company's on-line, real-time system tells the exact location of each package and estimates its arrival time. Federal Express also provides customers with personal computer software that allows them to track their own parcels.

INFORMATION OUTPUT

The final step in the data processing cycle is information output. In this section you will learn about the format, purpose, and user responsibilities associated with output.

Forms of Information Output

Information is presented in three forms: a document, a report, or a response to a query. Documents are records of transactions or other company data. Some, such as checks and invoices, are transmitted to external parties. Others, such as receiving reports and purchase requisitions, are used internally. Documents generated at the end of transaction processing activities are called **operational documents** to distinguish them from source documents, which are used at the beginning of a process.

Documents can be printed out or they can be stored as electronic images in a computer. For example, Toys 'R' Us uses electronic data interchange to communicate with its suppliers. Every year it processes over half a million invoices electronically, thereby eliminating paper documents and dramatically reducing costs and errors. This has resulted in higher profits and more accurate information.

Reports are prepared for both internal and external users. They are used by employees to control operational activities and by managers to make decisions and design strategies for the business. External users need reports for a wide variety of reasons, such as to evaluate company profitability, to judge creditworthiness, or to comply with regulatory requirements. For example, Eli Lilly, a large drug manufacturer, has applications that automatically gather, process, and display data in any form, such as text, spreadsheets, or easy-to-understand graphs or charts. When the Food and Drug Administration (FDA) mandated that it receive certain information electronically, Eli Lilly programmed its system to gather the needed data from its different systems, organize it, and submit it electronically to the FDA.

Some reports, such as financial statements and sales analyses, are produced on a regular basis. Others are produced on an exception basis to call attention to unusual conditions. For example, S&S could have its system produce a report to indicate when product returns exceed a certain percentage of sales. Finally, reports can be produced on demand. For example, Susan could produce a report to identify the S&S salesperson who sold the most items during a specific promotional period.

Increasingly, information needs cannot be satisfied entirely by documents or periodic reports. Instead, problems and questions that need rapid action or answers constantly arise. To respond to this problem, PCs or terminals are used to query the system. A user enters a request for a specific piece of information, and the system uses the indexes, lists, and pointers to find the information. Once found, the information is retrieved, displayed, or analyzed as requested. Since many queries are repetitive, most users will have a predetermined set of queries available to them. To shorten the time required to develop the queries and to improve their efficiency, these repetitive queries are often developed by information system (IS) specialists. Any unusual or one-time queries are usually developed by the users themselves. When displayed on a monitor, output is referred to as soft copy. When printed on paper, it is referred to as hard copy.

Some companies have even made it possible for their suppliers to query their own data bases. For example, Kmart allows Black & Decker to access any information in its data bases—excluding any data about Black & Decker's competitors—that will help it better serve Kmart's needs. Thus Black & Decker can gauge how well a product, such as a new electric drill, is selling in every Kmart store in the world. Kmart and Black & Decker can both maximize sales by stocking and promoting those items that are selling well. Customers are satisfied because the items they want are always available.

Purpose of Information Output

For external users, financial statements are produced to meet stewardship requirements. In addition, income tax returns and 10-K filings with the Securities and Exchange Commission are produced to comply with legal requirements. For internal users, budgets, sales forecasts, projected cash flow statements, and new product revenue and cost estimates are prepared for planning purposes. In addition, reports such as production and delivery schedules, open purchase orders, and inventory stock status reports are prepared to help effectively manage day-to-day operations.

Companies should periodically reassess the need for each report produced. All too often, reports continue to be prepared long after their need disappears, wasting time, money, and computer resources. For example, a team at Ameritech, a regional Bell telephone company, interviewed the preparers and users of every report. They found many duplicate and unnecessary reports, including a 25-page report that took five days to prepare yet sat unread. In the end, 6 million pages of reports were eliminated, a stack four times higher than Ameritech's 41-story headquarters in Chicago.

For control purposes, an organization must constantly monitor its progress so that problems can be corrected as soon as possible. Often monitoring consists of comparing standards or expected performances with actual performance. When variances get too far out of line, management takes corrective action to bring them back within an acceptable range. Examples of control reports include comparisons of standard and actual production rates, materials use, labor efficiency, profitability, and sales.

SUMMARY AND CASE CONCLUSION

The immediate need at S&S is to develop a computerized AIS. Based on his research, Ashton decided that on-line, real-time processing was appropriate for most applications. For example, it is vital that S&S capture and process data about sales transactions as they occur, so that Scott and Susan can make informed decisions concerning extending additional credit to customers. It is also important for S&S to have up-to-date accurate information about inventory levels. The only application that Ashton thinks might be appropriate for on-line batch processing is payroll, since the output (paychecks) need only be produced periodically.

Ashton realizes that developing a computer-based AIS for S&S will not be easy. The remaining chapters of this text cover the topics that need to be addressed in designing and running an AIS for any organization, including S&S, Inc. For example, Ashton is not sure that he wants to purchase a file-based system for S&S. His research indicates that most newer AIS are data base systems, and so he wants to learn more about them (see Chapters 5 and 6). Ashton is also unsure about S&S's needs in the area of electronic commerce, but he is confident that with a little more study (see Chapter 7) he will be able to make solid recommendations. He also wants to ensure that the system is adequately controlled and secure (see Chapters 8–11). In addition, Ashton knows that the system must capture and process the information needed in each business cycle (see Chapters 12–16). Finally, he realizes that it will require a great deal of time and effort to determine the needs of users and to ensure that the system meets those needs (see Chapters 17–19).

KEY TERMS

data processing cycle
source documents
turnaround document
source data automation
entity
attributes
field
record
data value
file
data base
master file
transaction file
primary key
secondary key
file organization
sequential access files
indexed sequential access method (ISAM) files
direct access files
file access
linked list
pointer field
chain
inverted lists
inverted file
batch processing
on-line, real-time processing
operational documents

CHAPTER QUIZ

1. The hierarchy of data elements, from largest to smallest, is
   a. field, record, file, data base.
   b. record, file, data base, field.
   c. file, data base, field, record.
   d. data base, file, record, field.

2. A permanent file that contains cumulative balances, such as quantity on hand, is called a(n)
   a. transaction file.
   b. master file.
   c. history file.
   d. accounting file.

3. The item that uniquely identifies a record in a file is called the
   a. foreign key.
   b. secondary key.
   c. primary key.
   d. identifying key.

4. A customer order form is an example of a
   a. source document.
   b. turnaround document.
   c. externally generated document.
   d. inverted file.

5. Electronically recording data about sales transactions at the time they occur and processing that data immediately is an example of
   a. batch processing.
   b. on-line batch processing.
   c. on-line, real-time processing.
   d. on-line processing.

6. Which type of file can be used for both batch and on-line, real-time processing?
   a. Sequential
   b. ISAM
   c. Random access
   d. All of the above

7. Which attribute would be the best primary key?
   a. Last name
   b. Major
   c. GPA
   d. ID number

8. A file containing data about all purchases made during the past month is a
   a. master file.
   b. transaction file.
   c. ISAM file.
   d. suspense file.

9. The data structure that would contain all the information (name, gpa, address, major, etc.) about one particular student is a
   a. field.
   b. record.
   c. file.
   d. attribute.

10. The concept of an entity corresponds to which data structure?
   a. A field
   b. A record
   c. A file
   d. A data base

DISCUSSION QUESTIONS

4.1 The following data items make up an accounts receivable record. Identify the data items within this record that are good candidates for secondary keys. Explain each of your choices.

Customer account number (primary key)
Customer name
Customer address
Location code
Credit rating code
Credit limit
Beginning account balance
Current transactions
Transaction type
Document number
Transaction date
Amount
Current balance

4.2 Computer data processing is based on the logical organization of data into files, records, and fields. State whether each of the following is a file, a record, or a field.

a. All data on one customer
b. Accounts receivable subsidiary ledger
c. Employee number
d. Amount owed to a particular vendor
e. General ledger
f. Accounts payable subsidiary ledger
g. Data on a particular vendor
h. The name of one vendor
i. All data on one inventory item

4.3 Indicate whether the following data would appear on a master file, a transaction file, or both:

a. Date
b. Account balance
c. Account number
d. Amount of payment
e. Customer name
f. Location of a sale
g. Phone number
h. Product number
i. Product description
j. Customer address
k. Invoice number
l. Credit limit
m. Vendor name
n. Quantity on hand
o. Amount of sale
p. Vendor number
q. Quantity received

4.4 For each of the following data processing applications, indicate which is more appropriate: batch or on-line, real-time processing. Explain your answers.

a. Weekly processing of employee time cards to prepare paychecks
b. Processing of customer reservation requests by a motel chain
c. Processing of credit checks by a retail credit bureau
d. Preparation of monthly customer bills by a utility company
e. Processing of customer transactions at a bank teller window
f. Scheduling of material and labor activity in an automated factory
g. Preparation of monthly financial statements
h. Processing of cash receipts on account from customers
i. Reordering of merchandise inventory in a high-volume retail store

4.5 Referring to the inverted lists in Table 4.3, describe the process the system would follow to answer the question, "Which parts supplied by RST Mfg. are used in the Lodix product line?" Retrieve the appropriate part numbers from Table 4.2.

PROBLEMS

4.1 This problem involves tracing the operations performed on a hypothetical set of master and transaction records through the sequential updating process shown in Table 4.4. Assume that a new master file is created to replace the old one and that any unmatched transaction records represent errors. Assume that the master file and the transaction file are composed of the following record numbers in the sequence given:

Required:

a. Construct a table similar to Table 4.4 to show how the transactions would be processed. Alternate as necessary among reading master file records, reading transaction file records, updating master file records, and writing records to the new master file. Number the steps as shown in Table 4.4. Continue until you have traced all records through the program.

Master File		**Transaction File**	
Account #	**Balance**	**Account #**	**Amount**
011	1400	011	+570
013	700	012	+700
014	250	014	+1400
015	2950	014	-250
016	1725	016	+275
017	885	018	-350
018	1150	EOF (end of file)	
019	2780		
EOF (end of file)			

b. Suppose that there was a transaction record with the account number 020 and a +625 amount after record number 018 and in front of the end-of-file record. Beginning at the point at which this change would first make a difference, trace the records through the program to the finish, recording the actions in your table as described in part (a).

4.2 The first few days of sales at S&S were excellent. Consumer demand for appliances exceeded all initial expectations. However, Scott arrived at the accounting office in a state of alarm. Apparently, the strong demand has rapidly diminished the inventory of S&S's most popular items. In fact, this afternoon a customer left the store quite upset that S&S would have to place a special order for an advertised appliance that would not be delivered for several weeks.

Scott is concerned with his inability as a manager to monitor the level of inventory on hand as sales are transacted. Scott encourages you to focus on the inventory problem and draft a potential solution aimed at integrating an inventory processing system into the future information system.

Required:

a. What are the underlying causes of S&S's inventory problem?
b. What information does Scott need to facilitate the flow of inventory? What impact does timeliness have on the value of information?
c. How effective would a manual system be in helping solve the inventory problem?
d. As you design a computerized information system, what data input and data processing methods should be used to deal with the inventory problem? Justify your selection.

4.3 On a day-to-day basis, students are involved with a number of transaction processing systems. On a college campus, transactions occur in the administration office, in the bookstore, and at the local pizza place.

Required:

Identify three transaction processing systems that you were involved in over the past month.

a. What are the outputs of the system? How are they used?
b. Identify the inputs and input methods used in each system. What role do source documents play in the data collection and input process for the information system?
c. What data processing and storage techniques are being used in each example?
d. Based on current technology, recommend two or more improvements to each existing information system. What types of benefits would these suggestions provide?

4.4 Ron Black, controller of Kessler Corporation, has been working with the Systems Department to revise and implement a data entry and data retention system. The departments involved and details of their data processing activities follow.

General Accounting

- Daily processing of journal entries submitted by various departments
- Weekly updating of file balances with subsystem data from areas such as payroll, accounts receivable, and accounts payable
- Sporadic requests for account activity and balances during the month, with increased activity at month's end

Accounts Receivable

- Daily processing of accounts receivable receipts
- Daily processing of customer sales
- Customer credit limit checks
- Daily identification of orders exceeding $20,000 per customer
- Daily requests for customer credit status
- Weekly reporting to the general accounting file

Accounts Payable

- Processing of payments to vendors three times per week
- Weekly expense distribution update to the general accounting file

Budget Planning and Control

- Monthly updating of flexible budgets
- Quarterly budget revisions based on sales forecast and production schedule changes
- Monthly inquiries for budget balances

Mary Crandall, manager of the Systems Department, has explained to Black and his staff the concepts of batch processing versus on-line, real-time processing, as well as off-line versus on-line file retention. Crandall has indicated that batch processing, along with off-line file retention, is the least expensive combination of techniques. A rough cost estimate reflecting alternative combinations has also been prepared:

Data Entry/File Retention Techniques	Cost in Relation to Batch/Off-line Processing
Batch/on-line	1.5 times
Real-time/on-line	2.5 times

Required:

a. Define and discuss the major differences between batch processing and real-time processing.
b. Define and discuss the major differences between off-line and on-line file retention.
c. For each of the four departments that report to Black, identify and explain (1) the type of data entry technique and (2) the type of file retention that should be used. Assume that the volume of transactions is not a key variable in the decision.
d. From a managerial perspective, Black feels that the Budget Planning and Control Department should be more effective in assisting operations with controlling costs. Of the data entry techniques identified in part (a), which technique will best help Black achieve this objective? Explain your answer.

(CMA Examination, adapted)

4.5 The MASI Corporation has decided to store its records using the indexing approach known as ISAM. Assume that 50 records with key values numbered sequentially from 500 to 549 are stored in blocks of five at 10 machine addresses numbered sequentially from 200 to 209. Each entry in the index contains the key of the last record in a block, as well as the address of that block.

Required:

a. Prepare an index for this file segment.
b. Assuming an indexed sequential file organization, explain how the system would access record number 522.

4.6 Assume that the hypothetical inventory records listed below are stored sequentially at machine addresses numbered from 1 to 9 and that we wish to use embedded pointers to chain together all items having the same color.

Part Number	Description	Color
1036	Refrigerator	White
1038	Refrigerator	Almond
1039	Refrigerator	Green
2061	Range	White
2063	Range	Black
3541	Washer	White
3544	Washer	Black
3785	Dryer	White
3786	Dryer	Black

Required:

a. Prepare a table with the column headings Machine Address, Part Number, Color, and Next C (for the pointer to the next item of the same color). Fill in this table according to the specifications just described.
b. Using an index, invert this file on the secondary key color.

4.7 Using the attributes "company" and "agent" as secondary keys, chain together the independent insurance broker records shown below. Set up a pointer field for each secondary key that contains the address of the next logical record in the list. (Hint: See Table 4.2.) Independent of your preceding answer, prepare an inverted list for the secondary keys. (Hint: See Table 4.3.)

Records of Independent Insurance Brokers

Address	Policy No.	Insured	Company	Agent
50	999	Joseph	ABCDE	Karina
51	888	Elizabeth	FGHIJ	Roxanne
52	777	Ruth	KLMNO	Jared
53	666	Joshua	ABCDE	David
54	555	Melody	QRSTU	Roxanne
55	444	Stephanie	KLMNO	Karina
56	333	Linda	FGHIJ	Jared

(continues)

Records of Independent Insurance Brokers *(continued)*

Address	Policy No.	Insured	Company	Agent
57	222	Chris	QRSTU	Roxanne
58	111	Nathanael	ABCDE	David
59	100	Isaiah	KLMNO	Jared
60	90	Eric	FGHIJ	Jared
61	80	Beth	QRSTU	Karina

CASE 4.1

Identify a local company (you may use the same company that you identified to complete Case 1.1) and answer the following questions:

1. Describe the data input processes of the company. How are data entered into the company's AIS? Does the company use batch input or on-line data entry? If it uses a combination, specify which data are entered using each process. Explain the company's use of any of the following: source or turnaround documents, batch totals, and source data automation.
2. Describe the company's data storage procedures. How large are the company's master files? How many records are in each master file? Which types of file organizations does the company use?
3. Describe the company's data processing procedures. Does it use batch or on-line, real time processing? If it uses the latter, describe its updating and inquiry processing procedures.
4. What are the major information outputs of each transaction cycle? What are the main outputs for planning, control, and operation? For each output, explain what output format is used.

CASE 4.2 S&S, INC.

You are a student accountant that S&S has hired to help with its accounting system. Although Ashton has not yet purchased a computerized system, he feels the need to do some advance planning and design work. At present, he is trying to analyze the input, storage, and output needs of S&S. Ashton would like you to prepare the following for your next meeting with him:

1. A list of the reports and documents S&S needs to ensure its business is properly managed. Specify how the data should be stored and organized. Make a list of the following:
   a. Relevant reports, documents, and other informational output (hard or soft copy) that you feel S&S will need to properly manage its business.
   b. Input forms that S&S will need to collect transaction and other input data; these inputs may take the form of source documents, computer data entry screens, or user prompts.
   c. Files that S&S needs to store all the data it will process.
2. Ashton would also like your recommendations on what data and information should be collected, processed, and reported. A complete list of all data elements for every single output, input, and file would be too much information for Ashton to assimilate, and so you have decided to provide him with some representative examples. List all of the data items (specific items of information such as company name, date, and amounts) that

should appear on the following output reports and documents to make them fully functioning system output:

a. Purchase order

b. Sales invoice (for sales on credit)

c. Stock status report (a report of inventory on hand)

Also list the data that should be captured on each of the following documents:

d. Receiving report

e. Employee time card for hourly employees

3. Scott would like to see what some of these system inputs and outputs will look like. He has asked you to design the following items:

a. Sales invoice

b. Receiving report

(Hint: You may find it helpful to refer to Chapters 12–16 for ideas.)

CASE 4.3 WEKENDER CORPORATION

Wekender Corporation owns and operates 15 large retail hardware stores. Each store carries a wide variety of merchandise, mostly geared toward the weekend do-it-yourselfer. The company has been successful in this field, almost doubling the number of stores in the chain since 1980.

The company wishes to maintain its competitive position with similar stores. However, Wekender has been having some difficulties with its purchasing and inventory procedures. Each retail store currently acquires its merchandise from the company's centrally located warehouse. The warehouse must maintain an up-to-date and well-stocked inventory so that stores can meet customer demands.

The number of stores, the number of inventory items carried, and the volume of business are creating pressure on the company to change from a manual to a computerized system. Recently, the company has been investigating two approaches to computerization—batch processing and on-line, real-time processing. No decision has been reached on which approach to use.

The current warehousing and purchasing procedures are as follows:

- Stock is stored in bins and is located by inventory number. The numbers are supposed to be listed sequentially on the bins, but this system is not always followed. As a result, some items are difficult to locate.
- Whenever a store needs merchandise, a three-part request form is completed—one copy is kept by the store, and two copies are mailed to the warehouse. If the merchandise is on hand, the goods are delivered to the store along with the third copy of the request. The second copy is filed at the warehouse. If goods are not in stock, the warehouse ships whatever quantity is available and notes the quantity shipped on the request form. Then a purchase memorandum for the shortage is prepared by the warehouse. At the end of each day, all the memos are sent to the Purchasing Department.
- When ordered goods are received, they are checked at the receiving area and a receiving report is prepared. One copy of the receiving report is retained at the receiving area, one is forwarded to Accounts Payable, and one is filed at the warehouse with the purchase memorandum.
- When the purchase memoranda are received from the warehouse, purchase orders are prepared. Vendor catalogs are used to select the best source for the requested goods, and the purchase order is filled out and mailed. Copies of the order are sent to Accounts Payable and the receiving area; one copy is retained in the Purchasing Department.
- When the receiving report arrives in the Purchasing Department, it is compared with the purchase order on file. Both documents are compared with the invoice before it is forwarded to Accounts Payable for payment.
- The Purchasing Department is supposed to evaluate vendors periodically for financial soundness, reliability, and trade relationships. However, because the volume of requests received from the warehouse is so high, this activity is given a low priority.
- Each week, a report of the open purchase orders is prepared to determine whether any action should be taken on overdue deliveries. This report is prepared manually by scanning the file of outstanding purchase orders.

Top management wants the new system to improve these four areas:

1. Rapid ordering to replenish warehouse inventory stocks with as little delay as possible. (Wekender buys from more than 1,500 vendors.)
2. Quick filling and shipping of merchandise to the stores. (This process involves determining whether sufficient stock exists.)
3. Some indication of inventory activity. (More than 800 purchase orders are prepared each week.)
4. Perpetual records that permit management to determine inventory levels by item number quickly. (Wekender sells more than 7,500 separate items.)

Required:

Given the current operations procedures and the goals of top management, answer the following questions:

1. How would an on-line, real-time computer system better meet the needs of Wekender Corporation?
2. Identify the master and transaction files Wekender would need for its new system, and briefly indicate the type of information that would be contained in each.
3. How should the files identified in question 2 be organized and accessed?

ANSWERS TO CHAPTER QUIZ

1. d **3.** c **5.** c **7.** d **9.** b
2. b **4.** a **6.** b **8.** b **10.** b

Appendix to Chapter 4

Information Technology Concepts

Many accountants think people are speaking a foreign language when they begin to talk about computers. Accountants who do not understand the terminology of information technology may encounter difficulty when it comes to understanding an AIS. Although they need not be technical experts, most accountants need to understand what computers are, what they are composed of, how they operate, and how they store and process data. This knowledge helps them use, develop, evaluate, and manage an AIS.

Accountants need to understand computer concepts for five key reasons. First, they are system users. Most employers expect accounting students to have a high degree of personal computer (PC) proficiency before they come to work. Most new hires receive a PC and are expected to know how to use it to access and analyze corporate data. Accountants also need to know how to use the computer as a stand-alone system to satisfy their own informational needs in a timely manner, without having to wait for the assistance of their programming staff. This allows programmers to concentrate on the complex, multiuser AIS needed by large organizations.

Second, information technology is a very powerful agent of change and is transforming the way companies operate and business is conducted. Companies that take advantage of new advancements and participate in the technological revolution are getting smarter, leaner, and closer to the customer, and they are capturing important competitive advantages. Companies that lag behind will be unable to compete; they will have to scramble to catch up or they will go out of business. Accountants must be major players in this technological revolution, or they too will be unable to compete. They must play a major role in systems development as members of AIS design and acquisition teams. An understanding of hardware and software concepts is essential in determining system requirements.

Third, accountants are AIS evaluators. Both internal and external auditors assess the strengths and weaknesses of an AIS. In doing so, they evaluate systems on the basis of criteria such as the adequacy of their internal controls and the effectiveness and usefulness of the overall system. It is difficult to assess systems effectively without an understanding of hardware and software concepts.

Fourth, accountants often manage computer resources. They may oversee the purchase of the systems, supervise those who use them, and evaluate the use of computer resources.

Finally, accountants will earn more if they are computer literate. A recent survey showed that college graduates earned over 50% more than high school graduates. Princeton economist Alan Kruegar found that over four-fifths of this increase was due to their knowledge of computers.

The remainder of this appendix is divided into two main sections: hardware and software. It emphasizes what computers are and how they work. The intent is to help you learn to speak "computerese."

SECTION A COMPUTER HARDWARE

Computer hardware is the physical equipment that performs the electronic data processing (EDP) tasks of a computer system. It includes the central processing unit (CPU) and the peripherals, the input, output, storage, and telecommunications devices. Figure 4A.1 shows the various data preparation, input, processing, storage, data communications, and output devices.

The speed, power, and storage capacities of computers have increased dramatically while their size and cost have decreased. For example, the first computers

FIGURE 4A.1
Computer Hardware

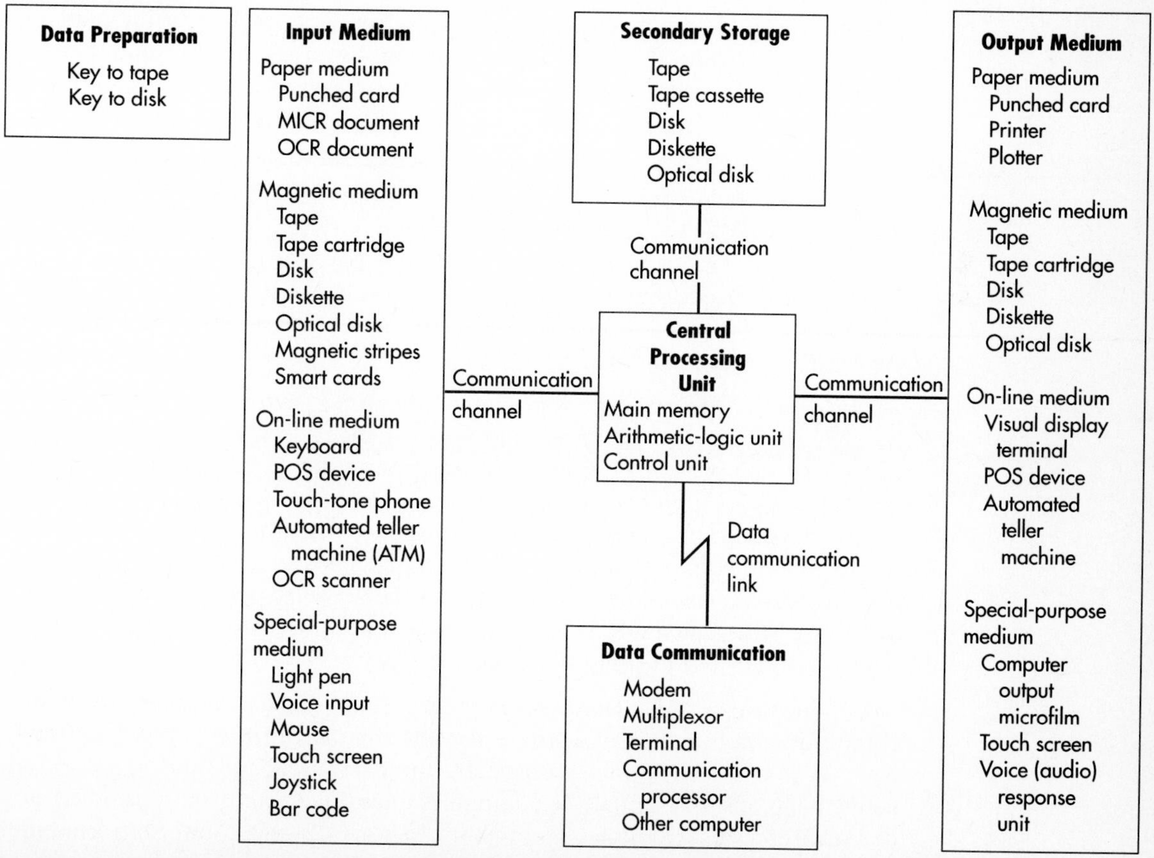

Data Preparation
Key to tape
Key to disk

Input Medium
Paper medium
Punched card
MICR document
OCR document
Magnetic medium
Tape
Tape cartridge
Disk
Diskette
Optical disk
Magnetic stripes
Smart cards
On-line medium
Keyboard
POS device
Touch-tone phone
Automated teller machine (ATM)
OCR scanner
Special-purpose medium
Light pen
Voice input
Mouse
Touch screen
Joystick
Bar code

Communication channel

Secondary Storage
Tape
Tape cassette
Disk
Diskette
Optical disk

Communication channel

Central Processing Unit
Main memory
Arithmetic-logic unit
Control unit

Data communication link

Data Communication
Modem
Multiplexor
Terminal
Communication processor
Other computer

Communication channel

Output Medium
Paper medium
Punched card
Printer
Plotter
Magnetic medium
Tape
Tape cartridge
Disk
Diskette
Optical disk
On-line medium
Visual display terminal
POS device
Automated teller machine
Special-purpose medium
Computer output microfilm
Touch screen
Voice (audio) response unit

were capable of processing hundreds of instructions per second; current computers can process hundreds of millions of instructions per second. Storage capacity has expanded from thousands to billions of characters. The cost of executing a million instructions has fallen from $10 to less than a tenth of a cent. Early computers filled a whole room; modern computers can fit in the palm of your hand.

The features of the modern computer were first proposed in 1834, by Charles Babbage. However, in 1842 the British prime minister labeled the calculating machine "worthless" and the British government refused further support of Babbage's invention. More than 100 years later, the British realized what a powerful tool they had passed on, and in 1991 they spent $600,000 to build the engine from Babbage's original design. That "computer" is 6 feet high and 10 feet long, contains 4,000 parts, and weighs 3 tons.

Sizes of Computers

Computers have been classified into four main categories based on their size and power: supercomputers, mainframes, minicomputers, and microcomputers. Power is measured by speed, memory capacity, computational power, and the number of users and peripherals the computer can support.

Supercomputers. **Supercomputers** are used for high-speed, number-crunching military and scientific tasks. They have enormous storage capacities and are up to ten times faster than mainframes. Recently, smaller supercomputers have been developed using powerful microprocessor chips. These supercomputers are small enough to sit by a desk, although they are only half as fast as their larger cousins.

Many supercomputers utilize massively parallel processing. Instead of using a single CPU to accomplish tasks sequentially, scores of CPUs are linked together to simultaneously work on different parts of a complex task. Massively parallel processing is especially useful for reducing the time required to search large data bases, because the entire data base can be partitioned and each part searched separately.

Mainframes. **Mainframe** computers are used extensively in business because they provide the speed and power needed to handle large, complex tasks. They can process millions of transactions a day in hundreds of different programs and respond to and coordinate *hundreds* of peripherals simultaneously. In addition to their higher performance and throughput, mainframe hardware and software is more reliable than that found in networks of PCs. Mainframes are so complex, however, that they require professional programmers, operators, and analysts. Mainframes and peripherals are housed in a controlled room called the data processing center.

Minicomputers. **Minicomputers** are larger and more powerful than microcomputers and smaller and less powerful than mainframes. IBM's AS/400 series is an example of a minicomputer. Minicomputers and mainframes often come in a family of compatible computers that differ mainly in size and capacity. Such cross-usage allows a company to start off small and then upgrade within the family as its needs increase. Moreover, minicomputers function in an ordinary office environment and do not need air-conditioning, special wiring, or a staff of computer experts, as do mainframes. Many organizations use them to handle all their data processing tasks. Other minicomputers are connected to mainframes to assist with time-consuming input and output tasks and telecommunications networks.

Microcomputers. **Microcomputers** range in size from a "computer on a chip" to a typewriter-sized, desktop unit. Microcomputers are used as stand-alone computers and as a part of a network. As a stand-alone, they allow users to maintain and use their own data and software for tasks such as word processing, spreadsheets, graphics presentations, and accounting. As part of a network, they allow documents, mail, and data to be transmitted electronically to other network users. Peripherals and computer files can be shared. For example, when users need data stored on a mainframe data base, they can access the appropriate computer files and download the data to their PC. They can also upload data or send it to someone else in the network.

Regardless of how computers are classified or used, they all have common ingredients. One of those, the central processing unit, is discussed next.

Central Processing Unit

Computer processing functions are performed by the **central processing unit (CPU).** It has three main components: the arithmetic–logic unit, the control unit, and the primary memory. The **arithmetic–logic unit (ALU)** performs all math calculations and logical comparisons. The **control unit** interprets program instructions and coordinates all input, output, and storage devices. Data and program instructions are stored in the primary memory. The relationships of these components to each other and to computer input, output, and storage are illustrated in Fig. 4A.2.

There are two types of primary memory: read-only and random-access. **Read-only memory (ROM)** can be read but not altered by other program instructions. ROM contains information that is stored permanently in the computer, such as all or part of the operating system. Computers temporarily store programs, data, and instructions in **random-access memory (RAM).** The amount of RAM a PC can hold determines how much data and how many programs it can handle at any one time. A semiconductor—a tiny silicon chip inscribed with a number of miniature circuits—is the most common form of RAM. RAM is temporary storage, as it is erased when power is shut off.

In contrast to conventional primary memory, a *flash memory chip* does not lose its contents when the power is shut off. Flash memory chips are used to replace hard disks in handheld computers and to store operating systems and application software. They eliminate the time it takes for software to load when a computer is turned on. These chips are easily erased and reprogrammed and do not require moving mechanical parts, which makes them more reliable, faster, lighter, smaller, more durable, and more power efficient than hard or floppy disks. However, they wear out after 100,000 cycles of data input, compared to billions for conventional RAM.

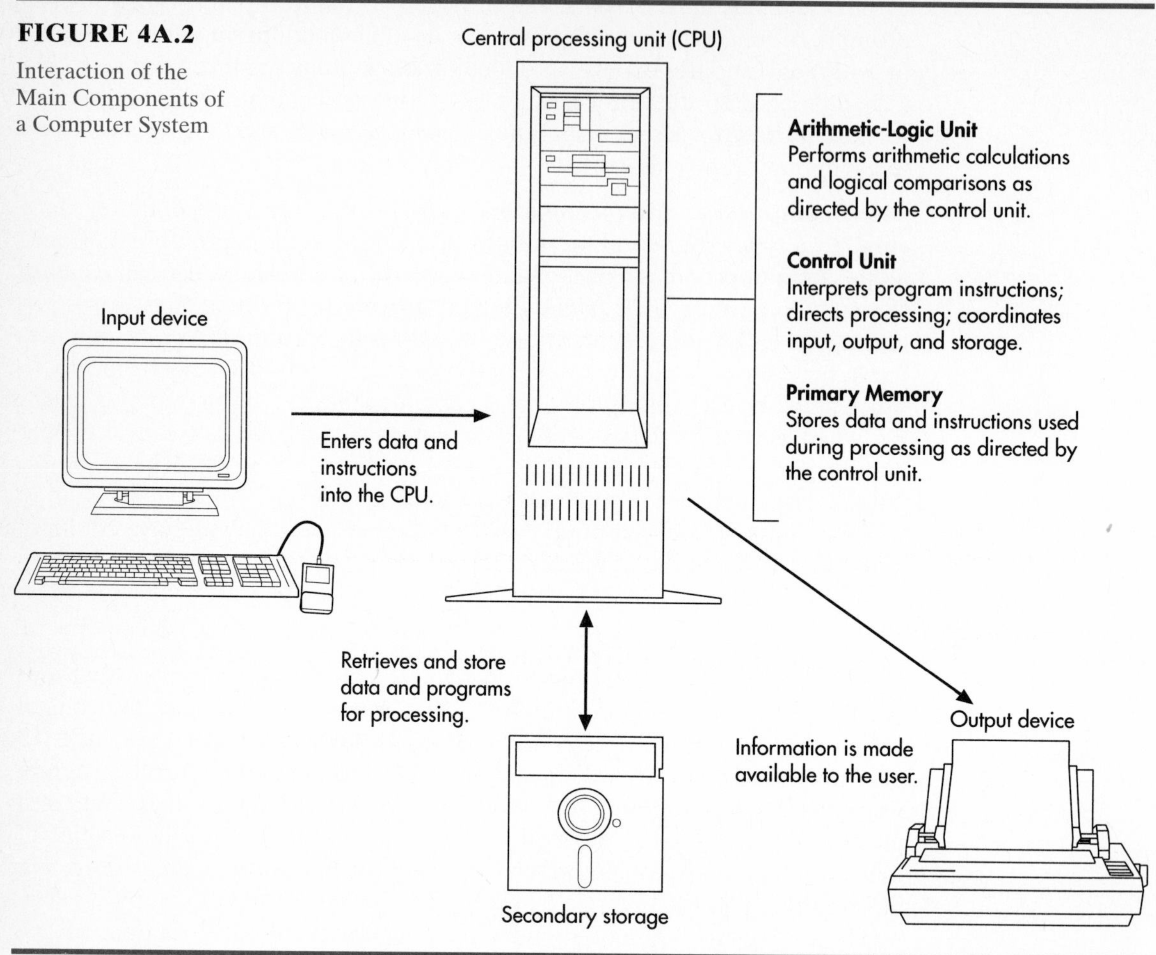
Central processing unit (CPU)
Arithmetic-Logic Unit
Performs arithmetic calculations and logical comparisons as directed by the control unit.
Control Unit
Interprets program instructions; directs processing; coordinates input, output, and storage.
Primary Memory
Stores data and instructions used during processing as directed by the control unit.
Input device
Enters data and instructions into the CPU.
Retrieves and store data and programs for processing.
Output device
Information is made available to the user.
Secondary storage

FIGURE 4A.2 Interaction of the Main Components of a Computer System

Peripheral devices connected to the CPU by cables or telephone lines are called *on-line devices* because they directly access the CPU. *Off-line devices* are not connected directly to the CPU and are used to prepare data input or output.

Storage Measurements. Computers execute and store data in **bits** (short for *binary digit*). A bit can assume one of two possible states, commonly referred to as *on* or *off*, or *0* or *1*. A group of 8 bits is called a **byte**. Each byte represents a different character, such as a number or letter of the alphabet. As shown in Table 4A.1, memory capacity is expressed in terms of kilobytes (K or KB), megabytes (MB), gigabytes (GB), and terabytes (TB).

Speed. The processing speed of a CPU is measured in terms of **MIPS** (millions of instructions per second). **Access time** is the time required to retrieve data from memory. **Execution time** is the time required to perform a computer instruction, such as add or compare. As shown in Table 4A.1, these times are measured in fractions of a second: **millisecond** (thousandth), **microsecond** (millionth),

TABLE 4A.1 Measuring Computer Speeds and Capacities

Time Measures	Storage Measures
Millisecond = 1,000th of a second Microsecond = 1,000,000th of a second Nanosecond = 1,000,000,000th of a second Picosecond = 1,000,000,000,000th of a second Megahertz = millions of cycles per second (measurement of processing speed of microcomputers) MIPS = million of instructions per second (measurement of speed of computers)	Bit = storage location that is on or off Byte = 8 bits that represent 1 character Kilobyte = 1,000 characters Megabyte = 1,000,000 characters Gigabyte = 1,000,000,000 characters Terabyte = 1,000,000,000,000 characters

nanosecond (billionth), or **picosecond** (trillionth). How fast are these speeds? If you took one step per nanosecond, you could circle the earth 20 times in one second!

Microcomputer CPUs. The central processing unit in a PC, called a **microprocessor,** is a large-scale integrated circuit on a silicon chip. It is about the size of a thumbnail. Other silicon chips constitute the computer's primary memory, where both instructions and data are stored. Still other chips govern the input and output of data and carry out control operations. Many PCs contain several processors. For example, an arithmetic processor can complete calculations up to 200 times faster than the main processor.

Microprocessor chips used to be identified by a number in the following series: 8086, 80286, 80386, and 80486. That changed when Intel called its 80586 chip the Pentium and gave the subsequent generation the name Merced.

The microprocessor chips are mounted on a main circuit board, or **motherboard.** Most PCs have expansion slots on the motherboard so that additional capabilities (such as increased memory or modems) and communication ports can be added. Communications between the computer's electrical components are in the form of digital electronic pulses that travel along a **data bus**, which connects the various components of the microcomputer.

Microcomputer Speed. There are three factors that affect the speed and computational power of microprocessors. The first is **word size,** which refers to the number of bits of data that can be processed in one cycle. The first generation of microcomputers had 4- or 8-bit microprocessors, which meant that they could process 4 or 8 bits of data at a time. Now 64-bit microprocessor chips are widely available and a number of companies are working on 128-bit chips. The second factor that affects the overall power and speed of a microcomputer is the frequency of the processor's electronic clock—that is, how many cycles a computer can execute per second. Microcomputer clock frequency speeds have increased from 1 **megahertz** (1 million cycles per second; abbreviated MHz) to hundreds of megahertz. The third factor affecting microcomputer speed and power is the **bus size**, or the number of bits transmitted at one time from one computer location to another.

Secondary Storage

Data stored in RAM is lost when the computer is turned off. Therefore, computer systems use secondary storage to save data and programs for future use. Commonly used secondary storage devices include magnetic tape and disks, diskettes, and optical disks. Magnetic tape is the most frequently used sequential-access medium; the others are frequently used direct-access media.

Magnetic Tape. Magnetic tape comes in two forms: reels and cartridges. Both need a tape drive for reading and writing purposes. Tape cartridges are much faster, store more information, take up less space, and are more convenient to use than reels.

Magnetic tapes have three properties that make them very useful for backup and archival purposes: They hold a lot of data, are inexpensive, and take up little storage space. For example, a standard 8-mm videotape can hold approximately 7 GB of data; 1,000 such tapes, holding 7,000 GB, can be stored in a box that is approximately 20 × 20 × 20 inches. When purchased in bulk, the tapes cost about $5 apiece. Thus the storage cost of magnetic tape is less than $1 per GB! The principal disadvantage of magnetic tape is that it must be read sequentially; this means it is only possible to add, delete, or update records by processing the entire file. Consequently, magnetic tape is used for backup and archival purposes, rather than as on on-line secondary storage media.

Magnetic Disks. **Magnetic disks** are the dominant direct-access storage device, providing optimal cost, access time, storage capacity, and flexibility. Those used in mainframes are similar in appearance to a stack of CDs, except for a space between each adjoining pair of disks for one or more read/write heads. The magnetic disk used in PCs and microcomputers is called a hard disk. Hard disks are packaged in clean, airtight, sealed boxes that contain one or more disks. This protective environment allows hard disks to be operated at high speeds and data to be packed close together on the disk.

The primary advantage of disks over tapes is their direct-access capability. An entire file need not be read to find a record, because the read/write head can move directly to any physical storage location. Thus accessing and updating data can be accomplished more efficiently than if the data were stored on tape. On the other hand, it costs more and takes more space to store the same amount of data on magnetic disk than on tape, which is why the latter is more commonly used for archival and backup purposes.

A *diskette,* or *floppy disk,* is a circular piece of flexible magnetic film enclosed in a protective cover. The most common size is 3.5 inches. Its greatest advantages are its ease of use, compactness, and low cost. Diskettes have a much smaller storage capacity and a slower access time than hard disks. The diskette is commonly used as a data entry medium and for secondary storage in smaller computer systems.

Optical Disks. Optical disks use laser technology to store and read data. They store data by burning microscopic holes in their recording surface. Most optical disks are **WORM (write-once, read-many)** devices and are often referred to as **CD-ROM (compact disk, read-only memory).** Some optical disks can also be rewritten on, although the number of rewrites is limited.

Laser optical disks offer significant advantages. First, they can hold a great deal of data. One optical disk can hold over a billion characters, which is roughly the equivalent of 70 floppy disks or 30 four-drawer file cabinets. Groliers has published its 21-volume Academic American Encyclopedia on a single optical disk. Second, unlike hard disks, laser disks can be removed from their drives, so that the disk unit can read or write to an almost unlimited number of disks. Third, disks can be mass-produced easily and inexpensively. Fourth, they are much less susceptible to data loss and disk crashes than are hard disks. Disadvantages are that they are more costly and have slower access times than magnetic disks. Also, it is impossible to alter data once it is stored on some CD-ROM disks.

A *videodisk* is an optical disk that stores audio, video, and text data. It can be accessed a frame at a time for motionless viewing or can be played like a videotape for moving action and sound. Any frame of the disk can be accessed in three seconds or less. These disks have many uses, including interactive training and marketing of products, such as cars, real estate, and vacation resorts.

Input Devices

Business systems have high input and output volumes and simple computations. Because input and output devices are much slower than CPUs, business systems are **input/output bound.** This characteristic reduces **throughput,** which is the amount of useful work performed during a given period of time. Most approaches to increasing throughput focus on utilizing data entry methods that minimize human interaction and that maximize the use of high-speed computer input devices. Several data entry approaches are taken.

Keying Data Captured on Source Documents. This approach is time-consuming, costly, and error-prone. It requires that data first be captured on paper and then transcribed to tape or disk. It involves several steps: data capture, keying onto a magnetic medium, and key verification.

On-Line Entry. Terminals and microcomputers can be used to key data directly into the computer. Although this process is time-consuming, costly, and error-prone, it avoids capturing data on paper.

Turnaround Documents. Turnaround documents, such as utility bills, are produced by the AIS, sent to the customer, and returned as inputs. This procedure reduces the input preparation workload and its potential for errors and is faster than keystroke entry. Because keying is slow and tedious, alternative methods for on-line data are continually being developed. Three of these are voice input, the use of penlike devices to handwrite information, and touchscreens.

Source Data Automation. **Source data automation** devices, such as the scanners used in grocery stores, automate the data capture and entry process. As a result, they decrease the time, effort, and errors associated with data entry.

Magnetic ink character recognition (MICR) devices read characters that have been encoded with a special magnetic ink. MICR is used by financial institutions to encode customer checks and deposit slips. For example, a blank check has the bank, account, and check number encoded on the lower-left portion. When a check is processed, the check amount is inscribed in the lower-right corner.

Optical character recognition (OCR) devices, which read printed or handwritten characters, are commonly used in many businesses. For example, American Express installed OCR equipment that reads 60% of the handwritten numbers on the 900,000 charge slips that it processes every day. The $10 million system will pay for itself in four years. The IRS uses OCR to read handwritten 1040EZ forms and by the year 2000 hopes to read all tax forms electronically. Other uses include reading turnaround documents such as insurance company premium notices and utility company billings.

Most students have used an automated teller machine (ATM) to withdraw cash from their bank accounts. However, ATMs dispense more than cash. Wells Fargo Bank customers use their ATMs to purchase additional shares of mutual funds and move cash between funds. ATMs also cash checks and sell bus passes, postage stamps, airline and event tickets, and travelers checks. ATMs can also be used to make mortgage or credit card payments and to dispense rolls of coins.

ATM cards are accepted by many businesses in lieu of credit and debit cards. In fact, Software Etc.'s stores in California no longer accept checks, preferring instead that customers pay using an ATM card. After the card is read by a countertop terminal, the customer enters his or her **personal identification number (PIN).** The account number, PIN number, and purchase amount are sent over phone lines to the customer's bank. If funds are available, the purchase amount is immediately withdrawn and placed in the store's account. Retail stores favor ATM cards because they eliminate the loss and hassle associated with bad checks and eliminate the float associated with charge cards and checks. Residents in some communities can even pay parking tickets and property taxes using ATM cards. Customers enjoy benefits such as the widespread acceptance of these cards (unlike checks, they can be used out-of-town), ease of use, and convenience.

Most debit, credit, and ID cards have a magnetic stripe that contains information such as the user's name, address, and account number. When the card is used, a point-of-sale (POS) terminal reads the information on the stripe, transmits it to the bank, and verifies its validity. Instead of a magnetic stripe, a **smart card** contains a microprocessor, memory chips, and software. Smart cards are used extensively in Europe and their use is increasing in the United States. A smart card can function as a credit or an ATM card as well as a storage center for costs and expense records. Since it can store up to three pages of text, it can contain vital personal data such as medical history and employment information. Marines at Parris Island boot camp receive their pay on smart cards that are good anywhere on base. At Loyola University, students can pay for almost everything on campus using smart cards, including books, meals, and traffic ickets.

Radio frequency identification tags track data from one location to another by sending and receiving radio signals that identify the objects attached to them. They track products such as Federal Express or UPS packages. Respiratory therapists at the University of California Medical Center use handheld computers and radio frequency devices to access the hospital mainframe where patients' records and treatment schedules are stored. After a treatment, therapists update patient records with these devices. This cuts down on the time and costs associated with paperwork and maximizes the appointment time between therapists and patients.

Radio frequency data communication transmits data through air waves rather than through wires. Costco discount warehouses use handheld computers and radio frequency to scan bar-coded items on the sales floor. For each scanned item, the system can retrieve information such as weekly sales, profitability, quantity on hand, and the reorder quantity. J. C. Penney utilizes radio frequency in its distribution centers to help receive and warehouse merchandise from vendors and then ship it to their stores.

Point-of-sale (POS) recorders, which read price or product code data, are usually built into counters or are used as handheld wands. One example is the optical scanner used in grocery stores to read the **universal product code (UPC),** one of many types of **bar codes** used to identify products. The scanner emits an intense light, recognizes the pattern of bars and spaces, retrieves the price of the item sold, and transmits it to the cash register. The computer also updates the quantity sold and the inventory balance of the product. For credit sales, after the clerk enters the customer's account number, the system will check the customer's credit, as well as update the accounts receivable record. Figure 4A.3 shows a UPC bar code and a terminal that reads the bar code.

Bar codes provide the advantages of improved accuracy of data entry, better customer service through faster checkout at the point of sale, and greater control and reliability of inventory records. They are used in industries and organizations that must count and track inventory, such as retail, medical, libraries, military and other government operations, transportation facilities,

FIGURE 4A.3
Data Collection Terminal Capable of Reading Bar Codes and Magnetic Stripes

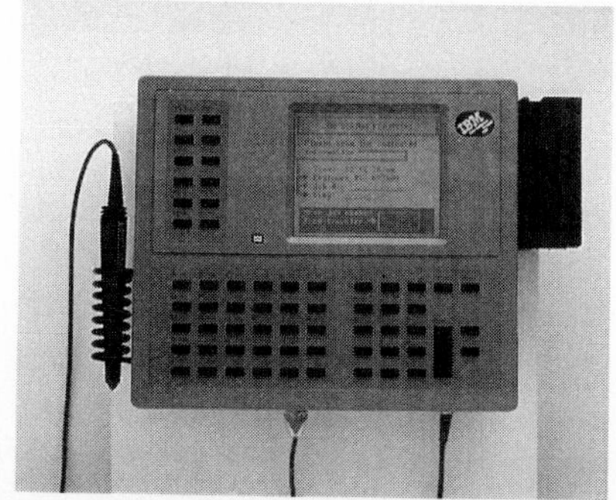

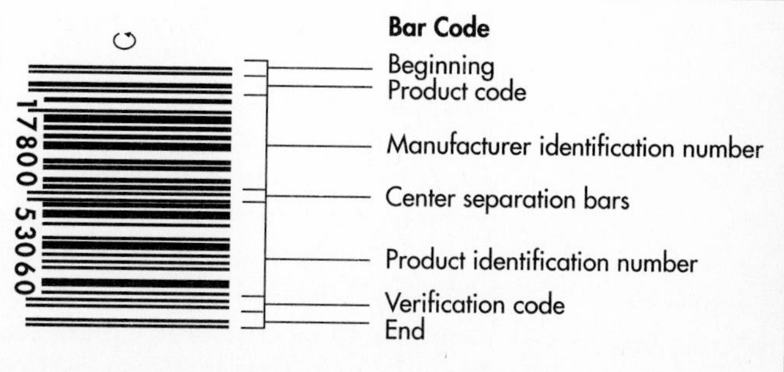

and the automotive industry. Because of the savings it provides, the Post Office gives discounts to companies that bar code their mail. Two people can sort 32,000 bar-coded letters in an hour, compared with 17 people using older sorting equipment and 40 people sorting by hand.

Two-dimensional (2D) bar codes have been developed that store the equivalent of two text pages in the same amount of space as a traditional UPC. One of the first uses of 2D bar coding was handing barrels of hazardous toxic waste. Now it is commonly used in a variety of industries. For example, every shipping carton sent to one of Wal-Mart's distribution centers must have a 2D bar code. The bar code contains the purchase order, stock numbers, the contents of each box, a product's origin, its destination, and how it should be handled during shipping. These bar codes automate many of the mundane and time-consuming shipping tasks.

Electronic Data Interchange. Electronic data interchange involves one company's computer talking to another company's computer—for example, a buyer electronically sending a purchase order to a supplier. This approach is attractive in terms of cost, speed, minimal human effort, and accuracy. Electronic data interchange is discussed in detail in Chapter 7.

Output Devices

Most input devices can also be used for output. For example, magnetic tapes and disks are often used not only to retrieve data, but also to store the results of processing that data. Similarly, not only can bar codes be read for input, they can also be created as output. This section discusses three other devices that are used primarily for output: monitors, printers, and computer output microfilm.

Computer monitors vary in price and quality. **Resolution** refers to how clear images are on the monitor; with higher resolution, the screen will be sharper, diagonal lines will be straighter, filled-in areas will be darker, and graphics will be clearer. The smaller the dot-pitch rating, the sharper the image. For example, a .28 dot-pitch rating is sharper than a .39 rating. In recent years a flat-panel display that uses liquid crystal or gas discharge technology has also been introduced. It is used on most portable systems.

A printer produces paper output, often referred to as hard copy. Printers vary widely in terms of quality, speed, graphics capabilities, and cost, which is directly affected by the first three elements. Color printing is also available. The best color printers can produce photographic-quality images on paper or transparencies.

Impact printers strike an embossed character against an inked ribbon. The most popular type of impact printer is the dot matrix printer, which forms characters by using a group of small wires to form dots. Nonimpact printers transfer images without striking the paper. The most common type are laser printers. They reflect laser beams off a rotating disk that contains the available characters onto paper, where an electrostatic image is formed. The paper is passed through a toner to produce high-quality images. Ink jet printers form letters by spraying ink on paper. Many devices have been developed that perform multiple functions, such as printing, scanning, faxing, and copying.

A **plotter** is a special type of printer that produces a graphical output by moving a writing arm across a paper surface. Modern plotters can produce three-dimensional and multicolored drawings.

Printers are connected to computers by a cable or a data communications line. If the computer sends the data along a single cable one bit at a time, the printer uses a *serial interface.* If the computer sends the bits simultaneously along parallel cables, the printer has a *parallel interface.* Serial transmission is slower but can be used over longer distances.

Computer output microfilm (COM) makes use of a photographic process to store noncurrent accounting records, copies of company documents, and other information on microfilm. For example, banks store copies of depositors' checks on microfilm. Microfilm is less expensive than paper and reduces storage requirements by up to 95%.

SECTION B SOFTWARE

Software is the detailed instructions that control the functions of hardware devices. A set of instructions that tell a computer how to accomplish a particular task is called a computer program. The process of writing software programs to accomplish these tasks is called computer programming. Software programs are written in a programming language.

Software programs can be divided into two categories. **Application software** is written to perform specific functions and to support users. Examples include programs to keep the accounts receivable, accounts payable, inventory, and payroll records up to date. **Systems software** interprets the application program instructions and tells the hardware how to execute them. The diagram shown in Fig. 4A.4 illustrates this relationship.

Levels of Computer Languages

Computer programs can be written in one of more than 200 programming languages, each with its own unique vocabulary, grammar, and usage rules. Languages are often classified as high- or low-level. The closer the language is to

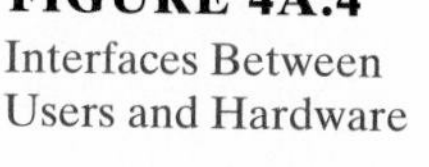

FIGURE 4A.4
Interfaces Between Users and Hardware

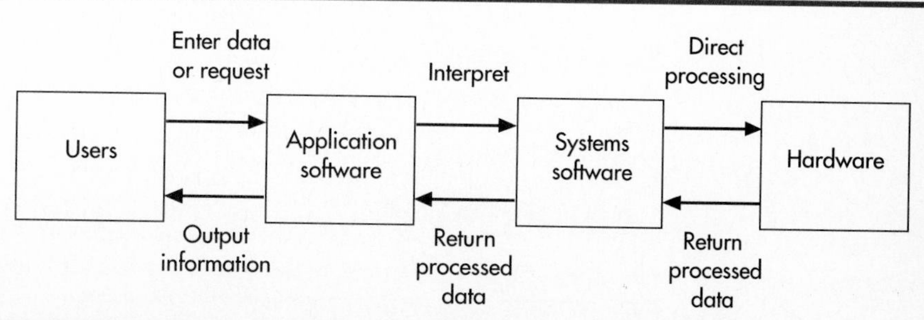

that used by the computer, the lower the language level; the closer the language is to English, the higher the level. This section briefly discusses four levels of languages: machine, symbolic, high-level, and fourth-generation. An example of each level is shown in Table 4A.2.

Each computer has its own **machine language,** which is interpreted by the computer's internal circuitry. A **symbolic language** represents machine instructions by symbols and is converted to machine language by an assembler. Machine and symbolic languages are seldom used today due to the availability of higher-level languages.

High-level languages are machine-independent languages, since many types of computers can use the same language. As shown in Fig. 4A.5, a program called a **compiler** converts high-level languages into machine language. The high-level language program, called the **source program,** and the compiler are input to the CPU. The compiler translates the entire source program into a machine language program, called the **object program.** Diagnostic messages inform the programmer of syntax errors (errors in the use of the language). Logic errors occur when the instructions given to the computer do not accomplish the desired objective. If there are no significant syntax errors, the object program and the input are read into the computer, the program is executed, and a printed report and a data file are produced according to the instructions of the program. Table 4A.3 lists some popular high-level languages and their uses.

Some high-level languages are translated by an **interpreter.** In contrast to a compiler, an interpreter translates and executes instructions one at a time. The interpreter does not produce object programs or diagnostics. The BASIC language used in PCs is an example of an interpreted language.

Fourth-generation languages (4GLs) have been developed so that programmers need not tell the computer the exact procedures to follow (multiply

TABLE 4A.2 Typical Instructions in the Four Levels of Programming Languages

Language	Instruction
Machine language	01011000001000000000100001110000 01011010001000000000100001110001 01010000001000000000100001110010
Symbolic assembly language	L 2,A A 2,B ST 2,C
High-level language	ADD SALARY, COMMISSION, GIVING TOTAL PAY
Fourth-generation language	COMPUTE THE TOTAL PAY OF ALL EMPLOYEES BY ADDING THEIR SALARY AND COMMISSION

FIGURE 4A.5
Compiling and Executing a High-Level Language Program

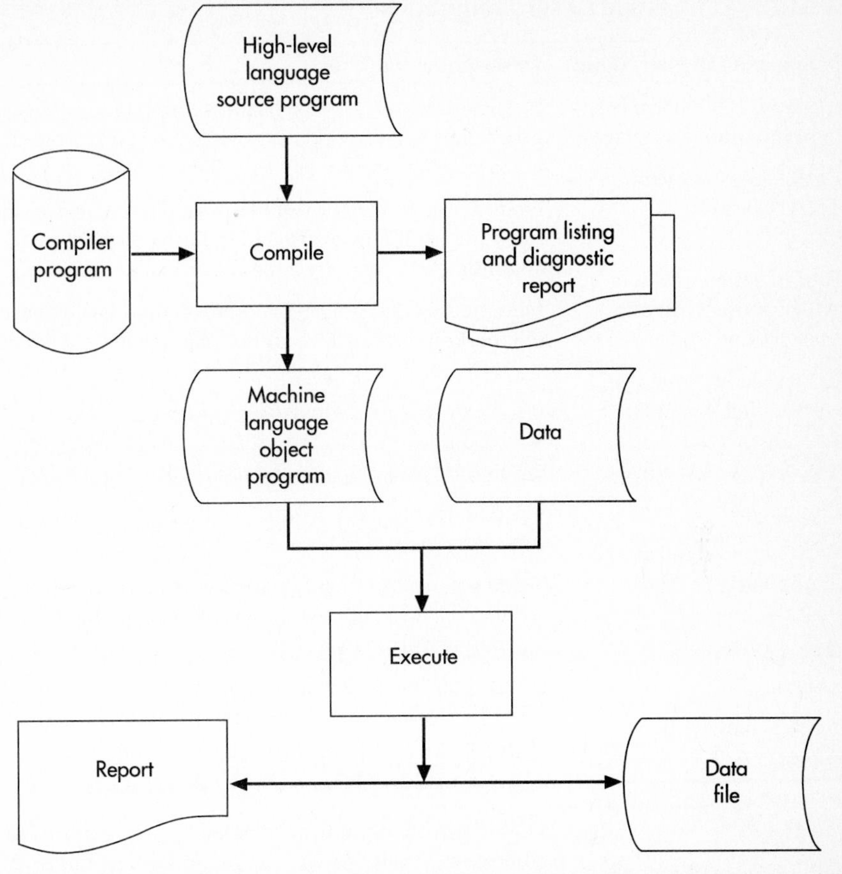

this, compare that). With a 4GL, users specify the information they want and the 4GL determines the sequence of instructions to follow. The result is a simpler, more efficient programming process that offers cost and time savings. Programs are shorter; easier to write, maintain, read, and understand; and more error-free. Some 4GLs so closely resemble English that they are referred to as *natural languages.*

Many 4GLs are simple enough that, with minimal training, end-users can satisfy many of their information needs in just a few minutes. Other 4GLs are so complex and powerful that they are used mainly by professional analysts and programmers. These are full-function, general-purpose languages used to develop application programs. Many users claim tremendous productivity gains; 5 to 10 lines in a 4GL program equal hundreds of lines of COBOL code. Table 4A.4 compares 3GLs and 4GLs and summarizes their differences.

Two powerful features of 4GL are report and application generators. To produce reports, a programmer must select and format data, specify titles and page

TABLE 4A.3 High-Level Languages

Name and Original Name	Description and Uses
COBOL (COmmon Business Oriented Language)	Designed specifically for business applications with large amounts of record processing and file updating. Most common programming language for business. English-like and self-documenting.
FORTRAN (FORmula TRANslation)	First high-level language to be widely used and accepted. Designed to solve scientific problems expressed in terms of mathematical formulas. Most common programming language for science and engineering.
BASIC (Beginner's All-Purpose Symbolic Instructions Code)	Designed so that nonprogrammers could easily learn it. Widely used on microcomputers and by on-line time-sharing services.
C^{++} (previous versions were called A and B)	Used extensively in developing software packages, especially for microcomputers. Has the executional efficiency of assembly language, yet has ease of use and machine independence of high-level languages.
ALGOL (ALGOrithmic Language)	Used internationally in place of FORTRAN for scientific and mathematical problems.
PASCAL (named after mathematician Blaise Pascal)	Allows a structured, modular approach to programming. Has a powerful data structuring and data manipulation feature. Very flexible and self-documenting. Used in mainframes and micros.
APL (A Programming Language)	Designed for efficient interactive programming of analytical business and scientific applications. Especially popular for time-sharing.
ADA (Named after Augusta Ada Byron)	Sophisticated multipurpose language designed for Department of Defense. Written to replace COBOL and FORTRAN.
PL/1 (Programming Language 1)	Highly flexible modular language for applications that require many computations and process large amounts of data records.
RPG (Report Program Generator)	Originally designed to produce reports. Has evolved into a powerful, prompt-driven programming language.
LISP (LISt Process)	Designed to manipulate symbols that are grouped into ordered lists. Widely used in artificial intelligence and expert system applications.
PROLOG	Artificial intelligence language especially suited to symbol manipulation. Is nonprocedural. Widely used in Japan for artificial intelligence.
JAVA	An object-oriented language that can run on any computer.
Visual Basic	A graphically oriented language frequently used to build front ends and forms for spreadsheet and database applications.

numbers, calculate totals, and specify the number and width of columns. **Report generators** were developed to make customizing reports easier and faster. These programs can access files and data bases, select the data desired, aggregate or manipulate it, and print it in the desired format. An **application generator** produces a program to accomplish tasks specified by its users. Application generators include a programming language; a code generator; a library of commonly used program code; tools for creating files, data bases, and a data dictionary; a screen painting feature to develop input and output layouts; a query language; and a graphics and report generator. IBM claims to have achieved a 27-fold improvement in productivity when ADF, its application generating program, was used instead of COBOL to write programs. At another company, a management reporting system that took six months to write was created in half a day using an application generator called FOCUS.

Object-Oriented Languages and Programming. With traditional programming approaches, developing a new program means writing entirely new code, one line at a time. The program may be hundreds of thousands of lines long and can take years to complete. Since each program is written from scratch, quality is often poor, productivity of programmers is low, and programs are usually behind schedule. When program modifications are needed, the code must be rewritten and tested. As programs become longer and more complex, achieving a reasonable quality level becomes a formidable task.

One solution to these problems is a new way of developing software using an object-oriented language (OOL). An **object** is a predefined set of program code that, after having been written and tested, will always behave the same way, so that it can be used for other applications. All programs consist of specific tasks such as saving or retrieving data and calculating totals. In object-oriented programming, an object is written for each specific task and saved in a library so that anyone can use it.

TABLE 4A.4 Major Differences Between 3GLs and 4GLs

Third-Generation Languages (3GLs)	Fourth-Generation Languages (4GLs)
Intended for use by professional programmers	May be used by a nonprogramming end-user as well as a professional programmer
Require specification of *how to perform task*	Require specification of *what task* to perform (system determines how to perform the task)
Require that all alternatives be specified	Have default alternatives built in; end-user need not specify these alternatives
Require large number of procedural instructions	Require far fewer instructions (less than one-tenth in most cases)
Code may be difficult to read, understand, and maintain	Code is easy to understand and maintain because of English-like commands
Language developed originally for batch operation	Language developed primarily for on-line use
Can be difficult to learn	Many features can be learned quickly
Difficult to debug	Errors easier to locate because of shorter programs, more structured code, and use of defaults and English-like language
Typically file-oriented	Typically data base–oriented

Source: Adapted from James A. Senn, *Information Systems in Management* (Belmont, Calif.: Wadsworth, 1990), p. 218. Reprinted with permission.

Using **object-oriented programming (OOP),** objects are combined and the small amount of code necessary for finishing the program is written. Rather than writing a program line by line, programmers select objects by pointing to a representative icon and then linking these objects together. Objects can be modified, reused, copied, or created, just like spreadsheet cells. When an object is updated, all programs using that object can be automatically updated as well.

These objects are then sent messages telling them what to do; the objects complete the task accordingly. For example, selecting an object that looks like a fax machine would mean that data are to be sent by fax. This programmer–machine interface is more natural, powerful, and easy to understand and use than more traditional methods.

The advantages of OOP are its graphical interface, ease of use, faster program development, and enhanced programmer productivity (up to tenfold increases). The programs produced by OOP are more reliable and contain fewer errors, since the modules being used have already been extensively tested. Its disadvantages are its steep initial development costs and a more extensive start-up time. OOP produces programs that are larger, slower, and use more memory and other computer resources than traditional methods. As a result, it requires powerful PCs and workstations. Investing in OOP is cheaper than hiring additional programming staff, however, and the increase in productivity makes up for the additional costs. Many companies are moving to OOP. For example, Florida Power and Light has seen a fourfold increase in developer productivity since it moved to object-oriented development.

Adherents of OOP claim that the future software market will deal in objects rather than in software packages. In other words, software applications will be sold as collections of objects. Eventually a do-it-yourself software situation will result that has users purchasing the necessary objects from a computer store, assembling them, and adding a little coding to tie up loose ends. Some common object-oriented languages are Smalltalk, C++ Visual Basic, and Java.

Systems Software

Systems software controls the use of the hardware, the application software, and other system resources used in executing data processing tasks. It also prepares user programs for execution by translating them into machine language. There are three basic types of systems software: operating systems, utility programs, and communications software.

Operating Systems. The **operating system (OS)** is the most important type of systems software. The OS manages the input, output, processing, and storage devices and operations in order to maximize the system's performance. It performs administrative functions such as scheduling jobs, allocating primary memory space, tracking all application programs and systems software, maintaining operating statistics, and communicating with equipment operators. The OS resides in main memory or in a readily accessible on-line storage device.

Windows NT and Windows 98 are two popular operating systems for PCs. Windows is an example of a **graphical user interface (GUI)** operating environment in which a mouse is used to point at icons and menu selections. Most

GUIs allow the screen to be divided into several windows so that the user can work with several programs.

Newer operating systems have a plug and play feature that identifies and configures the OS and the hardware so that the PC, peripherals, and software work together with minimal effort on the user's part. This feature minimizes user service and support, especially when a new hardware component or more software is added to a system. As a result, plug and play makes PC systems more economical to operate.

Two other important characteristics of operating systems are multitasking and virtual memory. In a **multitasking** environment, several jobs can be processed on the computer simultaneously. The OS can switch back and forth among a number of programs and keep the input/output devices for all the programs working at peak speed. In a **virtual memory** system, the operating system continually moves data back and forth between primary and secondary memory so that the system appears to have a virtually unlimited amount of primary memory.

Utility Programs. *Utility programs* handle common file, data manipulation, and housekeeping tasks. Debugging aids help correct programs. On-line users can employ text editors to modify the contents of data files and computer programs. Sort/merge programs sort files into a specific order and merge two or more sorted files into one. Media conversion programs transfer data from one medium to another, such as from tape to disk. Virus protection software helps to prevent infection by viruses. Utilities are easy to use, efficient, and inexpensive.

Communications Software. Most computer users transmit data electronically between computers and between terminals and computers, and they access corporate and public data bases to extract information. *Communications software* controls and supports these activities. The programs connect and disconnect communications links and terminals, automatically poll terminals or other computers for input/output activity, prioritize communication requests, and detect and correct data transmission errors. Communications software is discussed in Chapter 7.

Application Software

Hardware and systems software are not unique—they are available to anyone who can afford them. This is not the case with application software. It is a scarce commodity, and companies spend millions of dollars to develop application software that will give them a competitive edge. Application software is by far the most important software for accountants, because it performs specific data processing and accounting tasks. Application software of interest to accountants can be divided into three categories:

1. *General-purpose programs* handle common tasks such as word processing, spreadsheets, graphics, and data bases. They also include software packages that some of the major public accounting firms have developed to assist in auditing work.
2. *Business applications* update master files and data bases to include the effects of transactions. They also support the various business functions

of a company: accounting, marketing, production, finance, human resources, and management. Specific business applications programs in each of these areas are discussed in Chapters 12–16.

3. *Intelligent applications* focus on expanding the role of the computer beyond traditional data processing functions. Examples include decision support systems, expert systems, and artificial intelligence; each is discussed in more detail later in this appendix.

Image Processing

Businesses in the United States spend almost $400 billion a year to create, distribute, store, and update paper forms, and that figure is growing by up to 25% a year. Research has shown that filing and retrieving a document costs $20 in labor, finding a misfiled document costs $125, and re-creating a document costs $350. Many of these costs can be eliminated using document imaging systems.

Image processing captures an electronic image of data so that it can be stored and shared. Imaging systems can capture almost anything, including keystroked or handwritten documents (such as invoices or tax returns), flowcharts, drawings, and photographs. Many companies that use document imaging are making significant progress toward paperless offices. Table 4A.5 lists the benefits that can be derived from document imaging.

As shown in Fig. 4A.6, there are five distinct steps to document imaging:

- *Step 1: Data capture.* The most common means of converting paper documents into electronic images is to scan them. The scanning device converts the text and pictures into digitized electronic code. This scanner can range from a simple handheld device to a high-end, high-speed scanner capable of scanning more than 2,500 pages an hour. Fax modems are also used to receive electronic images of documents.
- *Step 2: Indexing.* Document images must be stored in a manner that facilitates their retrieval. Therefore, important document information, such as purchase order numbers or vendor numbers, is stored in an index. Great care is needed in designing the indexing scheme, as it affects the ease of subsequent retrieval of information.
- *Step 3: Storage.* Because images require a large amount of storage space, they are usually stored on an optical disk. One 5.25-inch optical platter can store 1.4 gigabytes, or about 25,000 documents (equivalent to 3 four-drawer filing cabinets). A 12-inch removable optical disk stores up to 60,000 documents, and up to 100 optical disks can be stored in devices called jukeboxes.
- *Step 4: Retrieval.* Keying in any information stored in an index can retrieve documents. The index tells the system which optical disk to search, and the requested information can be quickly retrieved.
- *Step 5: Output.* An exact replica of the original document is easily produced on the computer's monitor or on paper, or is transmitted electronically to another computer.

Image processing systems have produced significant benefits for many companies. Blue Cross and Blue Shield reduced insurance claims processing from

TABLE 4A.5 Advantages of Image Processing

It has been estimated that 90% of the work accountants and others do today is done using paper. It is also estimated that the volume of information required by companies doubles every three or four years. As a result we are faced with being buried by paper. One solution is to make better use of document imaging. More companies are moving to this technology and it is estimated that by 2004 only 30% of our work will be paper-based; 70% will be electronic. The move to document imaging provides the following advantages:

Accessibility. Documents can be accessed and reviewed simultaneously by many people, even from remote locations.

Accuracy. Accuracy is much higher because costly and error-prone manual data-entry processes are eliminated.

Availability. There are no more lost or misfiled documents.

Capacity. Vast amounts of data can be stored in very little space, which significantly reduces storage and office space.

Cost. When large volumes of data are stored and processed, the cost per document is quite inexpensive. As a result, the costs to input, file, retrieve, and refile documents are reduced significantly. For example, while the retail store Carter Hawley Hale was in bankruptcy proceedings the judge allowed it to spend $1.2 million dollars on an imaging system because he was convinced it was going to save rather than cost the company money.

Customer satisfaction. When waiting time is significantly reduced (due to lost or misfiled documents, queue time, etc.), customers can get the information almost immediately.

Security. Various levels of passwords (network, data base, files, etc.) and clearances can be assigned to restrict document access.

Speed. Data can be retrieved at fantastic speeds. Stored documents can be indexed using any number of identifying labels, attributes, or keywords. For example, Norfolk Southern railroad has decreased the time required to retrieve deeds from three days to a few seconds.

Versatility. Handwritten or typed text can be added to an image, as can voice messages. Documents can be added to word processing files; the data can be included in a spreadsheet or data base.

seven to two days and produced annual savings of $10 million. John Hancock secured new business because of tremendous improvements in customer service. Additional benefits include reduced processing and storage of paper, increased productivity, and fewer transcription errors and lost documents. UPS and Federal Express use image processing to facilitate the ability to track the status of customer shipments.

Decision Support Systems

A **decision support system (DSS)** helps managers make decisions in unstructured and semistructured problem situations where judgment, experience, and intuition are required. A DSS has a graphical orientation and provides the user with report and presentation flexibility.

A computer-based DSS consists of the following elements: (1) the decision maker's knowledge and experience, (2) decision models (such as quantity for ordering inventory), (3) internal and external data bases from which data can be quickly and efficiently retrieved, and (4) an interactive user interface that

FIGURE 4A.6
Document Image Processing

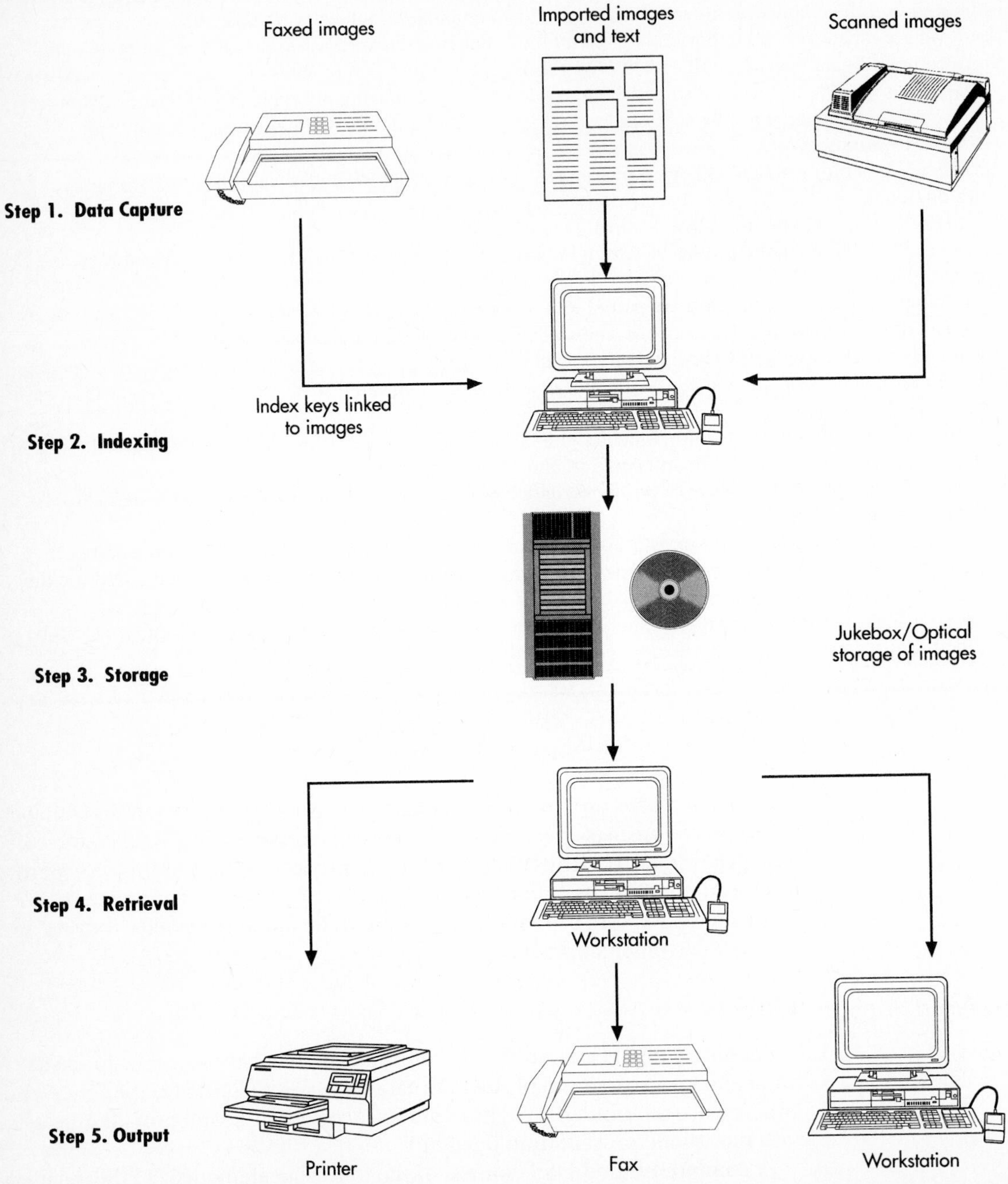

allows decision makers to communicate with a DSS's hardware and software. DSS software includes the following capabilities:

- *What-is.* DSS can be used to answer questions such as the following: What is S&S's best-selling appliance? Who are the top salespeople? How do the sales of wide-screen TVs compare with last year's? With the sales goal?
- *What-if.* DSS can be used to investigate questions such as the following: What effect would a 10% sales increase have on gross profit? What effect would a new incentive sales program have on net income?
- *Goal seeking.* DSS can be used to determine the tasks involved in accomplishing a specified goal. For example: What sales and expense levels would S&S have to achieve to reach a targeted net income?
- *Simulation.* These packages use different probabilities and expectations to simulate a particular situation.

The following two examples illustrate two types and various uses of DSS. The DSS developed by American Airlines, an Analytical Information Management System, is used by airlines, engine and aircraft manufacturers, consultants, and financial analysts. It supports planning, operations, marketing, and financial functions such as seating capacity and utilization, load factors, aircraft utilization, traffic growth, market share, operating statistics, and revenue and profitability. Citibank developed Managerial Analysis for Profit Planning to help bank managers make decisions about financial planning and budgeting. This DSS also helps them define and identify the costs of providing specific banking products, determine pricing, and allocate resources among products and services.

DSS have also been developed to facilitate working in groups. You have probably worked in groups and are familiar with some of their drawbacks. Some people dominate group discussions or decisions while others are reluctant to contribute or are excessively deferential. Often the discussion bounces around among topics, and by the time it is your turn to speak, the discussion has already shifted to another topic. Some people have axes to grind and return to the same topic repeatedly.

Group decision support software (GDSS) provides software support to overcome these problems. For example, a GDSS can keep a list of the topics being discussed, thereby reducing the likelihood that a topic is skipped over. Individual ideas can be submitted anonymously, making it easier for all participants to express their views. Moreover, the software can monitor whether everyone has contributed suggestions and prompt everyone to participate. GDSS can also be used to run totally electronic meetings, bringing groups of people together from all over the world at much less cost than would be required to meet face-to-face.

There are three types of GDSS:

1. A face-to-face session in a room equipped with the following: workstations connected to a coordinating computer; a large screen for displaying information such as tables, graphs, and charts; and video and other special equipment for recording the group's ideas. Seating is in a semicircle or a horseshoe so that everyone can see one another.

2. A configuration of two or more decision rooms linked together so that several groups can participate in the decision-making process.

3. A remote network of independent workstations. Networking technology and groupware software link individual users with a data base and GDSS tools. All users need not make use of the system at the same time. In fact, the decision making process may last several days as users respond to comments made by others at their convenience.

Artificial Intelligence

Artificial intelligence (AI) is software that tries to emulate aspects of human behavior, such as reasoning, communicating, seeing, and hearing. AI software can use its accumulated knowledge to reason and, in some instances, learn from experience and thereby modify its subsequent reasoning. There are several types of AI, including natural language, voice and visual recognition, robotics, neural networks, and expert systems.

Natural language and voice and visual recognition both focus on enabling computers to interact more easily and naturally with users. Robotics focuses on teaching machines to replace human labor. Both neural networks and expert systems aim to improve decision making.

Neural Networks. **Neural networks** are computing systems structured to emulate the brain's learning process. Like the brain, which uses a massively parallel network of interconnected neurons, the neural network uses interconnected processors that perform many operations simultaneously and interact dynamically to learn from data as it is processed. Although neural networks do not handle unexpected or one-of-a-kind events very well, they are very good at recognizing patterns that humans overlook and at uncovering emerging trends.

Like humans, neural networks learn by fine-tuning their accumulated knowledge using the facts present in each new case. For example, developing a neural network that detects fraudulent credit card transactions requires showing it enough examples of both valid and fraudulent transactions until it can reliably tell them apart. Developing a sufficiently large data base of examples is the most difficult and costly part of training a neural network.

Expert Systems. An **expert system (ES)** is a computerized information system that allows nonexperts to make decisions comparable to those of an expert. Expert systems are used for complex or ill-structured tasks that require experience and specialized knowledge in narrow, specific subject areas. As shown in Fig. 4A.7, expert systems typically contain the following components:

1. *Knowledge base.* This includes the data, knowledge, relationships, rules of thumb (heuristics), and decision rules used by experts to solve a particular type of problem. A knowledge base is the computer equivalent of all the knowledge and insight that an expert or a group of experts develop through years of experience in their field.

2. *Inference engine.* This program contains the logic and reasoning mechanisms that simulate the expert logic process and deliver advice. It uses data obtained from both the knowledge base and the user to make associations and inferences, form its conclusions, and recommend a course of action.

3. *User interface.* This program allows the user to design, create, update, use, and communicate with the expert system.

4. *Explanation facility.* This facility provides the user with an explanation of the logic the ES used to arrive at its conclusion.

5. *Knowledge acquisition facility.* Building a knowledge base, referred to as knowledge engineering, involves both a human expert and a knowledge engineer. The knowledge engineer is responsible for extracting an individual's expertise and using the knowledge acquisition facility to enter it into the knowledge base.

Expert systems can be example-based, rule-based, or frame-based. Using an example-based system, developers enter the case facts and results. Through induction the ES converts the examples to a decision tree that is used to match the case at hand with those previously entered in the knowledge base. Rule-based systems are created by storing data and decision rules as if-then-else rules. The system asks the user questions and applies the if-then-else rules to the answers to draw conclusions and make recommendations. Rule-based systems are appropriate when a history of cases is unavailable or when a body of

FIGURE 4A.7
Major Components of an Expert System

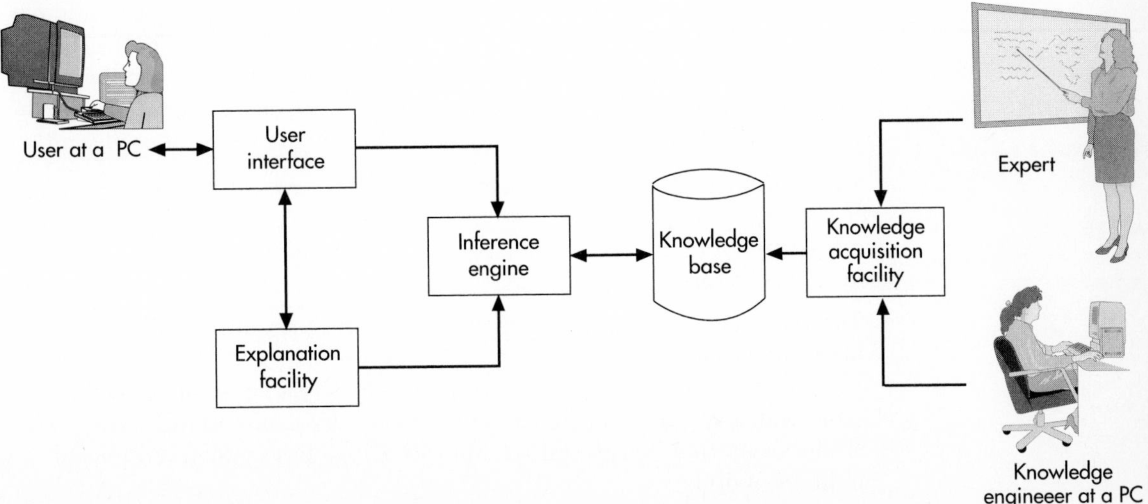

knowledge can be structured within a set of general rules. Frame-based systems organize all the information (data, descriptions, rules, etc.) about a topic into logical units called frames, which are similar to linked records in data files. Rules are then established about how to assemble or interrelate the frames to meet the user's needs.

Expert systems provide several levels of expertise. Some function as assistants that perform routine analysis and call the user's attention to tasks that require human expertise. Others function as colleagues, and the user "discusses" a problem with the system until both agree on a solution. When a user can accept the system's solution without question, the expert system can be referred to as a true expert. Developers of expert systems are still striving to create a true expert; most current systems function at the assistant or colleague level.

Expert systems offer the following benefits:

- They provide a cost-effective alternative to human experts.
- They can outperform a single expert because their knowledge is representative of numerous experts. They are faster and more consistent and do not get distracted, overworked, or stressed out.
- They produce better-quality and more consistent decisions. Expert systems assist users in identifying potential decision making problems, which increases the probability that sound decisions will be made.
- They can increase productivity.
- They preserve the expertise of an expert leaving the organization.

Although expert systems have many advantages and great promise, they also have a significant number of limitations:

- Development can be costly and time-consuming. Some large systems have required up to 15 years and millions of dollars to develop.
- It can be difficult to obtain knowledge from experts who have difficulty specifying exactly how they make decisions.
- Designers have not been able to program what humans consider common sense into current systems. Consequently, rule-based systems break down when presented with situations they are not programmed to handle.
- Until recently, developers encountered skepticism from businesses due to the poor quality of the early expert systems and the high expectations of users.

As technology advances, some of these problems will be overcome and expert systems will play an increasingly important role in accounting information systems. Here are specific examples of companies that have successfully used expert systems:

- The IRS analyzes tax returns to determine which should be passed on to tax fraud investigators.
- IBM designs and evaluates internal controls in both new and existing applications.
- American Express authorizes credit card purchases to minimize fraud and credit losses. Its ES replaced 700 authorization clerks and saved tens of millions of dollars.

- Xerox continually compares actual results against forecasts and updates its financial planning forecast as needed.
- Lockheed Missiles and Space Co. uses expert systems to eliminate procurement errors. For example, an ES examines each on-line request form. If an item has not been properly charged to overhead, the ES advises the requester of the mistake, explains why it is incorrect, and suggests a correction.

KEY TERMS

supercomputers
mainframe
minicomputers
microcomputers
central processing unit (CPU)
arithmetic-logic unit (ALU)
control unit
read-only memory (ROM)
random access memory (RAM)
bits
byte
MIPS
access time
execution time
millisecond
microsecond
nanosecond
picosecond
microprocessor
motherboard
data bus
word size
megahertz (MHz)
bus size
WORM (write-once, read-many)
CD-ROM (compact disk, read-only memory)
input/output bound
throughput
source data automation
magnetic ink character recognition (MICR)
optical character recognition (OCR)
personal identification number (PIN)
smart card
radio frequency identification tags
point-of-sale (POS) recorders
universal product code (UPC)
bar codes
resolution
plotter
computer output microfilm (COM)
application software
systems software
machine language
symbolic language
compiler
source program
object program
interpreter
fourth-generation languages (4GLs)
report generators
application generators
object
object-oriented programming (OOP)
operating system (OS)
graphical user interface (GUI)
multitasking
virtual memory
image processing
decision support systems (DSS)
group decision support system (GDSS)
artificial intelligence (AI)
neural networks
expert system (ES)

CHAPTER 5

Data Bases

LEARNING OBJECTIVES

After completing this chapter, you should be able to

- Describe what a relational data base is and how it organizes data.
- Explain the steps involved in designing a data base.

Integrative Case: S&S, Inc.

Ashton Fleming believes that the best way to provide Susan Gonzalez and Scott Parry with easy access to the information they need to run their business is to build S&S's new AIS as a data base system. Ashton has read that almost all new data base AIS are relational, but he is not quite sure exactly what a relational data base is. He knows that Scott and Susan are likely to have questions about whether a relational data base is appropriate for S&S. Therefore, he decides to prepare a brief report for them explaining why S&S's new AIS should be a relational data base system. He completes his report by addressing the following questions:

1. What is a data base system?
2. What is a relational data base system?
3. How do you design a relational data base?

INTRODUCTION

Many organizations are switching from the types of file-oriented transaction processing systems described in Chapter 4 to the data base approach. This chapter and the next will teach you about the design and construction of a data base AIS. This chapter explains what a data base is and how it differs from the file-oriented systems described in Chapter 4. It also describes the structure of a relational data base system, which is the most popular type of data base. This chapter concludes by discussing the basic steps involved in designing a data base. Chapter 6 then introduces two specific tools used by accountants to build data base AIS.

DATA BASES

For many years, companies created new files and programs each time an information need arose. The result was a significant increase in the number of master files stored by organizations. For example, Bank America at one time had 36 million customer accounts in 23 separate systems. One governmental agency had data stored in 22 separate systems.

This proliferation of master files created problems. Often the same data was stored in two or more separate files (see Fig. 5.1). Moreover, the specific data values stored in the different files may not always be consistent. For example, a customer's address may have been correctly updated in one file, but the old address may be still stored in another file. These problems make it difficult to effectively integrate data stored in different files and to obtain an organization-wide view of the data. Data base systems were developed to address these problems associated with the proliferation of master files. Figure 5.1 illustrates the differences between a file-oriented and a data base approach.

The data base approach views data as an organizational resource that should be used by and managed for the entire organization, not just the originating department or function. Its focus is data integration and data sharing

FIGURE 5.1
File-Oriented Approach Versus Data Base Approach

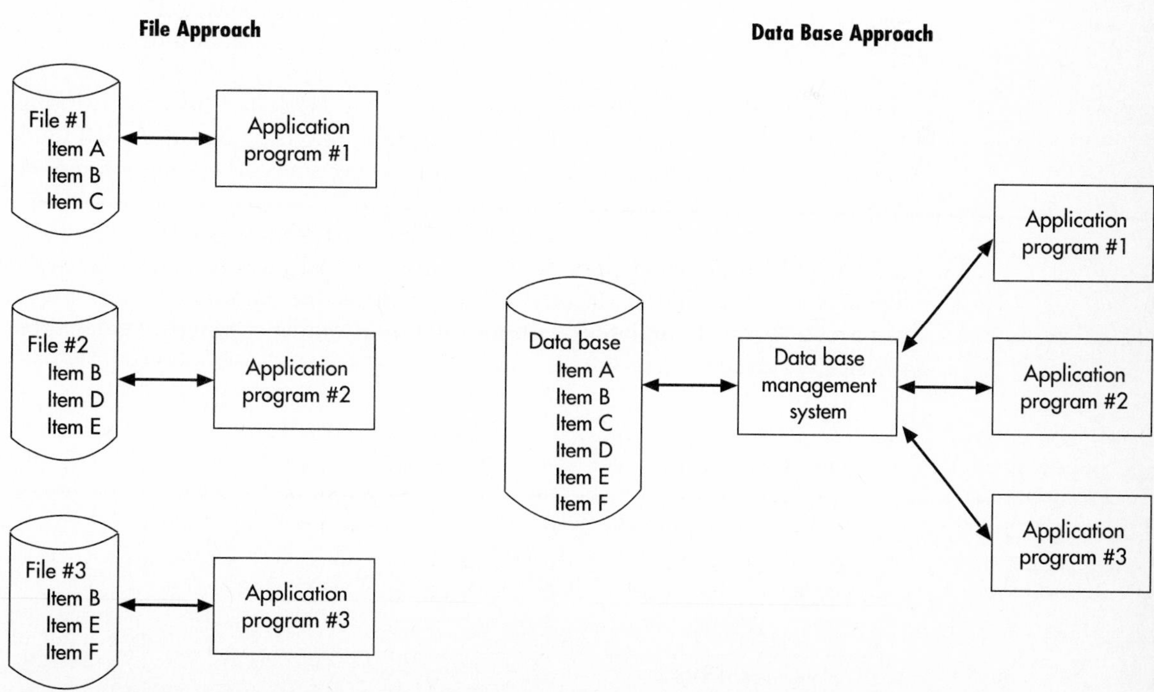

with all authorized users. Integration is achieved by combining master files into larger pools of data that can be accessed by many application programs. An example is an employee data base that consolidates data formerly contained in payroll, human resources, and job skills master files. The program that manages and controls access to the data base is the **data base management system (DBMS).** The combination of the data base, the DBMS, and the application programs that use the data base is the **data base system.** The person responsible for the data base is the **data base administrator (DBA).**

Logical and Physical Views of Data

A major advantage of data base systems over file-based systems is that the data base systems separate the logical and physical views of data. The **logical view** is how the user or programmer conceptually organizes and understands the data. For example, a sales manager may conceptualize all information about customers as being stored in the form of a table with each row containing all the relevant information about one customer. The **physical view** refers to how and where the data are physically arranged and stored on disk, tape, CD-ROM, or other media. For example, Fig. 5.2 shows a **record layout** of an accounts receivable file.

Separating the logical and physical views of data facilitates developing new applications, because programmers can concentrate on coding the application logic (what the program will do) and do not need to focus on how and where the various data items are stored or accessed. Referring back to Fig. 5.2, suppose a programmer wants a credit report showing the customer number, credit limit, and current balance. To write the program to produce such a report, she must understand the location and length of the fields needed (record positions 1 through 10 for customer number, for example) and the format of each field (alphanumeric or numeric). Clearly, the process becomes increasingly complex if data are needed from several files.

In contrast, Fig. 5.3 shows that the data base management system software deals with the link between the way data are physically stored and each user's logical view of that data. Thus the DBMS controls the data base so that users can access, query, or update it without reference to how or where the data are physically stored.

FIGURE 5.2
Accounts Receivable File Record Layout

Customer number A	Customer name A	Address A	Credit limit N	Balance N
1 – 10	11 – 30	31 – 60	61 – 68	69 – 76

A = alphanumeric field
N = numeric field

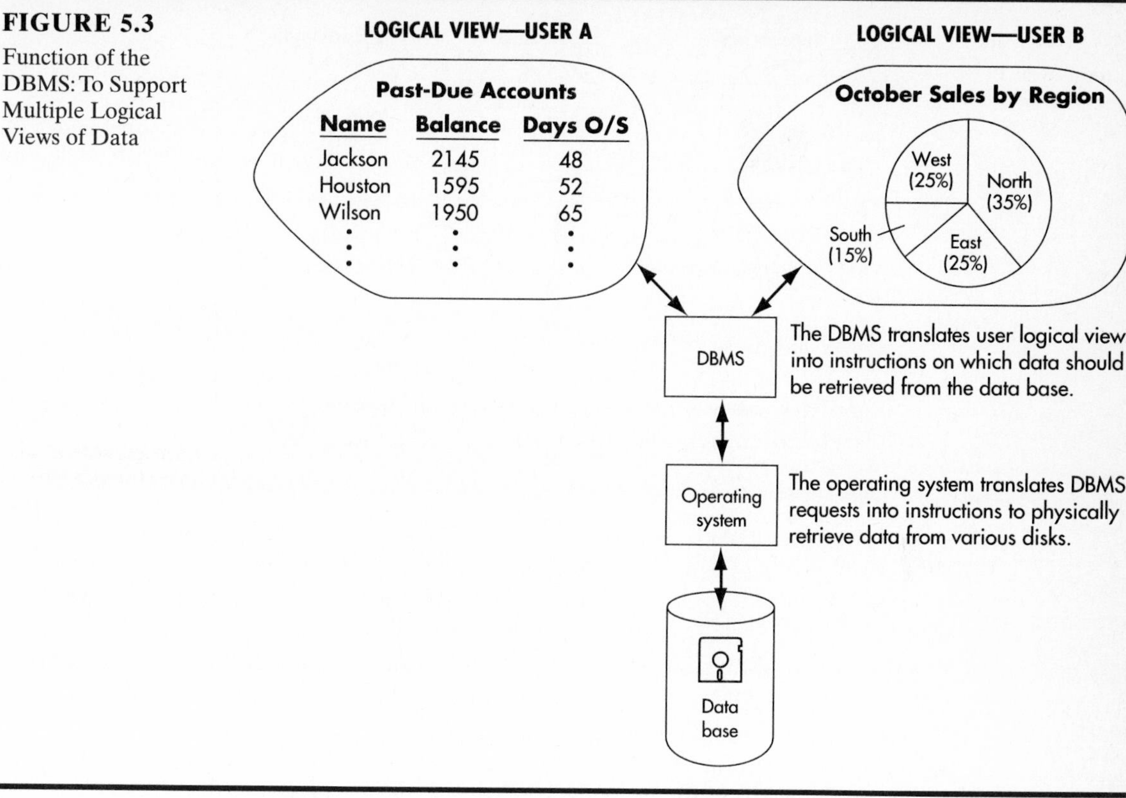

FIGURE 5.3 Function of the DBMS: To Support Multiple Logical Views of Data

Separating the logical and physical views of data also means that users can change their conceptualization about relationships among data items (their logical view of the task) without making changes in the way those data are physically stored. Likewise, the data base administrator can change the physical storage of the data to improve system performance, without affecting users or application programs. This separation of the logical and physical views of data is referred to as **program–data independence**.

Schemas

A **schema** describes the logical structure of a data base. There are three levels of schemas: the conceptual, the external, and the internal. Figure 5.4 shows the relationships between these three levels.

The **conceptual-level schema** is an organization-wide view of the entire data base. It lists all data elements and the relationships among them. The **external-level schema** consists of a set of individual user views of portions of the data base, each of which is also referred to as a **subschema**. The **internal-level schema** provides a low-level view of the data base. It describes how the data are actually stored and accessed, including information about pointers, indexes, record lengths, and so forth.

FIGURE 5.4
Three Levels of Schemas

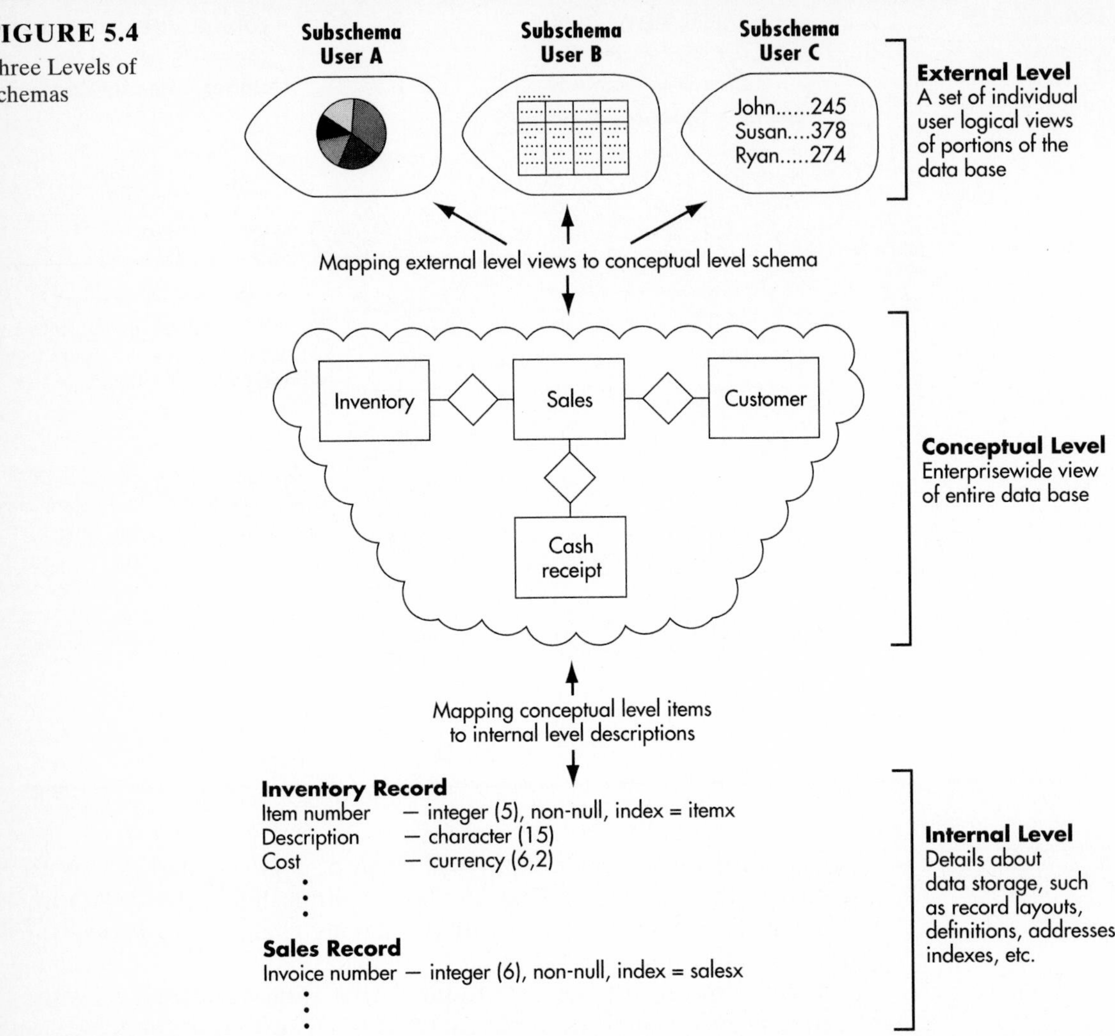

Figure 5.4 connects each of these levels with bidirectional arrows, which represent the mappings between the schemas. The DBMS uses these mappings to translate a user's or an application program's request for data (expressed in terms of logical names and relationships) into the corresponding pointers, indexes, and addresses needed to physically access the data.

Accountants are frequently involved in developing the conceptual- and external-level schemas, and they may also participate in developing the internal-level schema. Thus it is important to understand the difference between the conceptual- and external-level schemas. To illustrate this difference, consider the revenue cycle for S&S. The conceptual schema for the revenue cycle data base would contain information about customers, sales, cash receipts, sales staff, cash, and inventory. At the external level, a number of subschemas could be derived from this schema, each tailored to the needs of different users or application programs. Each subschema would also be designed to prevent access to those portions of the data base that are not relevant to a particular user's job. For example, the external-level subschema for the sales order entry staff would include information about customer credit limits and current balances, inventory quantities, and prices, but it would probably not include information about the costs of inventory or current company bank account balances. The external-level subschema for the delivery staff would include information about the customer's address, but would probably not include information about each customer's credit limit or employee pay rates. Similarly, additional subschema would define the relevant portions of the data base that other employees need to access to perform their jobs.

The Data Dictionary

One of the key components of a DBMS is a special file called the data dictionary. The **data dictionary** contains information about the structure of the data base. For each data element stored in the data base, such as the customer number, there is a corresponding record in the data dictionary describing it. Table 5.1 shows examples of the kind of information the data dictionary contains about each data element.

Accountants have a very good understanding of the data elements that exist in a business organization, where they originate, and where they are used. This knowledge is a result of the accountant's role in the design of the information system and in the processing of financial data. For this reason, accountants should participate in the development of the data dictionary.

The data dictionary is usually maintained automatically by the DBMS. In fact, this is often one of the first applications of a newly implemented data base system. Inputs to the data dictionary include records of any new or deleted data elements, as well as changes in names, descriptions, or uses of existing data elements. Outputs include a variety of reports useful to programmers, data base designers, and users of the information system. Sample reports include (1) a list of all programs in which a data item is used, (2) a list of all synonyms for the data elements in a particular file, (3) a list of all data elements used by a particular user, and (4) a list of all output reports in which a data element is used. These reports are useful in the design and implementation of a data base system, provide documentation of the system, and can become part of the audit trail.

DBMS Languages

Every DBMS must provide a means of performing the three basic functions of creating, changing, and querying the data base. The sets of commands used to perform these functions are referred to as the data definition, data manipulation, and data query languages, respectively.

The **data definition language (DDL)** is used to (1) build the data dictionary, (2) initialize or create the data base, (3) describe the logical views for each

TABLE 5.1 Example of a Data Dictionary

Data Element Name	Description	Records in Which Contained	Source	Field Length	Field Type	Programs in Which Used	Outputs in Which Contained	Authorized Users	Other Data Names
Customer number	Unique identifier of each customer	A/R record, customer record, sales analysis record	Customer number listing	10	Alphanumeric	A/R update, customer file update, sales analysis update, credit analysis	A/R aging report, customer status report, sales analysis report, credit report	No restrictions	None
Customer name	Complete name of customer	Customer record	Initial customer order	20	Alphanumeric	Customer file update, statement processing	Customer status report, monthly statement	No restrictions	None
Address	Street, city, state, and zip code	Customer record	Credit application	30	Alphanumeric	Customer file update, statement processing	Customer status report, monthly statement	No restrictions	None
Credit limit	Maximum credit that can be extended to customer	Customer record, A/R record	Credit application	8	Numeric	Customer file update, A/R update, credit analysis	Customer status report, A/R aging report, credit report	R. Drummond W. Francom H. Heaton	CR_limit
Balance	Balance due from customer on credit purchases	A/R record, sales analysis record	Various sales and payment transactions	8	Numeric	A/R update, sales analysis update, statement processing, credit analysis	A/R aging report, sales analysis report, monthly statement, credit report	O. Cherrington J. Hansen K. Stocks	Cust_bal

individual user or programmer, and (4) specify any limitations or constraints on security imposed on data base records or fields. Table 5.2 shows an example of a DDL command used to create a table to store information about vendors.

The **data manipulation language (DML)** is used for data maintenance, which includes such operations as updating, inserting, and deleting portions of the data base. The DML simplifies the writing of programs to accomplish these tasks by requiring references only to the names of data items, rather than to their physical storage locations. Table 5.3 shows examples of the three basic types of DML commands.

The **data query language (DQL)** is used to interrogate the data base. Whereas the DML is used to change the contents of the data base, the DQL merely retrieves, sorts, orders, and presents subsets of the data base in response to user queries. Most DQLs contain a fairly powerful, but easy to use, set of commands that enable users to satisfy many of their own information needs without the assistance of a programmer. Table 5.4 presents a sample query command written in a popular query language called SQL. Appendix A of this chapter presents more information about SQL and graphical query languages.

Many DBMSs also include a **report writer,** which is a language that simplifies report creation. Typically, users need only specify which data elements they

TABLE 5.2 Example of Data Definition Language (DDL) Command

The following command creates a table to store information about vendors:

```
CREATE TABLE            Vendor
     (Vendor#               INTEGER (5) NOT NULL,
     Name                   CHARACTER(15),
     Street_Address         CHARACTER(20),
     City                   CHARACTER(12),
     State                  CHARACTER(2),
     Zipcode                CHARACTER(10),
     Balance                FLOATING(10)   )
```

This command creates a vendor table with seven columns. The vendor number and balance columns must contain only numeric values; vendor# will take integer values, whereas balance can be any numeric value, including decimal format. The remaining columns may contain either numbers or letters. The number in parentheses indicates the maximum number of characters that can be stored in that column. Finally, the constraint NOT NULL indicates that vendor# cannot be left blank.

Result of the command:

Vendor

Vendor : Table

Vendor#	Name	Address	City	State	Zipcode	Balance
0	0	0	0	0	0	0

Record: 1 of 1

Note: This command creates an empty table. Filling the table requires the use of data manipulation language commands.

TABLE 5.3 Example of Data Manipulation Language (DML) Operations

This command inserts a new row, containing information about St. Louis Appliances, into the vendor table:

```
INSERT
INTO    Vendor (Vendor#, name, street_address, city, state, zipcode, balance)
VALUES  (10004, 'St. Louis Appliances', '2455 Chippewa', 'St. Louis', 'MO',
        '63109-2643', 0)
```

This command updates the address of St. Louis Appliances:

```
UPDATE  Vendor
SET     Street_address = '3542 Chippewa',
        Zipcode = '63110-2214'
WHERE   Vendor# = 10004
```

This command deletes from the vendor table the row containing information about St. Louis Appliances:

```
DELETE
FROM    Vendor
WHERE   Vendor# = 10004
```

TABLE 5.4 Example of Data Query Language (DQL) Command

Query:

```
SELECT     Name, Balance
FROM       Vendor
ORDER BY   Balance, Descending
```

Result:

5-4 : Table

Name	Balance
South Side Electronics	3987.00
St. Louis Electronics Supply	3250.67
St. Louis Computer Warehouse	2311.85
Oakville Electronics	954.95

Record: 5 of 5

This query specifies that the name and balance columns (the SELECT command) in the vendor table (the FROM command) be displayed. The result is arranged in descending order (the ORDER BY and the DESCENDING commands) by the amount owed.

want printed and how the report should be formatted. The report writer then searches the data base, extracts the specified data items, and prints them out according to the user-specified format.

All users generally have access to both the DQL and the report writer. Access to the DDL and DML, however, should be restricted to those employees with administrative and programming responsibilities. This helps to limit the number of people who have the capability to make changes to the data base.

RELATIONAL DATA BASES

A DBMS is characterized by the type of logical data model on which it is based. A **data model** is an abstract representation of the contents of a data base. The overwhelming majority of DBMSs used in AIS are called relational data bases because they use the relational data model. Therefore, this chapter focuses primarily on relational data bases. Appendix B discusses another increasingly popular type of data base that is built on the object-oriented data model.

The **relational data model** represents everything in the data base as being stored in the form of tables (see Table 5.5). Technically, these tables are called **relations** (hence the name relational data model), but we will use the two words interchangeably. Moreover, keep in mind that the relational data model only describes how the data appear in the conceptual- and external-level schemas. The data are not actually stored in tables, but rather in the manner described in the internal-level schema.

Each row in a relation, called a **tuple** (rhymes with couple), contains data about a specific occurrence of the type of entity represented by that table. Thus each row in Table 5.5 contains all the pertinent data about a particular inventory

TABLE 5.5 Sample Inventory Table for S&S

5-5 : Table

Item Number	Description	Color	Vendor Number	Quantity on Hand	Price
1036	Refrigerator	White	10023	12	1199
1038	Refrigerator	Almond	10023	7	1299
1039	Refrigerator	Hunter Green	10023	5	1499
2061	Range	White	10011	6	799
2063	Range	Black	10011	5	999
3541	Washer	White	10008	15	499
3544	Washer	Black	10008	10	699
3785	Dryer	White	10008	12	399
3787	Dryer	Almond	10019	8	499

Record: 10 of 10

item. Each column in the table contains information about one specific attribute of the represented object. Thus the columns in the inventory table in Table 5.5 represent specific characteristics about each inventory item carried by S&S.

Basic Requirements of the Relational Data Model

The relational data model imposes certain constraints on the structure of tables. We discuss six of the most important constraints here. The first two ensure the integrity, or accuracy, of the data base:

1. *Primary keys must be unique.* The primary key is the attribute, or combination of attributes, that uniquely identifies a specific row in a table. For example, the primary key in Table 5.5 is item number. Each different merchandise item sold by S&S can be uniquely identified by its item number. For this to be true, however, the primary key of any row in a relation cannot be null (blank), for there would never be a way to uniquely identify that row and retrieve the data stored there. A nonnull value for the primary key indicates that a specific object exists and can be identified by reference to its primary key value. Consequently, this constraint is referred to as the **entity integrity rule,** because it ensures that every row in every relation must represent data about some specific object in the real world.
2. *Every foreign key must either be null or have a value corresponding to the value of a primary key in another relation.* A **foreign key** is an attribute in one table that is the primary key of another table. In Table 5.5 vendor number is a foreign key. It is the primary key of the vendor table (not shown), uniquely identifying each vendor. Foreign keys are used to link tables together; in this example, the vendor number is used to identify the primary source for that particular inventory item. Additional information about that vendor, such as its address, can be obtained from the vendor table. This is possible only if the value in the vendor number column in the inventory table equals the value of the vendor number column in some row in the vendor table. Otherwise, the data base would be inconsistent. Consequently, this constraint is referred to as the **referential integrity rule.** Note, however, that the foreign key can be null if there is no existing relationship between the two tables. For example, a null value for vendor number in any row in Table 5.5 would indicate that there is no primary preferred vendor for that inventory item.

Four additional constraints contribute to the simplicity of a relational DBMS and enhance its efficiency and effectiveness for transaction processing:

3. *Each column in a table must describe a characteristic of the object identified by the primary key.* Look again at Table 5.5 and notice that every column in that table describes some property of the various inventory items carried by S&S. Facts about the vendors who supply those products and the customers who purchase them, however, are not included in the inventory table.

4. *Each column in a row must be single-valued.* Again, referring back to Table 5.5, notice that every column has one, and only one, value recorded in each row.

5. *The values in every row of a specific column must be of the same data type.* For example, in Table 5.5, the item number column has integer values in every row.

6. *Neither column order nor row order is significant.* Rearranging the sequence of rows or columns in Table 5.5 has no effect on data retrieval.

In the next section, we apply these constraints to designing a relational data base for S&S. Following these rules will result in a well-structured (normalized) data base. We will demonstrate the value of following the rules for producing a normalized data base, showing examples of the types of problems that can arise when these constraints are violated.

Case Study: Designing a Relational Data Base for S&S, Inc.

In its existing manual accounting system, S&S captures sales information on a sales invoice. This hard copy document provides both a logical and physical view of the data collected. Physical storage of sales invoice data is simple: S&S retains one or more copies of the invoice in a file cabinet. For example, one copy may be stored by invoice number to provide a chronological record of all sales and another is filed by customer name to facilitate analysis of specific customer accounts.

The procedure for storing the same data on computer is a little more complex. Suppose, for example, that S&S had five sales invoices (numbered from 101 to 105) that it wanted to store electronically. On several of these invoices, S&S records that the customer purchased more than one item (a television and a refrigerator, for example). Let us look at the effects of several potential ways of storing this information.

Option 1: Store All Data in One Uniform Table. S&S could store its sales data in one table, as illustrated in Table 5.6, but this approach has two disadvantages. First, it creates redundancy in terms of stored data. For example, examine sales invoice number 102 in Table 5.6. Since there are three separate inventory items sold, the invoice and customer data (the first nine columns) are recorded three times. Likewise, inventory descriptions and unit prices are repeated each time an item is sold. Because sales volume can be fairly high in a retail store (remember, this table represents only five invoices), such redundancy can make file maintenance unnecessarily time-consuming and error-prone. For example, recording a customer's address change requires searching the entire table and changing every occurrence of that customer's address. A similar process would be required to update the unit price of inventory items. In either case, it would be easy to overlook some occurrence and thereby create an inconsistency in the data base.

The second weakness of Table 5.6 is that customer and inventory data are not maintained independently of sales invoice data. Consequently, there is no

TABLE 5.6 Example of Storing All Sales Data Table for S&S in One Table

5-6 : Table

Sales Invoice #	Date	Salesperson	Customer #	Invoice Total	Customer Name	Street
101	10/15/1996	J. Buck	151	1447	D. Ainge	123 Lotus Lane
101	10/15/1996	J. Buck	151	1447	D. Ainge	123 Lotus Lane
102	10/15/1996	S. Knight	152	4394	G. Kite	40 Quatro Road
102	10/15/1996	S. Knight	152	4394	G. Kite	40 Quatro Road
102	10/15/1996	S. Knight	152	4394	G. Kite	40 Quatro Road
103	10/28/1996	S. Knight	151	898	D. Ainge	123 Lotus Lane
104	10/31/1996	J. Buck	152	789	G. Kite	40 Quatro Road
105	11/14/1996	J. Buck	153	3994	F. Roberts	401 Excel Way
105	11/14/1996	J. Buck	153	3994	F. Roberts	401 Excel Way
105	11/14/1996	J. Buck	153	3994	F. Roberts	401 Excel Way

Record: 11 of 11

way to store information about prospective customers until they actually make a purchase. Conversely, if a customer made only one purchase, consisting of a single item, deleting that row from the table would result in the loss of all information about that customer.

Option 2: Vary the Number of Columns. An alternative to the data storage scheme depicted in Table 5.6 is to record the sales invoice and customer information just once within the first nine columns and then add additional columns to record each item sold. Table 5.7 illustrates this approach.

Although this approach does reduce some of the data redundancy associated with the data storage scheme illustrated in Table 5.6, it still has its drawbacks. S&S would have to decide in advance how many item numbers to leave room for in each row. If room is left for only a few items, how would information about a sale involving many items be stored? If room is left for many items,

TABLE 5.7 Example of Modifying a Table's Structure in Order to Store S&S Sales Data by

5-7 : Table

Sales Invoice #	Columns 2-9	Item #	Quantity	Description	Unit Price	Extended Amount	Item #2	Quanity2
101	Same 8	10	2	Television	499	998	50	1
102	columns	10	1	Television	499	499	20	3
103	as in	50	2	Microwave	449	898		
104	Table 5.6	40	1	Range	789	789	789	
105	above	10	3	Television	499	1497	20	1

Record: 6 of 6

City	State	Item #	Quantity	Description	Unit Price	Extended Amount
Phoenix	AZ	10	2	Television	499	998
Phoenix	AZ	50	1	Microwave	449	449
Mesa	AZ	10	1	Television	499	499
Mesa	AZ	20	3	Freezer	699	2097
Mesa	AZ	30	2	Refrigerator	899	1798
Phoenix	AZ	50	2	Microwave	449	898
Mesa	AZ	40	1	Range	789	789
Chandler	AZ	10	3	Television	499	1497
Chandler	AZ	20	1	Freezer	699	699
Chandler	AZ	30	2	Refrigerator	899	1798

however, there will be a great deal of wasted space, as is the case for sales invoices 103 and 104.

The Solution: A Set of Tables. The problems associated with the data storage schemes from Tables 5.6 and 5.7 are a direct result of violating the six constraints presented earlier for designing relational tables. Table 5.8 shows the results of following those six constraints in designing a data base for S&S's sales invoice data.

Notice how the data storage scheme illustrated in Table 5.8 avoids the problems we discussed earlier. First, redundancy is greatly reduced. For example, in the schema shown in Table 5.8, customer addresses and inventory item unit prices are stored just once. This avoids potential inconsistencies that may arise from not changing every occurrence of a data item, a problem that is referred to as an *update anomaly.*

Adding Columns for Each Additional Item Sold

Description2	Unit Price2	Extended Amount2	Item#3	Quantity3	Description3	Unit Price3	Extended Amount3
Microwave	449	449					
Freezer	699	2097	30	2	Refrigerator	899	1798
Freezer	699	699	30	2	Refrigerator	899	1798

TABLE 5.8 Set of Relational Tables for Storing S&S Sales Data

Invoice : Table

Sales Invoice #	Date	Salesperson	Customer #	Invoice Total
101	10/15/96	J. Buck	151	1447
102	10/15/96	S. Knight	152	4394
103	10/28/96	S. Knight	151	898
104	10/31/96	J. Buck	152	789
105	11/14/96	J. Buck	153	3994

Record: 6 of 6

Line Item : Table

Sales Invoice #	Item #	Quantity	Extended Amount
101	10	2	998
101	50	1	449
102	10	1	499
102	20	3	2097
102	30	2	1798
103	50	2	898
104	40	1	789
105	10	3	1497
105	20	1	699
105	30	2	1798

Record: 11 of 11

Customer : Table

Customer #	Customer Nam	Street	City	State
151	D. Ainge	123 Lotus Lane	Phoenix	AZ
152	G. Kite	40 Quatro Road	Mesa	AZ
153	F. Roberts	401 Excel Way	Chandler	AZ

Record: 4 of 4

Inventory : Table

Item #	Unit Price	Description
10	499	Television
20	699	Freezer
30	899	Refrigerator
40	789	Range
50	449	Microwave

Record: 6 of 6

Note that redundancy is not entirely eliminated, however. Attributes that are foreign keys, such as sales invoice number and item number, appear in more than one table. This limited redundancy is not a problem because the referential integrity rule ensures that there will be no update anomaly problems with the foreign keys.

A second feature to notice about Table 5.8 is that data about various items of interest (customers, inventory, and sales) are stored in separate tables. This makes it easier to add new data to the system. For example, the schema represented in Table 5.8 allows information about prospective customers to be stored, simply by adding another row in the customer table. In the schemas represented by Tables 5.6 and 5.7, however, information about new customers could not be added until they had actually made a purchase. Otherwise, the sales invoice number column would be empty. The sales invoice number, however, is part of the primary key of Tables 5.6 and 5.7. Consequently, it cannot be null, for that would violate the entity integrity rule of a relational data base. This problem of not being able to insert new information without violating the basic integrity rules of a relational data base is referred to as an *insert anomaly.*

The schema shown in Table 5.8 also simplifies the deletion of information. For example, deleting sales invoice 105, representing the only sale to customer 153 (F. Roberts), would not result in the loss of all information about that customer. In contrast, deleting sales invoice 105 from Table 5.7 would have the unintended side effect of removing all information about customer 153 from the data base. This type of problem is referred to as a *delete anomaly.*

The third benefit of the schema depicted in Table 5.8 is that space is used efficiently. The line item table contains a row for each item sold on each invoice. There are no blank rows, yet all data about each sale is recorded. In contrast, the schema depicted in Table 5.7 results in much wasted space.

In summary, the process of following the guidelines for designing relational tables to create the data storage scheme illustrated in Table 5.8 is called **normalization.** The set of relational tables shown in Table 5.8 meet the requirements of what is referred to as *third normal form.*[1] Ensuring that every table in a relational data base is in third normal form produces a well-structured data base that is easy to maintain and free from update, insert, and delete anomalies.

DATA BASE DESIGN

The design and operation of a data base system consists of the six stages shown in Figure 5.5.

As Figure 5.5 shows, these six stages are repetitive. There will eventually come a time during the operation and maintenance stage when the need to redesign the data base, and possibly acquire a new DBMS, becomes apparent. At that point, the entire process starts over, beginning with a planning study to determine the feasibility of developing a new data base system. Let us now examine what occurs during each of these stages of data base design.

[1] For more information about normal forms and normalization, see any data base textbook. Chapter 6 will introduce a methodology for building an AIS data base in which all tables are in at least third normal form.

FIGURE 5.5
Stages of Data Base Design

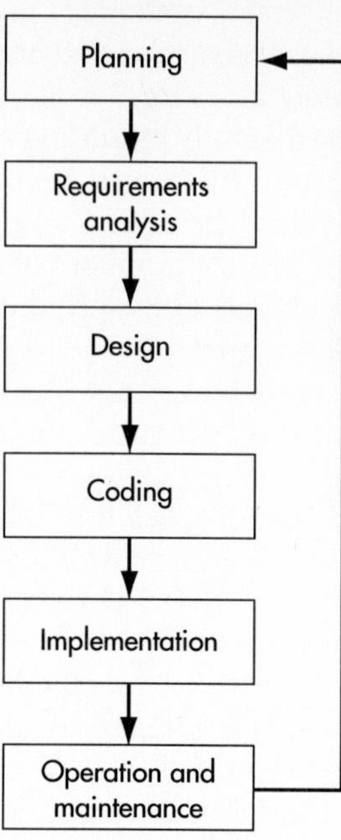

Planning

The first stage in data base design consists of initial planning to determine the need for and feasibility of developing a new database system. The objective is to determine whether the proposed system is technologically and economically feasible. If it is, then the project should proceed to the next stage: requirements analysis.

Requirements Analysis

Requirements analysis involves identifying user information needs, defining the scope of the proposed data base system, and determining preliminary hardware and software requirements. Data about user needs should be collected by a variety of methods, including interviews and questionnaires. The scope of the project should be defined in consultation with management so that it reflects the organization's information needs, strategic goals, and objectives. Once user information needs have been identified and the scope of the new data base system established, information about factors such as the number of users and expected transaction volume can be used to determine the preliminary hardware and software requirements.

Design

The third stage of the data base design process is when the structure of the data base is actually developed. The design stage can actually be broken down into three steps. The first step is referred to as **conceptual design,** which involves translating the data requirements of different users into a conceptual model (the conceptual schema) of the data base. This conceptual model can be implemented in any type of DBMS.

It is often easier to create the conceptual schema by subdividing it into major functional areas. This can be accomplished by identifying clusters of files and programs that are closely linked to each other in terms of processing and usage. For example, the different accounting cycles (revenue, expenditure, production, payroll, and general ledger) can be classified as naturally forming [functional] clusters within in an accounting data base. The revenue cycle schema would then include all data related to sales order processing, shipping, billing and accounts receivable, and cash collections.

Once the conceptual model has been developed, the next step involves choosing the type of DBMS that will be used and translating the conceptual model into a model that can be implemented in that type of DBMS. This step is referred to as **logical design.** For example, if Ashton decides to implement S&S's AIS in a relational DBMS, the logical design stage would involve developing a model, or schema, that could be implemented in any relational DBMS.

The third step in the design stage is to translate the logical schema into a model that describes the actual physical structures and access methods that will be used to implement the system using a specific DBMS package. This step, known as **physical design,** produces the physical schema. Thus it is during the physical design step that Ashton would designate both primary and secondary keys. The appropriate primary key for each record is generally obvious—for example, customer number for the customer file and invoice number for the invoice file. Identifying secondary keys is not as simple. Indeed, as explained in Chapter 4, secondary keys should be carefully selected because their use affects data base processing efficiency and information retrieval. The most appropriate secondary keys generally are those data elements that identify groups of records likely to be of interest to management. For example, invoice due date is often made a secondary key because it facilitates developing queries and reports about accounts receivable.

The data dictionary is also developed during the physical design stage. Finally, controls over access to and allowable operations on the data base should be specified at this time.

Coding

The fourth stage of the data base design process, coding, consists of translating the physical schema into actual data base structures (e.g., tables) that will be in the final system. This is also when new application programs are developed and modifications made to existing applications.

During this stage careful consideration is given to design alternatives, such as the use of pointers and indexes, that will maximize the efficiency and effectiveness of the system. Indeed, data base design must take into account a number of objectives (see Table 5.9). Unfortunately, it is not always possible to maximize every objective; thus, trade-offs are often required. For example, cost-effectiveness is often at odds with flexibility and accessibility. The data base designer's key task, therefore, is to try to achieve the best possible balance among these objectives.

Implementation

The fifth stage of the data base design process, implementation, consists of all the activities associated with getting the new data base system up and running. These include testing the new system, transferring data from existing files to the new data base, and training employees on how to use the new system.

Operation and Maintenance

The final stage of the data base design process, operation and maintenance, includes all the activities associated with running and maintaining the new system. This includes careful monitoring of system performance and user satisfaction with the system to determine the need for enhancements and modifications. Eventually, changes in business needs and practices, or new developments in information technology, initiate investigating whether there is a need to develop a new data base system. When that occurs, the data base design process starts over again with the initial planning stage.

TABLE 5.9 Data Base Design Objectives

Completeness	The data base should contain all the data (and the relationships between the data) needed by its various users. There should be proper integration and coordination of all users and suppliers of data. The data contained in the data base should be recorded in the data dictionary.
Relevance	Only relevant and useful data should be captured and stored.
Accessibility	Stored data should be accessible to all authorized users on a timely basis.
Up-to-dateness	Stored data should be kept current and up to date.
Flexibility	The data base should be flexible enough that a wide variety of users can satisfy their information needs.
Efficiency	Data storage should be accomplished as efficiently as possible, using the least amount of resources necessary. Data base update, retrieval, and maintenance time should be minimized.
Cost-effectiveness	Data should be stored in such a way that desired system benefits can be achieved at the lowest possible cost.
Integrity	The data base should be free from errors and irregularities.
Security	The data base should be protected from loss, destruction, and unauthorized access. Backup and recovery procedures should be in place so that the data base can be reconstructed if necessary.

Role of the Accountant

Accountants can and should be involved in all stages of the data base design process, although the level of their involvement in each stage is likely to vary. In the planning stage, accountants both provide some of the information used to evaluate the feasibility of the proposed project and participate in making that decision. In the requirements analysis and design stages, accountants participate in identifying user information needs, developing the logical schemas and designing the data dictionary, and specifying controls. Accountants with good AIS skills may participate in the coding stage. During the implementation stage, accountants are involved in testing the accuracy of the new data base and the application programs that will use that data. Finally, accountants use the data base system to process transactions, and sometimes they even help manage it.

DATA BASE SYSTEMS AND THE FUTURE OF ACCOUNTING

Data base systems may profoundly affect the fundamental nature of accounting. For instance, data base systems could lead to the abandonment of the double-entry accounting model. The basic rationale for the double-entry model is that the redundancy of recording the amount of a transaction twice provides a check on the accuracy of data processing. Every transaction generates equal debit and credit entries, and the equality of debits and credits is checked and rechecked at numerous points in the accounting process. Data redundancy, however, is the antithesis of the data base concept. If the amounts associated with a transaction are entered into a data base system correctly, it is necessary to store them only once, not twice. Computer data processing is sufficiently accurate to make an elaborate system of checks and double checks, which characterizes the double-entry accounting model, unnecessary.

Data base systems also have the potential to significantly alter the nature of external reporting. Considerable time and effort is currently invested in defining how companies should summarize and report accounting information to external users. Why not simply make a copy of the company's financial data base and make it available to external users in lieu of the traditional financial statements? Users would then be free to manipulate and analyze the raw data in whatever manner they see fit. Focus 5.1 discusses this possibility in more detail.

Perhaps the most significant effect of data base systems will be in the way that accounting information is used in decision making. The difficulty of formulating ad hoc queries in accounting systems based on traditional files or nonrelational DBMSs meant that accountants acted, in effect, as information gatekeepers. Financial information was readily available only in predefined formats and at specified times. The accountants specified the format of those reports and the times when they would be produced (usually monthly, quarterly, and annually).

Relational DBMSs, however, provide users with powerful yet easy-to-use query languages. These query languages make financial information available to managers whenever they want it. Financial statements can be easily prepared to cover whatever time periods managers want to examine, not just the time frames traditionally used by accountants. Relational DBMSs can also easily accommodate multiple views of the same underlying phenomenon. For exam-

FOCUS 5.1 Data Bases or Financial Statements?

ALTHOUGH information technology has dramatically changed the way that business is conducted, it has had relatively little effect on external reporting. Companies still produce periodic (quarterly and annual) financial reports of past activities based on historical costs. Moreover, they present that information at a highly aggregated level. It is estimated that the average financial data base of a typical large company is on the order of 100 gigabytes. Yet annual reports contain, on average, only about 100 KB of data! Consequently, users of annual reports see only a small portion of the data about the organization. On top of that, the information is presented in a predefined format (the financial statements).

Why not replace the annual report with a copy of the company's financial data base? Many companies already give their suppliers and customers limited access to their internal data bases. Suppliers, for example, may be given access to inventory data so that they can plan production and deliveries to replenish shortages. They are not, however, given access to human resource or payroll data. Companies could similarly define a view of their data base that excluded data too sensitive to be allowed to fall into the hands of competitors. This view of the data base could be placed on CD-ROMs or made available over the Internet to investors, creditors, and other external users.

The technical capability for providing such data base access exists. The computing power of current PCs makes processing such a data base feasible for a wide range of users. External users would get a fuller picture of the organization's performance, and the information would also be more timely.

In such a system, the company's primary financial reporting function would involve the definition of data elements and data base structure. Users would then be free to aggregate and classify that information using whatever decision model they believed to be appropriate.

Source: Robert K. Elliott, "Confronting the Future: Choices for the Attest Function," *Accounting Horizons* (September 1994): 106–124.

ple, tables storing information about assets can include columns not only for historical cost, but also for current replacement costs and market values. Thus managers will no longer be forced to look at data in ways predefined by accountants. Finally, relational DBMSs provide the capability of integrating financial and operational data. For example, data about customer satisfaction, collected by surveys or interviews, could be stored in the same table used to store information about current account balances and credit limits. Managers would thus have access to a richer set of data for making tactical and strategic decisions.

In all these ways, relational DBMSs have the potential to increase the use and value of accounting information for making the tactical and strategic decisions involved in running an organization. Accountants, however, must become knowledgeable about data base systems so that they can participate in designing the accounting information systems of the future. Such participation is important for ensuring that adequate controls are included in those systems to safeguard the data and assure the reliability of the information produced.

SUMMARY AND CASE CONCLUSION

Ashton prepared a report for Scott and Susan summarizing what he had learned about data base systems in general, and the relational data model in particular. His report explained that a data base management system (DBMS) is the software that makes a data base system work. A DBMS is based on a logical data model, which determines how users perceive the data as being stored.

For example, the relational data model represents data as being stored in the form of tables, which are called relations. Every row in a relational table has only one data value in each column. Neither row nor column position is significant. These properties support the use of simple, yet powerful, query languages for interacting with a relational data base. Users need specify only what data they want, and they need not be concerned with how that data is retrieved. The DBMS functions as an intermediary between the user and the data base, using a complex addressing scheme consisting of pointers, indexes, and other methods to retrieve and update the information stored in the data base.

After completing his research, Ashton examined a number of DBMS products at a local computer store. He invited Scott and Susan to a demonstration of the relational DBMS that he liked best. With the help of one of the computer store staff, Ashton built a sample data base for S&S, similar to that depicted in Table 5.8, and showed Scott and Susan how easy it was to query that data base. They were impressed with the demonstration and agreed with his recommendation to purchase a relational DBMS for S&S. They then asked Ashton to begin work on designing S&S's new AIS.

KEY TERMS

data base management system (DBMS)
data base system
data base administrator (DBA)
logical view
physical view
record layout
program–data independence
schema
conceptual-level schema
external-level schema
subschema
internal-level schema
data dictionary
data definition language (DDL)
data manipulation language (DML)
data query language (DQL)
report writer
data model
relational data model
relations
tuple
entity integrity rule
foreign key
referential integrity rule
normalization
requirements analysis
conceptual design
logical design
physical design

CHAPTER QUIZ

1. The relational data model portrays data as being stored in
   a. hierarchies.
   b tables.
   c. objects.
   d. files.
2. Users will most likely have access to the
   a. DML.
   b. DQL.
   c. DDL.
   d. DSL.
3. Which of the following is *not* a basic requirement (constraint) of the relational data model?
   a. All rows must be unique.
   b. In each row, there can only be one data value in each column.
   c. The data values in a column must be of the same data type.
   d. The order in which columns appear conveys important information.

4. An individual user's view of the data base is called the
   a. conceptual-level schema.
   b. external-level schema.
   c. internal-level schema.
   d. logical-data model.

5. Which language would be used by the DBA to create and maintain the data dictionary?
   a. DML
   b. DQL
   c. DDL
   d. DBMS

6. Who is responsible for developing general policies regarding the storage and maintenance of all organizational data?
   a. The data administrator
   b. The data base administrator
   c. Application programmers
   d. The controller

7. The software program that runs a data base system is called the
   a. DBA.
   b. DBMS.
   c. DML.
   d. DDL.

8. The constraint that all primary keys must have nonnull data values is referred to as
   a. the referential integrity rule.
   b. the entity integrity rule.
   c. normalization.
   d. requirements analysis.

9. The constraint that all foreign keys must have either null values or the value of a primary key in another table is referred to as
   a. the referential integrity rule.
   b. the entity integrity rule.
   c. normalization.
   d. requirements analysis.

10. The process of translating a conceptual schema into a model that can be implemented in a specific type of DBMS is called
   a. physical design.
   b. conceptual design.
   c. logical design.
   d. normalization.

DISCUSSION QUESTIONS

5.1 A data base allows two distinct views of data—a logical view and a physical view. Contrast the two views, and discuss why separate views are necessary in data base applications. Describe which perspective is most useful for each of the following employees: a programmer, a manager, and an internal auditor. How will understanding logical data structures assist accountants in designing and using data base systems?

5.2 The relational data model represents data as being stored in tables. Spreadsheets are another tool that accountants use that employs a tabular representation of data. What are some similarities and differences in the way that these two tools use tables? How might an accountant's familiarity with the tabular representation of spreadsheets facilitate or hinder learning how to use a relational DBMS?

5.3 The text explained how data base technology may eliminate the need for double-entry accounting. This creates three possibilities: (1) the double-entry model will be abandoned; (2) the double-entry model will not be used directly, but an external-level schema based on the double-entry model will be defined for use by accountants; or (3) the double-entry model will be retained in data base systems. Which alternative do you think is most likely to occur? Why?

5.4 Relational DBMS query languages provide easy access to information about the organization's activities. Does this mean that on-line, real-time processing should be used for all transactions? Are real-time financial reports needed by an organization? Why or why not?

PROBLEMS

5.1 The following data elements comprise the conceptual level schema for a data base:

ITEM NUMBER
COST
DESCRIPTION
QUANTITY ON HAND
INVOICE NUMBER
DATE
QUANTITY SOLD
TERMS
CUSTOMER NUMBER
CUSTOMER NAME
SHIPPING ADDRESS
BILLING ADDRESS
CREDIT LIMIT
ACCOUNT BALANCE
PRICE

Required:

Identify three potential users and design a subschema for each. Justify your design by explaining why each user needs access to that data element.

5.2 Most DBMS packages contain a data definition language, a data manipulation language, and a data query language. For each of the following examples, indicate which language would be used and why.

a. A data base administrator defines the logical structure of the data base.
b. The controller requests a cost accounting report containing a list of all employees being paid for more than ten hours overtime in a given week.
c. A programmer develops a program to update the fixed assets records stored in the data base.
d. The human resources manager requests a report noting all employees who are retiring within five years.
e. The inventory serial number field is extended in the inventory records to allow for recognition of additional inventory items with serial numbers containing more than ten digits.
f. A user develops a program to print out all purchases made during the past two weeks.
g. An additional field is added to the fixed asset records to record the estimated salvage value of each asset.

5.3 Ashton wants to store the following data about S&S's purchases of inventory:

ITEM NUMBER
DATE OF PURCHASE
VENDOR NUMBER
VENDOR ADDRESS
EXTENDED AMOUNT
VENDOR NAME
UNIT COST
QUANTITY PURCHASED
PURCHASING AGENT
PURCHASE ORDER NUMBER
DESCRIPTION
QUANTITY ON HAND
TOTAL AMOUNT OF PURCHASE

Required:

a. Design a set of relational tables to store this data.
b. Identify the primary key for each table.

5.4 Create the set of relational tables in Table 5.8 in any relational DBMS product to which you have access. Write queries to answer the following questions:

a. How many different kinds of inventory items does S&S sell?
b. How many sales were made during October?
c. What was the total amount of sales in October?
d. What was the average amount of a sales transaction?
e. Which salesperson made the largest sale?
f. How many units of each product were sold?
g. Which product was sold most frequently?

5.5 Implement the set of relational tables shown in Table 5.10 in a relational DBMS package to which you have access. Write queries to answer the following questions:

a. Which customers (show their names) made purchases from Martinez?
b. Who has the largest credit limit?
c. How many sales were made in October?
d. What were the item numbers, price, and quantity of each item sold on invoice number 103?
e. How much did each salesperson sell?
f. How many customers live in Arizona?
g. How much credit does each customer still have available?
h. How much of each item was sold? (Include the description of each item in your answer.)
i. Which customers still have more than $1,000 in available credit?
j. For which items are there at least 100 units on hand?

TABLE 5.10 Sample Relational Tables for Problem 5.5

Inventory : Table

Item_Number	Description	Unit Cost	Unit Price	QOH
1010	Blender	14	29.95	200
1015	Toaster	12	19.95	300
1020	Mixer	23	33.95	250
1025	Television	499	699.95	74
1030	Freezer	799	999.95	32
1035	Refrigerator	699	849.95	25
1040	Radio	45	79.95	100
1045	Clock	79	99.95	300

Record: 9 of 9

Customer : Table

Customer_Number	Name	City	State	Credit_Limit
1000	Smith	Phoenix	AZ	2500
1001	Jones	St. Louis	MO	1500
1002	Jeffries	Atlanta	GA	4000
1003	Gilkey	Phoenix	AZ	5000
1004	Lankford	Phoenix	AZ	2000
1005	Zeile	Chicago	IL	2000
1006	Pagnozzi	Salt Lake	UT	3000
1007	Arocha	Chicago	IL	1000

Record: 9 of 9

Sales : Table

Invoice_Number	Date	Salesperson	Customer_Number	Amount
101	10/3/96	Wilson	1000	1549.90
102	10/5/96	Mahomet	1003	299.85
103	10/5/96	Jackson	1002	1449.80
104	10/15/96	Drezen	1000	799.90
105	10/15/96	Martinez	1005	849.95
106	10/16/96	Martinez	1007	99.95
107	10/29/96	Mahomet	1002	2209.70
108	11/3/96	Martinez	1000	779.90

Record: 9 of 9

Sales-Inventory : Table

Invoice_Number	Item_Number	Quantity	Extension
101	1025	1	699.95
101	1035	1	849.95
102	1045	3	299.85
103	1010	1	29.95
103	1015	1	19.95
103	1025	2	1399.90
104	1025	1	699.95
104	1045	1	99.95
105	1035	1	849.95
106	1045	1	99.95
107	1030	1	999.95
107	1035	1	849.95
107	1040	2	159.90
107	1045	2	199.90
108	1025	1	699.95
108	1045	1	99.95

Record: 17 of 17

CASE 5.1 ANYCOMPANY, INC.—AN ONGOING COMPREHENSIVE CASE

Identify a local company (you may use the same company that you identified to complete Case 1.1) that uses a data base system, and write a report that includes the following information:

1. The type of logical data model used by the DBMS.
2. The reasons that particular product was chosen.
3. How the company transferred its data from its prior system to the data base system.
4. Advantages the company has reaped from using the DBMS.
5. Any problems encountered in implementing the data base system, and how those problems were dealt with.
6. The level of involvement of the company's accountants in converting to the data base system.

CASE 5.2 RESEARCH PROJECTS

As in all areas of information technology, DBMSs are constantly changing and improving. Research how businesses are using DBMSs and write a report of your findings. Address the following issues:

1. Which popular DBMS products are based on the relational data model?
2. What are differences between relational DBMSs designed for use on microcomputers and those designed for use on mainframes?
3. Which DBMS products are based on a logical model other than the relational data model? What are the relative strengths and weaknesses of those products in comparison with relational DBMSs? For what types of applications are they used?

APPENDIX A: QUERY LANGUAGES

QUERYING A RELATIONAL DATA BASE

The relational data model allows three fundamental types of operations to be performed on tables:

1. *PROJECT* creates a new table (or relation) by selecting specified columns from the original table.
2. *RESTRICT* creates a new table by selecting from the original table those rows that meet specified conditions.
3. *JOIN* creates a new table by selecting the designated columns from two or more tables and then choosing the rows that meet specified conditions. The JOIN operation is used frequently, since a single relation often does not contain all the data necessary to satisfy a user inquiry.

The key property of the relational data model is that each of these three basic operations always results in the creation of a new table. This means that the result of a query using these operations can itself be the object of additional queries. It is this possibility for nesting queries that makes relational data query languages so powerful.

Relational query languages can be classified into two broad categories: text-based query languages and graphical query languages. Let us examine how each type works.

Structured Query Language: A Text-Based Query Language

The standard text-based query language provided by most, but not all, relational DBMSs is called **structured query language (SQL).** Many popular microcomputer accounting packages also provide SQL access to the general ledger. SQL is powerful, yet simple to use. Its power and simplicity enable easy generation of special-purpose reports so corporate accountants can meet management's information requests. Similarly, SQL permits auditors easy retrieval of information from client data bases. Consequently, it is important to gain a basic understanding of how SQL works. In the remainder of this section, we introduce the principal SQL commands; additional information about SQL can be found in the reference manuals that accompany relational DBMS products.

SQL Syntax. Five basic keywords are used to construct most SQL queries:

1. *SELECT.* Used to list the columns that should be displayed in answering the query. This keyword implements the PROJECT operation.
2. *FROM.* Used to list the names of the tables that are referenced in answering the query. If two or more table names are listed, the JOIN operation is applied to them.

3. *WHERE.* Used to specify which rows to retrieve when answering the query. This keyword implements the RESTRICT operation.
4. *ORDER BY.* Used to specify how to format the answer. The column that serves as the basis for ordering is listed, along with the desired sequence (ascending or descending).
5. *GROUP BY.* Used to specify which rows in a table should be subject to basic mathematical operations (such as SUM, MINIMUM, and MAXIMUM). Referring back to Table 5.8, for example, applying GROUP BY to the salesperson column in the invoice table calculates total sales made by each salesperson. Alternatively, applying GROUP BY to the customer number column calculates total sales by customer.

Sample SQL Queries. Let us now see how these five keywords can be used to retrieve information from the data base shown in Table 5.8.

Query 1: Show the dates and invoice totals for all sales in October, arranged in descending order by amount of the sale.

This query would be written in SQL as follows:

```
SELECT    Date, Invoice Total
FROM      Invoice
WHERE     Date BETWEEN 10/01/96 and 10/31/96
ORDER BY            Invoice Total, DESCENDING
```

Table 5A.1 shows the original Invoice table and the response to this query.

Query 2: What are the invoice numbers of all sales made to D. Ainge, and who completed these sales?

This query would be written in SQL as follows:

```
SELECT    Sales Invoice #, Salesperson, Customer Name
FROM      Invoice, Customer
WHERE     Invoice.Customer # = Customer.Customer # AND Customer Name = 'D.
          Ainge'
```

Table 5A.2 shows the original tables and the result of the query.

Query 3: How many televisions were sold in October?

This query would be written in SQL as follows:

```
SELECT    Sum (quantity)
FROM      Line Item, Invoice, Inventory
WHERE     Line Item.Item # = Inventory.Item # AND Description = 'Television'
          AND Line Item.Sales Invoice # = Invoice.Sales Invoice # AND Date
          BETWEEN 10/01/96 and 10/31/96
```

This query shows that basic mathematical operators can be included in the SQL SELECT clause. In this case, the query is asking for the sum of the quantity sold column in the line item table. Table 5A.3 shows the result of this query.

Query 4: Display the names and addresses of all customers buying televisions in October.

TABLE 5A.1 Query 1
Show the dates and invoice totals for all sales in October, arranged in descending order by amount of the sale

Invoice : Table

Sales Invoice #	Date	Salesperson	Customer #	Invoice Total
101	10/15/96	J. Buck	151	1447
102	10/15/96	S. Knight	152	4394
103	10/28/96	S. Knight	151	898
104	10/31/96	J. Buck	152	789
105	11/14/96	J. Buck	153	3994

Record: 6 of 6

The SELECT clause in the query invokes the relational PROJECT operation to display only the date and invoice total columns. The FROM clause specifies that these columns are to be found in the Invoice table. The WHERE clause then invokes the relational RESTRICT operation to display only those rows representing sales made during October. The ORDER BY clause specifies that the answer should be displayed in descending order by the amount in the invoice total column.

Query Response : Table

Date	Invoice Total
10/15/96	4394.00
10/15/96	1447.00
10/28/96	898.00
10/31/96	789.00

Record: 4

This query would be written in SQL as follows:

```
SELECT   Customer Name, Street, City, State
FROM     Customer, Invoice, Line Item, Inventory
WHERE    Date BETWEEN 10/01/96 and 10/31/96 AND Description = 'Television'
         AND Invoice.Customer # = Customer.Customer # AND Invoice.Sales
         Invoice # = Line Item.Sales Invoice # AND Line Item.Item # = Inven-
         tory.Item #
```

The answer to this query is shown in Table 5A.4. Although only two lines long, the relational DBMS had to use all four tables to answer the query.

Query 5: How much did each salesperson sell so far this year?

This query would be written in SQL as follows:

```
SELECT     Sum (invoice total), Salesperson
FROM       INVOICE
GROUP BY   Salesperson
```

This query uses the GROUP BY keyword to instruct the DBMS to sum the invoice totals separately for each distinct value in the salesperson column. Table 5A.5 shows the result of this query.

TABLE 5A.2 Query 2

What are the invoice numbers of all sales made to D. Ainge, and who completed these sales?

Invoice : Table

Sales Invoice #	Date	Salesperson	Customer #	Invoice Total
101	10/15/96	J. Buck	151	1447
102	10/15/96	S. Knight	152	4394
103	10/28/96	S. Knight	151	898
104	10/31/96	J. Buck	152	789
105	11/14/96	J. Buck	153	3994

Record: 6 of 6

The SELECT clause in the query invokes the relational PROJECT operation to select the shaded columns in the invoice and customer tables. The FROM clause instructs the DBMS to apply the JOIN operator to the invoice and customer tables. The first WHERE clause specifies that customer #, the common column in both tables, is used to join them.

Customer : Table

Customer #	Customer Name	Street	City	State
151	D. Ainge	123 Lotus Lane	Phoenix	AZ
152	G. Kite	40 Quatro Road	Mesa	AZ
153	F. Roberts	401 Excel Way	Chandler	AZ

Record: 4 of 4

Temp : Table

Sales Invoice #	Salesperson	Customer Name
101	J. Buck	D. Ainge
102	S. Knight	G. Kite
103	S. Knight	D. Ainge
104	J. Buck	G. Kite
105	J. Buck	F. Roberts

Record: 6 of 21

Temp : Table

Sales Invoice #	Salesperson	Customer Name
101	J. Buck	D. Ainge
103	S. Knight	D. Ainge

Record: 3 of 21

The completed query looks like this. The customer name column can be deleted, if desired.

This temporary table is the result of executing the relational PROJECT and JOIN operations specified in the query. This temporary table would *not* appear on the screen; it is presented for illustrative purposes only. The second WHERE clause then invokes the relational RESTRICT operation to select only the shaded rows for display.

TABLE 5A.3 Query 3

How many televisions were sold in October?

Invoice : Table

Sales Invoice #	Date	Salesperson	Customer #	Invoice Total
101	10/15/96	J. Buck	151	1447
102	10/15/96	S. Knight	152	4394
103	10/28/96	S. Knight	151	898
104	10/31/96	J. Buck	152	789
105	11/14/96	J. Buck	153	3994

Record: 6 of 6

This query needs information from the invoice, line item, and inventory tables. The SELECT clause in the query invokes the relational PROJECT operation to select the shaded columns in all three tables. Those columns are joined to form a temporary table (not shown). The WHERE clause specifies the basis for linking the tables using columns common to each table (see arrows). It also invokes the relational RESTRICT operation to display only those rows that meet the query criteria.

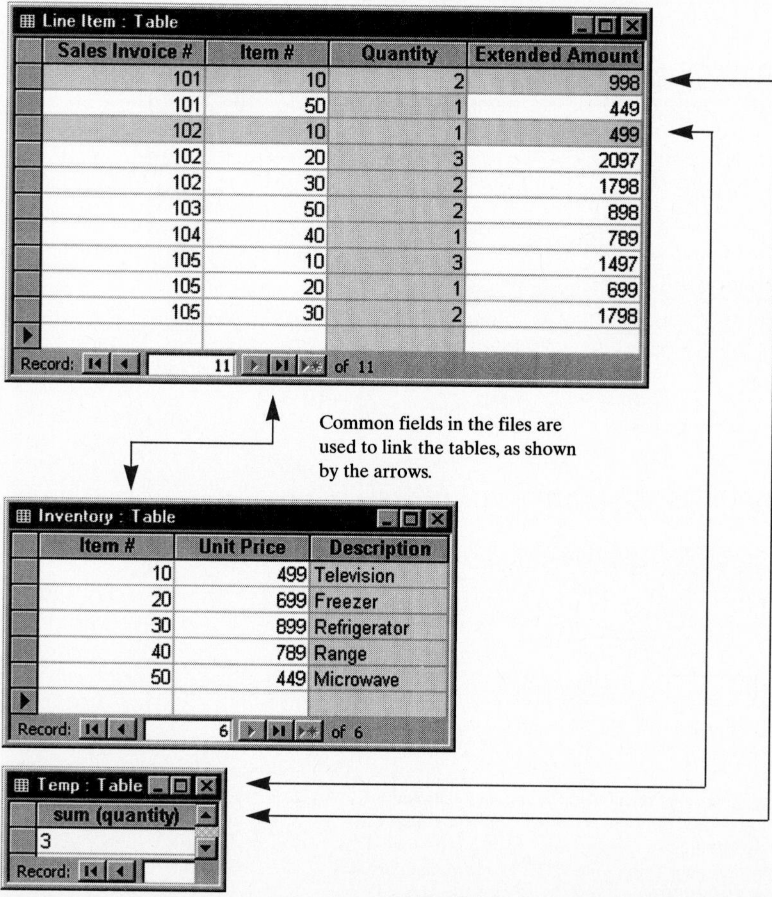

Line Item : Table

Sales Invoice #	Item #	Quantity	Extended Amount
101	10	2	998
101	50	1	449
102	10	1	499
102	20	3	2097
102	30	2	1798
103	50	2	898
104	40	1	789
105	10	3	1497
105	20	1	699
105	30	2	1798

Record: 11 of 11

Common fields in the files are used to link the tables, as shown by the arrows.

Inventory : Table

Item #	Unit Price	Description
10	499	Television
20	699	Freezer
30	899	Refrigerator
40	789	Range
50	449	Microwave

Record: 6 of 6

Temp : Table

sum (quantity)
3

Record:

TABLE 5A.4 Query 4

Display the names and addresses of all customers buying televisions in October

This query only displays data taken from the customer table. However, data from all four tables are used to answer the query. The data used in each table are shaded. The description column in the inventory table is used to decide what item number relates to televisions (10). The item number column in the line item table is used to identify on which invoice numbers televisions were sold (101, 102, and 105). The date column in the invoice table is used to narrow television sales to October sales (invoices 101, 102).

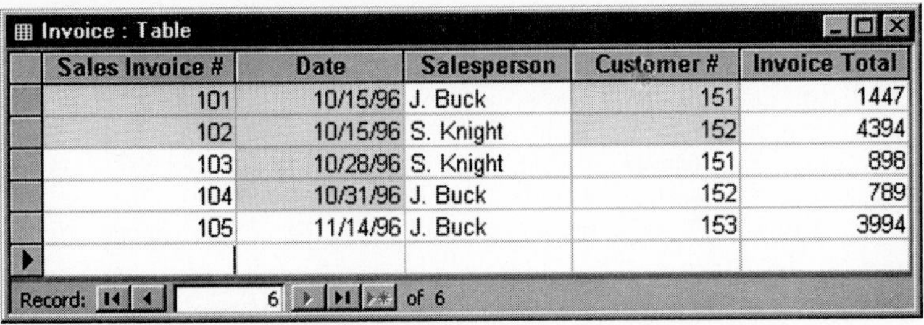

Invoice : Table

Sales Invoice #	Date	Salesperson	Customer #	Invoice Total
101	10/15/96	J. Buck	151	1447
102	10/15/96	S. Knight	152	4394
103	10/28/96	S. Knight	151	898
104	10/31/96	J. Buck	152	789
105	11/14/96	J. Buck	153	3994

Record: 6 of 6

Sales invoices 101 and 102 correspond to customers 151 and 152. Those names and addresses are retrieved from the customer table and displayed as shown here.

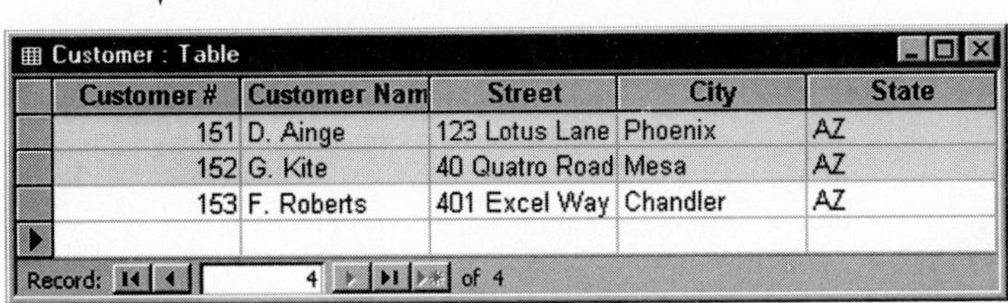

Customer : Table

Customer #	Customer Nam	Street	City	State
151	D. Ainge	123 Lotus Lane	Phoenix	AZ
152	G. Kite	40 Quatro Road	Mesa	AZ
153	F. Roberts	401 Excel Way	Chandler	AZ

Record: 4 of 4

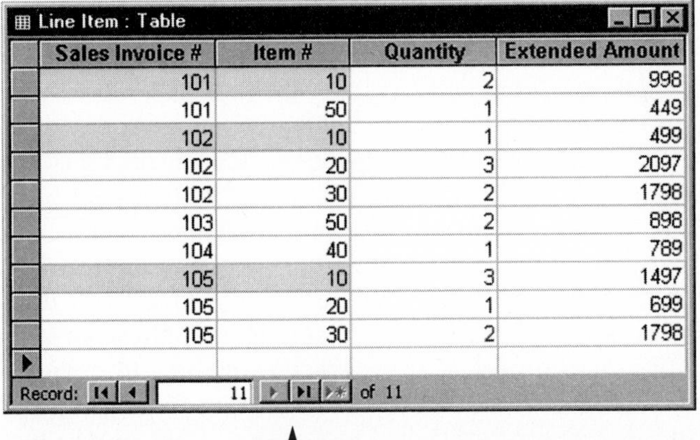

Line Item : Table

Sales Invoice #	Item #	Quantity	Extended Amount
101	10	2	998
101	50	1	449
102	10	1	499
102	20	3	2097
102	30	2	1798
103	50	2	898
104	40	1	789
105	10	3	1497
105	20	1	699
105	30	2	1798

Record: 11 of 11

Inventory : Table

Item #	Unit Price	Description
10	499	Television
20	699	Freezer
30	899	Refrigerator
40	789	Range
50	449	Microwave

Record: 6 of 6

Temp : Table

Customer Name	Street	City	State
D. Ainge	123 Lotus Lane	Phoenix	AZ
G. Kite	40 Quatro Road	Mesa	AZ

Record: 3 of 21

TABLE 5A.5 Query 5

How much did each salesperson sell?

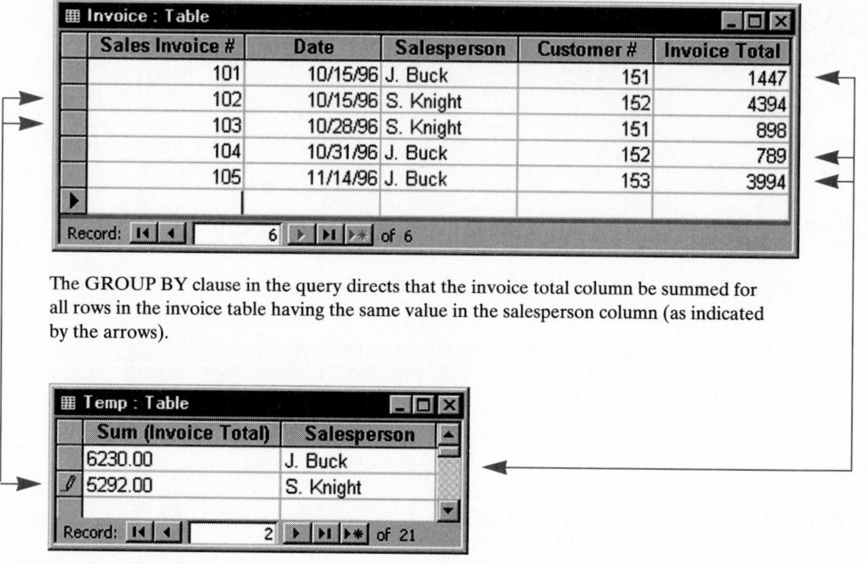

Invoice : Table

Sales Invoice #	Date	Salesperson	Customer #	Invoice Total
101	10/15/96	J. Buck	151	1447
102	10/15/96	S. Knight	152	4394
103	10/28/96	S. Knight	151	898
104	10/31/96	J. Buck	152	789
105	11/14/96	J. Buck	153	3994

Record: 6 of 6

The GROUP BY clause in the query directs that the invoice total column be summed for all rows in the invoice table having the same value in the salesperson column (as indicated by the arrows).

Temp : Table

Sum (Invoice Total)	Salesperson
6230.00	J. Buck
5292.00	S. Knight

Record: 2 of 21

Analysis of SQL. As seen from these five examples, SQL is simple to use yet quite powerful. SQL's simplicity allows users to specify the desired result without having to specify how the data are to be retrieved. All five example queries specified only the conditions to be met in providing the answer; no looping or procedural commands were required to tell the system how to search for the desired records.

The simplicity of SQL reflects the properties of the relational data model, especially the nonimportance of row and column order (constraint number 6). In contrast, the location of a data item in a nonrelational DBMS does provide important information. Consequently, users and application programmers working with nonrelational DBMSs must know how to navigate through the data base to find the answers to their queries. For example, a DBMS based on the hierarchical (or tree) data model (e.g., IBM's IMS) represents data as being stored in hierarchies. Users of a hierarchical DBMS must navigate up and down the hierarchy to retrieve the desired data. Although providing such specific navigational instructions may, in some cases, result in faster retrieval times, it poses an extra burden on the end-user to be aware of at least some aspects of the data base structure. It also requires that special operators be included in the query language for using pointers or otherwise navigating from one record to another. This makes it harder for users to write ad hoc queries, which in turn increases the demands placed on application programmers to write those queries for users.

SQL is powerful because it is set-based; every query inherently returns a subset of the tables referenced. In contrast, traditional programming languages such as COBOL, FORTRAN, and BASIC operate on just one record (row in a table) at a time. Consequently, using one of those languages to write these queries would have been much more complicated.

Graphical Query Languages

Most relational DBMSs also provide graphical query languages, which enable users to write queries by designing an example of what the desired answer should look like, instead of writing SQL code. (Figure 5A.1 shows an example

FIGURE 5A.1
Graphical Language Query and SQL Equivalent

SQL Query:

```
SELECT      Description, Sum(Qty Pur)
FROM        Inv-Pur, Inventory
WHERE       Inventory Item# = Inv-Pur Item#
GROUP BY    Description
```

The same query as written using the graphical language in ACCESS:

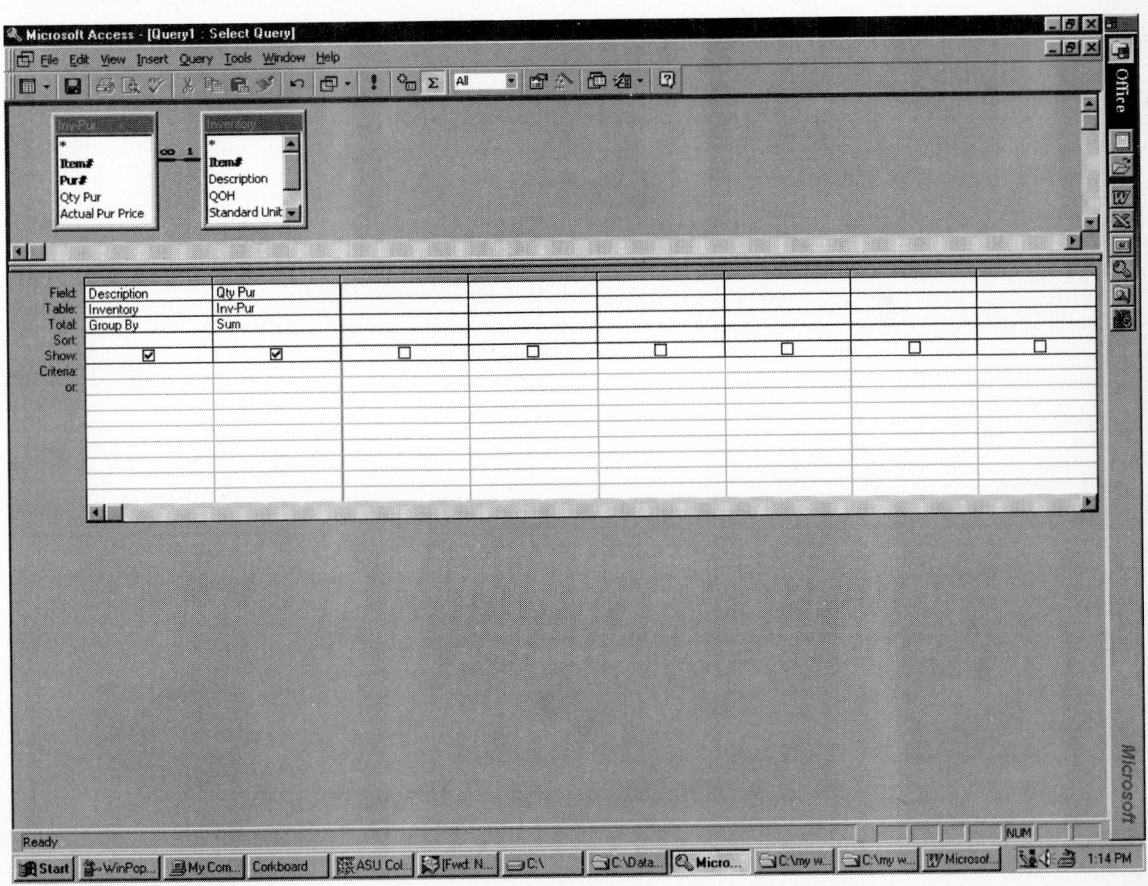

of a graphical language query and its SQL equivalent.) Usually, the DBMS translates these "query-by-example" queries into the equivalent set of SQL commands in order to retrieve the desired data.

KEY TERMS

structured query language (SQL)

APPENDIX B: OBJECT-ORIENTED DBMSs

Relational DBMSs have many strengths. A relational DBMS can significantly increase the speed and ease of accessing data. For example, it used to take up to 30 minutes for managers of the Coca-Cola Bottling Company of New York to retrieve details about individual journal entries from Coke's old file-based system. That dropped to about 10 seconds, after the company moved its general ledger data to a relational DBMS. The new system also lets managers create ad hoc reports whenever needed.

Relational DBMSs also make it easy to tailor accounting and other information systems to the needs of individual subunits of the organization. For example, R. P. Scherer, a Troy, Michigan, manufacturer of drug-delivery systems, has used a relational DBMS to integrate its regulatory, financial, and production systems. SQL enabled Scherer to define tables and user views that could be shared across applications. This made it easy to adapt the basic system to each of its manufacturing plants. Moreover, by integrating data across systems, Scherer can better manage the scheduling and production of customer orders. As a result, work-in-process inventories are greatly reduced.

Notwithstanding these benefits, a relational DBMS does have some limitations. It is generally less efficient for transaction processing and requires more memory than a file-based or nonrelational DBMS. These problems, however, are becoming less important as computers continue to increase in power and decrease in cost.

The most serious limitation of a relational DBMS is that current implementations of the relational data model do not easily accommodate the integration of complex data types, such as graphs, maps, sounds, and images, with the text and numeric data commonly associated with transaction processing. Proponents of the relational data model note that, theoretically, a relational DBMS can accommodate these complex data types. They argue that current difficulties in doing so merely reflect shortcomings in existing relational DBMS products, not in the underlying model. Nevertheless, the difficulties of representing such data in a relational DBMS are causing some companies to look at using an object-oriented DBMS for storing and processing such data.

OBJECT-ORIENTED DATA BASES

In the **object-oriented data model,** the basic conceptual building blocks are objects, rather than tables. An **object** is a reusable segment of program code that describes a data element and, further, contains instructions on how to manipulate that data. For example, the sales invoice object would not only store information about a particular sales transaction, it would also include instructions on how to (1) calculate extensions for each line item, (2) add sales tax to arrive at the total, and (3) update the appropriate customer account. This bundling together of data and instructions is called **encapsulation.**

Object-oriented data bases are hierarchical, as shown in Fig. 5B.1. All levels in the hierarchy, except the bottom one, represent object classes. Thus, in Fig. 5B.1, assets, current assets, and accounts receivable are all object classes. Entries at the bottom level of the hierarchy represent individual objects. For example, the accounts for Heather Powell and Rodney Washington represent individual objects. Each individual object is assigned a unique object identifier that serves the same function as the primary key in the relational data model. Pointers are used and explicitly included in the data model as a way to link objects and object classes. These pointers are then referred to in queries in order to navigate through the hierarchy to find the desired objects.

Each object class can be assigned its own properties or defining characteristics. An important feature of the hierarchical nature of the object-oriented data model is that each subclass inherits all the general properties of the classes above it in the hierarchy. Thus, referring to Fig. 5B.1, the accounts receivable subclass automatically possesses all the characteristics assigned to current assets. In turn, the current assets subclass possesses all the properties defined for the class called assets. Consequently, at each level only those properties or rules that are unique to that subclass need to be specified. This characteristic of inheriting the properties associated with nodes higher up in the hierarchy facilitates the quick design of new subschema in the object-oriented data model.

ADVANTAGES AND CRITICISMS OF OBJECT-ORIENTED DBMSs

One important property of object-oriented data bases is their ability to handle complex data types such as graphs, maps, sounds, and images, in addition to the

FIGURE 5B.1
Partial Schema for Object-Oriented Data Base

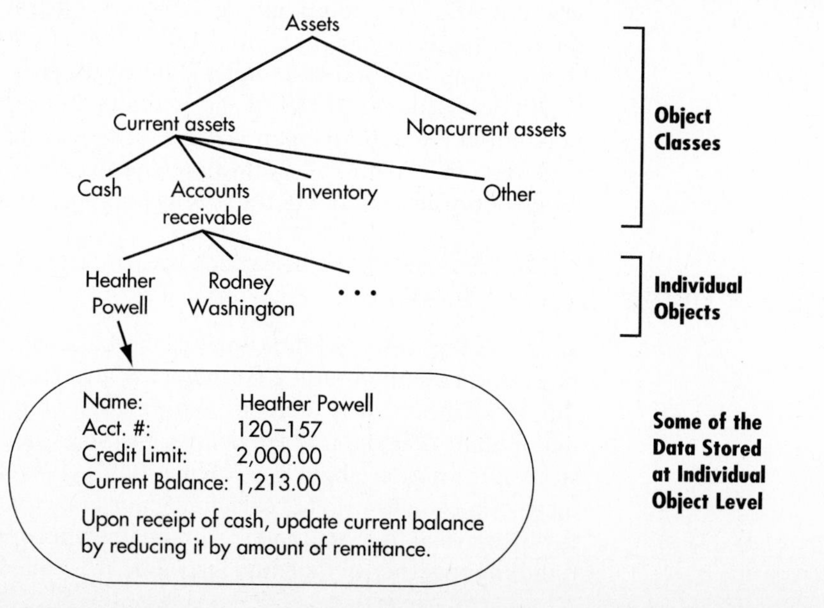

words and numbers that are manipulated and stored by the relational data model. Object-oriented DBMSs are especially useful for projects in which spatial relationships must be represented. For example, Ameritech, a Regional Bell Operating Company, uses an object-oriented DBMS to model its telecommunications network. This makes it easy to locate the source of problems. Florida Power & Light uses an object-oriented DBMS to help it design and lay out utility requirements in subdivisions.

Another important property of object-oriented DBMSs is that the reusability of object code speeds the development of new data base systems. Reusability is particularly important in fast-changing environments, such as financial services. Thus Fidelity Investments has used an object-oriented DBMS to model some of its new product offerings. Chemical Bank of New York used an object-oriented DBMS to build a data base system to track trading in derivatives when those new instruments began to appear.

There are some criticisms of the object-oriented data model, however. One criticism relates to the principle of encapsulation. Encapsulation permits object code to be reused in new applications, thereby improving programmer efficiency. If taken to the extreme, however, the principle of encapsulation can eliminate the ability to do ad hoc queries, because it limits the methods for accessing and manipulating an object to those that are predefined by the system designer when creating the object.

A second criticism concerns the explicit use of pointers in object-oriented DBMSs. This forces users to explicitly navigate through the data base to retrieve information. Proponents of the relational data model argue that this represents a step backward to a data base built to accommodate the programmer's, rather than the end-user's, view of the world. Finally, perhaps the most serious limitation of object-oriented DBMS is the lack of a standard, easy-to-use query language.

THE FUTURE OF RELATIONAL AND OBJECT-ORIENTED DBMSs

It is likely that businesses will continue to use both object-oriented and relational data bases. Some organizations currently use object-oriented DBMSs as the front end to integrate all organizational data, whether stored in a DBMS or in traditional files. For example, both the Federal Reserve and the Municipality of Metropolitan Toronto use an object-oriented DBMS to retrieve data currently stored in a variety of ISAM files, nonrelational DBMSs, and a number of different relational DBMS products. Using an object-oriented DBMS as an intelligent front-end is simpler and cheaper than trying to merge all those separate data stores into one unified data base.

It is also likely that the relational and object-oriented data models will merge. Indeed, software that combines the characteristics of both the relational and object-oriented data model is already beginning to appear. This product, called an object-oriented relational DBMS (ORDBMS), uses objects to support the storage and manipulation of complex data types while also maintaining the simplicity, flexibility, and easy-to-use query languages provided by the relational model. For example, Renaissance Technologies Corporation, in Stony Brook, New York, uses an ORDBMS for its stock trading data base. It chose an ORDBMS because a pure object-oriented DBMS would not have been compatible with its existing historical data base of stock price data, and a pure relational DBMS would have been too slow.

Thus businesses will likely use both object-oriented and relational DBMSs for the foreseeable future. Object-oriented DBMSs will be used to store and manipulate complex data types such as sound and images in tasks requiring such multimedia capabilities. Much routine business transaction data, however, consist of just words and numbers. Relational DBMSs have already proved to be ideal for handling such data and, therefore, will likely continue to be used for such applications.

KEY TERMS

object-oriented data model

object

encapsulation

ANSWERS TO CHAPTER QUIZ

1. b **3.** d **5.** d **7.** b **9.** a
2. b **4.** b **6.** b **8.** b **10.** c

CHAPTER 6

Data Modeling and Data Base Design

LEARNING OBJECTIVES

After studying this chapter, you should be able to

- Use the REA data model to design an AIS data base.
- Draw an Entity-Relationship (E-R) diagram of an AIS data base.
- Build a set of tables to implement an REA model of an AIS in a relational data base.
- Read an E-R diagram and explain what it reveals about the business activities and policies of the organization being modeled.

Integrative Case: S&S, Inc.

Ashton Fleming is frustrated. When S&S purchased a relational DBMS, it was with the intention that Ashton would have to design the data base himself, since Scott and Susan could not afford to hire an external consultant. Ashton had originally supported this plan. He had found it easy, with the help of the computer store salesperson, to build the sample data base that had convinced Scott and Susan to buy the package in the first place. Now, however, Ashton is learning that designing a relational data base for S&S is not as easy as the computer store salesperson made it seem. The software manuals did indeed provide "step-by-step" instructions for designing a relational data base, but they assumed a lot of background knowledge that Ashton did not possess. He wished that the instructor who had taught his accounting information systems class in college had spent more time on data bases.

While mulling over his situation, Ashton began to sort through his stack of mail from the AICPA and his state CPA society. Suddenly, he saw something that attracted his attention: a flyer announcing a two-day seminar on data modeling and data base design to be held next week at a downtown hotel. The seminar's objective was to teach accountants the basics on how to design a relational data base—for small businesses! Ashton immediately called and found that registration was still open. He then went to Susan and admitted he was having some difficulty in designing S&S's data base. Ashton explained the benefits he thought the seminar could provide and Susan agreed to send him.

Ashton hopes to have answers for the following questions by the end of the seminar:

1. What are the basic steps to follow when designing a data base?

2. When creating a relational data base, how exactly do you decide which attributes belong in which tables?

3. How can you document an AIS that is implemented as a relational data base?

INTRODUCTION

Like many companies, S&S is converting to the data base approach for storing its accounting data. In this chapter you will learn how to design and document a relational data base for an accounting information system. You will see that building a data base involves much more than simply learning the syntax of how to use a particular DBMS. As is the case for building reliable spreadsheet templates, building accurate data bases requires a great deal of careful planning and design *before* you even sit down at the computer.

This chapter focuses on one of the aspects of data base design with which accountants should be involved: data modeling. We introduce the REA accounting model and Entity-Relationship (E-R) diagrams and show how to use these tools to build a data model of an AIS. Then we describe how to implement the resulting data model in a relational data base. Keep in mind, however, that although our discussion focuses on relational data bases, the principles we discuss apply to building any type of data base.

THE REA DATA MODEL[1]

Data modeling is the process of defining a data base so that it faithfully represents all aspects of the organization, including its interactions with the external environment. As shown in Fig. 6.1, data modeling occurs during both the requirements analysis and design stages of data base design.

The **REA data model** is a conceptual modeling tool specifically designed to provide structure for designing AIS data bases. The REA data model provides structure in two ways: (1) by identifying what entities should be included in the AIS data base; and (2) by prescribing how to structure relationships among the entities in the AIS data base.

Types of Entities. Recall from Chapter 4 that an entity is any class of objects about which data is collected. The REA data model is so named because it classifies entities into three distinct categories: the *R*esources acquired and used by an organization, the *E*vents (business activities) engaged in by the organization, and the *A*gents participating in these events. **Resources** are defined as those things that have economic value to the organization. Cash, inventory,

---

[1] The material in this section is adapted from William E. McCarthy, "An Entity-Relationship View of Accounting Models," *The Accounting Review* (October 1979): 667–686; and William E. McCarthy, "The REA Accounting Model: A Generalized Framework for Accounting Systems in a Shared Data Environment," *The Accounting Review* (July 1982): 554–578.

FIGURE 6.1
Data Modeling in the Data Base Design Process

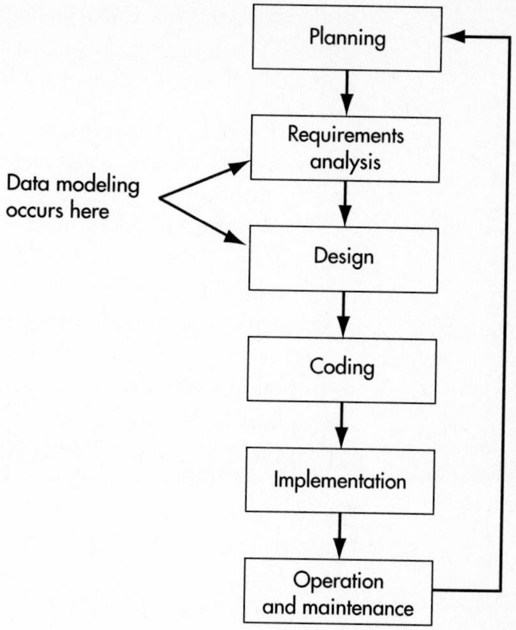

equipment, supplies, warehouses, factories, and land are examples of resources that would be included in an REA-based AIS data base.[2]

Events are the various business activities about which management wants to collect information for planning or control purposes.[3] Some events directly affect the quantity of resources. For example, the sales event decreases the quantity of inventory and the cash collections event increases the amount of cash. Other events, such as the activity of taking customer orders, do not directly change the quantity of a resource, but are necessary precursors to those events that do affect resources. Indeed, the taking customer order event provides important information that management can use to plan other activities, such as purchasing and production. Therefore, the AIS should be designed to explicitly capture and store information about both those events that directly alter the quantity of resources and those events, such as taking customer orders, that indirectly affect the quantity of resources.

---

[2] Recently, some researchers have proposed a fourth type of entity, which they call locations. Stores and warehouses would be examples of this fourth type of entity. Nevertheless, such location entities are usually also resources controlled by the organization. Therefore, the authors of this text see no compelling reason to create yet another type of entity, and model locations as resources.

[3] The discussion of events in this section is based on the work of Julie Smith David, "Three 'Events' that Define an REA Methodology for Systems Analysis, Design, and Implementation," working paper, Arizona State University, August 1997.

Agents are the third type of entity in the REA model. **Agents** are the people and organizations that participate in events and about whom information is desired for planning, control, and evaluation purposes. Thus employees, vendors, and customers are examples of agents that would appear in an REA model.

Structured Relationships. The REA data model prescribes a basic pattern for how the three types of entities (resources, events, and agents) should relate to one another. Figure 6.2 presents this basic pattern. Notice that every event entity is linked to a resource entity that it affects either directly or indirectly. Each event entity is also related to two agent entities. The internal agent is the employee who is responsible for the resource affected by that event; the external agent is the outside party to the transaction.

Figure 6.2 also shows that each event that changes the quantity of a resource is linked in a give-to-get duality relationship to another event that also changes the quantity of a resource. Such duality relationships reflect the basic business principle that organizations typically engage in activities that use up resources only in the hopes of acquiring some other resource in exchange. Indeed, Fig. 6.3 shows that each accounting cycle can be described in terms of such give-to-get duality relationships. For example, the sales event, which involves giving up (decreasing) inventory, is related to the cash collections event, which involves getting (increasing) cash.

ENTITY-RELATIONSHIP DIAGRAMS[4]

An **Entity-Relationship (E-R) diagram** is one method for portraying a data base schema. It is called an E-R diagram because it shows the various *entities*

[4] The material in this section is based P. Chen, "The Entity Relationship Model—Toward a Unified View of Data," *Transactions on Database Systems* (March 1976, 1:1): 9–36.

FIGURE 6.2

Basic REA Template

Source: Adapted from Fig. 6 (p. 566) in William E. McCarthy, "The REA Accounting Model: A Generalized Framework for Accounting Systems in a Shared Data Environment," *The Accounting Review* (July 1982): 554–578; and Fig. 1 (p. 35) in Cheryl L. Dunn and William E. McCarthy, "The REA Accounting Model: Intellectual Heritage and Prospects for Progress," *Journal of Information Systems* (Spring 1997): 31–51.

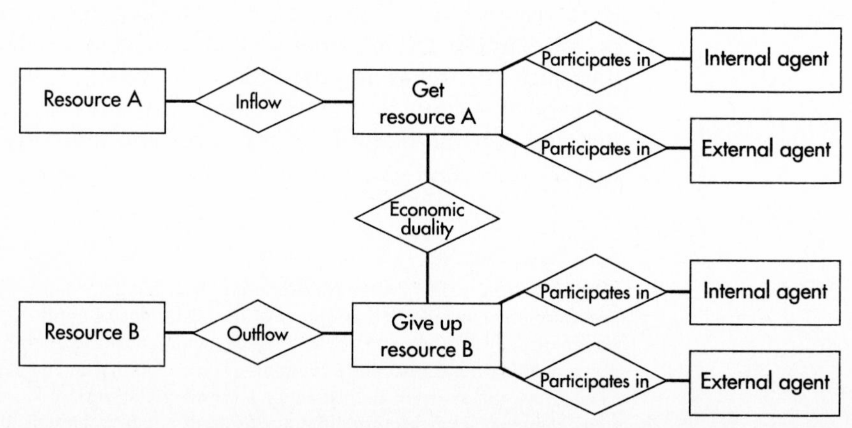

FIGURE 6.3
An AIS and Its Subsystems
Source: Adapted from classroom materials developed by Julie Smith David at Arizona State University, and based on ideas developed in the sources identified in footnote 1.

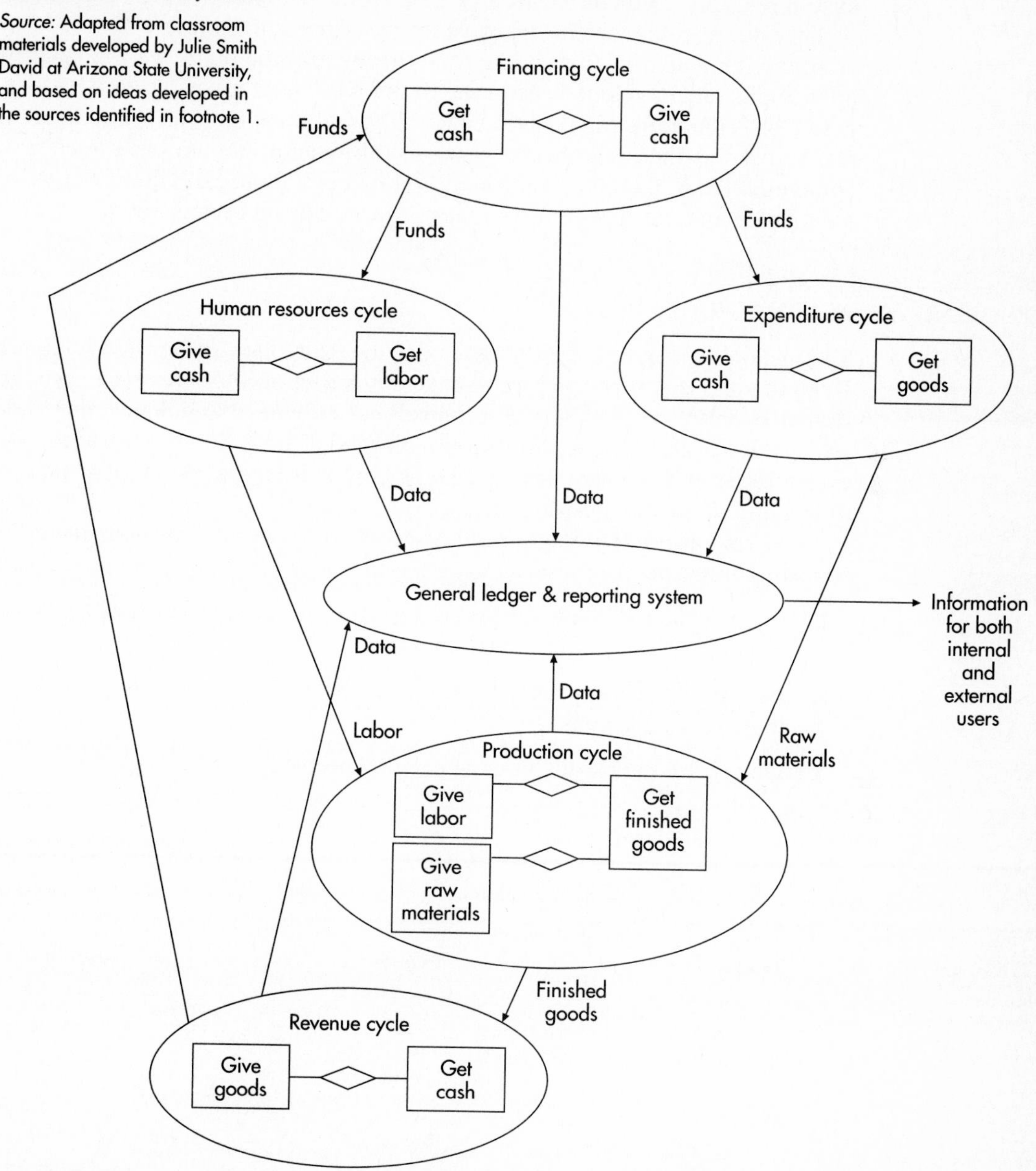

being modeled and the important *relationships* among them. In an E-R diagram, entities appear as rectangles and relationships between entities are represented as diamonds (see Fig. 6.4).

Figure 6.4 is an E-R diagram of part of S&S's revenue cycle. To simplify the figure, we have included only two events: (1) the sale of merchandise to customers, and (2) the collection of cash from customers. More complex E-R diagrams of each accounting cycle are presented in Chapters 12–16.

In the remainder of this chapter and throughout the book, we will refer to an E-R diagram developed according to the REA data model as an REA diagram. REA diagrams can be used in two different ways. First, an REA diagram can be used as the basis for designing a well-structured data base. Second, a completed REA diagram can be analyzed to learn about both the structure of a data base and the types of activities performed by an organization.

DEVELOPING AN REA DIAGRAM

This section explains how Ashton developed the REA diagram depicted in Fig. 6.4. Keep in mind that this diagram models only a part of S&S's revenue cycle. To design an entire AIS for S&S, Ashton will not only need to enhance this basic model, he will also have to develop similar models for S&S's other transaction cycles. Later in this chapter we will show how to integrate these separate diagrams into an enterprise-wide model.

Developing an REA diagram for a specific transaction cycle consists of the following three steps:

1. Identify the pair of events that reflect the basic economic exchange (give-to-get duality relationship) in that cycle.
2. Identify the resources affected by each event and the agents who participate in those events.
3. Determine the cardinalities of each relationship.

FIGURE 6.4
Simplified E-R Diagram of S&S Revenue Cycle: Retail Sales

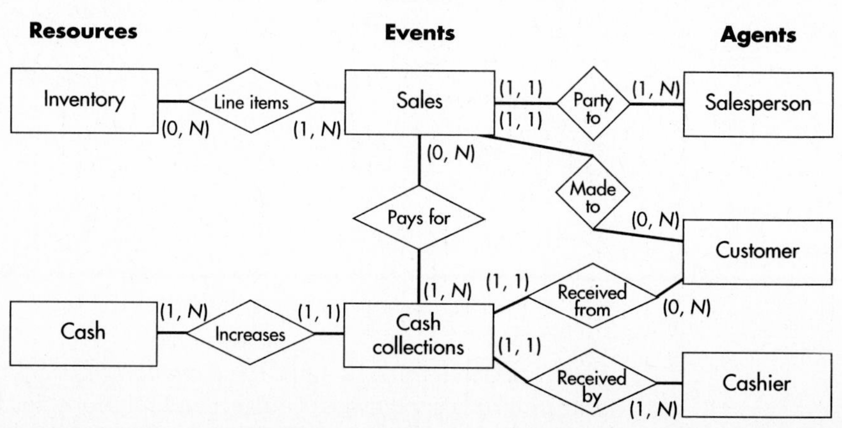

We now follow these three steps to show how Ashton developed Fig. 6.4 as a model of S&S's revenue cycle.

Step 1: Identify Economic Exchange Events

As shown in Fig. 6.2, the basic REA template consists of a pair of events, one that increases some resource and another that decreases some resource. The basic economic exchange in the revenue cycle involves the sale of goods or services and the subsequent receipt of cash in payment for those sales. Thus Ashton begins the REA diagram for S&S's revenue cycle by drawing the sales and cash collections events entities as rectangles, and the relationship between them as a diamond.

In drawing an REA diagram for an individual cycle, it is useful to divide the paper into three columns, one for each type of entity. Use the left column for resources, the middle column for events, and the right column for agents. Readability is further enhanced if the event entities are drawn from top to bottom corresponding to the sequence in which they occur. Thus Ashton begins to draw Fig. 6.4 by showing the sales event entity above the cash collections event entity in the middle column of the paper.[5]

It is also important to determine whether there are any other business events of interest in the cycle being modeled. For example, in the revenue cycle, many organizations may take orders from customers for items that either are currently out of stock or which may need to be specially produced. In such cases, the customer order event would be added to the REA diagram above the sales event. Information about business events is best obtained by interviewing management, because the set of activities that management is interested in planning, controlling, and evaluating differs for different organizations. To keep our example simple, assume that Scott and Susan have told Ashton that S&S does not take orders from customers and, therefore, that they are only interested in collecting information about the sales and cash collections events. Chapters 12–16 present more complex REA diagrams that include a number of additional business events in each cycle.

Step 2: Identify Resources and Agents

Once the events of interest have been specified, the resources that are affected by those events need to be identified. To continue our example, Ashton observed that the sales event involves the disposal of inventory and that the cash collections event involves the acquisition of cash. Thus he added the inventory and cash entities in the resources column and drew the relationships between those entities and the events that affected them.

[5] Placement conventions, such as the use of columns and sequential ordering of events, are not *required* in the REA model to design a data base. We suggest these rules only because following them often simplifies the process of drawing an REA diagram and produces REA diagrams that are easier to read.

What about accounts receivable? It is not included, because accounts receivable does not meet the REA data model's definition of a resource. Accounts receivable is not an independent object, but simply represents a timing difference between two events: sales and cash collections. Consequently, if data about both sales and cash collections is already stored in the data base, there is no need to redundantly store information about accounts receivable. Later, we will explain how to extract information about accounts receivable from an AIS data base built using the REA data model.

After specifying the resources affected by each event, the next step is to identify the agents who participate in those events. There will always be at least one internal agent (i.e., employee) and, in most cases, an external agent (i.e., customer or vendor) involved in each event. In the case of S&S's revenue cycle, customers and salespersons participate in the sales event; customers and the cashiers participate in the cash collection event. Thus Ashton included three agent entities in the REA diagram of S&S's revenue cycle: salespersons, customers, and cashiers. He then added relationships to indicate which agents participated in which events. To reduce clutter, he did not draw multiple copies of the customer entity.[6]

It is important to understand that the agents in an REA data model represent *functions,* not specific people. Thus, in Fig. 6.4, Ashton modeled both the salesperson and cashier agents as separate entities. It is possible, however, that the same person may fill both roles. For example, in a cash sale, the salesperson may also act as the cashier and collect payment from the customer. The REA diagram would still include two agents to model this situation, however.

Finally, add any other relationships of interest between entities. The REA model requires that each event be linked to at least one resource and to at least two agents. This information needs to be supplemented by interviews with management to identify other possible relationships of interest. For example, if the organization assigns customers to specific salespeople, in order to provide customized service, then a direct relationship between the salesperson and customer entities would be added.

Step 3: Specify Cardinalities

At this point, Ashton's REA diagram of S&S's revenue cycle looks like Fig. 6.5. All that remains is to add information about cardinalities. (Remember that to keep our example simple, we have focused on only a part of the revenue cycle; a complete data model would include many additional entities—deliveries, repairs, delivery staff, banks, etc.).

The **cardinality** of a relationship indicates how many occurrences of one entity in the relationship can be linked to a single occurrence of the other entity in the relationship. To better understand this, it helps to think in terms of the REA diagram being implemented in a relational data base.[7] In a relational data base, each entity would be implemented as a table. In this case, the cardinalities

---

[6] As the number of entities in an REA diagram increases, a point may be reached where the diagram is easier to read if there are multiple copies of the same entity.

[7] The REA data model can be used to design either relational or object-oriented data bases.

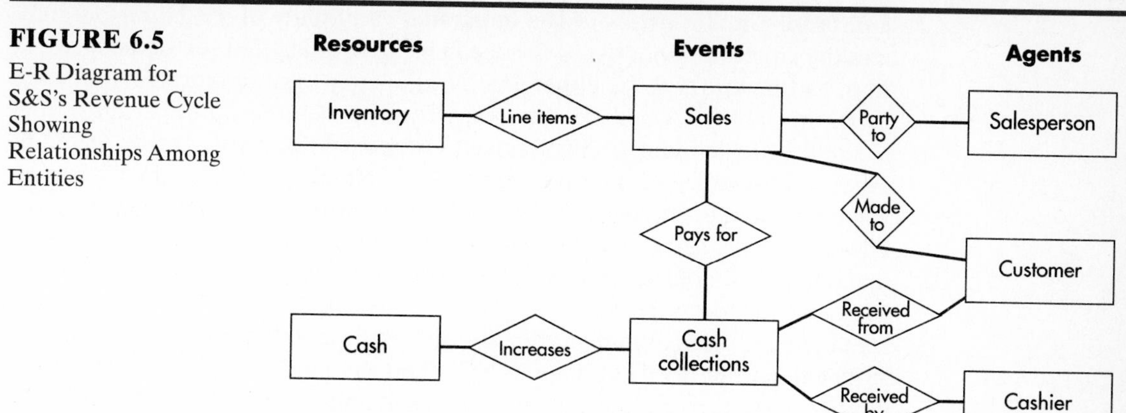

FIGURE 6.5
E-R Diagram for S&S's Revenue Cycle Showing Relationships Among Entities

then provide information about how many rows in the table on the other side of a relationship can be linked to each row in a given table.

Consider the relationship between sales and customers depicted in Fig. 6.4. The cardinality pair to the right of the sales entity indicates how many customers may participate in a single sales transaction; conversely, the cardinality pair to the left of the customer entity indicates the number of sales events that can be linked to a specific customer. Cardinalities are often expressed as a pair of numbers (see Fig. 6.4). The first number is called the minimum cardinality of the relationship; the second number is called the maximum cardinality.

Minimum Cardinalities. The **minimum cardinality** of a relationship indicates the fewest number of rows that can be involved in that relationship. Minimum cardinalities can be either 0 or 1. A minimum cardinality of zero means that each occurrence of the entity on the other side of the relationship (e.g., each row in that table) need not be linked to any occurrences of the entity on this side of the relationship. Thus, in Fig. 6.4, the minimum cardinality of zero in the (0,*N*) cardinality pair to the left of the customer entity in the customer–sales relationship indicates that a given customer (row in the customer table) need not be linked to any sales events (rows in the sales table). In other words, S&S's data base contains information about both current and *potential* customers.

Minimum cardinalities of zero are common for relationships between two temporally linked events, because at any given point in time the second event in the pair may not yet have occurred. Thus, in Fig. 6.4, the minimum cardinality below the sales event entity is zero; this indicates that there are likely to be some credit sales that are not yet paid for.

A minimum cardinality of 1 indicates that each instance of that entity *must* be associated with at least one instance of the other entity. For example, in Fig. 6.4 the minimum cardinality below the sales entity in the sales–customer relationship is represented as being 1. This reflects the general business rule that each sales event must be associated with some specific customer (either a person or an organization) who is responsible for paying for that purchase.

Maximum Cardinalities. The **maximum cardinality** of a relationship indicates the largest number of rows that can be involved in that relationship. Maximum cardinalities can be either 1 or *N;* the latter symbol indicates that each row in this table *may* be linked to many rows in the other table.[8] A maximum cardinality of one indicates that a given instance of that entity can be linked to *at most* one instance of the other entity. For example, in Fig. 6.4 the maximum cardinality next to the sales entity in the sales–customer relationship is 1. This reflects that a specific sales transaction can be associated with *only* one customer; S&S will hold some specific individual or organization legally responsible for paying for that sale.

In contrast, a maximum cardinality of *N* indicates that one instance of that entity can be, but does not have to be, linked to *more than one* instance of the other entity. Referring once again to Fig. 6.4, notice that the maximum cardinality next to the customer entity in the sales–customer relationship is *N*. This indicates that over time a given customer may, and hopefully will, participate in many different sales transactions with S&S.

Types of Relationships. Three basic types of relationships between entities are possible, depending on the *maximum* cardinality associated with each entity:

1. A one-to-one relationship exists when the maximum cardinality of each entity is 1 (Fig. 6.6A).
2. A one-to-many relationship exists when the maximum cardinality of one entity is 1 and the maximum cardinality of the other entity is *N* (Fig. 6.6B and C).
3. A many-to-many relationship exists when the maximum cardinality of both entities is *N* (Fig. 6.6D). (Many-to-many relationships are conventionally labeled as *M*:*N* instead of *N*:*N*.)

Figure 6.6 shows each of these different possible ways of modeling the relationship between the sales and cash collections events. Consider first Fig. 6.6A, which depicts a one-to-one (1:1) relationship. Note that each sale event (row in the sales table) is linked to *at most* one cash collection event. This would reflect a policy that customers are not allowed to make installment payments. Figure 6.6A also shows that each cash collection event is linked to *at most* one sale event. This indicates that customers must pay for each sales transaction separately.

A 1:1 relationship between sales and cash collections *may* model cash sales. Indeed, a minimum cardinality of one next to the sales event would indicate that all sales are cash sales. In Fig. 6.6A, however, the minimum cardinality next to the sales event is zero; this indicates that credit sales may also be made (a given sale may be linked to no cash collection event).

Now examine Fig. 6.6B and C, which depict two ways that one-to-many (1:*N*) relationships can occur. Figure 6.6B shows that each sales event may be

[8] Various authors use the symbols *n*, *, and ∞ to represent many.

FIGURE 6.6
Possible Cardinalities of the Sales–Cash Collections Relationship

A. One-to-One (1:1) Relationship

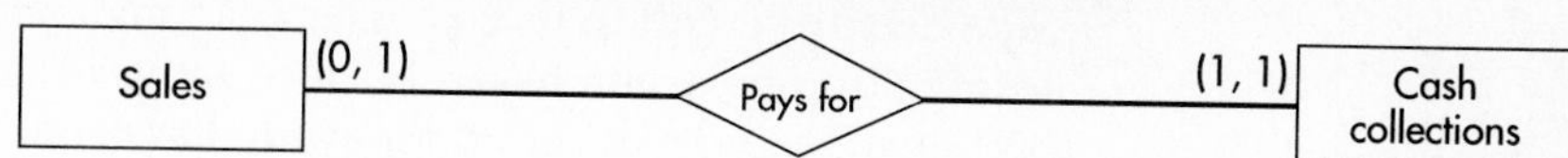

B. One-to-Many (1:*N*) Relationship Between Sales and Cash Collections

C. One-to-Many (1:*N*) Relationship Between Cash Collections and Sales

D. Many-to-Many (*M*:*N*) Relationship

linked to *many* cash collections events, but that each cash collection event is linked to at most one sales event. This indicates that customers *may* make installment payments (of course, they are not required to do so), but that each sales event must be paid for separately. In contrast, Fig. 6.6C shows that each sales event can be linked to at most one cash collection event, but that each cash collection event may be linked to many different sales events. This would reflect a policy that allowed customers to make one payment each month for all purchases made during that month, but did not allow them to make installment payments.

Finally, Fig. 6.6D depicts a many-to-many (*M*:*N*) relationship between the sales and cash collections events: each sales event may be linked to one or more cash collections events, and each cash collection event may be linked to one or more sales events. This reflects a situation where the organization makes some cash sales, makes some sales that are paid in installments, and also allows customers to pay for more than one sale with a single remittance.

Specifying Cardinalities. Cardinalities are not arbitrarily chosen by the data base designer. Instead, they reflect facts about the organization being modeled and its business practices obtained during the requirements analysis stage of the data base design process. Ashton used two types of information to add the cardinalities depicted in Fig. 6.4:

1. *Knowledge about the business policies followed by the company being modeled.* Figure 6.6 showed the three different possible ways to describe the relationship between the sales and cash collection events. To model

this relationship for a given company accurately, the data modeler must understand how that company conducts its business. Ashton knows that S&S extends credit to its customers and mails them monthly statements listing all unpaid purchases. He also knows that many customers send S&S one check to cover all their purchases during a given time period. Thus one cash receipt could be linked to many different sales events. S&S also allows its customers to make installment payments on large purchases. This means that a given sales event could be connected to more than one cash receipt. All of this information led Ashton to model the relationship between the sales and cash collections events as being many-to-many.

2. *General business knowledge.* Some cardinalities reflect general business policies common to most organizations. For example, Ashton modeled the relationship between customers and sales as being one-to-many. This reflects the fact that, although a specific customer can participate in many sales transactions over time, each sale is made to some *particular* customer or company who is responsible for paying for that sale. Ashton modeled the relationship between customers and cash collections similarly, and for the same reasons: a specific customer can send in many different payments, but a given remittance comes from just one specific customer.

Figure 6.4 shows what Ashton's REA diagram for S&S's revenue cycle looked like after adding information about cardinalities. In the next section, we explain how to implement this model in a relational data base.

IMPLEMENTING AN REA DIAGRAM IN A RELATIONAL DATA BASE

Once an REA diagram has been developed, it can be used to design a well-structured relational data base. A well-structured relational data base is one that satisfies the normalization requirements discussed in Chapter 5 and, consequently, is not subject to update, insert, and delete anomaly problems.

Step 1: Create Tables for Each Entity and Many-to-Many Relationship

A properly normalized relational data base has a table for each entity and each many-to-many relationship. In the case of S&S's revenue cycle, nine tables would be created from the REA diagram shown in Fig. 6.4: one for each of the seven entities (inventory, sales, salesperson, customer, cashier, cash collections, and cash) and one for each of the many-to-many relationships (sales–inventory, and sales–cash collections).

The title of each table should be the same as the name of the entity it represents. Tables representing many-to-many relationships, however, are often titled by joining the names of the two entities that are linked. Thus, in terms of Fig. 6.4, we would create tables labeled "sales–inventory" and "sales–cash collections" to represent the many-to-many relationships between sales and inventory, and sales and cash collections, respectively.

Step 2: Identify Attributes for Each Table

The next step is to identify the attributes to include in each table. Recall from Chapter 5 that each table must have a primary key that uniquely identifies each row in that table. In addition to the primary key, most relational tables will also contain other attributes.

Primary Keys. Companies often create numeric identifiers that uniquely identify specific resources, events, and agents; these numeric identifiers are good candidates for primary keys. For example, S&S might use invoice number as the primary key of the sales table and customer number as the primary key of the customer table.

Usually, the primary key of a table representing an entity is a single attribute. The primary key for many-to-many relationship tables, however, always consists of two attributes, representing the primary keys of each entity linked in that relationship. For example, the primary key of the sales–inventory table would consist of both the invoice number (the primary key of the sales entity) and item number (the primary key of the inventory entity). Such multiple-attribute primary keys are called **concatenated keys.**

Other Attributes. Additional attributes are included in each table to satisfy transaction processing requirements and management's information needs. Table 6.1 shows the attributes assigned to the various tables that were created to implement S&S's revenue cycle REA diagram. Some of these attributes, such as the date and amount of each sale, are necessary for complete and accurate transaction processing and the production of financial statements and managerial reports. Other attributes are stored because they facilitate the effective management of an organization's resources, events, and agents. For example, Scott and Susan can use data about the time when each sales transaction occurs to design staff work schedules.

Chapter 5 discussed several rules that must be followed for placing attributes in tables (refer to pp. 151-153). That discussion can be summarized in the following two principles:

1. Every attribute in a table must be single-valued.
2. Every attribute in a table must describe a characteristic of the object identified by the primary key, or it must be a foreign key.

The assignment of attributes to the relational tables shown in Table 6.1 follows both of these principles. It is easy to verify that every attribute in every row of every table has only one data value. It should also be clear how the placement of nonkey attributes in each of the seven entity tables satisfies the second principle.

Nonkey Attributes in Many-to-Many Relationship Tables. Let us now examine more closely the placement of the nonkey attributes in each of the many-to-many tables to see why they *must* be stored in those tables. Consider first the sales–cash collections table. Recall that S&S allows its customers to make multiple purchases on credit and to make installment payments on their outstanding balances. Thus one cash collection may need to be applied to several different

TABLE 6.1 Relational Tables for S&S's Revenue Cycle: Retail Sales

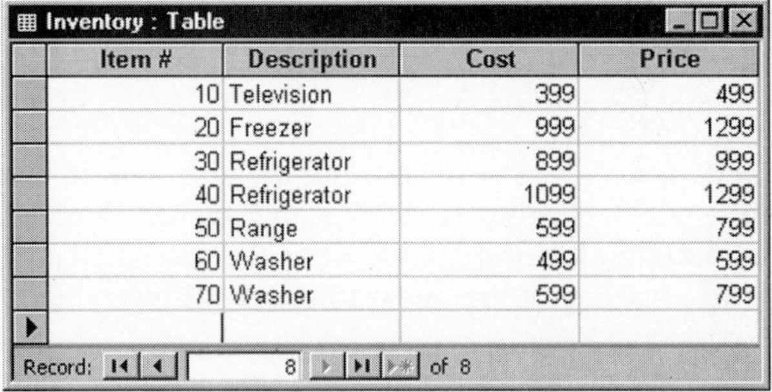

Inventory : Table

Item #	Description	Cost	Price
10	Television	399	499
20	Freezer	999	1299
30	Refrigerator	899	999
40	Refrigerator	1099	1299
50	Range	599	799
60	Washer	499	599
70	Washer	599	799

Record: 8 of 8

Sales-Inventory : Table

Invoice #	Item #	Quantity Sold	Replacement	Age
101	10	3	Yes	6
101	30	1	Yes	7
102	60	1	No	0
103	20	1	Yes	12
103	30	2	Yes	7
103	60	1	Yes	10
104	40	3	No	0
105	30	1	Yes	6
105	60	1	No	0

Record: 10 of 10

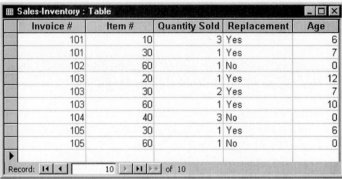

Sales : Table

Invoice #	Date	Salesperson #	Customer #	Amount	Time
101	10/9/97	101	10001	2655	930
102	10/10/97	102	10002	625	1045
103	10/10/97	101	10004	4295	1535
104	10/12/97	101	10001	4295	1230
105	10/13/97	102	10003	1735	1415

Record: 6 of 6

Salesperson : Table

Employee #	Name	Date hired	Salary
101	J. Buck	9/23/82	33000
102	M. Shannon	9/25/87	30000

Record: 3 of 3

Cashier : Table

Employee #	Name	Date hired	Salary
121	O. Smith	9/10/85	26000
122	T. Pagnozzi	5/18/75	32000

Record: 3 of 3

continued

TABLE 6.1 Continued

Sales-Cash Collections : Table

Invoice #	Remittance #	Amount
101	122	2655
103	123	4295
104	122	4295

Record: 4 of 4

Cash : Table

Account #	Type	Location
101	Checking	First Bank
102	Savings	First Bank

Record: 3 of 3

Cash_Collections : Table

Remittance #	Date	Customer #	Cashier #	Amount	Account #
122	10/28/97	10001	121	6950	101
123	10/31/97	10004	122	4295	101

Record: 3 of 3

Customer : Table

Customer #	Name	Street	City	State	Credit limit
10001	E. Banks	14 First	Chicago	IL	10000
10002	R. Santo	10 Third	St. Louis	MO	6000
10003	B. Williams	33 Left	Chicago	IL	7500
10004	G. Beckert	12 Second	Chicago	IL	3500

Record: 5 of 5

invoices (sales transactions). Therefore, the attribute "amount applied" cannot be placed in the cash collections table because it can have more than one value, which would violate a basic principle of normalization. Instead, the amount applied is a fact about the combination of a specific cash collection event and a specific sales event. Therefore, it belongs in the *M:N* table linking those events.

Now examine the sales–inventory table. S&S allows customers to buy several different kinds of appliances in one transaction. Each row in the sales–inventory table contains information about a line item in an invoice. Although many of S&S's sales will involve just one of each appliance bought, some customers, such as apartment owners or builders, may buy in larger quantities. Consequently, S&S needs to record the quantity sold of each item in a given sales transaction. Thus quantity sold is an attribute of each line item on a sales invoice and, therefore, belongs in the many-to-many table that stores data about those line items.

Price Data. Notice that in Table 6.1 price is stored as an attribute of the inventory table. This is because S&S, like most retail businesses, charges the same price to all customers. Thus, if price were included in the sales–inventory table, the same value would be stored many times.

But what about quantity discounts? In our example, we are assuming that S&S does not offer quantity discounts. If they did, however, the proper place to store the discount price attribute would depend on the basis for calculating the discount. If there was one discount rate for sales above a certain quantity, that attribute could be stored in the inventory table. If, however, there were a wide range of discount prices, then the actual selling price might have to be included as an attribute of the sales–inventory table.

In fact, prices of items usually do change over time. The price stored in the inventory table in Table 6.1 is the *current* selling price. There are several options for storing information about price changes over time. The choice of a particular approach is beyond the scope of this chapter. The interested reader is referred to any popular textbook on data base design for a discussion of such advanced topics.

Cumulative Data. What about cumulative data, like quantity on hand or cash account balances? It is not necessary to store these items separately in the data base, because the system can readily compute them whenever necessary. For example, information about the quantity sold for each item is stored in the sales–inventory table. Information about quantities purchased would be stored in a similar table linking purchases and inventory. To determine quantity on hand, the AIS could simply calculate the difference between the quantity sold and the quantity purchased. In a similar manner, the cash collections and cash disbursements tables contain information about cash inflows and outflows. The AIS can calculate the difference to display the current balance in the cash account.

Often, however, cumulative totals and balances are explicitly stored in order to improve response time to queries. That is why Table 6.1 shows several such summary attributes in appropriate tables. This is a compromise due to current technological limitations, and may not need to be made in the future as computer processing power and speed continue to increase.

Step 3: Implement One-to-One and One-to-Many Relationships

Many-to-many relationships *must* be implemented as separate tables in order to have a properly normalized relational data base. Both one-to-one and one-to-many relationships can also be implemented as separate tables, but they can also be implemented by means of foreign keys. Recall from Chapter 4 that a foreign key is an attribute of one entity that is itself the primary key of another entity. For example, if the attribute customer #, which is the primary key of the customer table, is also included as an attribute in the sales table, it would be labeled a foreign key in the sales table.

One-to-One Relationships. In a relational data base, one-to-one relationships between entities can be implemented by including the primary key of one entity as a foreign key in the table representing the other entity. For purposes of normalization, the choice of table in which to place the foreign key is arbitrary. Careful analysis of the minimum cardinalities of the relationship, however, may suggest which approach is likely to be more efficient.

Consider the 1:1 relationship between sales and cash collections depicted in Fig. 6.6A. The minimum cardinality for the sales event is zero, indicating the existence of credit sales, and the minimum cardinality for the cash collections event is one, indicating that cash collections only occur after a sale has been made (i.e., there are no advance deposits). In this case, including invoice number as a foreign key in the cash collections event may be more efficient, because then only that one table would have to accessed and updated to process data about the cash collection event. Moreover, for 1:1 relationships between two temporally related events, including the primary key of the event that occurs first as a foreign key in the event that occurs second may improve internal control. We will talk more about internal controls later, in Parts II and III of this text.

One-to-Many Relationships. As with one-to-one relationships, one-to-many relationships can be also implemented in relational data bases by means of foreign keys. To do this, the primary key of the entity participating once in the relationship appears as a foreign key in the table of the entity that participates many times in that relationship. For example, in Table 6.1 the primary keys of the salesperson and customer tables are included as foreign keys in the sales table. Similarly, the primary keys of the cash, customer, and cashier tables are included as foreign keys in the cash collections table.

A potential exception to this general rule for implementing one-to-many relationships may occur if the relationship involves two temporally related event entities, *and* the event that normally occurs first is also the one that can participate many times in that relationship. In that case, implementing the relationship as a separate table may improve internal control.

At this point, Ashton has almost completed the design of S&S's revenue cycle data base. All that remains is to document the structure of the data base in the data dictionary. Some of that information, especially information about the attributes associated with each entity and relationship, can then be included in the REA diagram, as shown in Fig. 6.7.

USING REA DIAGRAMS

In the previous sections, we used the REA data model to guide the design of an AIS. In that process, we developed an REA diagram for S&S. In this section, we discuss several uses of such completed REA diagrams.

Documentation

REA diagrams complement the other forms of documentation discussed in Chapter 3. They are especially useful, however, for documenting advanced AIS built using data bases. REA diagrams provide two important types of information about a data base AIS that are not reflected in other forms of documentation: information about the relationships among data items, and information about the organization's business practices.

FIGURE 6.7
Simplified E-R Diagram of S&S Revenue Cycle: Retail Sales

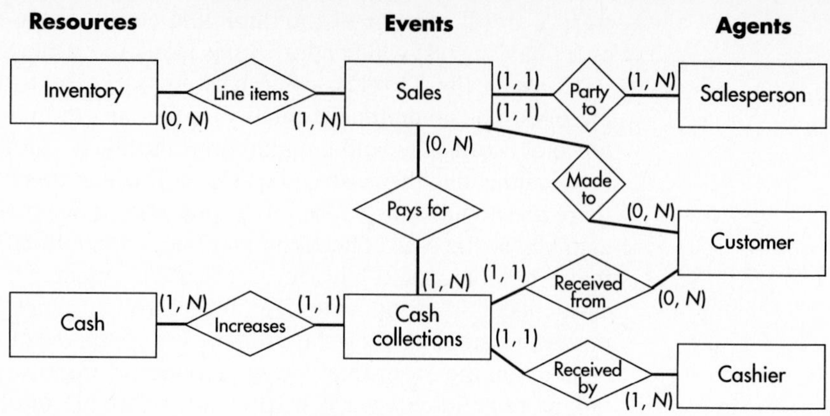

Table Name	**Contents (primary key**, *foreign keys*, other attributes)
Inventory	**Item #**, description, cost, price
Sales	**Invoice #**, *salesperson #*, *customer #*, date, amount, time
Salesperson	**Employee #**, name, date hired, salary
Cashier	**Employee #**, name, date hired, salary
Customer	**Customer #**, name, street, city, state, credit limit
Cash	**Account #**, type, location
Cash collections	**Remittance #**, *customer #*, *cashier #*, *account #*, date, amount
Sales—Inventory	**Invoice #**, **item #**, quantity sold, replacement, age
Sales—Cash collections	**Invoice #**, **remittance #**, amount

Information About Data Base Content. REA diagrams explicitly depict the relationships among the various data items that are stored in the accounting data base. In contrast, flowcharts only show which files exist and describe their basic characteristics, such as how they are organized (alphabetical, numerical, etc.) and stored (paper files, magnetic disk, etc.). Similarly, data flow diagrams (DFDs) describe the contents of each file in the system, but do not explicitly show how those files relate to one another. As Fig. 6.7 shows, however, REA diagrams explicitly show how the various items stored in the data base relate to one another.

Information About Business Practices. The cardinalities in REA diagrams provide useful information about the nature of the company being modeled and the business policies that it follows. For example, Fig. 6.7 indicates that S&S extends credit to its customers and also allows them to make installment payments on their purchases. It also indicates that S&S sells mass-produced goods.

Correctly interpreting what the cardinalities in an REA diagram mean requires understanding exactly what an occurrence of each entity represents. This is usually easy for both agent and event entities. Each occurrence of an agent entity represents a specific person or organization. Similarly, each occurrence of an event entity represents a specific business activity or transaction. For example, each occurrence of the sales event represents a specific sales transaction.

Understanding what each occurrence of a resource entity represents, however, can sometimes be more difficult. Consider inventory, for example. An individual occurrence of this entity might represent either a specific physical object or a class of objects, depending on the type of product being sold. Notice that information about the attributes stored with each entity and relationship is often included in REA diagrams (see Fig. 6.7). This information can be used to interpret what a resource entity, such as inventory, represents. In Fig. 6.7, the list of attributes for inventory includes quantity on hand. This indicates that each row in the inventory table represents a *kind* of inventory, not an individual object. Thus one row in S&S's inventory table may store data about a specific brand of a 60-inch big-screen TV, whereas another row may store data about a specific model of a DVD player. S&S would want to know how many of each of these products it has on hand; consequently, the attribute quantity on hand would be found in its inventory table.

In contrast, consider a dealer of rare art. Each product is unique; thus, each row in the inventory table would store data about a specific painting, sculpture, or other work of art. Consequently, the REA diagram for a rare art dealer would probably indicate that the attribute quantity on hand is not included in the inventory table. (Do you understand why not?)

We have already explained the meaning of most of the relationship cardinalities depicted in Fig. 6.7. Thus you should be able to explain how that REA diagram reveals that S&S

- Sells mass-produced items.
- Extends credit to its customers and allows them to either pay for several sales with one remittance or to make installment payments.
- Collects and stores data about potential customers.

Let us now examine the relationship between sales and inventory. This relationship is called line items and represents the fact that each sale consists of one or more items of merchandise, each of which appears as a separate line item on the sales invoice. In addition, the quantity sold indicates that a customer may buy more than one of a given item. Figure 6.7 also shows that two agents (a salesperson and a customer) must participate in any valid sales event.

Now examine the relationship between cash and cash collections. Each row in the cash entity represents a specific account. Thus one row stores data about S&S's regular checking account, another about its payroll account, another about a money market investment account, and so on. Figure 6.7 models the relationship between cash and cash collections as being one-to-many: all cash collections are deposited into the same account.

Finally, the cardinalities in an REA diagram provide information about business controls. For example, in Fig. 6.7 the minimum cardinality associated with the sales event in the sales–customer relationship is 1. This means that a sales transaction cannot be recorded unless the identity of the customer is also recorded. Part II of this text discusses the concept of internal control in more detail. In Part III of this text, where we discuss each cycle in more detail, we will discuss other examples of information about business controls that can be depicted in REA diagrams.

Organizational Specificity of REA Diagrams

Although the development of the REA diagram for S&S's revenue cycle may seem to have been fairly straightforward and intuitive, data modeling can be a complex and repetitive process. One common source of difficulty is the use of different terminology by various users. Therefore, Focus 6.1 highlights the importance of involving the eventual users of the system in the data modeling process.

In addition, keep in mind that an REA diagram is unique to the organization being modeled. S&S, for example, does not accept orders from customers. Instead, customers can only purchase whatever items are currently in stock. Consequently, S&S's revenue cycle includes only two basic events: sales and cash collections. In contrast, mail order companies take customer orders (by phone, Internet, mail, etc.), pick the items in the warehouse, and then ship the order to the customer. Therefore, the REA diagram for the revenue cycle of such companies would include four events: take order, fill order, ship order, and cash collections. Moreover, whereas an REA diagram for a retail organization like S&S only has one inventory entity, the REA diagram for a manufacturer will likely include separate entities for raw materials and finished goods inventories. Finally, because S&S sells mass-produced goods, its REA diagram models the relationship between sales and inventory as being many-to-many. In contrast, the REA diagram for a rare art dealer would depict the relationship between sales and inventory as being one-to-many, because although several different pieces of art may be sold as part of a single transaction, each piece of art is unique and, therefore, can be sold only once.

Extracting Information from the AIS

A completed REA diagram also serves as a useful guide for querying an AIS data base. We will illustrate this by referring to Table 6.1 and Fig. 6.7, which depict the data base AIS Ashton developed for S&S's revenue cycle using the REA data model. At first glance, it may appear that a number of elements found in a traditional AIS, such as journals, ledgers, and information about claims like accounts receivable, are missing. In reality, all that information is present, but it is stored in a different format.

Journals and Ledgers. Queries can be used to generate journals and ledgers from a relational data base built on the REA model. Let us consider journals first. The information normally found in a journal is stored in the tables used to record data about events. For example, a sales journal can be produced by writing a query that displays the appropriate entries in the sales table for a given period of time. A query can be written to display every entry in the sales table; this would produce a list of all sales events, both credit and cash sales. Traditionally, however, sales journals are used to record all *credit* sales. Therefore, the query to produce a credit sales journal would have to include both the sales and cash collections tables. The logic of the query would include restricting the output to display only those sales that are not linked to a corresponding cash collection event that occurred on the same day as the sale. Similar processes can be followed to produce cash collections, purchases, or cash disbursements journals.

FOCUS 6.1 Why Involve Users in Data Modeling?

DATA MODELING is not an easy task, as Hewlett-Packard learned when it began designing a new data base for its accounting and finance function. A major problem was that the same term meant different things to different people. For example, accounting used the term "orders" to refer to the total dollar amount of orders per time period, whereas the sales department used the same term to refer to individual customer orders. Moreover, such confusions existed even within the accounting and finance function. For example, the reporting group used the term "product" to refer to any good currently sold to customers. Thus the primary key for this entity was product number. In contrast, the forecasting group used the same term to refer to goods that were often still in the planning stage and that, therefore, did not even have a product number assigned yet.

To overcome these problems, Hewlett-Packard had to get the different user groups to actively participate in the data modeling process. The first step was to convince all users of the need for and benefits of creating a data model for their function. Then it was necessary to carefully define the scope of the modeling effort. Hewlett-Packard found that the time invested in these early steps was well worth the effort, because it facilitated the activities of clarifying definitions and developing attribute lists that took place later in the process. The latter activity was an iterative affair involving many revisions. Documentation was critical to this process. Each member of the modeling team and user groups had copies of the proposed lists, which made it easier to spot inconsistencies in definitions.

Hewlett-Packard credits the data modeling approach as contributing significantly to the overall success of the project. Data modeling allowed the participants to concentrate first on understanding the essential business characteristics of the new system, instead of getting bogged down in specifying the contents of relational tables. This helped them to identify and resolve conflicting viewpoints early in the process, and it paved the way for eventual acceptance of the resulting system. The key step, however, was in getting the different user groups to actively participate in the data modeling process. Otherwise, it is likely that the resulting data model would not have been accurate, or widely accepted.

Source: From C. Randall Byers and Lysa Beltz, "Financial Data Modeling at Hewlett-Packard," *Journal of Systems Management* (January 1994): 28–33.

The information traditionally contained in ledgers is often stored in a relational data base in a combination of resource and event tables. Let us consider first one of the most common types of subsidiary ledgers: accounts receivable. Examination of Table 6.1 and Fig. 6.7 does not show any explicit table called accounts receivable. The reason for this is that accounts receivable does not satisfy the REA model's definition of a resource. It is not an independent entity; rather, it represents an imbalance at any point in time between credit sales and cash collections. Thus accounts receivable does not need to be stored explicitly in the data base. Instead, the total amount of accounts receivable can be derived by calculating the total amount of sales for which cash collections have not yet occurred. Table 6.2 describes some of the ways to do this, depending on the cardinality of the relationship between the sales and cash collections events and how that relationship is implemented.

The query logic presented in Table 6.2 derives the *total* amount of accounts receivable. To derive account balances for each customer, the query logic needs to be expanded to reference the customer table and to include the appropriate command (e.g., GROUP BY in SQL) to perform the calculations separately for each customer. The result of such a query would be a table with a row for

TABLE 6.2 Query Logic for Calculating Total Accounts Receivable Under Various Relationship Cardinality Scenarios

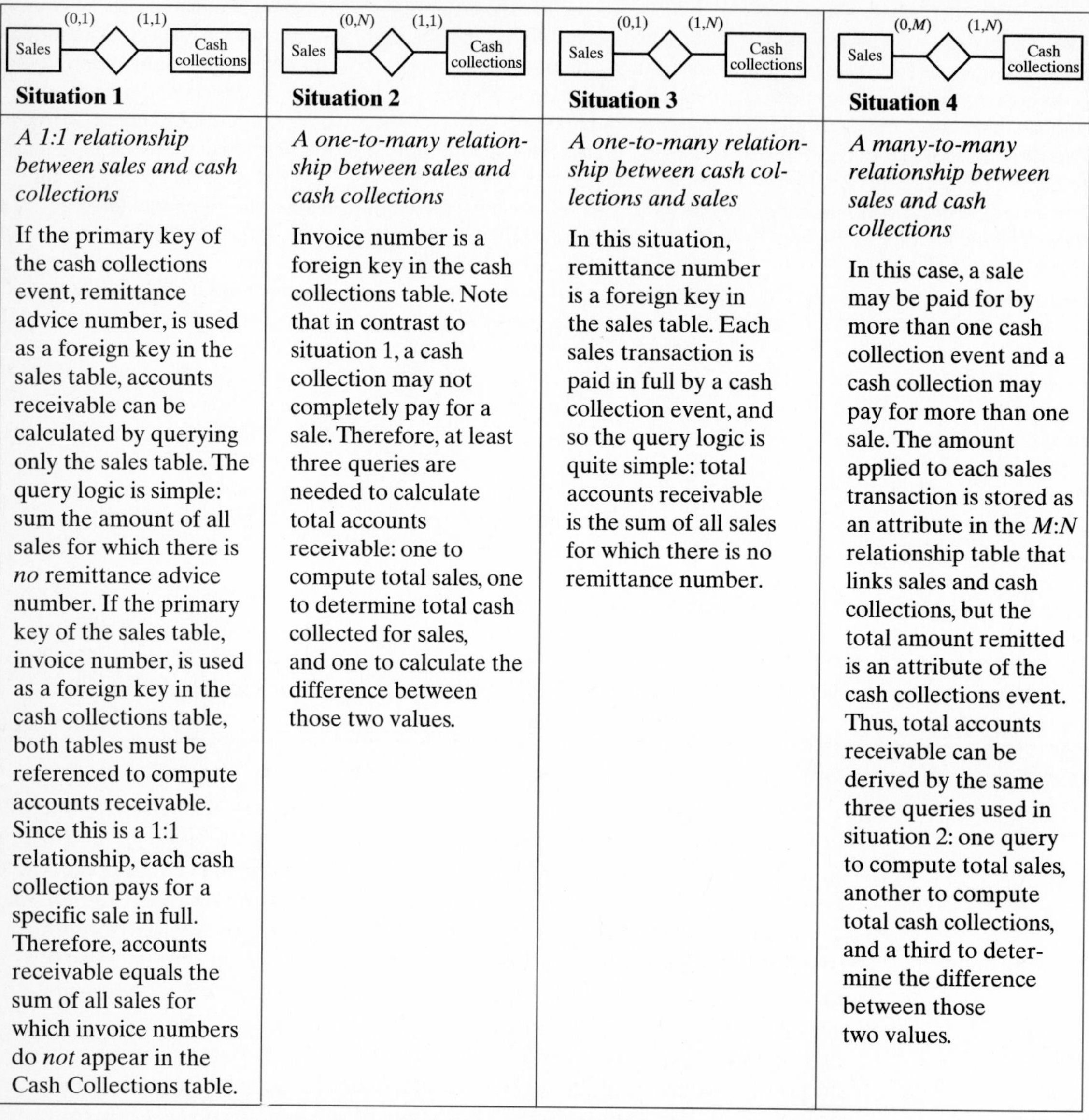

Sales (0,1) — (1,1) Cash collections **Situation 1**	Sales (0,*N*) — (1,1) Cash collections **Situation 2**	Sales (0,1) — (1,*N*) Cash collections **Situation 3**	Sales (0,*M*) — (1,*N*) Cash collections **Situation 4**
A 1:1 relationship between sales and cash collections If the primary key of the cash collections event, remittance advice number, is used as a foreign key in the sales table, accounts receivable can be calculated by querying only the sales table. The query logic is simple: sum the amount of all sales for which there is *no* remittance advice number. If the primary key of the sales table, invoice number, is used as a foreign key in the cash collections table, both tables must be referenced to compute accounts receivable. Since this is a 1:1 relationship, each cash collection pays for a specific sale in full. Therefore, accounts receivable equals the sum of all sales for which invoice numbers do *not* appear in the Cash Collections table.	*A one-to-many relationship between sales and cash collections* Invoice number is a foreign key in the cash collections table. Note that in contrast to situation 1, a cash collection may not completely pay for a sale. Therefore, at least three queries are needed to calculate total accounts receivable: one to compute total sales, one to determine total cash collected for sales, and one to calculate the difference between those two values.	*A one-to-many relationship between cash collections and sales* In this situation, remittance number is a foreign key in the sales table. Each sales transaction is paid in full by a cash collection event, and so the query logic is quite simple: total accounts receivable is the sum of all sales for which there is no remittance number.	*A many-to-many relationship between sales and cash collections* In this case, a sale may be paid for by more than one cash collection event and a cash collection may pay for more than one sale. The amount applied to each sales transaction is stored as an attribute in the *M*:*N* relationship table that links sales and cash collections, but the total amount remitted is an attribute of the cash collections event. Thus, total accounts receivable can be derived by the same three queries used in situation 2: one query to compute total sales, another to compute total cash collections, and a third to determine the difference between those two values.

each customer and with a column showing their outstanding balance. Another query could then be written to sum the account balances in this table, thereby calculating total accounts receivable. Similar procedures can be used to derive other accounting concepts, such as accounts payable, that represent imbalances between two events.

Keep in mind, however, that the procedures for calculating accounts receivable described in the preceding paragraphs would not have to be followed every time this information was desired. Instead, the queries would need only be written once and, after being tested for accuracy, they could be stored for subsequent use. Moreover, because information about temporal inter-event imbalances, such as accounts receivable and accounts payable, is needed so frequently, it is likely that an implementation compromise would be made so that account balance would be stored as a calculated attribute in the appropriate table. For example, the customer table depicted in Table 6.1 would have another column that stores that customer's account balance. In that case, the query logic required to derive accounts receivable would be greatly simplified because only the customer table need be accessed. To display the amount owed by a specific customer would involve writing a query that displayed a specific row in the customer table; calculating the total amount of accounts receivable would involve summing the account balance column.

Other Financial Statement Information. An REA diagram can guide the writing of queries to produce other information that would be included in financial statements. Some financial statement items can be derived by querying a single table. For example, summing the amount column in the sales table would yield sales for the current time period. Other information, however, such as accounts receivable, might require querying several tables. As shown in Table 6.2, correctly reading and understanding what the REA diagram says about how the data is stored is essential for knowing how to write such queries.

Preparing Managerial Reports. A major advantage of the REA data model is that it integrates nonfinancial and financial data in the AIS (see Table 6.1) and makes both types of data easily accessible for use in managerial decision making. For example, one of the attributes in the sales table is the time that the sale occurred. Scott and Susan can use this data to track sales activity during different times of the day, in order to better plan staffing needs. The sales–inventory table also includes two useful nonfinancial attributes: whether the purchase is a replacement or the first-time acquisition of a product, and the age of the appliance being replaced. Scott and Susan can use this data to improve their marketing efforts. For example, Scott and Susan can calculate the average frequency with which their customers replace appliances. Customized advertisements can then be mailed to those customers who are approaching the time when they may be considering replacing an appliance, describing the models and prices currently available at S&S.

In addition, the S&S revenue cycle data base shown in Fig. 6.7 and Table 6.1 can also be easily expanded to integrate data from external sources. For example, to better evaluate customer credit status, Scott and Susan may decide to collect information from a credit rating agency, such as Dun & Bradstreet. This information could be added to the data base by creating an additional column in the customer table to store the customer's credit rating. A similar process could be used to append information to the vendor table that could be used in the vendor selection process.

In contrast to the REA data model, the general ledger in a traditionally designed AIS uses the chart of accounts to store and organize data based on the structure of financial statements. In terms of the previous example, the traditional AIS contains only data about the financial aspects of a sales transaction, such as date and amount. Other data useful for evaluating operational performance, such as the time a sale occurred or whether the customer was replacing an old appliance, would have to be stored in a separate data base or information system. This would make it more difficult for management to access such information easily and quickly.

It is vitally important that an organization's AIS be capable of storing both traditional financial measures and other operational performance measures. As Robert Elliott explains[9]:

> Information technology (IT) is changing everything. It represents a new, post-industrial paradigm of wealth creation that is replacing the industrial paradigm and is profoundly changing the way business is done. Because of these changes in business, the decisions that management must make are very different from former decisions. *If the purpose of accounting information is to support business decision-making, and management's decision types are changing, then it is natural to expect accounting to change—both internal and external accounting.* [Emphasis added]

The REA data model can be used to build a data base that allows the AIS to change in response to management's changing information requirements.

The REA data model shows that accounting need not be limited to the traditional double-entry model with its journals, ledgers, and chart of accounts. Instead, the REA data model supports the view that accounting is a process or system for collecting and disseminating information about the business transactions engaged in by an organization. The means by which those objectives are accomplished, however, may change with new developments in information processing technology. Indeed, Focus 6.2 suggests that there may be some significant changes in store for *how* accounting is accomplished in many organizations. Nevertheless, although the *mechanics* of accounting may change, the need for the results (managerial reports and financial statements) of accounting remains.

INTEGRATING REA DIAGRAMS ACROSS CYCLES

In designing an AIS for S&S, Ashton modeled not only the revenue cycle, but also the expenditure cycles. Figure 6.8 shows the basic REA diagram he developed for the expenditure cycle.

Ashton then combined both REA diagrams in order to provide Scott and Susan with one high-level overview of what would be included in their AIS. To do this, he merged common entities found on the REA diagrams for each individual transaction cycle. Thus the final diagram (see Fig. 6.9) includes only one inventory and one cash entity.

---

[9] Robert K. Elliott, "The Third Wave Breaks on the Shores of Accounting," *Accounting Horizons* (June 1992): 61.

FIGURE 6.9
Integrated REA Diagram for Revenue and Expenditure Cycles of S&S

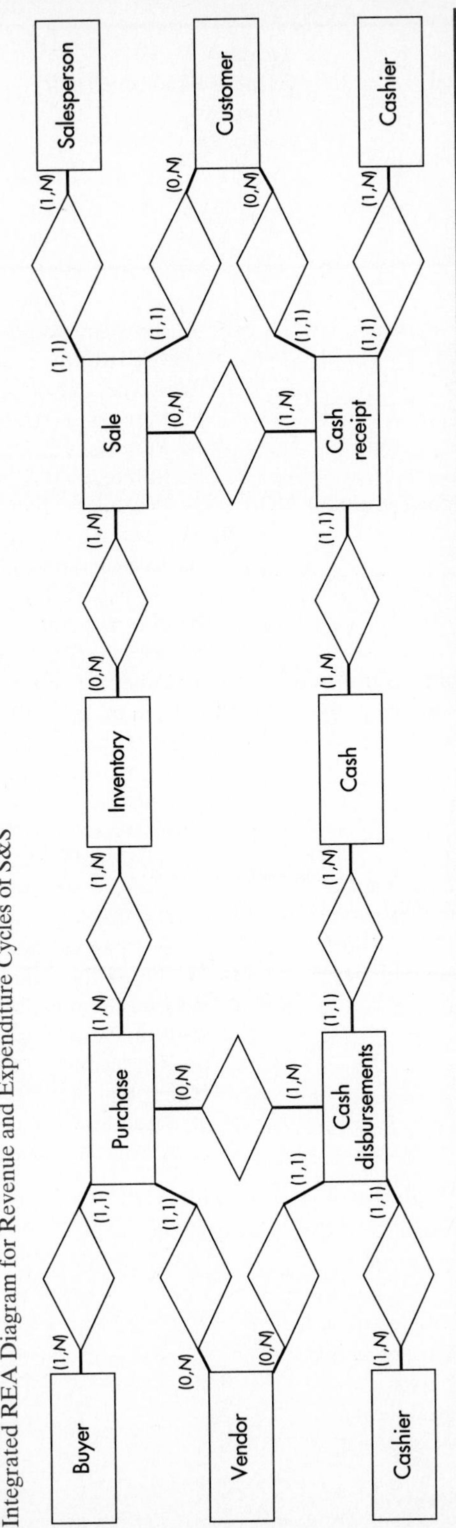

KEY TERMS

data modeling
REA data model
resources
events
agents
Entity-Relationship (E-R) diagram
cardinality
minimum cardinality
maximum cardinality
concatenated keys

CHAPTER QUIZ

1. Which of the following is not considered a resource in an REA data model?
a. Cash
b. Accounts Receivable
c. Inventory
d. Equipment

2. Which of the following is not a type of entity in the REA data model?
a. Customers
b. Sales
c. Invoices
d. Delivery trucks

3. Which type of relationship cardinality *must* be implemented in a relational data base as a separate table?
a. One-to-one
b. One-to-many
c. Many-to-many
d. All of the above

4. If a company pays for each purchase it makes with a separate check and does not make installment payments on any purchases, the relationship between cash disbursements and purchases would be modeled as being
a. one-to-one.
b. one-to-many.
c. many-to-many.
d. paid-in-full.

5. Which set of cardinality pairs most accurately models the sales of low-cost mass-produced items by a retail store?
a. Inventory (0,*N*)–(0,*N*) sales
b. Inventory (0,*N*)–(1,*N*) sales
c. Inventory (1,*N*)–(1,*N*) sales
d. Inventory (1,*N*)–(0,*N*) sales

6. Data modeling occurs during which stages of data base design?
a. Requirements analysis and physical design
b. Requirements definition and logical design
c. Logical design and coding
d. Physical design and implementation

7. A company wants to store information about both currently used and alternative suppliers. Which set of cardinality pairs allows this?
a. Purchases (0,*N*)–(0,1) suppliers
b. Purchases (1,*N*)–(1,1) suppliers
c. Purchases (0,1)–(1,*N*) suppliers
d. Purchases (1,1)–(0,*N*) suppliers

8. The key of a many-to-many relationship between the sales and inventory events would be
a. invoice number.
b. item number.
c. both invoice number and item number.
d. either invoice number or item number.

9. Which of the following statements about the REA data model is true?
a. Every event must be linked to at least two agents.
b. Every relationship must be implemented as relational table.
c. Every event must be linked to at least two resources.
d. Every agent must be linked to at least two events.

10. Which of the following elements of the REA data model must be implemented as tables in a relational data base?
a. Resources
b. Events
c. Agents
d. All of the above

DISCUSSION QUESTIONS

6.1 It has been argued that advances in information technology, especially the development of DBMSs, have made the double-entry model of accounting obsolete. Specifically, the ability of the computer to quickly and accurately sort and summarize transaction data has made the practice of maintaining ledgers in order to produce periodic reports unnecessary. Indeed, financial reports can now be produced at any time. What are the likely effects of these types of changes on the nature of accounting jobs in the future?

6.2 Traditional accounting systems are based on the chart of accounts, which establishes one predetermined basis for organizing and summarizing transaction data. How does the REA data model provide more flexibility in meeting the information needs of various decision makers? Provide specific examples.

6.3 A criticism of traditional accounting systems is that data is stored at too high a level of aggregation (summarization). That is, transaction data is recorded at the individual event level in journals, but once it is posted to ledgers it is kept in summarized form. Thus it is only easy for users to obtain information at three levels of aggregation: (1) individual transactions (from the journals or transaction files), (2) totals for a particular account for a particular time period (by summarizing transaction activity), or (3) the cumulative balance in the ledger accounts. In contrast, one objective of the REA model and the events-based approach is to store accounting data at a less aggregated level. How important is this objective in meeting user needs? Are the three levels of aggregation provided by the traditional AIS sufficient to support all of an organization's information needs? Why or why not?

6.4 The traditional chart of accounts only stores financial information about transactions. An objective of the REA accounting model is to facilitate the integration of financial and nonfinancial information. Is it necessary to abandon the chart of accounts to accomplish this objective? Why or why not? (Hint: Think about how operational data, such as average time to fill and ship customer orders, can be stored in an AIS that uses the chart of accounts.)

6.5 The REA data model does not treat activities such as mailing invoices, recording vendor invoices, and preparing reports as being events. Why not?

PROBLEMS

6.1 Revise the REA diagram in Fig. 6.7 to include the following:

a. *Sales calls on corporate customers.* Assume that not every call results in a sale, but that Scott and Susan want to record data about each call in order to evaluate sales staff effectiveness.
b. *Delivery of merchandise to customers.* Assume that deliveries are scheduled weekly, so that one delivery to a customer could include merchandise from several sales transactions. Also assume that deliveries occur independently of the cash collections event. In other words, sometimes products are delivered after the customer has paid for the merchandise, but other times deliveries occur before payment is collected.

6.2 Develop an REA data model for S&S's payroll and human resource management needs and express that model in the form of an E-R diagram. Then create a set of relational tables, complete with attributes, to implement your model. Put yourself in the Scott and Susan's place: what information about your employees do you need to collect and analyze?

6.3 The following information describes S&S's expenditure cycle in terms of purchasing inventory. The three principal events are (1) ordering of merchandise from vendors, (2) receipt of merchandise from vendors, and (3) payment of vendors for merchandise ordered and received. For the first two events, Scott and Susan wish to track the performance of their purchasing agents and receiving dock workers. Scott and Susan sign all checks. Vendor invoices are received for each delivery of inventory and are paid when due.

Required:

a. Develop an REA model for S&S's expenditure cycle and draw a corresponding E-R diagram for this model.
b. Develop a set of relational tables to implement your data model. Specify each table's primary key,

and list several other nonkey attributes that should be included as well.

6.4 Develop a data model of S&S's expenditure cycle activities related to the acquisition of office equipment and other fixed assets. Assume that S&S makes installment payments for most fixed asset acquisitions, but that it occasionally pays for some equipment in full at the time of purchase.

Required:

a. Draw an E-R diagram of your data model.
b. Develop a set of relational tables that implements your data model. Specify each table's primary key, and list several other nonkey attributes that should also be included in each table.

6.5 S&S has incorporated and issued shares of common stock.

Required:

a. Modify Fig. 6.9 to reflect this change in structure. Be sure to include both the inflow of funds from the initial sale of S&S's stock and the outflow of funds in the form of dividends to those shareholders.
b. Develop a set of relational tables to implement these modifications. Specify the primary key for each table, and list several other nonkey attributes that should also be included. Use your own judgment in selecting which attributes of common stock transactions should be collected and stored.

6.6 Provide an example (in terms of companies with which you are familiar) for each of the business situations described by the following relationship cardinalities:

a. Sales (0,*N*) to cash collections (1,*N*)
b. Sales (1,1) to inventory (0,1)
c. Purchases (0,*N*) to cash disbursements (1,*N*)
d. Purchases (0,1) to cash disbursements (1,*N*)
e. Purchases (1,*N*) to cash disbursements (1,1)
f. Employees (1,1) to departments (1,*N*)
g. Purchases (1,*N*) to inventory receipts (0,1)

6.7 Model the cardinalities of the following business policies:

a. The sales–cash collection relationship for installment purchases.
b. The sales–cash collection relationship at most self-service gasoline stations.
c. The customer order–sales relationship in a situation where sometimes several shipments are required to fill an order because some items were out of stock.
d. The sales–inventory relationship for a custom home builder.

6.8 The following tables and attributes exist in a relational data base:

Table	Attributes
Vendor	Vendor#, name, street_address, city, state, rating
Purchases	P.O.#, date, amount, vendor#, purchasing_agent
Cash_Disbursed	Check#, date, amount
Purchases-Cash_Disbursed	Check#, P.O.#

Assume that all purchases are paid for in full by one check.

Required:

Draw an REA diagram for this data base. State any assumptions you need to make about cardinalities.

6.9 Sparky's Amusement Park is an entertainment park run by recent college graduates. It caters to young people, and others who are just young at heart. The owners are very interested in applying what they have learned both in their Information Systems and Marketing classes to have a better park than any other in the area.

To accomplish these goals, every person who attends the park is given a personal membership card as they enter the park for the first time. This membership card will be used to identify each guest, and the owners would like to store information about each guest, such as their name, address, age, and the time the card is assigned. Assume that a new card is issued each time someone comes to the park. As a result, the system does not have to track one person over a period of time.

Similar to other parks, the guests will pay a flat fee for the day and will be able to ride all of the attractions (a double looping roller coaster, the merry-go-round, etc.) for no extra charge. The owners, however, want to track the rides each guest takes, and the attractions that each uses. They hope to do this by having the guest swipe their membership card through a computerized card reader, automatically entering information into the computer system. This should allow them to gather data about the following:

- The number of people who use each piece of equipment (How many people rode the Ferris wheel today?)
- How many times each piece of equipment is operated daily
- What times of day the attraction is busy or slow (When was the carousel the busiest?)

- The number of attractions each guest uses (How many different pieces of equipment did customer #1122 ride?)
- The number of rides each guest enjoys (How many different rides did #1122 enjoy? Did s/he go on any pieces of equipment more than once?)

Required:

Draw an REA diagram of Sparky's park. Use the following definitions in drawing the diagram:

- Piece of equipment: the equipment that is operated in the park (the Tilt-a-Whirl, roller coaster, etc.)
- Ride: a specific time that the attraction is run
- Guest: the people who enjoy the rides

(Adapted from a problem developed by Julie Smith David for classroom use at Arizona State University.)

6.10 The Mesa Veterinary Hospital is a sole proprietorship run by Brigitte Roosevelt. She has no employees and has asked you to develop a data base to help her better track her data. Dr. Roosevelt currently has a personal computer, but has only used it for word processing. She is interested in also using it to maintain pet histories and accounting information. While she has high hopes, she is counting on you to help her through this change. She describes her daily activities as follows:

When new customers come to Mesa veterinary hospital, the "parents" of the pets are required to complete an introductory form. This form includes the following:

- Parent name
- Address
- Day phone
- Night phone

They are also required to provide information about each pet. (Note: Some people own many pets!):

- Pet name
- Breed
- Color
- Birth date

Dr. Roosevelt would like to enter this information once, and then have the system retrieve for all subsequent visits.

Dr. Roosevelt sees only one pet during each appointment; if she is going to see one parent's two pets, two separate appointments are set up (but scheduled back-to-back). For each appointment, the pet's weight is recorded, the reason for the appointment is noted, and the doctor's diagnosis recorded. Depending on the diagnosis, the doctor will possibly prescribe any number of prescriptions to cure the pet. Parents are charged $25 for each appointment, and must pay additionally for any prescriptions needed.

Dr. Roosevelt concludes the interview by requesting that in addition to the aforementioned facts, she wants the system to also store the following attributes:

- Number of pets owned by each parent
- Total charge for the appointment
- Prescription Price
- Drug name
- Length of appointment
- Diagnosis
- Date of appointment

Required:

a. Given this brief overview, draw an REA diagram for the Mesa Veterinary Hospital. Include cardinalities in your diagram.
b. Assume you are going to implement your REA diagram using a relational data base. Draw the necessary tables. Be sure to include all attributes from the text and the additional ones listed. Only create additional attributes if the are absolutely needed. (Adapted from a problem developed by Julie Smith David for classroom use at Arizona State University.)

6.11 Imagine that you have been hired by your university to implement a data base system for the library network. You have interviewed several librarians, and the following summarizes these discussions.

- The main goal of the library is to provide students and professors with access to books and other publications. The library, therefore, maintains an extensive collection of materials that are available to anyone with a valid university identification card.
- The standard procedure for loaning materials is that the student or faculty member comes to one of the three campus libraries, and locates the book or journal on the shelves.
- Each book is assigned three unique numbers. First, the book is assigned a number by the publisher, which is called its ISBN number. This number allows the publishers to track each title, and the number changes with each new edition. The second number is the Dewey Decimal number, which is assigned to the title and is written on the outside spine of the book. This number is used to organize the library shelves and is very helpful to the students and faculty. Therefore, it is critical that this number is available to the users on the on-line inquiry screens. The last number is a university Book ID number. A different number is assigned to every book that is received so that the library can track every individual copy of each book. This is different from the other two numbers in that if the library has three copies of one book, each one will have a unique university Book ID number.

- When students or faculty check out books, the system must be able to track the specific copy that is being borrowed. Each book has a magnetic strip inserted in its spine, which is used as a security measure. If someone tries to take a book without checking it out, an alarm sounds.
- In general, students and faculty are treated the same way in the library. Both are able to check out most books, they may check out several books at one time, and neither is allowed to remove periodicals from any library. However, the length of time that the book may be borrowed varies depending on who checks it out; whereas students are only able to check a book out for several weeks, faculty may borrow them for more extended times.
- When anyone checks out a book (or books), they take the material they want to the circulation desk. At that time, the librarian scans in the book's university Book ID number and the borrower's ID. The system then assigns a Loan number to the transaction so that the system tracks each checkout uniquely (assume that each book is treated as a separate loan). At this time, each book's due date is calculated, and marked on a slip for each book's inner cover. Simultaneously, the magnetic strip is deactivated so that the book may be removed from the library.
- After anyone checks out a book, they are expected to return it by its due date. In reality, everyone is allowed 30 days after the due date recorded on the checkout slip before the book is officially overdue. At that point, the book must be returned, and a $10 fine is assessed to the borrower. If the book is permanently lost, the borrower is fined $75 for the book's replacement. All fines must be paid in cash, in full. Whenever a book is returned, the return must be entered into the system, and a unique Return number is used to log the transaction. At that time, the loan record is updated to show that the book has been returned.

The following is a list of attributes that have been identified as critical for the new system:

- University book ID
- Book publisher
- Due date
- Faculty address
- Loan #
- Student name
- Type of borrower (faculty, student)
- Loan status (still outstanding, or returned)
- Bank account number
- Library name
- Faculty number of dependents
- Actual return date
- Student ID
- Author name (consider the implications if there are more than one author for one book)
- Book status (on the shelf or checked out)
- Book title
- Fine receipt #
- Student address
- Library borrowed from
- Total # of books in specific library
- Librarian number
- Librarian college degree
- Book return #
- Dewey Decimal #
- Faculty ID
- Book copyright date
- Checkout date
- Faculty name
- Fine amount
- Default library where book is shelved
- ISBN #
- Student grade point average
- YTD number of loans processed by each librarian

Required:

a. Draw an E-R diagram, using the REA template as a starting point, for the library system. Do not forget cardinalities!
b. Draw the tables that would be required to implement your E-R diagram. Only use the attributes listed above, unless you *absolutely must* add any other attributes.

(Adapted from a problem developed by Julie Smith David for classroom use at Arizona State University.)

CASE 6.1 ANYCOMPANY, INC.—AN ONGOING COMPREHENSIVE CASE

Visit a local company (you may use the same company you selected in previous chapters) and study their revenue and expenditure cycles.

Required:

1. Develop an REA model for both cycles, using an E-R diagram for documentation.
2. Develop a set of relational tables to implement your data model. Interview management and employees to determine what attributes should be included in your model.

CASE 6.2 PRACTICAL DATA BASE DESIGN

Hands-on practice in data base design is important. Implement either the basic data model for S&S's revenue cycle that was presented in this chapter, or one of the enhanced data models from the homework problems, or some combination thereof, using a relational DBMS. Then perform the following tasks:

1. Create a user view of accounts receivable that is based on data stored in other tables.
2. Create a user view for sales order entry that includes information about the quantity on hand of inventory items.
3. Write queries to develop an income statement and a balance sheet from your data base (or at least those portions of each statement that are included in your data model).

ANSWERS TO CHAPTER QUIZ

1. b **2.** c **3.** c **4.** a **5.** b **6.** b **7.** d **8.** c **9.** a **10.** d

CHAPTER 7

Electronic Commerce

LEARNING OBJECTIVES

After studying this chapter you should be able to

- Explain what electronic commerce is and discuss its effect on business processes.
- Describe the information technology components required to conduct electronic commerce.
- Discuss the control issues related to electronic commerce and identify methods for addressing them.

Integrative Case: S&S, Inc.

The call from Dominican Electric (DE), one of S&S's largest customers, surprised Scott Parry. Ramon Lantigua, DE's controller, explained that DE is in the process of moving toward a paperless office. To achieve that goal, DE is now requiring all its suppliers to use electronic data interchange (EDI) to receive orders for goods, send invoices, and transfer funds electronically. Last year, the initial implementation of EDI with a few major suppliers saved DE over a million dollars. Consequently, DE is no longer willing to purchase from suppliers who are not fully EDI-capable. Ramon concludes the conversation by stating that DE has been highly satisfied with S&S and, therefore, is willing to work with them if they commit to becoming EDI-capable.

After he hangs up, Scott calls Ashton to his office. He tells Ashton about DE's request. He tells Ashton, "As you know, DE is one of our largest customers. We can't afford to lose their business." Scott then asked Ashton to research what S&S needs to do to meet DE's request. He also wants to know if doing so will enable S&S to not only retain DE as a customer, but whether it will provide other opportunities to both cut costs and increase revenues.

Ashton was overwhelmed with his assignment and was not sure he had the experience or expertise necessary to lead S&S into the world of electronic commerce. As he left Scott's office, he wished he had paid more attention to the discussions about the basics of electronic commerce and data communications in his AIS class.

INTRODUCTION

Electronic commerce is the systematic use of advances in networking and communications technology to *improve* the ways in which a company interacts with its suppliers and customers. Moreover, as the introductory case shows, electronic commerce is not an option, but a basic requirement for businesses today. This chapter provides accountants and systems professionals with a basic understanding of data communications and networking technologies so that they can actively participate in planning, designing, and managing the use of networks to carry out electronic commerce. This chapter also discusses the various threats associated with electronic commerce and the appropriate control activities that can be used to minimize those risks.

BASIC ELECTRONIC COMMERCE CONCEPTS

Types of Electronic Commerce

When most people think of electronic commerce, they think of business-to-consumer relationships. Indeed, you may regularly participate in this form of electronic commerce, buying books or music from a company like Amazon.com. Business-to-consumer electronic commerce receives a great deal of attention in the press, and it is a large and ever-growing market.

Business-to-consumer electronic commerce transactions are relatively simple. For example, a consumer will visit a company's web site, browse through their offerings, place an order, and pay for the purchase at the time the sale occurs, usually with a credit card. The company then ships the goods and the transaction is completed.

An important issue in business-to-consumer electronic commerce is trust. Consumers want to know that a company's web site represents the electronic storefront of a legitimate business; that their orders will be filled correctly; and that the company has procedures in place to safeguard their personal information. In response to such concerns, a number of organizations offer services designed to provide assurances about the company behind a web site. Focus 7.1 describes one such service, called WebTrust, which was developed by the AICPA.

Electronic commerce is not limited to business-to-consumer transactions, however. Indeed, the volume of business-to-business electronic commerce is many times larger than that of business-to-consumer transactions. Moreover, although there are many similarities between business-to-consumer and business-to-business electronic commerce, there are also some important differences. First, with the exception of miscellaneous purchases, most businesses engage in transactions with companies with whom they have established ongoing relationships. For example, automobile manufacturers have preferred suppliers for such items as car seats, brakes, and tires. Thus, because most transactions take place between companies that know each other, there is less need in business-to-business electronic commerce for web assurance services like WebTrust.

Business-to-business electronic commerce also differs from business-to-consumer electronic commerce in its emphasis on accountability and control. As a result, business transactions between companies have traditionally involved the exchange of a number of documents, such as purchase orders, bills of lading, receiving reports, and invoices. Various approval steps are also built into the process. Buyers and sellers may have relationships with different transportation companies and, therefore, may have to negotiate which carrier to use.

FOCUS 7.1 Providing Assurance for Electronic Commerce

CONSUMERS interested in shopping on-line have a number of concerns: Is the company legitimate? Will it protect the confidentiality of information I submit? What kind of post-sales service and support are provided? How are complaints resolved?

To address such concerns, the AICPA developed an assurance service called WebTrust. Companies that pass a WebTrust examination can place a distinctive seal on their web page, indicating that their web site and electronic commerce practices have been inspected by a CPA. Although other similar types of certification exist, WebTrust differs from them in several important ways.

First, WebTrust is broader in its scope. WebTrust not only certifies the legitimacy of the business, it also provides assurance about its business practices.

Second, the WebTrust seal is only awarded after a thorough examination of a company's electronic commerce practices. To get the WebTrust logo, sellers must disclose information about return procedures, customer service numbers, and performance data about such matters as delivery times. The CPA performing the WebTrust engagement then conducts tests to verify that the business does indeed follow those stated procedures. The CPA also examines the accuracy with which a company executes customer orders and whether it takes proper precautions to safeguard customers' personal information.

Third, WebTrust requires regular recertification. A WebTrust seal is only valid for 90 days. After that time, the company must undergo another examination to ensure that it continues to follow sound business practices.

More details about the WebTrust criteria, and the methods used to test compliance with them, can be found by visiting the AICPA's main web site at www.aicpa.org.

Source: Glen L. Gray and Roger Debreceny, "The Electronic Frontier," *Journal of Accountancy* (May 1998): 32–38.

Sellers frequently extend direct credit to the customers, and often bill them periodically for all sales transactions made during that time period. Customers remit payments to the seller, who must then reconcile the payments received against outstanding sales invoices.

All of this adds complexity. Traditionally, it also involved the processing of large volumes of paper documents. Business-to-business electronic commerce still requires much of the same information to be exchanged between companies, but now that information is exchanged electronically instead of via paper documents. Thus business-to-business electronic commerce requires electronic data interchange capabilities.

Electronic Data Interchange (EDI)

Electronic data interchange (EDI) is the electronic exchange of information between trading partners. By eliminating the need to manually enter data, EDI improves accuracy. It also cuts costs by eliminating the need to mail, process, and store paper documents. Moreover, the improved speed of information exchange enables companies to carry less inventory, because they do not need to maintain as large a buffer to cover the time lost in sending paper documents through the mail. The total savings can be significant. For example, it is estimated that using EDI with suppliers saves Chrysler about $100 per vehicle manufactured.

Although EDI has been available for over 20 years, until recently its use was primarily restricted to large companies. For example, by 1997 nearly 90% of Fortune 500 companies used EDI, but less than 10% of smaller businesses did so. Cost was the primary barrier; it could cost a company as much as $50,000 to join an existing EDI network. Two recent developments are removing that barrier. First, the Internet eliminates the need to use a special proprietary third-party network for EDI. Second, XML, a standard language for defining data on web pages, eliminates the need for complex software to translate documents created by different companies. Thus EDI can now be much more easily adopted and used by smaller businesses.

Reaping the full benefits of EDI, however, requires that it be fully integrated with the company's AIS. Figure 7.1 illustrates the difference between fully integrated and stand-alone EDI systems. Notice that a stand-alone EDI system is merely another alternative to toll-free telephone numbers or fax systems: in all three cases, incoming orders must still be separately entered into the AIS, just as outgoing documents must be separately entered into the EDI system. Not only does this arrangement fail to realize the full potential cost savings and accuracy improvements, but stand-alone EDI systems also fail to maximize

FIGURE 7.1
Stand-alone Versus Integrated EDI Systems

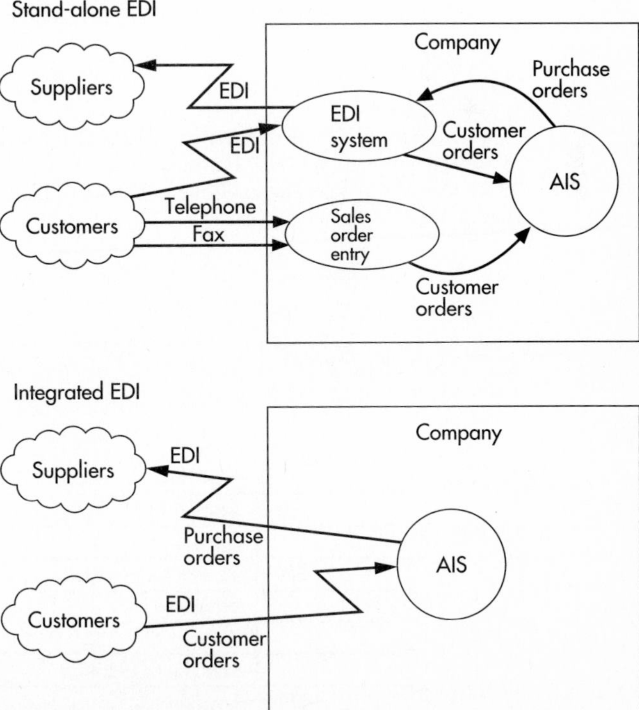

customer service. The problem is that because they are not integrated with the AIS, stand-alone EDI systems do not allow customers to know, at the moment they are placing an order, whether the requested items are in stock or will need to be back-ordered.

Financial Electronic Data Interchange (FEDI)[1]

Figure 7.2 shows that the use of EDI to exchange information is only part of the buyer–seller relationship in business-to-business electronic commerce. The complete transaction must also include the exchange of funds to pay for the goods or services that were purchased.

The term **electronic funds transfer (EFT)** refers to making cash payments electronically, rather than by check. EFT is usually accomplished through the banking system's Automated Clearing House (ACH) network. There are two types of ACH payments. An ACH *credit* is an instruction to your bank to transfer funds from your account to another account. An ACH *debit* is an instruction to your bank to transfer funds from another account into yours.

Although almost all banks can send and receive funds through the ACH network, not every bank possesses the EDI capabilities to process the accompanying remittance data. Consequently, many companies have had to use one network for EFT and a separate network for EDI (see top panel in Fig. 7.3). This complicates the seller's task of properly crediting customer accounts for payments, because information about the total amount of funds received arrives separately from information about which invoices that payment should

[1] The material on FEDI in this section is based on the articles Philip P. Grannan, "Electronic Commerce Today; Financial EDI Solutions for Tomorrow," *Management Accounting* (November 1997): 38–41; and Ann B. Pushkin and Bonnie W. Morris, "Understanding Financial EDI," *Management Accounting* (November 1997): 42–46.

FIGURE 7.2

Information Flows in Electronic Commerce

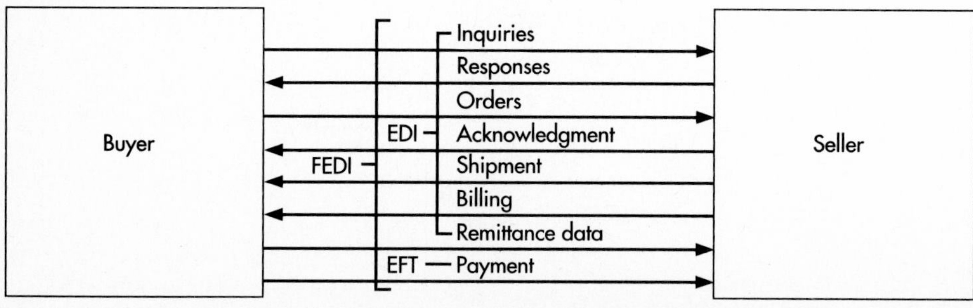

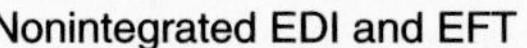

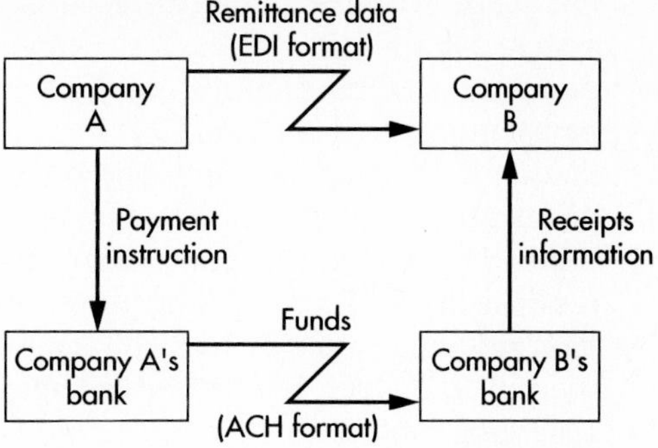

FEDI

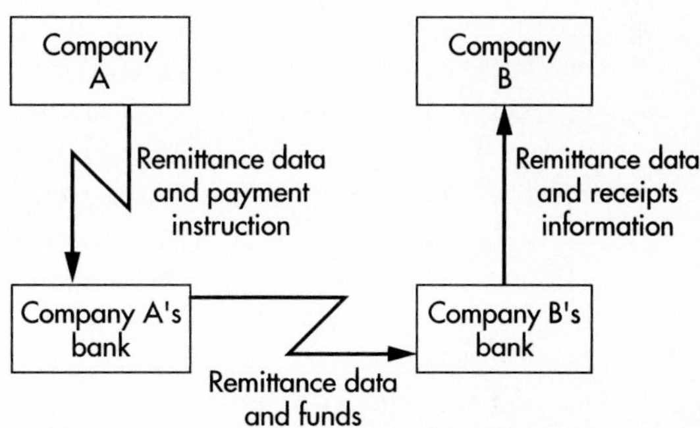

FIGURE 7.3
FEDI Versus EFT

be applied against. Similarly, the buyer's system must send information about payments to two different parties.

The ideal solution is to integrate EFT with EDI, which is referred to as **financial electronic data interchange (FEDI)**. With FEDI, the buyer's AIS can send both remittance data and funds transfer instructions in one package. Similarly, the seller's AIS receives both the remittance data and funds at the same time. The lower panel of Fig. 7.3 illustrates FEDI.

The full benefits of FEDI are realized when both the buyer's and seller's banks are EDI-capable. In this case, the buyer's AIS sends one message, containing both the remittance data and EFT instructions, to its bank. The buyer's bank forwards that message to the seller's bank, which credits the seller's account and then sends the remittance data and the notification of the funds transfer together to the seller.

Even if the seller's bank is not EDI-capable, however, the buyer still has two ways to implement FEDI. If the buyer's bank is EDI-capable, the buyer can still send the remittance data and funds transfer instructions together in one message to its bank. Alternatively, the buyer can contract with a **financial**

value-added network (FVAN) to implement FEDI. A FVAN is an independent organization that offers specialized hardware and software to enable the linking of various EDI networks with the ACH network used by the banking system for EFT. In this case, the buyer's AIS sends the remittance data and funds transfer instructions together to the FVAN. The FVAN translates the payment instructions from EDI format into ACH format and sends that information to the buyer's bank. The buyer's bank then makes a traditional EFT payment (an ACH credit) to the seller's bank. At the same time, the FVAN sends the remittance data to the seller in EDI format. Note that the seller receives the EFT and EDI portions separately; thus, both must contain a common reference number to facilitate proper matching. Consequently, although the buyer realizes the full advantage of FEDI under this arrangement, the seller does not.

Effects of Electronic Commerce

Electronic commerce can directly or indirectly affect every step in the value chain. The most obvious effect is on sales and marketing activities. Companies can create electronic catalogs on their web sites to totally automate sales order entry. For example, Cisco Systems' web site helps customers select the right components for their networking needs. The site generated around $4 billion in sales in 1998, which were processed by a staff of only ten salespeople.

Web sites designed to automate sales and marketing can also improve the efficiency of the operations step of the value chain. For example, Ford uses its internal data–voice–video communications network to facilitate communications among 120 designers throughout the world. Ford credits the network with helping to reduce the average time it takes to design a car from 36 to 24 months, while simultaneously avoiding the time and costs of flying people to meetings. Dell Computers credits its sophisticated web-based sale order entry system with helping it to minimize the amount of inventory it needs to carry. Other companies, like CDnow, have even completely eliminated inventories. CDnow simply takes orders at its web site and then arranges for distributors to ship the desired CD directly to the customer.

Electronic commerce applications can also significantly improve the quality of post-sales customer support. For example, setting up a web page ensures that all customers receive consistent information. Companies like AT&T and Nike use a sequence of menu-driven forms to electronically interview customers at their web site; only the most complex problems need to be routed to a customer service representative. Such practices can significantly reduce the costs of customer support. Wells Fargo, for example, found that customers with on-line access to their accounts made 40% fewer calls to the bank than did customers without such access. Focus 7.2 discusses how a web page can even be used as a significant public relations tool.

For products that can be digitized, such as books, software, and music, even the inbound and outbound logistics steps of the value chain can be performed electronically. This yields tremendous cost savings to both the acquiring and selling organizations. The buying organization is relieved of the time and cost

FOCUS 7.2 Using the Web for Public Relations

IN OCTOBER 1996, disaster struck Odwalla, Inc., a company that sells juices and other health foods. Some of their apple juice had gotten infected with a strain of *E. coli* bacteria, resulting in the death of one 16-month-old girl, with 61 other people becoming seriously ill. Thanks to its creative use of the Internet, Odwalla was able to survive this crisis.

Odwalla set up a special web site to dispense current information about the problem and what steps it was taking. The site also had links to other web sites where consumers could learn about reatments for illnesses caused by *E. coli*. Especially important was the ability to get the web site up by 4 P.M. the day after the first reports of contamination became public. During the first 48 hours, there were more than 20,000 hits on the site. Odwalla's ability to quickly provide information about what it was doing, and also provide links to other relevant sites, helped it to reestablish trust with its customers.

The Internet can also have negative effects, however, as Quigley Corporation learned. In 1996 news that one of its products, Cold-Eeze, shortened and reduced the intensity of colds, sent its stock skyrocketing. But shortly thereafter several Internet investor sites, such as Motley Fool and Silicon Investor, began publishing anonymous articles attacking the stock. Apparently, investors who had shorted the stock were trying to get it to crash. They succeeded in doing so after someone masquerading as the company's chairman in an AOL chat room spread false news about inventory shortages and other problems. Although the company responded to the disinformation campaign on its own web site, the negative PR drove the stock price down precipitously.

Source: Richard Rapaport, "PR Finds a Cool New Tool," *Forbes ASAP* (October 6, 1997): 101–108.

of receiving merchandise and then routing it to the person who ordered it. The selling organization avoids the time and expense of packing the goods for shipment and the associated shipping costs.

Electronic commerce applications can also significantly improve the efficiency and effectiveness of value chain support activities. For example, the purchasing activity benefits by being able to more easily compare prices across a larger number of potential vendors than would be possible to consider in a manual setting. General Electric, for example, estimates that such comparison shopping helped it save about 20% on materials costs associated with $1 billion of supplies it purchased in 1997. Even the human resource management function can benefit. A large proportion of the transactions processed in those systems result from changes initiated by employees, such as new withholdings, changes in retirement allocations, and name changes. Providing employees the ability to make those changes themselves can generate significant savings. For example, after enabling such employee self-service, Lawson Software realized a 93% reduction in the number of employee calls to the human resources department, resulting in an estimated savings of more than $15,000 a year.

Indeed, the capabilities provided by networking and communications technology is an important part of the infrastructure supporting globalization. For example, Lexmark Corporation manufactures its computer printers and related products in eight different countries on four continents, and sells those products in over 150 different countries. Lexmark's CIO believes that coordinating such dispersed activities would be impossible without an effective communications network. Many other companies, such as GM, similarly believe that an effective communications network is the key to globalization. Thus it is important to develop a basic understanding of the technology that underlies such networks and supports electronic commerce.

DATA COMMUNICATIONS SYSTEM MODEL

Types of Networks

The global networks used by many companies to conduct electronic commerce and to manage internal operations consist of two components: a private portion that is owned or leased by the company, and the Internet. The private portion can be further divided into two subsets: local area networks and wide area networks. A **local area network (LAN),** as its name implies, is a system of computers and other devices, such as printers, that are located in close proximity to each other (usually in the same building). In contrast, a **wide area network (WAN)** covers a wide geographic area; indeed, many large corporations have global WANs.

Companies typically own all the equipment that makes up their LANs, but they usually do not own the long-distance data communications connections of their WANs. Instead, they either contract to use a value-added network or use the Internet. A **value-added network (VAN)** is a long-distance communications system designed and maintained by an independent company. It offers specialized hardware and software to facilitate the exchange of data between various private networks. The **Internet** is an international network of computers (and smaller networks) all linked together. The connections that link those computers together are called the Internet's *backbone.* Although no one entity owns the Internet, portions of the backbone are owned and maintained by the major **Internet service providers (ISPs)** like MCI, GTE, and Sprint.

One of the biggest attractions of the Internet is its ease of use. Software called browsers enables users to easily navigate through vast amounts of information. Consequently, many companies have adapted their LANs to support these same basic Internet applications, including browsers. The term **intranet** refers to such internal networks that connect to the main Internet, can be navigated with the same simple browser software, but are closed off from the general public. Intranets can yield significant cost savings by enabling expertise to be shared by various units, instead of having a resident expert at each office. For example, Lehigh Valley hospital uses intranets to eliminate the need to employ radiologists at each of its outpatient clinics. Instead, X-ray data is sent over Lehigh's intranet to the hospital, where it is examined by staff radiologists. Focus 7.3 describes a similar use of intranet technology in public accounting.

Many companies have realized that there are significant benefits to letting some of their suppliers and customers access their intranets. This has led to the creation of **extranets,** which link the intranets of two or more companies. Either the Internet or a VAN can be used to connect the companies forming

FOCUS 7.3 Using Groupware and Intranets to Leverage Knowledge

KPMG (Peat Marwick) has installed worldwide more than 17,000 copies of FirstClass, a groupware system from Soft Arc Inc. This groupware supports Knowledge Manager, Peat Marwick's system containing a vast store of information and experience about almost everything associated with the firm. The system also allows every one of its 75,000 professionals worldwide to communicate via e-mail; access information stored in private and public bulletin boards, external data bases, and public networks; and process forms.

Most employees use the system almost daily to gain access to hundreds of gigabytes of information. The information is stored in different computer folders containing client experiences, proposals, resumes, methodologies, best practices, vendors, and demonstrations, among others. One of the most popular folders is Help Wanted. Auditors and consultants can post a request for help on a project and usually get feedback within an hour.

The system helps KPMG gather the best ideas from all over the world and allows the firm to be available to each individual client. Using the expertise of their entire staff of professionals, KPMG personnel can tailor a proposal to a user's exact needs. For example, Peat Marwick needed to create a proposal to bid on a job that required business planning, real estate, and information technology expertise. The partner in charge of preparing the bid used Knowledge Manager to review similar bids and to assemble a team of experts from Washington, Vancouver, and Chicago. Each team member prepared a portion of the proposal and reviewed and edited the entire draft. The result was a customized proposal for the prospective client. The entire proposal, including firm qualifications, partner resumes, and specific real estate project data, was prepared in just four days. Several team members never met until the day they made a formal in-person pitch to the client.

Auditors and consultants in CPA firms used to be rewarded primarily for their individual projects and contributions. Those with the biggest clients and projects had the most influence and were the most highly compensated. This practice led to information hoarding, a lack of cooperation, and an unwillingness to share expertise and other intellectual resources. That attitude is changing, and the emphasis at Peat Marwick is now on cooperation and sharing of resources and expertise. Groupware is facilitating this change, as it is one of the best ways to share data.

Source: Stephanie Stahl, "Hire On One, Get 'em All," *InformationWeek* (March 20, 1995): 120–124.

the extranet. VANs are more reliable and secure than the Internet, but they are also expensive. One way to improve reliability and security, while still taking advantage of the Internet, is to build what is called a virtual private network. As shown in Fig. 7.4, a **virtual private network (VPN)** uses encryption and authentication technology to control access to the extranet and to prevent eavesdropping. The ISPs used by each member of the extranet control access; encryption protects the data from eavesdropping while it is transmitted over the Internet.

Data Communications System Components

There are five basic components in any data communications network (whether it is the Internet, a LAN, a WAN, or a VAN):

1. The sending device
2. The communications interface device
3. The communications channel

FIGURE 7.4
A Virtual Private Network (VPN)

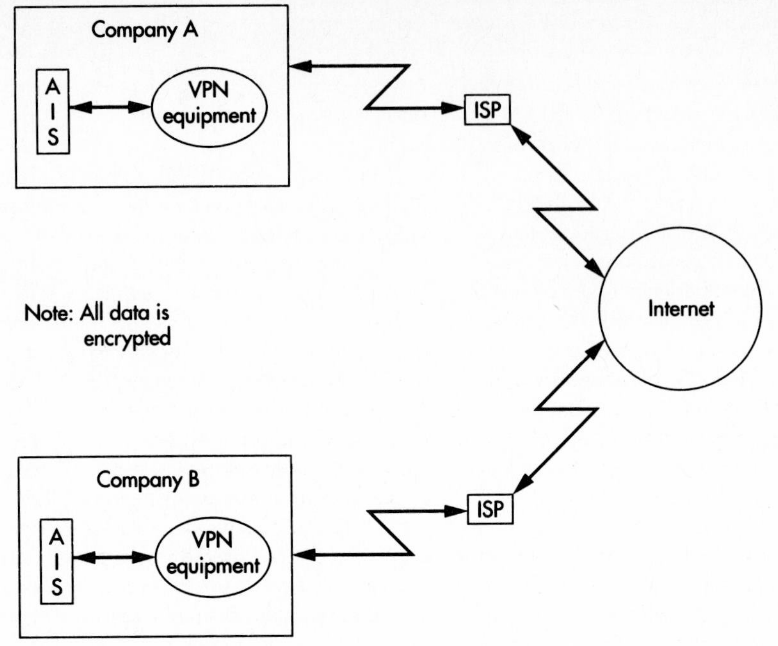

4. The receiving device
5. Communications software

Consider the example of a remote PC that transmits data to a centralized computer for processing. When the PC is ready to transmit the message or data, a communications interface device (such as a modem) converts the message to signals that are transmitted over a communications channel (such as a telephone line). At its destination, another communications interface device converts the message back to internal computer code and forwards it to the receiving computer. When the receiving unit returns a message to the source to verify the message has been received, the communications process is reversed. Communications software controls the entire process and manages all communication tasks.

You should already be familiar with the basic architecture of the computers that send and receive data. If you are not, or feel a need to refresh your knowledge, please refer to the appendix at the end of Chapter 4. The remainder of this section discusses the other components of the data communications model: interface devices, communications software, and channels.

Interface Devices

There are six basic communication interface devices that are used in most networks: network interface cards, modems, remote access devices, hubs, switches, and routers. Figure 7.5 shows the relationships among these different devices in a typical communications network.

Network Interface Cards. Every device (computer, printer, fax machine, etc.) connected to a data communications network needs a **network interface card (NIC)** to plug into the network. For example, your desktop PC may have an Ethernet card installed in it to connect it to an Ethernet LAN.

Modems. Computers store data internally in discrete, or digital, form as the presence or absence of an electronic pulse. Most networks, however, still use telephone lines at some point. Telephone lines were originally built to carry analog signals. A **modem** (modulator/demodulator) converts (modulates) a computer's digital signals into analog signals and then reconverts (demodulates) the analog signals back into digital signals at the destination (see Fig. 7.6). Thus a modem is needed at each end of the network that uses telephone lines or other analog transmission channels.

Modems can be internal (mounted on an expansion board within the computer) or external (a separate unit connected to the computer). External modems provide greater flexibility, since they can be used with more than one type of computer. Modem speeds are measured in bits per second (bps). The higher the bps, the lower the transmission costs but the higher the modem cost. Currently, modems are capable of speeds of up to 56,000 bps over regular telephone lines. Special modems designed for digital subscription lines (DSLs) can transmit at speeds of 256,000 bps or more. Cable modems may provide even faster speeds. Cable and DSL modems can also carry both voice and data simultaneously over the same physical line.

Most modems now also have fax capabilities. With the appropriate fax modem and accompanying software, users can send fully formatted documents and data files from their PC to a receiving fax machine or computer without having to print them first. A user merely selects the fax/modem feature, identifies the recipient (or their fax/modem phone number), and selects the print option. Optical character recognition (OCR) software can be used to convert faxes that are received into documents that can be edited and incorporated into word processing files. The visual appearance of the fax can subsequently be touched up with image processing software.

Remote Access Devices. **Remote access devices** are modem banks that serve as gateways to the Internet or to private corporate networks. Their function is to properly route all incoming and outgoing connections.

Hubs. A **hub** is a hardware device that provides a common wiring point in a LAN. Each node is connected to the hub by means of simple twisted-pair wires. The hub then provides a connection over a higher-speed link to other LANs, the company's WAN, or the Internet.

Switches and Routers. **Switches** and **routers** are hardware devices used to direct messages across a network. Switches create temporary point-to-point links between two nodes on a network and send all data along that link. In contrast, routers contain software that examines the header and contents of a message

FIGURE 7.5
Network Components

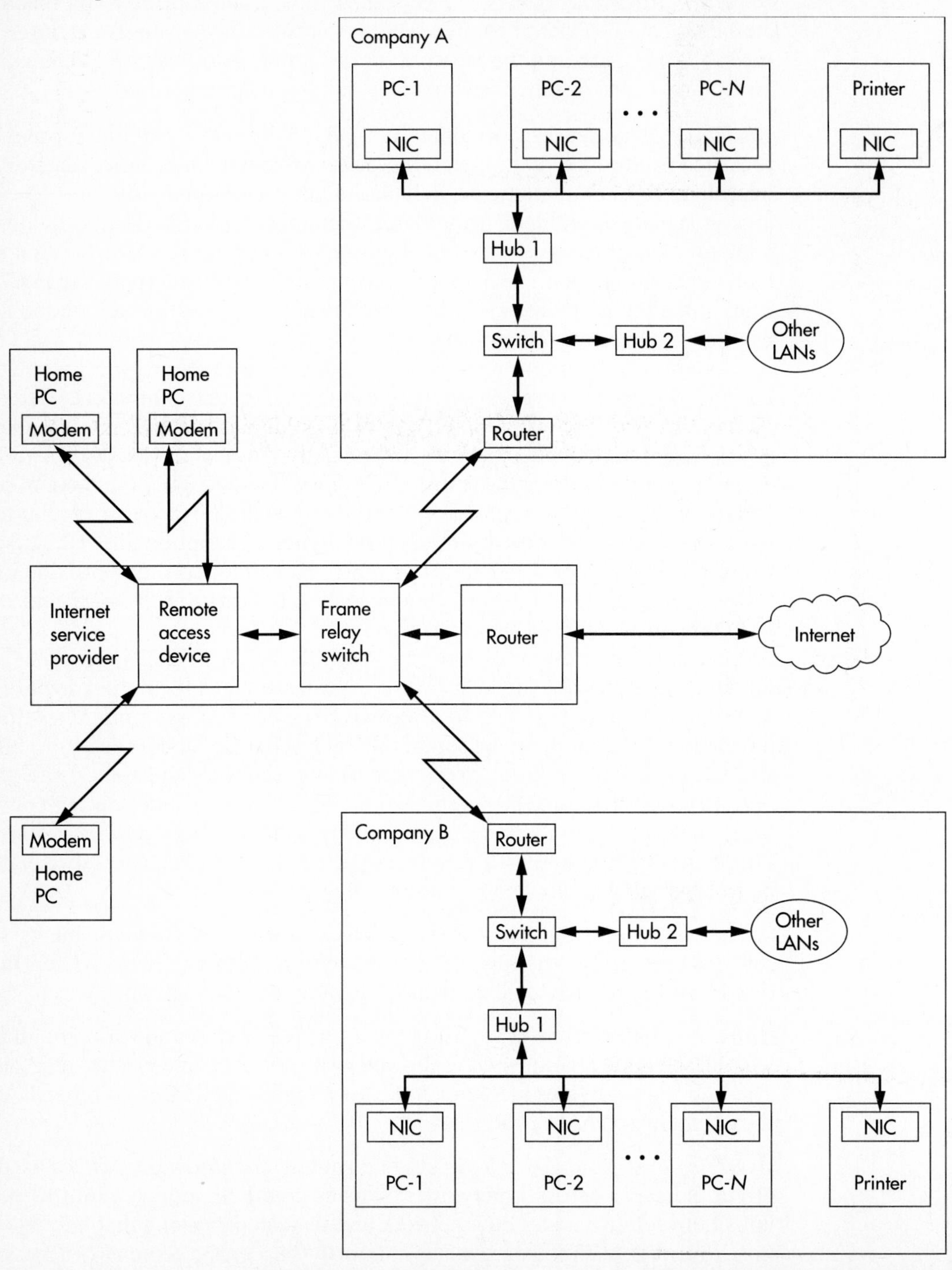

FIGURE 7.6
Digital and Analog Signals

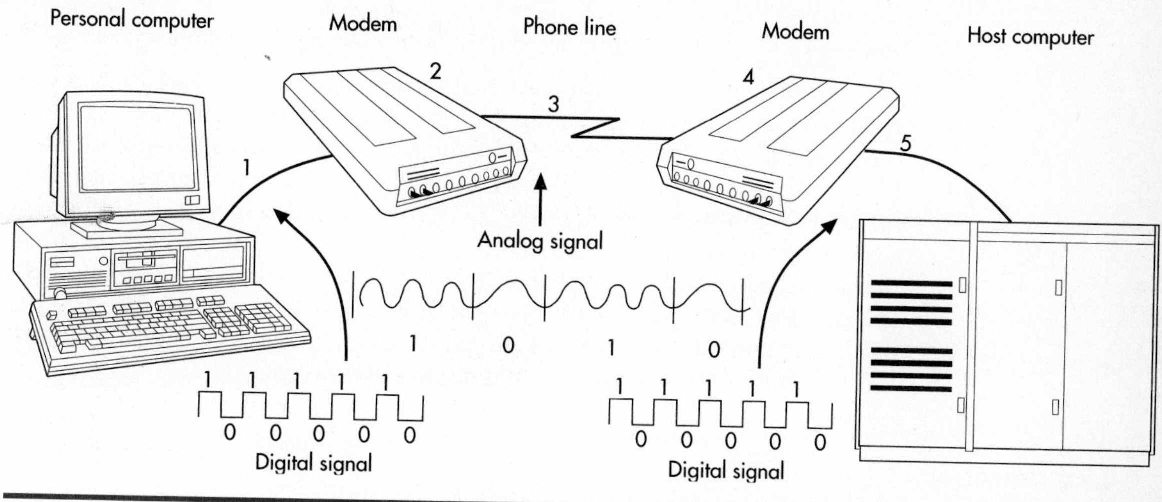

in order to direct it to its destination. This makes routers slower than switches. Routers, though, are less expensive and, because they inspect the contents of messages, can provide better control and security.

Not surprisingly, there are attempts to merge the advantages of routers and switches. One approach is the development of new hardware devices called routing switches, which combine the speed of hardware-based switching with the software intelligence built into routers. A second development is a software technique called *tag switching*. With tag switching, the first router or switch that encounters a packet adds a short tag to it that serves as a zip code to indicate where the message should be sent. Subsequent routers and switches then only have to examine the short tag, instead of the entire header or message, to determine where to send that packet next.

Communications Software

Communications software manages the flow of data across a network. It performs the following functions:

- *Access control.* Linking and disconnecting the different devices; automatically dialing and answering telephones; restricting access to authorized users; and establishing parameters such as speed, mode, and direction of transmission.
- *Network management.* Polling devices to see whether they are ready to send or receive data; queuing input and output; determining system priorities; routing messages; and logging network activity, use, and errors.

- *Data and file transmission.* Controlling the transfer of data, files, and messages among the various devices.
- *Error detection and control.* Ensuring that the data sent was indeed the data received.
- *Data security.* Protecting data during transmission from unauthorized access.

Communications software is written to work with a wide variety of protocols, which are rules and procedures for exchanging data. For example, the protocol used on the Internet is called TCP/IP (Transmission Control Protocol/Internet Protocol). TCP/IP creates what is called a packet-switching network. When a message, whether it is a file or just e-mail, is ready to be sent over the Internet, the TCP protocol breaks it up into small packets. Each packet is then given a header, which contains the destination address. The packets are then sent individually over the Internet. The IP protocol guides the packets so that they arrive at the proper destination. Once there, the TCP protocol reassembles the packets into the original message.

Communications Channels

A communications channel is the medium that connects the sender and the receiver in the data communications network. Common communications channels include telephone lines, fiber optic cables, terrestrial microwaves, satellite, and cellular radios. Indeed, as shown in Fig. 7.7, a communications network often uses several different media to minimize the total data transmission costs. Thus it is important to understand the basic characteristics, and costs, of different communications channels.

Characteristics of Alternative Communications Channels. The different communications channels each possess characteristics that affect the network's reliability, cost, and security. One of the most important characteristics of a channel is its bandwidth. **Bandwidth** refers to a channel's information carrying capacity. Technically, bandwidth, which represents the difference between the highest and lowest frequencies that can be used to transmit data, should be measured in cycles per second, called hertz (Hz). Nevertheless, bandwidth is usually measured in terms of bits per second (bps). All things else being equal, a communications channel with greater bandwidth will be more useful, because it can transmit more information in less time. For example, a web page that takes 15 seconds to download over a T-1 line that transfers data at approximately 1.5 megabits per second (Mbps) will take several minutes to download over normal telephone lines using a 56K modem. Higher bandwidth is essential for applications like real-time video. Table 7.1 compares the bandwidth and other characteristics of the most commonly used communications channels. It also provides information about the relative demands on bandwidth for different types of applications.

Standard Telephone Lines. Telephone lines are the most convenient communications channel because they are already installed just about everywhere. Most telephone lines consist of two insulated copper wires arranged in a spiral

FIGURE 7.7
Typical Communication Network Using Cables, Telephone Wires, Microwaves, and Satellites

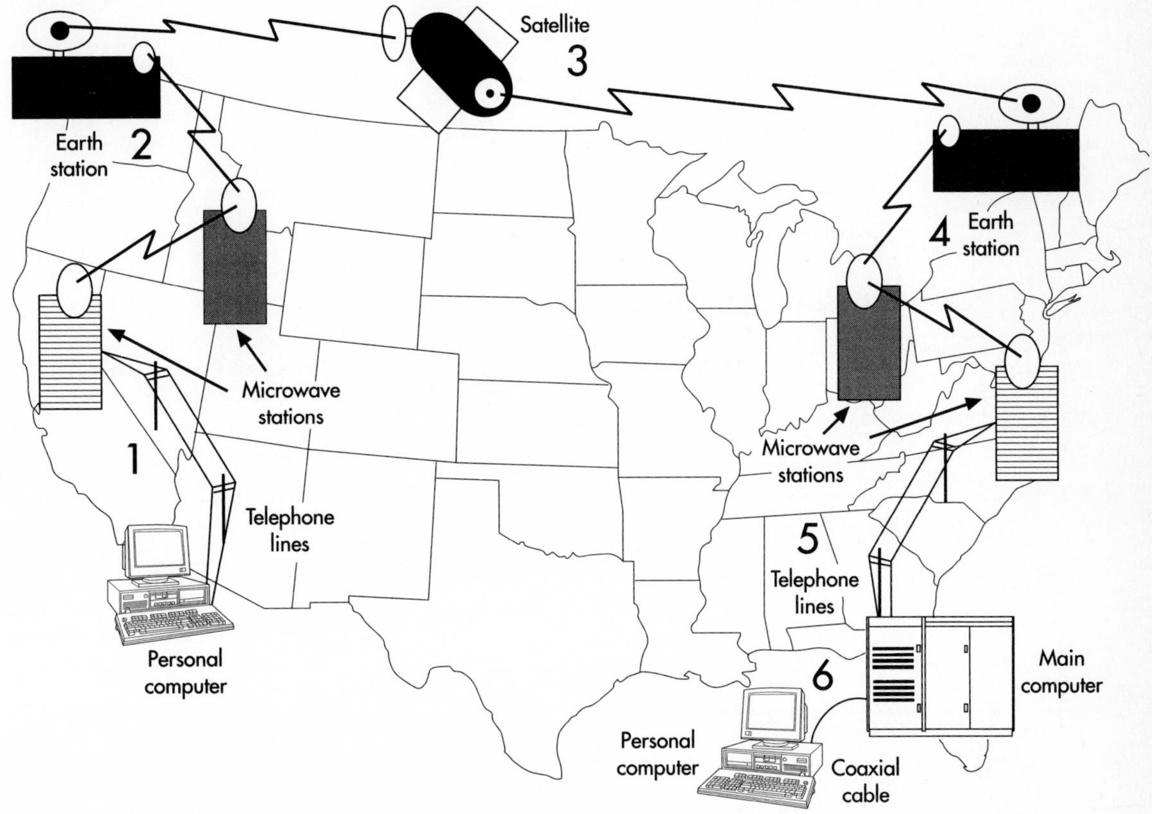

A West Coast corporate accountant for DE uses his PC to send e-mail to the corporate controller on the East Coast.

1. Lantigua's electronic e-mail message is sent over phone lines to a microwave transmitter.
2. The message is forwarded by several microwave stations to a satellite earth station.
3. The West Coast earth station forwards the message to a satellite, which relays the Message to an earth station on the East Coast.
4. The East Coast earth station forwards the message by microwave stations.
5. The last microwave station forwards the message by telephone wire to DE's main computer in Atlanta.
6. The host forwards the message by coaxial cable to the corporate controller's PC.

pattern (hence the term twisted-pair). Digital subscriber lines (DSL) provide the capability of carrying data at speeds of up to 1.5 Mbps over standard copper telephone wires. DSL also permits users to receive voice and data simultaneously.

Coaxial Cable. A coaxial cable consists of a stiff copper wire core that is surrounded by a protective sheath. The thicker wire and insulation make coaxial

TABLE 7.1 Panel A: Comparison of Communications Channels

Type of Channel	Cost	Transmission Quality	Speed	Capacity	Ease of Installation	Ease of Maintenance
Twisted-pair telephone wires	Low	Poorest	Slowest	Least	Easy	Easy
Coaxial cable	Medium	Good	Medium	Medium	Medium	Medium
Fiber optics	High	Excellent	Fastest	Highest	Difficult	Easy
Microwave	Medium	Good	Medium	High	Medium	Easy
Satellite	Medium	Good	Medium	High	Difficult	Easy

Panel B: Relative Bandwidth Demands for Various Applications

Application	Inbound Bandwidth Need	Outbound Bandwidth Need
Telnet	1 bps	1 bps
E-mail	10–300 bps	1 to 50 bps
File sharing	20–2,200 bps	20–2,200 bps
Web text mode	100–2,000 bps	5–50 bps
Web graphics mode	1,000–10,000 bps	10–100 bps
High-fidelity audio	10,000–50,000 bps	10–100 bps
High-grade video	100,000–350,000 bps	10–100 bps

cable less susceptible to interference and distortion than is twisted-pair telephone wire. Consequently, coaxial cable is capable of transmitting data at speeds of 1–2 gigabits per second (Gbps). There are two types of coaxial cable: baseband coaxial cable is used to carry digital signals, whereas broadband coaxial cable is used for analog transmission.

Fiber Optics. A fiber optic cable consists of thousands of tiny filaments of glass or plastic that transmit data using light waves. Fiber optics has many advantages over coaxial cable. It is much faster and has greater capacity, being able to transmit more than 100 Gbps. Fiber is practically immune to distortions and, therefore, has a lower error rate. It also provides greater data security than coaxial cable, because it is difficult to tap fiber optics cables. Thus it is not surprising that fiber optics has replaced coaxial cable for most long-distance applications.

Microwave Systems. Terrestrial microwaves are frequently used for long-distance data or voice transmission. Long-distance dish antennae with microwave repeater stations are placed about 30 miles apart. Each transmitter station receives a signal, amplifies it, and retransmits it to the next station. It is usually much less expensive to set up a series of microwave towers than it is to bury fiber optic cable (in part because no rights-of-way need to be acquired). Microwave systems may also save money by avoiding the charges associated with sending data over the telephone company's fiber network. Indeed, microwave communication is so widely used that there is a shortage of available spectrum.

Communications Satellites. Satellite transmission involves beaming a signal to a satellite in space. The satellite acts as a relay station and sends the transmission back to an earth station. Since the Iridium project by Motorola, many of these communications satellites are currently in use.

One advantage of satellites is that the cost of data transmissions is independent of the distance the message must travel. In addition, because satellite transmission is inherently broadcast in nature, it costs the same to send a message to one receiver as it does to send the same message to thousands of receivers. Although this feature is often useful, it means that sensitive data must be encrypted before transmission. Perhaps the most important niche for satellites is in establishing mobile communications networks. For example, most major trucking companies now use satellites to keep in constant touch with their drivers, thereby eliminating the time and expense of periodically stopping to make long-distance telephone calls.

Cellular Radio and Telephone. Cellular radios and cellular telephones use radio frequencies to send and receive messages. A radio frequency can be geographically divided into small sections, called cells, so that users in different locations can all use the same frequency. In this way, up to 25 times as many people can use the radio frequencies. A powerful central computer and sophisticated interface equipment coordinate and control the transmission between cells. Figure 7.8 compares microwave, satellite, and cellular transmission channels.

Network Configuration Options

LAN Configurations. Figure 7.9 shows that LANs can be configured in one of three basic ways: as a star, a ring, or a bus.

1. *Star configuration.* In a LAN configured as a star, each device is directly connected to the central server. All communications between devices are controlled by and routed through the central server. Typically, the server *polls* each device to see if it wants to send a message. If it does, the packet of data is sent to the server, which reads the destination address and routes it to the appropriate node. The star configuration is the most expensive way to set up a LAN, because it requires the greatest amount of wiring. Its principal advantage, however, is that if one node goes down, the performance of the rest of the network is not affected.

2. *Ring configuration.* In a LAN configured as a ring, each node is directly linked to two other nodes. As messages pass around the ring, each node checks the packet header to determine whether the data is intended for it. To control the flow of data, and to prevent collisions, a LAN configured as a ring uses a software code called a *token* (hence many LANs configured

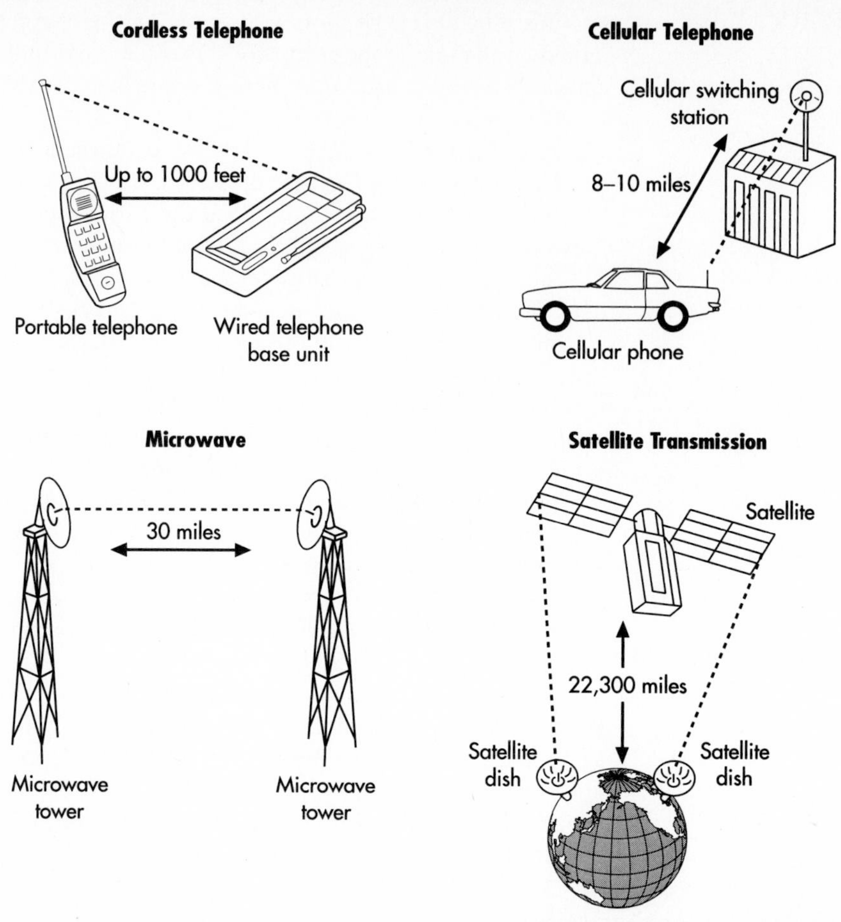

FIGURE 7.8
Four Examples of Wireless Transmission

Source: Adapted from Steve Alter, *Information Systems: A Management Perspective*, 2/E, Reading, Mass.: Addison-Wesley, 1996, p. 475. Reprinted with permission.

as rings are called *token ring networks*). The token continually passes around the ring. If a node wants to send a message, it grabs the token and attaches it to the message. The other nodes must then wait until the message reaches its destination and the token is once again free before they can send data. If one connection in the ring is broken, the network can still continue to function, albeit more slowly, by routing all messages in the opposite direction.

3. *Bus configuration.* In a LAN configured as a bus, each device is connected to the main channel, or bus. Communication control is decentralized on bus networks. A software algorithm known as *carrier sense multiple access with collision detection (CSMA/CD)* controls communications among devices. When a node wants to send a message, it checks to see if the bus is free. If it is, it sends the packets of data. The other nodes on the bus each check the header of the packet to determine whether the message is intended for them. If two nodes try to send a message at the

FIGURE 7.9

LAN Configurations. Note: Labeled nodes (A–H) represent devices connected to the LAN

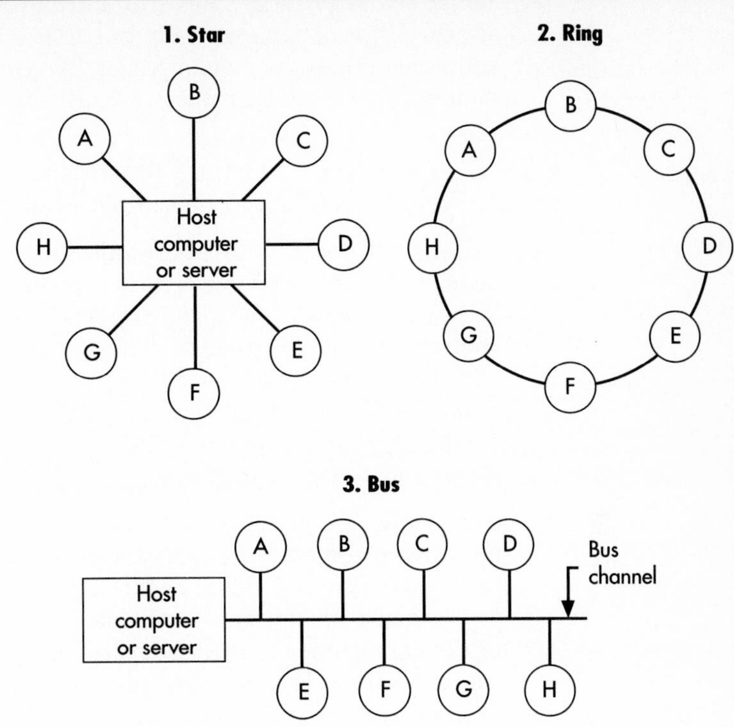

same time, the messages are likely to collide. In that case, one node is arbitrarily given priority to resend its message. Bus configurations are easy to expand and are cheaper to set up than stars. Performance decreases, however, as the number of nodes connected to the bus increases.

There is no simple answer to the question of which LAN configuration is best. Three basic factors affect the performance of any LAN, regardless of its configuration:

1. *Backbone bandwidth.* LAN backbones usually consist of coaxial cable or fiber optics. (In some cases, such as when an organization is housed in a historic building and does not want to or cannot install wiring in the walls, wireless backbones using infrared or radio waves are used.) The bandwidth of the backbone significantly affects LAN performance and reliability. Table 7.1A showed the characteristics of the different possible LAN backbones.

2. *Number of nodes.* As the number of nodes in a LAN increases, overall performance generally decreases. Thus, at some point, a LAN should probably be partitioned into separate LANs to improve performance.

3. *Server characteristics.* The size and power of the server significantly affects performance, especially in LANs configured as stars. To provide additional power, many companies, like Boeing, Wells Fargo Bank, J. C. Penney, and Lehman Brothers, are using their old mainframes as servers.

WAN Configurations. Figure 7.10 shows that there are three basic ways to configure a WAN: centralized, decentralized, or distributed.

1. *Centralized system.* In a centralized WAN, all terminals and other devices are connected to a central corporate computer, which is usually a large mainframe. Centralized systems provide the advantages of better control, more experienced IT staff, and some economies of scale. The disadvantages of centralized systems are greater complexity, higher communications costs (because all messages must be sent through the central computer), and less flexibility in meeting the needs of individual departments and users.
2. *Decentralized system.* In a decentralized WAN, each departmental unit has its own computer and LAN. Decentralized systems usually are better able to meet individual department and user needs than are centralized systems. In addition, communication costs are often lower, as much of the data needed is stored locally. The major disadvantages of decentralized systems are the complexity of coordinating data stored at many locations, increased hardware costs, and greater difficulty in implementing effective controls.
3. *Distributed data processing.* Figure 7.10 shows that a **distributed data processing (DDP)** system is essentially a hybrid of the centralized and decentralized approaches. Each location has its own computers to handle local processing, thus providing the advantages of decentralized systems. Each local system is also linked to the corporate mainframe, however, thus providing many of the benefits associated with centralized systems.

One advantage of DDP systems is that the various departmental computers back up one another; thus, there is less risk of catastrophic loss, since resources are in multiple locations. Another advantage is that each local system is treated as a module that can easily be added, upgraded, or deleted from the system. A disadvantage of DDP systems is that the multiple locations and varying needs complicate the tasks of coordinating the system and maintaining hardware, software, and data consistency. Standardizing documentation and control is also difficult, since authority and responsibility are distributed. Multiple locations and communications channels hinder adequate security controls and separation of duties. Another disadvantage of DDP is data duplication at multiple locations, which increases total storage costs and creates the opportunity for inconsistencies to arise.

Client/Server Configurations. Many WANs, and most LANs, are set up as client/server systems. Each desktop computer is referred to as a client. The clients send requests for data to the servers. The server performs preprocessing

FIGURE 7.10
Comparison of Centralized, Decentralized and Distributed Data Processing

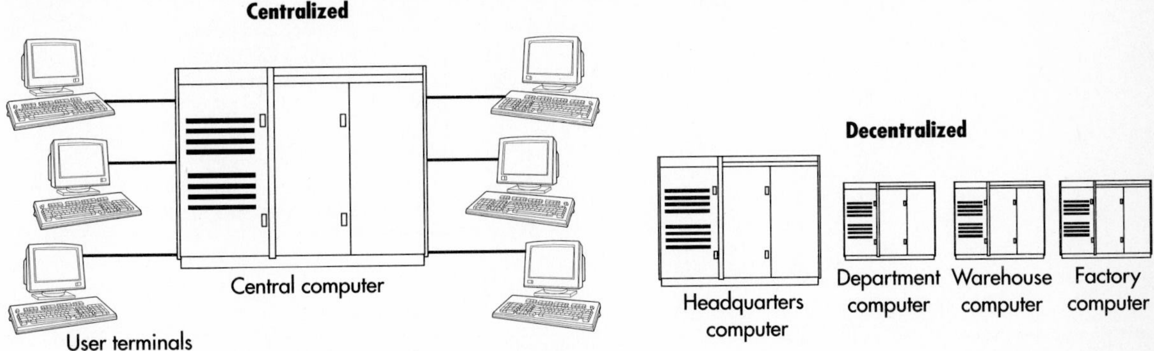

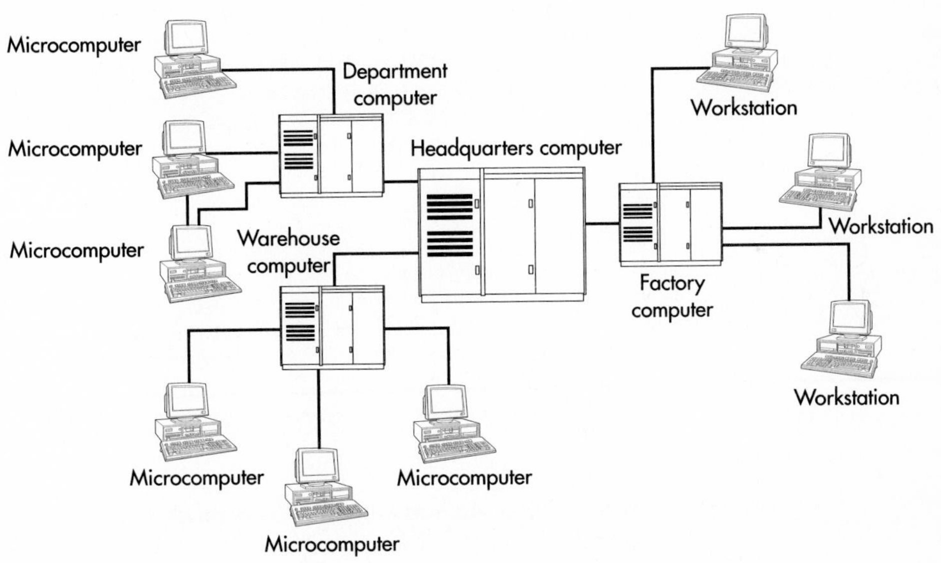

on the data base and sends only the relevant subset of data to the client for local processing.

Figure 7.11 shows that client/server systems can be configured as either a two-tier or three-tier architecture. In a two-tiered system, the central data base is stored on the server. Each client has its own copies of the necessary applications software and has a powerful enough CPU to do considerable local processing. For example, in a typical two-tier client/server network, many clients would be Pentium II desktop PCs with at least 64 MB of RAM. The major advantages of two-tier systems are flexibility in meeting individual user needs

FIGURE 7.11
Client/Server Architectures

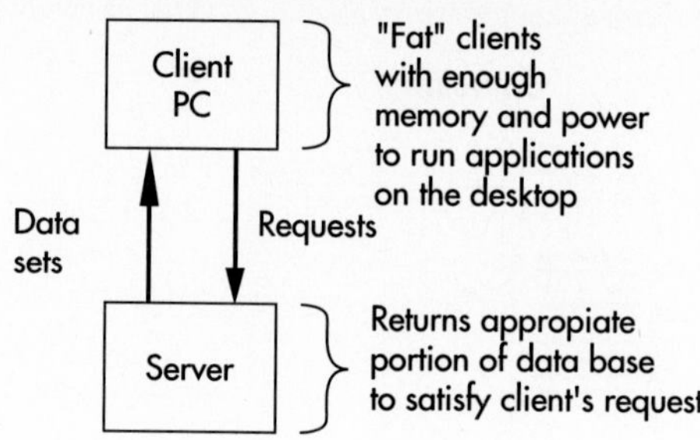
Two-Tier Client/Server Architecture
Client PC
"Fat" clients with enough memory and power to run applications on the desktop
Data sets
Requests
Server
Returns appropriate portion of data base to satisfy client's request

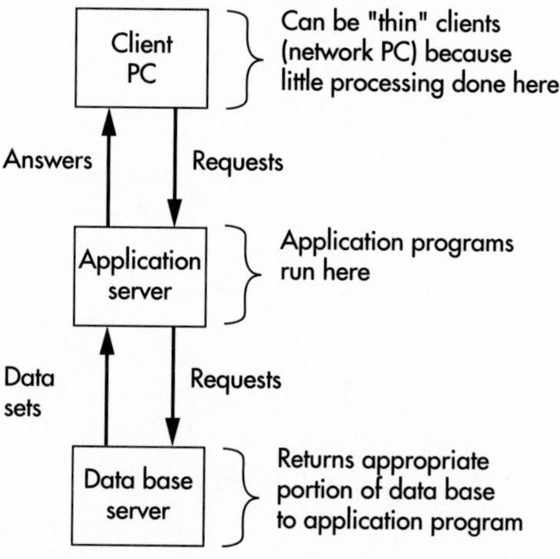
Three-Tier Client/Server Architecture
Client PC
Can be "thin" clients (network PC) because little processing done here
Answers
Requests
Application server
Application programs run here
Data sets
Requests
Data base server
Returns appropriate portion of data base to application program

and simplicity in overall design and control. The primary disadvantage is cost: users need powerful clients to perform tasks at the local level, and multiple copies of applications software must be purchased and maintained.

Three-tiered client/server systems attempt to reduce overall costs of corporate computing by having two levels of servers. The top-level server stores the central data base. The second-level servers store the applications software. Most processing takes place at this middle tier; the clients primarily are used as interfaces and for formatting the results in the desired manner. This three-tier arrangement can reduce costs in several ways. First, since little processing is done at the client level, inexpensive "thin clients" or network PCs, which have smaller CPUs and limited RAM and secondary storage, can be used. Second, fewer copies of applications software need to be purchased and maintained. Third, data transmission costs are reduced, because the large chunks of data are sent primarily between the two server levels, not to each individual client.

Setting up a three-tier client/server architecture is expensive, however. In addition, applications development is more complex. Thus, as with other configuration choices, there is no one best solution; instead, the optimal configuration depends on the needs of the specific organization.

CONTROL AND ACCOUNTING ISSUES IN ELECTRONIC COMMERCE

Electronic commerce is simply another method of doing business. In fact, in one sense the primary difference between electronic commerce and traditional business transactions is that trading partners exchange data electronically, instead of by phone, fax, or paper documents. Thus the same basic principles for efficiently and effectively executing and properly controlling business activities in traditional environments also apply to electronic commerce. Nevertheless, electronic commerce does raise new issues, which we discuss in this section.

Control Issues in Electronic Commerce

Electronic commerce creates control issues in three areas:

1. Validity of transactions
2. Authorization of transactions
3. Safeguarding of assets

Transaction Validity. One fundamental control objective of both electronic and traditional commerce is that all transactions are valid; in other words, assurance is needed that all transactions really occurred. In electronic commerce, transaction validity requires two things: (1) authenticating the identity of the other party to the transaction, and (2) ensuring that the information is not altered during transmission between the buyer and seller.

Authentication is essentially a question of trust: customers want assurance that the seller is a legitimate business; conversely, sellers want assurance that the customer exists and will not be able to repudiate the transaction. The manner in which customers can authenticate the seller depends, in part, on the type of electronic commerce being conducted. In business-to-business electronic commerce, companies can adapt the procedures they have already developed for identifying potential vendors in nonelectronic commerce settings. Indeed, most companies have established lists of preferred vendors and seldom make significant purchases from suppliers with whom they have never previously interacted. Therefore, authenticating the seller's identity may be of greater concern in business-to-consumer electronic commerce, because individuals may not have as easy access to independent sources of information. Consequently, a number of assurance services have been developed by third parties. Focus 7.1 described one such service, WebTrust.

A major concern of sellers, of course, concerns receiving payment from customers. In business-to-consumer electronic commerce this is seldom a problem, because payment is typically made at the time the transaction occurs before the merchandise is shipped. The situation is different in business-to-business electronic commerce, however, because companies frequently sell on credit to their customers. Consequently, the same procedures used to check the creditworthiness of new customers in nonelectronic commerce should be applied to electronic commerce.

It is also important to ensure that the information being exchanged in electronic commerce has not been altered during transmission between the trading partners. One way to reduce this risk is to use VPNs. If communication must be done over public networks, such as the Internet, the messages should be encrypted to make them difficult to read if intercepted by third parties. In addition, the use of digital signatures and message digests provides assurance that the message has not been altered. Chapter 9 discusses the mechanics of encryption, digital signatures, digital certificates, and message digests.

Proper Authorization of Transactions. One concern in any business transaction is providing a means to protect each party from unilateral repudiation of the transaction by the other party. Thus it is important to establish that transactions have been properly authorized. When paper documents are used, signatures provide proof that the transaction has been authorized and can be used to prevent unilateral repudiation of obligations. Digital signatures and digital certificates fulfill this function in electronic commerce.

Safeguarding Assets. Both organizations and individuals want to protect their assets. Electronic commerce creates a number of threats that must be addressed. In this section, we discuss three threats:

1. Loss of confidentiality
2. Unauthorized access
3. Loss of data

Loss of Confidentiality. One threat that arises in electronic commerce is the loss of confidentiality of data. This potential problem arises when using the Internet because it is a public packet-switching network, which means that there is no predetermined path that a message transverses. In other words, the sender cannot control or predetermine through which routers a message will go. This creates an opportunity for eavesdropping. The best way to protect confidential information that must be sent over the Internet is to encrypt the data prior to transmission to trading partners.

Unauthorized Access. Another threat is unauthorized access, either by outsiders or by employees, to parts of the system to which they should not have admittance. Passwords can provide some control over this threat. In addition, companies can build firewalls to insulate their internal systems from outside access through the Internet or VANs. As shown in Fig. 7.12, a **firewall** is a combination of hardware and software that controls the flow of data into and out of an organization's AIS.

Firewalls can and should be implemented at two levels. At the first level, routers should intercept all incoming and outgoing data packets, examine the source or destination information, and decide whether or not to let that packet proceed. Packets that pass this test should then routed to the appropriate application gateway, which provides a second level of security. The application gateway can be programmed to examine the contents of incoming and outgoing packets and determine whether or not they should be allowed to pass further.

Firewalls, like any locks, can be penetrated. Consequently, companies also need to implement intrusion detection systems to provide real-time warning that unauthorized access is occurring. In addition, firewalls can be bypassed by wireless communications links between the AIS and outside parties. Thus computer security and internal audit professionals need to continuously monitor and review *all* links in their organization's communications network.

Loss of Data. Another threat with electronic commerce concerns the loss of data. The best way to address this threat is to regularly create backup copies of all vital information and store one copy at another location. A related threat concerns the loss of services. Indeed, as businesses become increasingly dependent on electronic commerce, any disruption of that capability, however temporary, can create significant economic loss. Thus it is important to develop and practice disaster recovery plans. Backup and disaster recovery are discussed in more detail in Chapter 9.

Control Opportunities. Although electronic commerce introduces some new threats not present in traditional methods of conducting business, it also provides the possibility of more effective control. For example, the use of VANs and the Internet can create a more complete audit trail than in traditional paper-based systems, *if* the electronic logging capabilities of such networks are properly utilized. Therefore, an important responsibility of accountants is ensuring that adequate controls are designed and implemented in an organization's AIS. This section has provided an overview of control issues related to electronic commerce. Part II (Chapters 8–11) describes in greater detail the design and testing of controls in AIS.

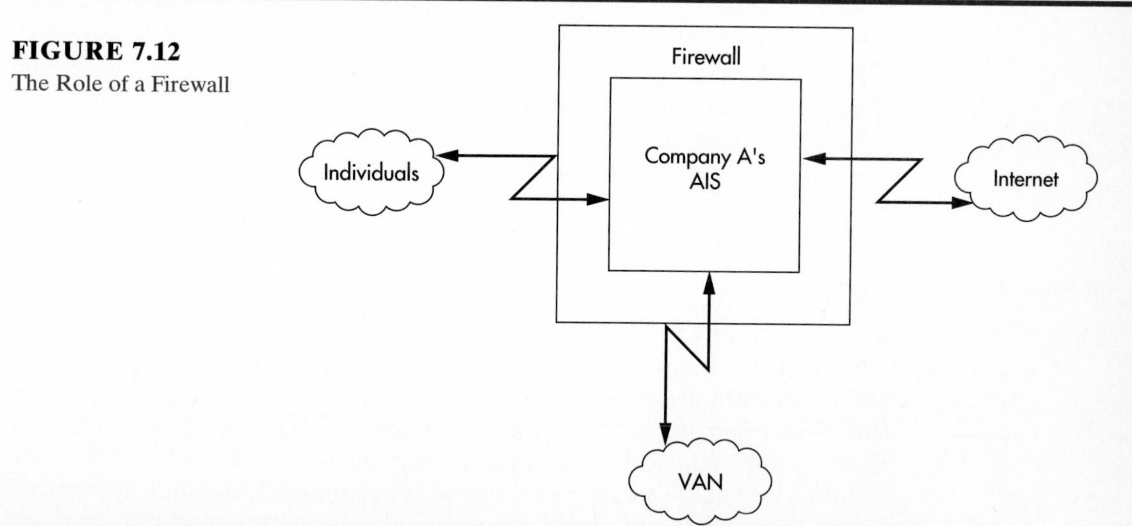

FIGURE 7.12
The Role of a Firewall

Accounting Issues

Two accounting issues related to electronic commerce are (1) the proper valuation of digital assets, and (2) taxation of electronic transactions.

Valuation of Digital Assets. Electronic commerce may involve the sale of digitized assets. For example, photographs can be digitized, stored, and distributed electronically. In the past, there were easily measurable costs associated with making copies of a photograph. In contrast, the marginal costs of making additional copies of a digitized image are close to zero. This raises questions about the cost of the goods sold. Moreover, when digitized assets are sold, the original item is not consumed. This raises questions about the cost of the digitized asset itself, and whether or not it should be depreciated.

Taxation. Taxation of electronic commerce is also a complex topic. One of the difficulties involves determining nexus, which is the legal term used to justify when and where a transaction can be taxed. The customer may live in Arizona, use an Internet service provider based in Maine to purchase items from a company located in Washington, and that company may use a shipping company headquartered in Tennessee to deliver the product. Which state(s) can properly tax that transaction is a complex question.

SUMMARY AND CASE CONCLUSION

S&S Today

Ashton spent as much time as he could spare learning about data communications. He soon realized S&S needed outside help and convinced Scott and Susan to hire some consultants. They hired Data Connections (DC), a firm specializing in data communications systems for small businesses.

After assessing their needs, DC suggested that S&S install a client/server LAN to facilitate the sharing of data internally. DC also suggested that S&S contract with an ISP to get access to the Internet. DC would help design S&S's web site. S&S's bank is EDI-capable, and so S&S will be able to implement FEDI with its suppliers, including DE.

Scott and Susan accepted DC's proposal and hired the firm to install the system, train employees, and prepare a recent accounting graduate for her role in maintaining and supporting the system. One of her key responsibilities will be ensuring that adequate controls are included in S&S's system.

S&S Five Years in the Future

Susan and Scott opened warehouse appliance clubs nationwide to sell high-volume and low-markup appliances. Each evening, a robot counts inventory in S&S's regional warehouses using a laser to scan the UPC on all merchandise. The robot enters the data into the warehouse computer, which reconciles the prior day's inventory, the current day's shipments and receipts, and the new inventory count. Discrepancies are sent to a manager's computer for investigation. The computer analyzes inventory on hand, daily usage, historical and seasonal trends, economic order quantities, and delivery times. It automatically orders goods from approved vendors and schedules their just-in-time arrival. All orders are sent to the inventory manager's computer for review. The computer reviews all store orders received and schedules appliance deliveries. Where appropriate, it arranges for goods to be sent directly from the suppliers to the individual stores. A similar system in the stores is linked to the warehouse computer. This is done electronically; there are no paper documents.

S&S encourages its customers to pay electronically, to provide instant access to cash and eliminate handling large amounts of currency. When merchandise is delivered, funds are electronically transferred to supplier accounts. Employees and most bills are also paid electronically. For instance, when the utility company sends an electronic notice showing energy consumption, the computer verifies that usage is within acceptable parameters before electronically transferring funds to the utility.

S&S subscribes to a personalized information service that focuses on individual information needs. The service remembers what subscribers like to read, combs information sources, and produces a personalized, electronic newspaper. Periodic feedback allows the system to learn each subscriber's needs and wants. One of the first things Scott and Susan do every day is read their personal newspaper. Articles they want to store are filed by the service, and items they want to act on are transferred to their personal productivity software (a combination spreadsheet, decision support system, graphics package, and word processor).

On a recent business trip, Susan received a message from the Appliance Vendors Association president telling her that Congress was proposing import restrictions on countries that were key appliance suppliers. Based on this information, he asked Susan to produce a report that he could take to a meeting scheduled with his representative. She used her laptop computer to access her files at S&S and download information. To get data on foreign imports and on pricing differences between their products and comparable U.S. ones, she downloaded data from a public data base. Susan then accessed the association's expert system to determine where appliances could be purchased most inexpensively when cost, freight, import duties, and several similar factors were included.

Susan used a special audiovisual room at the hotel to film a videotape presentation. She electronically sent a copy of her report and presentation to her office computer and directed that the report be printed and placed on her desk and that the presentation be stored on videotape. She sent a message on the S&S LAN scheduling a meeting with her buyers the day after her return. Finally, she sent the report and visual presentation to the association president with a note telling him where she could be reached for the remainder of the trip.

Two days later, the hotel clerk told her she had e-mail waiting and transferred it to the computer in her room. She found her report with requests for some minor changes. She made the corrections on the hotel's computer, sent a copy to the president and her office computer, and stored a copy on her laptop.

Does this sound farfetched? It shouldn't. Most of the technology required for such a scenario is already in place. It is just a matter of designing systems to take advantage of the technology. Remember that the personal computer is just a little over 20 years old. Think of all the progress that has been made in that time. If technology advances as quickly in the next 20 years as it has in the last 20, there are endless possibilities in store for the information systems of the future.

KEY TERMS

electronic commerce
electronic data interchange (EDI)
electronic funds transfer (EFT)
financial electronic data interchange (FEDI)
financial value-added network (FVAN)
local area network (LAN)
wide area network (WAN)
value-added network (VAN)
Internet
internet service providers (ISPs)
intranet
extranets
virtual private network (VPN)
network interface card (NIC)
modem
remote access devices
hub
switches
routers
bandwidth
distributed data processing (DDP)
firewall

CHAPTER QUIZ

1. Which of the following is not one of the five major components of a data communications system?
   a. Sending device
   b. Communications interface device
   c. Communications channel
   d. Communications software
   e. Message

2. Sending remittance data and payments together electronically is referred to as
   a. EDI.
   b. EFT.
   c. FVAN.
   d. FEDI.

3. Which of the following is not a control issue associated with electronic commerce?
   a. Invalid transactions
   b. Unauthorized transactions
   c. Lack of an audit trail
   d. Loss of confidentiality

4. The hardware device that provides a central wiring point for connecting many different computers and peripherals together is a
   a. router.
   b. hub.
   c. switch.
   d. modem.

5. Which of the following communications channels has the greatest bandwidth?
   a. Twisted-pair cables
   b. Coaxial cable
   c. Fiber optics cable
   d. T-1 lines

6. A network used to implement FEDI is
   a. the Internet.
   b. an FVAN.
   c. an intranet.
   d. an extranet.

7. In which of the following network configurations are all of the devices linked directly to a host computer?
   a. Ring
   b. Star
   c. Bus
   d. DDP

8. A network used to establish a secure link between two trading partners is
   a. the Internet.
   b. an intranet.
   c. a WAN.
   d. a VPN.

9. Assume S&S has expanded to six stores located in different parts of the country. It could link each store together by means of a
   a. LAN.
   b. extranet.
   c. WAN.
   d. VPN.

10. To prevent unauthorized access to its AIS, S&S should use
   a. encryption.
   b. firewalls.
   c. intrusion detection software.
   d. NIC.

DISCUSSION QUESTIONS

7.1 Communication is vital to any organization, especially to a multidivisional company spread over a wide geographic area. Corporate structure is often aligned along communications lines. Discuss the organizational structure that might conform to a centralized, decentralized, or DDP network configuration. If an improper configuration were chosen, what kind of organizational difficulties might arise?

7.2 Will the Internet replace shopping malls? Why or why not?

7.3 Do you think that electronic commerce is likely to provide more benefits to the customer or to the seller? Defend your answer.

7.4 Traditionally, vendors required payment within 30 days, but offered discounts for earlier payment. How will the use of EDI or FEDI likely affect such practices?

7.5 Firms that successfully digitize their assets can reap significant cost advantages. Consider, for example, the business of selling reproductions of famous photographs and paintings. How is digitalization likely to affect the structure of this market? Will it increase or decrease the number of competitors? Why?

7.6 Would the presence or absence of a third party—provided seal, such as WebTrust, influence your willingness to engage in electronic commerce with that company? Why or why not? Would your answer differ if you were a small business owner, rather than an individual consumer?

7.7 Privacy advocates argue that individuals own all the information about themselves and, therefore, have the right to control the distribution of that information to third parties. An opposing argument is that you cannot outlaw gossip and the creation of a reputation; indeed, such gathering and sharing of information about people is an essential part of commerce. What do you think? Do we need a coherent set of laws regarding the sharing and dissemination of information communicated by e-mail? Why or why not?

7.8 There is some evidence that many workers receive *too much* e-mail, thereby reducing their overall productivity. Discuss some ways to manage this problem.

PROBLEMS

7.1 Your friend owns a company that has offices in several locations and asks you whether she should implement a centralized, decentralized, or distributed data processing system. Prepare a one-page memo that explains the advantages and disadvantages of each approach. (SMAC Examination, adapted)

7.2 Colorgraph Printing is reviewing a proposal to acquire Puball Publishers. Puball's operations are located 300 miles from Colorgraph's headquarters. Colorgraph's recent success has been due in large part to its computerized AIS. Puball, however, has used a computer only for financial accounting applications such as payroll and inventory records. In considering the acquisition, Colorgraph's board of directors focused on two options for developing an AIS that would include Puball: a centralized or a distributed system.

Required:

a. Compare the information likely to be transmitted to headquarters in a centralized and in a distributed system.
b. Explain why Puball's management is more likely to be involved in and concerned with data processing in a distributed rather than a centralized system. Assume Puball is a separate profit center.
c. Explain briefly why a distributed system is less subject to a complete system breakdown.
(CIA Examination, adapted)

7.3 The Widget Manufacturing Company is installing a LAN at its San Francisco sales office that will be linked to its computer center in Los Angeles 400 miles away. One decision that must be made is whether to lease a line, obtain a WATS line, or use switched public lines for this long-distance connection. The monthly cost of a leased line includes a service charge of $83.50 plus mileage charges based on the following rates:

Mileage	Rate/Mile
0–100	$2.82
101–250	$1.48
251–300	$0.79
Over 300	$0.26

In computing total monthly mileage charges, a separate calculation is needed for each individual mileage segment, with the results then added to obtain a total cost. For example, a 300-mile line includes a fixed cost of $83.50 plus mileage charges of $2.82(100) + $1.48(150) + $0.79(50), for a total of $627.00.

The charge for a WATS line includes $30.50 per month for the service charge plus $18 per hour for the monthly use charge. Public telephone rates are $0.57 for the first minute and $0.34 for each additional minute. It is estimated that the time for entering a transaction over the terminal will average two minutes.

Required:

a. Compute the monthly cost of the leased line.
b. At what average monthly volume of transactions will the total cost of the leased line be equal to the cost of using (1) the WATS line and (2) the switched public lines? (Make each computation separately.)
c. Assume an average volume of 810 transactions per month. Which of the three alternatives is least expensive? Show supporting calculations.
d. If switched public lines are used, assume that the transactions will be entered in groups of three so that the extra rate for the first minute will be avoided for two-thirds of all transactions. How will this factor affect your answer to part (c)?

7.4 The Texas Machinery Distributing Company, a machinery products wholesaler, has its headquarters and a central warehouse in Houston, Texas. Sales offices are in Dallas, Waco, Austin, San Antonio, Laredo, Corpus Christi, and Abilene. The company plans to install a data communications system for processing sales orders. The computer center is located in Houston, and PCs will be located in each sales office. A major concern of the company is the cost of the data communications network. The company is considering four alternative configurations:

1. Voice-grade leased lines from Houston to each sales office
2. A wideband line from Houston to Austin and a modem bank in Austin to service six voice-grade leased lines from the other six sales offices
3. Normal telephone dial-up service from each sales office to Houston
4. A wideband line from Houston to Austin and modem bank in Austin to service dial-up lines from the other six sales offices

In addition to a monthly charge of $98.50, monthly cost figures for each voice-grade leased line are as follows:

Mileage	Rate/Mile
0–50	$2.20
51–150	$1.40
Over 150	$1.05

Monthly costs for wideband leased lines are as follows:

Mileage	Rate/Mile
0–50	$2.40
51–150	$1.60
Over 150	$1.20

In addition, there is a $165.20 monthly charge for each wideband line. (Note: For an explanation of how these rates are used, see Problem 7.3.)

The following table shows the distance in miles from Houston to the seven sales offices and from Austin to the other six sales offices:

	Houston	Austin
Waco	181	106
Austin	164	—
Dallas	244	198
San Antonio	195	79
Laredo	312	233
Corpus Christi	208	194
Abilene	349	217

The following table shows the cost of a two-minute long-distance call from Houston to the seven sales offices and from Austin to the other six sales offices:

	Houston	Austin
Waco	$0.88	$0.82
Austin	0.85	—
Dallas	0.91	0.88
San Antonio	0.88	0.76
Laredo	0.94	0.91
Corpus Christi	0.88	0.88
Abilene	0.94	0.91

It is assumed that each call will last approximately two minutes.

The following table shows the expected average monthly volume of calls from each of the seven sales offices.

Office	Monthly Volume
Waco	200
Austin	450
Dallas	650
San Antonio	500
Laredo	150
Corpus Christi	350
Abilene	200

If either alternative 2 or 4 is chosen, there will also be operating costs of approximately $500 per month.

Required:

Based on cost, which alternative should the company select?

7.5 The Savings Bank of California (SBC) is a large bank headquartered in Los Angeles. One of its selling points is a customer's ability to bank at offices throughout the state. SBC has regional offices in San Diego, Orange County, southern and northern Los Angeles, and San Francisco. Each region consists of between five and eight local banks.

SBC has established its own statewide real-time computer system. Each regional office maintains a data base for its local savings, checking, and loan customers. This data base can be accessed by the banks in that particular region, by other regional offices, and by corporate headquarters. Each local bank has 4 to 12 terminals that tie into a minicomputer. The minicomputers at each local bank are linked directly to computers located at SBC's regional offices. The lines between the local banks and the regional offices have fairly heavy use because of the number of transactions handled each day. Each regional computer is tied to two others, so that if one goes down, information can quickly be rerouted. In addition to being tied to two other regional computers, each one is tied directly to a mainframe computer at corporate headquarters.

Both the regional computers and the headquarters mainframe use front-end processors to help manage the data communications process. The regional computers are used during the day to process checks, bank card payments, and other transactions to customer accounts. During each day, the regional computers periodically update the mainframe data bases based on transactions processed during the last 24 hours. The mainframe computer at corporate headquarters coordinates the activities of the regional computers and maintains SBC's company-wide records. The headquarters mainframe also handles all fund transfers with the bank's office in New York. Communication between corporate headquarters and the New York office is through microwave transmission.

Tellers at each local branch use terminals hooked up to the bank's minicomputer to access the regional computer data base. If a customer is from the local region, his or her account is updated for the transaction. If not, the correct regional data base is accessed and updated. Funds from the local region are then transferred from or to the accessed region to cover the transaction.

Required:

a. What type of communications network is SBC using: centralized, decentralized, DDP, LAN, VAN, PBX, or other? How do you know?
b. Draw the communications network configuration used by SBC. Is this network a star, bus, ring, or some type of hybrid network?
c. What kinds of communications channels can SBC use in their data communications system? When is each most appropriate, and what are the advantages and drawbacks of each?
d. Should the channels that connect the local banks and the regional centers be narrowband, voiceband, or wideband? Why?

7.6 Visit several web pages for companies that are in the same industry. Select two: one that, in your opinion, is well designed, and one that is poorly designed. Write a brief memo to your instructor comparing and contrasting the two web pages. Include their URLs (Universal Resource Locators, also known as web addresses) in your report.

7.7 Design a web page for S&S. Write a brief report explaining and justifying your design choices. Describe how the web page can be used to support one of the strategic positions discussed in Chapter 1. Include the URL for your web page in your report.

7.8 Financial institutions face specific threats related to FEDI. Write a brief report describing the types of controls they use over both incoming and outgoing fund flows. Explain the purpose of each control activity.

7.9 A regional bank with offices in a four-state area wants to redesign its WAN. One decision involves the choice of a communications channel for long-distance links. Write a brief memo identifying the control threats that may arise if the bank uses each of the following as its primary long-distance communications channel:

a. Satellites
b. Microwave
c. The Internet
d. An FVAN
e. Leased telephone lines

7.10 Identify the control(s) that would best mitigate each threat:

a. Unauthorized entry to a company's payroll system by someone surfing the Internet.
b. Theft of a credit card number sent over the Internet.
c. Repudiation of a sale by a customer who claims that she did *not* order any merchandise from your company.
d. You order and pay for goods with your credit card at a company's web site, but never receive any merchandise from them because the company did not really exist.
e. The hard disk of the company's server crashed, destroying the accounts receivable master file.
f. A salesperson gained access to the company's human resource system and read his supervisor's annual performance evaluation of another employee.
g. A competitor intercepted your on-line bid for a county project and used the information to underbid and win the contract.

CASE 7.1 ANYCOMPANY, INC.—AN ONGOING COMPREHENSIVE CASE

Visit a local company and obtain permission to study its data communications system. Once you have lined up a company, write a report that summarizes the following information:

a. What is the general structure of the company's data communications network? Is processing and control centralized, decentralized, or distributed? Why does the company use this structure?
b. Identify the data communications hardware and software the company employs.
c. Identify the data communications channels the company uses by determining what the principal characteristics of each channel are and what channel configurations are used.
d. Does the company use EDI or FEDI? Why or why not?
e. What types of security procedures (firewalls, encryption, etc.) does the company employ?
f. Does the company have a web page? If so, how is it used? Critique the company's web page and offer suggestions for improvements.

CASE 7.2 ELECTRONIC PAYMENTS

Research the various methods of making payments electronically, such as smart cards, cybercash, credit cards, EFT, and others. Write a brief (maximum four pages, double-spaced) report that discusses the advantages and disadvantages of each approach.

CASE 7.3 ELECTRONIC COMMERCE OPPORTUNITIES

Research the use of electronic commerce in different industries. Write a report describing the extent to which electronic commerce is utilized in at least four different industries. Discuss the industry characteristics, such as nature of products or services being sold, that appear to encourage or discourage the use of electronic commerce.

ANSWERS TO CHAPTER QUIZ

1. e	**3.** c	**5.** c	**7.** b	**9.** c
2. d	**4.** b	**6.** b	**8.** d	**10.** b

PART TWO

CHAPTER 8

Control and Accounting Information Systems

Learning Objectives

After studying this chapter, you should be able to

- Describe the threats to an AIS and discuss why these threats are growing.
- Explain the basic concepts of control as applied to business organizations.
- Describe the major elements in the control environment of a business organization.
- Describe control policies and procedures commonly used in business organizations.
- Evaluate a system of internal accounting control, identify its deficiencies, and prescribe modifications to remedy those deficiencies.
- Conduct a cost–benefit analysis for particular threats, exposures, risks, and controls.

Integrative Case: Springer's Northwest Lumber & Supply

After completing his bachelor's degree in accounting at Idaho State, Jason Scott has been hired as an internal auditor for Northwest Industries, a diversified forest products company. He is assigned to audit Springer's Lumber & Supply, Northwest's building materials outlet in Bozeman, Montana. His supervisor, Maria Pilier, has asked him to trace a sample of purchase transactions from purchase requisition to cash disbursement to verify that proper control procedures were followed. By mid-afternoon Jason is frustrated with this task, and for good reasons:

- The purchasing system is poorly documented.
- He keeps finding transactions that have not been processed as Ed Yates, the accounts payable manager, said they should be.
- Purchase requisitions are missing for several items that had been personally authorized by Bill Springer, the purchasing vice president.
- Some vendor invoices have been paid without supporting documents, such as purchase orders or receiving reports.
- Prices charged for some items seem unusually high, and there are a few discrepancies in item prices between the vendor invoice and the corresponding purchase order. Yates seemed to have a logical answer for every question Jason raised. Yates ended the discussion by advising Jason that the real world is not always as tidy as the world portrayed in college textbooks. When Jason discussed his findings with Maria, he learned that she also has some concerns:
- Springer's is the largest supplier in the area and has a near monopoly.
- Management authority is concentrated in the company president, Joe Springer, and his two sons Bill (the purchasing VP) and

Ted (the controller). Several relatives and friends are on the payroll. Together the Springers own 10% of the company.

- Lines of authority and responsibility within the company are loosely defined and hard to understand.
- Maria feels that Ted Springer may have engaged in "creative accounting" to make Springer's one of Northwest's best-performing retail outlets.

After talking to Maria, Jason ponders the following issues:

1. Since Ed Yates had a logical explanation for every unusual transaction, should Jason describe these transactions in his report?
2. Is a violation of proper control procedures acceptable if it has been authorized by management?
3. Maria's concerns about Springer's loosely defined lines of authority and possible use of creative accounting are matters of management policy. With respect to Jason's control procedures assignment, does he have a professional or an ethical responsibility to get involved?

INTRODUCTION

Our society has become increasingly dependent on accounting information systems, which have grown increasingly more complex to meet our escalating needs for information. As system complexity and our dependence on them increase, companies face the growing risk of their systems being compromised. The four types of threats a company faces, which are summarized in Table 8.1, are discussed in the first part of this chapter.

AIS THREATS

One threat companies face is natural and political disasters such as fires, excessive heat, floods, earthquakes, high winds, and war. An unpredictable disaster can completely destroy an information system and cause a company to fail. When a disaster strikes, many companies can be affected at the same time. For example, a flood in Chicago destroyed or damaged 400 data processing centers. Examples of these types of disasters include the following:

- A few years ago unrelenting rains caused the Mississippi and Missouri rivers to overflow and flood parts of eight states. Many organizations lost their computer systems, including the city of Des Moines, Iowa, whose computers were buried by 8 feet of water.
- An earthquake in Los Angeles destroyed a number of systems and others were damaged by falling debris, water from ruptured sprinkler systems, dust, and severed communication lines. Companies in San Francisco suffered a similar fate a few years earlier.

TABLE 8.1 Threats to Accounting Information Systems

Threats	Examples
Natural and political disasters	Fire or excessive heat Floods Earthquakes High winds War
Software errors and equipment malfunctions	Hardware failures Power outages and fluctuations Undectected data transmission errors
Unintentional acts	Accidents caused by human carelessness, failure to follow established procedures, and poorly trained or supervised personnel Innocent errors or omissions Lost or misplaced data Logic errors Systems that do not meet company needs or are incapable of handling their intended tasks
Intentional acts (computer crimes)	Sabotage Computer fraud Embezzlement

- Terrorist attacks on the World Trade Center in New York City and the Federal Building in Oklahoma City destroyed or disrupted the systems in those buildings.
- The Defense Science Board has predicted that by 2005 attacks on information systems by foreign countries, espionage agents, and terrorists will be widespread.

A second threat to companies is software errors and equipment malfunctions such as hardware failures, power outages and fluctuations, and undetected data transmission errors. For example:

- Bugs in a new tax accounting system were to blame for the state of California's failure to collect $635 million in business taxes.
- At the Bank of New York, a field used to count the number of transactions was too small to handle the volume on a busy day. The error shut the system down and left the bank $23 million short when it tried to close its books. It had to borrow money overnight at a significant cost.

A third threat to companies is unintentional acts such as accidents or innocent errors and omissions. These are usually caused by human carelessness, failure to follow established procedures, and poorly trained or supervised personnel. Users often lose or misplace data and accidentally erase or alter files, data, and programs. Computer operators and users can enter the wrong input or erroneous input, use the wrong version of a program, use the wrong data files, or misplace the files. Systems analysts and programmers make logic errors, develop systems that do not meet the company's needs, or develop systems incapable of handling their intended tasks. Examples include the following:

- A data entry clerk at Giant Food, Inc. mistakenly keyed in a quarterly dividend of $2.50 instead of $0.25. As a result, the company paid over $10 million in excess dividends.
- In a bank, a programmer mistakenly calculated interest for each month using 31 days. In the five months before the mistake was discovered, over $100,000 in excess interest was paid out on the savings accounts.
- For years programmers have economized by using only the last two digits of the year (99 for 1999). As the year 2000 nears, problems due to this shortsightedness will increase. The Gartner Group, a consulting firm, estimates that 250 billion lines of code will have to be changed worldwide at a cost of $600 billion to $1 trillion; half of all companies will *not* be fully ready; and 30% of mission critical applications will not be ready. Companies that ignore the issue will face lawsuits and bankruptcy, or go out of business.

A fourth threat that companies face is intentional acts, typically referred to as computer crimes. This threat can take the form of **sabotage**, in which the intent is to destroy a system or some of its components. Or it can be a computer fraud, where the intent is to steal something of value such as money, data, or computer time or services. It can also involve **embezzlement,** which is the theft or misappropriation of assets by employees, accompanied by the falsification of records in order to conceal the theft. For example:

- A technology enthusiast, John Draper, discovered that the whistle offered as a prize in Cap'n Crunch cereal exactly duplicated the frequency of a WATS line. He used his discovery to defraud the phone companies by making a large number of free telephone calls.
- An AIS manager at a Florida newspaper went to work for a competitor when he was fired. Before long, the first employer realized that its reporters were constantly being scooped. The newspaper finally discovered that the AIS manager still had an active account and password and regularly browsed its computer files for information on its exclusive stories.

The greatest risks to information systems and the greatest dollar losses result from innocent errors and omissions. Carl Jackson, past president of the Information Systems Security Association, estimates that 65% of security problems are caused by human errors, 20% by natural and political disasters, and 15% by fraud.

Why AIS Threats Are Increasing

As a result of these problems, controlling the security and integrity of computer systems has become a very important issue. Most AIS managers indicate that control risks have increased in the last few years. For example, a recent study by Coopers & Lybrand found that more than 60% of organizations in the United Kingdom experienced a major control failure in the past two years. Studies in other countries have yielded similar statistics. Among the many reasons for the increase in security problems are these:

- Increasing numbers of client/server systems means that information is available to an unprecedented number of workers. Computers and servers are everywhere; there are PCs on most desktops, and laptop computers accompany people wherever they go. Chevron, for example, has 33,000 PCs.
- Because LANs and client/server systems distribute data to many users, they are harder to control than centralized, mainframe systems. At Chevron, information is distributed among many systems and thousands of employees working locally and remotely as well as nationally and internationally.
- WANs are giving customers and suppliers access to each other's systems and data, making confidentiality a major concern. For example, you learned in Focus 1.2 that Wal-Mart allows Procter & Gamble to have access to certain information in its computers as a condition of their alliance. Imagine the potential confidentiality problems if P&G also formed alliances with Wal-Mart competitors such as Kmart and Target.

Unfortunately, many organizations do not adequately protect their data due to one or more of the following reasons:

- Computer control problems are often underestimated and downplayed, and companies view the loss of crucial information as a distant, unlikely threat. For example, less that 25% of 1,250 participants in an Ernst & Young study thought computer security was an extremely important issue. That figure was down from about 35% in the prior year's survey.
- The control implications of moving from the centralized, host-based computer systems of the past to those of a networked system are not fully understood.
- Many companies do not realize that data security is crucial to their survival. Information is a strategic resource, and protecting it must be a strategic requirement. For example, one company lost millions of dollars over a period of several years because it did not protect its data transmissions. A competitor tapped into its phone lines and obtained faxes of new product designs sent to an offshore plant.
- Productivity and cost pressures motivate management to forgo time-consuming control measures.

Fortunately, companies are increasingly recognizing the problems and are taking positive steps to increase computer control and security. For example, they are becoming proactive in their approach. They are devoting full-time staff to security and control concerns and educating their employees about control measures. Many are establishing and enforcing formal information security policies. They are making controls a part of the applications development process and are moving sensitive data off the unsecured client servers to a more secure environment, such as a mainframe.

As a future accountant, you must understand how to protect systems from the threats they face. You must also have a good understanding of information technology (IT) and its capabilities and risks. This knowledge can help you use IT to achieve an organization's control objectives.

Achieving adequate security and control over the information resources of an organization should be a top management priority. Although internal control objectives remain the same regardless of the data processing method, a computer-based AIS requires different internal control policies and procedures. For example, while computer processing reduces the potential for clerical errors, it may increase the risks of unauthorized access to or modification of data files. In addition, segregating the authorization, recording, and asset custody functions within an AIS must be achieved differently, since computer programs may be responsible for two or all three of these functions. Fortunately, computers also provide opportunities for an organization to enhance its internal controls.

Assisting management in the control of a business organization is one of the primary objectives of an AIS. The accountant can help achieve this objective by designing effective control systems and by auditing (or reviewing) control systems already in place to assure that they are operating effectively.

Any potential adverse occurrence or unwanted event that could be injurious to either the AIS or the organization, such as one or more of these elements, is referred to as a **threat.** The potential dollar loss should a particular threat became a reality is referred to as the **exposure** from the threat, and the likelihood that the threat will actually come to pass is referred to as the **risk** associated with the threat.

As a future accountant, you must understand how to protect systems from threats. Management expects accountants to be their control consultants. That is, it is the accountant's job to (1) take a proactive approach to eliminating system threats and (2) detect, correct, and recover from threats if and when they occur.

The four chapters in Part IV focus on control concepts. This chapter explains general principles of control in business organizations and describes key control procedures most suitable for a typical AIS. Chapter 9 describes how control principles apply to a computer-based AIS and explains the control procedures most applicable to them. Chapter 10 provides an in-depth examination of the causes and remedies for fraud. Chapter 11 examines the processes and procedures used in auditing a computer-based AIS.

OVERVIEW OF CONTROL CONCEPTS

Internal control is the plan of organization and the methods a business uses to safeguard assets, provide accurate and reliable information, promote and improve operational efficiency, and encourage adherence to prescribed managerial policies. These internal control purposes are sometimes at odds with each other. For example, many people are pushing for radical business process reengineering so they can have better and faster information and improve operational efficiency. Others resist those changes because they impede the safeguarding of company assets and require significant changes in managerial policies.

Management control is broader than internal accounting control and encompasses the following three features:

1. It is an integral part of management responsibilities.
2. It is designed to reduce errors and irregularities and achieve organizational goals.
3. It is personnel-oriented and seeks to help employees attain company goals by following organizational policies.

The **internal control structure** is the policies and procedures established to provide a reasonable level of assurance that the organization's specific objectives will be achieved. The system only provides reasonable assurance, because a system that provides complete assurance would be difficult to design and prohibitively expensive.

Internal Control Classifications

The concepts of internal control and management control are broad in scope, aimed at describing entire control systems. The specific control procedures used in these systems may be classified using the following four internal control classifications.

Preventive, Detective, and Corrective. **Preventive controls** deter problems before they arise. Hiring highly qualified accounting personnel, appropriately segregating employee duties, and effectively controlling physical access to assets, facilities, and information are effective preventive controls. Because not all control problems can be prevented, **detective controls** are needed to discover control problems as soon as they arise. Examples of detective controls are duplicate checking of calculations and preparing bank reconciliations and monthly trial balances. **Corrective controls** remedy problems discovered with detective controls. They include procedures taken to (1) identify the cause of a problem, (2) correct resulting errors or difficulties, and (3) modify the system so that future problems are minimized or eliminated. Examples include maintaining backup copies of key transaction and master files, and adhering to procedures for correcting data entry errors as well as those for resubmitting transactions for subsequent processing.

General and Application. **General controls** are designed to ensure that an organization's control environment is stable and well managed to enhance the effectiveness of application controls. **Application controls** are used to prevent, detect, and correct errors and irregularities in transactions as they are processed. These two control classifications are discussed in Chapter 9.

Administrative and Accounting. **Administrative controls** help ensure operational efficiency and adherence to managerial policies. In contrast, **accounting controls** help safeguard assets and ensure the reliability of financial records.

Input, Processing, and Output. Controls can also be classified according to where they are implemented in the data processing cycle. **Input controls** are designed to ensure that only accurate, valid, and authorized data are entered into the system. For example, the computer could be programmed to reject payroll input for employees unless they are included on a list of authorized employees. **Processing controls** are designed to ensure that all transactions are processed accurately and completely and that all files and records are properly updated. An example is the batch totals described later in the chapter. **Output controls** are designed to ensure that system output is properly controlled. For example, unauthorized employees should be prevented from obtaining a copy of the report documenting top management's salaries.

The nature of a particular control procedure is less important than whether it effectively accomplishes its objective, which is to prevent losses to the organization resulting from a particular threat or hazard. In analyzing controls, one must first define an organization's control objectives. The next step is to determine whether effective control procedures (of any type) are in place to accomplish these control objectives.

The Foreign Corrupt Practices Act

In 1977 shock waves reverberated through the accounting profession when Congress incorporated language from an AICPA pronouncement into the **Foreign Corrupt Practices Act.** Specifically, all publicly owned corporations subject to the Securities Exchange Act of 1934 are now legally required to keep records that accurately and fairly reflect their transactions and assets in reasonable detail. They must also devise and maintain an internal accounting control system sufficient to provide reasonable assurances that (1) transactions are properly authorized and recorded; (2) assets are safeguarded and protected from unauthorized access; and (3) recorded asset values are periodically compared with actual assets and any differences are corrected.

The primary purpose of the act was to prevent the bribery of foreign officials in order to obtain business. A significant effect of the act, however, was to require corporations to maintain good systems of internal accounting control! Needless to say, this requirement has generated tremendous interest among management, accountants, and auditors in the design and evaluation of internal control systems. It is important to recognize that it is much easier to build controls into a system at the initial design stage than to add them after the system has been designed or built. For that reason, accountants and other control experts should be important members of the team that develops or modifies an information system.

Study by the Committee of Sponsoring Organizations

The **Committee of Sponsoring Organizations (COSO)** is a private sector group consisting of the American Accounting Association, the AICPA, the Institute of Internal Auditors, the Institute of Management Accountants, and the Financial Executives Institute. In 1992 COSO issued the results of a study to develop a definition of internal controls and to provide guidance for evaluating internal control systems. The report has been widely accepted as the authority on internal controls.

The study took three years and involved tens of thousands of hours of research, discussion, analysis, and due process. It involved hundreds of people, including members of the five COSO organizations, corporate chief executives and board members, legislators, regulators, lawyers, consultants, auditors, and academics. The report spells out employees' responsibilities for the proper functioning of controls and describes the external auditor's role in assessing controls. The report goes well beyond financial controls to incorporate the controls that management uses in running the company.

The COSO study defines internal control as the process implemented by the board of directors, management, and those under their direction to provide reasonable assurance that control objectives are achieved with regard to the following:

1. Effectiveness and efficiency of operations
2. Reliability of financial reporting
3. Compliance with applicable laws and regulations

Internal control is referred to as a *process,* because it permeates an organization's operating activities and is an integral part of basic management activities. Internal control provides reasonable, rather than absolute, assurance, because the possibilities of human failure, collusion, and management override of controls make this process an imperfect one.

COSO represents a significant move away from an internal control definition that is confined to accounting controls to one that addresses a wide range of board and management objectives. COSO's internal control model has five crucial components. These five components are summarized in Table 8.2 and are discussed in greater depth later in the chapter.

Study by the Information Systems Audit and Control Foundation

The Information Systems Audit and Control Foundation (ISACF) recently developed the Control Objectives for Information and related Technology (COBIT). COBIT is a framework of generally applicable IS security and control practices for information technology (IT) control. The framework allows (1) management to benchmark the security and control practices of IT environments, (2) users of IT services to be assured that adequate security and control exists, and (3) auditors to substantiate their opinions on internal control and to advise on IT security and control matters.

The framework addresses the issue of control from three vantage points, or dimensions:

1. To satisfy business objectives, information needs to conform to certain criteria that COBIT refers to as business requirements for information. The criteria are divided into seven distinct, yet overlapping categories, that map into the COSO objectives: effectiveness (relevant, pertinent, and timely), efficiency, confidentiality, integrity, availability, compliance with legal requirements, and reliability.
2. IT resources (people, application systems, technology, facilities, and data)

TABLE 8.2 Five Interrelated Components of COSO's Internal Control Model

Component	Description
Control environment	The core of any business is its people—their individual attributes, including integrity, ethical values, and competence—and the environment in which they operate. They are the engine that drives the organization and the foundation on which everything rests.
Control activities	Control policies and procedures must be established and executed to help ensure that the actions identified by management as necessary to address risks to achievement of the organization's objectives are effectively carried out.
Risk assessment	The organization must be aware of and deal with the risks it faces. It must set objectives, integrated with the sales, production, marketing, financial, and other activities so that the organization is operating in concert. It must also establish mechanisms to identify, analyze, and manage the related risks.
Information and communication	Surrounding the control activities are information and communication systems. They enable the organization's people to capture and exchange the information needed to conduct, manage, and control its operations.
Monitoring	The entire process must be monitored, and modifications made as necessary. In this way the system can react dynamically, changing as conditions warrant.

3. IT Processes (broken into four domains: planning and organization, acquisition and implementation, delivery and support, and monitoring)

COBIT, which consolidates standards from 36 different sources into a single framework, is having a big impact on the IS profession. It is helping managers learn how to balance risk and control investment in an IS environment. It provides users with greater assurance that the security and IT controls provided by internal and third parties are adequate. It guides auditors as they substantiate their opinions and as they provide advice to management on internal controls.

THE CONTROL ENVIRONMENT

A **control environment** consists of many factors, including the following:

1. Commitment to integrity and ethical values
2. Management's philosophy and operating style
3. Organizational structure
4. The audit committee of the board of directors
5. Methods of assigning authority and responsibility

6. Human resources policies and practices
7. External influences

Commitment to Integrity and Ethical Values

It is important for management to create an organizational culture that stresses integrity and ethical values. Companies can do this endorsing integrity as a basic principle of the company and by personally and actively teaching and practicing it. For example, top management should make it clear that honest reports are more important than favorable reports. Management should not assume that everyone accepts honesty. They should consistently reward and encourage honesty and give verbal labels to honest and dishonest behavior. If companies simply punish or reward honesty without giving it a label or explaining the principle, or if the standard of honesty is inconsistent, employees will most likely be inconsistent in their moral behavior.

Management should develop clearly stated policies that explicitly describe honest and dishonest behaviors. These policies should especially cover issues that are uncertain or unclear, such as conflicts of interest and the acceptance of gifts. For example, most purchasing agents would agree that accepting a $5,000 bribe from a supplier is dishonest, but a weekend vacation at a hunting cabin is not as clear-cut. A major cause of dishonesty comes from rationalizing these situations; it is natural for the criterion of expediency to replace the criterion of right versus wrong.

All dishonest acts should be thoroughly investigated and those found guilty should be dismissed. Enough dishonest employees should be prosecuted to let employees know that dishonesty will not be tolerated and will be punished.

Management's Philosophy and Operating Style

The more responsible management's philosophy and operating style are, the more likely it is that employees will behave responsibly in working to achieve the organization's objectives. If management shows little concern for internal controls, employees are less diligent and effective in achieving specific control objectives. For example, Maria Pilier found that lines of authority and responsibility at Springer's were loosely defined, and she suspected that management may have engaged in creative accounting to show its performance in the best light. Meanwhile, Jason Scott found evidence of poor internal control practices in the purchasing and accounts payable function. It is quite possible that these two conditions are related—that is, that management's loose attitude contributed to purchasing's inattentiveness to good internal control practices.

Management's philosophy and operating style can be assessed by answering questions such as the following:

- Does management take undue business risks to achieve its objectives, or does it assess potential risks and rewards prior to acting?
- Does management attempt to manipulate such performance measures as net income so that its performance can be seen in a more favorable light?

- Does management pressure employees to achieve results regardless of the methods, or do they demand ethical behavior? In other words, do they believe the ends justify the means?

Organizational Structure

A company's organizational structure defines its lines of authority and responsibility and provides the overall framework for planning, directing, and controlling its operations. Important aspects of organizational structure include the centralization or decentralization of authority, the assignment of responsibility for specific tasks, the way responsibility allocation affects management's information requirements, and the organization of the accounting and information system (IS) functions. An overly complex or unclear organizational structure may indicate more serious problems. ESM, a brokerage company dealing in government securities, used a multilayered organizational structure to hide a $300 million fraud. Company officers funneled cash to themselves and hid it by reporting a fictitious receivable from a related company in their financial statements.

In today's business world, drastic changes are occurring in management practices and in the organization of companies. Hierarchical organizational structures, with many layers of management who supervise and control the work of those under them, are disappearing. They are being replaced with flat organizations that have self-directed work teams composed of employees formerly assigned to separate and segregated departments. Team members are empowered to make decisions and no longer have to seek multiple layers of approvals to complete their work. There is an emphasis on continuous improvement rather than the periodic reviews and appraisals characteristic of earlier evaluators. These changes have an enormous impact on a company's organizational structure and on the nature and type of controls used in organizations.

The Audit Committee of the Board of Directors

All corporations listed on the New York Stock Exchange must have an **audit committee** composed entirely of outside (nonemployee) directors. The audit committee is responsible for overseeing the corporation's internal control structure, its financial reporting process, and its compliance with related laws, regulations, and standards. The committee works closely with the corporation's external and internal auditors. One of the committee's responsibilities is to provide an independent review of the actions of corporate managers on behalf of company shareholders. This review serves as a check on management integrity and increases the confidence of the investing public in the propriety of financial reporting.

Methods of Assigning Authority and Responsibility

Management should assign responsibility for specific business objectives to specific departments and individuals and then hold them accountable for achieving those objectives. Authority and responsibility may be assigned through formal job descriptions, employee training, and operating plans, schedules, and budgets. Of particular importance is a formal company code of conduct addressing such matters as standards of ethical behavior, acceptable business practices, regulatory requirements, and conflicts of interest.

A written **policy and procedures manual** is an important tool for assigning authority and responsibility. The manual spells out management policy with respect to handling specific transactions. In addition, it documents the systems and procedures employed to process those transactions. It includes the organization's chart of accounts and sample copies of forms and documents. The manual is a helpful on-the-job reference for employees and a useful tool in training new employees.

Human Resources Policies and Practices

Policies and practices dealing with hiring, training, evaluating, compensating, and promoting employees affect an organization's ability to minimize threats, risks, and exposures. Employees should be hired and promoted based on how well they meet written job requirements. Résumés, reference letters, and background checks are important means of evaluating the qualifications of job applicants. Training programs should familiarize new employees with their responsibilities as well as organization policies and procedures. Finally, policies with respect to working conditions, compensation, job incentives, and career advancement can be a powerful force in encouraging efficiency and loyal service.

The importance of thorough background checks is underscored by the case of Philip Crosby Associates (PCA), a consulting and training firm. PCA undertook an exhaustive search to select a financial director and hired John Nelson, an MBA and CPA with a glowing reference from his former employer. In reality, the CPA and reference were phony. Nelson was really Robert W. Liszewski, who had recently served an 18-month jail sentence for embezzling $400,000 from an Indiana bank. By the time PCA discovered this, Liszewski had embezzled $960,000 using wire transfers to a dummy corporation supported by forged signatures on contracts and authorization documents.

Additional control policies are needed for employees with access to cash or other property. They should be required to take an annual vacation, and during this time their job functions should be performed by other staff members. Many employee frauds are discovered when the perpetrator is suddenly forced by illness or accident to take time off. Periodic rotation of duties among key employees can achieve the same results. Of course, the very existence of such policies deters fraud and enhances internal control. Finally, fidelity bond insurance coverage of key employees protects companies against losses arising from deliberate acts of fraud by bonded employees.

External Influences

External influences that affect an organization's control environment include requirements imposed by stock exchanges, by the Financial Accounting Standards Board (FASB), and by the Securities and Exchange Commission (SEC). They also include regulatory agency requirements, such as those for banks, utilities, and insurance companies. Examples include enforcement of the internal control provisions of the Foreign Corrupt Practices Act by the SEC, and audits of financial institutions by the Federal Deposit Insurance Corporation.

CONTROL ACTIVITIES

The second component of COSO's internal control model (see Table 8.2) is control activities. Control activities are policies and rules that provide reasonable assurance that management's control objectives are achieved. Generally, control procedures fall into one of five categories:

1. Proper authorization of transactions and activities
2. Segregation of duties
3. Design and use of adequate documents and records
4. Adequate safeguards of assets and records
5. Independent checks on performance

Focus 8.1 discusses how a violation of specific control activities combined with control environment factors resulted in a fraud at a school district in the Midwest.

Proper Authorization of Transactions and Activities

Employees perform tasks and make decisions that affect company assets. Management does not have the time or resources to supervise each activity or decision. Instead, they establish policies for employees to follow and empower them to perform activities and make decisions. This empowerment, called **authorization,** is an important part of an organization's control procedures.

Authorizations are often documented by signing, initializing, or entering an authorization code on a transaction document or record. Computer systems are now capable of recording a **digital signature** (or fingerprint), a means of signing a document with a piece of data that cannot be forged.

Employees who process transactions should verify the presence of the appropriate authorization(s). Auditors review transactions to verify proper authorization, since their absence indicates that a control problem may exist. For example, when reviewing purchases, Jason Scott discovered that some did not have a purchase requisition. Instead, they had been "personally authorized" by Bill Springer, the purchasing vice president. In addition, Jason found that some vendor invoice payments had been authorized without proper supporting documents, such as purchase orders and receiving reports. These findings raise questions about the adequacy of Springer's internal control procedures.

Certain activities or transactions may be of such consequence that management grants **specific authorization** for them to occur. For example, management review and approval is often required for sales in excess of $20,000, capital expenditures in excess of $10,000, or uncollectible write-offs in excess

FOCUS 8.1 Control Problems in a School District

THE DIRECTOR of finance for a midwestern school district with 42 separate schools hired a CPA firm to audit the school district books. The audit was accompanied by a report that showed that the district's system had a number of serious internal control deficiencies. The director, a former auditor, went to work to improve the control system. The district (1) selected a new software package that all sites would use, (2) standardized accounting and bookkeeping procedures, (3) instituted consistent purchase order procedures, (4) implemented a separation of duties, and (5) created a control system for student vending machine cash and inventory.

As the changes were being made, the director noted that book collection fees for the middle school were low. He asked the district's internal auditor to investigate. The auditor contacted the middle school secretary responsible for making daily deposits of all student fees and writing checks to the central office for book fees. The secretary said the low amount was due to the increase in the number of fees waived by the principal for students who qualified for free or reduced lunches.

The principal denied that he was waiving the fee. The principal, the auditor, and the director examined the fee cards for each child. Their investigation showed that the daily deposits into the activity checking account did not agree with the dates stamped paid on the student fee cards. A search of the premises revealed no uncashed checks. So where did the money go, and how did the secretary manage to take it when most of the fees were paid with checks made out to the school?

They finally discovered that the secretary was also in charge of the faculty welfare and vending machine receipts fund. The district was not responsible for the fund, and so it was never audited or examined. Nor was the fund subject to the newly implemented system of internal controls. Deposits to the welfare fund consisted of checks from the faculty and cash from the vending machines.

An examination of the available records revealed how the $20,000 fraud took place. The secretary stole all cash received from the vending machines. She also wrote and recorded checks to vendors, and on some checks she erased the name of the payee and replaced it with her name. She deposited student fees into the faculty welfare fund to cover up the stolen money.

The secretary was immediately discharged for improper bookkeeping practices. The secretary was bonded, and so the district was able to recover all of its missing funds.

The school district made a number changes to strengthen control. Internal auditors now examine all funds at the schools. The control of faculty welfare funds was transferred to a faculty member. Since the investigation revealed that the secretary had a prior criminal record, a background check was implemented so that all future hires could be screened.

of $5,000. In contrast, management can authorize employees to handle routine transactions without special approval, a procedure known as **general authorization.** Management should have written policies on both specific and general authorization for all types of transactions. Table 8.3 shows some examples of authorization functions.

Segregation of Duties

Good internal control demands that no single employee be given too much responsibility. An employee should not be in a position to perpetrate *and* conceal fraud or unintentional errors. As shown in Fig. 8.1, effective segregation of duties is achieved when the following functions are separated:

- *Authorization*—approving transactions and decisions.

TABLE 8.3 Examples of Authorization Functions

Transaction Types	Examples of Authorization Functions
Sales orders	Approval of customer credit Approval of shipment Approval of sales returns and allowances
Purchases	Authorization to order goods or services Authorization of capital expenditures Selection of vendors Acceptance of delivered products
Production	Approval of products and quantities to be produced Approval of raw materials issued for use in production Approval of production schedules Approval of completed products
Human resources/payroll	Hiring of new employees Approval of increases in employee compensation Approval of records of time worked Approval of payroll withholdings
Cash receipts	Endorsement of checks for deposit in bank Write-offs of uncollectible accounts
Cash disbursements	Approval of vendor invoices for payment Approval of checks written to settle accounts payable Approval of petty cash fund replenishment

- *Recording*—preparing source documents; maintaining journals, ledgers, or other files; preparing reconciliations; and preparing performance reports.
- *Custody*—handling cash, maintaining an inventory storeroom, receiving incoming customer checks, writing checks on the organization's bank account.

If two of these three functions are the responsibility of a single person, problems can arise. For example, the former city treasurer of Fairfax, Virginia was convicted of embezzling $600,000 from the city treasury. When residents used cash to pay their taxes, she would keep the currency. She recorded tax collections on the property tax records but did not report them to the city controller. Eventually, an adjusting journal entry was made to bring her records into agreement with those of the controller. When cash was received to pay for business license fees or court fees, it was recorded on a cash register and deposited daily. She stole some of the cash and made up discrepancies in the bank deposit by substituting miscellaneous checks received in the mail that would not be missed when they went unrecorded. Because the controller was responsible both for the *custody* of cash receipts and for *recording* those receipts, she was able to steal cash receipts and falsify the accounts to conceal the theft.

The utilities director of Newport Beach, California who was responsible for *authorizing* transactions and had *custody* of cash, was charged with embezzling

FIGURE 8.1
Separation of Duties

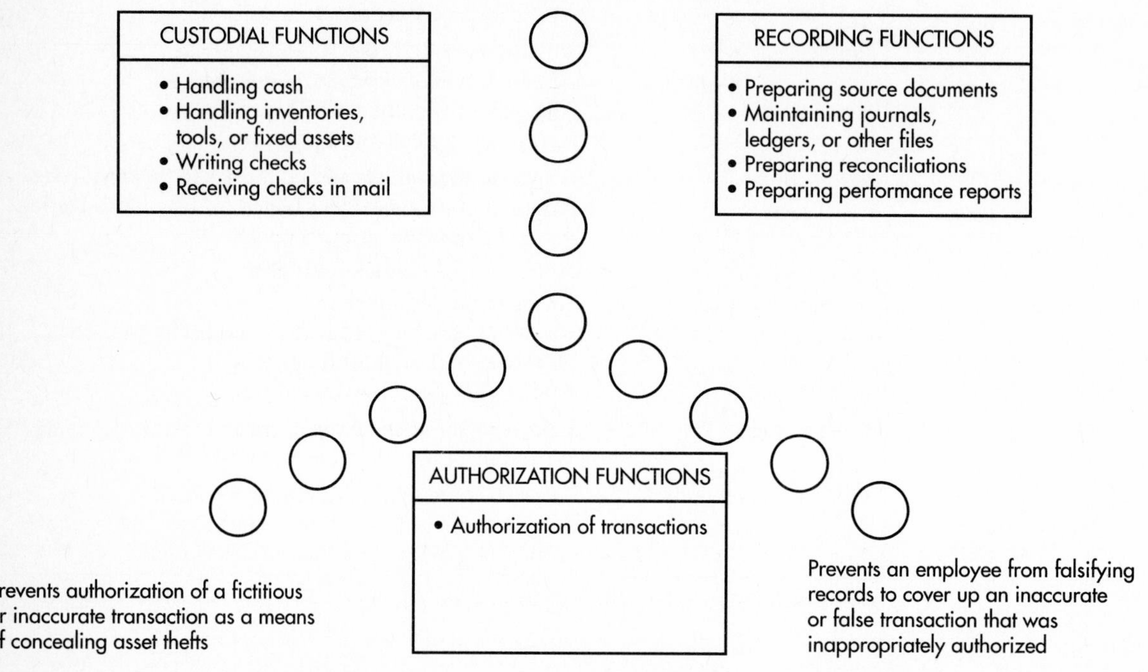
Prevents employees from falsifying records in order to conceal theft of assets entrusted to them
CUSTODIAL FUNCTIONS
• Handling cash
• Handling inventories, tools, or fixed assets
• Writing checks
• Receiving checks in mail
RECORDING FUNCTIONS
• Preparing source documents
• Maintaining journals, ledgers, or other files
• Preparing reconciliations
• Preparing performance reports
AUTHORIZATION FUNCTIONS
• Authorization of transactions
Prevents authorization of a fictitious or inaccurate transaction as a means of concealing asset thefts
Prevents an employee from falsifying records to cover up an inaccurate or false transaction that was inappropriately authorized

$1.2 million. He forged invoices or easement documents (the right to pass through a person's land) authorizing payments to a real or fictitious property owner. Finance department officials gave him the checks to deliver to the property owners. He forged signatures, endorsed the checks to himself, and deposited them in his own account. Because he was given physical custody of checks relating to transactions that he had authorized, he was able to authorize fictitious transactions and steal the payments.

The payroll director of the Los Angeles Dodgers, who was responsible for both *authorization* and *recording* functions, pleaded guilty to embezzling $330,000 from the team. He credited employees for hours not worked and then received a kickback of 50% of their extra compensation. He also added fictitious names to the Dodgers payroll and cashed the paychecks. The fraud was discovered when the payroll director became ill and another employee took over his duties. Since the perpetrator was responsible for both authorizing the hiring of new employees and for recording employee hours worked, he did not need to prepare or handle the actual paychecks. The club treasurer would simply mail the checks to an address specified by the payroll director.

In modern information systems, the computer often can be programmed to perform one or more of the already mentioned functions—in essence, replacing employees. The principle of separating duties remains the same; the only difference is that the computer, not a human, performs the function. For example, many gas stations are now equipped with pumps that allow customers to insert a credit card to pay for their gas. In such cases, the custody of the "cash" and the recording function are both performed by the computer. In addition to improving internal controls, these machines actually improve the process of serving the customer by increasing convenience and eliminating lines to pay for the gas.

In a system that incorporates an effective separation of duties, it should be difficult for any single employee to commit embezzlement successfully. Detecting fraud where two or more people are in **collusion** to override the controls is more difficult. For example, two women in a credit card company colluded to steal funds. One woman was authorized to set up credit card accounts, the other to write off unpaid accounts of less than $1,000. The first woman created a new account for each of them using fictitious data. When the amount outstanding neared the $1,000 limit, the woman in collections wrote them off. The first woman would then create two new cards, and the process would be repeated. The women were caught when the jilted boyfriend of one of them sought revenge; he called the credit card company and disclosed the fraudulent scheme.

Design and Use of Adequate Documents and Records

The proper design and use of documents and records helps ensure the accurate and complete recording of all relevant transaction data. Their form and content should be kept as simple as possible to promote efficient record keeping, minimize recording errors, and facilitate review and verification. Documents that initiate a transaction should contain a space for authorizations. Those used to transfer assets to someone else should have a space for the receiving party's signature. To reduce the likelihood of documents being used fraudulently, they should be sequentially prenumbered so each can be accounted for. A good audit trail facilitates tracing individual transactions through the system, the correction of errors, and the verification of system output.

Adequate Safeguards of Assets and Records

When people consider safeguarding assets, they most often think of cash and physical assets, such as inventory and equipment. In today's world, however, one of a company's most important assets is its information. Accordingly, steps must be taken to safeguard both information and physical assets. The following procedures safeguard assets from theft, unauthorized use, and vandalism:

- Effectively supervising and segregating duties.
- Maintaining accurate records of assets, including information.
- Restricting physical access to assets. Cash registers, safes, lockboxes, and safety deposit boxes limit access to cash, securities, and paper assets. Restricted storage areas are used to protect inventories. For example, over

$1 million was embezzled from Perini Corp. because of poor controls (blank checks were kept in an unlocked storeroom). It was easy for employees to take a check, make it out to a fictitious vendor, run it through the check signing machine (also left unlocked), and cash the check.
- Protecting records and documents. Fireproof storage areas, locked filing cabinets, and off-site backup locations are effective means of protecting records and documents. Access to blank checks and documents should be limited to authorized personnel. In Inglewood, California, a janitor was charged with stealing 34 blank checks while cleaning the city finance office. He forged the names of city officials on the checks and cashed them in amounts ranging from $50,000 to $470,000.
- Controlling the environment. Sensitive computer equipment should be located in a room with adequate cooling and special fire protection. The room should be elevated and reinforced to protect the equipment from flooding and falling objects.
- Restricting access to computer rooms, computer files, and information. Access controls are discussed in Chapter 9.

Independent Checks on Performance

Internal checks to ensure that transactions are processed accurately are another important control element. They should be independent because they are generally more effective if performed by someone other than the person responsible for the original operation. Various types of independent checks are discussed in the following subsections.

Reconciliation of Two Independently Maintained Sets of Records. One way to check the accuracy and completeness of records is to reconcile them with other records that should have the same balance. For example, a bank reconciliation verifies that company checking accounts agree with bank statements. Another example is comparing the accounts receivable subsidiary ledger total with the accounts receivable total in the general ledger.

Comparison of Actual Quantities with Recorded Amounts. The cash in a cash register drawer at the end of each clerk's shift should be the same as the amount recorded on the cash register tape. All inventories should be counted at least annually and the results compared with inventory records. High dollar value items, such as jewelry or furs, should be counted more frequently.

Double-Entry Accounting. The maxim that debits must equal credits provides numerous opportunities for internal checks. For example, debits in a payroll entry may be allocated to numerous inventory and/or expense accounts by the cost accounting department. Credits are allocated to several liability accounts for wages and salaries payable, taxes withheld, employee insurance, union dues, and so on, by the payroll department. At the conclusion of these two complex operations, the comparison of total debits with total credits provides a powerful check on the accuracy of both processes. Any discrepancy indicates the presence of one or more errors.

Batch Totals. In a batch processing application, source documents are assembled in groups and **batch totals** (also called **control totals**) are manually computed before source data are entered into the system. As the data is processed, the control totals should be generated during each processing step. An employee who was not involved in preparing the original batch totals should compare the two sets of totals. Otherwise, a person who generated the original control totals *and* reconciled the two sets of totals could easily hide errors or fraudulent transactions.

Discrepancies between the two totals indicate an error occurred during the previous processing step. Examples include lost records, unauthorized records added to the batch, or data transcription or data processing errors. The cause of discrepancies should be identified and the errors corrected before the transactions are processed further. Limiting batch sizes (such as to 50 records) reduces the time required to track down the cause of any individual discrepancy.

Five batch totals are used in computer systems:

1. A **financial total** is the sum of a dollar field, such as total sales or total cash receipts.
2. A **hash total** is the sum of a field that would usually not be added, such as the sum of customer account numbers or employee identification numbers.
3. A **record count** is the number of documents processed.
4. A **line count** is the number of lines of data entered. For example, the line count would be five if a sales order shows that five different products were sold to a customer.
5. A **cross-footing balance test.** Many worksheets have row totals and column totals. This test compares the grand total of all the rows with the grand total of all the columns to check that they are equal.

The business Sarah Robinson runs out of her home in Springville, Utah is used to illustrate the use of batch totals to prevent accounting and recording errors. Figure 8.2 illustrates the procedures Sarah uses to process customer payments.

1. When Sarah receives checks in the mail, she prepares a receipts list showing customer names and amounts received, computes a batch total (the total dollar amount of all checks) and writes it on the receipts list, and prepares a deposit slip.
2. After she deposits the checks, she compares the bank-validated copy of the deposit slip with her original batch total on the receipts list.
3. Using a copy of Sarah's receipts list, her CPA posts credits to the appropriate customer accounts and updates each customer's balance. He computes the new total balance of the accounts receivable file, determines the difference between the old and new file totals, and verifies that this difference agrees with Sarah's batch total. This comparison serves as an independent check on the accuracy of posting receipts to the customer accounts.
4. Her CPA prepares a summary journal entry and posts it to the general ledger, again verifying that the entry amount is equal to Sarah's batch total.

FIGURE 8.2
Example of the Use of Batch Totals in Processing Cash Receipts

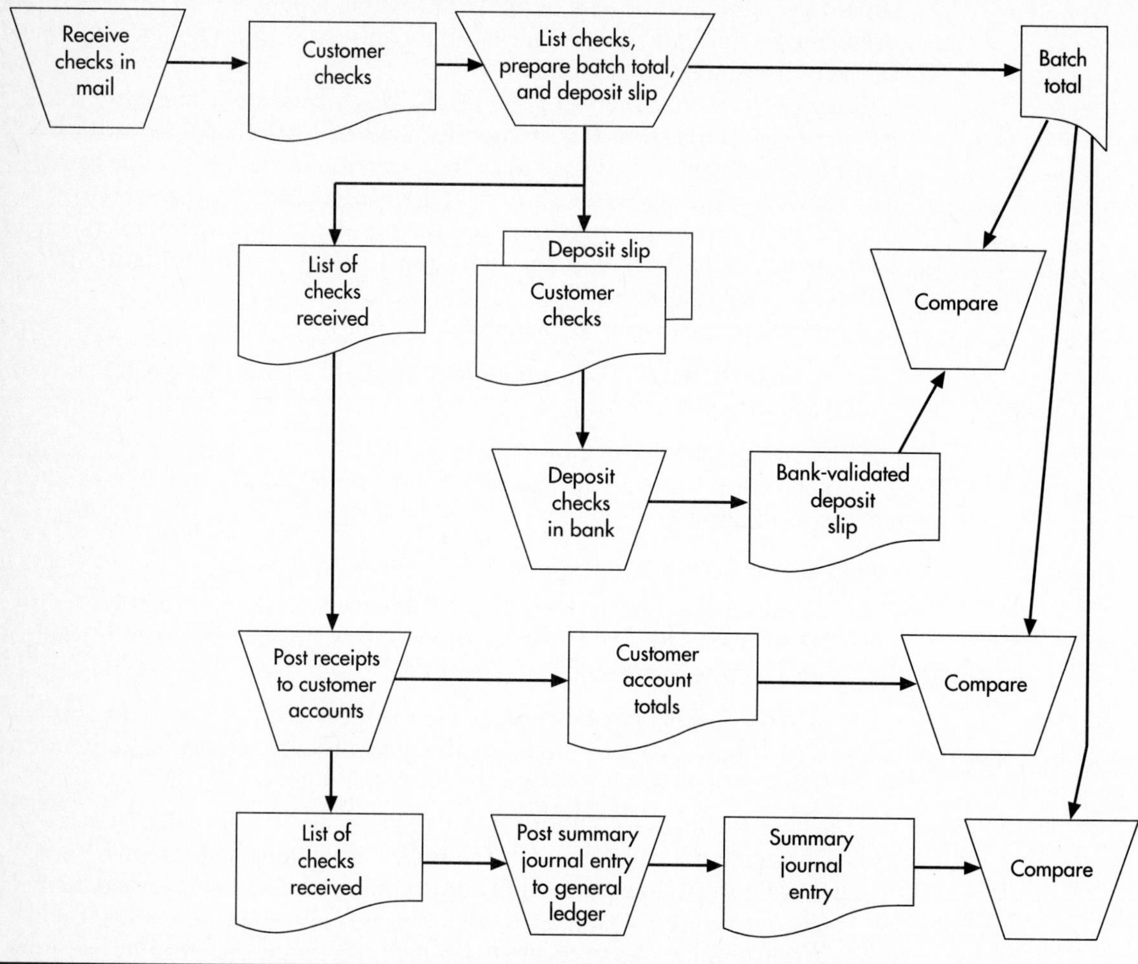

Batch totals provide an independent check on the accuracy of each processing step. If a discrepancy is discovered, the difference between the batch totals often provides a clue about where the error occurred. For example, if the difference equals a transaction amount, that transaction may have been omitted. If the difference is exactly double a transaction amount, it may have been incorrectly debited instead of credited or added instead of subtracted. If the discrepancy involves a nonzero digit, there may be a **transcription error,** in which a digit is entered incorrectly during processing (i.e., a 4 in the tens column entered as a 9, causing an error of 50). If it is evenly divisible by 9, the likely cause is a **transposition error,** in which two adjacent digits were inadvertently exchanged (e.g., 46 for 64).

Simple errors can have large financial consequences. For example, a single transposition error almost cost the U.S. Treasury $14 million. A clerk at the Federal Reserve Bank of Philadelphia transposed two digits while calculating the interest on newly issued five-year Treasury notes. The operator erroneously entered the interest rate as 8.67% rather than 6.87%. Fortunately, an investor detected the error when he received a notification of the amount to be paid. The bank was able to correct the error before the checks were issued and mailed. The bank quickly implemented new control procedures to make sure the problem did not reoccur.

Independent Review. After one person processes a transaction, a second person sometimes reviews the work of the first. The second person checks for proper authorization signatures, reviews supporting documents, and checks the accuracy of crucial data items such as prices, quantities, and extensions.

RISK ASSESSMENT

The third component of COSO's internal control model (see Table 8.2) is risk assessment. Accountants play an important role is helping management control a business by designing effective control systems and evaluating existing ones to ensure that they are operating effectively. Accountants can evaluate an internal control system using the risk assessment strategy shown in Fig. 8.3. We will now walk you through the major steps in this strategy. Focus 8.2 discusses how Dow Chemical assesses risk and designs control systems.

Identify Threats

Companies must identify the threats they face. These threats can be

- *Strategic*, such as doing the wrong things.
- *Operating*, such as doing the right things, but in the wrong way.
- *Financial*, such as having financial resources lost, wasted, or stolen or incurring inappropriate liabilities.
- *Information*, such as faulty or irrelevant information, unreliable systems, and incorrect or misleading reports.

For example, many organizations implement electronic data interchange (EDI) systems that provide instantaneous communications and eliminate paper documents. An EDI system allows them to create electronic documents, transmit them over private networks or the Internet to their customers' and suppliers' computers, and receive electronic responses back from them.

Companies that implement an EDI system must identify the threats the system will face, such as

1. *Choosing an inappropriate technology.* The company might move to EDI before their customers and suppliers are ready. They may also choose to use EDI when there is a more effective means of communicating with their customers and suppliers electronically.

FIGURE 8.3

Risk Assessment Approach to Designing Internal Controls

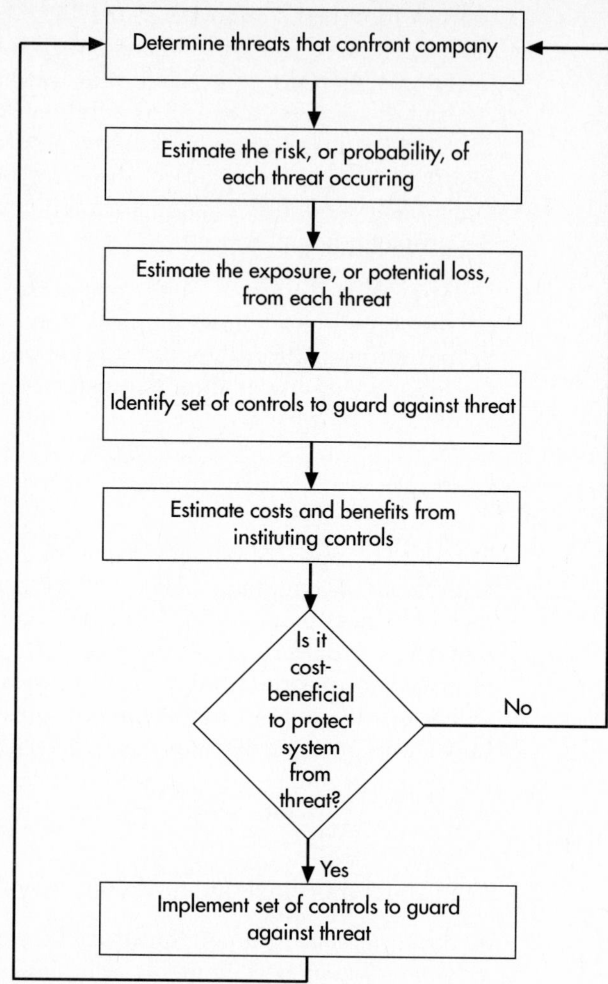

2. *Unauthorized system access.* Hackers can break into the system and steal data or sabotage the system.
3. *Tapping into data transmissions.* Hackers can eavesdrop on a data transmission and copy the transmission, distort it, or prevent it from arriving at its destination.
4. *Loss of data integrity.* Errors may be introduced into the data due to employee or software errors, erroneous input, faulty transmissions, etc.
5. *Incomplete transactions.* The receiving computer may not receive all of the data from the sending computer.

FOCUS 8.2 Risk Analysis at Dow Chemical

RISK ANALYSIS is often perceived as an expensive and lengthy process that outside consultants perform with a minimum of employee contact. Consequently, few end users actually understand or even desire the recommended controls and are reluctant to implement or enforce them. Dow Chemical is out to change this attitude; it has recently developed a simple and quick way to help users evaluate risk.

The key component of the Dow security program is the risk analysis matrix (RAM). The RAM is a grid-based question-and-answer chart that helps users identify potential threats and the associated data and assets that require protection. The first step in using the RAM is to classify undesirable events in terms of their effect. In the grid that follows, the vertical axis has three columns related to security objectives: data integrity (unauthorized data modification or destruction), data sensitivity (unauthorized data disclosure), and data availability (unavailability of data or system services).The horizontal axis pinpoints the accidental acts (such as an error or omission) and the deliberate acts (such as a hacker or employee fraud) from which data must be protected. After undesirable events are identified, employees affected by the system are then assembled. For example, if a regional sales office is to have a LAN installed, a salesperson, a LAN technician, and a clerk from the sales office are invited to a special meeting.

The manager of security prepares the matrix as a visual aid and asks each participant to think about the risks associated with each of its squares. For example, they might discuss what could happen if data were accidentally modified by an employee. Each square is considered in turn (reducing data integrity due to deliberate acts, unauthorized data disclosure due to an accident, etc.) until the chart is complete.

The next step is to determine which controls will address each security concern. For example, sensitive documents should be shredded to guard against their falling into the wrong hands. Another example is using a tape backup system to guard against the main server being accidentally destroyed. That is followed by management determining the economic feasibility of the controls. The last step is to assign implementation responsibilities to team members.

Many security managers find security to be a daunting proposition and do not know where to start. Dow Chemical claims that companies can now empower themselves and develop their own system of controls. No longer do they have to count on someone else to do it for them.

Risk Analysis Matrix

	Data Integrity	**Data Sensitivity**	**Data Availability**
Accidental Acts Errors and Omissions	Major or minor concern	Confidential or nonconfidential	Essential or nonessential
Deliberate Acts Fraud and Misuse	Major or minor concern	Confidential or nonconfidential	Essential or nonessential
	Data Destruction or Modification	**Data Disclosure**	**Data Inaccessibility**

6. *System failures.* Hardware or software problems, power outages, sabotage, employee mistakes, or other factors may make the EDI system fail or be unavailable for a period of time.
7. *Incompatible systems.* Some companies have difficulty interacting with other systems because of incompatible computer systems.

Estimate Risk

Some threats pose a greater risk because the probability of their occurrence is more likely. For example, a company is more likely to be the victim of a computer fraud than of a terrorist attack, and employees are more likely to make unintentional errors than they are to commit intentional acts of fraud.

Estimate Exposure

The risk of an earthquake may be very small but the exposure can be enormous; it could completely destroy a company and force it into bankruptcy. The exposure from a fraud is usually not as great, as most frauds do not threaten a company's existence. The exposure from unintentional errors could range from very small to very large, depending on the nature of the error and how long it persists. Risk and exposure must be considered together. As either increases, the materiality of the threat and the need to protect against it rises.

Identify Controls

Management must identify one or more controls that will protect the company from each threat. In evaluating the benefits of specific internal control procedures, management should consider their effectiveness and timing. All other factors being equal, a preventive control is superior to a detective one. However, if preventive controls fail, detective controls are essential for discovering the problem and recovering from it. Thus preventive and detective controls complement each other, and a good internal control system should employ both.

Estimate Costs and Benefits

No internal control system can provide foolproof protection against all internal control threats. The cost of a foolproof system would be prohibitively high. In addition, since many controls negatively affect operational efficiency, too many controls slow down the system and make it inefficient. Therefore, the objective in designing an internal control system is to provide reasonable assurance that control problems do not take place.

The benefit of an internal control procedure must exceed its cost. Costs are easier to measure than benefits. The primary cost element is personnel, including the time to perform control procedures, the costs of hiring additional employees to achieve effective segregation of duties, and the costs of programming controls into a computer system. Internal control benefits stem from reduced losses. One way to calculate benefits involves **expected loss,** the mathematical product of risk and exposure:

Expected loss = risk × exposure

The benefit of a control procedure is the difference between the expected loss with the control procedure(s) and the expected loss without it.

Determine Cost–Benefit Effectiveness

After estimating benefits and costs, management determines whether the control is cost beneficial. For example, at Atlantic Richfield data errors occasionally required an entire payroll to be reprocessed, at a cost of $10,000. Management determined that a data validation step would reduce error risk from 15% to 1%, at a cost of $600 per pay period. The cost–benefit analysis management used to determine if the validation step should be employed is shown in Table 8.4.

If the proposed payroll validation procedure is not employed, the expected loss to the company is $1,500. Since the expected loss with the validation step is $100, the control provides an expected benefit of $1,400. After deducting the control costs of $600, the validation step provides a net benefit of $800 and clearly should be implemented.

In evaluating the costs and benefits of internal control, management must consider factors other than those in the expected benefit calculation. For example, if an exposure threatens an organization's existence, it may be worthwhile to spend more than indicated by the cost–benefit analysis to minimize the possibility that the organization will perish. This extra cost can be viewed as a catastrophic loss insurance premium.

INFORMATION AND COMMUNICATION

The fourth component of COSO's internal control model (see Table 8.2) is information and communication. The primary purpose of an AIS is to record, process, store, summarize, and communicate information about an organization. This means that accountants must understand how (1) transactions are initiated, (2) data are captured in machine-readable form or converted from source documents to machine-readable form, (3) computer files are accessed and updated, (4) data is processed to prepare information, and (5) informa-

TABLE 8.4 Cost–Benefit Analysis of Payroll Validation Procedure

	Without Validation Procedure	With Validation Procedure	Net Expected Difference
Cost to reprocess entire payroll	$10,000	$10,000	
Risk of payroll data errors	15%	1%	
Expected reprocessing cost ($10,000 × risk)	$1,500	$100	$1400
Cost of validation procedure	$0	$600	$(600)
Net expected benefit of validation procedure			$800

tion is reported to internal users and external parties. Accountants must also understand the accounting records and procedures, supporting documents, and specific financial statement accounts involved in processing and reporting transactions.

All of these items make it possible for the system to have an audit trail. An **audit trail** exists when individual company transactions can be traced through the system from where they originate to where they end up on the financial statements. Likewise, the numbers on the financial statements can be traced back through the system to the individual transactions making up the balance.

According to the AICPA, an AIS has five primary objectives:

1. Identify and record all valid transactions. For example, if a company intentionally records a fictitious sale, it can overstate revenues and income. If a company forgets to record some expenses at the end of the year, expenses are understated and net income overstated.

2. Properly classify transactions. For example, improperly classifying an expense as an asset overstates assets and net income.

3. Record transactions at their proper monetary value. For example, an account receivable that becomes uncollectible should be written off.

4. Record transactions in the proper accounting period. Recording 2000 sales in 1999 overstates sales and net income for 1999 and has the opposite effect for 2000.

5. Properly present transactions and related disclosures in the financial statements. Failing to disclose a lawsuit or a contingent liability could mislead the reader of a financial statement.

Accounting systems generally consist of several accounting subsystems, each designed to process transactions of a particular type. Although they differ with respect to the type of transactions processed, all accounting subsystems follow the same sequence of procedures. These procedures are referred to as accounting cycles. The five major accounting cycles and their related control objectives and procedures are described in detail in Chapters 12–16.

MONITORING PERFORMANCE

The fifth component of COSO's internal control model (see Table 8.2) is monitoring. Key methods of monitoring performance include effective supervision, responsibility reporting, and internal auditing.

Effective Supervision

Effective supervision involves training and assisting employees, monitoring their performance, correcting errors, and safeguarding assets by overseeing employees who have access to them. Supervision is especially important in organizations that cannot afford elaborate responsibility reporting or are too small to have an adequate segregation of duties.

Responsibility Accounting

Responsibility accounting systems include budgets, quotas, schedules, standard costs, and quality standards; performance reports that compare actual with planned performance and highlight significant variances; and procedures for investigating significant variances and taking timely action to correct the conditions leading to such variances.

Internal Auditing

Internal auditing involves reviewing the reliability and integrity of financial and operating information and providing an appraisal of internal control effectiveness. It also involves assessing employee compliance with management policies and procedures and applicable laws and regulations, and evaluating the efficiency and effectiveness of management. Unlike external auditors, internal auditors place great emphasis on a company's management controls. Thus they can detect excess overtime, underused assets, obsolete inventory, padded travel expense reimbursements, excessively loose budgets and quotas, poorly justified capital expenditures, and production bottlenecks. Objectivity and effectiveness require that the internal audit function must be organizationally independent of accounting and operating functions. For example, the head of internal auditing should report to the audit committee of the board of directors rather than to the controller or chief financial officer.

One alert internal auditor noted that a department supervisor took the entire office staff out to lunch in a limousine on her birthday. During the remainder of the audit, he noted other evidences of an extravagant lifestyle. Questioning whether her salary could support her lifestyle, he began a more in-depth investigation. He found that she had set up several fictitious vendors, sent the company invoices from these vendors, and then cashed the checks when they were mailed to her. Over a period of several years, she had embezzled over $12 million.

SUMMARY AND CASE CONCLUSION

After three days in Bozeman, Jason and Maria returned to Northwest's main office and filed their audit report. One week later, they were summoned to the office of Roger Sawyer, Northwest's director of internal auditing, to explain their findings. Shortly thereafter, a high-level internal audit team was dispatched to Bozeman to take a closer look at the situation.

When the audit team returned, Jason and Maria inquired about their findings and were told the situation was still under investigation. Six months later, a company newsletter included an announcement that the Springer family had sold their remaining 10% interest in the Bozeman business to Northwest and had resigned from their management positions. Two Northwest executives were transferred in to replace them. Still, there was no word on the audit findings.

Two years later Jason and Maria were assigned to a job supervised by Frank Ratliff, a member of the high-level internal audit team. After-hours one evening, Ratliff told them the story. Based on Jason and Maria's reports, the investigation team had examined a large sample of purchasing transactions and all employee timekeeping and payroll records for a 12-month period. It had also taken a detailed physical inventory. The team discovered that the problems identified by Jason—including missing purchase requisitions, purchase orders, and receiving reports, as well as excessive prices—were widespread. They found that these problems occurred almost exclusively in transactions with three large vendors from whom Springer's had purchased several million dollars worth of inventories and supplies. The team discussed the unusually high item prices with the vendors, but did not receive a satisfactory explanation. However, a check of the county business licensing bureau revealed that Bill Springer held a significant ownership interest in each of these three companies. By authorizing excessive prices to companies he partially owned, Springer had earned a share of several hundred thousand dollars of excessive profits, all at the expense of Northwest Industries.

The investigation team had also found evidence that several of Springer's employees were paid for more hours than documented by timekeeping records. Finally, the team had determined Springer's inventory account was materially overstated. The physical inventory revealed that a significant portion of recorded inventory did not exist, and that other portions were obsolete. The adjusting journal entry reflecting Springer's real inventory wiped out much of the outlet's profits over the past three years.

When confronted, the Springers vehemently denied any laws had been broken. Northwest considered going to the authorities for a formal fraud investigation, but were concerned their case was not strong enough to prove in court. They were also worried that adverse publicity might damage the company's position in Bozeman. After months of negotiation, the Springers agreed to the settlement reported in the newsletter. Part of the settlement was that no public statement would be made about any alleged fraud or embezzlement involving the Springers. According to Ratliff, this was not unusual. In many cases of fraud, settlements are reached quietly, with no legal action taken, so the company can avoid adverse publicity.

KEY TERMS

sabotage
embezzlement
threat
exposure
risk
internal control
management control
internal control structure
preventive controls
detective controls
corrective controls
general controls
application controls
administrative controls
accounting controls
input controls
processing controls
output controls
Foreign Corrupt Practices Act
Committee of Sponsoring Organizations (COSO)
control environment
audit committee
policy and procedures manual
authorization
digital signature
specific authorization
general authorization
collusion
batch totals (control totals)
financial total
hash total
record count
line count
cross-footing balance test
transcription error
transposition error
expected loss
audit trail

CHAPTER QUIZ

1. The Committee on Sponsoring Organizations (COSO) identified five interrelated components of internal controls. Which of the following is *not* one of those five?
  a. Risk Assessment
  b. Internal Control Policies
  c. Monitoring
  d. Information and Communication

2. Which of the following statements is false?
  a. Administrative controls help ensure operational efficiency and adherence to managerial policies.
  b. Accounting controls help safeguard assets and ensure the reliability of financial records.
  c. Internal control encompasses both administrative and accounting controls.
  d. Management control has a narrower, less encompassing definition than internal accounting control.

3. Which of the following statements is true?
  a. The COSO report is narrow in scope and is limited to financial controls.
  b. The COSO report states internal control is a process that should provide reasonable assurance control objectives are achieved.
  c. The Foreign Corrupt Practices Act requires *all* U.S. companies to maintain a good system of internal accounting control.
  d. It is easier to add controls to an already designed system than to include them during the initial design stage.

4. All other things being equal,
  a. detective controls are superior to preventive controls.
  b. corrective controls are superior to preventive controls.
  c. preventive controls are equivalent to detective controls.
  d. preventive controls are superior to detective controls.

5. Which of the following statements about the control environment is *false?*
  a. Management's attitudes toward internal control and ethical behavior have little impact on employee beliefs or actions.
  b. An overly complex or unclear organizational structure may be indicative of more serious problems.
  c. A written policy and procedures manual is an important tool for assigning authority and responsibility in many organizations.
  d. Supervision is especially important in organizations that cannot afford elaborate responsibility reporting or are too small to have an adequate separation of duties.

6. To achieve effective segregation of duties, certain functions must be separated. Which of the following is the correct listing of the accounting-related functions that must be segregated?
  a. Control, recording, and monitoring
  b. Authorization, recording, and custody
  c. Control, custody, and authorization

d. Monitoring, recording, and planning

7. All of the following are independent checks *except*
a. bank reconciliation.
b. periodic comparison of subsidiary ledger totals to control accounts.
c. a trial balance.
d. re-adding the total of a batch of invoices and comparing it with your first total.

8. Which of the following is a control procedure relating to both the design and use of documents and records?
a. Locking blank checks in a drawer
b. Reconciling the bank account
c. Sequentially prenumbering sales invoices
d. Comparing actual physical quantities to recorded amounts

9. Which of the following is the correct order of the risk assessment steps discussed in the chapter?
a. Identify threats, estimate risk and exposure, identify controls, estimate costs and benefits
b. Identify controls, estimate risk and exposure, identify threats, estimate costs and benefits
c. Estimate risk and exposure, identify controls, identify threats, estimate costs and benefits
d. Estimate costs and benefits, identify threats, identify controls, estimate risk and exposure

10. Your current system is deemed to be 90% reliable. A major threat has been identified with an exposure of $3,000,000. Two control procedures exist to deal with the threat. Implementation of control A would cost $100,000 and reduce the risk to 6%. Implementation of control B would cost $140,000 and reduce the risk to 4%. Implementation of both controls would cost $220,000 and reduce the risk to 2%. Given the data and based solely on an economic analysis of costs and benefits, what should you do?
a. Implement control A only
b. Implement control B only
c. Implement both control A and control B
d. Implement neither control

DISCUSSION QUESTIONS

8.1 Answer the following questions about the audit of Springer's Northwest Lumber & Supply.
a. What deficiencies existed in the control environment at Springer's?
b. Do you agree with the decision to settle with the Springers rather than prosecute them for fraud and embezzlement? Why or why not?
c. Should the company have told Jason and Maria the results of the high-level audit? Why or why not?

8.2 Effective segregation of duties is sometimes not economically feasible in a small business. What internal control elements do you think can help compensate for this threat?

8.3 Craig Robinson has just purchased a PC and intends to computerize his sister Sarah's manual system (see Fig. 8.2). What effect will this have on the use of batch totals in cash receipts processing?

8.4 Some people feel that, instead of producing tangible benefits, business controls create resentment and loss of company morale. Discuss this position.

8.5 In recent years, Supersmurf's external auditors have given clean opinions on its financial statements and favorable evaluations of its internal control systems. Discuss whether it is necessary for this corporation to take any further action to comply with the Foreign Corrupt Practices Act.

8.6 When you go to a movie theater, you buy a prenumbered ticket from the window or counter cashier. This ticket is then handed to another person at the entrance to the movie. What kinds of irregularities is the theater trying to prevent? What controls is it using to prevent these irregularities? What remaining risks or exposures can you identify?

PROBLEMS

8.1 You are an audit supervisor who has recently been assigned to a new client, Go-Go Corporation, that is listed on the New York Stock Exchange. You recently visited Go-Go's corporate headquarters to become acquainted with key personnel and to conduct a preliminary review of the company's accounting policies and systems. During this visit, the following events occurred:

1. You met with Go-Go's audit committee, which consists of the corporate controller, treasurer, financial vice president, and budget director.
2. You recognized the treasurer as a former aide to John Boatsky, who was convicted of fraud in an insider-trading scandal three years ago.
3. Management explained its plans to change its method of accounting for depreciation from the accelerated method to the straight-line method. Management implied that, if your firm does not concur with this change, Go-Go will employ other auditors.
4. You learned that the financial vice president serves as the manager of a staff of five internal auditors.
5. You noted that all management authority seems to reside with three brothers, who serve as chief executive officer, president, and financial vice president.
6. You were told that the performance of division and department managers is evaluated on a subjective basis, because Go-Go's management believes that formal performance evaluation procedures are counterproductive.
7. You learned that the company has reported increases in earnings per share for each of the past 25 quarters. However, earnings during the current quarter have leveled off and may decline.
8. You reviewed the company's policy and procedures manual, which listed policies for dealing with customers, vendors, and employees.
9. Your preliminary assessment is that the accounting systems are well designed and employ effective internal control procedures.

Required:

The information you have obtained suggests potential problems relating to one or more of the elements of Go-Go's internal control structure. Identify these problems, and explain each in relation to internal control structure concepts.

8.2 The first column in Table 8.5 lists source document amounts that have been summed to obtain a batch total. You may assume that these amounts and the batch total are correct. Columns (a)–(d) contain batch totals computed from the same amounts after these source documents were processed in a subsequent processing step. One processing error occurred during each of these four cases.

For each case, you are to do the following:

a. Compute the difference between the batch total obtained after processing and the correct batch total shown on the left.
b. Explain specifically how this difference is helpful in discovering the processing error.
c. Identify the processing error.

8.3 Explain how the principle of separation of duties is violated in each of the following situations. Also suggest one or more procedures to reduce the risk and exposure highlighted in each example.

a. A payroll clerk recorded a 40-hour work week for an employee who had quit the previous week. He then prepared a paycheck for this employee, forged her signature, and cashed the check.
b. While opening the mail, a cashier set aside, and subsequently cashed, two checks payable to the company on account.
c. A cashier prepared a fictitious invoice from a company using his brother-in-law's name. He wrote a check in payment of the invoice, which the brother-in-law later cashed.
d. An employee of the finishing department walked off with several parts from the storeroom and recorded the items in the inventory ledger as having been issued to the assembly department.
e. A cashier cashed a check from a customer in payment of an account receivable, pocketed the cash, and concealed the theft by properly posting the receipt to the customer's account in the accounts receivable ledger.

8.4 McClain's Lumberyard uses the following procedures to sell lumber to its customers:

1. The customer tells an office clerk the sizes and quantities of lumber he wants to purchase.
2. The clerk records the items on a sales document, calculates the total cost, and collects the customer's payment.
3. A worker obtains the lumber from the yard and loads it into the customer's car or truck. If the purchase is large and the customer wishes, McClain's will deliver the order.

TABLE 8.5 Amounts from Source Documents

	(a)	(b)	(c)	(d)
$3,630.62	$3,630.62	$3,630.62	$3,630.62	$3,630.62
1,484.86	1,484.86	1,484.86	1,484.86	1,484.86
2,164.67	2,164.67	2,164.67	2,164.67	2,164.67
946.43	946.43	946.43	946.43	946.43
2,626.28	−2,626.28	2,626.28	2,626.28	2,626.28
969.97	969.97	969.97	969.97	969.97
2,772.42	2,772.42	2,772.42	3,772.42	2,772.42
934.25	934.25	934.25	934.25	934.25
1,620.94	1,620.94	1,620.94	1,620.94	1,620.94
4,566.86	4,566.86	4,656.86	4,566.86	4,566.86
1,249.32	1,249.32	1,249.32	1,249.32	1,249.32
1,070.27	1,070.27	1,070.27	1,070.27	1,070.27
2,668.51	2,668.51	2,668.51	2,668.51	2,668.51
1,762.62	1,762.62	1,762.62	1,762.62	873.26
873.26	873.26	873.26	873.26	$27,578.66
$29,341.28	$24,088.72	$29,431.28	$30,341.28	

Required:

Explain several aspects of the design and use of the sales document that will facilitate control of cash receipts and inventories by McClain's.

8.5 The Gardner Company, a client of your firm, has come to you with the following problem: It has three clerical employees who must perform the following functions.

1. Maintain the general ledger
2. Maintain the accounts payable ledger
3. Maintain the accounts receivable ledger
4. Prepare checks for signature
5. Maintain the disbursements journal
6. Issue credits on returns and allowances
7. Reconcile the bank account
8. Handle and deposit cash receipts

Assuming equal abilities among the three employees, the company asks you to assign functions 1–8 to them in order to maximize internal control. Assume that these employees will perform no accounting functions other than the ones listed.

Required:

a. List four possible unsatisfactory pairings of the functions.
b. State how you would distribute the functions among the three employees. Assume that with the exception of the nominal jobs of the bank reconciliation and the issuance of credits on returns and allowances, all functions require an equal amount of time.

(CPA Examination, adapted)

8.6 The Future Corporation is a small manufacturing company located in Aggie, Texas. It operates one plant and employs 50 workers in its manufacturing facility. Employees are paid weekly. Each week, the department supervisors supply the payroll clerk with signed time sheets and also with a list of any employees hired or terminated by the supervisor. The payroll clerk compares the time sheets with the time cards and prepares and signs payroll checks. The paychecks are then given in sealed envelopes to the supervisors, who in turn give them to the respective employees.

Required:

Identify several internal control weaknesses in Future's payroll system. For each weakness, describe how internal control could be improved.

8.7 You are auditing the Alaska Branch of Far Distributing Company. This branch has substantial annual sales, which are billed and collected locally. As a part of your audit, you find that the procedures for handling cash receipts are as follows.

Cash collections on over-the-counter sales and COD sales are received from the customer or delivery service by the cashier. Upon receipt of cash, the sales ticket is stamped "paid" and a copy is filed for future reference. The only record of COD sales is a copy of the sales ticket, which is given to the cashier to hold until the cash is received from the delivery service.

Mail is opened by the secretary to the credit manager, and remittances are given to the credit manager for review. The credit manager then places the remittances in a tray on the cashier's desk. At the daily deposit cutoff time, the cashier delivers the checks and cash on hand to the assistant credit manager, who prepares remittance lists and makes up the bank deposit, which the assistant manager also takes to the bank. The assistant credit manager also posts remittances to the accounts receivable ledger cards and verifies the cash discount allowable.

You also ascertain that the credit manager obtains approval from the executive office at Far Distributing Company, located in Chicago, to write off uncollectible accounts. In addition, the manager has retained in custody, as of the end of the fiscal year, some remittances that were received on various days during the last month.

Required:

a. Describe irregularities that might occur under the current procedures for handling cash collections and remittances.
b. List the procedures that you would recommend to strengthen internal control over cash collections and remittances.

(CPA Examination, adapted)

8.8 Your junior accountant has prepared the following description of the accounting and internal control procedures relating to purchases by the Branden Company, a medium-sized manufacturer of special order machinery.

After approval by Manufacturing Department supervisors, materials purchase requisitions are forwarded to the purchasing department supervisor, who distributes the requisitions to his employees. These employees prepare prenumbered purchase orders in triplicate, account for all numbers, and send the original purchase order to the vendor. One copy of the purchase order is sent to the receiving department, where it is used as a receiving report. The other copy is filed in the purchasing department.

When the materials are received, they are moved directly to the storeroom and issued to the supervisors on an informal request basis. The receiving department sends a receiving report (with its copy of the purchase order attached) to the purchasing department and forwards copies of the receiving report to the storeroom and to the accounting department.

Vendors' invoices for material purchases, received in duplicate in the mail room, are sent to the purchasing department and directed to the employee who placed the related order. He or she then compares (1) the invoice with the copy of the purchase order on file in the purchasing department for price and terms; and (2) the invoice quantity received as reported by the shipping and receiving department on its copy of the purchase order. The purchasing department employees also check discounts, footings, and extensions, after which they initial the invoice to indicate approval for payment. The invoice is then submitted to the voucher section of the accounting department, where it is coded for account distribution, assigned a voucher number, entered in the voucher register, and filed according to payment due date.

Required:

Discuss the internal control weaknesses at Branden Company. Suggest supplementary or revised procedures for remedying each weakness with regard to (a) requisition of materials and (b) receipt and storage of materials.

(CPA Examination, adapted)

8.9 During a recent review, ABC Corporation discovered that it has a serious internal control problem. It is estimated that the exposure associated with this problem is $1 million and that the risk is presently 5%. Two internal control procedures have been proposed to deal with this problem. Procedure A would cost $25,000 and would reduce risk to 2%. Procedure B would cost $30,000 and would reduce risk to 1%. If both procedures were implemented, risk would be reduced to a tenth of 1%.

Required:

a. What is the estimated expected loss associated with ABC Corporation's internal control problem before any new internal control procedures are implemented?
b. Compute the revised estimate of expected loss (1) if procedure A were implemented, (2) if procedure B were implemented, and (3) if both procedures were implemented.
c. Compare the estimated costs and benefits of procedure A, of procedure B, and of both procedures combined.
d. Considering only the estimates of cost and benefit, which procedure or procedures should be implemented? What other factors might be relevant to the decision?

CASE 8.1 ANYCOMPANY, INC.—AN ONGOING COMPREHENSIVE CASE

Visit a local company and obtain permission to study its system of internal controls. Once you have lined up a company, do the following:

1. Obtain copies of organizational charts, job descriptions, and related documentation on how authority and responsibility have been assigned within the organization. Evaluate whether lines of authority and responsibility seem to be clearly defined.
2. Determine whether the company has an internal audit function. If so, visit with an internal audit supervisor or manager and learn (a) to whom in the organization the head of internal auditing reports and (b) what kinds of jobs internal auditing generally performs.
3. If the company is a corporation whose equity securities are publicly traded,
   - **a.** Determine whether it has taken steps to document its compliance with the internal control provisions of the Foreign Corrupt Practices Act of 1977. If possible, examine and evaluate this documentation.
   - **b.** Determine whether an audit committee is part of the board of directors. If so, obtain a list of the members of the audit committee and a copy of the committee's charter or bylaws.
4. Interview someone who hires employees for positions in accounting and data processing. Find out the following information:
   - **a.** What sort of background checks are performed before these employees are hired?
   - **b.** Is fidelity bond coverage normally obtained for them?
   - **c.** Does the company require rotation of duties and enforced vacations for these employees?
5. Select any one of the five accounting data processing cycles described in Chapters 12–16 and examine the company's internal control procedures for that accounting cycle.
   - **a.** Identify the persons responsible for the transaction authorization, record keeping, and asset custody functions.
   - **b.** Learn how transaction documents and/or records are used to facilitate internal control.
   - **c.** Follow the audit trail by tracing one accounting transaction from its original source document through its entry in journals, ledgers, files, and so on, and ultimately the general ledger accounts.
   - **d.** Identify the policies and procedures used to safeguard assets and records.
   - **e.** Identify several internal check procedures.

CASE 8.2 THE GREATER PROVIDENCE DEPOSIT & TRUST EMBEZZLEMENT

On a Saturday afternoon in the spring of 1988, Nino Moscardi received an anonymous note in his mail. Moscardi, president of Greater Providence Deposit & Trust, was shocked to read the note's allegations: that an employee of the bank was putting through bogus loans. On the following Monday, he directed the bank's internal auditors to investigate certain transactions detailed in the note. The investigation led to James Guisti, manager of a North Providence branch office and a trusted 14-year employee who had once worked as one of the bank's auditors. Guisti was later charged with embezzling $1.83 million from the bank through 67 phony loans taken out over a three-year period.

Court documents revealed numerous details of Guisti's embezzlement scheme. For example, the first bogus loan was written in April 1985 for $10,000. The loans were 90-day notes requiring no collateral and ranged in amount from $10,000 to $63,500. Guisti originated the loans; when each one matured, he would take out a new loan, or rewrite the old one, to pay the principal and interest due. Some loans had been rewritten five or six times.

The 67 loans were taken out in various names, including his wife's maiden name, the name of his father, and the names of two of his friends. These people denied they received any stolen funds or knew anything about the embezzlement. In addition, one loan was in the name of James Vanesse, who police said did not exist. The Social Security number on Vanesse's loan application was issued to a female, and the phone number belonged to a North Providence auto dealer.

Court records also disclosed the details of police interviews with bank employees to determine how the loan money was dispensed. According to Lucy Fraioli, a customer service representative who cosigned checks to the five names to which Guisti had originated loans, Guisti was her supervisor and she thought nothing was wrong with the checks, though she did not know any of the five people. Marcia Perfetto, head teller at the branch, told police that she had cashed checks for Guisti made out to four of the five persons. Asked if she gave the money to Guisti when he gave her the checks to cash, she answered, "Not all of the time," though she could not recall ever having given the money directly to any of the four, whom she said she did not know.

According to news reports, Guisti was authorized to make consumer loans up to a certain dollar limit without loan committee approvals, which is a standard industry practice. Guisti's lending limit was $10,000 until January 1987, when it was increased to $15,000. In February 1988 it was increased again to $25,000. However, some of the loans, including the one for $63,500, far exceeded his lending limit. In addition, all loan applications should have been accompanied by a report on the applicant's credit history, purchased from an independent credit rating firm. The loan taken out in a fictitious name would not have had a credit report and should have been flagged by a loan review clerk at the bank's headquarters.

News reports raised several questions about why the fraud had not been detected earlier. State regulators had examined the bank's books in September 1986. The bank's own internal auditors also failed to detect the fraud. However, in checking for bad loans, bank auditors do not examine all loans and generally focus on loans much larger than the ones in question. In addition, Greater Providence had recently dropped its computer services arrangement with a local bank in favor of an out-of-state bank, and this changeover may have reduced the effectiveness of the bank's control procedures. Finally, the bank's loan review clerks were frequently rotated, making follow-up on questionable loans more difficult.

Court records indicate that Guisti was a frequent gambler and used the proceeds of the embezzlement to pay gambling debts. The bank's losses totaled $624,000, and its bonding company, Hartford Accident and Indemnity Company, covered the loss. The loss was less than the $1.83 million in bogus loans because Guisti used some of the borrowed money to pay back some loans as they came due.

According to financial reports made available by Greater Providence officials, the bank had assets of $220 million and outstanding loans of $184 million as of the end of 1987, and it earned a record $1.6 million for 1987. It had eight branches in the Providence area.

The bank had experienced other adverse publicity during that period. In 1985 it was fined $50,000 after pleading guilty to failure to report a series of cash transactions exceeding $10,000, which is a felony. In 1986, the bank was taken private by its current owners, but only after a lengthy public battle with State Attorney General Arlene Violet. The state charged that the bank had inflated its assets and overestimated its capital surplus to make its balance sheet look stronger. The bank denied this charge.

1. Discuss how Greater Providence Deposit & Trust might improve its control procedures over the disbursement of loan funds to minimize the risk of this type of fraud. In what way does this case indicate a lack of proper segregation of duties?
2. Discuss how Greater Providence might improve its loan review procedures at bank headquarters

to minimize their fraud risk. Was it a good idea to rotate the assignments of loan review clerks? Why or why not?

3. Discuss whether Greater Providence's auditors should have been able to detect this fraud.

4. Are their any indications that the control environment at Greater Providence may have been deficient? If so, could this have contributed in any way to this embezzlement? How?

Source: John Kostrezewa, "Charge: Embezzlement," *Providence Journal-Bulletin* (July 31, 1988): F-1.

ANSWERS TO CHAPTER QUIZ

1. b **3.** b **5.** a **7.** d **9.** a
2. d **4.** d **6.** b **8.** c **10.** b

CHAPTER 9

Computer-Based Information Systems Control

LEARNING OBJECTIVES

After studying this chapter, you should be able to

- Identify and explain the general controls that should exist within a computer-based information system.
- Identify and explain the application control procedures and techniques that should be incorporated into data processing applications of computer-based information systems.

Integrative Case: Seattle Paper Products (SPP)

During his fifth month at Northwest Industries, Jason Scott is assigned to audit Seattle Paper Products (SPP), a Northwest subsidiary. Jason's first task is to review 50 randomly selected payables transactions, track down all supporting documents, and verify that all the transactions have been properly authorized and correctly processed. Within a short time he locates vendor invoices and disbursement vouchers for all 50 transactions, and he finds purchase orders and receiving reports for 45 of them. After reviewing these documents, Jason is satisfied that these 45 transactions are valid and accurate.

The other five transactions involve the purchase of services, which are processed on the basis of vendor invoices approved by management. One particular invoice, from Pacific Electric Services, lists $450 for maintenance and repair work but does not have an authorization signature. Jason locates five more invoices from Pacific Electric, all for maintenance and repair services in amounts ranging from $300 to $500. These five bear the initials "JLC." JLC is Jack Carlton, the general supervisor of the plant. Much to Jason's surprise, Carlton denies initialing them and claims he has never heard of Pacific Electric. They find no such firm in the phone book.

Jason cannot believe he has found another hidden problem. After brooding over his bad luck, he begins to think about the following questions:

1. Is Jack Carlton telling the truth? If so, where did the Pacific Electric Services invoices come from?

2. If Carlton is not telling the truth, what is he up to?
3. If Pacific Electric Services is a fictitious company, how could SPP's control systems allow its invoices to be processed and approved for payment?

INTRODUCTION

Achieving adequate security and control over the information resources of an organization should be a top management priority. Although internal control objectives remain the same regardless of the data processing method, a computer-based AIS requires different internal control policies and procedures. For example, while computer processing reduces the potential for clerical errors, it may increase the risks of unauthorized access to or modification of data files. In addition, segregating the authorization, recording, and asset custody functions within an AIS must be achieved differently, since computer programs may be responsible for one or two or all three of these functions. Fortunately, computers also provide opportunities for an organization to enhance its internal controls.

This chapter discusses the many different types of controls that companies use to ensure the integrity of their AIS. The first section of the chapter discusses general AIS controls, which are applied at the organizational level or bear on all aspects of the AIS. The second section discusses application controls, which are used in specific AIS applications such as payroll and accounts receivable.

GENERAL CONTROLS

A company designs **general controls** to ensure that its overall computer system is stable and well managed. This portion of the chapter discusses 12 categories of general controls:

1. Developing a security plan
2. Segregation of duties within the systems function
3. Project development controls
4. Physical access controls
5. Logical access controls
6. Data storage controls
7. Data transmission controls
8. Documentation standards
9. Minimizing system downtime
10. Disaster recovery plans
11. Protection of personal computers and client/server networks
12. Internet controls

Management control of the AIS function, another general control, was discussed in Chapter 8.

Developing a Security Plan

In a Coopers & Lybrand study, 66% of those reporting problems with their systems said one of the reasons was inadequate monitoring of controls and security. Another 44% said insufficient understanding of control concepts and control design was a contributing factor. This highlights a significant problem in many companies—they do not have an effective security plan in place to ensure the integrity of their AIS.

Developing and continuously updating a comprehensive security plan is one of the most important controls a company can implement. A good way to develop the plan is to determine *who* needs access to *what* information, *when* they need it, and on *which* systems the information resides. This information can be used to determine information threats, risks, and exposures and to select the most cost-effective security measures. A top-level manager should be assigned to develop, supervise, and enforce the plan. The plan should be communicated to all company employees and continuously reviewed and updated.

Segregation of Duties Within the Systems Function

In a highly integrated AIS, procedures that used to be performed by separate individuals are combined. Therefore, any person who has unrestricted access to the computer, its programs, and live data could have the opportunity to both perpetrate and conceal fraud. To combat this threat, organizations must implement compensating control procedures such as the effective segregation of duties within the AIS function. Authority and responsibility must be clearly divided among the following functions:

1. *Systems analysis.* Systems analysts work with users to determine their information needs and then design an AIS to meet those needs.
2. *Programming.* Programmers take the design provided by systems analysts and create the AIS by writing the computer programs.
3. *Computer operations.* Computer operators run the software on the company's computers. They make sure that data is properly input to the computer, that it is processed correctly, and that the needed output is produced.
4. *Users.* User departments are the ones that record transactions, authorize data to be processed, and use the output produced by the system.
5. *AIS library.* The AIS librarian maintains custody of data bases, files, and programs in a separate storage area—the AIS library.
6. *Data control.* The data control group ensures that source data has been properly approved, monitors the flow of work through the computer, reconciles input and output, maintains a record of input errors to ensure their correction and resubmission, and distributes systems output.

It is important that different people perform these functions. Allowing a person to perform two or more of them exposes the company to the possibility of fraud. For example, if a programmer for a credit union were allowed to use actual data to test her program, she could erase her car loan balance while conducting the test. Likewise, if a computer operator has access to programming logic and documentation, he might, while processing the company payroll program, be able to alter the payroll program to increase his salary.

Project Development Controls

Examples abound of poorly managed development projects that have wasted large sums of money because certain basic principles of management control were ignored. For example, the Oklahoma State Insurance Fund terminated a development contract with Policy Management Systems for a software system that would issue policies and process and track claims and premiums. The contract was canceled when the project fell several months behind schedule and went $1 million over budget. As explained in Focus 9.1, Westpac Banking Corporation terminated a large-scale systems integration project after spending over $150 million.

To minimize failures, the basic principles of responsibility accounting should be applied to the AIS function. Adherence to these principles greatly reduces the potential for cost overruns and project failures while substantially improving the efficiency and effectiveness of the AIS. Project development control includes the following key elements:

1. *Long-range master plan.* A **master plan** is a multiyear (often 3–5 years) technological road map and lays out the projects the company needs to complete to achieve its long-range goals
2. *Project development plan.* A **project development plan** shows how a project will be completed, including the tasks to be performed, who will perform them, the dates they should be completed, the cost of each, and so forth. The plan should specify **project milestones**—or significant points when progress is reviewed and actual and estimated completion times are compared.
3. *Data processing schedule.* To maximize the use of scarce computer resources, all data processing tasks should be organized according to a **data processing schedule.**
4. *Assignment of responsibility.* Each project should be assigned to a manager and team. They should be held responsible for the success or failure of the project.
5. *Periodic performance evaluations.* Each job should be broken down into modules or tasks; a **performance evaluation** of the people performing the tasks should be done as each is completed.
6. *Postimplementation review.* After a development project is completed, a **postimplementation review** should be performed to determine whether the anticipated benefits were achieved. Reviews help control project development activities and encourage accurate and objective initial cost and benefit estimates.
7. *System performance measurements.* For a system to be evaluated properly, it must be assessed using **system performance measurements.** Common measurements include **throughput** (output per unit of time), **utilization** (percentage of time the system is being productively used), and **response time** (how long it takes the system to respond).

FOCUS 9.1 Harnessing Runaway Systems

WESTPAC Banking Corporation of Sydney, Australia instigated a five-year systems development project that was supposed to redefine the role of information technology. The project, designated Core System 90 (CS90), was budgeted at $85 million. Its objective was to decentralize Westpac's information systems by equipping branch managers with CASE (computer-aided software engineering) tools and expert systems, in order to generate new financial products. Decentralization would enable Westpac to respond more rapidly to customer needs while downsizing its internal AIS department.

Some three years after it began the project, Westpac took stock of CS90 and concluded that it was out of control. Despite an outlay of nearly $150 million on the project no usable results had been attained. In addition, bank officials determined that the scheduled completion date could not be realized. Facing serious problems with its loan portfolio and asset management programs, Westpac decided that it could not afford to risk several more million dollars on CS90. So, the bank fired IBM, the systems integrator* and primary software developer, and brought in Andersen Consulting to review the project and develop recommendations for salvaging it.

Westpac's CS90 boondoggle is merely one example of what has become an all-too-frequent story: a computer project that is over budget and behind schedule, often due to a systems integrator that is unable to deliver on lofty promises. Industry experts refer to such projects as runaways. Since 1988 KPMG has taken over some 50 runaway computer projects, and it estimates that, in about two-thirds of these cases, the problems arose from mismanagement by a systems integrator.

Computer systems built by a third party are subject to the same cost overruns and missed deadlines as systems developed internally. Therefore, it makes sense to use the same basic rules of project management and control, including close monitoring of system progress during development. Unfortunately, many companies are not doing this.

Instead, they rely on the integrator's assurance that the project will be completed on time. Too often, the integrator falls behind schedule but does not tell the client, figuring that the project can still be completed on time if a big push is made at the last minute. In such cases the CIO and other AIS executives are as much at fault as the systems integrator, according to experts in salvaging runaway systems.

These experts suggest that a systems integration project should be monitored by a sponsors committee, established by the CIO and chaired by the project's internal champion. Department managers for all units that will use the system should be on this committee. The role of this committee should be to establish formal procedures for measuring and reporting the status of the project. The best approach is to break the project down into manageable tasks, assign responsibility for each task, and then meet on a regular basis (at least monthly) to review progress and assess quality.

Equally important are steps that should be taken at the outset of the project. Before third parties are called in to bid on a project, clear specifications must be developed, including exact descriptions and definitions of the system, explicit deadlines, and precise acceptance criteria for each stage of the project. While specification development may seem expensive, it usually saves money in the long run. For example, Suffolk County, New York recently spent 12 months and $500,000 preparing detailed specifications for a new $16 million criminal justice information system before accepting bids. The county then hired Unisys Corporation and Grumman Data Systems to develop the system. County officials believe that their diligent upfront efforts helped ensure the success of their new system and saved the county $3 million in hardware costs.

Some systems integrators may object to detailed specifications and rigorous project control methods. For example, after reviewing Suffolk County's specifications, only 6 integrators out of 22 that had originally expressed interest bid on the project. This should be viewed as a blessing, rather than a problem. Those integrators who disdain a company's attempts to rigorously control the cost and quality of its systems projects are most likely the same ones responsible for most of the recent profusion of runaway systems.

*A systems integrator is a vendor that takes the responsibility for managing a cooperative systems development effort involving its own development personnel, those of the buyer, and possibly the systems development personnel of one or more other vendors, using common standards as much as possible.

Physical Access Controls

Both the physical ability to use computer equipment, referred to as **physical access,** and the ability to gain access to company data, called **logical access,** should be restricted. Physical access security can be achieved by the following controls:

- Placing computer equipment in locked rooms and restricting access to authorized personnel.
- Having only one or two entrances to the computer room. The entrances should be securely locked and monitored carefully by security guards and closed-circuit television systems.
- Requiring proper employee ID, such as a security badge, for passage through an access point. Modern security badges incorporate photos and magnetic, electric, or optical codes that can be read only by special badge readers. With advanced ID techniques, each employee's entry and exit may be automatically recorded in a log that is maintained on the computer and periodically reviewed by supervisory personnel.
- Requiring that visitors sign a log as they enter and leave the site. They should be briefed on company security policies, assigned visitor's badges, and escorted to their destination.
- Using a security alarm system to detect unauthorized access during off-hours.
- Restricting access to private, secured telephone lines or to authorized terminals or PCs.
- Installing locks on PCs and other computer devices.

Logical Access Controls

Users should be allowed access only to the data they are authorized to use and then only to perform specific, authorized functions such as reading, copying, and adding to and deleting data. It is also important to protect data from those outside the organization. For example, a manufacturing company's competitor broke into its system and browsed its data until it discovered a bid on a billion-dollar project. The competitor narrowly underbid the company and won the contract. The intrusion was discovered by an auditing system, but not before the bid was lost.

To restrict logical access, a system must differentiate between authorized and unauthorized users using what the user knows or possesses, where the user is accessing the system, or by some personal characteristic. Perhaps the most common approach is what a person knows. For example, the computer could ask users personal questions, such as their mother's maiden name. Or users could be asked to enter a personal identification number (PIN).

Passwords. The most frequent knowledge identifier is a user identification (ID) and authentication system. When signing on to a system, users identify themselves by entering an employee number, name, or account number. Users then enter a **password,** a series of characters that uniquely identifies the user and is known only to the user and the system. If the user-entered ID and password match those in the computer, the system assumes it is an authorized user.

The downside of passwords is that they can be guessed, lost, written down, or given away, creating the potential for unauthorized, and in some cases, dangerous persons to gain system access. For example, a convicted child rapist working in a Boston hospital used a former employee's password to gain access to confidential patient files. He proceeded to obtain telephone numbers of families that had children. The risks associated with passwords can be virtually eliminated by following the recommendations in Focus 9.2.

Physical Possession Identification. People can also be identified by what they physically possess, such as an ID card that records a person's name, ID number, picture, and other pertinent information. ID cards can be read by the

FOCUS 9.2 Ensuring Password Integrity

1. Require users to keep their ID number and password confidential. The system should not display ID numbers or passwords on the screen as they are entered. Users should never reveal passwords. At Pacific Bell, teenage hackers posed as company employees and persuaded system users to give them the passwords they needed to access the system.
2. Randomly assign passwords to users, since user-selected passwords are often easily guessed.
3. Change passwords frequently to maintain their confidentiality. Several months after she was fired, a woman in California logged on to her former company's computers to copy and damage files. The police raided her home and seized millions of dollars of company software. The company had invalidated her password, but since passwords were not changed regularly, one she stole just before she left allowed her access to the system.
4. Assign electronic ID numbers to each authorized device. Authorized devices should be the only ones allowed to interact with the system, and only to access certain data. For example, access to payroll records could be restricted to computers and terminals in the payroll department and appropriate top management.
5. Disconnect and deactivate the ID of anyone unable to provide a valid ID number or password within three attempts. This prevents hackers from programming a computer to try all combinations of user IDs and passwords. One company in Fort Worth had the ability to implement this control, but decided that it ate up too many system resources. After their internal auditors found evidence of repeated log-on attempts, they activated the software and found five employees who were trying to guess the passwords required to access confidential data. All five employees were terminated.
6. Immediately investigate devices from which repeated attempts to access the system with invalid ID numbers or passwords originate.
7. Require employees to log off their computers when they are not in use. It is especially important not to leave computers unattended during on-line interactions with confidential corporate data bases.
8. Restrict user or terminal transactions to specified times, such as normal business hours.
9. Immediately restrict employee access to data when they are transferred to another department. For example, someone leaving the payroll department should no longer have access to payroll data.
10. Immediately deactivate the user ID and password of any employee who is terminated. In a security review conducted by Ernst & Young, 240 ex-employees still retained access to their company's dial-in system.
11. Use password scanning programs to detect weak, or easily guessed, passwords.
12. Require the use of a smart card that uses an algorithm to generate a new and unique password every minute. The system uses the same algorithm and, since times are synchronized, generates the same password.

computer and security devices such as door locks. Unfortunately, they can also be lost, stolen, or given away. Security can be increased significantly if a user is required to have both an ID card and a password before receiving access to the system. However, even these systems can be compromised. For example, a hacker broke into the Motorola system by calling the help desk and saying he was an employee working at home who had forgotten his ID card (the card generated random passwords that change every few seconds). The help desk believed him and let him into the corporate network. Fortunately, he did no permanent damage to their system.

Focus 9.3 describes another physical possession ID, an active badge that transmits a radio signal picked up by special receivers.

Biometric Identification. **Biometric identification** devices identify unique physical characteristics such as fingerprints, voice patterns, retina prints, facial patterns and features, body odor, signature dynamics, and keyboarding patterns (the way a user types certain groups of characters). When a person desires access to the system, his or her biometric identifications are matched against those stored in the computer. For example, Oracle Corp. has a palm-sized device that compares a user's fingerprints to sets stored in a central data base. The device also tracks blood flow and pressure, which allows it to differentiate between a real fingerprint and one on a wax model or glove. Large banks are beginning to install retina scanners on their ATMs to prevent unauthorized access. The scanners capture and digitize the pattern of blood vessels produced when light is reflected off a retina, which contains about ten times more information than a fingerprint.

FOCUS 9.3 "Active Badges" Keep Silent Tabs on Employees' Whereabouts

GEORGE Orwell's Big Brother is watching more keenly than ever at the Olivetti Research Laboratory and the computer laboratory at Cambridge University in Cambridge, England. Employees there are sporting infrared tracking devices called active badges that allow a computer network to silently keep tabs on each person's whereabouts. In addition to enhancing physical security in corporate buildings, this automatic tracing system can be used to track objects in airports, ranging from luggage to lost children.

The small clip-on badges hanging from shirt pockets and dangling from belts are equipped with transceivers that emit uniquely coded signals every few seconds. The signals are picked up by infrared sensors located in each room and transferred to workstations and PCs that serve as nodes on a distributed computer network. When telephone calls come in to the facility, the receptionist can call up the system, locate the individual, and transfer the call to the nearest telephone.

The practical benefits of active badge tracing have turned some initial doubters into believers, according to Mark Chopping, a research engineer at the Olivetti lab. "We find we don't miss phone calls anymore," he said. "A lot of the people who refused to wear the badges at first came back after two months and asked for one."

One potential stumbling block is that the system responds to the badge, not the individual. Whoever wears that uniquely coded badge can assume the identity of the proper owner. Solving the authentication problem is the target of a related Olivetti/DEC research project.

The introduction of this technology raises a number of legal and ethical issues. Critics argue that the new technology sacrifices individual privacy in favor of convenience and efficiency. Some employees wearing active badges may feel like house arrest victims whose bracelets trigger an alarm when they leave home. Some people feel that it is great technology in the right hands, but that a bad manager could make an employee's life miserable.

U.S. Immigration has begun to use electronic hand readers to verify a person's identification. The handprint of a passport applicant is captured and stored on a wallet-sized card. When a cardholder enters the country, his or her card and hand are placed in a special reading device that matches the two. In airports equipped with hand readers, passports do not have to be shown when a cardholder reenters the country. The eventual goal is to put coded handprint data on machine-readable passports.

The ideal biometric device can adapt to slight personal changes, but will reject unauthorized users. Unfortunately, there are still some problems to work out. For example, voice recognition devices may reject a person with a head cold or whose voice is muffled over a phone line, while retina scanners may reject someone with bloodshot eyes. Another disadvantage is that, with the exception of voice scanners, users have to be physically present to use the system.

Compatibility Tests. When a valid user tries to operate the system, a compatibility test should be performed to determine if the user is authorized to perform the desired action. For example, factory employees would not be authorized to make entries involving accounts payable, and purchasing agents would not be allowed to enter sales orders. This procedure is necessary to prevent both unintentional errors and deliberate attempts to manipulate the system.

Compatibility tests utilize an **access control matrix,** which is a list of authorized user ID numbers and passwords, a list of all files and programs, and the access each user has to them. Figure 9.1 shows an access control matrix with codes for four types of access. User 12345-ABC is permitted only to read and display file C and is restricted from any kind of access to other files or programs. User 12389-RST, apparently a programmer, is authorized to make any type of change in program 2 and to read and display records in file B. User 12567-XYZ, probably a supervisor, is authorized to read and display the contents of all files and programs.

Data Storage Controls

Information is generally what gives a company a competitive edge and makes it viable. Because information is such a valuable resource, it must be protected from unauthorized disclosure and destruction. For example, a repairman working late to repair a printing press at Webco Press in Lapeer, Michigan was trusted to complete his assignment without supervision. The repairman gained access to Webco's mainframe computer and made a printout of the company's customer list, complete with prices. He attempted to sell the customer list to a Webco competitor for $5,000 but was apprehended. Mattel Corp. lost critical competitive information when the laptops of several of its executives were stolen.

A company should identify the types of data maintained and the level of protection required for each. A company must also document the steps taken to protect data. A company should keep track of security efforts; maintain records of confidential documents, records, and files; and implement audit trails to track those with access to confidential data. Employees should sign contracts that require them to maintain the confidentiality of company data.

A properly supervised file library is one essential means of preventing loss of data. The file storage area should also be protected against fire, dust, excess heat or humidity, and other conditions that could harm stored data.

FIGURE 9.1
Access Control Matrix

USER IDENTIFICATION		FILES			PROGRAMS			
Code Number	**Password**	**A**	**B**	**C**	**1**	**2**	**3**	**4**
12345	ABC	0	0	1	0	0	0	0
12346	DEF	0	2	0	0	0	0	0
12354	KLM	1	1	1	0	0	0	0
12359	NOP	3	0	0	0	0	0	0
12389	RST	0	1	0	0	3	0	0
12567	XYZ	1	1	1	1	1	1	1

Codes for type of access:
0 = No access permitted
1 = Read and display only
2 = Read, display, and update
3 = Read, display, update, create, and delete

File labels can protect data files from inadvertent misuse. An **external label,** a gummed paper label attached to a storage device (i.e., diskette), contains the file name, contents, and date processed. **Internal labels** are written in machine-readable form on the data recording media. There are three different internal labels. A **volume label** identifies the entire contents of each separate data recording medium, such as a hard disk, diskette, or tape reel. A **header label,** located at the beginning of each file, contains the file name, expiration date, and other identification data. A **trailer label,** located at the end of the file, contains file control totals, which are checked against those accumulated during processing.

Write protection mechanisms protect against users' accidentally writing over or erasing data files. A **tape file protection ring** is a plastic ring that, when removed, prevents a tape file from being written upon. Many diskettes have on/off switches that perform the same function. Unfortunately, these write protection mechanisms can easily be circumvented.

Data base systems use data base administrators, data dictionaries, and concurrent update controls to provide data protection. The administrator establishes and enforces procedures for accessing and updating the data base. The data dictionary ensures that data items are defined and used consistently. **Concurrent update controls** protect records from errors that occur when two or more users attempt to update the same record simultaneously. This is accomplished by locking out one user until the system has finished processing the update entered by the other.

Data Transmission Controls

To reduce the risk of data transmission failures, companies should monitor the network to detect weak points, maintain backup components, and design networks so that capacity is sufficient to handle peak processing periods. They should also establish multiple communication paths between crucial network components so the system can function if one of the paths fails. By way of preventive maintenance, companies can upgrade to conditioned telecommunications lines that are faster and more efficient, have fewer problems with static, and are less likely to fail.

Data transmission errors are minimized using data encryption, routing verification, parity checking, and message acknowledgment procedures.

Data Encryption (Cryptography). Due to the phenomenal growth of the Internet and electronic commerce, **data encryption (cryptography)** has become an extremely important control. Cryptography is the science of secret codes and is used to ensure that data transmissions and electronic commerce transactions meet three important security requirements—confidentiality, integrity, and authenticity. **Confidentiality** refers to limiting data access or use to authorized personnel. **Integrity** refers to protecting data from unauthorized tampering. **Authenticity** refers to being able to determine, with almost absolute certainty, who sent a message.

In data encryption, a Sender converts data into a scrambled format using a key and an algorithm. The encrypted data is transmitted over a network to a Receiver, who uses a key and algorithm to reverse the encryption process. Accordingly, encrypted data can be read only by someone with the appropriate decryption key.

There are two common encryption systems: private key and public key systems. In a **private key** system (also called secret key or symmetric key), both the Sender and the Receiver have access to the same key. A disadvantage of this system is that if the secrecy of the key is compromised, the system loses its effectiveness. Since secrecy is most likely to be compromised when the keys are initially delivered to the Sender and the Receiver, great care should be taken to see that they are not intercepted when delivered.

The industry standard for private key encryption systems is the 56-bit Data Encryption Standard (DES). A 56-bit encryption code has over 76 quadrillion possibilities for keys. Once thought to be unbreakable, a group of programmers and researchers needed only 5 months to decode a message sent using DES. They distributed code-breaking software over the Internet and used the idle time of tens of thousands of computers across the Internet to decode the message. Researchers and encryption developers are working on a 128-bit encryption system that will be many times harder to break than the 56-bit system.

Private key encryption systems are best suited for use within an organization or between closely related organizations. They are based on software and are up to 100 times faster than public key systems. However, private key systems are not appropriate for most electronic commerce applications, since both parties in a transaction must have access to the same private key. This means that (1) everyone who does business with a particular company must have the same key, which would negate the value of the system, or (2) there must be a separate key for each company you do business with, which would be confusing and very difficult to track.

Instead, electronic commerce systems use a public key encryption system. A **public key** system uses two separate keys: a public key that is available to everyone, and a private key known only to the user. Both keys are needed to encrypt or decrypt a message. An outgoing message is encrypted using the Receiver's public key and then further encrypted using the Sender's private key. After the message is transmitted, it is decrypted using the Sender's public key and then by the Receiver's private key.

The computer industry prevents public keys from being counterfeited by using an electronic document, called a **digital certificate,** that is issued by an independent organization called a **certificate authority.** The digital certificate for a company contains three things: a header (company name, ID number, expiration date, etc.), the company's public key, and the signature of the certificate authority.

To create the signature of the certificate authority, the other two items (header and company public key) are run through what is called a hash algorithm. The resultant hash number, called a **digital fingerprint,** identifies the certificate. The certificate authority encrypts the fingerprint using its own private key and "signs" the digital certificate by adding the encrypted fingerprint to the document. A change in either the header or the public key will invalidate the fingerprint.

The Receiver checks the certificate's validity by comparing the decrypted digital fingerprint with a recalculated digital fingerprint. The fingerprint that is part of the certificate is decrypted using the certificate authority's public key. The Receiver recalculates the fingerprint by taking the header and public key from the certificate and running them through the standard hash algorithm. If the decrypted and recalculated fingerprints match, the certificate is valid.

Without the certificate authority's private key, the digital signature could not have been encrypted properly. If someone had altered either the header or the company's public key on the certificate, the recalculated signature would not match the decrypted one. When used properly, digital certificates make it impossible for a person to impersonate someone by imitating their public key.

Routing Verification Procedures. Several **routing verification procedures** can ensure that messages are not routed to the wrong system address. Transmitted data can be given a header label that identifies its destination, which the system uses to verify that the destination is valid and authorized to receive it. **Mutual authentication schemes** require both computers to exchange their passwords before communication can take place. In a **callback system,** a user enters a password and is identified as an authorized user. Then the computer disconnects and calls the user back to verify the user's identity, password, telephone number, or location.

Parity. Computers use a combination of bits to represent a single character. For example, the digits 5 and 7 might be represented by 0101 and 0111, respectively. When data are transmitted, bits may be lost or received incorrectly. To detect these errors, a **parity bit** is added to every character. In even parity, each bit has an even number of 1s. The parity bit for 5 is 0 (0101 0), since 5 already has an even number of 1s. The parity bit for 7 is a 1 (0111 1) so there are an even number of 1s. In odd parity, there are an odd number of 1s.

Parity checking—verifying that there are an even (or odd) number of 1s—is performed by devices that receive data. Two-dimensional parity checking tests parity both vertically and horizontally. Dual checking is important in telecommunications, because noise bursts frequently cause two or more adjacent bits to be lost. A one-dimensional parity check will not detect all such errors.

Message Acknowledgment Techniques. A number of message acknowledgment techniques are used to let the sender of an electronic message know that a message was received.

- *Echo check.* When data is transmitted, the system calculates a summary statistic such as the number of bits in the message. The receiving unit performs the same calculation—a procedure known as an **echo check**—and sends the result to the sending unit. If the counts agree, the transmission is presumed to be accurate.
- *Trailer label.* The receiving unit can check for a trailer label to verify that the entire message was received.
- *Numbered batches.* If a large message is transmitted in segments, each can be numbered sequentially so that the receiving unit can properly assemble the segments.

Whenever a data transmission error is detected, the receiving unit will signal the sending unit and the data will be retransmitted. Generally, the system will do this automatically and the user is unaware that it has occurred. Occasionally, the system may not be able to accomplish automatic retransmissions and will request that the user at the sending end manually retransmit the data.

Data Transmission Controls for EDI and EFT. Data transmission controls take on added importance in organizations that utilize electronic data interchange (EDI) or electronic funds transfer (EFT) because of the risk of unauthorized access to proprietary data. EFT systems are also vulnerable to fraudulent fund transfers. In these types of environments, sound internal control is achieved using a number of control procedures. Physical access to network facilities should be strictly controlled. Electronic identification should be required for all authorized network terminals. Strict logical access control procedures are essential, with passwords and dial-in phone numbers changed on a regular basis. Encryption should be used to secure stored data as well as data being transmitted. Details of all transactions should be recorded in a log that is periodically reviewed for evidence of invalid transactions.

Documentation Standards

Another important general control is documentation procedures and standards to ensure clear and concise documentation. Quality documentation facilitates communication and regular progress reviews during systems development and can be used as a reference and training tool for newly hired systems employees. It also simplifies program maintenance, especially when updating applications written by someone else and eases problems related to job turnover, such as a programmer quitting in the middle of a major project.

Documentation may be classified into three basic categories:

1. **Administrative documentation** describes the standards and procedures for data processing, including the justification and authorization of new systems and system changes; standards for systems analysis, design, and programming; and procedures for file handling and storage.
2. **Systems documentation** describes each application system. It includes narrative material, flowcharts, and program listings. It shows application inputs, processing steps, outputs, and error handling procedures.
3. **Operating documentation** describes what is needed to run a program, including the equipment configuration, program and data files, procedures to set up and execute the job, conditions that may interrupt program execution, and corrective actions for program interruptions.

Minimizing System Downtime

Significant financial losses can be incurred if hardware or software malfunctions cause an AIS to fail. Among the methods to minimize system downtime are preventive maintenance, an uninterrupted power system, and fault tolerance. **Preventive maintenance** involves regular testing of system components and replacement of those in poor condition. An **uninterruptible power system (UPS)** is an auxiliary power supply that smooths the flow of power to the computer, preventing loss of data due to momentary surges or dips in power. In the event of a complete power failure, a UPS provides a backup power supply to keep the computer system operating. **Fault tolerance** is the ability to continue operating when system components (such as PCs, terminals, data transmission lines, and disk drives) fail. It is achieved using redundant components that take over in the event of failure.

Disaster Recovery Plans

Every organization should have a **disaster recovery plan** so that data processing capacity can be restored as smoothly and quickly as possible in the event of a major disaster. Being without an AIS can be very costly; some companies report losses as high as $500,000 per hour of downtime. John Alden Life Insurance estimates that, without its disaster recovery plan, Hurricane Andrew would have put them out of business in three days. Many of the 350 companies that had their systems destroyed in the World Trade Center bombing were unprepared; 150 of them went out of business.

A survey of 200 large U.S. businesses showed that only a third have a disaster recovery plan with off-site data storage for their client/server applications. As Focus 9.4 illustrates, those that have them are well rewarded for their planning and foresight when disaster strikes.

The objectives of a recovery plan are to (1) minimize the extent of the disruption, damage, and loss; (2) temporarily establish an alternative means of processing information; (3) resume normal operations as soon as possible; and (4) train and familiarize personnel with emergency operations. A sound disaster recovery plan should contain the following elements.

1. *Priorities for the recovery process.* The plan should identify the applications needed to keeping the organization running, the hardware and software necessary to sustain them, and the sequence and timing of all recovery activities.

2. *Backup data and program files.* Procedures should exist for recovering lost or destroyed files. All program and data files should be backed up regularly and frequently and stored at a secure site some distance from the main computer. The Federal Employees Credit Union offices were destroyed and 18 of its 33 employees killed in the bombing of the Federal Building in Oklahoma City. Even though all its records and computers were destroyed, duplicate copies of all crucial information had been stored off-site. Two days later, the company reopened its doors in a new location with new computer and phone systems.

   Backup files may be transported to the remote site physically or electronically using **electronic vaulting**. Many electronic vaulting services have users install their software on the user's computers so that they can use Internet connections to contact the computers and automatically backup data, usually in the middle of the night. If data is lost or needs to be accessed, the Internet connection provides prompt on-line access to the backup data. To protect data privacy, all data is encrypted before being transmitted.

   Batch processing files are backed up using the **grandfather–father–son** concept. In batch processing, when a master file is updated with a set of transactions a new master file is created. If a master file is destroyed, it can be re-created using prior generations of the master file and the appropriate transaction file. For example, suppose that on Wednesday night the current master file is destroyed. It could be re-created using the Tuesday master file (father file) and the Tuesday transaction file. If Tuesday's file was also destroyed, it could be re-created using the Monday master file (grandfather file) and Monday's transaction file. The Wednesday master file, as previously mentioned, could then be reconstructed with the new Tuesday master file and the Tuesday transaction file. When the update is complete on Thursday night, the Monday master file is no longer needed and the disk or tape can be reused.

   A similar procedure is employed to ensure that on-line master files can be reconstructed. Periodically during processing, a **checkpoint** is created; the system makes a copy of the master file at that point in time and the information needed to restart the system. The checkpoint file is stored on a separate disk or tape file. If a problem occurs, the system can be restarted by determining the last checkpoint and then reprocessing all subsequent transactions.

   Using a procedure called **rollback,** a preupdated copy of each record is created prior to processing a transaction. If a hardware failure occurs, the records are rolled back to the preupdate value and the transaction is reprocessed from the beginning.

   PC hard disks are often backed up on diskettes and tape files. However, if the backup copies are stored next to the PC, they can also be destroyed by a disaster that wipes out the PC. That is exactly what

FOCUS 9.4 A Model for Disaster Recovery Planning

THE VALUE of a disaster recovery plan is underscored by numerous case histories. Perhaps the best known is the story of the worst bank fire in history and how the bank recovered by following a plan that has since become a disaster recovery planning model.

On Thanksgiving Day, a huge fire swept through the offices of Northwest National Bank of Minneapolis, destroying bank transaction records and data processing facilities. It was described as one of the worst fires in the city's history. Yet the following Monday, bank employees were back on the job in new quarters—handling deposits, withdrawals, investments, loans, and other routine bank transactions. The fire could have threatened the bank's ability to remain in business, but it did not, thanks to a detailed disaster recovery plan. Because a record of nearly every bank transaction was stored elsewhere in computers or on microfilm, the bank lost few, if any, important records. The day after the fire, computers at a local service bureau were hard at work making new copies of the destroyed records. The recovery plan provided bank executives with a detailed blueprint for lining up new office space, replacing computer equipment and supplies, procuring new office equipment, and making other arrangements essential to the continuation of Northwest's banking operations.

An early morning fire struck the Bank of the Sierra in Porterville, California, destroying its corporate offices and melting its mainframe computer. Though the facility was seemingly well protected by a sprinkler system and a halon gas fire extinguishing system, this fire burned through the building's roof, which collapsed, crushing the sprinkler system and releasing the halon gas into the air. The bank's central data bases and related records, including all personal and mortgage loan records, credit card records, and unprocessed checks, were lost.

Using a 150-page disaster recovery plan grounded in Northwest National Bank's experience, Bank of the Sierra officials quickly identified team members, crucial tasks, and required equipment, and began an overnight effort to restore bank services. By 10:00 A.M. the following morning, nine hours after the fire started, backup files were on-line and tellers were conducting business at branch windows as if nothing had happened. For processing of the bank's 25,000 to 40,000 daily transactions, a data processing hot site in nearby San Ramon was utilized. Updated files were downloaded from the hot site to a mainframe computer provided by a Denver company, from which printouts were flown back to Porterville daily. Within six days after the fire, the bank had cleaned up its transaction processing backlog and its customer accounts were current.

happened when First Interstate Bancorp suffered a fire in its headquarters building in Los Angeles. First Interstate now repeatedly reminds employees to backup their files and take them home at the end of each day. Salomon, a large brokerage firm, has a system that creates weekly backup copies of all files on its 3,000 workstations worldwide. They also have a copy of all application programs on a duplicate computer system.

It is important to document the backup procedures and periodically practice restoring a system from the backup data. In this way, employees know how to quickly restart the system in the event of a failure.

3. *Specific assignments.* A disaster recovery coordinator responsible for implementing the plan should be appointed. The plan should assign responsibility for recovery activities to specific individuals and teams. These activities should include arranging for new facilities, operating the

computer, installing software, establishing data communications facilities, recovering vital records, and arranging for forms and supplies.

4. *Complete documentation.* The disaster recovery plan should be fully documented, with copies stored securely at multiple locations.

5. *Backup computer and telecommunications facilities.* Backup facilities can be arranged in several ways. One is to establish a reciprocal agreement with an organization that has compatible facilities, so that each party can temporarily use the other's data processing facilities in the event of an emergency. For example, four banks whose computers and data were damaged or destroyed in the World Trade Center bombing were able to use the New York Clearing House Association backup facilities to complete $90 billion of transactions on the day of the bombing.

   A second way is to contract with a vendor to provide contingent sites for emergency use. A **hot site** is a facility configured to meet the user's requirements. A **cold site** provides everything necessary to quickly install computer equipment (power, air conditioning, and support systems, etc.) but does not have the computers installed. A cold site user must contract with its vendor to ensure prompt delivery of equipment and software in the event of an emergency. For example, Brody White & Co., a brokerage, rerouted its distributed operations to a disaster recovery facility in New Jersey after the World Trade Center bombing.

   In a multilocation organization, you can distribute processing capacity so that other facilities can take over if one location is damaged or destroyed. In some cases, a system may be so important that a company invests in duplicate hardware, software, or data storage devices. For example, the system at Caesar's Palace in Las Vegas is so vital that an exact duplicate of the entire system, including an up-to-the-minute copy of the data base, is maintained 500 feet from the main system.

   Three other aspects of disaster recovery planning deserve mention. First, the recovery plan is incomplete until it has been satisfactorily tested by simulating a disaster and having each disaster recovery team carry out its prescribed activities. The plan should be retested twice a year. Most plans fail their initial test, and even tested plans rarely anticipate and deal with all problems that surface when a disaster strikes. Second, the recovery plan must be continuously reviewed and revised to ensure that it reflects current computer applications, equipment configurations, and personnel assignments. Third, the plan should include insurance coverage to defer costs of equipment replacement, recovery activities, and business interruption.

Protection of Personal Computers and Client/Server Networks

In the rush to move from mainframe to client/server networks, many companies have failed to develop adequate systems of internal controls for their client/server networks. They are now forced to go back and retrofit those applications with appropriate security features. Other companies have built mission-critical client/server applications that cannot be used because they lack adequate security features. PCs and networks of PCs are more vulnerable to security risks than are mainframes for several reasons:

1. PCs are everywhere, which means that it is difficult to restrict physical access to them. Each of these network PCs becomes a device that must be controlled. The more legitimate users there are, the greater the risk of an attack on the network. For example, Chevron distributes information to tens of thousands of employees using 33,000 PCs.
2. PC users are usually less aware of the importance of security and control.
3. Many more people are familiar with the operation of PCs and are proficient at using them.
4. Adequate segregation of duties is very difficult because PCs are located in user departments, and one person may be responsible for both development and operations.
5. Networks are accessed from remote locations using modems, EDI, and other communication systems. The sheer number and variety of these access points significantly increases the risks networks face.
6. PCs are portable and the most elaborate security system in the world cannot protect the data a PC contains if it is lost, stolen, or misplaced.

Many of the policies and procedures for mainframe control are applicable to PCs and networks. The following controls are also important:

- Train users in PC-related control concepts and their importance. Security should be an essential part of the application development process. Users who develop their own application programs should be taught how to test and document them.
- Restrict access by using locks and keys on PCs and, where appropriate, on the disk drives. Equipment should be clearly labeled with unremovable tags.
- Establish policies and procedures to (1) control the data that can be stored or downloaded to PCs, (2) minimize the potential that PCs removed from company premises are stolen, (3) prohibit users from loading personal software onto company PCs, copying company software for personal uses, or making unauthorized use of the system. It was a lack of these controls (or the failure to enforce them) that allowed employees at a major stock brokerage in San Francisco to use the company's computer system to buy and sell cocaine.
- Portable PCs should not be stored in cars and should be carried onto airplanes rather than checked. Those that contain confidential data should be locked up at night and otherwise secured when not in use. At the British Defense Ministry, a laptop was stolen that contained the entire war plan for Desert Storm.
- Keep sensitive data in the most secure environment possible, such as storing it on a server or mainframe, as opposed to a PC. Alternatively, sensitive data can be placed on removable diskettes or disk drives and stored in a locked safe. Someone used a screwdriver at Levi Strauss's main headquarters to remove a hard drive from a PC. It contained personal data (name, social

security number, birth dates, bank account numbers, etc.) for 20,000 of its employees. This data could be used to apply for fraudulent credit cards, to take money out of bank accounts, and so forth.

- Install software that automatically shuts down a terminal or a computer attached to a network after it has been idle for a predetermined amount of time.
- Back up hard disks regularly.
- Encrypt or password protect files so that data that is stolen will not be useful.
- Use a super erase utility program that actually wipes the disk clean when confidential data are deleted. The delete command on most PCs merely erases the index to the data rather than the data itself. Deleted (rather than erased) data can be retrieved by many common utility programs.
- Build protective walls around operating systems to keep users from altering crucial system files.
- Since PCs are most vulnerable when they are turned on, they should be booted up within a security system. Users should not be able to boot from a diskette, nor should they be able to use any part of the system until they have been properly authorized. Any attempt to remove security software from the system should render the keyboard inoperable.
- Where a physical segregation of duties is not possible, use multilevel password control to limit employee access to incompatible data and provide an effective segregation of duties.
- Use specialists or security programs to detect holes in a network. Security programs mimic an intruder and provide valuable information about how secure the network activity is and where improvements should be made. Care should be exercised to make sure these programs are not used improperly. For example, Satan (System Administrator Tool for Analyzing Networks), a free security program offered on the Internet, actually helps open networks to outsiders in certain situations.
- Audit and record what users do and when they do it, so that security breaches can be traced and corrected.
- Educate users about the risks of computer viruses and how they can be minimized (see Chapter 10).

In most organizations, PCs are electronically linked using local and wide area networks. One advantage of PC networks is improved security and control procedures and enforcement through the central network controller. In particular, password controls can be required, PC utilization can be centrally monitored, virus protection procedures can be enforced, and backup procedures can be performed automatically.

The development of an internal control strategy for PCs begins by inventorying all PCs and identifying their uses. Then each PC should be classified according to the risks and exposures associated with its applications. For example, a PC used to maintain accounts payable records and prepare cash disbursements is subject to more risk and exposure than one used for word processing. Next, a security program should be tailored to each PC according to the degree of risk and exposure and the nature of the system applications. Perhaps the most sensitive PC applications are accounting systems under the control of one individual, which implies an inadequate segregation of duties. In such cases sound human resource practices must be followed, such as background checks prior to hiring, fidelity bond coverage, enforced vacations, and periodic rotation of duties.

Internet Controls

There are a number of reasons that caution should be exercised when conducting business on the Internet:

- The sheer size and complexity of the Internet and the large and global base of people that depend on the Internet. The number of Internet users is growing dramatically and shows few signs of slowing.
- The tremendous variability in quality, compatibility, completeness, and stability of network products and services.
- Before an Internet message arrives at its destination, it can easily pass through six to ten computers. Anyone at one of these computers could read or make an electronic copy of the Internet message. Even messages sent on a company's secure **Intranet** (an internal Internet) can be read by others, as a large company found out recently during a security audit. The audit disclosed that confidential e-mail messages sent between executives in the main office could be read by a network administrator working in another building 30 miles away.
- Many web sites have security flaws. One study of 2,200 web sites found that between 70% and 80% had serious security flaws. High-profile sites were more likely to have serious flaws than less popular sites.
- Hackers are attracted to the Internet. For example, six young people were arrested in Denmark for using the Internet to break into the National Weather Service computers. Fortunately, the hackers did not bring the system to its knees, which could have grounded all commercial airline flights that depend on the center's weather forecasts. The hackers were discovered when obsolete employee passwords began appearing in the system. In another case, a 16-year-old hacker used his home computer and the Internet to break into more than 100 international networks. Although they have no proof, some investigators fear that the hacker was able to steal secret nuclear data.

A number of very effective controls can be used to secure Internet activity. Some of the most important have already been discussed, such as passwords, encryption technology, and routing verification procedures. Others, such as virus detection, are discussed in Chapter 10.

Another control is installing a **firewall,** hardware and software that control communications between a company's internal network, sometimes referred to as the trusted network, and an external network, or untrusted network, such as the Internet. The firewall is a barrier between the networks that does not allow unwanted information to flow into and out of the trusted network. Complex networks are sometimes divided into subnets, each with its own firewall. Organizations often use firewalls to separate internal networks, thereby protecting sensitive data from unauthorized internal use. Firewalls must be capable of protecting themselves from attack, hostile traffic, and unauthorized modification. Firewalls often use redundant hardware, software, and other technology to reduce outages and failures.

Control efforts are focused on constructing an impenetrable firewall to prevent unauthorized system access. It is much easier to have strong access controls at a single point of entry than to try controlling numerous points of entry. Digital Equipment Corp. installed a firewall, called SEAL (Screening External Access Link), between its internal corporate network and the Internet. SEAL has not allowed a single intruder in 11 years. To create secure Internet links between users of its Quicken software and banks, Intuit purchased 20 of Sun Microsystems' SunScreen firewall systems. However, other companies have not been so lucky. Over one Thanksgiving holiday, a hacker was able to bore through the firewall at General Electric and access proprietary information. GE had to shut down its Internet access for 72 hours to assess the damage and correct the problem.

Internet security can also be achieved using an approach called tunneling. In **tunneling,** networks are connected via the Internet—firewall to firewall—and data is divided into small segments called Internet Protocol (IP) packets, encrypted, mixed with millions of packets from thousands of other computers, and sent through the Internet. At the receiving end, the packets are decrypted and reassembled into the original message. This allows companies to use the Internet to create a virtual private network and avoid the cost of leasing private lines to connect the networks. Tunneling can also be used to safeguard individual networks within an organization.

E-mail messages can be protected by using an **electronic envelope.** The envelope is created using the private or public key encryption techniques discussed earlier in the chapter. If the secrecy of the keys is maintained, the authenticity and integrity of an encrypted e-mail can be guaranteed. The person receiving the e-mail opens the envelope by using the key to decrypt the message.

Some companies, such as Philip Morris, are so wary of hackers, viruses, and other undesirable aspects of Internet usage that they deny their employees access to the Internet and outside e-mail. Other companies have a one-way, outgoing Internet connection only, so that employees can get into the Internet to do research. There is no access into the system from the outside. However, this limits the effectiveness of the Internet, as people cannot receive e-mail.

Other companies take the opposite approach. They set up an Internet server that is not connected to their other computer systems in any way. The only items stored on the server are data that the company wants to make available to Internet users and is not afraid to lose. If hackers manage to bring the system to its knees, the company simply restarts the system and reloads the data stored in the system.

Internet security has a way to go before it can be considered secure. As a company introduces a new security program, a hacker often finds a way to compromise it. For example, security locks on Netscape's web browser were broken twice within a couple of months of the software's release. To motivate hackers to inform the company about future security problems, Netscape began offering prizes to anyone who finds new loopholes in its software.

Table 9.1 summarizes the key aspects of general controls that you have learned in this section.

TABLE 9.1 Controlling AIS Threat Using General Controls

Category of Controls	Threats/Risks	Controls
Segregation of duties	People perpetrate and conceal computer fraud	Clearly divide authority and responsibility among analysts, programmers, computer operators, user departments, AIS librarian, and data control group.
Project development controls	Systems development projects consume excessive resources	Long-range IS master plan, project development plans, data processing schedules, assignment of each project to a manager and team, periodic performance evaluations, postimplementation reviews, and system performance measurements.
Physical access controls	Damage to computers and files; unauthorized access to confidential data	Put computers in locked rooms, restrict access to authorized personnel, only one or two securely locked and carefully monitored entrances, require proper employee ID, require visitors to sign a log as they enter and leave the site, use a security alarm system, restrict access to private, secured telephone lines as well as authorized terminals and PCs, install locks on PCs and other computer devices.
Logical access controls	Unauthorized access to systems software, application programs, data files, and other system resources	Recognize users by what they know (passwords, PIN, answers to personal questions), or possesses (ID card, active badge), or by personal characteristics (fingerprints, voice patterns, retina prints, facial patterns, signature dynamics, and keyboarding patterns). Compatibility checks and access control matrix.
Data storage controls	Unauthorized disclosure or destruction of stored computer data	Identify data protection requirements; maintain records of confidential data; document protection efforts; audit trails for confidential data; employee confidentiality contracts; properly supervised file library protected against fire, dust, excess heat or humidity; file labels (external, internal, volume, header, trailer), write protection mechanisms (tape file protection ring, diskette on/off switches); data base administrators, data dictionaries, and concurrent update controls.
Data transmission controls	Unauthorized access to data being transmitted or to the system itself; system failures; errors in data transmission	Network monitoring, backup components, network designed to handle peak processing, multiple communication paths between network components, preventive maintenance, data encryption (private and public keys, digital certificates, certificate authorities, digital fingerprints), routing verification (header labels, mutual authentication schemes, callback systems), parity checking, message acknowledgment procedures (echo checks, trailer labels, numbered batches).

continued

TABLE 9.1 Continued

Category of Controls	Threats/Risks	Controls
Documentation standards	Ineffective design, operation, review, audit, and modification of application systems	Administrative (standards and procedures for data processing, analysis, design, programming, file handling and storage), systems (application inputs, processing steps, outputs, error-handling), operating (equipment configurations, programs, files, setup and execution procedures, corrective actions).
Minimizing system downtime	System failure that interrupts critical business operations	Regular preventive maintenance on key components, uninterruptible power system, fault tolerance.
Disaster recovery planning	Prolonged interruption of data processing and business operations due to fire, natural disaster, sabotage, or vandalism	Coordinator responsible for implementing plan, determining recovery priorities, assigning responsibility for recovery activities, documenting and testing plan, continuously reviewing and revising plan. Remote storage of backup data and program files (electronic vaulting, grandfather-father-son), procedures for recovering lost or destroyed files (checkpoint and rollback), insurance coverage, backup computer and telecommunications facilities (reciprocal agreements, hot and cold sites, duplicate hardware, software, and data storage devices).
Protection of personal computers	Damage to computer equipment and files; unauthorized access to confidential data; users who are not security conscious	Inventory PCs and uses, tailor security to risk and exposure, train users in PC controls, lock disk drives, label with unremovable tags, limit data stored or down-loaded, prohibit personal software or copying company software for personal uses, keep sensitive data in secure environment, automatically shut down idle network PCs, back up hard disks regularly, encrypt or password protect files, wipe disks clean with utility program, place protective walls around operating systems, boot PCs within a security system, use multilevel password control, employ specialists or security programs to detect holes in a network, audit and record security breaches.
Internet controls	Damage to computer files and equipment; unauthorized access to confidential data	Passwords, encryption, routing verification, virus detection software, firewalls, tunneling, electronic envelopes, deny an employees access to the Internet, an Internet server not connected to other company computers.

APPLICATION CONTROLS

The primary objective of **application controls** is to ensure the accuracy of a specific application's inputs, files, programs, and outputs, rather than to control the computer system in general. In the opening case, Jason Scott discovered several fictitious invoices at SPP that may have been processed by the accounts payable and cash disbursements system. If so, this represents a failure in the system's application controls. However, inadequate general controls also may have contributed to this control breakdown. General controls and application controls are important and necessary, because application controls will be much more effective in the presence of strong general controls.

If application controls are weak, AIS output is likely to contain errors. Erroneous data can lead to poor management decision making and can negatively affect a company's relationships with customers, suppliers, and other external parties. For example, Experian (formerly TRW), a large credit reporting bureau, was sued by several states for reporting inaccurate credit information and violating consumer privacy. These lawsuits were reportedly triggered by thousands of consumer complaints about inaccurate and negative information surfacing on their credit reports.

This section will discuss five categories of application controls:

1. Source data controls
2. Input validation routines
3. On-line data entry controls
4. Data processing and file maintenance controls
5. Output controls.

Batch totals, another application control, were discussed in Chapter 8.

Source Data Controls

There are a number of source data controls that regulate the accuracy, validity, and completeness of input:

- *Key verification.* **Key verification** is expensive and only used for crucial input such as customer numbers, amounts, and quantities ordered. It consists of an additional employee rekeying data into the computer, which compares the two sets of keystrokes and highlights discrepancies for correction.
- *Check digit verification.* Authorized ID numbers (such as an account number) can contain a **check digit** that is computed from the other digits. Data entry devices can be programmed to test the check digit each time an ID number is entered. **Check digit verification** will probably (but not certainly) detect errors in ID numbers and signal the operator.
- *Prenumbered forms sequence test.* When sequentially prenumbered forms are employed, the system identifies and reports missing or duplicate form numbers.

- *Turnaround documents.* Because turnaround documents are system output that comes back as a machine-readable input record, they are much more accurate than input records prepared by manual keying.
- *Authorization.* Data should not be entered into the system unless it has been properly authorized.
- *Cancellation of documents.* Documents that have been entered into the system should be defaced in some way so that they cannot be inadvertently or fraudulently reentered into the system.
- *Visual scanning.* Source documents should be scanned for reasonableness and propriety before being entered into the system.
- *Data control function.* When data is received for processing, data control personnel log the data in, check for user authorizations, monitor data processing, reconcile control totals after each processing step, notify users of any incorrect inputs, and reenter all error corrections.

Jason Scott discovered that prenumbered forms were not used at SPP. However, sequentially prenumbered vouchers could have been used, with a separate voucher attached to each vendor invoice and its supporting documents. In addition, supplier numbers were not controlled using check digits. In fact, there was no formal process of approving additions to the supplier (accounts payable) file. If a supplier's invoice was approved for payment, that supplier became an approved creditor. Jason noted in his report that the proper use of either sequentially prenumbered vouchers or check digit verification of supplier numbers could have helped prevent SPP from paying fictitious invoices.

Input Validation Routines

Input validation routines are programs that check the validity and accuracy of input data as it is entered into the system. These programs are called **edit programs,** and the accuracy checks they perform are called **edit checks.** In on-line processing, edit checks are performed during the source data entry process. As shown in Fig. 9.2, input validation in batch processing is performed by a separate program prior to regular processing. In on-line processing, the system should not accept the data until it has been corrected.

Information about data input or data processing errors (date they occur, cause of the error, date corrected and resubmitted, etc.) should be entered in an **error log.** Corrected data should be resubmitted with the next batch of transactions and reedited using the same input validation routine. Periodically, the error log should be used to prepare an **error report** summarizing errors by record type, error type, and cause.

Several edit checks are used in input validation routines:

- A **sequence check** tests whether a batch of input data is in the proper numerical or alphabetical sequence.
- A **field check** determines whether the characters in a field are of the proper type. For example, a check on a numerical field would indicate an error if it contained blanks or alphabetic characters.

FIGURE 9.2
Edit Program

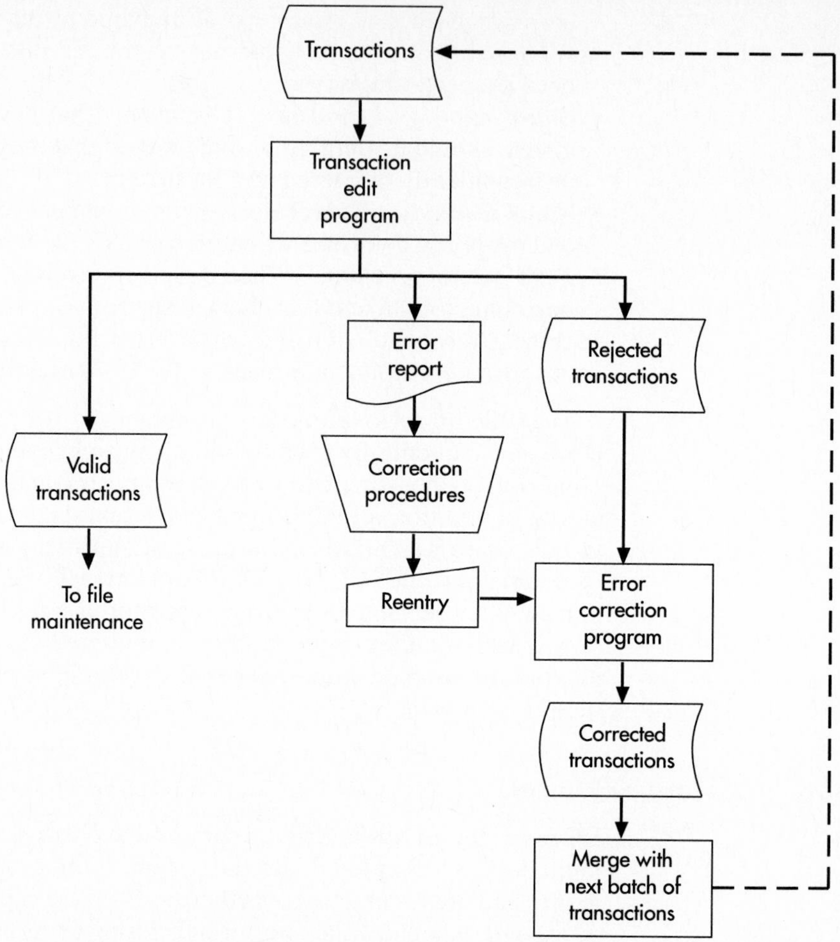

- A **sign check** determines whether the data in a field have the appropriate arithmetic sign. For example, data in an inventory balance field should never possess a negative sign.
- A **validity check** compares ID numbers or transaction codes with those already authorized. For example, if a sale to customer 65432 is entered, the computer must locate customer 65432 in the customer data base to confirm that the sale was indeed made to a valid customer.
- A **limit check** tests a numerical amount to ensure that it does not exceed a set predetermined upper or lower limit. For example, the hours worked field in weekly payroll input can be compared to a maximum amount, such as 60 hours.

- A **range check** is similar to a limit check except that it has both upper and lower limits. Range checks are used on transaction date fields, since a date should be within, but not in excess of, a few days of the current date.
- A **reasonableness test** determines the logical correctness of input and stored data. For example, a $1,000 monthly salary increase is reasonable for an executive with a current salary of $15,000 per month but not for a data entry clerk making $1,500 per month. Similarly, inventory receipts can be tested by checking whether they exceed twice the value of the quantity ordered.
- A **redundant data check** uses two identifiers in each transaction record to confirm that the correct data base record has been updated. For example, the customer account number and the first five letters of the customer's name can be used to retrieve the correct customer master record from the accounts receivable file.
- A **capacity check** to make sure that the data will fit into its assigned field. For example, 458,976,253 will not fit in an 8-digit field.

On-Line Data Entry Controls

The goal of on-line data entry controls is to ensure the accuracy and integrity of transaction data entered from on-line terminals and PCs. On-line data entry controls include the following:

- Field, limit, range, reasonableness, sign, validity, and redundant data checks, as described in the previous section.
- User ID numbers and passwords that limit data entry to authorized personnel.
- **Compatibility tests** to ensure that employees entering or accessing data are actually authorized to make those particular entries or view the data.
- **Prompting,** in which the system requests each input data item and waits for an acceptable response.
- **Preformatting,** in which the system displays a document with highlighted blank spaces and waits for the data to be entered.
- A **completeness check** on each input record to determine whether all required data items have been entered.
- Where possible, the system should automatically enter transaction data, which saves keying time and reduces errors. For example, the system can determine the next available document number and enter it into the transaction record. The system can also generate new ID numbers that satisfy the check digit algorithm and do not duplicate existing numbers, and then enter them into the input record.
- **Closed-loop verification** can be used to check the accuracy of input data. For example, if a clerk enters an account number, the system could retrieve and display the account name so that the clerk could determine if the correct account number had been entered. Closed-loop verification can be used instead of a redundant data check to protect against entry of a valid but incorrect identification number.

- A **transaction log** that includes a detailed record of all transaction data, the date and time of entry, the terminal and operator identification, and the sequence in which the transaction was entered. If an on-line file is damaged, the log can be used for reconstruction purposes. If a malfunction temporarily shuts down the system, the log can be used to ensure that transactions are not lost or entered twice.
- Clear **error messages** that indicate when an error has occurred, which item is in error, and what the operator should do to correct it.

Data Processing and File Maintenance Controls

Some of the more common controls that help preserve the accuracy and completeness of data processing and stored data are listed below.

- *Data currency checks.* Stored data become out of date, as when suppliers or customers move or go out of business and employees retire or quit. To identify such conditions, a "date of last transaction" field can be scanned periodically to identify records that are more than one year old.
- *Default values.* In certain instances, fields are left blank if a standard **default value** is to be used. For example, if the hours worked field in the payroll input is left blank an employee could be paid for 40 hours.
- *Data matching.* In certain cases, two or more items of data must be matched before an action can take place. For example, the AIS could check to see that the information on the vendor invoice matches the information on the purchase order and the receiving report before paying a vendor.
- *Exception reporting.* When files are scanned or processed, all unusual conditions should be listed. For example, the sign check might detect a negative inventory or customer account balance.
- *External data reconciliation.* Data base totals should periodically be reconciled with data maintained outside the system. For example, the number of employee records in the payroll file can be compared with the total from human resources to detect attempts to add fictitious employees to the payroll data base.
- *Control account reconciliation.* General ledger accounts should be reconciled to subsidiary account totals on a regular basis. For example, the inventory control account balance in the general ledger should equal the sum of the item balances in the inventory data base. This is true for the accounts receivable, capital assets, and accounts payable control accounts as well.
- *File security.* A file library, a librarian that logs files in and out, internal and external labels, write protection mechanisms, and backup copies of files stored at a secure off-site location all help ensure file integrity.
- *File conversion controls.* As data from old files are entered into new file structures, file conversion controls are needed to ensure that the new files are error-free. The old and new systems should be run in parallel at least once and the results compared to identify discrepancies. File conversion should be carefully supervised and reviewed by internal auditors.

Output Controls

The data control function should review all output for reasonableness and proper format and should reconcile corresponding output and input control totals. Data control is also responsible for distributing computer output to the appropriate user departments. Special care should be taken in handling checks and other sensitive documents and reports. Users are responsible for carefully reviewing the completeness and accuracy of all computer output that they receive. A shredder can be used to destroy highly confidential data such as obsolete customer listings, research data, and payroll registers. Error and exception reports should be printed and the items thereon investigated and corrected.

Special care should be taken when introducing new systems or new methods of providing information. For example, Experian developed a web site to let customers see their credit reports on the Internet that had excellent security: firewalls, encryption, and identity verifications so you could not order some one else's credit report. Two days after the site was launched, the *Washington Post* ran a story on the web site that resulted in more than 2,000 requests in a matter of hours. This load, which was much heavier than Experian had tested for, turned up a bug that caused the reports to queue up in the wrong order. As a result, people were sent the wrong credit report. Fortunately, the output controls Experian put into the system spotted the problem after only 213 reports were delivered. What could have been a major disaster was only a minor one because of the system controls.

Table 9.2 summarizes the key application controls discussed in this section.

Application Controls: An On-Line Processing Example

Many of the application controls described in the chapter can be illustrated using a credit sale as an example. The following transaction data are used: sales order number, customer account number, inventory item number, quantity sold, sale price, and delivery date. If the customer purchases more than one product, the inventory item number, quantity sold, and price fields will occur more than once in each sales transaction record. Processing these transactions includes the following steps: (1) Entering and editing the transaction data; (2) Updating the customer and inventory record. (The amount of the credit purchase is added to the customer's balance. For each inventory item, the quantity sold is subtracted from the quantity on hand); and (3) Preparing and distributing shipping and/or billing documents.

Data Entry. Data can be entered into the system through a keyboard or by capturing the data electronically using a source data automation device such as a scanner that reads Universal Product Codes. For adequate control, all significant transaction data are checked at least once. Generally, tests performed by the computer, such as edit checks, are less costly and more effective than tests performed by people, such as key verification and visual inspection. The earlier in the process a data entry error is caught, the easier and less costly it is to correct. A significant advantage of on-line systems is the immediate correction of any detected errors.

As needed, the following controls can be used to check the accuracy of transaction data that are entered into the system:

TABLE 9.2 Summary of Key Application Control Procedures

Category of Controls	Threats/Risk	Description and Examples
Source data controls	Invalid, incomplete, or inaccurate source data input	Examples include key verification; check-digit verification; sequentially prenumbered forms; turnaround documents; review for appropriate authorization; cancellation of documents; visual scanning; control log; and monitoring and expediting data entry by data control personnel.
Input validation routines	Invalid or inaccurate data in computer-processed transaction files	Transaction files are processed by edit programs that perform edit checks on key data fields, including sequence checks, field checks, sign checks, validity checks, limit checks, range checks, reasonableness tests, redundant data checks, and capacity checks.
On-line data entry controls	Invalid or inaccurate transaction input entered through on-line terminals	Examples include edit checks; user IDs and passwords; compatibility tests; prompting operators during data entry; preformatting; completeness test; automatic system data entry; closed-loop verification; a transaction log maintained by the system; and clear error messages.
Data processing and file maintenance controls	Inaccurate or incomplete data in computer-processed master files	Examples include checks on currency of stored data; default values; data matching; reporting exceptions identified by edit checks; reconciliation of data base totals with externally maintained totals; storage of files in secure file library; use of file labels and write protection mechanisms; backup file copies stored in secure off-site location; and file conversion controls.
Output controls	Inaccurate or incomplete computer output	Data control personnel perform visual review of computer output, reconciliation of batch totals, and proper distribution of output; users should review computer output for completeness and accuracy; shred output no longer needed; error and exception reports.

- When a user accesses an on-line system, logical access controls confirm the identity of the data entry device (personal computer, terminal, etc.) and the validity of the user's ID number and password.
- A compatibility test is performed on all user interactions to ensure that only authorized tasks are performed.
- The system automatically assigns the transaction the next sequential sales order number and the current date as the date of the invoice.

- To assist authorized personnel in entering sales data, the system asks for all required input (completeness test). After each prompt, the system waits for a response.
- Each response is tested using one of more of the following controls: validity checks (valid customer and inventory numbers), field and sign checks (only positive, numeric characters in the quantity, date, and price fields), and limit or range checks (delivery date).
- After the customer number is entered, the system retrieves the corresponding customer name from the database and displays it on the screen. The operator visually examines the customer name; if it matches the name on the sales order document, the operator signals the system to proceed with the transaction. If not, the operator rechecks the account and enters the correct value.
- After the inventory item number is entered, the system and the operator go through the same procedures as they do with the customer name.

File Updating. Because the file update program accesses the customer and inventory data base records, it performs additional input validation tests by comparing data in each transaction record with data in the corresponding data base record. These tests often include the following:

- Validity checks on the customer and inventory item numbers.
- Sign checks on inventory-on-hand balances (after subtracting sales quantities).
- Limit checks that compare each customer's total amount due with their credit limit.
- Range checks on the sale price of each item sold relative to the permissible range of prices for that item.
- Reasonableness tests on the quantity sold of each item relative to normal sales quantities for that customer and that item.
- At predetermined times (such as at the end of the day), backup copies of all transactions processed and the data base files are created and conveyed to a secure off-site location for storage purposes.

Preparing and Distributing Output. Outputs include billing and/or shipping documents and a control report. Some of the output controls that can be employed are the following:

- Billing and shipping documents are forwarded electronically to the appropriate users.
- Users in the shipping and billing departments perform a limited review of the documents by visually inspecting them for misaligned or incomplete data or other obvious deficiencies.
- The control report can be sent automatically to its intended recipients, or they can query the system for the report. If they query the system, logical access controls confirm the identity of the device making the query and the validity of the user's ID number and password.

Application Controls: A Batch Processing Example

Processing these transactions in a batch processing mode includes the following steps:

1. *Prepare batch totals.* These totals are recorded on batch control forms appended to each group of sales documents.
2. *Deliver the transactions to the Electronic Data Processing (EDP) department.* There each batch is checked for proper authorization and recorded in a control log.
3. *Enter the transaction data into the system.* Data entry errors generally fall into one of two types. Operator errors arise when an operator reads a source document incorrectly or accidentally strikes the wrong key. These errors are generally benign and can be corrected immediately. Incorrect source data, such as an unauthorized sales transaction or an invalid account number, is more problematic and should be corrected before the sales transaction data are processed any further.
4. *Edit the transaction file.* After the sales transaction file is sorted into customer number sequence, a program performs a number of edit checks. Rejected transactions are listed on a control report along with the computed batch totals. Data control reconciles the batch totals, investigates and corrects any errors, and submits the corrected transactions.
5. *Update the master files.* The sales transaction file is processed against customer (accounts receivable) and inventory master files. Care must be taken to ensure that the correct file copies are retrieved from the file library and loaded onto the system. The operator must check the file name and processing date on the external labels before loading the files. The file update program checks the internal header label before processing begins. Each file has a trailer label containing a record count and other file totals; these are checked and updated during the file updating run.
6. *Prepare and distribute output.* Outputs include billing and/or shipping documents and a control report. The control report contains batch totals accumulated during the file update run and a list of transactions rejected by the update program.
7. *User review.* Users in the shipping and billing departments perform a limited review of the documents for incomplete data or other obvious deficiencies.

Figure 9.3 illustrates these seven steps and identifies the application controls that should be employed in each one.

SUMMARY AND CASE CONCLUSION

Jason Scott and his supervisor were unable to identify the source of the fictitious invoices. They asked the police to identify the owner of the Pacific Electric Services bank account. The police discovered that Patricia Simpson, a data entry clerk at SPP, was the owner of the account. Under questioning by fraud investigators, Patricia admitted to an embezzlement scheme in which she created fictitious invoices, inserted them into batches of invoices submitted to her for data entry, modified the batch control totals, and destroyed the original batch control sheet. According to Patricia, the scheme had been initiated only three months previously, and no one else at SPP was involved. She also claimed that all fictitious invoices were in the name of Pacific Electric Services.

FIGURE 9.3
Flowchart of Sales Order Processing and Related Control Procedures

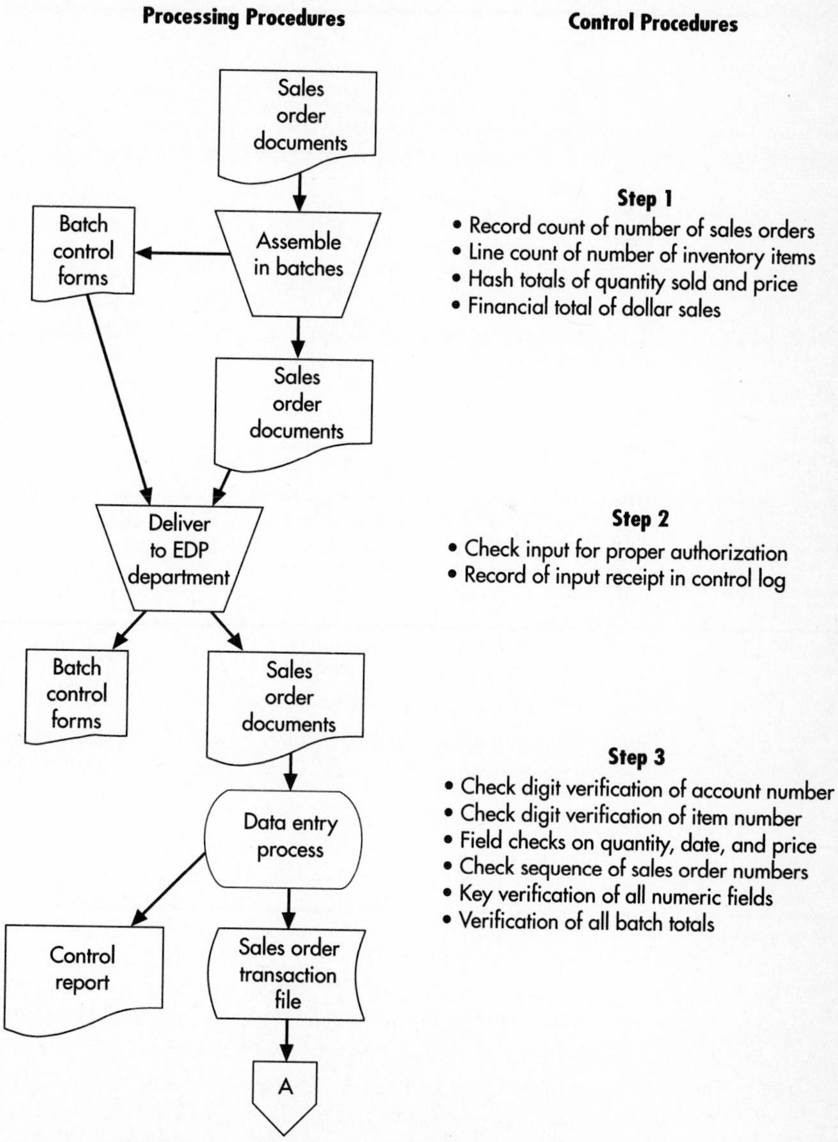

continued

FIGURE 9.3 Continued

Flowchart of Sales Order Processing and Related Control Procedures

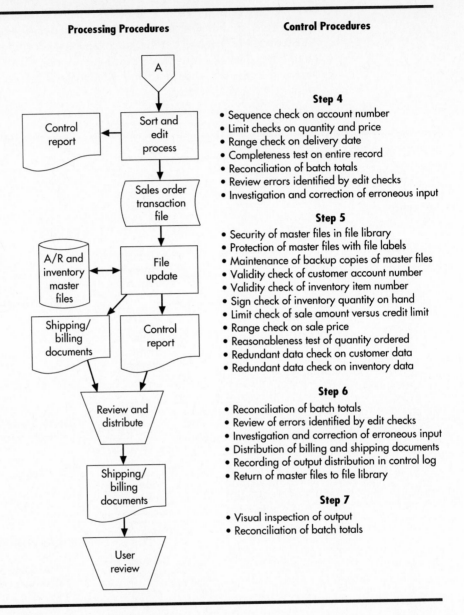

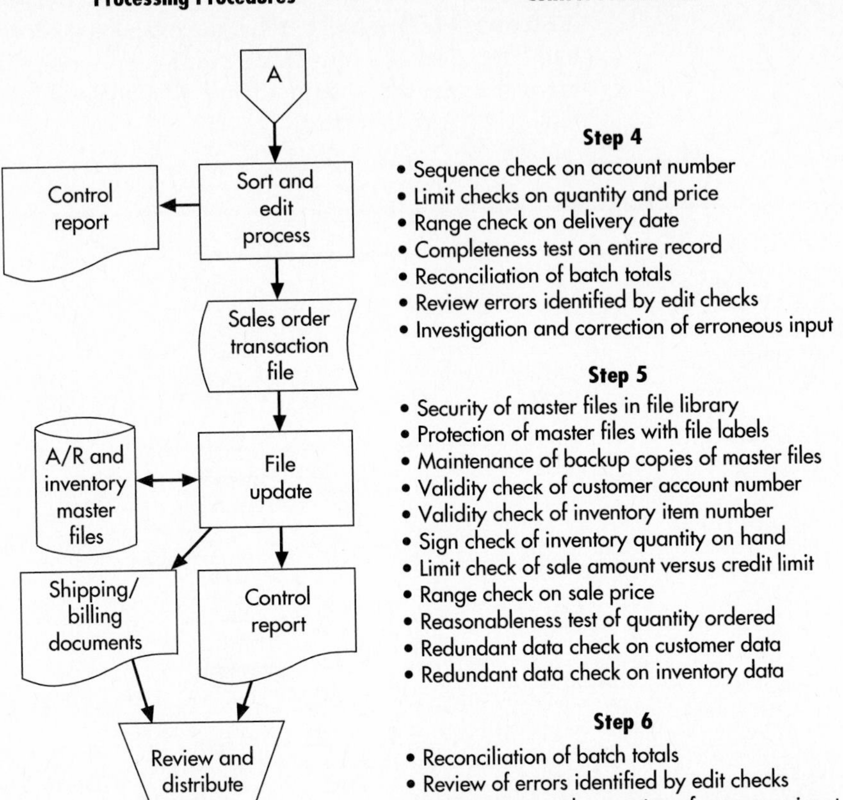

Jason examined SPP's cash disbursement records to corroborate Patricia's story. He wrote a program that reads cash disbursements transaction files and identifies disbursements to Pacific Electric Services. Then he undertook the daunting task of retrieving several hundred tape files containing disbursement transactions over the past two years from SPP's archives. He identified 40 fraudulent transactions totaling over $20,000. Contrary to Patricia's account, the first of these transactions occurred 18 months earlier.

Since Patricia had not been truthful about the duration of her scheme, Jason wondered whether she might also have used other fictitious company names. By this time, however, she was not supplying any further information, on the advice of her lawyer. So Jason wrote another computer program to scan the cash disbursement records and retrieve the supplier account number, name, address, and authorization code for every vendor invoice processed without a supporting purchase order or receiving report. This check eventually yielded a file containing 175 supplier records, payment authorizations for which had been granted by 23 different employees at SPP. Jason sorted this file by authorization code and prepared 23 printouts containing data about the suppliers with which each of these employees contracted. Each printout was sent to the corresponding employee, with a request to confirm the authenticity of every supplier on his or her list. After having received all of these printouts, Jason concluded that the embezzlement scheme was indeed confined to Pacific Electric Services.

SPP implemented several changes in its accounts payable and cash disbursements system in response to the auditors' recommendations:

1. There must be an approved purchase order for every disbursement, including those solely for service purposes.

2. Disbursements can be made only to approved suppliers, and every supplier must be approved by a purchasing agent who is not involved in the cash disbursements process. Approved suppliers are assigned an account number that contains a check digit. That account number must be included in every cash disbursement record. The purchasing department now maintains a count of the number of approved suppliers. This list is regularly compared with a computer-generated count of the number of supplier records in the accounts payable file.

3. When payment of vendor invoices is approved, a voucher record is prepared to document the approval. This voucher accompanies the invoice and any supporting documents through all subsequent processing steps. These vouchers are sequentially prenumbered, and all outstanding voucher numbers are accounted for on a regular basis.

4. Batch totals for the daily batch of cash disbursement transactions are prepared by an employee other than the person who approves the payments. The accounts payable department retains a copy of the batch control sheet for comparison with the final batch control report generated by the cash disbursement system.

As he learned about the changes SPP made to improve its internal control system, Jason reflected on how management rejected similar changes suggested by Northwest's internal audit staff, including those made by his supervisor, just one year ago. Jason realized he has learned an important truth about internal control: There are many companies and managers who do not realize the importance of internal control until they have been burned.

KEY TERMS

general controls
master plan
project development plan
project milestones
data processing schedule
performance evaluation
postimplementation review
system performance measurements
throughput
utilization
response time
physical access
logical access
password
biometric identification
access control matrix
external label
internal labels
volume label
header label
trailer label
tape file protection ring
concurrent update controls
data encryption
cryptography
confidentiality
integrity
authenticity
private key
public key
digital certificate
certificate authority
digital fingerprint
routing verification procedures
mutual authentication schemes
callback system
parity bit
parity checking
echo check
administrative documentation
systems documentation
operating documentation
preventive maintenance
uninterruptible power system (UPS)
fault tolerance
disaster recovery plan
electronic vaulting
grandfather–father–son
checkpoint
rollback
hot site
cold site
Intranet
firewall
tunneling
electronic envelope
application controls
key verification
check digit
check digit verification
input validation routines
edit programs
edit checks
error log
error report
sequence check
field check
sign check
validity check
limit check
range check
reasonableness test
redundant data check
capacity check
compatibility tests
prompting
preformatting
completeness check
closed-loop verification
transaction log
error messages
default value

CHAPTER QUIZ

1. Controls that are designed to ensure that an organization's computer-based control environment is stable and well managed are called
a. general controls.
b. application controls.
c. detective controls.
d. preventive controls.

2. All of the following are effective control procedures to ensure that operators do not make unauthorized changes to programs and files *except*
a. rotating duties.
b. having multiple operators in the computer room during processing.
c. requiring formal written authorization for and documentation of program changes.
d. maintaining and reviewing a log of all operator activity and interventions.

3. Password effectiveness is enhanced by all of the following *except*
a. frequent changes.
b. user selection of passwords.
c. not displaying the password on the screen.
d. automatic disconnection after several failed attempts.

4. The best method to reduce the risk of electronic eavesdropping is
a. the use of parity bits.
b. compatibility tests.
c. data encryption.
d. checkpoints and rollback procedures.

5. Descriptions of each application program, including narratives, flowcharts, and code, are called
a. administrative documentation.
b. accounting documentation.
c. operating documentation.
d. systems documentation.

6. Controls that are designed to prevent, detect, or correct errors in transactions as they flow through the various stages of a specific data processing program are referred to as
a. general controls.
b. application controls.
c. administrative controls.
d. data processing controls.

7. The computer industry prevents public keys from being counterfeited by using an electronic document, called a:
a. certificate authority.
b. digital certificate.
c. digital fingerprint.
d. data encryption document.

8. The computer sums the first four digits of a customer number to calculate the value of the fifth digit and then compares that calculation to the number typed during data entry. This is an example of a
a. field check.
b. parity check.
c. check digit verification.
d. batch total.

9. The edit check that would detect the entry of a customer number that does not exist is called a
a. check digit.
b. limit check.
c. sequence check.
d. validity check.

10. In an on-line system, the user enters the customer number and the system responds by displaying the customer name and asking the user for verification. This is called a
a. closed-loop verification test.
b. redundant data check.
c. compatibility test.
d. completeness test.

DISCUSSION QUESTIONS

9.1 A computer implementation project is often performed in a state of crisis, with the implementation group working feverishly to keep pace with the implementation schedule. In this atmosphere, corners are often cut with respect to documentation and application controls. What arguments do you feel would be effective to prevent these types of shortcuts?

9.2 Theoretically, a control procedure should be adopted if its benefit exceeds its cost. Explain how the benefits and costs of the following controls can be estimated:
a. Segregation of duties
b. Data protection procedures
c. Logical access controls
d. Input validation routines

9.3 Prudential-Bache Securities in New York contracted with Comdisco Computing Service Corporation in New Jersey to back up its data (more than 500,000 securities transactions per day) by transmitting it on a real-time basis to an electronic vaulting service. The service includes use of a high-speed data transmission line and an automated tape library. Comdisco also agreed to make a hot site available to Prudential-Bache in the event that a disaster shuts down their central data center. The hot site has a direct link to the vaulting system, ensuring that all but the last 15 minutes of trading data would be recovered.

Though terms of the contract were not disclosed, this arrangement is certainly a very expensive proposition for Prudential-Bache. Discuss how this contract could have been justified on a cost–benefit basis. In addition, name at least three steps that Prudential-Bache should take to prevent unauthorized access to its backup data.

9.4 For control purposes, the function of transaction authorization should be performed by employees outside the systems department. However, computers are increasingly being programmed to initiate transactions, such as issuing a purchase order when an inventory balance is low. Discuss whether such automatic transaction generation represents a violation of good internal control principles.

9.5 The Foster Corporation recently fired its AIS director after experiencing several years of budget overruns in systems development and computer operations. You have been appointed as interim director and are charged with investigating the problems the department has experienced. There is little written information about the activities of the department or the policies under which it was managed. The previous director communicated assignments, standards, and performance evaluations verbally. This management style was popular with some employees but unpopular with many others, some of whom have left the company.

The major systems project under development is an AIS. Objectives for the project are loosely defined, although a good deal of analysis, design, and programming has been completed. The project director estimates the project is half finished. The computer operations department runs jobs on an as-received basis. The operations supervisor suggests that a more reliable system is needed to satisfy demand during peak periods and cope with expected processing growth.

Identify and briefly describe several elements of control that appear to be lacking in this situation and that you feel should be implemented in the information systems department.

PROBLEMS

9.1 Your company has purchased a number of personal computers. One has been installed in the stores department, which is responsible for disbursing stock items and maintaining stores records. In your audit, you find that one employee, trained in computer applications, receives the requisitions for stores, reviews them for completeness and approvals, disburses the stock, maintains the records, operates the computer, and authorizes adjustments to the total amounts of stock accumulated by the computer.

When you discuss the applicable controls with the department manager, you are told that the personal computer is assigned exclusively to that department. Therefore, it does not require the same types of controls that are applicable to large computer systems.

Required:

Comment on the manager's contentions, discussing briefly five types of control that would apply to this personal computer application.
(CIA Examination, adapted)

9.2 You are the general manager of a manufacturing company in Woodbridge, Virginia. During the past six months, your company has consistently lost bids to a competitor whose bids always seem to be slightly lower. On a hunch that this could not keep happening by chance, you hire a private detective. She reports that one of your employees with access to the computer is stealing your bid data and selling it to the competitor for $25,000 per bid.

Required:

a. Identify the likely deficiencies in internal control over your company's computer systems that could have allowed this fraud to occur.
b. How else could bids have been stolen and sold?
c. How would you guard against each of these methods?

9.3 Consider the set of numeric computer input data in Table 9.3.

TABLE 9.3 Computer Input Data, Problem 14.3

Employee Number Col. 1–3	Pay Rate Col. 4–6	Hours Worked Col. 7–8	Gross Pay Col. 9–13	Deductions Col. 14–18	Net Pay Col. 19–23
121	250	38	$9500	01050	08450
123	275	40	11000	01250	09750
125	200	90	16000	02000	12000
122	280	40	11200	11000	00200

Required:

a. From the data in Table 9.3, calculate and show one specific example of the following:

   Hash total

   Record count

   Financial total

b. For each of the following controls, give a specific example from the four records in Table 9.3 of an error or probable error that would be caught by the control (list the error—do not merely describe it):

   Field check

   Sequence check

   Limit check

   Reasonableness test

   Cross-footing balance test

9.4 You are the data security administrator for a small company. Its system uses two programs: a payroll system and an inventory processing system. It maintains three files: a payroll master file, an inventory master file, and a transaction log. The following users should have the indicated access to the system:

User	Access Denied
Salesperson	Read and display records in the inventory file
Inventory control analyst	Read, display, update, create, and delete records in the inventory file

User	Access Denied
Payroll analyst	Read, display, and update records in the payroll file
Human resources manager	Read, display, update, create, and delete records in the payroll file
Payroll programmer	Perform all payroll system operations; Read and display payroll file records and transaction log records
Inventory programmer	Perform all operations on the inventory system; Read and display inventory file records and transaction log records
Data processing manager	Read and display all programs and files
Yourself	Perform all operations on all programs and files

continued

Required:

a. Create an access control matrix that allows the users to have the indicated levels of access. For each user, assign a six-character user code and select access authority codes. Use the following access authority coding system.

   0 = no access permitted

   1 = read and display only

   2 = read, display, and update

   3 = read, display, update, create, and delete

b. What changes would you make to the access privileges of the employees mentioned earlier?

9.5 What control or controls would you recommend to prevent the following situations from occurring?

a. The "time worked" field for salaried employees is supposed to contain a 01 for one week. One employee's field contained the number 40, and a check for $6,872.51 was accidentally prepared and mailed.
b. A programmer obtained the master payroll file, loaded it into the system, and changed his monthly salary from $4,400 to $6,000.
c. The accounts receivable file on disk was inadvertently destroyed and could not be reconstructed after being substituted for the accounts payable file in a processing run.
d. A company lost almost all its vital business data in a fire that destroyed the room in which it stored its magnetic disks and tapes.
e. A programmer quit the firm in the middle of an assignment. Because no other programmers could make sense of the work already completed, the project was started over from scratch.
f. A bank programmer obtained the disks containing the program that calculates interest on customer accounts. She loaded the program into the computer and modified it so the fractions of a cent from each interest calculation, which would otherwise be rounded off, were added to her account.

g. During keying of customer payment records, the digit 0 in a payment of $102.34 was mistakenly typed as the letter O. As a result, the transaction was not processed correctly, and the customer received an incorrect statement.

9.6 What control or controls would you recommend in an on-line computer system to prevent the following situations from occurring?

a. A teenager gained unauthorized access to the system by programming a PC to enter repeated user numbers until a correct one was found.
b. An employee gained unauthorized access to the system by observing her supervisor's user number and then correctly guessing the password after 12 attempts.
c. A salesperson for a PC manufacturer, keying in a customer order from a remote laptop computer, entered an incorrect stock number. As a result, an order for 50 monitors was placed for a customer who wanted to order 50 PCs.
d. A salesperson received a laptop computer to enter sales orders while calling on customers. She used it to increase her own monthly salary by $500.
e. A salesperson keying in a customer order from a remote computer inadvertently omitted the delivery address from the order.
f. A company's research and development center utilizes remote PCs tied into its computer center 100 miles away. Using a wiretap, the company's largest competitor stole secret plans for a major product innovation.
g. A $400 multiplexor at a bank served terminals at eight drive-in windows. When the multiplexor failed, the bank was forced to shut down the windows for two hours during a busy Friday afternoon.
h. A 20-minute power failure that shut down a firm's computer system resulted in loss of data for several transactions that were being entered into the system from remote terminals.

9.7 The headquarters of Gleicken Corporation, a private company with $3.5 million in annual sales, is located in California. For its 150 clients Gleicken provides an on-line legal software service that includes data storage and administrative activities for law offices. The company has grown rapidly since its inception three years ago, and its data processing department has mushroomed to accommodate this growth. Because Gleicken's president and sales staff spend a great deal of time out of the office soliciting new clients, planning the EDP facilities has been left to the data processing professionals.

Gleicken recently moved its headquarters into a remodeled warehouse on the outskirts of the city. While remodeling the warehouse, the architects retained much of the original structure, including the wooden-shingled exterior and exposed wooden beams throughout the interior. The company's hardware is situated in a large open area with high ceilings and skylights. This openness makes the data processing area accessible to the rest of the staff and encourages a team approach to problem solving. Before Gleicken began to occupy its new facility, city inspectors declared the building safe (i.e., adequate fire extinguishers, sufficient exits, etc.).

Gleicken wanted to provide further protection for its large data base of client information. Therefore, it instituted a tape backup procedure that automatically backs up the data base every Sunday evening to avoid interrupting daily operations and procedures. All the tapes are labeled and carefully stored on shelves in the data processing department reserved for this purpose. The departmental operator's manual has instructions on how to use these tapes to restore the data base should the need arise. In the event of an emergency, there is a home phone list of the individuals in the data processing department. Gleicken has recently increased its liability insurance for data loss from $50,000 to $100,000.

This past Saturday the Gleicken headquarters building was completely ruined by fire. The company must now inform its clients that all their information has been destroyed.

Required:

a. Describe the computer security weaknesses present at Gleicken Corporation that made it possible for a disastrous data loss to occur.
b. List the components that should have been included in the disaster recovery plan at Gleicken Corporation in order to ensure computer recovery within 72 hours.
c. What factors, other than those included in the plan itself, should a company consider when formulating a disaster recovery plan?
d. What threats, other than the fire, should Gleicken have protected itself from?

(CMA Examination, adapted)

9.8 The Moose Wings Cooperative Flight Club owns a number of airplanes and gliders. It serves less than 2,000 members, who are numbered sequentially from the founder, Tom Eagle (0001), to the newest member, Jacques Noveau (1368). Members rent the flying machines by the hour, and all planes must be returned on the same day. The club uses a computer on its premises and a dial-up line to send the billing data to a computer utility. The utility bills members monthly.

The following six records were among those entered for the flights taken on November 1, 1996.

Member #	Flight Date DDMMYY	Plane Used*	Takeoff Time	Landing Time
1234	311196	G	0625	0846
4111	011196	C	0849	1023
1210	011196	P	0342	0542
0023	011196	X	0159	1243
012A	011196	P	1229	1532
0999	011196	L	1551	1387

* G = glider; C = Cessna; P = Piper Cub; L = Lear Jet

Required:

a. For each of the five data fields, suggest one or more edit controls that could be included in the program for detecting possible errors.
b. Identify and describe any errors in the records.
c. Suggest other controls to prevent input errors if on-line entry were employed.

(SMAC Examination, adapted)

9.9 Talbert Corporation hired an independent computer programmer to develop a simplified payroll application for its newly purchased computer. The programmer developed an on-line data entry system that minimized the level of knowledge required by the operator. It was based on typing answers to input cues that appeared on the terminal's viewing screen. Examples of the cues follow.

a. Access routine:
   1. Operator access number to payroll file?
   2. Are there new employees?
b. New employees routine:
   1. Employee name?
   2. Employee number?
   3. Social Security number?
   4. Rate per hour?
   5. Single or married?
   6. Number of dependents?
   7. Account distribution?
c. Current payroll routine:
   1. Employee number?
   2. Regular hours worked?
   3. Overtime hours worked?
   4. Total employees this payroll period?

The independent auditor is attempting to verify that certain input validation (edit) checks exist. The checks should ensure that errors resulting from omissions, invalid entries, or other inaccuracies are detected as soon as the answers to the input cues are entered.

Required:

Identify the various types of input validation (edit) checks an auditor would expect to find in the EDP system. Describe the assurances provided by each identified validation check. Do not discuss the review and evaluation of these controls.

(CPA Examination, adapted)

9.10 Babbington-Bowles is an advertising agency that employs 625 salespersons, who travel and entertain extensively. Each month, salespersons are paid both salary and commissions. The nature of their job is such that expenses of several hundred dollars a day might be incurred. In the past these expenses were included in each monthly paycheck. Salespersons were required to submit their expense reports, with supporting receipts, by the 20th of each month. These reports would be reviewed and then sent to data entry in a batch. Suitable controls were incorporated on each batch during input, processing, and output. This system worked well from a company viewpoint, and the internal auditor was convinced that while minor padding of expense accounts might occur, no major losses had been encountered.

As interest rates began to climb, the salespersons became unhappy. They pointed out that they were often forced to carry several thousand dollars for an entire month. If they were out of town around the 20th, they might not be reimbursed for their expenses for two months. They requested that Babbington-Bowles provide a service whereby a salesperson or his or her representative could submit receipts and expense reports to the accounting department and receive a check almost immediately.

The data processing manager said that this procedure could be done. A computer terminal would be set up in the accounting office, along with a small printer. The salesperson's name would be entered along with the required expense amount broken down into the standard categories. A program would process these data to the proper accounts and, if everything checked out suitably, print the check on presigned check blank stock in the printer.

Required:

Identify five important controls, and explain why they might be incorporated in the system. These controls may be physical, they may relate to jobs and responsibilities, or they may be part of the program.

(SMAC Examination, adapted)

CASE 9.1 ANYCOMPANY, INC.—AN ONGOING COMPREHENSIVE CASE

Visit a local company and obtain permission to study its system of internal controls. Once you have lined up a company, do the following:

1. Obtain copies of organizational charts, job descriptions, and related documentation on how authority and responsibility have been assigned within the information systems function. Evaluate whether lines of authority and responsibility seem to be clearly defined and whether incompatible duties have been appropriately segregated.
2. Determine how the company evaluates the progress of systems development projects during the design and implementation stages.
3. Observe how the company controls physical access to its mainframe computer site, as well as to its personal computers and on-line terminals. Evaluate whether the company's access controls seem to be effective.
4. Determine the procedures used by the company to protect its stored program and data files from loss or destruction, including procedures for recovery of any program or data files that may be lost. Evaluate whether these procedures appear to be sound.
5. Examine the company's policies and procedures relating to the use of passwords to control logical access to its system resources. Evaluate these policies and procedures.
6. Briefly examine copies of the company's administrative, systems, and operating documentation. Evaluate the quality and completeness of this material.
7. Determine the techniques used by the company to minimize the risk of system downtime.
8. Ask whether the company has a written disaster recovery plan for its computer facilities. If so, examine a copy of the plan, and assess its strengths and weaknesses.

CASE 9.2 THE STATE DEPARTMENT OF TAXATION

The Department of Taxation in your state is developing a new computer system for processing individual and corporate income tax returns. The new system features direct data input and inquiry capabilities. Identification of taxpayers is provided by using the Social Security number for individuals and federal identification number for corporations. The new system should be fully implemented in time for the next tax season.

The new system will serve three primary purposes.

1. Data will be input directly into the system from tax returns using computer terminals located at central headquarters.
2. The returns will be processed using the main computer facilities at central headquarters. Processing will include four steps.
   a. Verifying mathematical accuracy
   b. Auditing the reasonableness of deductions, tax due, etc., through the use of edit routines, which also include a comparison of current and prior years' data
   c. Identifying returns that should be considered for audit by department revenue agents
   d. Issuing refund checks to taxpayers
3. Inquiry service will be provided to taxpayers upon request through the assistance of tax department

personnel at five regional offices. A total of 50 terminals will be placed at each regional office. A taxpayer will be allowed to determine the status of his or her return or get information from the last three years' returns by calling or visiting one of the department's regional offices.

The state commissioner of taxation is concerned about data security during input and processing, over and above protection against natural hazards such as fire and flood. This includes protection against the loss or damage of data during data input and processing as well as the improper input or processing of data. In addition, the tax commissioner and the state attorney general have discussed the general problem of data confidentiality that may arise from the nature and operation of the new system. Both individuals want to have all potential problems identified before the system is fully developed and implemented so that the proper controls can be incorporated into the new system.

Required:

1. Describe the potential confidentiality problems that could arise in each of the following three areas of processing, and recommend the corrective action(s) to solve each problem identified.
   a. Data input
   b. Processing of returns
   c. Data inquiry

2. The state tax commission wants to incorporate controls to provide data security against the loss, damage, improper input, or use of data during data input and processing. Identify the potential problems (outside of natural hazards such as fire or floods) for which the Department of Taxation should develop controls, and recommend the possible controls for each problem identified.

(CMA Examination, adapted)

ANSWERS TO CHAPTER QUIZ

1. a	**3.** b	**5.** d	**7.** b	**9.** d
2. c	**4.** c	**6.** b	**8.** c	**10.** a

CHAPTER 10

Computer Fraud and Security

LEARNING OBJECTIVES

After reading the chapter, you should be able to

- Understand what fraud is and the process one follows to perpetuate a fraud.
- Discuss why fraud occurs, including the pressures, opportunities, and rationalizations that are present in most frauds.
- Compare and contrast the approaches and techniques that are used to commit computer fraud.
- Describe how to deter and detect computer fraud.

Integrative Case: Northwest Industries

It was late on the last Sunday of March when Jason Scott finished his tax return. Before sealing the envelope, he reviewed his return for a final time. Jason quickly compared the documents used to prepare his return with the actual numbers. Everything was in order except his withholding amount. For some reason, the federal income tax withholdings on his final paycheck was $5 higher than on his W-2 form. He decided to use the W-2 amount and made a note to check with payroll to find out what happened to the other $5. The next day was a typical Monday at Northwest Industries and Jason was swamped. After reviewing his To Do list, he decided to dismiss the $5 difference because the amount was immaterial.

At lunch on April 16, several people were joking about their last-minute attempts to complete their tax returns. In the course of the conversation, one of Jason's coworkers grumbled about the company taking out $5 more from his check than he was given credit for on his W-2. No one followed up on the comment, and it was not until after lunch that the coincidence hit Jason: He was not the only one to have a $5 discrepancy between his withholdings and his W-2 statement. After obtaining the appropriate clearances, it was once again time to investigate. By the end of the following day, Jason was worried. Most of the 1,500 company employees had a $5 discrepancy between their reported withholdings and the actual amount withheld. Interestingly enough, the W-2 of Don Hawkins, one of the programmers in charge of the payroll system, showed that thousands of dollars more in withholdings had been reported to the IRS than had been withheld from his paycheck.

It certainly looked to Jason like Northwest had a serious problem. He knew that when he reported the situation, management was going to ask a lot of questions. For example:

1. What constitutes a fraud, and is the withholding problem a fraud?
2. If this is indeed a fraud, how was it perpetrated? What motivated Don to commit it?
3. Why did the company not catch these mistakes earlier? Was there a breakdown in controls?
4. What can the company do to detect fraud? To prevent fraud?
5. Just how vulnerable are computer systems to fraud?

INTRODUCTION

Fraud is any and all means a person uses to gain an unfair advantage over another person. Fraudulent acts include lies, suppressions of the truth, tricks, and cunning, and they often involve a violation of a trust or confidence. The economic losses to fraud each year are staggering; fraud losses in the United States are estimated to be about $500 billion a year.

A fraud can be committed by someone within an organization or by an external party. Not surprisingly, former and current employees (sometimes called knowledgeable insiders) are much more likely to perpetrate fraud than are nonemployees. Because employees understand the company's system and its weaknesses, they are better able to commit a fraud, evade detection, and cover their tracks. The controls most organizations use to protect corporate assets make it more difficult for an outsider to steal from a company. Fraud perpetrators are often referred to as **white-collar criminals,** to distinguish them from criminals who commit violent crimes.

Internal fraud can be broken down into two categories: misappropriation of assets and fraudulent financial reporting. **Misappropriation of assets,** or **employee fraud,** is committed by a person or group of persons for personal financial gain. The fraud discovered by Jason Scott is a misappropriation of assets.

The National Commission on Fraudulent Financial Reporting (the Treadway Commission) defines **fraudulent financial reporting** as intentional or reckless conduct, whether by act or omission, that results in materially misleading financial statements. Fraudulent financial reporting is of special concern to independent auditors; the Treadway Commission studied 450 lawsuits against auditors and found undetected fraud to be a factor in half of them. Financial statements can be falsified to deceive investors and creditors, to cause a company's stock price to rise, to meet cash flow needs, or to hide company losses and problems. The perpetrators receive indirect benefits: They keep their jobs, their stock rises, and they receive pay raises and promotions they do not deserve. They can also gain more power and influence than they should.

The Treadway Commission recommended four actions to reduce the possibility of fraudulent financial reporting:

1. Establish an organizational environment that contributes to the integrity of the financial reporting process.
2. Identify and understand the factors that lead to fraudulent financial reporting.
3. Assess the risk of fraudulent financial reporting within the company.
4. Design and implement internal controls to provide reasonable assurance that fraudulent financial reporting is prevented.

This chapter discusses fraud in four main sections. The first section describes the fraud process. Then the reasons that fraud occurs are explored. The third section describes the approaches to computer fraud and the specific techniques used to commit it. Finally, several ways companies can deter and detect computer fraud are analyzed.

THE FRAUD PROCESS

Most frauds involve three steps.

1. The *theft* of something of value, such as cash, inventory, tools, supplies, equipment, or data. Most employee fraud involves the theft of assets. Most fraudulent financial reporting involves the overstatement of assets or revenues. Few employees or companies are motivated to steal or overstate liabilities. Likewise, few frauds involve the theft or direct overstatement of equity accounts.
2. The *conversion* of the stolen assets into cash. For example, stolen inventory and equipment must be sold or otherwise converted into cash.
3. The *concealment* of the crime to avoid detection. When assets are stolen or overstated, the only way to balance the basic accounting equation is to inflate other assets or to decrease liabilities or equity. Unless perpetrators find some way to keep the accounting equation in balance, their theft or misrepresentation can be discovered. Concealment often takes more effort and time and leaves behind more evidence than the actual theft. For example, taking cash requires only a few seconds, whereas altering records to hide the theft can be more challenging and time-consuming.

A common and effective way to hide a theft is to charge the stolen item to an expense account. For example, one employee stole $10,000 and charged it to a miscellaneous expense account. Assets were reduced by $10,000 but so was equity, since expense accounts decrease net income as they are closed out, which in turn lowers the retained earnings amount. As another example, an enterprising payroll clerk added a fictitious name to his company's payroll records, intercepted the paycheck, and cashed it. Although the company was missing funds, its books were balanced because there was a debit to a wages expense and a credit to cash. In both cases, the perpetrator's exposure is limited to a year or less, because the expense accounts are zeroed out at the end of the year. On the other hand, perpetrators who hide a theft by affecting another balance sheet account must continue the concealment. Hence one of the most popular ways to cover up a fraud is to hide the theft in an income statement account.

Another way to hide a decrease in assets is by lapping. In a **lapping** scheme, the perpetrator steals cash received from customer A to pay its accounts receivable. Funds received at a later date from customer B are used to pay off customer A's balance. Funds from customer C are used to pay off B, and so forth. The cover-up must continue indefinitely unless the money is replaced, since the theft will be uncovered if the scheme is stopped.

In a **kiting** scheme, the perpetrator covers up a theft by creating cash through the transfer of money between banks. For example, the perpetrator creates cash by depositing a check from bank A into bank B and then withdraws the money. Since there are insufficient funds in bank A to cover the check, the perpetrator deposits a check from bank C to bank A before his check to bank B clears. Since bank C also has insufficient funds, money must be deposited to bank C before the check to bank A clears. The check to bank C is written from bank B or D, which also has insufficient funds. The scheme continues, with checks and deposits occurring as needed to keep the checks from bouncing.

WHY FRAUD OCCURS

Researchers have compared the psychological and demographic characteristics of three groups of people: white-collar criminals, violent criminals, and the general public. Although they found significant differences between violent and white-collar criminals, they found few differences between white-collar criminals and the general public. White-collar criminals tend to mirror the general public in education, age, religion, marriage, length of employment, and psychological makeup.

Fraud perpetrators share a number of common characteristics. Most spend their illegal income rather than invest or save it. Once they begin the fraud, it is very hard for them to stop. They usually begin to rely on the extra income. If the perpetrators are not caught shortly after they begin, they typically become brazen and their desire for even more money can cause them to increase the amount they take. As time passes, many perpetrators grow careless, overconfident, or greedy. Those who do usually make a mistake that leads to their apprehension.

Perpetrators of computer fraud tend to be younger and possess more computer knowledge, experience, and skills. Some computer fraud perpetrators are more motivated by curiosity and the challenge of "beating the system" than by the actual gain and view their actions as a game rather than as dishonest behavior. Others commit computer fraud to gain stature among others in the computer community. One study shows that computer crime is an equal opportunity employer; 32% of the perpetrators were women and 43% were minorities.

Some fraud perpetrators are disgruntled and unhappy with their job and are seeking to get even with their employer. Others are regarded as ideal employees who are dedicated, hard working, and in a position of trust. Most have no previous criminal record. Prior to their committing fraud, they were honest and upright citizens who were valued and respected members of their communities. Why, then, would they risk everything by committing a fraud? Fraud research shows that three conditions are necessary for fraud to occur: a pressure or motive, an opportunity, and a rationalization.

Pressures

A **pressure** is a person's motivation for committing a fraud. Three types of motivation that often lead to fraud are described next and are summarized in Table 10.1. Pressures can be financial, such as living beyond one's means or having heavy debts or unusually high bills. Oftentimes this pressure is nonshareable and the perpetrator feels it must be kept secret.

An illustration of financial pressures is Raymond Keller of Stockport, Iowa. Raymond was a local boy who worked his way up from driving a coal truck to owning a grain elevator. He made money by trading on commodities and built a lavish house overlooking the Des Moines River. No one knows why his financial situation declined. Some say he lost a lot of money speculating on the commodities markets; others say it was a grain embargo that virtually halted the buying and selling of grain. Whatever the reason, Raymond had a severe cash shortage and went deeply into debt. He asked some farmers to wait for their money, and he gave others bad checks. Finally, the seven banks to which he owed over $3 million began to call in their loans. So Raymond began to the sell grain that he stored for local farmers to cover his losses. When a state auditor

TABLE 10.1 Pressures that Can Lead to Fraud

Financial	Work-Related	Other
Living beyond means	Low salary	Challenge
High personal debt	Nonrecognition of performance	Family/peer pressure
"Inadequate" income	Job dissatisfaction	Emotional instability
Poor credit ratings	Fear of losing job	Need for power or control
Heavy financial losses	Overaggressive bonus plans	Excessive pride or ambition
Bad investments		
Health care expenditures		
Large gambling debts		
Need to support a drug or alcohol addiction		
Greed		

showed up at his door unexpectedly, Raymond chose to take his life rather than face the consequences of his fraud.

Pressures can also be work related. Some employees steal data so they can take it to a new job or to a company they are starting. Some employees turn to fraud because they have strong feelings of resentment or believe they have been treated unfairly. They may feel that their pay is too low, that their contributions to the company are not appreciated sufficiently, or that the company is taking advantage of them. Some fear losing their job and commit a fraud hoping to preserve their position by making themselves or their company look better. In one case, an accountant in California, passed over for a raise, increased his salary by 10%, the amount of an average raise. When apprehended, he defended his actions as being honest; he was only taking what was rightfully his. When asked how he would have felt if he had increased his salary by 11%, he responded that he would have been stealing 1%.

Other motivations that lead to fraudulent actions include family or peer pressure, emotional instability, and the challenge of beating the system. Many computer hackers commit fraud for the challenge of subverting the controls and breaking into a system. In one case, a company boasted in its advertisements that its new information system was so secure that outsiders would not be able to break into it. Within 24 hours of its implementation, a team of individuals had broken into the system and left a message that the impenetrable system had just been compromised.

Opportunities

An **opportunity** is the condition or situation that allows a person to commit and conceal a dishonest act. The list of opportunities that make fraud easy to commit and conceal is almost endless. Table 10.2 notes some of the more frequently mentioned opportunities noted in fraud research studies.

Opportunities often stem from a lack of internal controls. For example, a company might lack proper procedures for authorizations, clear lines of authority, or independent checks on performance. Likewise, there may not be a separation of duties among the authorization, custodial, and record-keeping functions. However, the most prevalent opportunity for fraud results from a company's failure to *enforce* its system of internal controls.

One control feature that many companies lack is a background check on all potential employees. A background check would have saved one company from the "phantom controller." In that case, the company president stopped by the office one night, saw a light on in the controller's office, and went over to see why he was working so late. He was surprised to find a complete stranger at work. An investigation showed the controller was not an accountant and had been fired from three of his previous five jobs in the last eight years. Because was unable to do the accounting work, he had hired someone to come in at night to do his work for him. Before his scam was discovered, the controller had defrauded the company of several million dollars.

A number of other situations make it easy for someone to commit a fraud: excessive trust in key employees, incompetent supervisory personnel, inattention to details, inadequate staffing, lack of training, and unclear company policies.

TABLE 10.2 Perceived Opportunities

Internal Control Factors	Other Factors
Failure to enforce internal controls	Too much trust in key employees
Lack of proper procedures for authorizations	Close association with suppliers/customers
No separation of duties between authorization, custody, and record-keeping functions	Incompetent supervisory personnel
No independent checks on performance	Operating on a crisis basis
No separation of accounting duties	Failure to discipline violators
Lack of clear lines of authority	Confusion about ethics
Lack of frequent reviews	Lack of explicit conflict-of-interest statements
Inadequate documentation	Inadequate physical security
No background checks	Inadequate staffing and/or training
	Poor management philosophy
	Lack of employee loyalty
	Unclear company policies
	Apathy
	Inattention to details

Also, many frauds arise when employees build mutually beneficial personal relationships with customers or suppliers. For example, a buyer could agree to purchase goods at an inflated price in exchange for a kickback from the vendor. Frauds can also occur when a crisis arises and the company disregards its normal control procedures. For instance, one *Fortune* 500 company was hit with three multimillion dollar frauds in the same year. All three took place when the company was trying to resolve a series of crises and failed to follow the standard internal control procedures.

Rationalizations

Most fraud perpetrators have an excuse or a **rationalization** that allows them to justify their illegal behavior. Perpetrators rationalize either that they are not actually being dishonest or that their reasons for committing fraud are more compelling than honesty and integrity. Perhaps the most frequently used rationalization is that the perpetrator is just "borrowing" the stolen assets. The perpetrator just needs a little money to tide her over a rough spot for a time. Therefore she is not really being dishonest, since she has every intention of paying it back.

Some perpetrators rationalize that they are not hurting a real person. It is just a faceless and nameless computer system that will be affected or a large, impersonal company that will not miss the money. For example, one perpetrator took pains to steal no more than $20,000, which was the maximum that the insurance company would reimburse the company for losses.

The list of rationalizations people use is lengthy. Here are some of the most frequently used:

- You would understand if you knew how badly I needed it.
- What I did was not that serious.
- It was for a good cause. (This is the Robin Hood syndrome, robbing from the rich to give to the poor.)
- I occupy a very important position of trust. I am above the rules.
- Everyone else is doing it, so it cannot be that wrong.
- No one will ever know.
- The company owes it to me, and I am taking no more than is rightfully mine.

Fraud occurs when people have high pressures, abundant opportunities, and the ability to rationalize away their personal integrity. Fraud is not likely to occur when people have few pressures, little opportunity to commit and conceal fraud, and high personal integrity that makes them less likely to rationalize fraud. This is illustrated in Fig. 10.1. Unfortunately, in most cases there is a mixture of these three forces that makes it very difficult to determine if a particular person is likely to commit a fraud.

COMPUTER FRAUD

The U.S. Department of Justice defines **computer fraud** as any illegal act for which knowledge of computer technology is essential for its perpetration, investigation, or prosecution. More specifically, computer fraud includes the following:

- Unauthorized theft, use, access, modification, copying, and destruction of software or data.
- Theft of money by altering computer records or the theft of computer time.

FIGURE 10.1
Fraud or Honesty?

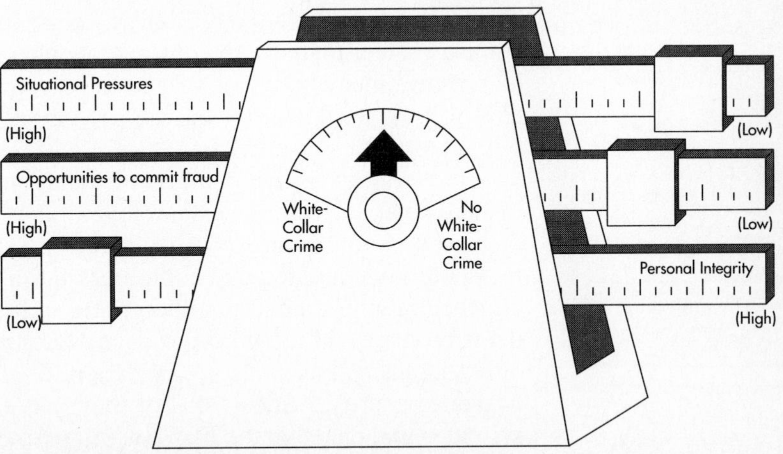

- Theft or destruction of computer hardware.
- Use or the conspiracy to use computer resources to commit a felony.
- Intent to illegally obtain information or tangible property through the use of computers.

Using a computer, fraud perpetrators are able to steal more, in much less time, and with much less effort. For instance, they can steal millions of dollars in less than a second. Perpetrators can commit a fraud and leave little or no evidence. Therefore, computer fraud is often much more difficult to detect than other types of fraud.

The Rise in Computer Fraud

Organizations that track computer fraud estimate that 80% of U.S. businesses have been victimized by at least one incident of computer fraud, at a cost of up to $9 billion per year. However, for the following six reasons no one knows for sure exactly how much companies lose to computer fraud.

1. Not everyone agrees on what constitutes computer fraud. For example, some people restrict the definition to a crime that takes place inside a computer or is directed at one. For others it is any crime where the perpetrator uses the computer as a tool. Many people do not believe that making an unlicensed copy of software constitutes computer fraud. Software publishers think otherwise, however, and prosecute those who make illegal copies. Similarly, some people do not think it is a crime to browse through someone else's computer if they have no intentions of harming the organization or its data.

2. Many computer frauds go undetected. At one time, the FBI estimated that only 1% of all computer crime is detected; other estimates are between 5% and 20%.

3. An estimated 80%–90% of the frauds that are uncovered are not reported. Only the banking industry is required by law to report all frauds. The most commonly cited reason for failure to report computer fraud is a company's fear that adverse publicity would result in copycat fraud and a loss of customer confidence that would cost more than the fraud itself. As a result, fraud estimates are based on the limited number of frauds that are both detected and reported.

   What is known is that computer fraud is large and growing. The dollar losses from unauthorized employee abuses in the United States increased 15-fold from 1997 to 1998, from $181,400 to $2.81 million per incident. It is estimated that computers at the Defense Department were attacked more than half a million times in 1998 and the number of incidents increases 50 to 100% per year. Defense Department staffers and outside consultants made 38,000 "friendly hacks" on their networks to evaluate security. Almost 70% of them were successful. Unfortunately, system management at the Defense Department were only able to detect 4% of the attacks; the others went unnoticed. At the Pentagon, which has the government's most advanced hacker-awareness program, only one in 500 break-ins was detected and reported.

As early as 1979, *Time* magazine labeled computer fraud a "growth industry." Some of the reasons attributed to the steady growth of fraud include the growing number of competent computer users, easier access to remote computers through both the Internet and other data networks, and the belief of many companies that "it won't happen to us."

4. Most networks have a low level of security. Dan Farmer, who wrote SATAN (a network security testing tool), tested 2,200 high-profile web sites at governmental institutions, banks, newspapers, and the like. Only three of the sites detected him and contacted him to find out what he was trying to do. His conclusions? Two out of three sites had serious vulnerabilities, and most firewalls and other protective measures at the sites were ineffective.

5. Many Internet pages give step-by-step instructions on how to perpetrate computer crimes and abuses. For instance, an Internet search found more than 17,000 matches for "denial of service," a rapidly growing form of computer abuse. There are also thousands of pages on how to break into routers and disable web servers.

6. Law enforcement is unable to keep up with the growing number of computer frauds. The FBI is one of two federal agencies (the other is the U.S. Secret Service) charged with investigating computer crime. Due to the lack of funding and people with the necessary skills, however, the FBI is only able to investigate one in 15 computer crimes.

One type of computer fraud, economic espionage, is growing especially fast. **Economic espionage,** the theft of information and intellectual property, increased by 323% during one 5-year period. Almost 75% of the estimated annual losses of $100 billion were to an employee, former employee, contractor, or vendor. At any point in time, the FBI is investigating about 800 separate incidents of economic espionage. One of the most noteworthy cases of industrial espionage is the allegations against Reuters Analytics. They are accused of breaking into the computers of their competitor, Bloomberg, and stealing lines of code. The lines were supposedly used in software that provides financial institutions with the ability to analyze historical data on the stock market.

Computer Fraud Classifications

Various studies have examined fraud to determine the types of assets stolen and the approaches used. As shown in Fig. 10.2, one way to categorize computer fraud is to use the data processing model: input, processor, computer instructions, stored data, and output.

Input. The simplest and most common way to commit a fraud is to alter computer input. It requires little, if any, computer skills. Instead, perpetrators need only to understand how the system operates so they can cover their tracks.

Paul Sjiem-Fat used desktop publishing technology to perpetrate one of the first cases of computer forgery. Sjiem-Fat created bogus cashier's checks and used

FIGURE 10.2
Computer Fraud Classifications

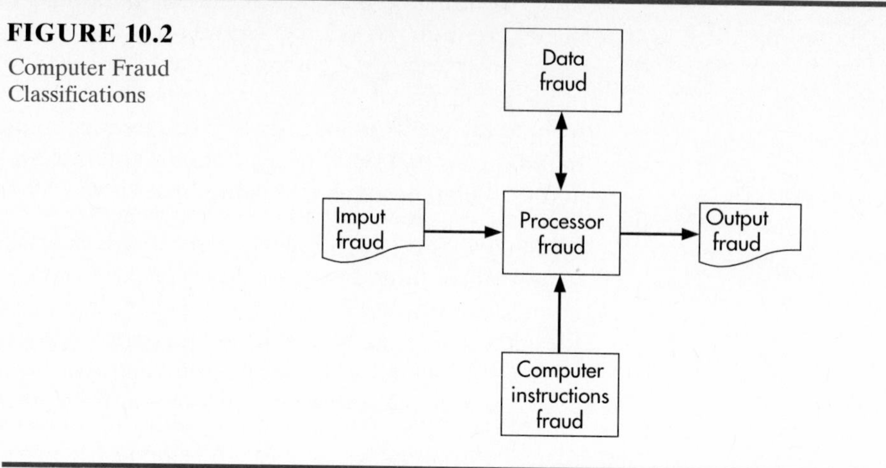

them to buy computer equipment, which he subsequently sold in the Caribbean. He was caught while trying to steal $20,000 from Bank of Boston. The bank called in the Secret Service, who raided his apartment and found nine bogus checks totaling almost $150,000. Sjiem-Fat was prosecuted and sent to prison.

Another perpetrator opened an account at a New York bank, then had a printer prepare blank deposit slips. The slips were similar to those available in bank lobbies, except that his account number was encoded on them. Early one morning he replaced all the deposit slips in the bank lobby with his forged ones. For three days, all bank deposits using the forged slips went directly into the perpetrator's account. After three days the perpetrator withdrew the money, then disappeared. He used an alias; his identity was never uncovered nor was he ever found.

In disbursement frauds, the perpetrator causes a company either to pay too much for ordered goods or to pay for goods never ordered. One perpetrator used a desktop publishing package to prepare fraudulent bills for office supplies that were never ordered, then mailed those bills to companies across the country. The perpetrator kept the dollar amount low enough ($300) so that most companies did not bother to require purchase orders or approvals. An amazingly high percentage of the companies paid the bills without question.

To commit inventory fraud, a perpetrator can enter data into the system to show that stolen inventory has been scrapped. For example, several employees at an East Coast railroad entered data into the company's system to show that more than 200 railroad cars were scrapped or destroyed. They removed the cars from the railway system, then repainted and sold them.

To commit payroll frauds, perpetrators can enter data to increase their salary, create a fictitious employee, or retain a terminated employee on the records. Under the latter two approaches, the perpetrator proceeds to intercept and cash the illegal checks.

In a cash receipts fraud, the perpetrator hides the theft by falsifying system input. For example, an employee at the Arizona Veteran's Memorial Coliseum sold customers full-price tickets, entered the sales as half-price tickets, and pocketed the difference.

Processor. Computer fraud can be committed through unauthorized system use, including the theft of computer time and services. For example, some companies do not permit employees to use company computers to keep personal or outside business records. Violating this policy would constitute a fraud. While most people would not call it fraud, **employee goofing** (surfing the Internet for personal entertainment on company time) has become a serious problem at many companies. One study estimates that employees with access to the Internet, on average, lose one to two hours of productivity a week goofing.

Computer Instructions. Computer fraud can be accomplished by tampering with the software that processes company data. This may involve modifying the software, making illegal copies, or using it in an unauthorized manner. It might also involve developing a software program or module to carry out an unauthorized activity. This approach to computer fraud used to be one of the least common, because it requires a specialized knowledge about computer programming that is beyond the scope of most users. Today, however, such frauds are much more frequent because there are many web pages with instructions on how to create viruses and other computer-instruction-based schemes.

Data. Computer fraud can be perpetrated by altering or damaging a company's data files or by copying, using, or searching them without authorization. There have been numerous instances of data files being scrambled, altered, or destroyed by disgruntled employees. In one instance, an employee removed all the external labels from hundreds of tape files. In another case, an employee used a powerful magnet to scramble all the data on magnetic files.

Company data can also be stolen. In one case, the office manager of a Wall Street law firm found information about prospective mergers and acquisitions in the firm's word processing files. He sold the information to friends and relatives, who made several million dollars by illegally trading securities. In another case, in Europe, a disgruntled employee removed all of a company's data files from the computer room. He then drove to the off-site storage location and removed the company's backup files. He demanded half a million dollars in return for the files, but was arrested while trying to exchange the tapes for the ransom. In another case, a software engineer stole secrets about manufacturing Intel microprocessors. Since the manufacturing plans could be read but not copied or printed, he videotaped the plans screen by screen.

Data can also be destroyed, changed, or defaced—particularly if stored on a company web site. For instance, vandals broke into the NCAA's web site just before the pairings were announced for the basketball tournament and posted swastikas, racial slurs, and a white-power logo. The Air Force, Central Intelligence Agency, and NASA have also been the victims of high-profile attacks on their web sites. An analyst at the Computer Security Institute described the problem as "cyberspace vandals with digital spray cans."

One noted hacker stated that all companies that use the web, especially those with important trade secrets or valuable information technology assets, are under constant attack. The attackers include disaffected employees, industrial spies, foreign governments, hackers and crackers, terrorist groups, and competitors.

Output. Computer fraud can be carried out by stealing or misusing system output. System output is usually displayed on monitors or printed on paper. Unless properly safeguarded, monitor and printer output is subject to prying eyes and unauthorized copying. A study by a Dutch engineer has shown that many computer monitors emit a television-like signal that can be picked up, restructured with the help of some very inexpensive electronic gear, and displayed on a standard TV screen. Under ideal conditions these signals can be picked up from terminals as far away as two miles. During one experiment the engineer was able to set up his equipment in the basement of an apartment building and read the screen on a terminal on the eighth floor.

Computer Fraud and Abuse Techniques

Over the years, perpetrators have devised many methods to commit computer fraud. This section discusses some of the more common techniques. These techniques are summarized in Table 10.3 on pages 342–343.

A **Trojan horse** is a set of unauthorized computer instruction s in an authorized and otherwise properly functioning program. It performs some illegal act at a preappointed time or under a predetermined set of conditions. Trojan horses are often placed in software that is billed as helpful add-ons to popular software programs. For example, several thousand America Online subscribers were sent messages containing an offer of free software. Users who opened the attachments unknowingly unleashed a Trojan horse that secretly copied the subscriber's account name and password and forwarded it to the sender. Another type of Trojan horse monitors a user's keystrokes, captures credit card numbers, and sends them by e-mail to the software's creator.

In another case, visitors to adult sites were told to download a special program to see the pictures. This program had embedded code that turned off the volume on their modem, disconnected them from their Internet service provider, and connected them to a service in the former USSR. The program kept them connected to this site, at $2 a minute, until they turned off their computer. Over 800,000 minutes were billed, with some phone bills as high as $3,000, before the scam was detected.

The **round-down technique** is used most frequently in financial institutions that pay interest. In the typical scenario, the programmer instructs the computer to round down all interest calculations to two decimal places. The fraction of a cent that is rounded down on each calculation is put into the programmer's account or one that he or she controls. No one is the wiser, since all the books balance. Over time these fractions of a cent can add up to a significant amount, especially when interest is calculated daily.

With the **salami technique,** tiny slices of money are stolen over a period of time. For example, a disgruntled chief accountant for a produce-growing company in California used the salami technique to get even with his employer. He used the company's computer system to falsify and systematically increase all the company's production costs by a fraction of a percent. These tiny increments were put into the accounts of dummy customers and then pocketed by the accountant. Every few months the fraudulent costs were raised another fraction of a percent. Because all expenses were rising together, no single account or expense would call attention to the fraud. The accountant eventually was caught when an alert bank teller brought to her manager's attention a check the perpetrator was trying to cash because she did not recognize the name of the company it was made out to.

A **trap door,** or back door, is a way into a system that bypasses normal system controls. Programmers use trap doors to modify programs during systems development and normally remove them before the system is put into operation. When a trap door is not removed before the program is implemented, anyone who discovers it can enter the program and commit a fraud. Programmers can also insert trap doors before they are terminated, allowing them access to the system after they leave.

Superzapping is the unauthorized use of special system programs to bypass regular system controls and perform illegal acts. The name of this technique is derived from a software utility, called Superzap, developed by IBM to handle emergencies, such as restoring a system that has crashed.

Software piracy is copying software without the publisher's permission. It is estimated that for every legal copy of software sold, between seven and eight illegal ones are made. Within days of being released, most new software is on a bulletin board and available free to those who want to download it illegally. An estimated 26% of software used in the United States is pirated; in some countries, this figure is over 90%. The software industry estimates the economic losses of piracy at between $15 and $18 billion a year.

Piracy is such a serious problem that the Software Publishers Association (which represents more than 500 software publishers) files lawsuits against companies and individuals. One lawsuit claimed the University of Oregon's Continuing Education Center violated copyright law by making illegal and unauthorized copies of programs and training manuals. The university settled the case by agreeing to (1) pay a $130,000 fine; (2) launch a campaign to educate its faculty, staff, and students on the lawful use of software; and (3) host a national conference on copyright law and software use. In another case, the Business Software Alliance found 1,400 copies of unlicensed software at an adult vocational school in the Los Angeles Unified School District. The district may have to pay up to $5 million to settle the case against it.

Individuals convicted of software piracy are subject to fines of up to $250,000 and jail terms of up to 5 years. However, the SPA often negotiates more creative punishments. For example, a Puget Sound student caught distributing copyrighted software over the Internet was required to write a 20-page paper on the evils of software piracy and copyright infringement. He will also have to perform 50 hours of community service wiring schools for Internet usage. Failure to comply with either item will subject him to a $10,000 fine and result in a lawsuit for copyright infringement.

Data diddling is changing data before, during, or after it is entered into the system. The change can be made to delete, alter, or add key system data. For

TABLE 10.3 Computer Fraud and Abuse Techniques

Technique	Description
Cracking	Unauthorized access to and use of computer systems, usually by means of a personal computer and a telecommunications network. Crackers are hackers with malicious intentions.
Data diddling	Changing data before, during, or after it is entered into the system in order to delete, alter, or add key system data.
Data leakage	Unauthorized copying of company data such as computer files.
Denial of service attack	Attacker sends e-mail bombs (hundreds of messages per second) from randomly generated false addresses; Internet service provider's e-mail server is overloaded and shuts down.
Eavesdropping	Listening to private voice or data transmissions, often using a wiretap.
E-mail forgery	Sending an e-mail message that looks as if it were sent by someone else.
E-mail threats	Sending a threatening message to try and get recipient to do something that would make it possible to defraud him
Hacking	Unauthorized access to and use of computer systems, usually by means of a personal computer and a telecommunications network. Hackers do not intend to cause any damage.
Internet misinformation	Using the Internet to spread false or misleading information about companies.
Internet terrorism	Using the Internet to disrupt electronic commerce and to destroy company and individual communications.
Logic time bomb	Program that lies idle until some specified circumstance or a particular time triggers it. Once triggered, the bomb sabotages the system by destroying programs, data, or both.
Masquerading or impersonation	Perpetrator gains access to the system by pretending to be an authorized user; enjoys same privileges as the legitimate user.
Password cracking	Intruder penetrates a system's defenses, steals the file containing valid passwords, decrypts them, and then uses them to gain access to system resources such as programs, files, and data.
Piggybacking	Tapping into a telecommunications line and latching on to a legitimate user before he logs into the system; legitimate user unknowingly carries perpetrator into the system.
Round-down	Computer rounds down all interest calculations to two decimal places. Remaining fraction of a cent is placed in an account controlled by perpetrator.
Salami technique	Tiny slices of money are stolen over a period of time. (Expenses are increased by a fraction of a percent; increments are placed in a dummy account and later pocketed by the perpetrator.)
Scavenging	Gaining access to confidential information by searching corporate records. Scavenging methods range from searching trashcans for printouts or carbon copies of confidential information to scanning the contents of computer memory.

continued

TABLE 10.3 Continued

Technique	Description
Social engineering	Perpetrator tricks an employee into giving out the information needed to get into a system.
Software piracy	Copying computer software without the publisher's permission.
Spamming	E-mailing the same message to everyone on one or more Usenet news groups or LISTSERV lists.
Superzapping	Unauthorized use of special system programs to bypass regular system controls and perform illegal acts.
Trap door	Perpetrator enters the system using a back door that bypasses normal system controls and perpetrates fraud.
Trojan horse	Unauthorized computer instructions in an authorized and properly functioning program.
Virus	Segment of executable code that attaches itself to software, replicates itself, and spreads to other systems or files. Triggered by a predefined event, a virus damages system resources or displays a message on the monitor.
War dialing	Programming a computer to search for an idle modem by dialing thousands of phone lines. Perpetrator enters the system though the idle modem, captures the personal computer attached to the modem, and gains access to the network to which the personal computer is attached.
Worm	Similar to a virus, except that it is a program rather than a code segment hidden in a host program. A worm also copies and actively transmits itself directly to other systems. It usually does not live very long, but it is quite destructive while it is alive.

example, a clerk for a Denver brokerage altered a transaction to record 1,700 shares of Loren Industries stock worth about $2,500 as shares in Long Island Lighting worth more than $25,000.

Data leakage refers to the unauthorized copying of company data. The Encyclopedia Britannica claimed losses in the millions of dollars when an employee made copies of its customer list and began selling them to other companies. Ten Social Security Administration employees sold 11,000 Social Security numbers (and other identifying information such as mother's maiden names) to credit card fraudsters.

Piggybacking is tapping into a telecommunications line and latching on to a legitimate user before the user logs into a system. The legitimate user unknowingly carries the perpetrator into the system.

In **masquerading** or **impersonation,** the perpetrator gains access to the system by pretending to be an authorized user. This approach requires a perpetrator to know the legitimate user's ID number and password. Once inside the system, the perpetrator enjoys the same privileges as the legitimate user being impersonated.

In **social engineering,** a perpetrator tricks an employee into giving him the information they need to get into the system. They might call saying they are conducting a security survey and lull the person into disclosing confidential information. They call help desks and claim to be an employee who has forgotten her password or call users and say they are from network engineering and are testing the system and need your password. They also pose as buyers or salespeople to get plant tours and obtain information that may help them break into the system.

A **logic time bomb** is a program that lies idle until some specified circumstance or a particular time triggers it. Once triggered, the bomb sabotages the system by destroying programs, data, or both. Most bombs are written by disgruntled programmers who want to get even with their company. Donald Burleson, a former security officer, set off a bomb that erased 168,000 sales commissions records. As a result, company paychecks were held up for a month. The program, which was attached to a legitimate one, was designed to go off periodically and erase more records. The bomb was discovered before it could go off again by a fellow programmer who was testing a new employee bonus system. The company's computers were shut down for two days while the bomb was located and diffused.

Timothy Lloyd detonated a logic time bomb three weeks after he was fired from Omega Engineering. The bomb caused an estimated $10 million in damages when it erased all of the network's software and the company's data. Lloyd, who functioned as both the system designer and its administrator, also disabled the network's automatic backup and recovery facilities. As a result, the company was unable to recover any of the software and data that were destroyed.

Hacking or **cracking** is the unauthorized access to and use of computer systems, usually by means of a personal computer and a telecommunications network. Hackers do not intend to cause any damage; they are usually motivated by the challenge of breaking and entering and are just browsing or looking for things to copy and keep. Crackers are hackers with malicious intentions. For example, during Desert Storm Dutch crackers broke into 34 different military computer sites and extracted confidential information. Among the information stolen were the troop movements and weapons used in the Iraq war. The group offered to sell the information to Iraq, but they declined, probably because they thought they were being set up.

Hackers and crackers have broken into the computers of governmental agencies such as the U.S. Department of Defense, NASA, and the Los Alamos National Laboratory. One 17-year-old cracker, nicknamed Shadow Hawk, was convicted of electronically penetrating the Bell Laboratories national network, destroying files valued at $174,000, and copying 52 proprietary software programs worth $1.2 million. He published confidential information, such as telephone numbers, passwords, and instructions on how to breach AT&T's computer security system, on underground bulletin boards. He was sentenced to nine months in prison and given a $10,000 fine. Like Shadow Hawk, many hackers are fairly young, some as young as 12 and 13.

Scavenging, or **dumpster diving,** is gaining access to confidential information by searching corporate records. Scavenging methods range from searching trash cans for printouts or carbon copies of confidential information to scanning the contents of computer memory. In one case, Jerry Schneider, a high school student, noticed a trash can full of papers on his way home from school. Rummaging through them, he discovered operating guides for Pacific Telephone computers. Over time his scavenging activities resulted in a technical library that later allowed him to steal a million dollars worth of electronic equipment. In another case, in South America, a man attached a video camera to a car battery, hid it in some bushes, and pointed it at the company president's window. The president had an office on the first floor and his computer monitor faced the window. A significant business acquisition almost fell through as a result of the information on the videotape.

Eavesdropping enables perpetrators to observe private communications or transmissions of data. One way to intercept signals is by setting up a **wiretap.** The equipment needed to wiretap an unprotected communications line is readily available at local electronics stores. One alleged wiretapping fraud involved Mark Koenig, a 28-year-old consultant to GTE, and four associates. Federal agents say they pulled personal identification numbers and other crucial information about Bank of America customers from GTE telephone lines. They used this data to make 5,500 fake ATM cards. They allegedly intended to use the cards over one weekend to withdraw money from banks all over the country. However, authorities were tipped off, and they were apprehended before they could use the cards.

Fraud perpetrators are beginning to use unsolicited **e-mail threats** to defraud people. For example, a company named Global Communications sent a message threatening legal action if an unspecified overdue amount is not paid within 24 hours. The message also said that court action could be avoided by calling Mike Murray at an 809 area code (which is for islands in the Carribean). People who called got a clever recording that sounded like a live person and responded to the caller's voice. The responses were designed to keep a caller on the phone as long as possible, since they are being billed at $25 per minute.

In another instance, a man posed as a woman on a chat line and lured men into erotic conversations. After a while she offered them very revealing pictures of herself. The men who asked for the pictures got, instead, a very angry letter from her "husband" threatening physical violence unless they paid him money.

It is also possible to commit **e-mail forgery.** One way to do so is to send an e-mail message through a re-mailer who removes the message headers, thereby making the message anonymous. Another way to commit e-mail forgery is to make the e-mail message look as if it was sent by someone else. For example, a former Oracle employee was charged with breaking into the company's computer network, falsifying evidence, and committing perjury for forging an e-mail message to support her charge that she was fired for breaking up a relationship with the company's chief executive. She faces up to six years in jail for her activities.

A **denial of service attack** occurs when an attacker sends **e-mail bombs:** so many messages (hundreds per second) from randomly generated false addresses that the Internet service provider's e-mail server is overloaded and shuts down. Other denial of service attacks involve sending so much data to a network or web server that it crashes. These attacks go by such creative names such as Bonk, Boink, Syn-flood, Ping of Death, WinNuke, and LandAttack. One Syn-flood attack shut down more than 3,000 web sites for 40 hours on one of the busiest shopping weekends of the year.

Internet terrorism is crackers using the Internet to disrupt electronic commerce and to destroy company and individual communications. For example, a cracker developed a program that erases messages and unleashed it at Usenet, an Internet bulletin board system. The program destroyed 25,000 messages before it could be removed from the system.

Internet misinformation is using the Internet to spread false or misleading information about companies. This can be done in a number of ways, including inflammatory messages in on-line chats, setting up web sites, and spreading urban legends. For example, Tommy Hilfiger Corp. was supposedly kicked off the Oprah Winfrey show for making racist remarks. This information, together with a call to boycott the company, quickly spread throughout the world on the Internet. This urban legend was totally false, and Hilfiger quickly went to the net to deny the story. McDonald's spent seven years fighting a large number of false accusations that were spread using pamphlets and web sites. McDonald's finally won the case after 313 days of testimony and an expenditure of $16 million. McDonald's was awarded $94,000. Immediately after the verdict, one anti-McDonald's web site mocked the verdict and called its campaign against McDonald's "unstoppable."

Crackers who search for an idle modem by programming their computers to dial thousands of phone lines are **war dialing.** Crackers can enter through the idle modem, capture the PC attached to the modem, and then gain access to the network to which it is connected. This approach got its name from the movie *War Games.*

Password cracking is when an intruder penetrates a system's defenses, steals the file containing valid passwords, decrypts them, and then uses them to gain access to system resources such as programs, files, and data.

Spamming is e-mailing the same message to everyone on one or more Usenet newsgroups or LISTSERV lists. The spammer may consider this a fun prank or a perfect, inexpensive, and legal way to reach potential customers. However, many in the Internet community take a dim view of these pranks and conducting business in this manner. In retaliation, some spammers have been spammed in return with thousands of messages, causing their e-mail service to fail. However, this is not a good idea, as it affects many innocent users of the same system and can result in your e-mail account being closed. A better approach is to e-mail the person in charge of the spammer's site. (If the spammer's address is gorilla@zoo.com, his administrator is postmaster@zoo.com.) An example of a spam is one called "MAKE.MONEY.FAST," which was sent to thousands of groups. It was nothing more that the Usenet equivalent of a chain letter.

Computer Viruses

A **computer virus** is a segment of executable code that attaches itself to software. Most viruses have two phases. In the first phase, the virus replicates itself and spreads to other systems or files. The replication phase is usually triggered by some predefined event, such as the computer being turned on; using or exiting software; creating, opening, or closing a document; reaching a specific date; or the software containing the virus being used a specific number of times. In the attack phase, also triggered by some predefined event, the virus carries out its mission. Both phases can be triggered at the same time, or the virus can be secretly replicated and set to go off at a later time. Many viruses lie dormant for extended periods of time without causing any specific damage, except to propagate themselves.

Viruses can destroy or alter data or programs, take control of the computer, destroy the hard disk's file allocation table, delete or rename files or directories, reformat the hard disk, change the content of files, or keep users from booting the system or accessing data on a hard disk. It can intercept and change transmissions, print disruptive images or messages on the screen or change its color, or cause the screen image to disappear. As the virus spreads, it takes up space, clogs communications, and hinders system performance. A particularly bad virus attack shut down a bank with 200 servers and 10,000 desktops for four days. During the downtime, the bank was locked out of its system and customer accounts could not be accessed. A firm that specializes in fixing virus attacks was eventually able to restore the system.

There are two ways computers become infected: (1) by booting, or starting, using an infected diskette (called a boot sector virus); and (2) by running a program that has been infected (a program file virus). There are a number of symptoms of a computer infected by a virus. These include computers that will not boot, programs that will not execute, unexpected read or write operations, an inability to save files to the A: drive, bad sectors on diskettes, long program load times, abnormally large file sizes, slow systems operation, and unusual screen activity, error messages, or file names.

Viruses are contagious and are easily spread from one system to another. For example, the National Computer Security Association estimated that in just one year the number of U.S. businesses infected by viruses tripled, even though the use of antivirus software increased. To spread rapidly, a virus must be introduced into a network with a large number of computers. In a relatively short time, the virus can spread to thousands of systems. When the virus is confined to a single machine or to a small LAN, it will soon run out of computers to infect. A virus also spreads when users share programs or diskettes or when they access and use programs from external sources such as bulletin boards and suppliers of free software. Research shows that e-mail containing hidden viruses is the fastest growing way to spread viruses. Macro viruses contained in common word processing and spreadsheet files are the most common viruses.

Many computer viruses have long lives because they can create copies of themselves faster than they can be destroyed. A number of viruses, such as Stone and Jerusalem-B, have spread so furiously that they have become epidemics. According to a survey conducted by Dataquest, 63% of the 600,000 personal computer users surveyed had experienced a virus and 38% of those affected had lost data. Virus creators are beginning to make viruses that mutate each time they infect a computer, making them much more difficult to detect and destroy.

A **worm** is like a virus, except that it is a program rather than a code segment hidden in a host program. A worm also copies and actively transmits itself directly to other systems. It usually does not live very long, but it is quite destructive while it is alive. One of the more destructive worms, written by Robert T. Morris, affected 6,000 computers in a very short time. Focus 10.1 details the impact of this worm on systems across the country.

FOCUS 10.1 A Worm Run Amok

SCIENTISTS at Berkeley's Experimental Computing Facility noticed a rash of unknown users trying to log into their system. The break-in attempts increased in frequency until they could no longer be monitored. Within minutes, the program invaded computer processing space and brought Berkeley's mammoth system to a halt. At this point they realized a program was trying to access the system.

Within a half hour, it was clear that the program was not limited to the Berkeley system; it was invading the *entire* Internet. Within hours, computer experts discovered the existence of a powerful "worm" in the Internet. While scientists attempted to stop the worm, law enforcement officials and the press were beginning their own investigations of the unauthorized entry. Information on a possible suspect was scarce until an unidentified phone caller tipped a *New York Times* writer by inadvertently referring to the criminal programmer as RTM.

Robert Tappan Morris loved computers and challenges. He acquired a passion for computer security issues while working with his father, a scientist at Bell Labs. At Harvard he received extensive recognition for problem-solving work using the school's main computer facility, which was linked to the Internet. Robert's most successful projects centered on improving the Bell systems Internet operations and its operating system, UNIX. At age 20 Robert's skills in UNIX security were so extensive that his father had him address a computer security conference at the National Security Agency. The next day he delivered the same address to the Naval Research Laboratory.

While Robert was attending graduate school at Cornell University, the first computer viruses were receiving national media attention. This sparked Robert's interest in developing an undetectable worm that would invade the Internet. His goal was to reach as many computers as possible. With Robert's background in UNIX security issues and his unlimited access to the Cornell computer, developing a worm was easy. Robert had discovered three programming flaws in the UNIX operating system that allowed him unauthorized access to any computer on the Internet. Robert developed a worm capable of entering a given system without authorization using a bug in the Sendmail subprogram. The worm was designed to replicate and use Sendmail to enter related systems entirely undetected.

When the worm was finished, Robert illegally logged on to the artificial intelligence lab computer at MIT from his system at Cornell and released his creation. After dinner Robert attempted to log on, but the computer did not respond. He immediately knew something was wrong and after several attempts to remedy the problem, the significance of the danger was clear. Robert had made a fatal programming error that allowed the worm to replicate out of control throughout the Internet.

Cleaning out the Internet system and re-creating the files destroyed by the worm took several months. On final tally, the worm had infected more than 6,000 computers, and the estimated costs to resolve the problem ranged from $150,000 to almost $200 million.

Robert was arrested and charged with a felony violation of the 1986 Counterfeit Access Device and Computer Fraud and Abuse Act, which prohibits unauthorized computer access. In 1990 he was convicted of computer crime and sentenced to three years probation, 400 hours of community service, and a $10,000 fine.

PREVENTING AND DETECTING COMPUTER FRAUD

Because fraud is such a serious problem, organizations must take every precaution to protect their information systems. A number of measures can significantly decrease the potential for fraud and any resulting losses. For example, a company can create a climate that makes fraud less likely, increase the difficulty of committing a fraud, reduce the amount of loss if a fraud occurs, increase the likelihood of detecting fraud, prosecute fraud perpetrators, and increase the penalty for committing fraud. These measures are summarized in Table 10.4.

TABLE 10.4 Summary of Ways to Prevent and Detect Computer Fraud

Make Fraud Less Likely to Occur
• Use proper hiring and firing practices • Manage disgruntled employees • Train employees in security and fraud prevention measures • Manage and track software licenses • Require signed confidentiality agreements
Increase the Difficulty of Committing Fraud
• Develop a strong system of internal controls • Segregate duties • Require vacations and rotate duties • Restrict access to computer equipment and data files • Encrypt data and programs • Protect telephone lines • Protect the system from viruses • Control sensitive data • Control laptop computers • Monitor hacker information
Improve Detection Methods
• Conduct frequent audits • Use a computer security officer • Set up a fraud hot line • Use computer consultants • Monitor system activities • Use forensic accountants • Use fraud detection software
Reduce Fraud Losses
• Maintain adequate insurance • Store backup copies of program and data files in a secure off-site location • Develop a contingency plan for fraud occurrences • Use software to monitor system activity and recover from fraud
Prosecute and Incarcerate Fraud Perpetrators

Make Fraud Less Likely to Occur

Some computer consultants claim that the most effective method of obtaining adequate system security is to rely on the integrity of company employees. At the same time, research shows that most fraud is committed by current and former employees. Thus employees are both the greatest control strength and weakness. Organizations can take steps to increase employee integrity and reduce the likelihood of employees committing a fraud, as described in the following sections.

Use Proper Hiring and Firing Practices. As discussed in Chapter 8, one of a manager's most important responsibilities is to hire and retain honest people.

Similarly, a company should be very careful when firing employees. Dismissed employees should be removed from sensitive jobs immediately and denied access to the computer system to prevent sabotage or copying confidential data before they leave.

One employee, after learning he had been terminated, lit a butane lighter under a smoke detector located just outside the computer room. It set off a sprinkler system that ruined most of the computer hardware in the room.

Some people intent on breaking into systems are posing as janitors or temporary employees because they are given access to the company's site and often to its AIS, but are not subjected to normal hiring practices such as background checks. Once they have legitimate access to the building or the system, they can use any number of techniques to commit fraud or sabotage the system. For this reason, all company personnel, including cleaning crews and temporary employees, should be subject to all hiring and firing policies. This technique was popularized by a story in *2600 Magazine* (a hacker quarterly) that explained how to get a job as a janitor so you can crack into a company's computers.

Manage Disgruntled Employees. Many employees who commit fraud are seeking revenge or "justice" for some wrong they perceive has been done to them. Hence companies should have procedures for identifying these individuals and either helping them resolve their feelings or removing them from jobs with system access. One way to avoid disgruntled employees and to maintain high company morale is to provide grievance channels and employee counseling. Employees need someone outside the normal chain of command to talk with about their grievances and problems. Having someone who will listen to them and help them resolve their problems can significantly decrease the number of dissatisfied employees. This is often not easy to accomplish, since most employees fear that airing their feelings could have negative consequences for their career.

Train Employees in Security and Fraud Prevention Measures. Many top executives believe that employee training and education is the most important element of any security program. Fraud is much less likely to occur in an environment where employees believe security is everyone's business. An ideal corporate culture for fraud deterrence exists when employees are proud of their company and are protective of its assets. They believe they have a responsibility to report fraud because what harms the company harms them. This culture does not just happen; it has to be created, taught, and practiced. To develop this type of culture, a company should educate and train employees in the following areas:

- *Security measures.* Employees should be well schooled in security measures, taught why they are important, and motivated to take them very seriously. Security should be monitored and enforced as a way of reinforcing this training.
- *Telephone disclosures.* Employees should be taught to not give out confidential information over the telephone without knowing for sure who is calling. The employees can be taught tactics such as dialing the caller back and verifying a person's identity by asking penetrating and specific questions that only they would be able to answer.

- *Fraud awareness.* Employees should be made aware of fraud, its prevalence, and its dangers. They should be taught why people commit fraud and how to deter and detect it.
- *Ethical considerations.* The company should promote its ethical standards in its practices and through company literature such as employee handouts. Acceptable and unacceptable behavior should be defined so that employees are aware of a company's ethical position should a problem arise. Many business practices fall into a gray area between right or wrong, and this problem is especially prevalent throughout the computer industry. For example, many professionals see nothing wrong with utilizing corporate computer resources for personal use or gaining unauthorized access to another company's data bases and browsing through them. One programmer, when arrested for unauthorized browsing, was shocked that he was prosecuted for his crime; he felt his activities were a common industry practice.
- *Punishment for unethical behavior.* Employees should be informed of the consequences of unethical behavior (reprimands, dismissal, prosecution, etc.). This information should be disseminated not as a threat but as the consequence of choosing to act unethically. For example, employees should be informed that using a computer to steal or commit fraud is a federal crime and anyone so doing faces immediate dismissal and/or prosecution. Likewise, the company should display notices of program and data ownership and inform employees of the penalties of misuse.

Educating employees in security issues, fraud awareness, ethical considerations, and the consequences of choosing to act unethically can make a tremendous difference. This education can be accomplished by conducting informal discussions and formal meetings, issuing periodic departmental memos, distributing written guidelines and codes of professional ethics, circulating reports of securities violations and their consequences, and promoting security and fraud training programs.

Manage and Track Software Licenses. Software license management, a fast-growing area of information technology management, helps companies make sure they comply with all their software licenses. Of key concern is making sure there are enough licenses to met user demands and that there are not more users than licenses. This protects them from software piracy lawsuits. It can also save the company money by ensuring that it does not pay for more licenses than they actually use or need.

Require Signed Confidentiality Agreements. All employees, vendors, and contractors should be required to sign and abide by a confidentiality agreement.

Increase the Difficulty of Committing Fraud

One way to deter fraud is to design a system with sufficient controls to make fraud difficult to perpetrate. These controls help ensure the accuracy, integrity, and safety of system resources. Many security consultants jokingly refer to a new "arms race," this one between those trying to protect systems from fraud and abuse and those trying to break into them. Unfortunately, the protectors seem to be losing the race. This section discusses how companies can develop a strong system of internal controls and details some of the more important fraud prevention techniques.

Develop a Strong System of Internal Controls. The overall responsibility for a secure and adequately controlled system lies with top management. Managers typically delegate the design of adequate control systems to systems analysts, designers, and end users. The corporate information security officer and the operations staff are typically responsible for ensuring that control procedures are followed.

To develop efficient and cost-effective controls, designers should follow the risk assessment strategy shown in Fig. 7.3. These controls are much more effective when placed in the system as it is built, rather than as an afterthought. Management must also establish a set of procedures to ensure that the controls are complied with and enforced.

It is especially important to make sure that internal controls are in place during the end-of-the-year holiday season. Research shows that a disproportionate amount of computer fraud and security break-ins takes place during the holidays. Some reasons for this are (1) extended employee vacations and hence fewer people to "mind the store," (2) students are out of school and have more time on their hands, and (3) counterculture hackers get lonely this time of year and increase their attacks on systems.

Segregate Duties. As discussed in Chapter 8, there must be an adequate segregation of duties to prevent individuals from stealing assets and covering up their tracks.

Require Vacations and Rotate Duties. Many fraud schemes, such as lapping and kiting, require the ongoing attention of the perpetrator. If mandatory vacations were coupled with a temporary rotation of duties, as explained in Chapter 9, such ongoing fraud schemes would fall apart. For example, when federal investigators raided an illegal gambling establishment, they found that Roswell Steffen, who earned $11,000 a year, was betting up to $30,000 a day at the racetrack. Investigators at Union Dime Savings Bank discovered he had embezzled and gambled away $1.5 million of their money over a three-year period. A compulsive gambler, Steffen started out by borrowing $5,000 to place a bet on a sure thing that did not pan out. He embezzled ever-increasing amounts trying to win back the original money he had "borrowed."

Steffen committed his fraud by transferring money from inactive accounts to his own account. If the owner of an inactive account complained, Steffen, who as the chief teller had the power to resolve these types of problems, replaced the money by taking it from some other inactive account. After being caught, and asked how the fraud could have been prevented, he said the bank could have coupled a two-week vacation period with several weeks of rotation to another job function. That would have made his embezzlement, which required his physical presence at the bank and his constant attention, almost impossible to cover up.

Restrict Access to Computer Equipment and Data Files. Computer fraud can be reduced significantly if access to computer equipment and data files is restricted. As explained in Chapter 8, physical access to computer equipment should be restricted, and legitimate users should be authenticated before they are allowed to use the system. Unfortunately, companies often fail to delete or change ID codes and passwords when employees leave or are transferred to another department. A favorite electronic espionage tactic is to gain access to a building and plug into an ethernet jack in the wall and talk to the system. This can be prevented by configuring the system to only respond to hardware that it recognizes.

Encrypt Data and Programs. Another way to protect data is to translate it into a secret code, thereby making it meaningless to anyone without the means to decipher it. Data encryption is explained in Chapter 9.

Protect Telephone Lines. Computer hackers (called **phreakers** when they attack phone systems) use telephone lines to transmit viruses and to access, steal, and destroy data. They also steal telephone services; one company lost $4.5 million in three days when their system was compromised and details on how to use their phone lines were published on the Internet. They also break into voice mail systems, as the New York Police Department learned. The phreakers changed the voice mail greeting to say that officers were too busy drinking coffee and eating doughnuts to answer the phone and to call 119 in case of an emergency.

One effective method to protect telephone lines is to attach an electronic lock and key to them. When one such device was tested, researchers concluded that it would take a hacker 188 days working nonstop to break the more than 1 trillion combinations. Few hackers would make the attempt; if they did, they would most likely be detected before they were successful. When a new phone system is installed, never use the default passwords as they are all published on the Internet. On established systems, change the passwords frequently.

Some crackers gain access to systems through dial-up modem lines. For example, a company in Silicon Valley refused to let workers have access to the Internet at work because they were afraid crackers would compromise their systems. Engineers at the company thought they needed Internet access to get their work done, and so they bought $50 modems for their analog telephone lines. Security took away their access by replacing their analog lines with digital lines. Not to be outdone, the engineers requested fax lines, which were analog. Security never found out about the "fax" lines until a disgruntled ex-employee had his computer dial all company numbers looking for the screech of a modem. The former employee entered through the modem line and caused considerable damage to the system. Another Silicon Valley company, Sun Microsystems, has made it a firing offense to use a modem on a desktop computer; employees caught using them are sent packing the day they are caught.

Protect the System from Viruses. There are hundreds of thousands of virus attacks every year, and an estimated 90% of the PCs that suffer a virus attack are reinfected within 30 days by the same virus or some other virus. A system can be protected from viruses by following the guidelines listed in Focus 10.2.

Fortunately, some very good virus protection programs are available. Virus *protection* programs are designed to remain in computer memory and search for viruses trying to infiltrate the system. The intrusion is usually detected when

FOCUS 10.2 Keeping Your Microcomputers Virus-Free

HERE ARE some practical suggestions for protecting computers from viruses.

- Install reliable antivirus software that scans for, identifies, and destroys viruses. There are some antivirus packages that use neural networks to seek out software that behaves like a virus. The suspected code is sent to a software lab via the Internet and tested. If the code is a virus, the lab develops an antidote and sends it back to the user via the Internet.
- Scan all incoming e-mail for viruses at the server level rather than when it hits users' desktops.
- Do not put your diskettes in strange machines; your diskette may become infected. Do not let others put their diskettes in your disk drives; your machine may become infected. Scan all new diskettes and all new files with antiviral software before any data or programs are copied to your machine.
- Use write-protect tabs that prohibit writing to diskettes; a virus cannot spread to a write-protected diskette.
- Obtain software and diskettes only from known and trusted sources. While the likelihood of contracting a virus in this manner is small, even this software may be infected.
- Be wary of software or diskettes from unknown sources. They may be virus bait, especially if their prices or functionality sound too good to be true.
- Deal with trusted software retailers. Some dealers rewrap and sell used software as if it were new.
- Some software suppliers use electronic techniques to make tampering evident. Ask whether the software you are purchasing has such protection.
- Write-protect new software diskettes before installing them. This will prevent infection and provide you with backup.
- Check new software on an isolated machine with virus detection software. Software direct from the publisher has been know to have viruses
- When you restart, use the "power-off–power-on" to clear and reset the system. It is possible for a virus to survive a warm start-up using the Ctrl–Alt–Del or Reset keys.
- It is safer to start up or boot the machine from a write-protected diskette than from a hard disk. This type of start-up will resist viruses that obtain control via the boot sector of the hard disk.
- Have two backups of all files. Data files should be backed up separately from programs to avoid contaminating backup data. Keep write-protected copies of original disks and restore from them.
- Restrict the use of public bulletin boards. All outside software should be certified as virus-free before loading it into the system.

Source: Deloitte & Touche, *Information Protection Review* 2(1): 6.

there is an unauthorized attempt to access an executable program. When an infection attempt is detected, the software freezes the system and flashes a message to the user. The user can then instruct the program to remove the virus. Virus *detection* programs, which spot an infection soon after it starts, are more reliable than virus protection programs. Virus *identification* programs scan all executable programs to find and remove all known viruses from the system. These programs work by scanning the system for specific characteristics of known virus strains.

Make sure that the latest versions of the antivirus programs are used. National City bank in Cleveland, Ohio installed some new laptops on their system. The laptops were checked for viruses by the manufacturer and by the bank, but not with the latest antivirus software. A virus spread from the hard drive of the laptops to 300 network servers and 12,000 workstations. It took the bank over two days to completely eradicate the virus from all bank systems.

Control Sensitive Data. To protect its sensitive data, a company should classify all of its data as to importance and confidentiality and then apply and enforce appropriate access restrictions. It should shred discarded paper documents. Controls can be placed over data files to prevent or discourage copying. Employees should be informed of the consequences of using illegal copies of software, and the company should institute controls to see that illegal copies are not in use. Sensitive and confidential information, backup tapes, and system documentation should be locked up at night and should not be left out on desks. Servers and PCs should also be locked when not in use. Companies should never store all of their data in one place or give an employee access to all of it. Local area networks can use dedicated servers that allow data to be downloaded but never uploaded to avoid infection by a network computer. Closed-circuit televisions can be used to monitor areas where sensitive data or easily stolen assets are handled.

Some organizations with particularly sensitive data are installing diskless PCs or workstations. All data are stored centrally in a network and users download the data they need to work on each day. At the end of the day all data to be saved must be stored in the network, thereby controlling the problem of unguarded information created and stored in desktop computers. Since users can delete or destroy only the data on their screens, the company's data is secure; the system is virtually immune to disasters a user might intentionally or unintentionally cause. In addition, without disks, users cannot introduce viruses into the system with contaminated diskettes. Nor does the company lose valuable data, because employees cannot copy company data on diskettes and remove them from the premises.

Control Laptop Computers. Special care should be given to laptops because thieves are increasingly breaking into cars and hotel rooms to steal laptops for the confidential information they contain. According to one insurance company, one out of 14 laptops purchased is stolen. To control laptops, companies should

- Make staff aware of the significant threats laptops face.
- Establish laptop security policies to require employees to back up data before traveling and to a separate source when on the road, and to never leave a laptop unattended or lock it to a large object when left unattended.
- Engrave the company name or logo and a phone number on the PC.
- Install software that makes it impossible for the computer to boot up without a password.
- Password protect and encrypt data on the hard disk so that if a laptop is stolen, the data cannot be used.
- Install motion detectors that can emit a loud shriek if the machine is moved.
- Install software that periodically disables the laptop's sound and dials a toll-free number to check in. Laptops reported stolen are told to call every five minutes so police can locate it.
- Store confidential data on a disk, rather than the hard drive, and always keeping the disk in your possession or locked in a safe place.

Monitor Hacker Information. Underground journals, books, and cracker web sites contain a great deal of information on how to break into systems. For example, there are articles on how to breach a server, how to generate virus code, and how to hide your identity in cyberspace. Details on how to take advantage of newly discovered security holes are published almost daily. It is important to monitor these sites and find any of these postings that pertain to systems that your company uses so they can be protected from hacker attacks.

Improve Detection Methods

Many companies are currently being defrauded and do not know it. The following steps can be taken to detect fraud as soon as possible.

Conduct Frequent Audits. One way to increase the likelihood of detecting fraud and computer abuses is to conduct periodic external and internal audits as well as special network security audits. Auditors should regularly test system controls and periodically browse data files looking for suspicious activities. However, care must be exercised to make sure employees' privacy rights are not violated. Informing employees that auditors will conduct a **random surveillance** not only helps resolve the privacy issue but also has a significant deterrent effect on computer crime. One large financial institution that implemented this strategy uncovered a number of abuses, including some that resulted in the termination of one employee and the reprimand of another. Systems auditing is addressed in depth in Chapter 11.

Use a Computer Security Officer. Most frauds are not detected by internal or external auditors. In a study published in the *Sloan Management Review,* only 4.5% of 259 cases of fraud were uncovered by auditors. Normal system controls uncovered 45%, accidental discovery uncovered 32%, and computer security officers found 8%. The study shows that assigning responsibility for fraud deterrence and detection to a **computer security officer** has a significant deterrent effect. This person should be independent of the information system function. The security officer can monitor the system and disseminate information about improper system uses and their consequences. Charles Schwab has implemented this strategy and has a fraud unit of more than 20 information technology people who constantly assess and monitor internal and external network traffic operations.

To prevent economic espionage, the computer security officer should head an information security committee that includes all departments that create, access, maintain, and use confidential information. The committee should develop procedures to identify, store, handle, transmit, and dispose of confidential information. They should also develop a comprehensive information security program, including things such as nondisclosure statements for employees, contractors, vendors, and visitors. It is especially important that the computer security officer work closely with the person in charge of building security, as that is often a company's weakest security leak.

Set Up a Fraud Hot Line. People witnessing fraudulent behavior are often torn between two conflicting feelings. They feel an obligation to protect company assets and turn in fraud perpetrators, yet they are uncomfortable in the whistle blower role and find it easier to remain silent. This reluctance is even stronger if they are aware of whistle blowers who in the past have been ostracized or persecuted by their coworkers or superiors, or have had their career damaged.

An effective way to resolve this conflict is to provide employees with hot lines so they can anonymously report fraud. In one study, researchers found that 33% of the 212 frauds studied were uncovered by anonymous tips. The insurance industry set up a hot line in an attempt to control an estimated $17 billion a year in fraudulent claims. In the first month, they received in excess of 2,250 calls; 15% of these resulted in investigative action. The downside of hot lines is that many of the calls are not worthy of investigation. Some are made seeking revenge, others are vague reports of wrongdoing, and others have no merit.

A potential problem with a hot line is that those who operate the hot line may report to people who are involved in top-management fraud. This threat can be overcome by using a fraud hotline set up by a trade organization or commercial company. Reports of management fraud can be passed by this company directly to the board of directors.

Use Computer Consultants. Many companies use outside computer consultants or in-house teams to test and evaluate their security procedures and computer systems. Each security weakness or means of breaching the system that is detected is closely evaluated, and corresponding protective measures are implemented. Some companies dislike this approach, because they do not want their weaknesses exposed nor do they want their employees to know that the system can indeed be broken into.

Arthur Anderson has more than 1,000 computer risk management specialists; more than half of their chargeable hours are spent on security matters. The Federal Reserve Bank of New York has three full-time people, called Tiger Teamers, that test their system for weaknesses. These teams try everything they can think of to compromise a company's system. To get into offices so they can they can look for passwords or get on computers, they masquerade as janitors, temporary workers, or confused delivery personnel. They also use sexy decoys to distract guards, climb through roof hatches, and drop through ceiling panels. Some outside consultants claim that they can thus get into 90% or more of the companies they attack.

In one documented case, a consultant was hired to find out who was leaking corporate secrets to a competitor. The culprit was found to be a young vice president who was not careful with his laptop and his passwords. When the CEO would not believe him, the consultant had a beautiful member of his staff put on a slinky little dress and talk her way past security guards by telling them she wanted to surprise her husband with her pregnancy test results. A few minutes later she left the building with the vice president's laptop.

There are "white-hat" organizations that monitor hackers and their activities and then publish their findings on web pages. The web pages explain in very simple language how to perpetrate all know hacking activities. The sites then explain how network administrators can protect themselves from each hacking approach. These sites provide information system managers with a valuable way to learn about the latest security threats and how to protect themselves from those threats.

Monitor System Activities. All system transactions and activities should be recorded in a log. The log should indicate who accessed what data, when, and from which terminal. These logs should be reviewed frequently to monitor system activity and trace any problems to their source.

There are a number of risk analysis and management software packages that can review computer systems and networks. These systems evaluate security measures already in place and test for weaknesses and vulnerabilities. A series of reports is then generated that explain the weaknesses found and suggest improvements. Cost parameters can be entered so that a company can balance acceptable levels of vulnerability and cost-effectiveness. There are also intrusion-detection programs and software utilities that can detect illegal entry into systems.

Use Forensic Accountants. **Forensic accountants** specialize in fraud auditing and investigation. In the past few years it has been the fastest-growing area in accounting. Many forensic accountants have degrees in accounting and have received specialized training with the FBI, the IRS, or other law enforcement agencies. A new professional designation has also been created to recognize this field. The Association of Certified Fraud Examiners in Austin, Texas has developed a Certified Fraud Examiner certification program. To become a CFE, candidates must pass a two-day exam. Today there are more than 15,000 CFEs scattered all over the world.

Use Fraud Detection Software. People who commit fraud tend to follow certain patterns and leave behind telltale clues, such as things that do not make sense. Software has been developed to search out these fraud symptoms. For example, a health insurance company could use fraud detection software to look at how often procedures are performed, whether a diagnosis and the procedures performed fit a patient's profile, how long a procedure takes, and how far patients live from the doctor's office. ReliaStar Financial used a fraud detection package from IBM to detect

- Hundreds of thousands of dollars in fraudulent claims from a Los Angeles chiropractor. The software noticed that all of the chiropractor's patients lived more than 50 miles from the doctor's office and flagged the bills for investigation.
- A Long Island ear, nose, and throat doctor who was submitting bills weekly for a rare and expensive procedure that is normally done only once or twice in a lifetime.
- A podiatrist who saw four patients and then billed ReliaStar for almost 500 separate procedures.

Other companies have **neural networks** (programs that mimic the brain and are able to learn new things) that are quite accurate in identifying suspected fraud. For example, the Visa and MasterCard operation at Mellon Bank uses neural network software to track 1.2 million accounts. Its neural network can spot the illegal use of a credit card and notify the owner shortly after it is stolen. The software can also spot trends before bank investigators do. For example, one investigator learned about a new scam from another bank. When he went to the system to have it check for the scam, he noticed that the neural network had already identified the scam and had printed out a list of transactions that fit its pattern. The software cost Mellon Bank less than $1 million and paid for itself in six months.

Reduce Fraud Losses

No matter how hard a company tries to prevent fraud, chances are that it will occur. Therefore, an important strategy is to seek to minimize potential fraud losses. Some of these methods include the following:

- Maintain adequate insurance.
- Keep a current backup copy of all program and data files in a secure off-site location.
- Develop a contingency plan for fraud occurrences and other disasters that might occur.
- Use special software designed to monitor system activity and help companies recover from frauds and malicious actions. One such software utility helped a company recover from a rampage caused by a disgruntled employee who had received a negative performance evaluation. The perpetrator ripped cards and cables out of PCs, changed the inventory control files, and edited the password file to stop people from logging onto the LAN. Shortly after the incident, the software identified the corrupted files and flashed an alert to company headquarters. The damage was undone by issuing simple commands to the utility software, which restored the corrupted file to its original status.

Prosecute and Incarcerate Fraud Perpetrators

Most fraud cases go unreported and unprosecuted for several reasons. First, many cases of computer fraud are as yet undetected. Second, companies are reluctant to report computer crimes because a highly visible computer fraud is a public relations disaster. Fraud also reveals the vulnerability of its system, possibly attracting more acts of fraud. Unreported fraud creates a false sense of security; people think systems are more secure than they really are.

Third, law enforcement officials and the courts are so busy with violent crimes that they have little time for fraud cases where no physical harm is present. All too often, prosecuting attorneys treat teen hacking and cracking as a childish prank and let them plea bargain down to a misdemeanor.

A fourth reason fraud goes unreported is that it is difficult, costly, and time-consuming to investigate. Successfully prosecuting computer fraud cases is difficult. Until 1986, law enforcement officials did not have a law that dealt specifically with computer crimes. As a result, they had to prosecute using laws written for other purposes. This problem was partially resolved when the U.S. Congress passed the Computer Fraud and Abuse Act of 1986. The law covers computers used by the federal government, financial institutions, and certain medical organizations. It also covers computers used in interstate or foreign commerce. The law makes it illegal to knowingly gain access to computers with intent to defraud. Trafficking in computer access passwords is also prohibited.

The crime is a felony if more than $1,000 worth of software is damaged or if money, goods, or services are stolen. The penalties are severe: 1–5 years for the first offense, 10 for the second, and 20 for the third and subsequent offenses. Fines can be up to $250,000 or twice the value of the stolen data. Although the law has resulted in increased prosecutions, many say it is vague and unclear and an easy target for defense attorneys. The laws are supplemented by computer fraud statutes in all 50 states.

A fifth reason for unreported fraud is that many law enforcement officials, lawyers, and judges lack the computer skills needed to investigate, prosecute, and evaluate computer crimes. Increased training, which is time-consuming and costly, is necessary in order for officials to understand and detect computer fraud.

Finally, when fraud cases are prosecuted and a conviction is obtained, the sentences received are often very light. For example, Judge John Lord, when sentencing convicted white-collar criminals, stated that the perpetrators were God-fearing, highly civic-minded men, who had spent their lifetimes in sincere and honest dedication and service to their families, churches, country, and communities. He said he could never send them to jail. One investigator noted that the average sentence for a fraud perpetrator was one year in jail for every $10 million stolen.

One of the most famous cases of a light sentence involved C. Arnoldt Smith, former owner of the San Diego Padres baseball team who was named Mr. San Diego of the Century. Smith was very involved in the community and made large political contributions. When investigations showed that he had stolen $200 million from his bank, he pleaded nolo contendere (no contest). He was given a sentence of four years probation and a fine of $30,000. The fine was to be paid at the rate of $100 a month for the following 25 years, with no interest. Mr. Smith was 71 at the time. The embezzled money was never recovered.

SUMMARY AND CASE CONCLUSION

Jason Scott believed Don Hawkins had committed a fraud, but he needed more details to support that conclusion. In preparation for his meeting with management, he expanded the scope of his investigation. A week later Jason presented his findings to the president of Northwest. To introduce the problem and to make it hit a little closer to home, Jason presented the president with a copy of his own withholding report filed with the IRS and pointed out the president's withholdings. Then he showed him a printout of withholdings from the payroll records and pointed out the $5 difference, as well as the difference of several thousand dollars in Don Hawkins's withholdings. This immediately got the president's attention, and Jason proceeded to tell him how he believed a fraud had been perpetrated.

During the latter part of the prior year, the payroll system had undergone some minor modifications. Don had been in charge of the project. Due to pressing problems with several other projects, the payroll project had been completed without the usual review by other systems personnel. Jason arranged for a member of the audit staff, who was a former programmer, to review the code changes. She found a few lines of unusual code in the program for generating the withholdings report for the IRS. The code subtracted $5 from most employee's withholdings and added it to Don's. Don got his hands on the money when the IRS sent him a huge refund check.

It appeared that Don intended to use the scheme every year, since he had not removed the incriminating code. He must have been fairly confident of his scheme, because he had not tried to modify the company's copy of the withholdings report. Somehow he knew there was no reconciliation of withholdings from the payroll records with the IRS report. It was a simple plan, and it could have gone undetected for years if Jason had not overheard someone in the cafeteria talk about a $5 difference.

Jason quietly investigated Don and found he had a reputation of being hard to work with. He had been passed over last year for a managerial position in the programming department and had been unhappy ever since. He made numerous comments to coworkers about favoritism and unfair treatment. He even mentioned getting even with the company somehow. Don had also recently purchased a fairly expensive sports car. No one knew where he got the money, but did mention to a coworker that he had made a sizable down payment when he bought the car in April.

When the president asked the inevitable question of how the company could prevent this type of thing from happening again, Jason suggested the following guidelines:

1. A review of the company's internal controls should be conducted to analyze their effectiveness in preventing fraud. One control that already existed, reviewing program changes, could have prevented Don's scheme had it been followed. As a result, Jason suggested a stricter enforcement of the existing controls.
2. New controls should be put into place to detect fraud. For example, he suggested a reconciliation of the withholdings on the IRS report with those on the payroll records.
3. Employees should be trained in fraud awareness, security measures, and ethical issues.

Jason also urged the president to prosecute the case. The president was reluctant to do so because of the adverse publicity and the problems it would cause for Don's wife and children. Jason's supervisor tactfully suggested that if other employees found out that Don was not prosecuted, it would send the wrong message to the rest of the company. The president finally conceded to prosecute if the company could prove that Don was guilty. The president agreed to hire a forensic accountant to build a stronger case against Don and try to get him to confess.

KEY TERMS

fraud
white-collar criminals
misappropriation of assets
employee fraud
fraudulent financial reporting
lapping
kiting
pressure
opportunity
rationalization
computer fraud
economic espionage
employee goofing
Trojan horse
round-down technique
salami technique
trap door
superzapping
software piracy
data diddling
data leakage
piggybacking
masquerading
impersonation
social engineering
logic time bomb
hacking
cracking
scavenging
dumpster diving
eavesdropping
wiretap
e-mail threats
e-mail forgery
denial of service attack
e-mail bombs
Internet terrorism
Internet misinformation
war dialing
password cracking
spamming
computer virus
worm
phreakers
random surveillance
computer security officer
forensic accountants
neural networks

CHAPTER QUIZ

1. A fraud in which later payments on account are used to pay off earlier payments that were stolen is called
   a. lapping.
   b. kiting.
   c. a Ponzi scheme.
   d. the salami technique.

2. Which type of fraud is associated with as many as 50% of all lawsuits against auditors?
   a. Kiting
   b. Fraudulent financial reporting
   c. Ponzi schemes
   d. Lapping

3. Which of the following statements is false?
   a. The psychological profiles of white-collar criminals differ from those of violent criminals.
   b. The psychological profiles of white-collar criminals differ from those of the general public.
   c. Computer fraud perpetrators are often different from other types of white-collar criminals.
   d. Computer fraud perpetrators often do not view themselves as criminals.

4. Which of the following conditions are usually necessary in order for a fraud to occur? (There is more than one right answer.)
   a. Pressures
   b. Opportunities
   c. Explanations
   d. Rationalizations

5. All of the following are examples of computer fraud except
   a. theft of money by altering computer records.
   b. intent to obtain information illegally through use of a computer.
   c. failure to perform preventive maintenance on a computer.
   d. unauthorized modification of a software program.

6. A set of instructions to increase a programmer's pay rate by 10% is hidden inside an authorized program. It changes and updates payroll files. This computer fraud technique is called a
   a. virus.
   b. worm.
   c. trap door.
   d. Trojan horse.

7. A set of instructions hidden inside a calendar utility that copies itself until memory is filled and the system crashes is a computer fraud technique called a
   a. logic bomb.
   b. worm.
   c. virus.
   d. Trojan horse.

8. Which of the following control procedures is most likely to deter lapping?

a. Encryption
b. Continual update of the access control matrix
c. A background check on employees
d. Periodic rotation of duties

9. Which of the following is the most important, basic, and effective control to deter fraud?

a. Enforced vacations
b. Logical access control
c. Segregation of duties
d. Virus protection controls

10. Which of the following are methods of reducing fraud losses? (There may be more than one right answer.)

a. Insurance
b. Regular backup of data and programs
c. A contingency plan
d. Segregation of duties

DISCUSSION QUESTIONS

10.1 Do you agree that the most effective method of obtaining adequate system security is to rely on the integrity of company employees? Why or why not? Does this seem ironic? What measures should a company take to ensure the integrity of its employees?

10.2 You are the president of a multinational company. One of your senior executives confessed to kiting $100,000. Explain what kiting is and what your company can do to prevent it. How would you respond to your employee's confession? What issues must you consider before pressing formal charges?

10.3 One December morning, the computers at U.S. Leasing Company began acting sluggish. Computer operators were relieved when a software troubleshooter from Digital Equipment called several hours later. They were more than happy to let him help correct the problem they were having with the Digital software. The troubleshooter asked for a phone number for the computers as well as a log-on number and passwords—a common procedure employed by Digital in handling software problems.

The next morning, the computers were worse. A call to Digital confirmed U.S. Leasing's suspicion: Someone had impersonated a Digital repairman to gain unauthorized access to the system and destroy the entire computer data base. U.S. Leasing was also concerned that the intruder had devised a program that would let him get back into the system even after all the passwords were changed.

What techniques might the imposter have employed to breach U.S. Leasing's internal security? What could U.S. Leasing do to avoid these types of incidents in the future?

10.4 To address the need for tighter data controls and lower support costs, Manufacturers Hanover has adopted a new diskless PC. It is little more than a mutilated personal computer described as a "gutless wonder." The concept behind the diskless PC is simple: A LAN server-based file system of high-powered diskless workstations is spread throughout an organization and connected with a central repository or mainframe. The network improves control by limiting user access to company data previously stored on desktop hard disks. Since the user can destroy or delete only the information currently on the screen, a company's financial data is protected from user-instigated catastrophes. The diskless computer also saves money in user support costs by distributing applications and upgrades automatically, as well by offering on-line help.

What threats in the information processing and storage system does the diskless PC minimize? Do the security advantages of the new system outweigh potential limitations?

10.5 Biometric security systems are becoming a cost-effective solution to the troubling problem of computer security. Biometric security devices measure our unique physical traits, such as speech patterns, eye and finger physiology, and written signature dynamics. The ideal system must be reliable and yet flexible enough to handle minor changes in physical characteristics such as a cut finger or a hoarse voice. The system also requires that the user be physically present to gain access to the system. Hertz and Security Pacific Bank are two companies seeking to use the new technology. For both companies the security devices will aid in ensuring that only authorized individuals have access to computer systems and their related operations.

Why are biometric security devices increasing in popularity? What are the advantages and disadvantages of these systems in comparison with traditional security measures (passwords, locked doors, etc.)?

10.6 A few days after the inventory control system for Revlon, the cosmetics giant, went down, officials discovered that the downtime was caused by Logisticon, a software developer. Seven months earlier, Revlon had signed an agreement to have Logisticon install a real-time invoice and inventory processing system. Prior to completion of phase I of the project, Revlon discovered a series of programming bugs. Revlon proceeded to withhold any additional payment on the contract to Logisticon. Logisticon contended that the software was fine but that the computer hardware was faulty. When Revlon refused payment, Logisticon sought repossession: It used a telephone dial-in feature in the software to make a disabling phone call and render the system unusable.

After a three-day standoff, Logisticon reactivated Revlon's inventory system. Revlon filed suit in California Superior Court charging Logisticon with trespassing, breach of contract, and misappropriation of trade secrets (use of Revlon passwords). Logisticon filed a countersuit for breach of contract. Revlon and Logisticon later settled out of court.

Would Logisticon's actions be classified as sabotage or repossession? Why? Would you find the company guilty of committing a computer crime? Be prepared to defend your position to the class.

10.7 Improved computer security measures create their own set of problems: user antagonism, sluggish response time, and hampered performance. Many professionals feel that the most effective way to promote computer security is to educate users about good moral conduct. According to Richard Stallman, president of the Free Software Foundation, MIT programmer, and computer activist, software licensing is antisocial because it prohibits the growth of the technology by keeping information away from your neighbors. He believes high school and college students should have unlimited access to computers without security measures in order to teach constructive and civilized behavior. He states that a protected system is a puzzle and, since it is human nature to solve puzzles, eliminating computer security so that there is no temptation to break in would reduce hacking.

Do you agree with Stallman's statements? Do you agree that software licensing is antisocial? Is ethical teaching the solution to computer security problems? Would the removal of computer security measures reduce the incidence of computer fraud? Why or why not?

10.8 Discuss the following statement by Roswell Steffen, a convicted embezzler: "For every foolproof system, there is a method for beating it." Do you believe a completely secure computer system is possible? Explain. If internal controls are less than 100% effective, why should they be employed at all?

10.9 What motives do people have for hacking? Why has hacking become so popular in recent years? Do you regard it as a crime? Explain your position.

PROBLEMS

10.1 An experienced senior auditor was assigned to investigate a possible fraudulent situation characterized by extremely high, unexplained merchandise shortages at one location of the company's department store chain. During the course of the investigation, the auditor determined the following:

1. The supervisor of the receiving department was the owner and operator of a small boutique carrying many of the same labels as the chain store. The chain store's general manager was unaware of the ownership interest.
2. The receiving supervisor signed receiving reports showing that the total quantity shipped by a vendor had been received. A total of 5% to 10% of each shipment was diverted to the boutique.
3. The chain's buyers were unaware of the short shipments, because the receiving supervisor would enter the correct quantity on the move ticket accompanying the merchandise to the sales areas.
4. The chain's accounts payable department paid vendors for the total quantity shown on the receiving report.
5. Based on the supervisor's instructions, quantities on the move tickets were not compared with those on the receiving report.

Required:

Classify each of the five situations as a fraudulent act, an indicator of fraud, or an event unrelated to the investigation. Justify your answers.

(CIA Examination, adapted)

10.2 A small but growing firm has recently hired you to investigate a potential fraud. The company heard through its hot line that the purchases journal clerk periodically enters fictitious acquisitions. The nonexistent vendor's address is given as a post office box, which is rented by the clerk. He forwards notification of the fictitious purchases for recording in the accounts payable ledger. Payment is ultimately mailed to the post office box. He then deposits the check in an account established in the name of the nonexistent vendor.

Required:

a. Define fraud, fraud deterrence, fraud detection, and fraud investigation.
b. List four red-flag indicators (personal as opposed to organizational) that might point to the existence of fraud in this example.
c. List two procedures you could follow to uncover the fraudulent behavior of the purchases journal clerk in this situation.

(CIA Examination, adapted)

10.3 Most experts maintain that the computer frauds publicly revealed represent only the tip of the iceberg. Although the major threat to computer security is perceived by many to be external, the more dangerous threats come from insiders. Management must recognize these problems and develop and enforce security programs to deal with the many types of computer fraud.

Required:

Explain how each of the following six types of fraud is committed. Also, identify a different method of protection for each and describe how it works. Use the following format.

Type of Fraud	Explanation	Identification and Description of Protection Methods

a. Input manipulation
b. Program alteration
c. File alteration
d. Data theft
e. Sabotage
f. Theft of computer time

(CMA Examination, adapted)

10.4 The Treadway Commission study shows that fraudulent financial reporting usually occurs as the result of environmental, institutional, or individual influences and opportune situations. These influences and opportunities, present to some degree in all companies, motivate individuals and companies to engage in fraudulent financial reporting. The prevention and detection of fraudulent financial reporting requires that these influences and opportunities be identified and evaluated in terms of the risks they pose to a company. These risk factors include internal ethical and control factors as well as external environmental conditions.

Required:

a. Identify two company situational pressures that would increase the likelihood of fraud.
b. Identify three corporate opportunities that make fraud easier to commit and detection less likely.
c. For each of the following, identify the external environmental factors that should be considered in assessing the risk of fraudulent financial reporting.
   1. The company's industry
   2. The company's business environment
   3. The company's legal and regulatory environment
d. According to the Treadway Commission, what can top management do to reduce the possibility of fraudulent financial reporting?

(CMA Examination, adapted)

10.5 The impact of employee and management fraud is staggering both in terms of dollar costs and the effect on the victims. For each of the following independent cases of employee fraud, describe the recommendations internal auditors should make to prevent similar problems from occurring in the future.

a. A retail store that was part of a national chain experienced an abnormal inventory shrinkage in its audiovisual department. The internal auditors, noting this shrinkage, included an in-depth evaluation of the department in the scope of their store audit. During their review the auditors were tipped off by an employee that a particular customer bought a large number of small electronic components and that the customer always went to a certain cashier's checkout line. The auditors' work revealed that the cashier and the customer had colluded to steal a number of electronic components. The cashier did not record the sale of several items the customer took from the store.

b. During an unannounced visit to a large hospital, internal auditors discovered a payroll fraud when they observed the distribution of paychecks. The supervisors of each department distributed paychecks to employees and were supposed to return unclaimed checks to the payroll department. When the auditors took control of, and followed up on, an unclaimed paycheck for an employee in the food service department, they discovered that the employee had quit four months previously. The employee and the supervisor had had an argument, and the employee had simply left and never returned. The supervisor had continued to turn in a time card for the employee and had taken the unclaimed checks and cashed them.

c. While performing an audit of cash disbursements at a manufacturing firm, internal auditors discovered a fraud committed by an accounts payable clerk. She made copies of supporting documents and used them to support duplicate payments to a vendor of manufacturing materials. The clerk, who had opened a bank account in a name similar to that of the vendor, took the duplicate checks and deposited them in her bank account.

(CMA Examination, adapted)

10.6 Rent-A-Wreck's policy requires a "sealed bid" to sell motor vehicles that are no longer efficient. In reviewing the sale of some vehicles that had been declared obsolete, the auditor found that management had not always complied with the stated policy. Records indicated that several vehicles on which major repairs had recently been performed were sold at negotiated prices. The auditor was assured by management that by performing limited repairs and negotiating with knowledgeable buyers, better prices had been obtained for the salvaged vehicles than had the required sealed-bid procedures been followed. The auditor suspected that there might be more involved than management indicated. Further investigation revealed that the vehicles had been sold to employees at negotiated prices well below market value. The auditor's work eventually resulted in three managers and five other employees pleading guilty to criminal charges and making restitution to the organization.

Required:

a. Based on this scenario, outline the symptoms or indications of possible fraud that would have aroused the auditor's suspicion.
b. Suggest audit procedures that the auditor could have employed to establish the fact that fraud had in fact occurred.

(CIA Examination, adapted)

10.7 On March 6, the computer world braced for a shock. News began circulating months before about a computer virus named Michelangelo that was set to "ignite" on the birthday of the famous Italian artist. The virus itself was spread via floppy disks used with IBM compatible PCs. When a software package containing the virus was introduced to the computer system, the virus would attach to the computer's operating system boot sector. On the magical date the virus would release itself, freezing the system's boot function and destroying all of its data.

When March 6 arrived, the virus did minimal damage. Preventive techniques limited the damage to isolated personal and business computers. Though the excitement surrounding the virus was largely illusory, Michelangelo helped the computer-using public realize their own system's vulnerability to outside attack.

Required:

a. What is a computer virus? Cite at least three reasons why no system is completely safe from a computer virus.
b. Why do viruses represent a serious threat to information systems? What damage can a virus do to a computer system?
c. Why is a virus often classified as a Trojan horse?
d. What steps can individuals and companies take to prevent the spread or propagation of a computer virus?

10.8 The auditor of a bank is called to a meeting with a senior operations manager because of a customer's report that an auto loan payment was not credited. According to the customer, the payment was made at a teller's window using a check drawn on an account in that bank. The payment was made on its due date, May 5. On May 10 the customer decided to sell the car and called the bank for a payoff on the loan. The payment had not been credited to the loan. The customer came to the bank on May 12 to inquire about the payment and meet with the manager. The manager found that the payment had been credited the night before the meeting (as of May 11); the customer was satisfied since no late charge would have been assessed until May 15. The manager asked whether the auditor was comfortable with this situation.

The auditor located the customer's paid check in the deposit department and found that it had cleared as of May 5. The auditor traced the item back through the computer entry records and found that the check had been processed by the teller as a cashed check. The auditor traced the payment through the entry records of May 11 and found that the payment had been made with cash instead of a check.

Required:

What type of embezzlement scheme does this appear to be, and how does that scheme operate?

(CIA Examination, adapted)

10.9 It was a typical Wednesday on the UCLA campus when everything began going wrong in the student computer lab. The computer lab was filled to capacity as the end of the semester neared. Nearly 70 students were logged into the UCLA computer network, run by Netware software, when the system came to a halt. Students tried running software without success, and many students could not even log in without getting a frustrating ABORT RETRY message from the Netware operating system.

System directors initially expected a cable break or an operating system failure as the culprit, but diagnostics revealed nothing. After several frustrating hours a staff member began running the SCAN virus detection program and uncovered a Jerusalem virus on the lab's main server. The virus was eventually traced to floppy disks used by unsuspecting UCLA students. When staff workers used the infected computers to gain supervisor access to the operating system, the virus spread.

The virus cost UCLA about 25 person-hours and disrupted the lives of frantic students preparing for finals. Later that evening the system was brought back on-line after infected files were replaced with backup copies.

Required:

a. What conditions made the UCLA system a potential breeding ground for the Jerusalem virus?
b. What symptoms indicated that a virus was present?
c. What advice would you give UCLA's director of computing to prevent the same incident from recurring?

CASE 10.1 KEVIN MITNICK: THE DARK-SIDE HACKER

No one is entirely certain when Kevin Mitnick's "professional" hacking career began. During his mid-teens, Kevin was a part of the phone phreak subculture in California. By their own definition, phone phreaks were telephone hobbyists more expert at understanding the workings of the Bell system than most Bell employees. Using their knowledge of the phone system and computers, phreaks would often arrange free phone service, long-distance calling, and airline tickets for friends.

In spite of his unique talents, Kevin never sought pay for his efforts. His reward came in defeating the computer system and gaining power and control over others in the process. The phone phreak logo said it all: If it could be done, it was legal. When Kevin's telecommunications hobby culminated in one of the boldest acts of computer piracy, no one was the least bit surprised.

As the manager of research and development for the University of Southern California's (USC) computer services, Mark Brown was all too familiar with the threat of unauthorized break-ins. Most of the hackers were harmless, many just wanting to take a look around. One day, Mark began a low-key investigation of some intruders and discovered that they were accessing the USC system through a modification in the Gatekeeper subprogram of the computer's VMS operating system.

A few days later Mark's amusement turned to concern as he noted that storage space was disappearing from the computer system at an alarming rate. After a more thorough investigation, Mark discovered that the intruders were storing vast amounts of information in bogus system index files. When Mark opened the files, he was alarmed to find a source code copy of the newest version of the Digital VMS operating system.

Source code represents the lifeblood of software development. Computer programs are written in a user-friendly source code language and then converted into unreadable binary code for distribution.

Such a process allowed software developers to protect the integrity of their programs from alterations and modifications from outside sources. Digital's source code had clearly been compromised.

Mark immediately called Digital Equipment to inform them of his discovery. He was surprised by the guarded reception he received from Digital representatives. Digital asked Mark to continue monitoring the intruders and keep careful logs of all suspicious activities.

Kevin and his friend Lenny DiCicco had years of experience with computers, networks, and VMS operating systems. They used that knowledge, the computer at Voluntary Plan Administrators (VPA), Lenny's workplace, and a list of stolen MCI long-distance accounts to exploit Digital's Easynet network. They gained access through an operating system bug in Easynet and sent a copy of the VMS operating system to the USC computer. With help from a friend the data was retrieved from the USC computer and stored on magnetic disk. From their viewpoint their actions were harmless; they were not really stealing because they never tried marketing the software.

However, Kevin was not satisfied with a copy of the VMS source code. He also wanted a copy of the source code for Doom, a lucrative game developed by Digital. When Lenny refused to help, Kevin became angry and began harassing him at work. When Lenny's boss called him into his office to discuss these problems, he came unglued. His boss, Ralph Hurley, was stunned when Lenny confessed to using VPA's computer to exploit Digital Equipment. Ralph convinced Lenny to call Digital and relate a similar confession to a Digital security team.

A Digital security expert, accompanied by an FBI agent, arrived the following morning to verify Lenny's claims and to compare them with the statements made by Mark Brown from USC. With Lenny's help the police spent the evening monitoring Kevin as he logged onto Digital's Easynet system with the VPA computer system.

Kevin kept much of his pirated software in a duffel bag in his car. Hoping to catch Kevin with stolen software and data, the FBI had Lenny ask if he could make copies of some of Kevin's pirated software. When Kevin went to the car and retrieved the duffel bag, the police made the arrest.

Kevin was charged with four felony counts, including unauthorized computer entry, theft of data, and software piracy. Hoping to avoid additional publicity, Digital sought a plea-bargain arrangement. Although the judge initially rejected the plea bargain, the arrangement was eventually made and Kevin was sentenced to one year in prison and six months in a rehabilitation program working to overcome his obsession with computer piracy. For his role in the crime Lenny received five years probation after pleading guilty to one felony count.

1. What is source code and what role does it play in software design and maintenance? What is the danger of having source code exposed to unauthorized users?
2. In what ways do Kevin and Lenny represent typical white-collar computer criminals? How are they different?
3. What were the hackers' motives for entering Digital's Easynet network without authorization? What rationale did Kevin and Lenny use to justify their invasion of the Easynet network?
4. How were the hackers so readily able to gain access to the USC computers as well as to Digital's Easynet? What steps should Digital take to minimize the impact of computer crime on its operations in the future?
5. Discuss whether or not Digital Equipment should have pressed charges against Kevin and Lenny for their piracy of Digital's VMS operating system source code.
   a. What charges should have been brought against the hackers?
   b. What impact would publicity have had on Digital Equipment?

Source: Katie Hafner and John Markoff, *Cyberpunk* (New York: Simon and Schuster, 1991).

CASE 10.2 DAVID L. MILLER: PORTRAIT OF A WHITE-COLLAR CRIMINAL

There is an old saying in crime-fighting circles: Crime doesn't pay. However, for David Miller crime has paid rich dividends. It paid for two Mercedes-Benz sedans, a $280,000 suburban house, a condominium at Myrtle Beach, South Carolina, $500 suits, and $75 tailored, monogrammed shirts. It also paid for diamond, sapphire, ruby, and emerald rings for his wife and a new car for his father-in-law. Though he has confessed to embezzling funds from six different employers over a 20-year period, he has never been prosecuted and has never been incarcerated. In large part Miller's freedom is the result of the fear that companies have about turning in employees who defraud them.

Miller's first employer was also his first victim. In 1965, after ten months of selling insurance in Wheeling, West Virginia, he was fired for stealing about $200. After an assortment of odd jobs he moved to Ohio and worked as an accountant for a local baker. Miller was caught embezzling funds and paid back the $1,000 he had stolen. Again, he was not reported to the authorities and was quietly dismissed.

Miller returned to Wheeling and went to work for Wheeling Bronze, Inc., a bronze-castings maker. In December 1971 the president of Wheeling Bronze discovered that several returned checks were missing and that there was a $30,000 cash shortfall. After an extensive search, workers uncovered a number of canceled checks with forged signatures in an outdoor sandpile. Miller was questioned and confessed to the scheme. He was given the choice of paying back the stolen amount or going to jail. Miller's parents took out a mortgage on their home to pay back the stolen money. No charges were ever filed, and Miller was dismissed.

Several months later Miller found a job in Pennsylvania working for Robinson Pipe Cleaning. When Miller was caught embezzling funds, he again avoided prosecution by promising to repay the $20,000 he had stolen.

In 1974 Crest Industries hired Miller as an accountant. Miller proved to be the ideal employee and was quickly promoted to the position of office manager. He was very dedicated, worked long hours, and did outstanding work. Soon after his promotion he purchased a new home, a new car, and a new wardrobe.

In 1976 Miller's world unraveled again when Crest's auditors discovered that $31,000 was missing. Once again there was a tearful confession and a promise to repay all money stolen. Miller confessed that he had written several checks to himself and had then recorded payments to vendors on the carbon copies of the checks. To cover his tracks, he intercepted and altered the company's monthly bank statements. He had used the money he had stolen to finance his lifestyle and to repay Wheeling Bronze and Robinson Pipe Cleaning.

Miller claimed in his confession that he had never before embezzled funds. He showed a great deal of remorse, so much so that Crest even hired a lawyer for him. He gave Crest a lien on his house, and he was quietly dismissed. Because the president of Crest did not want the publicity to harm Miller's wife and three children, Crest never pressed charges against him.

Miller next took a job as an accountant in Steubenville, Ohio with Rustcraft Broadcasting Company, a chain of radio and TV stations. Rustcraft was acquired in 1979 by Associated Communications, and Miller moved to Pittsburgh to become Associated's new controller.

Miller immediately began dipping into Associated's accounts. Over a six-year period he embezzled approximately $1.36 million, $445,000 of that in 1984 when Miller was promoted to CFO. Miller used various methods to embezzle the money. One approach to circumvent the need for two signatures on every check was to ask another executive who was leaving on vacation to sign several checks "just in case" the company needed additional cash while he was gone. Miller used most of these checks to siphon funds off to his personal account. To cover the theft, Miller retrieved the canceled check from the bank reconciliation and destroyed it. The amount stolen was then charged to an expense account of one of the units to balance the company's books.

While working at Associated, Miller was able to lead a very comfortable lifestyle. He bought a new house and several expensive cars. He bought vacation property and a very expensive wardrobe, and he was very generous with tips and gifts. The lifestyle could not have been supported by his $130,000 salary, yet no one at Associated ever questioned the source of his conspicuous consumption.

Miller's lifestyle came crashing down in December 1984 while he was on vacation. A bank officer called to inquire about a check written to Mr. Miller. An investigation ensued, and Miller confessed to embezzling funds. As part of the 1985 out-of-court settlement with Miller, Associated Communications received most of Miller's personal property.

Miller cannot explain why he was never prosecuted. He always insisted that he was going to pay the company back. Such statements would usually satisfy his employers and get him off the hook. He believes that these agreements actually contributed to his subsequent thefts. For example, one rationale for starting to steal from a new employer was to pay back the former one.

After leaving Associated, Miller was hired by a former colleague. Miller underwent therapy and believed he had resolved his problem with compulsive embezzlement.

When interviewed about his past activities, Miller said that he felt his problem with theft was an illness, just like alcoholism or compulsive gambling. The illness was driven by a subconscious need to be admired and liked by others. He thought that by spending money, others would like him. Ironically, he was universally well liked and admired at each job, and it had nothing to do with money. In fact, one associate at Associated was so surprised at the news of the thefts that he said that it was like finding out that your brother was an ax murderer. In the interview Miller also claimed that he is not a bad person. He says he never intended to hurt anyone, but once he got started, he just could not stop.

1. How does Miller fit the profile of the average fraud perpetrator? How does he differ? How did these characteristics make him difficult to detect?
2. Discuss the threefold fraud process (theft, conversion, concealment) Miller followed in embezzling funds from Associated Communications. What specific concealment techniques did Miller use?
3. What pressures motivated Miller to embezzle? What opportunities allowed him to steal and cover up his theft? How did Miller rationalize his actions?
4. Miller had a framed T-shirt in his office that said, "He who dies with the most toys wins." What does this tell you about Miller? What lifestyle red flags could have tipped off the company to the possibility of fraud?
5. Identify several reasons that companies hesitate in prosecuting white-collar criminals. What are the problems with such rationalizations? What could law enforcement officials do to encourage more rigorous prosecution of white-collar criminals?
6. Identify the primary action each of the victimized companies could have done to prevent Miller's embezzlement. What other controls could help in preventing future fraud?

Source: Bryan Burrough, "David L. Miller Stole from His Employer and Isn't in Prison," *Wall Street Journal* (September 19, 1986): 1.

CASE 10.3 LEXSTEEL CORPORATION

Lexsteel Corporation is a leading manufacturer of steel furniture. While the company has manufacturing plants and distribution facilities throughout the United States, the purchasing, accounting, and treasury functions are centralized at corporate headquarters in Fresno, California.

While discussing a recent management letter with the external auditors, Ray Landsdown, controller of Lexsteel, became aware of potential problems with the accounts payable system. The auditors had to perform additional audit procedures to attest to the validity of accounts payable and cutoff procedures. The auditors have recommended a detailed systems study of the current procedures to assess the company's exposure to potential embezzlement and fraud and to identify ways to improve management controls.

Landsdown has assigned the study task to Dolores Smith, a relatively new accountant in the department. Because Smith could not find adequate documentation of the accounts payable procedures, she interviewed those employees involved and constructed a flowchart of the current system. This flowchart is shown in Fig. 10.3, and descriptions of the current procedures follow.

Computer Resources

The host computer mainframe is located at corporate headquarters with interactive, remote job entry terminals at each branch location. In general, data entry occurs at the source and is transmitted to an integrated data base maintained on the host computer. Data transmission occurs over leased telephone lines between the branch offices and the host computer. The software allows flexibility for managing user access and editing data input.

Procedures for Purchasing Raw Materials

Production orders and appropriate bills of material are generated by the host computer at corporate headquarters. From these bills of material, purchase orders for raw materials are generated by the centralized purchasing function and mailed directly to the vendors. Each purchase order instructs the vendor to ship the materials directly to the appropriate

FIGURE 10.3
Accounts Payable Procedures at Lexsteel

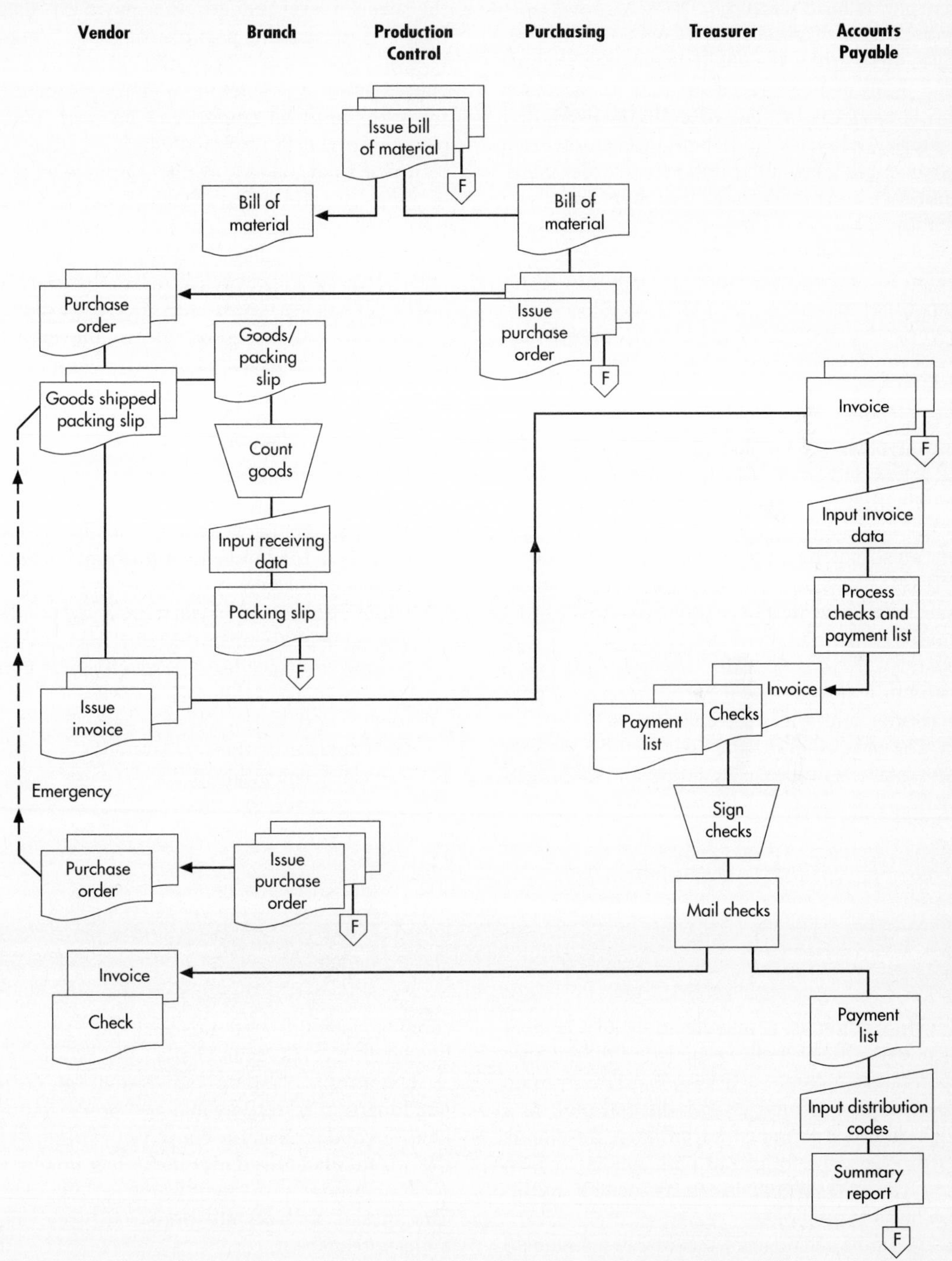

manufacturing plant. Assuming that the necessary purchase orders have been issued, the manufacturing plants proceed with the production orders received from corporate headquarters.

Upon receipt of goods, the manufacturing plant examines and verifies the count against the packing slip and transmits the receiving data to accounts payable at corporate headquarters. In the event that raw material deliveries fall behind production, each branch manager is given the authority to order materials and issue emergency purchase orders directly to the vendors. Data about the emergency orders and verification of materials receipt is transmitted via computer to accounts payable at corporate headquarters. Since the company employs a cost-effective computerized perpetual inventory system, physical counts of raw materials are not performed.

Accounts Payable Procedures

Vendor invoices are mailed directly to corporate headquarters and entered by accounts payable personnel when received. This often occurs before the receiving data are transmitted from the branch offices. The final day the invoice can be paid is entered as the payment due date. This due date must often be calculated by the data entry person using information listed on the invoice.

Once a week, invoices due the following week are printed in chronological entry order on a payment listing, and the corresponding checks are drawn. The checks and thepayment listing are sent to the treasurer's office for signature and mailing to the payee. The check number is printed by the computer, displayed on the check and the payment listing, and validated as the checks are signed. After the checks are mailed, the payment listing is returned to accounts payable for filing. When there is insufficient cash to pay all the invoices, certain checks and the payment listing are retained by the treasurer until all checks can be paid. When the remaining checks are mailed, the listing is then returned to accounts payable. Often weekly check mailings include a few checks from the previous week, but rarely are there more than two weekly listings involved.

When accounts payable receives the payment listing back from the treasurer's office, the expenses are distributed, coded, and posted to the appropriate plant/cost center accounts. Weekly summary performance reports are processed by accounts payable for each cost center and branch location reflecting all data entry to that point.

1. Identify and discuss three areas where Lexsteel Corporation may be exposed to fraud or embezzlement due to weaknesses in the procedures described. Recommend improvements to correct these weaknesses.
2. Describe three areas where management information could be distorted due to weaknesses in Lexsteel's procedures. Recommend improvements to correct these weaknesses.
3. Identify three strengths in Lexsteel's procedures, and explain why they are strengths.

(CMA Examination, adapted)

CASE 10.4 WARD CORPORATION

Ward Corporation is a manufacturer of cleaning products with three wholly owned subsidiaries that are operated as separate divisions. Ward's corporate headquarters are located in an industrial park in a Chicago suburb. The industrial products division is located in the same industrial park but in its own building. The other two divisions are located in Milwaukee and Indianapolis.

The operating and financial records are maintained on a mainframe computer at corporate headquarters. Each division has a small accounting department that submits operating and financial data to corporate headquarters on a regular basis.

The profit planning department at corporate headquarters is responsible for preparing special analyses and reports for Ward. To facilitate its work, the profit planning department has linked a personal computer to the mainframe to download data. The special analyses are prepared using this data and a spreadsheet.

Beth Simons recently joined the industrial products division as an accounting analyst. Simons is proficient in the use of personal computers and spreadsheet software. She has been assigned to work with Doug Laird, marketing manager of the industrial products division, to develop analyses and reports. One week into the assignment, she suggested that the perconal computers used in the marketing department for word processing could be valuable analytical tools if spreadsheet software were acquired. Laird knows little about computers, but he has received some of the special analyses prepared by the profit planning department at corporate headquarters. Laird wants Simons to try her idea, but he has suggested that she first borrow the software from the profit planning department.

Simons approached Tom Field, manager of profit planning, regarding the use of the software package. Field was very sympathetic to Simons's request, but he did not want to loan the original system disk, since the software is used extensively in his department and was copy-protected. However, Field did have a utility program that allowed him to make backup copies of most copy-protected software. Since there was no backup of the spreadsheet software, Field decided to make a copy and give it to Simons for her use during regular business hours. His instructions were as follows: "This is my only copy, but you may borrow it for your use only. Don't give it to anyone else. Once you have tried the software for your assignment, you must return it to me. Industrial product's accounting or marketing department will have to purchase its own copy."

Field did not give Simons a copy of the licensing agreement that accompanied the original software package. The license agreement that follows was affixed to the original sealed disk package. Although Simons was not aware of the specific provisions of the licensing agreement that pertained to the borrowed software, she knew that licensing agreements accompanied computer software packages.

Software License Agreement

IMPORTANT: Please read this agreement before opening the envelope.

Opening the disk envelope indicates the user's acceptance of the agreement to abide by these terms.

1. The software may be used on any compatible hardware that the purchaser owns or uses.
2. Backup copies of the software can be made provided that these copies are for exclusive use of the purchaser and only one copy of the software is in use at any one time.
3. No alterations to the software or the documentation are permitted.
4. The software may not be distributed on a permanent or temporary basis.
5. This license and the software may be transferred to another party provided that all copies of the software and documentation are transferred and the original party ceases to use the software after the transfer.

Consider the stipulations set forth in the license agreement for the spreadsheet software.

1. Did Field violate the agreement when he made a copy of the software disk using the utility program?
2. Did Field violate the agreement when he gave Simons the copy of the software disk he had made?
3. Without prejudice to your answer in number 1, assume that Field did violate the license agreement when he copied the software disk and gave it to Simons. Identify Field's alternatives in determining whether the spreadsheet software meets the needs of the industrial products division's marketing department without violating the license agreement.

(CMA Examination, adapted)

ANSWERS TO CHAPTER QUIZ

1. a	**3.** b	**5.** c	**7.** c	**9.** c
2. b	**4.** a,b,d	**6.** d	**8.** d	**10.** a,b,c

CHAPTER 11

Auditing of Computer-Based Information Systems

LEARNING OBJECTIVES

After studying this chapter, you should be able to

- Describe the scope and objectives of audit work, and identify the major steps in the audit process.
- Identify the objectives of an information system (IS) audit, and describe the four-step approach necessary for meeting these objectives.
- Design a plan for the study and evaluation of internal control in an AIS.
- Describe computer audit software, and explain how it is used in the audit of an AIS.
- Describe the nature and scope of an operational audit.

Integrative Case: Seattle Paper Products(SPP)

Shortly after learning how to use a computer audit software package, Jason Scott was assigned to a project at Seattle Paper Products (SPP). SPP is modifying its sales department payroll system to change the way it calculates sales commissions. Under the old system, commissions were a fixed percentage of dollar sales. The new system is considerably more complex, with commission rates varying according to the product sold and the total dollar volume of sales.

Jason's assignment is to use the audit software to write a parallel simulation test program to calculate sales commissions and compare them with those generated by the new system. Jason obtained the necessary payroll system documentation and the details on the new sales commission policy. After a few days his program was ready to run.

Jason obtained the file containing sales transaction data from the last payroll period and used it to run his program. To his surprise, his calculations were $5,000 less than those produced by SPP's new program; in fact, individual differences existed for about half of the company's salespeople. Jason double-checked his program code but could not locate any errors. He selected a salesperson for whom there was a discrepancy and recalculated the commission by hand. The result agreed with his program. He reviewed the new commission policy with the sales manager, line by line, and concluded that he understood the new policy completely. Jason is now convinced that his program is correct and that the error lies with the new program. Based on this conclusion, he ponders the following questions:

1. How could a programming error of this significance be overlooked by experienced programmers who thoroughly reviewed and tested the new system?
2. Is this an inadvertent error, or could it be another attempted fraud?
3. What can be done to find the error in the program?

INTRODUCTION

This chapter focuses on the concepts and techniques used in auditing an AIS. Auditors are employed for a wide range of tasks and responsibilities. Many organizations employ internal auditors to evaluate company operations. The General Accounting Office and state governments employ auditors to evaluate management performance and compliance with legislative intent in government departments. The Department of Defense employs auditors to review the financial records of companies with defense contracts. Publicly held companies hire external auditors to provide an independent review of their financial statements.

This chapter is written primarily from the perspective of the internal auditor. Internal auditors are directly responsible for helping management improve organizational effectiveness and efficiency, including assisting in the design and implementation of an AIS that contributes to the organization's goals. In contrast, external auditors are primarily responsible to corporate shareholders and investors and are only indirectly concerned with the effectiveness of a corporate AIS. Despite this distinction, many of the internal audit concepts and techniques discussed in this chapter apply to external audits.

The first section of this chapter provides an overview of auditing, the scope and objectives of internal audit work, and the steps in the auditing process. Then a methodology and a set of techniques for evaluating internal controls in an AIS are described. The third section discusses techniques for evaluating the reliability and integrity of information in an AIS. Finally, operational audits of an AIS are reviewed.

THE NATURE OF AUDITING

The American Accounting Association has formulated the following general definition of **auditing:**

> Auditing is a systematic process of objectively obtaining and evaluating evidence regarding assertions about economic actions and events to ascertain the degree of correspondence between those assertions and established criteria and communicating the results to interested users.[1]

Auditing requires a step-by-step approach characterized by careful planning and judicious selection and execution of appropriate techniques. Auditing

[1]Committee on Basic Auditing Concepts, *A Statement of Basic Auditing Concepts* (Sarasota, Fla.: American Accounting Association, 1973): 2.

involves the collection, review, and documentation of audit evidence. In developing recommendations, the auditor uses established criteria, such as the principles of management and control described in earlier chapters, as a basis for evaluation.

While the auditing principles have changed little in recent years, auditing methods and techniques have changed substantially. Auditors used to ignore the computer and its programs and merely examine the system's printed records and output. The assumption underlying auditing around the computer was: If output was correctly obtained from system input, then processing must be reliable. However, the technique of auditing around the computer was abandoned as better methods of auditing an AIS were developed. In addition, this approach was almost impossible to apply to a disappearing audit trail. The current approach, auditing through the computer, uses the computer to check the adequacy of system controls, data, and output. Most audit techniques discussed in this chapter involve auditing through the computer.

Internal Auditing Standards

According to the Institute of Internal Auditors (IIA), the purpose of an internal audit is to evaluate the adequacy and effectiveness of a company's internal control system and determine the extent to which assigned responsibilities are actually carried out. The IIA's five audit scope standards outline the internal auditor's responsibilities:

1. Review the reliability and integrity of operating and financial information and how it is identified, measured, classified, and reported.
2. Determine whether the systems designed to comply with operating and reporting policies, plans, procedures, laws, and regulations are actually being followed.
3. Review how assets are safeguarded, and verify the existence of assets as appropriate.
4. Examine company resources to determine how effectively and efficiently they are utilized.
5. Review company operations and programs to determine whether they are being carried out as planned and whether they are meeting their objectives.

Today's organizations use a computerized AIS to process, store, and control company information. To achieve the preceding five objectives, an internal auditor must be qualified to (1) examine all elements of the computerized AIS and (2) use the computer as a tool to accomplish these auditing objectives. In other words, computer expertise is essential to conducting an internal audit.

Types of Internal Auditing Work

Three different types of audits are commonly performed:

1. The **financial audit** examines the reliability and integrity of accounting records (both financial and operating information) and, therefore, correlates with the first of the five scope standards.

2. The **information systems (IS) audit** reviews the general and application controls of an AIS to assess its compliance with internal control policies and procedures and its effectiveness in safeguarding assets. Its scope roughly corresponds to the IIA's second and third standards.

3. The **operational,** or **management,** audit is concerned with the economical and efficient use of resources and the accomplishment of established goals and objectives. Its scope corresponds to the fourth and fifth standards. Operational audits are discussed in greater depth later in this chapter.

An Overview of the Auditing Process

All audits follow a similar sequence of activities and may be divided into four stages: planning, collecting evidence, evaluating evidence, and communicating audit results. Figure 11.1 presents an overview of the auditing process, specifying many of the procedures typically performed within each of these stages. This section discusses the four auditing stages and activities in greater detail.

Audit Planning. The purpose of audit planning is to determine why, how, when, and by whom the audit will be performed. The first step in audit planning is to establish the scope and objectives of the audit. For example, the audit scope of a publicly held corporation extends to its corporate stockholders with the purpose of evaluating the fairness of financial statement presentation. In contrast, an internal audit may examine an entire division, a specific department, or a computer application. It may focus on internal controls, financial information, operating performance, or some combination of the three.

An audit team with the necessary experience and expertise is formed. Team members become familiar with the auditee by conferring with supervisory and operating personnel, reviewing system documentation, and reviewing the findings of prior audits.

An audit should be planned so that the greatest amount of audit work focuses on the areas with the highest risk factors. There are three types of risk when conducting an audit:

1. **Inherent risk** is the susceptibility to material risk in the absence of controls. For example, a system that employs on-line processing, networks, data base software, telecommunications, and other forms of advanced technology has more inherent risk than a traditional batch processing system.

2. **Control risk** is the risk that a material misstatement will get through the internal control structure and into the financial statements. A company with weak internal controls has a higher control risk than one with strong controls. Control risk can be determined by reviewing the control environment and considering control weaknesses identified in prior audits and evaluating how they have been rectified.

3. **Detection risk** is the risk that auditors and their audit procedures will not detect a material error or misstatement.

FIGURE 11.1
Overview of the Auditing Process

Audit Planning
Establish scope and objectives
Organize audit team
Develop knowledge of business operations
Review prior audit results
Identify risk factors
Prepare audit program
Collection of Audit Evidence
Observation of operating activities
Review of documentation
Discussions with employees
Questionnaires
Physical examination of assets
Confirmation through third parties
Reperformance of procedures
Vouching of source documents
Analytical review
Audit sampling
Evaluation of Audit Evidence
Assess quality of internal controls
Assess reliability of information
Assess operating performance
Consider need for additional evidence
Consider risk factors
Consider materiality factors
Document audit findings
Communication of Audit Results
Formulate audit conclusions
Develop recommendations for management
Prepare audit report
Present audit results to management

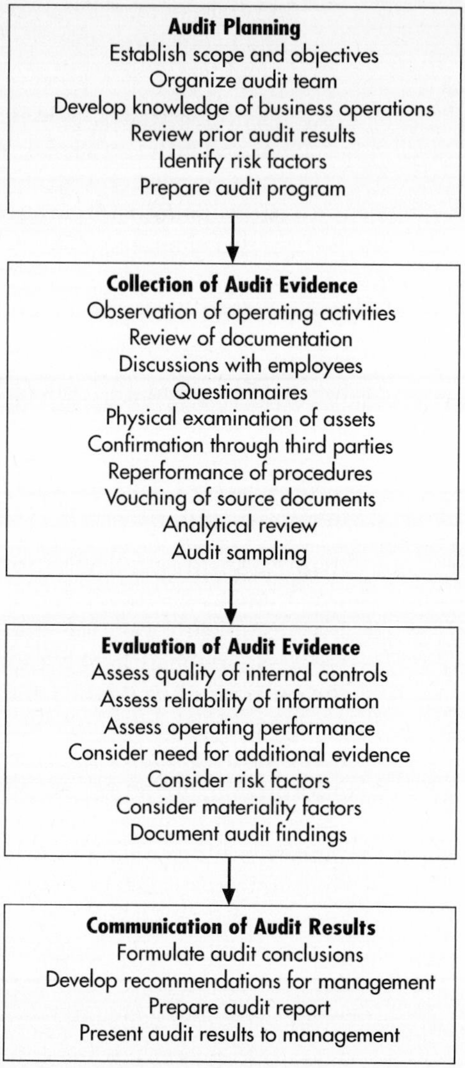

To conclude the planning stage, a preliminary audit program is prepared. It shows the nature, extent, and timing of the procedures necessary for achieving audit objectives and minimizing audit risks. A time budget is prepared, and staff members are assigned to perform specific audit steps.

Collection of Audit Evidence. Most audit effort is spent collecting evidence. The following are among the most commonly used methods of collecting audit evidence:

- *Observation* of the activities being audited. Examples include watching how employees enter the computer site or how data control personnel handle data processing work as it is received.

- *Review of documentation* to understand how a particular AIS or internal control system is supposed to function.
- *Discussions* with employees about their jobs and how they carry out certain procedures.
- *Questionnaires* that gather data about the system.
- *Physical examination* of the quantity and/or condition of tangible assets such as equipment, inventory, or cash.
- *Confirmation* of the accuracy of certain information, such as customer account balances, through communication with independent third parties.
- *Reperformance* of selected calculations in order to verify quantitative information on records and reports. For example, the auditor could recompute a batch total or recalculate the annual depreciation charge.
- *Vouching* for the validity of a transaction by examining all supporting documents, such as the purchase order, receiving report, and vendor invoice supporting an accounts payable transaction.
- *Analytical review* of relationships and trends among information to detect items that should be further investigated. For example, an auditor for a chain of dress shops discovered that at one shop the ratio of accounts receivable to sales was far too high. An investigation revealed that the manager had diverted funds from collections to her personal use.

Because many audit tests and procedures cannot feasibly be performed on the entire set of activities, records, assets, or documents under review, they are often performed on a sample basis. A typical audit will usually consist of a mix of audit procedures. For example, an audit designed to evaluate AIS internal controls would make greater use of observation, review of documentation, discussions with employees, and reperformance of control procedures. An audit of financial information would focus on physical examination, confirmation, vouching, analytical review, and reperformance of account balance calculations.

Evaluation of Audit Evidence. The auditor evaluates the evidence gathered in light of the specific audit objective and decides whether it supports a favorable or unfavorable conclusion. If inconclusive, the auditor plans and executes additional procedures until sufficient evidence is obtained to reach a definitive conclusion.

Materiality and reasonable assurance are important when deciding how much audit work is necessary and when evaluating evidence. Since errors are bound to exist in any system, auditors focus on detecting and reporting those that have a significant impact on management's interpretation of the audit findings. Determining **materiality,** what is and is not important in a given set of circumstances, is primarily a matter of judgment. Materiality is generally more important to external audits, where the overall emphasis is on the fairness of financial statement presentation, than to internal audits, where the focus is on determining adherence to management's policies.

The auditor seeks **reasonable assurance** that no material error exists in the information or process audited. Since it is prohibitively expensive to seek complete assurance, the auditor must be willing to accept some risk that the audit conclusion is incorrect. It is important to realize that when inherent or control risk is high, the auditor must obtain greater assurance to offset the greater uncertainty and risks.

At all stages of the audit, findings and conclusions are carefully documented in audit working papers. Documentation is especially important at the evaluation stage, when final conclusions must be reached and supported.

Communication of Audit Results. The auditor prepares a written (and sometimes oral) report summarizing the audit findings and recommendations, with references to supporting evidence in the working papers. This report is presented to management, the audit committee, the board of directors, and other appropriate parties. After the audit results are communicated, auditors often perform a follow-up study to ascertain whether or not recommendations have been implemented.

The Risk-Based Audit Approach

The following four-step approach to internal control evaluation, referred to as the risk-based audit approach, provides a logical framework for carrying out an audit:

1. Determine the threats (errors and irregularities) facing the AIS.
2. Identify the control procedures that should be in place to minimize each threat by preventing or detecting the errors and irregularities.
3. Evaluate the control procedures. Reviewing system documentation and interviewing appropriate personnel to determine whether the necessary procedures are in place is called a **systems review. Tests of controls** are conducted to determine whether these procedures are satisfactorily followed. These tests include activities such as observing system operations; inspecting documents, records, and reports; checking samples of system inputs and outputs; and tracing transactions through the system.
4. Evaluate weaknesses (errors and irregularities not covered by control procedures) to determine their effect on the nature, timing, or extent of auditing procedures and client suggestions. This step focuses on the control risks and whether the control system as a whole adequately addresses them. If a control deficiency is identified, the auditor asks whether there are **compensating controls,** or procedures that compensate for the deficiency. Control weaknesses in one area may be acceptable if they are compensated for by control strengths in other areas.

The risk-based approach to auditing provides auditors with a clear understanding of the errors and irregularities that can occur and the related risks and exposures. This understanding provides a sound basis for developing recommendations to management on how the AIS control system should be improved.

INFORMATION SYSTEMS AUDITS

The purpose of an AIS audit is to review and evaluate the internal controls that protect the system. When performing an IS audit, auditors should ascertain that the following objectives are met:

1. Security provisions protect computer equipment, programs, communications, and data from unauthorized access, modification, or destruction.
2. Program development and acquisition is performed in accordance with management's general and specific authorization.
3. Program modifications have the authorization and approval of management.
4. Processing of transactions, files, reports, and other computer records is accurate and complete.
5. Source data that is inaccurate or improperly authorized is identified and handled according to prescribed managerial policies.
6. Computer data files are accurate, complete, and confidential.

Figure 11.2 depicts the relationship among these six objectives and IS components. Each of these objectives is now discussed in detail. Each description includes an audit plan to accomplish each objective, as well as the techniques and procedures necessary for carrying out the plan.

Objective 1: Security

Table 11.1 contains a framework for auditing computer security. It shows the following:

1. *Types of security errors and fraud faced by companies.* These include accidental or intentional damage to system assets; unauthorized access, disclosure, or modification of data and programs; theft; and interruption of crucial business activities.
2. *Control procedures to minimize security errors and fraud.* These include developing an information security/protection plan, restricting physical and logical access, encrypting data, protecting against viruses, implementing firewalls, instituting data transmission controls, and preventing and recovering from system failures or disasters.
3. *Systems review audit procedures.* These include inspecting computer sites; interviewing personnel; reviewing policies and procedures; and examining access logs, insurance policies, and the disaster recovery plan.
4. *Tests of controls audit procedures.* Auditors test security controls by observing procedures, verifying that controls are in place and work as intended, investigating errors or problems to ensure they were handled correctly, and examining any tests previously performed. For example, one way to test logical access controls is to try to break into a system.

FIGURE 11.2
Information Systems Components and Related IS Audit Objectives

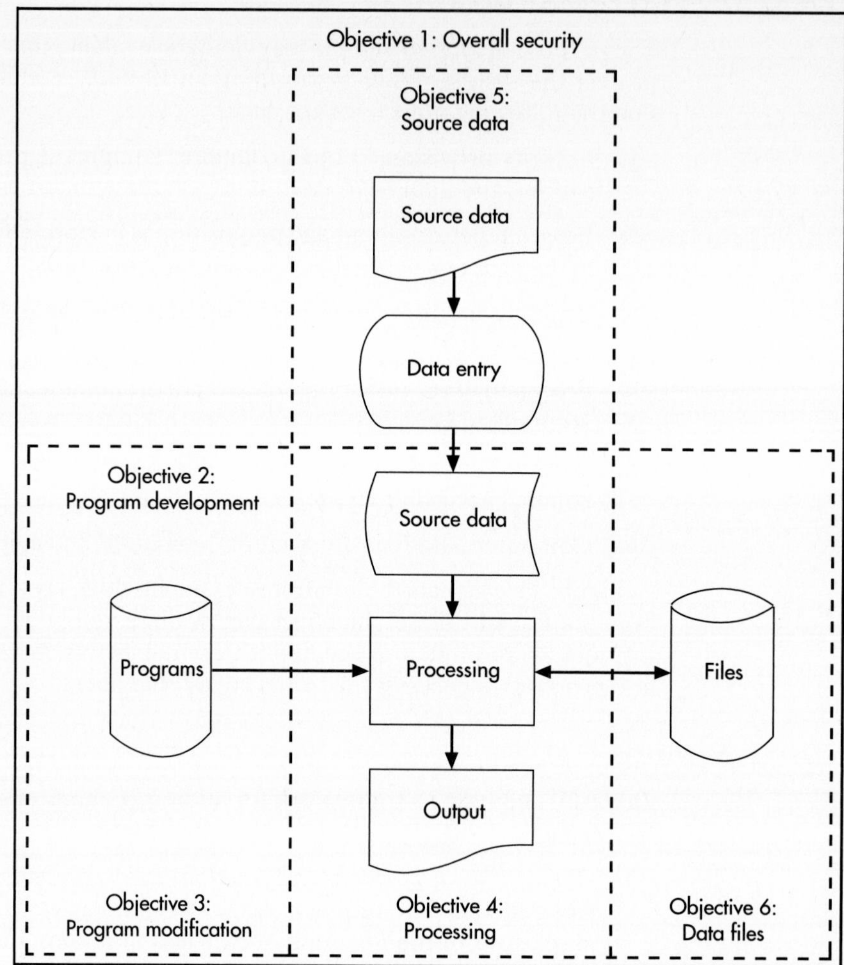

During a U.S. government agency security audit, auditors used agency terminals to gain unauthorized access to its computer system, disable its security-checking procedures, and control the system from the terminal. The security breakdown was possible because of poor administrative controls and inadequate security software.

5. *Compensating controls.* If security controls are seriously deficient, the organization faces substantial risks. Sound personnel policies and effective segregation of incompatible duties can partially compensate for poor computer security. Good user controls will also help, if user personnel can recognize unusual system output. However, it is unlikely these controls can compensate indefinitely for poor computer security. Hence auditors should strongly recommend that security weaknesses be corrected.

TABLE 11.1 Framework for Audit of Computer Security

Types of Errors and Fraud

- Theft of or accidental or intentional damage to hardware and files
- Loss or theft of or unauthorized access to programs, data files, and other system resources
- Loss or theft of or unauthorized disclosure of confidential data
- Unauthorized modification or use of programs and data files
- Interruption of crucial business activities

Control Procedures

- Information security/protection plan
- Restrictions on physical access to computer equipment
- Logical access controls based on password protection and other authentication procedures
- Data storage and transmission controls such as encryption
- Virus protection procedures
- File backup and recovery procedures
- Fault-tolerant systems design
- Disaster recovery plan
- Preventive maintenance
- Firewalls
- Information systems insurance

Audit Procedures: System Review

- Inspect computer sites
- Interview IS personnel about security procedures
- Review written documentation about physical access policies and procedures
- Review logical access policies and procedures
- Review file backup and recovery policies and procedures
- Examine data storage and transmission policies and procedures
- Review procedures employed to minimize system downtime
- Examine system access logs
- Examine disaster recovery plan
- Examine casualty insurance policies

Audit Procedures: Tests of Controls

- Observe computer site access procedures
- Observe the preparation and off-site storage of backup files
- Review records of password assignment and modification
- Investigate how unauthorized access attempts were dealt with
- Verify the extent of data encryption use
- Verify the effective use of data transmission controls
- Verify the effective use of firewalls
- Verify the effective use of virus protection procedures
- Verify the use of preventive maintenance and uninterruptible power
- Verify amounts and limitations on insurance coverage
- Examine the results of test simulations of disaster recovery plan

Compensating Controls

- Sound personnel policies
- Effective user controls
- Segregation of incompatible duties

Objective 2: Program Development and Acquisition

Table 11.2 provides a framework for reviewing and evaluating the program development process. Two things can go wrong in program development: (1) inadvertent errors due to misunderstanding system specifications or careless programming, and (2) unauthorized instructions deliberately inserted into the programs. These problems can be controlled by requiring both management and user authorization and approval, thorough testing, and proper documentation.

The auditor's role in systems development should be limited to an independent review of systems development activities. To maintain the objectivity necessary for performing an independent evaluation function, auditors should not be involved in developing the system. During the systems review, auditors should gain an understanding of development procedures by discussing them with management, system users, and IS personnel. They should also review the policies, procedures, standards, and documentation listed in Table 11.2.

To test systems development controls, auditors should interview managers and system users, examine development approvals, and review the minutes of

TABLE 11.2 Framework for Audit of Program Development

Types of Errors and Fraud
- Inadvertent programming errors
- Unauthorized program code

Control Procedures
- Management authorization for program development and approval of programming specifications
- User approval of programming specifications
- Thorough testing of new programs
- User acceptance testing
- Complete systems documentation, including approvals

Audit Procedures: System Review
- Independent and concurrent review of the systems development process
- Review systems development policies and procedures
- Review systems authorization and approval procedures
- Review programming evaluation standards
- Review program documentation standards
- Review program testing and test approval procedures
- Discuss systems development procedures with management, system users, and IS personnel
- Review final application system documentation

Audit Procedures: Tests of Controls
- Interview users about their involvement in systems design and implementation
- Review minutes of development team meetings for evidence of involvement
- Verify management and user sign-off at milestone points in the development process
- Review test specifications, test data, and results of systems tests

Compensating Controls
- Strong processing controls
- Independent processing of test data by auditor

development team meetings. The auditor should review thoroughly all documentation relating to the testing process and ascertain that all program changes were tested. The auditor should examine the test specifications, review the test data, and evaluate the test results. If unexpected test results were obtained, the auditor should ascertain how the problem was resolved.

Strong processing controls (see objective 4) sometimes can compensate for inadequate development controls. If compensatory processing controls are relied on, the auditor should obtain persuasive evidence of compliance, using techniques such as independent processing of test data. If this type of evidence cannot be obtained, the auditor may have to conclude that a material weakness in internal control exists and that the risk of significant errors or fraud in application programs is unacceptably high.

Objective 3: Program Modification

Table 11.3 presents a framework for auditing application programs and system software changes. The same errors and fraud that can take place during program changes can happen during program development. For example, one programmer assigned to modify his company's payroll system inserted a command to erase all company files if a termination notice was ever entered into his own payroll record. When the programmer was fired, his termination notice caused the system to crash and erase key files.

When a program change is submitted for approval, a list of all required updates should be compiled and then approved by management and program users. All program changes should be thoroughly tested and documented. During the change process, the developmental version of the program must be kept separate from the production version. After the amended program has received final approval, the change is implemented by replacing the production version with the developmental version.

During systems review, auditors should gain an understanding of the change process by discussing it with management and user personnel. The policies, procedures, and standards for approving, modifying, testing, and documenting the changes should be examined. A complete set of final documentation materials for recent program changes, including test procedures and results, should be reviewed. Finally, the auditor should review the procedures used to restrict logical access to the developmental version of the program.

An important part of an auditor's tests of controls is to verify that program changes were identified, listed, approved, tested, and documented. This step requires that the auditor observe how changes are implemented in order to verify that separate development and production programs are maintained and that changes are implemented by someone independent of the user and programming functions. The auditor should review the development program's access control table to verify that only those users assigned to carry out the modification had access to the system.

To test for unauthorized program changes, auditors can use a source code comparison program. After auditors thoroughly test a newly developed program (objective 2), they keep a copy of its source code. At any subsequent time,

TABLE 11.3 Framework for Audit of Program Modification Procedures

Types of Errors and Fraud
- Inadvertent programming errors
- Unauthorized progam code

Control Procedures
- Listing of program components that are to be modified
- Management authorization and approval of program modifications
- User approval of program change specifications
- Thorough testing of program changes, including user acceptance test
- Complete program change documentation, including approvals
- Separate development, test, and production versions of program
- Changes implemented by personnel independent of users and programmers
- Logical access controls

Audit Procedures: System Review
- Review program modification policies, standards, and procedures
- Review documentation standards for program modification
- Review program modification testing and test approval procedures
- Discuss program modification policies and procedures with management, system users, and IS personnel
- Review final documentation for some typical program modifications
- Review test specifications, test data, and results of systems tests
- Review logical access control policies and procedures

Audit Procedures: Tests of Controls
- Verify user and IS management approval for program changes
- Verify that program components to be modified are identified and listed
- Verify that program change test procedures comply with standards
- Verify that program change documentation complies with standards
- Verify that logical access controls are in effect for program changes
- Observe program change implementation and verify that
  –Separate development, test, and production versions are maintained
  –Changes are not implemented by either user or programming personnel
- To test for unauthorized or erroneous program changes, use
  –Source code comparison program
  –Reprocessing
  –Parallel simulation

Compensating Controls
- Independent audit tests for unauthorized or erroneous program changes
- Strong processing controls

the auditor may use the comparison program to compare the current version of the program with the original source code. If no changes have been authorized, these two versions should be identical. Therefore any unauthorized differences should result in an investigation. If the difference represents an authorized change, the auditor can refer to the program change specifications to ensure that the changes were authorized and correctly incorporated.

Two additional techniques detect unauthorized program changes. The **reprocessing** technique also uses a verified copy of the source code. On a surprise basis, the auditor uses the program to reprocess data and compare that output with the company's data. Discrepancies in the two sets of output are investigated to ascertain their cause. **Parallel simulation** is similar to reprocessing except that the auditor writes a program instead of saving a verified copy of the source code. The auditor's results are compared with the company's, and any differences are investigated. Parallel simulation can be used to test a program during the implementation process. For example, Jason used this technique to test a portion of SPP's new sales department payroll system.

Auditors should observe the testing and implementation, review related authorizations and documents, and, if necessary, perform independent tests for each major program change. If this step is skipped and program change controls are subsequently determined to be inadequate, it may not be possible to rely on program outputs. In addition, auditors should always test programs on a surprise basis as a precaution against unauthorized program changes being inserted after the examination is completed and then removed just prior to the next scheduled audit.

If internal controls over program changes are deficient, a compensating control is source code comparison, reprocessing, or parallel simulation performed by the auditor. In addition, the presence of sound processing controls, independently tested by the auditor, can partially compensate for such deficiencies. However, if the deficiencies are caused by inadequate restrictions on program file access, the auditor should strongly recommend actions that will strengthen the organization's logical access controls.

Objective 4: Computer Processing

Table 11.4 provides a framework for auditing computer processing controls. The focus of the fourth objective is the processing of transactions, files, and related computer records to update files and data bases and to generate reports.

During computer processing the system might fail to detect erroneous input, improperly correct input errors, process erroneous input, or improperly distribute or disclose output. The control procedures to detect and prevent these errors and the systems review and tests of control procedures the auditor employs are shown in Table 11.4. The purpose of these audit procedures is to gain an understanding of the controls, evaluate their adequacy, and observe operations for evidence that the controls are actually being followed.

Auditors must periodically reevaluate processing controls to ensure their continued reliability. If processing controls are unsatisfactory, user and source data controls may be strong enough to compensate. If not, a material weakness exists and steps should be taken to eliminate the control deficiencies.

Several specialized techniques allow the auditor to use the computer to test processing controls. They include processing test data, using concurrent audit techniques, and analyzing program logic. Each of these procedures is explained next.

Test Data Processing. One way to test a program is to process a hypothetical series of valid and invalid transactions. The program should process all of the valid transactions correctly and identify and reject all of the invalid ones. All logic paths should be checked for proper functioning by one or more of the

TABLE 11.4 Framework for Audit of Computer Processing Controls

Types of Errors and Fraud
- Failure to detect incorrect, incomplete, or unauthorized input data
- Failure to properly correct errors flagged by data editing procedures
- Introduction of errors into files or data bases during updating
- Improper distribution or disclosure of computer output
- Intentional or unintentional report inaccuracies

Control Procedures
- Computer data editing routines
- Proper use of internal and external file labels
- Reconciliation of batch totals
- Effective error correction procedures
- Understandable operating documentation and run manuals
- Competent supervision of computer operations
- Effective handling of data input and output by data control personnel
- File change listings and summaries prepared for user department review
- Maintenance of proper environmental conditions in computer facility

Audit Procedures: System Review
- Review administrative documentation for processing control standards
- Review systems documentation for data editing and other processing controls
- Review operating documentation for completeness and clarity
- Review copies of error listings, batch total reports, and file change lists
- Observe computer operations and data control functions
- Discuss processing and output controls with operators and IS supervisory personnel

Audit Procedures: Tests of Controls
- Evaluate adequacy of processing control standards and procedures
- Evaluate adequacy and completeness of data editing controls
- Verify adherence to processing control procedures by observing computer operations and the data control function
- Verify that selected application system output is properly distributed
- Reconcile a sample of batch totals, and follow up on discrepancies
- Trace disposition of a sample of errors flagged by data edit routines to ensure proper handling
- Verify processing accuracy for a sample of sensitive transactions
- Verify processing accuracy for selected computer-generated transactions
- Search for erroneous or unauthorized code via analysis of program logic
- Check accuracy and completeness of processing controls using test data
- Monitor on-line processing systems using concurrent audit techniques
- Re-create selected reports to test for accuracy and completeness

Compensating Controls
- Strong user controls
- Effective source data controls

test transactions. Examples of invalid data include records with missing data, fields containing unreasonably large amounts, invalid account numbers or processing codes, nonnumeric data in numeric fields, and records out of sequence.

Several resources are available when preparing test data. For example:

- A listing of actual transactions.
- The test transactions the programmer used to test the program.

- A **test data generator program,** which automatically prepares test data based on program specifications.

In a batch processing system, the company's program and a copy of relevant files are used to process the test data. The results are compared with the predetermined correct output; discrepancies indicate processing errors or control deficiencies that should be thoroughly investigated.

In an on-line system, auditors enter test data using a data entry terminal and observe and log the system's response. If the system accepts erroneous or invalid test transactions, the auditor reverses the effects of the transactions, investigates the problem, and corrects the deficiency.

Although processing of test transactions is usually effective, it does have the following disadvantages:

1. The auditor must spend considerable time developing an understanding of the system and preparing an adequate set of test transactions.
2. Care must be taken to ensure that test data does not affect the company's files and data bases. The auditor can reverse the effects of the test transactions or process the transactions in a separate run using a copy of the file or data base. However, a separate run removes some of the authenticity obtained from processing test data with regular transactions. Also, since the reversal procedures may reveal the existence and nature of the auditor's test to key personnel, it can be less effective than a concealed test.

Concurrent Audit Techniques. Millions of dollars of transactions can be processed in an on-line system without leaving a satisfactory audit trail. In such cases, evidence gathered after data processing is insufficient for audit purposes. In addition, since many on-line systems process transactions continuously, it is difficult or impossible to stop the system in order to perform audit tests. Thus the auditor uses **concurrent audit techniques** to continually monitor the system and collect audit evidence while live data are processed during regular operating hours. Concurrent audit techniques use **embedded audit modules,** which are segments of program code that performs audit functions. They also report test results to the auditor and store the evidence collected for the auditor's review. Concurrent audit techniques are time-consuming and difficult to use, but are less so if incorporated when programs are developed.

Auditors commonly use five concurrent audit techniques. An **integrated test facility (ITF)** technique places a small set of fictitious records in the master files. The records might represent a fictitious division, department, or branch office or a customer or supplier. Processing test transactions to update these dummy records will not affect the actual records. Because fictitious and actual records are processed together, company employees usually remain unaware that this testing is taking place. The system must distinguish ITF records from actual records, collect information on the effects of the test transactions, and report the results. The auditor compares processing and expected results in order to verify that the system and its controls are operating correctly.

In a batch processing system, the ITF technique eliminates the need to reverse test transactions and is easily concealed from operating employees. ITF is well suited to testing on-line processing systems because test transactions can be submitted on a frequent basis, processed with actual transactions, and traced throughout every processing stage. All this can be accomplished without disrupting regular processing operations. However, care must be taken not to combine dummy and actual records during the reporting process.

The **snapshot technique** examines the way transactions are processed. Selected transactions are marked with a special code that triggers the snapshot process. Audit modules in the program record these transactions and their master file records before and after processing. Snapshot data are recorded in a special file and reviewed by the auditor to verify that all processing steps have been properly executed.

SCARF (system control audit review file) uses embedded audit modules to continuously monitor transaction activity and collect data on transactions with special audit significance. The data are recorded in a SCARF file or **audit log.** Transactions that might be recorded in a SCARF file include those exceeding a specified dollar limit, involving inactive accounts, deviating from company policy, or containing write-downs of asset values. Periodically the auditor receives a printout of the SCARF file, examines the information to identify any questionable transactions, and performs any necessary follow-up investigation.

Audit hooks are audit routines that flag suspicious transactions. For example, internal auditors at State Farm Life Insurance determined that their policyholder system was vulnerable to fraud every time a policyholder changed his or her name or address and then subsequently withdrew funds from the policy. They devised a system of audit hooks to tag records with a name or address change. The internal audit department is now notified when a tagged record is associated with a withdrawal and can appropriately investigate the transaction for fraud. When audit hooks are employed, auditors can be informed of questionable transactions as soon as they occur. This approach, known as **real-time notification,** displays a message on the auditor's terminal. Additional information about State Farm's use of audit hooks, including how a major fraud was detected, is contained in Focus 11.1.

Continuous and intermittent simulation (CIS) embeds an audit module in a data base management system. The CIS module examines all transactions that update the DBMS using criteria similar to those of SCARF. If a transaction has special audit significance, the module independently processes the data (in a manner similar to parallel simulation), records the results, and compares them with those obtained by the DBMS. If any discrepancies exist, the details are written onto an audit log for subsequent investigation. If serious discrepancies are discovered, the CIS may prevent the DBMS from executing the update process.

Analysis of Program Logic. If an auditor suspects that a particular application program contains unauthorized code or serious errors, a detailed analysis of the program logic may be necessary. Since this process is time-consuming and requires programming language proficiency, it should be used only as a last resort. To perform the analysis, auditors refer to systems and program

FOCUS 11.1 Using Audit Hooks at State Farm Life

THE STATE Farm Life Insurance Company computer system has a host computer in Bloomington, Illinois and 26 minicomputers in regional offices. In the regional offices, more than 1,500 CRT input devices are used to update almost 4 million individual policyholder master records in the host computer. The system processes more than 30 million transactions per year. The system keeps track of policyholder funds valued at more than $6.7 billion.

The system is an on-line, real-time one, and all master record updating and transaction processing take place almost instantly. Paper audit trails have virtually vanished, and documents supporting changes to the policyholder master records have been virtually eliminated or are only held a short time before disposition.

Anyone with access and a working knowledge of the system could potentially commit fraud. The internal audit staff had the challenge of identifying the life insurance transactions where fraud was possible. To accomplish this, the internal auditors brainstormed ways to defraud the system and interviewed various system users, who provided extremely valuable insights.

Auditors currently have 33 embedded audit hooks monitoring 42 different types of transactions. One of the audit hooks monitors unusual transactions in transfer accounts, which are clearing accounts for temporarily holding funds that are to be credited to multiple accounts.

The audit hooks have been very successful. One employee fraudulently obtained cash by processing a loan for $250 on her brother's life insurance policy. She then forged her brother's endorsement and cashed the check. To cover up the fraud, she had to repay the $250 loan before the annual status report was sent to her brother. To do so, she used a series of fictitious transactions involving a transfer account. The fraud was uncovered almost immediately when the transfer account audit hook recognized the first of these fictitious transactions and sent a computer output notification to the auditor. Within a month after the notification was sent, the case had been investigated and the employee terminated.

Source: Linda Marie Leinicke, W. Max Rexroad, and John D. Ward, "Computer Fraud Auditing: It Works." *Internal Auditor* (August 1990).

flowcharts, program documentation, and a listing of the program source code. The following software packages serve as aids in this analysis:

- **Automated flowcharting programs,** which interpret program source code and generate a corresponding program flowchart.
- **Automated decision table programs,** which generate a decision table representing the program logic.
- **Scanning routines,** which search a program for occurrences of a specified variable name or other character combinations.
- **Mapping programs,** which identify unexecuted program code. This software could have uncovered the program code the unscrupulous programmer inserted to erase all computer files when he was terminated as detailed in an earlier example.
- **Program tracing,** which sequentially prints all application program steps (line numbers or paragraph names) executed during a program run. This list is intermingled with regular output so auditors can observe the precise sequence of events that unfold during program execution. Program tracing helps auditors detect unauthorized program instructions, incorrect logic paths, and unexecuted program code.

Objective 5: Source Data

Table 11.5 shows the internal controls that prevent, detect, and correct inaccurate or unauthorized source data. It also shows the systems review and tests of control procedures that auditors use for evaluation. In an on-line system, the source data entry and processing functions are one operation. Therefore source data controls such as proper authorization and editing data input are integrated with processing controls.

TABLE 11.5 Framework for Audit of Source Data Controls

Types of Errors and Fraud
- Inaccurate source data
- Unauthorized source data

Control Procedures
- Effective handling of source data input by data control personnel
- User authorization of source data input
- Preparation and reconciliation of batch control totals
- Logging of the receipt, movement, and disposition of source data input
- Check digit verification
- Key verification
- Use of turnaround documents
- Computer data editing routines
- File change listings and summaries prepared for user department review
- Effective procedures for correcting and resubmitting erroneous data

Audit Procedures: System Review
- Review documentation about responsibilities of data control function
- Review administrative documentation for source data control standards
- Review methods of authorization and examine authorization signatures
- Review accounting systems documentation to identify source data content and processing steps and specific source data controls used
- Document accounting source data controls using input control matrix
- Discuss source data control procedures with data control personnel, IS management, and system users

Audit Procedures: Tests of Controls
- Observe and evaluate data control department operations and specific data control procedures
- Verify proper maintenance and use of data control log
- Evaluate how items recorded in the error log are dealt with
- Examine samples of accounting source data for proper authorization
- Reconcile a sample of batch totals, and follow up on discrepancies
- Trace disposition of a sample of errors flagged by data edit routines

Compensating Controls
- Strong user controls
- Strong processing controls

FIGURE 11.3
Input Controls Matrix

Record Name: Employer Weekly Time Report	Employee number	Last name	Department number	Transaction code	Week ending (date)	Regular hours	Overtime hours		Comments
Input Controls									
Batch totals						✓	✓		
Hash totals	✓								
Record counts									Yes
Cross-footing balance									No
Key verification	✓					✓	✓		
Visual inspection									All fields
Check digit verification	✓								
Prenumbered forms									No
Turnaround document									No
Edit program									Yes
Sequence check	✓								
Field check	✓		✓			✓	✓		
Sign check									
Validity check	✓		✓	✓	✓				
Limit check						✓	✓		
Reasonableness test						✓	✓		
Redundant data check	✓	✓	✓						
Completeness test				✓	✓	✓	✓		
Overflow procedure									
Other:									

Auditors use an **input controls matrix,** such as the one depicted in Fig. 11.3, to document the review of source data controls. The matrix shows the control procedures applied to each field of an input record.

Auditors should make sure that the data control function is independent of other functions, maintains a data control log, handles errors, and ensures the overall efficiency of operations. It is usually not economically feasible for small businesses and PC installations to have an independent data control function. To compensate, user department controls over data preparation, batch control totals, edit programs, restrictions on physical and logical access to the system, and error handling procedures must be stronger. These procedures should be the focus of the auditor's systems review and tests of controls whenever the presence of an independent data control function is absent.

Although source data controls may not change often, the strictness with which they are applied may. Therefore auditors should test them on a regular basis. The auditor tests the system by evaluating samples of source data for proper authorization. A sample of batch controls should be reconciled. A sample of data edit errors should be evaluated to check that they were resolved and resubmitted into the system.

If source data controls are inadequate, user department and computer processing controls may compensate. If not, the auditor should strongly recommend steps to correct the source data control deficiencies.

Objective 6: Data Files

The sixth objective is concerned with the accuracy, integrity, and security of data stored in machine-readable files. Data storage risks include the unauthorized modification, destruction, or disclosure of data. Many of the controls discussed in Chapter 9 are used to protect the system against these risks. If file controls are seriously deficient, especially with respect to physical or logical access or to backup and recovery procedures, the auditor should strongly recommend they be rectified. Table 11.6 summarizes the errors, controls, and audit procedures for this objective.

The auditing-by-objectives approach is a comprehensive, systematic, and effective means of evaluating internal controls in an AIS. It can be implemented using an audit procedures checklist for each objective. The checklist should help the auditor reach a separate conclusion for each objective and suggest compensating controls when an objective is not fully achieved. A separate version of the checklist should be completed for each significant application.

Auditors should review system designs while there is still time to adopt their suggestions for control and audit features. Techniques like ITF, snapshot, SCARF, audit hooks, and real-time notification should be incorporated into a system during the design process, rather than as an afterthought. Similarly, most application control techniques are easier to design into the system than to add after the system is developed.

COMPUTER SOFTWARE

A number of computer programs, called **computer audit software (CAS)** or **generalized audit software (GAS),** have been written especially for auditors. They are available from software vendors and the larger public accounting firms. In essence, CAS is a computer program that, based on the auditor's specifications, generates programs that perform the audit functions. CAS is ideally suited for examination of large data files to identify records needing further audit scrutiny. For example, Focus 11.2 describes how the U.S. government uses CAS to battle the federal budget deficit. Table 11.7 contains a list of CAS functions and one or more audit examples for each function.

Figure 11.4 shows how CAS is used. The auditor's first step is to decide on audit objectives, learn about the files to be audited, design the audit reports, and determine how to produce them. This information is recorded on specification sheets and entered into the system via a data entry program. This program

TABLE 11.6 Framework for Audit of Data File Controls

Types of Errors and Fraud
- Destruction of stored data due to inadvertent errors, hardware or software malfunctions, and intentional acts of sabotage of vandalism
- Unauthorized modification or disclosure of stored data

Control Procedures
- Secure file library and restrictions on physical access to data files
- Logical access controls using passwords and access control matrix
- Proper use of file labels and write-protection mechanisms
- Concurrent update controls
- Use of data encryption for highly confidential data
- Use of virus protection software
- Maintenance of backup copies of all data files in an off-site location
- Use of checkpoint and rollback to facilitate system recovery

Audit Procedures: System Review
- Review documentation for functions of file library operation
- Review logical access policies and procedures
- Review operating documentation to determine prescribed standards for
  - –Use of file labels and write-protection mechanisms
  - –Use of virus protection software
  - –Use of backup data storage
  - –System recovery, including checkpoint and rollback procedures
- Review systems documentation to examine prescribed procedures for
  - –Use of concurrent update controls and data encryption
  - –Control of file conversions
  - –Reconciling master file totals with independent control totals
- Examine disaster recovery plan
- Discuss data file control procedures with IS managers and operators

Audit Procedures: Tests of Controls
- Observe and evaluate file library operations
- Review records of password assignment and modification
- Observe and evaluate file-handling procedures by operations personnel
- Observe the preparation and off-site storage of backup files
- Verify the effective use of virus protection procedures
- Verify the use of concurrent update controls and data encryption
- Verify completeness, currency, and testing of disaster recovery plan
- Reconcile master file totals with separately maintained control totals
- Observe the procedures used to control file conversion

Compensating Controls
- Strong user controls
- Effective computer security controls
- Strong processing controls

FOCUS 11.2 Battling Federal Budget Deficits with Audit Software

THE U.S. government is finding that computer audit software is a valuable tool in its attempts to reduce massive federal budget deficits. Audit software is being used to identify fraudulent Medicare claims, pinpoint excessive charges by defense contractors, and in many other ways.

A computer audit by the General Accounting Office (GAO) cross-checked figures with the IRS and discovered that thousands of veterans lied about their income to qualify for pension benefits. The audit revealed that 116,000 veterans receiving pensions on the basis of need failed to disclose $338 million in income from savings accounts, stock dividends, or rents. More than 13,600 veterans underreported their income by at least $4,000, $5,500, $10,000 or more, and one did not report over $300,000.

Before the computer check was instituted, the Veteran's Administration (VA) relied on the vets for accurate income reports. Once the VA notified beneficiaries that their income would be verified with the IRS and the Social Security Administration, the pension rolls dropped by more than 13,000, at a savings of $9 million a month, the GAO reported.

The VA plans to use the same system for checking income levels of those applying for medical care. If their income is found to be above a certain level, patients will be required to make copayments.

creates specification records that the CAS uses to produce one or more auditing programs. The auditing programs process the source files and perform the auditing operations needed to produce the specified audit reports. Frequently, an initial CAS computer run is performed to extract key auditing information and place it in an audit work file. Additional audit reports and analyses are generated by subsequent computer runs that use the audit work file as input.

The following case illustrates the value of audit software. In a small New England town, a new tax collector was elected, defeating the incumbent. The new tax collector requested an audit of the city's tax collection records. Using CAS, the auditor accessed the tax collection records for the past four years, sorted them by collection date, summed the amount of taxes collected monthly, and prepared a four-year summary report of monthly tax collections. The analysis revealed that tax collections during January and July, the two busiest months, had declined by 58% and 72%, respectively. Auditors used the CAS to compare the tax collection records, one by one, with the city's property records. The ensuing report identified several discrepancies, including one case where the former tax collector used another taxpayer's payment to cover her own delinquent tax bills. The former tax collector was arrested and charged with embezzlement.

The primary purpose of CAS is to assist the auditor in reviewing and retrieving information in computer files. When the auditor receives the CAS reports, most of the audit work still remains to be done. Items on exception reports must be investigated, file totals must be verified against other sources of information such as the general ledger, and audit samples must be examined and evaluated. Although the advantages of using CAS are numerous and compelling, CAS cannot replace the auditor's judgment or free her from other phases of the audit.

TABLE 11.7 General Functions of Computer Audit Software

Function	Explanation	Examples
Reformatting	Read data in different formats and data structures, and convert to a common format and structure	Read inventory records from purchasing data base and convert to an inventory file usable by the GAS program
File manipulation	Sort records into sequential order; merge files sequenced on the same sort key	Sort inventory records by location; merge customer transaction files with receivables master file
Calculation	Perform the four basic arithmetic operations: add, subtract, multiply, and divide	Foot client accounts receivable file; recalculate client inventory valuation; recalculate client depreciation; sum employee payroll by department
Data selection	Review data files to retrieve records meeting specified criteria	Identify customer accounts having a balance exceeding the credit limit; select all purchase transactions in excess of a specified dollar amount
Data analysis	Examine records for errors or missing values; compare fields in related records for inconsistencies	Perform data editing of client files; compare personnel and payroll files to verify consistency
File processing	Provide programming capability for file creation, updating, and downloading to a personal computer	Use parallel simulation to verify that client gross pay calculations are correct; download sample of client inventory records to personal computer for further analysis to support inventory test counts
Statistics	Stratify file records by item valuation; select statistical samples; analyze statistical sampling results	Stratify customer accounts by size of account balance and select a stratified sample of accounts for audit confirmation
Report generation	Format and print reports and documents	Prepare analysis of financial statement ratios and trends; prepare accounts receivable aging schedule; prepare audit confirmations

An Example of an Audit Software Application

Jason Scott was assigned to audit the accounts receivable information produced by the AIS at Northwest Builders Supply (NBS) in Tacoma, Washington. The system has an accounts receivable master file and transaction detail files for sales on account, cash collections, and credit memos. Copies of record layouts for these files are reproduced in Fig. 11.5. Jason's supervisor specified the following objectives for the CAS application:

1. Recalculate the current balance of every customer master record using the previous balance and the intervening transactions. Identify all accounts with an incorrect current balance.

FIGURE 11.4
Overview of GAS Processing

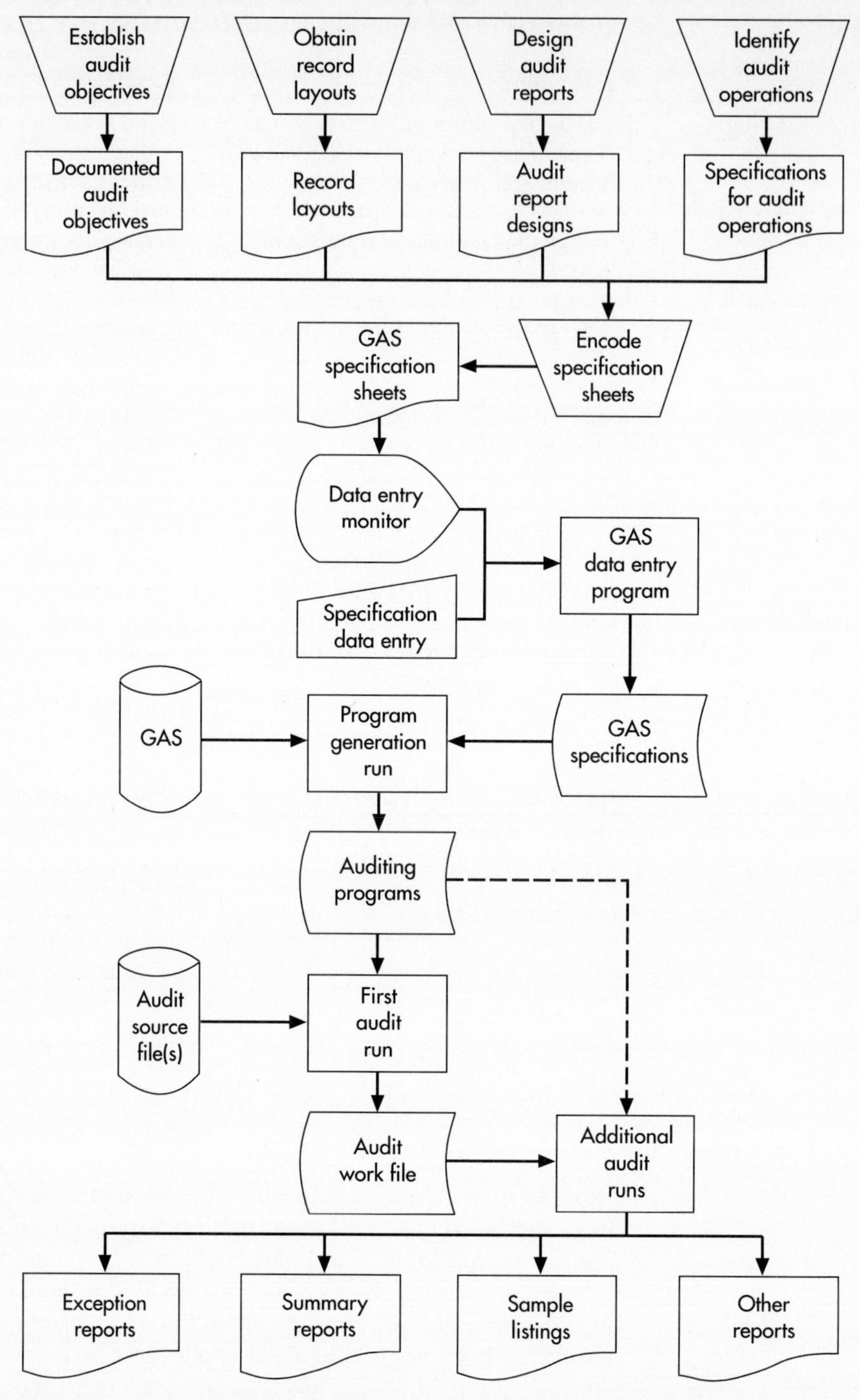

FIGURE 11.5
Record Layouts for Accounts Receivable System

Record Name: Accounts Receivable Master

Field Name	Account number	Name	Address				Credit code	Credit limit	Previous balance	Current balance
			Street	City	State	Zip				
Position	1 – 6	7 – 31	32 – 56	57 – 74	75 – 76	77 – 81	82 – 83	84 – 91	92 – 99	100 – 107

Record Name: Sales Detail

Field Name	Account number	Transaction code	Transaction date	Invoice number	Amount	
Position	1 – 6	7	8 – 13	14 – 18	19 – 26	

Record Name: Cash Collections Detail

Field Name	Account number	Transaction code	Transaction date	Reference number	Amount	
Position	1 – 6	7	8 – 13	14 – 18	19 – 26	

Record Name: Credit Memo Detail

Field Name	Account number	Transaction code	Transaction date	Credit memo number	Amount	
Position	1 – 6	7	8 – 13	14 – 18	19 – 26	

2. Sum the current balance, credit sales, cash collections, and credit memo amounts. They will be verified using independently maintained information.
3. Perform edit checks on selected fields in each file to confirm the reliability of data editing procedures.
4. Check transaction files for records that do not match a master record.
5. Prepare an accounts receivable aging schedule and an analysis of accounts having current balances in excess of their credit limit. These reports will be used to evaluate the sufficiency of NBS's allowance for uncollectible accounts and assess the performance of NBS's credit department.
6. Select a sample of accounts for confirmation. This will be used to verify the existence and accuracy of the receivables in NBS's customer master file.

7. Analyze cash collections and credit memos subsequent to the test date for those customers who do not respond to confirmation requests.

Figure 11.6 shows the sequence of computer operations Jason used to achieve the first six objectives. RUN 1 sorted the four source files into account number sequence and merged them into a combined master and transaction file. Details about the two transaction records lacking a matching master record were listed on the unmatched transaction report. Jason discovered that keying errors had caused invalid account numbers to be entered into these transaction records. Corrections were promptly recorded in NBS's records and in Jason's merged file.

During RUN 2 Jason completed the following functions:

- Extracted the records he needed from the merged file and placed them in sequential order in an audit work file.
- Created an audit record for each customer containing the account number, name, address, credit limit, current balance, last invoice (sale) date and amount, last credit payment or credit memo date, and last credit amount in the audit work file.
- Edited information on the merged master and transaction file and printed the exceptions on an exception report.
- Added sales to the previous balance and subtracted cash collections and credit memo amounts. If any results were not equal to the customer's current balance, all data pertaining to the account were printed on an exception report.
- Edited selected data fields and printed all erroneous records on the exception report. The edits included a validity check on the transaction codes and dates, a completeness test for each record, a sign test of the current balance, field checks of all numeric fields, and a sequence check based on account number. He investigated the errors and concluded that they were caused by inadvertent mistakes in data entry. Luckily, they had a negligible effect on NBS's accounts and did not affect the overall reliability of their accounts receivable information.
- Footed the amount fields for cash collections, sales, credit memos, and account balances and printed the totals on the edit exceptions report. He compared these totals with corresponding totals from NBS's sales and cash receipts journals and general ledger accounts.

RUN 3 processed the audit work file to generate an aging schedule for receivables. RUN 4 compared the current balance against the credit limit for each customer. If a limit was exceeded, the account was printed on the credit exceptions report. Jason gave the aging schedule and the exceptions report to his supervisor, who used them to evaluate the allowance for uncollectible accounts and the credit department's effectiveness in administering credit policies.

In RUN 5 the audit work file was sorted into sequence from high to low current balance and classified into a dollar range ($0 to $500, $501 to $1,000, and so on to all accounts over $20,000). A summary report was printed listing the number of accounts and the cumulative dollar amount for each range.

FIGURE 11.6
Application of Computer Audit Software to Accounts Receivable

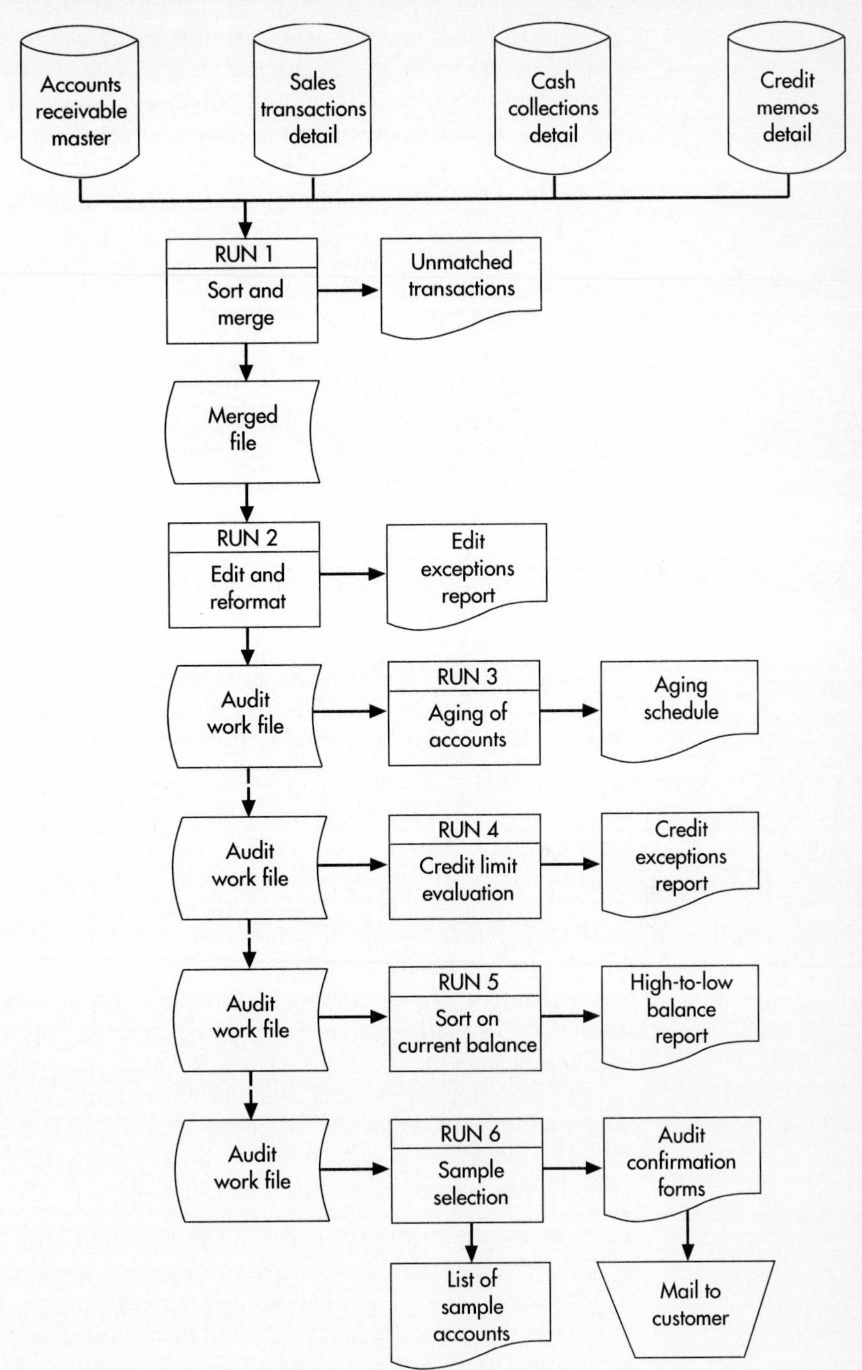

Jason used this report to select an accounts receivable confirmation sample. He selected all customer accounts above $15,000, 10% of accounts between $5,001 and $15,000, 1% of those $5,000 or less. This **stratified sampling** plan allows auditors to include a high percentage of the total dollars in the population, even though the sample may include a low percentage of the total number of accounts. The high-to-low-balance summary report helps the auditor decide how many sample strata (or ranges) to use and what their boundaries should be.

RUN 6 randomly selected and printed the accounts for the smaller strata and printed all of the confirmations as well. Although Jason mailed the confirmation forms to all of NBS's customers, several chose not to respond. Jason used the CAS to examine subsequent collections from these particular customers and verify that they paid off the amounts they owed NBS.

Once Jason obtained and examined confirmation responses and other related evidence, he would use the audit software to evaluate the results of the sample. Northwest's audit software program is capable of statistically evaluating sample results by computing means, variances, confidence intervals, and sampling risks.

The CAS allowed Jason to gather and evaluate evidence quickly and inexpensively. Note that Jason was able to perform these functions independently of NBS's IS personnel. The results Jason obtained from the CAS represented only the first step in the audit. Jason still had to investigate exceptions, audit sample items, independently verify file totals, evaluate the significance of summary reports, and perform other audit procedures.

OPERATIONAL AUDITS OF AN AIS

The techniques and procedures used in operational audits are similar to those of IS and financial audits. The basic difference is that the IS audit scope is confined to internal controls whereas the financial audit scope is limited to IS output. In contrast, the operational audit scope is much broader, encompassing all aspects of IS management. In addition, operational audit objectives include evaluating such factors as effectiveness, efficiency, and goal achievement.

The first step in an operational audit is audit planning, during which the scope and objectives of the audit are established, a preliminary review of the system is performed, and a tentative audit program is prepared.

Evidence collection includes the following activities:

- Reviewing operating policies and documentation
- Confirming procedures with management and operating personnel
- Observing operating functions and activities
- Examining financial and operating plans and reports
- Testing the accuracy of operating information
- Testing controls

At the evidence evaluation stage, the auditor measures the actual system against an ideal one, a system that follows all the best principles of systems management. One important consideration is that the results of management policies and practices are more significant than the policies and practices themselves. That is, if good results are achieved through policies and practices that are theoretically deficient, then the auditor must carefully consider whether recommended improvements would substantially improve results. In any event, the auditor should thoroughly document the findings and conclusions and communicate the audit results to management.

Being a good operational auditor requires some degree of management experience. Those with strong auditing backgrounds but weak or no management experience often lack the perspective necessary to understand the management process. Thus the ideal operational auditor is a person with auditing training and experience and a few years' experience in a managerial position.

SUMMARY AND CASE CONCLUSION

Jason was trying to figure out how his parallel simulation program generated sales commission figures that differed from those of SPP's program. When he studied the figures, he noticed that in all the differences the sales commission was higher than average. This meant there might have been a systematic error in one of the programs. After verifying that his program was correct, he asked to review a copy of SPP's program.

The program was very lengthy, so Jason used the scanning technique to search the code for a specified set of characters. Under the new commission policy, the commission rate changes when sales for the period exceed $40,000. Jason searched the code for occurrences of "40000," which directed him to the place where the commission rate structure resides. To his astonishment, he discovered a commission rate of 0.085 for sales in excess of $40,000, while the policy called for only 0.075. Some quick calculations confirmed this was the source of the differences between the two programs.

Jason reported his findings to his supervisor, who called in the audit manager. A meeting was arranged between the audit manager and the head of the systems development team. The meeting was quite embarrassing for the team head and her staff, but the coding error was acknowledged and corrected.

The audit manager called Jason to congratulate him and informed him that if the programming error had gone undetected, Seattle Paper would have paid over $100,000 per year in excess sales commissions. While Jason was grateful to receive the manager's praise, he also took the opportunity to point out deficiencies in the programming practices employed by the development team. First, the commission rate table had been embedded in the program code; good programming practice would require that it be stored in a separate table to be called by the program when needed. Second, he suggested that the incident called into question the quality of SPP's program development and testing practices. Jason asked whether a more extensive operational audit of those practices might be appropriate. The audit manager agreed that this might be worth looking into, and he promised to raise the issue at his next meeting with Northwest's director of internal auditing.

KEY TERMS

auditing
financial audit
information systems (IS) audit
operational audit
management audit
inherent risk
control risk
detection risk
materiality
reasonable assurance
systems review
tests of control
compensating controls
reprocessing
parallel simulation
test data generator program
concurrent audit techniques
embedded audit modules
integrated test facility (ITF)
snapshot technique
SCARF
audit log
audit hooks
real-time notification
continuous and intermittent simulation (CIS)
automated flowcharting programs
automated decision table programs
scanning routines
mapping programs
program tracing
input controls matrix
computer audit software (CAS)
generalized audit software (GAS)
stratified sampling

CHAPTER QUIZ

1. Which of the following is a characteristic of auditing?
a. Auditing is a systematic, step-by-step process.
b. Auditing involves the collection and review of evidence.
c. Auditing involves the use of established criteria to evaluate evidence.
d. All of the above are characteristic of auditing.

2. Which of the following is *not* one reason that an internal auditor should participate in internal control reviews during the design of new systems?
a. It is more economical to design controls during the design stage than to do so later.
b. It eliminates the need for testing controls during regular audits.
c. It minimizes the need for expensive postimplementation modifications.
d. It permits the design of audit trails while they are economical.

3. Which type of audit involves a review of general and application controls, with a focus on determining whether there is compliance with policies and adequate safeguarding of assets?
a. Information systems audit
b. Financial audit
c. Operational audit
d. Compliance audit

4. At what step in the audit process do the concepts of reasonable assurance and materiality enter into the auditor's decision process?
a. Planning.
b. Evidence collection.
c. Evidence evaluation.
d. Materiality is important in all three steps.

5. Examining whether the necessary controls have been designed into the system is called
a. risk analysis.
b. systems review.
c. tests of controls.
d. the risk-based approach to auditing.

6. Which of the following procedures is not used to detect unauthorized program changes?
a. Source code comparison
b. Parallel simulation
c. Reprocessing
d. Reprogramming code

7. The concurrent audit technique that monitors all transactions and collects data on those that meet certain characteristics specified by the auditor is called
a. an integrated test facility.
b. snapshot techniques.
c. SCARF.
d. audit hooks.

8. A computer technique that assists an auditor in understanding program logic by identifying all occurrences of specific variables is called
   a. a mapping program.
   b. program tracing.
   c. automated flowcharting.
   d. a scanning routine.
9. A computer program written especially for audit use is called
   a. GAS.
   b. SCARF.
   c. ITF.
   d. CIS.
10. The focus of an operational audit is on
   a. the reliability and integrity of the financial information.
   b. the efficient use of resources.
   c. internal controls.
   d. safeguarding assets.

DISCUSSION QUESTIONS

11.1 Auditing an AIS effectively requires that an auditor have some knowledge of computers and their accounting applications. However, it may not be feasible for every auditor to be a computer expert. Discuss the extent to which auditors should possess computer expertise in order to be effective auditors.

11.2 Should internal auditors be members of systems development teams that design and implement an AIS? Why or why not?

11.3 Berwick Industries is a fast-growing corporation that manufactures industrial containers. The company has a very sophisticated AIS utilizing advanced technology. Berwick's executives have decided to pursue listing the company's securities on a national stock exchange, but they have been advised that their listing application would be stronger if they were to create an internal audit department.

At present, Berwick does not have any employees with audit experience. To staff its new internal audit function, Berwick could (a) train some of its computer specialists in auditing, (b) hire experienced auditors and train them to understand Berwick's IS, (c) use a combination of the first two approaches, or (d) try a different approach. Which approach would you support, and why?

11.4 The assistant finance director for the city of Tustin, California was fired after city officials discovered that she had used her access to city computers to cancel her daughter's $300 water bill. An investigation revealed that she had embezzled a large sum of money from the city in this manner over a long period. She was able to conceal the embezzlement for so long because the amount embezzled always fell within a 2% error factor used by the city's internal auditors. Should Tustin's internal auditors have discovered this fraud earlier? Discuss.

PROBLEMS

11.1 You are the director of internal auditing at a university. Recently, you met with Issa Arnita, the manager of administrative data processing and expressed the desire to establish a more effective interface between the two departments. Arnita wants your help with a new computerized accounts payable system currently in development. He recommends that your department assume line responsibility for auditing suppliers' invoices prior to payment. He also wants internal auditing to make suggestions during system development, assist in its installation, and approve the completed system after making a final review.

Required:

Would you accept or reject each of the following? Why?

a. The recommendation that your department be responsible for the preaudit of suppliers' invoices.
b. The request that you make suggestions during development of the system.

c. The request that you assist in the installation of the system and approve the system after making a final review.

(CIA Examination, adapted)

11.2 As an internal auditor for the Quick Manufacturing Company, you are participating in the audit of the company's AIS. You have been reviewing the internal controls of the computer system that processes most of its accounting applications. You have studied the company's extensive documentation of its systems and have interviewed the MIS manager, operations supervisor, and other employees in order to complete your standardized computer internal control questionnaire.

You report to your supervisor that the company has designed a successful set of comprehensive internal controls into its computer systems. He thanks you for your efforts and asks for a summary report of your findings for inclusion in a final overall report on accounting internal controls.

Required:

Have you forgotten an important audit step? Explain. List five examples of specific audit procedures that you might recommend before reaching a final conclusion.

11.3 As an internal auditor, you have been assigned to evaluate the controls and operation of a computer payroll system. To test the computer systems and programs, you will be submitting independently created test transactions with regular data in a normal production run.

Required:

a. List four advantages of this technique.
b. List two disadvantages of this technique.

(CIA Examination, adapted)

11.4 You are involved in the internal audit of accounts receivable, which represent a significant portion of the assets of a large retail corporation. Your audit plan requires the use of the computer, but you encounter the following reactions.

a. The computer operations manager says that all time on the computer is booked for the foreseeable future and that it will not be available to help the auditor with his work.
b. The computer scheduling manager suggests that your computer program be cataloged into the computer program library (on disk storage) so that it can be run when computer time becomes available.
c. You are refused admission to the computer room.
d. The systems manager tells you that it will take too much time to adapt the computer audit program to the computer's operating system and that the computer installation programmers will write the programs needed for the audit.

Required:

For each of the four situations described, state the action the auditor should take to proceed with the accounts receivable audit.

(CIA Examination, adapted)

11.5 You are a manager for the regional CPA firm of Dewey, Cheatem, and Howe (DC&H). You are reviewing your staff's working papers of an audit of the state welfare agency. You find that the test data concept was used to test the agency's computer program that maintains accounting records. Specifically, your staff obtained a duplicate copy of the program and of the welfare accounting data file from the manager of computer operations and borrowed the test transaction data file used by the welfare agency's programmers when the program was written. These were processed on DC&H's home office computer. A copy of the edit summary report that listed no errors was included in the working papers, along with a notation by the audit senior that the test indicates good application controls.

You note that the quality of the audit conclusions obtained from this test is flawed in several respects, and you decide to ask your subordinates to repeat the test.

Required:

Identify three existing or potential problems with the way this test was performed. For each problem, suggest one or more procedures that might be performed during the revised test to avoid flaws in the audit conclusions.

11.6 You are auditing the financial statements of Aardvark Wholesalers, Inc. (AW), a wholesaler with operations in 12 western states and total revenues of about $125 million. AW uses a computer system in several of its major accounting applications. Accordingly, you are carrying out an IS audit to evaluate internal controls in their computer system.

You have obtained a manual containing job descriptions for key personnel in AW's IS division. Excerpts from these job descriptions follow.

Director of IS: Reports to administrative vice president. Responsible for defining the mission of the IS division and for planning, staffing, and managing a department that optimally executes this mission.

Manager of systems and programming: Reports to director of IS. Responsible for managing a staff of systems analysts and programmers whose mission is to design, program, test, implement, and maintain cost-effective data processing systems. Also responsible for establishing and monitoring documentation standards.

Manager of operations: Reports to director of IS. Responsible for cost-effective management of computer center operations, for enforcement of processing standards, and for systems programming, including implementation of operating system vendor upgrades.

Data entry shift supervisor: Reports to manager of operations. Responsible for supervision of data entry operators and monitoring of data preparation standards.

Operations shift supervisor: Reports to manager of operations. Responsible for supervision of computer operations staff and monitoring of processing standards.

Data control clerk: Reports to manager of operations. Responsible for logging and distributing computer input and output, monitoring source data control procedures, and custody of program and data files.

Required:

a. Prepare an organizational chart for AW's IS division.
b. Name two positive and two negative aspects (from an internal control standpoint) of this organizational structure.
c. What additional information, if any, would you require before you could make a final judgment on the adequacy of AW's separation of functions in the IS division?

11.7 Robinson's Plastic Pipe Corporation uses a computerized inventory data processing system. The basic input record to this system has the format shown in Table 11.8. You are performing an audit of source data controls for this system, and you have decided to use an input controls matrix for this purpose.

Required:

Prepare an input controls matrix using the same format and listing the same input controls as the one in Fig. 11.3. However, replace the field names shown in Fig. 11.3 with those of the inventory transaction file shown in Table 11.8. Place checks in the cells of the matrix that represent input controls you might expect to find for each field.

TABLE 11.8 Parts Inventory Transaction File

Field Name	Field Type	Positions
Item number	Numeric	1–6
Description	Alphanumeric	7–31
Transaction date	Date	32–37
Transaction type	Alphanumeric	38
Document number	Alphanumeric	39–46
Quantity	Numeric	47–51
Unit cost	Monetary	52–58

11.8 As an internal auditor for the state auditor's office, you have been assigned to review the implementation of a new computer system in the state welfare agency. The agency is installing an on-line computer system to maintain the state's data base of welfare recipients. Under the old system, state residents applying for welfare assistance completed a form giving their name, address, and other personal data, plus details about their income, assets, dependents, and other data needed to establish their eligibility. The data on these forms is checked by welfare examiners to verify its authenticity. The welfare examiners then certify the applicant's eligibility for assistance and determine the form and amount of aid.

Under the new system, welfare applicants will provide their case data to clerks, who will simultaneously enter the data into the system using on-line terminals. Each applicant record will be assigned a "pending" status until a welfare examiner can verify the authenticity of the crucial data used in determining eligibility for assistance. When this verification process has been completed, the welfare examiner will enter a change in the status code from "pending" to "approved," and then the system will execute a program to calculate the appropriate amount of aid.

Periodically, the circumstances (income, assets, dependents, etc.) of welfare recipients change and the data base needs to be updated accordingly. Welfare examiners will enter these change transactions into the system as soon as their accuracy has been verified. The system will then immediately recalculate the recipient's welfare benefit. At the end of each month, checks are generated and mailed to all eligible welfare recipients.

Welfare assistance in your state amounts to several hundred million dollars annually. You are concerned about the possibilities of fraud and abuse.

Required:

a. Describe how you could employ concurrent audit techniques within this system to reduce the risks of fraud and abuse.
b. Describe how computer audit software could be used to review the work of welfare examiners in verifying applicant eligibility data. For this purpose you may assume that the state auditor's office has access to computerized data bases maintained by other state and local government agencies.

11.9 You are an internal auditor for the Military Industrial Company. You are presently preparing test transactions for the company's weekly payroll processing program. Each input record to this program contains the following data items.

Spaces	Data Item
1–9	Social Security number
10	Pay code (1 = hourly; 2 = salaried)
11–16	Wage rate or salary
17–19	Hours worked, in tenths
20–21	Number of exemptions claimed
22–29	Year-to-date gross pay, including cents
30–80	Employee name and address

The program performs the following edit checks on each input record.

- Field checks to identify any records that do not have numeric characters in the fields for wage rate/salary, hours, exemptions, and year-to-date gross pay.
- A validity check of the pay code.
- A limit check to identify any hourly employee records with a wage rate higher than $20.00.
- A limit check to identify any hourly employee records with hours worked greater than 70.0.
- A limit check to identify any salaried employee records with a weekly salary greater than $2,000.00 or less than $100.00.

Records that do not pass these edit checks are listed on an error report. For those that pass the edit checks, the program performs a series of calculations. First, the employee's gross pay is determined. Gross pay for a salaried employee is equal to the salary amount contained within spaces 11–16 of the input record. Gross pay for an hourly employee is equal to the wage rate times the number of hours up to 40, plus 1.5 times the wage rate times the number of hours in excess of 40.

The program computes federal withholding tax for each employee by multiplying gross pay times a tax rate determined from Table 11.9. The program next computes state withholding tax for each employee by multiplying gross pay times a tax rate determined from Table 11.10.

The program next computes the employee's pension contribution, which is 3% of gross pay for hourly employees and 4% of gross pay for salaried employees. Finally, the program computes the employee's net pay, which is gross pay minus tax withholdings and pension contribution. Once all these calculations have been completed for one employee record, the program prints that employee's paycheck and summary earnings statement and then proceeds to the next employee input record to perform edit checks and payroll calculations, continuing this cycle until all input records have been processed.

Your short-term goal is to prepare a set of test transactions containing one of each possible type of error and another set of test transactions that will test each of the computational alternatives one at a time. Transactions to test for multiple errors in one record, or to test for multiple combinations of logic paths, are to be developed later.

The test transactions you prepare need not include a Social Security number or an employee name and address (your assistant will add those after reviewing a file printout). Accordingly, each of your test transactions will consist of a series of 20 characters representing data in spaces 10–29 of an input record. For example, for an hourly employee who has a wage rate of $9.50, worked 40.5 hours, claims two exemptions, and has a year-to-date gross pay of exactly $12,000, the test transaction would be 10009504050201200000.

Required:

a. Prepare a set of test transactions that contains one of the errors tested for by the edit checks. Determine the expected results of processing for each of these test transactions.
b. Prepare a set of test transactions that tests one of the ways in which gross pay may be determined. Determine the expected gross pay for each of these transactions.
c. Prepare a set of test transactions that tests one of the ways in which the federal withholding tax

TABLE 11.9 Computation of Federal Withholding Tax

Number of Exemptions	Gross Pay Range $0–$99.99	$100–$249.99	$250–$499.99	Over $500
0–1	0.06	0.12	0.18	0.24
2–3	0.04	0.10	0.16	0.22
4–5	0.02	0.08	0.14	0.20
Over 5	0.00	0.06	0.12	0.18

TABLE 11.10 Computation of State Withholding Tax

Number of Exemptions	Gross Pay Range $0–$249.99	Over $500
0–3	0.03	0.05
Over 3	0.01	0.03

may be computed. Determine the expected value of the federal withholding tax for each of these test transactions.

d. Prepare a set of test transactions that tests one of the ways in which the state withholding tax may be computed. Determine the expected value of the state withholding tax for each of these test transactions.

e. Prepare a set of test transactions that tests one of the ways in which the pension contribution may be computed. Determine the expected value of the pension contribution for each of these test transactions.

11.10 The internal audit department of Sachem Manufacturing Company is considering the purchase of computer software that will aid the auditing process. Sachem's financial and manufacturing control systems are completely automated on a large mainframe computer. Melinda Robinson, the director of internal auditing, believes that Sachem should acquire computer audit software to assist in the financial and procedural audits that her department conducts. Robinson is considering the following types of software packages:

- A generalized audit software package that assists in basic audit work such as the retrieval of live data from large computer files. The department would review this information using conventional audit investigation techniques. More specifically, the department could perform criteria selection, sampling, basic computations for quantitative analysis, record handling, graphical analysis, and the printing of output (i.e., confirmations).
- An integrated test facility (ITF) package that uses, monitors, and controls dummy test data as it is processed by existing programs. It also checks the programs and the existence and adequacy of program data entry and processing controls.
- A flowcharting package that graphically presents the flow of information through a system and pinpoints control strengths and weaknesses.
- A parallel simulation and modeling package that uses actual data to conduct the same tests using another program, a computer logic program developed by the auditor. The package can also be used to seek answers to difficult audit problems (involving many comparisons) within statistically acceptable confidence limits.

Required:

a. Without regard to any specific computer audit software, identify the general advantages of using computer audit software to assist with audits.

b. Describe the audit purpose facilitated and the procedural steps to be followed by the internal auditor in using the following:

1. Generalized audit software package

2. Integrated test facility package
3. Control flowcharting package
4. Program (parallel) simulation and modeling package

(CMA Examination, adapted)

11.11 The Thermo-Bond Manufacturing Company maintains its fixed asset records on its computer. The fixed asset master file includes the data items listed in Table 11.11.

Required:

Refer to Table 11.7, which describes the general functions of computer audit software. Then explain several ways such software could be used by an auditor in performing a financial audit of Thermo-Bond's fixed asset account.

11.12 An auditor is conducting an examination of the financial statements of a wholesale cosmetics distributor with an inventory consisting of thousands of individual items. The distributor keeps its inventory in its own distribution center and in two public warehouses. An inventory computer file is maintained on a computer disk, and at the end of each business day the file is updated. Each record of the inventory file contains the following data.

Item number	Location of item
Description of item	Cost per item
Quantity on hand	Date of last purchase
	Date of last sale
	Quantity sold during year

The auditor will have a CAS and a computer tape containing inventory data as of the date of the distributor's physical inventory count. The auditor will perform the following audit procedures:

1. Observe the distributor's physical count of inventories as of a given date, and test a sample for accuracy.
2. Compare the auditor's test counts with the inventory records.
3. Compare physical count data with the inventory records.
4. Test the mathematical accuracy of the distributor's final inventory valuation.
5. Test inventory pricing by obtaining item costs from buyers, vendors, or other sources.

TABLE 11.11 Fixed Asset Master File

Item Number	Location	Description
1	1–6	Asset number
2	7–30	Description
3	31	Type code
4	32–34	Location code
5	35–40	Date of acquisition
6	41–50	Original cost
7	51–56	Date of retirement*
8	57	Depreciation method code
9	58–61	Depreciation rate
10	62–63	Useful life (years)
11	64–73	Accumulated depreciation at beginning of year
12	74–83	Year-to-date depreciation

*For assets still in service the retirement date is assigned the value 99/99/99.

6. Examine inventory purchase and sale transactions on or near the year-end date to verify that all such transactions were recorded in the proper accounting period.
7. Ascertain the propriety of inventory items located in public warehouses.
8. Analyze inventory for evidence of possible obsolescence.
9. Analyze inventory for evidence of possible overstocking or slow-moving items.
10. Test the accuracy of individual data items listed in the distributor's inventory master file.

Required:

Describe how the use of the general-purpose software package and the tape of the inventory file data might be helpful to the auditor in performing each of these auditing procedures.

(CPA Examination, adapted)

CASE 11.1 ANYCOMPANY, INC.—AN ONGOING COMPREHENSIVE CASE

Select a local company with an internal auditing department, and obtain permission to study its internal auditing policies and procedures. Then complete the following steps and prepare a report describing your findings and conclusions:

1. Determine to whom internal auditing reports. Does this reporting arrangement provide the internal audit function with sufficient independence?
2. Does the internal audit function perform IS, financial, and operational audits? Does it perform other kinds of audits? About what percentage of its total audit work falls into each of these categories?
3. Determine how the internal auditors perform IS audits. If possible, obtain copies of audit programs, checklists, and/or questionnaires used in performing IS audits. Comment on the company's approach to IS auditing.
4. In performing IS audits, do the internal auditors use methods of auditing through the computer, such as reprocessing, parallel simulation, program tracing, test data processing, on-line testing, and concurrent audit techniques? Describe how the internal auditors use these methods.
5. In carrying out financial audits, does the internal audit function employ computer audit software? If so, obtain a copy of the documentation and describe the functions it can perform. If possible, observe how the audit software is used to carry out a financial audit, and examine copies of the output.
6. Ask the internal auditors to tell you about some specific audit jobs where they discovered something unusual and/or were able to recommend improvements in controls or operating procedures that saved the company substantial amounts of time or money.

CASE 11.2 PRESTON MANUFACTURING COMPANY

You are performing a financial audit of the general ledger accounts of the Preston Manufacturing Company. At the beginning of the current fiscal year, the company converted its general ledger accounting from a manual to a computer-based system. The new system uses two computer files, the contents of which are specified as follows:

General Journal

Field Name	Field Type	Size
Account number	Numeric	6
Amount	Monetary	9.2
Debit/credit code	Alphanumeric	1
Date (MM/DD/YY)	Date	6
Reference document type	Alphanumeric	4
Reference document number	Numeric	6

General Ledger Control

Field Name	Field Type	Size
Account number	Numeric	6
Account name	Alphanumeric	20
Beginning balance/year	Monetary	9.2
Beg-bal-debit/credit code	Alphanumeric	1
Current balance	Monetary	9.2
Cur-bal-debit/credit code	Alphanumeric	1

Each day as detailed transactions are processed by Preston's other computerized accounting systems, summary journal entries are accumulated; at the end of the day, they are added to the general ledger file. At the end of each week and each month, the general journal file is processed against the general ledger control file to compute a new current balance for each account and to print a trial balance.

The following resources are available as you complete the audit:

- Your firm's generalized computer audit software package, which can perform the general functions listed in Table 11.7.
- A complete copy of the general journal file for the entire year.
- A copy of the general ledger file as of the fiscal year-end (i.e., current balance = year-end balance).
- A printout of Preston's year-end trial balance listing the account number, account name, and balance of each account on the general ledger control file.

Design a series of procedures utilizing the CAS to analyze the data in these files, and prepare the reports needed to carry out your financial audit. Your application design should include the following:

1. A description of the data content of each output report, preferably in the form of a tabular layout chart of the report format.
2. A description of the auditing objectives of each report and how the report would be used in subsequent auditing procedures to achieve those objectives.
3. A detailed system flowchart showing each of the processing steps in the computer audit software application.

ANSWERS TO CHAPTER QUIZ

1. d	**3.** a	**5.** b	**7.** c	**9.** c
2. b	**4.** d	**6.** d	**8.** d	**10.** b

PART THREE

CHAPTER 12

The Revenue Cycle: Sales and Cash Collections

LEARNING OBJECTIVES

After studying this chapter, you should be able to

- Describe the major business activities and related data processing operations performed in the revenue cycle.
- Assess how developments in information technology affect the performance of revenue cycle activities.
- Document your understanding of the revenue cycle.
- Identify major threats in the revenue cycle, and evaluate the adequacy of various control procedures for dealing with those threats.
- Discuss the key decisions that need to be made in the revenue cycle, and identify the information needed to make those decisions.
- Read and understand a data model (REA diagram) of the revenue cycle.

Integrative Case: Alpha Omega Electronics

Alpha Omega Electronics (AOE) is a manufacturer of a variety of inexpensive consumer electronic products, including calculators, digital clocks, radios, pagers, toys, games, and small kitchen appliances. AOE's primary customers are discount retail stores, but the company has recently begun selling in bulk to mail order firms that advertise in catalogs and magazines. Figure 12.1 shows a partial organization chart for AOE.

Over the past three years, AOE has been steadily losing market share. At the last executive meeting, Trevor Whitman, vice president of marketing, explained that one reason for AOE's declining market share is its competitors' ability to provide better customer service. Currently, it takes AOE 24 hours to notify customers whether the items they ordered are in stock or need to be back-ordered. It also takes at least a full day to approve credit for new customers or to increase an existing customer's credit limit. Moreover, the sales staff estimates that they spend at least 10% of their time revisiting customers to collect data that is missing or erroneous on the original order.

Trevor suggested redesigning AOE's entire sales order entry system. He recommended supplying the sales force with portable computers so that they can check inventory availability from the field, thereby providing customers with more accurate delivery estimates. He also suggested increasing AOE's focus on the mail order business, which he perceived as being more lucrative and less volatile than the retail trade. In addition, Trevor wanted AOE to use the Internet to complement its mail order business.

FIGURE 12.1
Partial Organization Chart for AOE

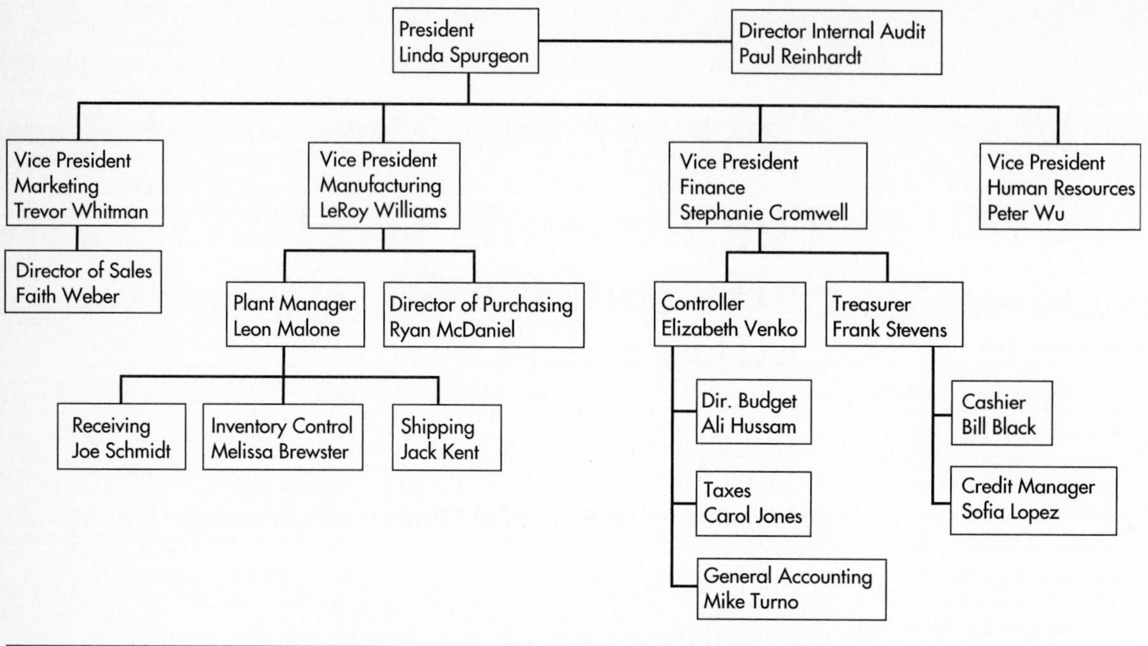

Linda Spurgeon, president of AOE, was skeptical of Trevor's proposals. She asked Elizabeth Venko, the controller, to investigate the costs and benefits of redesigning the sales order entry system around Trevor's suggestions and of increasing AOE's focus on the mail order and Internet markets.

Linda was also concerned about AOE's cash flow and asked Elizabeth to review the company's current cash collection procedures. The most recent accounts receivable aging schedule indicated a significant increase in the number of past due customer accounts. Consequently, AOE has had to increase its short-term borrowing because of delays in collecting customer payments. In addition, the Best Value Company, a retail chain that has been one of AOE's major customers, recently went bankrupt. Elizabeth admitted that she is not sure whether AOE will be able to collect the large balance due from Best Value.

Elizabeth began her assignment by listing the questions for which she needs answers:

1. How could AOE's sales order entry system be redesigned to provide better information to sales staff and reduce the time to fill customer orders? To improve customer service?

2. What opportunities exist in mail order sales and the Internet? What is the likely effect of the Internet and other technological advances on the mail order industry?

3. How can AOE improve its monitoring of credit accounts? How would any changes in credit policy affect both sales and uncollectible accounts?

4. How could information technology (IT) be used to improve cash collection procedures?

5. How can AOE identify its most profitable customers and markets?

As the AOE case indicates, deficiencies in the information system used to support revenue cycle activities can create significant problems for an organization. Accurate and timely information about inventory availability and customer credit status is essential. As you read this chapter, think about how AOE's information system can be redesigned to provide more efficient and effective support of its revenue cycle activities.

INTRODUCTION

The revenue cycle is a recurring set of business activities and related information processing operations associated with providing goods and services to customers and collecting cash in payment for those sales (see Fig. 12.2). As shown in Fig. 12.2, the primary external exchange of information is with customers. In addition, internal information flows between the revenue cycle and the other accounting cycles. For example, sales transaction data flows to the following cycles:

- The expenditure and production cycles, to initiate the purchase or production of additional inventory to meet demand.
- The human resource management/payroll cycle, to calculate sales commissions and bonuses.

FIGURE 12.2
The Context Diagram of the Revenue Cycle

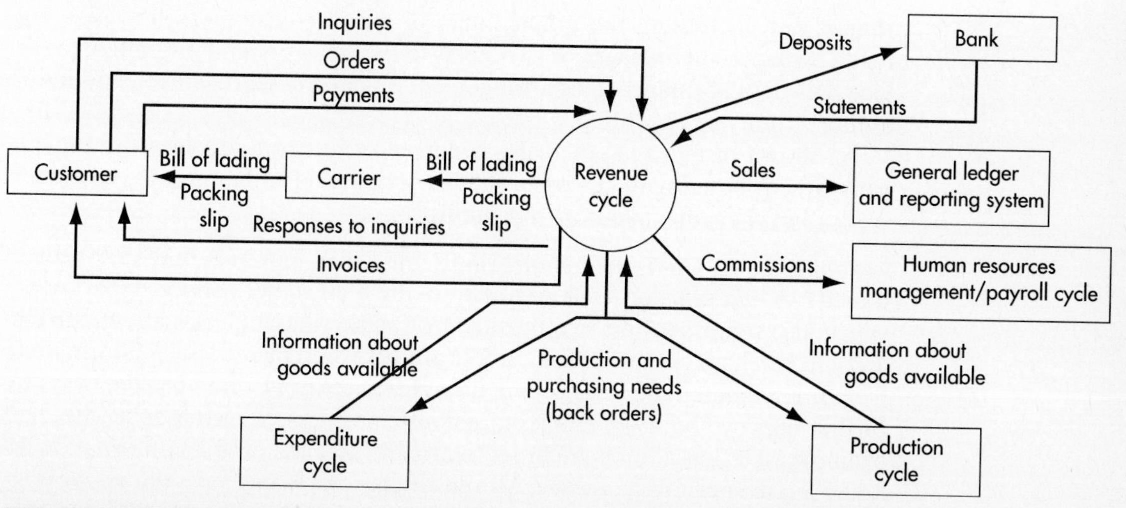

- The general ledger and reporting function, to prepare financial statements and performance reports.

This chapter is organized around the three basic functions of the AIS in the revenue cycle. The first section describes the basic business activities performed in the revenue cycle and how data about those activities is captured and processed by the AIS. The second section discusses the major control objectives in the revenue cycle and explains how the AIS can be designed to mitigate the threats associated with revenue cycle activities. The final section presents a data model that shows how the AIS can effectively and efficiently store and organize the information needed to make key revenue cycle decisions.

REVENUE CYCLE BUSINESS ACTIVITIES

One objective of the AIS in the revenue cycle is to support the performance of the organization's business activities by efficiently processing transaction data. Figure 12.3 shows the four basic revenue cycle business activities: sales order entry, shipping, billing, and cash collections. Although the remainder of this section discusses each of these activities separately, keep in mind that advances in IT often enable several of them to be performed simultaneously.

Sales Order Entry

The first step in the revenue cycle is sales order entry (circle 1.0 in Fig. 12.3). This function includes all the activities involved in soliciting and processing customer orders. These activities are performed by the sales order department, which reports to the vice president of marketing (refer back to Fig. 12.1).

Key Decisions and Information Needs. The sales order entry function obtains needed information about inventory availability and customer credit status from the inventory control and accounting functions, respectively. Decisions concerning credit policies, including the approval of credit for new customers and increasing the credit limits of existing customers, however, are made by the credit manager, who reports to the treasurer and ultimately to the vice president of finance. This arrangement effectively segregates the duties of authorization and recording.

As shown in Fig. 12.4, the sales order entry function involves three main activities: responding to customer inquiries, checking and approving customer credit, and checking inventory availability.

Responding to Customer Inquiries. Customer inquiries may be handled directly by the sales order department or by a customer service department, which also reports to the vice president of marketing. Inquiries about current account balances or the status of orders are answered by retrieving information from the customer and sales orders files. Advances in IT often provide ways to further improve both the efficiency and effectiveness of customer service. For example, web sites allow companies to provide detailed product information 24 hours a day, seven days a week. Moreover, customers can save the answers to their inquiries for future reference. Similarly, a company can use a record of a

FIGURE 12.3
Level 0 Data Flow Diagram of the Revenue Cycle

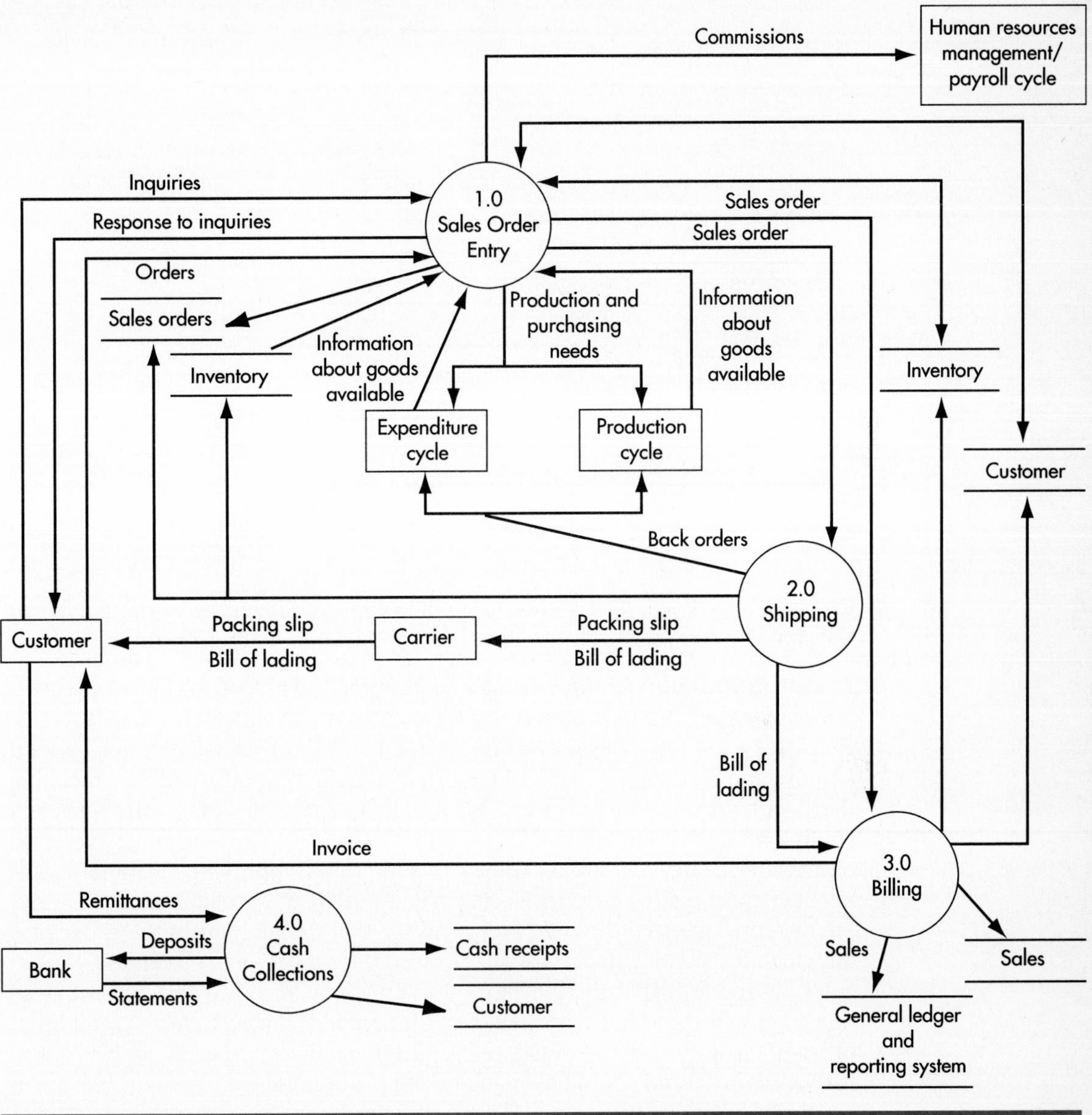

customer's past interaction with its web site to more effectively monitor how well customer problems are resolved.

The use of technologies like web sites and e-mail, instead of toll-free telephone numbers, can reduce the costs of customer service. Keep in mind, however, the value of the customer's time. A poorly designed, hard to use web site, for example, could actually hurt sales by frustrating customers and creating ill will.

FIGURE 12.4
Level 1 Data Flow Diagram: Sales Order Entry

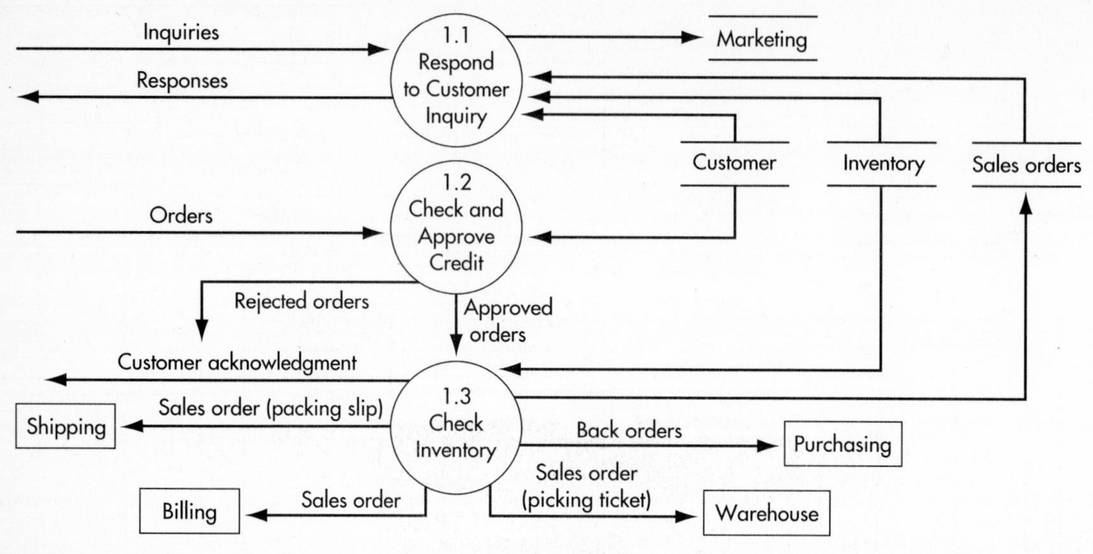

Conversely, as Focus 12.1 shows, using data captured from a well-designed web site can help companies better plan their production and thereby increase sales.

Credit Approval. Credit sales should be approved before they are processed. For existing customers with well-established payment histories, a formal credit check for each sale is usually unnecessary. Instead, order takers have general authorization to approve orders from "customers in good standing," meaning those without past due balances. This usually is accomplished by establishing a **credit limit** (maximum allowable account balance) for each customer based on past credit history and ability to pay. In such cases, approving customer credit involves checking the customer master file to verify the account exists, identifying the customer's credit limit, and verifying that the amount of the order plus any current account balance does not exceed this limit. Doing this efficiently and correctly requires that the customer master file be accurate and current at all times. For new customers, or when the order exceeds the customer's credit limit, or when the customer has outstanding, past due balances, specific authorization for approving credit should be made by the credit manager.

Checking Inventory Availability. Inventory quantities on hand must also be checked, so that customers can be informed about availability and expected delivery dates. This function is important because if inventory records are not accurate and up to date, customers may become justifiably upset when unexpected delays occur in filling their orders.

If sufficient inventory is on hand to fill the order, the sales order is completed and the shipping, inventory control, and billing departments are notified

FOCUS 12.1 Using Customer Inquiries Data to Improve Sales

NATIONAL Semiconductor a manufacturer of computer chips and other devices, credits improved management of customer inquiry data for dramatically increased sales of a heat-sensing device. Its web site gets millions of hits a month. Many of those are inquiries from engineers who want technical information about National's products.

National collected data about which products received the most attention from visitors to its web site and the number and frequency of e-mail inquiries about its various products. This information was then sent to product sales managers, along with traditional sales and order information. The web site and e-mail data alerted sales managers to a marked increase in interest in National's heat sensors. This allowed them to revise their sales forecasts and ramp up production in anticipation of increased demand. As a result, National was able to meet a surge of new orders for the product. Pat Brockett, National's vice president of sales and marketing, believes that without the analysis of customer inquiry data, the company would not have been prepared for the demand and, thereby, would have lost millions of dollars of sales to rivals.

Source: Mary J. Cronin, "Using the Web to Push Key Data to Decision Makers," *Fortune* (September 29, 1997): 254.

of the sale. An acknowledgment may also be sent to the customer. If there is not sufficient inventory on hand to fill the order, a **back order** for those items must be created. In manufacturing companies, this task involves notifying the production department to initiate the production of the requested items. In retail companies, the purchasing department would be notified about the need to order the required items.

Documents, Records, and Procedures. The receipt of a customer's order triggers the sales order entry process and produces several internal documents. To assist you in following the flow and purpose of these documents, Fig. 12.5 depicts a typical batch-oriented sales order entry process such as the one currently used at a typical manufacturing company like AOE.

As they complete calls, sales representatives write up orders on preprinted forms. These forms are faxed nightly to the sales order department, where they are assembled in batches of approximately 50 transactions for data entry. Before proceeding with data entry, batch totals (a record count and a hash total of quantities ordered) are manually calculated for each group of 50 transactions. Sales order clerks then enter only the following items for each transaction: customer account number, salesperson number, product numbers and quantities, and requested delivery date. The customer number is used to access the appropriate record in the customer file. The system then retrieves the customer's name and address to complete the sales order. Similarly, the product number is used to access the appropriate record in the inventory file and to retrieve the item description and price.

At this point a number of edit checks are performed to ensure input accuracy, including the following:

- *Validity checks* of the customer account and inventory item numbers are performed by matching them to information in the customer and inventory master files, respectively.

FIGURE 12.5
Sales Order Entry: Batch Processing

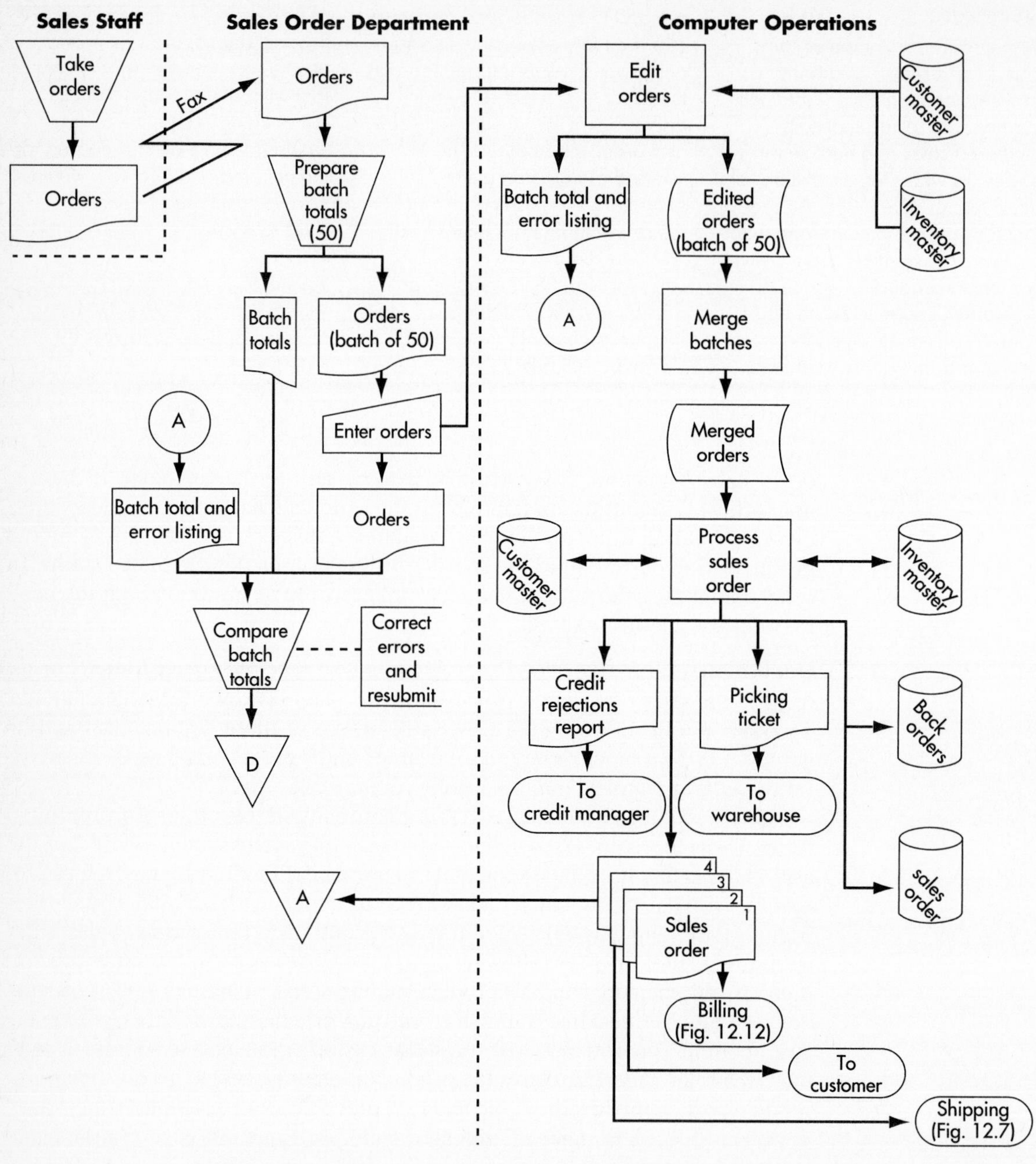

- *Redundant data checks* of customer account numbers and names and item numbers and descriptions are made to detect cases where a valid but incorrect account or item number was entered.
- *Field checks* are made to ensure that only numeric data are entered in all other numeric fields and to avoid subsequent processing errors.
- A *reasonableness test* is performed to verify the accuracy of the quantity ordered. The test compares the quantity ordered with the standard amounts normally ordered as indicated in the corresponding master inventory item record.
- *Range checks* on the order and delivery date are made to verify feasibility.
- A *completeness test* is run to verify that each transaction record contains all appropriate data items.

Transaction records that pass all these edit tests represent accurate and valid sales orders. Those that fail one or more tests are listed in an error and exception report for investigation and correction.

As the orders are entered, the system also automatically calculates batch totals. After processing, these system-generated batch totals are compared with those calculated manually to ensure that all transactions have been entered. Any discrepancies are investigated and corrected. The use of small batches facilitates identifying error sources.

The batches of valid sales orders are then merged into one large transaction file in order to process the orders and update the various master files. The system first calculates the sales amount and compares it with the customer's available credit (credit limit less any outstanding unpaid purchases). Orders that fail this credit check are printed on a *credit rejections report.* The credit manager evaluates this report and determines whether to increase the customer's credit limit or reject the order. Accepted orders are reentered with the next batch of orders; customers who are denied credit are notified that their order must be prepaid (these last two steps are not shown in Fig. 12.5).

Next the system checks whether the inventory is sufficient to fill accepted orders. If it is, the customer's account balance is debited for the amount of the sale and the "quantity available" field in the inventory file is reduced for the amount of the order. Otherwise, a back-order record is generated for the needed items.

At this point, several documents are printed. The primary internally generated document produced by sales order entry is the **sales order,** which lists the item numbers, quantities, prices, and terms of the sale (see Fig. 12.6). One copy of the sales order is filed in the sales order department, where it can be referenced to respond to customer inquiries, such as the status of open orders. Another copy is sent to the customer to acknowledge acceptance of the order. Copies of the sales order are also sent to the billing and shipping departments, to notify them of a pending shipment. The copy sent to the shipping department is often attached to the package, serving as a **packing slip** that identifies the contents of the shipment (note the columns for recording quantity shipped and quantity back-ordered).

The other document produced by sales order entry is the **picking ticket,** which authorizes the release of merchandise to the shipping department. The

FIGURE 12.6
Sample AOE Sales Order

12345

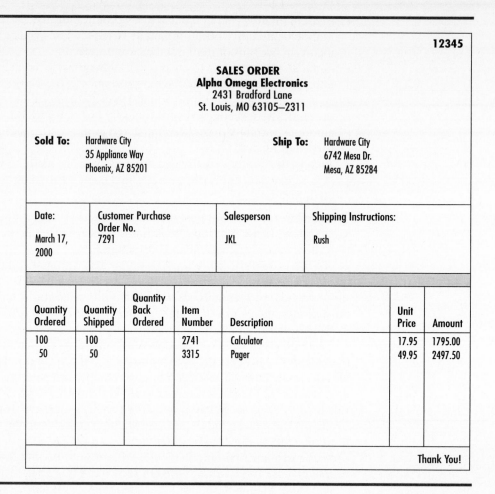

SALES ORDER
Alpha Omega Electronics
2431 Bradford Lane
St. Louis, MO 63105–2311

Sold To:	Hardware City 35 Appliance Way Phoenix, AZ 85201	**Ship To:**	Hardware City 6742 Mesa Dr. Mesa, AZ 85284

Date:	Customer Purchase Order No.	Salesperson	Shipping Instructions:
March 17, 2000	7291	JKL	Rush

Quantity Ordered	Quantity Shipped	Quantity Back Ordered	Item Number	Description	Unit Price	Amount
100	100		2741	Calculator	17.95	1795.00
50	50		3315	Pager	49.95	2497.50

Thank You!

picking ticket is often printed so that the item numbers and quantities are listed in the sequence in which they can be most efficiently retrieved from the warehouse.

Opportunities for Using Information Technology. At this point, you have probably noticed several inefficiencies with the batch processing of sales orders. For example, errors in customer orders are not caught until after they have been entered into the system, so that the customer will have to be recontacted to obtain the correct information. The credit approval process also requires considerable time.

To correct these inefficiencies, most organizations are switching to on-line processing of sales orders. For example, sales staff can be equipped with portable computers and modems so they can enter and edit customer orders from the field. Direct entry would enable them to catch and correct any mistakes in data entry as they occur, instead of having to revisit the customer. Sales representatives would also be able to inform the customer immediately whether the order had been approved and whether the items being ordered were in stock or had to be back-ordered.

Elizabeth Venko's research revealed that alternative types of portable computers could be used by AOE's sales force. The Gillette Company, for example, provides its sales force with pen-based computers instead of laptops with keyboards. Gillette claims that the pen-based computers are more useful because sales representatives can use the pen to check off items that need to be ordered and write short notes while walking down store aisles with the customer's purchasing agent. On the other hand, Ingersoll-Rand Corporation gives its sales representatives portable computers equipped with CD-ROM drives so that they can make multimedia presentations of technical products. The representatives can carry portable computers around more easily than lugging flip charts or boxes of slides. Moreover, their presentations are interactive because the multimedia software facilitates jumping to any topic raised by the customer simply by clicking on the appropriate icons. Presentations are further enhanced by including video clips of customer testimonials and demonstrations of how technical products work. Elizabeth decided to meet with Faith Weber, AOE's director of sales, to discuss which type of portable computer would be most appropriate for AOE's sales force.

Adding e-mail to the dial-in sales order entry system can further improve the effectiveness of the sales force. For example, Owens-Corning uses e-mail to provide sales representatives with detailed up-to-date data about each of the customers they are scheduled to call on that day, and about any new promotions or marketing strategies. Thus e-mail reduces the need for salespeople to return to the home office and enables them to spend more time with customers. E-mail also speeds up the approval of special deals for customers. For example, AT&T sales representatives use e-mail to simultaneously send proposals to all appropriate managers, thereby reducing overall approval time. Finally, e-mail streamlines the management of the sales force. For example, one e-mail message can inform the entire sales staff of last-minute price changes.

Elizabeth also learned that another way to improve the sales order entry process involves using electronic data interchange (EDI) to link directly with customers. With EDI, retail stores would send their orders directly to AOE's sales order system in a format that would eliminate the need for data entry. EDI would cut costs, eliminate errors, and reduce order processing time.

Linking EDI with customers' point-of-sale (POS) systems can provide additional service improvements. For example, Focus 12.2 describes how one manufacturer uses POS data from large retailers like Kmart for monitoring inventories of its products and for automatically replenishing stocks when they run low. Perhaps AOE could explore a similar arrangement with some of its major customers.

Sales order entry efficiency can also be improved by allowing customers to enter sales order data themselves. One way of doing this involves the use of optical character recognition (OCR) devices. For example, retail stores such as Service Merchandise and many mail order firms have customers mark item numbers and quantities on preprinted order forms that can be read by an OCR

FOCUS 12.2 Scotch Maid: Managing Your Customer's Inventory to Increase Your Sales

SCOTCH MAID is a manufacturer of stretchy women's garments known as bodywear. It is the largest private-label supplier of bodywear in the United States, supplying such retail giants as Kmart, Wal-Mart, Sears, and J. C. Penney.

Ivars Eichvalds, the chief information officer of the company, attributes the company's success to its philosophy that Scotch Maid does not just sell clothing, it sells both clothing and service, the service being information. Wal-Mart, Kmart, and other major retailers have pressured suppliers to use EDI to help better manage inventory. Scotch Maid has taken that system one step further. It provides value to its customers by performing sales analyses for them. For example, Scotch Maid downloads Kmart's current and historical sales figures for each of the approximately 140 items that it supplies and performs detailed sales analyses of each item. The company studies sales trends to spot any deviations from Kmart's projections. It uses that information to adjust its own production schedules so that it is able to meet Kmart's needs. This system has enabled Scotch Maid to almost always fill at least 99% of Kmart's weekly orders. That level of performance is not extraordinary, but expected. When the order fill rate once slipped to 97%, a Kmart buyer sent a fax asking what was going wrong.

Scotch Maid's success has led Kmart to include it in the selective vendor-managed inventory system. The system completely eliminates the need for ordering inventory. Kmart simply specifies the inventory levels that it wants to maintain. Scotch Maid will monitor sales at each Kmart store and inventories at Kmart's regional distribution centers and then automatically decide when it is time to replenish those inventories. Eichvalds believes that, although Scotch Maid's use of information technology currently provides it with a competitive advantage, in a few years such a capability will be necessary for all suppliers.

Source: David H. Freedman, "Why Big Retailers Love Little Scotch Maid," *Forbes ASAP* (February 28, 1994): 106–109.

reader. The Internet provides another method for direct customer order entry. Not only can customers place their orders, but as Focus 12.1 showed, companies can monitor what products in their catalog get the most attention, thereby improving sales projections and product line offerings.

An interactive web site can increase sales and reduce costs by providing customers the opportunity to customize the product to meet their needs and budgets. For example, visitors to Dell Computer's web site can try numerous combinations of components and features until they find a configuration that meets their needs at a price they can afford. Not only does this increase sales, but it also significantly cuts Dell's costs. The interactive web site eliminates the need for a salesperson to help customers configure their orders. It also enables Dell to build products in response to orders, thereby eliminating the need to carry a large inventory of finished goods. Moreover, since Dell receives payment at the time the customer orders the product, its need for working capital to finance production is drastically reduced.

Finally, Elizabeth learned that information technology can also be used to improve customer service and response to inquiries. For example, Norfolk Southern Corporation needed to provide its customers with current status reports about the location of more than 100,000 freight cars. It implemented a new information system that enabled customer service representatives to access a customer's file as soon as the telephone call was answered. The system automatically identifies the caller's telephone number. That number is then used to search the customer data base to retrieve the appropriate customer's file and display it on the service representative's computer screen. The entire process takes less time than asking for the customer's name or account number. It also eliminates errors associated with manually entering that data.

Shipping

The second step in the revenue cycle involves filling customer orders and shipping the desired merchandise (circle 2.0 in Fig. 12.3). Warehouse workers are responsible for filling customer orders by removing items from inventory according to the instructions on the picking ticket. The shipping department is responsible for the actual delivery of the merchandise to customers. As shown in Fig. 12.1, both of these functions, which involve the custody of inventory, report ultimately to the vice president of manufacturing.

Key Decisions and Information Needs. One major decision that needs to be made when filling and shipping customer orders concerns the choice of delivery method. Traditionally, many companies have maintained their own truck fleets for deliveries. Large companies such as GM have even assigned entire departments to this function. Increasingly, however, manufacturers are outsourcing this function to commercial carriers such as Ryder System, Inc., Roadway Services, Inc., and Schneider National Company. Outsourcing deliveries reduces costs and allows manufacturers to concentrate on their core business activity (the production of goods). Selecting the proper carrier, however, requires collecting and maintaining information about carrier performance (i.e., percentage of on-time deliveries, damage claims) and integrating that information in the AIS.

Globalization adds complexity to outbound logistics. The efficiency and effectiveness of different distribution methods, such as trucking or rail, differs around the world. Taxes and regulations in various countries can also affect distribution choices. For example, Harley-Davidson has a European distribution center. It ships directly from the United States to Norway, however, in order to avoid that country's 135% luxury tax on each motorcycle. Thus an organization's AIS must include logistics software that can help to maximize the efficiency and effectiveness of its shipping function.

Whichever delivery method is used, the shipping department needs accurate information about what to ship and where to send the merchandise. This information is provided on the documents that it receives from the sales order and warehouse departments.

Documents, Records, and Procedures. The picking ticket printed by sales order entry triggers the shipping process. Warehouse workers use the picking ticket to identify which products to remove from inventory. The quantities picked are marked on the picking ticket and then the inventory, along with the completed picking ticket, is brought to the shipping department.

Figure 12.7 illustrates the flow of documents in the shipping process. The shipping department compares the physical count of inventory with the quantities indicated on the picking ticket and with the quantities indicated on the packing slip (copy 3 of the sales order) that was sent directly to shipping from sales order entry. Discrepancies can arise either because the items were not stored in the location indicated on the picking ticket or because the perpetual inventory records were inaccurate. In such cases, the shipping department needs to initiate the back-ordering of the missing items and enter the correct quantities shipped on the packing slip (these steps are not shown in Fig. 12.7, because the process of ordering goods is part of the expenditure cycle and is discussed in Chapter 13).

After the shipping clerk counts the goods delivered from the warehouse, the sales order number, item number(s), and quantities are entered using on-line terminals. A variety of edit checks similar to those described earlier for sales order entry are used to ensure that the shipping data are valid, accurate, and complete. This process updates the quantity on hand field in the inventory master file and produces multiple copies of the bill of lading. The **bill of lading** is a legal contract that defines responsibility for the goods that are in transit. It identifies the carrier, source, destination, and any special shipping instructions, and it indicates who (customer or vendor) must pay the carrier (see Fig. 12.8).

Figure 12.7 shows that one copy of the bill of lading, along with the packing slip, accompanies the shipment. If the customer is to pay the shipping charges, this copy of the bill of lading sometimes serves as a **freight bill,** to indicate the amount the customer should pay to the carrier; in other cases, the freight bill is a separate document.

Figure 12.7 shows that a copy of the bill of lading is kept by the shipping department to track and confirm the transfer of goods to the carrier. Another copy of the bill of lading is sent to the billing department to indicate that the goods have been shipped and that an invoice should be prepared and mailed. The carrier also retains a copy of the bill of lading for its records.

Opportunities for Using Information Technology. Elizabeth's research suggested a number of ways that information technology could be used to streamline AOE's shipping and warehousing procedures. Automated warehouse systems consisting of computers, bar-code scanners, conveyer belts, and forklifts can reduce the time and cost of moving inventory into and out of the warehouse. For example, J. C. Penney equips its forklifts with radio frequency data communication (RFDC) terminals to provide drivers with information about which items to pick next and where they are located. Drivers no longer need to return to a central printer to receive instructions. Once picked, items are run through a bar-code scanner; this provides real-time and accurate recording of all inventory movements into and out of the warehouse, which is essential for perpetual inventory systems.

Automated warehouse systems not only cut costs and improve efficiency in handling inventory, but can also enable more customer-responsive shipments. For example, Levi Strauss & Company's advanced warehouse system uses bar-code scanners on conveyor belts to route jeans and shirts so that they can be

FIGURE 12.7
Shipping Procedures

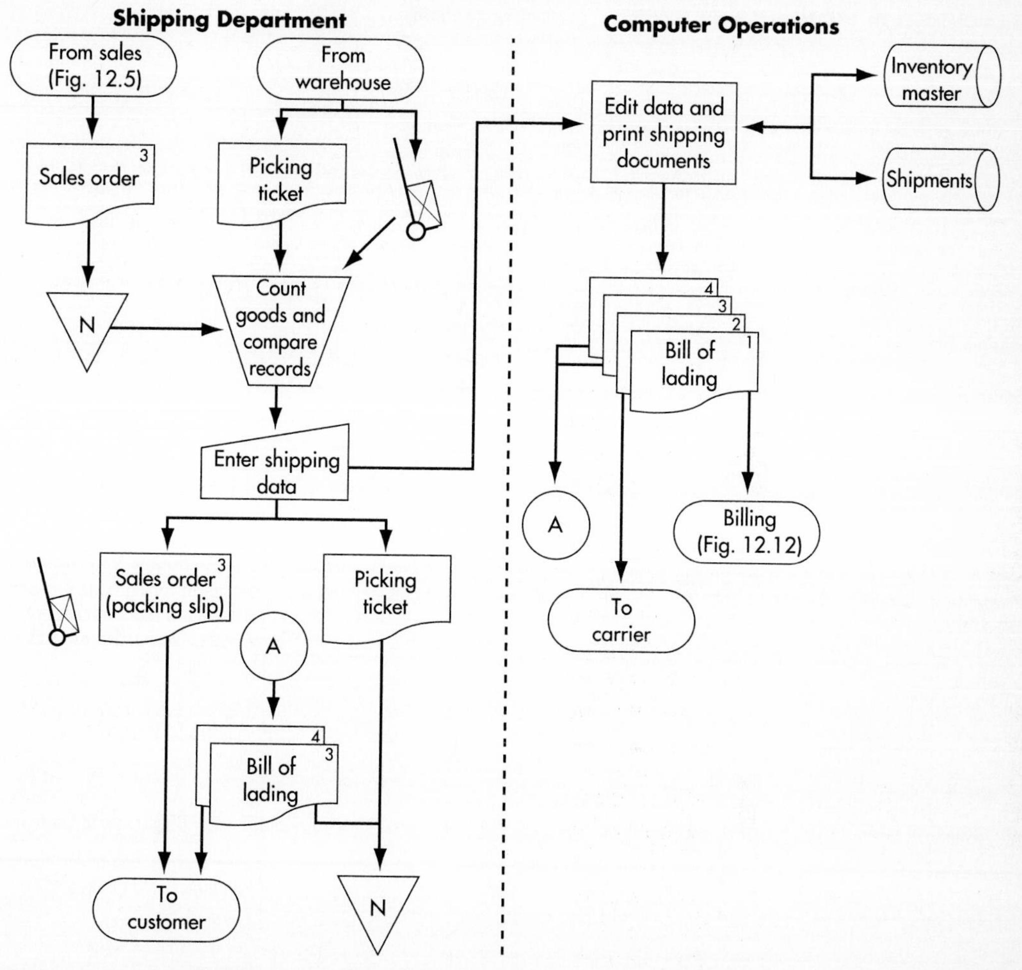

packed and shipped to customers in matched sets. Customers are also sent an electronic packing slip indicating the size, style, and colors of clothing in a pending shipment. The cartons are then bar-coded so retailers can quickly check in the merchandise and move it to the floor. All these services not only save retailers time and money, but also help improve turnover of Levi Strauss products, thereby increasing the manufacturer's sales.

Advanced communications systems can provide real-time information on shipping status. This can provide additional value to customers. For example, if the seller learns that a shipment is going to be late, prompt notification can help that customer revise its plans accordingly.

FIGURE 12.8
Sample Bill of Lading

STRAIGHT BILL OF LADING—SHORT FORM **Not Negotiable.**

Shipper's No.

Carrier **Carrier's No.**

RECEIVED, subject to the classifications and tariffs in effect on the date of the issue of this Bill of Lading.

at ____________________ **20**_____ **from** ____________________

the property described below, in apparent good order, except as noted (contents and condition of contents of packages unknown), marked, consigned, and destined as indicated below, which said carrier (the word carrier being understood throughout this contract as meaning any person or corporation in possession of the property under the contract) agrees to carry to its usual place of delivery at said destination, if on its route, otherwise to deliver to another carrier on the route to said destination. It is mutually agreed, as to each carrier of all or any of said property over all or any portion of said route to destination, and as to each party at any time interested in any or all of said property, that every service to be performed hereunder shall be subject to all terms and conditions of the Uniform Domestic Straight Bill of Lading set forth (1) in Uniform Freight Classification in effect on the date hereof, if this is a rail or a rail-water shipment, or (2) in the applicable motor carrier classification or tariff if this is a motor carrier shipment.

Shipper hereby certifies that he is familiar with all the terms and conditions of the said bill of lading, including those on the back thereof, set forth in the classification or tariff which governs the transportation of this shipment, and the said terms and conditions are hereby agreed to by the shipper and accepted for himself and his assigns.

Consigned to ____________________
(Mail or street address of consignee—For purposes of notification only.)

Destination ____________________ State _______ Zip Code _______ County _______

Delivery Address ★ ____________________
(★ To be filled in only when shipper desires and governing tariffs provide for delivery thereat.)

Route ____________________

Delivering Carrier Car or Vehicle Initials No.

No. Packages	Kind of Package, Description of Articles, Special Marks, and Exceptions	*Weight (Sub. to Cor.)	Class or Rate	Check Column

Subject to Section 7 of Conditions of applicable bill of lading, if this shipment is to be delivered to the consignee without recourse on the consignor, the consignor shall sign the following statement.

The carrier shall not make delivery of this shipment without payment of freight and all other lawful charges.

____
(Signature of Consignor.)

If charges are to be prepaid, write or stamp here, "To Be Prepaid."

Received $ __________ to apply in prepayment of the charges on the property described hereon.

____
Agent or Cashier

Per ____________________
(This signature here acknowledges only the amount prepaid.)

Charges advanced:
$

*If the shipment moves between two ports by a carrier by water, the law requires that the bill of lading shall state whether it is "carrier's or shipper's weight."

NOTE—Where the rate is dependent on value, shippers are required to state specifically in writing the agreed or declared value of the property.

The agreed or declared value of the property is hereby specifically stated by the shipper to be not exceeding

per

†"The fibre boxes used for this shipment conform to the specifications set forth in the box maker's certificate thereon, and all other requirements of Uniform Freight Classification."

†Shipper's imprint in lieu of stamp; not a part of bill of lading approved by the Interstate Commerce Commission.

____________________ Shipper, per ____________________ Agent, Per ____________________

Permanent post office address of shipper, ____________________

AOE, like many companies, uses common carriers for major deliveries, but also has its own trucks for local deliveries. On most days AOE makes between 100 and 200 local deliveries, using its fleet of eight trucks. Elizabeth has long believed that the costs of making those deliveries are higher than they need be. Therefore, she read with great interest an article about new logistical scheduling software that assigns deliveries to trucks in a manner that minimizes total time and miles traveled by the fleet. She decided to talk to Jack Kent, head of the shipping department, and Melissa Brewster, head of inventory control, about the possibility of acquiring such software and also applying some of the other automation techniques just discussed at AOE.

Billing and Accounts Receivable

The third step in the revenue cycle is billing (circle 3.0 in Fig. 12.3). Two activities are performed at this stage of the revenue cycle: invoicing customers and maintaining customer accounts. These processes are performed by the billing/accounts receivable department, which reports to the director of accounting and, ultimately, to the controller (see Fig. 12.1).

Key Decisions and Information Needs. Accurate billing for shipped merchandise is crucial, of course. This requires information from the shipping department identifying the items and quantities shipped, and information about prices and any special sales terms from the sales department. The **sales invoice** (see Fig. 12.9) notifies customers of the amount to be paid and where to send payment. The **monthly statement** summarizes all transactions that occurred during the past month and informs customers of their current account balance (see Fig. 12.10).

Sometimes adjustments to a customer's account are necessary. For example, customer accounts may be credited to reflect either the return of items or allowances granted for damaged goods. To credit a customer's account for returned goods, the credit manager must obtain information from the receiving dock that the goods were actually returned and replaced into inventory. Upon notification from the receiving department that the goods have been returned, the credit manager issues a **credit memo** (see Fig. 12.11), which authorizes the billing department to credit the customer's account. If the damage to the goods is minimal, the customer may agree to keep them for a price reduction. In such cases the credit manager issues a credit memo to reflect the amount that should be credited to the customer's account. One copy of the credit memo is sent to accounts receivable, to authorize an adjustment to the customer's account balance; the other copy is sent to the customer.

Occasionally, after all attempts to collect payment have failed, it may be necessary to write off a customer's account as uncollectible. The credit manager issues a credit memo to authorize the write-off. Unlike the cases involving damaged or returned goods, however, a copy of the credit memo is not sent to the customer.

To prevent fraud, decisions leading to the issuance of credit memos should be made by the credit manager. Otherwise, an employee with access to cash could steal a significant amount and then issue a fake credit memo to conceal the theft.

FIGURE 12.9
Sample AOE Sales Invoice

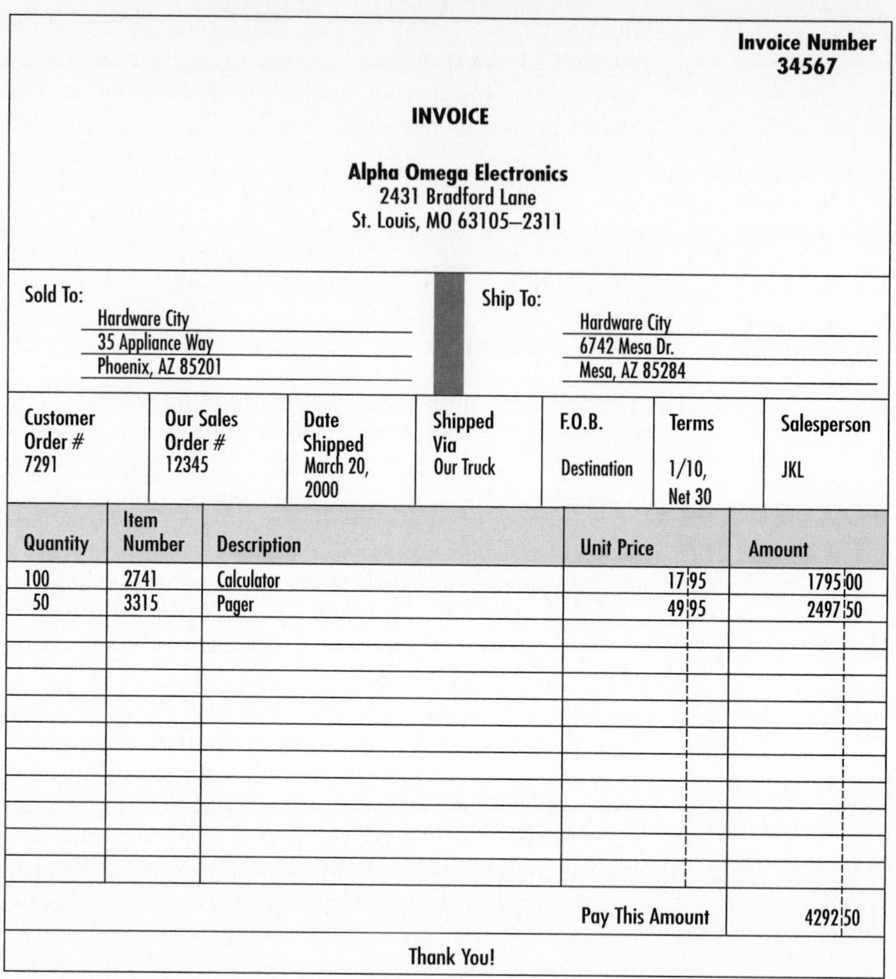

Invoice Number
34567

INVOICE

Alpha Omega Electronics
2431 Bradford Lane
St. Louis, MO 63105–2311

Sold To:
Hardware City
35 Appliance Way
Phoenix, AZ 85201

Ship To:
Hardware City
6742 Mesa Dr.
Mesa, AZ 85284

Customer Order #	Our Sales Order #	Date Shipped	Shipped Via	F.O.B.	Terms	Salesperson
7291	12345	March 20, 2000	Our Truck	Destination	1/10, Net 30	JKL

Quantity	Item Number	Description	Unit Price	Amount
100	2741	Calculator	17.95	1795.00
50	3315	Pager	49.95	2497.50
			Pay This Amount	4292.50

Thank You!

Types of Billing Systems. Most companies use either a prebilling or a postbilling system to generate invoices. At AOE, invoices are prepared after a copy of the bill of lading is received from the shipping department. This is an example of a **postbilling system,** because invoices are prepared after confirmation that the items were shipped. Postbilling systems are common in manufacturing companies, where there may often be a delay between the receipt of the order and shipment of the goods.

In contrast, mail order catalog companies, such as L.L. Bean and Spiegel, may use a **prebilling system,** in which invoices are prepared (but not sent) as soon as the order is approved (i.e., after credit has been approved and inventory availability checked). The inventory, accounts receivable, and general ledger files are also updated at this time. Prebilling systems eliminate the need

FIGURE 12.10
Sample AOE Monthly Statement

MONTHLY STATEMENT March 2000
Alpha Omega Electronics
2431 Bradford Lane
St. Louis, MO 63105–2311

Hardware City
35 Appliance Way
Phoenix, AZ 85201

Invoice Number	Date	Current	Past Due 1–30	Past Due 31–60	Past Due 61–90	Past Due Over 90
34567	3/20/2000	4292.50				
34591	3/27/2000	2346.50				
	Totals	6639.00				
				Total Amount Due	6639.00	

for some documents—for example, the invoice also fills the role of the sales order. Prebilling systems require extremely accurate inventory records, since all prebilled merchandise found to be out of stock requires accounting entries and file corrections and the addition of information about the back-ordered items to the invoice. In addition, customers are likely to be unhappy if their merchandise is not delivered when originally promised.

Figure 12.12 depicts a typical batch-oriented postbilling system such as the one used by AOE. When a copy of the bill of lading is received from the shipping department, the billing clerk matches it up with the corresponding copy of the sales order sent from sales order entry. The billing clerk then generates invoices by entering information about the item numbers and quantities shipped. The system performs a number of edit checks on the data entered, such as testing the validity of the item numbers entered and comparing the quantities with those listed in the open sales order file.

After these preliminary edit checks, the following operations are performed:

1. New records are created in the sales invoice file, and multiple copies of the sales invoice are printed.
2. The customer master file is accessed, and the customer's account is debited for the amount of the sale.
3. The open sales orders are closed to the sales order history file.

FIGURE 12.11
Sample AOE Credit Memo

11121

CREDIT MEMORANDUM

Alpha Omega Electronics
2431 Bradford Lane
St. Louis, MO 63105–2311

Credit To: Hardware City
35 Appliance Way
Phoenix, AZ 85201

Date April 7, 2000

Salesperson FRM

Apply To Invoice Number	Date	Customer's Order No.
34603	April 1, 2000	7413

3	4120	PCS	85.00	255.00

Reason Credit Issued: Units damaged during shipment. Returned on April 6, 2000

Received By: ALZ Authorized By: PJS

We Credit Your Account For This Amount 255.00

4. Finally, after all invoices have been processed, the system generates a summary journal entry reflecting the total amounts to be posted to the sales and accounts receivable accounts in the general ledger.

Methods for Maintaining Accounts Receivable. Most companies use either the open-invoice or the balance-forward method for maintaining accounts receivable. The two methods differ in terms of when customers remit payments, how those payments are applied to update the accounts receivable master file, and in the format of the monthly statement sent to customers.

Under the **open-invoice method,** customers typically pay according to each invoice. Usually, as shown in Fig. 12.12, two copies of the invoice are mailed to the customer, who is requested to return one copy along with the payment. This copy is a turnaround document called the **remittance advice.** Customer

FIGURE 12.12
Postbilling System

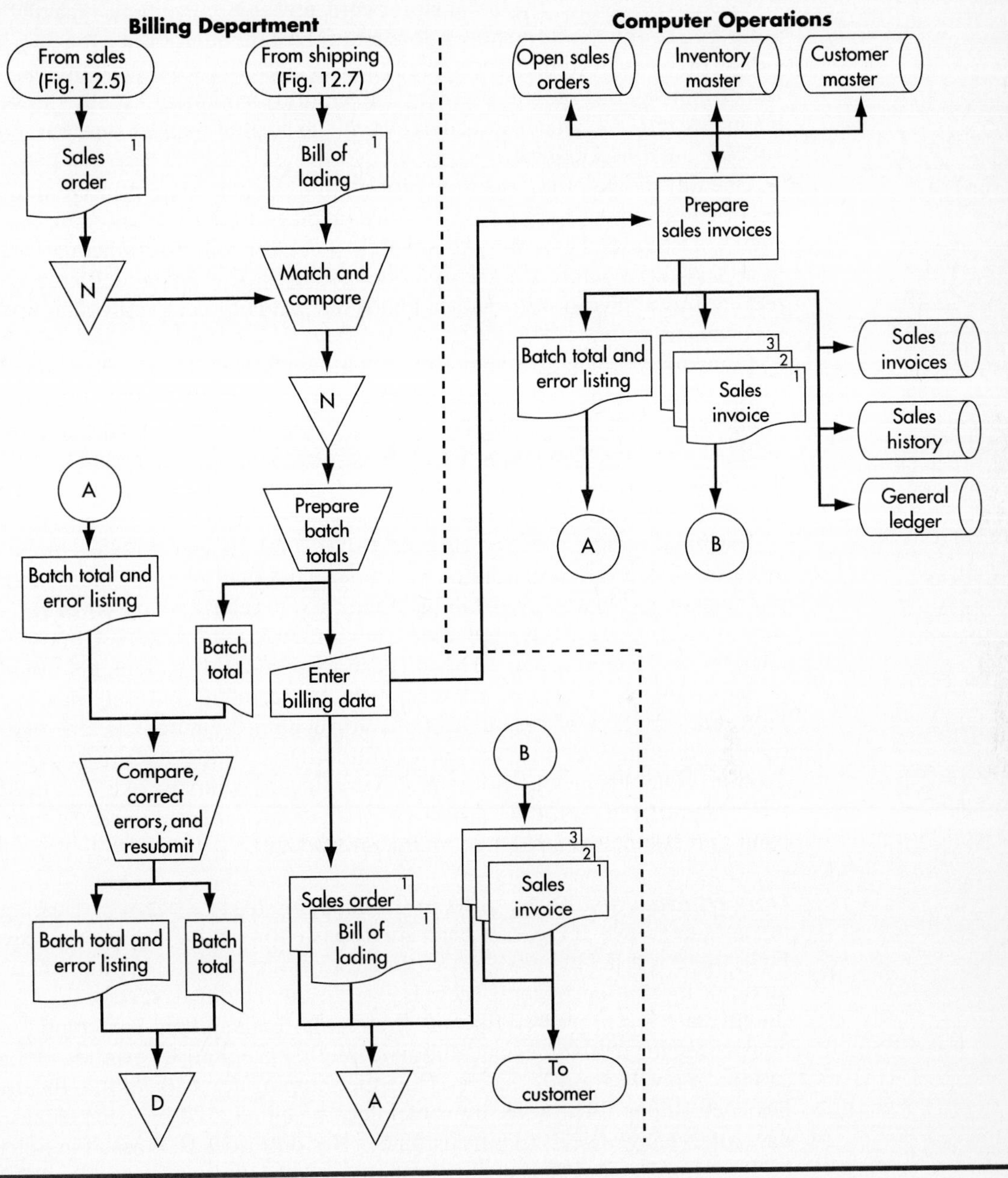

payments are then applied against specific invoices. The monthly statement produced under the open-invoice method lists all outstanding invoices and ages them individually (see Fig. 12.10).

In contrast, under the **balance-forward method,** customers typically pay according to the amount shown on a monthly statement, rather than by individual invoices. Remittances are applied against the total account balance, rather than against specific invoices. The monthly statement usually shows the beginning balance, all current charges, and the current balance due, but it does not age individual invoices.

One advantage of the open-invoice method is that it is conducive to offering discounts for prompt payment, since invoices are individually tracked and aged. It also results in a more uniform flow of cash collections throughout the month. A disadvantage of the open-invoice method is the added complexity required to maintain information about the status of each individual invoice for each customer.

Companies with large numbers of customers who make many small purchases each month, such as credit card companies like Visa and MasterCard or national retail chains like Sears and J. C. Penney, typically use the balance-forward method. For them, this method is more efficient and reduces costs by avoiding the need to process cash collections for each individual sale. It is also more convenient for the customer to make one monthly remittance.

To obtain a more uniform flow of cash receipts, many of these companies use a process called cycle billing to prepare and mail monthly statements to their customers. Under **cycle billing,** monthly statements are prepared for subsets of customers at different times. For example, the customer master file might be divided into four parts, and each week monthly statements would be prepared for one-fourth of the customers. Cycle billing not only produces a more uniform flow of cash collections throughout the month, it also reduces the time that the computer system is dedicated to printing monthly statements. To appreciate this benefit, note that if a credit card company like Visa or MasterCard prepared monthly statements for all its customers at the same time, its computer system would be tied up for several days.

Opportunities for Using Information Technology. Batch processing of invoices, as shown in Fig. 12.12, can create cash flow problems for two reasons. First, there is a delay between the time the goods are shipped and when the invoices are printed. Second, there is an additional delay of several days while the invoices are processed through the regular mail system. Switching to online processing of invoices can eliminate the first problem, by printing invoices as soon as notification is received from the shipping department that the order has been shipped. The second problem can be eliminated by using electronic data interchange (EDI) to bill customers. Not only does EDI result in quicker billing of customers, it also cuts costs by reducing paper handling and processing. For example, Sonoco Products Company estimates that EDI saves it \$0.70 to \$0.80 per invoice over processing of paper invoices. Depending on how many invoices are processed in a year, the savings can be significant. EDI invoices would also benefit customers by reducing their time and costs associated with processing paperwork.

An advanced AIS can even entirely eliminate the need to create and store invoices, at least with customers who have a sophisticated AIS. To understand this, reexamine the information included in a typical sales invoice (see Fig. 12.9). The invoice indicates the quantity of each item sold and the price charged for that item. But the price is usually set at the time the order is placed, and the actual quantity sold is known at the time the merchandise is shipped to the customer. Thus the selling company's AIS already contains all the information needed to calculate the amount of the sale at the time the goods are delivered. Conversely, the buyer knows the price at the time the order is placed, and knows the quantity purchased when the goods are received. Consequently, if both companies have accurate on-line systems, it may be possible to establish an agreement in which the buyer will automatically remit payments within a specified number of days after receiving the merchandise. Indeed, Ford has established such relationships with many of its main suppliers. Note that the seller can still monitor and determine accounts receivable by tracking shipments to cash remittances: accounts receivable represents all shipments that have not yet been paid for. The attraction of such *invoiceless* billing is that it saves both the seller and buyer considerable time and money, by eliminating the need to perform a traditional business process (billing).

Another information technology that can improve the billing and accounts receivable function uses imaging to create and store digital versions of all paper relating to a customer's account. The digital images can then be stored on an optical disk connected to a LAN, where they can be easily retrieved, manipulated, and integrated with other images and data to produce various types of output.

Image processing provides a number of advantages in managing customer accounts. First, employees have fast access to all documents relating to a customer—no more wasted time searching through file cabinets for lost paperwork. If a customer needs a duplicate copy of a monthly statement or an invoice to replace a lost original, it can be retrieved, printed, and faxed while talking to the customer on the phone. Second, image processing helps with resolving customer complaints, since the same image can be viewed simultaneously by more than one person. Thus a customer account representative and his credit manager could both review an image of a document in question while discussing the problem with the customer on the telephone. Finally, image processing reduces the space and cost associated with storing paper documents. The savings in this area can be substantial; one optical disk can store up to 20,000 documents in a fraction of the usual space.

An integrated AIS also provides the opportunity to merge the billing process with the sales and marketing function. This can be done by using data about a customer's past purchase history to send information about related products and services along with the monthly statement. Such customized advertising may generate additional sales with little, if any, incremental costs. Elizabeth Venko decided to talk to Faith Weber, AOE's director of sales, about this possibility.

Cash Collections

The fourth step in the revenue cycle is cash collections (circle 4.0 in Fig. 12.3). Two departments are involved in this activity. The cashier, who reports to the treasurer (see Fig. 12.1), handles the remittances and deposits them in the bank; the accounts receivable function, which reports to the controller, credits customer accounts for the payments received. This arrangement effectively segregates the custody and recording functions, thereby reducing the risk of theft.

Key Decisions and Information Needs. Because cash can be stolen so easily, it is important to take appropriate measures to reduce the risk of theft. One way to do this is to not let the billing/accounts receivable function, which is responsible for recording customer remittances, have physical access to cash or checks. Nevertheless, cash collections must be accurately recorded and customer accounts must be properly credited for all remittances. To do this, the accounts receivable function must be able to identify the source of any remittances and the applicable invoices that should be credited. One such method has already been discussed: mailing the customer two copies of the invoice and requesting that one be returned with the remittance. If this copy also contains a space for the customer to indicate the amount being remitted, the remittance data can be input by an OCR machine, thereby eliminating the potential for mistakes during data entry. An alternative solution is to have mail room personnel prepare a detailed listing of the names and amounts of all customer remittances, or photocopy those remittances, and send that information to accounts receivable.

Documents, Records, and Procedures. Figure 12.13 depicts a typical batch-oriented approach to processing cash collections, which is used by AOE. The cash collections process begins when two mail room clerks open the mail. One clerk restrictively endorses the checks received for deposit to one of the company's bank accounts. The other clerk prepares a **remittance list,** a document listing all checks received. The checks and one copy of the remittance list are then sent to the cashier, who prepares them for deposit. The second copy of the remittance list is sent to the internal audit department, where it is later used to reconcile the bank statements. The third copy of the remittance list and the remittance advices are sent to accounts receivable for use in updating customer accounts.

An accounts receivable clerk uses an on-line terminal to enter the sum of the remittance list as a batch total, the customer and invoice numbers, and the amount of each payment. The system performs a number of on-line edit checks to verify the accuracy of data entry, including the following:

1. Validity checks on the customer and invoice numbers.
2. Closed-loop verification to ensure that the proper account is credited. After the clerk enters the customer account number, the system displays the customer name corresponding to that account number and asks for confirmation that this is the correct person.

FIGURE 12.13
Cash Receipts Processing

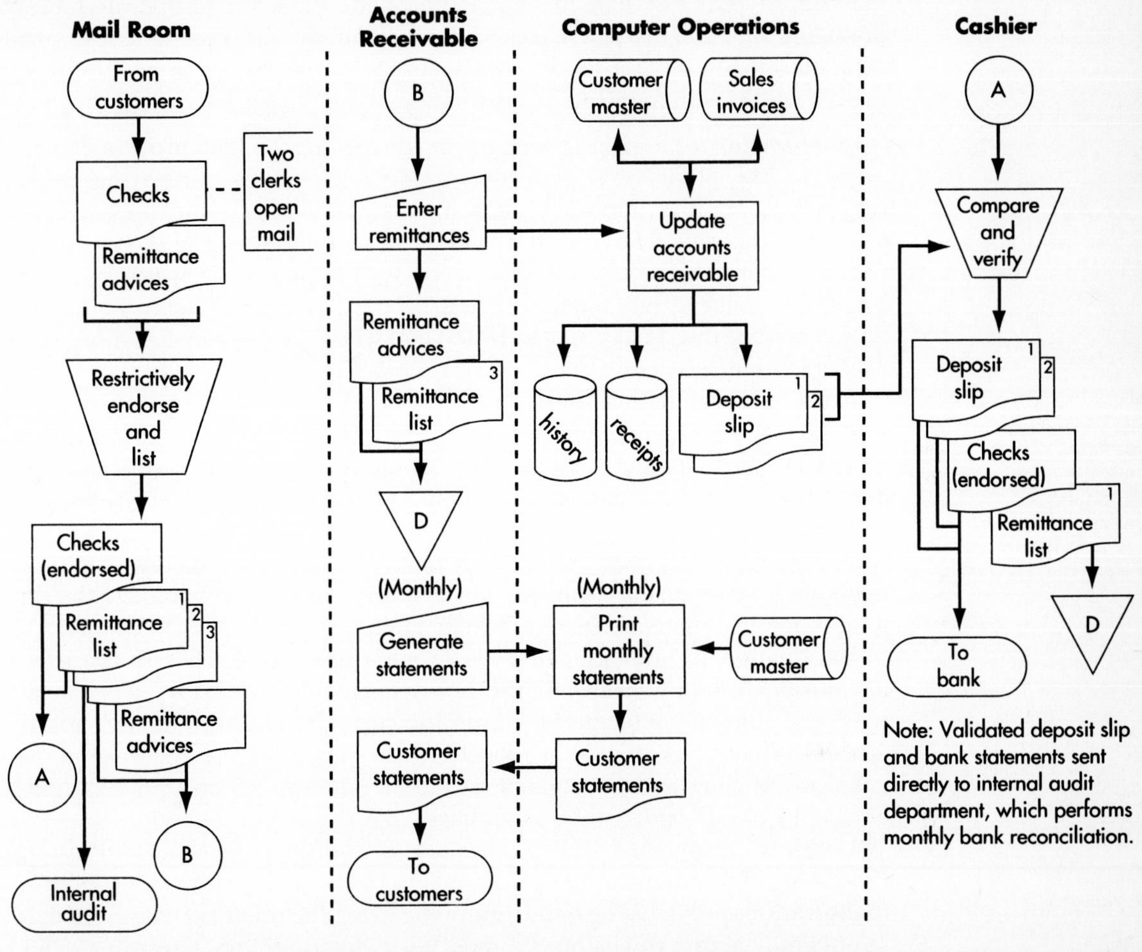

3. A field check to ensure that only numeric values are entered for payment amounts.
4. Summation of all amounts entered and a comparison of this total with the batch total entered by the clerk; if the two numbers agree, the batch is accepted and the respective files are then updated.

After these edit checks are performed, each customer's account in the customer master file is credited for the amount remitted, open sales invoices are marked "paid" and closed to the sales history file, and the total cash received is recorded in the cash receipts file. The system then prints two-part deposit slips and sends them to the cashier. The cashier compares the deposit slips with the checks and remittance list and, after verifying that all customer remittances are accounted for, sends the deposit to the bank. Someone not involved in processing cash collections (in this case, the internal audit department) receives the monthly bank statement and prepares the bank reconciliation, thereby providing an independent check on the accuracy and completeness of all deposits. Finally, once a month, the accounts receivable clerk generates and mails monthly statements to all customers.

Opportunities for Using Information Technology. The process depicted in Fig. 12.13 contains three steps that create a delay between the time when a sale is made and the time when the company obtains use of the funds remitted to pay for that sale. The first source of delay involves the time the customer's payment is in the mail system. The second is the time it takes to process the remittance once it has been received. A third source of delay is the time between when the checks are deposited and when the bank makes those funds available to the company.

Companies can reduce these time lags by setting up a lockbox arrangement with a bank. A **lockbox** is a postal address to which customers send their remittances. The participating bank picks up the checks from the post office box and deposits them to the company's account. The bank then sends the remittance advices, an electronic list of all remittances, and photocopies of all checks to the company. Typically, companies select several banks around the country to maintain lockboxes; the locations would be chosen so as to minimize the time it takes for customer checks to arrive by mail.

Information technology can provide additional efficiencies in the use of lockboxes. Under an **electronic lockbox** arrangement, the bank electronically sends the company information about the customer account number and the amount remitted as soon as it receives and scans those checks. This method enables the company to begin applying remittances to customer accounts before the photocopies of the checks arrive.

Lockbox arrangements only eliminate the delays associated with internal processing of remittances mailed directly to the company, however. Electronic funds transfer provides the opportunity to reduce the other two causes of delay in obtaining access to customer funds. With **electronic funds transfer (EFT),** customers send their remittances electronically to the company's bank. This arrangement eliminates the delay associated with the time the remittance is in the mail system. It also reduces the time lag before the bank makes the deposited funds available to the company by eliminating the time it takes the checks to clear the banking system. Integrating EFT with EDI, a process referred to as **financial electronic data interchange (FEDI),** completes the automation of both the billing and cash collections processes. To fully reap the benefits of FEDI, however, requires that both the selling company and its customers use banks that provide EDI services.

When dealing with customers who are not FEDI-capable, companies can also speed up the collection process by accepting the use of procurement cards (a special type of credit card, which will be discussed in Chapter 13) or credit cards. Accepting such methods of payment speeds up collection, because the card issuer usually transfers the funds within two days of the sale. Moreover,

FOCUS 12.3 Using Image Processing to Improve Cash Collections

BELL ATLANTIC processes more than 11 million customer remittances each month, sometimes receiving over 500,000 remittances in a single day. To reduce costs and improve accuracy, Bell Atlantic uses a high-speed image processing system.

The process begins when Bell Atlantic picks up the mail, which it does several times each day. The mail is electronically scanned; the scanners can detect the magnetic ink on the customer's check, thereby identifying how the checks are positioned in the envelopes. The scanner also determines the number of documents in and the presence of any metal objects (coins or staples) in each envelope. This information is used to sort the envelopes. Those that contain only one check and one return document are opened mechanically and run through a high-speed image capturing device. The remaining envelopes are also opened mechanically, but their contents are then inspected by hand for further sorting. Checks and remittance documents are then run through the image capturing device.

The system tries to read the handwriting on the check to match that against the customer's balance. The data on checks that cannot be read by the system is keyed in. The checks are then sent through high-speed machines that encode, endorse, and batch them for deposit.

The system cost Bell Atlantic $8 million. The cost savings in reduced clerical work and improved accuracy, however, yielded a payback in just two years.

Source: Scott Humphrey, "Bell Atlantic Reengineers Payment Processing," *Enterprise Reengineering* (October–November 1995): 1–22.

for sales in which the card is physically presented to the seller, the card issuer assumes the risks associated with nonpayment; thus, companies that accept credit or procurement cards can essentially eliminate the costs and risks associated with creating and maintaining accounts receivable. (For sales in which the card is not physically presented, such as telephone or Internet sales, however, the seller usually bears the risk of repudiation by the card issuer for any fraudulent use of the card.) These benefits must be weighed against the costs of accepting such cards, which are typically 2% to 4% of the gross sales price.

For companies that, due to either strategic or regulatory concerns, need to process a large number of remittances internally, image processing technology can provide significant performance improvements and cost savings. Focus 12.3 describes the use of image processing at Bell Atlantic.

This section described some methods, such as the use of lockbox arrangements, to not only improve the efficiency of processing cash collections, but also increase control by eliminating employee handling of customer remittances. In the next section, we discuss additional control procedures that can be used to ensure that revenue cycle activities are performed in accordance with management's policies and in a manner that safeguards the organization's assets.

CONTROL: OBJECTIVES, THREATS, AND PROCEDURES

A second function of a well-designed AIS is to provide adequate controls to ensure that the following objectives are met:

1. All transactions are properly authorized.
2. All recorded transactions are valid (actually occurred).

3. All valid, authorized transactions are recorded.
4. All transactions are recorded accurately.
5. Assets (cash, inventory, and data) are safeguarded from loss or theft.
6. Business activities are performed efficiently and effectively.

The documents and records described in the previous section play an important role in achieving these objectives. Simple, easy-to-complete documents with clear instructions facilitate the accurate and efficient recording of transaction data. The inclusion of appropriate application controls, such as validity checks and field (format) checks, further increases the accuracy of data entry when using electronic documents. Providing space on paper and electronic documents to record who completed and who reviewed the form provides evidence that the transaction was properly authorized. Finally, prenumbering the documents facilitates checking that all transactions have been recorded.

Table 12.1 lists the major threats and exposures in the revenue cycle and the additional control procedures, besides adequate documents and records, that should be in place to mitigate them. Every company, regardless of its line of business, faces these threats. Therefore, it is important to understand how the AIS can be designed to counter them. Our discussion will be organized around the four stages of the revenue cycle: sales order entry, shipping, billing, and cash collections.

Sales Order Entry

The primary objective of sales order entry is the efficient processing of customer orders. Threat 1 in Table 12.1 relates to this objective.

Threat 1: Sales to Customers with Poor Credit. The principal threat in sales order entry is the possibility of making sales that later turn out to be uncollectible. This threat is diminished by requiring proper authorization for each credit sale. For cases requiring specific authorization, such as new customers or the extension of additional credit to existing customers, approval should be granted by someone other than the sales representative, especially if the sales staff are paid on commission. The organization chart for AOE (see Fig. 12.1) shows this segregation of duties: the credit manager, who sets credit policies and approves the extension of credit to new customers and the raising of credit limits for existing customers, is independent of the marketing function.

Maintaining accurate and current records of customer account balances and credit limits further diminishes the risk of making uncollectible sales. Indeed, the concept of general authorization of credit sales cannot work effectively if the information about customer account balances and credit limits is inaccurate. Therefore edit checks and input validation routines must be in place to ensure the accuracy of sales transaction data used to update customer master files.

Shipping

The primary objective of the shipping function is the efficient and accurate delivery of goods to customers. Threats 2 and 3 in Table 12.1 relate to this objective.

TABLE 12.1 Threats, Exposures, and Control Procedures in the Revenue Cycle

Threat	Exposure	Applicable Control Procedures
1. Credit sales to customers with poor credit	Uncollectible sales and losses due to bad debts	Credit approval by credit manager, not by sales function Accurate records of customer account balances
2. Shipping errors: Wrong merchandise Wrong quantities Wrong address	Customer dissatisfaction	Reconciliation of sales order with picking ticket and packing slip Bar-code scanners Data entry application controls
3. Theft of inventory	Loss of assets Overstated inventory	Restrict physical access to inventory Documentation of all internal transfers of inventory Periodic physical counts of inventory and reconciliation of counts to recorded amounts
4. Failure to bill customers	Loss of inventory Loss of revenue (not collected) Overstated inventory and understated accounts receivable	Separation of shipping and billing functions Prenumbering of all shipping documents and periodic reconciliation of all bills of lading to invoices
5. Billing errors	Customer dissatisfaction Incorrect records and poor decision making	Reconciliation of picking tickets and bills of lading with sales orders Data entry edit controls Price lists
6. Theft of cash	Loss of assets Overstated accounts receivable	Segregation of duties Minimization of cash handling Lockbox arrangements Prompt endorsement and deposit of all receipts Periodic reconciliation of bank statement with records by someone not involved in cash receipts processing
7. Posting errors in updating accounts receivable	Customer dissatisfaction Incorrect records and poor decision making	Reconciliation of subsidiary accounts receivable ledger with general ledger Monthly statements to customers
8. Loss of data	Incorrect data for decision making Loss of confidential information	Backup and disaster recovery procedures Access controls (physical and logical)
9. Poor performance	Inefficient or ineffective processes	Preparation and review of performance reports

Retail stores and organizations that receive cash directly from customers should use cash registers that automatically produce a written record of all cash received. In these situations, customers can also play a role in controlling cash collections. For example, many stores use signs to inform customers that their purchase is free if they fail to get a receipt or that receipts marked with a red star entitle them to a discount. Such policies encourage customers to watch that employees actually do ring up the cash sale, and do so correctly.

All customer remittances should be deposited, intact, in the bank each day. Daily deposits reduce the amount of cash and checks at risk of theft. Depositing all remittances intact, and not using any of them for miscellaneous expenditures, facilitates reconciliation of the bank statement with the records of sales, accounts receivable, and cash collections.

Finally, the employee who reconciles the bank statements should be independent of any of the other activities involved in handling or recording the receipt of cash. This separation of duties provides an independent check on the cashier and prevents manipulating the bank statement to conceal the theft of cash.

Threat 7: Posting Errors in Updating Accounts Receivable. The other threat related to the cash collections step of the revenue cycle involves errors in maintaining customer accounts. Posting errors can be detected by reconciling the results of processing with both internal and external data. For example, after processing customer payments, the sum of all individual customer account balances (the accounts receivable subsidiary file) should equal the total balance of the accounts receivable control account in the general ledger. If the two are not equal, an error in posting has probably occurred and all transactions just entered should be reexamined.

To ensure that all remittances were processed, the number of customer accounts updated should be compared with the number of checks received. These reconciliations should be performed by someone other than the individual involved in processing the original transactions, because (1) it is easier to catch someone else's mistakes than your own and (2) it provides a means to identify irregularities. Finally, mailing monthly account statements provides an additional independent review of the accuracy of all postings to customer accounts, because customers will complain if their accounts have not been properly credited for payments remitted.

General Control Issues

Threats 8 and 9 in Table 12.1 are general threats that affect all phases of the revenue cycle.

Threat 8: Loss of Data. Another threat in the revenue cycle is loss of data about customer accounts. Accurate customer account and inventory records are important not only for external and internal reporting purposes, but also for responding to customer inquiries. Moreover, loss of all accounts receivable data could threaten a company's continued existence. Therefore those records must be protected from loss or damage.

The master accounts receivable, sales, and cash receipts files must all be backed up regularly. Two backup copies of key files, such as the accounts receivable master file, should be made; one should be kept on-site, the other stored off-site. Backup copies of the most recent transaction file should also be made. All disks and tapes should have both external and internal file labels to reduce the possibility of accidentally erasing important files.

Access controls are also important. Leakage of customer information to competitors can hurt sales and may even expose the company to legal liability. Unauthorized access also increases the risk of damage to important data files. A system of passwords and user IDs should be used to limit employees' access to and allowable operations on files. For example, only sales staff should be allowed to create sales orders. Moreover, sales staff should have read-only access to customer credit limits and current account balances. Access controls should also exist for individual terminals. For example, the system should be programmed to reject any attempts to enter sales orders from a terminal located at the shipping dock. Finally, logs of all activities, especially any actions involving managerial approval (e.g., extending credit limits) should be recorded and maintained for later review as part of the audit trail.

Threat 9: Poor Performance. In addition to ensuring accuracy and safeguarding assets, another objective of internal controls is to encourage efficient and effective performance of duties. The preparation and review of reports provides a basis for assessing the efficiency and effectiveness of revenue cycle activities and for diminishing the threat of substandard performance. The potential number of such reports is limited only by management's choice about what activities are important to monitor and control. For example, sales order entry efficiency can be monitored by preparing periodic reports of sales orders processed per individual in a given time period. The efficiency and effectiveness of the sales force can be assessed by **sales analysis reports,** which break down sales by salesperson, region, or product. Further insights about overall marketing performance can be provided by preparing **profitability analysis reports,** which break down the marginal profit contribution made by each territory, customer, distribution channel, salesperson, product, or other basis.

Reports on the frequency and size of back orders provide insight about the effectiveness of inventory management policies in satisfying customer demands. Similarly, reports that identify slow-moving products help to avoid excessive stockpiling. An **accounts receivable aging schedule** lists customer account balances by length of time outstanding; it provides useful information for evaluating current credit policies and for deciding whether to increase the credit limit for specific customers. It also provides information for estimating bad debts.

Carefully monitoring accounts receivables is extremely important. Indeed, cash flow problems are a major reason that many businesses fail. Therefore, a **cash budget,** which provides precise estimates of cash inflows (projected collections from sales) and outflows (outstanding payables), is essential. It can alert an organization to a pending short-term cash shortage, thereby enabling it to plan ahead to secure short-term loans at the best possible rates. Conversely, an organization that knows a surplus of cash is pending can take steps to invest those excess funds to earn the best possible returns. A cash budget could have helped AOE better manage its short-term borrowing needs.

In the next section, we discuss in more detail how the AIS can be designed to provide these various reports and other information useful for effectively managing revenue cycle activities.

REVENUE CYCLE INFORMATION NEEDS AND DATA MODEL

The third function of the AIS is to provide information useful for decision making. As discussed in the previous section, the AIS should provide the operational information needed to perform the following functions:

- Respond to customer inquiries about account balances and order status
- Decide whether to extend credit to a particular customer
- Determine inventory availability
- Decide what types of credit terms to offer
- Set prices for products and services
- Set policies regarding sales returns and warranties
- Select methods for delivering merchandise

In addition, however, the AIS should provide the following kinds of strategic and performance evaluation information:

- Response time to customer inquiries
- Time required to fill and deliver orders
- Percentage of sales that required back orders
- Customer satisfaction
- Analyses of market share and sales trends
- Profitability analyses by product, customer, and sales region
- Sales volume in both dollars and number of customers
- Effectiveness of advertising and promotions
- Sales staff performance
- Bad debt expenses and credit policies
- Expected cash collections and short-term borrowing needs
- Trends in days sales outstanding

Notice that both financial and operating information are needed to manage and evaluate revenue cycle activities. For example, evaluating the efficiency and effectiveness of sales order entry requires data not only about sales volumes, but also about order processing time. In addition, information from external sources, such as measures of customer satisfaction, is also needed. Traditionally, the AIS has provided the internally generated financial measures of performance and managers have turned to other sources for the internal operating and external information they need. This situation is costly and inefficient. It is also no longer necessary. With the use of data base systems, it is now possible to redesign the AIS to capture and store both financial and operating data about revenue cycle transactions and to integrate that internally generated data with information from external sources.

Revenue Cycle Data Model

As explained in Chapter 6, the REA data model provides one method for designing a data base that efficiently integrates both financial and operating data. Figure 12.14 shows a simplified REA data model for the revenue cycle of a manufacturing company such as AOE. It includes the following information:

- The two major resources (cash and inventory) used in the revenue cycle
- The four major business events in the revenue cycle (orders, filling the orders, shipping [sales], and cash collections)
- The primary external agent (customers) as well as the various internal agents involved in revenue cycle activities

If the data model depicted in Fig. 12.14 were implemented in a relational data base, there would be a table for each entity and for each many-to-many relationship. The bottom half of Fig. 12.14 lists many of the attributes that would be found in those tables.

As you recall, each box in an REA diagram represents a resource, an event, or an agent entity about which information is collected. The labeled diamonds between these entities represent the relationships of interest.

Recall also that the cardinalities of those relationships, which are shown in parentheses on the Entity-Relationship (E-R) diagram, reflect important information about the organization's policies and the nature of its business. For example, the many-to-many relationship in Fig. 12.14 between the customer order and fill order events indicates that for efficiency, AOE often batches customer orders to be picked in the warehouse. It also indicates that sometimes, if items are out of stock and must be back-ordered, it takes more than one picking and packing event to fill a particular customer order. The primary key of the shipping event is the sales invoice number, because the economic transaction of selling goods takes place when the goods are released to the customer. Therefore, each shipping event is linked to one and only one fill order event. The warehouse clerk, however, could be picking goods for several different customer orders at the same time; thus, each fill order event can be linked to many different shipping events. The one-to-one relationship between the shipping (sales) and cash collections events indicates that AOE expects its customers to pay by the invoice, rather than by a monthly statement. The minimum cardinality of zero associated with the cash collections event indicates that AOE does sell on credit. The one-to-many relationships between the various agent and event entities represent the fact that every event must involve both an internal and an external agent. Finally, the many-to-many relationships between inventory and the customer order, fill order, and shipping events represent the fact that AOE sells mass-produced items.

But where are data about accounts receivable stored? Accounts receivable represents sales for which payment has not yet been received. Therefore, recall from Chapter 6 that accounts receivable can be calculated by taking the difference between the total amount of sales and the amount of cash collections linked to those sales events. To improve query response time, however, the total outstanding balance is often stored as an attribute in the customer table.

FIGURE 12.14
Partial REA Diagram of the Revenue Cycle

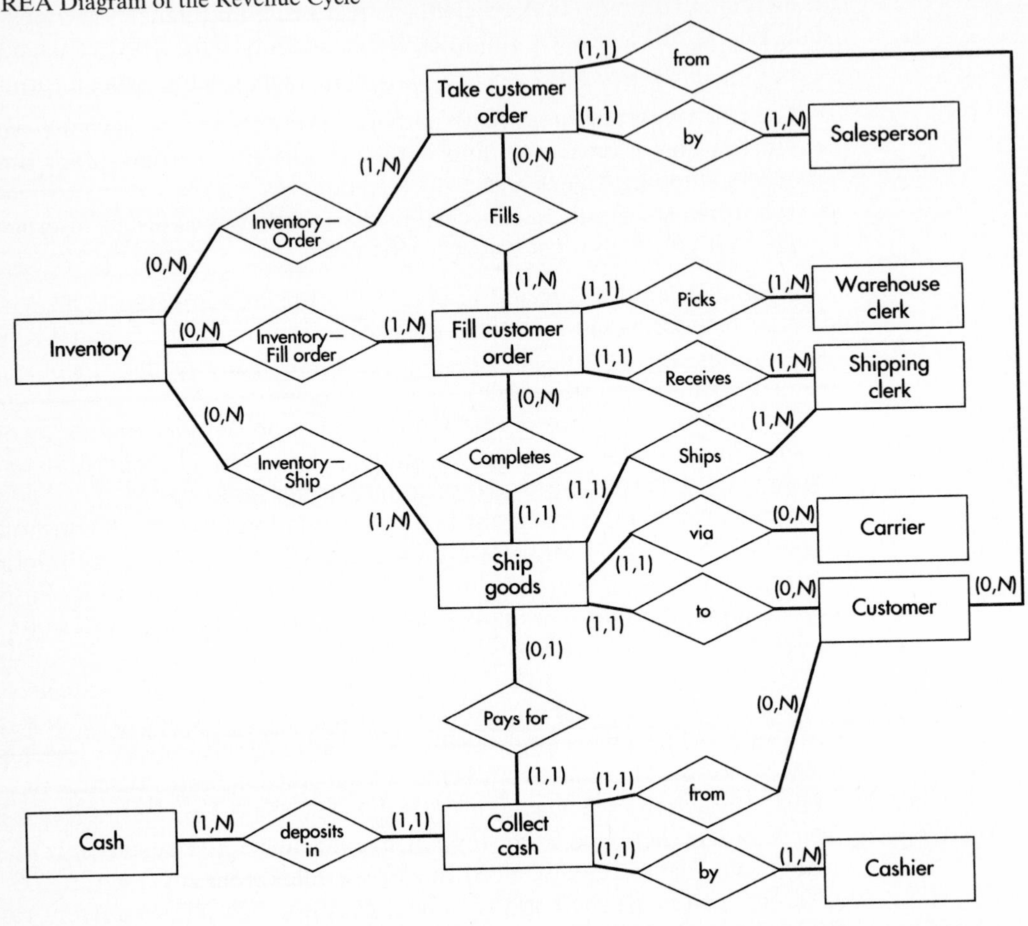

Benefits of the Data Model

Notice how the data model depicted in Fig. 12.14 effectively integrates both traditional accounting transaction data (for example, the date and amount of the sale) with other operational data (for example, information about the time the sale was made) that have not traditionally been captured by the AIS. Moreover, the system can capture some of this additional information, like the time of the sale, automatically without any extra data entry. An AIS based on the REA data model also dramatically increases the types of analyses that are possible. For example, sales can be analyzed by time of day to better plan for staffing needs.

It would also be easy to link this internal data with various types of external information. For example, credit rating data about current and potential customers could be downloaded from a commercial data base and stored in

FIGURE 12.14
Continued

Table Name	Attributes (**primary key**, *foreign keys*, other)
Inventory	**Product number**, description, unit cost, unit price, quantity on hand, weight, reorder point,...
Cash	**Account number**, *bank ID*, balance,...
Take cutomer order	**Sales order number**, date, *customer ID*, *salesperson number*, terms, desired delivery date,...
Fill customer order	**Picking ticket number**, date, time, *warehouse clerk number*, *shipping clerk number*,...
Ship goods	**Invoice number,** date, bill of lading number, *picking ticket number, shipping clerk number, carrier number, customer number,* amount due,...
Collect cash	**Remittance number**, date, amount, *customer number, cashier number, invoice number, bank account number*
Salesperson	**Employee number**, name, date hired, date of birth, salary, *manager number*,...
Warehouse clerk	**Employee number**, name, date hired, date of birth, salary, *manager number*,...
Shipping clerk	**Employee number**, name, date hired, date of birth, salary, *manager number*,...
Carrier	**Carrier number**, name, primary contact,...
Customer	**Customer number**, name, bill-to address,...
Cashier	**Employee number**, name, date hired, date of birth, salary, *manager number*,...
Inventory—Order	**Product number**, **sales order number**, quantity
Inventory—Fill order	**Product number**, **picking ticket number**, quantity
Inventory—Ship	**Product number**, **invoice number**, quantity
Take order—Fill order	**Sale order number**, **picking ticket number**

additional columns in the customer table. Similarly, information about customer satisfaction collected from surveys could also be stored in additional columns in the customer table.

Most importantly, decision makers can easily retrieve all this information with easy-to-use query languages. Thus implementing the REA data model in a relational data base significantly improves the ability of the AIS to provide management with the information necessary for effectively managing revenue cycle activities.

In addition to providing decision makers with quick and easy access to information, a well-designed data base can provide strategic benefits to a company's marketing efforts. Companies can "mine" their sales data to target advertising and sales promotions to the needs and desires of specific customers. Thus, instead of sending mass junk mail promotions to every potential customer in a geographic area, companies can send specific messages to targeted groups of people.

For example, General Motors Corporation uses data collected from its affinity program with Master Card and its own sales records to determine the type of vehicle information—makes, models, colors, and so on—it should send to specific customers. Similarly, Blockbuster Entertainment Corporation tracks a customer's rental history and mails promotions that suggest titles that may appeal to that customer. Kraft General Foods, Inc. uses information collected from surveys to prepare customized mailings that offer nutritional information and recipes featuring the very same Kraft products that a customer has purchased in the past. Siemens Rolm Communications Company tracks customer requests for moving, adding, or changing communications network switches. It uses this information to predict when a customer is approaching capacity limits and would therefore be receptive to a sales call recommending the purchase of additional capacity.

These examples illustrate how companies can use information about their customers to generate increased sales. The success of these strategies depends on two factors. First, data from both internal and external data sources must be integrated effectively, possibly by using the REA data model as the basis for redesigning the AIS. Second, adequate control procedures must also be built into the system to ensure that the data stored therein are accurate.

Internal Control Considerations

Data accuracy is vital when using a data base management system (DBMS). Fortunately, the relational data model provides some built-in controls to ensure data accuracy and consistency. One of the more important of these controls is support for foreign keys and referential integrity. It ensures, for example, that when a new row is added to the orders table, the system will verify that the customer number (which appears as a foreign key in that table) actually exists as primary key in the customer table (i.e., that there really is such a customer).

The use of a DBMS also increases the importance of having effective access controls. Most relational DBMSs provide a means to control access by letting different users see only a portion of the data base (called a *view*). For example, sales order entry clerks would see only the portion of Fig. 12.14, such as the tables for inventory, customers, and orders, relevant to their job duties. In addition, sales order entry clerks would be permitted to perform only certain operations on those tables. For example, sales order entry clerks should not be able to change customer credit limits.

Our discussion of the threats listed in Table 12.1 stressed the importance of properly segregating incompatible duties. REA diagrams are useful in evaluating the extent to which incompatible duties are segregated because they indicate which internal agents participate in each event. Moreover, if the REA model is implemented in a DBMS, the computer can be programmed to enforce segregation of duties by rejecting any employee attempts to perform incompatible functions. Conversely, the system can also be programmed to list all cases of an employee performing multiple roles, so that the auditors can investigate whether adequate compensating controls exist. Finally, the use of a DBMS makes adequate backup and disaster recovery procedures essential.

SUMMARY AND CASE CONCLUSION

The four basic functions in the revenue cycle are sales order entry, shipping, billing, and cash collections. The AIS should be designed to maximize the efficiency with which each of these functions is performed. The AIS must also incorporate adequate internal control procedures to mitigate threats such as uncollectible sales, billing errors, and lost or misappropriated inventory and cash. Control procedures are also needed to ensure that the information provided for decision making is both accurate and complete. Finally, to facilitate strategic decision making, the AIS should be designed to accommodate the integration of internally generated data with data from external sources.

Figure 12.15 depicts the new AIS that Elizabeth Venko has proposed for AOE. The proposal includes the following key points:

1. *On-line sales order entry.* Elizabeth plans to open a home page on the Internet. AOE's web site will use multimedia so that customers can test out simulated versions of the various products. It will also provide financial calculators and shipping cost information in order to help customers calculate the most cost-effective order size.

   The web site will not eliminate the need for a field sales force, however. Trevor Whitman, vice president of marketing, believes that AOE will still need its sales staff to visit existing customers to help identify which additional products can be profitably carried. Sales staff will also continue to make cold calls on prospective customers to try to convince them to carry AOE's products. Therefore, each salesperson will be equipped with a pen-based portable computer and a modem. As they walk down store aisles, sales representatives can check off the items that need to be restocked and then write in the appropriate quantities. When the order is complete, they can plug in their modem and transmit the order back to headquarters. The new system checks the customer's credit status and inventory availability and confirms orders within minutes, including an estimated delivery date. After the customer approves the order, the system immediately updates all affected files, so that current information about inventory status is available to other sales representatives.

2. *Electronic invoicing and cash receipts.* Whenever possible, EDI will be used to bill customers, although paper invoices will still be printed nightly for those customers not yet ready for EDI. EDI will speed up the

FIGURE 12.15

Proposed Revenue Cycle System for AOE. (a) Sales order entry, (b) Cash receipts

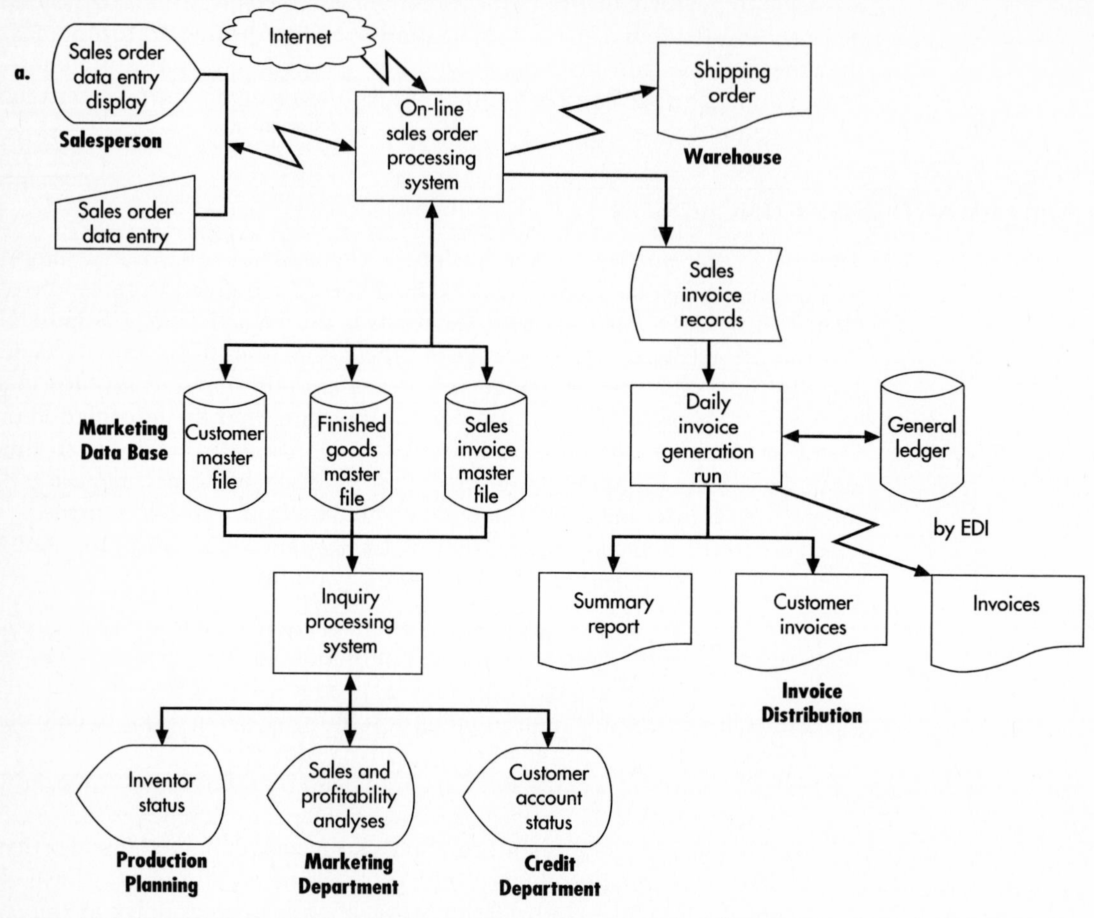

billing process and improve AOE's cash flow. Moreover, Elizabeth also plans to explore arrangements for invoiceless billing with AOE's major customers. In addition, once EDI links have been established with major customers, Elizabeth intends to obtain access to their POS data so that AOE can help them better manage their inventory of AOE products.

Several steps will be taken to speed up cash collections. To handle customers who still remit by check, electronic lockbox arrangements will been established with six regional banks. Customers who are EDI-capable will be encouraged to move to FEDI, so that both the funds and remittance data are received together. This will further improve AOE's cash flow and cut costs.

FIGURE 12.15 Continued

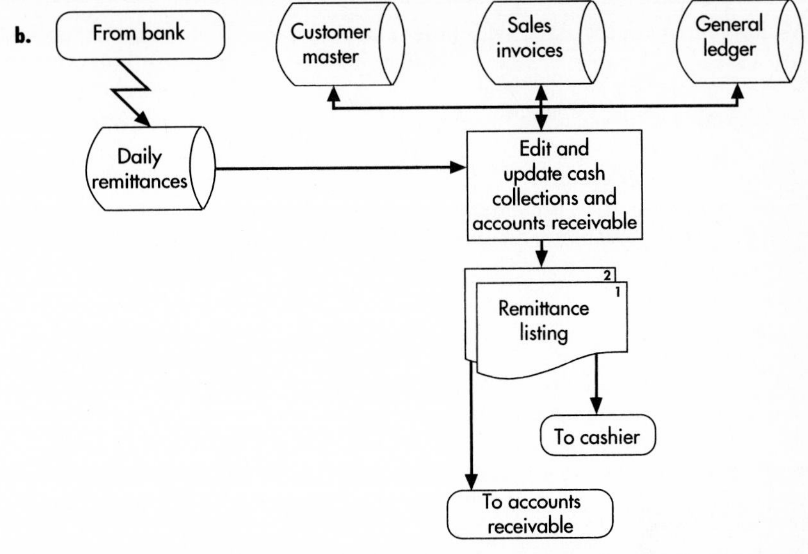

3. *Implementation of a relational data base.* A relational data base designed along the lines of the data model presented in Fig. 12.14 will pull together the internal and external information that Elizabeth Venko and other decision makers need to manage revenue cycle activities effectively. Moreover, easy-to-use relational query languages will give AOE's decision makers easy access to the information they require.

Linda Spurgeon, president of AOE, approved Elizabeth's proposal. She is impressed with the move to EDI and FEDI for invoicing and cash collections and asked Elizabeth to begin thinking about whether these techniques can also be used to streamline some of AOE's expenditure cycle activities.

KEY TERMS

revenue cycle
credit limit
back order
sales order
packing slip
picking ticket
bill of lading
freight bill
sales invoice
monthly statement
credit memo
postbilling system
prebilling system
open-invoice method
remittance advice
balance-forward method
cycle billing
remittance list
lockbox
electronic lockbox
electronic funds transfer (EFT)
financial electronic data interchange (FEDI)
sales analysis report
profitability analysis report
accounts receivable aging schedule
cash budget

CHAPTER QUIZ

1. Which activity is part of the sales order entry process?
a. Setting customer credit limits
b. Preparing a bill of lading
c. Checking customer credit
d. Approving sales returns

2. Which document often accompanies merchandise shipped to a customer?
a. Picking list
b. Packing slip
c. Credit memo
d. Sales order

3. Which approach to billing customers prepares invoices after merchandise has been shipped?
a. Open-invoice method
b. Prebilling system
c. Postbilling system
d. Cycle billing

4. Having customers send checks directly to a postal address, rather than to the company, is an example of
a. an EFT system.
b. an EDI system.
c. image processing.
d. a bank lockbox arrangement

5. Which of the following is not likely to be included in a data model of the revenue cycle?
a. Cash collections
b. Sales
c. Orders
d. Purchases

6. A(n) __________ would be most useful for determining which sales region needs to receive additional attention to improve sales.
a. accounts receivable aging schedule
b. profitability analysis
c. sales analysis
d. cash budget

7. The document used to authorize the release of merchandise from the inventory control (warehouse) to shipping is the
a. picking list.
b. packing slip.
c. shipping order.
d. sales invoice.

8. For a retail store like Wal-Mart, the relationship between sales and inventory items is most likely to be represented as being
a. one-to-one.
b. one-to-many.
c. many-to-one.
d. many-to-many.

9. For good internal control, credit memos should be approved by the
a. credit manager.
b. sales manager.
c. billing manager.
d. controller.

10. For good internal control over customer remittances, the mail room clerk should separate the checks from the remittance advices and send the checks to
a. billing.
b. accounts receivable.
c. the cashier.
d. the controller.

DISCUSSION QUESTIONS

12.1 The marketing department of the RSC Company maintains a computerized customer file that contains information on each customer, including the products in which the customer is interested, recent requests for information, recent contacts with sales personnel, recent order and delivery activity, reports on customer satisfaction, and customer service requirements. The accounting department currently maintains a separate customer file that contains accounting information on recent sales transactions and payments from customers, including the customer's current account balance.

The RSC Company has recently acquired a data base management system. The systems department has proposed building the new data base using the REA data model. One consequence of this approach is that a chart of accounts would no longer be used to record and store data. The controller is concerned about this change and argues that she will not be able to generate financial statements without a chart of accounts. Comment on the controller's concerns, and discuss the advantages and disadvantages of using the REA model, instead of a chart of accounts, as the basis for storing data about revenue cycle activities.

12.2 The Internet provides an example of how information technology is changing the nature of the sales process. Web sites enable companies to service customers 24 hours a day, seven days a week, without any human intervention. How does this capability affect a company's need for a sales force? For customer service representatives?

12.3 Consider an accounting package with which you are familiar. Does it provide the types of information needed to effectively manage and make strategic decisions in the revenue cycle?

12.4 Compare the relative advantages and disadvantages of using a prebilling versus a postbilling system.

12.5 Companies like Dell Computer Corporation are outsourcing their shipping functions to carriers like Roadway Services, Inc. The objective of such outsourcing deals is to cut costs. Discuss the advantages and disadvantages of outsourcing functions such as shipping. What control issues are raised by such an arrangement?

12.6 Advances in information technology make it possible to personalize mass advertising. To what extent is this effective? How can companies use IT to more completely personalize relationships with their customers?

12.7 Some types of products can actually be delivered over the Internet. What threats does this create? What control procedures can mitigate those threats?

12.8 Wholesalers have traditionally played an important role in the supply chain. To what extent is such a middleman role needed on the Internet?

PROBLEMS

12.1 Kids Choice Corporation is a manufacturer and distributor of children's toys. Over the past three years the company's sales volume has declined as several important distributors have dropped the Kids Choice product line. In response, the company's top management has just ordered every department within the company to reevaluate its operations, identify potential problems that may be contributing to the company's loss of business, and prepare recommendations for improvement. You have been asked to evaluate the revenue cycle activities.

At present, customers are sent catalogs, price lists, and order forms each quarter, and they mail completed order forms to a central data processing facility. There the orders are keyed into the computer system and processed in batches. Shipping documents are printed for approved orders and routed to the Kids Choice distribution center closest to the customer, where the merchandise is picked, packaged, and shipped to the customer. The process typically takes two to three weeks from time of receipt of the customer order to delivery.

The billing department prepares and mails invoices to customers after receiving notification from the shipping department that the order has been filled and shipped. Customers mail their remittances to the central Kids Choice office. Cash collections are processed and customer accounts are updated weekly. Several customers have complained that their account balances are incorrect and do not reflect recent payments.

Required:

Could Kids Choice Corporation's AIS be one of the factors contributing to the company's recent decline? Describe several ways to use information technology to improve the sales and cash collections procedures used by Kids Choice.

12.2 What internal control procedure(s) would provide protection against the following threats? If more than one control procedure could be used to solve a problem, rank the alternatives in terms of their effectiveness.

a. Theft of goods by the shipping dock workers, who claim that the inventory shortages reflect errors in the inventory records.
b. The posting of the amount of a sale to the wrong customer account, because a customer account number was incorrectly keyed into the system.
c. A credit sale to a customer who is already four months behind in making payments on his account.
d. Authorization of a credit memo for a sales return when the goods were never actually returned.
e. Writing off a customer's accounts receivable balance as uncollectible in order to conceal the theft of subsequent collections.

f. Billing customers for the quantity ordered when the quantity shipped was actually less due to back-ordering of some items.
g. Theft of checks by the mail room clerk, who then endorsed the checks for deposit into the account of a fictitious company.
h. Theft of funds by the cashier, who cashed several checks and did not record their receipt.
i. Theft of cash by a waiter who destroyed the customer sales ticket for customers who paid cash.

12.3 Refer to Fig. 12.14 to answer the following questions:

a. If the relationship between shipping and cash collections were one-to-many, what would that reveal about the company's sales policy? What if the relationship were many-to-one? What if it was many-to-many? Think of real examples of companies that reflect each of these options.
b. What would a one-to-one relationship between inventory and sales imply about the types of products sold by the company?
c. Can the relationship between sales and customers ever be one-to-many or many-to-many? Why or why not?

12.4 Your company has just acquired a data base management system and wants to develop an REA data model for its revenue cycle activities.

Required:

a. Use the following facts, plus the generic description of the revenue cycle included in the chapter, to modify Fig. 12.14:
   1. The company uses the balance-forward method to bill its customers.
   2. The company carries its own credit; customers may pay all or only a portion of their bill each month.
   3. There are no back orders.
   4. The company wants to track the performance of its customer service representatives in terms of responding to customer inquiries.
   5. Customers can return unsatisfactory merchandise for credit.
b. In addition to modifying the REA diagram, list the attributes that should be stored about the customer service event. Indicate which of these attributes should be the primary key and which, if any, are foreign keys.
c. List the attributes that should be stored about the sales return event. Identify the primary key and foreign keys, if any.

12.5 Table 12.2 shows some of the relational tables used to implement an REA model of a company's revenue cycle.

Required:

a. Identify the primary key of each table.
b. Identify the foreign key(s), if any, of each table.
c. Which tables represent resources? Events? Agents?
d. Draw an REA diagram of the system. List any assumptions you made in assigning cardinalities to relationships.

12.6 The Quality Building Supplies Company operates six wholesale outlets that sell roofing materials, electrical and plumbing supplies, lumber, and other building materials to general contractors in a large metropolitan area. The company is studying the feasibility of introducing a guaranteed same-day delivery plan, under which it would guarantee delivery within four hours for orders received from approved customers by noon of that day. For orders received in the afternoon, delivery would be guaranteed by 8 A.M. the next day. The company believes that this system would give it a substantial competitive advantage relative to other regional building wholesalers, because it would enable contractors to maintain smaller inventories yet still be assured of having building supplies when needed.

You have been asked to assist in designing the proposed system. It will be designed to receive customer orders by phone, so that contractors can call from the construction site. Customers will be billed monthly for all purchases. You want to streamline the processing of cash collections and minimize the time it takes to deposit those funds in the company's bank account.

Required:

a. Specify all the factors that should be used to qualify customers for this new service.
b. Identify the input transactions that this system must process and the output documents (excluding reports) that it should produce.
c. Draw an E-R diagram based on the REA data model to describe the information that must be captured and maintained by the new system.
d. Describe several reports that would be useful to management's implementation of the new credit sales policy. What data needs to be collected to produce these reports? What application controls should be in place to ensure that these reports contain complete, accurate, and valid information?
e. Draw a systems flowchart of your proposed system.

TABLE 12.2 Relational Tables for Problem 12.5

Inventory

Part Number	Description	Cost	Price
101	Monitor	899	1295
102	CPU	2150	2599
103	CD-ROM drive	95	199
104	Printer	345	499
105	Tape unit	195	259

Inventory-Sales

Part Number	Invoice Number	Quantity
101	25	1
102	25	1
103	25	1
104	26	2

Cash Collections

Remittance Number	Amount	Invoice Number	Customer Number
120	499	23	1001
121	4851	24	1003
122	4851	27	1001

Sales

Invoice Number	Date	Customer Number	Salesperson Number
23	11/05	1001	12
24	11/05	1003	10
25	11/06	1002	8
26	11/07	1003	12
27	11/07	1001	8
28	11/07	1003	12

Salesperson

Salesperson Number	Name
8	Jones
10	Brown
12	Alawi

Customer

Customer Number	Name	Address
1001	Agrawal	Chicago
1002	Chen	Memphis
1003	Finney	St. Louis

f. Describe the threats that need to be protected against and the control procedures that should be included in the new system to address those threats.

12.7 O'Brien Corporation is a medium-sized, privately owned industrial instrument manufacturer supplying precision equipment manufacturers in the Midwest. The corporation is ten years old and operates a centralized AIS. The administrative offices are located in a downtown building, and the production, shipping, and receiving departments are housed in a renovated warehouse a few blocks away. The shipping and receiving areas share one end of the warehouse.

The marketing department consists of four sales representatives. Upon obtaining an order, usually over the telephone, a salesperson manually prepares a prenumbered, two-part sales order. One copy of the order is filed by date, and the second copy is sent to the shipping department. All sales are on credit, FOB destination. Because of the recent increase in sales, the sales representatives have not had time to check credit histories. As a result, 15% of credit sales are either late collections or uncollectible.

The shipping department receives the sales orders and packages the goods from the warehouse, noting any items that are out of stock. The terminal in the shipping department is used to update the perpetual inventory records of each item as it is removed from the shelf. The packages are placed near the loading dock door in alphabetical order by customer name. The sales order is signed by a shipping clerk, indicating that the order is filled and ready to send.

The sales order is forwarded to the billing department, where a two-part sales invoice is prepared. The sales invoice is prepared only upon receipt of the sales order from the shipping department, so that the customer is billed just for the items that were sent, not for back orders. Billing sends the customer's copy of the invoice back to shipping; shipping then inserts it into a special envelope on the package in order to save postage.

The carrier of the customer's choice is then contacted to pick up the goods. In the past, goods were shipped within two working days of the receipt of the customer's order; however, shipping dates now average six working days. One reason for this slippage is that two new shipping clerks are still undergoing training. Because they have fallen behind, the two clerks in the receiving department, who are experienced, have been assisting them.

The receiving department is located adjacent to the shipping dock, and merchandise is received daily by many different carriers. The clerks share a computer terminal with the shipping department. The date, vendor, and number of items received are entered upon receipt in order to keep the perpetual inventory records current.

Hard copies of the changes in inventory (additions and shipments) are printed once a month. The receiving supervisor makes sure that the additions are reasonable and forwards the printout to the shipping supervisor, who is responsible for checking the reasonableness of the deductions from inventory (shipments). The inventory printout is stored in the shipping department by date. A complete inventory list is printed only once a year, when the entire inventory is counted.

The diagram in Fig. 12.16 presents the document flows employed by O'Brien Corporation.

Required:

a. Identify at least five weaknesses in O'Brien Corporation's marketing, shipping, billing, and receiving information system. Describe the exposure resulting from each weakness. Recommend control procedures that should be added to the system to correct each weakness. Format your answer as follows:

Weakness	Threat	Recommended Control Procedure(s)

b. Discuss how O'Brien Corporation could use information technology to improve both control and efficiency during sales order processing.

(CMA Examination, adapted)

12.8 Parktown Medical Center, Inc. is a small health care provider that is owned by a publicly held corporation. It employs seven salaried physicians, ten nurses, three support staff, and three clerical workers. The clerical workers perform such tasks as reception, correspondence, cash receipts, billing, and appointment scheduling. All are adequately bonded.

Most patients pay for services by cash or check at the time services are rendered. Credit is not approved by the clerical staff. The physician who is to perform the respective services approves credit based on an interview. When credit is approved, the physician files a memo with the billing clerk (clerk #2) to set up the receivable from data generated by the physician.

The servicing physician prepares a charge slip that is given to clerk #1 for pricing and preparation of the patient's bill. Clerk #1 transmits a copy of the bill to clerk #2 for preparation of the revenue summary and for posting in the accounts receivable subsidiary ledger.

The cash receipts functions are performed by clerk #1, who receives cash and checks directly from patients and gives each patient a prenumbered cash receipt. Clerk #1 opens the mail and immediately stamps all checks "for deposit only" and lists cash and checks for deposit. The cash and checks are deposited daily by the office manager. The list of cash and checks together with the related remittance advices are forwarded by clerk #1 to clerk #2. Clerk #1 also serves as the office receptionist with general correspondence duties.

Clerk #2 prepares and sends monthly statements to patients with unpaid balances. He also prepares the cash receipts journal and is responsible for the accounts receivable subsidiary ledger. No other clerical employee is permitted access to the accounts receivable subsidiary ledger. Uncollectible accounts are written off by clerk #2 only after the physician who performed the respective services believes the account is uncollectible and communicates the write-off to the office manager. The office manager then issues a write-off memo that clerk #2 processes.

The office manager supervises the clerks, issues write-off memos, schedules appointments for the doctors, makes bank deposits, reconciles bank statements, and performs general correspondence duties.

Additional services are performed monthly by a local accountant who posts summaries prepared by the clerks to the general ledger, prepares income statements, and files the appropriate payroll forms and tax returns. The accountant reports directly to the parent corporation.

Required:

a. Identify at least four control weaknesses at Parktown. Describe the potential threat and exposure associated with each weakness. Also recommend how to best correct each weakness.

(CPA Examination, adapted)

FIGURE 12.16
Revenue Cycle Activities for O'Brien Corporation

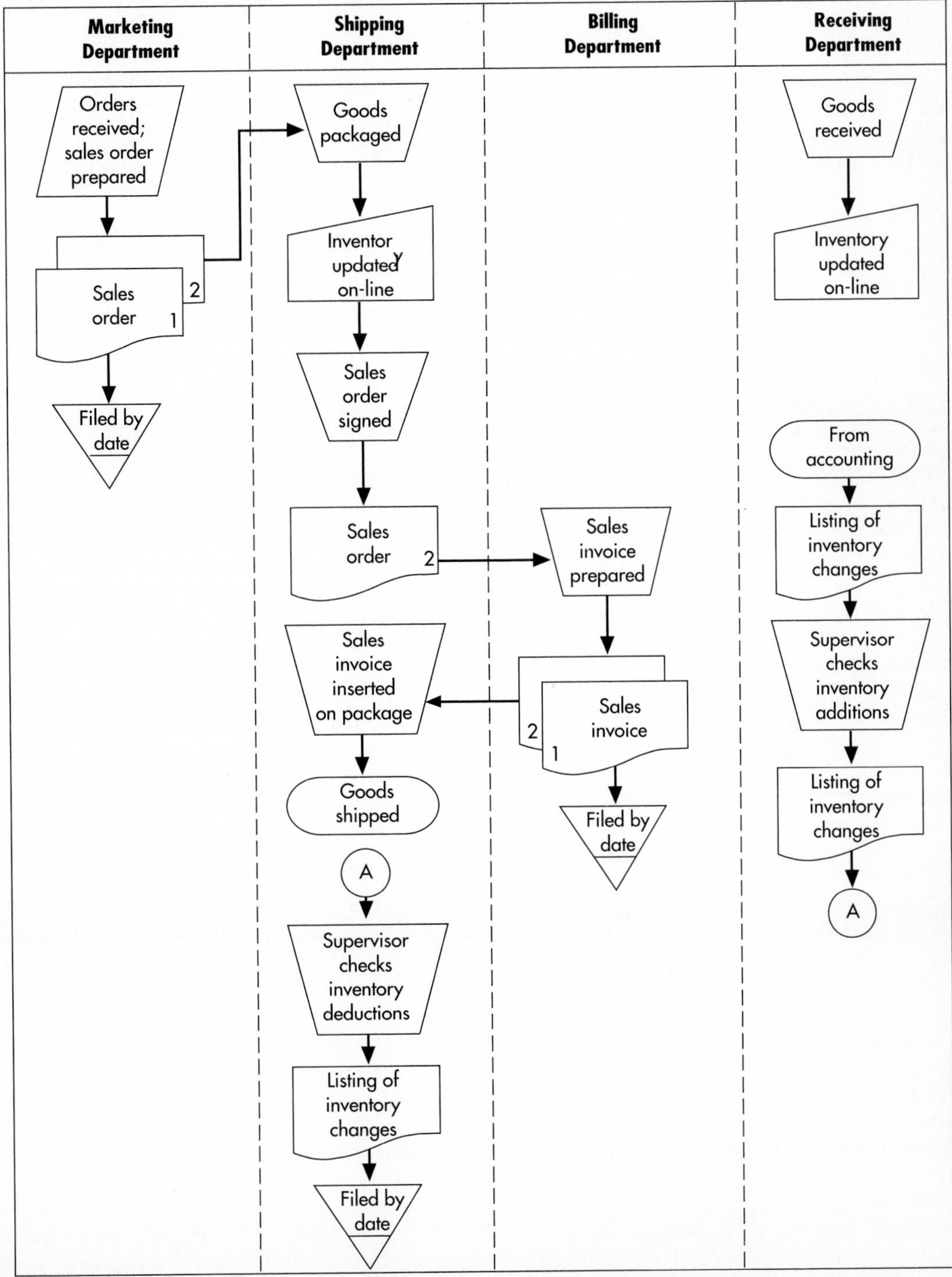

b. Identify opportunities for using information technology to streamline procedures at Parktown. Also discuss the control procedures that need to be included in any such new system.

12.9 Figure 12.17 depicts all the activities performed in the revenue cycle by the Newton Hardware Company.

Required:

a. Identify the weaknesses in Newton Hardware's revenue cycle. Explain the resulting threats and suggest methods to correct the weaknesses. Organize your answer as follows:

Weakness	Threat	Recommended Improvement

(CPA Examination, adapted)

b. Identify ways to use information technology to streamline Newton's revenue cycle activities. Describe the control procedures that should be included in the new system.

12.10 Complete the cell entries in Table 12.3, which lists the various activities performed in the revenue cycle and the journal entries, documents, data, and control issues associated with them.

(Adapted from teaching materials developed by Martha Eining at the University of Utah)

CASE 12.1 ANYCOMPANY, INC.—AN ONGOING COMPREHENSIVE CASE

Identify a local company (you may use the same company that you identified to complete this case in prior chapters), and answer the following questions:

1. Who are the individuals responsible for sales order preparation, credit checks, safeguarding of physical inventories, shipping, billing, maintaining accounts receivable, and handling cash collections? How are these duties segregated to diminish the threat of errors or irregularities?
2. What documents are used in the system? Are they designed in a manner that makes them easy to complete? Do they collect all the information needed to manage the various revenue cycle business activities? Do the reports generated by the system provide adequate information for decision making?
3. Are data stored in separate files or in a data base? How is this information updated? What process is used to update the general ledger? What application controls are in place to ensure accuracy, completeness, and validity of data entry, processing, and output?
4. Document your understanding of the system using flowcharts, data flow diagrams, and REA diagrams. Discuss how current developments in information technology could be used to improve the efficiency and effectiveness of existing procedures.

CASE 12.2 ELITE PUBLISHING COMPANY

Elite Publishing Company has established Business Book Club, Inc. (BBC), a subsidiary that operates as follows: BBC's editors select from among recently published business books those they feel will be most interesting to businesspeople. BBC will purchase these books in large quantities at approximately 40% of list price and then sell them to their club members at approximately 75% of list price.

Both direct mail and advertisements in selected publications are used to solicit new customers. The advertisements offer an introductory membership bonus whereby new members who purchase one book will receive four free titles. Each month, club members are sent a list of new selections and a book order form. For every four books they purchase, members earn one free book.

You have been called on to design a computerized billing and book inventory system for BBC. The advertising manager wants to know which advertising media are most effective, the credit manager wants to

TABLE 12.3 Overview of Revenue Cycle Business Activities

	Revenue Cycle							
	Contact Customer	**Customer Agrees to Sale**	**Approve Credit**	**Transfer Goods**	**Bill Customer**	**Receive Remittance**	**Credit Accounts Receivable**	**Deposit Cash**
Accounting transaction				Sale				
Journal entry							Dr. Cash Cr. A/R	
Documents		Purchase order from customer						
Data collected	Name Address Contact person							
Department					Accounting			
Control issues			Only approved customer get credit					
Information required								
Information generated								
Effect of automation								

Source: Adapted from teaching materials developed by Martha Eining, University of Utah. Reprinted with permission.

FIGURE 12.17
Newton Hardware Company: Revenue Cycle Procedures

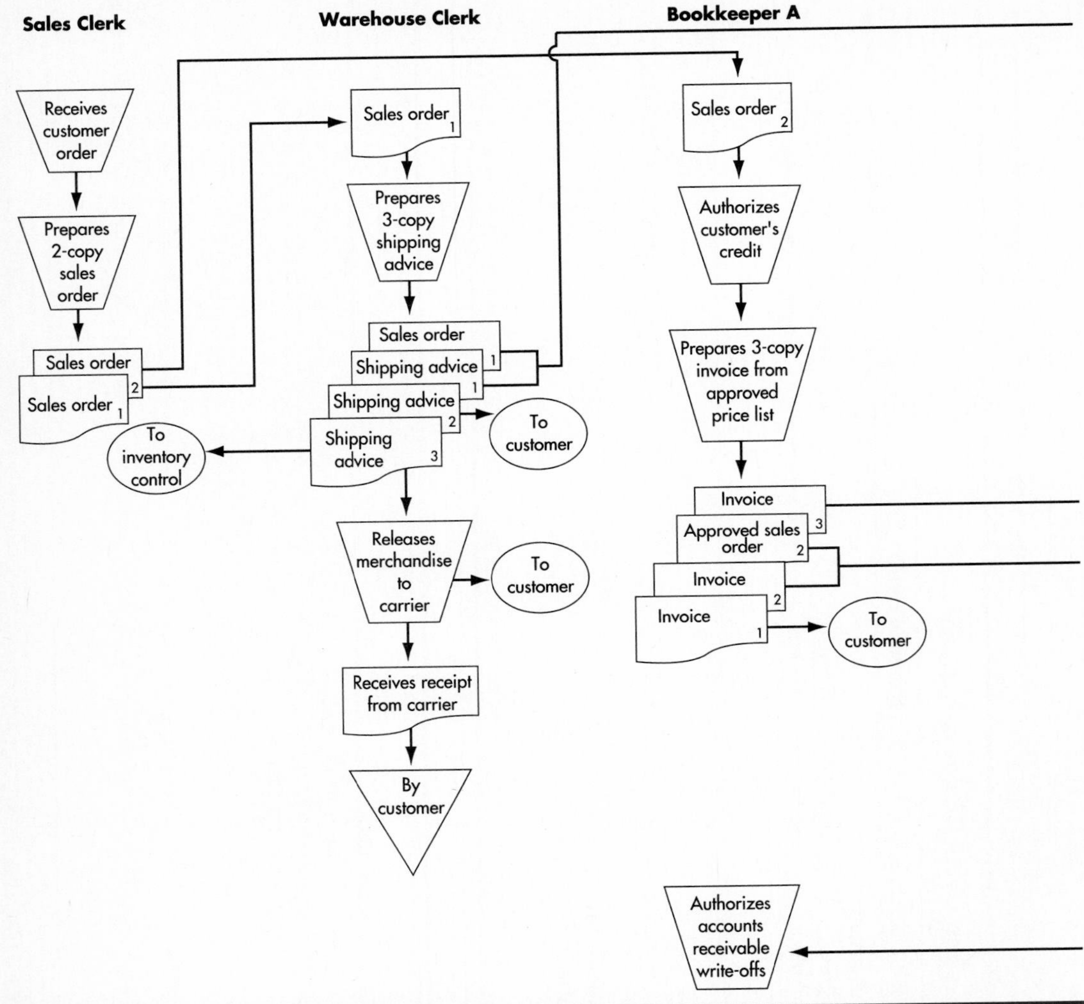

know which accounts are more than 90 days past due, and the editors want to know which books are best-sellers for the club.

Required:

1. Draw an REA diagram of the system, and prepare a list of attributes that should be stored in the system.
2. Identify the input transactions that this system must process and the output documents and reports that the system should be designed to produce.
3. Describe how information technology can be used to maximize the efficiency of sales order entry, shipping, billing, and cash collections. Draw a systems flowchart of your proposal.
4. Describe the control procedures that should be included in this system.

FIGURE 12.17
Continued

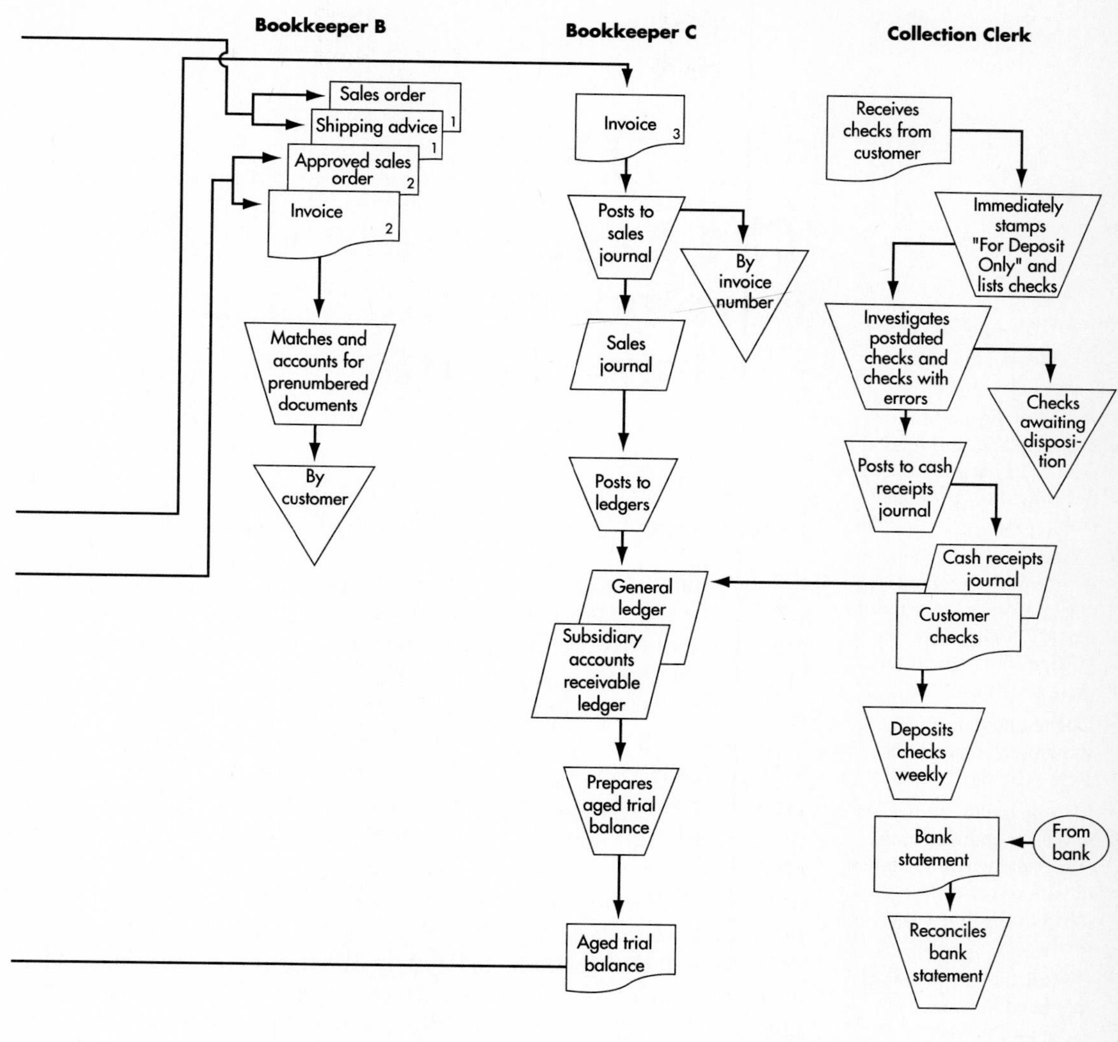

ANSWERS TO CHAPTER QUIZ

1. c **3.** c **5.** d **7.** a **9.** a
2. b **4.** d **6.** c **8.** d **10.** c

CHAPTER 13

The Expenditure Cycle: Purchasing and Cash Disbursements

LEARNING OBJECTIVES

After studying this chapter, you should be able to

- Describe the major business activities and related data processing operations performed in the expenditure cycle.
- Assess the relative benefits of alternative methods for using information technology (IT) to improve the efficiency of expenditure cycle activities.
- Document your understanding of expenditure cycle activities.
- Identify the major threats in the expenditure cycle, and evaluate the adequacy of various control procedures for dealing with them.
- Discuss the key decisions that need to be made in the expenditure cycle, and identify the information needed to make those decisions.
- Read and understand a data model (REA diagram) of the expenditure cycle.

Integrative Case: Alpha Omega Electronics

Sales volume for Alpha Omega Electronics (AOE) has leveled off the past two years after strong growth. Surveys indicate product pricing and quality are significant concerns among AOE's customers.

LeRoy Williams, vice president of manufacturing for AOE, is disappointed with the second quarter financial results. He is especially distressed with escalating production costs at both the Dayton and Wichita plants. Several production runs were delayed at the Wichita plant because components were unavailable that, according to inventory records, should have been in stock. The problems at the Dayton plant arose because of numerous instances when suppliers either did not deliver components on a timely basis or delivered substandard products. LeRoy is also concerned about AOE's failure to take advantage of the discounts offered by its suppliers for prompt payment of invoices. The combined effect of these problems was a 15% drop in AOE's gross margin, compared with the previous year.

LeRoy asked Elizabeth Venko, the controller, for some recommendations on how AOE's information system could be used to solve these problems. Specifically, he asked Elizabeth to address the following issues:

1. What must be done to ensure that AOE's inventory records are current and accurate? To prevent unexpected components shortages like those experienced at the Wichita plant?
2. How could the problems at the Dayton plant be avoided in the future? What can be done to ensure timely delivery of quality components?

3. Is it possible to reduce AOE's investment in materials inventories?
4. What must be done to ensure that available vendor discounts are taken?
5. How could the information system provide better information to guide planning and production?
6. How could IT be used to reengineer expenditure cycle activities?

As this case suggests, deficiencies in the information system used to support expenditure cycle activities can create significant financial problems for an organization. The availability of current and accurate information about inventories, vendors, and the status of outstanding purchase orders is crucial for effective management of the expenditure cycle. As you read this chapter, think about how changes in AOE's information system could improve the effectiveness and efficiency of its expenditure cycle activities.

INTRODUCTION

The **expenditure cycle** is a recurring set of business activities and related data processing operations associated with the purchase of and payment for goods and services (see Fig. 13.1). This chapter focuses on the acquisition of raw materials, finished goods, supplies, and services. Chapters 14 and 15 address two other special types of expenditures: the acquisition of fixed assets and labor services, respectively.

In the expenditure cycle, the primary external exchange of information is with vendors. Internally, the expenditure cycle receives notification from the revenue and production cycles, inventory control, and various departments about the need to purchase goods and materials; it then notifies them when

FIGURE 13.1
Context Diagram of the Expenditure Cycle

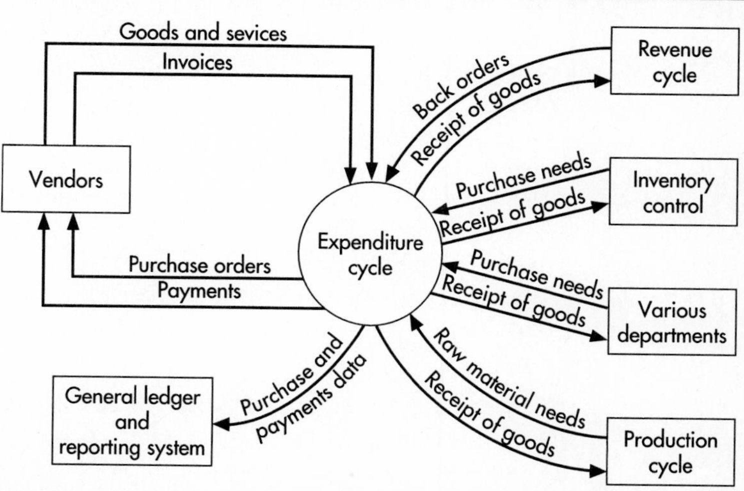

those goods have been received. The expenditure cycle also sends expense data to the general ledger and reporting function for inclusion in financial statements and performance reports.

This chapter is organized around the three basic objectives of the AIS in the expenditure cycle. The first section describes the basic business activities performed in the expenditure cycle and explains how data about those activities is captured and processed by the AIS. Opportunities for using information technology (IT) to improve the effectiveness and efficiency of those activities are also discussed. The second section discusses the major control objectives in the expenditure cycle and explains how the AIS can be designed to mitigate the threats associated with each expenditure cycle business activity. The final section discusses the key decisions that need to be made and presents a data model that shows how the AIS can effectively and efficiently store and organize the information needed to make those decisions.

EXPENDITURE CYCLE BUSINESS ACTIVITIES

One function of the AIS is to support the effective performance of the organization's business activities by efficiently processing transaction data. Figure 13.2 shows the five basic business activities in the expenditure cycle:

1. Requesting the purchase of needed goods
2. Ordering goods to be purchased
3. Receiving ordered goods
4. Approving vendor invoices for payment
5. Paying for goods purchased

Notice that the last four activities in the expenditure cycle are mirror images of the basic activities performed in the revenue cycle:

- The order goods activity (circle 2.0 in Fig. 13.2) generates the purchase order that serves as the customer input to the sales order entry process (circle 1.0 in Fig. 12.3).
- The receive goods activity (circle 3.0 in Fig. 13.2) handles the goods sent by the vendor's shipping function (circle 2.0 in Fig. 12.3).
- The approve vendor invoice for payment activity (circle 4.0 in Fig. 13.2) processes the invoices generated by the vendor's bill customer activity (circle 3.0 in Fig. 12.3).
- The pay for goods activity (circle 5.0 in Fig. 13.2) generates the payments that are processed by the vendor's cash collection activity (circle 4.0 in Fig. 12.3).

As we will see later in the chapter, these close linkages between the buyer's expenditure cycle activities and the seller's revenue cycle activities have important implications for the design of an AIS. Specifically, by applying new IT developments to reengineer expenditure cycle activities, companies create the

FIGURE 13.2
Level 0 DFD for the Expenditure Cycle

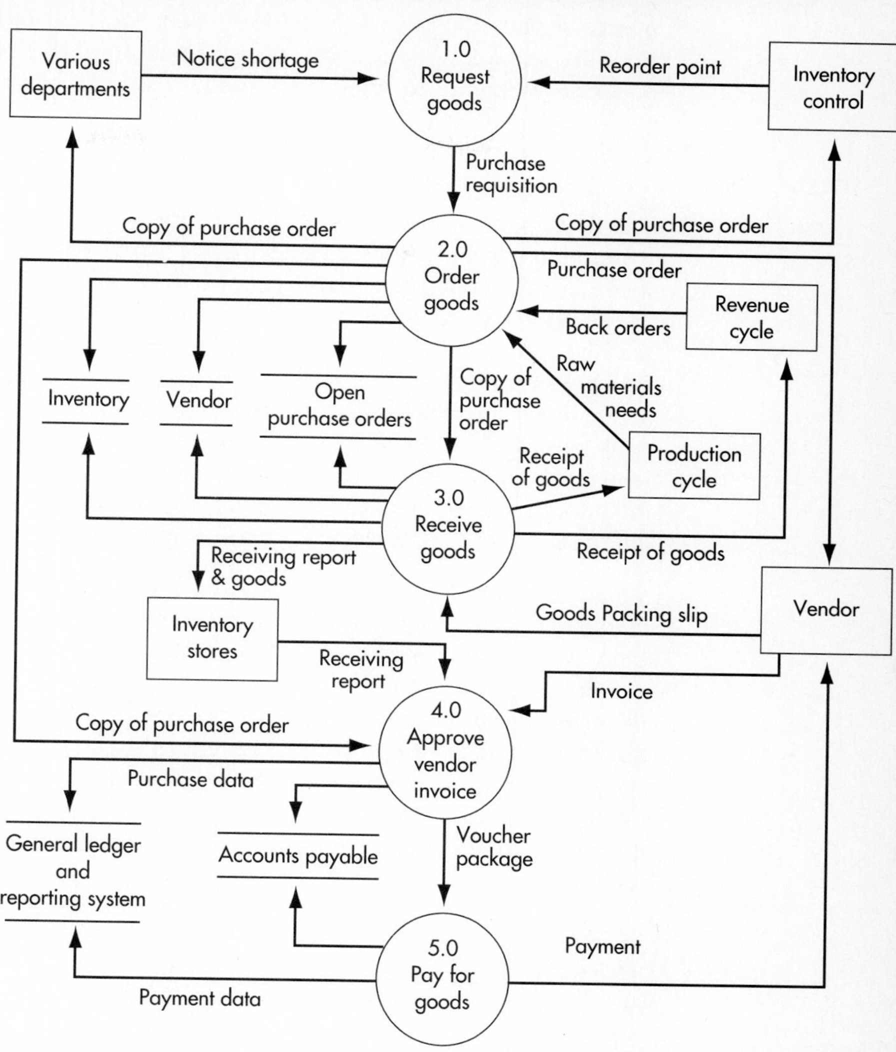

opportunity for their suppliers to reengineer their revenue cycle activities. Conversely, the use of IT to redesign a company's revenue cycle can create opportunities for customers to modify their own expenditure cycles. Indeed, in many cases the changes in one company's operations may *require* changes in the AIS of other companies with which it does business. For example, the major automobile manufacturers require that suppliers transmit invoices via EDI—or they will not do business with them.

The remainder of this section discusses how the AIS captures and processes transaction data about each of the basic activities in the expenditure cycle.

Although each activity is discussed separately, keep in mind that IT developments often enable several activities to be performed simultaneously. In addition, the same key data about transactions must still be collected, whether paper or electronic documents are used.

Request Goods

The first major business activity in the expenditure cycle involves the request to purchase inventory or supplies (circle 1.0 in Fig. 13.2). The key decisions made in this process are identifying what, when, and how much to purchase. These decisions are normally made by the inventory control function, although the need to reorder items is sometimes noticed by various user departments. Purchase requests are also sometimes generated in the production cycle or arrive in the form of back orders from the revenue cycle.

Weaknesses in the inventory control function can create significant problems, as the introductory AOE case demonstrated. Specifically, inaccuracies in inventory records caused AOE's inventory shortages at the Wichita plant, and led to the failure to purchase needed components in a timely manner.

The Traditional Inventory Control Method. The traditional approach to managing inventory is to maintain sufficient stock so that production can continue without interruption even if inventory use is greater than expected or if suppliers are late in making deliveries. This traditional approach is often called the **economic order quantity (EOQ)** approach, because it is based on calculating an optimal order size so as to minimize the sum of ordering, carrying, and stockout costs. *Ordering costs* include all expenses associated with processing purchase transactions. *Carrying costs* are the costs associated with holding inventory. *Stockout costs* represent costs that result from inventory shortages, such as lost sales or production delays.

Actual application of the EOQ approach varies depending on the type of item. For high-cost or high-use items, such as the computer chips and displays used by AOE, all three types of costs are included in the formula. For low-cost or low-use items, such as the screws and springs used by AOE to assemble its products, ordering and carrying costs are usually ignored and the sole objective is to maintain sufficient inventory levels.

The EOQ formula is used to calculate how much to order. The **reorder point** specifies when to order. Companies typically set the reorder point based on considerations involving delivery time and desired levels of safety stock to handle unexpected fluctuations in demand.

Alternative Inventory Control Methods. The traditional EOQ approach to inventory control often results in carrying significant amounts of inventory. In recent years many large U.S. manufacturing companies, including Xerox, Ford, Motorola, NCR, Intel, McDonnell Douglas, and Delco Electronics, have adopted alternative methods of inventory control that seek to minimize or even eliminate the amount of inventory that must be carried.

One alternative approach to managing inventory is called **materials requirements planning (MRP).** MRP seeks to reduce required inventory levels by *scheduling* production, rather than *estimating* needs. For example, the production planning department of a company using MRP would prepare a detailed schedule specifying the quantities of each finished product that it wants to manufacture in a specified time period, such as the next three months. Using this schedule and the engineering specifications for each product, the quantities of raw materials, parts, and supplies that will be needed in production, and the point in time when they will be needed, can be determined. Thus MRP systems reduce uncertainties about when raw materials are needed and, therefore, require less inventory to be carried.

A **just-in-time (JIT) inventory system** is another alternative approach to managing inventory. JIT systems attempt to minimize, if not totally eliminate, both carrying and stockout costs. JIT systems are characterized by frequent deliveries of small amounts of materials, parts, and supplies directly to the specific locations that require them, when they are needed, rather than by infrequent bulk deliveries to a central receiving and storage facility. Thus a factory utilizing a JIT system will have multiple receiving docks, each assigned to accept deliveries of items needed at nearby work centers.

A major difference between MRP and JIT systems involves the scheduling of production. MRP systems schedule production to meet estimated sales needs, thereby creating a stock of finished goods inventory. JIT systems, in contrast, schedule production to meet customer demands, thereby virtually eliminating finished goods inventory. Both MRP and JIT systems can reduce costs and improve efficiency. Choosing between them depends, in part, on the types of products a company sells. MRP systems are more effectively used with products, such as consumer staples, with fairly predictable patterns of demand. JIT inventory systems are especially useful for products, such as fashion apparel, for which demand cannot be accurately predicted and that also have relatively short life cycles. In such cases, it is important to be able to quickly ramp up production to meet unanticipated demand and also to be able to quickly stop production to avoid accumulating large inventories that must be marked down for clearance because the product is no longer in demand.

Documents and Procedures. The request to purchase goods or supplies is triggered either by the inventory control function or by employees noticing a shortage of materials. The advanced inventory control systems used in large manufacturing companies, such as IBM and Ford, automatically generate purchase requisitions whenever the quantity of an item on hand falls below its reorder point. In contrast, in smaller companies the employees who use the items note when stock is running low and request that it be reordered. For example, your neighborhood hair stylist will order shampoos, hairbrushes, and other supplies when he or she notices the supply is low. Moreover, even in large companies, office supplies such as copier paper and pencils are often ordered by the employees who use those items whenever they notice that stock is running low.

Regardless of its source, the need to purchase goods or supplies usually results in the creation of a purchase requisition. The **purchase requisition** (Fig. 13.3) is a document that identifies the requisitioner; specifies the delivery location and date needed; identifies the item numbers, descriptions, quantity, and price of each item requested; and may suggest a vendor. The person

FIGURE 13.3
Sample AOE Purchase Requisition (items in boldface are preprinted)

ALPHA OMEGA ELECTRONICS
PURCHASE REQUISITION
No. 89010

Date Prepared: 07/02/2000	**Prepared by:** Harold Brown *HB*		**Suggested Vendor:** Best Office Supply
Deliver To: Copy Center		**Attention:** Harold Brown	**Date Needed:** 7/15/2000

Item Number	**Quantity**	**Description**	**Price/Unit**
32047	15 boxes	Xerox 4200 paper, 20 wt., 10 ream box	$33.99
80170	5 boxes	Moore 2600 continuous form, 20 lb	$31.99
81756	20 boxes	Dysan 100 HD diskettes, box of 10	$ 6.49
10407	10	IBM 4207 Proprinter ribbon, black	$ 8.99

Approved by: Susan Chen	**Department:** Admin. Services	**Date Approved:** 07/02/2000	**Account No.:** 91887

approving the purchase requisition indicates the department number and account number to which the purchase should be charged.

Opportunities for Using Information Technology. One way to improve the efficiency of the purchase requisition process involves the use of on-line data entry instead of paper documents. Electronic documentation reduces the time required to process purchase requisitions, as well as the costs of storing the data. The incorporation of appropriate edit controls can also increase accuracy.

The use of on-line processing systems and integrated data bases linking sales, purchasing, and production information is necessary for implementing alternative methods of inventory control, such as JIT or MRP systems. Both systems require accurate perpetual inventory records so that the computer can be programmed to monitor inventory levels and automatically generate purchase requisitions whenever quantities on hand fall below the reorder point.

Bar-code technology facilitates the maintenance of accurate perpetual inventory records. The printed lines in a bar code contain information such as the item's number, location, cost, and price. This information is read by an optical scanner, thereby eliminating the need for human data entry. Bar coding not only reduces the time and cost associated with taking inventory, it also virtually eliminates data entry errors. The effect on accuracy can be dramatic: Studies have found that even expert typists make one mistake for every 300 keystrokes.

Bar coding is not a panacea, however. Errors can still occur due to human mistakes, most likely when bar-code scanning is used to record the sale of assorted varieties of a product. For example, if you purchase 24 cans of store-brand soda at a grocery store, the clerk may scan only one can and then manually enter the number purchased. Since the flavors are all priced the same, the amount of the sale is correctly calculated. The perpetual inventory records will be incorrect, however, because the exact count of the flavors sold is not correctly recorded. Consequently, the grocery store may not be able to use point-of-sale (POS) data to maintain its perpetual inventory records, but must still rely on counting what is actually on the shelves. Nevertheless, because bar coding makes it easier and faster to count inventory, such counts can be more frequent, thereby reducing the risk of running out of stock. For example, employees at many retailers use portable bar-code scanners to track inventory status on the floor and to initiate the replenishment process.

Order Goods

The second major business activity in the expenditure cycle involves the ordering of supplies and materials (circle 2.0 in Fig. 13.2). The purchasing activity is usually performed by purchasing agents (sometimes called buyers) within the purchasing department. In manufacturing companies, such as Alpha Omega Electronics, the purchasing function is closely related to the production cycle. Consequently, Ryan McDaniel, the head of the purchasing department at AOE, reports directly to LeRoy Williams, the vice president of manufacturing (see Fig. 12.1, p. 414).

Key Decision: Vendor Selection. The crucial operating decision in the purchasing activity involves the selection of vendors for inventory items. Several factors should be considered in making this decision:

- Price
- Quality of materials
- Dependability in making deliveries

In terms of quality and dependability vendor reliability is very important, especially to JIT systems, because a late delivery or defective parts can bring the entire system to a halt. Consequently, vendor certification is a key component of most JIT systems, and many companies require that their suppliers meet ISO 9000 quality standards. Focus 13.1 introduces the concept of vendor certification and explains what ISO 9000 does, and does not, imply about vendor quality.

Once a vendor has been selected for a product, that company's identity should normally become part of the product inventory master record. This avoids having to repeat the vendor selection process for every subsequent order. (In some cases, however, such as for the purchase of high-cost and low-use items, management may explicitly want to reevaluate all potential vendors each time that product is ordered.) A list of potential alternative vendors for each item should also be maintained, in case the primary vendor is ever out of stock of a needed item.

Vendor performance should also be tracked and periodically evaluated to determine whether there is a need to switch suppliers. Properly evaluating suppliers requires more than just data about prices. Companies also incur costs, such as rework and scrap, related to the quality of the products purchased. There are also costs associated with vendor delivery performance. The AIS can

FOCUS 13.1 ISO 9000 Certification

IN 1987 the International Organization for Standardization issued a set of five standards, referred to as ISO 9000, for assessing potential suppliers' quality control systems. These standards set guidelines for the procedures that should be included in a company's quality control systems. They cover such matters as documentation, inspection, and complaint resolution. The specific requirements vary across companies, with different standards for companies that merely purchase and resell products as opposed to companies that design and manufacture goods. To obtain ISO certification, companies must document their quality control process and hire an accredited company to inspect and evaluate their quality control system.

The continuing globalization of business makes ISO 9000 standards increasingly important. For example, the European Economic Community requires suppliers of certain products to have ISO 9000 certification. So does the U.S. Department of Defense and many large American companies, including Ford, IBM, and Motorola. Thus it is not surprising to learn that most U.S. manufacturing plants now meet those standards.

Meeting ISO 9000 standards may help improve a company's effectiveness and efficiency. For example, the defect rate at one DuPont manufacturing plant fell from 30% to 8%. Similarly, a Rockwell International plant reported that complying with ISO 9000 standards resulted in a productivity increase of 21% while reducing product defect rates by 32% and cycle times by 18%.

Nevertheless, it is important to note that ISO 9000 addresses process, not product quality standards. Therefore ISO 9000 certification does not say anything about product quality. It only means that a company has a total quality control system in place, that the system is adequately documented, and that the system functions as documented. Thus it is possible for a company with poor product quality, but with a good customer complaint resolution system, to obtain ISO 9000 certification.

Sources: Peter C. Brewer and Tina Y. Mills, "ISO 9000 Standards: An Emerging CPA Service Area," *Journal of Accountancy* (February 1994): 63–67; and "Focus on: ISO 9000," *Journal of Accountancy* (February 1994): 60–61.

be designed to capture and track this information. For example, AOE could measure the quality of a vendor's products by tracking how often its items fail to pass inspection in the receiving department. Data on the amount of production that had to be reworked or scrapped because of substandard materials could also be collected. AOE could also measure vendor dependability by matching and tracking actual delivery dates versus those promised. Finally, to ensure that all these factors are considered by purchasing agents, the purchasing function should be evaluated and rewarded by how well it minimizes the total costs, not just the purchase price, of the items acquired.

Documents and Procedures. As shown in Fig. 13.2, the receipt of a purchase requisition triggers the process of ordering goods and supplies. The principal document produced by this process is the purchase order. A **purchase order** is a document that formally requests a vendor to sell and deliver specified products at designated prices. It is also a promise to pay and becomes a contract once it is accepted by the vendor. The purchase order includes the names of the vendor and purchasing agent; the order and requested delivery dates; the delivery location and method of shipment; and information about the items ordered (see Fig. 13.4). Frequently, several purchase orders are

FIGURE 13.4
Sample AOE Purchase Order (items in boldface are preprinted)

Alpha Omega Electronics **No. 2463**

Billing Address: **2431 Bradford Lane**
St. Louis, MO 63105–2311
(314) 467-2341

Reference the above number on all invoices and shipping documents

PURCHASE ORDER

To: Best Office Supply
4567 Olive Blvd.
St. Louis, MO 63112–2345

Ship To: AOE, Inc.
1735 Sandy Dr.
Dayton, OH 33421–2243

Vendor Number:	**Order Date:**	**Requisition Number:**	**Buyer:**	**Terms:**
121	07/03/2000	89010	Fred Mozart	1/10, n/30

F.O.B.	**Ship Via:**	**Delivery Date:**	**Remarks:**
Destination	Your choice	07/15/2000	

Item	**Item Number**	**Quantity**	**Description**	**Unit Price**
1	32047	15 boxes	Xerox 4200 paper, 20 wt., 10 ream box	$33.99
2	80170	5 boxes	Moore 2600 continuous form, 20 lb.	$31.99
3	81756	20 boxes	Dysan 100 HD Diskettes, box of 10	$6.49
4	10407	10	IBM 4207 Proprinter ribbon, black	$8.99

Approved by: *Susan Beethoven*

generated to fill one purchase requisition because different vendors may be the preferred suppliers for the various items requested.

Figure 13.5 shows a typical on-line purchasing system, like that used by AOE. Approved purchase requisitions arrive daily from inventory control and various user departments. The purchasing agent uses an on-line terminal to enter the requisition data and create a purchase order. After the item number is entered, the system searches the inventory master file to identify the preferred vendor for that item. The system then proceeds to create a purchase order record by retrieving data from the inventory and vendor master files and prompting the purchase agent to enter the remaining data, such as quantity needed and desired delivery date. The purchase requisition is then temporarily filed in numerical order.

The system stores the completed purchase order record in a temporary disk file. At the end of the day, all items to be ordered from the same vendor are consolidated into a single purchase order record. Each of these records is

FIGURE 13.5
Flowchart of the Purchasing System

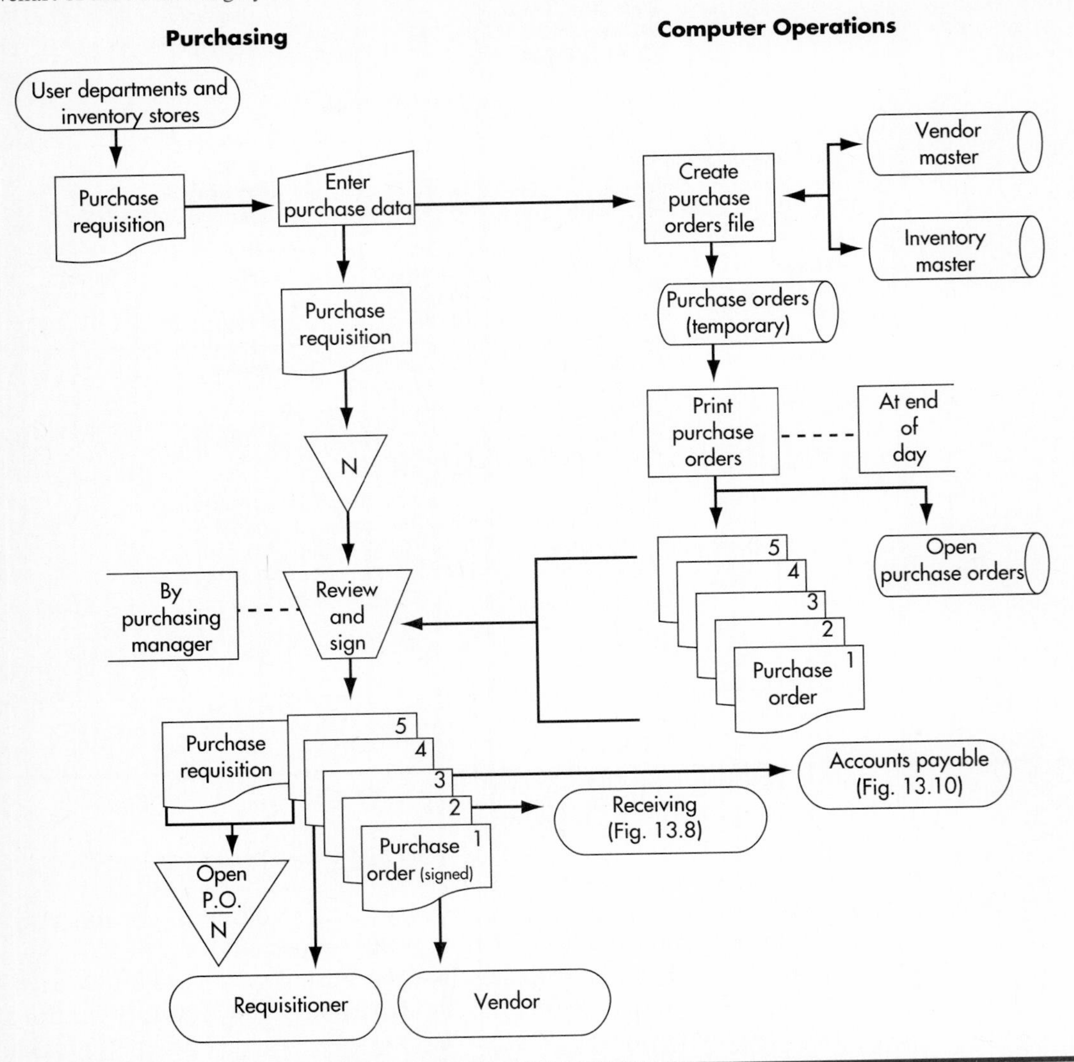

assigned a purchase order number and added to the open purchase order file, and five copies of the purchase order are printed.

The five copies of the purchase order are sent to the purchasing manager for review and approval. After the purchase orders have been signed, the original is sent to the vendor. Copy 2 goes to the receiving department to inform them of anticipated deliveries. Copy 3 goes to accounts payable to notify them of a pending financial commitment. A fourth copy of the purchase order goes to the department that generated the purchase requisition, to let them know their request has been acted on. The final copy is retained in purchasing, where it is attached to the purchase requisition and filed numerically, by purchase order number, in the open purchase order file.

Many companies maintain special purchasing arrangements with important vendors. One such arrangement involves the use of blanket purchase orders. A **blanket purchase order** is a commitment to purchase specified items at designated prices from a particular supplier for a set time period, often one year. The use of blanket purchase orders reduces the buyer's uncertainty about reliable sources of raw materials and provides the vendor with a better basis for planning its capacity and operations. For example, Steelcase Company has an agreement with Cannon Mills to purchase large volumes of fabrics for upholstered furniture. Steelcase provides detailed weekly reports to Cannon listing the quantities of various fabrics that it will need for the next several weeks. Steelcase can make these commitments only because it has a reliable purchasing and inventory control information system.

Opportunities for Using Information Technology. The major cost driver in the purchasing function is the number of purchase orders processed. Thus, finding ways to reduce the number of orders processed and to streamline the steps involved can yield significant savings. One way to improve the purchasing process involves the use of EDI. EDI reduces costs by eliminating the clerical work associated with printing and mailing paper documents. It also reduces the time between recognizing the need to reorder an item and subsequently receiving it. Consequently, the risk of running out of stock is lessened, which can significantly increase profitability. Some companies, such as Kmart, have gone even further in their use of EDI to streamline the inventory control and purchasing process by linking EDI for purchasing with their POS systems and letting suppliers manage and automatically replenish inventory (refer back to Focus 12.2, on p. 424).

It is also important to improve the efficiency of the purchasing process for miscellaneous supplies. These purchases usually involve such small dollar amounts that the cost of processing the orders through the same system used to purchase inventory can exceed the cost of the supplies themselves. Moreover, the quantities involved are often too small to justify using a JIT system. Therefore many companies are exploring alternative methods for processing purchases of miscellaneous supplies. Focus 13.2 describes one such alternative that is growing in favor: procurement cards.

Procurement cards not only reduce costs and improve efficiency, they can also help combat employee fraud. For example, one New Jersey service company used procurement cards provided by Portland, Maine-based Wright Express to detect and stop hundreds of thousands of dollars of theft by its union drivers. The magnetic strip on the back of the cards identified the vehicle for which fuel was being purchased. To get a purchase authorized, drivers had to enter their personal identification number and odometer reading. The system then automatically recorded the location of the filling station, the

FOCUS 13.2 Using Procurement Cards to Streamline Purchasing at ITT Automotive

IN 1993 ITT Automotive conducted a detailed study of its accounts payable function. The results indicated that 59% of the manufacturing unit's invoices were for noninventory items, such as office and shop supplies. Moreover, 91% of those purchases totaled less than $1,000. Nevertheless, ITT Automotive, like many companies, applied the same set of stringent controls to all purchases, regardless of size. Consequently, the average cost to requisition, order, receive, and pay for each invoice was $142, even though almost 34% of all purchases cost less than $100! Clearly, something needed to be done to streamline these procedures.

ITT Automotive's solution was to use procurement cards for all noninventory purchases below $1,000. Procurement cards are like credit cards in that employees can use them to charge purchases up to a set dollar limit. Unlike credit cards, however, ITT Automotive receives just one monthly bill summarizing all employee purchases. Moreover, unique monthly and per-transaction limits can be assigned to each employee. Card usage can even be restricted to vendors in specific SIC industry codes.

The use of procurement cards creates savings in a number of ways. For example, the purchasing department is no longer involved in negotiating and ordering miscellaneous supplies. A single electronic funds transfer exchange replaces the writing of tens of thousands of monthly checks. Postage costs decrease as fewer checks are mailed. Overall, less paper is processed internally. Indeed, ITT Automotive anticipates that procurement cards could eliminate up to 75% of all noninventory purchase orders and 81% of related invoices. In effect, ITT Automotive is outsourcing its paperwork to the banks that issue the procurement cards!

In addition to cost savings, procurement cards have had a positive effect on employee morale and business practices. Employees are empowered to make small-dollar purchases as they see fit. In addition, the time lag between recognition of supply need and its acquisition is reduced.

Source: Richard J. Palmer, "Reengineering Payables at ITT Automotive," *Management Accounting* (July 1994): 38–42.

amount and type of fuel purchased, and the time of the transaction. All this information was used to document numerous cases in which union drivers purchased more gas than the tank of the truck could hold. In these cases, drivers had convinced gas station attendants to pad the amount purchased and had split the excess with them. The procurement card data gave the company the evidence it needed to fire those union drivers. It also deterred future thefts of that nature.

Another way to streamline and automate the purchasing process for supplies and other noninventory items involves the use the Internet. Software exists to create a custom catalog of all authorized suppliers for various products. When employees want to order some supplies, they navigate through this catalog, which shows the various products they are authorized to order. The catalog provides information about price and terms. Clicking on a specific product automatically links to that supplier's web site for additional details. To order, employees fill out an electronic form, which is then routed to the appropriate supervisor for digital approval. Savings come from eliminating paperwork and by consolidating purchases with fewer vendors, who often offer volume discounts.

The Internet may also be used to reduce the prices paid for raw materials by conducting an auction among potential suppliers. In these reverse auctions, vendors bid on-line, competing on prices and other terms they are willing to offer. Caterpillar, Inc. claims that such auctions have helped it shave an average of 6% on purchasing costs.

Receive and Store Goods

The third major business activity in the expenditure cycle involves the receipt and storage of ordered items (circle 3.0 in Fig. 13.2). The receiving department is responsible for accepting vendor deliveries; it usually reports to the warehouse manager, who in turn reports to the vice president of manufacturing (see Fig. 12.1, p. 414). The inventory stores department, which also reports to the warehouse manager, is responsible for storage of the goods. Information about the receipt of ordered merchandise must also be communicated to the inventory control function, to update the inventory records.

Key Decisions and Information Needs. Figure 13.6 shows that the receiving department has two major responsibilities: deciding whether to accept a delivery, and verifying the quantity and quality of the goods delivered. The first decision is made based on information provided by the purchasing function: The existence of a valid purchase order indicates that the delivery should be accepted. This decision is important, because the acceptance of unordered goods would result in wasted time and space in handling and storing those items until they can be returned.

Verifying the quantity of goods delivered is extremely important to ensure that the company pays only for goods actually received and that inventory records are accurately updated. To encourage the receiving clerk to accurately count what was delivered, many companies black out the quantity ordered field

FIGURE 13.6
Level 1 DFD of the Receiving Function

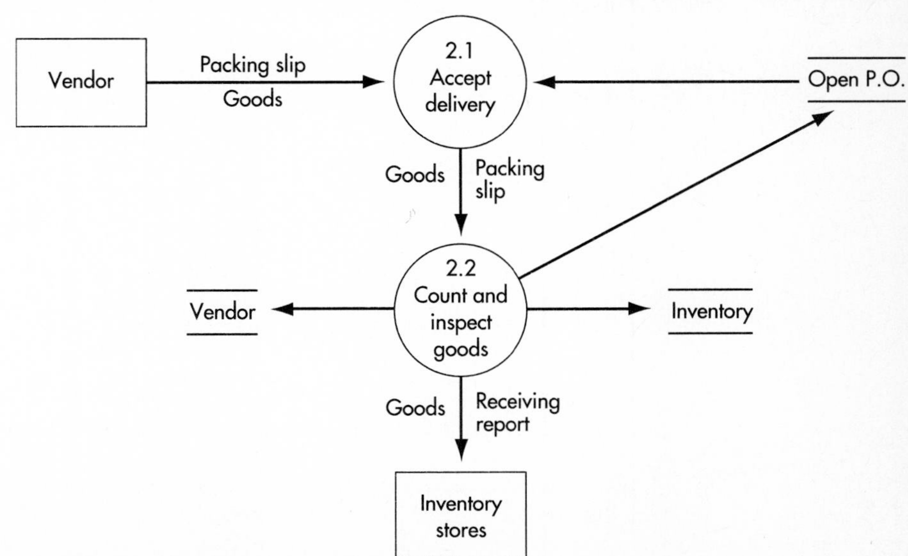

on the receiving department's copy of the purchase order. Nevertheless, the receiving clerk still knows the expected quantity of goods because vendors usually include a packing slip with each order. Consequently, there is a temptation to do just a quick visual comparison of quantities received with those indicated on the packing slip, in order to quickly route the goods to where they are needed. Therefore, companies must clearly communicate to receiving clerks the importance of carefully and accurately counting all deliveries. An effective means of communication is to require the receiving clerk not only to record the quantity received, but also to sign the receiving report. Signing a document indicates an assumption of responsibility, which usually results in more diligent work.

Before routing the inventory to the warehouse, the receiving clerk should also carefully examine each delivery for signs of obvious damage. Information about the delivery time and condition of the goods is added to the vendor file, the inventory file is updated to reflect the quantity of goods received, and the receipt of goods is noted on the purchase order. Upon transfer of the goods to the warehouse, the inventory stores department verifies the count of the items placed into inventory.

Documents and Procedures. The primary document used in the receiving subsystem of the expenditure cycle is the receiving report. The **receiving report** documents details about each delivery, including the date received, shipper, vendor, and purchase order number (Fig. 13.7). For each item received, it shows the item number, description, unit of measure, and count of the quantity received.

FIGURE 13.7
Sample AOE Receiving Report (items in boldface are preprinted)

Alpha Omega Electronics
RECEIVING REPORT **No. 3113**

Vendor: Best Office Supply	**Date Received:** 07/13/2000
Shipped via: UPS	**Purchase Order Number:** 2463

Item Number	**Quantity**	**Description**
32047	15	Xerox 4200 paper, 20 wt., 10 ream box
80170	5	Moore 2600 continuous form, 20 lb.
81756	20	Dysan 100 HD diskettes, box of 10
10407	10	IBM 4207 Proprinter ribbons, black

Remarks:
Two boxes of Moore 2600 paper received with water damage on outside, but the paper appears to be okay

Received by:	**Inspected by:**	**Delivered to:**
Nathan Hale	*Nathan Hale*	*Harold Brown*

It also contains space to identify the persons who received and inspected the goods as well as for remarks concerning the quality of the items received.

A receiving report is typically not used to document the receipt of services, such as advertising and cleaning. Instead, receipt of such services is usually documented by supervisory approval of the vendor's invoice.

Figure 13.8 depicts an on-line receiving process used by a manufacturing company such as AOE. The copy of the purchase order sent from the purchasing department is filed alphabetically by vendor. When a delivery arrives, a receiving clerk verifies that the goods were indeed ordered by comparing the purchase order number referenced on the vendor's packing slip with the copy of the purchase order from the purchasing department. The receiving clerk then counts and inspects the goods and uses an on-line terminal to enter the inventory item numbers, count, and purchase order number. The system checks that data against the open purchase order file; any discrepancies are immediately displayed on the screen and must be resolved.

FIGURE 13.8
Flowchart of the Receiving System

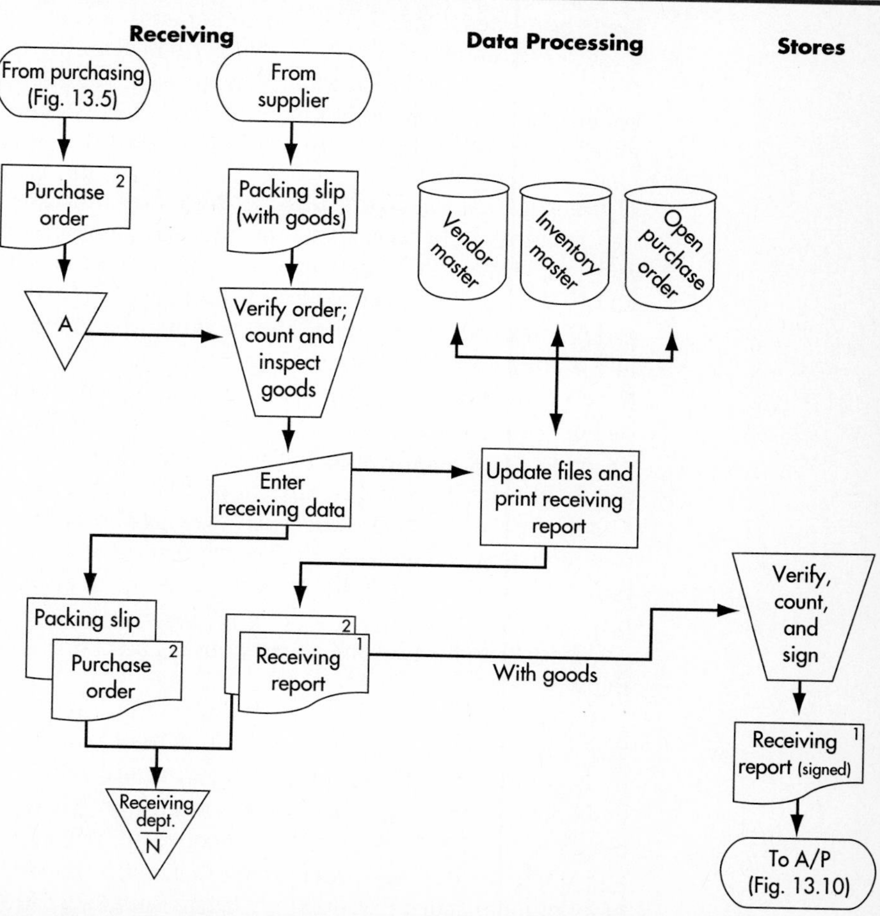

Once the goods are accepted, the system updates the quantity on order and quantity on hand fields in the inventory master file, records the date of receipt in the vendor master file, and notes the quantity received in the open purchase order file. Two copies of a prenumbered receiving report are also printed in the receiving department. One of these accompanies the goods to the inventory stores department, where a clerk signs off to acknowledge transfer of the goods into inventory. This signed copy of the receiving report is then sent to accounts payable, where it is used to approve the vendor invoice. The other copy of the receiving report is filed in the receiving department, along with the related purchase order and packing slip.

Three possible exceptions to this process are not shown in Fig. 13.8: (1) receiving a quantity of goods different from the amount ordered, (2) receiving damaged goods, or (3) receiving goods of inferior quality that fail inspection. In all three cases, the purchasing department must resolve the situation with the vendor. Usually, the vendor will give the buyer permission to correct the invoice for any discrepancies in quantity. In the case of damaged or poor-quality goods, a document called a debit memo is prepared after the vendor agrees to take back the goods or to grant a price reduction. The **debit memo** records the adjustment being requested. One copy of the debit memo is sent to the vendor, who subsequently creates and returns a credit memo in acknowledgment. Another copy of the debit memo goes to accounts payable, where it is used to adjust the account balance owed to that vendor. A third copy of the debit memo accompanies the goods to the shipping department to authorize their return to the vendor.

Opportunities for Using Information Technology. Counting and recording inventory deliveries is a labor-intensive task. One way for companies like AOE to improve the efficiency of this process is to require vendors to bar-code all of their products. Bar coding would enable receiving clerks to scan in the product number, description, and quantity of all items received, thereby virtually eliminating data entry errors. Moreover, although the goods would still have to be manually inspected to ensure they meet quality standards, the use of bar-code scanners can significantly reduce delivery processing time. For example, Sea-Land Service, Inc. uses handheld bar-code scanners to enter data about the quantities and conditions of cargo containers at its Charleston, South Carolina port. The data is then sent over a radio-based communications system to a SQL server data base. Previously, it took 50 to 55 minutes to inspect containers moving through the shipyard; with the new system, most containers are inspected in 30 minutes. J. C. Penney uses a similar system of radio-transmission bar-code scanners in its warehouses and claims to have increased productivity by 23%.

Passive radio frequency identification tags provide the opportunity to further streamline the receiving process. These batteryless tags are attached to each crate of goods and emit a signal that can be read by a receiving unit embedded in the gates near a company's warehouse unit. This eliminates the need for employees to scan the bar codes on items.

Satellite technology provides another opportunity to improve the efficiency of inbound logistics. By equipping trucks with data terminals linked to satellites, companies can track the exact location of all incoming shipments and ensure that adequate staff will be there to unload the trucks. Truck drivers can also be directed to pull up to specific loading docks closest to the place where the goods will be used.

Approve Vendor Invoices

The fourth activity in the expenditure cycle entails approving vendor invoices for payment (circle 4.0 in Fig. 13.2). This process is performed by the accounts payable department, which reports to the controller (see Fig. 12.1, p. 414). This is an example of an important segregation of duties. The purchase transaction was authorized when the purchase order was issued; the accounts payable department records the obligation to pay the vendor.

Key Decision and Information Needs. Legally, an obligation to pay vendors arises at the time goods are received. For practical reasons, however, most companies record accounts payable only after receipt and approval of the vendor's invoice (as shown in Fig. 13.2). This timing difference is usually not important for daily decision making, but it does require making appropriate adjusting entries to prepare accurate financial statements at the end of a fiscal period.

The objective of accounts payable is to authorize payment only for goods and services that were ordered and actually received. Accomplishing this objective requires internally generated information from both the purchasing and receiving functions. The copy of the purchase order sent from purchasing confirms that the goods or services listed on the vendor invoice were actually ordered. The copy of the receiving report that came from inventory stores confirms the quantity and condition of the goods received and also documents that they were either placed into inventory or released to production.

Documents and Procedures. There are two basic ways to process vendor invoices, referred to as nonvoucher or voucher systems. In a **nonvoucher system,** each approved invoice is posted to individual vendor records in the accounts payable file and then is stored in an open-invoice file. When a check is written to pay for an invoice, the invoice is removed from the open-invoice file, marked "paid," and then stored in the paid-invoice file.

In a **voucher system,** a document called a disbursement voucher is also prepared. The **disbursement voucher** identifies the vendor, lists the outstanding invoices, and indicates the net amount to be paid after deducting any applicable discounts and allowances (see Fig. 13.9). Thus a disbursement voucher summarizes the information contained in a set of vendor invoices. It also specifies the general ledger accounts to be debited.

The use of disbursement vouchers offers three advantages. First, it reduces the number of checks that need to be written, because several invoices may be included on one voucher. Second, because the disbursement voucher is an internally generated document, it can be prenumbered to simplify tracking all payables. Third, because the voucher provides an explicit record that a vendor invoice has been approved for payment, it facilitates separating the time of

FIGURE 13.9
Sample AOE Disbursement Voucher (items in boldface are preprinted)

Alpha Omega Electronics **DISBURSEMENT VOUCHER**				**No. 16123**	
Date Entered: **07/22/2000**				**Debit Distribution**	
Prepared by: BC				**Account No.**	**Amount**
Vendor Number: 109				22-140 22-145 20-699 20-799	$868.33 629.01 30.56 98.45
Remit To: Avalon Electronics 1401 East Grand St. Louis, MO 63106–2211					
Vendor Invoice					
Number	**Date**	**Amount**	**Returns & Allowances**	**Purchase Discount**	**Net Remittance**
5386	07/15/2000	$984.50	$98.45	$17.72	$868.33
5389	07/20/2000	641.85	0.00	12.84	629.01
Voucher Totals:		$1626.35	$98.45	$30.56	$1497.34

invoice approval from the time of invoice payment. This makes it easier to schedule both activities to maximize efficiency.

Figure 13.10 depicts the accounts payable process used at AOE, which is typical of traditional voucher systems. When an invoice is received from a vendor, it is compared with the information contained in copies of the purchase order and receiving report to ensure accuracy and validity. For purchases of supplies or services, which do not usually involve purchase orders and receiving reports, the invoice is sent to the appropriate supervisor for approval. The vendor invoice itself is also checked for mathematical accuracy.

The accounts payable clerk then enters the approved invoice data into the open-invoice file. At this time the system also updates the open purchase order file to reflect the receipt of the vendor invoice. At the end of each day, the system uses the open-invoice file to update the balances due to each vendor in the vendor master file. At this time disbursement vouchers are printed and the accounts payable control account in the general ledger is updated.

The accounts payable clerk compares the disbursement vouchers with the supporting documents (vendor invoice, purchase order, and receiving report) and files them by due date in an unpaid-vouchers file. Prior to the due date, the disbursement voucher and supporting documents, which are often referred to as a **voucher package,** are sent to the cashier for payment.

Opportunities for Using Information Technology. The vouching process, which matches invoices to purchase orders and receiving reports, is a prime

FIGURE 13.10
Flowchart of the Accounts Payable System

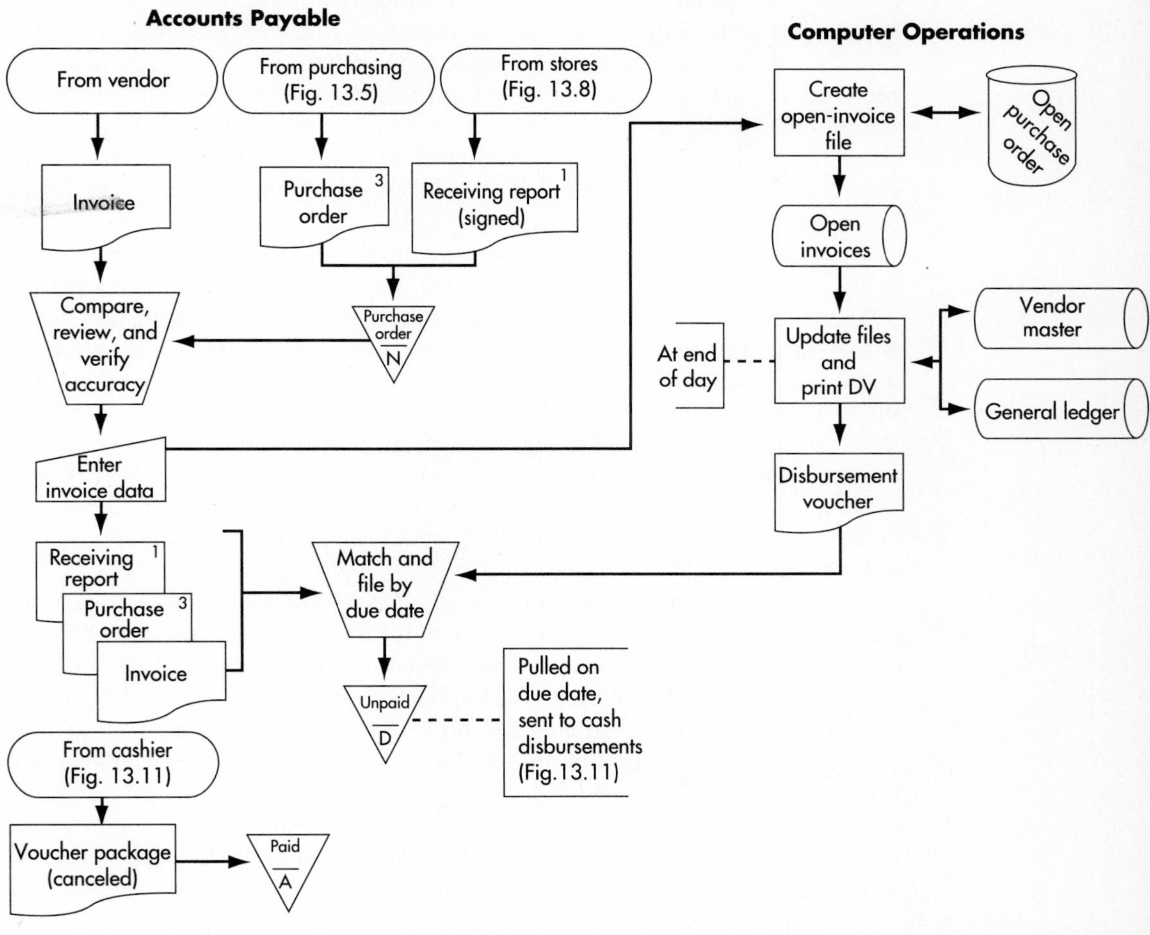

candidate for automation. Companies like AOE can improve the efficiency of their accounts payable system by requiring vendors to send invoices by EDI. EDI eliminates the need to enter invoice data manually, saving time and the associated clerical costs while also removing the chance for errors. Additional time and cost savings can be realized by having the system automatically match the EDI invoice to the computer files of purchase orders and receiving reports. Together, these steps would enable companies to approve vendor invoices more quickly, allowing them to take advantage of any vendor discounts offered for prompt payment.

Another option is to eliminate vendor invoices entirely. After all, for most recurring purchases companies usually know the prices of goods and services at the time they are ordered. Thus, as soon as receipt of the goods or services is verified, all the information required to pay the vendor is already in the AIS. One company that has done so is the industrial products division of the Lord Corporation in Erie, Pennsylvania. Lord wrote a vouchering program that automatically generates a disbursement voucher upon the receipt of goods. The program matches information about quantities received with price information on the purchase order. This system requires 100% accuracy from the receiving department in counting and inspecting goods received and relies on the purchasing department's ability to negotiate firm prices upon issuance of the purchase order. These requirements, however, have produced amazing results for Lord: Paper flow was reduced by 80% and the time and cost associated with processing invoices was cut in half.

For companies that still use paper invoices, image processing and optical character recognition (OCR) provide yet another method for improving the efficiency and effectiveness of the accounts payable function. Image processing works similarly to a fax machine. The paper document (in this case, the vendor invoice) is scanned into the system and converted into a binary representation, thereby creating an electronic image of the original document. The image is then run through an OCR program to capture individual data elements, such as item numbers, prices, and quantities, for further processing. Image processing can reduce costs and improve access to information. As Focus 13.3 shows, however, reaping the benefits of image processing requires both careful planning and good data base design.

Perhaps the biggest opportunity to improve the efficiency of accounts payable is in the area of noninventory purchases. As discussed earlier in the section on purchasing, the use of procurement cards eliminates the need to process hundreds of small invoices. Similarly, issuing corporate credit cards to employees who travel frequently also reduces the number of invoices that need to be processed. It also shifts the burden of reconciling invoices with supporting documents to the employees who incurred the expenses. In addition, electronic forms can be developed for submitting travel expenses. Such forms prevent delays due to math errors, eliminate the need for accounts payable staff to enter the travel expense data, and speed up the reimbursement process.

Pay for Goods

The final activity in the expenditure cycle is the payment of approved invoices (circle 5.0 in Fig. 13.2). This activity, referred to as the cash disbursements function, is performed by the cashier, who reports to the treasurer (see Fig. 12.1, p. 414). This segregates the custody function, performed by the cashier, from the authorization and recording functions, performed by the purchasing and accounts payable departments, respectively.

Key Decision: Taking Vendor Discounts. A key decision in the cash disbursement process is determining whether to take advantage of any vendor discounts offered for prompt payment. A short-term cash flow budget is useful for making this decision. This report lists projected inflows and outflows of cash for a period of time, up to a year in advance. The information in this budget

FOCUS 13.3 Image Processing: Creating a Paperless Office

CHAPARRAL STEEL Company, a subsidiary of Texas Industries, Inc., uses a document imaging system to reduce costs and improve access to information. The system has two input workstations, each equipped with scanners that can be set to different resolution levels, depending on the type of document being scanned. Large 19-inch color monitors are used so clerks can easily check image quality; if an image is not readable, the document needs to be rescanned at another time. All documents related to a transaction (purchase orders, receiving reports, and vendor invoices) are grouped together and scanned consecutively. Related reports produced by the accounting system, such as journal listings, are electronically merged into the scanned data base. The documents are indexed as they are scanned; the accounting reports are stored as text and can be searched just like any other word processing document. The images are stored on optical disks; the index, however, which is already 400 MB and growing, is stored on a hard drive because it provides faster access. To retrieve a document, the data base server searches the index, finds the access keys, and sends them to the jukebox server, which retrieves the document from the appropriate optical drive.

Chaparral learned by experience that proper design of the index scheme is as crucial to the success of a document imaging system as the design of the chart of accounts is to an effective accounting system. When the document imaging system was first implemented, documents were scanned and indexed by department, since that was the traditional way they had been processed. The result was chaos: Some documents that crossed departmental boundaries, such as purchase orders, were lost in the system. Linking related documents was almost impossible. After carefully working through the problems, the current approach of grouping documents by transaction, rather than department, was developed.

Two years after initial implementation, the system is saving the company an estimated $18,500 annually by reducing the time and costs associated with processing paper documents. In addition, productivity has greatly increased, because the accounting staff can now easily locate and examine copies of any document needed to resolve a question with either suppliers or customers.

Source: James E. Hunton, "Setting up a Paperless Office," *Journal of Accountancy* (November 1994): 77–85.

comes from a number of sources. Accounts receivable provides projections of future cash collections. The accounts payable and open purchase order files indicate the amount of current and pending commitments to vendors, while the human resources function provides information about payroll needs. If the cash flow budget indicates that sufficient cash is available, vendor discounts for prompt payment should be taken because they provide substantial savings. For example, a 1% discount for paying within 10 days, instead of 30, represents a savings of 18% annually.

Documents and Procedures. Figure 13.11 depicts the cash disbursements process used by AOE, which reflects a typical batch-oriented accounts payable system. The cashier receives the voucher package, which consists of the vendor invoice, purchase order, receiving report, and disbursements voucher, from the accounts payable department. The cashier reviews each voucher package, computes a batch total of the amounts to be paid, and enters the disbursement data.

The system then uses the disbursement voucher file to update the accounts payable, open-invoice, and the general ledger files. For each vendor, the totals of

FIGURE 13.11
Flowchart of the Cash Disbursements System

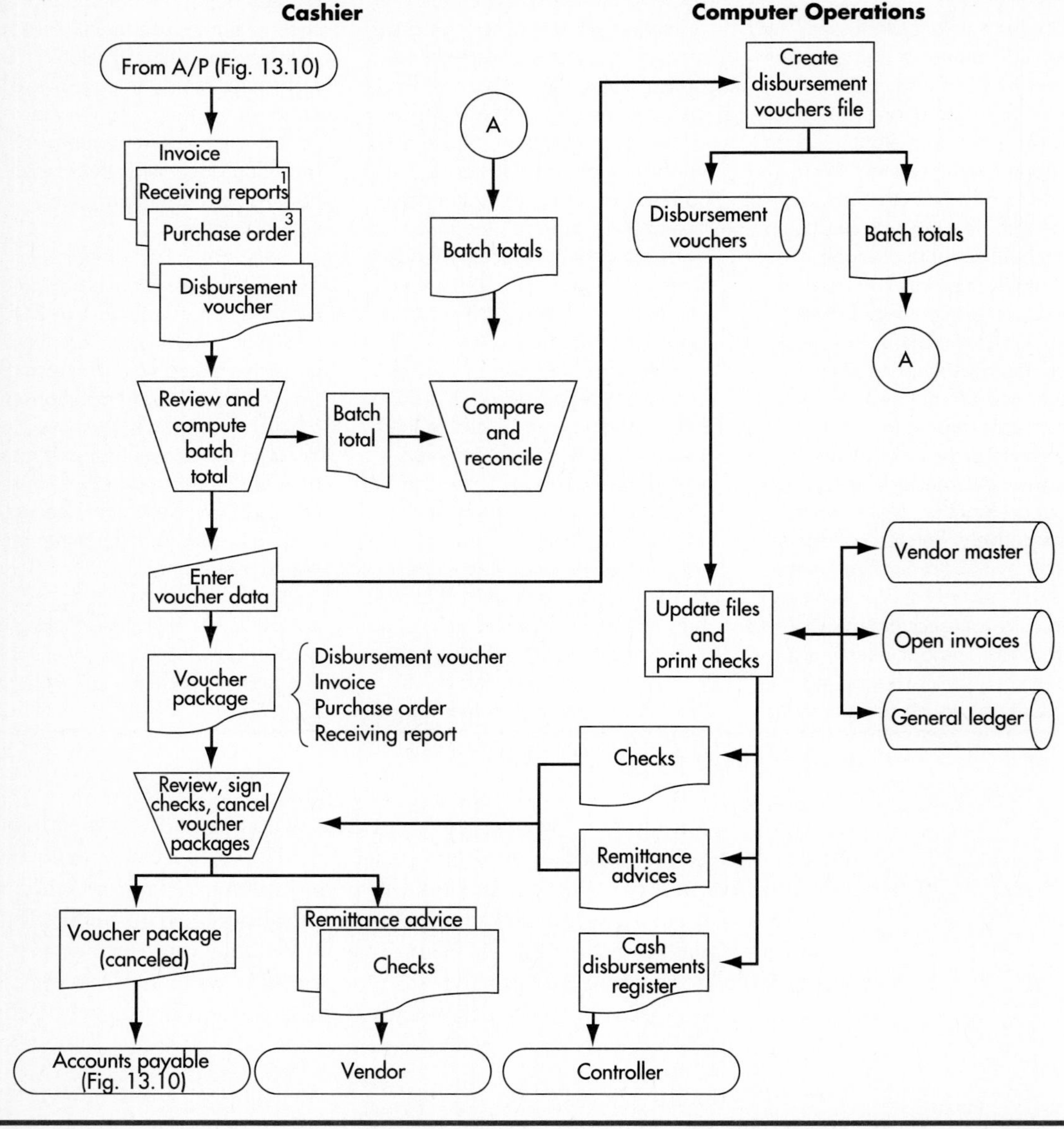

all vouchers are summed and that amount is subtracted from the balance field in that vendor's master file record. The invoices being paid are then deleted from the open-invoice file. A remittance advice is prepared for each vendor, listing each invoice being paid and the amounts of any discounts or allowances taken. The checks and remittance advices are then printed. After all disbursement transactions have been processed, the cash disbursements register is printed and sent to the controller. At the same time, the system generates a summary journal entry debiting accounts payable and crediting cash, and posts that entry to the general ledger.

The checks and remittance advices are then returned to the cashier for signing. After reviewing the checks against the voucher package, the cashier signs the checks. (Checks above a specified amount may also require the treasurer's signature.) The cashier then mails the checks and remittance advices to the vendors, and cancels supporting documents before returning them to accounts payable, where they are filed alphabetically by vendor.

Opportunities for Using Information Technology. IT can be used to improve the cash disbursement process by paying vendors through electronic funds transfer (EFT) instead of by check. With EFT, companies provide instructions to their bank about transferring funds out of their bank account and into the vendor's account. EFT can generate considerable cost savings because the time and expenses associated with preparing, signing, and mailing checks, as well as storing canceled checks, are eliminated. Additional savings can be generated by using FEDI, thereby combining the remittance and EFT data. Indeed, many large companies, such as Chevron, Mobil, and DuPont, have begun to use FEDI for remittances, which is a natural extension of using EDI for purchase orders and invoices.

The use of EFT or FEDI does create new exposures, however, which in turn require additional control procedures. The next section discusses the control procedures for addressing all the expenditure cycle threats, including those arising from the use of EFT or FEDI.

CONTROL OBJECTIVES, THREATS, AND PROCEDURES

A second function of a well-designed AIS is to provide adequate controls to ensure meeting the following objectives:

1. All transactions are properly authorized.
2. All recorded transactions are valid (actually occurred).
3. All valid, authorized transactions are recorded.
4. All transactions are recorded accurately.
5. Assets (cash, inventory, and data) are safeguarded from loss or theft.
6. Business activities are performed efficiently and effectively.

The documents and records described in the previous section play an important role in achieving these objectives. Simple, easy-to-complete documents with clear instructions facilitate the accurate and efficient recording of transaction data. The inclusion of appropriate application controls, such as validity checks and field (format) checks, further increases the accuracy of data entry when using electronic documents. Providing space on paper and electronic documents to record who completed and who reviewed the form provides evidence that the transaction was properly authorized. Finally, prenumbering the documents facilitates checking that all transactions have been recorded.

Table 13.1 lists the major threats and exposures in the expenditure cycle and the additional control procedures, besides adequate documents and records, that should be in place to mitigate them. Every company, regardless of its line of business, faces these threats. Therefore it is important to understand how the

TABLE 13.1 Threats, Exposures, and Control Procedures in the Expenditure Cycle

Threat	Exposure	Applicable Control Procedures
1. Stockouts	Production delays lost sales	Inventory control system Vendor performance analysis
2. Purchasing unnecessary goods or in too great a quantity	Increased inventory costs	Accurate perpetual inventory Approved purchase requisitions Restricted access to blank purchase requisitions Prenumbered purchase requisitions
3. Purchasing goods at inflated prices	Cost overruns	Price list consultation Solicitation of written bids Approved purchase orders Budgetary controls
4. Purchasing goods of inferior quality	Production delays Cost overruns	Use of approved vendor lists Review of purchase orders Vendor performance analyses
5. Purchasing from unauthorized vendors	Inferior quality of purchased goods Inflated prices Violation of laws or import quotas	Approval of purchase orders Restricted access to approved vendor list and approval of any changes made to that list Prenumbered purchase orders
6. Kickbacks	Inferior quality of purchased goods Inflated prices Violation of law	Prohibition of gifts from vendors Requirement that purchasing agents disclose financial interest in suppliers Vendor audits
7. Receiving unordered goods	Increased inventory costs	Approved purchase order for all deliveries
8. Errors in counting goods received	Payment for items not received Inaccurate inventory records	Blank quantity field on copy of the purchase order sent to receiving Incentives to count all deliveries
9. Theft of inventory	Loss of assets Inaccurate records	Physical access controls Documentation of all internal transfers of inventory Periodic physical counts of inventory and reconciliation with recorded amounts
10. Errors in vendor invoices	Inaccurate records Inaccurate payment	Recheck of invoice accuracy Comparison of invoice to purchase order and receiving report

continued

TABLE 13.1 Continued

Threat	Exposure	Applicable Control Procedures
11. Paying for goods not received	Loss of cash Overstated costs	Requirement of voucher package to support payment of invoices
12. Failure to take available purchase discounts	Increased expenses	Procedures to track invoice due dates Cash flow budgets
13. Paying the same invoice twice	Cash flow problems Erroneous records (overstated expenses)	Approval of invoices for payment only when accompanied by complete voucher package Payment of only original invoices that are accompanied by original copies of supporting documents Cancellation of voucher package once checks are signed
14. Errors in recording and posting purchases and payments	Incorrect financial statements Erroneous decisions	Data entry controls Periodic reconciliation of subsidiary accounts payable with general ledger
15. Misappropriation of cash by (a) Payments to fictitious vendors (b) Alteration of checks	Loss of assets	Restricted access to cash, blank checks, and check signing machine Prenumbered checks Imprinted amounts on checks Bank check protection services (Positive Pay) All purchases paid by check Impress petty cash fund Segregation of duties Independent bank account reconciliation
16. Theft associated with use of EFT		Strict access controls Frequent changing of user IDs and passwords Encryption of transmissions
17. Loss of data	Incorrect data for decision making Loss of confidential information	Backup and disaster recovery procedures Access controls (logical and physical)
18. Poor performance	Inefficient or ineffective processes	Preparation and review of performance reports

AIS can be designed to counter them. Our discussion will be organized around the stages of the expenditure cycle.

Request Goods

The primary objective of the purchase requisition process is to maintain an adequate supply of all needed materials. The first two threats listed in Table 13.1 pertain to this objective.

Threat 1: Stockouts. To guard against the threat of stockouts, companies need to establish an accurate inventory control system. The perpetual inventory method should be used to ensure that information about inventory stocks is always current. Companies should select vendors that are known to meet their delivery commitments. The AIS should prepare a vendor performance report that highlights deviations in product quality, prices, and delivery commitments. As explained earlier in the chapter, this report should be reviewed periodically and new vendors selected whenever a supplier's performance falls below acceptable levels.

Threat 2: Purchasing Unnecessary Goods or in Too Great a Quantity. Companies must also beware of purchasing items that are not currently needed. Accurate perpetual inventory records ensure the validity of purchase requisitions generated automatically by the inventory control system. Purchase requisitions initiated by individual employees should be reviewed and approved by appropriate supervisors. Access to blank purchase requisitions should be restricted. In addition, purchase requisitions should be prenumbered and accounted for periodically.

A related problem is multiple purchases of the same item by different subunits of the organization. As a result, the organization may be carrying a larger inventory than desired, and may also be failing to take advantage of volume discounts that might be available. This usually occurs because different subunits have different numbering systems for the parts they use. To overcome this, the AIS must be designed in a manner that facilitates integrating the data bases of various subunits. Then reports linking item descriptions to part numbers can be produced.

Order Goods

The primary objective of the purchasing activity is to secure the most reasonable prices for ordered items while satisfying quality standards. Threats 3–6 in Table 13.1 relate to this objective.

Threat 3: Purchasing Goods at Inflated Prices. Companies strive to secure the best prices for raw materials and inventory. Price lists for frequently purchased items should be stored in the computer and consulted when ordering. The prices of many low-cost items can be readily determined from catalogs. Competitive, written bids should be solicited for high-cost and specialized items. Purchase orders should be reviewed to assure that these policies have been followed.

Budgetary controls are also helpful in controlling expenses. Purchases should be charged to an account that is the responsibility of the person or department approving the requisition. Actual costs should be compared periodically with budget allowances. To facilitate control, these reports should highlight any significant deviations from budgeted amounts for further investigation (the principle of management by exception).

Threat 4: Purchasing Goods of Inferior Quality. In their quest to obtain the lowest possible prices, companies must beware of purchasing inferior-quality products. Substandard products can result in costly production delays; moreover, the costs of scrap and rework often result in higher total production costs than if better-quality materials, at higher prices, had been initially purchased.

Buyers, through experience, often learn which vendors provide the best-quality goods at competitive prices. Such informal knowledge should be incorporated into formal control procedures so that it is not lost when a particular employee leaves the company. Establishing lists of approved vendors known to provide goods of acceptable quality will achieve this goal. Purchase orders should be reviewed to ensure that only these approved vendors are being used. In addition, vendor performance data should be collected and periodically reviewed to maintain the accuracy of these approved vendor lists. Finally, purchasing managers should be held responsible for the total cost of purchases, which includes not just the purchase price, but also the quality-related costs of rework and scrap. Doing this requires the AIS to track the latter costs so that they can be allocated back to the purchasing department.

Threat 5: Purchasing from Unauthorized Vendors. Purchasing from unauthorized vendors can result in a number of problems. Items may be of inferior quality or may be overpriced. The purchase may even cause legal problems, such as violating import quotas. Consequently, all purchase orders should be reviewed to ensure that only approved vendors are used. It is especially important to restrict access to the approved vendor list, and to periodically review the list for any unauthorized changes. Purchase orders should also be prenumbered and accounted for periodically, to ensure that no unauthorized purchases have been made. If procurement cards are used for minor purchases, the company should work with the card issuer to limit the types of vendors at which the card will be accepted.

Threat 6: Kickbacks. **Kickbacks** are gifts from vendors to purchasing agents for the purpose of influencing their choice of suppliers. Kickbacks may result in the purchase of goods at inflated prices or of inferior quality. Even if neither of these problems occurs, kickbacks impair the objectivity of buyers. Moreover, employees should not profit from performing their regular business duties.

To prevent kickbacks, companies should prohibit purchasing agents from accepting any gifts from potential or existing suppliers. (Trinkets that are clearly of inconsequential value, such as pens or calendars, may be allowed.) In addition, purchasing agents should also be required to sign annual conflict of interest statements, disclosing any financial interests they may have in current or potential suppliers. Admittedly, kickbacks are difficult to prevent. Consequently, detective controls are also needed. Focus 13.4 discusses one particularly effective detection control: the vendor audit.

EDI-Related Threats. The use of EDI for purchase orders requires additional control procedures. Access to the EDI system should be controlled and limited to authorized personnel through the use of passwords, user IDs, access control matrices, and physical access controls. Procedures to verify and authenticate EDI transactions are also needed. Most EDI systems are programmed to send an acknowledgment for each transaction, which provides a rudimentary accuracy check. Further protection against transmission problems, which can result in the loss of orders, is provided by time-stamping and numbering all

FOCUS 13.4 Vendor Audits: A Means to Control Purchasing

RAY MIZE, a consulting auditor in Kenner, Louisiana, believes that vendor audits may be one of the most effective tools for assessing the effectiveness of expenditure cycle controls. A vendor audit entails visiting a supplier's office to check its records. It is designed to answer a number of questions. Who determines the business requirements for a good or service? How is the good or service consumed, and how is this documented? What is the procurement process, and how is the company assured that the best-quality goods or services were obtained at the best price? Were any gifts or favors provided to purchasing agents?

After doing a number of vendor audits, Mize developed a list of red flags that identify vendors likely to represent potential problems:

1. A large percentage of the vendor's gross sales was to one company.
2. The vendor's pricing methods differ from standard industry practice.
3. The vendor does not own the equipment it rents to customers, but is itself renting that equipment from a third party.
4. Entertainment expenses are high as a percentage of the vendor's gross sales.
5. Third-party invoices submitted by the vendor are altered or fictitious.
6. The vendor's addresses on their invoices are fictitious.

Vendor audits can yield substantial returns. Mize reports that the first six vendor audits he performed helped his former employer recover more than $250,000 for such failures as duplicate billings. Audits also uncovered a major violation of the company's conflict of interest policy. Interestingly, Mize notes that virtually all of the suppliers he has audited support the idea of vendor audits because the process gives them a "good excuse" for not offering purchasing agents gifts or entertainment. This reduces the vendor's costs and results in better procurement terms for the buyer.

Source: B. Ray Mize, Jr., "Vendor Audits," *The CPA Journal* (February 1994): 18–22.

EDI transactions. Companies should maintain and periodically review a log of all EDI transactions to ensure that all have been processed and that established policies are being followed. Encryption can be used to ensure the privacy of EDI transactions, which is especially important for competitive bids. Digital signatures should also be used to ensure the authenticity of transactions.

Numerous policy-related threats also arise with the use of EDI, each of which must be covered in the trading agreement. Additional complexity arises when vendors are linked to the purchasing company's POS system in order to automatically manage inventory (as was described in Focus 12.2). Examples of these types of issues include the following:

- At what point in the process can the order be canceled?
- Who is responsible for return freight if contract terms are not followed?
- Which party is responsible for errors in bar codes and labels?
- What happens if errors in the purchasing company's POS system cause errors in the amount of goods provided by vendors?
- Can vendors ship more inventory than ordered if doing so reduces total freight costs by having a full, rather than partial, truck load?

Purchase of Services. Thus far, the discussion has centered on the purchase of inventory items. Different procedures are needed to control the purchase of services, such as painting or maintenance work. The major challenge in this area is establishing that the services were actually performed. This is not always easy to do. For example, visual inspection can indicate whether a room has been painted. It does not, however, reveal whether the walls were appropriately primed, unless the inspection was done during the painting process, which may not always be feasible.

One way to control the purchase of services is to hold the appropriate supervisor responsible for all such costs incurred by that department. The supervisor is required to acknowledge receipt of the services, and the related expenses are then charged to accounts for which he or she is responsible. Actual versus budgeted expenses should then be routinely compared, and any discrepancies investigated.

Receive and Store Goods

The primary objectives of the receiving and storage function are to verify the receipt of ordered inventory and to safeguard it against loss or theft. Threats 7–9 in Table 13.1 apply to the receipt and storage of inventory.

Threat 7: Receiving Unordered Goods. Accepting delivery of unordered goods results in costs associated with storing, and later returning, those items. The best control procedure to mitigate this threat is to instruct the receiving department to accept only deliveries for which it has an approved copy of the purchase order. Effective control requires that a copy of every purchase order be sent to the receiving department upon issuance and that these copies be filed in a manner that facilitates their subsequent retrieval.

Threat 8: Errors in Counting Goods Received. Accurate counting of goods received is crucial for maintaining accurate perpetual inventory records. It also ensures that the company pays only for goods actually received. This threat is best dealt with by the procedures discussed earlier for encouraging receiving clerks to count all deliveries accurately: blacking out the quantities ordered on their copy of the purchase order and requiring them to sign each receiving report. Some companies also offer bonuses to receiving clerks for catching discrepancies between the packing slip and actual quantity received before the delivery person leaves. Additional control is provided by requiring inventory stores, or the appropriate user department, to count the items transferred from receiving and then hold that department responsible for any subsequent shortages.

Threat 9: Theft of Inventory. Several control procedures can be used to safeguard inventory against loss. First, inventories should be stored in secure locations to which access is restricted. Second, all transfers of inventory within the company should be documented. For example, both the receiving department and the inventory stores department should acknowledge the transfer of goods from the receiving dock into inventory. Similarly, the release of inventory into production should be acknowledged by both the inventory stores and the production departments. This documentation provides the necessary information for establishing responsibility for any shortages, thereby encouraging employees to take special care to record all inventory movements accurately.

Finally, it is important to take periodic physical counts of inventory on hand and to reconcile those counts with the inventory records.

One annual physical inventory count will generally not be sufficient to maintain accurate inventory records, especially for MRP and JIT systems. Instead, an ABC cost analysis should be used to classify items according to their importance: The most critical items (A items) should be counted most frequently, and the least critical items (C items) can be counted less often. Note that use of this approach might have alerted management at AOE's Wichita plant about shortages of key components early enough to avoid production delays.

Approve Vendor Invoices

The objective of this activity is to ensure that the company pays only for goods that were ordered and received. Threats 10–14 in Table 13.1 apply to this objective.

Threat 10: Errors in Vendor Invoices. Vendor invoices may contain various errors, such as discrepancies between quoted and actual prices charged or miscalculations of the total amount due. Consequently, the mathematical accuracy of vendor invoices must be verified and the prices and quantities listed thereon compared with those indicated on the purchase order and receiving report. For procurement card purchases, users should be required to keep receipts and verify the accuracy of the monthly statement.

Freight expenses require special consideration, because their complexity creates numerous opportunities for mistakes to occur. The best way to reduce freight-related threats is to provide the purchasing and accounts payable staffs with adequate training on transportation practices and terminology. For example, if the purchase contract says "full freight allowed," that means that the vendor is responsible for the freight costs. When the purchasing organization is responsible for freight expenses, costs can be reduced by using a designated carrier for all incoming shipments. The discounts will only be realized, however, if vendors comply with requests to use that carrier. Therefore, an important detective control is to capture data on all incoming carriers so that reports can be prepared identifying vendors who fail to comply with shipping instructions.

Threat 11: Paying for Goods Not Received. The best control to prevent paying for goods not received is to compare the quantities indicated on the vendor invoice with the quantities indicated on the copy of the receiving report that was signed by the person accepting the transfer of those goods from the receiving department.

Threat 12: Failure to Take Available Purchase Discounts. Failure to take advantage of purchase discounts can cost a company money. Proper filing can significantly reduce the risk of this threat. Approved invoices should be filed by due date, and the system should be designed to track invoice due dates and to print a periodic list of all outstanding invoices. A cash flow budget, indicating expected cash inflows as well as outstanding commitments, can also help companies plan to take advantage of any available purchase discounts.

Threat 13: Paying the Same Invoice Twice. The same invoice can be submitted for payment more than once for a variety of reasons. It may be a duplicate invoice that was sent after the company's check was already in the mail, or it may have become separated from the other documents in the voucher package. Although paying invoices a second time is usually detected by the vendor and results in a credit to the company's account, it can affect a company's cash flow needs. In addition, the financial records will be incorrect, at least until the duplicate payment is detected.

Three control procedures can mitigate this threat. First, invoices should be approved for payment only when accompanied by a complete voucher package (purchase order and receiving report). Second, only the original copy of an invoice should be paid. Most duplicate invoices sent by vendors clearly indicate that they are not originals; therefore, payment should never be authorized for a photocopy of an invoice. Third, when the check to pay for an invoice is signed, the invoice and the voucher package should be canceled (marked "paid") in a manner that would prevent their resubmission. If paper documents are not used, the computer records of accounts payable should be marked with a code indicating that the invoice has been paid.

Automating and streamlining accounts payable is not a panacea, however. Automated systems do eliminate most clerical errors associated with processing invoices, and invoiceless accounts payable systems cut costs and improve efficiency. Yet computers can only catch the types of errors that they have been programmed to identify, whereas there are an infinite number of errors that can exist in vendor invoices. In addition, unscrupulous vendors continually devise new ways to fool automated accounts payable systems. Therefore companies must use detective controls to minimize the risk of overpayments to vendors. Such investigative work can be done either by internal auditors or by hiring a consulting firm that specializes in helping companies to detect and recover overpayments to suppliers.

Finally, in invoiceless accounts payables systems, it is important to control access to the vendor master file and monitor all changes made to it. The reason is that the vendor master file now contains information about the prices of the various items being purchased. Upon entry of data about the quantity of goods received, those prices are used by the system to establish the amount to be paid the vendor. Thus unauthorized changes to those prices can result in overpayments to vendors.

Threat 14: Errors in Recording and Posting Purchases and Payments. Errors in recording and posting payments to vendors will result in errors in financial and performance reports, which in turn can contribute to poor decision making. Appropriate data entry and processing controls are necessary to prevent these types of problems. One such control involves comparing the difference in vendor account balances before and after processing checks with the total value of invoices processed. The total of all vendor account balances (or unpaid vouchers, whichever exists) should also be reconciled periodically with the amount of the accounts payable control account in the general ledger.

Pay for Goods

The primary objective of this activity is to safeguard cash by ensuring that all disbursements are legitimate. Threats 15 and 16 in Table 13.1 apply to the cash disbursement function.

Threat 15: Misappropriation of Cash. Cash is the easiest asset to steal; consequently, access to cash and blank checks should be restricted. Checks should be sequentially numbered and periodically accounted for by the cashier. If a check signing machine is used, access to it should be restricted as well.

Fraudulent disbursement, particularly the issuance of checks to fictitious vendors, is one of the most common types of fraud. Proper segregation of duties can significantly reduce the risk of this threat. The authorization of payment, including the assembling of a voucher package, should be performed by the accounts payable function; checks should be signed, however, only by the treasurer or cashier. Checks in excess of a certain amount, such as $5,000–$10,000, should require two signatures, thereby providing yet another independent review of the expenditure. Finally, access to the approved vendor list should be restricted, and any changes to that list should be carefully reviewed and approved. In addition, internal auditors should periodically review the vendor master file to ensure that there are no duplicate entries for vendors. Many companies that have done this have discovered that, over time, there may be three or four entries for the same vendor, each entered by a different clerk with a slightly different spelling. For example, the same vendor may be listed twice, once as AZBest Ltd and another time as AZBest Limited.

Once signed, the checks should be mailed by the cashier and not returned to accounts payable, to ensure that they are indeed sent to the intended payee. The cashier should also cancel all documents in the voucher package to prevent their being resubmitted to support another disbursement. Finally, all bank accounts should be reconciled by someone who did not participate in processing either cash collections or disbursements. This control provides an independent check on accuracy and prevents someone from misappropriating cash and then concealing the theft by adjusting the bank statement.

Check alteration and forgery are also major problems. Check-protection machines can reduce the risk of this threat by imprinting the amount in distinctive colors, typically using a combination of red and blue ink. Using special inks that change colors if altered, and printing checks on special papers that contain watermarks, can further reduce the probability of alteration. Many banks also provide special services to help protect companies against fraudulent checks. One such service, called Positive Pay, involves sending a daily list of all legitimate checks to the bank; the bank will then clear only checks appearing on that list. Finally, bank reconciliations are an important detective control for identifying check fraud. Moreover, if done in a timely manner they facilitate recovery from banks; indeed, many banks will only cover bad check losses if a company notifies them promptly of any such checks it discovers.

Whenever possible, expenditures should be made by check. Nevertheless, it is often more convenient to pay for minor purchases, such as coffee or pencils, in cash. A petty cash fund, managed by an employee who has no other cash-handling or accounting responsibilities, should be established to handle such expenditures. The petty cash fund should be set up as an imprest fund. An **imprest fund** has two characteristics: (1) it is set at a fixed amount, such as $100, and (2) it requires vouchers for every disbursement. At all times the sum of cash plus vouchers should equal the preset fund balance. When the fund balance gets low, the vouchers are presented to accounts payable for replenishment. After accounts payable authorizes this transaction, the cashier then writes a check to restore the petty cash fund to its designated level. As with the supporting documents used for regular purchases, the vouchers used to support replenishment of the petty cash fund should be canceled at the time the fund is restored to its preset level.

The operation of an imprest petty cash fund technically violates the principle of segregation of duties, because the same person has custody of the cash, authorizes disbursements from the fund, and maintains a record of the fund balance. The threat of misappropriation is more than offset, however, by the convenience of not having to process small miscellaneous purchases through the normal expenditure cycle. Moreover, the risk of misappropriation can be mitigated by having the internal auditor make periodic unannounced counts of the fund balance and vouchers and by holding the person in charge of the petty cash fund responsible for any shortages discovered during those counts.

Threat 16: Theft Associated with the Use of EFT. The use of EFT (either by itself or as part of FEDI) requires additional control procedures. Because EFT involves the movement of funds, strict access controls are needed. Passwords and user IDs should be used and changed regularly. The user as well as the location of the originating terminal should be recorded so that the adequacy of access controls can be monitored. All EFT transmissions should be encrypted, to prevent alteration. In addition, all EFT transactions should be time-stamped and numbered, to facilitate subsequent reconciliation. A control group should also be established and given responsibility for monitoring EFT transactions for validity and accuracy and maintaining the adequacy of the controls outlined here. Special programs, called embedded audit modules, can also be designed into the system to monitor all transactions and identify any that possess specific characteristics. A report of those flagged transactions can then be given to management for review and, if necessary, more detailed investigation.

General Control Issues

Threats 17 and 18 in Table 13.1 are general threats that affect all phases of the expenditure cycle.

Threat 17: Loss of Data. Data about pending cash disbursement obligations and open orders must be safeguarded from loss or corruption. Both external and internal file labels should be used to reduce the possibility of accidentally erasing important files and to ensure that the most recent version of the master file is being updated. In addition, the purchases, receipts, master accounts payable, and cash disbursements files should be backed up regularly.

Two backup copies should be made: one to be stored on-site and the other off-site. These backups should include not only the current and previous versions of the master file, but also the most recent transaction file.

Access controls are also important. A system of passwords and user IDs should be used to limit employee access to various files. For example, only the cashier should be able to alter the field indicating whether an invoice has been paid. Access controls should also exist for individual terminals. For example, the system should be programmed to accept approval of invoices only from terminals located in the accounts payable department. When image processing is used, access controls are extremely important to prevent alteration of the source document.

Threat 18: Poor Performance. In addition to ensuring accuracy and safeguarding assets, another objective of internal controls in the expenditure cycle is to encourage efficient and effective performance of business activities. The preparation and review of performance reports is effective in achieving this objective. Several have already been discussed in this chapter, such as reports on vendor performance and lists of outstanding invoices. Reports that help manage inventory are especially valuable. For example, organizations should carefully monitor the percentage of requisitions that are filled from inventory on hand. For critical items this should be close to 100%, but for most items such a high fill rate is undesirable because it requires carrying too much inventory.

The number of additional performance reports that can be developed is limited only by the ingenuity of the controller and by management's decisions about what factors are important to monitor and control. The ease with which such reports can be produced, however, is affected by the methods used to store and maintain expenditure cycle data.

EXPENDITURE CYCLE INFORMATION NEEDS AND DATA MODEL

A third function of the AIS is to provide information useful for decision making. Usefulness in the expenditure cycle means that the AIS must provide the operational information needed to perform the following functions:

- Determine when and how much additional inventory to order.
- Select the appropriate vendors from whom to order.
- Verify the accuracy of vendor invoices.
- Decide whether purchase discounts should be taken.
- Monitor cash flow needs to pay outstanding obligations.

In addition, the AIS needs to provide the following kinds of strategic and performance evaluation information:

- Efficiency and effectiveness of the purchasing department
- Analyses of vendor performance such as on-time delivery, quality, and so on
- Time taken to move goods from the receiving dock into production
- Percentage of purchase discounts taken

Notice that these decisions require both financial and operating data. For example, vendor selection should take into consideration not only price, but also information about vendor performance in meeting delivery dates and quality of goods. Traditionally, the AIS has provided the financial information needed to make expenditure cycle decisions, and other information systems have generated the operating data about expenditure cycle activities. One problem with using separate information systems, however, is that the two sets of resulting data may be inconsistent. For example, many companies are not aware that different subunits may be purchasing the same items, because each unit uses a slightly different name and part number for those items. Consequently the organization as a whole may be failing to take advantage of potential discounts for volume purchases. Thus the existence of multiple, overlapping systems increases costs and reduces effectiveness. Fortunately, the advent of relational DBMSs makes the need to maintain separate information systems for financial and operating data obsolete.

Many expenditure cycle decisions also require externally generated information. For example, data about vendor financial characteristics may be useful in selecting vendors that are stable and likely to be able to meet future commitments. A well-designed data model facilitates the integration of such externally generated information with internally generated financial and operating data about expenditure cycle activities.

Expenditure Cycle Data Model

Figure 13.12 shows a simplified example of an REA data model for the expenditure cycle of a manufacturing company such as AOE. It includes information about the following activities:

- The two major resources (cash and inventory) used in the expenditure cycle and the location in which they are stored (bank and warehouse).
- The four major business events in the expenditure cycle (request goods, order goods, receive goods, and pay for goods).
- The primary external agent (vendors) as well as the various internal agents involved in expenditure cycle activities.

If the data model depicted in Fig. 13.12 were implemented in a relational data base, there would be a table for each entity (box) and for each many-to-many relationship. Figure 13.12 lists many of the attributes that would be found in those relational tables. Most of these attributes and their placement in specific tables should be self-explanatory. The placement of standard and actual costs, however, deserves some explanation.

Standard cost is stored as an attribute of the inventory table because it is the same for all units of a given inventory item. In contrast, the actual cost of inventory is stored in the order–inventory table. This reflects the fact that purchase prices can vary over time. By storing the cost of each order along with the quantity purchased, the system can easily calculate the actual cost of ending inventory and the cost of goods sold according to any accepted inventory valuation method (LIFO, FIFO, weighted-average, or specific identification). If, on the

FIGURE 13.12
Partial REA Diagram for the Expenditure Cycle

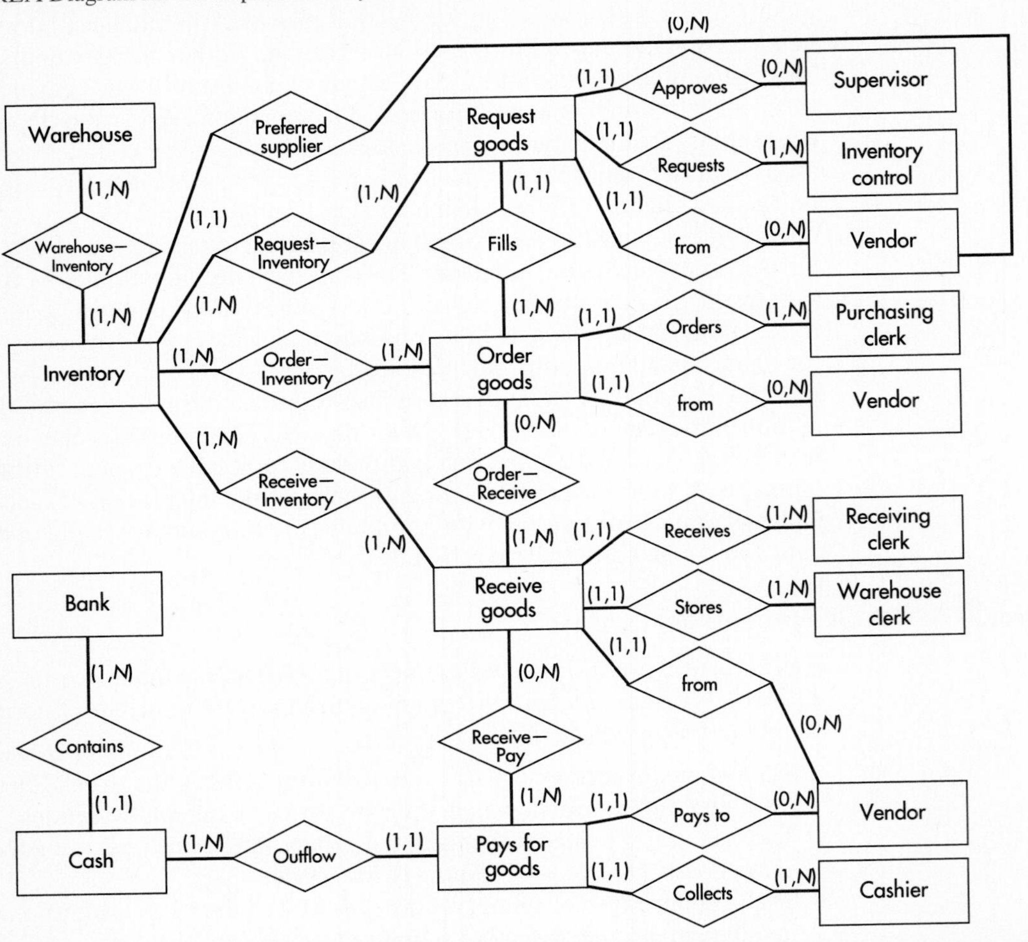

other hand, actual cost were stored as an attribute of the inventory table, it would necessitate the use of the weighted-average method because all units of a given inventory item would be assigned the same cost. In addition, cost data would be available only in this format; it would be impossible to compute alternative values for inventory because the detailed data about the cost associated with each purchase would not be stored in the data base.

Reading the REA Diagram

Figure 13.12 provides a great deal of information about AOE's business policies. The figure models the relationship between the request goods and order goods events as being many-to-one. This reflects the fact that AOE sometimes issues

FIGURE 13.12
Continued

Table Name	Attributes (**primary key**, *foreign keys*, other attributes)
Warehouse	**Warehouse number**, address, number of employees, *manager number*,...
Inventory	**Item number**, description, standard cost, reorder point, quantity on hand, quantity available, *preferred vendor*,...
Bank	**Bank ID**, name, address,...
Cash	**Account number**, balance, *bank ID*,...
Request goods	**Requisition number**, date, date needed, *supervisor, inventory control clerk, vendor number*,...
Order goods	**Purchase order number**, date, total amount, *vendor number, clerk number*,...
Receive goods	**Receiving report number**, date, condition of goods, *receiving clerk number, warehouse number*,...
Pay for goods	**Check number**, date, amount, *cashier number, vendor number, account number*,...
Cashier*	**Employee number**, name, date hired, date of birth, number of dependents, *supervisor*,...
Vendor	**Vendor number**, name, address, performance rating, accounts payable balance,...
Warehouse—Inventory	**Warehouse number**, **item number**, quantity
Request—Inventory	**Requisition number**, **item number**, quantity
Order—Inventory	**Purchase order number**, **item number**, quantity, unit cost,....
Receive—Inventory	**Receiving report number**, **item number**, quantity
Order—Receive	**Purchase order**, **receiving report number**
Receive—Pay	**Receiving report number**, **check number**, amount applied to invoice

*Similar tables would exist for all other employees, but are omitted to save space.

purchase orders for individual purchase requests, but at other times it takes advantage of volume discounts by issuing one purchase order for a set of requests.

Figure 13.12 depicts a many-to-many relationship between the order goods and receive goods events. This reflects the fact that vendors sometimes make several separate deliveries to fill one purchase order, at other times fill several purchase orders with one delivery, and sometimes make a delivery to fill a single purchase order in full.

The relationship between the receive goods and cash disbursements events is depicted as being many-to-many. This reflects the fact that although vendors bill AOE for each delivery, AOE sometimes pays vendor invoices individually, at other times it writes one check to pay for several invoices, and occasionally it makes installment payments for purchases. Finally, there is always some amount of time lag between events, as depicted in Fig. 13.12 by the minimum cardinality of 0 associated with the later of the two events linked in a relationship.

Events must always involve internal or external agents; consequently, Fig. 13.12 shows that both the minimum and maximum cardinalities associated with the various agent entities is 1. Each agent, however, can potentially be involved in zero or many instances of an event; this is depicted by the (0, *N*) cardinality attached to the event entity in each event–agent relationship.

AOE manufactures and sells mass-produced items from a limited set of component parts; consequently, each component part (represented by a row in the inventory table) can be linked to many different request, order, and receipt events. At the same time, each of those events can involve many different component parts. Thus the relationships between inventory and those three events are all depicted in Fig. 13.12 as being many-to-many.

AOE has several warehouses; consequently, a given inventory item can be stored at more than one warehouse, and each warehouse can store many different inventory items. This is reflected in the many-to-many relationship between the inventory and warehouse entities. Note, however, that the minimum cardinality associated with each entity in that relationship is 1; this reflects the fact that a given inventory item must be stored somewhere, and each warehouse must contain at least one kind of component part.

AOE uses one bank account to pay for its purchases; this is reflected in the one-to-many relationship in Fig. 13.12 between the cash resource entity and the pay for goods event. AOE does, however, have several different bank accounts and sometimes has more than one account at a given bank. This is reflected in Fig. 13.12 by the many-to-one relationship between the cash and bank entities. Notice, moreover, that the minimum cardinality for both entities is 1; AOE maintains information only about banks at which it has accounts, and each account must be associated with one and only one particular bank. Figure 13.12 also includes a relationship between the inventory resource entity and the vendor agent entities. This relationship represents the fact that AOE has developed a list of preferred vendors for each component part that it purchases.

Why is there no entity for approving vendor invoices? The reason is that this is just an information processing activity. All the information included on the vendor invoice is already in the system: purchase prices were set when the order was placed, and the quantity received was identified when the goods were delivered. Thus no additional data is provided when the vendor invoice is received (indeed, as we discussed earlier, many companies are moving to invoiceless accounts payable systems).

Also notice that data about the amount owed to specific vendors is stored as an attribute in the vendor table. This is done only to improve query efficiency, however. Accounts payable represents those purchases that have not yet been paid for. Therefore, as explained in Chapter 6, accounts payable could be calculated by computing the difference between total purchases and the cash disbursements linked to those purchase events.

Benefits of the Data Model

Notice that the data model in Fig. 13.12 effectively integrates both traditional accounting transaction data (for example, the date and amount of each purchase) with other operational data (for example, information about where that item is stored and vendor performance measures, such as the delivery date). It would also be easy to link this internally generated data with various types of external information. For example, information about the financial position and credit rating of vendors could be downloaded from a commercial data base, appended as additional columns in the vendor table, and used in the vendor selection process. Most importantly, implementing the data model shown in Fig. 13.12 in a relational DBMS would enable LeRoy Williams and other decision makers at AOE to directly access and manipulate the information they need by using powerful but easy-to-use query languages.

Internal Control Considerations

Our discussion of the threats listed in Table 13.1 stressed the importance of properly segregating incompatible duties. REA diagrams are useful for this task because they indicate which internal agents participate in each event. In addition, if the REA model is implemented in a DBMS, the computer can be programmed to enforce segregation of duties by preventing the same person from performing incompatible functions. Conversely, the system can be programmed to list all cases of an employee performing multiple roles, so that the auditors can investigate whether adequate compensating controls exist.

The use of a DBMS also increases the importance of having effective access controls. Most relational DBMSs provide a means to control access by letting users see only a portion of the data base (called a *view*). For example, purchasing agents should see only the portion of Fig. 13.12 relevant to their job duties, such as the tables for inventory, vendors, and purchases. Moreover, purchasing agents should be allowed to perform only a restricted set of operations on those tables. For example, they should have read-only rights to the vendor table, to prevent them from making any unauthorized changes to the list of approved vendors.

Data accuracy is vital when using a DBMS. Fortunately, the relational data model provides some built-in controls to ensure data accuracy and consistency. One of the more important of these controls is support for foreign keys and referential integrity. For example, when a new row is added to cash disbursements table, the system should automatically verify that the vendor number (which appears as a foreign key in that table) actually exists as a primary key in the vendor table. This control ensures that there really is such a vendor. Finally, the use of a DBMS makes adequate backup and disaster recovery procedures crucial.

SUMMARY AND CASE CONCLUSION

Activities performed in the expenditure cycle include the following:

- Requesting the purchase of needed goods
- Ordering goods from vendors
- Receiving goods from vendors
- Approving vendor invoices for payment
- Disbursing cash to pay for purchases

The efficiency and effectiveness of these activities can significantly affect a company's overall performance. For example, deficiencies in requesting and ordering necessary inventory and supplies can create production bottlenecks and result in lost sales due to stockouts of popular items. Problems in the procedures related to receiving and storing inventory can result in a company's paying for items it never received, accepting delivery and incurring storage and return costs for unordered items, and experiencing theft of inventory. Problems in approving vendor invoices for payment can result in overpaying vendors or failing to take available discounts for prompt payment. Weaknesses in the cash disbursement process can result in the misappropriation of cash.

IT can help improve the efficiency and effectiveness with which expenditure cycle activities are performed. In particular, the use of EDI, bar coding, and EFT can significantly reduce the time and costs associated with ordering, receiving, and paying for goods. In addition, the use of a well-designed data model can allow for the integration of internally generated financial and operating data with externally generated information so that all three types of data can be considered when making important operating and strategic decisions. Finally, proper control procedures, especially segregation of duties, are needed to mitigate the various threats, such as errors in performing expenditure cycle activities and the theft of inventory or cash.

Figure 13.13 depicts the new system recommended by Elizabeth Venko to help solve AOE's expenditure cycle problems. This proposed system is typical of the systems used by many large manufacturing companies such as Ford, IBM, and McDonnell Douglas.

The proposed system puts on-line terminals in each of AOE's departments. A JIT inventory control system will be implemented, to minimize inventory carrying costs. EDI will be used to send purchase orders to vendors, thereby improving the efficiency of the ordering process and also reducing the lead time between ordering and receiving goods. On-line data entry by receiving dock workers and by the warehouse clerk will improve the accuracy and timeliness of AOE's perpetual inventory records. Vendors will be asked to bar-code their shipments so that the use of handheld bar-code scanners can further improve the speed and accuracy of recording inventory receipts and movements. Vendors will also be asked to send invoices via EDI, which should improve the efficiency and accuracy of processing invoices and also reduce the costs associated with handling and storing paper invoices. The system will automatically match the EDI invoices with the

FIGURE 13.13
Flowchart of AOE's Proposed New Expenditure Cycle

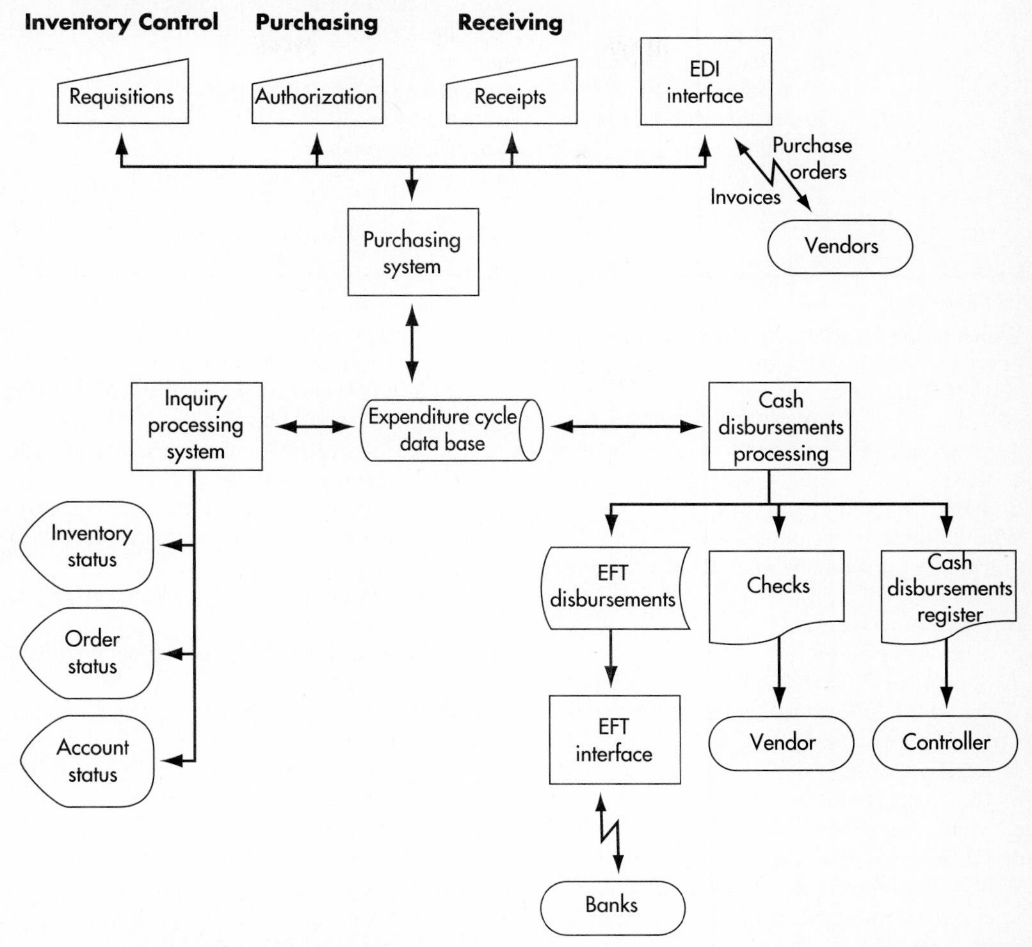

related purchase orders and receiving reports. It will also track invoice due dates so that AOE will not miss out on any available discounts for prompt payment. Finally, EFT will be used as much as possible to streamline the cash disbursements process and reduce the costs associated with processing payments by check.

The proposed system will also use a relational data base built on a data model similar to that shown in Fig. 13.12. Query languages will make it easy for LeRoy Williams, Elizabeth Venko, and other AOE managers to retrieve the information needed to make purchasing and payment decisions. Appropriate access controls will be used to limit the tables that individual employees can see and the operations that they can perform on those tables.

KEY TERMS

expenditure cycle
economic order quantity (EOQ)
reorder point
materials requirements planning (MRP)
just-in-time (JIT) inventory system
purchase requisition
purchase order
blanket purchase order
receiving report
debit memo
nonvoucher system
voucher system
disbursement voucher
voucher package
kickbacks
imprest fund

CHAPTER QUIZ

1. Which of the following inventory control methods is least likely to require maintenance of perpetual inventory records?
a. JIT
b. Economic order quantity
c. MRP
d. ABC

2. Who should prepare purchase orders?
a. Factory personnel who notice the need for items
b. Purchasing agents
c. Accounts payable
d. Supervisors of any department needing items

3. Which of the following documents is *not* always a part of the voucher package?
a. Purchase order
b. Receiving report
c. Vendor invoice
d. Disbursement voucher

4. Which document is used to establish a contract for the purchase of goods or services from a vendor?
a. Vendor invoice
b. Purchase requisition
c. Purchase order
d. Disbursement voucher

5. Which method would provide the greatest efficiency improvements for cash disbursements?
a. Bar coding
b. EDI
c. EFT
d. Vendor certification

6. Which of the following is *not* one of the events that would be included in the REA data model of the expenditure cycle?
a. Purchasing
b. Cash receipts
c. Receiving
d. Cash disbursements

7. The best control procedure to prevent paying the same invoice twice is
a. segregation of check preparation and check signing functions.
b. preparing checks only for invoices that have been matched to receiving reports and purchase orders.
c. requiring two signatures on all checks above a certain limit.
d. canceling all supporting documents when the check is signed.

8. For good internal control, who should sign checks?
a. Cashier
b. Accounts payable
c. Purchasing
d. Controller

9. Which of the following procedures is least effective in preventing the purchasing agent from receiving kickbacks?
a. Maintaining a list of approved vendors and requiring all purchases to be made from vendors on that list
b. Requiring purchasing agents to disclose any financial investments in potential suppliers
c. Requiring approval of all purchase orders
d. Prenumbering and periodically accounting for all purchase orders

10. Which document is used to record adjustments to accounts payable based on the return of unacceptable inventory to the vendor?
a. Receiving report
b. Credit memo
c. Debit memo
d. Purchase order

DISCUSSION QUESTIONS

13.1 In both Chapters 12 and 13, the controller of AOE played a major role in evaluating and recommending ways to use IT to improve efficiency and effectiveness. Shouldn't these decisions be made by the company's chief information officer instead? Should the controller be involved in making these types of decisions? Why or why not?

13.2 Some companies, like IBM and Ingersoll-Rand, have moved beyond JIT to JIT-II systems. In JIT-II systems, vendor sales representatives work on-site so that they can monitor inventory levels and have access to current sales data and forecasts. The vendor representatives use this information to reorder goods automatically and meet production needs. Discuss the potential advantages and disadvantages of this arrangement. What special controls, if any, need to be developed to monitor JIT-II systems?

13.3 A standard control procedure that ensures an organization pays only for inventory actually received is to require that all vendor invoices be matched with purchase orders and receiving reports. How can an organization verify that services, such as cleaning and painting, for which no receiving report is prepared, were actually performed?

13.4 Will the use of EFT reduce the opportunity for fraud by eliminating the problems associated with the use of checks, such as forgery? Why or why not?

13.5 Some people argue that if total quality control principles are followed, there should be little or no "shrinkage" of inventory and therefore little need for periodic inventory counts. Comment on this argument.

13.6 In what ways can you apply the control procedures discussed in this chapter to paying your own personal debts (e.g., credit card bills)?

13.7 Discuss examples of the kinds of products for which a JIT inventory system is appropriate, and examples when an MRP inventory system may be more appropriate.

PROBLEMS

13.1 Which internal control procedure would be most cost-effective in dealing with the following expenditure cycle threats?

a. A purchasing agent orders materials from a vendor that he partially owns.
b. Inventory was stolen by receiving dock personnel; they claim the inventory was sent to the warehouse.
c. An unordered supply of laser printer paper was delivered to the office; it was accepted and paid for because the "price was right." After jamming all of the laser printers, however, it became obvious that the "bargain" paper was of inferior quality.
d. A vendor's invoice overcharged for items ordered and delivered.
e. A company was late in paying a particular invoice. Consequently, a second invoice that crossed the first invoice's payment in the mail was sent. The second invoice was submitted for processing and also paid.
f. Inventory records showed that an adequate supply of copy paper was supposed to be in stock, but none was available on the supply shelf.
g. The inventory records were incorrectly updated when a receiving dock employee entered the wrong product number at the terminal.
h. A clerical employee obtained a blank check and wrote a large amount payable to a fictitious company.
i. A fictitious invoice was received and used to pay for goods that were never ordered or delivered.
j. The petty cash custodian confessed to having "borrowed" $12,000 over the last five years.

13.2 The data models for both the revenue and expenditure cycles (Chapters 12 and 13) contain some common elements, such as inventory and cash. Discuss how the two cycles interact with each other. Sketch out a combined E-R diagram to cover both cycles.

13.3 Refer to Fig. 13.12 to answer the following questions:

a. If the relationship between cash disbursements and receipts was one-to-many, what would that reveal about the company's payment policy?
b. Why is the relationship between inventory and purchases many-to-many? What other possible cardinalities can exist between inventory and purchases? What would those other possibilities indicate about the company's business practices?
c. Why is the relationship between purchases and receipts many-to-many?

d. If a company regularly bought inventory on an installment payment plan, how would that be reflected in Fig. 13.12?
e. Modify Fig. 13.12 to include the event of returning defective merchandise. Create any additional tables needed, and identify the attributes that would go in those tables.
f. Modify Fig. 13.12 to include the purchase of services, such as rent and utilities. Create any additional tables needed and identify the attributes that would go in those tables.

13.4 The following documents are used in the expenditure cycle:

- Vendor invoice
- Purchase order
- Disbursement voucher
- Purchase requisition
- Packing slip
- Receiving report
- Check

Required:

a. Identify which of these documents are internally generated and which are externally generated.
b. For each internally generated document, how many copies are needed? What is the purpose of each copy? Where does each copy go?
c. Describe the application controls that should be in place if each of these paper documents were replaced by electronic forms.

13.5 The receiving department at Culp Electronics Company processes inventory deliveries upon arrival by means of on-line data terminals located on the receiving dock. Each inventory receipt entered into the system is processed to update both the inventory master file and the open purchase order file. The system then automatically generates a voucher to authorize a cash disbursement for each receipt.

Required:

a. What items of data should be entered by receiving department employees?
b. Describe several application controls that should be programmed into the system to check the accuracy and validity of the data entered by the receiving department employees. Relate your answer specifically to the data items mentioned in part a.

13.6 This problem consists of two parts.

Part I. What is the purpose of each of the following control procedures?

a. Cancellation of the voucher package by the cashier after signing the check.
b. Separation of duties of approving invoices for payment and signing checks.
c. Prenumbering and periodically accounting for all purchase orders.
d. Periodic physical count of inventory.
e. Requiring two signatures on checks for large amounts.
f. Requiring that a copy of the receiving report be routed through the inventory stores department prior to going to accounts payable.
g. Requiring a regular reconciliation of the bank account by someone other than the person responsible for writing checks.
h. Maintaining an approved vendor list and checking that all purchase orders are issued only to vendors on that list.

Part II. How can the objectives of the control procedures listed in part I be accomplished in an automated AIS?

13.7 The systems flowchart presented in Fig. 13.14 and the following description summarize ConSport Corporation's cash disbursements system:

1. The accounts payable department approves all invoices for payment by matching them with the related purchase requisitions, purchase orders, and receiving reports. The accounts payable clerks focus on matching the vendor names on all documents and skim the remaining information.
2. The vendor file is searched daily for the disbursement vouchers of invoices due to be paid. Both copies of these vouchers are sent to the treasury department, along with the other supporting documents. The cashier prepares and signs a check for each vendor and records the check in the check register.
3. The cashier receives the monthly bank statement with canceled checks and prepares the bank reconciliation. If an adjustment is required as a consequence of the bank reconciliation, a two-copy journal voucher is prepared. A copy of the bank reconciliation is sent to the internal audit department.

Required:

Identify weaknesses in ConSport's expenditure cycle, explain the resulting problem(s), and suggest a control procedure that would best prevent or detect and correct each weakness. Use the labels next to each figure to reference your answer.

(CMA Examination, adapted)

FIGURE 13.14
Cash Disbursements System for ConSport Corporation

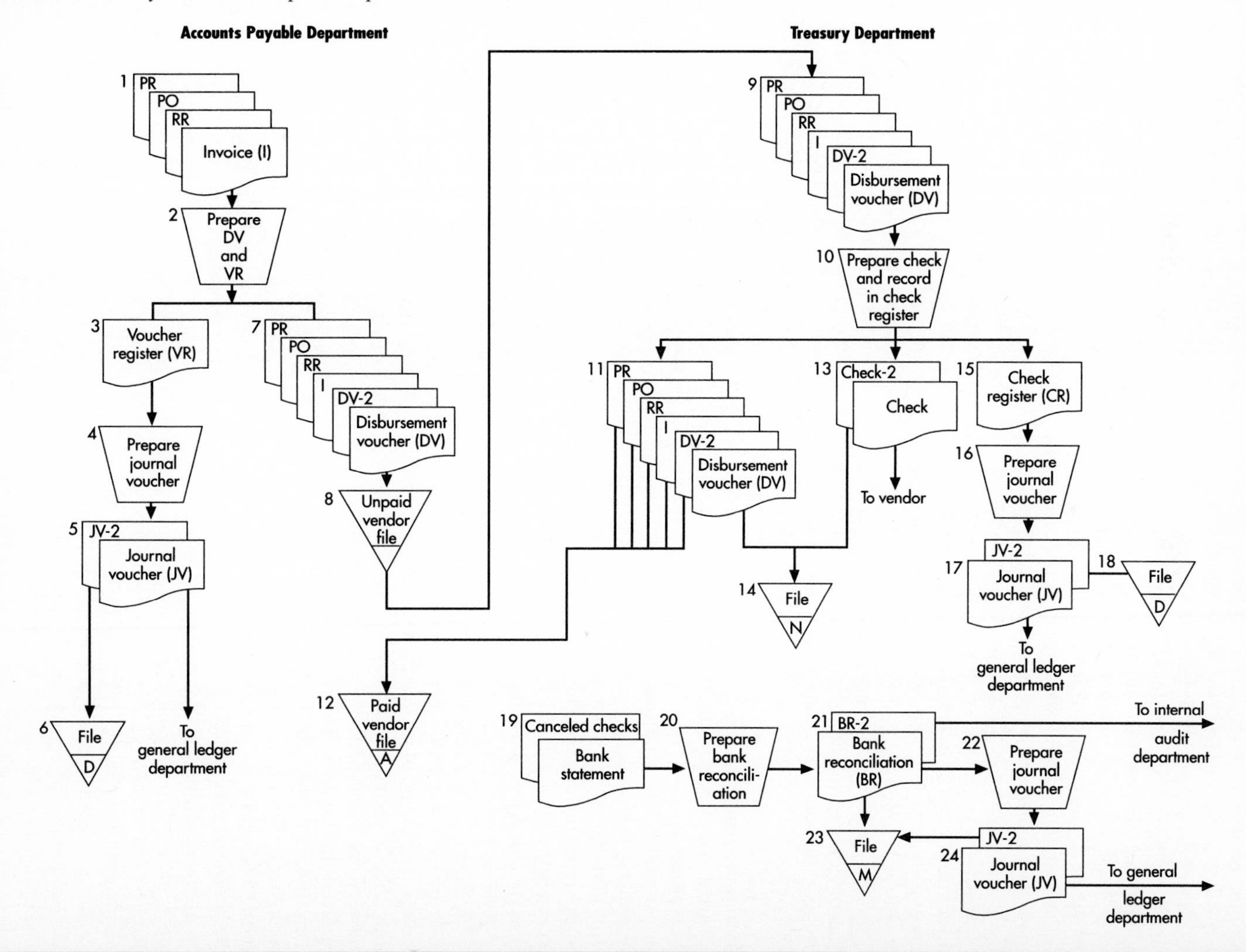

13.8 In 1995 the Diamond Manufacturing Company purchased over $10 million worth of office equipment under its "special" ordering system, with individual orders ranging from $5,000 to $30,000. Special orders entail low-volume items that have been included in an authorized user's budget. As part of their annual budgets, department heads request equipment and specify estimated costs. The budget, which limits the types and dollar amounts of office equipment a department head can requisition, is approved at the beginning of the year by the board of directors. A purchase requisition form for all approved equipment purchases must be prepared and forwarded to the purchasing department. The special ordering system functions as follows:

Purchasing. Upon receiving a purchase requisition, one of the five purchasing agents (buyers) verifies that the requester is indeed a department head. The buyer next selects the appropriate vendor by searching the various catalogs on file. The buyer then phones the vendor, requests a price quote, and places a verbal order. A prenumbered purchase order is then processed, with the original sent to the vendor and copies to the department head, receiving, and accounts payable. One copy is also filed in the open-requisition file. When the buyer is verbally informed by the receiving department that the item has been received, the purchase order is transferred from the open to the filled file. Once a month, the buyer reviews the unfilled file to follow up on open orders.

Receiving. The receiving department is sent a copy of each purchase order. When equipment is received, that copy of the purchase order is stamped with the date and, if applicable, any differences between the quantities ordered and the quantities received are noted in red ink. The receiving clerk then forwards the stamped purchase order and equipment to the requisitioning department head and verbally notifies the purchasing department that the goods were received.

Accounts Payable. Upon receipt of a purchase order, the accounts payable clerk files it in the open purchase order file. When a vendor invoice is received, it is matched with the applicable purchase order, and a payable is created by debiting the equipment account of the requisitioning department. Unpaid invoices are filed by due date. On the due date, a check is prepared and forwarded to the treasurer for signature. The invoice and purchase order are then filed by purchase order number in the paid invoice file.

Treasurer. Checks received daily from the accounts payable department are sorted into two groups: those over and under $10,000. Checks for less than $10,000 are machine signed. The cashier maintains the check signature machine's key and signature plate and monitors its use. All checks over $10,000 are signed by both the cashier and the treasurer.

Required:

a. Describe the weaknesses relating to purchases and payments of special orders by the Diamond Manufacturing Company.
b. Recommend control procedures that need to be added to overcome the weaknesses identified in step a.
c. Describe how the control procedures you recommended in step b should be modified if Diamond reengineered its expenditure cycle activities to make maximum use of current IT (e.g., EDI, EFT, bar-code scanning, and electronic forms in place of paper documents).

(CPA Examination, adapted)

13.9 Lecimore Company has a centralized purchasing department managed by Tawanda Mason. Mason has established policies and procedures to guide the clerical staff and purchasing agents in daily department operations. She is satisfied that these guidelines conform with company objectives and that no major problems exist in the regular operations of the purchasing department.

Lecimore's internal audit department recently performed a routine operational audit of the purchasing department. Mason's policies and procedures that were first reviewed are described here:

- All significant purchases are made on a competitive basis. The probability of timely delivery and vendor reliability are taken into account on a subjective basis.
- Quality acceptability requirements are provided to all potential vendors.
- Vendor adherence to quality specifications is checked by the materials manager of the inventory stores department, not by the purchasing department. The materials manager inspects the goods upon arrival and ensures that only goods meeting minimum quality standards are transferred to the storeroom.
- All purchase requests are prepared by the materials manager and are based on the production schedule for the next four months.

The internal audit staff then observed the purchasing department's operations and noted the following:

- One vendor provides 90% of the crucial raw materials used by Lecimore. This vendor has a good delivery record and has been the low bidder for several years.
- As production plans change, rush and expedite orders are made by production directly to the purchasing department. Materials ordered for canceled production runs are stored for future use. The purchasing department absorbs the costs associated with both types of changes because Mason believes this is a way of being a "good team player."
- As soon as the production department announces changes, purchasing orders the appropriate materials. Mason is very proud of her staff's quick response time to such orders. Materials on hand are not reviewed before these orders are placed, however.
- Partial and advance shipments are accepted by the materials manager, who notifies the purchasing department of the receipt of the goods. The purchasing department is responsible for following up on partial shipments; no action is taken to discourage advance shipments.

Required:

a. Identify weaknesses and inefficiencies in the purchasing procedures that Mason developed for Lecimore.

b. Suggest ways to overcome those weaknesses or inefficiencies.

(CMA Examination, adapted)

13.10 You have been hired by the management of Alden, Inc. to review its internal controls over the purchase, receipt, storage, and issuance of raw materials. You observed the following:

- Raw materials, which consist mainly of high-cost electronic components, are kept in a locked storeroom. Storeroom personnel include a supervisor and four clerks. All are well trained, competent, and adequately bonded. Raw materials are removed from the storeroom only upon written or oral authorization by a production supervisor.
- No perpetual inventory records are kept; hence the storeroom clerks do not keep records for goods received or issued. To compensate, a physical inventory count is performed monthly by the storeroom clerks. The clerks are supervised during this count, and other appropriate procedures are followed.
- After the physical count, the storeroom supervisor matches the quantities on hand against a predetermined reorder level. If the count is below the reorder level, the supervisor enters the part number on a materials requisition list that is sent to the accounts payable clerk. The accounts payable clerk prepares a purchase order for each item on the list and mails it to the vendor from whom the part was last purchased.
- When ordered materials arrive, they are received by the storeroom clerks. The clerks count all items and verify that the counts agree with the quantities on the bill of lading. The bill of lading is then initialed, dated, and filed in the storeroom, to serve as a receiving report.

Required:

a. Describe the weaknesses that exist in Alden's expenditure cycle.

b. Suggest control procedures to overcome the weaknesses noted in step a.

c. Discuss how those control procedures would be best implemented in an automated AIS utilizing the latest developments in IT.

(CPA Examination, adapted)

13.11 Table 13.2 lists the various activities performed in the expenditure cycle and the journal entries, documents, data, and control issues associated with them. Complete each of the cell entries in this table. (Adapted from teaching materials developed by Martha Eining at the University of Utah)

13.12 The purchasing procedures followed by the Branden Company, a medium-sized manufacturer of specialized machinery, are as follows:

- Materials purchase requisitions are approved by manufacturing supervisors and then forwarded to the purchasing department.
- Purchasing clerks prepare prenumbered purchase orders in triplicate. The original copy is sent to the vendor. The second copy is sent to the receiving department to notify them of an incoming shipment. The third copy is filed in the purchasing department.
- When materials are delivered, they are moved directly to the storeroom, along with a copy of the receiving report. The receiving department sends another copy of the receiving report, along with its copy of the purchase order, to the purchasing department. The third copy of the receiving report is sent to the accounting department.

TABLE 13.2 Overview of Expenditure Cycle Business Activities

	Expenditure Cycle						
	Request Purchase of Goods	**Approve Purchase**	**Receive Goods**	**Receive Invoice**	**Approve Vendor Invoice**	**Prepare Check**	**Pay Vendor**
Accounting transaction							
Journal entry					Dr. Purchases Cr. A/P		
Documents		Purchase order					
Data collected	• Name • Item #						
Department					Accounting		
Control issues	Order only what is needed						
Information required							
Information generated							
Effect of automation							

Adapted from teaching materials developed by Martha Eining, University of Utah. Reprinted with permission.

- Vendor invoices are sent to the purchasing department and directed to the employee who placed that order. He or she checks the invoice for accuracy in terms of discounts, extensions, and footings. The purchasing clerk then compares the invoice with (1) the copy of the purchase order and (2) the copy of the receiving report to verify the quantities ordered and received and approves it for payment.
- The approved invoice is then sent to the accounting department, where it is coded for account distribution, assigned a voucher number, entered in the voucher register, and filed according to payment due date.

Required:

Identify weaknesses in Branden's expenditure cycle activities, explain the resulting problems that may occur, and recommend control procedures that should be implemented to correct those weaknesses.

(CPA Examination, adapted)

CASE 13.1 ANYCOMPANY, INC.—AN ONGOING COMPREHENSIVE CASE

Identify a local company (you may use the some company you identified to complete this case in previous chapters) and do the following:

1. Identify who is responsible for decisions involving (a) requisitioning, ordering, and receiving inventories; (b) authorizing cash disbursements; and (c) making cash disbursements. Assess whether there is adequate segregation of duties regarding these activities.
2. Describe the paper documents and electronic

forms used by the company. Evaluate the design of each document or electronic form, and assess its appropriateness for its intended use.

3. Draw a data model, in the form of an REA diagram, of the organization's expenditure cycle.
4. Describe how the system updates the master files (or data base) after each type of transaction (purchase, receipt, cash disbursement). Draw a systems flowchart of these processes.
5. Identify and evaluate the adequacy of the control procedures used to ensure the accuracy and validity of all transaction processing.
6. Examine copies of the reports produced by the system. Identify the major decisions that must be made in the expenditure cycle. Evaluate the adequacy of existing reports in assisting good decision making.

CASE 13.2 BLACKWELL INDUSTRIES

Blackwell Industries manufactures sporting goods. You have been asked to evaluate the proposed redesign of Blackwell's purchasing system. The new system will utilize a materials inventory master file, an open purchase order master file, and a vendor history file, all organized and stored in a relational data base system. System inputs will include materials inventory receipt and issue transactions, which will be keyed in as they occur from on-line terminals located in the appropriate departments. System outputs will include batches of purchase orders and periodic reports of overdue deliveries, vendor performance, and cash flow commitments. These reports will be generated by programs that are separate from the main update program and also by on-line queries.

The main update program will begin by reading a transaction record and determining whether it is a receipt or issue transaction. Then it will update the appropriate inventory master record. As each issue transaction is processed, the program will also check the quantity on hand in the master inventory record; if it falls below the reorder point, a reorder record will be written to a temporary file on a separate disk. This file will be processed at the end of each day, to prepare purchase orders. For each inventory receipt transaction, the program will update not only the quantity on hand in the inventory master record but also the corresponding open purchase order and vendor history records.

The purchase order preparation program will process the temporary reorder file by first sequencing it by vendor code number. All reorder records for the same vendor will be consolidated into one purchase order. When all reorder records for a vendor have been processed, a purchase order will be generated and transmitted by EDI. The order will also be added to the open purchase order file.

At the end of each day, the open purchase order file will be processed to identify any purchase orders for which delivery is past due, and an overdue deliveries report will be generated. At the end of each month, the vendor history and open purchase order files will be processed to generate vendor performance and cash flow commitments reports.

Required:

1. Prepare a systems flowchart of the main update program.
2. Prepare a systems flowchart of the purchase order preparation program.
3. Draw an REA diagram of the data included in the proposed system.
4. Suggest potential ways that IT could be used to further improve the efficiency of the proposed system.
5. Identify the data that will be input on each transaction record. Suggest appropriate application controls to ensure accurate and reliable input.
6. Identify potential threats relating to the proposed system and suggest appropriate internal control procedures for mitigating them.

ANSWERS TO CHAPTER QUIZ

1. b	**3.** d	**5.** c	**7.** d	**9.** d
2. b	**4.** c	**6.** b	**8.** a	**10.** c

CHAPTER 14

The Production Cycle

LEARNING OBJECTIVES

After studying this chapter, you should be able to

- Describe the major business activities and related data processing operations performed in the production cycle.
- Document your understanding of production cycle activities.
- Explain how a company's cost accounting system can help it achieve its manufacturing goals.
- Identify major threats in the production cycle, and evaluate the adequacy of various control procedures for dealing with those threats.
- Discuss the key decisions that need to be made in the production cycle, and identify the information needed to make those decisions.
- Read and understand a data model (REA diagram) of the production cycle.

Integrative Case: Alpha Omega Electronics

LeRoy Williams, vice president for manufacturing at Alpha Omega Electronics (AOE), is concerned about problems associated with AOE's change in strategic mission. Two years ago, AOE's top management decided to shift the company from its traditional position as a low-cost producer of consumer electronic products (see Chapters 12 and 13). Under the new strategy AOE is positioning itself as a producer of top-quality products sold at moderate prices. As part of this strategy, AOE increased the variety of sizes, styles, and features within each of its product lines.

To support its shift in strategic focus, AOE has invested heavily in factory automation. AOE's cost accounting system has not been changed, however. For example, manufacturing overhead is still allocated on the basis of direct labor hours, even though automation has drastically reduced the amount of direct labor used to manufacture a product. Consequently, investments in new equipment and machinery have resulted in dramatic increases in manufacturing overhead rates. This situation has created a number of problems:

1. Production supervisors complain that the accounting system "does not make sense" and that they are being "penalized" for making investments that improve overall efficiency. Indeed, some products now "cost" more to produce using state-of-the-art equipment than they did before the new equipment was purchased. Yet use of the new equipment has increased production quantity while reducing defects.

2. The marketing and product design executives have all but dismissed the system's product cost figures as useless for setting prices or determining the potential profitability of new products. Indeed, some competitors have begun to price their products below AOE's reported cost to produce that item!

3. Although a number of steps have been taken to improve quality, the cost accounting system does not provide adequate measures to evaluate the effect of those steps and to indicate areas that need further improvement.

4. Performance reports continue to focus primarily on financial measures. Line managers in the factory, however, need accurate information on physical activities, such as units produced, defect rates, and production time.

LeRoy has expressed these concerns to Linda Spurgeon, AOE's president, who agrees that these problems are serious. Linda then called a meeting with LeRoy; Stephanie Cromwell, AOE's vice president of finance; and Elizabeth Venko, AOE's controller. At the meeting, Elizabeth agreed to undertake a study of how to modify the cost accounting system to more accurately reflect AOE's new production processes. To begin this project, LeRoy agreed to take Elizabeth on a tour of the factory so that she could see and understand how the new technology has affected production cycle activities.

As this case suggests, deficiencies in the information system used to support production cycle activities can create significant problems for an organization. The availability of current and accurate information about product costs is crucial for effective management of the production cycle. As you read this chapter, think about how the introduction of new technology in the production cycle may require corresponding changes in a company's cost accounting system.

INTRODUCTION

The **production cycle** is a recurring set of business activities and related data processing operations associated with the manufacture of products. Figure 14.1

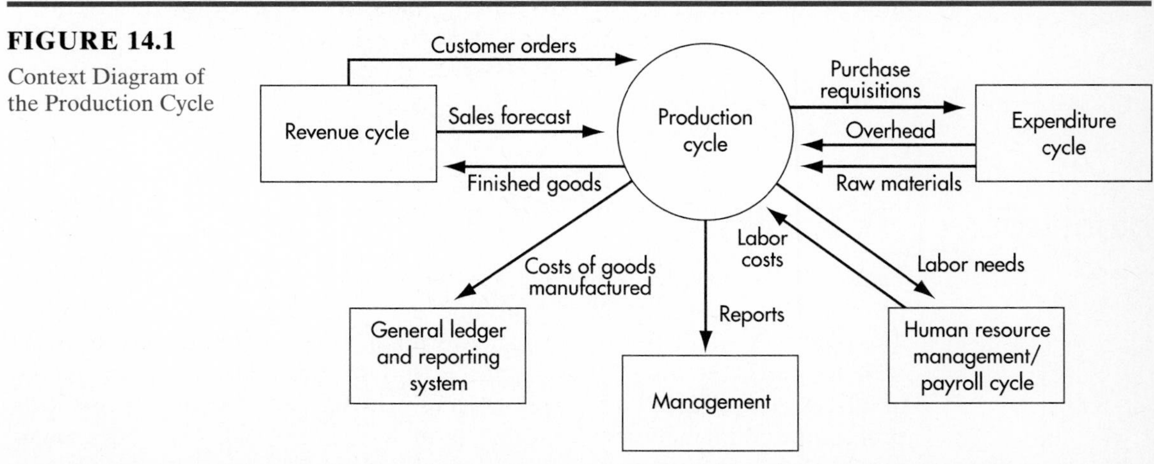

FIGURE 14.1
Context Diagram of the Production Cycle

shows how the production cycle is linked to the other subsystems in a company's AIS. The revenue cycle information system (see Chapter 12) provides the information (customer orders and sales forecasts) used to plan production and inventory levels. In return, the production cycle information system sends the revenue cycle information about finished goods that have been produced and are available for sale. Information about raw materials needs is sent to the expenditure cycle information system (see Chapter 13) in the form of purchase requisitions. In exchange, the expenditure cycle system provides information about raw material acquisitions and about other expenditures included in manufacturing overhead. Information about labor needs is sent to the human resources cycle (see Chapter 15), which in return provides data about labor costs and availability. Finally, information about the cost of goods manufactured is sent to the general ledger and reporting information system (see Chapter 16).

A company's AIS plays a vital role in the production cycle. Accurate and timely cost accounting information is essential input to decisions about the following:

- Product mix (what to produce)
- Product pricing
- Resource allocation and planning (e.g., whether to make or buy a product, relative profitability of different products)
- Cost management (planning and controlling manufacturing costs, evaluating performance)

These decisions require much more detailed information about costs than the data needed to prepare financial statements in accordance with GAAP. Thus the design of a company's production cycle AIS must go beyond simply meeting external financial reporting requirements.

This chapter is organized around the three major functions of the AIS in the production cycle. The first section describes production cycle activities and discusses how data about their costs are collected and processed. The second section discusses the major control objectives in the production cycle and explains how the AIS can be designed to achieve them. The final section discusses the key production cycle decisions and presents a data model that shows how the AIS can effectively and efficiently store and organize the information needed to make those decisions.

PRODUCTION CYCLE ACTIVITIES

Figure 14.2 shows the four basic activities in the production cycle: product design, planning and scheduling, production operations, and cost accounting. The figure also depicts the principal information flows between each of those activities and the other AIS cycles. Although accountants are primarily involved in the fourth step, cost accounting, they need to understand the processes and information needs of the other steps as well. It is the accountant's role to ensure that the AIS can provide the information needed to manage the four activities of the production cycle.

FIGURE 14.2
Level 0 DFD of the Production Cycle

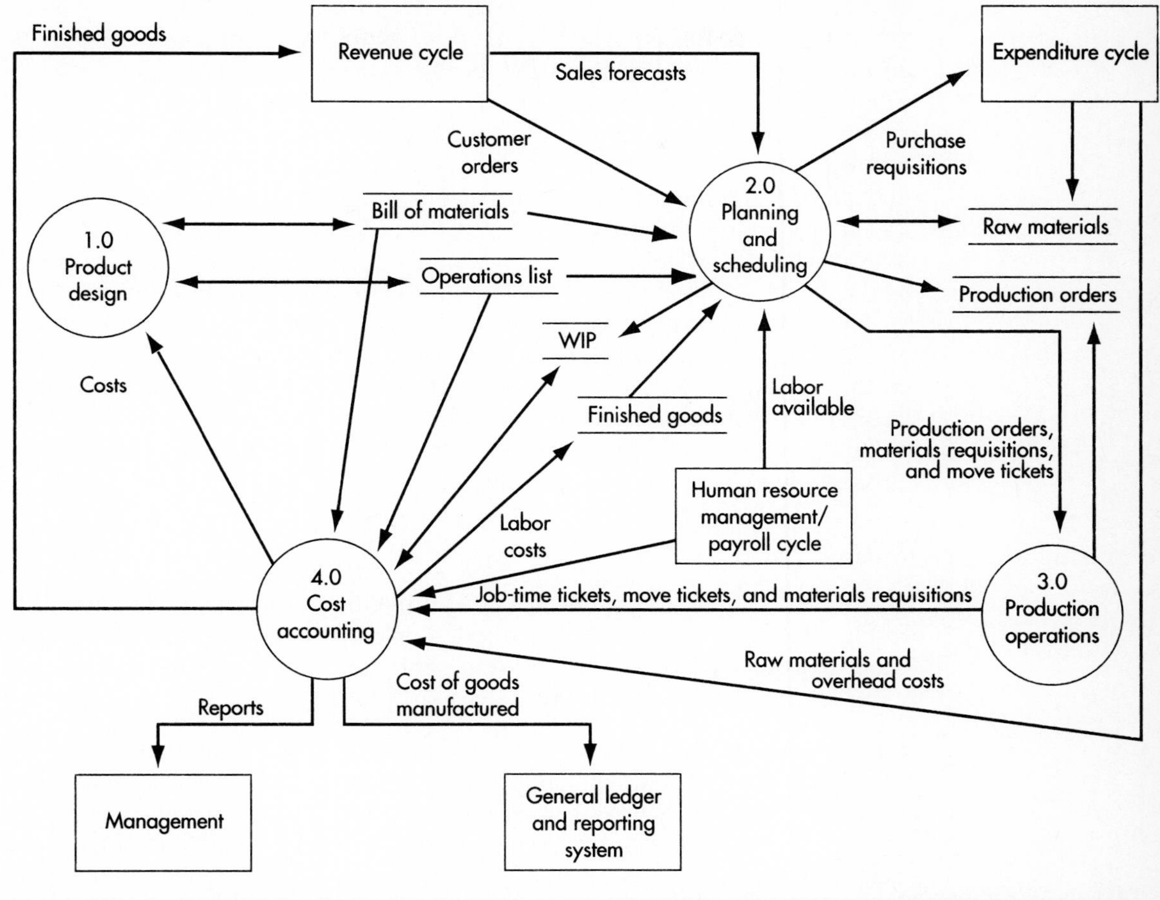

Product Design

The first step in the production cycle is product design (circle 1.0 in Fig. 14.2). The objective of this activity is to design a product that meets customer requirements for quality, durability, and functionality while simultaneously minimizing production costs. Some of these criteria conflict with one another, making the product design task a challenging one.

Documents and Procedures. The product design activity creates two main documents. The first, a **bill of materials,** specifies the part number, description, and quantity of each component used in a product. The second is an **operations list,** which specifies the labor and machine requirements needed to manufacture the product. The operations list is also referred to as a *routing sheet* because it indicates how a product moves through the factory, specifying what is done at each step and how much time each operation should take.

Role of the Accountant. Accountants should play an important role in product design, because 65% to 80% of product costs are determined at this stage of the production process. Accountants can become involved in product design by showing how various design trade-offs affect production costs and thereby profitability. For example, it is possible to significantly reduce the costs of producing a line of related products by increasing the number of common components used in each product. The AIS should be able to provide data about current component usage in various products and the projected costs of using alternative components. Similarly, aspects of product complexity, such as the number of different components and manner of assembly, can significantly affect production time and costs. Again, the accountant should ensure that the AIS is designed to collect and provide information about the machine setup and materials handling costs associated with alternative product designs.

Finally, data about repair and warranty costs associated with existing products can be useful for designing better products. This data should be collected in the revenue cycle; the key is to design the AIS so that the information is accessible to product designers. Notice that in all of these examples the accountant adds value not by merely measuring costs, but by using cost information proactively to improve long-run profitability.

Planning and Scheduling

The second step in the production cycle is planning and scheduling (circle 2.0 in Fig. 14.2). The objective of this step is a production plan efficient enough to meet existing orders and anticipated short-term demand without creating excess finished goods inventories.

Planning Methods. Two common methods of production planning are manufacturing resource planning and just-in-time manufacturing. **Manufacturing resource planning (MRP-II)** is an extension of materials resource planning (see Chapter 13) that seeks to match existing production capacity and raw materials needs with forecasted sales demands. MRP-II systems are often referred to as *push manufacturing*, because goods are produced in expectation of customer demand.

Just as MRP-II is an extension of MRP inventory control systems, **just-in-time (JIT) manufacturing systems** extend the principles of just-in-time inventory systems (see Chapter 13) to the entire production process. The goal of JIT manufacturing is to minimize or eliminate inventories of raw materials, work-in-process, and finished goods. The use of JIT is often referred to as *pull manufacturing*, because goods are produced in response to customer demand. Theoretically, JIT manufacturing systems produce only in response to customer orders. In practice, however, most JIT manufacturing systems develop short-run production plans. For example, Toyota develops monthly production plans so that it can provide a stable schedule to its suppliers. This strategy enables the suppliers to plan their production schedules so that they can deliver their products to Toyota at the exact time they are needed for production. Otherwise, production will come to a halt. Thus both MRP-II and JIT manufacturing systems plan production in advance; they differ, however, in the length of the planning horizon. MRP-II systems may develop production plans for up to 12 months in advance, whereas JIT manufacturing systems use much shorter planning horizons.

Documents and Procedures. The **master production schedule (MPS)** specifies how much of each product is to be produced during the planning period and when that production should occur (see Fig. 14.3). Information about customer orders, sales forecasts, and finished goods inventory levels is used to determine production levels. Although the long-range part of the MPS may be modified in response to changes in market conditions, production plans must be frozen a few weeks in advance to provide sufficient time to procure the necessary raw materials, supplies, and labor resources. Moreover, the complexity of scheduling increases dramatically as the number of factories grows. For example, Thomson Consumer Electronics must coordinate production at ten different plants in four different countries. Some of those plants produce basic components like picture tubes and circuit boards; others assemble the final products. The production information system must coordinate these activities to minimize bottlenecks and partially completed inventories.

The MPS is used to develop a detailed timetable that specifies daily production. It is also used to determine whether any raw materials need to be purchased, by exploding the bill of materials to determine the immediate raw materials requirements for meeting the production goals listed in the MPS (see Table 14.1). These requirements are compared with current inventory level

FIGURE 14.3
Sample Master Production Schedule (MPS)

MASTER PRODUCTION SCHEDULE

Product Number 120 **Description:** VCR

Lead time[a]:	**Week Number**							
1 week	**1**	**2**	**3**	**4**	**5**	**6**	**7**	**8**
Quantity on hand	500	350[b]	350	300	350	300	450	300
Scheduled production	150[c]	300	250	300	250	400	250	300
Forecasted sales	300	300	300	250	300	250	400	250
Net available	350[d]	350	300	350	300	450	300	350

[a]Time to manufacture product (1 week for VCR).
[b]Ending quantity on hand (net available) from prior week.
[c]Calculated by subtracting quantity on hand from sum of this week's and next week's forecasted sales, plus a 50-unit buffer stock. For example, begin week 1 with 500 units. Projected sales for weeks 1 and 2 total 600 units. Adding 50-unit desired buffer inventory yields 650 units needed by end of week 1. Subtracting beginning inventory of 500 units results in planned production of 150 units during week 1.
[d]Beginning quantity on hand plus scheduled production less forecasted sales.

TABLE 14.1 Example of "Exploding" a Bill of Materials

Step 1: Multiply the component requirements for ONE product by the number of products to be produced next period (from the MPS).

Components in Each VCR				
Part No.	Description	Quantity	Number of VCRs	Total Requirements
105	Control Unit	1	2000	2,000
125	Back Panel	1	2000	2,000
148	Side Panel	4	2000	8,000
173	Timer	1	2000	2,000
195	Front Panel	1	2000	2,000
199	Screw	6	2000	12,000

Components in Each CD Player				
Part No.	Description	Quantity	Number of CD Players	Total Requirements
103	Control Unit	1	3000	3,000
120	Front Panel	1	3000	3,000
121	Back Panel	1	3000	3,000
173	Timer	1	3000	3,000
190	Side Panel	4	3000	12,000
199	Screw	4	3000	12,000

Step 2: Calculate total component requirements by summing products.

Part No.	VCR	CD Player	Total
103	0	3,000	3,000
105	2,000	0	2,000
120	0	3,000	3,000
121	0	3,000	3,000
125	2,000	0	2,000
148	8,000	0	8,000
173	2,000	3,000	5,000
190	0	12,000	12,000
195	2,000	0	2,000
199	12,000	12,000	24,000

Step 3: Repeat steps 1 and 2 for each week during planning horizon.

Part No.	Week 1	Week 2	Week 3	Week 4	Week 5	Week 6
103	3,000	2,000	2,500	3,000	2,500	3,000
105	2,000	2,000	2,500	2,500	2,000	3,000
120	3,000	2,000	2,500	3,000	2,500	3,000
121	3,000	2,000	2,500	3,000	2,500	3,000
125	2,000	2,000	2,500	2,500	2,000	3,000
148	8,000	8,000	10,000	10,000	8,000	12,000
173	5,000	4,000	5,000	5,500	4,500	6,000
190	12,000	12,000	10,000	12,000	10,000	12,000
195	2,000	2,000	2,500	2,500	2,000	3,000
199	24,000	20,000	25,000	27,000	22,000	30,000

and, if additional materials are needed, purchase requisitions are generated and sent to the purchasing department to initiate the acquisition process.

Figure 14.2 shows that three other documents are produced by the planning and scheduling step: production orders, materials requisitions, and move tickets. A **production order** authorizes the manufacture of a specified quantity of a particular product. It lists the operations that need to be performed, the quantity to be produced, and the location where the finished product should be delivered (see Fig. 14.4).

A **materials requisition** authorizes the removal of the necessary quantity of raw materials from the storeroom to the factory location where production operations are to begin. This document contains the production order number, date of issue, and, based on the bill of materials, the part numbers and quantities of all necessary raw materials (see Fig. 14.5). Subsequent transfers of raw materials throughout the factory are documented on **move tickets,** which identify the parts being transferred, the location to which they are transferred, and the time of the transfer (see Fig. 14.6).

FIGURE 14.4

Sample Production Order for AOE

4587

Alpha Omega Engineering

PRODUCTION ORDER

Order No. 2289	**Product No.** 4430	**Description:** Cabinet Side Panel		**Production Quantity** 1000
Approved by: PJS	**Release Date:** 02/24/2000	**Issue Date:** 02/25/2000	**Completion Date:** 03/09/2000	**Deliver to:** Assembly Department

Work Station No.	**Product Operation No.**	**Quantity**	**Operation Description**	**Start Date & Time**		**Finish Date & Time**	
MH25	100	1003	Transfer from stock	02/28	0700	02/28	0800
ML15-12	105	1003	Cut to shape	02/28	0800	02/28	1000
ML15-9	106	1002	Corner cut	02/28	1030	02/28	1200
S28-17	124	1002	Turn & shape	02/28	1300	02/28	1700
F54-5	142	1001	Finish	03/01	0800	03/01	1100
P89-1	155	1001	Paint	03/01	1300	03/02	1300
QC94	194	1001	Inspect	03/02	1400	03/02	1600
MH25	101	1000	Transfer to assembly	03/02	1600	03/02	1700

Explanation of numbers in Quantity column:

1. Total of 1003 sheets of raw material used to produce 1000 good panels and 3 rejected panels.
2. One panel not cut to proper shape, thus only 1002 units had operations 106 and 124 performed on them.
3. One panel not properly turned and shaped; hence only 1001 panels finished, painted, and received final inspection.
4. One panel rejected during final inspection; thus only 1000 good panels transferred to assembly department.

FIGURE 14.5
Sample Materials Requisition for AOE

MATERIALS REQUISITION					No. 2345
Issued To: Assembly		**Issue Date:** 08/15/2000		**Production Order Number:** 62913	
Part Number	**Description**	**Quantity**	**Unit Cost**	**Total Cost**	
115	Calculator Unit	2000	2.95	5900.00	
135	Lower Casing	2000	.45	900.00	
198	Screw	16000	.02	320.00	
178	Battery	2000	.75	1500.00	
136	Upper Casing	2000	.80	1600.00	
199	Screw	12000	.02	240.00	
Issued by: AKL				10,460.00	
Received by: GWS		**Costed by:** ZBD			

Note: Cost information is entered when the materials requisition is turned in to the cost accounting department. Other information, except for signatures, is printed by the system when the document is prepared.

FIGURE 14.6
Sample Move Ticket for AOE

MOVE TICKET			No. 8753
Production Order Number: 2345	**Date Transferred:** 08/18/2000		
From: Assembly *KLS*	**To:** Finishing *NRC*		
Operation To Perform	**Completed**	**Date**	**Time**
Clean	X	08/19/2000	0900
Polish			
Package			
Comments:			

Role of the Accountant. The accountant must ensure that the AIS collects and reports costs in a manner consistent with the production planning techniques used by the company. This may require making changes to the AIS whenever new planning techniques are adopted. For example, AOE is thinking about adopting the JIT approach to manufacturing. JIT manufacturing emphasizes working in teams and seeks to maximize the efficiency and synergy of all teams involved in making a particular product. Consequently, Elizabeth Venko realizes that collecting and reporting labor variances at the individual or team level may create dysfunctional incentives to maximize local performance at the expense of plantwide performance. Therefore she plans to redesign AOE's AIS so that it collects and reports costs in a manner that highlights the joint contributions of all teams involved in making a particular product.

Accountants can also help a company choose whether MRP-II or JIT is more appropriate for planning and scheduling its production. If demand for a company's product is predictable and the product has a long life cycle, then an MRP-II approach may be justified. On the other hand, a JIT approach may be more appropriate if a company's products are characterized by short life cycles, unpredictable demand, and frequent markdowns of excess inventory. Thus the accountant should design the AIS to provide this kind of detailed information about product sales.

Production Operations

The third step in the production cycle is the actual manufacture of products (circle 3.0 in Fig. 14.2). The manner in which this activity is accomplished varies greatly across companies, differing according to the type of product being manufactured and the degree of automation used in the production process.

The use of various forms of information technology (IT) in the production process, such as robots and computer-controlled machinery, is referred to as **computer-integrated manufacturing (CIM).** CIM can significantly reduce production costs. For example, Northrop Corporation used to collect 16,000 sheets of paper containing shop-floor work instructions related to the manufacture of plane fuselages. When on-line terminals were installed at each assembly station, the elimination in paper flow and improved efficiency reduced costs by 30%!

Accountants do not need to be experts on every facet of CIM, but they do need to understand how it affects the AIS. One effect of CIM is a shift from mass production to custom order manufacturing. For example, every Northrop Grumman product is assembled to order. Each product, however, can use any of about 256,000 separate components. Thus, to minimize inventory carrying costs, Northrop's AIS must maintain accurate perpetual inventory records. Its AIS must also be able to integrate sales orders with the production system and track the status of all orders. Thus its AIS must fully integrate information from the revenue, expenditure, and production cycles. Enterprise resource planning (ERP) systems provide such integration.

Although both the nature of the production process and the extent of CIM vary across companies, every firm needs to collect data about the following three facets of its production operations: raw materials used, labor hours expended, and machine operations performed and other manufacturing overhead costs incurred. In the next section, we discuss the methods used to collect and process this data.

Cost Accounting

The final step in the production cycle is cost accounting (circle 4.0 in Fig. 14.2). The two principal objectives of the cost accounting system are (1) to provide information for planning, controlling, and evaluating the performance of production operations; and (2) to provide accurate cost data about products for use in pricing and product mix decisions. In addition, the cost accounting system provides the information used to calculate the inventory and cost of goods sold values that appear in the company's financial statements.

To accomplish these objectives, the AIS collects costs by various categories and then assigns those costs to specific products and organizational units. Careful coding of cost data during collection is important, because often the same costs may be allocated in multiple ways, for several different purposes. For example, factory supervisory costs may be assigned to departments for performance evaluation purposes, but to specific products for pricing and product mix decisions.

Types of Cost Accounting Systems. Most companies use either job-order or process costing to assign production costs. **Job-order costing** assigns costs to specific production batches, or jobs; it is used whenever the product or service being sold can be distinctly identified. For example, construction companies use job-order costing for each house being built. Similarly, public accounting and law firms use job-order costing to account for the costs of individual audits or cases, respectively. AOE currently uses job-order costing.

In contrast, **process costing** assigns costs to each process, or work center, in the production cycle and then calculates the average cost for all units produced. Process costing is used whenever similar goods or services are produced in mass quantities. For example, breweries accumulate the costs associated with the various steps (e.g., mashing, primary fermentation, filtering, bottling) in producing a batch of a particular kind of beer and then compute the average total unit cost for that product. Similarly, mutual funds accumulate the costs associated with handling customer deposits and withdrawals and then compute the per-unit costs of those transactions.

Information Processing. Figure 14.7 depicts a typical on-line AIS for the production cycle, such as the one used by AOE. Engineering department specifications for new products result in the creation of new records in both the bill of materials and operations list files. To develop those specifications, engineering accesses both files to examine the design of similar products. It also accesses the general ledger and inventory files for information about the costs of alternative product designs. Sales forecasts and customer special order information are entered by the sales department. That information, and data about current inventory levels, is used by the production planning department to develop the master production schedule. New records are then added to the production order file to authorize the production of specific goods. At the same time, new records are added to the work-in-process file, to accumulate cost data. The list of operations to be performed is displayed at the appropriate workstation. Corresponding instructions are also sent to the CIM interface to guide the operation of computerized machinery and robots. Finally, materials requisitions are sent to the inventory stores department to authorize the release of raw materials to production.

The system shown in Fig. 14.7 could be used to implement either a job-order or process costing system. Both systems require accumulating data about three

FIGURE 14.7
On-Line Production Cycle Information System

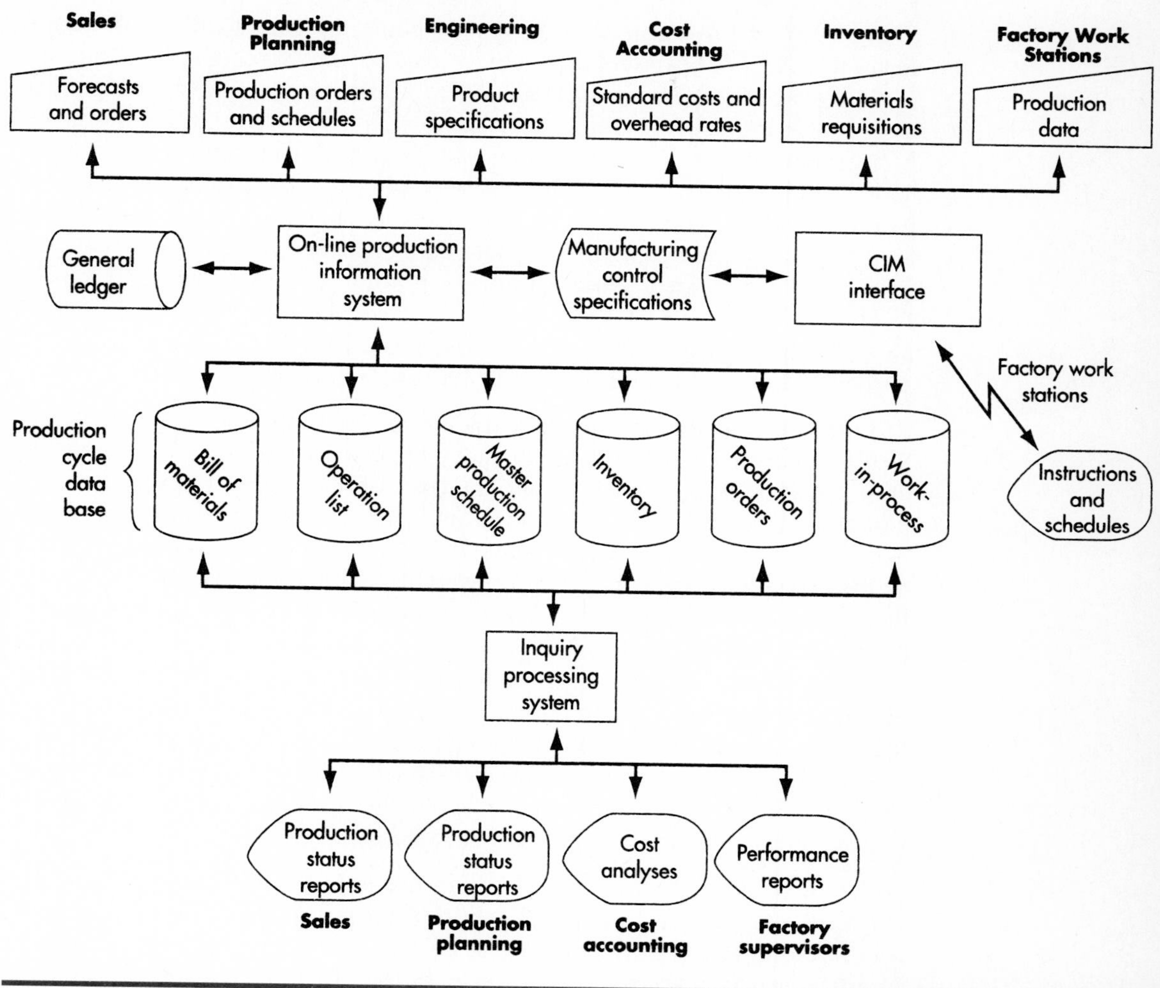

basic kinds of costs: raw materials, direct labor, and manufacturing overhead. The choice of job-order or process costing affects only the method used to assign those costs to products, not the methods used for data collection. Let us now examine how these three types of cost data are collected.

Raw Materials. When production is initiated, the issuance of a materials requisition triggers a debit to work-in-process for the raw materials sent to production. If additional materials are needed, another debit is made to work-in-process; conversely, work-in-process is credited for any materials not used and returned to inventory. Most raw materials are bar-coded; this enables usage data to be collected by scanning the products when they are released from, or returned to, inventory. Inventory clerks use on-line terminals to enter usage data for those items that are not bar-coded.

Direct Labor. In the past, AOE used a paper document called a **job-time ticket** to collect data about labor activity. This document recorded the amount of time a worker spent on each specific job task. Now, as shown in Fig. 14.7, workers enter this data using on-line terminals at each factory workstation. To further improve the efficiency of this process, AOE is considering switching to coded identification cards, which workers would run through a badge reader or bar-code scanner when they start and finish any task. The time savings associated with using bar coding to automate data collection can be significant. For example, Consolidated Diesel Company, a joint venture between Cummins Engine Company and J. I. Case, found using bar-code scanners to capture data about materials usage and labor operations saved about 12 seconds per workstation, resulting in a permanent 15% increase in productivity.

Manufacturing Overhead. **Manufacturing overhead** consists of all manufacturing costs that are not economically feasible to trace directly to specific jobs or processes. Examples include the costs of water, power, and other utilities; miscellaneous supplies; rent, insurance, and property taxes for the factory plant; and the salaries of factory supervisors. Most of these costs are collected by the expenditure cycle information system (see Chapter 13), with the exception of supervisory salaries, which are processed by the human resources cycle information system (see Chapter 15).

Accountants can play a key role in controlling costs by carefully assessing how changes in product mix affect the total manufacturing overhead. They should go beyond merely collecting such data, however, and identify the factors that drive the changes in total costs. This information can then be used to adjust production plans and factory layout. As Focus 14.1 explains, this may require redesigning the cost accounting system.

Accounting for Fixed Assets. Thus far we have focused on accounting for the costs associated with the production of inventory. The AIS also needs to collect and process information about investments in the property, plant, and equipment used in the production cycle. Indeed, such fixed assets represent a significant portion of total assets for many companies. Thus it is important to monitor this investment.

Fixed assets should be bar-coded. Bar coding enables quick and accurate periodic updating of the fixed asset data base. At a minimum, every organization should maintain the following information about each of its fixed assets: identifying number, serial number, location, cost, date of acquisition, vendor name and address, expected life, expected salvage value, depreciation method, depreciation charges to date, improvements, and maintenance services performed.

The procedures involved in authorizing the purchase of fixed assets vary, depending on the size of the purchase request. Large capital expenditures should first be recommended by a supervisor or manager, who provides details about expected cash flows and other costs and benefits of the proposed expenditure.

FOCUS 14.1 JIT + A New Cost Accounting System = Success For Harley-Davidson

THE ADOPTION of a JIT manufacturing system saved Harley-Davidson more than $22 million in less than one year by reducing its work-in-process inventory. After it switched to JIT, however, Harley-Davidson did not initially modify its cost accounting system to reflect the changes in the production process. This created several problems. Overhead, for example, continued to be allocated on the basis of direct labor. This meant that the overhead rate increased even though the amount of labor required to make a product decreased. Consequently, products with small differences in labor content were assessed large differences in total costs.

Another problem involved the practice of measuring plant performance based on period-end inventory absorption. This measure implied that as long as monthly goals were met, daily production goals were not that important. In a JIT environment, however, period-end performance measures are of little value for controlling operations. For example, failure to meet daily goals could cause an entire assembly line to shut down. Consequently, plant managers wanted continuous performance measures.

By the end of the second year following implementation of the JIT system, Harley-Davidson's accountants realized that the cost accounting system needed a major overhaul. They toured the factory to observe firsthand how the new production processes worked. This led to the following changes in the cost accounting system:

1. Detailed accounting for direct labor was eliminated. Direct labor now represented only 10% of product costs, and so it was combined with overhead into one account called conversion costs. Conversion costs were then applied to cost products according to process hours. This change not only simplified the accounting system, it reduced administrative costs dramatically (almost 62% of administrative costs under the old system related to collecting and reporting on direct labor!). In place of direct labor costs, plant managers received reports about the number of employees at work each day and daily overtime hours. This information was easy to collect and report on a daily basis; it also represented the most important controllable aspects of labor use in a JIT manufacturing system.
2. A *backflush* costing system was adopted. Backflush costing begins with the outputs of production and works backward to apply production costs to finished goods inventory and cost of goods sold. Costs are applied upon completion of production. In contrast, conventional cost accounting tracks costs through a work-in-process account as they are incurred. Thus backflush costing essentially eliminates the use of a separate work-in-process inventory account.

Together, these two changes greatly simplified Harley-Davidson's cost accounting system. They reduced the administrative costs of the system and made it possible to provide timely information to plant managers.

Source: William T. Turk, "Management Accounting Revitalized: The Harley-Davidson Experience," in *Readings in Management Accounting* (edited by S. Mark Young) (Englewood Cliffs, N.J.: Prentice-Hall), 1995, pp. 135–144.

All such recommendations should be reviewed by a senior executive or by an executive committee, and the various projects ranked in order of priority. Smaller capital expenditures (e.g., those costing $10,000 or less) can usually be purchased directly out of departmental budgets, which avoids a formal approval process. In either case, the output of this process is a document that provides formal authorization to acquire a particular fixed asset.

Due to the size of fixed asset purchases, most companies invite several competing vendors to provide bids. A document called a *request for proposal*

(RFP), which specifies the desired properties of the asset, is sent to each vendor. The capital investments committee reviews vendor responses and selects the best one.

Once a vendor has been selected, the acquisition of the asset may be handled through the regular expenditure cycle process, as described in Chapter 13. Specifically, a formal purchase order is prepared, receipt of the asset is formally documented using a receiving report, and a disbursement voucher is used to authorize payment to the vendor. The same set of processing controls and edit checks employed for other purchases should also be used for fixed asset acquisitions (for details, refer back to the discussion in Chapter 13). In the next section we will discuss the controls that should be in place for transactions involving the disposal of fixed assets, as well as all other production cycle activities.

CONTROL OBJECTIVES, THREATS, AND PROCEDURES

A second function of a well-designed AIS is to provide adequate controls in order to meet the following production cycle objectives:

1. All production and fixed asset acquisitions are properly authorized.
2. Work-in-process inventories and fixed assets are safeguarded.
3. All valid, authorized production cycle transactions are recorded.
4. All production cycle transactions are recorded accurately.
5. Accurate records are maintained and protected from loss.
6. Production cycle activities are performed efficiently and effectively.

The documents and records described in the previous section play an important role in achieving these objectives. Simple, easy-to-complete documents with clear instructions facilitate the accurate and efficient recording of transaction data. The inclusion of appropriate application controls, such as validity checks and field (format) checks, further increases the accuracy of data entry when using electronic documents. Providing space on paper and electronic documents to record who completed and who reviewed the form provides evidence that the transaction was properly authorized. Finally, prenumbering the documents facilitates checking that all transactions have been recorded.

Table 14.2 lists five major threats and exposures in the production cycle and the additional control procedures, besides adequate documents and records, that should be in place to mitigate them. As you will see in the following discussion, every company, regardless of its line of business, faces these threats. Therefore it is important to understand how the AIS can be designed to counter them.

Threat 1: Unauthorized Transactions

Unauthorized production can result in a supply of goods in excess of short-run demands, thereby creating potential cash flow problems because resources are tied up in inventory. Overproduction also increases the risk of carrying inventory

TABLE 14.2 Threats, Exposures, and Control Procedures in the Production Cycle

Threat	Exposure	Applicable Control Procedures
1. Unauthorized transactions	Overproduction and excess inventories Obsolescence Underproduction, stockouts, and lost sales Excess investment in fixed assets	Accurate sales forecasts Accurate inventory records Authorization of production Restricted access to production planning program and to blank production order documents Review and approval of capital asset expenditures
2. Theft or destruction of inventories and fixed assets	Loss of assets Overstated inventory records	Restricted physical access Documentation of all internal movements of inventory Proper segregation of duties Periodic physical counts of inventory, reconciled to records Assignment of accountability and responsibility for fixed assets Proper approval and documentation of all disposals of fixed assets Insurance
3. Recording and posting errors	Ineffective scheduling and planning Decision errors (product mix, product pricing, over/underproduction) Increased expenses and taxes on fixed assets that are incorrectly valued	Source data automation On-line data entry edit controls Periodic physical counts of inventory and fixed assets, and reconciliation of those counts to corresponding records
4. Loss of data	Loss of assets Ineffective decision making	Backup and disaster recovery procedures File labels Access controls Creation and review of logs of all computer activity
5. Inefficiencies and quality control problems	Increased expenses (scrap, rework, warranty repairs, sales returns and allowances) Loss of customer goodwill and future sales	Regular performance reports Exception reports highlighting variances from budget plan Measure throughput Measure cost of quality control

that becomes obsolete. In addition, the associated costs of storing and handling inventory increase expenses and reduce profitability. These problems can have significant negative effects on a company's finances. For example, in the early 1990s Herman's Sporting Goods, Inc. was turning over its inventory only 4 times a year; one of its competitors, Sports Authority, boasted turnover rates ranging from 8 to 12 times annually at each of its stores. The result? Herman's lost $18.5 million on $580 million in sales in 1993, whereas Sports Authority earned $10 million on only $412 million in sales.

A related threat is failing to produce enough goods to meet demand. This can result in lost sales and customer dissatisfaction. For example, Apple underestimated demand for its new Power Mac computers in 1995. Consequently, it could not follow its planned strategy of reducing prices to increase market share. Indeed, Apple's market share plummeted drastically due to the shortage of its new machines.

Over- and underproduction can be prevented by more accurate production planning. Improvement requires accurate and current sales forecasts and data about inventory stocks, information that can be provided by the revenue and expenditure cycle systems. In addition, information about production performance, particularly that concerning trends in total time to manufacture each product, should be collected regularly. All these sources of data should be used periodically to review and adjust the master production schedule.

Proper approval and authorization of production orders is another control to prevent overproduction of specific items. One means is to restrict access to the production scheduling program using passwords and an access control matrix. It is also important to ensure that the correct production orders are released. Closed-loop verification can accomplish this control: The production planner enters the product number and the system retrieves the description, order quantity, and other relevant data, and requests the user to verify that the correct production order is being released. Finally, if blank production order documents are used, access to them should be restricted. These documents should also be prenumbered and periodically accounted for to ensure that all production is authorized.

Unauthorized acquisition of fixed assets can result in overinvestment and reduced profitability. The procedures discussed earlier for reviewing, approving, and documenting fixed asset purchases can prevent this threat. Holding managers accountable for their department's return on the fixed assets provides additional incentive to control such expenditures.

Threat 2: Theft or Destruction of Inventories and Fixed Assets

Theft of inventories and fixed assets is a major threat to manufacturing companies. In addition to the loss of assets, thefts also result in overstated asset balances, which can lead to erroneous analyses of financial performance and, in the case of inventory, underproduction.

To reduce the risk of inventory loss, physical access to inventories should be restricted and all internal movements of inventory should be documented. Thus materials requisitions should be used to authorize the release of raw materials to production. Both parties involved should sign the requisition to acknowledge release of the goods to production. Requests for additional materials in excess of the amounts specified in the bill of materials should be documented and authorized by supervisory personnel. Move tickets should then be used to document subsequent movement of inventory through various stages of the production process. The return of any materials not used in production should also be documented.

Proper segregation of duties is also important to safeguard inventory. Maintaining physical custody of the raw materials and finished goods inventories is the responsibility of the inventory stores department; department or factory supervisors have primary responsibility for work-in-process inventories. The authorization function, represented by the preparation of production orders, materials requisitions, and move tickets, is the responsibility of the production planners or, increasingly, of the production information system itself. Bar-code scanners and on-line terminals are used to record movement of inventory, thereby maintaining accurate perpetual inventory records. Consequently, proper access controls and compatibility tests are important, to ensure that only authorized personnel have access to those records. Finally, inventory on hand should be periodically counted by an employee without any custodial responsibility. Any discrepancies between these physical counts and recorded amounts should be investigated.

Similar controls are needed to safeguard fixed assets. All fixed assets should be identified and recorded. Managers should be assigned responsibility and accountability for fixed assets under their control. Security measures should be in place to control physical access to fixed assets. Their disposal should be properly authorized and documented. A report of all fixed asset transactions should be printed periodically and sent to the controller, who should verify that each transaction was properly authorized and executed.

Finally, inventories and fixed assets are also subject to loss due to fire or other disasters. Therefore adequate insurance should be maintained to cover such losses and provide for replacement of those assets.

Threat 3: Recording and Posting Errors

Inaccurate recording and processing of production activity data can diminish the effectiveness of production scheduling and undermine management's ability to monitor and control manufacturing operations. For example, inaccurate cost data can result in inappropriate decisions about which products to make and how to set current selling prices. Errors in inventory records can lead to either over- or underproduction of goods. Inaccuracies in financial statements and managerial reports can distort analyses of past performance and the desirability of future investments or changes in operations.

The best control procedure to ensure that data entry is accurate is to automate data collection using bar-code scanners, badge readers, and other devices. When this is not feasible, on-line terminals should be used for data entry. Passwords and user IDs should be used to restrict access to authorized employees. In addition, an access control matrix should be used to limit access to only those portions of the data base that a particular employee needs to perform his or her job. Check digits and closed-loop verification should be used to ensure that information about the raw materials used, operations performed, and employee number are entered correctly. Validity checks, such as comparing raw materials part numbers with those listed in the bill of materials file, provide further assurance. Finally, to verify the accuracy of data base records, periodic physical counts of inventories should be made and compared with recorded quantities.

As with inventory, periodic inspections and counts of all fixed assets should be made, and those figures should be reconciled with recorded amounts. Overstated fixed assets increase expenses, through extra depreciation and higher property taxes. Understated fixed assets can also cause problems. For example, inaccurate counts of the number of personal computers in use can cause a company to unknowingly violate software license requirements.

Threat 4: Loss of Data

Loss of production data hinders the monitoring of inventory and fixed assets and makes it difficult to ensure that manufacturing activities are being performed efficiently and effectively. Therefore inventory and work-in-process records must be protected from loss or damage, both intentional and accidental. Regular backup of all data files is imperative. Additional copies of key master files, such as open production orders and raw materials inventory, should be stored off-site. All disks and tapes should have both external and internal file labels, to reduce the possibility of accidentally erasing important files.

Access controls are also important. The loss of production trade secrets can destroy a company. That is what happened to Recon Optical of Barrington, Illinois. One of its customers obtained access to its production data base, stole the company's trade secrets, and used that information to become a competitor of Recon. As a result, Recon Optical was forced to lay off 800 of its 1,000 employees. Although companies that are victimized in this manner can sue the perpetrator, any financial compensation may come too late to restore the business itself.

Unauthorized access also increases the risk of damage to important data files. A system of passwords and user IDs should be used to limit access to sensitive files. Moreover, access controls should also apply to terminals. For example, the system should be programmed to reject any attempts to alter inventory records from a terminal located in the engineering department. Finally, logs of all activities, especially any actions involving managerial approval, such as requests for additional raw materials or overtime, should be recorded and maintained for later review as part of the audit trail.

Threat 5: Inefficiencies and Quality Control Problems

Inefficiencies in production operations result in increased expenses. Quality control problems also increase expenses and may even reduce future sales. Thus manufacturing activities must be closely monitored and prompt action taken to correct any deviations from standards. It is sometimes possible to enlist customers as part of the quality control process. For example, after Netscape corrected a security weakness in its Internet access software, it offered rewards to any customer who found additional problems.

The AIS can help control efficiency and quality by preparing appropriate performance reports. In addition to traditional comparisons of actual and budgeted performance, measures of throughput and quality control should also be produced by the AIS.

Throughput: A Measure of Production Effectiveness. **Throughput** represents the number of good (nondefective) units produced in a given period of time. It consists of three factors, each of which can be separately controlled, as shown in the following formula[1]:

Throughput = (total units produced/processing time)
X (processing time/total time)
X (good units/total units)

Productive capacity, the first term in the formula, shows the maximum number of units that can be produced using current technology. Productive capacity can be increased in a number of ways, such as by improving labor or machine efficiency, by rearranging the factory floor layout to smooth the flow of materials, or by simplifying product design specifications.

Productive processing time, the second term in the formula, indicates the percentage of total production time used to manufacture the product. Productive processing time can be improved in a number of ways, such as by improving maintenance to reduce machine downtime or by better scheduling of material and supply deliveries to reduce wait time.

Yield, the third term in the formula, represents the percentage of nondefective units produced. Yield can be improved by such actions as using better-quality raw materials or improving worker skills.

Information About Quality Control. Information about quality costs can help companies determine the effects of actions taken to improve yield and identify areas for further improvement. Quality control costs can be divided into four areas:

1. *Prevention costs* are incurred to ensure that products are created without defects the first time.
2. *Inspection costs* are associated with testing to ensure that products do indeed meet quality standards.
3. *Internal failure costs* represent the costs incurred in producing units that are identified as being defective prior to their sale.
4. *External failure costs* result when defective products were sold to customers, such as product liability, loss of customer satisfaction, and damage to the company's reputation.

The ultimate objective of quality control is to minimize the sum of these four types of costs. This objective recognizes that there are trade-offs between categories. For example, increasing prevention costs can lower inspection costs as

---

[1]This formula was developed by Carole Cheatham in "Measuring and Improving Throughput," *Journal of Accountancy* (March 1990): 89–91.

well as internal and external failure costs. The experiences of Lockheed Martin at its Pike County plant in Troy, Alabama illustrate the potential benefits of increased attention to quality. Factory workers are organized in teams. Team members continuously monitor a number of quality measures and discuss ways to save time and money. Each new step in the manufacturing process begins by verifying the quality of the previous step. In this way, any quality problems are immediately brought to the attention of the person who made the mistake. Both workers then work together to fix the problem, thereby teaching each other how to do their jobs better. Management credits such procedures with cutting the defect rate by 82%, so that defects now occur only 0.0003 times per million operations. The bottom line effect of such quality is that the plant has never had a customer reject a single shipped product!

Elizabeth Venko agreed with LeRoy Williams that production managers at AOE should receive both throughput and cost of quality reports. She also discussed with him the behavioral effects of performance reporting. For example, measuring total production may encourage the buildup of inventories. Similarly, reimbursing departments for scrap and rework may be less effective in promoting quality control efforts than measuring and rewarding departments on the basis of yield. As a result of this discussion, LeRoy realized that he and Elizabeth will probably need to closely monitor the effects of any new performance reports and make appropriate modifications to them.

PRODUCTION CYCLE INFORMATION NEEDS AND DATA MODEL

A third function of the AIS is to provide information useful for decision making. In the production cycle, cost information is needed by internal and external users. Internally, management uses information about costs to make decisions about product pricing and product mix and to evaluate performance. Externally, costs must be properly matched with revenues when preparing financial statements. Traditionally, most cost accounting systems have been designed primarily to meet financial reporting requirements and have given only secondary attention to meeting the needs of production management. Consequently, in recent years traditional cost systems have been criticized for not providing adequate information to manage production operations in a modern manufacturing environment.

Criticisms of Traditional Costing Systems

The two major criticisms of traditional cost accounting systems are reflected in the issues raised in the chapter opening case for AOE: Overhead costs are inappropriately allocated to products, and performance measures do not accurately reflect the effects of factory automation.

Inappropriate Allocation of Overhead Costs. Traditional cost systems use volume-driven bases, such as direct labor or machine hours, to apply overhead to products. Many overhead costs, however, do not vary directly with production volume. Purchasing and receiving costs, for example, vary with the number of purchase orders processed and the number of shipments received from suppliers respectively. Setup and materials handling costs vary with the number of different batches that are run, not with the total number of units that are produced. Thus allocating these types of overhead costs to products on the basis of output volume overstates the costs of products manufactured in large quantities. It also understates the costs of products manufactured in small batches.

In addition, allocating overhead on the basis of direct labor input can distort costs across products. As investments in factory automation increase, the amount of direct labor used in production decreases. Consequently, the amount of overhead charged per unit of labor increases dramatically. As a result, small differences in the amount of labor used to produce two products can result in significant differences in computed product costs.

Inaccurate Performance Measures. In the modern manufacturing environment, the focus is on total quality management. Thus managers need more than information about the standard costs of inventory and variances. They also need information about how well the production process is functioning, including defect rates, breakdown frequency, percentage of finished goods completed without any rework, and percentage of defects discovered by customers. Although much of this information is collected in the production cycle information system, it is not integrated with cost data. Therefore operational performance measures are not directly linked with their financial consequences.

Indeed, in many companies the cost accounting system has been separate from the production operations information system. The former collects data about the costs of production, storing that information in the work-in-process file; the latter collects data about the physical aspects of manufacturing operations, storing that information in the open production order file. Both types of data are closely related, however, and both are needed for effectively managing the production process. For example, real-time information about production quality enables defects to be spotted and corrected immediately, before additional labor and materials are used. Therefore both cost and operational data should be integrated into one system.

The next two sections discuss two potential solutions to these criticisms. The first topic, activity-based costing, addresses the criticisms about the allocation of overhead costs. The second topic, an integrated data model, addresses the criticisms about the lack of integration of financial and operational measures of production cycle activities.

Activity-Based Costing[2]

Both job-order and process cost systems can be refined and improved by adopting activity-based costing. **Activity-based costing** is so named because it attempts to trace costs to the activities, such as grinding or polishing, that create them and only subsequently allocates those costs to products or departments.

---

[2] In this section, we provide an overview of activity-based costing, its effects on the AIS, and its benefits. For additional details on the mechanics of activity-based costing, see any leading cost accounting textbook.

An underlying objective of activity-based costing is to link costs to corporate strategy. Corporate strategy results in decisions about what goods and services to produce. Activities must be performed to produce these goods and services, which in turn incur costs. Thus corporate strategy determines costs. Consequently, by measuring the costs of basic activities, such as materials handling or processing purchase orders, activity-based costing provides information for evaluating the consequences of strategic decisions.

Activity-Based Costing Versus Traditional Cost Accounting. There are three significant differences between activity-based costing and traditional approaches to product costing:

1. Activity-based costing (ABC) systems attempt to directly trace a larger proportion of costs to products. Advances in information technology make this feasible. For example, bar coding facilitates tracking miscellaneous parts used in each product or process stage. ABC systems accountants observe production operations and interview factory workers and supervisors to obtain a better understanding of how costs relate to production.

2. ABC systems use a greater number of cost pools to accumulate indirect costs (manufacturing overhead). Whereas most traditional cost systems lump all overhead costs together, ABC systems distinguish three separate categories of overhead:

   - *Batch-related overhead.* Examples include setup costs, inspections, and materials handling. ABC systems accumulate these costs for a batch and then allocate them to the units produced in that batch. Thus products produced in large quantities have lower batch-related overhead costs per unit than do products produced in small quantities.

   - *Product-related overhead.* These costs are related to the diversity of the company's product line. Examples include research and development, expediting, shipping and receiving, complying with environmental regulations, and purchasing. ABC systems try to link these costs to specific products whenever possible. For example, if a company produces three products, one of which generates hazardous waste, an ABC system would charge only the latter product for all the costs of complying with environmental regulations. Other costs, such as purchasing raw materials, might be allocated across products on the basis of the relative number of purchase orders required to make each end product.

   - *Company-wide overhead.* This category includes such costs as rent or depreciation. These costs apply to all products; thus, ABC systems typically allocate them using departmental or plant rates.

3. The bases used to allocate manufacturing overhead in ABC systems are more likely to be cost drivers. A **cost driver** is anything that has a cause-and-effect relationship on costs. For example, the number of purchase

orders processed is one cost driver of purchasing department costs. That is, the total costs of processing purchase orders (e.g., purchasing department salaries, postage) vary directly with the number that are processed. As in this example, cost drivers in ABC systems are often nonfinancial variables. In contrast, traditional costing systems often use financial variables, such as dollar volume of purchases, as the bases for allocating manufacturing overhead.

Benefits of ABC Systems. ABC systems cost more to run than traditional cost systems because they require the collection of more production-related data, and in greater detail. ABC systems are also more complex, in part because more bases are used to allocate manufacturing overhead. Proponents of ABC systems argue that the increased costs and complexity provide two important benefits: (1) more accurate cost data results in better product mix and pricing decisions; and (2) more detailed cost data improves management's ability to control and manage total costs.

Better Decisions. Traditional cost systems tend to apply too much overhead to some products and too little to others, because too few cost pools are used. This leads to two types of problems, both of which AOE experienced. First, companies may accept sales contracts for some products at prices below their true cost of production. Consequently, although sales increase, profits decline. Second, companies may overprice other products, thereby inviting new competitors to enter the market. Ironically, if more accurate cost data were available, companies would find that they could cut prices to keep competitors out of the market and still make a profit on each sale. ABC systems avoid these problems because overhead is divided into three categories and applied using cost drivers that are causally related to production. Therefore product cost data is more accurate.

ABC data can also be used to improve product design. For example, Elizabeth Venko discovered that the costs associated with processing purchase orders can be used to calculate the purchasing-related overhead associated with each component used in a finished product. Engineering can then use this information, along with data on relative use of components across products, to identify unique components that could be replaced by lower-cost, more commonly used parts.

Improved Cost Management. Proponents argue that another advantage of ABC is that it clearly measures the results of managerial actions on overall profitability. Whereas traditional cost systems only measure spending to acquire resources, ABC systems measure both the amount spent to acquire resources and the consumption of those resources. This distinction is reflected in the following formula:

Cost of activity capability = cost of activity used + cost of unused capacity

To illustrate, consider the receiving function at a manufacturing firm like AOE. The total monthly employee cost in the receiving department, including salaries and benefits, represents the cost of providing this function—receiving shipments from suppliers. Assume that the salary expense of the receiving department is $100,000. Further, assume that the number of employees is sufficient to handle 500 shipments. The cost per shipment then would be $200. Finally, assume that 400 shipments are actually received. The ABC system would report that the cost of the receiving activity used is $80,000 ($200 times 400 shipments) and that the remaining $20,000 in salary expense represents the cost of unused capacity.

In this way, performance reports generated by ABC systems help direct managerial attention to how policy decisions made in one area affect costs in another area. For example, a purchasing department manager may decide to increase the minimum size of orders to obtain larger discounts for bulk purchases. This would also reduce the number of incoming shipments that must be handled by the receiving department, thereby increasing its unused capacity. Similarly, actions taken to improve the efficiency of operations, such as requiring vendors to send products in bar-coded containers, increase practical capacity and also create additional unused capacity. In either case, ABC performance reports highlight this excess capacity for managerial attention. Management can then try to improve profitability by applying that unused capacity to other revenue generating activities. If that is not possible, the excess capacity should be eliminated.

AIS Design Requirements for ABC Systems. Elizabeth Venko's research indicates that ABC systems impose several requirements on the AIS. First, the general ledger must be redesigned to fit the additional cost categories used by ABC. As shown in Focus 14.2, this task is not necessarily easy to accomplish. Second, ABC systems require extensive use of information technology in order to accumulate more precise data about cost drivers. Third, and perhaps most important, ABC systems require that both financial and nonfinancial measures of production activity be stored in an integrated manner. In the next section we discuss how the REA data model can be used to accomplish this integration.

Production Cycle Data Model

Figure 14.8 presents a simplified example of a data model for the production cycle of a manufacturing company, such as AOE. Four types of resources are shown: equipment and inventory accounts for raw materials, work-in-process, and finished goods. Two event entities are depicted: job operations captures data about labor activities, and machine operations tracks equipment usage. There are also two agent entities: factory workers and their supervisors. Finally, the figure also includes four abstract entities—bill of materials, production orders, job operations list, and machine operations list—that we will explain shortly.

Reading the E-R Diagram. To maximize its usefulness for cost management and decision making, production cycle data must be collected at the lowest possible level of aggregation. Therefore the event entities depicted in Fig. 14.8 do not correspond to the processes depicted in the level 0 DFD for the production cycle presented earlier. Rather, they represent the detailed activities that occur during the production operations stage (circle 3.0 in Fig. 14.2).

FOCUS 14.2 Adapting the General Ledger to ABC

THE ORIGINAL Bradford Soap Works Company manufactures private-label bar soap. It makes more than 20 different bases, which can then be combined with various additives and colors to produce about 5,000 types of soap each year. Until 1989 this complex manufacturing process was run on the expertise and "gut feel" of key employees. As the number of new products grew, however, Bradford began to experience wide swings in profitability even as total sales volume increased. In addition, management lost confidence in its ability to accurately estimate the profitability of new products.

These problems were solved by using a relational DBMS to support an ABC system. It took more than three years for Bradford to implement a successful ABC management system. One crucial and time-consuming step involved recasting the general ledger to match the ABC system's cost pool structure. This led to an almost 30% increase in the number of general ledger accounts. For example, instead of a single account for salaries, separate accounts were created for each major soap-making activity, such as milling and perfuming, as well as for indirect activities such as machine setup. Moreover, mapping ABC cost pools to general ledger accounts was not always a straightforward process, but involved many judgment calls and compromises. For example, there was no logical way to set up direct accounts linking utility use, such as electricity, to individual machines. Consequently, a single general ledger account was retained and a formula in the ABC system was created to allocate those costs to various machine pools.

Eventually, Bradford succeeded in mapping its ABC system to its general ledger. Twice each year, the ABC numbers are closed to the general ledger accounts. This allows Bradford to update its estimating data base (used to bid on new business) with the actual financial results of prior periods. In this way, Bradford can continuously learn from experience and refine the accuracy of its bidding process.

Although pleased with these results, Bradford's accounting staff plans to continuously improve and change its ABC management system. Specifically, they recognize that the accounting system must always reflect the production processes used on the shop floor. Otherwise, even the best ABC system will eventually become obsolete and useless.

Source: Francis Gammell and C. J. McNair, "Jumping the Growth Threshold Through Activity-Based Cost Management," *Management Accounting* (September 1994): 37–46.

Let us now examine Fig. 14.8 more closely, to see what it reveals about the nature of this production cycle. The abstract entity "bill of materials" is used to store information about the raw materials used to make a finished product. It includes data about the standard quantity of each raw material that should be used to make that product. Similarly, the abstract entities "job operations list" and "machine operations list" specify the labor and machine activities that need to be performed to manufacture each finished product. Both entities also store data about the standard time it should take to perform those operations.

Data about actual raw materials used in production is stored in the "raw material issuance" entity. Similarly, information about the actual job and machine operations performed, including the actual amount of time each activity took, are stored in the "job operations" and "machine operations" entities. Performance can be evaluated by comparing the data in these three event entities with the information about standards that is stored in the abstract type entities.

The "work-in-process" resource entity is used to collect and summarize data about the raw materials, labor, and machine operations used to produce a batch

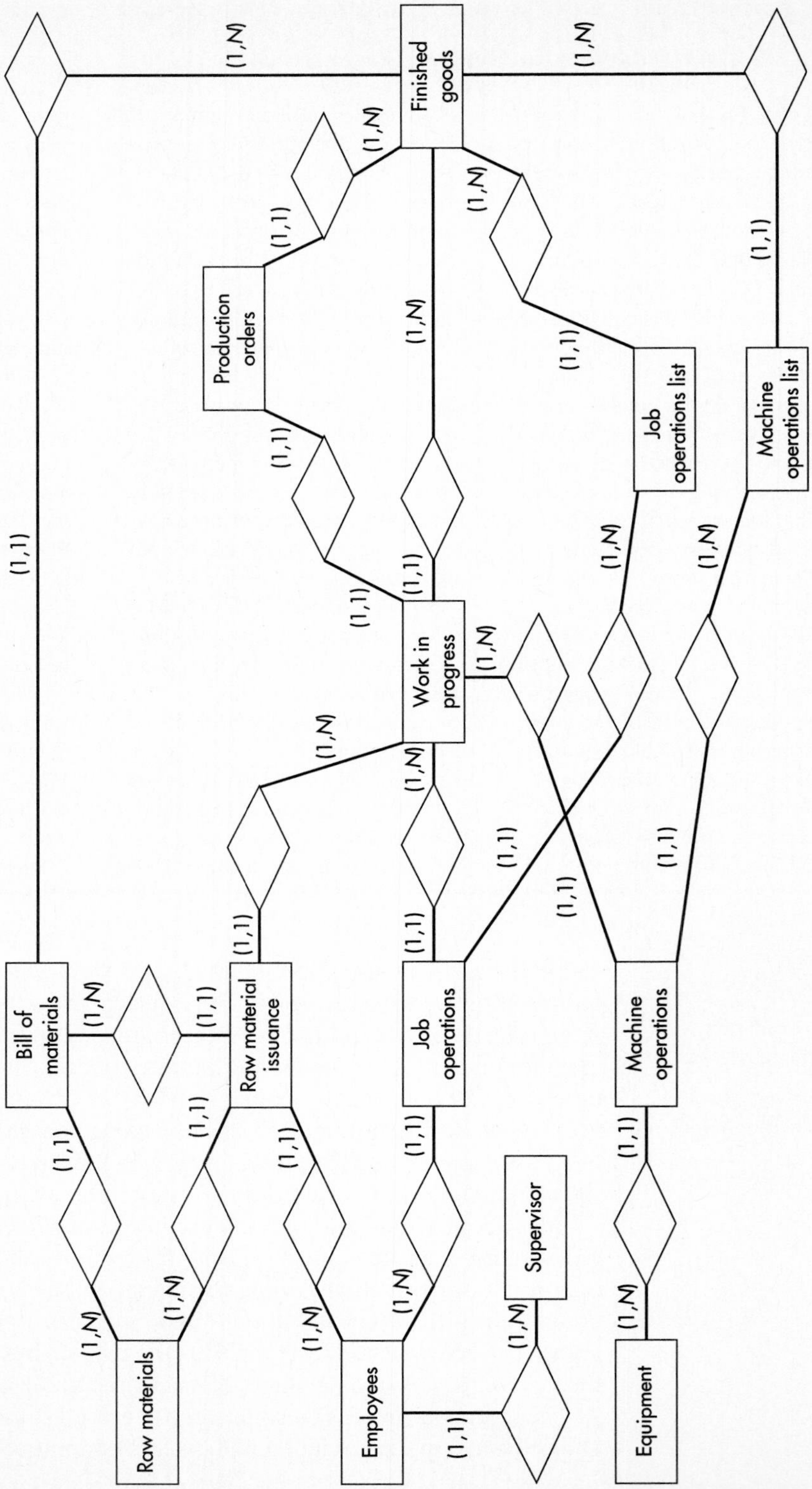

FIGURE 14.8
Partial REA Diagram for the Production Cycle

FIGURE 14.8 Continued

Table Name	Attributes (**primary key**, *foreign keys*, other attributes)
Raw materials	**Item number**, description, quantity on hand,...
Employees	**Employee number**, name, date hired,wage rate, *supervisor number*,...
Supervisor	**Employee number**, name, date hired, number of employees supervising,...
Equipment	**Equipment ID**, description, cost, depreciation method, accumulated depreciation, salvage value, estimated life,...
Bill of materials	**Bill of materials number**, *item number, finished goods number*, standard quantity needed,...
Raw materials issuance	**Raw materials issuance number**, date, time, *item number, employee number, WIP job number*, quantity issued,...
Job operations	**Job operation number**, description, *performing employee,WIP job number, job operations list number*, start time, stop time,...
Job operations list	**Operations list number**, description, standard time, activity level for standard, *finished good #*,...
Machine operation	**Machine operation number**, description, start time, stop time, *WIP job number, machine operations list number, equipment ID*,...
Machine operations list	**Machine operations list number**, description, standard time, *finished goods number*,...
Work in progress	**WIP job number**, start date, start time, end date, end time, quantity ordered, quantity produced, *production order number, finished goods number*,...
Finished goods	**Product number**, description, quantity on hand,...
Production order	**Production order number**, date, date needed, *finished good number*,...

of goods. The relationships between work-in-process and those three event entities are all one-to-many, reflecting the fact that each production run may involve a number of raw materials issuances, labor operations, and machine operations; each of those activities, however, is linked to a specific production run.

Figure 14.8 shows that there is a many-to-one relationship between employees and supervisors. This reflects the fact that currently at AOE each employee is assigned to a specific supervisor; each supervisor, however, is responsible for many employees. Should AOE change to a matrix style of organization, where each employee reports to several supervisors, the relationship between factory employees and supervisors would be modeled as being many-to-many.

Finally, the abstract "production orders" entity stores data about planned production activity. The relationship between it and the "finished goods" entity is modeled as being many-to-one, reflecting the fact that over time there are many production runs for each item. Although not shown in the diagram, the production order entity is also linked to customer order event in the revenue cycle.

Benefits of the Data Model. Examination of the table of attributes for the data model depicted in Fig. 14.8 shows that it effectively integrates both financial and nonfinancial measures of production cycle activities. Thus it facilitates multifaceted analyses of performance. For example, management can easily track variances related to raw materials usage, labor activities, and machine operations. Analyses of the "bill of materials" entity can identify which components are used in only a few finished products. This information can then be used to explore possible design modifications that would use more commonly used components. Thus the REA data model provides managers with access both to traditional financial cost data that can be used to evaluate performance and to operational data that can be used to plan changes in production methods. In addition, the data model depicted in Fig. 14.8 supports activity-based costing because it captures performance and cost data by each activity.

Figure 14.9 shows another advantage of the REA data model: the ability to easily share data across the revenue, expenditure, production, and human resource management cycles. Thus, when a new customer order is received, the system can quickly check current inventory levels. If additional production is needed to fill the order, the data is immediately routed to the planning and scheduling module. Once this is done, labor needs can be determined. This information is shared with the human resource management system to identify any needs for hiring temporary help or scheduling overtime. At the same time, information in the bill-of-materials is used to identify raw materials needs. That data is sent to the inventory control system, which compares it with current inventory levels and, if necessary, initiates purchase orders for required items. Thus well-designed data models facilitate the integration of a company's various information systems so that it can optimally respond to new customer orders.

The benefits of such coordination and information sharing can be dramatic. For example, Foxboro, a manufacturer of process controls and systems for oil and chemical refineries, cut its production cycle time from 16 to 6 weeks after it implemented an integrated production cycle data base. The new software enabled the design, engineering, purchasing, and manufacturing departments to share a wide range of data, including information about product specifications, the status of purchase orders, and production schedules. With more accurate and timely information, unforeseen delays in production schedules were all but eliminated. It was also easier to adjust the production schedule in response to changes in customer requirements. Moreover, the reduction in cycle time not only improved customer satisfaction, it also reduced work-in-process inventory levels by 76%.

In addition, such integrated systems enable retailers and manufacturers to share information in a manner that facilitates the move toward mass customization of products in the apparel industry. Instead of producing large lots of shoes or clothing, manufacturers can link their production and purchasing

FIGURE 14.9
Enterprise Resource Planning (ERP) System for Manufacturing

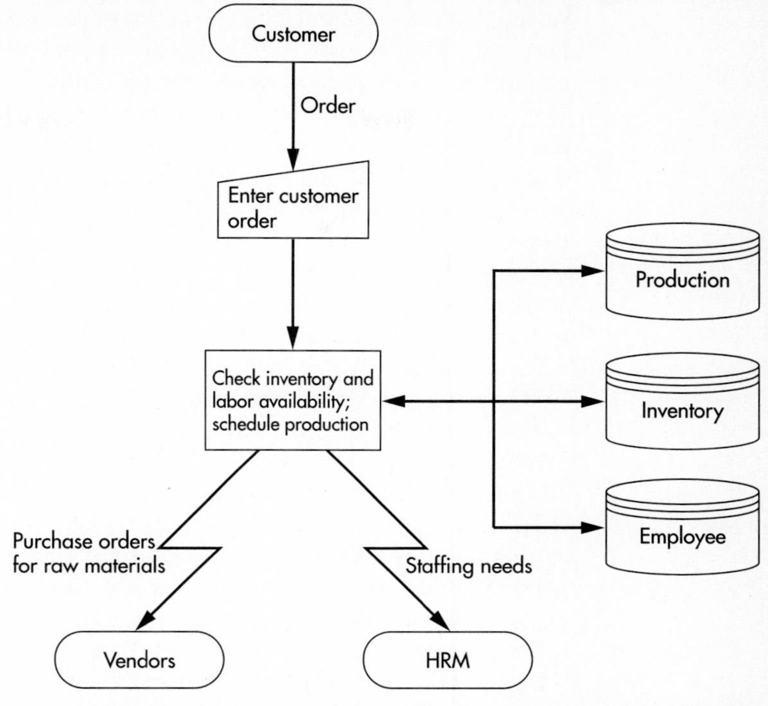

systems to a retailer's revenue cycle system. Actual production begins only after the retailer sends precise customer measurement data to the manufacturer.

Realization of these benefits, however, depends on the accuracy of the information in the data model. In a data base environment, this means that data entry edit and data base update controls are extremely important. Indeed, accuracy, or the lack thereof, can be costly. For example, Elizabeth Venko recalled reading that Red Devil, a manufacturer of tools and supplies for the do-it-yourself home remodeler, routinely overstocked inventory because it did not trust the accuracy of its inventory figures. After implementing a new integrated data base system that accurately tracked inventory, Red Devil was able to reduce its inventory by $2 million. Elizabeth wondered whether improving the accuracy of AOE's production cycle data base could yield similar savings.

SUMMARY AND CASE CONCLUSION

The production cycle consists of four basic activities: product design, production planning and scheduling, production operations, and cost accounting. Companies are continually investing in information technology to improve the efficiency of the first three activities. However, for a business to reap the full benefit of these changes, corresponding modifications must be made to the cost accounting portion of the AIS.

Indeed, upon completing her tour of the factory, Elizabeth Venko was convinced that some major changes were required in AOE's cost accounting system. For example, although AOE's production operations were highly automated, manufacturing overhead was still being allocated on the basis of direct labor hours. This resulted in distorted product costs due to small differences in the amount of direct labor used to assemble each item. Elizabeth decided that the solution was to do more than merely change the allocation base. Instead, AOE would implement activity-based costing. A number of different pools would be used to accumulate overhead costs, and the appropriate cost drivers would be identified for use in assigning those costs to specific products. Based on her research, including conversations with a controller at another company that had recently implemented an ABC system, Elizabeth believed that these changes would solve AOE's problems with product pricing and mix decisions. In addition, reports prepared by the ABC system would more fairly represent factory supervisor actions.

Elizabeth also decided that two major changes were needed in the reports produced by the AIS. First, data about all the costs associated with quality control, not just those involving rework and scrap, should be collected and reported. Second, performance reports should include nonfinancial as well as financial measures. Elizabeth realized that both of these changes would necessitate a redesign of AOE's production cycle data base. Based on her previous experience with redesigning AOE's revenue and expenditure cycle information systems, she decided that the best way to implement the required modifications would be to adopt a data model similar to the one depicted in Fig. 14.8.

Elizabeth discussed her plans in an executive meeting. LeRoy Williams was satisfied that the changes would indeed address his complaints about AOE's current production cycle information system. Stephanie Cromwell, vice president of finance, stated that resources were available to assign Elizabeth to carry out this project. Linda Spurgeon, AOE's president, supported the proposal and agreed to fund the necessary changes. Peter Wu, the vice president of human resources, was also impressed with Elizabeth's plans. In fact, he left the meeting resolved to secure Elizabeth's cooperation in revamping AOE's human resource management/payroll cycle information system, as soon as she completed her work on the production cycle.

KEY TERMS

- production cycle
- bill of materials
- operations list
- manufacturing resource planning (MRP-II)
- just-in-time (JIT) manufacturing systems
- master production schedule (MPS)
- production order
- materials requisition
- move tickets
- computer-integrated manufacturing (CIM)
- job-order costing
- process costing
- job-time ticket
- manufacturing overhead
- throughput
- activity-based costing
- cost driver

CHAPTER QUIZ

1. Most costs are locked in at which stage in the production cycle?
   a. Product design
   b. Production planning
   c. Production operations
   d. Cost accounting

2. Which report or measure provides the most information about production efficiency?
   a. Cost of quality report
   b. Activity-based cost reports
   c. Throughput
   d. MPS

3. The list of all components, and their quantities, used to make a finished good is found in the
   a. operations list.
   b. master production schedule.
   c. bill-of-materials.
   d. production order.

4. Information about labor used in production is captured on the
   a. move ticket.
   b. job-time ticket.
   c. operations list.
   d. bill-of-materials.

5. In an REA data model, information about standard labor hours is stored in which entity?
   a. Job operations
   b. Job operations type
   c. Work-in-process
   d. Employee

6. Activity-based costing can be used to refine
   a. job-order costing.
   b. process costing.
   c. both job-order and process costing.
   d. neither job-order nor process costing.

7. Which system is most likely to be used by a company that mass produces large batches of standard items in anticipation of customer demand?
   a. Job-order costing
   b. Standard costing
   c. Activity-based costing
   d. Process costing

8. The development of an MPS would be most effective in preventing which of the following threats?
   a. Recording and posting errors
   b. Loss of inventory
   c. Production of poor-quality goods
   d. Excess production

9. Which control procedure is probably least effective in reducing the threat of inventory loss?
   a. Limiting physical access to inventory
   b. Documenting all transfers of inventory within the company
   c. Regular materials usage reports that highlight variances from standards
   d. Periodically counting inventory and investigating any discrepancies between those counts and recorded amounts

10 The number of good units produced in a given period of time is called
   a. productive capacity.
   b. productive processing time.
   c. yield.
   d. throughput.

DISCUSSION QUESTIONS

14.1 When ABC reports indicate that excess capacity exists, management should either find alternative revenue enhancing uses for that capacity or eliminate it through downsizing. What factors influence management's decision? What are the likely behavioral side effects of each choice? What implications do those side effects have for the long-run usefulness of ABC systems?

14.2 How might some financial reporting requirements mandated by GAAP, such as absorption accounting, lead to undesirable behaviors by line managers?

14.3 American manufacturing efficiency is improving. Part of the credit is due to a form of CIM called soft manufacturing that increases production. Soft manufacturing entails the use of software and computer networks, rather than robots, to improve efficiency. Indeed, one of its tenets is that there can be too much automation of the manufacturing process. An often-cited example is that of a robot repeatedly trying to jam a bolt into an opening that is obviously too small. Do you think that soft manufacturing, with its emphasis on augmenting human workers with software, is a viable long-term strategy? Or do you see it as only a short-term solution until further research in artificial intelligence improves robot performance? Give reasons to support your opinion.

14.4 Some companies have eliminated the collection and reporting of detailed analyses on direct labor costs broken down by various activities. Instead, first-line supervisors are responsible for controlling the total costs of direct labor. The justification for this argument is that labor costs represent only a small fraction of the total costs of producing a product and are therefore not worth the time and effort to trace to individual activities. Do you agree or disagree with this argument? Why?

14.5 Typically, McDonald's produces menu items in advance of customer orders, based on anticipated demand. In contrast, Burger King produces menu items only in response to customer orders. Which system (MRP-II or JIT) does each company utilize? What are the relative advantages and disadvantages of each system?

14.6 Describe some of the trade-offs likely to arise when attempting to reduce the quality control costs associated with prevention, inspection, internal failure, and external failure.

14.7 Products for which demand is predictable and relatively stable are called staples; products for which demand is unpredictable and that have relatively short life cycles are referred to as innovative products. Identify examples of staples and innovative products. Discuss whether MRP-II or JIT manufacturing is appropriate for each type of product. What other implications does the type of product have on the value chain activities of inbound logistics, production, and outbound logistics?

PROBLEMS

14.1 Write a memo discussing the relationships and trade-offs among the concepts of accuracy, precision, and fairness in terms of allocating manufacturing overhead costs.

14.2 What internal control procedure(s) would best prevent or detect the following problems?

a. A production order was initiated for a product that was already overstocked in the company's warehouse.
b. Items of work-in-process inventory were stolen by a production employee.
c. The "rush order" tag on a partially completed production job became detached from the materials and lost, resulting in a costly delay.
d. A production employee prepared a materials requisition and used the document to steal $300 worth of parts from the raw materials storeroom.
e. A production worker entering job time data using an on-line terminal mistakenly entered 3,000 instead of 300 in the quantity completed field.
f. A production worker entering job-time data using an on-line terminal mistakenly posted the completion of operation 562 to production order 7569 instead of production order 7596.
g. A parts storeroom clerk issued parts in quantities 10% lower than those indicated on several materials requisitions and stole the excess quantities.
h. A parts storeroom clerk stole electronics components and covered up the loss by submitting a form to the accounting department indicating that the missing parts were obsolete and should be written off as worthless.
i. The quantity-on-hand balance for a key component shows a negative balance.
j. Materials requisitions are used to authorize the release of the standard quantities of raw materials needed to manufacture a product. At times, production employees use a lesser amount of materials to finish the product and steal the remaining parts.
k. A factory supervisor accesses the operations list file and inflates the standards for work completed in his department. Consequently, future performance reports show favorable budget variances for that department.

14.3 Refer to Fig. 14.8 to answer the following questions:

a. The job operations list entity stores information about the standard time it should take to perform a specific job operation. It also indicates whether this operation takes place at the unit, batch, or production run level. The work-in-process entity collects data by production runs. How would you calculate the labor time standards for each production run? How could the data model be modified to make this calculation easier?

b. The diagram shows that information about the bill-of-materials is stored as an entity. Why not store that information as a many-to-many relationship between raw materials and finished goods?
c. The relationship between employees and activities is one-to-many. Is any other type of relationship cardinality possible? For which types of companies?
d. Adopting a product life cycle approach to product costing would include linking marketing and sales costs to specific products. Expand Fig. 14.8 to show how this approach could be accomplished.
e. Modify the REA diagram to include information about equipment repairs and maintenance.
f. Specify the set of on-line application controls that should be used to control updates to the assembly event table.
g. Specify the access controls that should be designed into a system based on this data model. Specifically, which employees should be allowed to access each table, and what operations (read, write, update, delete) should they be permitted to perform?

14.4 You have been hired to design a production information system for a new company that will manufacture custom automobile wheels. List all the documents (paper and electronic) that should be included in the system, and specify the purposes they serve.

14.5 You are a management consultant for a large public accounting firm. One of your firm's clients is the Willard Corporation, a medium-sized manufacturer of karaoke machines and other audio equipment. You have been hired to advise on the following problems:

- Customer order fulfillment has declined from 90% to 50% during the past year.
- Production costs have risen dramatically because of increased charges for overtime and rework. In addition, idle time due to materials shortages and machine downtime has increased.

Required:

Develop a questionnaire that could be used to interview the controller and obtain a better understanding of these problems and their potential causes.

14.6 You have recently been hired as the controller for a small manufacturing firm. One of your first tasks is to develop a report measuring throughput for each of the company's three production departments.

Required:

Describe what data you will need to collect and how you could most efficiently and accurately collect it.

14.7 Table 14.3 represents the first draft of a report on quality control costs developed by one of your assistants.

Required:

a. Based on the data sources used for this report, what are the most efficient and effective ways to collect the key information needed?
b. Suggest improvements in the design of this report.

14.8 What is the purpose of each of the following control activities?

a. Periodic reconciliation of the work-in-process subsidiary ledger to the work-in-process control account.
b. Documentation of the return of any scrapped products to inventory stores.
c. Use of an MPS to schedule production.
d. Periodic counts of fixed assets and reconciliation of those counts with the fixed asset subsidiary ledger.
e. The use of move tickets to document transfers of work-in-process between factory departments.
f. The prenumbering and periodic accounting of all materials requisitions.
g. Access to the system that generates production orders is controlled by the use of passwords.
h. A list of all transactions involving the acquisition or disposal of fixed assets is printed monthly and reviewed by the controller.

TABLE 14.3 Quality Cost Report for Problem 14.7

Quality Cost Report				
June 2000				
Cost Type	**June 2000**	**June 1999**	**YTD 2000**	**YTD 1999**
Prevention:				
QC Admin.	350	450	1800	1700
QC Services	400	550	2100	2200
Training	750	900	4300	4000
Work Safety	400	200	2500	1000
Total Prevent	1900	2100	10,700	8900
Appraisal:				
Inspection	900	1200	5000	5300
Analysis	600	800	4000	4900
Supplier	800	400	4200	2500
Total Appraise	2300	2400	13,200	12,700
Internal Failure:				
Rework	700	1000	3000	4000
Scrap	800	1100	6000	6500
Work. Comp.	500	800	2800	3500
Overtime	600	200	3400	1000
Overruns	500	900	4500	5300
Total Internal	3100	4000	19,700	20,300
External Failure:				
Complaints	800	1200	5600	6500
Returns	900	1300	6300	9000
Freight on returns	500	750	3400	5400
Total External	2200	3250	15,300	20,900

CASE 14.1 ANYCOMPANY, INC.—AN ONGOING COMPREHENSIVE CASE

Visit a local company and obtain permission to study its production information system (you may use the same company you identified to complete this case in previous chapters). Write a report that includes the following:

1. DFDs of each of the four major steps in the production cycle (design, planning, operations, and cost accounting).
2. A list of all paper and electronic documents used by the company, with copies if possible. Evaluate the design of each document.
3. A data model, in the form of an REA diagram, of all the information stored in the system.
4. A description of how the system updates the master files (or data base) after each type of transaction occurs (materials requisition, machine operation, etc.). Draw a systems flowchart for each step in the production cycle.
5. A list and evaluation of the adequacy of the control procedures used to ensure transaction processing accuracy and validity.
6. Your opinion of whether the cost accounting reports produced by the system help managers make good decisions. Suggest changes to improve the use of cost accounting data to help the company attain its strategic objectives.

CASE 14.2 THE CONTROLLER AND CIM

Examine the issues of the *Journal of Accountancy* and *Management Accounting* for the last two years. Write a brief report on one current development in factory automation and its effects on the AIS. Be sure to describe the controller's role in either initiating or responding to the change. In addition, discuss its effect on the risk of the various production cycle threats.

CASE 14.3 JOSEPH BRANT MANUFACTURING

The Joseph Brant Manufacturing Company makes athletic footwear. Processing of production orders is as follows: At the end of each week, the production planning department prepares a list of shoes and quantities to be produced during the next week. Using this list as a source, data entry clerks key in production order release records onto a temporary disk file. Once data entry has been completed, a production order preparation program accesses the operations list (stored on a permanent disk file) and prepares a production order for each shoe to be manufactured. For each new production order, the program (1) prints three copies of a production order document, (2) writes the production order to the open production order master file stored on disk, and (3) prints an operations card identifying each operation that needs to be performed to manufacture that style of shoe.

The operations cards are used as turnaround documents. Each card is sent to the factory department where the operation will be performed. After completing an operation, factory employees mark the elapsed time, quantity completed, and other pertinent data on the card and return it to computer operations. A scanner is then used to read and write the operations data onto a temporary disk file. At the end of each day, this file is processed to update the open production order master file. Once this update has been completed, the program generates departmental production schedules for the next day.

Required:

1. Prepare both a data flow diagram and a systems flowchart of all operations described.
2. Describe a comprehensive set of control procedures that should be included in each system. Organize your answer by listing the potential threats and specifying the control procedures that would best address them.

ANSWERS TO CHAPTER QUIZ

1. a **2.** c **3.** c **4.** b **5.** b **6.** c **7.** a **8.** d **9.** c **10.** d

CHAPTER 15

The Human Resources Management/Payroll Cycle

LEARNING OBJECTIVES

After studying this chapter, you should be able to

- Describe the major business activities and related data processing operations performed in the human resources management (HRM)/payroll cycle.
- Assess the relative benefits of using new developments in information technology to improve the efficiency of HRM/payroll cycle activities.
- Document HRM/payroll cycle activities.
- Describe basic governmental reporting requirements relating to HRM and payroll activities, and explain what information must be collected to meet those requirements.
- Identify the major threats in the HRM/payroll cycle, and evaluate the adequacy of various internal control procedures for dealing with them.
- Explain the key decisions that need to be made in the HRM/payroll cycle, and identify the information required to make those decisions.
- Read a data model (REA diagram) of the HRM/payroll cycle.

Integrative Case: Alpha Omega Electronics

Peter Wu has just been hired as the new vice president for human resources at Alpha Omega Electronics (AOE). When hired, Peter was told that his first priority was to correct two weaknesses in AOE's existing human resources management (HRM)/payroll system. First, payroll processing costs have been rising steadily for years, yet the current system does not provide adequate service. For example, employees are unhappy with the lengthy delays required to obtain information about their benefits and retirement plans. Moreover, Linda Spurgeon, AOE's president, wants to provide employees with an expanded flexible benefits plan. Doing so, however, will further increase the demands on the existing system. Thus Peter must find a way to improve the efficiency and responsiveness of AOE's payroll system.

A second weakness with AOE's current HRM/payroll system is its inability to track employee skill development. Consequently, department managers have tended to hire externally to meet new staffing needs, rather than promoting or transferring existing employees. This practice has hurt employee morale. It also impedes evaluating the effectiveness of AOE's investment in training and continuing education. Thus Peter's other task is to find a way to improve the effectiveness of AOE's HRM system.

Peter noted that AOE, like many companies, has separate HRM and payroll systems. The payroll system, which is under the control of the accounting department, produces employee paychecks and maintains the related records required by government regulations. The payroll system uses batch processing: Hourly employees are paid biweekly, and salaried employees and those on commission are paid monthly. The HRM system, which is run by the human resources department, maintains files on employee job history, skills, and benefits; these files are updated weekly. Each system maintains its own separate files, sometimes storing the same data, such as pay rates, in different formats. Thus Peter was not surprised to learn that it was difficult to prepare reports that combined HRM and payroll data.

Peter decided to begin by examining how to improve the payroll processing system, because it handles the routine transactions affecting human resources. He met with Elizabeth Venko, AOE's controller, to discuss how to improve the efficiency of the payroll system. Elizabeth explained how the new methods being used to collect factory labor time data (see Chapter 14) should streamline the initial stages of payroll processing. She added that it may be possible to use information technology to improve the efficiency of other stages of the payroll process. Peter then inquired about the likelihood of redesigning the payroll data base in order to integrate it with the HRM system. Elizabeth said this was possible and agreed to develop a plan to address the following issues:

1. How can AOE use recent advances in information technology (IT) to process payroll more efficiently, while still meeting all government regulations?
2. How can the payroll system be modified to provide employees with direct access to information about their benefits and retirement plans, without creating new threats to the system's integrity?
3. How can a skills inventory system be implemented to provide operating managers with the information they need to make staffing assignments? Can this skills inventory system be integrated with the payroll system so that AOE can track the costs and benefits of training programs?

As you read this chapter, think about how AOE's HRM and payroll systems could be improved in order to resolve these questions.

INTRODUCTION

The **human resources management (HRM)/payroll cycle** is a recurring set of business activities and related data processing operations associated with effectively managing the employee work force. Some of the more important activities include the following tasks:

1. Recruitment and hiring
2. Training
3. Job assignment
4. Compensation (payroll)
5. Performance evaluation
6. Discharge

In addition, as discussed in Chapter 14, payroll costs are also allocated to products and departments, for use in product pricing and mix decisions and to evaluate performance.

Tasks 1 and 6 are performed once for each employee; tasks 2–5 are performed repeatedly for as long as the employee works for the company. Moreover, in most companies these six activities are split between two separate systems. Task 4, compensating employees, is the primary function of the payroll system. The other five steps are performed by the HRM system. In many companies, these two systems are organizationally separate: The HRM system is usually the responsibility of the director of human resources, and the payroll system is managed by the controller.

This chapter focuses primarily on the payroll system, because it is one of the largest and most important components of the AIS. Moreover, the payroll system must be designed to meet government regulations as well as management's information needs. Indeed, incomplete or erroneous payroll records not only impair decision making but can also result in fines and imprisonment! Thus the design of an efficient and effective payroll system is vital.

It is also important to have a well-designed HRM system. Employees' knowledge and skills are an extremely valuable asset and must be carefully managed, developed, and maintained. Therefore companies need effective HRM systems to help assign appropriate employees to different tasks and to facilitate monitoring the continuous development of the organization's intellectual assets.

OVERVIEW

Figure 15.1 presents a context diagram of the payroll system, depicting its relationships with the HRM system and with the other parts of the AIS. This figure shows five major sources of inputs to the payroll system. The HRM department provides information about hirings, terminations, and pay-rate changes due to

FIGURE 15.1
Context Diagram of the Payroll Portion of the HRM/Payroll Cycle

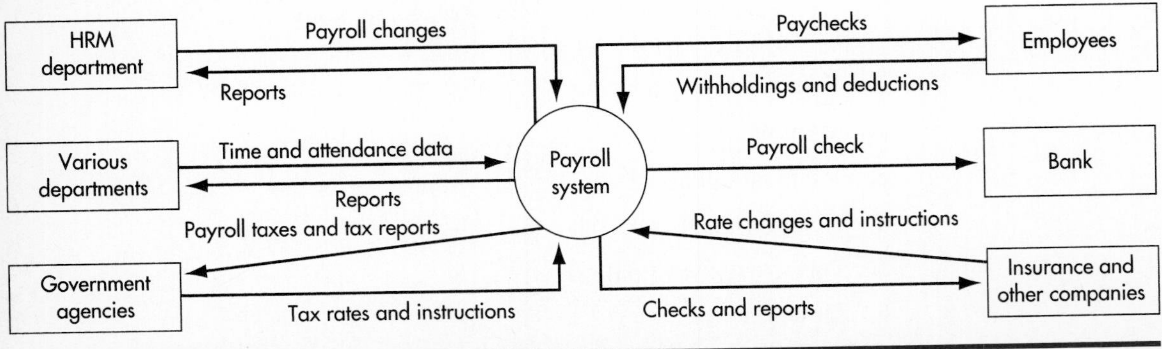

raises and promotions. Employees initiate changes in their discretionary deductions (e.g., contributions to retirement plans). The various departments provide data about actual hours worked by employees. Government agencies provide tax rates and instructions for meeting regulatory requirements. Similarly, insurance companies and other organizations provide instructions about how to calculate and remit various withholdings.

Checks are the principal output of the payroll system. Employees receive individual paychecks in compensation for their services. A payroll check is sent to the bank to transfer funds from the company's regular accounts to its payroll account. Checks are also issued to government agencies, insurance companies, and other organizations to meet company obligations (e.g., taxes and insurance premiums). In addition, a variety of reports, which we discuss later in the chapter, are prepared for internal and external use.

As noted earlier, an organization's most valuable asset is its employees. Their knowledge and skills affect the quality of the goods and services provided to customers. Indeed, research indicates that employees' attitudes toward their jobs and the company predicts the quality of their interaction with customers, which in turn predicts future financial performance. Moreover, in professional service organizations, such as accounting and law firms, labor costs represent the major expense incurred in generating revenues. Even in manufacturing firms, where direct labor costs represent only a fraction of total direct costs, employees are a key cost driver in that the quality of their work affects both overall productivity and product defect rates. Thus it is not surprising to find that some stock analysts believe that a company's human resources may be worth several times the value of its tangible assets, such as inventory, property, and equipment.

Nevertheless, the AIS has not traditionally been used to measure or report on the status of a company's human resources. One reason is that the assets reported in financial statements represent resources the organization owns but has not yet consumed. Human resources, however, are not owned by the company. Consequently, the value of human resources has traditionally been recognized only when they are used, at which time they are either recorded as wages and salary expenses or, in the case of direct labor in manufacturing firms, included as part of the cost of inventory.

This situation is in the process of changing. Companies like Dow Chemical have created new executive positions with such titles as director of intellectual assets. Among their responsibilities is the measurement and development of the organization's human resources. Moreover, as Focus 15.1 shows, some companies, like Skandia Group, Scandinavia's largest financial services company, have even begun to include human resources information in their annual reports. Indeed, some banks, including the Canadian Imperial Bank of Commerce, are beginning to request and use information about a company's employees in making loan decisions. These banks want this data because they believe that such "soft" assets often represent a better credit risk than "hard" assets like office buildings and land. Indeed, many information technology companies, such as Microsoft, own relatively few hard assets; instead, their market value reflects primarily the skills and knowledge of their employees.

FOCUS 15.1 Measuring and Reporting "Soft" Capital

SKANDIA GROUP, a financial services company, represents what is probably the most innovative and advanced approach to measuring and reporting the value of its human intellectual resources. In 1991 the company hired the corporate world's first director of intellectual capital, and in 1993 it released its first annual report on the value of those assets.

Skandia divides intellectual capital into two categories: human and structural. Human capital is the company's employees and their knowledge, which can be increased and developed through hiring and training. Structural capital represents the organizational resources used to leverage individual human capital so that it can be effectively used throughout the organization. Structural capital includes such assets as information systems, knowledge of market channels and customers, and managerial skills. It is increased by finding ways to institutionalize individual knowledge or by capturing it in the form of expert systems, decision rules, or new procedures. For example, Skandia has captured the basic knowledge required to open an office in a new country and formalized it as a set of standard procedures. This process has allowed it to cut in half the time and costs associated with entering a new country. Skandia's director of intellectual capital believes that structural capital is even more valuable than the human capital, because it will not quit or hire on with a competitor and can be used over and over again.

Skandia's director of intellectual capital works closely with the controller to develop multiple measures of intellectual capital. For example, both the number of new products resulting from employee suggestions and the number of suggestions are recorded. The ratio of the former to the latter is then used as one measure of the quality of employee suggestions. A number of measures have been developed to measure the efficiency and effectiveness with which the company's intellectual capital is being used: (1) administrative expenses as a percentage of revenues and compared with the revenue generated per employee, (2) the investment in information technology per employee, and (3) both the number and average size of new accounts. Eventually, Skandia hopes to be able to correlate trends in these measures with changes in traditional measures of financial performance.

Source: Thomas A. Stewart, "Your Company's Most Valuable Asset: Intellectual Capital," *Fortune* (October 3, 1994): 68–74.

Unfortunately, many companies only realize the value of such intellectual capital after they have lost it through overaggressive downsizing. For example, in the mid-1990s Digital Equipment Corp. eliminated hundreds of sales and marketing jobs in its health industries group as part of a major reorganization. In doing so, Digital disrupted longstanding customer relationships and lost valuable customer service knowledge. Consequently, many Digital customers turned to IBM and other competitors.

These examples underscore the need to effectively manage and develop a company's intellectual resources. To do this, the AIS must be designed to do more than just record time and attendance data and prepare paychecks. Instead, the payroll system should be integrated with the HRM system so that management has easy access not only to data about employee-related costs, but also to information about skills and knowledge.

The remainder of this chapter is organized in terms of the three basic functions provided by the AIS: processing transactional data, safeguarding the organization's assets, and providing information for decision making. We begin by describing the basic activities in the payroll cycle. In this section we also explore opportunities for using new developments in information technology (IT) to improve the effectiveness and efficiency of those activities. Next we discuss the control objectives of the HRM/payroll cycle and describe applicable control procedures for mitigating the major potential threats in this cycle. We conclude this chapter with a discussion of key decisions in the HRM/payroll cycle and identify the information needed to make those decisions. Then we present a data model that effectively integrates payroll data with the information produced by and maintained in the HRM system.

PAYROLL CYCLE ACTIVITIES

Figure 15.2 shows the seven basic activities performed in the payroll cycle. Payroll is one AIS application that continues to be processed in batch mode, because (1) paychecks are prepared periodically (either weekly, biweekly, or monthly) and (2) most employees are paid at the same time. Figure 15.3 depicts a typical batch-oriented HRM/payroll system like that used by AOE. We will refer to Fig. 15.3 as we discuss the seven activities depicted in Fig. 15.2, to show the opportunities for using developments in IT to improve the efficiency and effectiveness of payroll processing.

Update Master Payroll File

The first activity in the HRM/payroll cycle involves updating the payroll master file to reflect various types of payroll changes: new hires, terminations, changes in pay rates, or changes in discretionary withholdings (circle 1.0 in Fig. 15.2). This information is provided by the HRM department. Although payroll is processed in batch mode, Fig. 15.3 shows that the HRM department has on-line access to make these changes to the payroll master file. Appropriate edit checks, such as validity checks on employee numbers and reasonableness tests for the changes being made, are applied to all payroll change transactions.

It is important that all payroll changes are entered in a timely manner and are properly reflected in the next pay period. Records of employees who quit or are fired should not be deleted immediately, however, because some year-end reports require data about all employees who worked for the organization at any time during the year.

Update Tax Rates and Deductions

The second activity in the HRM/payroll cycle involves updating information about tax rates and other withholdings (circle 2.0 in Fig. 15.2). These changes are made by the payroll department but are not shown in Fig. 15.3 because they occur infrequently. They happen whenever updates about changes in tax rates and other payroll deductions are received from various government units and insurance companies.

FIGURE 15.2
Level 0 DFD for the Payroll Cycle

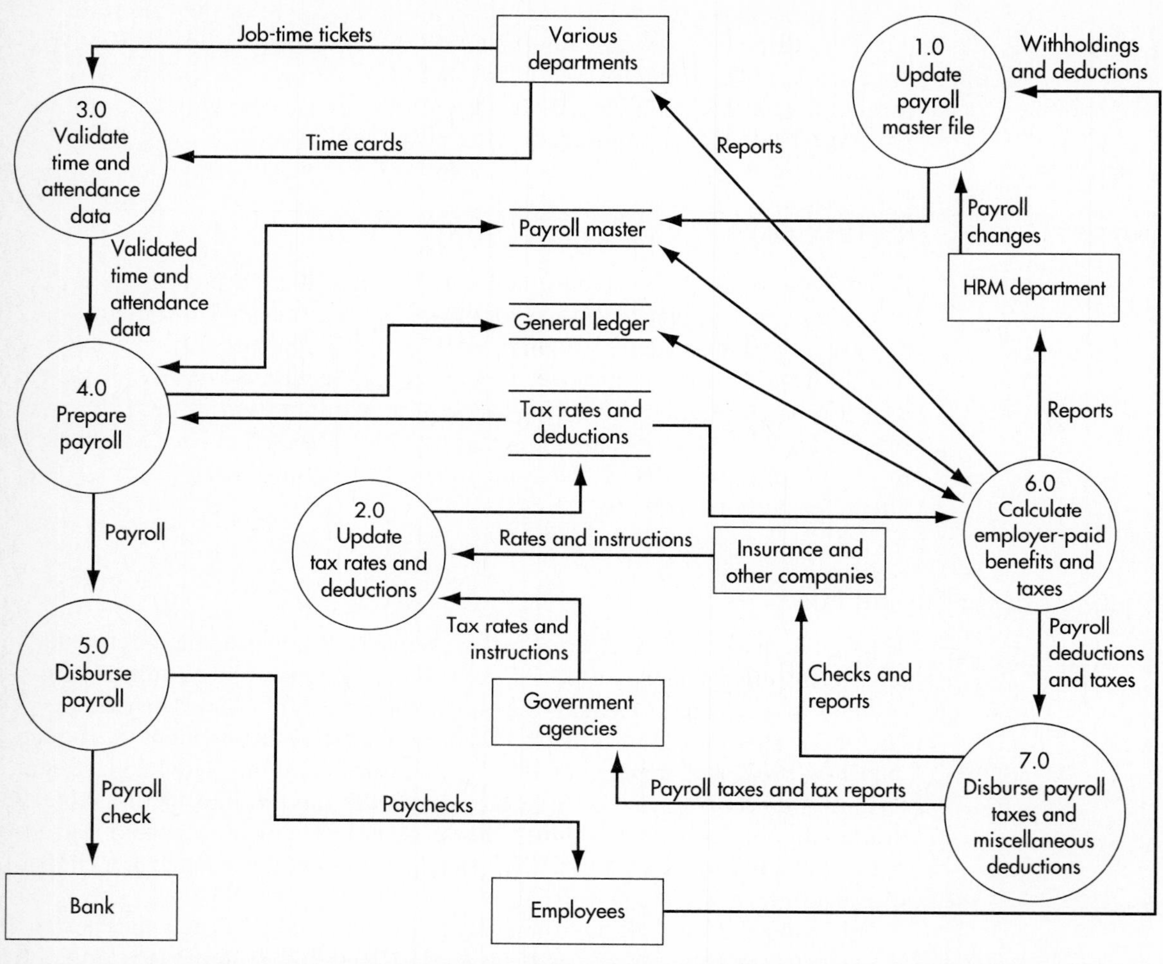

Validate Time and Attendance Data

The third step in the payroll cycle is to validate each employee's time and attendance data (circle 3.0 in Fig. 15.2). This information comes in various forms, depending on an employee's pay status.

Pay Schemes. For those paid on an hourly basis, most companies use an employee **time card,** which records the employee's arrival and departure times for each work shift and totals the hours worked during a pay period. As discussed in Chapter 14, manufacturing companies also use job-time tickets to record data about the time spent on each job. This data is used to allocate labor costs among various departments, cost centers, and production jobs. The total

FIGURE 15.3
Flowchart of the Payroll System–Batch Processing at AOE

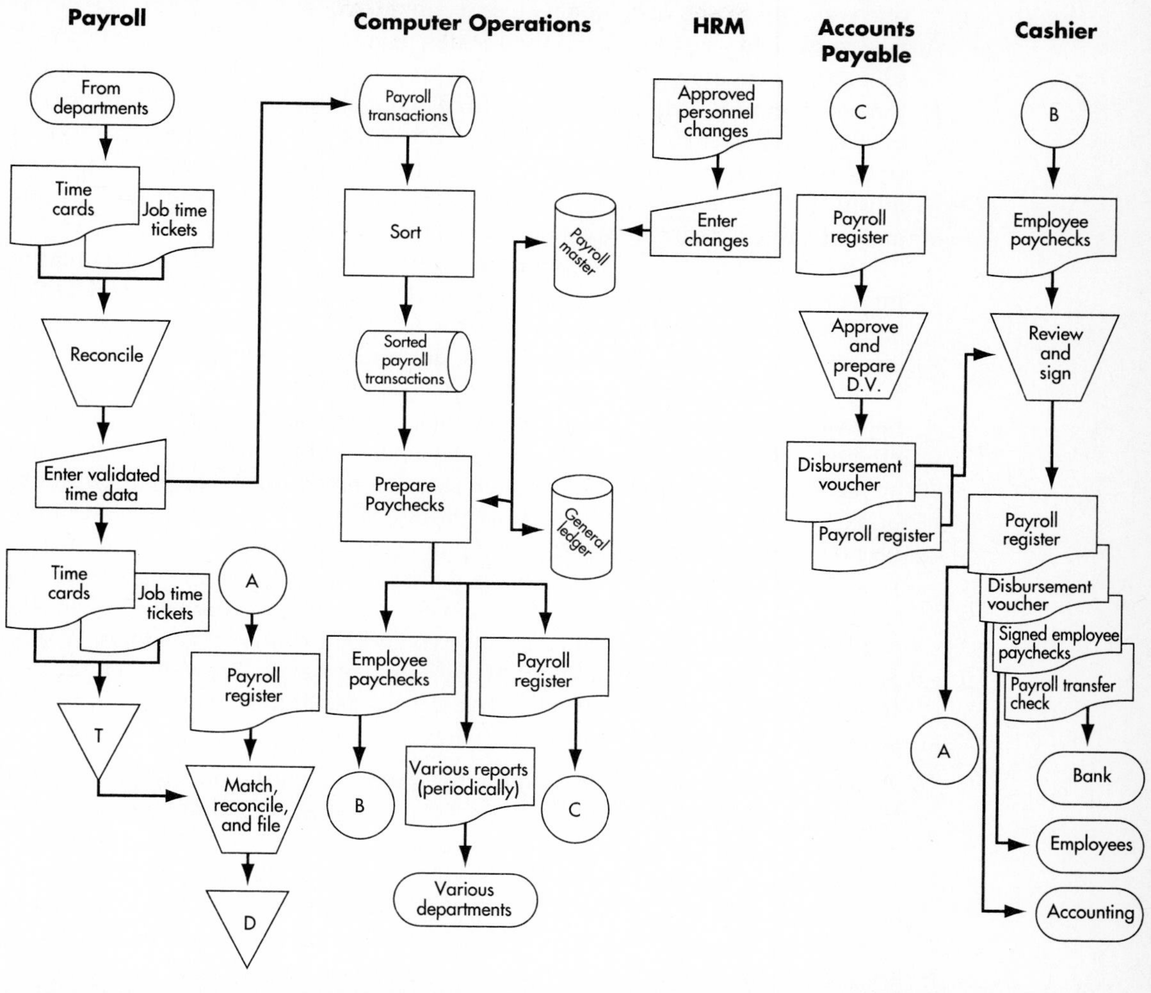

hours on the job-time ticket should equal those on the time card. The reconciliation of these two documents is an important control function performed by the payroll system.

Employees who are paid a fixed salary, such as managers and professional staff, seldom record their labor efforts on time cards. Instead, their presence on the job is usually informally monitored by their supervisors. Professionals in many service organizations, such as accounting, law, and consulting firms, usually self-report the time they spend on each client. This data is the basis for billing clients.

Sales staff often are paid either on a straight commission or on a salary plus commission basis. This requires careful recording of the amount of sales made by each employee. In addition, some sales staff are paid bonuses for exceeding targets. Increasingly, U.S. companies are extending the use of such incentive bonuses to employees other than sales staff, in order to motivate greater productivity and better work quality. For example, Nucor Corporation, one of the largest steel producers in the United States, pays its steel workers an hourly rate set at approximately 60% of the industry average, plus a bonus based on the tons of steel produced and shipped. Many companies are also offering nonexecutive employees stock options. Indeed, Starbucks, the coffee store chain, gives stock options to all employees. It claims that doing so has affected employee attitudes and behavior, as they now actively look for ways to improve service and cut costs, so that the value of their compensation package rises.

The use of incentives and bonuses requires that the payroll system and the information systems of sales and other cycles be linked in order to collect the data used to calculate bonuses. Moreover, as Focus 15.2 shows, if they are to be effective, bonus incentive systems must be carefully designed.

Indeed, poorly designed incentive pay schemes can result in undesirable behavior. For example, Sears Automotive experienced unintended negative effects from implementing a new incentive plan. In the early 1990s it instituted an incentive system that paid its repair staff a commission based on the amount of parts sold and labor performed. The intent was to focus employee attention on how their efforts affected the company's bottom line. The result, however, was a scandal in which it was alleged that Sears employees recommended unnecessary repairs in order to boost their own pay. The alleged abuses reduced public trust in Sears Automotive and led to lower revenues. Wisely, Sears finally abandoned this incentive system. This story illustrates that the key to a successful incentive plan is careful consideration of how the incentive scheme is likely to affect employee behavior.

Procedures. Figure 15.3 shows that the payroll department is responsible for validating employee time records. For factory workers, validation involves comparing the total time worked, as recorded on the time cards, with the time spent on each job, as recorded on the job-time tickets. The payroll clerk calculates batch totals, such as record counts and hash totals of hours worked, and enters them along with the time data. The batch totals are recalculated by the computer after subsequent processing steps, to ensure that payroll is processed for all employees.

Payroll transaction data are entered through on-line terminals. This enables errors to be detected at the time the data is being entered. The edit checks performed on each time and attendance record include the following:

- Field checks for numeric data in the employee number and hours worked fields
- Limit checks on the hours worked field
- Range checks on pay rates
- A validity check of the employee number

Opportunities for Using Information Technology. Payroll processing can be made more efficient by collecting employee time and attendance data electronically, instead of on paper documents. This can reduce the time, and potential errors, associated with manually recording, verifying, and finally entering employee time and attendance data. For example, badge readers can be used

FOCUS 15.2 Designing Effective Bonus Pay Schemes

EXECUTIVE compensation has long included bonuses and incentives linked to corporate performance. Increasingly, companies are beginning to extend such plans to all their employees. In 1988, slightly over half of medium- and large-sized U.S. companies had some form of incentive or bonus pay scheme for their nonsales staff employees; by 1994, this number had jumped to almost two-thirds. The major objective of extending bonus pay plans beyond the executive level is to motivate all employees to increase their productivity and quality.

Incentive pay schemes can be quite effective. For example, after Xel Communications, a Colorado manufacturer of telecommunications equipment, implemented an incentive system that included team-based goals, such as improving on-time delivery, average production time dropped from 30 days to 3. Novadyne Computer Company implemented an incentive plan to encourage its service engineers to solicit continuing maintenance contracts while providing on-site repair calls. In its second year, the program brought in over $800,000 of additional revenue. One of the greatest success stories involving the use of incentive plans is Nucor Corporation. The North Carolina–based company, which began making steel in the 1970s, credits its success in becoming the fifth-largest U.S. steel producer to the fact that all of its employees, whether they work in the factory or the office, are covered by some form of incentive pay.

The key to achieving such success, however, depends on how the incentive plan is designed. To be effective, an incentive pay scheme should have the following characteristics:

1. *Attainable goals.* Unrealistic targets can reduce morale and performance.
2. *Controllable goals.* Employees must believe their efforts will influence achievement of the established goal. For example, Monsanto Company faced resistance when it tried to link incentives for factory workers to overall plant financial performance, because that factor was affected by too many things beyond the direct control of the employees.
3. *Goals congruent with corporate objectives.* Incentive plans must be designed to motivate the appropriate behavior. For example, linking bonuses to plant safety measures could encourage employees to cover up any on-site accidents or injuries. Similarly, basing bonuses on individual or work-cell output in a JIT manufacturing plant is counter to the JIT philosophy of maximizing throughput and minimizing work in process. To combat this, Nucor rewards production work cells on the basis of tonnage actually shipped to customers.
4. *Measurable goals.* It can be difficult to quantify productivity for many office tasks. One approach, adopted by companies like American Express and GTE, is to survey customer satisfaction periodically. Although such measures may be subjective, they at least provide some basis for measuring performance.
5. *Periodic review of goals.* In accordance with Total Quality Management (TQM) philosophy, performance goals need periodic increases in order to achieve additional productivity gains. Change must be done in a manner, however, that does not create unrealistic expectations regarding base standards. Otherwise, employees may be motivated to produce at a level near, but below, existing standards so that those standards are not raised.

Sources: Howard Gleckman, Sandra Atchison, Tim Smart, and John A. Byrne, "Bonus Pay: Buzzword or Bonanza?" *Business Week* (November 14, 1994): 62–64; and Gillian Flynn, "Non-sales Staffs Respond to Incentives," *Personnel Journal* (July 1994): 33–38.

to collect job-time data for production employees. That data is then automatically fed to the payroll processing system. Similarly, electronic time clocks can transmit time and attendance data directly to the payroll processing program. As discussed in Chapter 14, AOE is planning to implement these techniques to automate collection of time and attendance data for its factory workers.

Similar procedures can be used for professional service staff. For example, AT&T's internal service staff use Touch-Tone telephones to log in time spent on various tasks, thereby eliminating the use of paper time sheets. The payroll program applies edit checks to verify the accuracy, and reasonableness, of the data at the time it is entered.

Prepare Payroll

The fourth step in the payroll cycle involves preparing payroll (circle 4.0 in Fig. 15.2). Data about the hours worked is provided by the department in which the employee works and usually is confirmed or signed off by his or her direct supervisor. Pay rate information is obtained from the payroll master file. As shown in Fig. 15.3, this information can be updated only by the HRM department. Thus file maintenance (updating the payroll master file) is performed by someone other than the person responsible for actual transaction processing (payroll preparation). This separation of duties helps to prevent payments being made to nonexistent workers. Paychecks can be prepared only for employees who are listed in the payroll master file, but the person responsible for preparing paychecks cannot add new records to this file.

Procedures. Figure 15.3 shows that payroll processing is performed in the computer operations department. First, the payroll transaction file is sorted by employee number, so that it is in the same sequence as the payroll master file. If the organization is processing payrolls from several divisions, each of these payroll transaction files must also be merged (this step is not shown in Fig. 15.3).

The sorted time data file is then used to prepare employee paychecks. For each employee, the payroll master file record and corresponding transaction record are read and gross pay is calculated. For hourly employees, this process involves multiplying the number of hours worked by the wage rate and then adding any applicable premiums for overtime or bonuses. For salaried employees, gross pay is a fraction of the annual salary, where the fraction reflects the length of the pay period. For example, a salaried employee paid monthly would receive 1/12 of his or her annual salary each pay period.

Next, all payroll deductions are summed and the total is subtracted from gross pay to obtain net pay. Payroll deductions fall into two broad categories: payroll tax withholdings and voluntary deductions. The former include federal, state, and local income taxes, as well as Social Security taxes. Voluntary deductions include contributions to a pension plan; premiums for group life, health, and disability insurance; union dues; and contributions to various charities.

At this time the year-to-date fields for gross pay, deductions, and net pay in each employee's record in the payroll master file are updated. Maintaining accurate cumulative earnings records is important for two reasons. First, because Social Security tax withholdings and other deductions have cutoffs, the company must know when to cease deductions for individual employees. Second, this information is needed to ensure that the appropriate amounts of taxes and other deductions are remitted to government agencies, insurance companies, and other organizations (such as the United Way). In addition, this information needs to be included in the various reports that must be filed with those entities.

Finally, the payroll register and employee paychecks are printed. The **payroll register** is a report that lists each employee's gross pay, payroll deductions, and net pay in a multicolumn format; it is often accompanied by a separate **deduction register,** which lists the miscellaneous voluntary deductions for each employee. Figure 15.4 provides examples of both reports. The payroll register is also used to authorize the transfer of funds to the company's payroll bank account. Employee paychecks also typically include an earnings statement. The **earnings statement** lists the amount of gross pay, deductions, and net pay for the current period, as well as year-to-date totals for each category.

As each payroll transaction is processed, the system also allocates labor costs to the appropriate general ledger accounts by checking the code on the job-time ticket record. The system maintains a running total of these allocations until all employee payroll records have been processed. These totals, along with the column totals in the payroll register, form the basis for the summary journal entry, which is posted to the general ledger after all paychecks have been printed. Table 15.1 describes some of the additional reports produced by the payroll system.

Opportunities for Using Information Technology. One way to cut costs and improve efficiency is to produce and distribute payroll reports electronically, rather than on paper. In addition, IT can also be used to improve

FIGURE 15.4

Sample Payroll and Deduction Registers

Alpha Omega Electronics				**PAYROLL REGISTER**				**Period Ended 12/03/2000**	
					Deductions				
Employee No.	Name	Hours	Pay Rate	Gross Pay	Fed. Tax	FICA	State Tax	Misc.	Net Pay
37884	Jarvis	40.0	6.25	250.00	35.60	18.75	16.25	27.60	151.80
37885	Burke	43.6	6.50	295.10	42.40	22.13	19.18	40.15	171.24
37886	Lincoln	40.0	6.75	270.00	39.20	20.25	17.55	27.90	165.10
37887	Douglass	44.2	7.00	324.10	46.60	24.31	21.07	29.62	202.50

Alpha Omega Electronics				**DEDUCTION REGISTER**		**Period Ended 12/03/2000**	
		Miscellaneous Deductions					
Employee No.	Name	Health Ins.	Life Ins.	Retirement	Union Dues	Savings Bond	Total Misc.
37884	Jarvis	10.40	5.50	7.50	4.20	0.00	27.60
37885	Burke	11.60	5.50	8.85	4.20	10.00	40.15
37886	Lincoln	10.40	5.20	8.10	4.20	0.00	27.90
37887	Douglass	10.20	5.50	9.72	4.20	0.00	29.62

TABLE 15.1 Examples of Commonly Generated HRM/Payroll Cycle Reports

Report Name	Contents	Purpose
Cumulative earnings register	Cumulative year-to-date gross pay, net pay, and deductions for each employee	Used for employee information and annual payroll reports
Work force inventory	List of employees by department	Used in preparing labor-related reports for government agencies
Position control report	List of each authorized position, job qualifications, budgeted salary, and position status (filled or vacant)	Used in planning future work force needs
Skills inventory report	List of employees and current skills	Useful in planning future work force needs and training programs
Form 941	Employer's quarterly federal tax return (showing all wages subject to tax and amounts withheld for income tax and FICA)	Filed quarterly
Form W-2	Report of wages and withholdings for each employee	Sent to each employee for use in preparing their individual tax returns; due by January 31
Form W-3	Summary of all W-2 forms	Sent to federal government along with a copy of all W-2 forms; due by February 28
Form 1099-Misc.	Report of income paid to independent contractors	Sent to recipients of income for use in filing their income tax returns; due by January 31
Various other reports to government agencies	Data on compliance with various regulatory provisions, state and local tax reports, etc.	To document compliance with applicable regulations

employee access to their benefits and earnings records. For example, employees at many companies, such as Bristol-Myers Squibb and Sears, can use the telephone to find out about their current benefits options and make changes in withholdings, profit sharing, and medical coverage. Employees at Federal Express can make similar changes through on-line terminals. Increasingly, many companies are also providing access to HRM data through corporate intranets. As explained in Focus 15.3, providing such capabilities to employees improves the quality and reduces the costs of HRM services.

Disburse Payroll

The next step is actual disbursement of paychecks to employees (circle 5.0 in Fig. 15.2). Most employees are paid either by check or by direct deposit of the net pay amount into the employee's bank account because, unlike cash payments, both methods provide a means to document the amount of wages paid.

Procedures. Figure 15.3 shows that once paychecks have been prepared, the payroll register is sent to the accounts payable department for review and approval. A disbursement voucher is then prepared to authorize the transfer of funds from the company's general checking account to its payroll bank account. Payroll checks should not be drawn on the organization's regular bank account. Instead, for control purposes, a separate payroll bank account should be used. This limits the company's loss exposure to the amount of cash in the separate payroll account.

The disbursement voucher and payroll register are then sent to the cashier. The cashier reviews the payroll register and disbursement voucher and then prepares and signs a check transferring funds to the company's payroll bank account. The cashier also reviews, signs, and distributes the employee paychecks. Thus the duties of authorizing and recording payroll transactions are segregated from the actual distribution of paychecks. Any unclaimed paychecks are promptly redeposited in the company's bank account by the cashier. As an added control to prevent the creation and distribution of fraudulent paychecks, a list of unclaimed paychecks is sent to the internal audit department for further investigation.

FOCUS 15.3 Using Technology to Boost HRM Productivity

MANY FIRMS are finding that their HRM function is using the corporate intranet to improve efficiency and effectiveness. Significant gains can be realized because much of the work traditionally done by HRM departments involves record keeping and administrative tasks. Indeed, experts estimate that about 80% of employee questions are routine enough to be answered through an intranet without requiring any direct involvement of the HRM staff. Moreover, corporate intranets and extranets allow many transactions traditionally processed by the HRM department to be outsourced to the employees themselves. For example, Compaq Computer Corporation lets employees use browser software and the corporate intranet to manage their 401(k) accounts. Volkswagen of North America lets its workers make decisions about health care coverage by going directly to Aetna's web site. Such uses of technology not only cut costs, but also enable the transactions to be completed more quickly than they would be if the HRM department had to be involved.

Web technology also makes hiring and internal reassignment tasks easier. For example, Allied Signal has assembled a data base of approximately 100,000 resumes, which it can quickly search to find employees or potential employees who possess the specific skills required for a new project. The company estimates that during the first six months of use the system cut its recruiting costs by $750,000.

In addition to cutting costs, the use of intranets improves the accuracy of the HRM data base because employees can easily check and correct any errors. But perhaps the greatest benefit is the ability to more effectively share knowledge. Information posted on the corporate intranet can be quickly accessed by anyone who needs it. For example, all of Motorola's employees throughout the world can easily search the intranet to find the information they need, or to locate the individual who might be able to help them solve a particular problem.

Source: Samuel Greengard, "HR's Great Enabler," *IndustryWeek* (September 15, 1997), URL: http://www.industryweek.com/internet/091597/ihr0915.html.

Finally, the payroll register is returned to the payroll department, where it is filed by date along with the time cards and job-time tickets. The disbursement voucher is sent to the accounting clerk, who uses it to update the general ledger.

Opportunities for Using Information Technology. Direct deposit is one way to improve the efficiency and reduce the costs of payroll processing. Employees who are paid by direct deposit generally receive a copy of the paycheck indicating the amount deposited along with an earnings statement. The payroll system must generate a series of payroll deposit files, one for each bank through which payroll deposits are made. Each file contains a record for each employee whose account is maintained at a particular bank. Each record includes the employee's name, Social Security number, bank account number, and net pay amount. These files are sent electronically, using EDI, to each participating bank. The funds are then electronically transferred from the employer's bank account to the employee's. Thus direct deposit eliminates the need for the cashier to sign individual payroll checks. The cashier does, however, have to authorize the release of funds from the organization's regular checking account.

Direct deposit provides several cost savings to employers. First, the cost of purchasing, processing, and distributing paper checks is eliminated. Second, bank fees and postage expenses are reduced. Third, payroll bank reconciliations can be done more quickly. These savings are partially offset by the loss of float, which represents the employer's use of the funds between the time the checks are drawn and when they are presented for payment. On balance, however, the savings associated with direct deposit generally exceed its costs; consequently, most companies now offer their employees the option of direct deposit payment and encourage them to elect this form of payment.

Payroll Service Bureaus. Another way to reduce payroll processing costs is by outsourcing this function to a payroll service bureau. A **payroll service bureau** maintains the payroll master file for each of its clients and performs the payroll processing activities described in this section. At the end of each pay period, each client sends time and attendance data to the payroll service bureau, along with information about personnel changes. The payroll service bureau uses that data to prepare employee paychecks, earnings statements, and a payroll register. It also periodically produces employee W-2 forms and other tax-related reports.

Payroll service bureaus are especially attractive to small- and medium-sized businesses, for the following reasons:

- *Reduced costs.* Payroll service bureaus benefit from the economies of scale associated with preparing paychecks for a large number of companies. They can charge fees that are typically less than the cost of doing payroll in-house. The use of a payroll service bureau also saves money by eliminating the need to develop and maintain the expertise needed to comply with the constantly changing tax laws.
- *Privacy.* To prevent potential morale problems, many companies do not want employees to know the salaries of their coworkers. Use of a payroll service bureau provides increased control over access to payroll data.

- *Freeing up of computer resources.* The use of a payroll service bureau eliminates a major AIS application: payroll. The freed up computing resources can then be used to improve service in other areas, such as sales order entry.

The major drawback associated with the use of a payroll service bureau is the difficulty of fully integrating the payroll system with the HRM system. Thus, as the number of employees grows, the cost and time required to prepare management reports on the utilization of human resources increases. Consequently, many large organizations continue to process payroll in-house.

Calculate Employer-Paid Benefits and Taxes

Some payroll taxes and employee benefits are paid directly by the employer (circle 6.0 in Fig. 15.2). For example, employers must pay Social Security taxes, in addition to the amounts withheld from employee paychecks. Circular E, the *Employer's Tax Guide* published by the IRS, provides detailed instructions about an employer's obligations for withholding and remitting payroll taxes and for filing various reports.

Federal and state laws also require employers to contribute a specified percentage of each employee's gross pay, up to a maximum annual limit, to federal and state unemployment compensation insurance funds. In addition, employers often contribute some or all of the amounts to pay for their employees' health, disability, and life insurance premiums. Many companies also offer their employees **flexible benefit plans,** under which each employee receives some minimum coverage in medical insurance and pension contributions, plus additional benefit credits that can be used to acquire extra vacation time or additional health insurance. These plans are sometimes called cafeteria-style benefit plans because they offer a menu of options. Finally, many employers offer and contribute toward a choice of retirement savings plans.

Providing these additional services and benefits places increased demands on a company's HRM/payroll system. For example, the HRM staff of a large company with thousands of employees can spend a considerable amount of time just responding to 401(k) plan inquiries. Moreover, employees want to be able to make changes in their investment decisions on a timely basis. The use of information technology, such as that discussed in Focus 15.3, provides a means to satisfy employee demands for such service without increasing costs.

Disburse Payroll Taxes and Miscellaneous Deductions

The final activity in the payroll process involves paying the payroll tax liabilities and the other voluntary deductions of each employee (circle 7.0 in Fig. 15.2). An organization must periodically prepare checks or use electronic funds transfer to pay the various tax liabilities incurred. The timing of these payments is specified by the respective government agencies. In addition, the funds voluntarily withheld from each employee's paycheck for various benefits, such as a payroll savings plan, must be disbursed to the appropriate organizations.

CONTROL OBJECTIVES, THREATS, AND PROCEDURES

A second major function of the AIS in the HRM/payroll cycle is to provide adequate internal controls to ensure meeting the following objectives:

1. All payroll transactions are properly authorized.
2. All recorded payroll transactions are valid.
3. All valid, authorized payroll transactions are recorded.
4. All payroll transactions are accurately recorded.
5. Applicable government regulations regarding remittance of taxes and filing of payroll and HRM reports are met.
6. Assets (both cash and data) are safeguarded from loss or theft.
7. HRM/payroll cycle activities are performed efficiently and effectively.

The various documents and records (e.g., time cards, payroll register) described in the previous section play an important role in achieving these objectives. Simple, easy-to-complete documents with clear instructions facilitate the accurate and efficient recording of payroll transactions. The use of appropriate application controls, such as validity checks and field (format) checks, further increases the accuracy of data entry when using electronic documents. Providing space on both paper and electronic documents to record who completed and who reviewed the form provides evidence that the transaction was properly authorized. Finally, prenumbering all documents facilitates checking to verify that all transactions have been recorded.

Table 15.2 lists the major threats in the HRM/payroll cycle and the applicable control procedures for mitigating those threats. Every company, regardless of its line of business, faces these threats. Therefore it is important to understand how the AIS can be best designed to counter them.

Threat 1: Hiring Unqualified or Larcenous Employees

Hiring unqualified employees can increase production expenses; hiring a larcenous employee can result in the theft of assets. Both threats are best dealt with by appropriate hiring procedures. Skill qualifications for each open position should be stated explicitly in the position control report. Candidates should be asked to sign a statement on the job application form that confirms the accuracy of the information being submitted and consents to a thorough background check of their credentials and employment history. It is especially important to verify job applicants' skills and references, including possession of college degrees, because research suggests that approximately 30% of resumes contain false or embellished information. The presence of any misstatements on resumes should be a warning sign about the applicant's honesty.

TABLE 15.2 Threats, Exposures, and Control Procedures in the HRM/Payroll Cycle

Threat	Exposure	Control Procedures
1. Hiring of unqualified or larcenous employees	Increased expenses Lower productivity Theft	Sound hiring practices, including verification of job applicants' skills, references, and employment history
2. Violation of employment law	Fines Civil suits	Thorough documentation of hiring procedures
3. Unauthorized changes to the master payroll file	Increased expenses Inaccurate records and reports Loss of assets (cash)	Segregation of duties Access controls
4. Inaccurate time data	Incorrect expenses and internal reports Over/underpayment of employees	Automation of data collection Application controls Reconciliation of time card and job time tickets
5. Inaccurate processing of payroll	Inaccurate records and poor decision making Penalties for violation of tax law Reduced morale, if all employees not paid	Batch totals and other application controls Payroll clearing account
6. Theft or fraudulent distribution of paychecks	Increased expenses Loss of assets (cash)	Direct deposit Paycheck distribution by someone independent of payroll process Investigation of all unclaimed paychecks Restricted access to blank paychecks Prenumbering and periodic accounting for all paychecks Separate payroll checking account, run as an imprest fund Independent reconciliation of the payroll bank account
7. Loss or unauthorized disclosure of payroll data	Loss of assets Reduced morale Employee lawsuits	Access controls Backup procedures Encryption

Threat 2: Violation of Employment Law

The government imposes stiff penalties on firms that violate provisions of employment law. In addition, organizations can also be subject to civil suits by alleged victims of employment discrimination. In this case, the best control procedure is careful documentation of all actions involved in advertising, recruiting, and hiring new employees in order to demonstrate compliance with the applicable government regulations.

Threat 3: Unauthorized Changes to the Payroll Master File

Unauthorized changes to the payroll master file can result in increased expenses if wages, salaries, commissions, or other base rates used to determine employee compensation are falsified. These problems also result in inaccurate reports on labor costs, which in turn can lead to erroneous decisions.

Proper segregation of duties is the key control procedure for dealing with this threat. As shown in Fig. 15.3, only the HRM department should be able to update the payroll master file for hirings, firings, pay raises, and promotions. This restriction prevents someone with access to paychecks from creating fictitious employees or altering pay rates and then intercepting those fraudulent checks. In addition, all changes to the payroll master file should be reviewed and approved by someone other than the person recommending the change. Traditionally, such approval has involved reading and signing a transaction document. For changes processed through on-line terminals, the system must be designed to verify the identity and authority of the persons making and approving the request. A report documenting these changes should also be sent to each department supervisor for review.

Controlling access to the payroll system is also important. Indeed, in a data base environment, access controls are vital because many previously separate functions are now performed solely by the system. The system should be programmed to compare user IDs and passwords to an access control matrix that (1) defines what actions each employee is allowed to perform and (2) confirms what files he or she is allowed to access. Payroll clerks, for example, should not be permitted to change employee pay rates.

Threat 4: Inaccurate Time Data

Inaccuracies in time and attendance records can result in increased labor expenses and erroneous labor expense reports. Moreover, inaccuracies can either hurt employee morale (if paychecks are incorrect or missing) or result in payments for labor services not rendered. Automation can reduce the risk of unintentional inaccuracies in time data. Badge readers and bar-code scanners can be used to collect data on employee time and attendance in machine-readable form. If their use is not feasible, on-line terminals should be utilized. The data entry program should include a variety of edit checks, including the following:

- *Validity checks* on employee numbers
- *Limit checks* on hours worked
- *Reasonableness tests* of production data, such as comparing the quantity produced with the master production schedule

Proper segregation of duties can reduce the risk of intentional inaccuracies. Reconciliations are also useful. Job-time ticket data should be reconciled with employee time cards. The total time spent on all tasks, as recorded on the job-time tickets, should not exceed the attendance time indicated on an employee's time card. Conversely, all time spent at work should be accounted for on the job-time tickets. In addition, time cards and job-time tickets should be approved by the employee's supervisor.

Threat 5: Inaccurate Processing of Payroll

The complexity of payroll processing, especially the various tax law requirements, makes it susceptible to errors. Errors obviously can hurt employee morale, particularly if paychecks are late. In addition to incorrect payroll expense records and reports, processing errors can lead to penalties if the errors result in failure to remit the proper amount of payroll taxes due the government. Similarly, failure to accurately assess garnishments on employees' wages and remit those funds to the appropriate party can also lead to financial penalties.

Three types of control procedures address the threat of payroll errors:

1. *Batch totals.* Even advanced HRM/payroll systems will continue to use batch processing for payroll. Consequently, batch totals should be calculated at the time of data entry and then checked against comparable totals calculated during each stage of processing. Hash totals of employee numbers, for example, are particularly useful. If the original and subsequent hash totals of employee numbers agree, it means that (1) all payroll records have been processed, (2) data input was accurate, and (3) no bogus time cards were entered during processing.
2. *Cross-footing the payroll register.* The total of the net pay column should equal the total of gross pay less total deductions.
3. *A payroll clearing account.* The **payroll clearing account** is a general ledger account that is used in a two-step process to check the accuracy and completeness of recording payroll costs and their subsequent allocation to appropriate cost centers. First, the payroll control account is debited for the amount of gross pay; cash is credited for the amount of net pay, and the various withholdings are credited to separate liability accounts. Second, the cost accounting process distributes labor costs to various expense categories and credits the payroll control account for the sum of these allocations. The amount credited to the payroll control account should equal the amount it was previously debited when net pay and the various withholdings were recorded. This particular internal check is called a *zero balance check,* because the payroll control account should equal zero once both entries have been posted.

The tax status of workers should be properly classified as either employees or independent contractors, because misclassification can cause companies to owe substantial back taxes, interest, and even penalties. This issue often arises when department managers attempt to circumvent a general hiring freeze by using independent contractors. Any decisions to hire outside help should always be reviewed by the HRM department. The IRS provides a checklist of questions that can be used to determine whether a worker should be classified as an employee or an independent contractor.

Threat 6: Theft or Fraudulent Distribution of Paychecks

Another major threat is the theft of paychecks or the issuance of paychecks to fictitious or terminated employees. This can result in increased expenses and the loss of cash. Proper segregation of duties relating to the preparation and distribution of paychecks can reduce the risk of this threat.

Payroll Check Writing Controls. The controls related to other cash disbursements, discussed in Chapter 13, also apply to payroll:

- Access to blank payroll checks and to the check signature machine should be restricted.
- All payroll checks should be sequentially prenumbered and periodically accounted for.
- The cashier should sign all payroll checks only when supported by proper documentation (the payroll register and disbursement voucher).
- The payroll bank account should be reconciled by someone independent of the payroll process.

The use of a separate payroll bank account provides additional protection against forgery or alteration by limiting the total amount of cash at risk. This account should be operated as an imprest fund; that is, the amount of the check written to replenish the fund should equal the amount of net pay for that period. Thus, when all paychecks have been cashed, the payroll account should have a zero balance. The use of a separate payroll checking account also makes it easier to spot any fraudulent checks when the account is reconciled.

Paycheck Distribution Controls. Paychecks should be distributed by someone who is not involved in authorizing or recording payroll. To see why this segregation of duties is so important, assume that the person responsible for hiring and firing employees also distributes paychecks. This combination of duties could enable that person to conveniently "forget" to report the termination of an employee and subsequently keep that employee's future paychecks. Additional control over paycheck distribution is provided by requiring that the person distributing paychecks positively identify each person picking up a paycheck. Furthermore, the paycheck distribution process should be observed periodically by the internal audit department.

Special procedures should be used to handle unclaimed paychecks, because they indicate the possibility of a problem, such as a nonexistent or terminated employee. Unclaimed paychecks should be returned to the treasurer's office for prompt redeposit. They should also be traced back to time records and matched against the employee master payroll file to verify that they are indeed legitimate.

Threat 7: Loss or Unauthorized Disclosure of Data

The HRM/payroll data base is a valuable resource that must be protected from loss or destruction. It is also important to protect the privacy of employee data. For example, morale may suffer if employees learn the salaries of other workers. In addition, unauthorized disclosure of performance evaluation data may subject the organization to lawsuits.

The best control procedure for reducing the risk of unauthorized disclosure of payroll data is the use of passwords and physical security controls to restrict access to authorized persons. Encryption provides additional control by making HRM/payroll information unintelligible to anyone who succeeds in obtaining unauthorized access to the payroll master file. The use of a payroll service bureau also mitigates this threat.

Backup and disaster recovery procedures provide the best controls for reducing the risk of payroll data loss. Both internal and external file labels should be used to ensure that the data base is not inadvertently erased or processed by the wrong program. Backup copies of the payroll master file and recent transaction files should be created; one should be stored on-site, the other off-site.

KEY DECISIONS, INFORMATION NEEDS, AND DATA MODEL

The previous two sections discussed how the AIS fulfilled the functions of processing payroll transactions and providing controls to safeguard assets. A third function of the AIS in the payroll/HRM cycle is to provide information for managing business activities. The traditional payroll system was designed primarily to meet the needs of external decision makers. Investors, creditors, and various government agencies were generally satisfied with information about a company's periodic salary expenses. As mentioned earlier, however, banks and other external users are beginning to demand additional information about a company's human resources. In response, as Focus 15.1 indicates, some companies are beginning to include more detailed information about their human resources in their annual reports.

Designing the payroll system to satisfy the needs of external users, however, does not ensure the production of all the information management needs to use and develop the company's human resources. Instead, the payroll system must be designed to collect and integrate cost data with other types of information in order to enable management to make the following kinds of decisions:

- *Future work force staffing needs.* How many employees are needed in the next five years to accomplish the organization's strategic plans? Which employees possess the needed skills? Which skills are in short supply? Which skills are in oversupply? How effective are current training programs in maintaining and improving employee skill levels?
- *Employee performance.* Which employees should be promoted or receive pay raises? Which should be discharged? Is overall performance improving or declining? Is turnover excessive? Is tardiness or absenteeism a problem?
- *Employee morale.* What is the overall level of employee morale and job satisfaction? How can the compensation scheme be used to improve morale, satisfaction, and performance? What additional fringe benefits, if any, should be offered?

- *Payroll processing efficiency and effectiveness.* How frequently should employees be paid? Are labor costs being accurately allocated to products and other cost centers? Are all applicable tax reporting requirements being met? How easily can employee requests for information be answered?

Some of the information needed to answer these questions, such as data about labor costs, has traditionally been provided by the payroll system. Other information, such as data about employee skills, has normally been provided and maintained by the HRM system. Still other information, such as data about employee morale, has traditionally not been collected by either the payroll or the HRM system. Finally, note that externally generated information, such as data about tax rates and industry averages for turnover and absenteeism, is also needed to make these decisions. Let us now examine how a well-designed data model facilitates the effective integration of all this information.

Data Model

Figure 15.5 presents a partial REA data model for the HRM/payroll cycle. Notice that the employees entity is linked to almost every other entity in the diagram, reflecting the importance of employees to the organization.

If the data model depicted in Fig. 15.5 were implemented in a relational data base, there would be a table for each entity (box) and for each many-to-many relationship. Figure 15.5 lists many of the attributes that would be found in each table. Most of these attributes and their placement should be self-explanatory. Let us briefly discuss several key points.

The recruiting event entity stores data about activities performed to notify the public of job openings. The data recorded in this entity is useful for documenting compliance with employment laws and also for evaluating the effectiveness of various methods used to announce job opportunities. The one-to-many relationship between skills and recruiting reflects the fact that each advertisement seeks a specific skill and that, over time, there may be several advertisements for a given skill. The relationship between the recruiting event and job applicants is modeled as being many-to-many, because many people typically apply for each job opening but a given individual may also respond to more than one recruiting event.

The interview event stores detailed data about each job interview. It is linked to the hire employees event in a many-to-one relationship, reflecting the fact that the hiring event occurs only once, but may result from either one or a number of preceding interviews.

The next two events, get employee service and pay employees, represent the basic economic exchange in the HRM/payroll cycle: the company obtains the services of employees and must pay them for those services. The get employee service entity captures the data traditionally found on time cards. The employee services entity represents the resource being acquired: an individual employee's time. Although this resource cannot be inventoried, organizations may wish to track how much is acquired and how it is used. Therefore, it would be linked to another event (not shown) showing how employees spend their time. For factory workers, that data would be stored in the job operations event (see Fig. 14.8, p. 540). Recall that the job operations event captures data corresponding to what would be found on a job-time ticket and is used for cost accounting purposes. Thus an important control involves comparing the total hours allocated to various jobs with the total time worked during that pay period (stored in the get employee services table).

The employees entity stores much of the data typically found in the employee (payroll) master file. The skills entity contains data about the different job skills of interest to the organization. The relationship between skills and employees is modeled as being many-to-many, because an employee may possess a number of job skills and, conversely, the same skill may be possessed by several employees.

The training event entity represents the various workshops, training programs, and other opportunities provided for employees to develop and maintain their skills. Thus this entity stores data that can be used to evaluate the effectiveness and cost of training and development efforts. The relationship between the employees and training entities is many-to-many, because a given employee will, over time, attend numerous training courses and, conversely, a number of employees will attend a specific training class. The relationship between the skills and training entities is one-to-many, because each course is designed to develop a specific skill but a specific skill can be acquired and enhanced by several different training courses.

Benefits of the Data Model

If the data model shown in Fig. 15.5 were implemented in a relational data base, managers could use query languages to easily retrieve the data they need to manage their employees. For example, Peter Wu could write a query to identify which employees at AOE possess a specific skill, such as knowledge of SQL. He could use this type of query to staff special projects or create task forces. The information retrieved by such queries could also be combined with projected future skill needs to plan hiring strategies and to influence the scheduling of future training courses.

Creating a data model for the HRM/payroll cycle like the one depicted in Fig. 15.5 can also provide an organization with several strategic benefits. First, because it makes information more easily accessible to managers, it should result in better decisions concerning the use and development of human resources. For example, detailed travel expense data can alert management to employees who are not using preferred providers with whom the company has negotiated discounts. The potential savings for monitoring and enforcing compliance with travel policies can be quite large. Moreover, an integrated data model facilitates automating the travel and expense reimbursement process, which can save companies additional hundreds of thousands of dollars annually and improve employee morale.

A second benefit is that many HRM activities can be performed more efficiently, thereby reducing costs. For example, notice that Fig. 15.5 includes information about job applicants. On-line resume data bases now exist for many professional fields. That information can be downloaded and automatically stored in the job applicant entity, thereby saving considerable time and expense as compared with traditional manual collection and entry of this data. Moreover, once in the system, that information can be quickly distributed. For

FIGURE 15.5
Partial REA Diagram for the HRM/Payroll Cycle

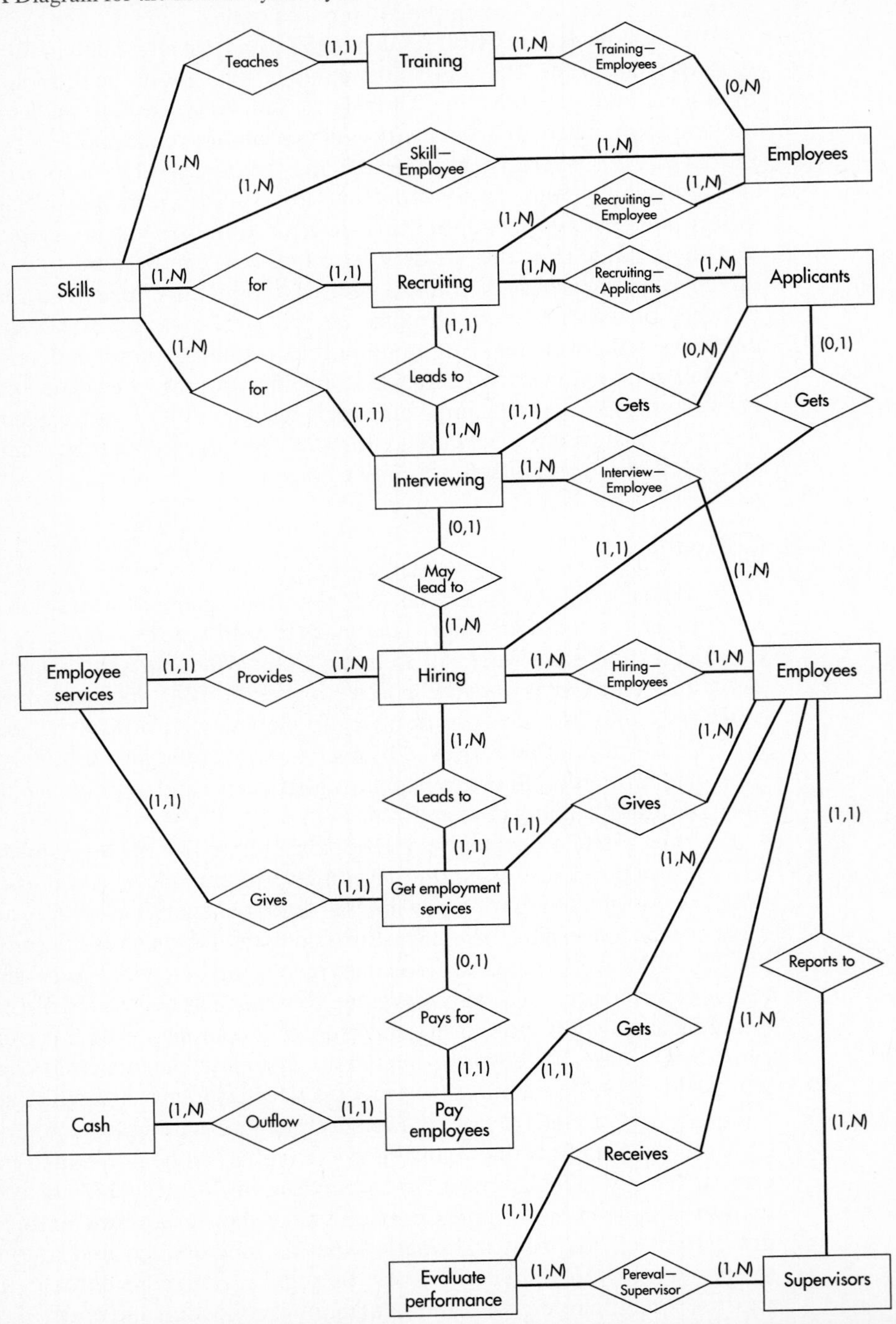

FIGURE 15.5
Continued

Table Name	Attributes (**primary key**, *foreign keys*, other attributes)
Skills	**Skill number**, description, pay rate,...
Employees	**Employee number**, name, date hired, wage rate, *supervisor number*,...
Supervisor	**Employee number**, name, date hired, number of employees supervising,...
Employee services	**Payperiod**, **employee number**, total hours worked, total hours allocated to jobs
Cash	**Account number**, *bank number*, balance,...
Training	**Course number**, date, location, *skill number*,...
Recruiting	**Recruiting number**, description, date, media, *skill number*,...
Interviewing	**Interview number**, date, *skill number, recruiting number, applicant number*,...
Hiring	**Hiring number**, date, *applicant number*,...
Get employee services	**Timecard number**, pay period, hours worked, *employee number*,...
Pay employees	**Paycheck number**, date, amount, *checking account number, employee number, time card number*,...
Evaluate performance	**Performance evaluation number**, date, time period, *employee number*,...
Applicants	**Applicant number**, name, date of birth,...
Training—Employees	**Course number**, **employee number**, rating,...
Skills—Employees	**Skill number**, **employee number**
Recruiting—Employees	**Recruiting event number**, **employee number**
Recruiting—Applicants	**Recruiting event number**, **applicant number**,...
Interview—Employees	**Interview number**, **employee number**, evaluation
Hiring—Employees	**Hiring number**, **employee number**
Pereval—Supervisor	**Performance evaluation number**, **supervisor number**, evaluation comments

example, Federal Express now scans all resumes and stores them in an image processing data base. This system allows managers who are making hiring decisions to access and print out relevant resumes immediately, rather than waiting for days for the paper documents to be routed to them.

It is also not uncommon for several related job openings to arise over a short period of time. If data about previous applicants is stored in an easily accessible data base, much of the clerical work associated with processing applications for subsequent job openings can be avoided. National Semiconductor Corporation, for example, typically receives 50,000 resumes each year, many from applicants qualified to fill several different positions. Consequently, National Semiconductor has created a data base containing more than 82,000 resumes. Now when a job opening occurs, the data base can be quickly searched to produce a short list of potential applicants. Similar systems are used by many companies. Such data bases not only improve recruiting efforts, but also significantly slash costs.

A well-designed HRM data base can also be used to reduce recruiting costs. For example, Cisco Systems now lists its HRM web site address in its print help-wanted ads. On the web site, potential new employees can access detailed descriptions of hundreds of job openings. Maintaining and presenting this information on its web site is much less costly than using traditional print media. It also enables Cisco to track interest levels more accurately by monitoring visits to the site.

A third strategic benefit of a well-designed HRM/payroll data base is that it can help companies more effectively utilize existing employee skills. AT&T, for example, has developed an internal temporary professional services staff, called Resource Link. The key to Resource Link is a data base of employee skills. Many of the employees assigned to Resource Link have had their previous positions eliminated due to ongoing restructuring and downsizing efforts. Whenever a department needs temporary help, it first contacts Resource Link to determine whether those needs can be met by existing AT&T employees. AT&T benefits by being able to retain these employees and to avoid paying severance pay.

Similarly, each of the Big 5 public accounting firms are creating data bases of employee expertise. Using these data bases, professional staff can quickly identify and solicit the advice of colleagues who have had prior experience in addressing a given problem. This saves considerable time in developing solutions to client problems and enables geographically dispersed staff to learn from each other. Well-designed and easily accessible data bases are the key to such effective sharing and leverage of knowledge.

A fourth strategic benefit of a well-designed HRM/payroll database is that it makes it easier for companies to monitor that employees are indeed attending the proper training classes and upgrading their skills. The experience of the Lockheed Martin plant in Pike County, Alabama shows the potential benefits of ensuring that continuous training occurs. The plant requires employees to undergo 96 hours of training when initially hired, and 24 hours of additional training each year. The goal is to have employees become skilled in as many different jobs as possible. Plant management credits this policy with enabling it to achieve an in-plant defect rate on finished products of 0.0003 per million opportunities. Even more impressive is the fact that the plant has never had a customer reject a shipped order!

Control Considerations

Our discussion of the threats listed in Table 15.2 stressed the importance of properly segregating incompatible duties. REA diagrams are particularly useful in assessing these controls because they indicate which internal agents participate in each event. In addition, if the REA model is implemented in a DBMS, the computer can be programmed to enforce segregation of duties by preventing one person from performing incompatible functions. Conversely, the system can also be programmed to list all cases of one employee performing multiple roles, so that the auditors can investigate whether adequate compensating controls exist.

The use of a DBMS also increases the importance of effective access controls. Most relational DBMSs provide a means to control access by letting users see only a portion of the data base (called a *view*). For example, the view defined for payroll clerks would probably not include access to the data pertaining to the hiring or performance evaluation events. In addition, they would have read-only access to pay rate data in the employee table; this restriction would enable them to obtain the information needed to prepare payroll but would prevent them from making unauthorized changes to that data.

Data accuracy is vital when using a DBMS. Fortunately, the relational data model provides some built-in controls to ensure data accuracy and consistency. One of the more important of these controls is support for foreign keys and referential integrity. This ensures, for example, that when a new row is added to the Services Provided table, the system verifies that the employee number (which appears as a foreign key in that table) actually exists as primary key in the employee table (i.e., there really is such an employee). Finally, with a DBMS, adequate backup and disaster recovery procedures become crucial.

SUMMARY AND CASE CONCLUSION

The HRM/payroll cycle information system consists of two related, but separate, subsystems: HRM and payroll. The HRM system records and processes data about the activities of recruiting, hiring, training, assigning, compensating, evaluating, and discharging employees. The payroll system records and processes data used to pay employees for their services.

The HRM/payroll system must be designed to comply with myriad government regulations related to both taxes and employment practices. In addition, adequate controls must exist to prevent (1) overpaying employees due to invalid (overstated) time and attendance data and (2) disbursing paychecks to fictitious employees. These two threats can be best minimized by proper segregation of duties, specifically by having the following functions performed by different individuals:

1. Authorizing and making changes to the payroll master file for such events as hirings, firings, and pay raises

2. Recording and verifying time worked by employees
3. Preparing paychecks
4. Distributing paychecks

Although the HRM and payroll systems have traditionally been separated, many companies, like AOE, are trying to integrate them to manage their human resources more effectively and to provide employees with better benefits and service. Elizabeth Venko explained to Peter Wu that in this regard, the key to success involves designing the payroll data base so that it can be easily linked with the nonpayroll data, such as the employee skills data base, maintained in the HRM system. Working together, Elizabeth and Peter developed a data model for AOE similar to that shown in Fig. 15.5. Elizabeth showed Peter how easily data about employee skills and attendance at training classes could be retrieved from this data base. Peter agreed that this would satisfy the needs of department managers for quick and easy access to such information. He also realized that the HRM staff could similarly use this query capability to provide quick responses to employee requests for information about their benefits, deductions, or retirement plans. He was even more impressed when Elizabeth explained that the new system would also allow employees to make direct changes in their retirement savings allocations, medical plan choices, and other benefit options. Freeing the HRM staff from these routine clerical tasks would allow his people to devote more time to strategic activities such as planning for future work force needs, career counseling, and employee development.

Elizabeth then described her plans to use IT to improve the efficiency of payroll processing. One source of productivity gains would be achieved through electronic collection and entry of time and attendance data. As discussed in Chapter 14, new time clocks would be installed in the factory that would transmit data directly to the payroll system. Similarly, bar-code scanners would be used to collect job-time ticket data at each factory workstation and send it directly to the payroll system. The computer will be programmed to reconcile the time clock data with the job-time ticket information. This would eliminate the time and expense associated with manually reconciling these two information flows in the payroll department (refer back to Fig. 15.3).

Elizabeth explained that payroll processing itself could continue to be performed in batch mode, because there is no need for on-line processing (employees would continue to be paid only at periodic intervals). Reports, such as the payroll register, however, would be distributed electronically to improve efficiency. Elizabeth also wants to encourage employees to sign up for direct deposit of their paychecks, thereby reducing the number of checks that need to be printed.

Finally, an access control matrix would be created to maintain adequate segregation of duties in the new system and protect the integrity of the HRM/payroll data base. For example, pay rate changes would be entered only by HRM employees from terminals located in the HRM department. Similarly, various department managers would have read-only access to the employee skills and work assignment portions of the HRM/payroll data base. These controls would provide protection against unauthorized changes to payroll data.

KEY TERMS

human resources management (HRM)/payroll cycle
time card
payroll register
deduction register
earnings statement
payroll service bureau
flexible benefits plans
payroll clearing account

CHAPTER QUIZ

1. Which is the best way to validate time worked by employees?
  a. Cross-foot the payroll register.
  b. Reconcile job-time tickets to time cards.
  c. Create batch totals during paycheck preparation.
  d. Electronically capture time worked at each factory station.

2. Which is the key entity in an REA data model of the HRM/payroll cycle?
  a. Payroll
  b. HRM
  c. Employees
  d. Skills

3. Which document lists the current amount and year-to-date totals of gross pay, deductions, and net pay for one employee?
  a. Payroll register
  b. Time card
  c. Paycheck
  d. Earnings statement

4. On-line processing is most useful for which of these tasks?
  a. Preparing payroll checks
  b. Reconciling job-time tickets and time cards
  c. Paying payroll tax obligations
  d. Making changes in employee job status and pay rate

5. Use of a payroll service bureau provides all of these benefits *except*
  a. integration of payroll and personnel data, such as job skills.
  b. lower cost of processing payroll.
  c. less need for developing and maintaining payroll tax expertise.
  d. fewer staff needed to process payroll.

6. Which control procedure would be most effective in detecting the failure to prepare a paycheck for a new employee prior to when paychecks are distributed?
  a. Validity checks on the employee number on each time card
  b. Record counts of time cards submitted and time cards processed
  c. A zero balance check
  d. Use of a separate payroll bank account

7. Which department should have responsibility for authorizing pay rate changes?
  a. Timekeeping
  b. Payroll
  c. HRM
  d. Accounting

8. To maximize effectiveness of internal controls over payroll, which of the following persons should be responsible for distributing employee paychecks?
  a. A departmental secretary
  b. The cashier
  c. The controller
  d. A departmental supervisor

9. Unclaimed paychecks should be returned to
  a. the HRM department.
  b. the cashier.
  c. the payroll department.
  d. the absent employee's supervisor.

10. All of the following provide a means to improve the efficiency of payroll processing *except*
  a. direct deposit.
  b. the use of badge readers to collect time worked data.
  c. the use of a payroll clearing account.
  d. the use of a payroll service bureau.

DISCUSSION QUESTIONS

15.1 This chapter noted many of the benefits that can arise by integrating the HRM and payroll data bases. Nevertheless, many companies maintain separate payroll and HRM information systems. Why do you think this is so? (Hint: Think about the differences in the backgrounds of employees and the functions performed by the HRM and payroll departments.)

15.2 Focus 15.1 described how some companies are beginning to measure the value of their human resources. Those attempts have generally been separate from the company's financial statements. Some accountants have advocated that a company's human assets be measured and included directly in the financial statements. For example, the costs of hiring and training an employee would be recorded as an asset that is amortized over the employee's expected term of service. What do you think about this proposal? Should information about human resources appear in a company's published financial statements? Why or why not?

15.3 Focus 15.1 also discussed how companies like Skandia Group are attempting to capture employees' knowledge and preserve it. (Skandia refers to this as transforming human intellectual capital into structural intellectual capital.) To what extent can this be done? To what extent should it be done? When an employee develops specialized skills and knowledge on the job, who "owns" that knowledge?

15.4 You are responsible for implementing a new employee performance measurement system that will provide factory supervisors with detailed information about each of their employees on a weekly basis. In conversation with some of these supervisors, you are surprised to learn they do not believe these reports will be useful. They explain that they can already obtain all the information they need to manage their employees simply by observing the shop floor. Comment on that opinion. How could formal reports supplement and enhance what the supervisors learn by direct observation? Why is it difficult to get people to agree to formally document what they think they already know?

15.5 In some aspects, the acquisition and use of employee services is similar to the purchase and use of other resources, such as raw materials and supplies. Discuss the similarities and differences between the way that the purchasing and payroll cycles account for the acquisition of and payment for resources used.

15.6 Direct deposit both reduces the costs of and improves control over payroll distribution. Does this mean that all companies should require their employees to be paid by direct deposit? Why or why not?

15.7 With e-mail and Internet access, employees can "moonlight" while on the job. How should, and can, companies deal with this?

15.8 Throughout the 1990s, many companies have undergone several rounds of downsizing. Research indicates, however, that downsizing has little, if any, long-term positive impact on either earnings or stock market performance. It does, however, frequently lead to serious morale problems. In light of such evidence, why do companies continue to downsize?

15.9 The importance of human intellectual capital has focused increasing attention to managing employee relationships. Some companies have begun to experiment with using internal auditors to periodically measure and evaluate the quality of interemployee relationships. To do so, the internal auditor conducts structured interviews with management, asking the interviewee to explicitly rate the quality of his or her relationships with other managers. This process identifies problematic relationships so that action can be taken to improve the relationship and, eventually, overall managerial effectiveness. Do you think such "relationship audits" have value? Why or why not? What are the advantages and disadvantages of having internal auditors conduct such interviews?

PROBLEMS

15.1 What internal control procedure(s) would be *most effective* in preventing the following errors or fraudulent acts?

a. An inadvertent data entry error caused an employee's wage rate to be overstated in the payroll master file.
b. A fictitious employee payroll record was added to the payroll master file.
c. During data entry, the hours worked on an employee's time card for one day were accidentally entered as 80, instead of 8.
d. A computer operator used an on-line terminal to increase her own salary.
e. A factory supervisor failed to notify the HRM department that an employee had been fired. Consequently, paychecks continued to be issued

for that employee. The supervisor pocketed and cashed those paychecks.

f. A factory employee punched a friend's time card in at 1:00 P.M. and out at 5:00 P.M. while the friend played golf that afternoon.

g. A programmer obtained the payroll master file and increased his salary.

h. Some time cards were lost during payroll preparation; consequently, when paychecks were distributed, several employees complained about not being paid.

i. A large portion of the payroll master file was destroyed when the disk pack containing the file was used as a scratch file for another application.

15.2 Refer to Fig. 15.5 to answer the following questions:

a. Explain the meaning of the relationship cardinalities that were not discussed in the text.

b. Explain how to include data about teams of employees assigned to projects.

15.3 Assume that the data model depicted in Fig. 15.5 is used to store HRM/payroll data. List the programmed application controls that should be used for adding data to the services provided, performance evaluation, and pay employees tables. Your answer should state which controls should be applied to each data item and the purpose of each control.

15.4 You have been hired to evaluate the payroll system for the Skip-Rope Manufacturing Company. The company processes its payroll in-house. Prepare a list of questions that you would need answered in order to evaluate Skip-Rope's internal control structure as it pertains to payroll processing for its factory employees. Each question should be phrased so that it can be answered with either a yes or a no; all no answers should indicate potential internal control weaknesses. Include a third column listing the potential problem that could arise if that particular control was not in place.

15.5 The internal audit department of the Newberry Manufacturing Company was assigned to review the payroll department of the Galena, Illinois plant. The internal audit consisted of (1) various tests to verify the numerical accuracy of the payroll department's records and (2) the determination of the procedures used to process payroll.

The internal audit team found that all numerical items were accurate. The proper hourly rates were used and the wages and deductions were calculated correctly. The payroll register was properly footed, totaled, and posted.

Interviews with plant personnel revealed the following information:

- The payroll clerk receives the time cards from the various department supervisors at the end of each pay period, checks the employee's hourly rate against information provided by the HRM department, and records the regular and overtime hours for each employee.
- The payroll clerk sends the time cards to the plant's computer operations department, where the payroll is processed.
- The computer operations department returns the time cards along with the printed checks and payroll register to the payroll clerk. The payroll clerk then verifies the hourly rate and hours worked for each employee by comparing the detail in the payroll register with the time cards.
- If errors are found, the payroll clerk voids the computer-generated check, prepares another check for the correct amount, and adjusts the payroll register accordingly.
- The payroll clerk obtains the plant's check signature plate from the accounting department and signs the payroll checks.
- An employee of the HRM department picks up and holds the checks until they are delivered to the department supervisors for distribution to employees.

Required:

Identify the shortcomings in the payroll procedures at the Newberry Manufacturing Company and suggest steps to correct those weaknesses.
(CMA Examination)

15.6 Rose Publishing Company devotes the bulk of its work to the development of high school and college textbooks. The printing division has several production departments and employs 400 people. Approximately 95% of the staff is paid hourly rates and can earn overtime pay; the remainder earn fixed salaries. All employees are paid weekly.

A manual time card system is used. Each employee punches in and out when entering or leaving the plant. The timekeeping department audits the time cards daily and prepares input sheets for the computerized functions of the payroll system.

Currently, a daily report of the previous day's clock card information, organized by department, is sent to each supervisor in the printing division for verification and approval. Any changes are made directly on the report, signed by the supervisor, and returned to timekeeping. The altered report serves as the input

FIGURE 15.6

Arlington Industries Flowchart of Payroll Processing

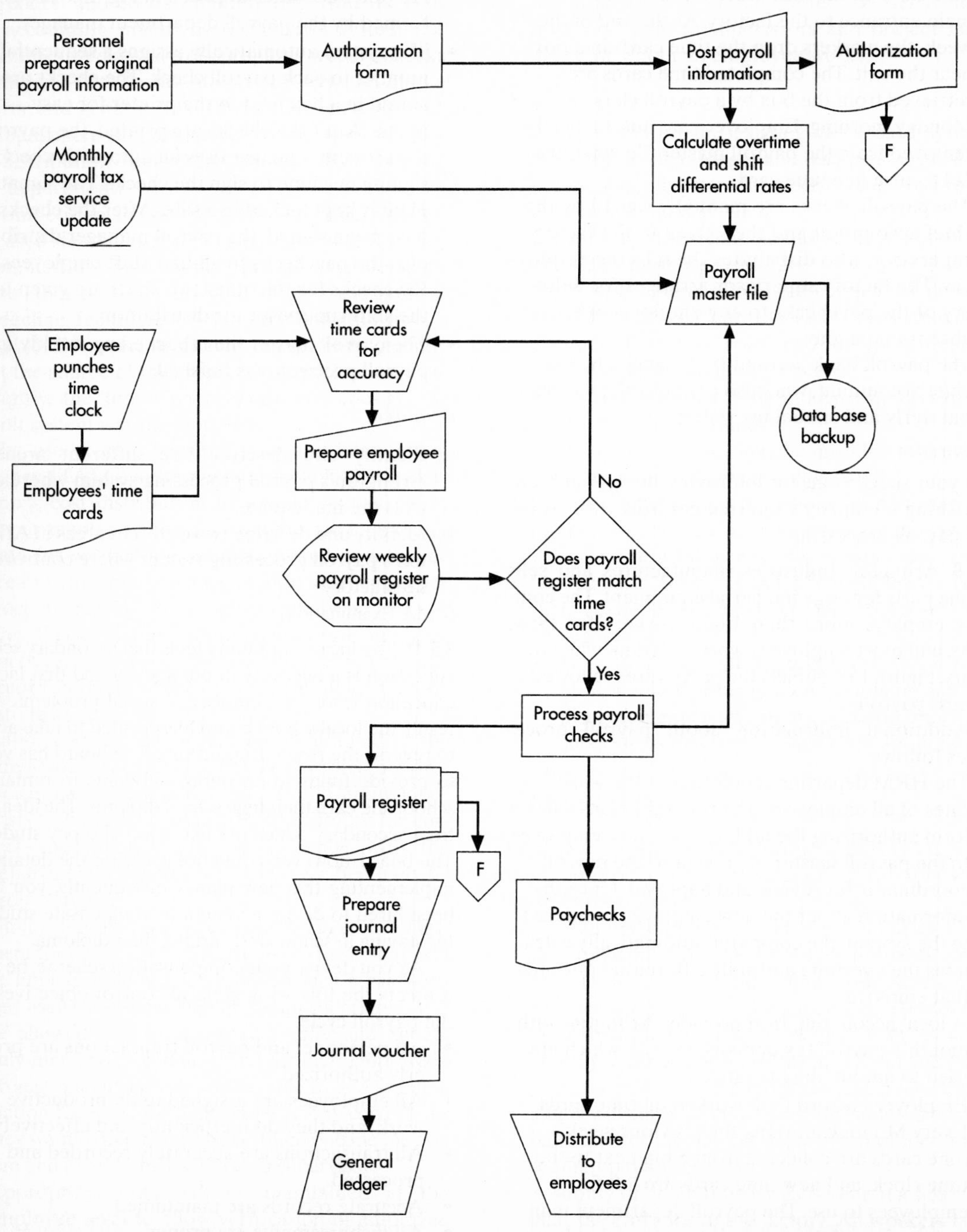

Required:

Write a proposal that addresses these five questions:

a. How should the students be compensated (i.e., attendance, grades, etc.)?
b. How and by whom will the payments be authorized?
c. How will the payments be processed?
d. How should the payments be made (e.g., in cash or other means)?
e. When will the payments be made?

(Adapted from "Development of Diversity Awareness and Critical Thinking" by Carol F. Venable, Proceedings of the Lilly Conference on Excellence in College and University Teaching–West, Lake Arrowhead, Calif., March 1995; and American Accounting Association Teaching and Curriculum Demonstration Session, Orlando, Fla., August 1995. Reprinted with permission of Carol Venable.)

CASE 15.1 ANYCOMPANY, INC.—AN ONGOING COMPREHENSIVE CASE

Select a local company and study its payroll system (you may use the same company you identified to complete this case in previous chapters). Prepare a report that contains the following:

1. A DFD of the payroll system.
2. A flowchart of the payroll system. Comment on the company's use, or lack thereof, of IT in payroll processing.
3. A list of the various paper and electronic documents used to process payroll. Evaluate the design of each document and assess its appropriateness for its intended use.
4. A list of the various threats and the control procedures employed to mitigate them. Assess the overall adequacy of internal controls.
5. A list of the reports produced by the system. Evaluate how well those reports meet management's information needs.
6. An REA data model for the company's HRM/payroll processes.

CASE 15.2 PAYROLL SERVICE BUREAUS

Write a brief report describing the advantages and disadvantages of using a payroll service bureau, rather than processing payroll internally. Perform the following research to collect the data for your report:

1. Contact a local payroll service bureau. Find out what services it provides and how it charges for those services. Ask about the bureau's client base—what size companies does it serve? In what industries?
2. Contact two companies that use a payroll service bureau and two that process their own payroll. Ask them to explain why they do (or do not) use a payroll service bureau.

CASE 15.3 DARWIN DEPARTMENT STORE

The Darwin Department Store pays all of its employees on a salaried basis. Payroll processing is done internally. The payroll master file is maintained on disk. At periodic intervals every month, the HRM department uses on-line terminals to enter batches of payroll file change transactions. After those changes pass the appropriate data entry controls, they are posted to the payroll master file. This run produces a printed report listing all file changes processed.

The payroll run takes place on the last day of each month. Because all employees are paid a fixed salary, there is no transaction input. This run produces printed employee paychecks, earnings registers, a printed summary report, and a payroll register file recorded on disk. The payroll register file is later processed to print a payroll register.

1. What is meant by the term "payroll file change transactions"? Give four examples of these types of transactions.
2. Prepare a flowchart of the processes described.
3. The summary report that is generated by the payroll run includes accounting journal entries. Describe the contents of these journal entries. What other information is likely to be found on the summary report?
4. Describe a comprehensive set of internal control procedures and policies for this payroll application. Relate each control procedure to a specific objective and explain what threats it is designed to mitigate.
5. Suppose that Darwin decides to pay commissions to its sales staff. What changes would be required in (a) the payroll master file, (b) the payroll run, and (c) the internal control procedures you developed in step 4?

ANSWERS TO CHAPTER QUIZ

1. b **3.** d **5.** a **7.** c **9.** b
2. c **4.** d **6.** b **8.** b **10.** c

CHAPTER 16

General Ledger and Reporting System

LEARNING OBJECTIVES

After studying this chapter, you should be able to

- Describe the information processing operations required to update the general ledger and to produce other reports for internal and external users.
- Discuss methods for improving the efficiency and effectiveness of general ledger and reporting activities.
- Identify the major threats in general ledger and reporting activities, and evaluate the adequacy of various control procedures for dealing with them.
- Read and explain an integrated REA data model.

Integrative Case: Alpha Omega Electronics

During the past two years, Elizabeth Venko, AOE's controller, has participated in the successful redesign of the company's various AIS subsystems (see Chapters 12–15). She has now been asked by Stephanie Cromwell, AOE's chief financial officer, to redesign AOE's general ledger and reporting system. She has two primary goals:

1. To speed up the closing process. Currently, it takes two weeks to complete monthly closings and to distribute the financial performance reports to AOE's divisional managers. Last week Stephanie almost had to postpone her scheduled presentation of AOE's quarterly financial results to Wall Street security analysts because of delays in preparing the interim financial statements.
2. To make financial performance data more accessible to divisional managers. Currently, divisional managers receive printed monthly financial performance reports. Consequently they have to reenter the data into personal computers in order to do "what if" analyses or to prepare graphical summaries.

As you read this chapter, think about how Elizabeth can utilize recent developments in information technology to improve the efficiency of AOE's general ledger processing and the effectiveness of its reporting systems.

INTRODUCTION

This chapter discusses the information processing operations involved in updating the general ledger and preparing reports that summarize the results of an organization's activities. As shown in Fig. 16.1, the general ledger and reporting system plays a central role in a company's AIS. One of its primary functions is to collect and organize data from a variety of sources:

- Information about regular transactions is provided by each of the accounting cycle subsystems described in Chapters 12–15. (Only the principal data flows from each subsystem are depicted, to keep the figure uncluttered.)
- Information about financing and investing activities, such as the issuance or retirement of debt and equity instruments and the purchase or sale of investment securities, is provided by the treasurer.
- Budget numbers are provided by the budget department.
- Adjusting entries are provided by the controller.

All this information must be organized and stored in a manner that facilitates meeting the varied information needs of internal and external users. Managers need detailed information about the results of operations in their area of responsibility. Investors and creditors want periodic financial statements to help them assess the organization's performance. Increasingly, they are demanding more detailed and more frequent reports. Government agencies also have periodic information requirements that must be met.

Consequently, the general ledger and reporting system needs to be designed not only to produce regular periodic reports, but also to support real-time inquiry needs. For example, departmental managers should be able to assess actual versus planned performance at any time so that deviations can be identified early enough to take corrective actions. Likewise, the treasurer must be able to closely monitor cash flows so that deviations from forecasts can be identified in time to adjust short-term borrowing plans.

A logical question to ask at this point, however, concerns the need for a general ledger system. After all, in Chapters 12–15 we presented REA data models for the various subsystems of the AIS. Theoretically, implementation of these REA data models in each subsystem of the AIS precludes the need for a separate general ledger. Some general ledger accounts, such as inventory and sales, would be represented explicitly as relational tables. Other general ledger accounts, such as accounts receivable and accounts payable, could be derived from data stored in several tables, but would also probably be stored as summary attributes in the customer and vendor tables, respectively.

Nevertheless, we describe a separate general ledger system in this chapter because the organization you begin to work for after graduation will likely still be using a separate general ledger package. Many organizations have not yet implemented relational data base systems to integrate their operational and financial data. Instead, they continue to use separate files, as illustrated in the flowcharts in Chapters 12–15. Moreover, even companies that have created relational data bases typically continue to maintain a

FIGURE 16.1
Context Diagram of the General Ledger and Reporting System

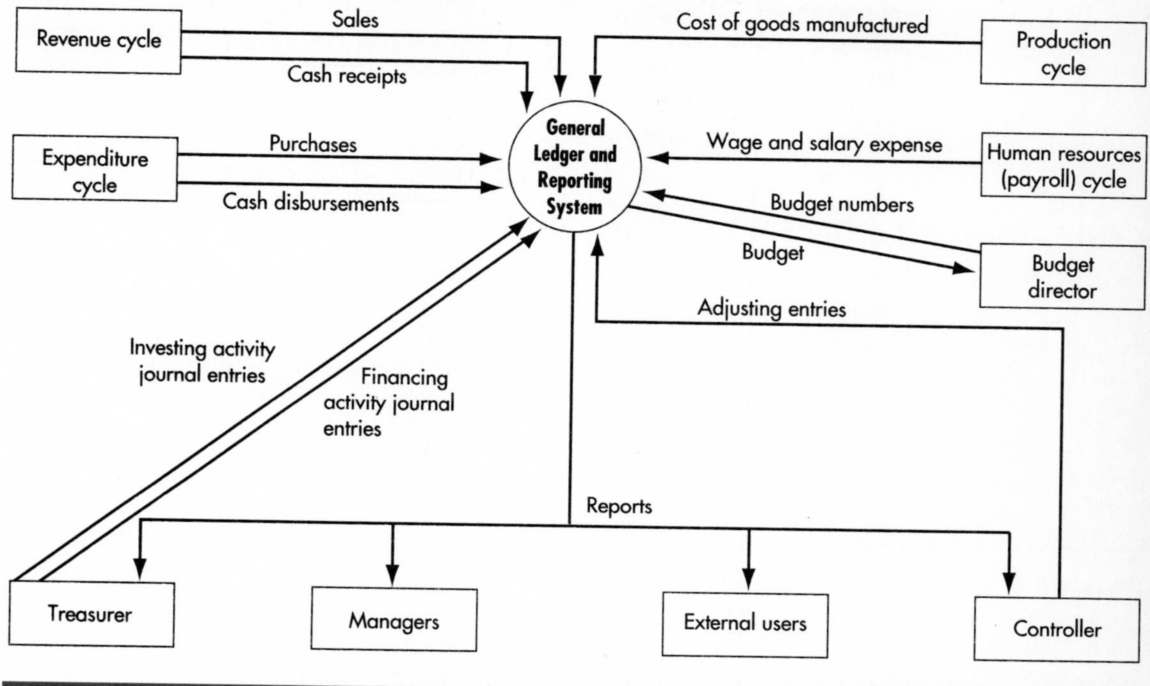

separate general ledger, usually for reasons of organizational tradition and politics. Note that this practice not only creates redundancy, it also continues the separation of financial from nonfinancial operating data. One unfortunate result is that accountants are often tempted to think that the only important data is that representing the financial aspects of operations. As we discussed in Chapters 12–15, such thinking seriously limits the opportunity for accountants to take a proactive value-added role in providing managers with all the information they need to make sound decisions.

What you learned in previous chapters about relational data bases and the REA model is still useful, however. A growing number of general ledger packages are based on the relational data model and support SQL access to financial data. In addition, many larger companies are acquiring **enterprise resource planning (ERP) systems,** which successfully integrate the traditionally separate functional subsystems of an AIS. Thus the skills you have developed in earlier chapters can be applied productively to designing and using the general ledger. Moreover, it is likely that over time, as accountants become more comfortable with the concept of producing financial statements directly from a relational data base, the use of separate general ledger packages may ultimately disappear.

In the first section of this chapter, we describe the basic information processing operations performed to update the general ledger and to prepare reports for both internal management and external users. Next we explore opportunities for using information technology to improve the efficiency and effectiveness of those activities. Then we discuss major control threats in the general ledger and reporting cycle and the control procedures that can be used to mitigate them. We conclude the chapter by examining an integrated REA data model for an organization's AIS.

GENERAL LEDGER AND REPORTING ACTIVITIES

Figure 16.2 shows the four basic activities performed in the general ledger and reporting system. The first three activities represent the basic steps in the accounting cycle, and they culminate in the production of the traditional set of financial statements. The fourth activity indicates that, in addition to financial reports for external users, the AIS produces reports for internal management as well. We now examine each of these activities in more detail.

FIGURE 16.2
Level 0 DFD for the General Ledger and Reporting System

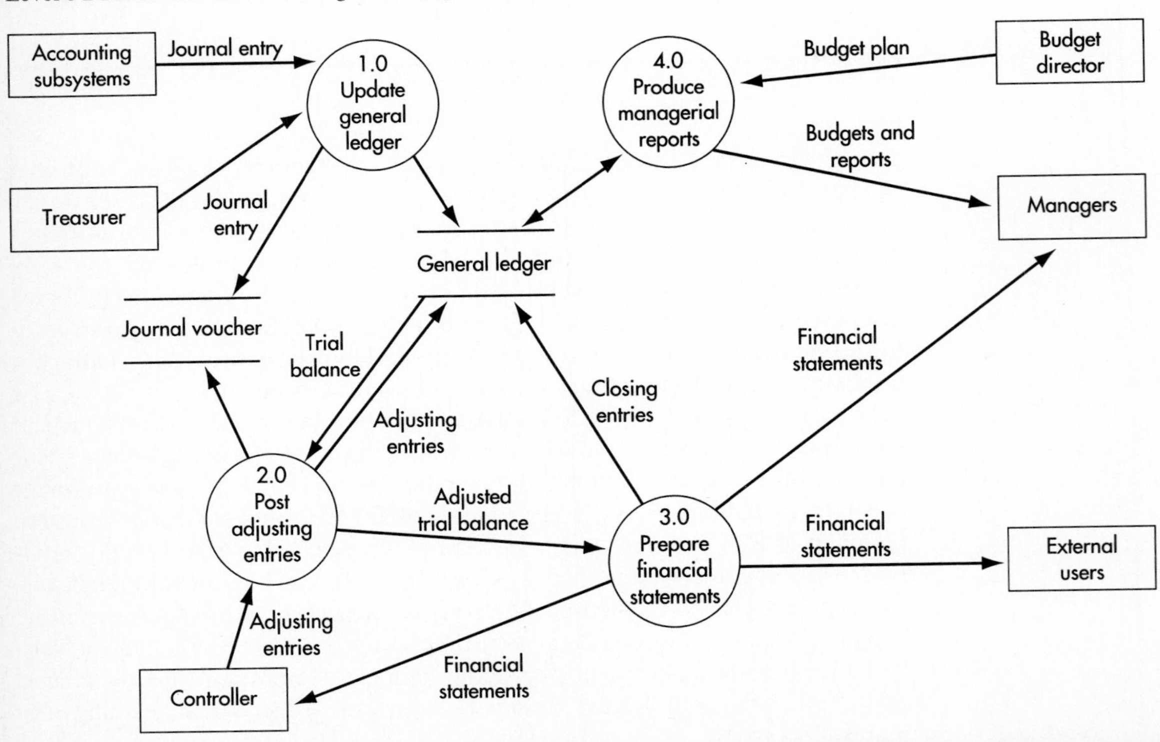

Update General Ledger

As shown in Fig. 16.2, the first activity in the general ledger system (circle 1.0) is to update the general ledger. Updating consists of posting journal entries that originate from two sources:

1. *Accounting subsystems.* Each of the accounting subsystems described in Chapters 12–15 creates a journal entry to update the general ledger. In theory, the general ledger could be updated for each individual transaction. In practice, however, the various accounting subsystems usually update the general ledger by means of summary journal entries that represent the results of all transactions that occurred during a given period of time (day, week, or month). For example, the revenue cycle subsystem would generate a summary journal entry debiting accounts receivable and cash and crediting sales for all sales made during the update period. Similarly, the expenditure cycle would generate summary journal entries to record the purchase of supplies and inventories and to record cash disbursements in payment for those purchases.
2. *The treasurer.* The treasurer's office creates individual journal entries to update the general ledger for nonroutine transactions such as the issuance or retirement of debt, the purchase or sale of investment securities, or the acquisition of treasury stock.

Journal entries to update the general ledger may be documented on a form called a **journal voucher.** Figure 16.2 shows that the individual journal entries used to update the general ledger are then stored in the journal voucher file. Thus this file contains the information that would be found in the general journal in a manual AIS. Note, however, that the journal voucher file is a by-product of, not an input to, the posting process. As we will explain later in the chapter, in our discussion of internal controls, the journal voucher file forms an important part of the audit trail.

Post Adjusting Entries

The second activity in the general ledger system involves posting various adjusting entries (circle 2.0 in Fig. 16.2). These adjusting entries originate from the controller's office, after the initial trial balance has been prepared. Adjusting entries fall into five basic categories:

1. *Accruals* represent entries made at the end of the accounting period to reflect events that have occurred but for which cash has not yet been received or disbursed. Examples include the recording of interest revenue earned and wages payable.
2. *Deferrals* represent entries made at the end of the accounting period to reflect the exchange of cash prior to performance of the related event. Examples include recognizing the portion of advance payments from customers earned during a specific period and expensing the portion of prepaid assets (e.g., rent, interest, and insurance) used this period.

3. *Estimates* represent entries that reflect a portion of expenses that occur over a number of accounting periods. Examples include depreciation and bad debt expenses.
4. *Revaluations* represent entries made to reflect either differences between the actual and recorded value of an asset or a change in accounting principles. Examples include a change in the method used to value inventory or a writing down of inventory to reflect obsolescence or shrinkage noted during a physical count of inventory.
5. *Corrections* represent entries made to counteract the effects of errors found in the general ledger.

As shown in Fig. 16.2, information about these adjusting entries is stored in the journal voucher file, forming another part of the audit trail. After all adjusting entries have been made, an adjusted trial balance is prepared. It serves as the input to the next step in the general ledger and financial reporting cycle, the preparation of financial statements.

Prepare Financial Statements

The third activity in the general ledger and reporting system involves the preparation of financial statements (circle 3.0 in Fig. 16.2). The income statement is prepared first, using data from the revenue and expense account balances in the adjusted trial balance. The balance sheet is prepared next. This activity requires closing entries that zero out all revenue and expense accounts and transferring the net income or loss to retained earnings. In manual systems, this was typically performed only once each year. Automated general ledger systems, however, simplify the monthly and annual closing process. The former zeroes out the current month's revenue and expense account balances but leaves the year-to-date totals intact. Thus an income statement generated immediately after a monthly closing would display all zeroes in the current month column but would store cumulative numbers in the year-to-date column. Finally, the statement of cash flows is prepared, using data from both the income statement and balance sheet, along with other information about the organization's investment and financing activities.

Produce Managerial Reports

The final activity in the general ledger and reporting system (circle 4.0 in Fig. 16.2) involves the production of various managerial reports. These fall into two main categories: general ledger control reports and budgets. Examples of control reports include lists of journal vouchers by numerical sequence, account number, or date and listings of general ledger account balances. These reports are used to verify the accuracy of the posting process.

A number of budgets are produced for use in planning and evaluating performance. The operating budget depicts planned revenues and expenditures for each organizational unit. The capital expenditures budget shows planned cash inflows and outflows for each project. Cash flow budgets compare estimated cash inflows from operations with planned expenditures and are used to determine borrowing needs.

Budgets and performance reports should be developed on the basis of responsibility accounting. **Responsibility accounting** involves reporting financial results on the basis of managerial responsibilities within an organization. The result is a set of correlated reports that break down the organization's overall performance by specific subunits, as shown in Fig. 16.3. Note that each report shows actual costs and variances from budget for the current month and the year to date, but only for those items that are controllable by the manager of that subunit. Note also the hierarchical nature of the reports: The total cost of each individual subunit is displayed as a single line item on the next-higher-level report.

The contents of the budgetary performance reports should be tailored to the nature of the unit being evaluated. For example, many production, service, and administrative departments are treated as cost centers. Accordingly, as shown in Fig. 16.3, their performance reports should highlight actual versus budgeted performance in regard to controllable costs (those that can be directly affected by the actions of the unit manager). In contrast, sales departments are often evaluated as revenue centers; consequently, their performance reports should compare actual and forecasted sales, broken down by appropriate product and geographic categories. Some departments, like Information Technology (IT) and utilities, charge other units for their services and are evaluated as profit centers; in this case, performance reports should appropriately compare actual revenues, expenses, and profits with their corresponding budgeted amounts. Finally, if plants, divisions, and other autonomous operating units are treated as investment centers, their performance reports should provide data for calculating that unit's return on investment.

No matter which basis is used to prepare a unit's budgetary performance report, the method used to calculate the budget standard is crucial. The easiest approach is to establish fixed targets for each unit, store those figures in the data base, and compare actual performance with those preset values. One major drawback to this approach is that the budget number is static and does not reflect unforeseen changes in the operating environment. Consequently, individual managers may be penalized or rewarded for factors beyond their control. For example, assume that the budgeted amounts in Fig. 16.3 for the general superintendent are based on planned output of 2,000 units. If, however, due to greater than anticipated sales, actual production is 2,200 units, then the negative variances for each expense category may not really indicate inefficiency, but merely reflect the increased level of output.

A solution to such problems is to develop a flexible budget, in which the budgeted amounts vary in relation to some measure of organizational activity. In terms of our previous example, flexible budgeting would entail dividing the budget for each line item in the general superintendent's department into its fixed and variable cost components. In this way, budget standards

FIGURE 16.3
Sample Set of Reports for a Responsibility Accounting System

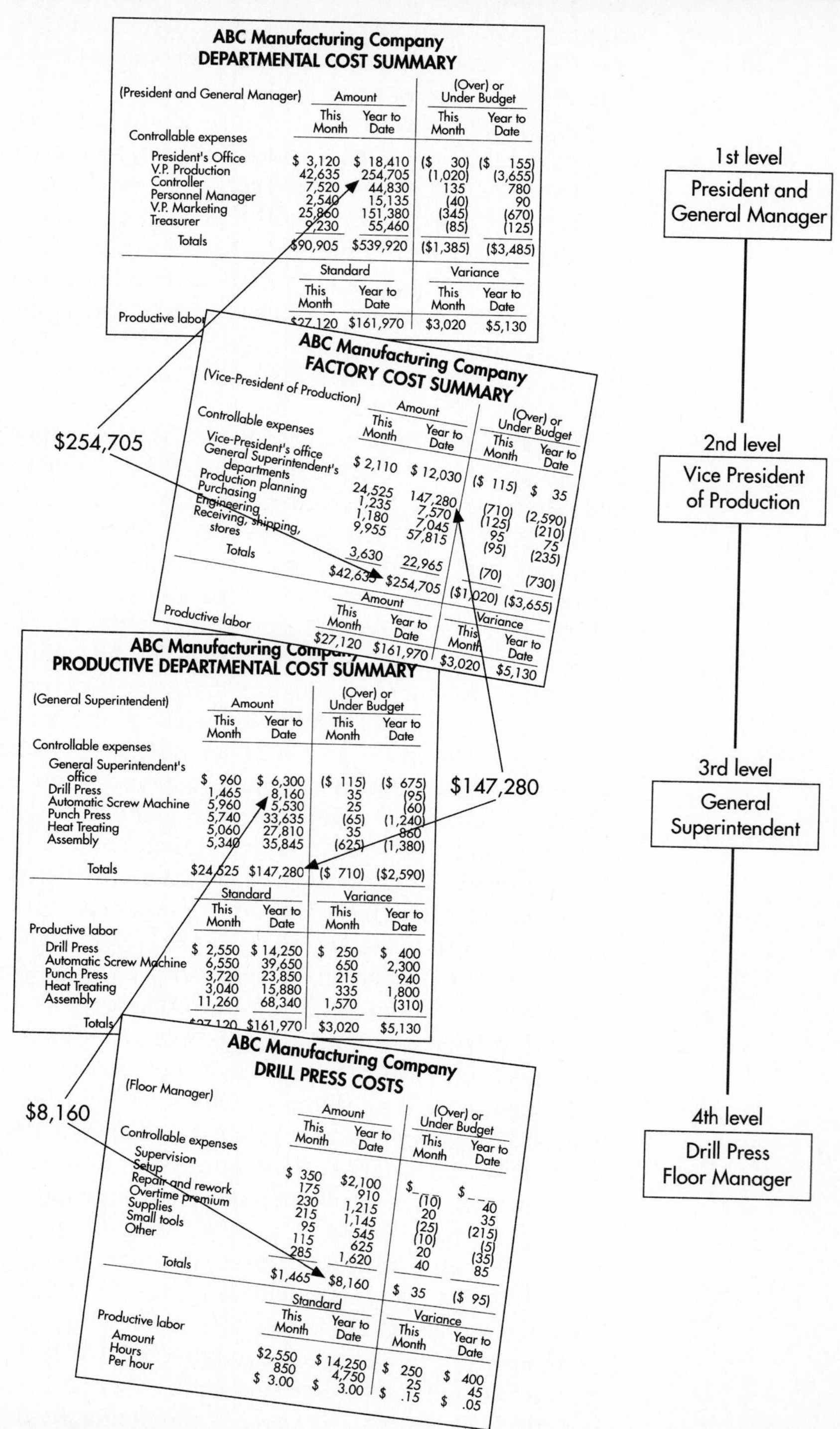

ABC Manufacturing Company
DEPARTMENTAL COST SUMMARY

(President and General Manager)

Controllable expenses	Amount This Month	Amount Year to Date	(Over) or Under Budget This Month	(Over) or Under Budget Year to Date
President's Office	$ 3,120	$ 18,410	($ 30)	($ 155)
V.P. Production	42,635	254,705	(1,020)	(3,655)
Controller	7,520	44,830	135	780
Personnel Manager	2,540	15,135	(40)	90
V.P. Marketing	25,860	151,380	(345)	(670)
Treasurer	9,230	55,460	(85)	(125)
Totals	$90,905	$539,920	($1,385)	($3,485)
	Standard This Month	**Standard** Year to Date	**Variance** This Month	**Variance** Year to Date
Productive labor	$27,120	$161,970	$3,020	$5,130

ABC Manufacturing Company
FACTORY COST SUMMARY

(Vice-President of Production)

Controllable expenses	Amount This Month	Amount Year to Date	(Over) or Under Budget This Month	(Over) or Under Budget Year to Date
Vice-President's office	$ 2,110	$ 12,030	($ 115)	$ 35
General Superintendent's departments	24,525	147,280	(710)	(2,590)
Production planning	1,235	7,570	(125)	(210)
Purchasing	1,180	7,045	95	75
Engineering	9,955	57,815	(95)	(235)
Receiving, shipping, stores	3,630	22,965	(70)	(730)
Totals	$42,635	$254,705	($1,020)	($3,655)
	Amount This Month	**Amount** Year to Date	**Variance** This Month	**Variance** Year to Date
Productive labor	$27,120	$161,970	$3,020	$5,130

ABC Manufacturing Company
PRODUCTIVE DEPARTMENTAL COST SUMMARY

(General Superintendent)

Controllable expenses	Amount This Month	Amount Year to Date	(Over) or Under Budget This Month	(Over) or Under Budget Year to Date
General Superintendent's office	$ 960	$ 6,300	($ 115)	($ 675)
Drill Press	1,465	8,160	35	(95)
Automatic Screw Machine	5,960	5,530	25	(60)
Punch Press	5,740	33,635	(65)	(1,240)
Heat Treating	5,060	27,810	35	860
Assembly	5,340	35,845	(625)	(1,380)
Totals	$24,525	$147,280	($ 710)	($2,590)
Productive labor	**Standard** This Month	**Standard** Year to Date	**Variance** This Month	**Variance** Year to Date
Drill Press	$ 2,550	$ 14,250	$ 250	$ 400
Automatic Screw Machine	6,550	39,650	650	2,300
Punch Press	3,720	23,850	215	940
Heat Treating	3,040	15,880	335	1,800
Assembly	11,260	68,340	1,570	(310)
Totals	$27,120	$161,970	$3,020	$5,130

ABC Manufacturing Company
DRILL PRESS COSTS

(Floor Manager)

Controllable expenses	Amount This Month	Amount Year to Date	(Over) or Under Budget This Month	(Over) or Under Budget Year to Date
Supervision	$ 350	$2,100	$—	$—
Setup	175	910	(10)	40
Repair and rework	230	1,215	20	35
Overtime premium	215	1,145	(25)	(215)
Supplies	95	545	(10)	(5)
Small tools	115	625	20	(35)
Other	285	1,620	40	85
Totals	$1,465	$8,160	$ 35	($ 95)
Productive labor	**Standard** This Month	**Standard** Year to Date	**Variance** This Month	**Variance** Year to Date
Amount	$2,550	$ 14,250	$ 250	$ 400
Hours	850	4,750	25	45
Per hour	$ 3.00	$ 3.00	$ .15	$ .05

would be automatically adjusted for any unplanned increases (or decreases) in production. Thus any differences between these adjusted standards and actual costs can more appropriately be interpreted.

OPPORTUNITIES FOR USING INFORMATION TECHNOLOGY

Information technology provides opportunities for improving the efficiency and effectiveness of the general ledger and reporting system in terms of (1) the timing of general ledger updates, (2) the monthly closing process, and (3) financial reporting.

Timing of General Ledger Update

As described in Chapters 12–15, modern AIS systems often use on-line processing to update the subsidiary ledgers as each transaction occurs. (In an REA data model, subsidiary ledgers take the form of relational tables.) This immediate updating keeps the subsidiary ledger balances current and can improve the quality of subsequent decisions. For example, updating an individual customer's account balance immediately after a sale facilitates subsequent decisions about whether to extend additional credit to that customer.

General ledger account balances, however, traditionally have not been updated immediately because they are not directly used to make operational decisions. For example, decisions about extending credit are based on information about the individual customer's current account balance and credit limit. That information is found in the subsidiary accounts receivable ledger; the general ledger accounts receivable control account only stores information about the total outstanding account balances of all customers.

The information in the general ledger is used to produce periodic performance reports. Traditionally, most organizations have prepared these reports for internal use on a monthly basis, and for external users on a quarterly basis. Consequently, many general ledger systems traditionally have been updated only once a month. Such a policy, however, creates two problems. First, because the general ledger is accurate only immediately after posting the summary monthly journal entries, it cannot be used as a source of data for interim "what if" analyses by management. In the past, the need for such continuous planning was less important. In today's fast-paced global economy, however, management must constantly monitor and reevaluate the organization's financial performance in light of its strategic goals. Firms must be able to alter their plans quickly in response to changes in their environment. A second problem with periodic updates to the general ledger is that any delays or problems encountered in the monthly update process will cause delays in producing those interim financial statements. This is the situation that arose at AOE, as explained in the introductory case.

Consequently, many organizations are adopting on-line general ledger systems similar to that depicted in Fig. 16.4. Each individual application program in these systems, such as sales order entry or cash receipts, posts summary journal entries to the general ledger at least daily. The treasurer's staff uses on-line

FIGURE 16.4
Flowchart of an On-Line General Ledger and Reporting System

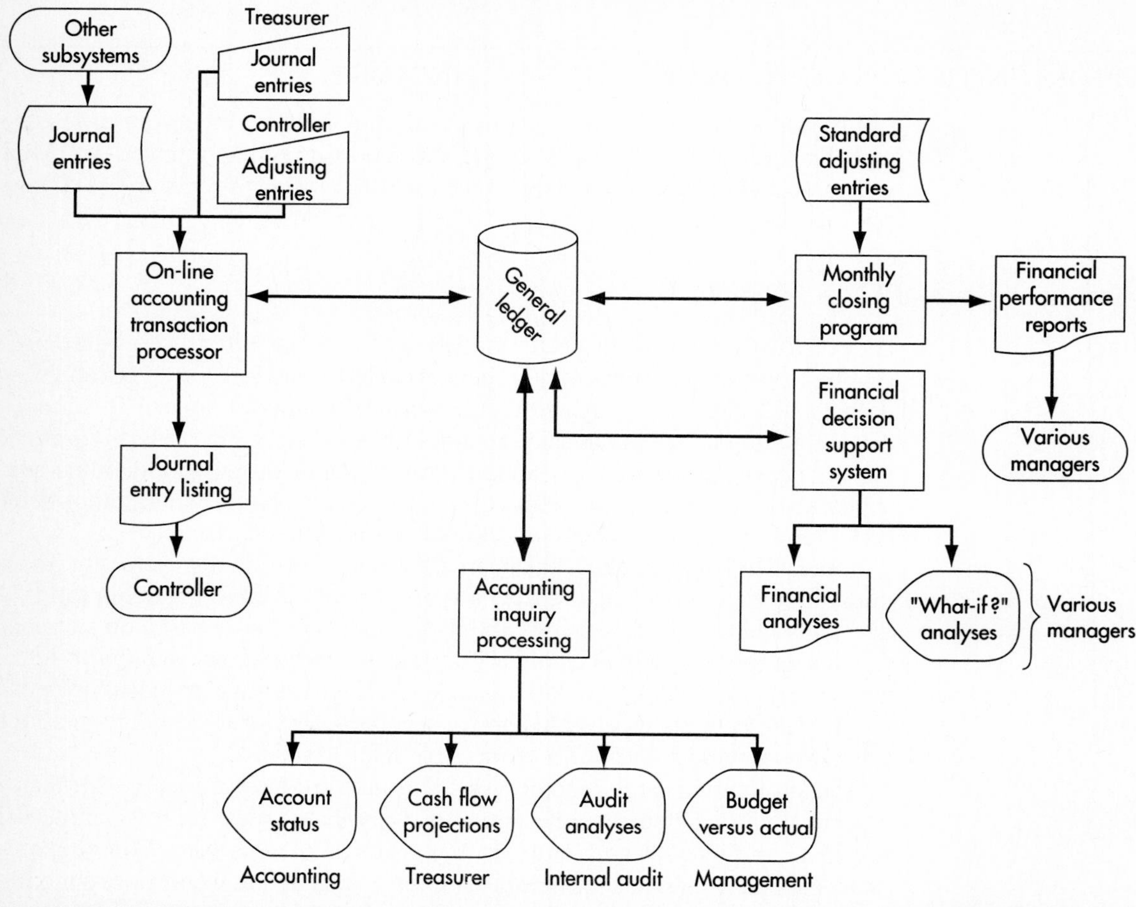

terminals to enter data about nonroutine transactions on the day they occur. Thus the general ledger is kept more current, thereby increasing its usefulness as a source of data for managers to perform "what if" analyses of the effects of policy changes. In addition, the on-line general ledger system supports inquiries by various users, as depicted at the bottom of the figure.

Monthly Closing Process

Many organizations, such as AOE, are interested in finding ways to speed up the monthly closing process. After all, two-week-old monthly income statements are of limited usefulness for taking prompt, corrective actions. In addition, reducing the closing process frees up more time for the accounting staff to analyze the data and advise operating managers about important trends. The potential time savings can be substantial. For example, in 1987 it took Motorola eight days to perform monthly closings; by 1995 the process was completed in just two days.

One way to speed up the monthly closing process is to consolidate overlapping AIS subsystems. Over the years, many organizations have found that their AIS subsystems have proliferated as a result of mergers and acquisitions or internal growth into new markets. For example, IBM once had 315 separate AIS subsystems worldwide. The CFO and the controller worked together to consolidate them into 36 subsystems, which not only sped up the closing process but also substantially reduced costs.

Client/server systems provide another way to improve the closing process and to disseminate financial performance reports more quickly. Focus 16.1 describes the benefits Microsoft derived from putting its general ledger on the corporate LAN and creating internal home pages to access it.

Financial Reporting

Communications technology can also be used to reduce both the time and costs of preparing and disseminating financial statements. For example, controllers can access public financial reporting data bases, such as NAARS and EDGAR, to find examples of how other companies disclose various items. Similarly, tax forms and regulations can be accessed from the IRS on the Internet. Conversely, a

FOCUS 16.1 How an IT-Savvy Accountant Reengineered Microsoft's General Ledger and Reporting System

REMEMBER the old joke about the shoemaker's children being the last to have shoes? Well, in 1993 when Scott Boggs joined Microsoft as assistant corporate controller, he found that it was using a terribly inefficient and inflexible mainframe-based general ledger and reporting system. It took two weeks to get the monthly profit and loss statements to Microsoft's 60 worldwide subsidiaries. Half of that time was spent in printing, mailing, and faxing the reports because the mainframe-based data could not be distributed electronically.

Boggs worked with the IT group to make several significant improvements to the system. First, the general ledger data was extracted from the mainframe and stored in a client/server relational data base. This made it possible to disseminate the data over Microsoft's Ethernet network. This step alone reduced the monthly closing process to one week. Next, data from 30 other management systems around the world were consolidated into one relational transaction data base built on an SQL server. Now Microsoft divisional managers can easily access subsets of the financial data that are most relevant to their individual needs.

Nevertheless, the amount of data available was overwhelming. The daily revenue data base, for example, was 1.4 gigabytes and contained 1.1 million records. Consequently, Boggs borrowed an idea from the Internet to improve the interface to Microsoft's internal financial network: The accounting department created an internal home page. This "Controller's Financial Information" home page provides users with graphic-enhanced information about Microsoft's cost centers, accounting policies, and corporate financial planning, thereby helping managers to find the data they need.

Source: Peggy Wallace, "Microsoft's Finance Department Gets Up to Speed," *Infoworld* (June 5, 1995): 58.

company's financial statements can be made available to the public via the Internet. A company can also submit required financial and tax filings electronically to the SEC and the IRS, respectively.

Graphs Spreadsheets and graphics packages can improve the financial reporting process by facilitating the creation of graphs to highlight key trends. The utility of graphical analysis, however, depends on the accuracy with which the graphs are designed. A properly designed graph should lead to the same conclusions as a detailed analysis of the data on which the graph is based. Focus 16.2 summarizes basic principles for designing accurate graphs and reports the results of a study indicating how often those principles are violated in published financial statements.

FOCUS 16.2 Accurately Graphing Financial Data

THE FOLLOWING four principles are crucial to designing accurate graphs:

1. *Start the vertical axis at zero.* Failure to do so exaggerates the magnitude of changes because the upper intervals of the graph do not represent the same amount of change as the lower intervals.
2. *Do not extend the vertical scales far beyond the upper limit of the variable being graphed.* This principle is most commonly violated when graphing two variables that differ greatly in their data values, such as income and sales. Although sales and income are related, using one scale to depict both variables on the same graph can hide the actual magnitude of the change in income, because the heights of the columns for income are so small.
3. *Order time series from left to right on the horizontal axis.* Although comparative financial statements may place the most recent year's data on the left, people normally read graphs and text from left to right. Violating this principle can lead to misleading interpretations of trends.
4. *Avoid using three-dimensional column charts.* These type of graphs look dramatic, but they are difficult to interpret correctly. It is hard to note accurate changes in height across columns, because the back of the column is itself higher than the front. Moreover, the change in the volume of each columnar bar is much greater than the change in height.

These principles are easily violated. A detailed study of more than 250 annual reports of *Fortune* 500 companies revealed that 10% contained graphs that violated one or more of these four basic principles of graph design, thereby distorting the data in a manner favorable to the company.

The most common problem was overstating the magnitude of a change. Specifically, 13 annual reports contained graphs that exaggerated the magnitude of an increase in sales, income, or dividends by 100% or more. In other words, the graph made the amount of change appear to be at least twice as large as it really was. Three other annual reports contained graphs that understated the numerical decline in sales, income, or dividends. On the other hand, the study also found that another 12 annual reports contained graphs that distorted financial results in a manner unfavorable to the company (for example, by understating the magnitude of an increase in sales, income, or dividends).

Interestingly, every annual report that contained an improperly drawn graph contained other graphs that followed the principles of good graph design. In addition, companies that had experienced a decrease in net income from the prior year were twice as likely to have improperly drawn graphs in their annual reports than were companies that had experienced an increase in net income.

Source: Paul John Steinbart, "The Auditor's Responsibility for the Accuracy of Graphs in Annual Reports: Some Evidence on the Need for Additional Guidance," *Accounting Horizons* (September 1989): 60–70.

Data Warehouses An on-line general ledger system like that depicted in Fig. 16.4 typically contains detailed data for only the current year. Consequently, a financial data warehouse, which contains both current and historical data, can provide additional support for strategic decision making.

On-line analytical processing (OLAP) tools provide one way to access the information stored in a data warehouse. **On-line analytical processing (OLAP)** involves the use of queries to investigate hypothesized relationships. For example, management may begin with a query that breaks down sales by region for the last three years. This may be followed by additional queries that "drill down" to lower levels (similar to the hierarchy of reports depicted in Fig. 16.3) by, for example, grouping sales by different customers and by quarters. Companies can use such drill down capabilities to develop profit and loss statements for individual customers and then use that information to renegotiate contracts.

Data mining is another way to access the information stored in a data warehouse. **Data mining** involves the use of sophisticated statistical analysis, including artificial intelligence techniques like neural networks, to discover relationships in the data. For example, credit card companies use data mining to identify patterns of use indicative of fraud. Similarly, data mining techniques can be used to identify previously unknown relationships in sales data that can then be used as the basis for future promotions.

CONTROL OBJECTIVES, THREATS, AND PROCEDURES

The control objectives in the general ledger and reporting system are similar to those in the other AIS cycles discussed in previous chapters:

1. All updates to the general ledger are properly authorized.
2. All recorded general ledger transactions are valid.
3. All valid, authorized general ledger transactions are recorded.
4. All general ledger transactions are accurately recorded.
5. General ledger data are safeguarded from loss or theft.
6. General ledger system activities are performed efficiently and effectively.

Well-designed documents and records play an important role in achieving these objectives. If paper journal vouchers are used, they should contain clear instructions about how to complete them. On-line data entry of transactions by the treasurer and the controller, as depicted in Fig. 16.4, facilitates the accurate and efficient recording of general ledger journal entries. In such situations, the use of appropriate application controls, such as validity checks and field (format) checks, enhances the accuracy of data entry. Providing space on both paper and electronic documents to record who completed and who reviewed the form provides evidence that the journal entry was properly authorized. Finally, prenumbering all documents facilitates checking to verify that all transactions have been recorded.

Table 16.1 lists the major threats and exposures in the general ledger and financial reporting system, along with applicable control procedures for mitigating them. Because the general ledger and reporting system involves only information processing activities, there are fewer threats than in the other AIS cycles. Moreover, the threats in the general ledger and reporting system primarily relate to the corruption, loss, or destruction of data. Let us now examine the control procedures that can be used to deal with these threats.

Threat 1: Errors in Updating the General Ledger

Errors made in updating the general ledger can lead to poor decision making based on erroneous information in financial performance reports. The control procedures for dealing with this threat fall into three categories: (1) input edit and processing controls, (2) reconciliations and control reports, and (3) maintenance of an adequate audit trail.

Input Edit and Processing Controls. Two types of journal entries are used to update the general ledger shown in Fig. 16.4: (1) summary journal entries from the other AIS cycles and (2) direct entries made by the treasurer or controller. The former are themselves the output of a series of processing steps, each of which was subject to a variety of application control procedures designed to ensure accuracy and completeness. Consequently, the primary input edit control for summary journal entries involves checking their date to ensure that they represent activity for the most recent, unposted time period.

Journal entries made by the treasurer and controller, however, are original data entry. Consequently, the following types of input edit and processing controls are needed to ensure that they are accurate and complete:

1. A validity check to ensure that general ledger accounts do exist for each account number referenced in a journal entry.

TABLE 16.1 Threats, Exposures, and Control Procedures in the General Ledger and Reporting Cycle

Threat	Exposure	Control Procedures
1. Errors in updating the general ledger: (a) Inaccurate/incomplete journal entries (b) Inaccurate/incomplete posting of journal entries	Inaccurate records and reports, resulting in bad decisions based on erroneous information	Input, edit, and processing controls Reconciliations and control reports Audit trail
2. Unauthorized access to the general ledger	Leak of confidential data Corruption of general ledger Cover-up of theft	Access controls Adequate audit trail
3. Loss or destruction of general ledger data	Loss of data Loss of assets	Proper backup procedures Disaster recovery plan

2. Field (format) checks to ensure that the amount field in the journal entry contains only numeric data.
3. Zero-balance checks to verify that total debits equals total credits in a journal entry.
4. A completeness test to ensure that all pertinent data are entered. It is especially important that the source of the journal entry be identified, because this information forms a key part of the audit trail.
5. A redundant data check to match account numbers with account descriptions, to ensure that the correct general ledger account is being accessed. For on-line data entry, this would be referred to as closed-loop verification.
6. The creation of a standard adjusting entry file for recurring adjusting entries made each period, such as depreciation expenses. Input accuracy is improved without repeatedly keying in these entries. The possibility of forgetting to make a recurring adjusting entry is also reduced, thereby ensuring input completeness.
7. A sign check of the general ledger account balance once updating is completed, to verify that the balance is of the appropriate nature (debit or credit).
8. Calculation of run-to-run totals, to verify the accuracy of journal voucher batch processing. The computer calculates the new balance of the general ledger account, based on its beginning balance and the total debits and credits applied to that account, and then compares that with the actual account balance in the updated general ledger. Any discrepancies indicate a processing error that must be investigated.

Reconciliations and Control Reports. The use of reconciliations and control reports can detect whether any errors were made during the process of updating the general ledger. One form of reconciliation used in manual systems is the preparation of a trial balance. It indicates whether the total of the debit balances in the general ledger equals the total credit balances; if not, an error in posting has occurred. In automated systems, the use of clearing and suspense accounts ensures that the general ledger is always in balance. At the close of a period, all these special accounts should have zero balances; otherwise, an error was made in updating the general ledger.

To illustrate, assume that one clerk is responsible for recording the release of inventory to customers and another is responsible for recording the billing of customers. The first clerk would make the following journal entry:

Unbilled shipments	xxx	
Inventory		xxx

The second clerk would make this entry:

Accounts receivable	yyy	
Unbilled shipments		yyy

Once both entries have been completed, the special clearing account, unbilled shipments, should have a zero balance. If not, an error has been made that needs to be investigated and corrected.

Two other forms of reconciliation are used in both manual and automated systems. One involves comparing the general ledger control account balances with the total balance in the corresponding subsidiary ledger. If these two totals do not agree, the difference must be investigated and corrected. The second involves examining all transactions occurring near the end of an accounting period to verify that they are recorded in the proper time period.

Control reports can help identify the source of any errors that occurred in the general ledger update process. Listing journal vouchers by general account number facilitates identifying the cause of errors affecting a specific general ledger account. Listing the journal vouchers by sequence can indicate the absence of any journal entry postings. Finally, the **general journal listing** shows the details (account number, source reference code, description, and amount debited or credited) of each entry posted to the general ledger. This report indicates whether the total debits equal the total credits posted to the general ledger.

The Audit Trail. In Chapter 2 we explained that the audit trail depicts the path of a transaction through the accounting system. Specifically, it provides the information needed to perform the following tasks:

1. Trace any transaction from its original source document to the general ledger and to any report or other document using that data.
2. Trace any item appearing in a report or other output document back through the general ledger to its original source document.
3. Trace all changes in the general ledger from its beginning balance to its ending balance.

Figure 2.3 (p. 36) illustrated the elements of the audit trail in a manual system. Although the format of the various journals and ledgers may look different in a conventional computer-based AIS, the same basic information is preserved and can be displayed on control reports. For example, the general journal transaction file indicates the source of all entries made to update the general ledger. The customer master file contains information about the account balances of individual customers; these can be summed and compared with the accounts receivable control account in the general ledger. A similar process can be followed to reconcile accounts payable, inventory, and equipment balances. In an advanced AIS, however, there may no longer be any paper source documents. Thus it is important to create periodic copies of transaction and master files and to ensure that those files cannot be altered.

Threat 2: Unauthorized Access to the General Ledger

Access to the general ledger by unauthorized persons can result in confidential data leaks to competitors or corruption of the general ledger. It can also provide a means for concealing the theft of assets. Consequently, it is important to have adequate controls to prevent unauthorized access to the general ledger.

User IDs and passwords should be used to control access to the general ledger and to enforce the proper segregation of duties by limiting the functions that each legitimate user may perform. For example, employees who have custody of assets or the ability to authorize the release of assets should be prevented from updating the general ledger. Similarly, management should be given read-only access to the general ledger, as depicted in the bottom of Fig. 16.4. The access control matrix should also limit the functions that can be performed at various terminals. Adjusting entries, for example, should be allowed only from terminals in the controller's office.

Controls over the creation of journal voucher records are also important because they authorize changes to general ledger account balances. Thus the system should check for the existence of a valid authorization code for each journal voucher record before posting that transaction to the general ledger. Otherwise, the integrity of the general ledger may be compromised. Note that this authorization code also forms a part of the audit trail. Indeed, inspection of the audit trail provides a means to detect unauthorized access to the general ledger.

Threat 3: Loss or Destruction of General Ledger Data

The general ledger is a key component of the organization's accounting information system. Therefore, it is important to provide adequate backup and disaster recovery procedures to protect this asset. Backup controls include the following:

1. The use of internal and external file labels to protect against inadvertent destruction of the current general ledger.
2. Regular backup of the general ledger. At least two backup copies of the general ledger should exist. One copy should be kept on-site where it can be immediately accessed. The other copy should be stored elsewhere to provide protection against a major disaster, such as a fire or an earthquake.

Disaster recovery planning is also crucial. Given the increasing reliance on EDI, EFT, and the Internet to conduct daily business activities, no organization can survive for long if its computers go down. As you learned in Chapter 9, organizations need to prepare and periodically practice a plan for dealing with a major disaster that has the potential to shut down their computer systems.

INTEGRATED ENTERPRISE-WIDE DATA MODEL

Figure 16.5 presents an integrated enterprise-wide data model for AOE. Most of this figure represents a merging of the data models that were presented in Chapters 12–15. Note that this merging primarily involved linking each resource that appeared in those separate data models with the events that increase and decrease that resource. For example, the cash resource is linked to both cash disbursements and cash receipts. Similarly the raw materials inventory is linked to both purchases and uses in production. Figure 16.5 also models the major events in the financing cycle: the issuance of equity and debt instruments, and related periodic payments to investors and creditors.

FIGURE 16.5
Integrated REA Diagram

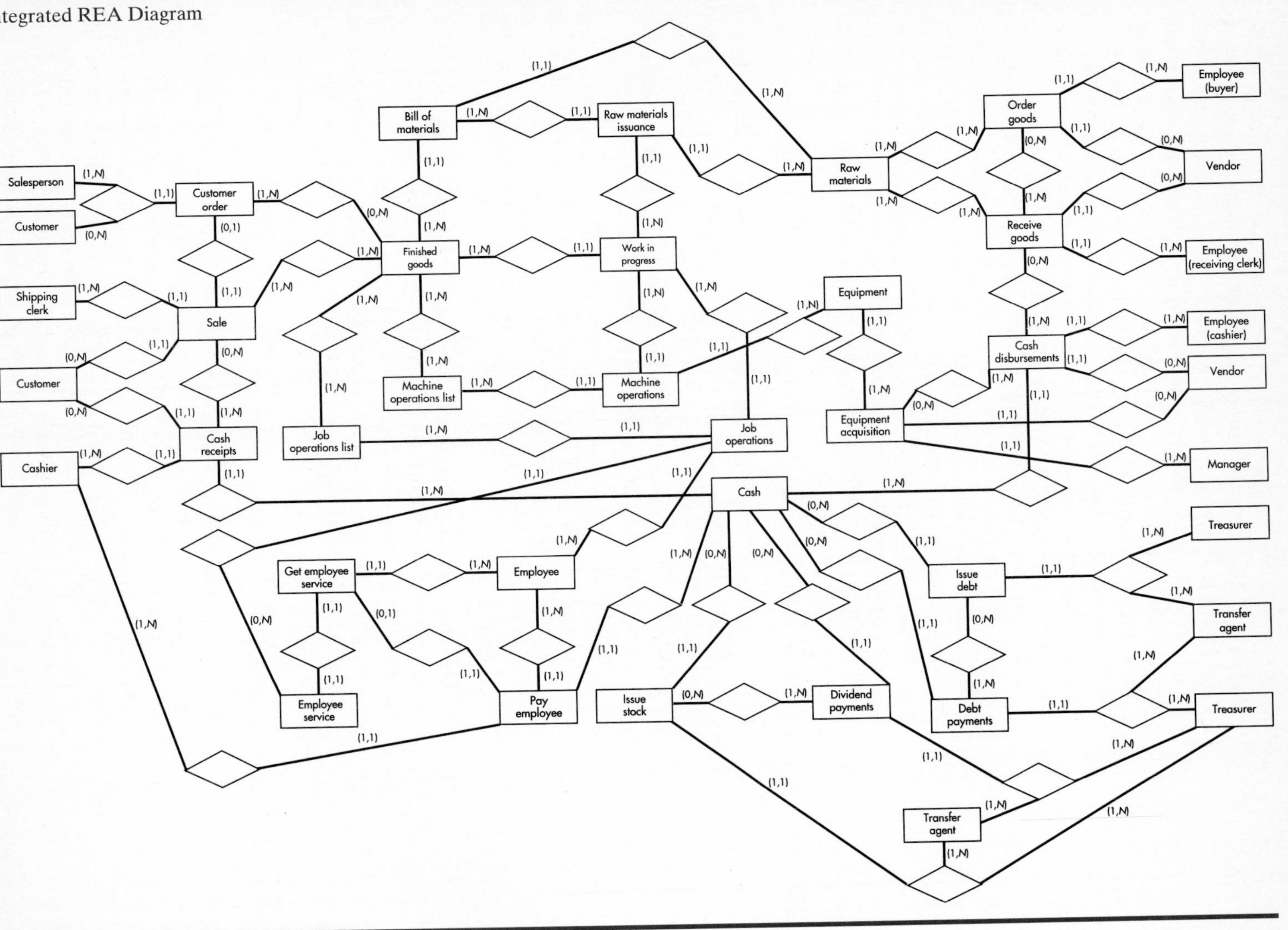

Examination of Figure 16.5 shows the linkages among different subsystems of the AIS. For example, customer orders for finished goods may, if there is insufficient quantity on hand, trigger additional production of those goods. In turn, this may necessitate ordering additional raw materials. ERP systems are designed to automatically trigger these types of related actions across subsystems. This is accomplished by linking each subsystem to a common enterprise-wide data base. Thus, even though most ERP systems are not specifically based on the REA data model, a model like that depicted in Fig. 16.5 can be useful in representing the contents of the ERP data base.

Most of Fig. 16.5 is simply an integration of figures from previous chapters. The lower-right-hand corner, however, contains some new entities that represent two important types of financing activities.

The event issue debt event is a special kind of cash receipt. It is modeled as a separate entity because it contains distinctly different attributes from those associated with cash receipts from sales–face amount of debt issued, total amount received, date issued, maturity date, interest rate, and so forth. Usually, most companies do not deal directly with individual creditors. Instead, they sell their debt instruments through a financial intermediary, which is depicted in Fig. 16.5 as the transfer agent. The transfer agent maintains all the necessary information about individual debtholders in order to properly direct both the periodic interest payments and eventual repayment of principal. Therefore, each occurrence of an issue debt event contains data about the aggregate amount received from issuing a set of debt instruments. For example, the issuance of $10,000,000 of 5% bonds, which were ultimately purchased by several thousand different individuals for a total of $9,954,000, constitutes one issue debt event.

The debt payments in art event is a special type of cash disbursement. Each debt payment event reflects the sending of funds to the transfer agent for the total amount of interest due at that time. Thus, to continue our example, the company would send $125,000 to the transfer agent to make the first quarterly payment on that $10,000,000 of bonds. The transfer agent, in turn, would then send individual checks to each debtholder.

Equity transactions are modeled in a similar manner as debt transactions. The issue stock event is a special kind of cash receipt associated with the issuance of stock, and the dividend payments in art event is a special kind of cash disbursement. As with debt, most companies do not deal directly with individual stockholders. Thus Fig. 16.5 shows that both types of equity transactions involve participation by an external transfer agent.

Benefits of an Integrated Data Model

Improved Support for Decision Making. An integrated enterprise-wide data model like that depicted in Fig. 16.5 can significantly improve the support provided for managerial decision making. To appreciate this fact, consider how the chart of accounts in a traditional general ledger system limits subsequent analyses of expense data. Expenses are typically recorded and stored in an account that reflects either the nature of the expense, such as travel, or its function, such as campus recruiting visits. With the first alternative, it is easy to prepare reports of total travel expenses but difficult to identify how much travel expense is associated with campus recruiting. With the second alternative, it is easy to prepare reports that show the costs associated with campus recruiting but difficult to prepare reports that track total travel costs.

A common response to this problem in file-based general ledger systems is to create more detailed account numbers that identify both the nature and purpose of each expense. Thus there would be separate accounts for campus recruiting travel expenses, sales travel expenses, and so on. The drawback of this approach, however, is that it results in an exponential expansion of the chart of accounts and an increase in the length of each account code. Both of these factors make it more difficult for coding clerks and managers to learn the chart of accounts and apply it correctly. In addition, the ability to further analyze the data remains limited to those categories that were considered when the chart of accounts was designed.

In contrast, an integrated enterprise-wide data model avoids these problems and provides greater flexibility for analyzing data. Tables can be created for basic account categories, such as travel expenses. These tables can also include a text attribute for describing the purpose of that expenditure. Managers can then use queries to extract travel expenses by category, such as campus recruiting or trade shows. Moreover, these categories can be easily changed over time in response to different needs simply by changing the condition specified in the query. Thus users are not limited to predetermined expense classification schemes. Yet reports of total travel expenses for all purposes can also be easily generated by querying travel expenses without any clauses that restrict the scope of the query.

Integration of Financial and Nonfinancial Information. A second benefit of an integrated enterprise-wide data model is that it facilitates the integration of financial and nonfinancial information. The importance of this feature is underscored by increasing pressure to expand the scope of the information presented in financial statements. For example, the AICPA Special Committee on Financial Reporting (the Jenkins Committee) recommends that financial reports prepared for external users include nonfinancial information such as measures of customer satisfaction and product cycle times. Similarly, in Chapter 15 we discussed the trend toward including measures of the value of a company's human capital in annual reports. This information can also be easily incorporated in an integrated enterprise-wide data model. Indeed, this and the other benefits discussed in this section explain the growing popularity of ERP systems, such as those marketed by SAP, PeopleSoft, Baan, J. D. Edwards, and other software vendors.

Effective integration of financial and nonfinancial data also enables improved internal reporting. Traditionally, internal reports have focused primarily on financial performance measures. Effective management of an organization, however, requires measuring performance on multiple dimensions; no one measure alone is sufficient. Instead, top management needs a "balanced scorecard" that provides a multidimensional perspective on performance.

A **balanced scorecard**[1] is a report that measures four dimensions of performance: financial, internal operations, innovation and learning, and customer perspectives of the organization. On each dimension, the balanced scorecard shows the organization's goals and specific measures that reflect performance in attaining those goals. Figure 16.6 shows an example balanced scorecard for AOE.

The financial dimension provides several measures that reflect the financial performance of the organization. This provides information about how the organization looks to shareholders. The internal operations dimension presents several measures that focus on how efficiently and effectively the organization is performing key business processes. The specific activities that are measured reflect those that top management believes are critical to the long-run success of the organization. The innovation and learning dimension provides measures on actions taken to ensure future success. Finally, the customer dimension provides explicit information about customer perspectives.

Together, these four dimensions provide a much more comprehensive overview of organizational performance than that provided by financial measures alone. Moreover, each of these four dimensions affects the others. Innovation and learning should improve efficiency and effectiveness, which should

FIGURE 16.6
Sample Balanced Scorecard for AOE

Dimension/goal	Measure	Current period	Last period	Year ago
Financial:				
Profitability	Income (000s)	104	103	100
Return	ROA (%)	12.5%	12.6%	12.2%
Liquidity	Current ratio	2.04	2.06	2.01
Customer:				
Satisfaction	Rating (0–100)	95	93	92
Preferred supplier	% purchased from us	20%	20%	18%
Internal:				
Product quality	Defect rate (%)	1.00%	1.01%	1.10%
Speed of delivery	Cycle time (days)	10.4	10.5	11.2
Process efficiency	Setup time (hours)	3.1	3.15	4.0
Innovation & learning:				
New products	Number new products	4	4	3
Employee learning	% attending advanced training courses	10%	25%	9%

[1] The concept of a balanced scorecard was introduced by Robert S. Kaplan and David P. Norton, "The Balanced Scorecard–Measures that Drive Performance," *Harvard Business Review* (January–February 1992): 71–79; and it was further developed by the same authors in "Using the Balanced Scorecard as a Strategic Management System," *Harvard Business Review* (January–February 1996): 75–85.

be reflected in the internal operations measures in future periods. Efficient and effective internal operations are likely to improve customer satisfaction. Efficient and effective internal operations, coupled with favorable customer perceptions, should eventually be reflected in improved financial performance. Indeed, it can be argued that the financial dimension measures are lagging indicators, whereas the other three dimensions are predictive indicators of future financial performance.

Enabling Exploitation of the Virtual Value Chain.[2] An integrated enterprise-wide data model is a prerequisite for successfully exploiting a new source of revenue: the virtual value chain. Chapter 1 introduced the concept of the physical value chain, consisting of the five basic activities involved in providing value to customers: inbound logistics, production, outbound logistics, sales and marketing, and post-sale support and service. Information plays a vital role in the physical value chain by supporting decision making to ensure that each activity is performed as efficiently and effectively as possible.

Information, however, not only can be used to support decision making, but can also be a direct source of value itself. Reaping that value results from performing the three basic activities in the **virtual value chain:**

1. gathering information,
2. synthesizing, organizing, and
3. distributing the information to customers.

The information can either be sold, thereby providing a new source of revenue, or can be provided to customers to enhance services and build loyalty. For example, common carriers like Federal Express and UPS must monitor the location of packages to effectively manage their daily operations. This information is also valuable to customers because it can allow them to better plan their shipping and receiving activities.

Development of a virtual value chain occurs in three stages. The first stage, *visibility,* occurs when an organization has easy access to information about its physical activities. This requires an integrated enterprise-wide data base so that management can have ready access to information about all business activities. The second stage, *mirroring,* involves using information technology to perform processes in the virtual world that were formerly performed only physically. For example, Boeing and other airline manufacturers now use simulation, rather than physical wind tunnels, to test new designs. This makes it possible to test many more variations, at a much lower cost, than would be possible if a physical model of each design had to be built. Software vendors can deliver their products electronically, over the Internet, instead of by means of magnetic disks or CDs, thereby almost eliminating the costs of outbound logistics.

The third stage of development of the virtual value chain, *building new customer relationships,* occurs when companies use the information they possess

[2] The material in this section is based on Jeffrey F. Rayport and John J. Sviokla, "Exploiting the Virtual Value Chain," *Harvard Business Review* (November–December 1995): 75–85.

to provide new services to customers. For example, automobile manufacturers can configure their home pages to let customers "test drive" new models. The greatest potential gains come, however, if companies can figure out some way to create new digital assets. For example, once a digital copy of a photograph has been created, it can be sold on the Internet. A significant advantage of such digital assets is that they are not used up when sold; innumerable digital copies of the same photograph can be sold. Moreover, unlike physical copies of a photograph, there is almost no variable cost for each digital copy that is made. Thus companies that can successfully create digital assets have significant cost advantages over competitors who only have physical assets.

Note again that the first stage of developing a virtual value chain is having easy access to information about operations. Indeed, the ability of companies like Federal Express and UPS to exploit the virtual value chain only became possible *after* they had developed the comprehensive information systems that enabled them to gather and organize detailed, up-to-the-minute information about their daily operations. They needed the ability to track the location of every package in order to monitor the efficiency and effectiveness of their own internal operations. Once this information was available, it could then be provided to customers as an additional value-added service. Thus development of an integrated enterprise-wide data model is essential to exploiting the virtual value chain.

Internal Control Considerations

As noted earlier, most ERP systems use centralized data bases similar to that depicted Fig. 16.5 to share data across functions. ERP systems affect internal controls in several ways. Such systems typically empower many different individuals to enter data relating to a specific business activity. This makes it harder to assign responsibility for maintaining data integrity. Moreover, ERP systems often produce process efficiencies by enabling one individual to perform multiple steps in a business process, thereby reducing segregation of duties. Finally, the integrated and all-encompassing nature of ERP systems increases the exposure resulting from a system crash.

ERP systems, however, also provide several features that, if properly utilized, can mitigate many of the threats just described. First, ERP systems typically provide sophisticated access controls that not only validate user identities but also limit authorized users to specific tasks. Second, the ability of ERP systems to link transactions offers the possibility for accountants to create well-controlled transaction flows. Finally, ERP systems typically provide a detailed trace capability that enables internal auditors to easily follow a transaction through each stage of processing.

To illustrate the potential power, let us examine the process for validating the updates to the sales account in the general ledger. Referring to Fig. 16.5, the first step would involve writing queries against the data model for the revenue cycle. One such query would sum the amount of all sales during the time period of interest. Other queries would link the sales, shipments, and orders tables to verify the completeness and validity of all recorded sales. Additional queries could be written to trace sales to specific customers and sales staff. In fact, the number of such cross-table links that can be easily generated is limited only by the investigator's imagination. In addition, extensive log files can be created to make it easy to identify who authorized a transaction. Thus there is the potential to create a much richer and more complete audit trail than that typically provided by conventional AIS (whether manual or computer-based).

SUMMARY AND CASE CONCLUSION

The general ledger and financial reporting system integrates and summarizes the results of the various accounting subsystems for the revenue, expenditure, production, and human resource cycles. The general ledger is the central master file in the accounting information system. Consequently, it is important to implement control procedures to ensure its accuracy and security. Important controls include edit checks of the journal voucher records posted to the general ledger, access controls, an adequate audit trail, and appropriate backup and disaster recovery procedures.

The reports produced by the general ledger system fall into two primary categories: financial statements and managerial reports. The former are prepared periodically in accordance with GAAP and are distributed to both internal and external users. The latter are prepared for internal use only and, therefore, often include comparisons between actual and budgeted performance. The usefulness of these reports, whether presented in the form of tables or graphs, is affected by how well they are designed.

In addition to printed reports, the general ledger system should also support inquiry processing by decision makers. This requires adequate controls that limit access to, and permissible operations on, the data in the general ledger. Designing the general ledger in accordance with the relational data model facilitates inquiry processing by making the data more easily accessible to desktop tools found on most personal computers.

Although many organizations have traditionally used batch processing to update their general ledger, there is a movement to switch to on-line systems. Indeed, on-line systems are necessary to provide useful inquiry processing capabilities. They also speed the period-end closing process. Consequently, Stephanie Cromwell and Elizabeth Venko decided that AOE needs to switch to an on-line general ledger system similar to that depicted in Fig. 16.4, set up on a client/server network.

Elizabeth tells Stephanie that her ultimate goal is to eliminate the use of a separate general ledger. She and Stephanie agree, however, that AOE will first acquire a general ledger package that is built on a relational data base, similar to that shown in Fig. 16.5. This will enable the accounting department to gain experience in using a relational data base. It will also provide time to explore the control issues involved with providing managers with increased access to the general ledger.

This chapter concludes our examination of the various cycles in an AIS. You have learned that accounting information systems have three main objectives: (1) to process transactions for accountability purposes, (2) to maintain adequate controls to ensure the integrity of the organization's data and the safeguarding of its assets, and (3) to provide information to support decision making. We would like to close by reiterating one other theme that appears throughout this book: the need for accountants to move beyond the traditional role of scorekeeper and actively seek to add value to their organization. It is especially important that accountants participate in decisions concerning the adoption of new technology. Chapters 17 through 19 discuss these activities.

Accountants should participate in decisions about adopting new technology because they have the training to properly evaluate the relative costs and benefits, as well as the economic risks, underlying such investments. Effective evaluation requires that accountants not only keep abreast of current accounting developments, but also stay informed about advances in information technology. Thus you must make a commitment to lifelong learning. We wish you well in this endeavor.

KEY TERMS

enterprise resource planning (ERP) systems
journal voucher
responsibility accounting
on-line analytical processing (OLAP)
data mining
general journal listing
balanced scorecard
virtual value chain

CHAPTER QUIZ

1. Adjusting entries are normally provided by
a. the treasurer.
b. the controller.
c. the various accounting cycle subsystems, such as sales order entry.
d. unit managers.

2. Preparing performance reports that contain data only about items that a specific organizational unit controls is an example of
a. a flexible budget system.
b. a responsibility accounting system.
c. closing the books.
d. management by exception.

3. Which of the following is *not* a stage of development of the virtual value chain?
a. Visibility
b. Mirroring
c. Distribution
d. Establishing new customer relationships

4. The first step in the virtual value chain is
a. visibility.
b. gathering information.
c. mirroring.
d. organizing information.

5. Writing a query to identify which salesperson made a specific sale is an example of
a. data mining.
b. responsibility accounting.
c. mirroring.
d. use of on-line analytical processing.

6. Measures of cycle time would most likely appear in which part of the balanced scorecard?
a. Innovation and learning
b. Customer
c. Internal operations
d. Financial

7. Which of the following would be a good measure of innovation and learning?
a. Percentage of on-time deliveries
b. Percentage of sales from products less than two years old
c. Market share percentage
d. Customer satisfaction ratings

8. Traditionally, the general ledger is updated
a. when each transaction occurred.
b. at year-end.
c. monthly.
d. on demand.

9. Which of the following factors is most likely to result in a graph that distorts the magnitude of a trend in financial numbers?
   a. Not starting the vertical axis at zero
   b. Using 3-D bar charts to illustrate sales growth
   c. Ordering the years from left to right
   d. Failing to include a chart title

10. In performance reports, setting the comparison standards on the basis of the actual level of activity that occurred is an example of
   a. responsibility accounting.
   b. long-range planning.
   c. variance analysis.
   d. flexible budgeting.

DISCUSSION QUESTIONS

16.1 The data model shown in Fig. 16.5 is supposed to accommodate the unified storage of financial and nonfinancial operating data. How can you effectively combine both types of information in one report? For example, how can you compare and relate a 15% reduction in scrap and rework costs with an 8% increase in customer satisfaction and a 10% increase in sales?

16.2 What effect does the classification of an organizational unit as a cost, revenue, profit, or investment center have on the types of managerial reports produced for that unit?

16.3 It has been proposed that companies should provide users with a computer-readable copy, either on disk or through the Internet, of the organization's general ledger instead of its financial statements. This would permit users to analyze the data in whatever manner they desire. Assuming that this approach is technologically feasible, should it be done? Why or why not?

16.4 Digital assets are not used up when they are consumed. Moreover, the variable costs associated with distributing those assets may be close to zero. What implications do these properties have for accounting for digital assets? (Hint: Think about depreciation and cost of goods sold.)

16.5 Many companies are participating in studies to develop benchmarks for evaluating the efficiency of their accounting departments. These studies typically report such statistics as the total costs of the accounting department as a percentage of revenues, documents processed per accounting clerk each month, and monthly closing times. Both "best" and "average" figures are usually reported for these categories. Discuss the usefulness and limitations of using such measures to evaluate the accounting department of a specific company.

16.6 Some companies are abandoning the practice of budgeting, because they claim that the costs outweigh the benefits. They argue that instead of comparing actual performance with budgeted standards, closely monitoring trends in actual performance over time would be more effective. Deviations from historical trends would signal the need to take corrective actions. Discuss the advantages and disadvantages of this practice.

16.7 The balanced scorecard measures organizational performance along four dimensions. Is it possible that measures on the customer, internal operations, and innovation and learning dimensions could all be improving without any positive change in the financial dimension? If so, what are the implications of such a pattern?

PROBLEMS

16.1 Which control procedure would be most effective in addressing the following problems?

a. When entering a nonroutine journal entry, the accounting clerk inadvertently transposes two digits in the debit amount.
b. When entering a nonroutine journal entry, the accounting clerk inadvertently transposes two digits in the account code.
c. Last Tuesday an accounting clerk forgot to mark the source journal voucher as being entered after keying in the data for the issuance of debt. Consequently, another accounting clerk entered that same data on Wednesday.
d. The credit manager makes an entry authorizing the write-off of a friend's account.
e. The general ledger master file is stored on disk. For some reason, the disk is no longer readable. It takes the accounting department a week to reenter the past month's transactions from source documents in order to create a new general ledger master file.

f. An accounting clerk, unsure as to which department to charge for a loss on the disposition of some fixed assets, debited a suspense account in order to make the entry balance. Consequently, performance evaluation reports did not correctly show the results of this transaction.
g. The budget director accessed the payroll file and discovered the salaries of every other financial executive.
h. The treasurer inadvertently omitted the credit portion of the journal entry submitted to account for the repurchase of treasury stock.
i. During data entry, the controller transposed two digits in the debit portion of the adjusting entry for bad debt expense.
j. The treasurer forgot to submit a journal entry to record the accrual of interest on a short-term CD.
k. A nonexistent customer account number is entered during the posting of cash receipts. Consequently, the accounts receivable subsidiary ledger is out of balance with the general ledger control account.

16.2 Obtain an annual report that contains several graphs and answer the following questions:

a. Which financial and nonfinancial variables are graphed?
b. Do all the graphs satisfy the general principle that the portrayed magnitude of change equal the actual magnitude of change? If not, which of the rules for accurate graphs were violated? Which variables are not graphed correctly?
c. Redraw any graphs identified in part b so that they accurately portray the magnitude of change in the variable being graphed.
d. Draw a pie graph, a line graph, and a column graph for data in the annual report that have not already been graphed. Design each graph to communicate one essential point about the organization's performance. Defend your choices of graph–variable pairings and your design.

16.3 Give two specific examples of nonroutine transactions that may occur in processing cash receipts and updating accounts receivable. Also specify the control procedures that should be in place to ensure the accuracy, completeness, and validity of those transactions.

16.4 An important control procedure involves the periodic reconciliation of general ledger accounts with their subsidiary ledgers. Explain how this control procedure works in the context of accounts payable. Your answer should specify how to verify the accuracy, completeness, and validity of all entries involving purchases, purchase returns, purchase discounts, and cash disbursements.

16.5 Figure 16.1 is a context diagram for the general ledger and reporting cycle that shows the principal data flows to and from the general ledger.

Required:

a. List the source documents or journals underlying each data flow into the general ledger.
b. Identify at least two additional data flows resulting from the revenue and expenditure cycle systems, and specify the source documents or journals that would support those flows.

16.6 Refer to the example of responsibility accounting coding depicted in Fig. 16.3.

Required:

a. Design a coding scheme that will support the production of this set of reports. Make and state any assumptions you believe are necessary.
b. Write a brief (half-page) explanation of how your coding scheme works.
c. Suggest improvements in the set of reports depicted in Fig. 16.3.

16.7 The manager of a local pizza parlor wants to develop a balanced scorecard to help her more effectively monitor the restaurant's performance. She has asked you to help her design the scorecard.

Required:

a. Propose at least two goals for each dimension. Justify those goals.
b. Suggest specific measures for each goal you developed in step a.
c. Write a brief explanation of how to gather the data needed for each of the measures you suggested in step b.

CASE 16.1 ANYCOMPANY, INC.—AN ONGOING COMPREHENSIVE CASE

Select a local company and obtain permission to study its general ledger and financial reporting system. Write a report that addresses the following issues:

1. Analyze the structure of its general ledger. How does it reflect the nature of the company's line of business? Is the system file-based or is it organized as a data base?
2. How often is the general ledger updated? Why?
3. Is an operating budget used for performance evaluation purposes? If so, what is the basis for setting the budget?
4. What control procedures are in place to safeguard the integrity of the general ledger?
5. How often do various unit managers receive reports on their unit's financial performance? Do any of those reports combine financial with non-financial data? If so, how?
6. Evaluate the tabular reports produced by the system. Are they easy to understand? Appropriate for their intended use?
7. Are graphs used to supplement or present performance results? If so, analyze the graphs in light of the principles of graph design discussed in this chapter.
8. Does the company prepare a balanced scorecard? If it does, evaluate it. If it does not, develop one.

CASE 16.2 EVALUATING A GENERAL LEDGER PACKAGE

Accounting magazines like the *Journal of Accountancy* and *Management Accounting* periodically publish reviews of accounting software. Obtain a copy of a recent software review article and read its comments about a general ledger package to which you have access. Using the software, write a report that indicates whether, and why, you agree or disagree with the review's opinions about the following features of the general ledger package:

1. Ease of installation.
2. Flexibility in the initial setup of the chart of accounts and during subsequent modifications.
3. Frequency of updates from subsystems (sales, cash receipts, etc.).
4. Control procedures available to restrict access.
5. Control procedures to ensure accuracy of input and processing.
6. Report flexibility—how easy it is to design reports, change report content, alter output format, etc.
7. Adequacy of the audit trail. For example, what reference data is automatically provided versus how much of the audit trail has to be manually constructed?

CASE 16.3 RESEARCHING THE VIRTUAL VALUE CHAIN

Write a brief report on how a particular company is successfully exploiting the virtual value chain. Your report should clearly explain the following:

1. The product being sold.
2. The types of mirroring activities and new customer relationships that exist.
3. Accounting implications.
4. Control issues and how the company is addressing them.

ANSWERS TO CHAPTER QUIZ

1. b **2.** b **3.** c **4.** b **5.** d **6.** c **7.** b **8.** c **9.** a **10.** d

PART FOUR

CHAPTER 17

Introduction to Systems Development and Systems Analysis

LEARNING OBJECTIVES

After studying this chapter, you should be able to

- Explain the five phases of the systems development life cycle.
- Discuss the people involved in systems development and the role they play.
- Explain the importance of systems development planning and describe planning techniques.
- Discuss the various types of feasibility analysis, and calculate economic feasibility.
- Explain why systems change triggers behavioral reactions, what form this resistance to change takes, and how to avoid or minimize the resulting problems.
- Discuss the key issues and steps in systems analysis.

Integrative Case: Shoppers Mart

Several months ago Ann Christy, a successful accountant, was promoted to controller of Shoppers Mart (SM), a small but rapidly growing regional chain of discount stores. Since her promotion she has been assessing how the accounting function could better serve Shoppers Mart. She has held meetings with the president and CEO and with other key managers at headquarters. She has also spent several weeks visiting various SM stores, talking one on one with store managers and employees. Here are her findings:

1. Store managers cannot obtain information other than what is contained on SM's periodic, preformatted reports. As soon as information is needed from several functional areas, the system bogs down.
2. The sales and purchasing department cannot get timely information about what products are or are not selling well. As a result, stores are often out of popular items and overstocked with ones that customers are not buying.
3. Top management is concerned that SM is losing market share to larger rivals with better prices and selection. The current system cannot provide management with the information it needs to analyze and solve this problem.

After analyzing the situation, Ann is convinced that Shoppers Mart needs a new information system—one that is flexible, efficient, and responsive to user needs. Ann knows that a new system will never be successful unless it has the complete support of top management. Before she asks for approval and funding for the new system, Ann schedules a meeting with the head of systems development. She has the following questions:

1. What process must the company go through to obtain and implement a new system?
2. What types of planning are necessary to ensure the system's success? Who will be involved, and how? Do any special committees need to be formed? What resources need to be planned for? How should all of the planning be documented?
3. How will employees react to a new system? What problems might this changeover cause, and how can they be minimized?
4. How should the new system be justified and sold to top management? How can expected costs and benefits be quantified to determine whether the new system will indeed be cost-effective?

INTRODUCTION

Because we live in a highly competitive and ever-changing world, organizations continually face the need for new, faster, and more reliable ways of obtaining information. To meet this need, an information system must continually undergo changes, ranging from minor adjustments to major overhauls. Occasionally, the needed changes are so drastic that the old system is scrapped and replaced by an entirely new one. Change is so constant and frequent that at any given time most organizations are involved in some system improvement or change. Companies usually change their systems for one of the following reasons:

- *Changes in user or business needs.* Increased competition, business growth or consolidation, mergers and divestitures, new regulations, or changes in regional and global relationships can alter an organization's structure and purpose. To remain responsive to company needs, the system must change as well.
- *Technological changes.* As technology advances and becomes less costly, an organization can make use of the new capabilities or existing ones that were previously too expensive.
- *Improved business processes.* Many companies have inefficient business processes that need to be updated. For example, the ordering system at Nashua, an office supply manufacturer, caused customer frustration and dissatisfaction. When a customer called, a clerk would take information and promise to call back. Before doing so, the clerk had to access two separate systems: a mainframe system to verify customer information and perform a credit check, and a PC-based system to calculate pricing. If the customer was still interested, the clerk accessed another centralized system to determine inventory availability. When the system was redesigned, it took three minutes to process a telephone order instead of two days.

- *Competitive advantage.* Increased quality, quantity, and speed of information can result in an improved product or service and may help lower costs. For example, Wal-Mart invests heavily in technology to provide information about customers and their purchases in order to increase sales. Bell Atlantic increased revenues by investing $2.1 billion in a new system. This is a shift in management focus, since previously 90% of new systems were to automate labor and reduce expenses.
- *Productivity gains.* Computers automate clerical and repetitive tasks and significantly decrease the performance time of other tasks. Expert systems place specialized knowledge at the disposal of many others. Carolina Power and Light was able to eliminate 27% of its IS staff when it installed a new system that significantly outperformed the old one.
- *Growth.* Companies outgrow their systems and need to either upgrade or replace them entirely.
- *Downsizing.* Companies often move from centralized mainframes to networked PCs to take advantage of their price/performance ratios. This places decision making and its corresponding information as far down the organization chart as possible. For example, Consolidated Edison of New York downsized from a mainframe-based system to a client/server system and eliminated 100 clerical positions. The new system does much more than the old one, including handling work-flow management, user contact, data base queries, automatic cash processing, and voice/data integration.

This chapter discusses five major topics. The first is the systems development life cycle, the process that organizations must go through to obtain and implement a new AIS. The second is the planning activities that are necessary during the development life cycle. The third is the process that one goes through to demonstrate that a new AIS is feasible. The fourth is the behavioral aspects of change that companies must deal with to successfully implement a new system. The last topic is a discussion of systems analysis, the first step in the development life cycle.

SYSTEMS DEVELOPMENT

Whether systems changes are major or minor, most companies go through a systems development life cycle. The steps in that cycle and the people involved in systems development are discussed in this section.

The Systems Development Life Cycle

Ann Christy asked the manager of systems development to explain the process Shoppers Mart would go through to design and implement a new system. This five-step process, known as the **systems development life cycle (SDLC),** is shown in Fig. 17.1 and briefly explained next.

Systems Analysis. As organizations grow and change, management and employees recognize the need for more or better information and request a new or improved information system. The first step in systems development is systems analysis. During **systems analysis,** the information needed to purchase

FIGURE 17.1
The Systems Development Life Cycle}

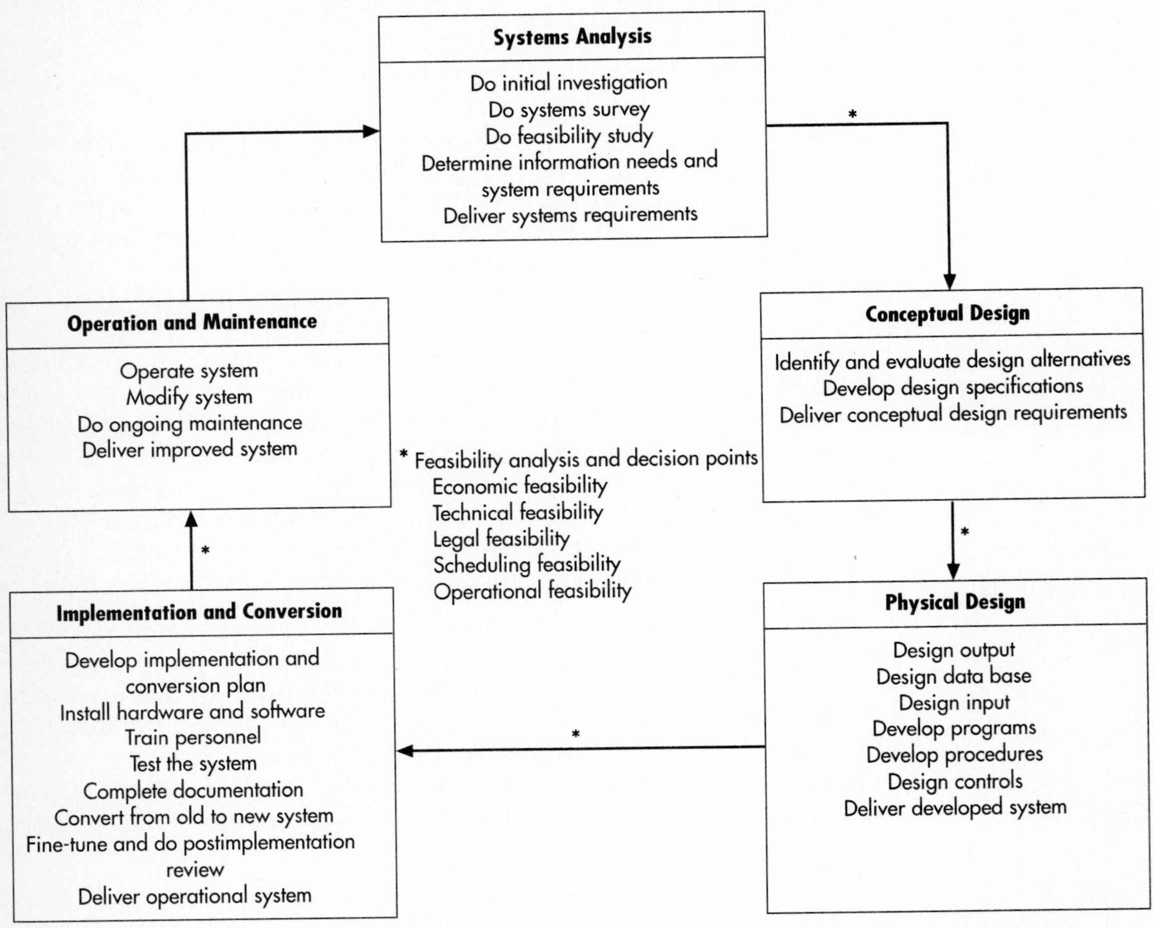

or develop a new system is gathered. Requests for systems development are prioritized to maximally utilize limited development resources. If a project passes the initial screening, the current system is surveyed to define the nature and scope of the project and understand its strengths and weaknesses. Then an in-depth study of the proposed system is conducted to determine its feasibility.

If the proposed system is feasible, the information needs of system users and managers are identified and documented. This is the most important part of systems analysis, as these needs are used to develop and document system requirements. System requirements are used to select or develop a new system.

A systems analysis report is prepared and submitted to the information systems steering committee.

Conceptual Design. During **conceptual systems design,** the company decides how to meet user needs. The first task is to identify and evaluate appropriate design alternatives. There are many different ways to obtain a new system, including buying software, developing it in-house by the IS staff or users, or outsourcing the system to someone else. Detailed specifications outlining what the system is to accomplish and how it is to be controlled must be developed. This phase is complete when conceptual system design requirements are communicated to the information systems steering committee.

Physical Design. During **physical design,** the company translates the broad, user-oriented requirements of the conceptual design into detailed specifications that are used to code and test the computer programs. Input and output documents are designed, computer programs are written, files are created, procedures are developed, and controls are built into the new system. This phase is complete when physical system design results are communicated to the information systems steering committee.

Implementation and Conversion. The **implementation and conversion** phase is the capstone phase where all the elements and activities of the system come together. Because of this phase's complexity and importance, an implementation and conversion plan is developed and followed. As part of implementation, any new hardware or software is installed and tested. New employees may need to be hired and trained, or existing employees relocated. New processing procedures must be tested and perhaps modified. Standards and controls for the new system must be established and system documentation completed. The organization must convert to the new system and dismantle the old one. After the system is up and running, any fine-tuning adjustments needed are made and a postimplementation review is conducted to detect and correct any design deficiencies. The final step in this phase is to deliver the operational system to the organization, at which time the development of the new system is complete. A final report is prepared and sent to the information systems steering committee.

Operations and Maintenance. The new—and now operational—system is used as needed in the organization. During its life, the system is periodically reviewed. Modifications are made as problems arise or as new needs become evident, and the organization uses the improved system. This is referred to as **operations and maintenance.** Eventually a major modification or system replacement is necessary and the SDLC begins again.

In addition to these five phases, three activities (planning, managing the behavioral reactions to change, and assessing the ongoing feasibility of the project) are performed throughout the life cycle. These three activities, as well as systems analysis, are discussed in this chapter. The different approaches to obtaining an AIS are discussed in Chapter 18. The other four SDLC phases are explained in Chapter 19.

The Players

Many people must cooperate to successfully develop and implement an AIS. This section discusses those involved and their roles.

Management. One of the most effective ways to generate systems development support is a clear signal from top management that involvement is important. With respect to systems development, top management's most important roles are providing support and encouragement for development projects and aligning information systems with corporate strategies. Other key roles include establishing system goals and objectives, reviewing IS department performance and leadership, establishing project selection and organizational structure policies, and participating in important IS decisions. The principal roles of user management are to determine information requirements for departmental projects, assist systems analysts with project cost and benefit estimations, assign key staff members to development projects, and allocate appropriate funds to support systems development and operation.

Accountants. Accountants may play three roles during systems design. First, as AIS users they should determine their information needs and system requirements and communicate them to system developers. Second, they may be members of the project development team and IS steering committees and help manage systems development. Third, accountants should take an active role in designing system controls and periodically monitoring and testing the system to verify that the controls are implemented and functioning properly. All systems should contain sufficient controls to ensure the accurate and complete processing of data. The system should also be easy to audit. If addressed at the start of development, auditability and control concerns can be maximized; trying to achieve them after a system has been designed is inefficient, time-consuming, and costly. Control and audit issues are discussed in depth in Chapters 8–11.

Information Systems Steering Committee. Because AIS development spans functional and divisional boundaries, organizations usually establish an executive-level **steering committee** to plan and oversee IS function. The committee often consists of high-level management people, such as the controller and IS and user department management. The steering committee sets policies that govern the AIS; ensures top-management participation, guidance, and control; and facilitates the coordination and integration of IS activities to increase goal congruence and reduce goal conflict.

Project Development Team. Each development project has a team of systems specialists, managers, accountants and auditors, and users that guides its development. They plan each project, monitor it to ensure timely and cost-effective completion, make sure proper consideration is given to the human element, and communicate project status to top management and the steering committee. Team members should communicate frequently with users and hold regular meetings to consider ideas and discuss progress so there are no surprises upon project completion. A team approach usually produces more effective results and facilitates user acceptance of the implemented system.

Systems Analysts and Programmers. **Systems analysts** study existing systems, design new ones, and prepare specifications that are used by computer programmers. Analysts interact with employees throughout the organization and systems technology in order to successfully bridge the gap between the user and technology. It is their responsibility to ensure that the system meets user needs.

Computer programmers write computer programs using the specifications developed by the analysts. They also modify and maintain existing computer programs.

External Players. There are many people outside an organization that play a role in systems development. These include customers, vendors, auditors, and governmental entities. For example, Wal-Mart has told its vendors that if they want to do business with them they must implement and use electronic data interchange (EDI).

PLANNING SYSTEMS DEVELOPMENT

As shown in Fig. 17.1, there are several activities that must be performed at various times throughout the SDLC. One of these is planning. The organization must have a long-range plan, each systems development project requires a plan, and each phase of each development plan must also be planned. This section discusses these plans and a number of techniques used in developing them.

Imagine that you built a two-bedroom house for your first home. Several years later you add a bedroom, then another bedroom and a bathroom. Over the years you add a family room, recreation room, deck, and two-car garage; in addition, you expand the kitchen and the dining area. Without prior thought to what you eventually want in a home, your house will end up as a poorly organized patchwork of rooms surrounding the original structure. In addition, the cost of the house can end up greatly exceeding its value. This scenario also applies to an AIS that is not properly planned. The result is a costly and poorly integrated system that is difficult to operate and maintain.

Systems development planning is an important step for a number of key reasons:

- *Consistency.* Planning enables the system's goals and objectives to correspond to the overall strategic plan of the organization.
- *Efficiency.* Systems are more efficient, subsystems are coordinated, and there is a sound basis for selecting new applications for development.
- *Cutting edge.* The company remains abreast of the ever-present changes in information technology.
- *Lower costs.* Duplication, wasted efforts, and cost and time overruns are avoided. The system is less costly and easier to maintain.
- *Adaptability.* Management is better prepared for future resource needs, and employees are better prepared for the changes that will occur.

When development efforts are poorly planned, a company must often return to a prior phase and correct errors and design flaws, as shown in Fig. 17.2. Such a process is very costly, and it also results in delays, frustration, and low morale. Two types of systems development plans are needed: individual project plans prepared by project teams, and a master plan developed by the information system steering committee.

1. *Project development plan.* The basic building block of IS planning is the **project development plan.** Each project development plan contains a cost/benefit analysis; developmental and operational requirements, including human resource, hardware, software, and financial resource requirements; and a schedule of the activities required to develop and operate the new application.
2. *The master plan.* A **master plan** is a long-range planning document that specifies what the system will consist of, how it will be developed, who will develop it, how needed resources will be acquired, and where the AIS is headed. The master plan should also provide the status of projects in process, prioritize planned projects, describe the criteria used for prioritization, and provide timetables for development. The projects

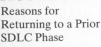

FIGURE 17.2
Reasons for Returning to a Prior SDLC Phase

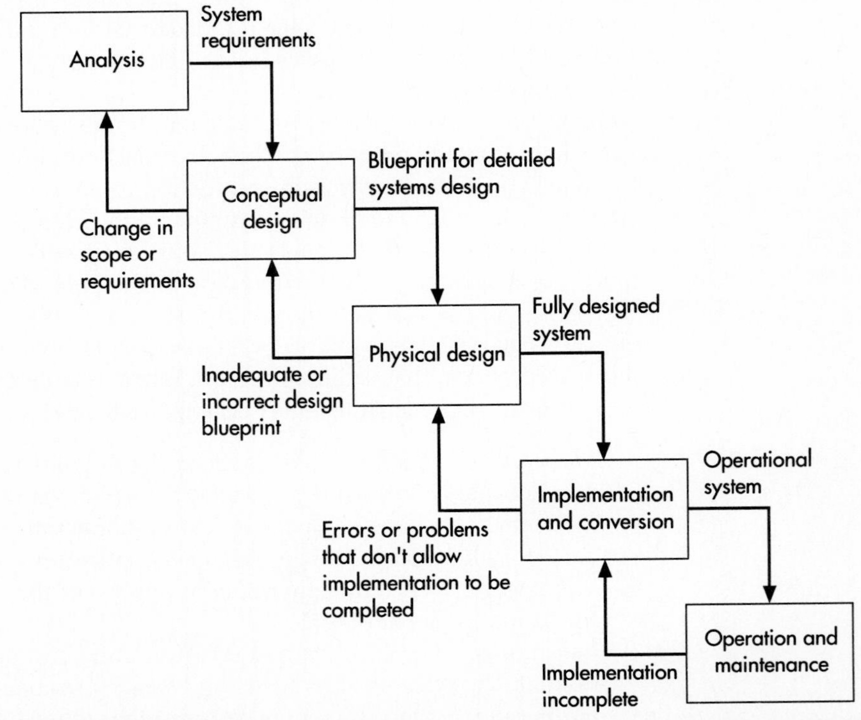

with the highest priority should be the first to be developed. The importance of this decision dictates that it be made by top management and not by computer specialists. A planning horizon of approximately five years is reasonable for any master plan. The plan should be updated at least once each year. MCI, which uses a five-year plan, updates parts of its plan as often as biweekly. The table of contents of the master plan used at Shoppers Mart is shown in Table 17.1.

Systems planning at MCI has been an important factor in their success, as explained in Focus 17.1.

Planning Techniques

Two techniques for scheduling and monitoring systems development activities are PERT and the Gantt chart. **PERT (program evaluation and review technique)** requires that all activities and the precedent and subsequent relationships among them be identified. The activities and relationships are used to draw a PERT diagram, which consists of a network of arrows and nodes representing, respectively, project activities that require an expenditure of time and resources and the completion and initiation of activities. Completion time estimates are made and the **critical path**—the path requiring the greatest amount of time—is determined. A PERT diagram is shown in Fig. 17.3. Its critical path is activities B, C, F, H, I, J, K, and M. Project completion time is 83 weeks. If any of activities on the critical path is delayed, the whole project is delayed. If possible, resources are shifted to critical path activities to reduce project completion time.

A **Gantt chart** (Fig. 17.4) is a bar chart with project activities listed on the left-hand side and units of time (days or weeks) across the top. For each activity a

TABLE 17.1 Components of Systems Master Plan at Shoppers Mart

Organizational goals and objectives	Status of systems being developed
Company mission statement and goals	Proposed systems priorities
IS strategic plan and goals	Approved systems development
Organizational constraints	Proposals under consideration
Organizational approach to AIS	Development timetables and schedules
Organizational and AIS priorities	Forecast of future developments
Inventory and assessments	Forecasts of information needs
Current systems	Technological forecasts
Approved systems	Environmental/regulatory forecasts
Current hardware	Audit and control requirements
Current software	External user needs
Current AIS staff	
Assessment of current strengths and weakness	

FOCUS 17.1 Planning Helps MCI Cope with Popular New Service

WHEN MCI's Friends & Family service was introduced, order entry transaction volume soared 70% in three months. Fortunately, MCI was able to keep response times for the order entry system within acceptable bounds. One reason MCI was prepared was due to planning. Computer capacity planning and performance management are vital activities at MCI, where double-digit annual growth is the norm and computing does not just support the business—it *is* the business. Five-year plans are updated annually, annual plans are revised quarterly, and quarterly plans may change biweekly. MCI's capacity planning staff has such a good track record that top management will accept, with little question, a recommendation to spend millions on a system.

The planning process takes input from three sources. Sales projections go into a computer model developed by MCI, as do service-level objectives such as response time. Out of the model flows capacity requirements for each of MCI's five data centers, indicating the need for hardware resources such as off-line and on-line storage, main memory, and processor power. Capacity planners also factor in advance notice of new software coming from MCI's applications developers and forecasts of new technology from industry research firms and vendors.

Once applications are in production, MCI uses a variety of automated tools to spot abnormal patterns, looming bottlenecks, and other trouble spots. When they are found, the consulting group works with users and software developers to fine-tune applications or to smooth work loads.

FIGURE 17.3
PERT Network of the AIS Implementation Process

Activity	Time (weeks)	Predecessor Activities	Activity Description
A	36	None	Physical preparation (including vendor lead time)
B	4	None	Organizational planning
C	2	B	Personnel selection
D	2	A	Equipment installation
E	10	C	Personnel training
F	15	C	Detailed systems design
G	9	F	File conversion
H	4	F	Standards and controls development
I	9	H	Program preparation
J	9	I	Program testing
K	20	D,E,G,J	Parallel operations
L	8	I	System documentation completion
M	20	K,L	Follow-up

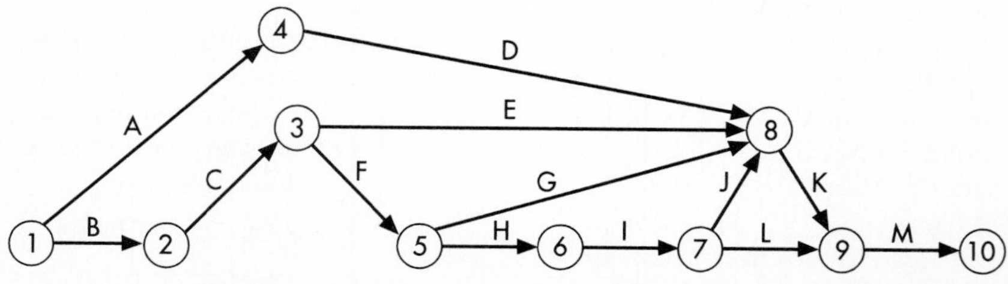

FIGURE 17.4
Sample Gantt Chart

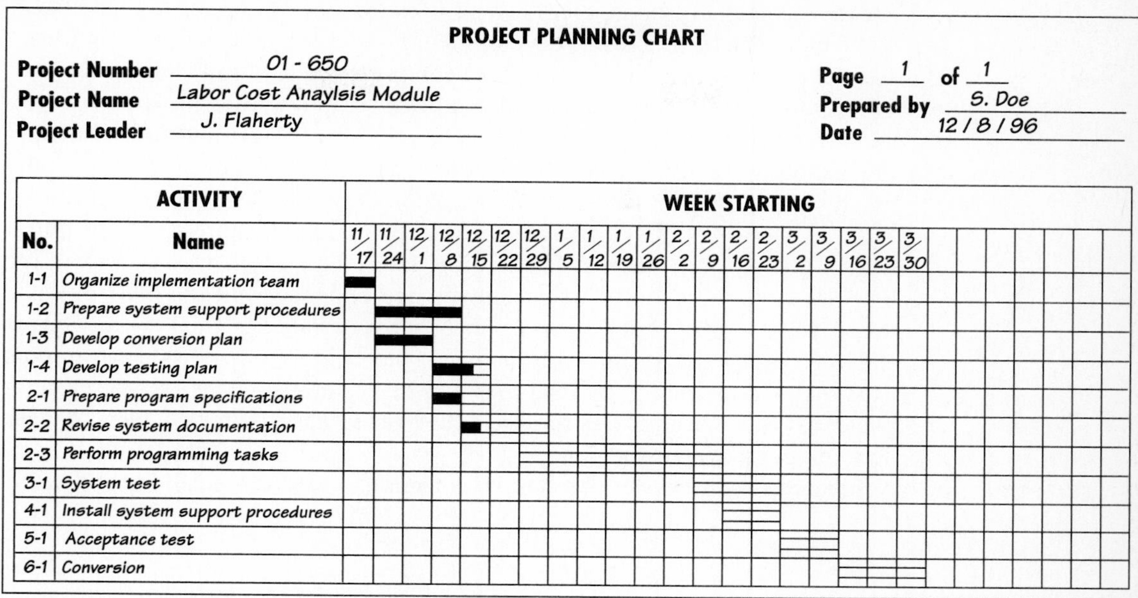

PROJECT PLANNING CHART

Project Number 01 - 650
Project Name Labor Cost Anaylsis Module
Project Leader J. Flaherty

Page 1 **of** 1
Prepared by S. Doe
Date 12 / 8 / 96

ACTIVITY		WEEK STARTING																								
No.	**Name**	11/17	11/24	12/1	12/8	12/15	12/22	12/29	1/5	1/12	1/19	1/26	2/2	2/9	2/16	2/23	3/2	3/9	3/16	3/23	3/30					
1-1	Organize implementation team																									
1-2	Prepare system support procedures																									
1-3	Develop conversion plan																									
1-4	Develop testing plan																									
2-1	Prepare program specifications																									
2-2	Revise system documentation																									
2-3	Perform programming tasks																									
3-1	System test																									
4-1	Install system support procedures																									
5-1	Acceptance test																									
6-1	Conversion																									

bar is drawn from the scheduled starting date to the ending date, thereby defining expected project completion time. As activities are completed they are recorded on the Gantt chart by filling in the bar. Thus at any time it is possible to determine quickly which activities are on schedule and which are behind. The capacity to show, in graphical form, the entire schedule for a large, complex project, including progress to date and current status, is the primary advantage of the Gantt chart. Gantt charts do not show, however, the relationships among various project activities.

FEASIBILITY ANALYSIS

As shown in Fig. 17.1, a **feasibility study** (also called a business case) is prepared during systems analysis and updated as necessary during the remaining steps in the SDLC. The extent of these studies varies, depending on the size and nature of the system. For example, the study for a large-scale system is generally quite extensive, whereas one for a desktop system might be conducted informally. The feasibility team should include management, accountants skilled in controls and auditing, systems personnel, and users.

At major decision points (see Fig. 17.1), the steering committee uses the study to decide whether to terminate a project, proceed unconditionally, or proceed if specific problems are resolved. Although a project can be terminated at any time, the early go/no go decisions are particularly important as each subsequent SDLC step requires more time and monetary commitments. As the project proceeds, the study is updated and the project's viability is reassessed. The further into a development project, the less likely it is to be canceled if a proper feasibility study has been prepared and updated.

Although uncommon, systems have been scrapped after they were implemented because they did not work or failed to meet an organization's needs. For example, Bank America hired a software firm to replace a 20-year-old batch system used to manage billions of dollars in institutional trust accounts. After two years of development, it was implemented despite warnings that it was not adequately tested. Ten months later the system was scrapped, the bank's top systems and trust executives had resigned, and the company had taken a $60 million write-off to cover expenses related to the system. During the 10 months the system was in place the company lost 100 institutional accounts with $4 billion in assets. As another example, Focus 17.2 describes a project at Blue Cross and Blue Shield that was scrapped after six years of work and a $120 million investment.

Five important aspects need to be considered during a feasibility study:

FOCUS 17.2 Blue Cross Abandons Runaway

BLUE CROSS and Blue Shield of Massachusetts hoped that its new information system would usher in a new era. After six years and $120 million, however, the System 21 project was behind schedule and significantly over budget. The project was canceled, and Blue Cross turned its computer operation over to Electronic Data Systems Corporation (EDS), an outside contractor.

Although information system failures of this magnitude are unusual, they happen more often than one would expect. According to a KPMG (Peat Marwick) survey, 35% of all major information system projects become a runaway—a project that is millions of dollars over budget and months or years behind schedule. Other surveys show that almost every *Fortune* 200 company has had at least one runaway.

One major reason for the development problems was Blue Cross's failure to properly supervise the project. Blue Cross hired an independent contractor to develop the software but neglected to appoint someone to coordinate and manage the project in-house. Top management did not establish a firm set of priorities regarding essential features and the sequence of application development.

When the developers presented the claims processing software to Blue Cross, the developers thought it was a finished product. The managers and users at Blue Cross had other ideas. They were not happy with the software and requested numerous changes. As a result, the whole project was delayed. This led to ever-increasing cost overruns. By the time System 21 was launched, Blue Cross had fallen far behind its competitors in its ability to process an ever-swelling load of paperwork. In fact, between 1985 and 1991 it lost a million subscribers and came close to bankruptcy. It also had a poorly integrated system—nine different claims processing systems running on hardware dating back to the early 1970s.

The lesson that Blue Cross learned with System 21 was a painful one. The system it spent six years working on was abandoned, and it turned its hardware over to EDS. Fortunately, although the system died, the patient survived.

1. **Technical feasibility.** Can the planned system be developed and implemented using existing technology?
2. **Operational feasibility.** Does the organization have access to people who can design, implement, and operate the proposed system? Can and will the system be used by those it is intended to serve?
3. **Legal feasibility.** Does the system comply with all applicable federal and state laws and statutes, administrative agency regulations, and the company's contractual obligations?
4. **Scheduling feasibility.** Can the system be developed and implemented in the time allotted? If not it will have to be modified, postponed, or replaced by an alternative selection.
5. **Economic feasibility.** Will system benefits justify the time, money, and other resources required to implement it?

Economic feasibility, the most important and frequently analyzed of the five aspects, is now discussed in greater depth. The feasibility analysis that Ann performed for Shoppers Mart will be shown in Table 17.8.

Calculating Economic Feasibility Costs and Benefits. Determining economic feasibility requires a careful investigation of the costs and benefits of a proposed system. Because accountants are familiar with cost concepts, they provide a significant contribution to this evaluation. The basic framework for feasibility analysis is the **capital budgeting model** in which cost savings and other benefits, as well as initial outlay costs, operating costs, and other cash outflows, are translated into dollar estimates. The estimated benefits are compared with the costs to determine whether the system is cost beneficial. Where possible, benefits and costs that are not easily quantifiable should be estimated and included in the feasibility analysis. If they cannot be accurately estimated, they should be listed and the likelihood of their occurring and the expected impact on the organization evaluated.

Some of the tangible and intangible benefits a company might obtain from a new system are cost savings; improved customer service, productivity, decision making, and data processing; better management control; and increased job satisfaction and employee morale.

Equipment costs are an initial outlay cost if the system is purchased and an operating cost if rented or leased. Equipment costs vary from $1,000 for PC systems to millions of dollars for enormous mainframes. Equipment costs are usually less than the cost of acquiring software and maintaining, supporting, and operating the system. Software acquisition costs include the purchase price of software as well as the time and effort required to design, program, test, and document software. The human resource costs associated with hiring, training, and relocating staff can be substantial. Site preparation costs may also be incurred for large computer systems. In addition, there are costs involved in installing the new system and converting files to the appropriate format and storage media.

The primary operating cost is maintaining the system. Studies show that between 65% and 75% of an organization's systems efforts are spent in maintaining current information systems. In addition, there may be significant annual cash outflows for equipment replacement and expansion and software updates. Human resource costs include the salaries of systems analysts, programmers, operators, data entry operators, and management. Costs are also incurred for supplies, overhead, and financial charges. Initial outlay and operating costs are summarized in Table 17.2.

Capital Budgeting. During systems design, several alternative approaches to meeting system requirements are developed. Various feasibility measures are then used to narrow the list of alternatives. Capital budgeting techniques are used to evaluate the economic merits of the alternatives. Three capital budgeting techniques are commonly used:

1. **Payback period.** This figure represents the number of years required for the net savings to equal the initial cost of the investment. The project with the shortest payback period is usually selected.

TABLE 17.2 Initial Outlay and Operating Costs

Hardware	Maintenance/backup
Central processing unit	Hardware/software maintenance
Peripherals	Backup and recovery operations
Communications hardware	Power supply protection
Special input/output devices	Documentation
Upgrade and expansion costs	Systems documentation
Software	Training program documentation
Application, system, general-purpose, utility, and communications software	Operating standards and procedures
Updated versions of software	Site preparation
Application software design, programming, modification, and testing	Air-conditioning, humidity, and dust controls
Staff	Physical security (access)
Supervisors	Fire and water protection
Analysts and programmers	Cabling, wiring, and outlets
Computer operators	Furnishing and fixtures
Input (data conversion) personnel	Installation
Recruitment and staff training	Freight and delivery charges
Consultants	Setup and connection fees
Supplies and overhead	Conversion
Preprinted forms	Systems testing
Data storage devices	File and data conversions
Supplies (paper, ribbons, toner)	Parallel operations
Utilities and power	Financial
	Finance charge
	Legal fees
	Insurance

2. **Net present value (NPV).** With the NPV method all estimated future cash flows are discounted back to the present, using a discount rate that reflects the time value of money. The initial outlay costs are deducted from the discounted cash flows to obtain the net present value. A positive NPV indicates the alternative is economically feasible. When comparing projects, the one with the highest positive NPV is usually accepted.
3. **Internal rate of return (IRR).** The IRR is the effective interest rate that results in an NPV of zero. A project's IRR is compared with a minimum acceptable rate to determine acceptance or rejection. When comparing projects, the proposal with the highest IRR is usually selected.

Payback, NPV, and IRR are illustrated in Ann's feasibility analysis for Shoppers Mart, which will be shown in Table 17.8.

BEHAVIORAL ASPECTS OF CHANGE

Individuals involved in systems development are agents of change who are continually confronted by people's reaction and resistance to change. The **behavioral aspects of change** are crucial because the best system will fail without the support of the people it serves. Niccolo Machiavelli discussed resistance to change some 400 years ago:[1]

> It must be considered that there is nothing more difficult to carry out, nor more doubtful of success, not more dangerous to handle, than to initiate a new order of things. For the reformer has enemies in all those who could profit by the old order, and only lukewarm defenders in all those who could profit by the new order. This lukewarmness arises partly from fear of their adversaries, who have the laws in their favor, and partly from the incredulity of mankind, who do not truly believe in anything new until they have had an actual experience of it.

Organizations must be sensitive to and consider the feelings and reactions of persons affected by change. They should also be aware of the type of behavioral problems that can result from changes, as discussed in this section.

Why Behavioral Problems Occur

An individual's view of change as good or bad will usually depend on how he or she is personally affected by it. For example, management views change positively if it increases profits or performance or reduces costs. An employee, on the other hand, will view the same change as bad if his or her job is terminated or adversely affected.

To minimize adverse behavioral reactions, one must first understand why resistance takes place. Some of the more important factors include the following:

[1] Niccolo Machiavelli, *The Prince*, translated by Luigi Rice, revised by E. R. P. Vincent (New York: New American Library, 1952).

- *Personal characteristics and background.* Generally speaking, the younger and more highly educated people are, the more likely they are to accept change. Likewise, the more comfortable people are with technology, the less likely they are to oppose changes in an AIS.
- *Manner in which change is introduced.* Resistance is often a reaction to the methods of instituting change rather than to change itself. For example, the rationale used to sell the system to top management may not be appropriate for lower-level employees. The elimination of menial tasks and the ability to advance and grow are often more important to users than are increasing profits and reducing costs.
- *Experience with prior changes.* Employees who had a bad experience with prior changes are more reluctant to cooperate when future changes occur.
- *Top-management support.* Employees who sense a lack of top-management support for change wonder why they themselves should endorse it.
- *Communication.* Employees are unlikely to support a change unless the reasons behind it are explained.
- *Biases and natural resistance to change.* People with emotional attachments to their duties or coworkers may not want to change if those elements are affected.
- *Disruptive nature of the change process.* Requests for information and interviews are distracting and place additional burdens on people. These disturbances can create negative feelings toward the change that prompted them to occur.
- *Fear.* Many people fear the unknown and the uncertainty accompanying change. They also fear loss of their jobs, loss of respect or status, failure, technology, and automation.

How People Resist AIS Changes

Behavioral problems may begin as soon as people find out that a system change is being made. Initial resistance is often subtle, manifested by tardiness, subpar performance, or failure to provide developers with information. Major behavioral problems often occur after the new system has been implemented and the change has become a reality. Major resistance often takes one of three forms: aggression, projection, or avoidance.

Aggression. **Aggression** is behavior that is usually intended to destroy, cripple, or weaken the effectiveness of a system. It may take the form of increased error rates, disruptions, or deliberate sabotage. One organization introduced an on-line AIS, only to discover soon thereafter that the data input devices were inoperable; some had honey poured into them, others had been mysteriously run over by forklifts, and still others had paper clips inserted in them. Employees had also entered erroneous data into the system. More subtle forms of aggression can also undermine the system's intended use. In another organization, disgruntled workers used the new system to gang up on an unpopular foreman. Instead of clocking in and out as they moved from one station to another, they punched in at the foreman's department for the entire day and proceeded to work in different areas. This adversely affected the foreman's performance evaluation, as he was charged for hours that did not belong to his operation.

Projection. **Projection** involves blaming the new system for any and every unpleasant occurrence. For example, missing and incorrect data, which were present but undetected in a manual system, are blamed on the fact that there is a new automated system until the actual cause is determined. In essence, the system becomes the scapegoat for all real and imagined problems and errors. If these criticisms are not controlled or answered, the integrity of the system can be damaged or destroyed.

Avoidance. Dealing with problems through **avoidance** is a common human trait. For example, a person who cannot decide between two job offers may delay a decision until one company withdraws its offer and the decision is made for him. Likewise, one way for employees to deal with a new AIS is to avoid using it in the hope that the problem (the system) can be ignored or that it will eventually go away.

Preventing Behavioral Problems

The human element is often thought to be the most significant problem a company encounters in designing, developing, and implementing a system. Although there is no one best way to overcome behavioral problems, people's reactions can be improved by observing the following guidelines:

- *Meet the needs of the users.* It is essential that the form, content, and volume of system output be designed to satisfy user needs.
- *Keep communication lines open.* Managers and users should be fully informed of system changes as soon as possible. They should be told what changes are being made and why, and they should be shown how the new system will benefit them. The objective is to help employees identify with the company's efforts to improve the system. This helps ensure that employees feel they are indeed key players in the company's future goals and plans. Open communication also helps prevent the spread of damaging and inaccurate rumors and misunderstandings. Employees should be told who they can contact if they have questions or concerns.
- *Maintain a safe and open atmosphere.* It is vital that everyone affected by systems development have an attitude of trust and cooperation. If employees become hostile, it will be very difficult to change their attitude or to implement the system successfully.
- *Obtain management support.* Where possible, a powerful champion, who can provide resources for the system and motivate others to assist and cooperate with systems development, should be utilized.
- *Allay fears.* The organization should provide assurances (to the extent possible) that no major job losses or responsibility shifts will occur. These goals can be achieved through relocation, attrition, and early retirement. If employees are terminated, severance pay and outplacement services should be provided.
- *Solicit user participation.* Those who will use or be affected by the system should participate in its development by providing data, making suggestions, and helping make decisions. Participation is ego enhancing,

challenging, and intrinsically satisfying. Users who participate in development are more knowledgeable, better trained, and more committed to using the system.

- *Provide honest feedback.* To avoid misunderstandings, users should be told which suggestions are being used and how, which suggestions are not being used and why, and which ones will be incorporated at a later date.
- *Make sure users understand the system.* Effective use or support cannot be obtained if users are confused about or do not understand the system. Generally, those who have a working knowledge of computers often underestimate user training needs.
- *Humanize the system.* System acceptance is unlikely if individuals believe the computer is controlling them or has usurped their positions.
- *Describe new challenges and opportunities.* System developers should emphasize important and challenging tasks that can be performed with the new system. It should also be emphasized that the system may provide greater job satisfaction and increased opportunities for advancement.
- *Reexamine performance evaluation.* Users' performance standards and criteria should be reevaluated to ensure that they are satisfactory in view of changes brought on by the new system.
- *Test the system's integrity.* The system should be properly tested prior to implementation to minimize initial bad impressions.
- *Avoid emotionalism.* When logic vies with emotion, it rarely stands a chance. Emotional issues related to change should be allowed to cool, handled in a nonconfrontational manner, or sidestepped.
- *Present the system in the proper context.* Users are vitally interested in how system changes affect them personally. Relevant explanations should be presented that address their concerns, rather than the concerns of managers or developers.
- *Control the users' expectations.* A system is sold too well if users have unrealistic expectations of its capabilities and performance. Be realistic when describing the merits of the system.
- *Keep the system simple.* Avoid complex systems that cause radical changes. Make the change seem as simple as possible by conforming to existing organizational procedures.

Observing these guidelines is both time-consuming and expensive. As a result, there is a tendency to skip the more difficult steps in order to speed up systems development and installation. However, the problems caused by not following these guidelines are usually more expensive and time-consuming to fix than preventing behavioral problems in the first place.

SYSTEMS ANALYSIS

When a new or improved system is needed, a written **request for systems development** is prepared. The request describes the current system's problems, why the change is needed, and the proposed system's goals and objectives as well as its anticipated benefits and costs. The analysis is conducted by the project development team. The five steps in the analysis phase and their objectives are shown in Fig. 17.5 and discussed in this section.

Initial Investigation

An **initial investigation** is conducted to screen projects. The person conducting an initial investigation must gain a clear picture of the problem or need, determine the project's viability and expected costs and payoffs, make an initial evaluation of the extent of the project and the nature of the new AIS, and recommend whether the development project should be initiated as proposed, modified, or abandoned.

During the initial investigation the exact nature of the problem/problems under review must be determined. In some instances what is thought to be the cause is not the real source of the problem. For example, a governmental accountant once asked a consultant to develop an AIS to produce the infor-

FIGURE 17.5
Steps in Systems Analysis

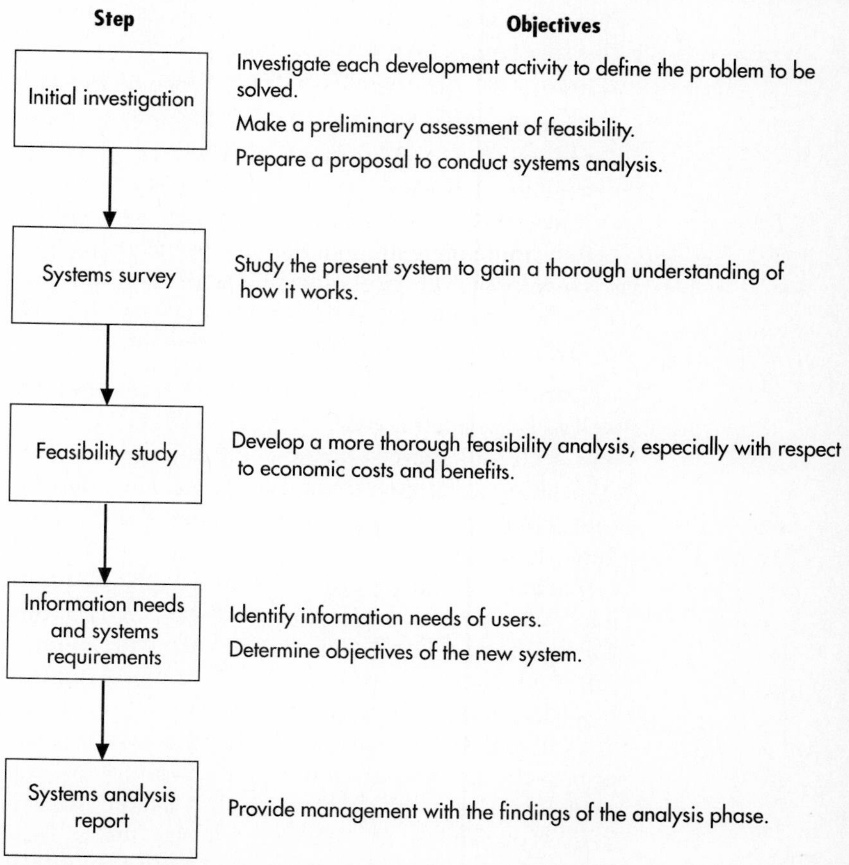

Step	Objectives
Initial investigation	Investigate each development activity to define the problem to be solved. Make a preliminary assessment of feasibility. Prepare a proposal to conduct systems analysis.
Systems survey	Study the present system to gain a thorough understanding of how it works.
Feasibility study	Develop a more thorough feasibility analysis, especially with respect to economic costs and benefits.
Information needs and systems requirements	Identify information needs of users. Determine objectives of the new system.
Systems analysis report	Provide management with the findings of the analysis phase.

mation he needed on fund expenditures and available funds. Further investigation showed that the agency's system already provided the information; the accountant simply did not understand the reports he was receiving.

The scope of a project (what it should and should not seek to accomplish) must also be determined. A new AIS is useful when problems are a result of lack of information, inaccessibility of data, and inefficient data processing. However, a new AIS is *not* the answer to organizational problems, such as the controller managing too many employees. Likewise, if a manager lacks organization skills or if control problems are caused by a failure to enforce existing procedures, a new AIS is not the answer.

If a project is approved, a **proposal to conduct systems analysis** is prepared, it is assigned a priority and added to the master plan, and the development team begins the survey of the existing AIS. As the investigation progresses, the proposal will be modified as more information becomes available. The table of contents for the Shoppers Mart proposal, shown in Table 17.3, is representative of the information in a proposal to conduct systems analysis.

Systems Survey

During the **systems survey** an extensive study of the current AIS is undertaken. This survey may take weeks or months, depending on the complexity and scope of the system. The objectives of a systems survey are as follows:

- Gain a thorough understanding of company operations, policies, and procedures; data and information flow; AIS strengths and weaknesses; and available hardware, software, and personnel.
- Make preliminary assessments of current and future processing needs, and determine the extent and nature of the changes needed.
- Develop working relationships with users and build support for the AIS.
- Collect data that identifies user needs, conduct a feasibility analysis, and make recommendations to management.

Data about the current AIS can be gathered internally from employees as well as from documentation such as organization charts and procedures manuals. External sources include consultants, customers and suppliers, industry associations, and government agencies. The advantages and disadvantages of four common methods of gathering data are summarized here and in Table 17.4.

An *interview* helps gather answers to "why" questions: Why is there a problem? Why does the AIS work this way? Why is this information important? Care must be taken, however, to ensure that an interviewee's personal biases, self-interests, or desire to say what he or she thinks the interviewer wants to hear does not produce inaccurate information.

Ann Christy's interviews at Shoppers Mart were successful because of her approach and preparation. For each interview, she made an appointment, explained the purpose beforehand, indicated the amount of time needed, and arrived on time. Before each session she studied the interviewee's responsibilities and listed the points she wanted to cover. She put each interviewee at ease by being friendly, courteous, and tactful. Her questions dealt with the person's

TABLE 17.3 Table of Contents for Reports Prepared During Systems Analysis at Shoppers Mart

Shoppers Mart
Proposal to Conduct Systems Analysis

Table of Contents

I. Executive Summary
II. System Problems and Opportunities
III. Goals and Objectives of Proposed System
IV. Project Scope
V. Anticipated Costs and Benefits
VI. Participants in Development Project
VII. Proposed Systems Development Tasks and Work Plan
VIII. Recommendations

Shoppers Mart
Systems Survey Report

Table of Contents

I. Executive Summary
II. System Goals and Objectives
III. System Problems and Opportunities
IV. Current System Operations
  A. Policies, Procedures, and Practices Affecting System
  B. Systems Design and Operation (Intended and Actual)
  C. System Users and Their Responsibilities
  D. System Outputs, Inputs, and Data Storage
  E. System Controls
  F. System Strengths, Weaknesses, and Constraints
  G. Costs to Operate System
V. User Requirements Identified During Survey

Shoppers Mart
Systems Analysis Report

Table of Contents

I. Executive Summary
II. System Goals and Objectives
III. System Problems and Opportunities
IV. Project Scope
V. Relationship of Project to Overall Strategic Information Systems Plan
VI. Current System Operations
VII. User Requirements
VIII. Feasibility Analysis
IX. System Constraints
X. Recommendations for New System
XI. Proposed Project Participants and Work Plan
XII. Summary
XIII. Approvals
XIV. Appendix of Documents, Tables, Charts, Glossary of Terms

responsibilities, how the person interacted with the AIS, how the system might be improved, and the person's information needs. She let the interviewee do most of the talking and paid special attention to nonverbal communication, since subtle overtones and body language can be as significant as direct responses to questions. She took notes and augmented them with detailed impressions shortly after the interview. She asked permission to tape especially important interviews.

Questionnaires are used when the amount of information to be gathered is small and well defined, is obtained from many people or from those who are

TABLE 17.4 Advantages and Disadvantages of Data Gathering Methods

	Advantages	Disadvantages
Interviews	Can answer "why" questions Interviewer can probe and follow up Questions can be clarified Builds positive relationships with interviewee Builds acceptance and support for new system	Time-consuming Expensive Personal biases or self-interest may produce inaccurate information
Questionnaires	Can be anonymous Not time-consuming Inexpensive Allows more time to think about responses	Does not allow in-depth questions or answers Cannot probe or follow up on responses Questions cannot be clarified Impersonal; does not build relationships Difficult to develop Often ignored or completed superficially
Observation	Can verify how system *actually* works, rather than how it *should* work Results in greater understanding of system	Time-consuming Expensive Difficult to interpret properly Observed people may alter behavior
System documentation	Describes how system should work Written form facilitates review, analysis	Time-consuming May not be available or easy to find

physically removed, or is intended to verify data from other sources. Questionnaires take relatively little time to administer, but developing a quality questionnaire can be challenging and require significant time and effort.

Observation is used to verify information gathered using other approaches and to determine how a system actually works, rather than how it should work. It can be difficult to interpret observations properly because observed people may change their normal behavior or make mistakes. Observation effectiveness is maximized by identifying what is to be observed, estimating how long it will take, obtaining permission, and explaining what will be done and why. The observer should not make value judgments, and notes and impressions should be formally documented as soon afterward as possible. For example, a systems analyst could observe a customer representative interacting with customers in order to better understand what they do and what information they need.

System documentation describes how the AIS is intended to work. Throughout the systems survey, the project team should be alert to differences between intended and actual system operation. These differences provide important insights into problems and weaknesses. If documentation is unavailable or incomplete, it may be worthwhile to develop it.

Document Findings and Model the Existing System. The information gathered during the analysis phase must be documented so it can be used throughout the systems development project. Documentation consists of questionnaire copies, interview notes, memos, and document copies. Another way of documenting a system is to model it. **Physical models** illustrate *how* a system functions by describing the flow of documents, the computer processes performed and the people performing them, the equipment used, and any other physical elements of the system. **Logical models** illustrate *what* is being done, irrespective of how that flow is actually accomplished. The logical model focuses on the essential activities and the flow of information, not on the physical processes of transforming and storing data. Table 17.5 contains a list of the analysis and design tools and techniques used by accountants and system developers to create an AIS and identifies the chapter where each is discussed in this text.

Analyze the Existing System. Once data gathering is complete, the survey team evaluates the AIS's strengths and weaknesses to develop ideas for how to design and structure the new AIS. Where appropriate, strengths should be retained and weaknesses corrected. For example, if output is being duplicated, consolidating reports might produce cost savings. Sometimes, however, revolutionary rather than evolutionary change is needed and an entirely new system is developed. This process, called *reengineering*, is discussed in Chapter 18.

Prepare Systems Survey Report. The systems survey culminates with a **systems survey report**. Table 17.3 shows the table of contents for the Shoppers Mart systems survey report. The report is supported by documentation such as memos, interview and observation notes, questionnaire data, file and record layouts and descriptions, input and output descriptions, copies of documents, flowcharts, and data flow diagrams.

Feasibility Study

At this point in systems analysis, a more thorough feasibility analysis is conducted to determine the project's viability. Especially important is economic

TABLE 17.5 Systems Analysis and Design Tools and Techniques

CASE (Chapter 18)	Forms design checklist (Chapter 2)
Data dictionary (Chapter 5)	Gantt charts (Chapter 17)
Data flow diagrams (Chapter 3)	PERT charts (Chapter 17)
Data modeling (Chapter 6)	Program flowcharts (Chapter 3)
Decision tables (Chapter 3)	Prototyping (Chapter 18)
Document flowcharts (Chapter 3)	Record layouts (Chapter 5)
E-R diagrams (Chapter 6)	System flowcharts (Chapter 3)

feasibility, as discussed earlier in the chapter. The feasibility analysis is updated regularly as the project proceeds and costs and benefits become clearer.

Information Needs and Systems Requirements

Once a project is deemed to be feasible, the company identifies the information needs of AIS users and documents system requirements. Table 17.6 lists some of the items that a systems requirements list should contain.

Determining information needs can be a challenging process due to the sheer quantity and variety of information that must be specified, even for a relatively simple AIS. In addition, it may be difficult for employees to articulate their information needs or they may identify them incorrectly. Figure 17.6 is a humorous view of the types of communication problems associated with this process.

To illustrate the importance of accurately determining system requirements, consider the example of Corning Corporation. When the company began investigating the quality of the ophthalmic pressings it manufactures and sells to the makers of prescription lenses, it found that 35% of its drafting documents contained errors. Corning also found that the drafting errors became increasingly expensive to correct at each subsequent stage of the manufacturing process. It cost $250 if discovered before the toolmakers cut the tools, $20,000 if discovered before the assembly line began production, and up to $100,000 after it was sent to the customer. As a result of the study, a number of corrective actions were undertaken that reduced the error rates

TABLE 17.6 Possible Contents of Systems Requirements

Processes	A description of all processes in the new system, including what is to be done and by whom
Data elements	A description of the data elements needed, including their name, size, format, source, and significance
Data structure	A preliminary data structure, showing how the data elements will be organized into logical records
Outputs	A copy of system outputs and a description of their purpose, frequency, and distribution
Inputs	A copy of system inputs and a description of their contents, source, and who is responsible for them
Documentation	A description of how the new system and each subsystem will operate
Constraints	A description of constraints such as deadlines, schedules, security requirements, staffing limitations, and statutory or regulatory requirements
Controls	Controls to ensure the accuracy and reliability of inputs, outputs, and processing
Reorganizations	Organizational reorganization needed to meet the users' information needs, such as increasing staff levels, adding new job functions, restructuring, or terminating existing positions or jobs

FIGURE 17.6

Communications Problems in Systems Analysis and Design

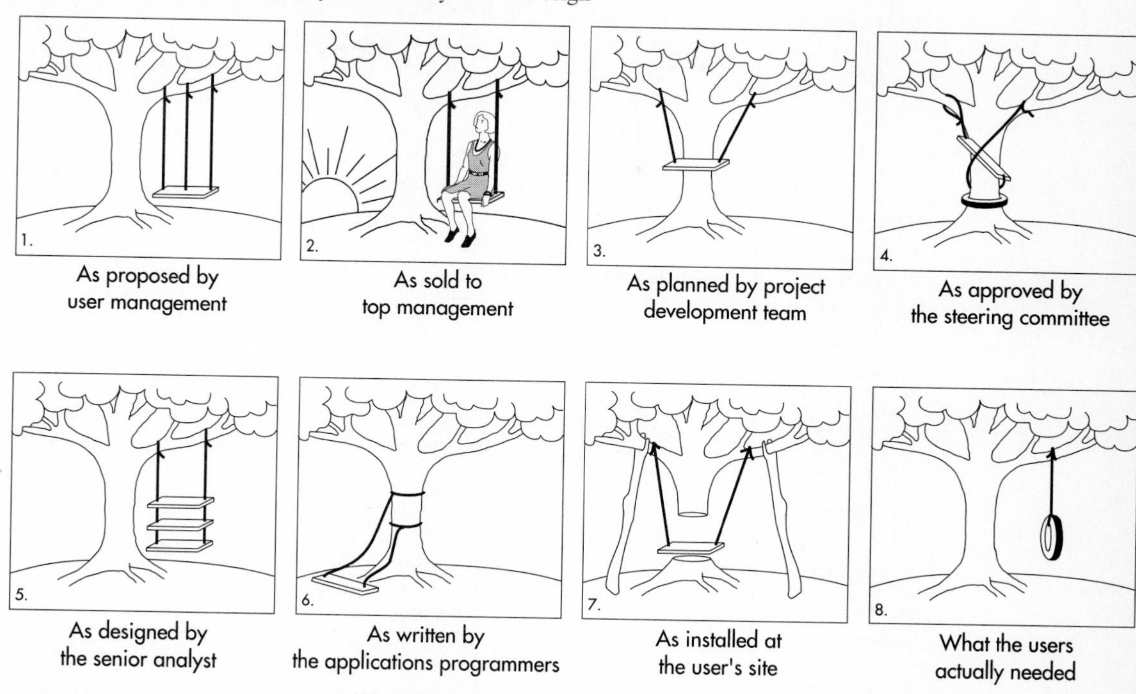

from 35% to 0.2%. The same type of cost relationship exists in IS development; the cost to correct an error increases as development proceeds through the SDLC phases.

1.
As proposed by user management
2.
As sold to top management
3.
As planned by project development team
4.
As approved by the steering committee
5.
As designed by the senior analyst
6.
As written by the applications programmers
7.
As installed at the user's site
8.
What the users actually needed

Systems Objectives and Constraints. Many organizations take a **systems approach** to determining information needs and system requirements; problems and alternatives are viewed from the standpoint of the entire organization, rather than from any single department or interest group.

It is important to determine system objectives so that analysts and users can focus on those elements most vital to the AIS's success (see Table 17.7). However, it is difficult for a system to satisfy every objective. For example, designing adequate internal controls must be viewed as a trade-off between the objectives of economy and reliability. Similarly, cutting clerical costs must balance the objectives of capacity, flexibility, and customer service.

Organizational constraints usually make it impossible to develop all parts of a new AIS simultaneously. Therefore the system is divided into smaller subsystems, or modules, that are analyzed, developed, and installed independently. When changes are made to the system, only the affected module needs to be changed. Great care should be taken to ensure that the modules are properly integrated into a workable system.

TABLE 17.7 AIS Objectives

Usefulness	Information produced by the system should help management and users in decision making.
Economy	The benefits of the system should exceed the cost.
Reliability	The system should process data accurately and completely.
Availability	Users should be able to access the system at their convenience.
Timeliness	Crucial information should be produced first and then less important items as time permits.
Customer service	Courteous and efficient customer service should be provided.
Capacity	System capacity should be sufficient to handle periods of peak operation and future growth.
Ease of use	The system should be user-friendly.
Flexibility	The system should accommodate reasonable operating or system requirements changes.
Tractability	The system should be easily understood by users and designers and facilitate problem solving and future systems development.
Auditability	Auditability should be built into the system from the beginning of systems development.
Security	Only authorized users should be granted access or allowed to change system data.

A system's success often depends on the project team's ability to cope with the constraints under which the organization is operating. Common constraints include governmental agency requirements, management policies and guidelines, lack of sufficiently qualified staff, the capabilities and attitudes of system users, available technology, and limited financial resources. To maximize system performance, the effects of these constraints on system design must be minimized.

Strategies for Determining Requirements. One or more of the following four strategies are used to determine AIS requirements:

1. *Ask users what they need.* Though this is the simplest and fastest strategy, many people do not realize or understand their true needs. Although they may know how to do their job, they may not be able to break it down into the individual information elements they use. It is sometimes better to ask users questions pertaining to what decisions they make and what processes they are involved in and then help them design a system to address their answers. Users must think beyond their current information needs so that the new system does not simply replicate the current information in a new and improved format.

2. *Analyze existing systems.* Both internal and external systems should be analyzed. A partial solution may already exist, thus eliminating the problem of "reinventing the wheel."

3. *Examine existing system utilization.* This strategy differs from the previous one by taking into account that users may not use the existing AIS as intended. Certain modules may not be used as intended, may be augmented by manual tasks, or may be avoided altogether. This approach helps determine whether a system can be modified or must indeed be replaced.

4. *Prototyping.* When it is difficult to identify a usable set of requirements, a developer can quickly rough out a system for users to critique. Once users see something on the screen, they can begin to identify what they like and dislike and request changes. This iterative process of looking at what is developed and then improving it continues until users agree on their needs. Prototyping is discussed in Chapter 18.

Documentation and Approval of User Requirements. Detailed requirements for the new AIS that explain exactly what the system must produce should be created and documented. How to produce the required features is determined during the design phase of the SDLC. The requirements list should be supported by sample input and output forms as well as charts to make it easier for readers to conceptualize the system. A nontechnical summary is often prepared for management that captures important user requirements and development efforts to date.

When user requirements have been determined and documented, the project team meets with the users, explains the requirements, and obtains their agreement and approval. When an agreement is reached, user management should sign the appropriate system requirements documents to indicate approval.

Systems Analysis Report

Systems analysis is concluded by preparing a **systems analysis report.** This report summarizes and documents the analysis activities and serves as a repository of data from which systems designers can draw. The report shows the goal and objectives of the new system, the scope of the project, how it fits into the company's master plan, processing requirements and the information needs of users, the feasibility analysis, and recommendations for the new system. The Shoppers Mart report, shown in Table 17.3, shows in more detail the information typically contained in the report.

A go/no go decision is generally made three times during systems analysis: (1) during the initial investigation, to determine whether to conduct a systems survey; (2) at the end of the feasibility study, to determine whether to proceed to the information requirements phase; and (3) at the completion of the analysis phase, to decide whether to proceed to the design phase.

After systems analysis is completed, projects developed using the SDLC approach move to the conceptual design phase and then to physical design, implementation and conversion, and operation and maintenance. These topics are discussed in the next two chapters.

SUMMARY AND CASE CONCLUSION

An extensive analysis of Shoppers Mart's current system and core business processes was conducted. After the analysis Ann Christy, in consultation with the IS steering committee, decided they wanted the corporate office to gather daily sales data from each store. Analyzing the prior day's sales will help Shoppers Mart adapt quickly to customer needs. Providing sales data to suppliers will help avoid stockouts and overstocking.

Coordinating buying at the corporate office will help Shoppers Mart to minimize inventory levels and negotiate lower wholesale prices. Stores will send orders electronically the day they are prepared. Based on store orders, the previous day's sales figures, and warehouse inventory, Shoppers Mart will send purchase orders to suppliers. Suppliers will process orders and ship goods to regional warehouses or directly to the stores the day orders are received. Each store will have the flexibility to respond to local sales trends and conditions by placing local orders. Accounts payable will be centralized so the firm can make payments electronically.

Ann reviewed the system with the legal department and the AIS staff and was assured that it complied with all legal considerations and was technologically feasible. Top management and the IS steering committee will decide how to allocate time and resources for this massive project and will communicate all staff assignments to systems management and personnel.

Ann's team conducted an economic feasibility study and determined that the project makes excellent use of funds. As shown in Table 17.8, they estimated that initial outlay costs for the system are $5 million (new hardware and initial systems design $2 million each, software $400,000, and training, site preparation, and conversion $200,000 each).

The team estimated what it would cost to operate the system for its estimated six-year life, as well as what the system would save the company. The following recurring costs were identified: hardware expansion, additional software and software updates, systems maintenance, added personnel to operate the system, communication charges, and overhead. The system will also save Shoppers Mart money by eliminating clerical jobs, generating working capital savings, increasing sales and profits, and decreasing warehouse costs. The costs and savings for years 1 through 6, which are expected to rise from year to year, are shown in Table 17.8.

Ann calculated the annual savings minus the recurring additional costs and then calculated the after-tax cash savings for each year. The $5 million system can be depreciated over the six-year period (see Table 17.8 for the rates). For example, the depreciation in year 1 of $1 million reduces net income by that amount. Since the company does not have to pay taxes on the $1 million, at their tax rate of 34% they end up saving an additional $340,000 in year 1. Finally, Ann calculated the net savings for each year.

Shoppers Mart has a 10% cost of capital. Ann used this rate to calculate the net present value of the investment, which is over $3 million. The internal rate of return is a lofty 25%. Ann realized how advantageous it would be for the company to borrow the money (at 10% interest rates) in order to produce a 25% return on that borrowed money. In addition, payback (the point at which benefits exceed costs) occurs in the fourth year.

TABLE 17.8 Economic Feasibility Study for Shoppers Mart's New Information System

	Initial Outlay	Year 1	Year 2	Year 3	Year 4	Year 5	Year 6
Initial outlay costs							
Hardware	$2,000,000						
Software	400,000						
Training	200,000						
Site preparation	200,000						
Initial systems design	2,000,000						
Conversion	200,000						
Total initial outlays	$5,000,000						
Recurring costs							
Hardware expansion			$260,000	$300,000	$340,000	$380,000	$400,000
Software			150,000	200,000	225,000	250,000	250,000
Systems maintenance		$ 60,000	120,000	130,000	140,000	150,000	160,000
Personnel costs		500,000	800,000	900,000	1,000,000	1,100,000	1,300,000
Communication charges		100,000	160,000	180,000	200,000	220,000	250,000
Overhead		300,000	420,000	490,000	560,000	600,000	640,000
Total costs		$960,000	$1,910,000	$2,200,000	$2,465,000	$2,700,000	$3,000,000
Savings							
Clerical cost savings		$600,000	$1,200,000	$1,400,000	$1,600,000	$1,800,000	$2,000,000
Working capital savings		900,000	1,200,000	1,500,000	1,500,000	1,500,000	1,500,000
Profits from sales increases			500,000	900,000	1,200,000	1,500,000	1,800,000
Warehousing efficiencies			400,000	800,000	1,200,000	1,600,000	2,000,000
Total savings		$1,500,000	$3,300,000	$4,600,000	$5,500,000	$6,400,000	$7,300,000
Savings minus recurring costs		540,000	1,390,000	2,400,000	3,035,000	3,700,000	4,300,000
Less income taxes (34% rate)		(183,600)	(472,600)	(816,000)	(1,031,900)	(1,258,000)	(1,462,000)
Cash savings (net of tax)		$356,400	$917,400	$1,584,000	$2,003,100	$2,442,000	$2,838,000
Savings on taxes due to depreciation deduction		340,000	544,000	326,400	195,500	195,500	98,600
Net savings	($5,000,000)	696,400	1,461,400	1,910,400	2,198,600	2,637,500	2,936,600

Payback occurs in the fourth year when the savings net of taxes of $6,266,800 exceed the costs of $5,000,000

Net present value (interest rate of 10%):

(5,000,000)		(5,000,000)
696,400	× 0.9091 =	633,097
1,461,400	× 0.8265 =	1,207,847
1,910,400	× 0.7513 =	1,435,284
2,198,600	× 0.6830 =	1,501,644
2,637,500	× 0.6209 =	1,637,624
2,936,600	× 0.5645 =	1,657,711
Net present value		3,073,206

Internal rate of return is 25.04%

Depreciation on initial investment of $5,000,000

Tax rate			34%
Year	MACRS rate	Depreciation	Tax savings
1	20.00%	1,000,000	340,000
2	32.00%	1,600,000	544,000
3	19.20%	960,000	326,400
4	11.50%	575,000	195,500
5	11.50%	575,000	195,500
6	5.80%	290,000	98,600

Ann presented the system to top management and described its objectives. Challenges to her estimates were plugged into the spreadsheet model so that management could see the effect of the changed assumptions. Even the stiffest challenges to Ann's numbers showed a positive return. As a result of the meeting, top management was very supportive of the new system. They requested a number of changes and gave Ann the approval to proceed.

Ann soon found the enthusiastic support of management to be crucial to the system's success. Several employees with vested interests in the current system felt it was adequate and were critical of her ideas. Some employees remembered the problems Shoppers Mart had when the current system was implemented a few years ago. Ann concluded that those who were resistant to the new system were afraid of the change and its effect on them personally. To counter the negative behavioral reactions, Ann took great pains to explain to all employees how the new system would benefit them individually and the company as a whole. With management's approval, she assured employees they would not lose their jobs and that all affected employees would be retrained. She involved the two most vocal opponents to the system change in planning activities, and soon they became two of its biggest advocates.

Ann set up a steering committee and was granted approval to put the managers of all affected departments on the committee. A master plan for developing the system was formulated, and the system was broken down into manageable projects. The projects were prioritized, and project teams were formed to begin work on the highest-priority projects. Documentation standards were developed and approved.

KEY TERMS

- systems development life cycle (SDLC)
- systems analysis
- conceptual systems design
- physical design
- implementation and conversion
- operations and maintenance
- steering committee
- systems analysts
- computer programmers
- project development plan
- master plan
- PERT (program evaluation and review technique)
- critical path
- Gantt chart
- feasibility study
- technical feasibility
- operational feasibility
- legal feasibility
- scheduling feasibility
- economic feasibility
- capital budgeting model
- payback period
- net present value (NPV)
- internal rate of return (IRR)
- behavioral aspects of change
- aggression
- projection
- avoidance
- request for systems development
- initial investigation
- proposal to conduct systems analysis
- systems survey
- physical models
- logical models
- systems survey report
- systems approach
- systems analysis report

CHAPTER QUIZ

1. Which of the following is *not* one of the reasons that companies make changes to their AIS?
   a. To gain a competitive advantage
   b. To increase productivity
   c. To keep up with company growth
   d. To downsize
   e. All of the above are reasons that companies change an AIS

2. The planning technique that identifies implementation activities and their relationships, constructs a network of arrows and nodes, and then determines the critical path through the network is referred to as a
   a. Gantt diagram.
   b. PERT diagram.
   c. physical model.
   d. data flow diagram.

3. The purchasing department is designing a new AIS. The person or group best able to determine departmental information requirements is
   a. the steering committee.
   b. the controller.
   c. top management.
   d. the purchasing department.

4. Which of the following is the correct order of the steps in systems analysis?
   a. Initial investigation, determination of information needs and system requirements, feasibility study, system survey
   b. Determination of information needs and system requirements, system survey, feasibility study, initial investigation
   c. System survey, initial investigation, determination of information needs and system requirements, feasibility study
   d. Initial investigation, system survey, feasibility study, determination of information needs and system requirements

5. The long-range planning document that specifies what the system will consist of, how it will be developed, who will develop it, how needed resources will be acquired, and its overall vision is referred to as the
   a. steering committee agenda.
   b. master plan.
   c. systems development life cycle.
   d. project development plan.

6. Resistance is often a reaction to the methods of instituting change rather than to change itself.
   a. True
   b. False

7. Increased error rates, disruptions, and sabotage are examples of
   a. aggression.
   b. avoidance.
   c. projection.
   d. payback period.

8. The most significant problem a company encounters in designing, developing, and implementing a system is
   a. the human element.
   b. technology.
   c. legal challenges.
   d. planning for the new system.

9. Determining whether the organization has access to people who can design, implement, and operate the proposed system is referred to as
   a. technical feasibility.
   b. operational feasibility.
   c. legal feasibility.
   d. scheduling feasibility.
   e. economic feasibility.

10. Which of the following is *not* one of the tangible or intangible benefits a company might obtain from a new system?
   a. Cost savings
   b. Improved customer service and productivity
   c. Improved decision making
   d. Improved data processing
   e. All are benefits of a new system

DISCUSSION QUESTIONS

17.1 The approach to long-range AIS planning described in this chapter is important for large organizations with extensive investments in computer facilities. Should small organizations with far fewer IS employees attempt to implement planning programs? Why or why not? Be prepared to defend your position to the class.

17.2 Assume you are a consultant advising a firm on the design and implementation of a new system. Management has decided to let several employees go after the system is implemented. Some have many years of company service. How would you advise management to communicate this decision to the affected employees? To the entire staff?

17.3 While reviewing a list of benefits from a computer vendor's proposal, you note an item that reads "improvements in management decision making—$50,000 per year." How would you interpret this item? What influence should it have on the economic feasibility and the computer acquisition decision?

17.4 This chapter suggests that an organization should make special efforts to ease fears among its employees about potential job or seniority loss. One advantage of mechanizing a system, however, is a reduction of clerical costs, which often results in job losses. Are these two concepts inconsistent? What policies should be consistent with both concepts?

17.5 The president of Monteer Signature Homes is perplexed by requests for computers from three different areas of the firm. The EDP manager wants $4.5 million to upgrade the mainframe computer. The vice president of engineering wants $450,000 to buy a client/server system. The vice president of finance wants $200,000 to purchase laptop computers. Rapid growth is putting a strain on computer resources and keeping profits down. Payroll, accounting, inventory, and engineering functions are computerized; other tasks are manual. The firm is organized by business functions, with vice presidents for manufacturing, marketing, engineering, finance, and human resources. The president wonders whether a steering committee is needed. Discuss the objectives, responsibilities, and composition of an information systems steering committee. Justify your recommendations concerning its membership and the selection of a chairperson.
(CIA Examination, adapted)

17.6 Describe some examples of systems analysis decisions that involve a trade-off between each of the following pairs of objectives:

a. Economy and usefulness
b. Economy and reliability
c. Economy and customer service
d. Simplicity and usefulness
e. Simplicity and reliability
f. Economy and capacity
g. Economy and flexibility

17.7 For years Jerry Jingle's dairy production facilities led the state in total sales volume. However, recent declines left Jerry wondering what his company was doing wrong. When he asked several customers to rate his products, they seemed satisfied but did note several areas of concern. First on the list was the dairy company's record of late deliveries and incomplete orders. Further discussion with some of the company's production employees (not the cows) revealed several problems, including bottlenecks in milk pasteurization and homogenization due to a lack of coordination in job scheduling; mix-ups in customers orders; and improperly labeled products. How would you suggest Jerry begin addressing the company's problems? What types of data gathering techniques would be helpful at this early stage?

17.8 The following problem situations could arise in any manufacturing firm. What questions should you ask to understand the problem?

- Customer complaints about product quality have increased.
- Accounting sees an increase in the number and dollar value of bad debt write-offs.
- Operating margins have risen the past four years due to higher-than-expected production costs from idle time, overtime, and reworking of products.

17.9 For each of the following items, discuss which data gathering method(s) are most appropriate and why.

a. Surveying the adequacy of internal controls in the purchase requisition procedure
b. Identifying the controller's information needs
c. Determining how cash disbursement procedures are actually performed
d. Surveying the opinions of employees concerning the move to a total quality management program
e. Investigating an increase in uncollectible accounts

PROBLEMS

17.1 Yuping Chai has seen the future, and so far she wants no part of it. The offices at Sierra Manufacturing Company, where Chai is vice president, have just been automated. Sitting at her desk in Sacramento, Chai can push buttons on the keyboard of a computer terminal and staff memos will appear on the screen. She can respond with her own memos, which will instantly be sent to colleagues, either for immediate viewing or for storage and later retrieval. By pressing a few other buttons, she can view company financial data stored in the corporate computer. Chai can do all that and more, but instead she has unplugged the terminal. "I think most managers, including me, are talkers," she states. "I would much rather talk than push buttons." Chai's resistance exemplifies the reaction of some professionals and executives who are being forced to make major psychological and behavioral adjustments as they begin to move into a paperless world.

Required:

a. What do you believe is the real cause of Chai's resistance to the computer system?
b. As a colleague of Chai, how could you help her realize the benefits of computerization and overcome her computer phobia?

17.2 Mary Smith is the bookkeeper for Dave's Distributing Company, a distributor of soft drinks and juices. Because the company is rather small, Mary performed all the daily accounting tasks by herself. Dave, the president and owner of the company, supervises the warehouse/delivery and front office staff, but he also spends much of his time jogging and skiing.

For several years profits were good and sales grew faster than industry averages. Although the accounting system was working well, Dave was being pressured by bottlers to computerize. With a little guidance from a CPA friend and with no mention to Mary, Dave bought a new personal computer and some accounting software. Only one day was required to set up the hardware, install the software, and convert the files. The morning the vendor installed the computer, Mary's job performance changed dramatically. Although the software company provided two full days of training, she had trouble learning the new system. As a result, Dave decided she should run both the manual and computer systems for a month to verify the accuracy of the new system.

Mary continually complained that she lacked the time and expertise to run both systems by herself. She also complained that she did not understand how to run the new computer system. To keep accounts up to date, Dave spent two to three hours a day running the new system himself. Dave found that much of the time spent running the system was devoted to identifying discrepancies between the computer and manual results. When the error was located, it was almost always in the manual system. This significantly increased Dave's confidence in the new system.

At the end of the month Dave was ready to scrap the manual system, but Mary said she was not ready. Dave went back to skiing and jogging, and Mary went on with the manual system. When the computer system fell behind, Dave again spent time catching it up. He also worked with Mary to make sure she understood how to operate the computer system.

Months later Dave was still keeping the computer system up to date and training Mary. He was at the height of frustration. "I know Mary *knows* how to run the system, but she doesn't seem to *want* to. I can do all the accounting work on the computer in two or three hours a day, but she can't even do it in her normal eight-hour workday. What should I do?"

Required:

a. What actions and lack of actions may have contributed to the new system's failure?
b. In retrospect, how should Dave have handled the computerization of the accounting system?
c. At what point in the decision-making process should Mary have been informed? Should she have had some say in whether the computer was purchased? If so, what should have been the nature of her input? If Mary had not agreed with his decision to acquire the computer, what should Dave have done?
d. A hard decision needs to be made about what to do with Mary. Significant efforts have been made to train her, but they have been unsuccessful. What would you recommend at this point? Should she be fired? Threatened with the loss of her job? Moved somewhere else in the business? Given additional training?

17.3 Wright Company employs a computer-based data processing system to maintain company records. The present system was developed in stages over the past five years and has been fully operational for the past two. During the design process, department heads were asked to specify the types of information and reports they would need. Company management also asked for a number of reports. By the time the development stage began, there were several staff changes and the new department heads requested additional reports. The IS department complied with these changes, and reports were discontinued only upon the request of a department head. Few reports were actually discontinued, and a large number of reports are generated each period.

Company management is concerned about the quantity of information produced by the system. Internal auditing was asked to evaluate the effectiveness of the system and determined that more information was being generated than could be used effectively. They noted the following reactions to this information overload.

- Many department heads did not act on certain reports during periods of peak activity. They let them accumulate in the hope of catching up later.

- Some department heads had so many reports they did not act at all, or misused the information.
- Frequently, no action was taken until another manager needed a decision made. Department heads did not develop a priority system for acting on the information.
- Department heads often developed information from alternative, independent sources. This was easier than searching the reports for the needed data.

Required:

a. Indicate whether each of the observed reactions is a functional or dysfunctional behavioral response. Explain your answer in each case.
b. Recommend procedures to eliminate any dysfunctional behavior and prevent its recurrence.

(CMA Examination, adapted)

17.4 The controller of Tim's Travel (TT), a rapidly growing travel corporation, is deciding between upgrading the company's existing computer system or replacing it with a new MANTIS XIT-470. The present system is four years old. Upgrading will cost $97,500 and will extend its useful life for another seven years. The book value is $19,500, although it would sell for $24,000. Upgrading will eliminate one employee at a salary of $19,400; the MANTIS will eliminate two employees. Annual operating costs are estimated at $15,950 per year. Upgrading is expected to increase profits 3.5% above last year's level of $553,000.

The BetaTech Company has quoted a price of $224,800 for the new MANTIS, which has a useful life of seven years. Annual operating costs are estimated to be $14,260. The average processing speed of the MANTIS is 12% faster than that of other systems in its price range, which would increase TT's profits by 4.5%.

Tim's present tax rate is 35% and money is worth 11%. Also assume that after seven years the salvage value, net of tax, would be $12,000 for the MANTIS and $7,500 for the present system. For tax purposes, computers are depreciated over five full years (six calendar years; a half year the first and last year) and the cost recovery percentages are as follows:

Year	Percent
1	20.00
2	32.00
3	19.20
4	11.52
5	11.52
6	5.76

Required:

Use a spreadsheet package to perform an economic feasibility analysis to determine whether TT should rehabilitate the old system or purchase the MANTIS. As part of the analysis, compute the after-tax cash flows for years 1 through 7 and the payback, NPV, and IRR of each alternative.

17.5 Rossco Incorporated is considering purchasing a new Z-660 computer to maximize office efficiency. The proposal estimates that initial systems design would cost $54,000; hardware, $74,000; and new software, $35,000. One-time initial training costs are expected to be $11,000, an additional $20,000 will be required to install the system, and $12,000 will be required to convert the files. A net reduction of three employees, whose average salaries are $40,000 per year, is expected if the new machine is acquired. A special study was just completed that found that computerization could decrease average yearly inventory by $150,000. Annual operating costs, other than employee wages, are expected to be $30,000 per year higher than those for the current manual system.

The expected life of the machine is four years, with an estimated salvage value of zero. The effective tax rate is 40%. For purposes of the feasibility study, assume that all costs associated with the computer purchase will be depreciated equally over the four-year life using the straight-line method. Assume that Rossco can invest money made available from the reduction in inventory at 11% annually. Also, assume that all cash flows, except for the initial investment and start-up costs, are at the end of the year. Assume 365 days in a year.

Required:

Use a spreadsheet to perform a feasibility analysis to determine whether Rossco should purchase the computer. Compute the following as part of the analysis:

a. Initial investment
b. After-tax cash flows for years 1–4
c. Payback period
d. Net present value
e. Internal rate of return

17.6 XYZ Conglomerate Company has completed a feasibility study to upgrade its computer system. Management received the information in Table 17.9, which shows the benefits of the new system.

TABLE 17.9 Benefits to Be Derived from the New System

1. Production		
a. Marketing forecasting is presently in dollars per product line. Calculation of units by product line takes an estimated two man-days, a total of $80. This saving would be repeated each time the market forecast was updated, presumably monthly. The program to calculate the forecast in units would be more accurate than the present method of applying factors to dollar value.	$ 960	
b. More effective inventory control would permit an overall reduction in inventory. The ability to quickly establish total requirements would help to overcome parts stockout situations. For this calculation we estimate a 10% inventory reduction. The cost of capital at XYZ Conglomerate Company approximates 20%, and the benefit then approximates 20% of $100,000.	$20,000	
c. Evaluation of changes to plans will be possible in detail. This is not so under our manual system. Parts explosions are time-consuming and can only be done monthly. The impact here would be increased production flexibility and the reduction of sales losses due to finished goods stockouts. We estimate that this can be valued as the equivalent of hiring two clerks.	$15,000	$35,960
2. Engineering		
a. Use of the computer in filing and updating bills of material would save 40% of the industrial engineer's time.	$ 4,000	
b. The improved updating of files, which includes the bills of material and product structure files, which affect many areas, should save a minimum 25% of one clerk (if we took all areas, this would probably be closer to 50%).	$ 1,500	
c. Estimated clerical savings in labor calculations, rates, and bonus detail is two days per week, or 40% of one person.	$ 2,000	$ 7,500
3. Sales		
a. Improved reporting will enable sales staff and sales management to react more quickly to prevailing conditions. The implied benefit would be sales increases, especially during promotions, and a better sales/expense ratio. We are assuming an improvement in sales of only $1000 per person, for a total of $5000.		$ 5,000
4. Marketing		
a. Revised reports and an improved forecasting system will help in establishing sales trends and will help the production department in flexibility and inventory control.		
5. Accounting		
a. Standard costing of all bills of material, and in fact, the side effect of being able to cost new products quickly, can be expressed as the equivalent of saving 30%–40% of the plant accountant's time.	$ 3,000	
b. A revised incentive earnings and payroll system installed on the computer should reduce the payroll department clerical labor from three days to one day—possible benefit of 40% of one clerk.	$ 2,400	$ 5,400
Total		$53,860

Required:

As a board member, which of the benefits would you accept as relevant to the cost justification of the system? Defend your answer.

(SMAC Examination, adapted)

17.7 The Alkin Chemical Company manufactures and sells chemicals for agricultural and industrial use. The company has grown significantly over the past five years. However, the company's AIS is the original one developed and installed by the former president's son while he was in college. Much of the information generated by the system is irrelevant, and more appropriate and timely information is needed.

The controller is concerned that actual monthly cost data for most production processes are compared with actual costs of the same processes for the previous year. However, the production supervisors contend that the system is adequate because it accounts for discrepancies. The current year's costs seldom vary from the previous year's costs when adjusted for inflation. Thus they feel that costs are under control.

The vice president of manufacturing has found that preparing even the simplest of cost analyses requires that she spend days compiling information generated by the current system. She feels that the system should be flexible enough for each manager to develop quickly his or her own recurring reports.

As a result of these concerns, the new president has appointed a committee to review the system. It will determine management's information needs for cost control and decision purposes and ensure that the behavioral needs of the company and its employees are met. The committee is chaired by the vice president of finance and administration.

Shortly after announcing the formation of this committee, the vice president of finance overheard a cost accountant say, "I've been doing it this way since the company began and now this committee plans to make my job redundant." Several employees in the general accounting department also felt that their positions would be eliminated or changed significantly. Several days later, the vice president of finance and administration overheard one of the production managers state that he believed the system was in need of revision because the most meaningful information that he was receiving came from a junior salesperson.

Required:

a. Identify the behavioral implications of utilizing an AIS that does not appear to meet management's needs.
b. Identify and explain the problems that employees have with the AIS.
c. Identify policies or practices the company could follow during systems implementation that would reduce costs without laying off employees.

(SMAC Examination, adapted)

17.8 Recent years have brought an explosive growth in electronic communication. Computers, photocopiers, fax machines, word processors, electronic mail, teleconferencing, and sophisticated management information systems have changed the way information is received, processed, and transmitted. With the decreasing costs of computer equipment and the increasing power of automation, the full impact of computerization has not yet been felt. Although the development of computer applications is directed at being user-friendly or user-oriented, the integration of computers into the organization has had both positive and negative effects on employees.

Required:

a. Describe the benefits that companies and their employees can receive from electronic communication.
b. Discuss the organizational impact of introducing new electronic communication systems.
c. Explain (1) why an employee might resist the introduction of electronic communication systems and (2) the steps an organization can take to alleviate this resistance.

(CMA Examination, adapted)

17.9 PWR Instruments is a manufacturer of precision nozzles for fire hoses. The company was started by the president, Ronald Paige, an engineer. This closely held corporation has been very successful and has experienced steady growth. Reporting to Paige are six vice presidents representing the company's major functions—marketing, production, research and development, information services, finance, and human resources. The information services department was just established during the past fiscal year, when PWR began developing a new computer-based information system. The new data base system employs a server connected to several terminals and personal computers in each of the six departments. The personal computers can both download data from and upload data to the main computer. For example, financial analysts can access the data stored on the main computer through the personal computers and use the latter as smart terminals on a stand-alone basis. PWR is still in the process of designing and developing new applications for its computer system.

Paige has recently received the management letter prepared by the company's external audit firm, and he has called a meeting with his vice presidents to review the recommendations. One major item that Paige wants to discuss is the recommendation that PWR form an IS steering committee.

Required:

a. Explain why the external auditor would recommend that PWR establish an IS steering committee, and discuss its specific responsibilities. What advantages can an IS steering committee offer PWR?
b. Identify the PWR managers who would be most likely to serve on the committee.

(CMA Examination, adapted)

17.10 Over four hundred years ago, Machiavelli wrote in *The Prince*, "It must be considered that there is nothing more difficult to carry out, nor more doubtful of success, nor more dangerous to handle, than to initiate a new order of things." This statement is as applicable today as it was in 1520.

Implementing organizational change is one of the most demanding assignments faced by any executive. It has been suggested that every change requires three steps: unfreezing the current situation, implementing the change, and finally refreezing the effected change. This view, however, lacks the specific details needed by an operating manager who must initiate the change.

Required:

a. Identify and describe the specific steps a manager must take to implement an organizational change.
b. Suppose an organization does make a change that affects employees directly or affects how they conduct their operations.
   1. Explain why employees generally resist change.
   2. Outline and describe the ways a manager can reduce the resistance to change.

(CMA Examination, adapted)

17.11 Don Richardson, vice president of marketing for the JEM Corporation, has just emerged from another strategic planning session aimed at developing a new line of business. The company's management team has been discussing these plans for several months, since major organizational changes will be required to implement the strategic plan. Rumors about the plans have been circulating the office for months, and Richardson has already been confronted by several employees who are anxious about the expected changes. His only response has been to tell them that an official announcement of this new business plan is expected shortly.

When he returns to his office, Richardson is met by an ad hoc committee composed of his department managers. The sales manager, Susan Williams, has been the most vocal of the group and, as expected, is acting as spokesperson. "Mr. Richardson, it is imperative that we speak to you right away. The employees are becoming very apprehensive about the proposed changes, and lately their job performance has slacked off."

"That's right," adds George Sussman, accounting manager. "My subordinates are asking me all sorts of questions concerning this new line of business, and I don't have any answers for them. They're not buying the 'official announcement' line any longer. I suspect that some of them are already looking for jobs in the event that department 'changes' phase out their positions."

Required:

a. Describe the general steps in the decision-making process that a company should follow before choosing to implement a major organizational change.
b. Explain why employees generally resist organizational change.
c. Discuss ways JEM Corporation can alleviate employee resistance to change.

(CMA Examination, adapted)

17.12 Remnants, Inc. is a large company that manufactures and markets designer clothing throughout the United States. From its St. Louis headquarters, Remnants has developed a regional system for marketing and servicing its products. Each region functions as a profit center because of the authority given to regional managers within their territories.

Each regional organization consists of an accounting and a budget department, a human resources and training department, and several area offices to market and service the products. Each area office consists of sales, service, and administrative departments, the managers of which ultimately report to one area manager.

The New York area office departed from the standard organizational structure by establishing a branch office to market and service the firm's products in the

Boston area. The local office is headed by a branch manager who reports directly to the area manager.

In recent years the Boston branch manager has encouraged the area manager to consider a new information system to handle the local branch's growing information needs. The New York area manager and the eastern regional manager have concluded that they should establish a project team with employees from the regional office, the area office, and the branch office to (1) assess the information needs at the Boston branch office and (2) develop system recommendations, if necessary. The following employees have been appointed to the project team, with Keith Nash acting as chairperson:

Eastern Region Office
Kurt Johnson, Budget Supervisor
Sally Brown, Training Director

New York Office
Keith Nash, Administrative Director

Boston Branch
Heidi Meyer, Branch Manager and Sales Manager
Bobby Roos, Assistant Branch Manager and Service Manager
Joe Gonzalez, Salesperson
Juana Martinez, Serviceperson

Required:

a. A project team, similar to the one organized at Remnants, Inc., is organized to contribute their skills to accomplish a given objective. Characteristics of group members can influence the functioning and effectiveness of a project team. Identify some of these characteristics.
b. Due to the team's composition, what sources of conflict can you see arising among its members? Do you think the group will succeed in its objective to develop an information system for the Boston branch office? Why or why not?
c. What contribution would a person who holds a position as budget supervisor make in a project team such as this one?

17.13 Managers face a continual crisis in the systems development process: IS departments develop systems that businesses cannot use. At the heart of the problem is a proverbial "great divide" that separates the world of business from the world of information systems. Few departments seem able or ready to cross this gap.

A major reason for the resulting information systems development crisis is that many large systems currently handling corporate information needs are seriously out of date. As a result, companies are looking for ways to improve existing systems or to build new ones.

Another reason for the crisis is the widespread use of PC-based systems that have spawned a high level of user expectation that is not being met by IS departments. As computer education increases, users are seeking more powerful applications that are not available on many older systems.

The costs of the great divide can be devastating for unprepared companies. An East Coast chemical company spent more than $1 million on a budgeting and control system that was never used. The systems department created an administrative budgeting system; the company's expertise was technical excellence, not budgets. As a result, the new system completely missed the mark when it came to meeting business needs.

Another example of poor systems development comes from a midwestern bank. It used an expensive computer-aided software engineering (CASE) tool to develop a system that users ignored because there had been no design planning. A senior analyst for Franklin Savings Association said, "They built the system right; but, unfortunately, they didn't build the right system."

So what is the solution? The first step in effective systems design is a thorough business analysis, not a systems analysis. A business analysis includes a thorough review of how a business operates and how the functions of the business relate. Only with this understanding can systems professionals and business managers communicate effectively when developing an integrated system.

In addition, businesses are seeking managers that have a systems background, because they provide a liaison between the systems department and the finance and accounting departments, helping business managers to clearly communicate their needs.

What is still missing is more involvement between systems staff and end users. Systems designers must take more time to interact with end users. In addition, business managers must provide their employees with the training time required to make the system work right.

Required:

a. What is the great divide in the systems development process? What are the reasons for this gap?
b. What are the suggested solutions to the information crisis? How will the systems approach to development help?

c. Discuss the role that a systems designer, a business manager, and an end user can take to narrow the great divide.
d. Who plays the most vital role in the effective development of the system?

17.14 Joanne Grey, a senior consultant, and David Young, a junior consultant, were assigned by their firm to conduct a systems analysis for a client. The objective of the study was to consider the feasibility of integrating and automating certain clerical functions. Grey had previously worked on jobs for this client, but Young had been hired only recently.

On the morning of their first day on the job, Grey directed Young to interview a departmental supervisor and learn as much as he could about the operations of the department. Young went to the supervisor's office, introduced himself, and made the following statement: "Your company has hired my firm to study the way your department works and to make recommendations as to how its efficiency could be improved and its cost lowered. I would like to interview you to determine what goes on in your department."

Young questioned the supervisor for about thirty minutes but found him to be uncooperative. He then gave Grey an oral report on how the interview had gone and what he had learned about the department.

Required:

Describe several flaws in the approach taken to obtain information about the operation of the department under study. How should this task have been performed?

17.15 Business organizations often are required to modify or replace a portion or all of their financial information system in order to keep pace with their growth and take advantage of improved information technology. The process involved in modifying or replacing an AIS requires a substantial commitment of time and resources. When an organization undertakes a change in its AIS, a systems analysis takes place.

Required:

a. Explain the purpose and reasons for surveying an organization's existing system during a systems study.
b. Identify and explain the general activities and techniques that are commonly used during the systems analysis.
c. Systems analysis is often carried out by a project team composed of a systems analyst, a management accountant, and other persons in the company who would be knowledgeable and helpful in the systems study. What would be the role of the management accountant in systems analysis?

(CMA Examination)

17.16 The following list presents specific project activities and their scheduled starting and completion times:

Activity	Starting Date	Ending Date
A	Jan. 5	Feb. 9
B	Jan. 5	Jan. 19
C	Jan. 26	Feb. 23
D	Mar. 2	Mar. 23
E	Mar. 2	Mar. 16
F	Feb. 2	Mar. 16
G	Mar. 30	Apr. 20
H	Mar. 23	Apr. 27

Required:

a. Using a format similar to that illustrated in Fig. 17.4, prepare a Gantt chart for this project. Assume that each activity starts on a Monday and ends on a Friday.
b. Assume today is February 16 and activities A and B have been completed, C is half completed, F is a quarter completed, and the other activities have not yet commenced. Record this information on your Gantt chart. Is the project behind schedule, on schedule, or ahead of schedule? Explain.
c. Discuss the relative merits of the Gantt chart and PERT as tools for project planning and control.

17.17 Refer to the PERT network of the computer implementation process shown in Fig. 17.3. Using months as the basic unit of time, prepare a Gantt chart for the project like that in Fig. 17.4. Assume that each activity is scheduled to begin immediately following the scheduled completion of any preceding activities. To simplify your analysis, you may assume that four weeks equal one month.

CASE 17.1 ANYCOMPANY, INC.—AN ONGOING COMPREHENSIVE CASE

Identify a local company (you may use the same company that you identified to complete Case 1.1) and perform the following steps:

1. Schedule a visit with a member of the AIS staff. With help, identify the most significant revision in the company's AIS (for some, this may mean the initial design and implementation). Discuss the following issues.
   a. What groups were organized to oversee systems design/revision and implementation? How was the implementation strategy developed?
   b. What problems did the company run into when it was developing/revising its system? How did the company handle these problems?
   c. Which staff members were affected by the change in the AIS? In general terms, how did employees react to the changes? What did the project development team do to minimize potential negative effects of the system change?
   d. If the company were starting the project over again, what would it do differently? Why?
2. Review the documentation that covers system design/revision and implementation. Take a few moments to review any project development plans and the master plan, if available.
3. If appropriate, ask to review the feasibility analysis surrounding the implementation of the AIS.
4. From your interview and your observations, write a brief report summarizing your findings. Consider the following issues:
   a. How well did the company organize the design/revision and implementation of the AIS?
   b. What suggestions do you have for improving the company's development and implementation procedures?

CASE 17.2 AUDIO VISUAL CORPORATION

Audio Visual Corporation (AVC) manufactures and sells visual display equipment. The company is headquartered outside of Boston. The majority of sales are made through seven geographical sales offices located in Los Angeles, Seattle, Minneapolis, Cleveland, Dallas, Boston, and Atlanta. Each sales office has a warehouse located nearby that carries an inventory of new equipment and replacement parts. The remainder of the sales are made through manufacturers' representatives.

AVC's manufacturing operations are conducted in a single plant, which is highly departmentalized. In addition to the assembly department, there are several departments responsible for various components used in the visual display equipment. The plant also has maintenance, engineering, scheduling, and cost accounting departments.

Early in 1996 management decided that its AIS needed upgrading. As a result, the company installed a mainframe at corporate headquarters and local area networks at each of the seven sales offices.

The integration of the new computer and the LANs into the AVC AIS was carried out by the IS staff. The IS manager and the four systems analysts who had the major responsibility for the integration were hired by the company in the spring of 1997. The department's other employees—programmers, machine operators, and keypunch operators—have been with the company for several years.

During its early years AVC had a centralized decision-making organization. Top management formulated all plans and directed all operations. As the company expanded, some of the decision making was decentralized, although the information processing was still highly centralized. Departments had to coordinate their plans with the corporate office, but they had more freedom in developing their sales programs. However, information problems developed, and the IS department was assigned the task of improving the company's information processing system once the new equipment was installed.

The IS analysts reviewed the current AIS prior to the acquisition of the new computer and identified its weaknesses. They then designed new applications to overcome these problems. During the 18 months since the acquisition of the new equipment, the following applications have been redesigned or developed and are now operational: payroll, production scheduling, financial statement preparation, customer billing, raw material use in production, and finished goods inventory by warehouse. The operating departments of Audio Visual affected by the systems changes were rarely consulted or contacted until the system was operational and the new reports were distributed to the operating departments.

AVC's president is very pleased with the work of the IS department. During a recent conversation with an individual who was interested in AVC's new system, the president stated, "The IS people are doing a good job and I have full confidence in their work. I touch base with them frequently, and they have encountered no difficulties in doing their work. We paid a lot of money for the new equipment and the IS people certainly cost enough, but the combination of the new equipment and new IS staff should solve all of our problems."

Recently, two additional conversations regarding the computer and the AIS have taken place. One was between Jerry Adams, plant manager, and Bill Taylor, the IS manager; the other was between Adams and Terry Williams, the new human resources manager.

Taylor–Adams Conversation

ADAMS: Bill, you're trying to run my plant for me. I'm supposed to be the manager, yet you keep interfering. I wish you would mind your own business.

TAYLOR: You've got a job to do, but so does my department. As we analyzed the information needed for production scheduling and by top management, we saw where improvements could be made in the work flow. Now that the system is operational, you can't reroute work and change procedures, because that would destroy the value of the information we're processing. And while I'm on that subject, it's getting to the point where we can't trust the information we're getting from production. The documents we receive from production contain a lot of errors.

ADAMS: I'm responsible for the efficient operation of production. Quite frankly, I think I'm the best judge of production efficiency. The system you installed has reduced my work force and increased the work load of the remaining employees, but I don't see that this has improved anything. In fact, it might explain the high error rate in the documents.

TAYLOR: This new computer cost a lot of money, and I'm trying to ensure that the company gets its money's worth.

Adams–Williams Conversation

ADAMS: My best production assistant, the one I'm grooming to be a supervisor when the next opening occurs, came to me today and said he was thinking of quitting. When I asked him why, he said he didn't enjoy the work anymore. He's not the only one who is unhappy. The supervisors and department heads no longer have a voice in establishing production schedules. This new computer system has taken away the contribution we used to make to company planning and direction. We seem to be going way back to the days when top management made all the decisions. I have more production problems now than I used to. I think it boils down to a lack of interest on the part of my management team. I know the problem is within my area, but I thought you might be able to help me.

WILLIAMS: I have no recommendations for you now, but I've had similar complaints from purchasing and shipping. I think we should explore your concerns during tomorrow's plant management meeting.

Evaluate the preceding information, and answer the following questions:

Case Questions

1. Apparently the development of and transition to the new computer-based system has created problems among AVC's staff. Identify and briefly discuss the apparent causes of these problems.
2. How could the company have avoided these problems in the first place? How could they prevent them from happening in the future?

(CMA Examination, adapted)

ANSWERS TO CHAPTER QUIZ

1. e **3.** d **5.** b **7.** a **9.** b
2. b **4.** d **6.** a **8.** a **10.** e

CHAPTER 18

AIS Development Strategies

LEARNING OBJECTIVES

After studying the chapter, you should be able to

- Describe how organizations purchase application software, vendor services, and hardware.
- Explain how information system departments develop custom software.
- Explain how end users develop, use, and control computer-based information systems.
- Explain why organizations outsource their information systems, and evaluate the benefits and risks of this strategy.
- Explain the principles and challenges of business process reengineering.
- Describe how prototypes are used to develop an AIS, and discuss the advantages and disadvantages of doing so.
- Explain what computer-aided software engineering is and how it is used in systems development.

Integrative Case: Shoppers Mart

Ann Christy was elated that the new system Shoppers Mart so badly needed was approved and that she and her team had accurately assessed the needs of the company. As she turned her attention to designing the new system, she realized she needed to determine if it would be better to purchase a software system from an outside vendor, develop the system in-house, or go to a company that specialized in systems like the one she envisioned and hire them to develop and operate it. More specifically, she needed answers to the following questions:

1. Was the software she needed available for her to purchase? If so, how should she approach the process of buying hardware and software and selecting a vendor?
2. How do companies go about developing software in-house, and is this the best approach for Shoppers Mart?
3. How extensively should the system make use of end-user-developed software?
4. Should Shoppers Mart just make the needed improvements to its existing system, or should it consider reengineering its business processes and then develop a system to support the new processes?
5. Was outsourcing the information system a viable alternative to obtaining a new system? Did the benefits of outsourcing outweigh its risks?
6. If the company decided to develop the system in-house, should it try and speed up the development process by using

advanced techniques such as prototyping or computer-assisted software engineering?

Ann decided to investigate the various design alternatives in order to determine what course of action was best for Shoppers Mart.

INTRODUCTION

Traditionally, accountants have experienced a number of difficulties in developing an AIS:

- Demands for development resources are so numerous that AIS projects can be backlogged for several years.
- A newly designed AIS does not always meet user needs. The problem may not be discovered until the system is in use, often after a lengthy development process. It is hard for users to visualize how the AIS will look or how it will operate by reviewing design documentation. In addition, when systems developers do not understand the company's business needs or user needs, it is hard for them to make meaningful suggestions for improvement.
- The development process can take so long that the system no longer meets company needs. For example, Fannie Mae spent eight years and $100 million developing the largest loan accounting system in the world. Unfortunately, when it was finally completed it no longer met most of Fannie Mae's business needs.
- Users are unable to specify their needs adequately. Often they do not know exactly what they need; and when they do, they sometimes cannot communicate these ideas to systems developers.
- Changes to the AIS are often difficult to make after requirements have been frozen into specifications. If users are able to keep changing the requirements, the AIS may take forever to finish and costs increase each time the AIS is reworked.

In today's fast-changing world, many companies find themselves in the position of Shoppers Mart. They must meet user information needs quickly and efficiently. In this chapter you will learn about three ways to obtain a new information system: purchasing prewritten software, developing software in-house (either by the development staff or by the system users themselves), and hiring an outside company (outsourcing) to develop and operate the system. You will also learn about three ways of speeding up or improving the development process: business process reengineering, prototyping, and computer-aided software engineering (CASE) tools.

PURCHASE SOFTWARE

In the early days of computers it was rare that a company was able to buy software that could meet their needs from a vendor. However, as the software industry has matured, more companies have begun to purchase software.

Because of its easy availability and lower cost, an estimated 80% of companies currently installing computers are either using or considering canned software packages.

Written by computer manufacturers or software development companies, **canned software** is sold on the open market to a broad range of users with similar requirements. Some companies combine software and hardware and sell them as a package. These are referred to as **turnkey systems** because the vendor installs the entire system and the user only needs to "turn the key." Many turnkey systems are written by vendors who specialize in a particular industry. For example, there are systems geared to doctors, dentists, and others in the medical fields; others to automobile repair and service, full-service restaurants, fast-food outlets, video rentals, and other retail stores.

Not too many years from now it is likely that application systems will be developed in-house only by very large organizations or companies with unique requirements. However, even today many large organizations purchase software from outside suppliers. For example, Pacific Gas & Electric Company signed a $750,000 contract that calls for the license and installation of Dun & Bradstreet's General Ledger software to replace its in-house-developed general ledger system. A recent Deloitte & Touche survey found that most chief information officers expect to replace their current systems with commercially available packages rather than custom-developed systems.

A major problem with canned software is that it oftentimes does not meet all of a company's information or data processing needs. This disadvantage can sometimes be overcome by modifying canned software. Generally, the best way to accomplish this is to have the software vendor make the modifications rather than the in-house programming staff. Any modifications not authorized by the vendor will not be supported and may make the program unreliable and unstable. Some companies have used this approach quite successfully. For example, about 90% of Dow Chemical's software are canned packages that have been modified to match their businesses processes; the rest is custom software written in-house.

Purchasing Software and the SDLC

Companies that buy rather than develop AIS software still go through the SDLC process:

- *Systems analysis.* Companies must conduct an initial investigation, system survey, and feasibility survey. They must also determine AIS requirements.
- *Conceptual systems design.* An important part of conceptual design is determining whether software that meets AIS requirements is already available. If it is, a make-or-buy decision must be made.
- *Physical design.* If software is purchased, some of the physical design phase, such as designing and coding the program, can be omitted. However, it may be necessary to modify the purchased software to better meet company needs. Even when software is purchased, companies often design output, input, files, and control procedures.

- *Implementation and conversion.* Companies must plan implementation and conversion activities, select and train personnel, install and test the hardware and software, document their procedures, and convert from the old to the new AIS. However, they do not have to develop and test software modules or document the computer program itself.
- *Operation and maintenance.* The AIS has to be operated just like any other software. The software is usually maintained by the vendor.

Selecting a Vendor

The decision to make or purchase software can be made independently of the decision to acquire hardware, service, maintenance, and other AIS resources. Likewise, these resources can be purchased independently of the software, although the hardware and vendor decisions may depend on the software decision. The flowchart in Fig. 18.1 summarizes the process of acquiring software, hardware, and vendor services.

FIGURE 18.1
The Systems Acquisition Process

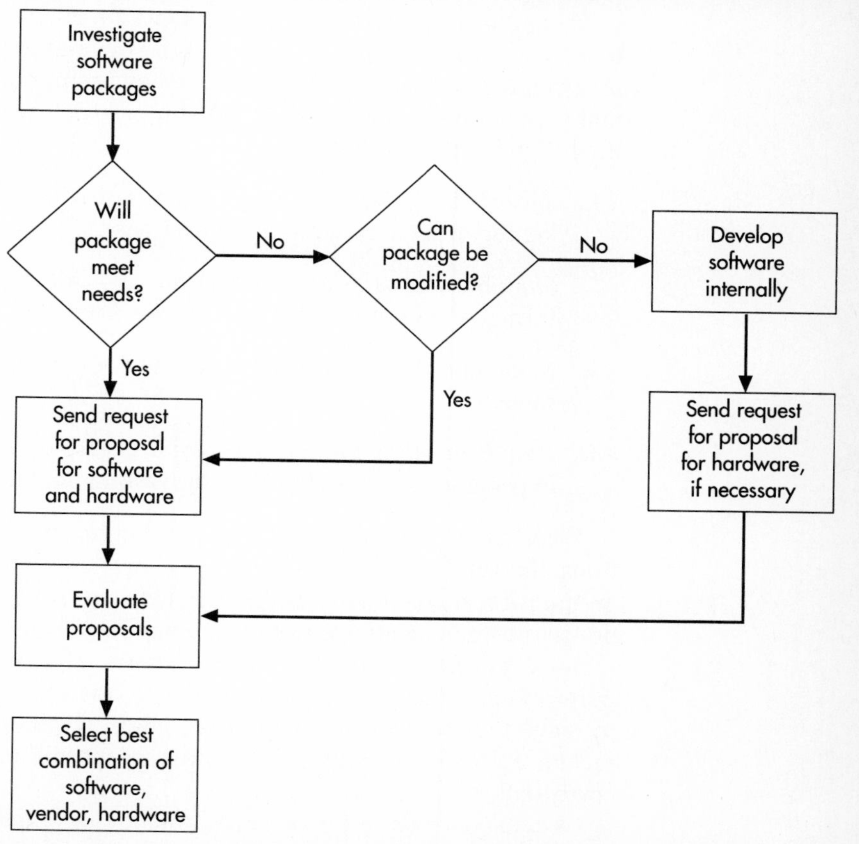

Vendors can be found by looking in the phone book, obtaining referrals, scanning computer or trade magazines, attending conferences, or using search organizations. Some vendors flourish for a while and then go out of business. For example, Ashton-Tate was once the supplier of the best-selling data base package, until product development problems and economic hardships forced the firm to sell out to Borland. Later, Borland also fell on hard times. Osborne Computers produced the first portable PC, but it, too, went out of business. Additionally, many companies offer computer services but have little experience or capital. When vendors go out of business, they often leave the companies that use their products high and dry. As a result, it is important to be very selective when choosing a vendor.

Acquiring Hardware and Software

Once AIS requirements have been defined, an organization is ready to purchase software and hardware. Companies requiring only a PC, a word processor, and a spreadsheet can usually complete their own research and make a selection. Companies buying large or complex systems, however, send vendors a **request for a proposal (RFP),** an invitation to propose a system by a specified date. Each proposal is evaluated, with the best systems investigated in depth to verify that company requirements can be met. A formal approach to acquiring system resources, such as an RFP, is important for the following reasons:

1. *Saves time.* The same information is provided to all vendors, eliminating repetitive interviews and questions.
2. *Simplifies the decision-making process.* All responses are in the same format and based on the same information.
3. *Reduces errors.* The chances of overlooking important factors are reduced.
4. *Avoids potential for disagreement.* Both parties possess the same expectations and pertinent information is captured in writing.

When an RFP is solicited based on exact hardware and software specifications, the total costs are usually lower and less time is required for vendor preparation and company evaluation. However, this does not permit the vendor to recommend alternative technology. In contrast, a generalized RFP contains a problem definition and requests a system that meets specific performance objectives and requirements. This allows the requesting company to leave the technical issues to the vendor. Disadvantages of this approach include a greater difficulty in evaluating proposals and the potential for more costly bids.

Generally speaking, the more information a company provides to a vendor, the better the chances of receiving a system that meets its requirements. Vendors need detailed specifications for the new AIS, including the required applications, inputs and outputs, files and data bases, frequency and methods of file updating and inquiry, and unique characteristics or requirements. It is also essential to distinguish between mandatory and desirable requirements.

Evaluating Proposals and Selecting a System

Proposals that are missing important information, fail to meet minimum requirements, or are ambiguous should be eliminated. Proposals that pass this preliminary screening should be carefully compared against the proposed AIS requirements to determine (1) whether they meet all mandatory requirements and (2) how many of the desirable requirements they meet. The top vendors can be invited to demonstrate their system using company-supplied data. This measures the system's performance and validates the vendor's claims. Table 18.1 presents criteria that can be used to evaluate hardware, software, and vendors.

One way to compare system performance is to use a **benchmark problem**—a data processing task with input, processing, and output jobs typical of those the new AIS will be required to perform. Processing times are calculated and compared; the AIS with the lowest time is judged the most efficient.

Another approach is **point scoring,** which is illustrated in Table 18.2. For each system evaluation criterion, a weight is assigned based on its relative importance. Vendors are assigned a score for each criterion based on how well its proposal measures up to the standard. The total of the weighted scores provides a basis for comparing and contrasting the various systems. Based on the point-scoring approach in this example, vendor 3 offers the best system. Its system scored 190 points more than vendor 2, the second place candidate.

Requirements costing estimates the cost of purchasing or developing features that are not present in a particular AIS. The total cost for each AIS is computed by adding the acquisition cost and the purchasing or developing costs. The resulting totals represent the costs of systems with all required features and provides an equitable basis for comparison.

Neither point scoring nor requirements costing is totally objective. In points scoring, the weights and the points used are assigned subjectively and dollar estimates of costs and benefits are not included. Requirements costing overlooks intangible factors such as reliability and vendor support. In any event, the final choice among vendor proposals is not likely to be clear-cut, because it must rely to some extent on subjective factors and cost considerations.

Once the best AIS has been identified, the software should be thoroughly test-driven, other users contacted, vendor personnel evaluated, and proposal details confirmed. In essence, the company wants to verify that the AIS that appears to be the best on paper actually is the best in practice. The lessons that Geophysical Systems Corporation learned from its vendor selection process highlight the importance of a thorough vendor evaluation (see Focus 18.1).

TABLE 18.1 Hardware, Software, and Vendor Evaluation Criteria

Hardware evaluation	Is the cost of the hardware reasonable based on its capabilities and features? Can the hardware run the desired software? Are the CPU's processing speed and capabilities adequate for the intended use? Are the secondary storage capabilities adequate? Are the input and output speeds and capabilities adequate? Does the system have adequate communication capabilities? Is the system expandable? Is the hardware based on the most recent technology, or on technology that is old or soon to be out of date? Is the hardware available now? If not, when? Is the system under consideration compatible with existing hardware, software, and peripherals? How do evaluations of the system's performance compare to those of its competitors? What is the availability and cost of support and maintenance? What guarantees and warranties come with the system? Are financing arrangements available? (if applicable)
Software evaluation	Does the package meet all mandatory specifications? How well does the package meet desirable specifications? Will program modifications be required to meet company needs? Does the software contain adequate controls? Is the performance (speed, accuracy, reliability, etc.) adequate? How many other companies use the software? Are other users satisfied with the package? Is the package well documented? Is the software compatible with existing corporate software? Is the software user-friendly? Can the software be demonstrated and test driven? Does the software have an adequate warranty? Is the software flexible and easily maintained? Is on-line inquiry of files and records possible? Will the vendor keep the package up to date?
Vendor evaluation	How long has the vendor been in business? How large is the vendor? Is the vendor financially stable and secure? How much experience does the vendor have with the hardware and software ? How well does the vendor stand behind its products? How good is its guarantee? Does the vendor regularly update its products? Does the vendor provide financing? Will the vendor put promises in a contract? Will the vendor supply a list of customers as references? Does the vendor have a reputation for reliability and dependability? Does the vendor provide hardware and software support and maintenance? Does the vendor provide implementation and installation support? Does the vendor have high-quality, responsive, and experienced personnel? Does the vendor provide training? How responsive and timely is vendor support?

TABLE 18.2 Point Scoring Evaluation of Vendor Proposals

		Vendor 1		Vendor 2		Vendor 3	
Criterion	**Weight**	**Score**	**Weighted Score**	**Score**	**Weighted Score**	**Score**	**Weighted Score**
Hardware compatibility	60	6	360	7	420	8	480
Hardware speed	30	6	180	10	300	5	150
Memory expansion	60	5	300	7	420	8	480
Hardware current	30	9	270	9	270	6	180
Software compatibility	90	7	630	7	630	9	810
On-line inquiry capabilities	40	9	360	10	400	8	320
Controls	50	7	350	6	300	9	450
Positive references	40	10	400	8	320	6	240
Documentation	30	9	270	8	240	7	210
Easily maintained; updated regularly	50	7	350	8	400	9	450
LAN and WAN capabilities	50	8	400	7	350	8	400
Vendor support	70	6	420	9	630	10	700
Totals	600		4,290		4,680		4,870

FOCUS 18.1 A Software Purchase that Went Awry

GEOPHYSICAL SYSTEMS Corporation (GSC), which specializes in developing drilling equipment, developed a device that uses sonar to analyze the production potential of oil and gas discoveries. GSC needed a software program to analyze the data generated by the company's sonar device. GSC hired Seismograph Service Corporation and paid it $20 million to write the computer system. To its dismay, Geophysical found that the Seismograph system could not accurately process the massive volume of data and perform the complex computations needed. When this failing became apparent, Geophysical's clients canceled their contracts. As a result, the company went from yearly sales of $40 million and profits of $6 million to filing for bankruptcy two years later.

Geophysical sued Seismograph, claiming that the supplier's system failed to perform as promised. In addition, it claimed that Seismograph knew the system would not be able to perform as desired before it began the development project. The jury agreed, awarding Geophysical over $48 million as compensation for lost profits and the cost of the computer system. Seismograph appealed on the basis that its system did work and that Geophysical's sales decline resulted from a slump in oil prices.

Geophysical's experience is not uncommon; there are many systems development projects that do not produce the intended results.

Despite the availability of many good software packages, many organizations meet their information needs by writing their own software. The next section discusses software development by the in-house IS department. The section after that discusses software that is developed by the users themselves.

DEVELOPMENT BY IN-HOUSE IS DEPARTMENT

In the past most organizations had their information system departments develop **custom software,** because canned software that fit their specific needs was not available. Despite the availability of many good canned software packages today, many organizations still develop their own software because their requirements are unique or their size and complexity necessitate a custom package.

Developing custom software is difficult and error-prone, and it consumes a great deal of time and resources. After end users define their requirements, analysts work with them to determine the format of paper and screen outputs. The analysts then identify the data required for each input and the data to be retained in the files. Analysts also develop detailed program specifications to be interpreted and coded by a programmer. Because of the many and varied development tasks, the process requires a significant amount of discipline and management supervision. Accountants often help develop custom software, either as project supervisors, users, or development team members.

Custom software is usually developed and written in-house. Chapter 19 discusses in more depth the process used to develop software. Alternatively, organizations may engage an outside company, such as Andersen Consulting or EDS, to develop a package or assemble it from their inventory of program modules. These modules are adapted, combined, and organized to form a customized product that meets a company's specific requirements. When contracting with an outside organization, a company should maintain control over the development process. The following guidelines are recommended:

- *Carefully select a developer.* The outside developer should have experience in the company's industry, a good understanding of business in general, and an in-depth understanding of how the company conducts its business.
- *Sign a contract.* The contract should place responsibility for meeting the company's requirements on the developer and allow the company to discontinue the project if certain key conditions are not met.
- *Plan and monitor each step.* All aspects of the project should be designed in detail, and there should be frequent checkpoints for monitoring the project.
- *Maintain effective communication.* The relationship between the company and the developer should be rigorously defined: frequent communication is necessary.
- *Control all costs.* Costs should be tightly controlled and cash outflows minimized until the project has been completed and accepted.

Arthur D. Little and other information systems consultants tell clients to develop custom software only if it provides a significant competitive advantage.

For example, there is usually no measurable benefit to having a custom-written payroll or accounts receivable system. On the other hand, there may be significant benefits to sophisticated, just-in-time inventory management or product manufacturing software. If a software application will not provide a competitive advantage, Little advises its clients to buy software from an outside supplier.

There is no single right answer to the build-or-buy decision. Different companies come to different conclusions. For example, Gillette used to develop its own software but recently decided to move from proprietary systems to off-the-shelf software wherever possible. Its rationale is that it gains a greater competitive advantage from deciding *how* software should be used than from determining *what* software should be used and then creating it. If canned software does not meet all of Gillette's needs, it is modified using high-level development tools. Pepsi Cola, on the other hand, has moved in the opposite direction. It used to buy most of its mainframe software but, after moving to a client/server architecture, it could not find software sophisticated enough to meet its needs. Although Pepsi still buys software when it can find it, it has had to create most of its newly installed software.

This section has discussed why many organizations have IS staff develop their software. Organizations are also finding it productive to allow users to develop systems to meet their own information needs. The next section discusses this approach.

End-User-Developed Software

End-user computing (EUC) is the hands-on development, use, and control of computer-based information systems by users. In other words, EUC is people using information technology to meet their information needs rather than having to rely on IS professionals. For example, a savings and loan in California wanted a system to track loan reserve requirements. Their IS department said the system would take 18 months to develop. Rather than wait, the loan department used a PC and a data base program to develop a functional program in a single day. Enhancing the program took several more days. Not only did the loan department cut the development time from 18 months to a few days, they ended up with the exact information they needed since they developed the system themselves.

After the automobile was introduced, a famous sociologist predicted that the automobile market would not exceed 2 million cars, because only that many people would be willing to serve as chauffeurs. Instead, tens of millions of cars are sold annually to people who drive themselves. It was also once predicted that the telephone system would collapse because the geometric growth in calls would require everyone to be telephone operators. Instead, equipment was developed that automated many of the functions previously performed by operators.

Since the introduction of the computer, the demand for information systems has grown astronomically. If a company wanted to eliminate all its information backlogs, almost everyone would have to become a programmer. Doesn't this sound similar to the automobile and the telephone examples? The solution? End users meeting their own information needs. As with telephones, technology is being developed to automate much of the process for us. Just as most people learn to drive automobiles, increased computer literacy and easier-to-use programming languages will allow almost everyone to operate powerful computers.

With the advent of inexpensive PCs and a wide variety of powerful and inexpensive software, users began developing their own systems to create and store data, access company data and download it, and share data and computer resources in networks. As end users began to meet their initial needs, two things happened. First, users realized computers could be used to meet more and more information needs. Second, increased access to data created many new uses and needs for information. The result has been a tremendous growth in end-user computing, a growth that is expected to continue to accelerate through the next century.

The growth in end-user computing has significantly altered the role of the IS staff. They continue to develop and maintain the transaction processing systems and company-wide data bases that end users draw on to meet their information needs. In addition, they provide technical advice and operational support and make as much information available to end users as possible. While this has resulted in more work for the IS staff, it has been counterbalanced by a lessened demand for their traditional services.

If the end-user computing trend continues, it will represent 75% to 95% of all information processing by the turn of the century. Since you will be an end user or have a significant involvement with end-user computing no matter where you work, it is essential you understand end-user computing concepts.

Appropriate End-User Development and Use

End-user development (EUD) occurs when information users, such as managers, accountants, and internal auditors, develop their own applications using computer specialists as advisors. End-user development is inappropriate for complex systems, such as those that process a large number of transactions or update data base records. Therefore, it is not used for processing payroll, accounts receivables and payables, general ledger, or inventory. A few examples of the many appropriate end user development uses are

- Retrieving information from company data bases to produce simple reports or to answer one-time queries.
- Performing "what if," sensitivity, or statistical analyses.
- Developing applications using prewritten software such as a spreadsheet or a data base system.
- Preparing schedules and lists, such as depreciation schedules, accounts receivable aging, and loan amortizations.

Benefits of End-User Computing

One reason end-user computing has increased so significantly is it offers the following advantages.

User Creation, Control, and Implementation. Accountants and other end users, rather than the IS department, control the development process. They can decide for themselves what information needs are important and whether a system should be developed. The sense of ownership that comes with end-user development helps users develop better systems.

Systems that Meet User Needs. When end users develop their own systems they are more likely to meet their needs. They can also discover flaws in systems the IS people would not catch. The user–analyst–programmer communication problems inherent in traditional program development are avoided since the users develop the system.

Timeliness. Much of the lengthy delay inherent in the traditional system development process is avoided, such as expensive and time-consuming cost–benefit analysis, detailed requirements definitions, and the inevitable delays and red tape inherent in the approval process.

Freeing Up IS Resources. The more information needs users can meet, the more time the IS department has to spend on other information and maintenance activities. This reduces both the visible and the invisible backlog of systems development projects.

Versatility and Ease of Use. Most end-user computing software is easy to understand and use. Users can change the information they produce or modify their application anytime their requirements change. With a laptop, work can be completed at home, on a plane, or almost anywhere else.

As the foregoing paragraphs explain, there are a number of significant advantages to end-user computing. There are also a number of important disadvantages; these are discussed in the next section. The benefits and risks associated with end-user computing are summarized in Table 18.3.

TABLE 18.3 Benefits and Risks of End-User Computing

Benefits	Risks
Users control development process and decide what systems are created and implemented.	End-user systems are more likely to contain errors or be flawed in some way.
The systems that are developed are more likely to meet user needs.	Systems are implemented that have not been adequately tested.
Systems are developed when they are needed.	Systems are more likely to be inefficient or use more resources than they should.
IS resources are freed up for other tasks.	Systems are often poorly controlled and documented.
Systems are usually easy to use and modify.	Systems are more likely to be incompatible with other systems in the organization.
	Greater likelihood of producing duplicate systems or wasting organization resources.
	Often results in greater overall system costs.

Risks of End-User Computing

Some significant drawbacks to end-user computing and to eliminating analyst/programmer involvement in the development process are discussed next.

Logic and Development Errors. End users have little experience in systems development and are more likely to make errors and are less likely to recognize when errors have occurred. The user–developer may solve the wrong problem, poorly define system requirements, apply an inappropriate analytical method, use the wrong software, or use incomplete or outdated information. Often the error is caused by faulty logic or by incorrectly using formulas or software commands.

For example, an oil and gas company developed a complex spreadsheet to analyze a proposed acquisition. Based on the results, the company scheduled a meeting to propose the acquisition to the board of directors. Before making the presentation consultants from their CPA firm tested the model to see if they agreed with its results and gave their approval. Shortly before his speech, one of presenters performed his own tests so he would understand how the model worked and could answer any tough questions the board threw at him. He discovered a few formulas he thought distorted the projections of what the company could attain by selling properties of the acquired company, the restatement of oil and gas reserves, and the consolidated balance sheet of the two combined entities. He called in the group that developed the spreadsheet and several partners of the CPA firm. The formulas were wrong, and when corrected they showed the acquisition would have led to significant losses. They called off the presentation to the board, the person who developed the spreadsheet was fired, and the CPA firm no longer does any audit or consulting work for the company.

Inadequately Tested Applications. Users are not as likely to rigorously test their applications, either because they do not recognize the need to do so or because of the difficulty or time involved. One result is an application with the types of errors mentioned previously.

Inefficient Systems. Most end users are not programmers and have not been trained in systems development. Although the systems they develop may get the job done, they are not always efficient. For example, a bank clerk spent three weeks developing a program that examined each cell in a spreadsheet and changed its value to zero if it was a negative amount. When the 60-page program began returning a "too many nested ifs" error message, he called in a computer consultant. Within 5 minutes the consultant developed a finished application using a built-in spreadsheet function.

Poorly Controlled and Documented Systems. Many end users do not implement controls to protect their system. User-created systems are often poorly documented because the user considers the task boring or unimportant. They fail to realize that without documentation, others cannot understand how their system works.

System Incompatibilities. Some companies add end-user equipment without considering the technological implications. As a result, they have a diversity of hardware and software that is very hard to support or to network. For example, Aetna Life & Casualty spent more than $1 billion a year on information technology in an attempt to gain a competitive advantage. The result was 50,000 PCs from a few dozen manufacturers, 2,000 minicomputers and servers, 108 word processing systems, 19 incompatible e-mail systems, and 36 different communications networks. They finally realized they needed to shift their emphasis from trying to own the latest technology to the effective *use* of technology. They standardized their systems and now use only a few different types of PCs, Microsoft software products, 2 electronic mail systems, and one network. The result is compatibility across all systems and significantly less cost.

Duplication of Systems and Data and Wasted Resources. If end users are unaware that other users have similar information needs, duplicate systems occur. Inexperienced users also may take on more than they are able to accomplish, which ends up wasting time and resources.

Increased Costs. A single PC purchase is inexpensive, but buying them for hundreds or thousands of workers is costly. Updating the hardware and software every few years is also expensive. End-user computing also has a high opportunity cost if it diverts users' attention from their primary job. In addition, it increases time and data demands on the company mainframe and on IS people for support and assistance.

A proper balance between maximizing the benefits and minimizing the risks of end-user systems can be achieved by providing systems analysts as advisers and by requiring user-created systems to be reviewed and documented prior to use. In addition, users can be trained in the systems analysis process so they can identify and adequately meet their needs and review the work of other users.

Managing and Controlling End-User Computing

Organizations use several different approaches to manage and control end-user computing. Giving the IS department control over end-user computing discourages its growth, denies the organization of most of its benefits, and is not in the best long-term interests of the company. However, if there are no controls over end users, such as what end-user computing tools are purchased or how they are used, chaos can easily result. It can also be very difficult to support the system. It is best to provide enough guidance and standards to adequately control the system yet allow users the flexibility they need.

One way to do this is to have a **help desk** to encourage, support, coordinate, and control end-user activities. The 60 help desk analysts and technicians at Schering-Plough handle more than 9,000 calls a month. The front-line analysts use expert system software to quickly find the answers to their questions and then provide callers with scripted answers. The second-line technicians handle the more complicated queries. Other companies use multimedia software with animation or videos to help first-line staffers walk callers through a complicated process. Duties of the help desk include

- Providing hot-line assistance to help resolve problems.
- Serving as a clearinghouse for information, coordination, and assistance.

- Training end users how to use specific hardware and software, and providing corresponding technical maintenance and support.
- Evaluating new end-user hardware and software products.
- Assisting with application development.
- Developing and implementing standards for (1) hardware and software purchase to ensure compatibility; (2) documentation and application testing; and (3) controlling security issues such as fraud, software piracy, and viruses.
- Controlling corporate data so (1) authorized end users can access and share it; (2) it is not duplicated; and (3) access to confidential data is restricted.

OUTSOURCE THE SYSTEM

We have discussed two approaches to obtaining software: buying it and developing it in-house. A third way to acquire software is to outsource the information system.

Outsourcing is hiring an outside company to handle all or part of an organization's data processing activities. In a mainframe outsourcing agreement, the outsourcers buy their client's computers and hire all or most of the client's employees. They then operate and manage the entire system on the client's site, or they migrate the system to the outsourcer's computers. Most mainframe outsourcing contracts are for ten years or more and cost from hundreds of thousands to millions of dollars a year. For example, the natural gas producer Enron signed a $750 million agreement with EDS to outsource its entire information system. EDS bought Enron's computers, software, and transmission network. It also hired all 550 of Enron's information systems staff at comparable wages and benefits. Enron pays EDS a fixed annual fee, plus additional fees based on processing volume. During the ten-year life of the contract Enron expects to save $200 million, which is almost 25% of its computing costs.

In a client/server or a PC outsourcing agreement, an organization outsources a particular service, a segment of its business, a particular function, or PC support. Most *Fortune* 2000 companies outsource anywhere from 10% to 80% of their PC support functions. For example, Taco Bell outsourced its PC help desk services to Coopers & Lybrand. Royal Dutch Shell, the international oil company, has 80,000 PCs worldwide and has outsourced most of its installation, maintenance, training, help desk, and technical support.

The Growth in Outsourcing Applications

Outsourcing was initially used for standardized applications such as payroll, accounting, and purchasing or by companies that were struggling to survive and wanted a quick infusion of cash from selling their hardware. However, in 1989 Eastman Kodak surprised the business world by hiring three different companies to operate its computer systems. Kodak outsourced its data processing operations and sold its mainframes to IBM. It outsourced its telecommunications functions to DEC and its PC operations to Businessland (and later Entek Information Services). When the performance of DEC and Entek began to slip in 1994, Kodak opened those services to new bids. Kodak continues to perform its own information systems strategic planning and development, but the system implementation and operation are the responsibility of the outsourcers. The results have been dramatic. Capital expenditures for computers fell 90% while operating expenses decreased between 10% and 20%. Kodak expects the annual information systems savings to reach approximately $130 million over the ten-year period of the agreement.

In 1994 Xerox signed what was then the largest outsourcing deal in history: a $3.2 billion, ten-year contract with EDS to outsource its computing, telecommunications, and software management in 19 countries. The company moved to outsourcing to cut costs, to speed up the move from a mainframe architecture to client/server computing, and to free management to focus on strategic management issues rather than on day-to-day concerns. However, Xerox did retain control over its IS functions, such as IS strategic planning and new application development, in order to support its reengineering efforts.

The decisions by Kodak and Xerox have motivated other organizations to consider outsourcing their information systems. For example, 10 of the top 25 *Fortune* 500 companies outsource some or all of their information systems. The five largest outsourcers (EDS, IBM, Andersen Consulting, Digital Equipment, and Computer Sciences Corporation) have captured half of the worldwide outsourcing market.

The Benefits of Outsourcing

This section discusses the benefits of outsourcing; the disadvantages are discussed in the next section. The advantages and disadvantages of outsourcing are summarized in Table 18.4.

A Business Solution. Outsourcing is a plausible business solution, rather than just an IS solution. Kodak and Enron believe outsourcing is a viable approach, strategically and economically, because it allows them to concentrate on their core competencies. Kodak believes in focusing its efforts on what it does best—selling film and cameras—and leaving data processing to more qualified computer companies. Kodak treats outsourcers as partners and works closely with them to meet its strategic and operational data processing objectives.

Asset Utilization. Organizations with millions of dollars tied up in information technology can improve their cash position and reduce annual expenses by selling those assets to an outsourcer. With technology changing so rapidly, the AIS function can drain a company's cash reserves as it tries to keep up with the latest advancements. For example, Health Dimensions, a hospital management company, outsourced the data processing functions of its four hospitals so it could use its limited monetary resources for revenue generating purchases.

Access to Greater Expertise and More Advanced Technology. Many companies cannot afford to retain a staff to manage and develop the increasingly complex networks required in today's businesses. Continental Bank and Del Monte Foods turned to outsourcing because the cost and time involved in staying at the cutting edge of technology were rising significantly. Washington Water Power Company began outsourcing when the prospect of upgrading and replacing its obsolete computer system seemed too daunting a task.

TABLE 18.4 Advantages and Disadvantages of Outsourcing

Advantages	Disadvantages
It is a business as well as an information system solution.	Outsourcing contracts are not very flexible due to their length.
It allows a company to better utilize its assets and scarce resources.	Companies may lose control of their system and data. This may result is abuse, such as confidential data shared with competitors.
It provides access to greater expertise and more advanced technology.	Over time, company may lose sight of its information needs and how the system can provide it with competitive advantages.
It can lower a company's overall IS costs.	It is expensive and difficult to reverse the outsourcing decision and replace the hardware, software, and people.
It can result in faster and more efficient systems development.	Many outsourcing goals and benefits are never realized.
It helps eliminate the peaks and valleys of system usage.	
It facilitates downsizing.	

Lower Costs. Outsourcing can decrease IS costs by 15% to 30%. Outsourcers can pass along some of the savings achieved from standardizing users' applications, buying hardware at bulk prices, splitting development and maintenance costs between projects, and operating at higher volumes. Continental Bank will save $100 million (20% of information technology costs) during the life of its ten-year contract. However, companies such as Occidental Petroleum and USX have rejected outsourcing as costing more than internal AIS development and operation.

Improved Development Time. Experienced industry specialists often can develop and implement a system faster and more efficiently than in-house staff. Outsourcers can also help a company cut through much of the internal politics surrounding systems development.

Elimination of Peaks and Valleys Usage. Many companies have seasonal businesses that requires heavy computer power during part of the year but very little the remainder of the year. For example, from January to March, W. Atlee Burpee & Company processes mail order and wholesale requests for its seeds and gardening products. During this period its IBM mainframe operated at 80% capacity; it functioned at 20% the rest of the time. IS personnel were underutilized most of the time. Burpee turned to outsourcing and now pays Computer Science Corporation according to how much the system is used. In doing so, Burpee cut its processing costs in half.

Facilitation of Downsizing. Companies that downsize are often left with an unnecessarily large AIS function. General Dynamics downsized dramatically in the early 1990s due to reduced spending in the defense industry. They sold their data centers to Computer Sciences Corporation (CSC) for $200 million and transferred 2,600 employees to CSC. They signed a $3 billion, ten-year outsourcing contract even though their IS function was rated number one in the aerospace industry.

The Risks of Outsourcing

Companies that outsource often experience one or more of the following drawbacks.

Inflexibility. Most outsourcing contracts are signed for ten years. If problems arise during this time, if the company is dissatisfied, or if the company goes through extensive structural changes, the contract is difficult or costly to break. In such cases companies may find themselves in a technological straitjacket. Before they merged, Integra Financial Corp. and Equimark Corp. held contracts with different outsourcers. After the merger one of the contracts had to be eliminated, at a cost of $4.5 million.

Loss of Control. A company that outsources a significant portion of its AIS runs the risk of losing control of its system and data. In addition, when an external party processes its business data, the company is exposed to possible abuse such as sharing confidential data. For that reason, Ford's outsourcing agreement with Computer Sciences Corporation excludes CSC from taking on other automobile manufacturers as clients.

Reduced Competitive Advantage. Over the long run a company can lose a fundamental understanding of its own IS needs and how the system can provide it with competitive advantages. A system that does not evolve and improve cannot add value and help achieve corporate objectives. In addition, outsourcers cannot be expected to be as motivated as their clients in trying to meet a particular industry's competitive challenges.

Locked-In System. Once a company outsources its system and sells its data processing centers, it is very expensive and difficult to reverse the process. If the company is unable to buy back the data processing facilities, it will have to buy new equipment and hire a new data processing staff, often at prohibitive costs. Blue Cross of California decided that the performance of its outsourcer, EDS, was so poor that it would end their agreement. However, when Blue Cross started to initiate the change it realized that it knew virtually nothing about its system and could not afford to discharge EDS.

Unfulfilled Goals. Critics point out that many outsourcing goals and benefits are never realized. At least one study has shown that some alleged benefits, such as increased efficiency, are a myth. USF&G Corporation canceled its $100 million contract with Cigna Information Services after 18 months because Cigna could not implement the changes needed to make the system work properly.

A problems with some systems is that they are simply automated ways of doing business the same way it was done before computers. A radical approach to introducing massive changes into information systems and improving the development process, called business processing reengineering, is discussed in the next section.

BUSINESS PROCESSES REENGINEERING

Despite the trillion-plus dollars spent on information technology in the past decade, productivity has not increased significantly. One reason is that many business processes are relics from precomputer days when work was based on economies of scale and specialization of labor. Work was organized as a sequence of narrowly defined tasks, flowing between specialists who did not have to do much thinking or reasoning. Workers simply had to carry out their assigned tasks as efficiently as possible. When computers came along, businesses used them to speed up their manual and paper flow processes and procedures.

In recent years the work environment has changed drastically. Many current systems are not designed to handle the flood of new information available today. Nor can they take advantage of the steady stream of new technology that makes it possible to do things differently. With powerful data bases and almost unlimited storage, we have access to more and better information than ever before. In summary, an approach is needed that, instead of "paving cow-paths" blazes new trails.

Many management gurus now advocate radical change, or what they refer to as **business process reengineering (BPR).** BPR is the thorough analysis and complete redesign of business processes and information systems to achieve dramatic performance improvements. It is a revolutionary process that challenges traditional organization structures, rules, assumptions, work flows, job descriptions, management procedures, controls, and organizational values and cultures associated with underperformance.

BPR reduces a company to its essential business processes and focuses on *why* they are done rather than on the details of *how* they are done. It then completely reshapes organizational work practices and information flows to take advantage of technological advancements. This is done to simplify the system, to make it more effective, and to improve a company's quality and service.

CSC Index, a consulting firm, measured the cost and time savings and the reduction in defects before and after helping 15 clients complete reengineering efforts. CSC found that fundamentally changing business processes produced an average improvement of 48% in cost, 80% in time, and 60% in defects. After Citibank reengineered a credit analysis system, employees spent 43% of their time (instead of 9%) recruiting new business instead of completing paperwork on closed deals. Profits increased by over 750% over a two-year period. By reengineering its customer service operations, Datacard Corporation increased its sales by sevenfold. A process that took a full day and five phone calls was replaced with one that took one hour.

The Principles of Reengineering

What are the secrets to reengineering? How can a company minimize the costs and maximize the benefits received? Michael Hammer, a leading proponent of reengineering, set forth seven principles that help organizations successfully reengineer business processes.[1] These principles are summarized in Table 18.5.

Organize Around Outcomes, Not Tasks. In a reengineered system, the traditional approach of assigning different parts of a business process to many people is not appropriate. This approach, with its numerous handoffs, results in delays and errors. Instead, wherever possible, one person is given responsibility for the entire process. Each person's job is designed around an objective or an outcome, such as a finished component or a completed process, rather than one of many tasks necessary to produce the finished component or complete the process.

At Mutual Benefit Life (MBL), an insurance company, approving an insurance application previously included 30 steps performed by 19 people in five departments. Because paperwork had to be transferred among so many people, an approval took anywhere from 5 to 25 days. When MBL reengineered its business processes, it eliminated existing job descriptions and departmental boundaries. It created the position of case manager and gave each one the authority to perform all application approval tasks. Case managers are supported by a number of information systems, including an expert system, and can call on specialists for help with any particularly difficult application. Because one person is in charge of the entire process, there is no handing off of files. This has resulted in fewer errors, decreased costs, and a dramatically improved turnaround time. Case managers now handle more than twice the volume of new applications, allowing the company to eliminate 100 field positions. A new application can now be processed in as little as four hours, with an average turnaround of only two to five days.

TABLE 18.5 Seven Principles of Business Processing Reengineering

1. Organize around outcomes, not tasks.
2. Have output users perform the process.
3. Have those who produce information process it.
4. Centralize and disperse data.
5. Integrate parallel activities.
6. Empower workers, use built-in controls, and flatten the organizational chart.
7. Capture data once, at its source.

[1] Much of this section is adapted from Michael Hammer, "Reengineering Work: Don't Automate, Obliterate," *Harvard Business Review* (July–August 1990): 104–112.

Have Output Users Perform the Process. Owners and managers often organize their company into separate departments, each specializing in a separate task. Because each department passes its completed product off to someone else, departments are customers of one another. This strategy may work well for specialized projects, but it can hurt a company's performance when it comes to less significant tasks. For example, consider the problem when accounting wants to order nonstrategic or inexpensive goods such as office supplies. It must requisition the supplies from purchasing, which is responsible for selecting suppliers and ordering goods. This system is slow, cumbersome, and can actually cost the company more, in time and money, than the supplies are worth.

One large manufacturer had this exact problem before reengineering its business processes. The manufacturer took advantage of information technology and set up a computerized data base of approved vendors (maintained by purchasing), developed an expert system for purchasing nonstrategic items, and linked all departments in a network. The new process enables users, with the help of the expert system and the data base, to order their own supplies. The purchasing process is now much faster, simpler, and less costly because the department that orders the supplies is the one that actually uses them.

Have Those Who Produce Information Process It. Most organizations process their acquisition/payment information the way Ford Motor used to. Previously, Ford's purchasing department prepared a multicopy purchase order, sending one copy to the vendor and another to accounts payable and keeping one itself. When goods were received, the receiving department prepared a multicopy receiving report and sent one copy to accounts payable and kept the other. The vendor prepared a multicopy invoice and sent one copy to accounts payable. Accounts payable processed all three documents and matched 14 different data items on the three documents before a payment could be processed. Accounts payable spent most of its time trying to reconcile all of the mismatches. Payments were delayed, vendors were unhappy, and the process was time-consuming and frustrating. It took more than 500 employees to process Ford's accounts payable.

In Ford's reengineered system, the people who produce the information also process it. Purchasing agents create and process their purchase orders by entering them into an on-line data base. Vendors ship goods but do not send an invoice. When the goods arrive, the receiving clerk enters three items of data into the system: part number, unit of measure, and supplier code. The computer compares the receiving information with the outstanding purchase order data. If they do not match, the goods are returned. If they do match, the goods are accepted and the computer prepares the vendor's check, which is sent by accounts payable. The reengineered system saves a significant amount of money, much of it achieved through a 75% reduction of accounts payable staff.

Centralize and Disperse Data. To achieve economies of scale and to eliminate bureaucracy and redundant resources, companies centralize operations. To be more responsive to their customers and to provide better service, they decentralize operations. With current technology, companies no longer have to choose between these two approaches. Corporate-wide data bases can centralize data, and telecommunications technology can then disburse it to the necessary locations. In effect, companies can have the advantages of both approaches.

Hewlett-Packard (HP) had a decentralized purchasing system that successfully served the needs of its 50 manufacturing units. However, HP could not take advantage of its extensive buying power to negotiate quantity discounts. HP reengineered its system and introduced a corporate-wide purchasing department that developed and maintained a shared data base of approved vendors. Each plant continued to meet its unique needs by making its own purchases from the approved vendors. The corporate office tracked the purchases of all 50 plants, negotiated quantity discounts and other vendor concessions, and resolved disputes with vendors. The result was a significantly lower cost of goods purchased, a 50% reduction in lead times, a 75% reduction in failure rates, and a 150% improvement in on-time deliveries.

Integrate Parallel Activities. Certain processes, such as product development, are performed in parallel and then integrated at the end. For example, Chrysler had one department that worked exclusively on designing engines, another on transmissions, another on frames, and so on. Unfortunately, the departments often did not communicate as well as they should. At the integration and testing phase they often found that the components did not fit together properly. As a result, they had to be redesigned at considerable expense.

Chrysler reengineered its product development process to place at least one person from each department area on a team. Each team was put in charge of a particular automobile. As a result, Chrysler was able to decrease its product development time significantly and reduce costly redesigns.

Empower Workers, Use Built-In Controls, and Flatten the Organizational Chart. Most organizations have a layer of employees who do the work and several layers who record, manage, audit, or control the efforts of the former group. The logic behind this organization is that the workers are not able either to make correct decisions, to monitor and control the process themselves, or both. In a reengineered system, the people who do the work are empowered with this type of decision-making responsibility. This results in a faster response time to problems and increases the quality of the task performed. Information technology, such as expert systems, can help workers make correct decisions and avoid mistakes. This same principle also states that controls should be built into the process itself. For example, the system could be programmed with preventive controls so that it would proceed only when all relevant data have been entered and edited by the system for validity, correctness, and reasonableness. Controls could also be placed in the system to detect and correct any errors that might make their way into the system.

When Mutual Benefit Life empowered its case managers with decision-making ability, it was able to eliminate several layers of managers. Those who were retained changed their focus from supervision and control to support and facilitation.

Capture Data Once, at Its Source. Historically, each functional area has designed and built its own AIS. As a result, information was entered into several different applications. For example, a vendor number was entered in the accounts payable system as well as the purchasing system. Each application had to collect the same piece of information (usually on different forms), enter it into their system, and store it. This is both inefficient and expensive. In addition, there were discrepancies between the individual systems as a result of data capture and data entry errors. EDI and source data automation devices such as bar coding now allow data in a reengineered system to be captured electronically at its source. The data can be entered once in an on-line data base and made available to all who need it. This approach reduces errors, eliminates data processing delays, and reduces clerical and other costs.

A few years ago management at Sun Microsystems decided to solve the problem of its information systems not being able to easily communicate with each other. In addition, certain data needed to be entered as many as ten times into incompatible systems. The system was reengineered and now data that is entered into any system worldwide is entered only once and made available to whomever needs it.

Underlying each of these seven principles is the efficient and effective use of the latest information systems technology. Future advances will allow even more powerful reengineering efforts. Radio- and satellite-based communications technology, coupled with very powerful handheld computers, will have a significant impact on the way companies do business. With image processing, a document can be used by multiple users simultaneously. *Active documents* that automatically know where to go will also have an impact. For example, suppose you are buying a mail order computer. After the sales clerk creates the *active order*, it will automatically be sent to shipping, inventory control, sales and marketing, the credit card company, and your customer record. With an active document, the decision about where the information on the document is to go need only be made once. From then on, all orders will automatically be sent to the appropriate location.

Challenges Faced by Reengineering Efforts

Business process reengineering is a very difficult venture. Not only must a company be rethought and completely reorganized, but people must abandon the old ways of doing things and learn new jobs and new ways of operating. As a result, many reengineering efforts fail or do not accomplish all they set out to do. To successfully complete the reengineering process, a company must face and overcome the following obstacles:

- *Tradition.* The inefficient business processes that are being reengineered oftentimes are decades old. Traditional ways of doing things do not often die easily, especially practices associated with the culture of an organization. Successful reengineering requires changes in employee culture and beliefs.

- *Resistance.* Change, especially radical change, is always met with a great deal of resistance. Throughout the process, managers must continually reassure, persuade, and provide support to those affected so that the necessary changes will work.
- *Time requirements.* Reengineering is a lengthy process, almost always taking two or more years to complete.
- *Cost.* It is costly to thoroughly examine and question a company's business processes in order to find a faster and more efficient way of operating.
- *Lack of management support.* Reengineering is still in its infancy and, since few companies have completed full-blown reengineering projects, many top managers have not yet been converted to its benefits. Many are afraid of the "big hype, few results" syndrome. Without top management support, reengineering has little chance of succeeding. IS management does not have enough power and influence to push a reengineering project successfully.
- *Risk.* IS management is aware that pushing a reengineering project can be a risky career move. If it is a success, they will be looked on with great favor in the organization. If not, they may very well be looking for new jobs.
- *Skepticism.* Some in the IS community are skeptical about reengineering. Some view it as traditional systems development, but in a brand new wrapper with a fancy name. One of the biggest obstacles to reengineering is outlasting the nonbelievers and the cynics who say it cannot be done.
- *Retraining.* Many reengineering efforts dramatically change the way work is done. That means employees have to be retrained, which is time-consuming and expensive.
- *Controls.* An important element of an information system is the controls that ensure system reliability and integrity. People involved in reengineering efforts need to be careful that they do not reengineer important controls out of the system. For example, a key element of internal control is a separation of duties and if that control is reengineered out of the new system, compensating controls have to be built into the system to take its place.

Sometimes systems under development do not need to be reengineered, but the development team would like to speed up the development process significantly. A good way to do that, called prototyping, is discussed in the next section.

PROTOTYPING

Prototyping is an approach to systems design in which a simplified working model of a system is developed. This **prototype,** or "first draft," is quickly and inexpensively built and provided to users for testing. Experimenting with the prototype allows users to determine what they do and do not like about the system. Based on their reactions and feedback, the developers modify the system and again present it to the users. This iterative process of trial usage and modification continues until the users are satisfied that the system adequately meets their needs.

The basic premise of prototyping is that it is easier for people to express what they like or dislike about a prototype than to imagine what they want in a system. In other words, if users can try out an actual application, they can provide feedback as to what they do and do not like about it. Even a simple system that is not fully functional demonstrates features far better than diagrams, drawings, verbal explanations, or volumes of documentation.

UNUM Life Insurance used prototyping to show how a new system using image processing would work. UNUM wanted to use new technologies to link its system with all external and internal systems and their users. However, top management had a hard time getting middle managers to envision how they wanted to use image processing and to understand the issues involved in the change. After viewing a prototype, the managers caught on to the possibilities and issues associated with image processing. Up until that point, all image processing meant to these managers was replacing file cabinets; only after viewing the prototype did they realize its business potential.

Developers who use prototyping still go through the systems development life cycle discussed in Chapter 17. However, prototyping allows developers to condense and speed up parts of the analysis and the design phases. For example, prototyping does a good job of capturing user needs and helps developers and users make many of the conceptual and physical design decisions.

Steps in Developing a Prototype

As shown in Fig. 18.2, four steps are involved in developing a prototype. The first step is to identify basic system requirements by meeting with the user to agree on the size and scope of the system and to decide what the system should include and exclude. The developer and user also determine decision-making and transaction processing outputs, as well as the inputs and data needed to produce these outputs. The emphasis is on *what* output should be produced rather than *how* it should be produced. The developer must ensure that user expectations are realistic and that the user's basic information requirements can be met. The designer uses the information requirements to develop cost, time, and feasibility estimates for alternative AIS solutions. Because only general requirements are identified, determining requirements for the prototype is less formal and time-consuming than in the traditional SDLC approach. Detailed system requirements are developed by users as they interact with the prototype.

The second step is to develop an initial prototype that meets the agreed-on requirements. The emphasis is on speed and low cost rather than efficiency of operation. The goal is to implement the prototype within a short time period, perhaps days or weeks. Because of these time limitations, some aspects of the system are sacrificed in the interests of simplicity, flexibility, and ease of use. Therefore nonessential functions, system controls, exception handling, validation of input data, processing speed, and efficiency considerations are ignored at this point. It is critical, however, that users see and use tentative versions of data entry display

FIGURE 18.2
The Steps to Developing a System from a Prototype

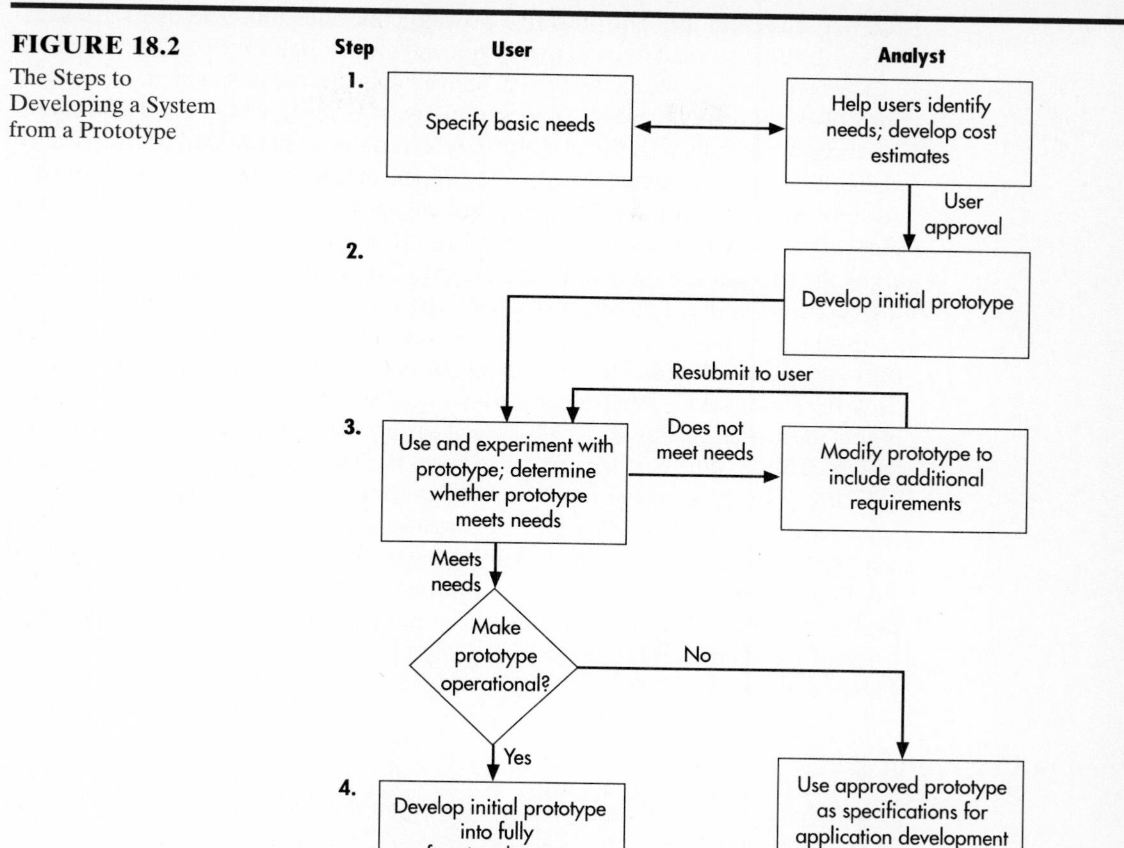

screens, menus, input prompts, and source documents. They must also respond to prompts, query the system, judge response times, and issue commands.

A number of tools help designers develop prototypes. These tools are efficient, are easy to use, and can create files, screens, reports, and program code much faster and with much less effort than conventional programming languages. They include fourth-generation languages (4GLs), CASE tools, data bases, high-level query languages, generalized report writers, and various application software packages.

When the prototype is finished, the developer returns to the user and demonstrates the system. The user is instructed to experiment with the system and comment on what he or she does and does not like about its content and performance.

The third step is an iterative process in which users identify changes, developers make changes, and the system is again turned over to the user for evaluation and experimental use. This iterative process continues until the users are satisfied with the system. A typical prototype will go through four to six iterations.

The fourth step is to use the system approved by the users. As shown in Fig. 18.2 an approved prototype is typically used in one of two ways. Half of all prototypes are turned into fully functional systems referred to as **operational prototypes.** To make the prototype operational, the developer must incorporate needed controls, improve operational efficiency, provide backup and recovery, and integrate the prototype with the systems with which it interfaces. Changes may be necessary to allow the program to accept real input, access real data files, process data, make the necessary computations and calculations, and produce real output.

In many instances it is not practical to modify the prototype to make it a fully functional system. These **nonoperational** or **throwaway prototypes** can be used in several ways. The prototype may be discarded, and the system requirements identified during the prototyping process can be used to develop a new system. The system development life cycle is followed to develop the system, with the prototype as the model for development. The prototype can also be used as the initial prototype for an expanded system designed to meet the needs of many different users. Finally, if the user and the developer decide that the system under consideration is unsalvageable, the prototype can be discarded completely. In this instance, the company has saved itself years of development work and a lot of money by avoiding the much more costly traditional SDLC process.

When to Use Prototyping

In most cases prototyping supports rather than replaces the SDLC. Prototyping is appropriate when there is a high level of uncertainty about the AIS; it is unclear what questions to ask; the final AIS cannot be clearly visualized because the decision process is still unclear; speed is an issue; or there is a high likelihood of failure. Systems that are especially good candidates for prototyping are decision support systems, executive information systems, expert systems, and information retrieval systems. Prototyping is also appropriate for systems that involve experimentation and trial-and-error development or where the requirements evolve as the system is used. Prototyping is not usually appropriate for large or complex systems that serve major organizational components or cross a number of organizational boundaries. Nor are they commonly used for developing standard AIS components such as accounts receivable and payable, or inventory management. A summary of the conditions that make prototyping an appropriate design methodology is presented in Table 18.6.

Advantages of Prototyping

The advantages of prototyping are discussed in the following subsections. The advantages and disadvantages are summarized in Table 18.7.

Better Definition of User Needs. Because of intensive end-user involvement, prototyping usually results in a good definition of user needs. Many users

TABLE 18.6 Conditions that Favor the Use of Prototyping

Users do not understand their needs very well, or their needs change rapidly.
System requirements are hard to define.
System inputs and outputs are not known.
The task to be performed is unstructured or semistructured.
Designers are uncertain about what technology to use.
The system to be developed is crucial and needed quickly.
The risk associated with developing the wrong system is high.
The users' reactions to the new system are important development considerations.
Many design strategies must be tested.
The development staff is experienced with 4GL and other prototyping tools.
The design staff has little experience developing the system or application under consideration.
The system will be used infrequently (and therefore processing efficiency is not a major concern).

TABLE 18.7 Advantages and Disadvantages of Prototyping

Advantages	**Disadvantages**
Usually produces a better definition of user needs than other approaches.	Requires a significant amount of user time.
Greater user involvement and satisfaction and less risk the system will not be used.	Shortcuts used in developing a prototype may result in inefficient systems.
Systems can be developed much more quickly.	May not lead to a comprehensive and thorough requirements analysis.
Errors are more likely to be detected and eliminated.	Developers may shortchange the testing and documentation process.
Users can see and use system and have more opportunities to make changes.	May result in a number of negative behavioral reactions.
Less costly than other approaches.	Unending iterations and revisions may be proposed because changes are so easy to make.

find that systems developed using prototypes do not have to be modified for quite some time because they were done right the first time. When significant changes are needed, it is usually because business requirements have changed.

Higher User Involvement and Satisfaction. Better meeting user requirements results in greater user satisfaction and less risk that the AIS will not be used. Early user involvement also helps to build a climate of acceptance rather than skepticism and criticism about the new AIS.

Faster Development Time. It only takes a few days or weeks to get a prototype system up and running, which allows users to immediately evaluate significant changes in the way business is transacted. In contrast, it may take a year or more under the traditional approach before the new system can be evaluated. After that time the system may no longer be useful, and enough time has passed for user resistance to build. John Hancock Mutual Life Insurance developed the prototype of an executive information system in only one month, as described in Focus 18.2.

Fewer Errors. Because the user experiments with and uses each version of the prototype, errors are detected and eliminated early in the development process. In addition, it is much easier to identify and terminate an infeasible AIS before a great deal of time and expense are incurred.

More Opportunity for Changes. Under the traditional SDLC approach, the design team is responsible for identifying AIS requirements the first time around. These requirements are then frozen so that the team can complete the

FOCUS 18.2 Prototyping: The Third Dimension

AN ARCHITECT develops two-dimensional blueprints that show how a custom home will look. But that is not the same as walking through a model of the proposed home. That third dimension, walking through the home, lets you actually see the rooms and get a feel for the layout. Creating customized software provides a similar challenge. Users must try to visualize the look and feel of their software from written specifications. Prototypes are very helpful to users who have ideas or plans but do not know how to turn them into reality, as well as to users who have a problem but do not know how to begin solving it. A prototype lets them walk through the proposed system and experiment with its look and feel before committing to the expense of application development.

John Hancock Mutual Life Insurance Company was dissatisfied with the traditional development process: determining user specifications (getting information from high-level executives was especially difficult), writing them up, developing the system, and presenting it to the end users. The typical reaction from a user was, "I may have said that this is what I wanted, but it isn't."

To counter these problems, Hancock used a prototyping approach to develop an executive information system (EIS). The EIS was needed because the company was dissatisfied with its inability to obtain data quickly and easily from the existing system.

A team was formed that included systems development consultants from IBM, user representatives, systems analysts, and programmers. The prototyping process was highly interactive, and the continual involvement of the end users eliminated a great deal of misunderstanding. The programmers on the team started programming almost immediately. They prepared sample screens for the first interview session with users. The development staff sat down with users and showed them how the system would work. Users were then given a chance to try the screens. Almost immediately, users could determine whether what they said they wanted was really what they needed.

The result was a prototype for an EIS that took only one month to build. The prototype allows top management at Hancock to access and query current and historical financial data and measurements. Top managers who had been skeptical when the project began were impressed by how much the team was able to accomplish in one short month.

AIS. With prototyping, users can continue to suggest changes until the system is exactly what they want.

Less Costly. Some prototype systems can be developed for 10% to 20% of the cost of systems developed using the traditional approach. For example, one utility company claimed a 13-to-1 improvement in development time over traditional methods using COBOL when prototyping was used to develop ten major applications.

Disadvantages of Prototyping

Prototyping has the following disadvantages.

Significant User Time. Prototyping can be successful only if users are willing to devote a significant amount of time to working with the AIS and providing the developer with feedback and suggestions. Prototyping may require a greater involvement and commitment than busy users are willing to give.

Less Efficient Use of System Resources. The shortcuts that make rapid prototyping iterations possible do not always allow for efficient use of computer resources. As a result, poor performance and reliability and high maintenance and support costs may be incurred. As systems become less expensive and faster, however, the exposure from this limitation is reduced.

Incomplete Systems Development. In large or complex systems with many users, prototyping may not lead to a comprehensive and thorough requirements analysis.

Inadequately Tested and Documented Systems. Because prototypes are used heavily before acceptance, developers are often tempted to shortchange the testing and documentation process.

Negative Behavioral Reactions. If a prototype is a throwaway, users may react negatively to learning the system and then not being able to use it. They may also become dissatisfied if all their demands for improvements are not met or if they have to go through too many iterations.

Neverending Development. If prototyping is not managed properly, the prototype may never be completed. Unending iterations and revisions may be proposed because changes are so easy to make.

Another tool for improving the development process is a set of software tools referred to as CASE. They are discussed in the next section.

COMPUTER-AIDED SOFTWARE ENGINEERING (CASE)

Software developers have been compared to the shoemaker's children who had to go barefoot; they develop software for others, yet fail to create software to simplify their own work. That has changed with the development of powerful **computer-aided software** (or **systems**) **engineering (CASE)** tools, an integrated package of computer-based tools that automate important aspects of the software development process. CASE tools are used to plan, analyze, design, program, and maintain an information system. They are also used to enhance the efforts of managers, users, and programmers in understanding information needs.

Many companies are currently using CASE tools. For example, Florida Power's new $86 million customer information system was created using a CASE tool sold by Andersen Consulting. The system has been so successful that Andersen Consulting is packaging it for other utility companies. America West Airlines has more than half of its 90 programmers developing applications using a PC-based CASE tool. Its employees use the tool to model data and business processes; then the tool uses this information to design and construct a system.

CASE tools do not replace skilled designers; instead they provide a host of well-integrated tools that give developers effective support for all SDLC phases. CASE software typically has tools for strategic planning, project and system management, data base design, screen and report layout, and automatic code generation.

Advantages and Disadvantages of CASE Technology

CASE tools provide several important advantages:

- *Improved productivity.* Sony reported that CASE tools increased productivity by over 600%. CASE can generate bug-free code from system specifications as well as automate repetitive tasks. A programmer at Baptist Medical System, using an integrated CASE tool, developed a system in one week that was estimated to take four months!
- *Improved program quality.* CASE tools simplify the enforcement of structured development standards, thus improving the quality of development and reducing the threat of serious design errors. CASE tools also can check the internal accuracy of the design and detect inconsistencies.
- *Cost savings.* Savings of 80% to 90% are possible. At DuPont, an application estimated to require 27 months at a cost of $270,000 was finished in 4 months for $30,000. Over 90% of the code was generated directly from design specifications.
- *Improved control procedures.* CASE tools encourage the development of system controls, security measures, and system auditability and error handling procedures early in the design process.
- *Simplified documentation.* CASE tools automatically document the system as the development process progresses.

Some of the more serious problems with CASE technology include the following:

- *Incompatibility.* Some CASE tools do not interact effectively.
- *Cost.* CASE technology is expensive, with some packages in excess of $300,000. As a result, most small companies cannot afford integrated CASE tools.

- *Unmet expectations.* According to a recent Deloitte & Touche survey, only 37% of the chief information officers using CASE believe they achieved the expected benefits.

SUMMARY AND CASE CONCLUSION

There are a number of different strategies that a company can use to obtain a new AIS. First, as the quality and quantity of vendor-written software increases, more and more companies are purchasing canned software. Second, they can use their information systems departments to develop their software or allow end-users to develop their own software. When vendor-written software does not meet all of their needs, some companies buy the software and then modify it themselves or, preferably, have the vendor make the needed modifications. Third, they can hire an outsourcing company to handle data processing activities.

There are a number of approaches that help speed up or improve the development process. One way to improve the development process is called business process reengineering. It is the thorough analysis and complete redesign of business processes and information systems to achieve dramatic performance improvements. It is a revolutionary process that challenges traditional organization structures, rules, assumptions, work flows, job descriptions, management procedures, controls, and organizational values and cultures associated with underperformance.

A second way to improve the development process is to design a simplified working model of a system. This prototype is quickly and inexpensively built and given to users to test drive so they decide what they like and dislike about the system. Their reactions and feedback are used to modify the system, which is again given to the user to test. This iterative process of trial usage and modification continues until the users are satisfied that the system adequately meets their needs.

A third way to improve the development process is to use computer-aided software engineering (CASE) tools to automate important aspects of the software development process. CASE tools are used to plan, analyze, design, program, and maintain an information system. They are also used to enhance the efforts of managers, users, and programmers in understanding information needs. CASE software typically has tools for strategic planning, project and system management, data base design, screen and report layout, and automatic code generation.

Ann considered the different strategies discussed in the chapter and eliminated a number of them. She decided against outsourcing the AIS because she did not feel that option would provide Shoppers Mart with the type of system that management was looking for. She also believed her team could do a better and faster job developing the system than an outsourcer. Ann did not think that prototyping would work well because Shoppers Mart needed a large and complex system that would serve the needs of many users in many functional areas. Ann discussed the new system with top management and the IS staff and decided that the company's business processes did not need to be radically overhauled—that is, the system does not need to be reengineered.

Ann narrowed her options down to purchasing a system or designing one in-house. If Shoppers Mart decides to develop its own software, Ann will investigate the various CASE packages on the market to see if they will add value to the development process.

No matter which approach she chose, Ann wanted to facilitate as much end-user development as was practical and useful. Ann will make the final decision during the conceptual design phase (Chapter 19). To gather the information she needed to decide whether or not to purchase software, Ann prepared and sent an RFP to vendors. The RFP asked them to propose software and hardware to meet the company needs that were identified during systems analysis.

KEY TERMS

canned software
turnkey systems
request for a proposal (RFP)
benchmark problem
point scoring
requirements costing
custom software
end-user computing (EUC)
end-user development (EUD)
help desk
outsourcing
business process reengineering (BPR)
prototyping
prototype
operational prototypes
nonoperational (throwaway) prototypes
computer-aided software (*or* systems) engineering (CASE)

CHAPTER QUIZ

1. Which of the following is *not* one of the difficulties accountants have experienced using the traditional systems development life cycle?
a. AIS development projects are backlogged for years.
b. Changes are not possible after requirements have been frozen.
c. The AIS that is developed does not meet their needs.
d. All of the above are difficulties with the SDLC.

2. Companies that buy rather than develop an AIS must still go through the systems development life cycle.
a. True
b. False

3. Which of the following statements is *false?*
a. As a general rule, companies should buy rather than develop software if they can find a package that meets their needs.
b. As an AIS increases in size and complexity, there is a greater likelihood that canned software can be found that meets user needs.
c. A company should not attempt to develop their own custom software unless experienced, in-house programming personnel are available and the job can be completed less expensively on the inside.
d. As a general rule, a company should develop custom software only when it will provide a significant competitive advantage.

4. When buying large and complex systems, vendors are invited to submit systems for consideration. Such a solicitation is referred to as a
a. request for a quotation.
b. request for a system.
c. request for a proposal.
d. good faith estimate.

5. To compare system performance, a company can create a data processing task with input, processing, and output jobs. This task is performed on the system under consideration and the processing times are compared. The AIS with the lowest time is the most efficient. This process is referred to as
a. benchmarking.

b. requirements costing.
c. point scoring.
d. performance testing.

6. Which of the following statements is true?
a. Because the AIS is so crucial, companies never outsource the entire AIS.
b. Most mainframe outsourcing contracts are for two to three years and cost thousands of dollars a year.
c. In elaborate agreements, outsourcers often buy their clients' computers and hire all or most of their employees.
d. Outsourcing is used only by companies struggling to survive and wanting a quick infusion of cash from selling their hardware.

7. Which of the following is *not* a benefit of outsourcing?
a. It offers a great deal of flexibility because it is relatively easy to change outsourcers.
b. It can provide access to the expertise and special services provided by outsourcers.
c. It allows companies to move to a more sophisticated level of computing at a reasonable cost.
d. It is a cost-effective way to handle the peaks and valleys found in seasonal businesses.

8. Which of the following is a true statement with respect to prototyping?
a. In the early stages of prototyping, system controls and exception handling may be sacrificed in the interests of simplicity, flexibility, and ease of use.
b. A prototype is a scaled-down, first draft model that is quickly and inexpensively built and given to users to evaluate.
c. The first step in prototyping is to identify system requirements.
d. All of the above statements are true.

9. All of the following are advantages of prototyping *except*
a. better definition of user needs.
b. adequately tested and documented systems.
c. higher user involvement and satisfaction.
d. faster development time.

10. It is most appropriate to use prototyping when
a. there is a little uncertainty about the AIS.
b. it is clear what user needs are.
c. the final AIS cannot be clearly visualized because the decision process is still unclear.
d. there is a low likelihood of failure.

DISCUSSION QUESTIONS

18.1 What is the role of the accountant in the computer acquisition process? Should the accountant play an active role, or should all the work be left to computer experts? In what aspects of computer acquisition might an accountant provide a useful contribution?

18.2 A city in the Midwest, with a population of 45,000, purchased a computer and began developing application programs with in-house programmers. Four years later, only one major application had been developed and it was neither complete nor functioning properly. Moreover, none of the application software running on the system met the users' minimum requirements. Both the hardware and the software frequently failed. A similarly configured system, fully programmed with canned software, would have saved the city nearly half a million dollars. Moreover, the city's annual data processing costs exceeded the annual costs of a brand-new turnkey system with packaged software.

Why do you think the city was unable to produce quality, workable systems? Would the city have been better off purchasing canned software? Do you think the city would have been able to find software to adequately meet their needs? Why or why not?

18.3 Custom, canned, and modified canned software all have advantages and disadvantages. In this age of increasing computerization, which do you feel will become predominant? Will any of the methods will be phased out? Does your response vary depending on the type and size of user organizations?

18.4 You are a systems consultant for Cooper, Price, and Arthur, CPAs. During your country club's annual golf tournament, your partner is Frank Fender, owner of an automobile dealership. He describes a proposal he received from Turnkey Systems and asks for your opinion. The system will handle inventories, receivables, payroll, accounts payable, and general ledger accounting. Turnkey personnel would install the $70,000 system and train Fender's employees. Identify the major themes you would touch on in responding to Fender. Identify the advantages and disadvantages of using a turnkey system to operate the organization's accounting system.

18.5 Sara Jones is the owner of a rapidly growing department store and faces stiff competition. The store is using an out-of-date AIS, resulting in poor customer service, late and error-prone billing, and inefficient control and monitoring of inventory. If the store is to continue growing, its AIS must be upgraded. However, the company is not exactly sure what it wants the AIS to accomplish. Sara has heard about prototyping, but she does not know what it is and whether it would help her. What would you tell Sara if she asked you to define and explain prototyping? Include an explanation of the advantages and disadvantages of prototyping and the circumstances in which it would be most appropriate.

18.6 Clint Grace is the owner of a chain of regional department stores and has been in the business for more than 30 years. He has definite ideas about how department stores should be run. He is financially conservative and is reluctant to make expenditures that do not have a clear financial payoff.

In recent years the stores' profitability has declined sharply and customer dissatisfaction is at an all-time high. Store managers never know exactly how much inventory is on hand and when purchases are needed until a shelf is empty. Grace asks you to study the reason for the profitability decline and to recommend a solution. During your research you find that the current AIS is inefficient and unreliable and that the company's processes and procedures are old and out of date.

You believe that the solution is to reengineer the business processes at the department stores and in the central office. What are some of the challenges you might face in reengineering Grace's stores? Knowing what you do about Grace's personality, how will you present your recommendation?

PROBLEMS

18.1 Don Otno is confused. He has been researching software options but cannot decide among three alternatives. He has come to you for help.

Otno started his search at Computers Made Easy (CME), a computer store in his office complex. He almost wished he had looked no further. Steve Young, the manager of CME, appeared to be knowledgeable and listened attentively as Otno explained his problems, needs, and concerns. Young stated that he had a series of software packages that would, with a few exceptions, come close to meeting Otno's needs. He could fix Otno up with both hardware and software, and Otno could start implementing the package almost immediately. The system's price was unexpectedly reasonable.

Impressed but wanting to shop around, Otno visited Custom Designed Software (CDS). After three hours, he left convinced that CDS could produce a program that was exactly what he needed. Cost and time estimates had not been established, but CDS assured him that the cost would be reasonable and that the programs would only take a few months to complete.

Seeking a third opinion, Otno visited Modified Software Unlimited (MSU). The MSU representative said customized packages were very good but expensive, whereas canned software was inexpensive, but rarely met more than a few needs. The best of both worlds could be achieved by having MSU modify the package that came closest to meeting Otno's needs.

On his way back to his office Otno stopped by CME and asked Young about customized and modified software. Steve expressed enough concerns about both that Otno came full circle; he began thinking canned software was best. Late that night Otno realized that he was not able to make an objective decision. He was swayed by whichever vendor he was talking to at the time. The next morning he called you for help.

Required:

a. At Otno's request you agree to conduct a study and submit a report showing the advantages and disadvantages of each vendor's approach. Outline the report's contents, identifying the advantages and disadvantages of each approach.
b. Recommend the course of action that you feel would be best for Otno, and support your decision.

18.2 One unhappy federal agency spent almost $1 million on a development contract for an integrated human resources/payroll system that produced no usable software. The original contract was for

$445,158 and 15 months; the agency terminated the contract after 28 months and $970,000. The agency had not fully developed user requirements or system specifications for the proposed software when it issued the RFP. There were a number of problems:

- The contractor did not understand the desired software systems.
- User requirements were never adequately defined and frozen. Changes delayed completion schedules and caused disagreements about whether new requirements were included in the original scope of work.
- The contract did not specify systems requirements or performance criteria and the terminology was vague. The contract was amended 13 times to add or delete requirements and to reimburse the contractor for the extra costs resulting from agency-caused delays. The amendments increased the cost of the contract to $1,037,448.
- The contractor complained of inexcusable agency delays, such as taking too much time to review items submitted for approval. The agency blamed the delays on the poor quality of the documentation under review.
- The agency did not require each separate development phase to be approved before work continued. When the agency rejected the general system design, the contractor had to scrap work already completed.

The agency eventually became convinced that the contractor could not deliver the software at an acceptable time and cost, canceled the contract, and tried to withhold payment for poor performance. A negotiated settlement price of $970,000 was agreed on. None of the software was ever used by the agency.

Required:

a. Who is to blame for the agency's problems? How could the agency have done a better job of managing the systems development project? What about the contractor?

b. Can we generalize from this case that organizations and governmental agencies should not try to have custom software written for them? Why or why not?

18.3 Wong Engineering Corporation (WEC) operates in 25 states and three countries. WEC faced a crucial decision: choosing a network operating system and software that would maximize functionality, manageability, and acceptance of the system by end users. WEC developed and followed a four-step approach:

Step 1: Develop the evaluation criteria. WEC organized a committee to develop proper evaluation criteria. Committee members interviewed users and developed the following criteria:

Menu or graphical user interface
Ease of use
Scope of vendor support
Ease of LAN management and administration
Cost, speed, and performance
Wide area communications abilities
Ability to access other computing platforms
Security
Fault tolerance and recovery abilities
Ability to connect workstations to the network
Global naming services
Printing capabilities
Upgrade and enhancement options
Stability of the vendor

WEC organized the criteria into the following four categories and prioritized them.

1. *Business criteria* refer to overall business, economic, and competitive issues.
2. *Operational criteria* refer to tactical issues and operating characteristics.
3. *Organizational criteria* refer to people issues such as the LAN's impact on the IS structure.
4. *Technical criteria* refer to hardware, software, and communications issues.

The evaluation committee used a weighting scale of 1 to 5, with 5 as the highest, to select the top three evaluation criteria for each category. Criteria vital to short-term and long-term business goals were given a 5. "Wish list" criteria were weighted a 3. Inapplicable criteria were given a 1.

Step 2: Define the operating environment. A number of data gathering techniques were used to collect information from which an IS model was developed. The model revealed the need to share accounting, sales, marketing, and engineering data at three organizational levels: the district, division, and home office. In addition, district offices needed access to centralized financial information to handle payroll. WEC decided it needed a distributed network that allows users throughout the organization access to company data.

Step 3: Identify the operating alternatives. Using the criteria developed in step 1, WEC evaluated each package identified. Each committee member established personal matrices for each product, and then members compared notes during a roundtable discussion.

Step 4: Test and prototype products. The highest-scoring products were tested further using prototypes. Finally, WEC selected the product that fit the organization's needs most completely.

Required:

a. Discuss the role of the evaluation committee in the selection process. How should members of the committee be selected? What advantages and problems result from using a committee to make the selection?
b. What data gathering techniques could WEC use to assess user needs? To select a vendor?
c. What is the benefit of analyzing the operating environment before selecting the software? What data gathering techniques should a company employ in understanding the operating environment?
d. In selecting a system using the point-scoring method, how should the committee resolve scoring disputes? List at least two methods.
e. Assume the point-scoring approach narrowed the process to three candidates. Should a purchase decision be made on the point-scoring process alone? What other procedure(s) should the committee employ in making the final selection?

18.4 Mark Mitton is the accountant acting as liaison to the IS department for a medium-sized retail firm in Salem, Oregon. Mark has been investigating several computer systems and has narrowed the selection to three turnkey systems. Mark developed a shopping list of features the system needs. He carefully reviewed each system, talked to other users, and interviewed appropriate system representatives. Using a point-scoring system, Mark assigned weights to each factor to coincide with his evaluation. Mark developed Table 18.8 to help him select the best turnkey system.

Required:

a. Use a spreadsheet program to develop a point-scoring matrix and determine which of the three systems Mark should select.
b. Mark's coworker, Susan Shelton, did not agree with Mark's weightings. Susan suggested the following changes:

Flexibility	60
Reputation and reliability	50
Quality of support utilities	10
Graphics capibility	10

On the basis of the changes, which vendor should Mark recommend?
c. Mark's manager suggested the following changes to Susan's weightings:

Reputation and reliability	90
Installation assistance	40
Experience with similiar systems	40
Training assistance	65
Internal memory size	10

Will the manager's changes affect the decision about which system to buy?
d. What can you conclude about point scoring from the changes made by Susan and Mark's manager? Develop your own weighting scale to evaluate the selection of the three software packages. Be prepared to discuss your results with the class.
e. What are the weaknesses of the point-scoring method?

18.5 Nielsen Marketing Research USA (NMR), with operations in 29 countries, is the recognized world leader in the production and dissemination of marketing information. Nielsen was a pioneer in the development of the decision support information business and has been the primary supplier for more than 70 years. NMR's most recognizable product is the Nielsen television ratings.

Nielsen is one of the largest users of computer capacity in the United States. Its information system has consistently ranked above average in efficiency for its industry. However, it commissioned IBM's Integrated Systems Solutions Corporation (ISSC) to evaluate outsourcing NMR's information processing. NMR wants to know whether outsourcing will allow it to concentrate on giving its customers value-added services and insights and whether outsourcing can increase its flexibility, promote rapid growth, and provide it with more real-time information.

Required:

What are the benefits and risks of outsourcing for NMR? Do you think the benefits of outsourcing outweigh the risks? Why or why not?

18.6 The Pedaler, one of the largest bicycle manufacturers in the world, has grown significantly in the 20 years since it was formed. Eighteen years ago the company began using a computer to handle its data processing needs. Since then, several million dollars have been spent on hardware and software.

TABLE 18.8 An Alternative Evaluation Matrix

Selection Criteria	Weight	System 1	System 2	System 3	Selection Criteria	Weight	System 1	System 2	System 3
Software					*Vendor*				
Fulfillment of business needs	100	6	8	9	Reputation and reliability	10	3	9	6
Acceptance in marketplace	30	6	7	6	Experience with similar systems	20	5	5	6
Quality of documentation	50	7	9	8	Installation assistance	70	9	4	6
Quality of warranty	50	4	8	7	Training assistance	35	4	8	6
Ease of use	80	7	6	5	Timeliness of maintenance	35	5	4	4
Control features	50	9	7	9	*Hardware*				
Flexibility	20	4	5	9	Internal memory size (RAM)	70	5	6	8
Security features	30	4	4	8	Diskette capacity	40	9	9	5
Modularity	30	8	5	4	Graphics capabilities	50	7	7	8
Integration with other software	30	8	9	6	Processing speed	30	8	8	5
Quality of support utilities	50	9	8	5	Overall performance	40	9	4	4
					Expandability	50	7	2	5
					Support for LAN technology	30	3	4	7

For the past several years the IS department has effectively handled company needs. During the slow season IS employees have light schedules, work on special projects, and spend one to two weeks at training seminars. During the peak season employees average five hours of overtime per week. Recently, the Pedaler has grown so fast that IS is having a hard time keeping up. Management realizes the benefit IS provides and is thinking of expanding the department at a cost of $1 million over the next three years. Due to their rapid expansion, the Pedaler would have to borrow the money for this project. Investing in a new system, however, may slow the company's growth or, worse, add significantly to debt.

At the last board of directors meeting, outsourcing was suggested as a possible solution. Brian Cycle, the president, has asked you, an independent consultant specializing in AIS strategies, for your advice.

Required:

Write a one-page memo explaining outsourcing and summarizing the benefits and drawbacks of outsourcing the Pedaler's IS functions. Address the issues of whether outsourcing fits the Pedaler's situation, whether it can save the Pedaler money, and whether it can effectively meet the needs of a growing company.

18.7 Meredith Corporation publishes books and magazines, owns and operates television stations, and provides a real estate marketing and franchising service. Meredith is dissatisfied with its ability to retrieve correct and timely inventory information from its AIS. Each division either developed its own inventory system or already had one in place when it was acquired by Meredith. As a result, Meredith has 11 different inventory systems, which are unable to communicate with each other. Management wants to tie the systems together and have one consistent inventory pool from which to extract the information needed for making good business decisions. Meredith has decided to use prototyping to develop the system.

Required:

a. What three key questions would you ask when interviewing Meredith's personnel to determine system requirements? What type of information are you attempting to elicit from each question?

b. What do you think Meredith's basic information needs are?

c. Explain how the prototyping process would work for Meredith. What would the system developer do during the iterative process step? Why would you want the fewest iterations possible?

d. What tools will you use to design your prototype? Why would you use them instead of conventional programming languages?

e. Would you want this prototype to be operational or nonoperational? Why? If it were an operational prototype, what would have to happen? If it were a nonoperational prototype, how would the prototype be used?

f. Suppose the company decides the prototyped system is not practical, abandons the system, and takes some other approach to solving its inventory problem. Does that mean prototyping is not a valid systems development approach? Why or why not?

18.8 The following list outlines the activities a company may perform in the process of reengineering its business. Match each activity with one of the seven principles of reengineering.

Reengineering Activities

a. One person processes an employment application from beginning to end.

b. The department manager using the yearly budget is also the one who prepared it.

c. The purchasing manager has the authority to handle every aspect of purchase making.

d. Each plant issues its own purchase orders, and a new corporate department coordinates purchasing across all the plants.

e. All customer service representatives share a corporate-wide data base that contains customer sales data.

f. A sales clerk enters a customer's order into a computer terminal. The order is then automatically sent over the network to shipping, inventory control, and the credit manager. In addition, the data base is updated immediately.

Seven Principles of Reengineering

1. Organize the business and information system around outcomes, not individual tasks.
2. Individuals who need to use the output from a process should be the ones performing it.
3. Individuals who produce information should process it as well.
4. Use information technology to achieve the benefits of both centralization and decentralization of data.
5. Integrate parallel processes instead of performing them separately and trying to integrate them at the end of the process.
6. Flatten the organizational chart by giving workers the power to make decisions and utilize built-in controls.
7. Capture data only once, at its source, using source data automation.

18.9 The management of Quickfix would like to decrease costs and increase customer service by reengineering its computer repair procedures. Currently, when a defective or broken computer needs servicing, the customer calls one of five regional customer service centers. A customer service representative manually logs in the relevant customer information and then searches through a list to find the closest qualified technician. That technician is then contacted by phone to see whether the repair fits into his or her schedule. If not, the representative finds the next closest technician. When a technician who can perform the service is located, the customer and repair information is provided over the phone. The technician then calls the customer and makes arrangements to pick up the broken computer and replace it with a loaner. Making these arrangements takes one to two days and sometimes more if technicians are not available or do not promptly return calls.

The broken computer is sent to a repair depot. Typically, the entire repair process takes another four to seven days. Overall, it can take up to three weeks for an item to be repaired. When a customer calls to see whether their computer is ready, the customer service representative must then call the technician, find out the status of the item, and call the customer back. Throughout the entire repair process, usually five phone calls take place between the customer, the customer service representative, and the technician.

There are three main problems with this process: (1) it is time-consuming; (2) it is an inconvenience for customers to have their computer removed, a new one installed, and then the old one reinstalled; and (3) customer service representatives do not have immediate access to information about items currently being repaired.

Required:

a. Identify the most basic activities that occur when an item is repaired and around which the reengineered process should be developed.
b. Describe how the current repair process can be reengineered to achieve the goal of more timely repair and increased customer service.
c. What will be the specific benefits of reengineering the repair process?

18.10 Selling goods to a manufacturer that employs a just-in-time (JIT) inventory system requires immediate and reliable information from a company's AIS—just ask Sony Corporation of America. The need for faster information is partially a result of Sony's shift in business strategies. Over the past decade Sony has increased market penetration by supplying electronic parts to computer manufacturers. However, the AIS, originally built for the consumer market, was simply not prepared to handle this shift in information needs.

The problems with the system are readily apparent. One of Sony's biggest obstacles is that it does not get the information it needs, when it needs it, from its factories. As a result, it cannot provide good delivery information to its customers. And that causes a big problem—if Sony is not responsive to its customers' needs, it will probably lose them.

To speed system development, the IS organization at Sony is employing a computer-aided software engineering (CASE) tool from Texas Instruments. The tool lets systems designers use local workstations linked to a mainframe and uses artificial intelligence features to develop program code.

To use the CASE tool, the designer enters statements that describe the data the company will use and the relationships among the data files that will store this information. The CASE tool checks the data relationships to ensure that they are consistent. After any inconsistencies have been corrected, the CASE tool produces code that describes the relationships. The information is then stored in a global encyclopedia of corporate information. This process continues until a model of how the company operates is developed. The CASE tool allows this model to be updated and altered as relationships change.

Sony is finding several advantages to using CASE technology. For instance, the use of CASE technology requires that developers possess a certain business expertise; this expertise makes designers more effective in translating business problems into systems solutions. The CASE system has also provided a significant productivity boost. Recent smaller development projects at Sony have seen sixfold increases in programming productivity. CASE tools also require significant planning long before any source code is written. Such planning minimizes wasted programming time and the possibility of a runaway system.

Required:

a. What are the benefits of CASE technology? How does CASE technology improve the systems development process?
b. Discuss why CASE technology might not be used in systems development.

CASE 18.1 ANYCOMPANY, INC.—AN ONGOING COMPREHENSIVE CASE

Visit a local company and obtain permission to study its systems development approach. Once you have lined up a company, do the following:

1. With a member of the information systems staff, discuss the following issues:
   a. What procedures does the company follow in determining its hardware and software needs? How does the company select software, hardware, and vendors?
   b. Does the company outsource any of its data processing activities? If so, what benefits is it now deriving, and what risks is it exposed to? Does the company think the decision was a good one? If it does not outsource, has it considered the option? If so, why was it rejected?
   c. Has the company used prototyping? If so, what benefits did it derive? What were the disadvantages? Does the company continue to use prototypes, or has it discontinued their use? If it has not used prototypes, was it the approach considered? If so, why was it rejected?
2. Summarize your findings in a written report and be prepared to share your findings with the class.

CASE 18.2 WIDGET MANUFACTURING COMPANY

The Widget Manufacturing Company is a major producer of widgets, with total sales of $50 million annually. Its AIS department currently has an ABC Model 115 computer, which operates 12 hours per day, five days a week. It processes payroll, general accounting, inventory control, and accounts receivable using a batch mode. This equipment also supports an on-line order entry system with four workstations located in the sales department. This application processes an average of 240,000 transactions per year.

The company prepared a two-year information systems plan. D. MacTavish, Widget's AIS director, determined that the present computer could absorb any additional work load caused by rapidly increasing sales. This increase could be handled by scheduling a full second shift and possibly a third shift. The present computer would not have sufficient memory or be fast enough, however, to handle a new production scheduling system that was planned and that would require more workstations be added in the production planning department and at several locations throughout the plant. This new system would increase the number of workstation transactions by approximately 720,000 per year but would require approximately one year to develop and implement following the availability of a new system.

After a presentation to the president and executive committee, MacTavish was authorized to prepare the hardware and software specifications for a system that would meet the needs of Widget for the next two years. Also, because the company was expanding so quickly, the president asked MacTavish to include the cost of renting space in a nearby office building in which the entire AIS department could be relocated. This would provide space in the Widget head office building for additional staff that were needed by other company departments. The AIS department currently occupies approximately 3,300 square feet of space in the basement of the Widget head office building. MacTavish was asked to prepare a financial summary showing the cost of the present and proposed systems for presentation to the company's board of directors.

MacTavish prepared the specifications for the new systems and sent them to the ABC Computer Company, the supplier of the present computer. He also invited the PQR Company to submit a proposal for its equipment and software, and he decided to ask XYZ, an outsourcing company, to respond with the prices it would charge to process Widget's information. Included in the specifications were all processing volumes and transaction rates for existing and proposed applications. Also included was the fact that Widget uses 75 magnetic tapes for backup storage of important disk files. This figure was expected to increase to 100 tapes with the implementation of the production scheduling system.

The important facts from each of the three proposals MacTavish received are as follows.

The ABC Proposal

The ABC representative recommended a Model 138 computer that leased for $273,478 per year. This system would have sufficient memory and speed to handle all current applications plus the new system. Because it is also a member of the same family of computers as Widget's Model 115, it would use the same software as the 115 and therefore require the same amount of training as was needed on the present equipment. He pointed out, however, that the larger 138 could use a new series of workstations that ABC had recently announced and would enable Widget to acquire the additional workstations it needed to replace its present terminals at a total cost of $14,100 per year for the two years. This new system would require the same space as the present Model 115.

The PQR Proposal

The PQR Company recommended a Model 906 system. The equipment that would be located in the Widget computer center would cost $213,660 per year, and all of the necessary workstations would be supplied at a cost of $9,468. PQR's marketing policy differed from that of ABC in that all software and staff training costs were included in the price of the equipment. It also was willing to provide a discount of $66,000 during the second year if Widget would sign a two-year lease for the equipment. The PQR proposal indicated that its equipment would fit into an area equivalent to that occupied by the present computer.

The XYZ Proposal

The XYZ outsourcing proposal involved the installation of a minicomputer at the Widget computer center that would be used for editing and balancing all batch input. The data would be sent over a telephone line several times a day to a large computer located at the outsourcing company, where it would be processed. Output would be returned to Widget over the same communications line to the minicomputer, where it would be stored on a disk until it could be printed out and distributed. The on-line order entry system and the new production scheduling system would use workstations connected to the large computer at XYZ, and any printed output from these systems would be sent by telephone line to the minicomputer for printing and distribution. The cost to Widget for leasing the minicomputer would be $32,724 per year, and workstations would be leased for $11,000 annually. The cost of the communications line between the minicomputer at the Widget offices and the large system at XYZ would be $21,420 each year, with an installation charge of $4,020 the first year.

On the basis of benchmark tests using existing Widget programs, XYZ estimated that the cost of running all batch programs would be $132,000 per year. The cost of storing the backup tapes for Widget would be $1 per tape per year.

XYZ used a price schedule for on-line applications based on the number of transactions entered through the workstations. Its price was quoted at 10 cents per transaction, which included software charges. As an incentive to Widget, XYZ offered a volume discount of $109,800 during the second year and agreed to provide all necessary training of Widget staff during the first year of the agreement at no cost. Widget would have to pay for training during the second year. Since XYZ used an ABC computer, Widget's staff could take the same courses at the same cost as the ones required for the larger ABC machine.

In the opinion of XYZ, the installation of a minicomputer by Widget would reduce the computer center space requirements by 450 square feet.

During negotiations for a nearby office building MacTavish was able to negotiate the lease of space for his department at a rate of $10 per square foot per year, the amount of space depending on the alternative selected by Widget's board of directors.

Present computer costs are as follows:

Central Site Hardware (monthly)	$16,764.00
Software (monthly)	1,516.00
Workstations (monthly)	1,292.50
Training costs (annually)	7,000.00

Note: All hardware and software is leased. The company follows the policy of capitalizing lease payments for financial statement purposes.

As MacTavish, write a report to the board of directors recommending which proposal to accept. Include the quantitative and qualitative aspects of each proposal. Indicate what impact, if any, the decision regarding the development of the proposed production scheduling system would have on your recommendation.

(SMAC Examination, adapted)

CASE 18.3 PROFESSIONAL SALON CONCEPTS

Steve Cowan is the owner of Professional Salon Concepts (PSC), a distribution company for hair salon products, in Joliet, Illinois. Steve started working for his father, a distributor of barber and beauty salon products, at age 16 and a decade later decided to start his own business. He rented a small warehouse, hired four people, and began selling products carrying the name of famous hairstylist Paul Mitchell. Unfortunately, hairstylists ignored the products and did not buy them. Steve eventually had to let his people go and move his products to an inexpensive basement location.

The tables turned for Steve when he put on a free two-hour seminar at a local hair salon demonstrating how hairstylists could successfully use his products. He left with a $1,000 order and the realization that he had found his niche. He decided to sell only to salons that allowed him to put on a seminar and demonstrate his products.

PSC has done very well using Steve's strategy. Sales took off, reaching $7 million in 1993, as PSC grew to 45 employees and 3,000 salon customers. Warehouse operations ran smoothly due to Paul Mitchell's specialized product line, which was 75% of

PSC's business. PSC carried 1,000 products, compared with 10,000 for the average salon distributor. This more focused product line enabled PSC to achieve a 24-hour turnaround on orders, in contrast to more than two days for the competition. To achieve this quick turnaround, Steve sometimes worked late packing orders so he could drive them to the UPS hub a few towns away by the 2 A.M. deadline.

In 1985 Steve bought PSC's first computer, and installed a $3,000 accounting package, which served his accounting needs very well. In fact, Steve thought everything was going great until Terri Klimko, a consultant from PSC's second largest supplier, stopped by. Terri asked Steve some questions designed to reveal how well he knew his business:

- Do you know exactly to whom you ship each month?
- Do you know how much each customer bought, by supplier?
- Can you rank your customer sales?
- Can you break your sales down by product?
- Do you know how the profit per client breaks down into product lines?
- Do you know how revenues per salesperson vary over the days of the week?

Steve's answer was an uncomfortable no to each question. Terri told him that people who cannot answer these questions are losing money. That upset Steve and he terminated the session, politely dismissing Terri. While Steve was not impressed with Terri's advice, he was impressed with her. They started dating and were soon married. Shortly after the marriage, she joined the company.

Steve realized that Terri's skills could be used either to help PSC's business grow or to help PSC internally. Believing it was more important to grow the business, he asked Terri to help make the salons more profitable. She developed a template to break down and, with PSC's help, analyze every aspect of their business. The template helped salon owners determine such statistics as how much each hairstylist brings in per client, whether enough clients receive extra services, and how many clients, and which ones, buy hair products. The Cowans soon became more like partners to their customers than trainers and educators. If a salon had employee problems, the Cowans would help settle the issues. If a salon fell behind in a grand opening, the Cowans lent a hand. The only catch was the salons had to buy PSC's products. The better the customer, the more time the Cowans gave.

PSC began selling turnkey systems and support services at cost to help salons answer questions like those Terri posed to Steve. Unfortunately, PSC's computer could not answer those same questions. Steve asked Mike Fenske, a consultant with Arthur Andersen, for help, and sent to Mike as much raw data as could be extracted from his PC-based accounting system. Mike entered it into a data base and wrote programs to produce the information Steve wanted. The system worked, but it was very slow—so slow that accounts payable and purchasing information was handled manually. Nor did the system answer all of Terri's questions, and her list was getting longer. To make matters worse, only a few months of detailed information was available at any time. To partially alleviate some of these problems, Steve hired Mike, who had married Steve's sister, as the company's controller.

After reading a special industry report, Steve realized that his company was well positioned in every aspect, except investment in technology. Steve and Mike realized it was time to purchase a new system. They considered outside consultants but felt they would take too much time trying to understand PSC's special needs. In addition, Mike believed consultants knew little about the detailed workings of the software they recommend. They decided to evaluate and select the software themselves and rely on the vendor for installation help.

Steve and Mike spent months researching software and attending demonstrations before settling on a generic AIS software program. They paid the $20,000 price tag and the vendor began installing the system and training PSC personnel. Three days prior to conversion, Steve met a distributor from North Dakota at a social gathering. The distributor described how his system not only provided all the detailed accounting and customer reporting features but also met his distributorship's inventory management and order fulfillment needs. Steve was so impressed that he excused himself and called Mike, telling him to halt the conversion. They immediately went to North Dakota to check out the system, then flew to Minneapolis to visit DSM, the software developer.

DSM did a great job of demonstrating the software and provided Steve and Mike with several great references. The only hitch was DSM's inability to demonstrate two features that were particularly important to Steve. The first was the ability to adjust orders automatically to reflect outstanding customer credits and back orders. The second was the ability to determine the least expensive way to pack and ship each order. DSM's salespeople assured Steve and Mike that those features would be up and running on the package by the time it was delivered to PSC.

Before committing to the system, Steve and Mike sat down to determine whether it was economically feasible. They estimated $234,000 in yearly savings:

$144,000 Most of PSC's orders consisted of several boxes, 95% of which were sent COD. PSC's old system had no way of writing orders for shipments of more than one box; in other words, an order shipped in five boxes had required five sales invoices and five separate COD tickets. The new system would allow PSC to generate one sales order and ship one box COD. The other four would be shipped by regular delivery, which was much less costly than COD delivery. Eliminating the need to ship every box COD would save the company $144,000 a year.

$50,000 PSC paid an outside accounting firm $40,000 a year to prepare their financial statements. The new software would prepare most of those statements automatically.

$40,000 Because the old system did not have credit managing capabilities, it was hard to detect past due accounts. Steve believed earlier detection of past due accounts would result in faster collections, fewer lost customers, and fewer write-offs.

Unknown The major reason for acquiring the system was to improve customer service by making more detailed customer information available.

Steve and Mike estimated annual maintenance costs of $10,000 and an annual return on investment of $224,000. Since the system would pay for itself in less than a year, Steve bought it and wrote off his $20,000 investment in the other system.

At the end of 1993 DSM technicians arrived at PSC to install the software. To Steve's dismay, the promised features were not part of the package and there was no immediate plan to add them. Although Steve and Mike were upset, they realized they had to shoulder some of the blame for not insisting on seeing the two features before signing the deal. A subsequent search found a program that automatically determined the cheapest way to pack and ship an order. DSM agreed to pay half of the $10,000 cost to integrate it into the program. DSM also offered to create the module to reflect customer credits and back orders for another $20,000, but Steve declined. These problems pushed the conversion date back several months.

PSC spent the first three months of 1994 preparing to implement the new system. Training PSC employees to use the new system was particularly important. For example, adding a customer to the data base required only one screen with the old system; the new software required six screens. Employees were taught to shout "Fire!" if they came upon a problem they could not handle. Mike, or one of the DSM programmers, would come to their assistance and explain what they had done wrong and how to fix the problem. During implementation the new system was tested for glitches by processing real data. Looking back, Mike admits three months was not nearly long enough for the training and testing; they should have used twice as much time to identify and eliminate glitches.

PSC dismantled the old system and converted over to the new one on April 20, 1994. Before long, telephone operators grew confused and forgot how to move from one part of the system to another. They began bumping up against unfamiliar error messages and getting themselves into situations they had not been trained to handle. Soon everyone was yelling "Fire!" at the same time. In less than an hour so many people were waiting for help that the programmers stopped explaining the correct procedures and simply ran from operator to operator correcting problems. Mistakes were repeated over and over again, and the situation intensified. Some employees, feeling embarrassed and ashamed at their inability to work the new system, broke down and cried openly.

Steve was running the warehouse area and was not having much fun either. On a normal day PSC has 200 to 300 boxes ready for 3:30 P.M. shipment. On conversion day only one box was ready to go. Facing the first default on his 24-hour turnaround promise since he started PSC, Steve, along with Terri, Mike, and a few others, stayed long after midnight packing boxes and loading them on trucks. They just barely made it to the nearest UPS hub on time.

The next day, order entry and shipping ran much smoother. However, when Steve sat down to retrieve the data he needed to monitor sales, he could not get the system to work. It wasn't that the system did not have the information, Steve just didn't know how to get it. Needless to say, he was not feeling too kindly toward his $200,000 system or the company who sold it to him.

It took Steve several weeks to figure out how to get the data he needed to monitor sales. When he did, he was horrified that sales had dropped nearly 15%. They had focused so hard at getting the system up and running that they had taken their eyes off the customers. To make matters worse, Steve could not get information on sales by customer, salesperson, or product, and he could not figure out why or where sales were falling.

However, things quickly improved after "Hell Week." Orders are now entered just as quickly as before, and printed copies are not needed for filing purposes. Warehouse operations are improved thanks to the integrated add-in program. The new system provides pickers with the most efficient path to follow when picking orders. It also tells them which items to pack in which boxes based on destination and weight. The system selects a carrier and prints out labels for the boxes. Order turnaround time was shaved to 20 minutes from 5 hours.

Months after the system was installed, it still does not do everything Steve needs it to do, including some things the old system did. Nor does it answer all of Terri's questions. However, Steve is confident that the system will eventually provide PSC with a distinct competitive advantage. He is negotiating with DSM to write the credit and back-order module.

With all that has happened, Steve believes that the step up to the new system was necessary, even the right move, for his growing company. With the exceptions of taking the DSM salesperson's word and not taking enough time to practice with the system, Steve feels PSC did as good a job as they could have in selecting, installing, and implementing a new system.

Write a memo to address the following questions. Be prepared to defend your position to the class.

1. Do you agree with Steve's assessment that PSC did a good job selecting, installing, and implementing the new system considering the exceptions he noted? If so, why? Or do you feel PSC could have done a better job? If so, what did they do wrong and what should they have done differently?
2. How could PSC have avoided the problem of the missing features?
3. How could PSC have avoided some of the conversion and reporting problems they faced?
4. Based on what you read about economic feasibility in Chapter 17, evaluate Steve's analysis. Do you agree with his numbers and his conclusions? Why or why not?
5. How could PSC's customers use the new multi-box shipping approach to defraud PSC?
6. On a scale of 1 to 5, with 1 being the best, how would you rate the service that PSC received from DSM? Could it have been improved? If so, how?

Source: Adapted from David H. Freedman, "Computer Upgrade: To Hell and Back," *INC. Technology:* 46–53.

ANSWERS TO CHAPTER QUIZ

1. d **3.** b **5.** a **7.** a **9.** b
2. a **4.** c **6.** c **8.** d **10.** c

CHAPTER 19

Systems Design, Implementation, and Operation

LEARNING OBJECTIVES

After studying this chapter, you should be able to

- Discuss the conceptual systems design processes and the activities undertaken in this phase.
- Discuss the physical systems design processes and the activities undertaken in this phase.
- Discuss the systems implementation and conversion process and the activities undertaken in this phase.
- Discuss the systems operation and maintenance process and the activities undertaken in this phase.

Integrative Case: Shoppers Mart

Ann Christy, the controller at Shoppers Mart, presented the results of her systems analysis to top management and received permission to develop a new AIS (Chapter 17 conclusion). The following week she sat in her office planning the rest of the project. Ann is concerned because many development projects bog down during the design and implementation phases. She certainly does not want to have a runaway project on her hands—one that she cannot control. She feels that her staff has adequately determined the requirements for the new system and wants to make sure that the rest of the development process is completed correctly. She decides to schedule another meeting with the head of systems development to discuss the following questions:

1. She has to determine what type of system will best meet Shoppers Mart's needs and to make a proposal to management. Should her team develop what they consider to be the best approach to meeting Shoppers Mart's needs, or should they develop several approaches?
2. What can be done to ensure that system output will meet user needs? When and how should input, such as accounting transactions, be captured and who should capture it? Where should AIS data be stored and how should it be organized and accessed?

3. How should Shoppers Mart convert from its current to its new AIS? How much time and effort will be needed to maintain the new AIS? How should Ann's accounting staff be involved?

INTRODUCTION

Developing quality, error-free software is a very difficult and time-consuming task. However, most companies that seek to implement a new system want their new system immediately. As developers feel the pressure to perform system miracles, they begin skipping the basic steps of systems analysis and design and start writing code. Omitting systems analysis steps only leads to disaster, as they develop nice, well-structured systems that do not meet user needs and have nothing to do with the business problems they were trying to solve. An American Management Systems study revealed that 75% of all large systems either are not used, are not used as intended, or generate meaningless reports.

In a recent survey KPMG Peat Marwick found that 35% of all major IS projects were classified as runaways—hopelessly incomplete and over budget. Although not the only cause of runaways, skipping or skimping on systems analysis and design steps is a major factor in their occurrence. Runaways can consume a great deal of time and money and in the end produce no usable results, as illustrated by the following examples:

- Pacific Gas & Electric (PG&E) pulled the plug on a client/server information system for all of its residential and commercial customers. The system, five years in development, was labeled a financial disaster with no end product by people in and out of the utility. In an effort to fix the problem PG&E used several consulting firms, including 3 of the Big 5 CPA firms.
- California's Department of Motor Vehicles decided to overhaul its system, which was originally developed in 1965. The system was so difficult to maintain that it took the equivalent of 18 programmers working for an entire year to add a Social Security number file to the drivers license and vehicle registration file. After seven years, $44 million, and not a single usable application, the state canceled the project.

Many of these problems can be attributed to ineffective or incomplete systems analysis and design efforts. Effective systems analysis and design can ensure that developers correctly define the business problem and design the appropriate solution. As discussed in Chapter 17, systems analysis is a crucial phase in the systems design life cycle (SDLC). It begins with problem recognition, feasibility analysis, and a study and documentation of the existing system. The goal is to define the new system's requirements so it will take the organization where it needs to go. This chapter discusses the other four steps (see Fig. 17.1) in the systems development life cycle: conceptual systems design, physical systems design, systems implementation and conversion, and operation and maintenance. Chapter 18 discusses how some of the steps in the SDLC can be shortened or made more effective.

Accountants must understand the development process. They are involved in this process in several ways—as users helping to specify their needs, as members of the development team, and as auditors after the system is complete. Accountants should help keep the project on track by evaluating and measuring benefits, monitoring costs, and ensuring that the project is on schedule.

CONCEPTUAL SYSTEMS DESIGN

In the **conceptual systems design** phase, a general framework is developed for implementing user requirements and solving problems identified in the analysis phase. As shown in Fig. 19.1, there are three main steps in conceptual design: evaluate design alternatives, prepare design specifications, and prepare the conceptual systems design report. We will now discuss these three steps.

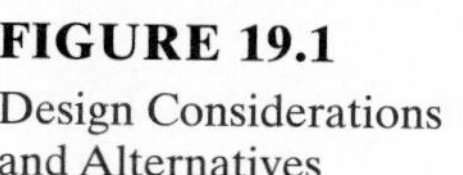

FIGURE 19.1
Design Considerations and Alternatives

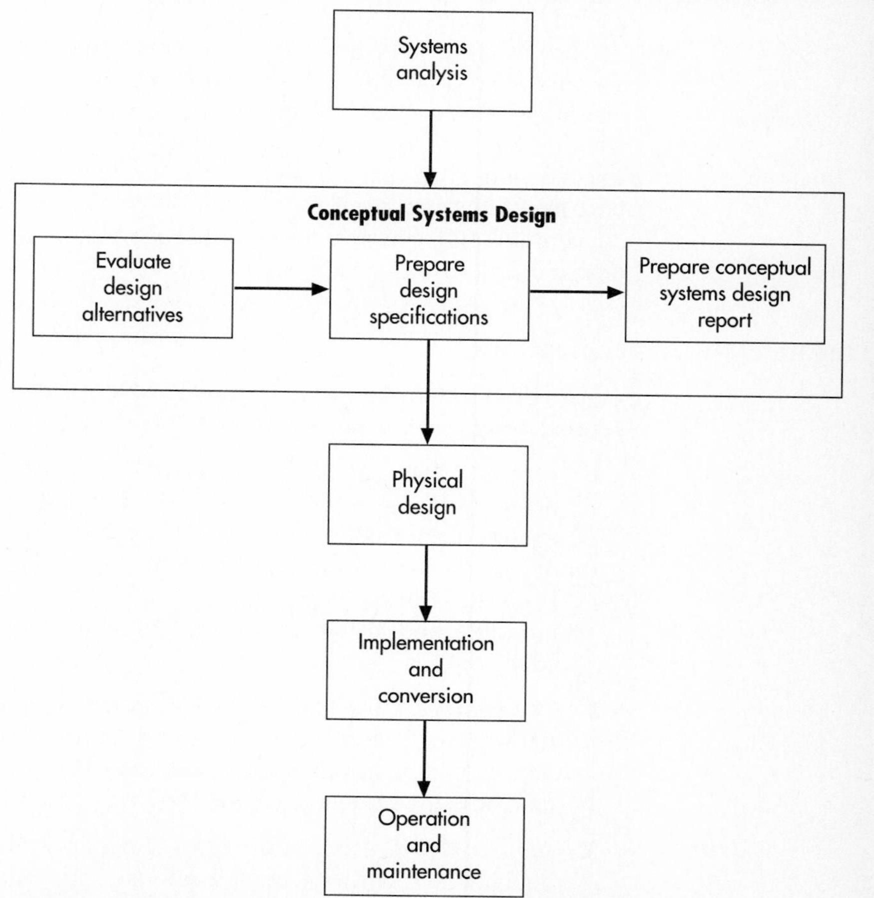

Evaluate Design Alternatives

There are many ways to design an AIS, so accountants and others involved in systems design must continually make design decisions. For example: Should the company mail hard copy purchase orders or use EDI? Should the company have a large centralized mainframe and data base, or distribute computer power to the stores using minicomputers, PCs, distributed data bases, LANs, and WANs? Should data entry be through keyboard, optical character recognition, point-of-sale devices, or some combination of these?

In addition, there are many different ways that a company can approach the systems development process. They could purchase software from a vendor, have the in-house information systems staff develop the software, have the people who are going to use the system design it, or hire an outside company to develop and manage their information system. The company could modify, enhance, or replace existing software or completely reengineer all of its business processes and develop software to support these new processes. These alternatives, which must all be considered in conceptual systems design, are discussed in more detail in Chapter 18.

The design team should identify a variety of design alternatives and evaluate each with respect to the following standards: (1) how well it meets organizational and system objectives, (2) how well it meets users' needs, (3) whether it is economically feasible, and (4) its advantages and disadvantages. The steering committee evaluates the alternatives and selects the one that best meets the organization's needs. Table 19.1 presents some examples of conceptual and physical design considerations and their corresponding design alternatives.

Prepare Design Specifications

Once a design alternative has been selected, the project team develops the **conceptual design specifications** for the following elements:

1. *Output.* Because the system is designed to meet users' information needs, output specifications *must* be prepared first. For example, to evaluate store sales using a sales analysis report, Shoppers Mart must decide (a) how often to produce the report (daily or weekly), (b) what it should contain (store number, sales volume, etc.), (c) what it will look like, and (d) whether users will need a hard copy or screen (or both) output.

2. *Data storage.* Development decisions for Shoppers Mart include which data elements must be stored to produce the sales report, whether the data should be stored in sequential or random order, what type of file or data base to use, and which field size is appropriate for the data items.

3. *Input.* Design considerations for Shoppers Mart include which sales data to enter, sale location and amount, and where, when, and how to collect data. Inputs are considered only after the desired output is identified.

TABLE 19.1 Design Considerations and Alternatives

Design Consideration	Design Alternatives
Communications channel configuration	Point to point, multidrop, or line sharing
Communications channels	Telephone lines, coaxial cable, fiber optics, microwave, or satellite
Communications network	Centralized, decentralized, distributed, or local area
Data storage medium	Tape, floppy disk, hard disk, or hard copy
Data storage structure	Files or data base
File organization and access	Random or sequential
Input medium	Keying, OCR, MICR, POS, EDI, or voice
Operations	In-house or outsourcing
Output frequency	Instantaneous, hourly, daily, weekly, or monthly
Output medium	CRT, hard copy, voice, or turnaround document
Output scheduling	Predetermined times or on demand
Printed output	Preprinted forms or system-generated forms
Processing	Manual, batch, or real-time
Processor	Personal computer, minicomputer, or mainframe
Software acquisition	Canned, custom, or modified
Transaction processing	Batch or on-line
Update frequency	Instantaneous, hourly, daily, weekly, or monthly

4. *Processing procedures and operations.* Design considerations for Shoppers Mart include how to process the input and stored data in order to produce the sales report, and also the sequence in which the processes must be performed.

Prepare the Conceptual Systems Design Report

At the end of the conceptual design phase, the project development team prepares and submits a **conceptual systems design report.** The purpose of this report is to (1) guide physical systems design activities, (2) communicate how management and user information needs will be met, and (3) help the steering committee assess system feasibility. The main component is a description of one or more recommended system designs. This description contains the contents of each output, data base, and input; processing flows and the relationships among the programs, files, inputs, and outputs; hardware, software, and resource requirements; and audit, control, and security processes and procedures. Any assumptions or unresolved problems that may affect the final systems design should be discussed. The table of contents of the Shoppers Mart report is shown in Table 19.7, in the chapter summary on page 721.

PHYSICAL SYSTEMS DESIGN

During the **physical systems design** phase, the company determines *how* the conceptual AIS design is to be implemented. Physical design translates the broad, user-oriented AIS requirements of conceptual design into detailed specifications that are used to code and test the computer programs. As shown in Fig. 19.2, the steps that occur during this phase include designing output,

FIGURE 19.2
Physical Systems Design

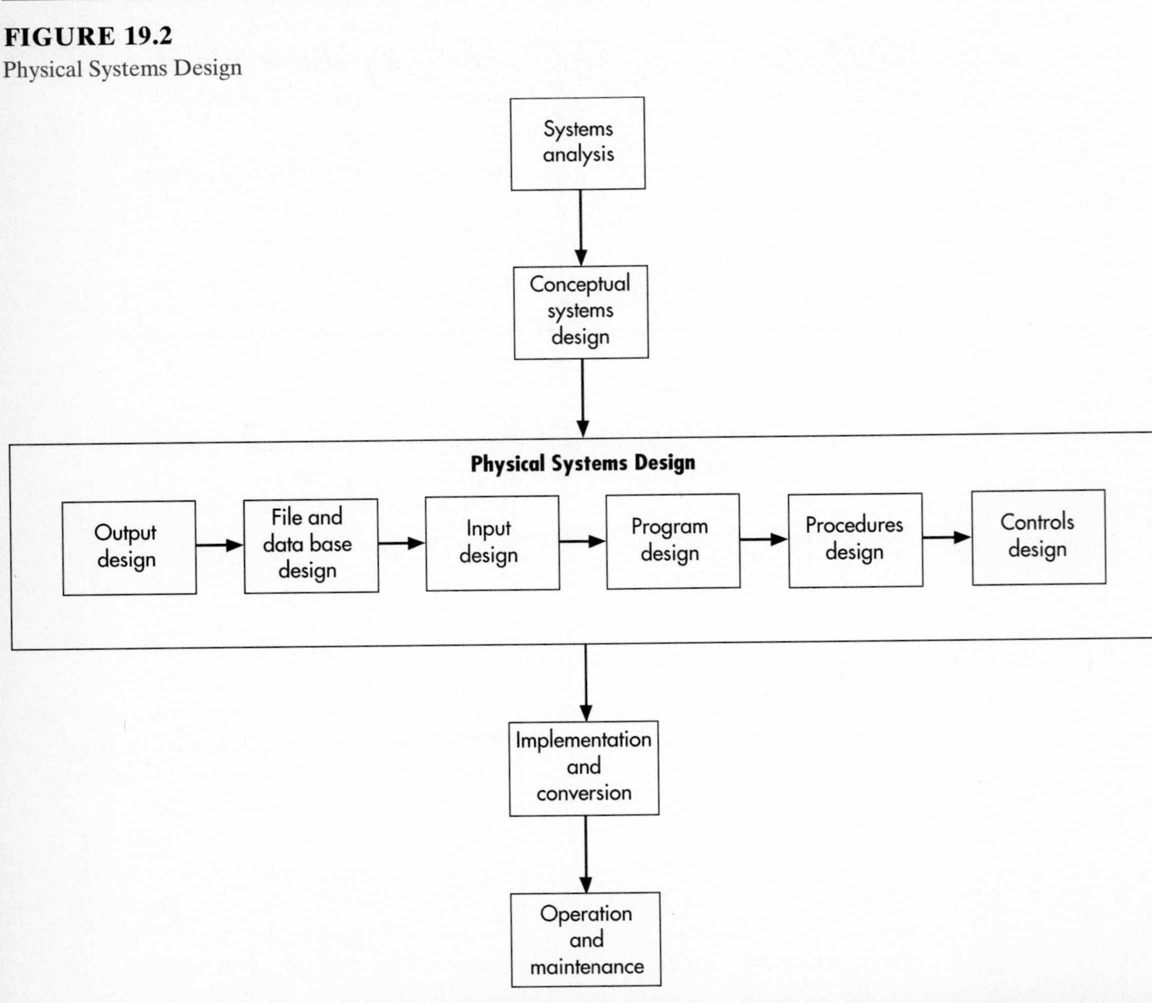

creating files and data bases, designing input, writing computer programs, developing procedures, and building controls into the new AIS. The following subsections describe these activities in detail.

Output Design

The objective of output design is to determine the nature, format, content, and timing of printed reports, documents, and screen displays. Tailoring the output to user needs requires cooperation between users and designers. Some important output design considerations are summarized in Table 19.2.

Output usually fit into one of the following four categories:

1. **Scheduled reports** have a prespecified content and format and are prepared on a regular basis. Examples include monthly performance reports, weekly sales analysis, and annual financial statements.
2. **Special-purpose analysis** have no prespecified content or format and are not prepared on a regular schedule. They are prepared in response to a management request to evaluate an issue, such as which of three new products would provide the highest profits.
3. **Triggered exception reports** have a prespecified content and format but are prepared only in response to abnormal conditions. Excessive absenteeism, cost overruns, inventory shortages, and situations requiring immediate corrective action trigger such reports.

TABLE 19.2 Output Design Considerations

Consideration	Concern
Use	Who will use the output, why do they need it, and what decisions will they need to make based on it?
Medium	Should output be on paper, screen, voice response, diskette, microfilm, or some combination of these?
Format	The format that clearly conveys the most information should be selected (table, narrative, graphic); for example, large volumes of data can be easily condensed into graphs that are easy to read and interpret.
Preprinted	Should paper output be on a preprinted form, such as a check or purchase order?
Location	Where should AIS output be sent?
Access	Who should have access to hard copy and computer screen output?
Detail	Lengthy output should be preceded by an executive summary and a table of contents. Headings and legends organize data and highlight important items. Detailed information is placed in an appendix.
Timeliness	How often should AIS output be produced?

4. **Demand reports** have a prespecified content and format but are prepared only on request. Both triggered exception reports and demand reports can be used effectively to facilitate the management process.

The AIS developers prepare an output sample, and users evaluate it to ensure that it is complete, relevant, and useful. Unacceptable output is modified and reviewed as many times as necessary to make it acceptable. To avoid the expense and time delays resulting from changes made later in the SDLC, many organizations require users to sign a document stating that the form and content are acceptable.

File and Data Base Design

It is important that the various divisions or departments of a company store data in compatible formats. This helps companies avoid the problem currently facing AT&T: 23 business units and a jumble of incompatible systems. Some of these units find it difficult to share e-mail with other units. Perhaps more importantly, the business units do not maintain customer records in formats that allow them to be easily shared. AT&T has undertaken a five-year project to create a "single view" of each customer so that customer data can be shared across all business units.

In Chapters 4 and 5 you learned about files and data bases and how to design them. Some of the more important file and data base design considerations are summarized in Table 19.3.

Input Design

When evaluating input design, the design team must identify the different types of data input and optimal input methods. There are two principal types of data input: forms and computer screens. These two types of input are discussed in the next two subsections. Considerations in input design are shown in Table 19.4.

TABLE 19.3 File and Data Base Design Considerations

Consideration	Concern
Medium	Should data be stored on disk, diskettes, optical disk, or tape?
Organization and access	Should sequential, indexed-sequential, or random-access methods be used?
Processing mode	Should batch or real-time processing be used?
Maintenance	What procedures are needed to maintain data effectively?
Size	How many records will be stored in the data base and how large are they? How fast is the number of records expected to grow?
Activity level	What percentage of the records will be added or deleted each year? What percentage will need to be updated?

TABLE 19.4 Input Design Considerations

Consideration	Concern
Medium	Should AIS data be entered using key-to-disk methods; a keyboard; an OCR, MICR, or POS terminal; or voice input?
Source	Where does data originate (a computer, customer, remote location, etc.), and how does that affect data entry?
Format	What format (source or turnaround document, screen) efficiently captures the data with the least effort and cost?
Type	What is the nature of AIS data?
Volume	How much data are to be entered?
Personnel	What are the data entry operators' abilities, functions, and expertise? Is additional training necessary?
Frequency	How often does AIS data need to be entered?
Cost	How can costs be minimized without adversely affecting efficiency and accuracy?
Error detection and correction	What errors are possible, and how can they be detected and corrected?

Forms Design. Many information systems still capture input data on paper and later transfer that data to a computer medium. Although more and more systems are moving away from the use of paper documents and toward source data automation techniques, forms design is still a very important topic. Forms design was discussed in detail in Chapter 2, and a number of important forms design principles are summarized in Table 2.3 (p. 34). This checklist is a useful tool for evaluating existing forms and designing new ones.

Designing Computer Screens. When data must be keyed into a system, it is more efficient to enter it directly on a computer screen than to put it on paper for subsequent entry. As a result, it is important to understand how to design computer screens for input as well as for output. Computer screens are most effective when the following principles are followed:

- Organize the screen in such a way that data can be entered quickly, accurately, and completely. Minimize data input by retrieving as much information as possible from the system. For example, entering a customer number could automatically cause the system to retrieve the customer's name, address, and other key information.
- Enter data in the same order it is displayed on paper forms used to capture the data.
- Fill the screen out from left to right and top to bottom. Group logically related data together.
- Design the screen so that users either can jump from one data entry location to another using a single key, or go directly to screen locations.

- Make it easy to correct mistakes. Clear and explicit error messages that are consistent across all screens are essential. There should be a help feature to provide on-line assistance.
- Restrict the amount of data on a screen to avoid clutter. Limit the number of menu options on a single screen.

Program Design

Program development is one of the most time-consuming activities in the entire SDLC. Programs should be subdivided into small, well-defined modules to reduce complexity and enhance reliability and modifiability. This is referred to **structured programming.** Modules should interact with a control module rather than with each other. Each module should have only one entry and exit point, to facilitate testing and modification.

To improve the quality of their software, organizations should develop programming standards (rules for writing programs). This contributes to consistency among programs, making them easier to read and maintain. They should also conduct a structured program walk-through to find incorrect logic, errors, omissions, or other problems.

Procedures Design

Everyone who interacts with the newly designed AIS should follow procedures that answer the who, what, when, where, why, and how questions related to all AIS activities. Procedures should cover input preparation, transaction processing, error detection and correction, controls, reconciliation of balances, data base access, output preparation and distribution, and computer operator instructions. Procedures may take the form of system manuals, user instruction classes, training materials, or on-line help screens. They may be written by development teams, users, or teams representing both groups.

Controls Design

An often-heard saying in the computer industry is, "Garbage in, garbage out." This adage emphasizes that improperly controlled input, processing, and data base functions produce information of little value. Controls must be built into an AIS to ensure its effectiveness, efficiency, and accuracy. They should minimize errors and detect and correct them when they do occur. Accountants play a vital role in this area. Some of the more important control concerns that must be addressed are summarized in Table 19.5. Controls are discussed in greater detail in Chapters 8–10.

Physical Systems Design Report

At the end of the physical design phase the team prepares a **physical systems design report.** (Table 19.7, on page 725, shows a table of contents for the report prepared at Shoppers Mart.) This report becomes the basis for management's decision whether to proceed to the implementation phase.

TABLE 19.5 Controls Design Considerations

Consideration	Concern
Validity	Are all system interactions valid? For example, how can the AIS ensure that cash disbursements are made only to legitimate vendors?
Authorization	Are input, processing, storage, and output activities authorized by the appropriate managers? For example, how can the AIS ensure that payroll additions have been authorized?
Accuracy	Is input verified to ensure accuracy? What controls are in place to ensure that data passed between processing activities is not lost?
Access	Is access to data adequately controlled? For example, how are hackers denied access to data files?
Numerical control	Are documents prenumbered to prevent errors or intentional misuse and to detect when documents are missing or stolen?
Audit trail	Can transaction data be traced from source documents to final output (and vice versa)? For example, if a customer calls with a question, can transaction details be easily accessed?

SYSTEMS IMPLEMENTATION

Systems implementation is the process of installing hardware and software and getting the AIS up and running. This process generally consists of developing a plan, developing and testing software, preparing the site, installing and testing hardware, selecting and training personnel, developing documentation, and testing the system. These activities are illustrated in Fig. 19.3 and are discussed in this section.

The state of Virginia has been especially successful in designing and implementing its AIS. In fact, it serves as a model for other governmental agencies. Focus 19.1 describes the improvements the state has made to its AIS.

Implementation Planning

An **implementation plan** consists of implementation tasks, expected completion dates, cost estimates, and the person or persons responsible for each task. The plan specifies when the project should be complete and when the AIS is operational. The implementation team should identify risk factors that decrease the likelihood of successful implementation, and the plan should contain a strategy for coping with each of the identified risk factors.

Plan for Organizational Changes. AIS changes may require adjustments to a company's existing organizational structure. New departments may be created and existing ones eliminated or reduced in size. The structure and status

FIGURE 19.3
Systems Implementation

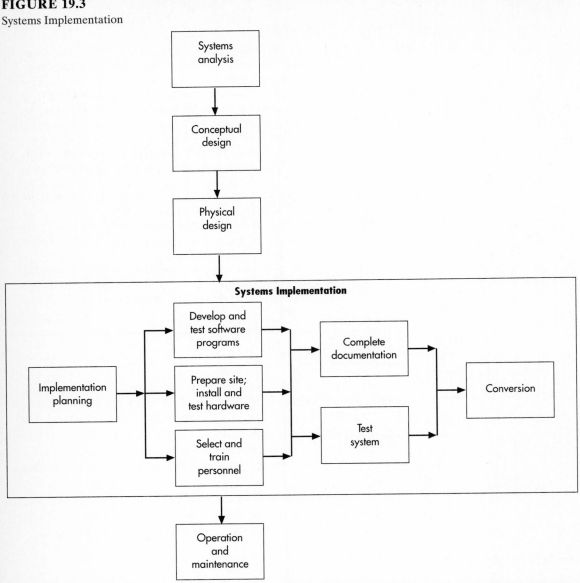

of the data processing department itself may change. For example, Blue Cross and Blue Shield of Wisconsin contracted for a new $200 million system. The system—initiated by technical staff who did not understand the company's business or vision—did not work properly. It sent hundreds of checks to a nonexistent town, made $60 million in overpayments, and resulted in the loss of 35,000 clients. One reason the system failed was that its implementation should have included an organizational restructuring.

FOCUS 19.1 Stars Saves Virginia $80 Million

HUNDREDS of thousands of Virginia taxpayers now receive tax refunds within a week of filing instead of the two to three months it previously took. They owe the quick turnaround to Jane Bailey, director of AIS at the Department of Taxation. Bailey managed the development of the State Tax Accounting and Reporting System (STARS), a multisystem project requiring nine years for completion. STARS has been so successful that the IRS, 27 states, and a Canadian province have sent teams to Richmond to see whether a little magic might rub off on their own systems development and implementation efforts.

The state's central information technology group strongly recommended that the department engage outside contractors for the job, saying Bailey's six-person staff was far too small and unsophisticated to overhaul the vast and motley collection of manual and batch systems formerly in place. But Bailey insisted on going with an inside job. She was able to convince management by letting them know that once it was developed, the system would be maintained by her and that she would be able to respond quickly to tax law changes.

Bailey's staff eventually swelled to 45 people. She insisted that these employees be first-rate; if she could not hire the experts and specialists she needed, she retained them as consultants and then used them to train her existing staff. In addition, she recruited five management analysts to redesign business processes, write user documentation, and train users. Ten people from her staff are management analysts who work full-time on user procedures and issues. Seeing user involvement as crucial, Bailey succeeded in getting six managers from user areas assigned full-time to the project.

Over the years the scope of STARS expanded to encompass more functions and more users, and its budget climbed from its original $3 million to $11 million. A major new piece of software was installed every three to six months. Users had to adapt, often getting 15 new screens at a time. The megaproject eventually involved putting together 1,500 COBOL programs, 40 IBM IMS data bases, and 350 on-line screens in 25 applications for 1,800 users.

The state, which asked for a Chevrolet, got a Cadillac and the payoff has been impressive. STARS' users estimate that it saved the state $80 million over five years, most of it from added collections from would-be tax cheats.

Develop and Test Software Programs

Although accountants need not be computer programmers, they should understand how software is created. Program preparation time may range from a few days to a few years, depending on program complexity. Seven steps are followed when developing software:

1. *Determine user needs.* The team should consult with users and draw up an agreement about software requirements.

2. *Develop a plan.* A development plan should be developed and documented.

3. *Write program instructions (code).* The overall program approach and major processing tasks should be identified first, before each program step is planned in greater detail. Designing a program from the top down to more detailed levels is referred to as **hierarchical program design.**

4. *Test the program.* **Debugging** is the process of discovering and eliminating program errors. The process begins after a program is coded, when a visual and mental review, referred to as **desk checking,** is conducted to

discover keying or programming errors. During program compilation, syntax errors are uncovered. A program is tested for logic errors using test data that simulate as many real processing situations or input data combinations as possible. Test data should include all valid transactions and all possible error conditions. Large programs are often tested in three stages: individual program modules, the linkages between modules and a control module, and interfaces between the program being tested and other application programs.

Focus 19.2 discusses the difficulty of testing software and the consequences of releasing software with undetected errors. Many software developers state that 20% to 30% of software development costs should be allocated to testing, debugging, and rewriting software.

5. *Document the program.* Because documentation explains how the program works, it can assist in correcting and resolving errors. Flowcharts, record layouts, decision tables, and related items should be retained as part of program documentation and organized into a meaningful documentation manual.
6. *Train program users.* Training begins toward the end of the test phase. Program documentation is often used to train users.
7. *Install and use the system.* The process of revising an existing program is referred to as **program maintenance.** Factors that necessitate this type of change include requests for new or revised reports; changes in input, file content, or values such as tax rates; error detection; and conversion to new hardware.

Site Preparation

A PC, or minicomputer, requires little site preparation. A large system may require extensive changes, such as additional electrical outlets, data communications facilities, raised floors, humidity controls, special lighting, and air-conditioning. Security measures, such as fire protection and an emergency power supply, may also be necessary. Space is needed for equipment, storage, and offices. Site preparation is a lengthy process and should begin well in advance of the installation date.

Select and Train Personnel

Employees can be hired from outside the company or transferred internally. Hiring from within the company is the less costly, more effective alternative, since employees already understand the firm's business and operations. Transferring employees who are displaced as a result of the new system could boost employee loyalty and morale.

Studies of large companies show that over 90% of employees have computers but more than a third do not feel they have the skills to use them adequately. Because effective training is time-consuming and expensive, companies take

FOCUS 19.2 Software Bugs Take Their Toll

AN $18.5 MILLION rocket explodes seconds after lift-off. Telephone networks mysteriously crash in three cities, leaving 10 million customers without service. A nuclear plant releases hundreds of gallons of radioactive water near Lake Huron. These three events have one disturbing fact in common: They were caused by tiny errors (bugs) buried in computer programs. The term bug was coined during World War II when a researcher, puzzled by a computer shutdown, removed a moth stuck between two electric relays. Lately, these electronics pests have been on a rampage.

- Without warning, Washington, D.C., Los Angeles, and Pittsburgh residents lost local phone service at almost the same time each morning. The culprit? Three missing digits in several million lines of programming that controls the phone companies' call-switching computers.
- During the Persian Gulf War, a software error prevented a Patriot missile from destroying an incoming Iraqi Scud missile that killed 28 people.
- American Airlines' reservations system shut down for almost 12 hours, crippling 14,000 travel agencies nationwide and forcing American's agents to write tickets by hand.
- A bug in a linear accelerator—a device that uses X rays to treat cancer victims—caused the accelerator to deliver a radiation overdose, killing one patient and leaving two others deeply burned and partly paralyzed.
- Ashton-Tate, a powerhouse in PC software, never recovered after it shipped bug-filled software.

Where do these bugs come from? To create software, a programmer writes millions of lines of code. One incorrect letter or punctuation mark in a line of code—even a missing period—can cause a computer to issue an incorrect command or no command at all. For instance, a flaw in DSC's call-switching computers sent hundreds of erroneous messages to other DSC computers, asking for assistance in rerouting calls when no help was necessary. The flood of messages shut down the computers and gave callers busy signals for hours.

Bugs exist in most software and are almost impossible to get rid of. A program containing bugs can work just fine for quite some time until suddenly, with no warning—zap—the bug triggers something and the computer suddenly goes haywire.

Programmers go to great pains to detect and eliminate bugs before software is shipped. But no one has the time or money to find every bug—or to simulate the exact situations the computer program will encounter in the real world. It would take 3,000 years to completely test a program with several hundred instructions if one performed 1,000 tests a second. Instead, software is tested with assumptions about how it will be used. Only a certain amount of information—for instance, the number of paychecks to be sent out each Friday—is used to test the program. No one can predict that a few enterprising customers will add more information than the software can handle.

A former Lotus Development product manager estimated that Lotus often found 5,000 bugs in each product. The company would fix serious flaws before shipping the product and ignore minor or cosmetic flaws and those that were highly unlikely to ever cause a problem. If software developers took the time to find every one of these flaws, they would miss getting their product out to market on a timely basis and they would lose market share to competitors able to get their products out on time.

Software developers also cannot predict whether computer users will work faster than the software itself. The linear accelerators that killed and maimed cancer patients were controlled by an operator who typed extremely fast. She accidentally selected the X-ray mode and then switched to the electron beam. The software was not quick enough to recognize the change and the machine beamed radiation at full power to a tiny spot on the patients' bodies. The bug was so subtle it took programmers a year to detect and eliminate it.

The sheer volume of software code needed in a complex program makes finding bugs difficult. There are over 2.5 million lines of code in systems that check for cracks in the engine wheel of a space shuttle and 12 million in a phone company's call-switching computer. Finding a flaw in this code is as difficult as looking for one misspelled name in the New York City phone book.

Source: Adapted from John Schneidawind, "Getting the Bugs Out," *USA Today* (August 29, 1991): #1–2.

shortcuts. In addition, those who understand the system are so busy trying to maintain and upgrade it that they lack the time to provide training. When users are not adequately trained, the company will not achieve the expected benefits and return on their investment. The hidden cost of inadequate training is that users turn to coworkers who have mastered the system for help, resulting in less productive coworkers and increased company costs.

Effective AIS training must consist of more than just the hardware and software skills needed to use the new AIS. Employees must be oriented to new policies and operations, and training should be planned and scheduled so it occurs just before systems testing and conversion. Many types of training programs are available to companies: technical training from vendors, self-study manuals, computer-assisted instruction, videotape presentations, role playing, case studies, and experimenting with the AIS under the guidance of experienced users.

Boots the Chemists, a London-based international pharmacy chain with more than 1,000 stores, came up with a novel approach to training. Store employees, nervous about a forthcoming computer system, were invited to a party at a store where a new point-of-sale (POS) system had been installed. They were asked to try to harm the system by pushing the wrong buttons or fouling up a transaction. Employees quickly found they could not harm the system and that it was easy to use.

Complete Documentation

Three types of documentation must be prepared for new systems:

1. *Development documentation* describes the new AIS. It includes a system description; copies of output, input, and file and data base layouts; program flowcharts; test results; and user acceptance forms.
2. *Operations documentation* includes operating schedules; files and data bases accessed; and equipment, security, and file retention requirements.
3. *User documentation* teaches users to operate the AIS. It includes a procedures manual and training materials.

Test the System

One reason for the Blue Cross and Blue Shield system failure, described earlier, was inadequate system testing. The developers underestimated the complexity of the system and promised an overly optimistic delivery time of 18 months. One of the shortcuts they took to meet that deadline was to deliver an untested system.

Documents and reports, user inputs, operating and control procedures, processing procedures, and computer programs should all be given a trial run in realistic circumstances. In addition, capacity limits and backup and recovery procedures should be tested. There are three common forms of testing:

1. **Walk-throughs** are step-by-step reviews of procedures or program logic. Walk-throughs early in system design are attended by the development team and system users. The focus is on the inputs, files, outputs, and data flows of the organization. Subsequent walk-throughs, attended by programmers, address logical and structural aspects of program code.

2. **Processing of test transactions** determines whether a program operates as designed. Valid and erroneous data are processed to determine whether transactions are handled properly and errors are detected and dealt with appropriately. To evaluate test results, the correct system response for each test transaction must be specified in advance.
3. **Acceptance tests** use copies of real transaction and file records rather than hypothetical ones. Users develop the acceptance criteria and make the final decision whether to accept the AIS.

Chemical Bank suffered the consequences of not adequately testing an upgrade to its ATM system. Shortly after its installation, New York customers who withdrew cash from one of Chemical's 900 ATMs found their accounts were debited twice. Before the problem could be corrected, 150,000 withdrawals with a total value of $8 million were posted twice to customer accounts. Thousands of small accounts were overdrawn or emptied, which annoyed and angered customers. Chemical lost a great deal of credibility with its customers as a result of the glitch.

Even software purchased from an outside vendor must be tested thoroughly before being installed. Kane Carpets learned this lesson after it installed an AIS custom-tailored to the floor covering industry. No sooner was the software up and running when Kane began experiencing serious problems. For example, its inventory control system told its salespersons that orders could not be filled when the product was in fact available, and vice versa. As a result Kane lost many of its customers.

SYSTEMS CONVERSION

Conversion is the process of changing from the old AIS to the new. Many elements must be converted: hardware, software, data files, and procedures. The process is complete when the new AIS has become a routine, ongoing part of the system.

Conversion Approaches

As shown in Fig. 19.4, four conversion approaches are used to change from an old to a new system.

Direct conversion is an immediate discontinuance of the old AIS when the new one is introduced. For example, Shoppers Mart could discontinue its old system on Saturday night and use its new AIS on Monday morning. Direct conversion is appropriate when the old AIS has no value or the new one is so different that comparisons between the two are meaningless. The approach is inexpensive, but it provides no backup AIS. Unless a system has been carefully developed and tested, therefore, direct conversion carries a high risk of failure.

Parallel conversion operates the old and new systems simultaneously for a period of time. For example, Shoppers Mart could process transactions with both systems, compare the outputs, reconcile the differences, and correct problems with the new AIS. After the new system proves itself, Shoppers Mart could discontinue the old one. Parallel processing protects companies from errors,

FIGURE 19.4
Comparison of Conversion Methods

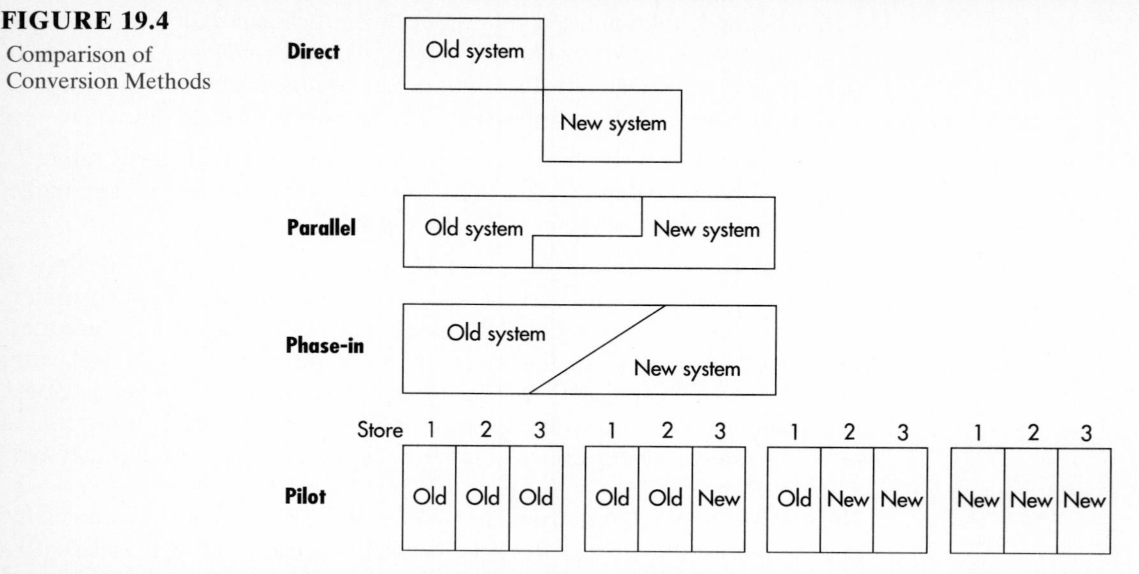

but it is costly and stressful for employees to process all transactions twice. However, because companies often experience problems during conversion, parallel processing has gained widespread popularity.

Phase-in conversion gradually replaces elements of the old AIS with the new one. For example, Shoppers Mart could implement its inventory system, then disbursements, followed by sales collection, and so forth, until the whole system is functional. These gradual changes mean that data processing resources can be acquired over time. The disadvantages are the cost of creating the temporary interfaces between the old and the new AIS and the time required to make the gradual changeover.

Pilot conversion implements a system in just one part of the organization, such as a branch location. For example, Shoppers Mart could install its new POS system at one of its stores using a direct, parallel, or phase-in approach. When problems with the system are resolved, the new system could be implemented at the remaining locations. This approach localizes conversion problems and allows training in a live environment. The disadvantages are the long conversion time and the need for interfaces between the old and the new systems, which coexist until all locations have been converted. Owens-Corning Fiberglass implemented its accounts payable, travel and expense, and payroll systems by getting the system up and running in one plant and then moving it to all the others one by one.

Data Conversion

Data conversion can be time-consuming, tedious, and expensive. The difficulty and magnitude of the task can be easily underestimated. Data files may need to be modified in three ways. First, files may be moved to a different storage medium—for example, from tapes to disks. Second, data content may be changed; for example, fields and records may be added or deleted. Third, file format may be changed.

The first step in the data conversion process is to decide which data files need to be converted. They then must be checked for completeness and any data inaccuracies and inconsistencies removed. Actual data conversion is next. Validating the new files, to ensure data were not lost during conversion, follows. If the file conversion is lengthy, the new files must be updated with the transactions that occurred during data conversion. Once the files and data bases have been converted and tested for accuracy, the new system is functional. The system should be monitored for a time to make sure it runs smoothly and accurately. The final activity is to document the conversion activities.

OPERATION AND MAINTENANCE

The final step in the SDLC is to operate and maintain the new system. A **postimplementation review** should be conducted on a newly installed AIS to ensure it meets its planned objectives. Some important factors to consider and questions to answer during the postimplementation review are listed in Table 19.6. Any problems uncovered during the review should be brought to the attention of management and the necessary adjustments made. When the review has been completed, a **postimplementation review report** is prepared. The table of contents in Table 19.7 illustrates what this report should contain. User acceptance of the postimplementation review report is the concluding activity in the systems development process. Control of the AIS is passed to the data processing department. Work on the new system is not finished, however. Studies show that, over the life of a system, only 30% of the work takes place during development; the other 70% is spent maintaining the system. Most maintenance costs relate to software modifications and updates.

The experience of the Hartford Insurance Group illustrates the cost of maintenance. Approximately 70% of its personnel resources are devoted to maintaining existing systems. Hartford must maintain an inventory of 34,000 program modules containing 24 million lines of COBOL code. The job is even more difficult because recent changes in insurance regulations and business strategies have reduced the structure of the code and increased its complexity.

SUMMARY AND CASE CONCLUSION

Ann tackled the sales processing portion of the AIS first. She gave the project development team her systems analysis report and accompanying data. During conceptual systems design, the team visited stores with similar operations and identified ways to meet AIS requirements. Alternative approaches were discussed with users, management, and the steering committee and were narrowed down to Ann's original approach. Ann considered buying software but did not find any that did what she and the company wanted to accomplish. The team developed conceptual design specifications for the output, input, processing, and data storage elements.

TABLE 19.6 Factors to Investigate During Postimplementation Review

Factors	Questions
Goals and objectives	Does the system help the organization meet its goals, objectives, and overall mission?
Satisfaction	Are the users satisfied with the system? What would they like changed or improved?
Benefits	How have users benefited from the system? Were the expected benefits achieved?
Costs	Are actual costs in line with expected costs?
Reliability	Is the system reliable? Has the system failed and, if so, what caused its failure?
Accuracy	Does the system produce accurate and complete data?
Timeliness	Does the system produce information on a timely basis?
Compatibility	Are the hardware, software, data, and procedures compatible with existing systems?
Controls and security	Is the system safeguarded against unintentional errors, fraud, and unauthorized intrusion?
Errors	Do error-handling procedures exist, and are they adequate?
Training	Are systems personnel and users adequately trained to support and use the system?
Communications	Is the communications system adequate?
Organization changes	Are any organizational changes brought about by the system beneficial or harmful? If harmful, how can they be resolved?
Documentation	Is system documentation complete and accurate?

The company decided to utilize screen-based output as much as possible and to capture data electronically using POS devices. Data that cannot be captured electronically will be entered using PCs. Each store will have a LAN that connects all their PCs and POS devices to a local data base. The POS cash registers will be used to capture and feed sales data electronically to this data base. Each store will be linked electronically to the central office using a wide area network (WAN). All sales data, store orders, and other summary-level information will be uploaded to the corporate data base daily. The corporate data base will download the information needed to manage the store. The central office will use EDI to order goods and pay suppliers. The table of contents for the conceptual systems design report is shown in Table 19.7.

During physical design, the development team designed each report identified during conceptual design in screen or hard copy format. The reports were shown to users and reworked until everyone involved was satisfied. The team then designed all files, data bases, and input screens. Next came the detailed design of the software programs needed to collect and process data and produce the output. The team also developed new procedures for handling data and operating the AIS. The accountants and the internal audit staff were especially helpful during the design of the controls needed to protect the system against errors and fraud. The physical systems design report table of contents is shown in Table 19.7.

TABLE 19.7 Table of Contents for Shoppers Mart Documentation Reports

Shoppers Mart Conceptual Systems Design Report	Shoppers Mart Physical Systems Design Report	Shoppers Mart Postimplementation Review Report
Table of Contents I. Executive Summary of Conceptual Systems Design II. Overview of Project Purpose and Summary of Findings to Date III. Recommended Conceptual Design(s) of Proposed System A. Overview of Recommended Design(s) B. Objectives to Be Achieved by Design(s) C. Impact of Design(s) on Information System and Organization D. Expected Costs and Benefits of Design(s) E. Audit, Control, and Security Processes and Procedures F. Hardware, Software, and Other Resource Requirements G. Processing Flows: Relationships of Programs, Data Bases, Inputs, and Outputs H. Description of System Components (Programs, Data Bases, Inputs, and Outputs) IV. Assumptions and Unresolved Problems V. Summary VI. Appendixes, Glossary	Table of Contents I. Executive Summary of Physical Systems Design II. Overview of Project Purpose and Summary of Findings to Date III. Major Physical Design Recommendations A. Output Design B. Input Design C. Data Base Design D. Software (Processing) Design E. Hardware Design F. Controls Design G. Procedures Design IV. Assumptions and Unresolved Problems V. Summary VI. Appendixes, Glossary	Table of Contents I. Executive Summary of Postimplementation Review II. Overview of Project Development Project III. Evaluation of the Development Project A. Degree to Which System Objectives Were Met B. Analysis of Actual Versus Expected Costs and Benefits C. User Reactions and Satisfaction IV. Evaluation of Project Development Team V. Recommendations A. Recommendations for Improving the New System B. Recommendations for Improving the System Development Process VI. Summary

Ann and her staff started implementation planning early. A location for the new mainframe was identified, and site preparation began during the design phase. First the hardware and then the software was installed and tested, followed by testing the entire AIS. The new AIS was staffed almost exclusively with existing employees trained as the system was tested. System documentation was completed before data from the old AIS was converted to the new one.

Ann and her staff used a variety of conversion approaches. Because corporate-wide mainframe data were vitally important, Ann used a parallel conversion strategy. The new and old systems were operated together for a month, and the results were compared. When the bugs in the new AIS were ironed out, the old AIS was discontinued. A pilot approach was used for the store AIS. The AIS was installed at several stores and all problems were resolved before implementing the system at the remaining Shoppers Marts. Conversion was not easy and required a fair amount of overtime and duplicate processing. After a few months Ann and her staff conducted a postimplementation review and made some adjustments to enhance the already high user acceptance and satisfaction of the new AIS. The table of contents for the postimplementation report is shown in Table 19.7

Ann made a final presentation to top management after the AIS was installed and operating. She was widely congratulated and even heard the president mention to an executive vice president that she "was worth keeping an eye on" for even more responsibility in the firm.

KEY TERMS

conceptual systems design
conceptual design specifications
conceptual systems design report
physical systems design
scheduled reports
special-purpose analysis
triggered exception reports
demand reports
structured programming
physical systems design report
systems implementation
implementation plan
hierarchical program design
debugging
desk checking
program maintenance
walk-throughs
processing of test transactions
acceptance tests
conversion
direct conversion
parallel conversion
phase-in conversion
pilot conversion
postimplementation review
postimplementation review report

CHAPTER QUIZ

1. The developers of your new system have proposed two different AIS designs and have asked you to evaluate them. This evaluation process is *most* likely to be a part of which SDLC step?
   a. Systems analysis
   b. Conceptual design
   c. Physical design
   d. Implementation and conversion
   e. Operation and maintenance
2. The purpose of the conceptual systems design report is to
   a. guide physical systems design activities.
   b. communicate how management and user information needs are met.
   c. help the steering committee assess system feasibility.
   d. a and b
   e. a, b, and c
3. Which of the following is the correct order of the steps in physical systems design?
   a. Input, file and data base, output; controls, procedures, program
   b. File and data base, output, input, procedures, program, controls
   c. Output, input, file and data base, procedures, program, controls
   d. Output, file and data base, input, program, procedures, controls

4. A monthly payroll register showing all hourly employees, the number of hours they worked, their deductions, and their net pay is *most* likely a
   a. scheduled report.
   b. special-purpose analysis.
   c. triggered exception report.
   d. demand report.

5. Considerations in input design include all of the following *except*
   a. which errors are possible and how they can be detected and corrected.
   b. how data are entered (key-to-disk, keyboards, OCR, or POS terminal).
   c. which format efficiently captures the input data with the least effort and cost.
   d. how often the system should produce reports and forms.

6. Which of the following procedures is most likely to help improve program development?
   a. Physical model
   b. IT Strategic plan
   c. Walk-through
   d. Record layout

7. Which of the following statements is true?
   a. An American Management Systems study revealed that 95% of all large systems either are not used, are not used as intended, or generate meaningless reports.
   b. Peat Marwick found that 65% of all major IS projects were classified as runaways—hopelessly incomplete and over budget.
   c. Many software developers state that 35% to 40% of software development costs should be allocated to testing, debugging, and rewriting software.
   d. Studies show that, over the life of a system, only 30% of IS work takes place during development; the other 70% is spent maintaining the system.

8. The systems testing approach that uses real transaction and file records rather than hypothetical ones is called
   a. a walk-through.
   b. processing of test transactions.
   c. an acceptance test.
   d. a parallel conversion test.

9. The process of discontinuing an old system as soon as a new one is introduced is called
   a. direct conversion.
   b. parallel conversion.
   c. phase-in conversion.
   d. pilot conversion.

10. Designing a program from the top down to more detailed levels is referred to as
   a. hierarchical program design.
   b. top-down program design.
   c. parallel program design.
   d. unstructured program design.

DISCUSSION QUESTIONS

19.1. Prism Glass Company is currently in the process of converting from a manual data processing system to a computerized one. To expedite the implementation of the system, the CEO has asked your consulting team to postpone establishing standards and controls until after the system is fully operational. How should you respond to the president's request?

19.2 When a company converts from one system to another, many areas within the organization are affected. Explain how conversion to a new system will affect the following groups, both individually and collectively.
a. Personnel
b. Data storage
c. Operations
d. Policies and procedures
e. Physical facilities

19.3 The following notice was posted in the employee cafeteria on Monday morning.

To: All Accounting and Clerical Employees
From: I.M. Krewel, President
Subject: Termination of Employee Positions

Effective this Friday, all accounting and clerical employees not otherwise contacted will be terminated. Our new computer system eliminates the need for most of these jobs. We're grateful for the loyal service you've rendered as employees and wish you success. You may wish to pick up your final checks on Friday before you go.

Discuss the president's approach to human resource management. What are the possible repercussions of this episode? Assuming that job termination is the best alternative available, how would you approach the situation?

19.4 In which phase of the systems development cycle would each of the following positions be most actively involved? Justify your answers.

a. Managerial accountant
b. Programmer
c. Systems analyst
d. Financial vice president
e. Information systems manager
f. Auditor

19.5 During which of the five SDLC stages is each task labeled a–m performed? More than one answer may apply for each activity.

1. Systems analysis
2. Conceptual (general) system design
3. Physical (detailed) systems design
4. Implementation and conversion
5. Operation and maintenance

a. Write operating procedures manuals
b. Develop program and process controls
c. Identify alternative systems designs
d. Develop a conceptual model of the system
e. Identify external and administrative controls
f. Test the system
g. Train personnel
h. Evaluate the existing system
i. Analyze the achievement of systems benefits
j. Modify and alter programs
k. Analyze total quality management (TQM) performance measures
l. Conduct a feasibility analysis
m. Align AIS development plans with business objectives

PROBLEMS

19.1 The Glass Jewelry Company manufactures costume jewelry. You have just been hired as the management accountant in charge of the accounting and control functions. During your introductory meeting with the president, he outlined your first project: the design and implementation of a new AIS for the company. He stated that the new system must be fully implemented within 6 months. Total company sales for the past year were $10 million. Sales are expected to double within the next 18 months.

Required:

a. Outline the procedures you would follow to complete your assigned project. Your response should include a description of the following:
   1. The various sources of information
   2. The methods of documenting information collected
   3. The methods of verifying the information collected
b. One of the subsystems that you plan to design is the accounts payable system. This system will contain a number of programs, two of which include Enter Invoices and Print Payable Checks. For each of these programs, describe its purpose and outline the application control considerations.

(SMAC Examination, adapted)

19.2 Chaotic order processing at Wang Laboratories had long been accepted by its customers as the cost of doing business with the computer giant. The tremendous growth of Wang throughout the 1970s left the company with a serious revenue tracking problem: Customers would often wait months for Wang to fill orders and process invoices. Repeated attempts by Wang's understaffed AIS department to solve these problems always met with failure.

Finally, Wang Laboratories hired a small consulting organization in 1980 to solve its revenue tracking problems and expedite prompt receipt of payments. The 18-month project turned into a doubly long nightmare. After three years and $10 million, the consultants were dismissed from the unfinished project.

The reasons for the project failure were clear. First, the project was too large and far too complex for the appointed consulting team. According to one consultant, the systems development process was so dynamic that the failure to complete the project quickly was self-defeating, as modifications took over the original design.

Second, management had no clear vision of the new AIS system and lacked a strong support staff. As a result, a number of incompatible tracking systems sprang up throughout the company's distributed computer system.

Third, the consulting firm had little experience with the desired technology: a complex data base that represented the heart of the new system.

Finally, the project had too many applications. Interdependencies among subprograms and subroutines left consultants with few completed programs. Every program was linked to several subprograms, which in turn were linked to several other programs. Programmers would begin an initial program only to find that several subroutines were necessary. They eventually found themselves lost in a morass of subroutines with no completed program.

Wang's ultimate solution to the crisis came from the internal AIS department. However, the revenue tracking system that the internal staff developed suffered quality problems for years.

Required:

The president of Wang Laboratories has asked you, as a member of the AIS staff, to write a memo explaining the failure of the systems development project.

a. Outline the specific reasons for the development failure. What role did the consultants play in the project's failure?
b. Identify the organizational issues that management must address in the future.
c. Recommend any future steps the company could take to guarantee the quality of consulting services.

19.3 Tiny Toddlers Company, a large multinational manufacturer of children's toys and furniture, is planning the design and implementation of a distributed data processing system to assist its sales force. The company has 10 sales offices in Canada and 20 in the United States. The company's sales departments have been set up in a regional structure: Each sales office maintains its own customers and is responsible for granting credit and collecting receivables.

The proposed system will not only permit inquiries, but will also allow entry of daily sales and maintenance of the customer master file. Reports used by each sales office to maintain the customer master file and to enter the daily sales orders are shown in Figs. 19.5 and 19.6.

Required:

Evaluate the reports shown in Figs. 19.5 and 19.6 using the following format:

Report Weakness	**Explanation**	**Recommendation(s)**

(SMAC Examination, adapted)

19.4 Mickie Louderman is the new assistant controller of Pickens Publishers, a growing company with sales of $35 million. She was formerly the controller of a smaller company in a similar industry, where she was in charge of accounting and data processing and had considerable influence over the entire computer center operation. Prior to Louderman's arrival at Pickens, the company revamped its entire computer operations center, placing increased emphasis on decentralized data access, personal computers with mainframe access, and on-line systems.

John Richards, the controller of Pickens, has been with the company for 28 years and is near retirement. He has given Louderman managerial authority over both the implementation of the new system and the integration of the company's accounting-related functions. Her promotion to controller will be dependent on the success of the new AIS.

Louderman began to develop the new system by using the same design characteristics and reporting format that she had used at her former company. She sent details of the new AIS to the departments that interfaced with accounting, including inventory control, purchasing, human resources, production control, and marketing. If they did not respond with suggestions by a prescribed date, she would continue the development process. Louderman and Richards determined a new schedule for many of the reports, changing the frequency from weekly to monthly. After a meeting with the director of computer operations, she selected a programmer to help her with the details of the new reporting formats.

Most of the control features of the old system were maintained to decrease the initial installation time, while a few new ones were added for unusual situations; however, the procedures for maintaining the controls were substantially changed. Louderman appointed herself the decisive authority for all control changes and program testing that related to the AIS, including screening the control features that related to batch totals for payroll, inventory control, accounts receivable, cash deposits, and accounts payable.

As each module was completed, Louderman told the corresponding department to implement the change immediately, in order to take advantage of the labor savings. However, incomplete instructions accompanied these changes, and specific implementation responsibility was not assigned to departmental personnel. Louderman believes that operations people should "learn as they go," reporting errors as they occur.

Accounts payable and inventory control were the initial areas of the AIS to be implemented; several problems arose in both of these areas. Louderman was disturbed that the semimonthly runs of payroll, which were weekly under the old system, had abundant

FIGURE 19.5 Customer Maintenance Form for Tiny Toddlers

CUSTOMER MAINTENANCE FORM

New Customer?	☐ Yes ______
	☑ No 24671
Name	The Little Ones Furniture Store
New Address	5 St. Antoine Street N. Quebec City
Old Address	305 St. Antoine Street S. Quebec City
Salesperson #	02
Requested Credit Limit	50,000
Sales Office	Eastern Canada
Pricing Code	25
Estimated Sales	300,000
Credit Limit	10,000
Currency	U.S.A. ☐, Canada ☐
Bank	Canadian Credit Bank 50 St. Antoine Street Quebec City
Bank Line	______
Rating	Satisfactory

____
Sales Manager

____
Credit Manager

errors and, consequently, required numerous manual paychecks. Frequently, the control totals of a payroll run would take hours to reconcile with the computer printout. To expedite matters, Louderman authorized the payroll clerk to prepare journal entries for payroll processing.

The new inventory control system failed to improve the carrying level of many stock items, causing several critical raw material stockouts that resulted in expensive rush orders. The primary control procedure under the new system was the availability of ordering and use information. It was available by direct-access terminals to both inventory control and purchasing personnel so that both departments could issue purchase orders on a timely basis. The inventory levels were updated daily, and so the previous weekly report was discontinued by Louderman.

Because of these problems, system documentation is behind schedule and proper backup procedures have not been implemented in many areas. Louderman has requested budget approval to hire two systems analysts, an accountant, and an administrative assistant to help her implement the new system. Richards is disturbed by her request, since her predecessor had only one part-time employee as his assistant.

Required:

a. List the steps Louderman should have taken during the design of the AIS to ensure that end-user needs were satisfied.

FIGURE 19.6
Sales Order Form for Tiny Toddlers

SALES ORDER FORM

Customer: 24671
The Little Ones Furniture Store
5 St. Antoine Street N.
Quebec City

Date:

Product Code	Description	Quantity
24571	Crib	4
M0002	Mattress	102
HG730	High chair – white	32
HG223	High chair – natural wood	22
CT200	Change table	300
D0025	Desk – modern design	2
C9925	Chair – modern design	5
BP809	Bumper pads	1200

Salesperson No.:

Entered by:

b. Identify and describe three areas where Louderman has violated the basic principles of internal control during the implementation of the new AIS.

c. Refer to Louderman's approach to implementing the new AIS.
   1. Identify and describe its weaknesses.
   2. What recommendations do you have that would improve the situation and allow development to continue on the remaining areas of the AIS?

(CMA Examination, adapted)

19.5 Columbia Corporation is a medium-sized, diversified manufacturing company. Ryon Pulsipher has been promoted recently to manager of the company's property accounting division. Pulsipher has had difficulty responding to requests from other departments for information about the company's fixed assets. Five of the requests and problems Pulsipher has been involved with follow:

1. The controller has requested schedules of individual fixed assets to support the balance in the general ledger. Although Pulsipher has furnished the necessary information, it has always been late. The manner in which the records are organized makes it difficult to obtain information easily.
2. The maintenance manager wishes to verify the existence of a punch press that he thinks was repaired twice. He has asked Pulsipher to confirm the asset number and location of the press.
3. The insurance department wants data on the cost and book values of assets to include in its review of current insurance coverage.
4. The tax department has requested data that can be used to determine when Columbia should switch depreciation methods for tax purposes.

5. The company's internal auditors have spent a significant amount of time in the property accounting division in a recent attempt to confirm the annual depreciation expense.

The property account records that are at Pulsipher's disposal consist of a set of manual books. These records show the date the asset was acquired, the account number to which the asset applies, the dollar amount capitalized, and the estimated useful life of the asset for depreciation purposes.

After many frustrations Pulsipher realized that his records are inadequate and that he cannot supply data easily when it is requested. He has decided to discuss his problems with the controller, Gig Griffith.

PULSIPHER: Gig, something has to give. My people are working overtime and can't keep up. You worked in property accounting before you became controller. You know that I can't tell the tax, insurance, and maintenance people everything they need to know from my records. Also, the internal auditing team is living in my area and that slows down the work pace. The requests of these people are reasonable, and we should be able to answer their questions and provide the needed data. I think we need an automated property accounting system. I would like to talk with the AIS people to see if they can help me.

GRIFFITH: Ryon, I think you have a great idea. Just be sure you are personally involved in the design of any system so that you get all the information you need. Keep me posted on the project's progress.

Required:

a. Identify and justify four major objectives Columbia Corporation's automated property accounting system should possess in order to respond to departmental requests for information.
b. Identify the data that should be included in the computer record for each asset included in the property account.

(CMA Examination, adapted)

19.6 A savings and loan association has decided to develop a new AIS. The internal auditors have suggested planning the systems development process in accordance with the SDLC concept. The following nine items have been identified as major systems development activities that will have to be undertaken.

1. System test
2. User specifications
3. Conversion
4. System planning study
5. Technical specifications
6. Postimplementation planning
7. Implementation planning
8. User procedures and training
9. Programming

Required:

a. Arrange the nine items in the sequence in which they should logically occur.
b. One major subactivity that will occur during system implementation is the conversion of data files from the old system to the new one. Indicate three types of documentation for a file conversion work plan that would be of particular interest to an auditor.

(CMA Examination, adapted)

CASE 19.1 ANYCOMPANY, INC.—AN ONGOING COMPREHENSIVE CASE

Visit a local company and obtain permission to study its systems development approach. Once you have lined up a company, do the following:

1. With a member of the IS staff, discuss the procedures the company follows in designing and implementing AIS changes.
   a. When a decision is made to change an existing system, how does the company approach conceptual systems design? Who determines which design alternatives are selected? What are the outputs from conceptual systems design?
   b. How does the company handle the physical design procedures involved in the development of the system? If available, view any documentation or flowcharts used in the development of a prior system.
   c. What implementation strategy does the company employ? What conversion procedures does the company find most effective in making the transition from an old system to a new one?

2. Obtain the documentation manual for one of the company's software programs. Evaluate the effectiveness of the documentation and identify its strengths and weaknesses. What suggestions do you have for improvement?

3. Summarize the results of your findings in a memo report.
   a. How effective are the company's conceptual and physical design procedures?
   b. How effective are the company's implementation, conversion, operation, and maintenance procedures?
   c. What recommendations do you have for improving the company's AIS development procedures?

CASE 19.2 CITIZEN'S GAS COMPANY

Citizen's Gas Company is a medium-sized gas distribution company that provides natural gas service to approximately 200,000 customers. The customer base is divided into three revenue classes. Data by customer class is as follows:

Class	Customers	Sales in Cubic Feet	Revenues
Residential	160,000	80 billion	$160 million
Commercial	38,000	15 billion	25 million
Industrial	2,000	50 billion	65 million
		145 billion	$250 million

Residential customer gas use is primarily for residential heating and so is highly correlated with the weather. Commercial and industrial customers, on the other hand, may or may not use gas for heating purposes, and so consumption does not necessarily depend on the weather.

The largest 25 out of the company's 2,000 industrial customers account for $30 million of the industrial revenues. Each of these 25 customers uses gas for both heating and industrial purposes and has a consumption pattern governed almost entirely by business factors.

The company obtains its gas supply from ten major pipeline companies. The pipeline companies provide gas in amounts specified in contracts that extend over periods ranging from 5 to 15 years. For some contracts the supply is in equal monthly increments, whereas for others the supply varies in accordance with the heating season. Supply over and above the contract amounts is not available, and some contracts contain take-or-pay clauses—that is, the company must pay for the volumes specified in the contract, whether or not it uses that amount of gas.

To assist in matching customer demand with supply, the company maintains a gas storage field. Gas can be pumped into the storage field when supply exceeds customer demand; likewise, gas can be obtained when demand exceeds supply. There are no restrictions on the use of the gas storage field except that the field must be filled to capacity at the beginning of each gas year (September 1). Consequently, whenever the contractual supply for the remainder of the gas year is less than that required to satisfy projected demand and replenish the storage field, the company must curtail service to the industrial customers (except for quantities that are used for heating). The curtailments must be carefully controlled so that an oversupply does not occur at year-end. Similarly, care must be taken to ensure that curtailments are adequate during the year to protect against the need to curtail commercial or residential customers in order to replenish the storage field at year-end.

In recent years the company's planning efforts have not provided a firm basis for the establishment of long-term contracts. The current year has been no different. Planning efforts have not been adequate to control the supply during the current gas year. Customer demand has been projected only as a function of the total number of customers. Commercial and industrial customers' demand for gas has been curtailed. This has resulted in lost sales and caused an excess of supply at the end of the gas year.

In an attempt to correct the problems of Citizen's Gas, the president has hired a new director of corporate planning. The director has been presented with a conceptual design for a system to assist him in the analysis of the supply and demand of natural gas. The system should provide a monthly gas plan for each year for the next five years, with particular emphasis on the first year. The plan should provide a set of reports that assists in the decision-making process and that contains all necessary supporting schedules. The system must provide for the use of actual data during the course of the first year to project demand for the rest of the year and the year in total. The president has indicated to the director that he will base his decisions on the effect alternative plans have on operating income.

1. Discuss the criteria that must be considered in specifying the basic structure and features of Citizen's Gas Company's new system to assist in planning its natural gas needs.
2. Identify the major data items that should be incorporated into Citizen's Gas Company's new system to provide adequate planning capability. For each item identified, explain why the data item is important, and describe the level of detail that would be necessary for the data to be useful.

(CMA Examination, adapted)

ANSWERS TO CHAPTER QUIZ

1. b	**3.** d	**5.** d	**7.** d	**9.** a
2. e	**4.** a	**6.** c	**8.** c	**10.** a

GLOSSARY

Acceptance Tests. Tests of new systems using specially developed transactions and acceptance criteria. The test results are evaluated to determine whether the system is acceptable.

Access Control Matrix. An internally maintained list that a computer uses to verify that the person attempting to access system resources is authorized to do so. The matrix usually consists of a list of user codes, a list of all files and programs maintained on the system, and a list of the accesses each user is authorized to make.

Access Time. The time required to transfer data to or from a storage device.

Accounting Controls. The plan of organization and the procedures and records concerned with the safeguarding of assets and the reliability of financial records.

Accounting Cycle. The activities corresponding to an organization's major accounting transactions. There are five major accounting cycles: acquisition and cash disbursements; payroll and personnel; sales and collection; capital acquisition and repayment; and inventory and warehousing.

Accounting Information System (AIS). The human and capital resources within an organization that are responsible for (1) the preparation of financial information and (2) the information obtained from collecting and processing company transactions. The AIS is a subset of the management information system

Accounts Receivable Aging Schedule. A report listing customer account balances by length of time outstanding; it provides useful information for evaluating current credit policies and for deciding whether to increase the credit limit for specific customers. It also provides information for estimating bad debts.

Activity-Based Costing. A cost system that attempts to trace costs to the activities, such as grinding or polishing, that create them, and only subsequently allocates those costs to products or departments.

Ad Hoc Queries. Nonrepetitive requests for reports or answers to specific questions about the contents of the system's data files.

Address. The unique identifier of a computer storage location.

Adjusted Trial Balance. A trial balance prepared after all adjusting entries have been made. The income statement can be produced from the adjusted trial balance.

Administrative Controls. The plan of organization and all methods and procedures that are concerned with operational efficiency and adherence to managerial policies.

Administrative Documentation. A description of the overall standards and procedures for the data processing facility, including policies relating to justification and authorization of new systems or systems changes; standards for systems analysis, design, and programming; and procedures for file handling and file library activities.

Agents. In the REA data model, the people and organizations that participate in events.

Aggression. Resisting change by activities intended to destroy, cripple, or lessen the effectiveness of a system. Aggression may take the form of increased error rates, disruptions, or deliberate sabotage.

Application. The problem or data processing task to which a computer's processing power is applied.

Application Controls. Controls that relate to the data inputs, files, programs, and outputs of a specific computer application, rather than the computer system in general. Contrast with *general controls.*

Application Generator. Software that produces a program to accomplish tasks specified by its users. Programming languages and tools for creating data bases are application generators.

Application Programmer. A person who formulates a logical model, or user view, of the data to be processed and then writes an application program using a programming language.

Application Software. Programs that perform the data or information processing tasks required by the user. Common types of applications software in accounting include accounts receivable and payable, inventory control, and payroll.

Application Suites. End-user software programs that are packaged and sold together. They usually include spreadsheets, word processors, data bases, graphics, and e-mail.

Arithmetic Processor. A microprocessor especially designed for arithmetic computations; it can complete such computations up to 200 times as fast as a regular microprocessor.

Arithmetic–Logic Unit. The portion of the CPU that executes arithmetic calculations and logic comparisons.

Artificial Intelligence (AI). A field of study in which researchers are attempting to develop computers with the ability to reason, think, and learn like a human being.

ASCII. An acronym for American Standard Code for Informational Interchange, a standard seven-bit code that facilitates the interchange of data between data processing, data communications, and related equipment. Also known as the ASCII character set.

Assembler. A special program that converts a symbolic language program to a machine language.

Assembler Language. A programming language in which each machine-level instruction is represented by mnemonic characters that bear some relation to the instruction. It is also called a symbolic language.

Asynchronous Transmission. Data transmission in which each character is transmitted separately. A start bit is required before the character and a stop bit after it, because the interval of time between transmission of characters can vary. Contrast with *synchronous transmission.*

ATM Card. A bank card that many businesses accept in lieu of credit and debit cards.

Attribute. Characteristics of interest in a file or data base; the different individual properties of an entity. Examples of attributes are employee number, pay rate, name, and address.

Audio Response Unit. A hardware device that converts computer output into spoken output (e.g., as in telephone directory assistance).

Audio Teleconferencing. A conference call where several locations are linked together so that they can hear and consult with each other.

Audit Committee. The committee responsible for overseeing a corporation's internal control structure, financial reporting process, and compliance with related laws and regulations. It is made up of outside members of the board of directors.

Audit Hooks. Concurrent audit techniques that embed audit routines into application software to flag certain kinds of transactions that might be indicative of fraud.

Audit Log. A log, kept on magnetic tape or disk, of all computer system transactions that have audit significance.

Audit Trail. A traceable path of a transaction through a data processing system, from source documents to final output.

Auditing. A systematic process of (1) objectively obtaining and evaluating evidence regarding assertions about economic actions and events to ascertain the degree of correspondence between those assertions and established criteria and (2) communicating the results to interested parties.

Authenticity. Refers to being able to determine, with almost absolute certainty, who sent a message.

Authorization. The empowerment of an employee to perform certain functions within an organization, such as to purchase or sell on behalf of the company. Authorization can be either general or specific. **General** authorization is when regular employees are authorized to handle routine transactions without special approval. **Specific** authorization is when an employee must get special approval before handling a transaction.

Automated Decision Table Program. A program that interprets the logic used in a computer program and displays the logic in the form of a decision table.

Automated Flowcharting Program. A program that interprets the source code of a program and generates a flowchart of the logic used by the program.

Automated Teller Machine (ATM). A special-purpose, intelligent terminal used by financial institutions to provide remote banking services.

Avoidance. Resisting change by not using the new system.

Back order. A document authorizing the purchase, or production, of items for which sufficient quantity is not available to meet customer orders.

Back-End (or **Lower**) **CASE.** These CASE tools support the later system development life cycle phases. Programmers generate structured program code from data base specifications and from screen and report layouts.

Backup File. Duplicate copy of a current file.

Balanced Scorecard. A management report that measures four dimensions of performance: financial, internal operations, innovation and learning, and customer perspectives of the organization.

Balance-Forward Method. Method of maintaining accounts receivable in which customers typically pay according to the amount shown on monthly statement, rather than by individual invoices. Remittances are applied against the total account balance, rather than against specific invoices.

Bandwidth. The difference between the highest and the lowest frequency of a communications channel, usually expressed in cycles per second (hertz).

Bar Codes. Special identification labels found on most merchandise. A code includes vertical lines of differing widths that represent binary information that is read by an optical scanner.

Batch Processing. Accumulating transaction records into groups or batches for processing at some regular interval, such as daily or weekly. Batched records are usually sorted into some sequence (such as numerically or alphabetically) before processing.

Batch Totals. Sums of the instances of numerical items, calculated for a batch of documents. These totals are calculated prior to processing the batch and are compared with machine-generated totals at each subsequent processing step to verify that the data were processed correctly.

Baud Rate. The speed with which data are electronically transferred from one location to another. In many data communications transmissions, it is equal to one bit per second.

BBS. See *bulletin board system.*

Behavioral Aspects of Change. Refers to the fact that systems development causes changes in organizations that may result in people changing their behavior. Organizations must be sensitive to and consider the feelings and reactions of persons affected by such changes.

Benchmark Problem. A data processing task that is executed by different computer systems. The results are used to measure systems performance and to make comparative evaluations among systems.

Bill of Lading. A legal contract that defines responsibility for the goods while they are in transit. It identifies the carrier, source, destination, any special shipping instructions, and indicates which party (customer or vendor) must pay the carrier.

Bill of Materials. A document that specifies the part number, description, and quantity of each component used in a product.

Biometric Identifications. Using unique physical characteristics such as fingerprints, voice patterns, retina prints, signature dynamics, and they way people type certain groups of characters to identify people.

BIPS. Billions of instructions per second; a way of measuring CPU speed.

Bits. Binary digits, which are the smallest storage location in a computer. A bit may be either "on" or "off," or "magnetized" or "nonmagnetized." A combination of bits (usually eight) is used to represent a single character of data.

Bits per Second (BPS). A unit of measurement describing the number of bits of data transmitted electronically in one second.

Blanket Purchase Order (or **Blanket Order**). A commitment to purchase specified items at designated prices from a particular supplier for a set time period, often one year.

Broadband Lines. Communications channels that can handle high-speed data transmissions, usually in the range of 20,000 to 500,000 bits per second. Their primary use is for high-speed data transmission between computer systems.

Budget. The formal expression of goals in financial terms. Budgets are financial planning tools. Contrast with *performance report.*

Bulletin Board System (BBS). An information sharing service that allows computer user to meet and share ideas and information. Most BBSs are free and cater to specialized interests.

Bus. The path for moving data, instructions, or other signals between the various components of the CPU. The bus could be in the form of a cable or in the form of the connecting paths within a microcomputer chip.

Bus Network. Type of network organization where all devices are attached to a main channel, called a bus. Each network device can access the other devices by sending a message to its address. Each device reads the address of all messages sent on the bus and responds to the messages sent to it.

Bus Size. The number of bits transferred at one time from one computer location to another.

Business Cycle. The five major business cycles are marketing, purchasing and inventory control, production, personnel, and finance.

Business Process Reengineering (BPR). The thorough analysis and complete redesign of business processes and information systems to achieve dramatic performance improvements.

Byte. A group of adjacent bits that is treated as a single unit by the computer. The most common size for a byte is eight bits. An eight-bit byte can be used to represent an alphabetic, numeric, or special character, or two numeric characters can be "packed" into a single eight-bit byte.

Callback System. A routing verification procedure. After the user dials in and is authenticated, the computer disconnects and calls the user back as an additional security precaution.

Canned Software. Programs written by computer manufacturers or software development companies for sale on the open market to a broad range of users with similar needs.

Capacity Check. An input validation routine that ensures that data will fit into its assigned field.

Capital Budgeting Model. An estimate of funds to be appropriated for the acquisition of major capital assets and for investment in long-term projects. The estimated benefits are compared with the costs to determine whether the system is cost beneficial.

Cardinality. A property of a data base relationship, indicating the number of occurrences of one entity that may be associated with a single occurrence of the other entity. Three types of cardinalities are one-to-one (1:1), one-to-many (1:*N*), and many-to-many (*M*:*N*).

Carrying Costs. The costs associated with holding inventory.

CASE Encyclopedia. See *data repository.*

Cash Budget. A budget that shows projected cash inflows and outflows. A cash budget can provide advance warning of cash flow problems in time for corrective action to be taken.

Cathode Ray Tube (CRT). Another name for the monitor on a computer. Sometimes, terminals are referred to as CRTs as well.

CD-ROM. A storage device that uses laser optics for reading data rather then magnetic storage devices. Although CD-ROM discs are "read only," the discs are useful for storing large volumes of data (roughly 600 megabytes per disc).

Cells. (1) The intersections of rows and columns in an electronic spreadsheet. (2) Small sections of a larger metropolitan area in which cellular radio is used.

Cellular Radios. A means of making greater use of radio frequencies. A large area is divided into smaller sections called cells, and each radio frequency is assigned to a different user in each cell. A powerful central computer controls transmission between cells.

Cellular Telephones. Telephones that use radio frequencies to send and receive messages. These radio frequencies are divided into geographic regions called cells so that users in different locations can share the same frequency.

Central Processing Unit (CPU). The hardware that contains the circuits controlling the interpretation and execution of instructions; it serves as the principal data processing device. Its major components are the arithmetic–logic unit, the memory, and the control unit.

Centralized Data Processing System. A data processing system in which all the data processing equipment, personnel, and controls are located in the same geographical area.

Centralized Network. A large, centralized computer system that handles a company's data processing needs. Such a system requires complex software and is designed to provide a company with an economy-of-scale advantage in data processing operations.

Centralized System. A data processing system in which data processing is done at a centralized location. User terminals are linked to the centralized host computer so that users can send data to the host computer for processing and access data as needed.

Certificate Authority. An independent organization that issues digital certificates.

Chain. A group of records connected by pointer fields, as in a linked list.

Channel. (1) A path that electronic signals follow when traveling between electronic devices. (2) A hardware device that acts as a communication interface between the CPU and input/output devices.

Character. Letters, numeric digits, or other symbols used for representing data to be processed by a computer.

Chart of Accounts. A listing of all balance sheet and income statement account number codes for a particular company.

Check Digit. A redundant digit in a data field that provides information about the other digits in the data field. It is used to check for errors or loss of characters in the data fields as a result of data transfer operations. If data are lost or erroneously changed, the fact that the check digit does not match the other data in the field will signal that an error has occurred.

Check Digit Verification. The edit check in which a check digit is recalculated to verify that an error has not been made. This calculation can be made only on a data item that has a check digit.

Checkpoint. Any one of a series of points during a long processing run at which an exact copy of all the data values and status indicators of a program is captured. Should a system failure occur, the system could be backed up to the most recent checkpoint and processing could begin again at the checkpoint rather than at the beginning of the program.

Client–Server System. An arrangement of a LAN where information requested by a user is first processed as much as possible by the server and then transmitted to the user. Contrast with *file–server.*

Closed-Loop Verification. An input validation method in which data that have just been entered into the system are sent back to the sending device so that the user can verify that the correct data have been entered.

Coaxial Cable. A group of copper or aluminum wires that have been wrapped and shielded to reduce interference. The cables are used to transmit electronic messages between hardware devices.

Coding. (1) Assigning numbers, letters, or other symbols according to a systematic plan so that a user can determine the classifications to which a particular item belongs. (2) Writing program instructions that direct a computer to perform a specific data processing task.

Cold Site. A location that provides everything necessary to quickly install computer equipment in the event that a disaster strikes an organization.

Collusion. Cooperation between two or more people in an effort to thwart internal controls.

Committee of Sponsoring Organizations (COSO). A private sector group consisting of the American Accounting Association, the AICPA, the Institute of Internal Auditors, the Institute of Management Accountants, and the Financial Executives Institute.

Common Carriers. Governmentally regulated private organizations that provide telecommunications equipment and services to the public.

Communications Channel. The line, or link, between the sender and the receiver in a data communications network.

Communications Network. An information system consisting of one or more computers, a number of other hardware devices, and communication channels all linked together into a network.

Communications Software. A program that controls the transmission of data electronically over communications lines.

Compatibility Check (or **Compatibility Test**). A procedure for checking a password to determine whether its user is authorized to engage in the type of transaction or inquiry he or she is attempting to initiate.

Compensating Controls. Control procedures that will compensate for the deficiency in other controls.

Compilers. Programs that convert all high-level language commands (source code) into machine language commands (object code) before any commands are executed. Contrast with *interpreter.*

Completeness Test. An on-line data entry control in which the computer checks to see whether all of the data required for a particular transaction have been entered by the user.

Computer Audit Software. See *generalized audit software.*

Computer Conferencing. Personal interaction using computers at remote sites linked through communications facilities.

Computer Configuration Chart. A type of flowchart that shows the different hardware devices in a computer system.

Computer Console. A hardware device that computer operators use to interact with large computer systems.

Computer Crime. Any illegal act for which knowledge of a computer is essential for the crime's perpetration, investigation, or prosecution.

Computer Fraud. See *computer crime.*

Computer Hardware. See *hardware.*

Computer Integrated Manufacturing (CIM). A manufacturing approach in which much of the manufacturing process is performed and monitored by computerized equipment, in part through the use of robotics and real-time data collection on manufacturing activities.

Computer Output Microfilm (COM). A hardware device that uses a photographic process to record computer output on photosensitive film in microscopic form.

Computer Program. See *program.*

Computer Programmers. Persons who develop, code, and test computer programs.

Computer Programming. The process of writing software programs to accomplish a specific task or set of tasks.

Computer Security. All of the policies, procedures, tools, and other means of safeguarding information systems from unauthorized access or alteration and from intentional or unintentional damage or theft.

Computer Security Officer. An employee independent of the information system function who monitors the system and disseminates information about improper system uses and their consequences.

Computer System. The input/output devices, data storage devices, CPU, and other peripheral devices that are connected together to provide an organization's computing capability. The software necessary to operate the computer is also considered a part of the system.

Computer System Flowchart. A type of flowchart that shows the inputs to a computer system or program, the program modules that process the data, and the output from the system.

Computer Virus. A segment of executable code that attaches itself to an application program or some other executable system component. When the hidden program is triggered, it makes unauthorized alterations to the way a system operates.

Computer-Aided Software (or **Systems**) **Engineering (CASE).** This type of software is used by analysts to document and manage a systems development effort.

Computer-Based Information System. Information system in which a computer is used as the data processor. All the equipment, programs, data, and procedures for performing a set of related tasks on a computer.

Concatenated Key. The combination of two fields in a data base table that together become a unique identifier or key field.

Concentrator. A communications device that combines signals from several sources and sends them over a single line. The concentrator also performs such tasks as data formatting, data validation, and data backup.

Conceptual Design Specifications. The systems requirements that are specified for systems output, data storage, input, and processing procedures and operations once a conceptual design alternative has been selected.

Conceptual Systems Design. A phase of the systems development life cycle in which the systems designer proposes a systems design without considering the physical restrictions of particular hardware and software.

Conceptual Systems Design Report. A document specifying the details of the conceptual systems design, which is used by physical systems designers to identify the hardware, software, and procedures necessary to deliver the system.

Conceptual-Level Schema. The organization-wide schema of the entire data base. It lists all data elements in the data base and the relationships between them. Contrast with *external-level schema* and *internal-level schema.*

Concurrent Audit Techniques. A software routine that continuously monitors an information system as it processes live data in order to collect, evaluate, and report to the auditor information about the system's reliability.

Concurrent Update Controls. Controls that lock out one user to protect individual records from potential errors that could occur if two users attempted to update the same record simultaneously.

Confidentiality. Refers to the limiting of data access or use to authorized personnel.

Configuration. For a network, a configuration is the entire interrelated set of hardware. For a microcomputer, the configuration references the complete internal and external components of the computer including peripherals.

Context Diagram. The highest level of a data flow diagram. It provides a summary-level view of a system. It shows the data processing system, the inputs and outputs of the system, and the external entities that are the sources and destinations of the system's inputs and outputs.

Continuous and Intermittent Simulation (CIS). A concurrent audit technique that embeds an audit module into a data base management system, rather than into the application software.

Control Account. The general ledger account that summarizes the total amounts recorded in subsidiary ledger. Thus, the accounts payable control account in the general ledger represents the total amount owed to all vendors. The balances in the subsidiary accounts payable ledger indicate the amount owed to each specific vendor.

Control Environment. The organization's environment as related to controls. It consists of many factors, including management's philosophy, the audit committee, and the organizational structure.

Control Risk. The risk that a significant control problem will fail to be prevented or detected by the internal control system.

Control Totals. Batch totals used to ensure that all data is processed correctly. Examples are the number of transactions processed and the dollar amount of all updates.

Control Unit. The CPU component that interprets program instructions and controls and coordinates the system's input, output, and storage devices.

Conversion. The process of changing from one form or format to another.

Corrective Controls. Procedures established to remedy problems that are discovered through detective controls.

Cost Driver. Anything that has a cause-and-effect relationship on costs. For example, the number of purchase orders processed is one cost driver of purchasing department costs.

Cracking. See *hacking.*

Credit Limit. The maximum allowable account balance for each customer, based on past credit history and ability to pay.

Credit Memo. A document authorizing the billing department to credit the customer's account. Usually issued for sales returns, allowances granted for damaged goods kept by the customer, or to write off uncollectible accounts. Approved by the credit manager.

Cross-Footing Balance Test. A procedure in which worksheet data are totaled both across and down and then the total of the horizontal totals is compared with the total of the vertical totals to make sure the worksheet balances.

Cryptography. See *data encryption.*

Cumulative Data. Data that does not need to be stored because it can be calculated using data already in the data base. For example, quantity on hand can be calculated by finding the difference between the quantity sold and the quantity purchased.

Custom Software. Computer software that is developed and written in-house to meet the unique needs of a particular company.

Cycle Billing. A procedure for producing monthly statements for subsets of customers at different times. For example, the customer master file might be divided into four parts, and each week monthly statements would be prepared for one-fourth of the customers.

Data. Characters that are accepted as input to an information system for further storing and processing. After processing, the data become information.

Data Administrator (DA). The person responsible for developing general policies and procedures governing all organizational data, not just what is stored in the data base. The DA is ultimately responsible for understanding the information needs of the organization in order to decide what should be included in the data base.

Data Base. A set of interrelated, centrally controlled data files that are stored with as little data redundancy as possible. A data base consolidates many records previously stored in separate files into a common pool of data records and serves a variety of users and data processing applications.

Data Base Administrator. The person responsible for coordinating, controlling, and managing the data in the data base.

Data Base Management System (DBMS). The specialized computer program that manages and controls the data and interfaces between the data and the application programs.

Data Base Query Languages. Easy-to-use programming language that lets the user ask questions about the data stored in a data base.

Data Base Retrieval System (DBRS). Public data bases, or electronic libraries, that contain millions of items of data that can be retrieved, reviewed, and analyzed for a fee.

Data Base System. The combination of the data base, the data base management system, and the application programs that access the data base through the data base management system.

Data Bus. The path, or circuitry, that the computer uses to move data and instructions between the different parts of the CPU, and to and from the input/output devices.

Data Communications. The transmission of data from a point of origin to a point of destination.

Data Communications Networks. Communication system that bridges geographical distances, giving users immediate access to a company's computerized data. It also allows multiple companies or computer services to be linked together for the purpose of sharing information.

Data Definition Language (DDL). A data base management system language that ties the logical and physical views of the data together. It is used to create the data base, to describe the schemas and subschemas, to describe the records and fields in the data base, and to specify any security limitations or constraints imposed on the data base.

Data Destination. A component of data flow diagrams that represents an entity outside of the system that receives data produced by the system.

Data Dictionary. An ordered collection of data elements that is essentially a centralized source of data about data. For each data element used in the organization, there is a record in the data dictionary that contains data about that data element.

Data Diddling. Changing data before it enters, as it enters, or after it has already been entered into the system. The change can be made to delete data, to change data, or to add data to the system.

Data Encryption. The translation of data into a secret code for storage or data transmission purposes. Encryption is particularly important when confidential data are being transmitted from remote terminals, because data transmission lines can be electronically monitored without the user's knowledge.

Data Flow. A component of a data flow diagram that represents a piece of data flowing into or out of a process.

Data Flow Diagram. A diagram that concentrates on identifying the types of data and their flow through various types of processing. The physical nature of the data (e.g., physical document, electronic) is ignored; the diagram simply identifies the content of the data, the source, and the destination.

Data Independence. A data organization approach in which the data and the application programs that use the data are independent—one may be changed without affecting the other.

Data Leakage. The unauthorized copying of company data, often without leaving any indication that it was copied.

Data Maintenance. The periodic processing of transactions to update stored data. The four types of data maintenance are additions, deletions, updates, and changes.

Data Manipulation Language (DML). A data base management system language that is used to update, replace, store, retrieve, insert, delete, sort, and otherwise manipulate the records and data items in the data base.

Data Mining. A method for accessing information stored in a data warehouse by using statistical analysis or artificial intelligence techniques to discover relationships in the data.

Data Model. An abstract representation of the contents of a data base.

Data Modeling. The process of defining a data base so that it faithfully represents all key components of an organization's environment. The objective is to explicitly capture and store data about each and every business activity that the organization wishes to plan, control, or evaluate.

Data Processing Center. The location that houses a company's computer system (the hardware, software, and people who operate the system).

Data Processing Cycle. The operations performed on data in computer-based systems in order to generate meaningful and relevant information. The data processing cycle has four stages: data input, data processing, data storage, and information output.

Data Processing Schedule. A schedule of data processing tasks designed to maximize the use of scarce computer resources.

Data Query Language (DQL). A high-level, English-like command language that is used to interrogate a data base. Most DQLs contain a fairly powerful set of commands that are easy to use, yet provide a great deal of flexibility.

Data Redundancy. The storage of the same item of data in two or more files within an organization.

Data Repository (or **CASE Encyclopedia**). Stores and manages project data dictionaries. It contains information about the system and is cross-referenced to other system components.

Data Source. A component of a data flow diagram that represents a source of data outside the system being modeled.

Data Store. A component of a data flow diagram that represents the storage of data within a system.

Data Transmission Controls. Methods of monitoring the network to detect weak points, maintain backup components, and ensure that the system can still communicate if one of the communications paths should fail.

Data Value. The actual value stored in a field. It describes a particular attribute of an entity.

Data Warehouses. Very large data bases.

Debit Memo. A document used to record an adjustment to the balance due a vendor, reflecting a reduction in the amount owed.

Debugging. The process of checking for errors in a computer program and correcting the errors that are discovered.

Decentralized System. An information processing system that has an independent CPU and a data processing manager at each location.

Decision Rule. The vertical columns in a decision table that represent a combination of logical relationships and the actions that should be taken for each of those conditions.

Decision Scope. The range of influence and effect a decision has on an organization.

Decision Structure. The degree to which a decision is either routine or requires subjective judgment.

Decision Support Systems (DSS). An interactive computer system designed to help with the decision-making process by providing access to a computer-based data base or decision-making model.

Decision Table. A tabular representation of program logic that indicates the possible combinations of logic conditions and the courses of action taken by the program for each condition.

Deduction Register. A report listing the miscellaneous voluntary deductions for each employee.

Delete Anomaly. A problem that can arise in a poorly designed relational data base, when attributes that are not characteristics of the primary key of a relation are stored in that table. Deleting a row from that table may result in the loss of all information about those attributes that are not characteristics of the primary key. For example, if customer addresses are only stored in the sales invoice table, then deleting the row representing the only sale to a particular customer results in the loss of all information about that customer.

Demand Reports. Reports that have a prespecified content and format but are prepared only in response to a request from a manager or other employee.

Denial of Service Attack. An attack that bombards the receiving server with so much information that it shuts down.

Desk Checking. A visual and mental review of a newly coded program to discover keying or program errors.

Desktop Publishing (DTP). Software that provides an end user with the ability to design, develop, and produce professional-quality printed documents containing text, charts, pictures, graphs, spreadsheets, photographs, and illustrations.

Detection Risk. The risk that the auditors and their audit procedures will not detect a material misstatement.

Detective Controls. Controls designed to discover control problems soon after they arise.

Diagnostic Messages. Messages that inform the programmer of syntax errors.

Digital Fingerprint. A hash number that identifies and validates a digital certificate.

Digital Signature. A piece of data signed on a document by a computer. A digital signature cannot be forged and is useful in tracing authorization.

Direct Access. An access method that allows the computer to access a particular record without reading any other records. Since each storage location on a direct access storage device has a unique address, the computer can find the record needed as long as it has the record's address.

Direct Access Processing. Updating the master file immediately as transactions occur. With each transaction, the master file is retrieved, updated, and stored.

Direct Access Storage Device (DASD). A storage device (such as a disk drive) that can directly access individual storage locations to store or retrieve data.

Direct Conversion. An approach to converting from one system to another in which the old system is altogether discontinued, after which the new system is started (also known as "burning the bridges" or "crash conversion").

Disaster Recovery Plan. Plan that prepares a company to recover its data processing capacity as smoothly and quickly as possible in response to any emergency that could disable the computer system.

Disbursement Voucher. A document that identifies the vendor, lists the outstanding invoices, and indicates the net amount to be paid after deducting any applicable discounts and allowances.

Diskette. A round piece of flexible magnetic film enclosed within a protective cover. It is a popular storage medium for microcomputers.

Distributed Data Processing (DDP) System. A system in which computers are set up at remote locations and then linked to a centralized mainframe computer.

Document Flowchart. A diagram illustrating the flow of documents through the different departments and functions of an organization.

Documentation. Written material consisting of instructions to operators, descriptions of procedures, and other descriptive material. Documentation may be classified into three basic categories: (1) administrative, (2) systems, and (3) operating.

Documents. Records of transaction or other company data such as checks, invoices, receiving reports, and purchase requisitions.

Download. To transmit data or software maintained on a large host (mainframe) computer to a personal computer for use by an individual working at the personal computer.

Downsizing. Shifting data processing and problem solving from mainframes to smaller computer systems. Downsizing saves money and allows the end user to be more involved in the processing of the data.

Earnings Statement. A report listing the amount of gross pay, deductions, and net pay for the current period; year-to-date totals for each category are also listed.

Eavesdropping. An event in which a computer user observes transmissions intended for some one else. One way unauthorized individuals can intercept signals is by setting up a wiretap.

Echo Check. A hardware control that verifies transmitted data by having the receiving device send the message back to the sending device so that the message received can be compared with the message sent.

Economic Espionage. The theft of information and intellectual property.

Economic Exchange Event. An event in which one agent gives a resource to another agent.

Economic Feasibility. The dimension of feasibility concerned with whether the benefits of a proposed system will exceed the costs.

Economic Order Quantity (EOQ). The optimal order size so as to minimize the sum of ordering, carrying, and stockout costs. Ordering costs include all expenses associated with processing purchase transactions. Carrying costs are the costs associated with holding inventory. Stockout costs represent costs, such as lost sales or production delays, that result from inventory shortages.

Edit Checks. Accuracy checks performed by an edit program.

Edit Programs. Computer programs that verify the validity and accuracy of input data.

Electronic Commerce. The use of advances in networking and communications technology to improve the ways in which a company interacts with its suppliers and customers.

Electronic Data Interchange (EDI). The use of computerized communication to exchange business data electronically in order to process transactions.

Electronic Data Processing (EDP). Processing data utilizing a computer system. Little or no human intervention is necessary while data are being processed.

Electronic Envelope. A method for protecting e-mail messages by using public or private key techniques to encrypt and decrypt the messages.

Electronic Funds Transfer (EFT). The transfer of funds between two or more organizations or individuals using computers and other automated technology.

Electronic Lockbox. A lockbox arrangement in which the bank electronically sends the company information about the customer account number and the amount remitted as soon as it receives and scans those checks. This enables the company to begin applying remittances to customer accounts before the photocopies of the checks arrive.

Electronic Mail (or **E-mail**). A system that allows a person to use a computer to send a message to another person.

Electronic Spreadsheet. An applications program used for analysis, planning, modeling, and decision support. It is a worksheet, or matrix of rows and columns, containing blank cells into which numeric data, alphabetic data, or formulas can be entered.

Electronic Vaulting. Electronically transmitting backup copies of data to a physically different location. Electronic vaulting permits on-line access to backup data when necessary.

E-mail Bomb. A type of denial of service attack in which the receiver's e-mail server is bombarded with hundreds of e-mail messages per second.

E-mail Forgery. Altering e-mail to make it appear that it came from a different source.

E-mail Threats. Unwarranted threats sent to victims by e-mail. The threats usually require some follow-up action, often at great expense to the victim.

Embedded Audit Modules. Special portions of application programs that keep track of items of interest to auditors, such as any unauthorized attempts to access the data files.

Embezzlement. The fraudulent appropriation of business property by an employee to whom it has been entrusted. It is often accompanied by falsification of records.

Employee Fraud. Type of internal fraud where an employee or group of employees use company resources for their own personal gain.

Employee Goofing. Surfing the Internet for personal entertainment on company time.

Encapsulation. The bundling together of data and instructions in the object-oriented data model.

End-User Computing (EUC). The creation, control, and implementation by end users of their own information system.

End-User Development. A process in which information users develop applications on their own, rather than going through the IS department.

End-User System (EUS). Information system developed by the users themselves, rather than professionals in the IS department, to meet their own operational and managerial information needs. An EUS draws on the information in existing corporate data bases to meet users' information needs.

Enterprise Resource Planning (ERP) System. A system that integrates all aspects of an organization's activities into one accounting information system.

Entity. The item about which information is stored in a record. Examples of an entity include an employee, an inventory item, and a customer account.

Entity Integrity Rule. A design constraint in a relational data base, requiring that the primary key have a nonnull value. This ensures that a specific object exists in the world and can be identified by reference to its primary key value.

Entity-Relationship (E-R) diagram. A graphical depiction of a data base's contents. It shows the various entities being modeled and the important relationships among them. An entity is any class of objects about which data is collected. Thus, the resources, events, and agents that make up the REA data model are all entities. An E-R diagram represents entities as rectangles; lines and diamonds represent relationships between entities.

Error Log. The record of data input and data processing errors.

Error Message. A message from the computer indicating that it has encountered a mistake or malfunction.

Error Report. A report summarizing errors by record type, error type, and cause.

Ethernet. A bus configuration that allows LAN devices to put messages on the network and to take them off. In addition, it regulates traffic on the network.

Events. In the REA data model, the various business activities about which management wants to collect information.

Execution Time. The time required to perform a computer instruction.

Executive Information System (EIS). An information system designed to provide executives with the needed information to make strategic plans, to control and operate the company, to monitor business conditions in general, and to identify business problems and opportunities.

Expected Loss. A measure of loss based on the potential loss associated with a control problem and the risk, or probability, that the problem will occur.

Expenditure Cycle. A recurring set of business activities and related data processing operations associated with the purchase of and payment for goods and services.

Expert System (ES). A computerized information system that allows nonexperts to make decisions about a particular problem that are comparable to those of experts in the area.

Explanation Facility. A component of an expert system that provides the user with an explanation of the logic that the ES used to arrive at its conclusion.

Exposure. A measure of risk derived by multiplying the potential magnitude of an error, in dollars, by the error's estimated frequency (probability) of occurrence.

External Label. A label on the outside of a magnetic storage medium (e.g., tape, disk) that identifies the data contained on the storage medium.

External Players. Customers, vendors, government entities, and other people outside of the organization that play a role in systems development.

External-Level Schema. An individual user's or application program's view of a subset of the organization's data base. Each of these individual user views is also referred to as a subschema. Contrast with *conceptual-level schema* and *internal-level schema.*

Extranet. The linked intranets of two or more companies.

Facsimile (Fax) Transmission. The electronic transmission of pictures, contracts, signatures, and so forth over data communications lines.

Fault Tolerance. The capability of a system to continue performing its functions in the presence of a hardware failure.

Fax Modem. A type of modem that, in conjunction with accompanying software, allows users to send fully formatted documents and data files from their PC to a receiving fax machine or computer without having to print them first.

Feasibility Study. An investigation to determine whether the development of a new application or system is practical. This is one of the first steps in the systems evaluation and selection process.

Feedback. Informational output of a process that returns as input to the process, initiating the actions necessary for process control.

Feedback Controls. Controls that measure some aspect of the process being controlled and adjust the process when the measure indicates that the process is deviating from the plan.

Feedforward Controls. Controls that monitor both process operations and inputs in an attempt to predict potential deviations, in order that adjustments can be made to avert problems before they occur.

Femtosecond. One-quadrillionth (10^{-15}) of a second.

Fiber Optics Cable. A data transmission cable consisting of thousands of tiny filaments of glass or plastic.

Field. The part of a data record that contains the data value for a particular attribute. All records of a particular type usually have their fields in the same order. For example, the first field in all accounts receivable records may be reserved for the customer account number.

Field Check. An edit check in which the characters in a field are examined to make sure they are of the correct field type (e.g., numeric data in numeric fields).

File. A set of logically related records, such as the payroll records of all employees.

File Access. The way the computer finds or retrieves each record it has stored.

File Maintenance. The periodic processing of transaction files against a master file. This maintenance, which is the most common task in virtually all data processing systems, includes record additions, deletions, updates, and changes. After file maintenance, the master file will contain all current information.

File Organization. The way data are stored on the physical storage media. File organization may be either sequential or direct (random, nonsequential, or relative).

File–Server. An arrangement of a LAN where an entire file is sent to the user and then processed by the user, not the server. Contrast with *client–server system.*

Financial Audit. A review of the reliability and integrity of financial and operating information and the means used to identify, measure, classify, and report such information.

Financial Electronic Data Interchange (FEDI). The combination of EFT and EDI. It enables both remittance data and funds transfer instructions to be included in one electronic package.

Financial Total. The total of a dollar field, such as total sales, in a set of records. It is usually generated manually from source documents prior to input and compared with machine-generated totals at each subsequent processing step. Any discrepancy may indicate a loss of records or errors in data transcription or processing.

Financial Value-Added Network (FVAN). An independent organization that offers specialized hardware and software to link various EDI networks with the banking system for EFT.

Financing Cycle. A recurring set of business activities and related data processing operations associated with obtaining the necessary funds to run the operations, repaying creditors, and distributing profits to investors.

Firewall. A combination of security algorithms and router communications protocols that prevent outsiders from tapping into corporate data bases and e-mail systems.

Flash Memory Chip. A memory chip that does not lose its contents when the power is shut off. Used to replace hard disks in handheld computers and to store operating systems and application software.

Flat File. A file structure in which every record is identical to every other record in terms of attributes and field lengths.

Flexible Benefit Plans. Plans under which each employee receives some minimum coverage in medical insurance and pension contributions, plus additional benefit credits that can be used to acquire extra vacation time or additional health insurance. These plans are sometimes called cafeteria-style benefit plans because they offer a menu of options.

Flexible Manufacturing System (FMS). A system in which a computer is used to automate and integrate the performance of all major production tasks within a factory, including production planning, stock control, materials handling, machine scheduling and operation, and quality control.

Floppy Disk. A 3 1/2-inch diskette.

Flowchart. A diagrammatic representation of the flow of information and the sequence of operations in a process or system.

Flowcharting Symbols. A set of standard objects that are used in flowcharts to show how and where data moves. Each symbol has a special meaning that is easily conveyed by its shape.

Flowcharting Template. A piece of hard, flexible plastic on which the shapes of flowcharting symbols have been cut out.

Foreign Corrupt Practices Act (1977). Among other things, requires all publicly owned corporations subject to the Securities Exchange Act of 1934 to keep reasonably detailed records and maintain an internal accounting control system.

Foreign Key. An attribute appearing in one table that is itself the primary key of another table.

Forensic Accountants. Accountants that specialize in fraud auditing and investigation. Upon qualification, forensic accountants may receive a Certified Fraud Examiner (CFE) certificate.

Fourth-Generation Languages (4GL). High-level, application, or user-oriented languages that are easy to learn and do not require the user to understand the details of the computer.

Fraud. Any and all means a person uses to gain an unfair advantage over another person.

Fraudulent Financial Reporting. Intentional or reckless conduct, whether by act or omission, that results in materially misleading financial statements.

Freight Bill. A document that indicates the amount the customer should pay to the carrier for delivered goods. May be either a separate document or a copy of the bill of lading.

Front-End (or **Upper**) **CASE.** These CASE tools support the early stages of the systems development life cycle, such as analysis and design.

Front-End Processor (FEP). A dedicated communications computer that is connected to a host CPU. It handles the communications tasks so that the CPU can spend its time processing data.

Full-Duplex Channel. A data transmission channel that allows data transmissions in both directions at the same time. Contrast with *half-duplex channel* and *simplex channel.*

Gantt Chart. A bar graph used for project planning and control. Project activities are shown on the left, and units of time are shown across the top. The time period over which each activity is expected to be performed is represented with a horizontal bar on the graph.

Gateway. A communications interface device that allows a local area network to be connected to external networks and to communicate with external mainframes and data bases.

General Authorization. Refers to a situation in which regular employees are authorized to handle routine transactions without special approval.

General Controls. Controls that relate to all or many computerized accounting activities, such as those relating to the plan of organization of data processing activities and the separation of incompatible functions. Contrast with *application controls.*

General Journal. The journal that is used to record infrequent or nonroutine transactions, such as loan payments and end-of-period adjusting and closing entries.

General Journal Listing. A report showing the details (account number, source reference code, description, and amount debited or credited) of each entry posted to the general ledger.

General Ledger. The general ledger contains summary-level data for every asset, liability, equity, revenue, and expense account of the organization.

General Ledger and Reporting Cycle. The information processing operations involved in updating the general ledger and preparing reports that summarize the results of the organization's activities.

Generalized Audit Software (GAS). A software package that performs audit tests on the data files of a company.

Gigabyte. One billion characters of data.

Goal Conflict. The situation in which a decision or action of one subgoal or subsystem is inconsistent with another subgoal or subsystem.

Goal Congruence. The situation in which employees can achieve their assigned subgoals while contributing to the achievement of their organization's overall goals.

Gopher. Used to quickly move from one place on the Internet to another.

Grandfather–Father–Son. A method for maintaining backup copies of files on magnetic tape or disk. The three most current copies of the data are retained, with the son being the most recent.

Graphical User Interface (GUI). Operating environment where the user selects commands, starts programs, or lists files by pointing to pictorial representations (icons) with a mouse. A Macintosh computer, Microsoft's Windows, and IBM's OS/2 are all GUI environments.

Group Decision Support Software (GDSS). Software that encourages and allows everyone in a group to participate in decision making. A GDSS brings a group of people together to share information, exchange ideas, explore differing points of views, examine proposed solutions, arrive at a consensus, or vote on a course of action.

Groupware. Software that combines the power of computer networks with the immediacy and personal touch of the face-to-face brainstorming session. Groupware lets users hold computer conferences, decide when to hold a meeting, make a calendar for a department, collectively brainstorm on creative endeavors, manage projects, and design products.

Hacking. Unauthorized access and use of computer systems, usually by means of a personal computer and telecommunications networks.

Half-Duplex Channel. A data transmission channel that allows transmissions in both directions, but in only one direction at a time. Contrast with *full-duplex channel* and *simplex channel.*

Hard Disk. A magnetic storage disk made of rigid material and enclosed in a sealed disk unit to cut down on the chances of the magnetic medium's being damaged by foreign particles. A hard disk has a much faster access time and greater storage capacity than a floppy disk.

Hardware. Physical equipment, or machinery, that is used in a computer system.

Hash Total. A total generated from values for a field that would not usually be totaled, such as customer account numbers. It is usually generated manually from source documents prior to input and compared with machine-generated totals at each subsequent processing step. Any discrepancy may indicate a loss of records or errors in data transcription or processing.

Header Label. Type of internal label that appears at the beginning of each file and contains the file name, expiration date, and other file identification information.

Help Desk. An in-house group of analysts and technicians that answer employees' questions with the purpose of encouraging, supporting, coordinating, and controlling end-user activity.

Hierarchical Network. A variation of the star network. The configuration looks like a hierarchical organization chart.

Hierarchical Organization Structure. An organizational structure created by subdividing organizational goals and tasks into a graded series of lower-level goals and tasks.

Hierarchical Program Design. The process of designing a program from the top level down to the most detailed level.

History File. A file that contains records of account balances and of past transactions that have already been processed to update appropriate master files. These records are retained for reference purposes.

Home Page. A storefront or site on the Internet that is set up by individuals and firms to provide useful and interesting information about the individual or firm.

Hot Site. Completely operational data processing facility configured to meet the user's requirements that can be made available to a disaster-stricken organization on short notice.

Hub. A hardware device that provides a common wiring point in a LAN and a connection over a higher-speed link to other LANs, WANs, or the Internet.

Human Resource Management (HRM)/Payroll Cycle. The recurring set of business activities and related data processing operations associated with effectively managing the employee work force.

Hybrid Network. A combination of both star and ring network configurations.

Icons. Pictures on a computer screen that represent functions.

Image Processing. Using scanning and photographic techniques to capture the exact image of a document. The scanning device converts the text and pictures into a digitized electronic code that can be displayed on a computer monitor and stored on laser optical disks.

Impact Printers. Printers that strike an embossed character against an inked ribbon. Dot matrix printers are the most popular type of impact printer.

Impersonation. See *masquerading.*

Implementation. The process of installing a computer system. It includes selecting and installing the equipment, training personnel, establishing operating policies, and getting the software onto the system and functioning properly.

Implementation and Conversion. The capstone phase in the systems development life cycle, where all the elements and activities of the system come together. Implementation includes installing and testing new hardware and software, hiring and training employees, and testing new processing procedures. Standards and controls must be established and documented. The final step, conversion, consists of dismantling the old system and converting it into the new one.

Implementation Plan. A written plan that outlines how a new system will be implemented. The plan includes a timetable for completion, who is responsible for each activity, cost estimates, and task milestones.

Imprest Fund. A cash account with two characteristics: (1) it is set at a fixed amount, such as $100, and (2) vouchers are required for every disbursement. At all times, the sum of cash plus vouchers should equal the preset fund balance.

Index File. A master file of record identifiers and corresponding storage locations.

Index Sequential Access Method (ISAM). A file organization and access approach in which records are stored in sequential order by their primary key on a direct access storage device. An index file is created, which allows the file to be accessed and updated randomly.

Inference Engine. A component of an expert system; it is a program containing the logic and reasoning mechanisms that simulate the expert logic process and deliver advice.

Information. Data that has been processed and organized into output that is meaningful to the person who receives it. Information can be mandatory, essential, or discretionary.

Information Center (IC). A department or division in a company with the purpose of facilitating, coordinating, and controlling end-user activities and support.

Information Overload. The state in which additional information cannot be used efficiently and has no marginal value.

Information Processing. The process of turning data into information. This process has four stages: data input, data processing, data storage, and information output.

Information System. An organized way of collecting, processing, managing, and reporting information so that an organization can achieve its objectives and goals. A formal information system has an explicit responsibility to produce information. In contrast, an informal information system is one that arises out of a need that is not satisfied by a formal channel. It operates without a formal assignment of responsibility.

Information Systems (IS) Audit. Reviews the general and application controls of an accounting information system to assess its compliance with internal control policies and procedures and its effectiveness in safeguarding assets.

Inherent Risk. The susceptibility of a set of accounts or transactions to significant control problems in the absence of internal control.

Initial Investigation. A preliminary investigation to determine whether a proposed new system is both needed and possible.

Input. Data entered into the computer system either from an external storage device or from the keyboard of the computer.

Input Controls. Controls that ensure only accurate, valid, and authorized data is entered into the system.

Input Controls Matrix. A matrix that shows the control procedures applied to each field of an input record.

Input Device. Hardware used to enter data into a computer system.

Input Validation Routines. Computer programs or routines designed to check the validity or accuracy of input data.

Input/Output Bound. Describes a system that can process data faster than it can receive input and send output. Consequently, the processor has to wait on the input and output devices.

Inquiry Processing. Processing user information queries by searching master files for the desired information and then organizing the information into an appropriate response.

Insert Anomaly. A problem that can arise in a poorly designed relational data base, when attributes that are not characteristics of the primary key of a relation are stored in that table. The problem is that new information about those attributes cannot be entered in the data base without violating the integrity rules. For example, assume that information about vendors is only stored as part of the purchases table. Data about potential new vendors, or about alternative suppliers, could not be added until a purchase from them was made. Otherwise, the purchase order # column, the primary key of the purchases table, would have a null value, violating the entity integrity rule.

Integrated CASE. A software package that combines upper and lower CASE tools, linked by the data repository.

Integrated Circuits. Small silicon chips that contain the circuitry used by the computer.

Integrated Services Digital Network (ISDN). An extensive digital network with built-in intelligence to permit all types of data (voice, data, images, facsimile, video, etc.) to be sent over the same line.

Integrated Test Facility. A testing technique in which a dummy company or division is introduced into the company's computer system. Test transactions may then be conducted on these fictitious master records without affecting the real master records. These test transactions may be processed along with the real transactions, and the employees of the computer facility need not be aware that testing is being done.

Integration. The combining of subsystems.

Integrity. Protecting data from unauthorized tampering.

Interface. The common boundary between two pieces of hardware or between two computer systems. It is the point at which the two systems communicate with each other.

Interface Devices. Devices used by computer systems to communicate with each other. Examples include modems, hubs, and network interface cards.

Internal Control. Controls within a business organization that ensure information is processed correctly.

Internal Control Flowcharts. A type of flowchart that shows the internal control structure of a company. Often used by auditors in the planning stage of an audit.

Internal Control Structure. The plan of organization and all the coordinate methods and measures adopted within a business to safeguard its assets, check the accuracy and reliability of its accounting data, promote operational efficiency, and encourage adherence to prescribed managerial policies.

Internal Labels. Labels written in machine-readable form on a magnetic storage medium (e.g., tape, disk) that identify the data contained on the storage medium. Internal labels include volume, header, and trailer labels.

Internal Rate of Return (IRR). The effective interest rate that equates the present value of the total costs to the present value of the total savings.

Internal-Level Schema. A low-level view of the entire data base, describing how the data is actually stored and accessed, including information about pointers, indexes, record lengths, and so forth. Contrast with *external-level schema* and *conceptual-level schema.*

Internet. An international network of independently owned computers that operate as a giant, seamless computing network. No one owns it and no single organization controls its use. Data are not centrally stored but are stored on computers called web servers.

Internet Misinformation. Using the Internet to spread false or misleading information.

Internet Service Providers (ISPs). Companies that provide connections to the Internet for individuals and other companies. Major ISPs include MCI, GTE, and Sprint.

Internet Terrorism. Crackers using the Internet to disrupt electronic commerce and destroy company and individual communications.

Interpreter. A program that, one statement at a time, translates the source language into machine code and then executes it. Contrast with *compilers.*

Intranet. An internal network that can connect to the main Internet and be navigated with simple browser software. It is usually closed off from the general public.

Inventory Control. The function of determining what, when, and how much inventory to purchase.

Inverted File. A file containing inverted lists for selected attributes.

Inverted List. A method for organizing records in a database. An inverted list has an index containing pointers to each record.

Job-Order Costing. A cost system that assigns costs to specific production batches, or jobs; it is used whenever the product or service being sold can be distinctly identified.

Job-Time Ticket. A document used to collect data about labor activity, recording the amount of time a worker spends on each specific job task.

Journal Voucher. Form that is used to summarize a group of transactions. For example, a group of documents would be gathered and their total entered on the journal voucher.

Joystick. An input device consisting of a stick that can be tilted in any direction to position the cursor on a graphics screen. A joystick is usually used in conjunction with a computer game.

Just-in-Time (JIT) Inventory System. A system that minimizes or virtually eliminates manufacturing inventories by scheduling inventory deliveries at the precise times and locations needed. Instead of making infrequent bulk deliveries to a central receiving and storage facility, suppliers deliver materials in small lots at frequent intervals to the specific locations that require them.

Key. A unique identification code assigned to each data record within a system.

Key Verification. A way to check the accuracy of data entry by having two people enter the same data using a key-operated device. The computer then compares the two sets of keystrokes to determine if the data was entered correctly.

Key-to-Disk Encoder. Several keying stations are linked to a minicomputer that has an attached disk memory. Data may be entered simultaneously from each of the keying stations and pooled on the disk file.

Key-to-Tape-Encoder. A device for keying in data and recording the data on magnetic tape.

Kickbacks. Gifts given by vendors to purchasing agents for the purpose of influencing their choice of suppliers.

Kilobyte (K). 1,024 bytes of memory capacity. K is usually expressed in terms of 1,000 characters of memory; that is, 64K represents approximately 64,000 characters of memory.

Kiting. Fraud scheme where the perpetrator covers up a theft of cash by creating cash through the transfer of money between banks.

Knowledge Acquisition Facility. A component of an expert system. It is used to enter knowledge and expertise into the knowledge base.

Knowledge Base. A component of an expert system that includes data, knowledge, relationships, rules of thumb (heuristics), and decision rules used by experts to solve a particular type of problem.

Knowledge Engineering. The process of building a knowledge base. It involves both a human expert and a knowledge engineer.

LAN. See *local area network.*

LAN Interface. The hardware device that interfaces between the local area network (LAN) cable and the hardware devices (computers, printers, etc.) connected to the LAN.

Language Translator. A software program that is used to convert instructions written in a programming language into machine language. There are three types: assemblers, compilers, and translators.

Lapping. Concealing a cash shortage by means of a series of delays in posting collections to accounts.

Legal Feasibility. The dimension of feasibility that determines if there will be any conflicts between the system under consideration and the organization's ability to discharge its legal obligations.

Light Pens. Pencil-shaped devices that use photoelectric circuitry to enter data through the video display terminal of the computer system. Their principal use is in graphics applications.

Limit Check. An edit check to ensure that a numerical amount in a record does not exceed some predetermined limit.

Line Count. Total number of lines entered during a data processing session.

Line-Sharing Device. A device that combines the data from several terminals or computers and sends the data over a single line to the host computer.

Linked List. A method for organizing records in a database. Each record includes a pointer field containing the address of the next record on the list.

Local Area Network (LAN). A network that links together microcomputers, disk drives, word processors, printers, and other equipment that is located within a limited geographical area, such as one building.

Lockbox. A postal address to which customers send their remittances. This post office box is maintained by the participating bank, which picks up the checks several times each day and deposits them to the company's account. The bank then sends the remittance advices, an electronic list of all remittances, and photocopies of all checks to the company.

Logic Errors. Errors that occur when the instructions given to the computer do not accomplish the desired objective. Contrast with *syntax errors.*

Logic Time Bomb. A program that lies idle until some specified circumstance or a particular time triggers it. Once triggered, the bomb sabotages the system by destroying programs or data.

Logical Access. The ability to use computer equipment to access company data.

Logical Design. The third stage in the data base design process. It entails completing the external-level schemas and translating the data requirements of different users and application programs into the conceptual-level schema.

Logical Models. Descriptions of a system that focus on the essential activities and flow of information in the system, irrespective of how the flow is actually accomplished.

Logical View. The manner in which users conceptually organize, view, and understand the relationships among data items. Contrast with *physical view.*

Logistics Management. The planning and control of the physical flow of materials through an organization, through purchasing, inventory management, and production management.

Machine Language. Binary code that can be interpreted by the internal circuitry of the computer.

Machine-Independent Language. A programming language that can be used on many different types of computer platforms. The language does not depend on the type of computer being used.

Macro. (1) A series of keystrokes or commands that can be given a name, stored, and activated each time the keystrokes must be repeated. (2) A programming command.

Magnetic Disks. Magnetic storage media consisting of one or more flat round disks with a magnetic surface on which data can be written.

Magnetic Ink Character Recognition (MICR). The recognition of characters printed by a machine that uses a special magnetic ink.

Magnetic Stripe. Found on debit, credit, and ID cards; used to store information such as name, address, and account number.

Magnetic Tape. A secondary storage medium that is about 1/2 inch in width and that has a magnetic surface on which data can be stored. The most popular types are seven-track and nine-track tapes.

Main Memory. The internal memory directly controlled by the CPU, which usually consists of the ROM and RAM of the computer.

Mainframe Computers. (1) Same as CPU. (2) Large-size digital computers, typically with a separate stand-alone CPU. They are larger than minicomputers.

Management Audit. A review of how well management is utilizing company resources and how well company operations and programs follow established objectives and are being carried out as planned.

Management by Exception. A method for interpreting variances displayed on performance reports. If the performance report shows actual performance to be at or near budgeted figures, a manager can assume that the item is under control and that no action needs to be taken. On the other hand, significant deviations from budgeted amounts, in *either* direction, signal the need to investigate the cause of the discrepancy and take whatever action is appropriate to correct the problem.

Management Control. Activities by management designed to motivate, encourage, and assist officers and employees to achieve corporate goals and objectives as effectively and efficiently as possible and observe corporate policies.

Management Information System (MIS). The set of human and capital resources within an organization that is responsible for collecting and processing data so that all levels of management have the information they need to plan and control the activities of the organization.

Manual Information System. Information system in which most of the data processing load is completed by people without the use of computers.

Manufacturing Overhead. All manufacturing costs that are not economically feasible to trace directly to specific jobs or processes.

Manufacturing Resource Planning (MRP-II). A comprehensive, computerized planning and control system for manufacturing operations. It is an enhancement of Materials Requirements Planning that incorporates capacity planning for factory work centers and scheduling of production operations.

Mapping Programs. Programs activated during regular processing that provide information as to which portions of the application program were not executed.

Masquerading. Describes the activity of a perpetrator who gains access to a system by pretending to be an authorized user. This approach requires that the perpetrator know the legitimate user's identification numbers and passwords.

Massively Parallel Processing (MPP). Performing multiple processing tasks at the same time. MPP is made possible by linking multiple microprocessors.

Master File. A permanent file of records that reflects the current status of relevant business items such as inventory and accounts receivable. The master file is updated with the latest transactions from the current transaction file.

Master Plan. A document specifying the overall information system plan of an organization.

Master Production Schedule (MPS). The schedule that specifies how much of each product is to be produced during the planning period, and when that production should occur.

Materiality. The concept that an auditor should focus on detecting and reporting only those errors, deficiencies, and omissions that could have a significant impact on decisions.

Materials Requirements Planning (MRP). An approach to inventory management that seeks to reduce required inventory levels by *scheduling* production to meet sales forecast demands, rather than *estimating* needs.

Materials Requisition. Authorizes the removal of the necessary quantity of raw materials from the storeroom to the factory location in which production operations are to begin.

Maximum Cardinality. The second symbol in a cardinality pair next to an entity in the REA data model. It represents the maximum number of occurrences on the other side of the relationship that can be linked to each occurrence on the entity's side.

Megabyte (M). One million characters of data.

Megahertz (MHz). One million computer cycles per second.

Memory Unit. The part of the CPU where data and instructions are stored internally.

Menu. A list of computer commands or options that is displayed by a program. The user chooses the option that will cause the desired action to take place.

Message. (1) The data transmitted over a data communications system. (2) The instructions that are given to an object in object-oriented languages.

Microcomputers. Small computer systems anywhere from a "computer on a chip" to a system that covers a desk top. Often called a personal or desktop computer, this type of computer usually sells for less than $5,000.

Microprocessor. A large scale or very large scale integrated circuit on a silicon chip. Some of the more common microprocessors in use are the 8088, 8086, 80286, 80386, 80486, Pentium (80586), Z80, 68000, and 8080.

Microsecond. One-millionth of a second.

Millisecond. One-thousandth of a second.

Minicomputers. Digital computers that usually are larger than microcomputers but smaller than mainframe computers. They have a higher performance, a more powerful instruction set, higher prices, more input/output capability, a greater variety of programming languages, and a more powerful operating system than a microcomputer does. However, they have less of the above than a mainframe computer does.

Minimum Cardinality. The first symbol in the cardinality pair next to an entity in the REA data model. It represents the minimum number of occurrences on the other side of the relationship that need to be linked to each occurrence on the entity's side.

MIPS. Millions of instructions per second. Unit for measuring CPU speed.

Misappropriation of Assets. See *employee fraud.*

Modem. Modulator/demodulator. A communications device that converts the computer's digital signals into analog signals that can be sent over phone lines. The modem can be internal (mounted on a board within the computer) or external (a freestanding unit).

Modified Canned Software. Canned software that has been modified to meet the particular needs of the user.

Modular Conversion. An approach for converting from an old system to a new system in which parts of the old system are gradually replaced by the new until the old system has been entirely replaced.

Monitor. (1) A video display unit or CRT. (2) Software that controls how a system operates.

Monthly Statement. A document summarizing all transactions that occurred during the past month and informing customers of their current account balance.

Mosaic. A GUI program that uses menus to help users navigate the Internet by pointing and clicking a mouse on a highlighted piece of text, causing a jump from one web server to another.

Motherboard. The main circuit board of a microcomputer. It usually contains the memory, the CPU, and the input/output circuitry.

Mouse. A small device that is connected to a computer, usually by a cord. When the user moves the mouse, the movement is translated into a movement of the screen's cursor; the user issues a command by pressing a button on the mouse when the cursor is positioned on the desired command.

Move Tickets. Documents that identify the internal transfer of parts, the location to which they are transferred, and the time of the transfer.

MS-DOS. An acronym for MicroSoft/Disk Operating System, the operating system used by IBM and many IBM-compatible microcomputers.

Multiattribute Search File Organization. A file organization scheme that allows data records to be accessed by means of secondary keys. Examples include linked lists and inverted lists.

Multidrop Lines. Communications channel configurations in which most terminals are linked together, with only one or a few terminals linked directly to the CPU.

Multimedia. Computer-based applications that combine text, 3-D graphics, full-screen video, sound, and animation.

Multiplexor. A communications device that combines signals from several sources and sends them out over a single line. Multiplexors can also split the signals back into the individual messages.

Multiprocessing. The simultaneous execution of two or more tasks, usually by two or more processing units that are part of the same system.

Multiprogramming. Switching execution back and forth between two or more programs so that the processing unit seems to be executing them simultaneously.

Multitasking. Processing several jobs on a computer at the same time. Multitasking is possible in the Windows 95 environment, for example.

Mutual Authentication Scheme. A routing verification procedure that requires both computers to exchange their passwords before communication takes place.

Nanosecond. One-billionth of a second.

Narrative Description. Written, step-by-step explanation of the system components and how these components interact.

Narrowband Lines. Phone lines designed to accept data transmissions of up to 300 bits per second. This type of line is not suitable for transmitting audible or voicelike signals.

Natural Languages. Fourth-generation languages that closely resemble English.

Net Present Value (NPV). A value determined by discounting all estimated future cash flows back to the present, using a discount rate that reflects the time value of money to the organization.

Netscape. A GUI program that uses menus to help users navigate the Internet by pointing and clicking a mouse on a highlighted piece of text, causing a jump from one web server to another.

Network. (1) A group of interconnected computers and terminals; a series of locations tied together by communications channels. (2) A data structure involving relationships among multiple record types.

Network Administrator. One who installs, manages, and supports a LAN. The network administrator also controls access to the system and maintains the shared software and data.

Network Interface Card (NIC). The device needed to connect a computer or peripheral to a data communications network.

Network Switching. The routing of all data and messages through a central computer for forwarding to the correct location.

Neural Networks. Computing systems that imitate the brain's learning process by using a network of interconnected processors that perform multiple operations simultaneously and inter-

act dynamically. Neural networks recognize and understand voice, face, and word patterns much more successfully than do regular computers and humans.

Nonimpact Printers. Printers that transfer images without striking the paper. The most common are laser printers.

Nonoperational (or **Throwaway**) **Prototypes.** Prototypes that are discarded, while the system requirements identified from the prototypes are used to develop a new system.

Nonvoucher System. A method for processing accounts payable in which each approved invoice is posted to individual vendor records in the accounts payable file and is then stored in an open-invoice file. Contrast with *voucher system.*

Normalization. The process of following the guidelines for properly designing a relational data base that is free from delete, insert, and update anomalies.

Object. An element of data and a set of instructions that specify the actions that are to be performed on the data. Used in object-oriented languages.

Object Program. A compiled or assembled machine-level program that can be executed by the computer. The source program and the translator are inputs to the computer translation process, and the output is the machine-executable object program.

Object-Oriented Data Model. An data model in which the basic conceptual building blocks are objects, rather than tables. An object is a reusable segment of program code that not only describes a data element, but also contains instructions on how to manipulate that data. For example, the sales invoice object would not only store information about a particular sales transaction, but would also include instructions on how to (1) calculate extensions for each line item, (2) add sales tax to arrive at the total, and (3) update the appropriate customer account.

Object-Oriented Language (OOL). A programming language in which the user selects objects instead of writing procedural code. Each object can then be modified, reused, or copied. The objects are then sent messages telling them what to do.

Object-Oriented Programming (OOP). A programming method that involves linking different objects (see *object*) and writing only a small amount of code.

Off-Line Devices. Devices that are not connected to or controlled by the main CPU. Off-line devices are usually used to prepare data for entry into the computer system (e.g., key-to-tape encoder, keypunch/verification equipment). Contrast with *on-line devices.*

On-Line Analytical Processing (OLAP). Tools that provide access to information stored in a data warehouse by using queries to investigate hypothesized relationships.

On-Line Batch Processing. Processing in which a computer captures the data electronically and stores it so that it can be processed later.

On-Line Devices. Hardware devices that are connected directly to the CPU by cable or telephone line (e.g., CRT terminal, disk drive).

On-Line Processing. Processing individual transactions as they occur and from their point of origin rather than accumulating them to be processed in batches. On-line processing requires the use of on-line data entry terminals and direct access file storage media so that each master record can be accessed directly.

On-Line, Real-Time Processing. Processing in which a computer system processes data immediately after it is captured and provides updated information to the user on a timely basis. On-line, real-time processing usually entails one of two forms of processing: on-line updating and inquiry processing.

Open-Invoice Method. Method for maintaining accounts receivable in which customers typically pay according to each invoice. Usually, two copies of the invoice are mailed to the customer, who is requested to return one copy along with the payment.

Operating Budget. A report that projects an organization's revenues and expenses for a given time period, usually a month or a year. Typically, operating budgets are structured along the lines of financial statements.

Operating Documentation. All information required by a computer operator to run a program, including the equipment configuration used, variable data to be entered on the computer console, and descriptions of conditions leading to program halts and related corrective actions.

Operating Environment. A software program that runs on top of the operating system to provide the system with desirable enhancements. For example, Microsoft's Windows is an operating environment that runs on top of DOS.

Operating System. A software program that controls the overall operation of a computer system. Its functions include controlling the execution of computer programs, scheduling, debugging, assigning storage areas, managing data, and controlling input and output.

Operational Audit. See *management audit.*

Operational Control. Decisions that are concerned with the efficient and effective performance of specific tasks in an organization.

Operational Document. A document that is generated as an output of transaction processing activities. Examples include purchase orders, customer statements, and employee paychecks. Contrast with *source documents.*

Operational Feasibility. The dimension of feasibility concerned with whether a proposed system will be used by the people in an organization. It also is concerned with how useful the system will be within the operating environment of the organization.

Operational Prototypes. Prototypes that are further developed into fully functional systems.

Operations and Maintenance Phase. The last phase of the system development life cycle, where follow-up studies are conducted to detect and correct design deficiencies. Minor modifications will be made as problems arise in the new system.

Operations List. A document that specifies the labor and machine requirements needed to manufacture the product. Also referred to as a routing sheet because it indicates how a product moves through the factory, specifying what is done at each step and how much time each operation should take.

Opportunity. The condition or situation that allows a person to commit and conceal a dishonest act.

Optical Character Recognition (OCR). The use of light-sensitive hardware devices to convert characters readable by humans into computer input. Since OCR readers can read only certain items, a special machine-readable font must be used.

Optical Disk. A mass storage medium that can store billions of bits. Lasers are used to write to and read from an optical disk.

Ordering Costs. Include all expenses associated with processing purchase transactions.

Output. The information produced by a system. Output is typically produced for the use of a particular individual or group of users.

Output Controls. Controls that regulate system output.

Outsourcing. Hiring an outside company to handle all or part of the data processing activities.

Packing Slip. A document identifying the contents of the shipment.

Parallel Conversion. A systems conversion approach in which the new and old systems are run simultaneously until the organization is assured that the new system is functioning correctly.

Parallel Interface. A way of connecting peripherals (such as a printer) to a computer. Data is transferred simultaneously along several parallel cables at the same time.

Parallel Port. A communications interface that allows data to be transmitted a whole character (eight bits) at a time. Contrast with *serial port.*

Parallel Processing. Performing two or more processing tasks simultaneously within a single CPU.

Parallel Simulation. An approach auditors use to detect unauthorized program changes and data processing accuracy. The auditor writes his or her own version of a program and then reprocesses data. The outputs of the auditor's program and the client's program are compared to verify that they are the same.

Parallel Transmission. The transmission of data in groups of two or more bits. Contrast with *serial transmission.*

Parity Bit. An extra bit added to a byte, character, or word. The parity bit is magnetized as needed to ensure that there is always an odd (or even) number of magnetized bits. The computer uses the odd (or even) parity scheme to check the accuracy of each item of data.

Parity Checking. As a computer reads or receives a set of characters, it sums the number of 1-bits in each character to verify that it is an even number. If not, the corresponding character must contain an error.

Password. A series of letters, numbers, or both that must be entered in order to access and use system resources. Password use helps prevent unauthorized tampering with hardware, software, and the organization's data.

Password Cracking. Using illicit means to steal a file containing passwords and then using them.

Payback Period. The number of years required for the net savings to equal the initial cost of the investment.

Payroll Clearing Account. A general ledger account used to check the accuracy and completeness of recording payroll costs and their subsequent allocation to appropriate cost centers.

Payroll Register. A listing of payroll data for each employee for the current payroll period.

Payroll Service Bureau. An organization that maintains the payroll master file for each of its clients and performs their payroll processing activities for a fee.

Performance Evaluations. A project development control that requires evaluating each module or task as it is completed.

Performance Report. Lists the budgeted and actual amounts of revenues and expenses and also shows the variances, or differences, between these two amounts. Used for financial control. Contrast with *budget.*

Peripherals. The hardware devices (such as those used for input, output, processing, and data communications) that are connected to the CPU.

Personal Computer (PC). See *microcomputers.*

Personal Digital Assistant (PDA). A new type of handheld computer that is expected to have a significant impact on personal productivity.

Personal Identification Number (PIN). A confidential code, known only to an individual and a financial institution, that allows the individual to conduct banking transactions at automated teller machines.

Personal Information Manager. Software that helps end users organize their daily activities. Some components are a calendar, calculator, electronic notepad, electronic name and address system, e-mail, and a to-do list.

Personal Information System. One type of information system where individuals use a personal computer, data they have created and stored themselves, and corporate data to meet their own personal information needs.

PERT (Program Evaluation and Review Technique). A commonly used technique for planning, coordinating, controlling, and scheduling complex projects such as systems implementation.

Phase-In Conversion. See *modular conversion.*

Phreaker. A hacker who attacks phone systems.

Physical Access. Ability to physically use computer equipment.

Physical Design. (1) A phase of the system development life cycle where the broad, user-oriented requirements of the conceptual design are implemented by creating a detailed set of specifications that are used to code and test the computer programs. (2) The fourth stage of the data base design process. It consists of taking the conceptual design and converting it into physical storage structures.

Physical Model. The description of physical aspects of a data base (e.g., field and file sizes, storage and access methods, security procedures).

Physical Possession Identification. A method of identifying people by what an item they physically possess, such as an ID card.

Physical Systems Design. The phase of the systems development life cycle in which the designer specifies the hardware, software, and procedures for delivering the conceptual systems design.

Physical Systems Design Report. Report that is prepared at the end of the physical design phase; it describes the system. Management uses this report to decide whether or not to proceed to the implementation phase.

Physical View. The way data are physically arranged and stored on disks, tapes, and other storage media. Electronic data processing personnel use this view to make efficient use of storage and processing resources. Contrast with *logical view.*

Picking Ticket. A document authorizing the release of merchandise to the shipping department. The picking ticket is often printed so that the item numbers and quantities are listed in the sequence in which they can be most efficiently retrieved from the warehouse.

Picosecond. One-trillionth (10^{-12}) of a second.

Piggybacking. When a perpetrator latches on to a legitimate user that is logging into a system. The legitimate user unknowingly carries the perpetrator with him/her as he/she is allowed into the system.

Pilot Conversion. The implementation of a system in just one part of the organization, such as a branch location. This approach localizes conversion problems and allows training in a live environment. Disadvantages are the long conversion times and the need to interface the old system with the new system.

Pixel. The smallest particle of information that appears on a monitor's screen. The greater the number of pixels displayed, the better the monitor's resolution.

Plotter. A hard-copy output device that produces drawings and other graphical output by moving an ink pen across a page.

Plug and Play. A feature, found in newer operating systems, that identifies and configures the OS and the hardware so that the PC, peripherals, and software work together with minimal effort on the user's part.

Point Scoring. An objective procedure in which weighted selection criteria are used to evaluate the overall merits of vendor proposals.

Pointer Field. The field containing the address of the next record in a linked list.

Point-of-Sale (POS) Recorders. Electronic devices that function as both a terminal and a cash register. They are used commonly in retail stores to record sales information at the time of the sale and to perform other data processing functions.

Point-to-Point Lines. Communications channel configurations that use a separate line between each terminal and the central computer.

Policy and Procedures Manual. A management tool for assigning authority and responsibility. It details management's policy for handling specific transactions.

Post-billing System. A system in which invoices are prepared *after* confirmation that the items were shipped. Contrast with *pre-billing system.*

Postimplementation Review. Review made after a new system has been operating for a brief period. The purpose of this review is to ensure that the new system is meeting its planned objectives, identify the adequacy of system standards, and review system controls.

Postimplementation Review Report. A report that analyzes a newly delivered system to determine whether the system achieved its intended purpose and was completed within budget.

Pre-billing System. A system in which invoices are prepared (but not sent) as soon as the order is approved (i.e., after credit has been approved and inventory availability checked). Contrast with *post-billing system.*

Preformatting. An on-line data entry control in which the computer displays a form on the screen and the user fills in the blanks in the form as needed.

Pressure. A person's motivation for committing a fraud.

Preventive Controls. A control system that places restrictions on and requires documentation of employee activities so as to reduce the occurrence of errors and deviations. Because preventive controls operate from within the process being controlled, they are perhaps the type of control most consistent with the original meaning of the term internal control.

Preventive Maintenance. A program of regularly examining the hardware components of a computer and replacing any that are found to be weak.

Primary Activities. Activities in the value chain that are performed to create, market, and deliver products and services to customers and provide post-delivery service and support. Primary activities include production, shipping and receiving, and marketing.

Primary Key. A unique identification code assigned to each record within a system. The primary key is the key used most frequently to distinguish, order, and reference records.

Primary Memory. See *memory unit.*

Printer. An output device that produces a hard copy of computer output.

Private Branch Exchange (PBX). Special-purpose computer that manages a company's telephone network.

Private Key System. An encryption system in which both the sender and the receiver have access to the key but do not allow others access to the same key.

Procedure-Oriented Language. A high-level language such as COBOL or FORTRAN, in which the programmer must specify the logic necessary to accomplish a specific task.

Process. A set of actions, automated or manual, that transforms data into other data or information.

Process Costing. A cost system that assigns costs to each process, or work center, in the production cycle, and then calculates the average cost for all units produced. Process costing is used whenever masses of similar goods or services are sold.

Processing Controls. Controls that ensure that all transactions are processed accurately and completely and that all files and records are properly updated.

Processing of Test Transactions. Running hypothetical transactions through a new system to test for processing errors.

Production Cycle. The recurring set of business activities and related data processing operations associated with the manufacture of products.

Production Order. A document authorizing the manufacture of a specified quantity of a particular product. It lists the operations that need to be performed, the quantity to be produced, and the location to which the finished product is to be delivered.

Productive Capacity. The maximum number of units that can be produced using current technology.

Productive Processing Time. The percentage of total production time that was actually used to manufacture the product.

Profitability Analysis. Reports used to assess overall marketing performance by breaking down the marginal profit contribution made by each territory, customer, distribution channel, salesperson, product, or other basis. Contrast with *sales analyses.*

Program. A set of instructions that can be executed by a computer.

Program Flowchart. A diagrammatic representation of the logic and sequence of processes used in a computer program.

Program Generators. Computer programs designed to speed up the process of writing programs. The user specifies certain information, such as what the screen layouts should look like and what processing procedures need to be performed, and the program generates program instructions.

Program Maintenance. The revision of a computer program in order to meet new program instructions, satisfy system demands such as the need for a new report, correct an error, or make changes in file content.

Program Tracing. A technique used to obtain detailed knowledge of the logic of an application program, as well as to test the program's compliance with its control specifications.

Program–Data Independence. The separation of the logical and physical views of data. Because of this separation, the way a computer stores data does not affect the way a user views or manipulates the data.

Programming Language. The language the programmer uses to write a computer program (e.g., COBOL, BASIC, PASCAL, LOGO).

Project Development Plan. A proposal to develop a particular computer system application. It contains an analysis of the requirements and expectations of the proposed application.

Project Development Team. A group of people consisting of specialists, management, and users that develop a project's plan and direct the steps of the systems life cycle. The team monitors costs, progress, employees, and gives status reports to top management and to the steering committee.

Project Management Software. A software program that is used to plan, schedule, track, control, and evaluate projects to ensure they are completed within the budget and on time.

Project Milestones. Significant points in a development effort at which a formal review of progress is made.

Projection. Resisting change by blaming anything and everything on the new system. The system becomes the scapegoat for all real and imagined problems and errors.

Prompting. An on-line data entry control that uses the computer to control the data entry process. The system displays a request to the user for each required item of input data and then waits for an acceptable response before requesting the next required item.

Proposal to Conduct Systems Analysis. A document calling for the analysis of either an existing or a proposed system. This document is prepared by a user or department, requesting the information systems function to analyze the feasibility of developing a system to perform a specific function.

Protocol. The set of rules governing the exchange of data between two systems or components of a system.

Prototype. A simplified working model of an information system used in prototyping.

Prototyping. An approach to systems design in which a simplified working model, or prototype, of an information system is developed. The users experiment with the prototype to determine what they like and do not like about the system. The developers make modifications until the users are satisfied with the system.

Pseudocode. An informal design language oriented toward structured programming. It uses English language phrases to describe the processing logic of a computer program.

Public Data Bases. Electronic libraries containing millions of items of data that can be reviewed, retrieved, analyzed, and saved by the general public.

Public Key System. An encryption system that uses two separate keys: a public key that is available to everyone and a private key known only to the user.

Purchase Order. A document that formally requests a vendor to sell and deliver specified products at designated prices. It is also a promise to pay and becomes a contract once it is accepted by the vendor.

Purchase Requisition. A document that identifies the requisitioner; specifies the delivery location and date needed; identifies the item numbers, descriptions, quantity and price of each item requested; and may suggest a vendor.

Query. A request for specific information from a computer. Queries are often used with a data base management system to extract data from the data base.

Query Languages. Languages used to process data files and to obtain quick responses to questions about those files.

Query-by-Example (QBE) Languages. Graphical query languages for retrieving information from a relational data base.

Radio Frequency Data Communication. The transmission of data through air waves rather than through wires.

Radio Frequency Identification. The use of tags that track data from one location to another by sending and receiving radio signals.

Random Access Memory (RAM). A temporary storage location for computer instructions and data. RAM may have data both written to it and read from it.

Random Surveillance. Way of detecting fraud by having auditors periodically audit the system and test system controls. Informing employees that the auditors will conduct random surveillance is a deterrent to computer crime.

Range Check. An edit check designed to verify that a data item falls within a certain predetermined range of acceptable values.

Rationalization. The excuse that fraud perpetrators use to justify their illegal behavior.

REA Data Model. A data model developed explicitly for use in designing AIS data bases. The name *REA* is an acronym signifying that the data model contains information about three fundamental types of objects: resources, events, and agents. Resources represent identifiable objects that have economic value to the organization. Events represent all of an organization's business activities. Agents represent the people or organizations about which data is collected.

Read Only Memory (ROM). Internal CPU memory that can be read but usually may not be changed.

Real-Time Notification. A variation of the embedded audit module in which the auditor is notified of each transaction as it occurs by means of a message printed on the auditor's terminal.

Real-Time System. A system that can respond to an inquiry or provide data fast enough to make the information meaningful to the user. Real-time systems are usually designed for very fast response.

Reasonable Assurance. The concept that an auditor cannot seek complete assurance that an item is correct, since to do so would be prohibitively expensive. Instead, the auditor accepts a reasonable degree of risk that the audit conclusion is incorrect.

Reasonableness Test. An edit check of the logical correctness of relationships among the values of data items on an input record and the corresponding file record. For example, a journal entry that debits inventory and credits wages payable is not reasonable.

Receiving Report. A document that records details about each delivery, including the date received, shipper, vendor, and purchase order number.

Record. A set of logically related data items that describe specific attributes of an entity, such as all payroll data relating to a single employee.

Record Count. A total of the number of input documents to a process or the number of records processed in a run.

Record Layout. A document that illustrates the arrangement of items of data in input, output, and file records.

Recovery Procedures. A set of procedures that is followed if the computer quits in the middle of processing a batch of data. The procedures allow the user to recover from hardware or software failures.

Redundant Data Check. An edit check that requires the inclusion of two identifiers in each input record (e.g., the customer's account number and the first five letters of the customers name). If these input values do not match those on the record, the record will not be updated.

Reengineering. The thorough analysis and complete redesign of all business processes and information systems to achieve dramatic performance improvements. Reengineering seeks to reduce a company to its essential business processes.

Referential Integrity Rule. A constraint in relational data base design requiring that any nonnull value of a foreign key must correspond to a primary key in the referenced table. For example, if vendor number is a foreign key in the inventory table, to indicate the preferred source of that item, then any vendor number appearing in that table must appear as a primary key value in the vendor table. This constraint ensures consistency in the data base. Note, however, that the foreign key can be null, if there is no existing relationship between the two tables. For example, a null value for vendor number in any row in the inventory table would indicate that there is no preferred vendor for that inventory item.

Relational Data Base. A data base model in which all data elements are logically viewed as being stored in the form of two-dimensional tables called relations. These tables are, in effect, flat files where each row represents a unique entity or record. Each column represents a field where the record's attributes are stored. The tables serve as the building blocks from which data relationships can be created.

Relations. The tables used to store data in a relational data base.

Remittance Advice. An enclosure included with a customer's payment that indicates the invoices, statements, or other items paid.

Remittance List. A document listing all checks received in the mail.

Remote Access Devices. Modem banks that act as gateways to the Internet or to private corporate networks. Their function is to properly route all incoming and outgoing connections.

Remote Batch Processing. Accumulating transaction records in batches at some remote location and then transmitting them electronically to a central location for processing.

Reorder Point. The level to which the inventory balance of an item must fall before an order to replenish stock is initiated.

Report. System output organized in a meaningful fashion. Used by employees to control operational activities, by managers to make decisions, and by investors and creditors. Prepared for both internal and external use.

Report File. A temporary file generated as an intermediate step in the preparation of a report.

Report Generators. Computer programs designed to make report writing easier and faster.

Report Writers. Software that lets a user specify the data elements to be printed. The report writer searches the database, extracts the desired items, and prints them out in the user-specified format.

Reprocessing. An approach auditors use to detect unauthorized program changes. The auditor verifies the integrity of an application program and then saves it for future use. At subsequent intervals, and on a surprise basis, the auditor uses the previously verified version of the program to reprocess data that have been processed by the version in current use by the company. The output of the two runs is compared and discrepancies are investigated.

Request for a Proposal (RFP). A request by an organization or department for vendors to bid on hardware, software, or services specified by the organization or department.

Request for Systems Development. A written request for a new or improved system. The request describes the current system's problems, why the change is needed, and the proposed system's goals and objectives as well as its anticipated benefits and costs.

Requirements Costing. A system evaluation method in which a list is made of all of the required features of the desired system. If a proposed system does not have a desired feature, the cost of developing or purchasing that feature is added to the basic cost of the system. This method allows different systems to be evaluated based on the costs of providing the required features.

Requirements Definition. The second step in the data base design process. It entails defining the scope of a proposed data base system, determining general hardware and software requirements, and identifying user information needs.

Resolution. Describes the density and overall quality of the video display on a terminal or monitor.

Resources. Those things that have economic value to an organization, such as cash, inventory, supplies, factories, and land.

Response Time. The amount of time that elapses between making a query and receiving a response.

Responsibility Accounting. A system of reporting financial results on the basis of managerial responsibilities within an organization.

Revenue Cycle. The recurring set of business activities and related information processing operations associated with providing goods and services to customers and collecting cash in payment for those sales.

Ring Network. A configuration in which the data communications channels form a loop or circular pattern when the local processors are linked together. Contrast with *star network.*

Risk. The likelihood that a threat or hazard will actually come to pass.

Rollback. A process whereby a log of all preupdate values is prepared for each record that is updated within a particular interval. If there is then a system failure, the records can be restored to the preupdate values and the processing started over.

Rounding-Down Technique. A fraud technique used in financial institutions that pay interest. The programmer instructs the computer to round down all interest calculations to two decimal places. The fraction of a cent that was rounded down on each calculation is put into the programmer's own account.

Router. A communications interface device that connects two LANs of the same type.

Routing Sheet. See *operations list.*

Routing Verification Procedures. Controls to ensure that messages are not routed to the wrong system address. Examples are header labels, mutual authentication schemes, and dial-back.

Sabotage. An intentional act where the intent is to destroy a system or some of its components.

Salami Technique. A fraud technique where tiny slices of money are stolen from many different accounts.

Sales Analyses. Reports used to assess the efficiency and effectiveness of the sales by breaking down sales by salesperson, region, or product. Contrast with *profitability analysis.*

Sales Invoice. A document notifying customers of the amount to be paid and where to send payment.

Sales Order. The document created during sales order entry, listing the item numbers, quantities, prices, and terms of the sale.

Satellite Transmission. A data transmission system that transmits data from earth stations to satellites and back to earth again.

Scanning Routines. Software routines that search a program for the occurrence of a particular variable name or other combinations of characters.

SCARF (System Control Audit Review File). A concurrent audit technique that embeds audit modules into application software to continuously monitor all transaction activity and collect data on transactions having special audit significance.

Scavenging. The unauthorized access to confidential information by searching corporate records. Scavenging methods range from searching trash cans for printouts or carbon copies of confidential information to scanning the contents of computer memory.

Scheduled Reports. Reports that are generated by a system at specified time intervals.

Scheduling Feasibility. The dimension of feasibility that determines if the system being developed can be implemented in the time allotted.

Schema. A description of the types of data elements that are in the data base, the relationships among the data elements, and the structure or overall logical model used to organize and describe the data.

Secondary Key. A field that can be used to identify records in a file. Unlike the primary key, it does not provide a unique identification.

Secondary Storage. Storage media, such as magnetic disks or magnetic tape, on which data that are not currently needed by the computer can be stored. Also called auxiliary storage.

Security Measures and Controls. Controls that are built into an information system to ensure that the data is accurate and free from errors. Security measures also protect the data from unauthorized access.

Segregation of Duties. The separation of assigned duties and responsibilities in such a way that no single employee can both perpetrate and conceal errors or irregularities.

Semiconductor. A tiny silicon chip on which a number of miniature circuits have been inscribed.

Semistructured Decisions. Decisions that require subjective assessment and judgment to supplement formal data analysis.

Sequence Check. An edit check that determines whether a batch of input data is in the proper numerical or alphabetical sequence.

Sequential Access. An access method that requires data items to be accessed in the same order in which they were written.

Sequential File. A way of storing numeric or alphabetical records according to a key—for example, customer numbers from 00001 to 99999. To access a sequential file record, the system starts at the beginning of the file and reads each record until the desired record is located.

Sequential File Processing. Processing a master file sequentially from beginning to end. The master and transaction files are processed in the same predetermined order, such as alphabetically.

Serial Interface. Way of connecting peripherals (such as a printer) to a computer. Data are transferred along a single cable one bit at a time.

Serial Port. A communications interface that allows data to be sent only one bit at a time. Contrast with *parallel port.*

Serial Transmission. The transmission of data one bit at a time. Contrast with *parallel transmission.*

Server. High-capacity computer that contains the network software to handle communications, storage, and resource sharing needs of other computers in the network. The sever also contains the application software and data common to all users.

Service Bureau. An organization that provides data processing services on its own equipment to users for a fee.

Sign Check. An edit check that verifies that the data in a field have the appropriate arithmetic sign.

Simplex Channel. A data transmission channel that allows data transmissions in only one direction. Contrast with *half-duplex channel* and *full-duplex channel.*

Smart Cards. Plastic cards that contain a microprocessor, memory chips, and software; can store up to three pages of text. Used in Europe as a credit or ATM card.

Snapshot Technique. An audit technique that records the contents of both a transaction record and a related master file record before and after each processing step.

Social Engineering. Fraudulently gaining information to access a system by fooling an employee.

Software. A computer program that gives instructions to the CPU. Also used to refer to programming languages and computer systems documentation.

Software Agents. Computer programs that learn how to do often-performed, tedious, time-consuming, or complex tasks.

Software Piracy. The unauthorized copying of software.

Source Code (or **Source Program**). A computer program written in a source language such as BASIC, COBOL, or assembly language. The source program is translated into the object (machine language) program by a translation program such as a compiler or assembler.

Source Data Automation (SDA). The collection of transaction data in machine-readable form at the time and place of origin. Examples of SDA devices are optical scanners and automated teller machines.

Source Documents. Documents containing the initial record of a transaction that takes place. Examples of source documents, which are usually recorded on preprinted forms, include sales invoices, purchase orders, and employee time cards. Contrast with *operational document.*

Spamming. E-mailing the same message to everyone on one or more Usenet newsgroups or LISTSERV lists.

Specialized Journals. Specialized journals are used to simplify the process of recording large numbers of repetitive transactions. Specialized journals are most commonly used for the following types of transactions: credit sales, cash receipts, purchases on account, and cash disbursements.

Special-Purpose Analyses. Reports that have no prespecified content or format and are not prepared according to any regular schedule; rather, they are generally prepared in response to a management request to investigate a specific problem or opportunity.

Specific Authorization. Describes the situation in which an employee must get special approval before handling a transaction.

Star Network. A configuration in which there is a centralized real-time computer system to which all other computer systems are linked. Contrast with *ring network.*

Steering Committee. An executive-level committee to plan and oversee the information systems function. The committee typically consists of management from the systems department, the controller, and other management affected by the IS function.

Stockout Costs. The costs, such as lost sales or production delays, that result from inventory shortages.

Storage. Placement of data in internal memory or on a medium such as magnetic disk or magnetic tape, from which they can later be retrieved.

Strategic Planning. Decisions that establish the organization's objectives and the policies for accomplishing those objectives.

Stratified Sampling. A sampling approach in which a population is divided into two or more groups to which different selection criteria can be applied.

Structure Chart. A document showing the hierarchical organization of computer program modules. The idea is that each module should be able to be developed and tested independently of the other processing modules.

Structured Decisions. Decisions that are repetitive, routine, and understood well enough that they can be delegated to the lower-level employees of an organization.

Structured Programming. A modular approach to programming in which each module performs a specific function, stands alone, and is coordinated by a control module. Also referred to as "GOTO-less" programming, because modular design makes GOTO statements unnecessary.

Structured Query Language (SQL). The standard text-based query language provided by most, but not all, relational DBMS. Powerful queries can be built using three basic keywords: SELECT, FROM, and WHERE.

Structured Relationships. Relationships in the REA data model in which every event entity is linked to a resource entity and two agent entities.

Structured Walkthrough. A formal review process in program design in which one or more programmers walk through the logic and code of another programmer to detect weaknesses and errors in program design.

Stylus. A penlike device used to write directly on a computer screen.

Subschema. (1) A subset of the schema that includes only those data items used in a particular application program or by a particular user. (2) The way the user defines the data and the data relationships.

Subsidiary Ledgers. A ledger used to record all the detailed data for any general ledger account that has many individual subaccounts. Subsidiary ledgers are commonly used for accounts receivable, inventory, fixed assets, and accounts payable.

Subsystem. Smaller system that is a part of the entire information system. Each subsystem performs a specific function that is important to and that supports the system of which it is a part.

Supercomputers. Very large, high-speed computers used by businesses and organizations that have high-volume needs.

Superzapping. The use of a special system program to bypass regular system controls to perform unauthorized acts. A superzap utility was originally written to handle emergencies, such as restoring a system that has crashed.

Support Activities. Activities in the value chain that enable the primary activities to be performed efficiently and effectively. Examples include administration, purchasing, and human resources.

Suspense File. A file containing records that have been identified as erroneous or are of uncertain status.

Switch. Creates temporary point-to-point links between two nodes on a network.

Switched Line. A regular dial-up telephone line. The charges for line usage are usually based on the amount of time used and the length of line used.

Symbolic Language. A language in which each machine instruction is represented by symbols that bear some relation to the instruction. For example, the symbol "A" might represent the Add command.

Synchronous Transmission. Data transmission in which start and stop bits are required only at the beginning and end of a block of characters. Contrast with *asynchronous transmission.*

Syntax. The rules of grammar and structure that govern the use of a programming language.

Syntax Errors. Errors that result from using the programming language improperly or from incorrectly typing the source program. Contrast with *logic errors.*

System. (1) An entity consisting of two or more components or subsystems that interact to achieve a goal. (2) The equipment and programs that make up a complete computer installation. (3) The programs and related procedures that perform a single task on a computer.

System Flowchart. A diagrammatic representation that shows the flow of data through a series of operations in an automated data processing system. It shows how data are captured and input into the system, the processes that operate on the data, and system outputs.

System Review. A step in internal control evaluation in which it is determined whether the necessary control procedures have been prescribed.

Systems Analysis. (1) A rigorous and systematic approach to decision making, characterized by a comprehensive definition of available alternatives and an exhaustive analysis of the merits of each alternative as a basis for choosing the best alternative. (2) Examination of the user information requirements within an organization in order to establish objectives and specifications for the design of an information system.

Systems Analysis Report. Comprehensive report prepared at the end of the systems analysis and design phase that summarizes and documents the findings of analysis activities.

Systems Analysts. The people within an organization who are responsible for developing the company's information system. The analyst's job generally involves designing computer applications and preparing specifications for computer programming.

Systems Approach. Way of handling systems change by recognizing that every system must have an objective, a set of components, and a set of interrelationships among the components. The systems approach proceeds step by step, with a thorough exploration of all implications and alternatives at each step.

Systems Concept. A systems analysis principle that states that alternative courses of action within a system must be evaluated from the standpoint of the system as a whole rather than that of any single subsystem or set of subsystems.

Systems Design. The process of preparing detailed specifications for the development of a new information system.

Systems Development Life Cycle (SDLC). Six procedures and steps that a company goes through when it decides to design and implement a new system. The six steps are systems analysis, systems acquisition, conceptual design, physical design, implementation and conversion, and operation and maintenance.

Systems Documentation. A complete description of all aspects of each systems application, including narrative material, charts, and program listings.

Systems Implementation. The task of delivering a completed system to an organization for use in day-to-day operations.

Systems Software. Software that interfaces between the hardware and the application program. Systems software can be classified as operating systems, data base management systems, utility programs, language translators, and communications software.

Systems Survey. The systematic gathering of facts relating to the existing information system. This task is generally carried out by a systems analyst.

Systems Survey Report. The culmination of the systems survey. It contains documentation such as memos, interview and observation notes, questionnaire data, file and record layouts and descriptions, input and output descriptions, copies of documents, flowcharts, and data flow diagrams.

Table File. A file of reference data (generally numeric) that is retrieved during data processing to facilitate performing calculations or other processing tasks.

Tagging. An audit procedure in which certain records are marked with a special code before processing. During processing, all data relating to the marked records are captured and saved so that they can be verified later by the auditors.

Tape Drive. The device that controls the movement of the magnetic tape and that reads and writes on the tape.

Tape File Protection Ring. A circular plastic ring that determines when a tape file can be written on. When the ring is inserted on a reel of magnetic tape, data can be written on the tape. If the ring is removed, the data on the tape cannot be overwritten with new information.

Technical Feasibility. The dimension of feasibility concerned with whether a proposed system can be developed given the available technology.

Telecommunications System. An information system that uses data communications technology.

Teleconferencing. Linking a number of different people in different locations together electronically or through telecommunications so that they can confer.

Terabyte. One trillion (10^{15}) characters of memory.

Terminal. An input/output device for entering or receiving data directly from the computer. Also referred to as cathode ray tube (CRT) or visual display terminal (VDT).

Terrestrial Microwave. A microwave data transmission system that utilizes transmission facilities located on the earth instead of satellites.

Test Data. Data that have been specially developed to test the accuracy and completeness of a computer program. The results from the test data are compared with hand-calculated results to verify that the program operates properly.

Test Data Generator. A program that takes the specifications describing the logic characteristics of the program to be tested and automatically generates a set of test data that can be used to check the logic of the program.

Tests of Controls. A test whose objective is to determine if control procedures are being followed correctly.

Threats. Potential losses to an organization arising from hazards such as embezzlement, employee carelessness or theft, or poor management decisions.

Throughput. (1) The total amount of useful work performed by a computer system during a given period of time. (2) A measure of production efficiency representing the number of "good" units produced in a given period of time.

Time Card. A document that records the employee's arrival and departure times for each work shift. The time card records the total hours worked by an employee during a pay period.

Time-Sharing. The use of small slices of CPU time from a large mainframe computer by a number of small users, for a fee.

TIPS. Trillions of Instructions Per Second. A unit for measuring CPU speed.

Token Ring. A LAN configuration that forms a closed loop. A token is passed around the ring to indicate that a device is free to send or receive a message.

Touch-Sensitive Screens. Sensitized video display screens that allow users to enter data or select menu items by touching their surface with a finger or a special pointer.

Trailer Label. Type of internal label that appears at the end of each file and serves as an indicator that the end of the file has been reached.

Transaction Cycles. A group of related business activities. For example, the set of business activities consisting of sales order entry, shipping, billing, and cash receipts constitutes the revenue cycle. The five major transaction cycles are revenue, expenditure, production, human resource management/payroll, and general ledger and reporting.

Transaction File. A temporary data file containing transaction data that are typically used to update a master file.

Transaction Log. A detailed record of every transaction entered in a system through data entry.

Transaction Processing. A process that begins with capturing transaction data and ends with an informational output.

Transcription Error. An error occurring during data conversion from a manual to an automated environment in which one digit of a number is written incorrectly during the conversion (e.g., a "4" in the tens position transcribed as a "9," which would cause an error of 50 in the value of the number).

Transposition Error. An error that results when the numbers in two adjacent columns are inadvertently exchanged (for example, 64 is written as 46).

Trap Door. A set of computer instructions that allows a user to bypass the system's normal controls.

Tree. A data structure or logical data model in which relationships among data items are expressed in the form of a hierarchical structure.

Trial Balance. A report listing the balances of all general ledger accounts. It is so named because one of its purposes is to allow the accountant to verify that the total debit balances in various accounts equal the total credit balances in other accounts.

Triggered Exception Reports. Preformatted reports, generated only when certain conditions exist (e.g., the amount of raw materials on hand falls below the safety stock amount), that brings this information to the attention of a decision maker.

Trojan Horse. A set of unauthorized computer instructions in an authorized and otherwise properly functioning program. It performs some illegal act at a preappointed time or under a predetermined set of conditions.

Tunneling. An Internet security approach in which the data is sent between firewalls in small encrypted segments called packets.

Tuple (pronounced to rhyme with the word *couple*). A row in a relation. A tuple contains data about a specific occurrence of the type of entity represented by that data base table. For example, each row in the inventory table contains all the pertinent data about a particular inventory item.

Turnaround Document. A document readable by humans that is prepared by the computer as output, sent outside the system, and then returned as input into the computer. An example is a utility bill.

Turnkey System. A system that is delivered to customers ready (theoretically) to be turned on. A turnkey system supplier buys hardware, writes applications software that is tailored both to that equipment and to the specific needs of its customers, and then markets the entire system.

Uninterruptible Power System. An alternative power supply device that protects against the loss of power and fluctuations in the power level.

Universal Product Code (UPC). A machine-readable code that is read by optical scanners. The code consists of a series of bar codes and is printed on most products sold in grocery stores.

UNIX. A flexible and widely used operating system for 16-bit machines.

Unstructured Decisions. Nonrecurring and nonroutine decisions that require considerable judgment and intuition.

Update Anomaly. A problem that can arise in a poorly designed relational data base. If attributes that are not characteristics of the primary key of a relation are stored in that table, then that data item is stored in many different rows. For example, if customer addresses are stored in the sales invoice table, then the address for a given customer is stored many times (once for each sale). Consequently, if the value of that data item is not changed in every row in which it is stored, inconsistencies in the data base will result.

Updating. Changing stored data to reflect more recent events (e.g., changing the account receivable balance because of a recent sale or collection).

Upload. To send data to someone else on the network.

User Interface. A component of an expert system that is a program allowing the user to design create, update, use, and communicate with the expert system.

Users. All the people that interact with the system. Users are the people that record data, manage the system, and control the system's security. Those who use information from the system are end users.

Utility Programs. A set of prewritten programs that perform a variety of file and data handling tasks (e.g., sorting or merging files) and other housekeeping chores.

Utilization. The percentage of time a system is being productively used.

Validity Check. An edit test in which an identification number or transaction code is compared with a table of valid identification numbers or codes maintained in computer memory.

Value Chain. The linking together of all the primary and support activities in a business. Value is added as a product passes through the chain.

Value of Information. The net value added to an organization in acquiring information—that is, the benefit of that information minus the costs of acquiring it. VALUE OF INFORMATION = BENEFIT – COST.

Value System. The combination of several value chains into one system. A value system includes the value chains of a company, its suppliers, its distributors, and its customers.

Value-Added Network (VAN). Public network that adds value to the data communications process by handling the difficult task of interfacing with the multiple types of hardware and software used by different companies.

Vendor Performance Report. A report that highlights deviations in product quality, prices, and delivery commitments.

Very Large Scale Integration (VLSI). A process in which a large number (1,000 or more) of integrated circuits are placed on one chip.

Video Teleconferencing. A conference where people in several different locations can both see and hear each other.

Videodisk. A special type of optical disk that can store audio, video, and text data. The disk can be accessed a frame at a time for motionless viewing or can be played like a videotape for moving action and sound.

Virtual Memory (or **Virtual Storage**). On-line secondary storage that is used as an extension of primary memory, thus giving the appearance of a larger, virtually unlimited amount of internal memory. Pages of data or program instructions are swapped back and forth between secondary and primary storage as needed.

Virtual Private Network (VPN). A network that controls access to an extranet by encryption and authentication technology.

Virtual Value Chain. The process of gathering and organizing information and using it as a source of revenue or to enhance customer service.

Visual Display Terminal (VDT). See *terminal.*

Voice Input. A data input unit that recognizes human voices and converts spoken messages into machine-readable input.

Voice Mail (V-mail). A service that converts voice messages into computer data and stores them so that they can be retrieved later by the person for whom they were intended.

Voice Recognition. A system that understands spoken words and transmits them into a computer at speeds faster than most users can type.

Voice Response Unit. See *audio response unit.*

Voiceband Lines. Phone lines designed to accept data transmissions of between 300 and 9,600 bits per second. They can be used for transmitting voice or data communications.

Volume Label. A type of internal label that identifies the contents of each separate data recording medium, such as a tape, diskette, or disk pack.

Voucher. A document that summarizes the data relating to a disbursement and represents final authorization of payment.

Voucher Package. The set of documents, consisting of a purchase order, receiving report, and vendor invoice, used to authorize payment to a vendor.

Voucher System. A method for processing accounts payable in which a document called a disbursement voucher is prepared, instead of posting invoices directly to vendor records in the accounts payable subsidiary ledger. The disbursement voucher identifies the vendor, lists the outstanding invoices, and indicates the net amount to be paid after deducting any applicable discounts and allowances. Contrast with *nonvoucher system.*

WAIS (Wide Area Information Servers). Tools for searching the Internet's huge information libraries.

Walkthroughs. Meetings, attended by those associated with a project, in which a detailed review of systems procedures and/or program logic is carried out in a step-by-step manner.

War Dialing. Searching for an idle modem by programming a computer to dial thousands of phone lines. Finding an idle modem often enables a cracker to gain access to the network to which it is connected.

WATS Line. An acronym for Wide Area Telephone Service line, a phone line for which the customer pays both a fixed charge and an additional charge that varies directly with the amount of extra usage.

Web Servers. Large computers on the Internet that are scattered worldwide and contain every imaginable type of data. Each web server can have thousands of networks and users attached to it.

White-Collar Criminals. Typically, business people who commit fraud. White-collar criminals usually resort to trickery or cunning, and their crimes usually involve a violation of trust or confidence.

Wide Area Network (WAN). A telecommunications network that covers a large geographic area anywhere from a few cities to the whole globe. A WAN uses telephone lines, cables, microwaves, or satellites to connect a wide variety of hardware devices in many different locations.

Wiretapping. Listening (eavesdropping) on an unprotected communications line.

Word. A group of bytes moved and processed by a computer. The most common word size for large computers is 32 bits; for smaller computers, it is 16 bits.

Word Processing. A program that facilitates creating, processing, editing, formatting, and printing text data.

Word Size. The number of bits of data that can be processed in one CPU cycle.

World Wide Web. An advanced Internet navigation system that organizes its contents by subject matter.

Worm. Similar to a virus except that it is a program rather than a code segment hidden in a host program. A worm also copies itself and actively transmits itself directly to other systems.

WORM. Write Once, Read Many. For example, an optical disk can be written on once, but later read many times.

Yield. The percentage of total units produced that are not defective.

Zero-Balance Check. An internal check that requires the balance of the payroll control account to be zero after all entries to it have been made.

REFERENCES

CHAPTER 1

Ackoff, R. L. "Management Misinformation Systems." *Management Science* (December 1, 1967): 147–156.

American Institute of Certified Public Accountants. *Information Technology Competencies in the Accounting Profession. AICPA Implementation Strategies for IFAC International Education Guideline No. 11.* AICPA Technology Curriculum and Competency Task Force, June 1996.

Baker, Stephen, and Gary McWilliams. "Now Comes the Corporate Triathlete." *Business Week* (January 31, 1994): 71–72.

Berton, Lee. "Accountants Expand Scope of Audit Work." *Wall Street Journal* (June 17, 1996): B1, B8.

Cook, Gail Lynn, and Martha M. Eining. "Will Cross Functional Information Systems Work?" *Management Accounting* (February 1993): 53–57.

Deloitte Touche Tohmatsu International. *Leading Trends in Information Services.* Information Technology Consulting Services Seventh Annual Survey of North American Chief Information Executives, 1995.

Dunn, Cheryl L., and William E. McCarthy. "Conceptual Models of Economic Exchange Phenomena: History's Third Wave of Accounting Systems." *Collected Papers of the Sixth World Congress of Accounting Historians, Volume 1, Kyoto, Japan:* 133–164.

Eisenstodt, Gale. "Information Power." Forbes (June 21, 1993): 44–45.

Elliott, Robert K., and Don M. Pallais. "Are You Ready for the New Assurance Services?" *Journal of Accountancy* (June 1997): 47–51.

Financial Accounting Standards Board. *Statement of Financial Accounting Concepts No. 2: Qualitative Characteristics of Accounting Information,* 1980.

Geerts, Guido, and William E. McCarthy. "Modeling Business Enterprises as Value-Added Process Hierarchies with Resource-Event-Agent Object Templates." *Business Object Design and Implementation: OOPSLA 1995 Workshop Proceedings* (October 16, 1995).

Institute of Management Accountants. *The Practice Analysis of Management Accounting: An IMA Research Project.* Institute of Management Accountants, Montvale, NJ, 1996.

Keen, Peter G. W., and Michael S. Scott Morton. *Decision Support Systems: An Organizational Perspective.* Reading, MA: Addison-Wesley, 1978.

King, Julia. "Techno MBAs Pay Off." *Computerworld* (October 7, 1996): 77.

Porter, Michael E. "What Is Strategy?" *Harvard Business Review* (November–December 1996): 61–78.

Porter, Michael E., and V. E. Millar. "How Information Gives You Competitive Advantage." *Harvard Business Review* (July–August 1985): 149–160.

Scrupski, Susan. "Severe Talent Drought Ahead." *Datamation* (May 15, 1995): 30.

Shirouzu, Norihiko, and Jon Bigness. "7-Eleven Operators Resist System to Monitor Managers." *Wall Street Journal* (June 16, 1997): B1, B3.

Siegel, Gary, C. S. Kulesza, and James E. Sorensen. "Are You Ready for the New Accounting?" *Journal of Accountancy* (August 1997): 42–46.

Stewart, Thomas A. "Welcome to the Revolution." *Fortune* (December 13, 1993): 66–77.

Taylor, Alex, III. "How Toyota Defies Gravity." *Fortune* (December 8, 1997): 100–108.

Thompson, Arthur A., Jr., and A. J. Strickland, III. *Strategic Management—Concepts and Cases.* 6th ed. Boston: Irwin, 1992, 955–987.

Wreden, Nick. "Sharpening the Corporate Vision." *Beyond Computing* (March–April 1994): 29–32.

Zachary, G. Pascal. "Computer Data Overload Limits Productivity Gains." *Wall Street Journal* (November 11, 1991): B1.

Zarowin, Stanley. "The Future of Finance." *Journal of Accountancy* (August 1995): 47–49.

CHAPTER 2

Anand, Vikas, et al. "An Organizational Memory Approach to Information Management." *Academy of Management Review* (October 1998): 796.

Curley, John. "How a Clerk Built Up a Brokerage Business by Hook or by Crook." *Wall Street Journal* (February 7, 1985): A1, A22.

Hibbard, Justin. "Not Much Transacting Going On." *Computerworld* (March 10, 1997): 61.

Kaplan, Robert S., and David P. Norton. "The Balanced Scorecard—Measures that Drive Performance." *Harvard Business Review* (January–February 1992): 71–79.

———. "Putting the Balanced Scoreboard to Work." *Harvard Business Review* (September–October 1993): 134–147.

Keys, E. Theodore, Jr. (Editor of Roundtable column). "'Free' Maintenance Service." *Internal Auditor* (October 1993): 74.

———. (Editor of Roundtable column). "Altered Checks." *Internal Auditor* (October 1993): 77.

———.(Editor of Roundtable column). "Return to Sender." *Internal Auditor* (June 1995): 64.

———. (Editor of Roundtable column). "Budget-Busting Leases." *Internal Auditor* (June 1995): 66.

Koch, Christopher. "The Middle Ground." *CIO* (January 15, 1999): 48–54.

Labrack, Bonnie D. "Small Business Controller." *Management Accounting* (November 1994): 38–41.

Porter, Anne. "Automation Fails to Free Purchasing from Transactions." *Purchasing* (October 8, 1998): 20–21.

Rehnberg, Stephen M. "Keep Your Head Out of the Cockpit." *Management Accounting* (July 1995): 34–37.

Rossett, Alison. "First Things Fast." Jossey-Bass Inc.: January 1998.

Schulte, Roy. "Rapid Response." *Forbes* (October 19, 1998): 38.

Tayi, Giri Kumar. "Examining Data Quality." *Communications of the ACM* (February 1998): 54.

Tracey, Brian. "The Color of Money." *Wall Street Journal* (November 16, 1998): R28.

CHAPTER 3

Aktas, A. Ziya. *Structured Analysis and Design of Information Systems*. Englewood Cliffs, NJ: Prentice-Hall, 1987.

American National Standard Institute. *Flowchart Symbols and Their Usage in Information Processing*. Publication No. ANSI X3.5. New York: American National Standards Institute, 1970.

Atre, Shaku. "The Art Of Data Design." Computerworld (June 29 1998).

Broad, Maureen. "Information Analysis." *Accountancy* (January 1997): 62–66.

Bull, Katherine. "Making Magic." *InfoWorld* (June 22, 1998): 33.

Carbone, John P., and Joseph R. Hudicka. "Layered Systems Deployment." *Management Accounting* (December 1998): 27.

DeMarco, Tom. *Structured Analysis and System Specification*. Englewood Cliffs, NJ: Prentice-Hall, 1979.

Faye, David, and Theodore J. Mock. "How to Prepare Better Accounting Systems Flowcharts." *Practical Accountant* (November 1986): 106–118.

Ferguson, Tim W. "Drawing Room." *Forbes* (December 14, 1998): 227–228.

Gibbs, Mark. "Documentation." *Network World* (August 4, 1997): 70.

Hay, David C. "Making Data Models Readable." *Information Systems Management* (Winter 1998): 21.

Kievit, K., and M. Martin. "Systems Analysis Tools—Who's Using Them?" *Journal of Systems Management* (July 1989): 26–30.

McMenamin, Stephen M., and John F. Palmer. *Essential Systems Analysis*. Englewood Cliffs, NJ: Yourdon Press, 1984.

Quinn, Juanita C. "Flow Chart Eases Planning Process for Hospitals." *Health Care Strategic Management* (April 1991): 16–18.

Zeigler, Heather, and Alexia Marcous. "Business Process Modeling Leads to Web Warehouse Success." *e-Business Advisor* (July 1998): 14.

CHAPTER 4

Alpert, Mark. "Building a Better Bar Code." *Fortune* (June 15, 1992): 101.

Ambrosio, Johanna. "UPS 'Dials' Up Fast Data on Deliveries." *Computerworld* (September 14, 1992): 79.

American Institute of Certified Public Accountants. *Image Processing and Optical Character Recognition: How They Work and How to Implement Them.* Technology Bulletin, Information Technology Division, 1993.

American Institute of Certified Public Accountants. *Memory Management.* Technology Bulletin, Information Technology Division, 1993.

Anthes, Gary H. "Postal Service Sorts Through Automation." *Computerworld* (October 4, 1993): 1, 26.

Bartholomew, Doug. "B of A's Data Warehouse." *InformationWeek* (July 25, 1994): 16.

Baum, David. "Au Bon Pain Gains Quick Access to Sales Data." *InfoWorld* (August 10, 1992): 46.

Berry, Jonathan, John Verity, Kathleen Kerwin, and Gail DeGeorge. "Database Marketing: A Potent New Tool for Selling." *Business Week* (September 5, 1994): 56–62.

Booker, Ellis. "Pizza Hut: Making It Great with Imaging, EDI." *Computerworld* (January 27, 1992): 67, 72.

Boudette, Neal. "Pen PCs Help Utility Trim Costs." *PC Week* (August 10, 1992): 19.

Daly, James. "Insurer Sees Future in Imaging Strategy." *Computerworld* (January 6, 1992): 41.

Elliston, James. "Image Processing: Bright Picture for the Future." *Management Accounting* (August 1991): 23–26.

Fitzgerald, Michael. "Laptops Make Sales Force Shine." *Computerworld* (August 12, 1991): 35.

Hackathorn, Richard. "Data Warehousing Energizes Your Enterprise." *Datamation* (February 1, 1995): 38–45.

Hamilton, Rosemary. "Chase Banks on 'Info' Access." *Computerworld* (January 27, 1992): 6.

Hunton, James E. "Setting Up a Paperless Office." *Journal of Accountancy* (November 1994): 77–85.

Lazar, Jerry. "The Object Is Productivity." *InformationWeek* (January 3, 1994): 36–38.

Levick, Diane. "A New Weapon for Car Insurers: Database Allows Companies to Check Drivers' Records." *New York Newsday* (February 20, 1990): 49.

Luzi, Andrew D., and R. K. McCabe. "Harnessing the Power of Databases." *Journal of Accountancy* (July 1993): 71–75.

Nolan, Richard L. "Computer Databases: The Future Is Now." *Harvard Business Review* (September–October 1973): 98–114.

Port, Otis, Neil Gross, Robert Hof, and Gary McWilliams. "Wonder Chips: How They'll Make Computing Power Ultrafast and Ultracheap." *Business Week* (July 4, 1994): 86–92.

Richman, Dan. "Let Your Agent Handle It." *InformationWeek* (April 17, 1995): 44–56.

Rifkin, Glenn. "The Future of the Document." *Forbes ASAP* (October 9, 1995): 42–60.

Sadhwani, Arjan T., and Thomas Tyson. "Does Your Firm Need Bar Coding?" *Management Accounting* (April 1990): 45–48.

CHAPTER 5

Andren, Emily. "Scherer Gets System to Gel." *InformationWeek* (March 6, 1995): 60–62.

Bozman, Jean S. "Coke Plans to Add Life with Relational Data Base Move." *Computerworld* (January 13, 1992): 35.

Cushing, Barry E. "On the Feasibility and the Consequences of a Database Approach to Corporate Financial Reporting." *Journal of Information Systems* (Spring 1989): 29–52.

DePompa, Barbara. "Objects Drive a New Market." *InformationWeek* (November 7, 1994): 48–52.

Eldred, Eric. "Entering the Realm of Complex Data." *Client/Server Today* (May 1994): 47–54.

Elliott, Robert K. "Confronting the Future: Choices for the Attest Function." *Accounting Horizons* (September 1994): 106–124.

Garry, Greg. "How the Object-Oriented World Translates into Reality." *Client/Server Today* (May 1994): 56–63.

Hooper, Paul, and John Page. "Relational Databases: An Accountant's Primer." *Management Accounting* (October 1996): 48–53.

"Hot Seat." *Infoworld* (January 20, 1997): 33, 36.

Hunton, James E., and M. K. Raja. "When Is a Database Not a Database? (When It's a Spreadsheet.)" *Journal of Accountancy* (June 1995): 89–93.

Leon, Mark. "Object-Relational Databases May Be Ahead of Their Time." *Infoworld* (May 19, 1997): 51, 56.

Levick, Diane. "A New Weapon for Car Insurers: Database Allows Companies to Check Drivers' Records." *New York Newsday* (February 20, 1990): 49.

"The Relational World of Chris Date." *Interface: Candle's View on IBM's Database World* (Summer 1993): 1–5.

Ricciuti, Mike. "Object Databases Find Their Niche." *Datamation* (September 15, 1993): 56–58.

Soat, John. "Forging the Future." *InformationWeek* (February 21, 1994): 42–50.

The, Lee. "Wedding Bells Sound for Objects and Relational Data." *Datamation* (March 1, 1994): 49–52.

Wilson, Linda. "Bank Systems Earn Credit." *InformationWeek* (May 30, 1994): 70–72.

CHAPTER 6

Andros, David P., J. Owen Cherrington, and Eric L. Denna. "Reengineering Your Accounting, the IBM Way." *Financial Executive* (July–August 1992): 28–31.

Berton, Lee. "Finance Executives Criticize Software for Accounting," *Wall Street Journal* (February 2, 1995): B2.

Byers, C. Randall, and Lysa Beltz. "Financial Data Modeling at Hewlett–Packard." *Journal of Systems Management* (January 1994): 28–33.

Chen, Peter. "The Entity Relationship Model—Toward a Unified View of Data." *Transactions on Database Systems* (March 1976): 9–36.

David, Julie Smith. "Three Events that Define an REA Methodology for Systems Analysis." Unpublished working paper, Arizona State University, 1997.

Dunn, Cheryl L., and William E. McCarthy. "The REA Accounting Model: Intellectual Heritage and Prospects for Progress." *Journal of Information Systems* (Spring 1997): 31-51.

Elliott, Robert K. "The Third Wave Breaks on the Shores of Accounting." *Accounting Horizons* (June 1992): 61–85.

Hollander, Anita S., Eric L. Denna, and J. Owen Cherrington. *Accounting, Information Technology, and Business Solutions.* 1st ed. Chicago: Irwin, 1996.

McCarthy, William E. "An Entity–Relationship View of Accounting Models." *Accounting Review* (October 1979): 667–686.

McCarthy, William E. "The REA Accounting Model: A Generalized Framework for Accounting Systems in a Shared Data Environment." *Accounting Review* (July 1982): 554–578.

Winsberg, Paul, and Daniel Richards. "Data Modeling Isn't Dead." *ComputerWorld* (April 4, 1994): 85.

Zarowin, Stanley. "The Future of Finance." *Journal of Accountancy* (August 1995): 47–49.

CHAPTER 7

Aggarwal, Rajesh, and Zabihollah Rezaee. "Introduction to EDI Internal Controls." *IS Audit & Control Journal* (Volume II, 1994): 64-68.

Akasie, Jay. "Imagine, No Inventory." *Forbes* (November 17, 1997): 144-145.

American Institute of Certified Public Accountants. *Client/Server Computing and Cooperative Processing.* Technology Bulletin, Information Technology Division, 1994.

Anthes, Gary H. "Army Enlists Client/Server." *Computerworld* (March 29, 1993): 12.

"At the Pump: A Special Report." *Wall Street Journal* (May 21, 1992): 1.

Baum, David. "Transcending EDI." *Infoworld* (March 24, 1997): 67-68.

Booker, Ellis. "Motorola to Provide Remote E-mail."

Borthick, A. Faye, and Harold P. Roth. "Understanding Client/Server Computing." *Management Accounting*
(August 1994): 36–41.

Brull, Steven V. "Networks that Do New Tricks." *Business Week* (April 6, 1998): 100.

Burrows, Peter. "Instant Info Is Not Enough." *Business Week* (June 22, 1998): 144.

Caldwell, Bo. "Gearing Up to Integrate Voice and Data." *InfoWorld* (January 13, 1992): S67–S70.

Champlain, Jack J. "Is Your Wire Transfer System Secure?" *Internal Auditor* (June 1995): 56–59.

Den Boef, Anthonie. "Assessing Electronic Funds Transfer (EFT) Security Vulnerabilities in SAP R/3 Environments." *IS Audit & Control Journal* (Volume I, 1999): 25–28.

Flynn, Laurie. "Hotels Speed Reservations with PC Network Linking." *InfoWorld* (November 11, 1991): S72.

Grannan, Philip P. "Electronic Commerce Today; Financial EDI Solutions for Tomorrow." *Management Accounting* (November 1997): 38–41.

Gray, Glen L., and Roger Debreceny. "The Electronic Frontier." *Journal of Accountancy* (May 1998): 32–38.

Gunther, Lisa J. "Implementing EDI in a Controlled Environment." *IS Audit & Control Journal* (Volume II, 1994): 42–46.

Hatlestad, Luc. "Hospital Upgrades ATM Network to Overcome Bottlenecks." *Infoworld* (March 4, 1996): 65.

Higgins, Kelly Jackson. "Safer Nets?" *Communications Week* (March 17, 1997): 52–55.

Hof, Robert, Gary McWilliams, and Gabrielle Saveri. "The Click Here Economy." *Business Week* (June 22, 1998): 122–128.

"Information Strangles Productivity." *Internal Auditor* (August 1998): 13.

Jenks, Andrew. "Groupware Fosters Shared Info, Ideas." *USA Today* (October 21, 1991): 10E.

Johnson, Richard A. "The Facts on PC-Based Faxing and Winfax Pro." *New Accountant* (January 1995): 18–20.

"May I Take Your Order?" *Computerworld* (October 7, 1991): 29.

Joseph, Gilbert W., Terry J. Engle, and Justin Childs. "All VANs Are Not Created Equal Regarding Internal Control." *IS Audit & Control Journal* (Volume I, 1999): 41–47.

Lawson, Richard. "Achieving 'Net' Results." *Management Accounting* (January 1998): 51–54.

Lawson, Stephen. "Fortify Your Backbone." *Infoworld* (May 4, 1998): 113–114.

Leibs, Scott. "Spreading the Nets." *IndustryWeek* (December 15, 1997).

Martin, Richard J. "Two Tiers or Three?" *Journal of Systems Management* (August 1994): 32–33.

Mukhopadhyay, Tridas, Sunder Kekre, and Suresh Kalathur. "Business Value of Information Technology: A Study of Electronic Interchange. *MIS Quarterly* (June 1995): 137–156.

O'Leary, Daniel E. "The Internet and Accountants." *AICPA InfoTech Update* (Summer 1994): 10–11.

Postrel, Virginia. "The Politics of Privacy." *Forbes ASAP* (June 1, 1998): 130.

Pushkin, Ann B., and Bonnie W. Morris. "Understanding Financial EDI." *Management Accounting* (November 1997): 42–46.

Rapaport, Richard. "PR Finds a Cool New Tool." *Forbes ASAP* (October 6, 1997): 101–108.

Rayport, Jeffrey F., and John J. Sviokla. "Managing in the Marketspace." *Harvard Business Review* (November–December, 1994): 141–150.

Reinhardt, Andy. "Log On, Link Up, Save Big." *Business Week* (June 22, 1998): 132–138.

Sager, Ira. "IBM Swings into the On-Line Fast Lane." *Business Week* (December 5, 1994): 100–102.

Schultz, Keith. "Taming the Flames." *CommunicationsWeek* (March 10, 1997): 53–60.

Sevcik, Peter J. "Tightening the Access Strings." *CommunicationsWeek* (September 1996): S21–S22.

Stahl, Stephanie. "Hire on One, Get 'Em All." *InformationWeek* (March 20, 1995): 120–124.

Tanenbaum, Andrew S. *Computer Networks.* 3rd ed. Upper Saddle River, NJ: Prentice-Hall, 1996.

Verity, John W., Peter Coy, and Jeffrey Rothfeder. "Special Report: Taming the Wild Network." *Business Week* (October 8, 1990): 142–148.

Wallace, Bob. "National Fuel Gas Migrates SCADA Net to LAN Platform." *Network World* (April 15, 1991): 24.

Wilder, Clinton. "Codex Goes Paperless with EDI." *Computerworld* (January 13, 1992): 6.

Wilder, Clinton. "The Internet Pioneers." *InformationWeek* (January 9, 1995): 38–48.

Woolley, Scott. "I Got It Cheaper than You." *Forbes* (November 2, 1998): 82–84.

CHAPTER 8

Aggarwal, Rajesh, and Zabihollah Rezaee. "EDI Risk Assessment." *Internal Auditor* (February 1996): 40–44.

American Institute of Certified Public Accountants. *Statement on Auditing Standards No. 1-69.* New York: AICPA, 1992

Casson, Peter. "Framework for the Evaluation of Internal Controls." *Financial Regulation Report* (February 1998): 12–13.

Committee of Sponsoring Organizations of the Treadway Commission. *Internal Control—Integrated Framework*. New York: Committee of Sponsoring Organizations of the Treadway Commission, 1992.

Coughlan, John W. "The Fairfax Embezzlement." *Management Accounting* (May 1983): 32–39.

Curtis, Mary. "Internal Control Issues for Data Warehousing." *IS Audit & Control Journal* (1997, vol. IV): 40–45.

Daly, James. "The 30-Minute Risk Analysis." *Computerworld* (November 29, 1993): 68.

Davia, H. R., P. C. Coggins, J. C. Wideman, and J. T. Kastantin. *Management Accountant's Guide to Fraud Discovery and Control*. New York: Wiley, 1992.

Elliott, Robert K., and John J. Willingham. *Management Fraud: Detection and Deterrence*. New York: Petrocelli Books, 1980.

Foltz, Ronald. "Monitoring a Small Firm." *Journal of Accountancy* (June 1997): 54.

Foreign Corrupt Practices Act of 1977. U.S. Code, 1976 edition, Supplement II, Title 15, Selection 78. Washington, D.C.: U.S. Government Printing Office, 1979.

Goldstein, Leslie M. "Favorite Frauds." *Internal Auditor* (August 1992): 35–39.

Hawkins, Kyleen W., and Bill Huckaby. "Using CSA to Implement COSO." *Internal Auditor* (June 1998): 50–55.

Hogg, Joseph D. "How Much Does an Error Cost—And How Much Does It Cost to Prevent It?" *Internal Auditor* (August 1992): 67–69.

McArthur, Larry. "Countdown to 2000: Millenium Bug Risk Assessment and Management." *Risk Management* (October 1997): S6.

Robertson, Michael. "Getting Perspective on Risk." *CMA—The Management Accounting Magazine* (June 1997): 4.

Root, Steven J. "Beyond COSO: International Control to Enhance Corporate Governance." John Wiley & Sons (May 1998).

Rose, Frederick. "Risk Guru." *Wall Street Journal* (January 20, 1998): A1.

Roth, Jim. "A Hard Look at Soft Controls." *Internal Auditor* (February 1998): 30–33.

Siegel, Joel, and Anique Qureshi. "Risk Analysis and Management Software and the CPA." *CPA Journal* (December 1997): 65.

Thompson, Courtenay. "Fraud Findings." *Internal Auditor* (October 1995): 50–52.

Tongren, John, and Slemo Warigon. "A Preliminary Survey of COBIT Use." *EDPACS* (The EDP Audit, Control, and Security Newsletter) (September 1997): 17–19.

Willis, Alan, and William Bradshaw. "Risky Business." *CA Magazine* (August 1998): 37.

CHAPTER 9

American Institute of Certified Public Accountants. *Statements on Auditing Standards No. 1-69*. New York: AICPA, 1992.

Baker, Richard H. *Computer Security Handbook*. 2nd ed. Blue Ridge Summit, PA: TAB Books, 1991.

Booker, Ellis. "Data Dowsed in Midwest Floods." *Computerworld* (July 19, 1993): 6.

Bozman, Jean S. "Quake Shakes IS, Leaves Networks in Disarray." *Computerworld* (January 24, 1994): 1, 14.

Caldwell, Bruce, and Doug Bartholomew. "Glitch Zaps Bank Accounts: Chemical ATMs Have Bad Reaction." *InformationWeek* (February 21, 1994): 13–14.

Coderre, Dave. "Testing Application Controls." *Internal Auditor* (December 1996): 18.

Cone, Edward. "Taking No Chances." *InformationWeek* (December 12, 1994): 30–40.

Dash, Julekha. "Crash!" *Software Magazine* (February 1997): 48–51.

Davis, Beth. "In Certificates We Trust." *InformationWeek* (March 23, 1998): 60–64.

Davis, Charles. "An Assessment of Accounting Information Security." *CPA Journal* (March 1997): 28.

DePompa, Barbara. "Date with Disaster." *InformationWeek* (May 2, 1994): 48–58.

Edwards, John. "A Sure, Secure Thing." *CIO* (July 1996): 106–110.

Garceau, Linda R., Jack Matejka, Santosh K. Misra, and Etzmun Rozen. "The Electronic Envelope." *Internal Auditor* (December 1998): 24–30.

Groenfeldt, Tom. "The Online Safety Net." *InformationWeek* (January 30, 1995): 74–84.

Hayes, Frank. "Tip of the Day: Be Paranoid." *Computerworld* (August 5, 1997): 8.

________. "Just a Number." *Computerworld* (February 1, 1999): 69.

Hoffman, Thomas. "Explosion Spotlights LAN Vulnerability." *Computerworld* (March 15, 1993): 67.

Institute of Internal Auditors Research Foundation. *Systems Auditability and Control Report.* Altamonte Springs, FL: Institute of Internal Auditors Research Foundation, 1991.

Keeton, Laura E. "In the Wake of Bombing, One Business Rises from Its Own Ashes." *Wall Street Journal* (April 26, 1995): A1, A9.

Kring, Richard. "Systems Control Strategies." *Internal Auditor* (April 1998): 60–63.

Machlis, Sharon. "Thief Walks Off with Employee Data on Hard Disk." *Computerworld* (May 5, 1997): 1–2.

McHugh, Josh. "Politics for the Really Cool." *Forbes* (September 8, 1997): 172–179.

Microcomputer Security. New York: American Institute of Certified Public Accountants (Information Technology Division), 1994.

Oster, Patrick. "A Better Passport: The Human Hand." *Business Week* (May 2, 1994): 132.

Panettieri, Joseph, and Chuck Appleby. "Survival of the Fittest." *InformationWeek* (January 10, 1994): 22–30.

Parker, Robert. "Access Control Software: What It Will and Will Not Do." *EDPACS* (February 1991): 1–8.

Patrowicz, Lucie Juneau. "A River Runs Through IT." *CIO* (April 1, 1998): 36–44.

Phillips, Mark. "Planning Speeds Bank's Recovery from Fire." *Disaster Recovery Journal* (January–March 1992): 56–58.

Riley, W. D. "Encrypt This!!" *Datamation* (May 1, 1996): 27–35.

Rodetis, Susan. "Can Your Business Survive the Unexpected?" *Journal of Accountancy* (February 1999): 27–32.

Ross, Philip E. "I Can Read Your Face." *Forbes* (December 19, 1994): 304–305.

Semer, Lance J. "Disaster Recovery Planning in Distributed Environments." *Internal Auditor* (December 1998): 40–47.

Sherizen, Sanford. "The Net's Safety Net: Encryption." *Beyond Computing* (April 1996): 16–18.

Socka, George. "When Disaster Strikes." *CMA—The Management Accounting Magazine* (November 1998): 12.

Storkman, Wayne D. "Before Disaster Strikes: 12 Steps to Minimize Compuer Losses." *Technology Alert,* American Institute of Certified Public Accountants (July 1994).

Summers, Rita C. "Secure Computing: Threats and Safeguards." McGraw-Hill: January 1997.

Verity, John W., and Rob Hof. "Bullet-proofing the Net." *Business Week* (November 13, 1995): 98–99.

Warigon, Slemo. "Data Warehouse Control and Security." *Internal Auditor* (February 1998): 54–60.

Wilder, Clinton, Bruce Caldwell, Joseph C. Panettieri, and Marianne Kolbasuk McGee. "Hackers' Break-in at General Electric Raises Questions About the Net's Security." *InformationWeek* (December 12, 1994): 13–14.

Wilder, Clinton, Mitch Wagner, and Jason Levitt. "Satan's Surprise." *InformationWeek* (April 24, 1995): 22.

Yasin, Rutrell. "Assessing and Reducing Security Risks." *Internetweek* (February 8, 1999): 12.

CHAPTER 10

Albrecht, W. Steve, Marshall B. Romney, et al. *How to Detect and Prevent Business Fraud.* Englewood Cliffs, NJ: Prentice-Hall, 1982.

Albrecht, W. Steve, Marshall B. Romney, and Keith Howe. *Deterring Fraud: The Internal Auditor's Perspective.* Altamonte Springs, FL: Institute of Internal Auditors, 1984.

Alexander, Michael. "Prison Term for First U.S. Hacker-Law Convict." *Computerworld* (February 29, 1989): 1, 12.

————. "Hacker Stereotypes Changing." *Computerworld* (April 3, 1989): 101.

————. "Strong Scruples Can Curb Computer Crime." *Computerworld* (April 3, 1989): 100.

————. "Biometric System Use Widening." *Computerworld* (January 8, 1990): 16.

————. "Computer Crime: Ugly Secret for Business." *Computerworld* (March 12, 1990): 1, 104.

Allen, Brandt. "Embezzler's Guide to the Computer." *Harvard Business Review* (July–August 1975): 79–89.

————. "The Biggest Computer Frauds: Lessons for CPAs." *Journal of Accountancy* (May 1977): 52–62.

Anthes, Gary H. "'Stealth E-Mail' Poses Corporate Security Risk." *Computerworld* (February 12, 1996): 1.

BloomBecker, Jay J. Buck. "My Three Computer Criminological Sins." *Communications of the ACM*, (November 1994): 15–16.

________. *Spectacular Computer Crimes*. Homewood, IL: Dow-Jones-Irwin, 1990.

Bozman, Jean S. "Bell Tolls for the Shadow Hawk." *Computerworld* (August 15, 1988): 104.

Burrough, Bryan. "The Embezzler David L. Miller Stole from His Employers and Isn't in Prison." *Wall Street Journal* (September 19, 1986): 1.

Cobb, Stephen, and David Brussin. "Hackers in White Hats." *Byte* (June 1998): 112.

Coderre, David G. "Full Service Fraud." *Internal Auditor* (April 1998): 77–78.

Coffee, Peter. "What You Don't Know Will Hurt You." *PC Week* (February 8, 1999): 43.

Corbin, Terry. "Detecting White Collar Crime." *Management Accounting* (November 1998): 64–65.

Doney, Lloyd D. "The Growing Threat of Computer Crime in Small Businesses." *Business Horizons* (May 15, 1998): 81.

Elliot, Lance B. "AI Crime Busters." *AI Expert* (January 1992): 11.

Field, Tom. "Sweat About the Threat." *CIO* (December 1, 1998): 35–43.

Finch, Peter. "Confessions of a Compulsive High-Roller." *Business Week* (July 29, 1991): 78–79.

Frank, Craig. "How to Face Down Fraud." *Security Management* (September 1998): 73.

Furnell, S. M., and M. J. Warren. "Computer Hacking and Cyber Terrorism." *Computers and Security* (1999): 28–34.

Hafner, Katie, and John Markoff. *Cyberpunk*. New York: Simon & Schuster, 1991.

Hoffer, Jeffrey A., and Detmar A. Straub, Jr. "The 9 to 5 Underground: Are You Policing Computer Crimes?" *Sloan Management Review* (Summer 1989): 35–43.

Horowitz, Alan S., and Michael Cohn. "Ensuring the Integrity of Your Data." *Beyond Computing* (May 1998): 27–30.

Information Protection Review **2** (1) Deloitte & Touche, 1–6.

Keefe, Patricia. "Doing Away with Hard Disks." *Computerworld* (March 12, 1990): 39.

Knowles, Anne. "The Enemy Within." *CIO* (June 15, 1996): 84–89.

Menkus, Belden. "Eight Factors Contributing to Computer Fraud." *Internal Auditor* (October 1990): 71–74.

Moukheiber, Zina. "Cybercops." *Forbes* (March 10, 1997): 170–172.

________. "Got a Hacker Policy?" *Forbes* (November 16, 1998): 77.

Pasternak, Douglas, and Bruce B. Auster. "Terrorism at the Touch of a Keyboard." *U.S. News & World Report* (July 13, 1998): 37.

Romney, Marshall B., David Cherrington, and W. Steve Albrecht. "Red-Flagging the White-Collar Criminal." *Management Accounting* (March 1980): 51–57.

________. "Auditors and the Detection of Fraud." *Journal of Accountancy* (May 1980): 63–69.

________. "The Role of Management in Reducing Fraud." *Financial Executive* (March 1981): 28–34.

Russell, Harold F. *Foozles and Frauds*. Altamonte Springs, FL: Institute of Internal Auditors, 1977.

Savage, J. A. "Computer Time Bomb Defused: Felon Nailed." *Computerworld* (September 26, 1988): 2.

"Special Report: Security." *Computerworld* (February 10, 1997): 65–84.

Teach, Edward. "Look Who's Hacking Now: Securing Computer Systems." *CFO* (February 1998): 38.

"University of Oregon Settles Suit Brought by Software Publishers." *Wall Street Journal* (August 23, 1991): B2.

Vistica, Gregory L., and Evan Thomas. "The Secret Hacker Wars." *Newsweek* (June 1, 1998): 60–61.

Wells, J. T. "Six Common Myths About Fraud." *Journal of Accountancy* (February 1990): 82–88.

Whiteside, Thomas. *Computer Capers*. New York: Crowell, 1978.

www.cert.org. The CERT Coordination Center at the Carnegie Mellon Software Engineering Institute.

www.ciac.org. Computer Incidence Advisory Capability of the U.S. Department of Energy.

CHAPTER 11

American Institute of Certified Public Accountants. *Computer-Assisted Audit Techniques*. New York: AICPA, 1979.

________. *Audit and Control Considerations in an On-Line Environment*. New York: AICPA, 1983.

———. *Statements on Auditing Standards No. 1-69.* New York: AICPA, 1992.

Arens, Alvin A., and James K. Loebbecke. *Auditing: An Integrated Approach.* 6th ed. Englewood Cliffs, NJ: Prentice-Hall, 1994.

Austin, Gary R. "Moving into the Next Millenium: Systems Auditing Capability Development for Internal Auditing." *Internal Auditing* (September–October 1998): 21–26.

Babcock, Charles. "Software Development: A Glimpse Ahead." *Computerworld* (June 20, 1994): 6.

Champlain, Jack J. "Demystifying Computer Systems Auditing." *Internal Auditor* (December 1995): 28–33.

Chapman, Christy. "Just Wired About Software." *Internal Auditor* (August 1995): 24–36.

Coderre, Dave, and Jim Kaplan. "Computers and Auditing: Pulling It All Together." *Internal Auditor* (June 1995): 20–22.

Elliott, Robert K. "The Future of Audits." *Journal of Accountancy* (September 1994): 74–82.

Flesher, Dale L., and Roberto De Magalhaes. "Electronic Workpapers." *Internal Auditor* (August 1995): 38–43.

Helms, Glenn L., and Jane Mancino. "The Electronic Auditor." *Journal of Accountancy* (April 1998): 45–48.

Institute of Internal Auditors Research Foundation. *Systems Auditability and Control Report.* Altamonte Springs, FL: Institute of Internal Auditors Research Foundation, 1991.

Jenne, Stanley E. "Microcomputers Present a New Internal Control Challenge." *National Public Accountant* (June 1998): 34.

Lanza, Richard B. "Take My Manual Audit, Please." *Journal of Accountancy* (June 1998): 33–36.

Robertson, Jack C. *Auditing.* 8th ed. Homewood, IL: BPI Irwin, 1996.

Roesch, Laura, and Laurie J. Henry. "Client/Server Systems." *Internal Auditor* (August 1997): 40–43.

Shields, Greg. "Non-stop Auditing." *CA Magazine* (September 1998): 39–40.

Simmons, Mark R. "COSO Based Auditing." *Internal Auditor* (December 1997): 68–73.

Sriram, Ram S., and Glenn E. Sumners. "Understanding Concurrent Audit Techniques." *EDPACS* (July 1992): 1–8.

Weber, Ron. "Information Systems Control and Audit." Prentice-Hall: November 1998.

Wilson, Linda. "Insurer Gets a Quality Check on Decision Support." *Computerworld* (August 18, 1997): 71–72.

www.isaca.org. The Information Systems Audit and Control Association and Foundation.

Zarowin, Stanley. "The Future of Finance." *Journal of Accountancy* (August 1995): 47–49.

CHAPTER 12

Askelson, Kenneth. D. "Automatic Identification Technologies." *AICPA InfoTech Update* (Summer 1994): 7–9.

Berry, Jonathan, Kathleen Kerwin, and Gail DeGeorge. "Database Marketing: A Potent New Tool for Selling." *Business Week* (September 5, 1994): 56–62.

Bigness, Jon. "In Today's Economy, There Is Big Money to Be Made in Logistics." *Wall Street Journal* (September 6, 1995): A1, A9.

Cronin, Mary J. "Using the Web to Push Key Data to Decision Makers." *Fortune* (September 29, 1997): 254.

DeJong, Jennifer. "Smart Marketing." *Computerworld* (February 7, 1994): 113–118.

Freedman, David H. "Why Big Retailers Love Little Scotch Maid." *Forbes ASAP* (February 28, 1994): 106–109.

Gelinas, Ulric J., Jr., and Allan E. Oram. *Accounting Information Systems.* 3rd ed. Cincinnati, OH: South-Western College Publishing, 1996.

Halper, Mark. "JC Penney Warehouses Do Away with Paper." *Computerworld* (September 12, 1994): 64.

Harrar, George. "Levi's: Cool Brand, Lousy Distribution, IT to the Rescue." *Forbes ASAP* (February 28, 1994): 140–142.

Heidkamp, Martha M. "Reaping the Benefits of Financial EDI." *Management Accounting* (May 1991): 39–43.

Henderson, Angelo B. "Bilked of Batteries, Exide Corp. Says It'll Take A Charge." *Wall Street Journal* (March 26, 1996): A3, A4.

Hollander, Anita S., Eric L. Denna, and J. Owen Cherrington. *Accounting, Information Technology, and Business Solutions.* 1st ed. Chicago: Irwin, 1996.

Humphrey, Scott. "Bell Atlantic Reengineers Payment Processing." *Enterprise Reengineering* (October–November 1995): 1–22.

Jenkins, Avery. "Get Connected." *Computerworld Premier 100* (September 19, 1994): 26–32.

Kay, Emily. "Selling Enters the Information Age." *Datamation* (May 1, 1995): 38–42.

King, Julia. "Big Brother Mans Help Desk." *Computerworld* (October 17, 1994): 1, 28.

Maglitta, Joseph E. "Best Face Forward." *Computerworld* (May 16, 1994): 100–107.

McCartney, Scott. "Companies Go On-Line to Chat, Spy and Rebut." *Wall Street Journal* (September 15, 1994): B1, B6.

Montgomery, M. R. "The Genie of Jeans." *Boston Globe* (January 4, 1995): 52–58.

Moskal, Brian S. "Captain to Navigator." *IndustryWeek: International* (September 15, 1997). URL: www.industryweek.com/intl/091597/intern0915.html

Seideman, Tony. "Who Needs Managers?" *Sales & Marketing Management—Part 2* (June 1994): 14–17.

Seideman, Tony. "On the Cutting Edge." *Sales & Marketing Management—Part 2* (June 1994): 18–23.

Serwer, Andy. "Michael Dell Rocks." *Fortune* (May 11, 1998): 59–70.

Trumfio, Ginger. "The Case for E-mail." *Sales & Marketing Management* (July 1994): 94–98.

Trumfio, Ginger. "The Future Is Now." *Sales & Marketing Management* (November 1994): 74–80.

Tully, Shawn. "How Cisco Mastered the Net." *Fortune* (August 17, 1998): 207–210.

Verity, John W. "The Gold Mine of Data in Customer Service." *Business Week* (March 21, 1994): 113–114.

Wilkinson, Joseph W. *Accounting Information Systems: Essential Concepts and Applications.* 2nd ed. New York: John Wiley & Sons, 1993.

Wilson, Linda. "One Leg at a Time." *InformationWeek* (April 18, 1994): 52.

CHAPTER 13

Askelson, Kenneth D. "Automatic Identification Technologies." *AICPA InfoTech Update* (Summer 1994): 7–9.

Berton, Lee. "Downsize Danger: Many Firms Cut Staff in Accounts Payable and Pay a Steep Price." *Wall Street Journal* (September 15, 1996): A1, A6.

Brewer, Peter C., and Tina Y. Mills. "ISO 9000 Standards: An Emerging CPA Service Area." *Journal of Accountancy* (February 1994): 63–67.

Churbuck, David C. "Don't Leave Headquarters Without It." *Forbes* (December 20, 1993): 242–243.

Cohen, Eric E. "Reading Between the Lines." *Journal of Accountancy* (August 1994): 59–64.

Cronin, Mary J. "Ford's Intranet Success." *Fortune* (March 30, 1998): 158.

Fisher, Marshall L. "What Is the Right Supply Chain for Your Product?" *Harvard Business Review* (March–April 1997): 105–116.

Gelinas, Ulric J., Jr., and Allan E. Oram. *Accounting Information Systems.* 3rd ed. Cincinnati, OH: South-Western College Publishing, 1996.

Halper, Mark. "JC Penney Warehouses Do Away with Paper." *Computerworld* (September 12, 1994): 64.

Hoffman, Thomas. "Sea-Land Finds Gateway to Excellence Through Automation." *Computerworld* (August 8, 1994): 39–42.

Hollander, Anita S., Eric L. Denna, and J. Owen Cherrington. *Accounting, Information Technology, and Business Solutions.* 1st ed. Chicago: Irwin, 1996.

Hunton, James E. "Setting Up a Paperless Office." *Journal of Accountancy* (November 1994): 77–85.

Kalstrom, David J. "Slaying the Paper Dragon." *Financial Executive* (September–October 1993): 37–39.

Mize, B. Ray, Jr. "Vendor Audits." *CPA Journal* (February 1994): 18–22.

Palmer, Richard J. "Reengineering Payables at ITT Automotive." *Management Accounting* (July 1994): 38–42.

Pavlinko, Jean L. "Paperless Payables at Lord." *Management Accounting* (July 1993): 32–34.

Vollmann, Thomas E., William L. Berry, and D. Clay Whybark. *Manufacturing Planning and Control Systems.* 3rd ed. Homewood, IL: Irwin, 1992: 191–193.

Wilder, Clinton. "A Penney Saved." *InformationWeek* (December 20–27, 1993): 24–30.

Wilkinson, Joseph W. *Accounting Information Systems: Essential Concepts and Applications.* 2nd ed. New York: John Wiley & Sons, 1993.

Wooley, Scott. "Double Click for Resin." *Forbes* (March 10, 1997): 132–134.

Wooley, Scott. "E-muscle." Forbes (March 9, 1998): 204.

CHAPTER 14

Brinkman, Stephen L., and Mark A. Appelbaum. "The Quality Cost Report: It's Alive and Well at Gilroy Foods." *Management Accounting* (September 1994): 61–65.

Cheatham, Carole. "Measuring and Improving Throughput." *Journal of Accountancy* (March 1990): 89–91.

Fisher, Marshall L. "What Is the Right Supply Chain for Your Product?" *Harvard Business Review* (March–April 1997): 105–116.

Fletcher, P. "Performing a Multi-plant Ballet." *IndustryWeek* (December 15, 1997), URL: www.industryweek.com/minc/121597/mc1215.html

Gammell, Frances, and C. J. McNair. "Jumping the Growth Threshold Through Activity-Based Cost Management." *Management Accounting* (September 1994): 37–46.

Garner, Rochelle. "Open Insecurities." *Computerworld* (September 12, 1994): 121–122.

Gelinas, Ulric J., Jr., and Allan E. Oram. *Accounting Information Systems.* 3rd ed. Cincinnati, OH: South-Western College Publishing, 1996.

Hollander, Anita S., Eric L. Denna, and J. Owen Cherrington. *Accounting, Information Technology, and Business Solutions.* 1st ed. Chicago: Irwin, 1996.

Horngren, Charles T., George Foster, and Srikant M. Datar. *Cost Accounting.* 8th ed. Englewood Cliffs, NJ: Prentice-Hall, 1994.

Keegan, Daniel P., and Robert G. Eiler. "Let's Reengineer Cost Accounting." *Management Accounting* (August 1994): 26–31.

LaPlante, Alice. "New Software = Faster Factories." *Forbes ASAP:* 36–41.

Luternow, Bonnie A. "Serving Two Masters with IT." *Financial Executive* (September–October 1994): 39–42.

Marion, Larry. "Product Data Management." *Beyond Computing* (September–October 1994): 55–56.

Montgomery, M. R. "The Genie of Jeans." *Boston Globe* (January 4, 1995): 52–58.

"Netscape Awards Bounties to Successful Bug Hunters." *Wall Street Journal* (December 11, 1995): C2.

Panchak, Patricia. "Lockhee Martin Pike County Troy, Ala.: Profiles in Excellence." *IndustryWeek* (March 24, 1998), URL: www.industryweek.com/IwinPrint/BestPlants/profiles/pwp032498.html

Turk, William T. "Management Accounting Revitalized: The Harley-Davidson Experience." In *Readings in Management Accounting* (edited by S. Mark Young). Englewood Cliffs, NJ: Prentice-Hall, 1995, 135–144.

Wilkinson, Joseph W. *Accounting Information Systems: Essential Concepts and Applications.* 2nd ed. New York: John Wiley & Sons, 1993.

Wilson, Linda. "Two Outs, Bottom of the Ninth . . . ." *InformationWeek* (October 4, 1993): 30–34.

CHAPTER 15

Danilewicz, Dennis. "How Technology Has Changed the Payroll Function." *Management Accounting: Human Resources/Payroll Supplement* (June 1997): 6–9.

Flynn, Gillian. "Non-Sales Staffs Respond to Incentives." *Personnel Journal* (July 1994): 33–38.

Geer, Carolyn T. "For a New Job, Press #1." *Forbes* (August 15, 1994): 118–119.

Gelinas, Ulric J., Jr., and Allan E. Oram. *Accounting Information Systems.* 3rd ed. Cincinnati, OH: South-Western College Publishing, 1996.

Gleckman, Howard, Sandra Atchison, Tim Smart, and John A. Bryne. "Bonus Pay: Buzz-word or Bonanza?" *Business Week* (November 14, 1994): 62–64.

Grant, Linda. "Happy Workers, High Returns." *Fortune* (January 12, 1998): 81.

Greengard, Samuel. "New Technology Is HR's Route to Reengineering." *Personnel Journal* (July 1994): 32c–32o.

Greengard, Samuel. "HR's Great Enabler." *IndustryWeek* (September 15, 1997). URL: www.industryweek.com/internet/091597/ihr0915.html

Hollander, Anita S., Eric L. Denna, and J. Owen Cherrington. *Accounting, Information Technology, and Business Solutions.* 1st ed. Chicago: Irwin, 1996.

Imberman, Woodruff. "Is Gainsharing the Wave of the Future?" *Management Accounting* (November 1995): 35–39.

Markels, Alex, and Matt Murray. "Call It Dumbsizing: Why Some Companies Regret Cost-Cutting." *Wall Street Journal* (March 14, 1996): A1, A6.

McCormick, Steven C. "The Virtual HR Organization." *Management Accounting* (October 1998): 48–51.

Meadows, Jim L. "AT&T Workers Form an Internal Contingent Labor Pool." *Personnel Journal* (December 1994): 90.

Nakache, Patricia. "Cisco's Recruiting Edge." *Fortune* (September 29, 1997): 275–276.

Panchak, Patricia. "Lockhee Martin Pike County Troy, Ala.: Profiles in Excellence." *IndustryWeek* (March 24, 1998), URL: www.industryweek.com/IwinPrint/BestPlants/profiles/pwp032498.html

Patterson, Gregory A. "Distressed Shoppers, Disaffected Workers Prompt Stores to Alter Sales Commissions." *Wall Street Journal* (July 1, 1992): B1, B6.

Schulz, Howard. "Starbucks: Making Values Pay." *Fortune* (September 29, 1997): 261–272.

Stamler, Michael. "Screening for Fraud." *Internal Auditor* (October 1997): 67–69.

Stewart, Thomas A. "Your Company's Most Valuable Asset: Intellectual Capital." *Fortune* (October 3, 1994): 68–74.

Stewart, Thomas A. "Taking on the Last Bureaucracy." *Fortune* (January 15, 1996): 105–108.

Stewart, Thomas A. "A New Way to Think About Employees." *Fortune* (April 13, 1998): 169–170

Thornburg, Linda. "Accounting for Knowledge." *HRMagazine* (October 1994): 50–56.

Wilkinson, Joseph W. *Accounting Information Systems: Essential Concepts and Applications.* 2nd ed. New York: John Wiley & Sons, 1993.

Yin, Tung. "Sears Is Accused of Billing Fraud at Auto Centers." *Wall Street Journal* (June 12, 1992): B1, B5.

CHAPTER 16

AICPA. *Improving Business Reporting.* A Customer Focus Report of the AICPA Special Committee on Financial Reporting, 1994.

Allen, Kenneth A. "The One-Day Close." *Management Accounting* (November 1995): 18.

Andros, David P., J. Owen Cherrington, and Eric L. Denna. "Reengineering Your Accounting, the IBM Way." *Financial Executive* (July–August 1992): 28–31.

Brachel, John von. "Interpreting Financial Statements: How One Firm Uses the Language of Graphics." *Journal of Accountancy* (April 1995): 42–43.

Flaherty, Daniel J., Raymond A. Zimmerman, and Mary Ann Murray. "Benchmarking Against the Best." *Journal of Accountancy* (July 1995): 85–88.

Gelinas, Ulric J., Jr., and Allan E. Oram. *Accounting Information Systems.* 3rd ed. Cincinnati, OH: South-Western College Publishing, 1996.

Heid, Jim. "Graphs that Work." *Macworld* (February 1994): 155–156.

Kabak, Irwin, and Thomas J. Beam. "Two-Dimensional Accounting: A New Management Demand." *Industrial Management* (November–December 1990): 25–29.

Kaplan, Robert S., and David P. Norton. "The Balanced Scorecard—Measures that Drive Performance." *Harvard Business Review* (January–February 1992): 71–79.

Kaplan, Robert S., and David P. Norton. "Using the Balanced Scorecard as a Strategic Management System." *Harvard Business Review* (January–February 1996): 75–85.

Karon, Paul. "Hallmark Welcomes Change in Handling Finances." *InfoWorld* (December 19, 1994): 6.

Lee, John Y. "How to Make Financial and Nonfinancial Data Add Up." *Journal of Accountancy* (September 1992): 62–66.

Ramanathan, Kavasseri V., and Douglas S. Schaffer. "How Am I Doing?" *Journal of Accountancy* (May 1995): 79–82.

Rayport, Jeffrey F., and John J. Sviokla. "Exploiting the Virtual Value Chain." *Harvard Business Review* (November–December 1995): 75–85.

Shank, John K. "How Safe Is Your Job?" *Journal of Accountancy* (October 1993): 72–80.

Steinbart, Paul John. "The Auditor's Responsibility for the Accuracy of Graphs in Annual Reports: Some Evidence on the Need for Additional Guidance." *Accounting Horizons* (September 1989): 60–70.

Wallace, Peggy. "Microsoft's Finance Department Gets Up to Speed." *InfoWorld* (June 5, 1995): 58.

Wilkinson, Joseph W. *Accounting Information Systems: Essential Concepts and Applications.* 2nd ed. New York: John Wiley & Sons, 1993.

Zarowin, Stanley. "Motorola's Financial Closings: 12 'Non-events' a Year." *Journal of Accountancy* (November 1995): 59–63.

CHAPTER 17

Anthes, Gary H. "Planning Spells Results at MCI." *Computerworld* (January 27, 1992): 31.

Atre, Shaku. "Nailing Down User Requirements." *Computerworld* (June 1, 1998): 51–54.

Blodgett, Mindy. "Separation Anxiety." *CIO* (November 15, 1998): 32–38.

Booker, Ellis. "IS Trailblazing Puts Retailer on Top." *Computerworld* (February 12, 1990): 69, 73.

Borthick, A. Faye, and George P. Wentworth. "Will Your Company by Year-2000 Compliant?" *Management Accounting* (July 1998): 31.

Bozman, Jean S. "Red Cross Re-vamp Slowly Takes Shape." *Computerworld* (June 8, 1992): 63.

Champy, James. "Have Your Computer Call My Computer." *Forbes* (January 26, 1998): 95.

Coy, Peter, and Chuck Hawkins. "The New Realism in Office Systems." *Business Week* (June 15, 1992): 128–132.

Field, Tom. "When Bad Things Happen to Good Projects." *CIO* (October 15, 1997): 62.

Gilpin, Linda. "Learning From Past Projects So History Isn't Repeated." *Computerworld* (November 18, 1996): T16.

Gwynne, Peter. "Involving Users in Software Development." *Beyond Computing* (January–February 1998): 21–24.

Hamilton, Rosemary. "Met Life Finds Dividend in Automation System." *Computerworld* (January 6, 1992): 41.

Hammer, Michael. "Making the Quantum Leap." *Beyond Computing* (March–April 1992): 10–14.

Harrington, H. James, et al. "Business Process Improvement Workbook." McGraw-Hill: April 1997.

Hubbard, Douglas. "Everything is Measurable." *CIO* (November 15, 1997): 68–70.

Hunton, James E., and Jesse D. Beeler. "Effects of User Participation in Systems Development." *MIS Quarterly* (December 1997): 359.

Kara, Dan. "Get It Right the First Time: Identifying Requirements Early in the Development Process." *Software Magazine* (November 1997): 112.

Keen, Peter G. W. "Get the Right Process Right." *Harvard Business Review* (Boston, 1997): 4–8.

Laplante, Alice. "For IS, Quality Is 'Job None.'" *Computerworld* (January 6, 1992): 57–59.

Nash, Kim S. "Trucking Firm Seeks Faster Dispatching." *Computerworld* (January 2, 1991): 33.

Ramos, Lee. "How to Do a Great Needs Analysis." *Network VAR* (February 1998): 40.

Reimus, Byron. "The IT System that Couldn't Deliver." *Harvard Business Review* (May–June 1997): 22–35.

Ryan, Alan J. "Banks Assess IS' Worth." *Computerworld* (October 7, 1991): 113–116.

Smith, Geoffrey. "The Computer System that Nearly Hospitalized an Insurer." *Business Week* (June 15, 1992): 133.

Thackara, John. "Does Your Technology Fit?" *Inc.* (March 19, 1996): 31.

"To Hell and Back." *CIO* (December 1, 1998): 45–61.

Warren, Liz. "Basic Instinct." *Computing* (March 13, 1997): 34.

Wilde, Cande. "Staying Aligned: Five Tales." *Computerworld* (May 25, 1992): 78.

Wreden, Nick. "Model Business Processes." *InformationWeek* (September 28, 1998).

CHAPTER 18

Appleby, Chuck, John P. McPartlin, and Linda Wilson. "The Human Face of Outsourcing." *InformationWeek* (January 17, 1994): 30–34.

Antonucci, Yvonne L. "The Pros and Cons of IT Outsourcing." *Journal of Accountancy* (June 1998): 26.

Black, George. "Simplify End-User Computing: Outsource It." *Datamation* (September 15, 1995): 67–69.

Bowman, Bob. "How To . . . Develop Applications Rapidly." *Computing* (May 22, 1997): 55.

Caldwell, Bruce. "Going Against the Grain: USF&G Takes Network Back from Outsourcer." *InformationWeek* (April 11, 1994): 15.

———. "Xerox Outsources to EDS: A Case of Dollars and Sense." *InformationWeek* (March 28, 1994): 15.

———. "Farming Out Client-Server." *InformationWeek* (December 12, 1994): 46–56.

———. "Special Counsel." *InformationWeek* (October 31, 1994): 40–48.

———. "Who Needs Programmers?" *InformationWeek* (April 25, 1994): 23–30.

Caldwell, Bruce, Bob Violino, and Marianne Kolbasuk McGee. "Hidden Partners, Hidden Dangers." *InformationWeek* (January 20, 1997): 38–52.

Caldwell, Bruce, Mary E. Thyfault, and Mike Fillon. "Moving Out." *InformationWeek* (March 14, 1994): 12–13.

Carr, David F. "Outsourcing Revisited: Will the Net Replace IT at Small Firms?" *Internet World* (October 26, 1998).

Crowley, Aileen. "Taming the Ferocious Outsourcing Beast." *PC Week* (February 15, 1999): 85.

Fabris, Peter. "The Perfect Host." *CIO* (March 1, 1999): 46–52.

Field, Tom. "Caveat Emptor." *CIO* (April 1, 1997): 47–58.

Foxman, Noah. "Succeeding in Outsourcing." *Information Systems Management* (Winter 1994): 77–80.

———. "The Power of Enterprise Computing." *Internal Auditor* (February 1997): 34–37.

Frieswick, Kris. "Turning Inside Out: Intranet Outsourcing." *CFO* (October 1998): 73.

Halper, Mark. "Weather Drives Burpee to Outsourcing." *Computerworld* (October 12, 1992): 77, 80.

Halvey, John. "No Longer a Last Resort." *InformationWeek* (August 1, 1994): 84.

Hammer, Michael. "Reengineering Work: Don't Automate, Obliterate." *Harvard Business Review* (July–August 1990): 104–112.

———. "Making the Quantum Leap." *Beyond Computing* (March–April 1992): 10–14.

Jorgensen, Jim. "Managing the Risks of Outsourced IT." *Internal Auditor* (December 1996): 54–59.

Kleinschrod, Walter A. "Outsourcing: Weighing the Issues." *Beyond Computing* (October–November 1992): 44–50.

Koch, Christopher. "Staying Alive." *CIO* (February 16, 1999): 38–43.

Lee, Louise. "Rent-a-Techs: Hiring Outside Firms to Run Computers Isn't Always a Bargain." *Wall Street Journal* (May 18, 1995): A1, A13.

McGee, Marianne. "Strategic Applications." *InformationWeek* (November 23, 1998).

Ricciuti, Mike. "Outsourcing as a Survival Tactic." *Datamation* (April 15, 1994): 48–52.

Schroeder, Erica. "I Have Seen the Future, and It Is Outsourcing." *PC Week* (February 22, 1999): 77.

Scrupski, Susan. "Take my PCs, Please." *Datamation* (February 1, 1995): 32.

Slater, Derek. "An ERP Package for You . . . and You . . . and You . . . and Even You." (February 15, 1999): 30–37.

Tinnierello, Paul C. "Can Your Vendor Pass a Physical?" *PC Week* (December 1996): E8.

Van Name, Mark L., and Bill Catchings. "Rules of Thumb for System Purchases." *PC Week* (September 2, 1996): N12.

Wakin, Eric. "Outsource Partnering." *Beyond Computing* (March 1997): 35–40.

Wilder, Clinton. "80% Satisfied with Outsourcing, Survey Says." *Computerworld* (January 27, 1992): 77.

CHAPTER 19

Anthes, Gary H. "Triumph Over a Taxing Project." *Computerworld* (November 4, 1991): 65–69.

Appleby, Chuck. "Agency's Drive to Nowhere." *InformationWeek* (June 13, 1994): 72.

———. "Power Failure: Five Years into a Client-Server Conversion, Pacific Gas & Electric Backs Up and Starts Over." *InformationWeek* (February 21, 1994): 12–13.

Bartholomew, Doug. "Strategic Bungling." *InformationWeek* (October 4, 1993): 12–13.

Bartholomew, Doug, and Frank Hayes. "Utility's Bright Idea." *InformationWeek* (March 13, 1995): 28.

Bozman, Jean S. "DMV Disaster: California Kills Failed $44M Project." *Computerworld* (May 9, 1994): 1, 16.

Caldwell, Bruce, and Doug Bartholomew. "Glitch Zaps Bank Accounts: Chemical ATMs Have Bad Reaction." *InformationWeek* (February 21, 1994): 13–14.

DePompa, Barbara. "Waging War on the Applications Backlog." *Beyond Computing* (July–August 1993): 40–44.

Dryden, Patrick. "Support Staffers Get Holiday Hangovers." *Computerworld* (January 12, 1998): 47.

Epstein, Harry. "Technology Redux: Sometimes the Best Way to Upgrade Is to Resurrect the Tried and True." *Inc.* (March 18, 1997): 27.

Gullo, Karen. "Stopping Runaways in Their Tracks." *InformationWeek* (November 13, 1989): 63–70.

Hayes, Frank. "Of Big Projects and Back Burners." *Computerworld* (May 19, 1997): 111.

Henry, Jacqueline. "Is Your System Ready?" *InformationWeek* (October, 17, 1994): 38–46.

Jacobsen, Ivar, et al. "Unified Software Development Process." Addison-Wesley: January 1999.

Joslin, Douglas E. "Installing a New System: 11 Commandments." *Management Accounting* (December 1998): 32.

Kirchner, Jake. "GAO Tells a $970,000 Horror Story." *Computerworld* (December 3, 1979): 12.

Lozinsky, Sergio. "Enterprise Wide Software Solutions: Integration Strategies and Policies." Addison-Wesley: April 1998.

Marenghi, Catherine. "Nashua Keeps Quality Flame Burning in Customer Service." *Computerworld* (January 6, 1992): 61.

McPartlin, John P. "$11M System Development Failure: Arizona Begins the Postmortem." *InformationWeek* (September 6, 1993): 13.

Messmer, Max. "Pay Per Project." *Management Accounting* (June 1998): 36–41.

Nelson, Anthony C., and Joe Rottman. "Before and After CASE Adoption." *Information and Management* (December 15, 1996): 193.

Rigdon, Joan E. "Frequent Glitches in New Software Bug Users." *Wall Street Journal* (January 18, 1995): B1, B5.

Ross, Philip E. "The Day the Software Crashed." *Forbes* (April 25, 1994): 142–156.

Rothfeder, Jeffrey. "Using the Law to Rein in Computer Runaways." *Business Week* (April 3, 1989): 70–76.

Ryan, Alan J. "D & B Scores Contracts." *Computerworld* (May 13, 1991): 29.

Schneidawind, John. "Getting the Bugs Out." *USA Today* (August 29, 1991): 1–2.

Thyfault, Mary E. "The AT&T Dream Team." *InformationWeek* (March 6, 1995): 26–38.

Vijayan, Jaikumar. "Platform Overhauls Need Careful Planning." *Computerworld* (December 9, 1996): 49.

Wreden, Nick. "Build, Buy or Modify?" *Beyond Computing* (January–February 1995): 47–49.

www.hissa.ncsl.nist.gov. The U.S. Department of Commerce's National Institute of Standards and Technology—High Integrity Software and Systems Assurance.

Yang, Heng-Li. "Adoption and Implementation of CASE Tools in Taiwan." *Information and Management* (February 8, 1999): 89–112.

INDEX